W9-BZM-172

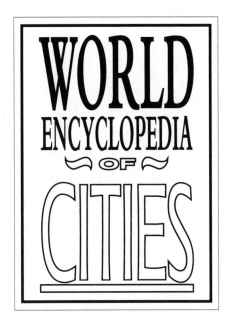

WORLD
ENCYCLOPEDIA
~ OF ~
CITIES

WORLD ENCYCLOPEDIA ~OF~ CITIES

VOLUME II
NORTH AMERICA
(United States N–Z, and Canada)

George Thomas Kurian

ABC-CLIO

Library of Congress Cataloging-in-Publication Data

Kurian, George Thomas.
   World encyclopedia of cities / George Thomas Kurian.
     p. cm.
   Includes bibliographical references.
   Contents: v. 1. North America (United States A–M) — v. 2. North
America (United States N–Z and Canada)
   1. Cities and towns—Encyclopedias. I. Title.
HT108.5.K87 1993   307.76′03—dc20   93-43133

ISBN 0-87436-650-X (Volume I, United States A–M)
ISBN 0-87436-651-8 (Volume II, United States N–Z, and Canada)
ISBN 0-87436-649-6 (set)

00 99 98 97 96 95 94   10 9 8 7 6 5 4 3 2   (hc)

ABC-CLIO, Inc.
130 Cremona Drive, P.O. Box 1911
Santa Barbara, California 93116-1911

This book is printed on acid-free paper ⊖ .
Manufactured in the United States of America

Contents

Volume II: North America
(United States N–Z, and Canada)

Preface, vii
Cities Listed by State or Province, xi

Nashua, New Hampshire, 611
Nashville, Tennessee, 619
New Haven, Connecticut, 629
New Orleans, Louisiana, 639
New York, New York, 649
Newark, New Jersey, 667
Newport, Rhode Island, 677
Oklahoma City, Oklahoma, 687
Omaha, Nebraska, 695
Peoria, Illinois, 703
Philadelphia, Pennsylvania, 711
Phoenix, Arizona, 723
Pittsburgh, Pennsylvania, 731
Portland, Maine, 741
Portland, Oregon, 749
Portsmouth, New Hampshire, 759
Providence, Rhode Island, 767
Richmond, Virginia, 775
Rochester, New York, 785
Rutland, Vermont, 795
Sacramento, California, 803
St. Louis, Missouri, 811
St. Paul, Minnesota, 823
St. Petersburg, Florida, 831
Salt Lake City, Utah, 839
San Antonio, Texas, 849
San Diego, California, 859
San Francisco, California, 869
San Jose, California, 881
Scranton, Pennsylvania, 889
Seattle, Washington, 897
Sioux Falls, South Dakota, 907
South Bend, Indiana, 915
Spokane, Washington, 923

Springfield, Illinois, 931
Springfield, Massachusetts, 939
Springfield, Missouri, 947
Stamford, Connecticut, 955
Syracuse, New York, 963
Tacoma, Washington, 973
Tampa, Florida, 981
Toledo, Ohio, 989
Topeka, Kansas, 999
Trenton, New Jersey, 1007
Tucson, Arizona, 1015
Tulsa, Oklahoma, 1023
Washington, District of Columbia, 1031
Waterbury, Connecticut, 1041
Wichita, Kansas, 1049
Wilmington, Delaware, 1057
Worcester, Massachusetts, 1067

CANADA
Calgary, Alberta, 1077
Edmonton, Alberta, 1085
Halifax, Nova Scotia, 1091
Hamilton, Ontario, 1097
London, Ontario, 1103
Montreal, Quebec, 1107
Ottawa, Ontario, 1115
Quebec, Quebec, 1121
Regina, Saskatchewan, 1129
St. John's, Newfoundland, 1135
Saskatoon, Saskatchewan, 1141
Toronto, Ontario, 1147
Vancouver, British Columbia, 1155
Winnipeg, Manitoba, 1163

Preface

The first volumes of the *World Encyclopedia of Cities,* covering North America north of Mexico, were designed for ease-of-use and accessibility for the general researcher. Information compiled from hundreds of books, government documents, and other sources has been gathered within these volumes to provide a one-stop source of information on urban areas across the continent. Information categories vary from history and climate to public finance and parks and recreation. The data chosen reflect the various information needs of different library patrons, whether they are travelers, students, geography teachers, public officials, or simply interested laypersons. Our purpose is to provide a balanced picture of the cities, the history that has influenced and continues to shape them, and the social and economic conditions that bear on them.

The criteria for including or excluding cities in these volumes evolved during the writing and development of the work. The list of cities to be covered was originally compiled on the basis of population—all cities in North America with populations over 100,000—yet this proved to be problematic in presenting a balanced geographical reference work. For example, was the work to include many cities from one heavily populated state, yet completely exclude whole regions with generally lower populations? Should every state capital be included, even though there are other cities in the region both more populous and more economically or socially significant? Such questions eventually led to the modification of the inclusion criteria, and cities were added to help round-out and balance the work geographically.

Both statistical data and narrative information are provided for each city. The problem of gathering statistics that are both current and internally consistent was difficult and in the last analysis not entirely solvable; thus, some of the statistics boxes are sprinkled with the abbreviation *NA*, Not Available or Not Applicable. In general, the smaller the city, the larger the problem of obtaining detailed statistical information. In some cases, the only available statistics were internally inconsistent; where the inconsistencies could not be resolved but were not egregious,

they were preserved as a better alternative than excluding the information altogether. Also included for each city are maps, a history narrative, and a brief chronology to assist the reader in placing a city's development in historical perspective.

Inevitably, as in any work of this scope, there will be some errors of fact and omission. The reader is invited to submit corrections or suggestions to the publisher so that such oversights might be corrected in future editions.

Sources for U.S. Statistics

The statistical data summarized in the boxes that appear within the text for each U.S. city are from a variety of sources. The categories of information and their sources are listed below.

Basic Data

Information for the Name, Name Origin, Year Founded, and Status of cities is primarily from city chambers of commerce, supplemented by a variety of secondary sources. Data for Area, Elevation, Time Zone, and road mileage between cities are from the 1993 *Rand McNally Road Atlas.* The Population and Population of Metro Area statistics are from the 1992 *County and City Extra.* Sister Cities listings are from the 1992 *Directory of Sister Cities, Counties and States by State and Country.*

Environment

The Environmental Stress Index data are from the April 1991 *ZPG Reporter.* The Green Cities Index Rank and Score statistics are from the 1992 *Information Please Environmental Almanac.* The Parkland as % of Total City Area statistic is from *The Livable Cities Almanac.* Information for the % of Waste Landfilled/Recycled and the Annual Parks Expenditures per Capita statistics are provided by the National Urban League.

Weather

The weather statistics are from the National Oceanic and Atmospheric Administration and its annual publication, *Comparative Climatic Data for the United States*.

Population

Population statistics, including the information on composition of households, are compiled from the 1992 *County and City Extra*.

Ethnic Composition

Data on the ethnic composition of cities are from the 1992 *County and City Extra*. Please note that in some cases the percentages of the various ethnic groups can total more than 100 percent. This apparent anomaly is due to some persons in the survey data being counted twice, as, for example, when an individual is black and hispanic.

Government

Most government information is provided courtesy of the city chambers of commerce. The City Government Employment Total and Rate per 10,000 statistics are from the 1992 *County and City Extra*.

Public Finance

The statistical data for Total Revenue, Intergovernmental Revenue–Total, Federal Revenue per Capita, % Federal Assistance, % State Assistance, Sales Tax as % of Total Revenue, Local Revenue as % of Total Revenue, City Income Tax, and Fiscal Year Begins are from the U.S. Bureau of the Census publication *Government Finances. City Government Finances: 1989-90*.

Data for Taxes Total, Taxes per Capita (Total and Property), Sales and Gross Receipts, General Expenditures–Total, General Expenditures per Capita, Capital Outlays per Capita, % of Expenditures (for Public Welfare, Highways, Education, Health and Hospitals, Police, Sewage and Sanitation, Parks and Recreation, and Housing and Community Development), Debt Outstanding per Capita, Federal Procurement Contract Awards, and Federal Grant Awards are from the 1992 *County and City Extra*.

Economy

Statistical data for Total Money Income, % of State Average, Per Capita Annual Income, and % of Population below Poverty Level are from the 1992 *County and City Extra*. The information on Fortune 500 companies is from the 19 April 1993 issue of *Fortune* magazine. The data on Banks, Passenger Autos, Electric Meters, and Gas Meters are from the 1992 *Editor & Publisher Market Guide*.

Manufacturing, Wholesale Trade, Retail Trade, and Service Industries data are from the 1992 *County and City Extra*.

Labor

Data for Civilian Labor Force (including % Change), Total Unemployment (including Rate %), and Federal Government Civilian Employment are from the 1992 *County and City Extra*. Information on Work Force Distribution is from the U.S. Department of Labor publication, *Employment, Hours, and Earnings, States and Areas, Data for 1987-92*.

Education

Most of the education data are from the National Center for Education Statistics' June 1991 survey report, *Key Statistics on Public Elementary and Secondary Education Reported by State and by Regional, Locale, and Wealth Clusters, 1988-89*. The Educational Attainment (Age 25 and Over) data are from the 1992 *County and City Extra*. Information for Four-Year and Two-Year Colleges and Universities is from the 1992 *Higher Education Directory*.

Libraries

All information on libraries is from the 1991–92 *American Library Directory*.

Health

The numbers and rates for Deaths and Infant Deaths are from the 1992 *County and City Extra*. Information for Health Expenditures per Capita is from the U.S. Bureau of the Census publication, *Government Finances: City Government Finances, 1989-90*. All other health statistics are from *The Livable Cities Almanac*.

Transportation

Data for Interstate Highway Mileage, Total Urban Mileage, and Total Daily Vehicle Mileage are provided by the U.S. Department of Transportation. Information for Daily Average Commute Time and Number of Buses is from *Places Rated Almanac*. All statistics on air transportation are from the Federal Aviation Administration's 1991 publication, *Airport Activity Statistics of Certified Route Air Carriers*.

Housing

All housing data are from the 1992 *County and City Extra* except the data for Tallest Buildings, which are from the 1993 World Almanac.

Crime

Information for Police and Fire Expenditures per Capita is from the 1992 *County and City Extra.* Data for Number of Police and Police per Thousand are from the 1992 *City and County Extra.* Other statistical information for Crime is from the Federal Bureau of Investigation's publication, *Crime in the United States 1991: Uniform Crime Reports.*

Religion

All statistical information on religion is from the 1992 *Churches and Church Membership in the United States.*

Media

Media data are from the *Gale Directory of Publications and Broadcast Media.*

Travel and Tourism

The statistical data on Hotel Rooms, Convention and Exhibit Space, Convention Centers, and Festivals are provided by city chambers of commerce.

Sources for Canadian Statistics

Information for the Name, Year Founded, Status, Area, and Elevation is primarily from *The Canadian Encyclopedia,* 1988. Data for Time Zone and road mileage between cities are from the 1993 *Rand McNally Road Atlas.* Information in all other categories is from the 1992 *Canadian Markets.*

Cities Listed by State or Province

UNITED STATES

Alabama
Birmingham
Mobile

Alaska
Anchorage

Arizona
Phoenix
Tucson

Arkansas
Little Rock

California
Los Angeles
Sacramento
San Diego
San Francisco
San Jose

Colorado
Colorado Springs
Denver

Connecticut
Bridgeport
Hartford
New Haven
Stamford
Waterbury

Delaware
Wilmington

Florida
Miami
St. Petersburg
Tampa

Georgia
Atlanta

Hawaii
Honolulu

Idaho
Boise

Illinois
Chicago
Peoria
Springfield

Indiana
Evansville
Fort Wayne
Indianapolis
South Bend

Iowa
Cedar Rapids
Davenport
Des Moines

Kansas
Kansas City
Topeka
Wichita

Kentucky
Lexington
Louisville

Louisiana
Baton Rouge
New Orleans

Maine
Augusta
Lewiston
Portland

Maryland
Baltimore

Massachusetts
Boston
Lowell
Springfield
Worcester

Michigan
Ann Arbor
Detroit
Grand Rapids
Lansing

Minnesota
Duluth
Minneapolis
St. Paul

Mississippi
Jackson

Missouri
Kansas City
St. Louis
Springfield

Montana
Billings

Nebraska
Lincoln
Omaha

Nevada
Las Vegas

New Hampshire
Concord
Manchester
Nashua
Portsmouth

New Jersey
Atlantic City
Jersey City
Newark
Trenton

New Mexico
Albuquerque

New York
Albany
Buffalo
New York City
Rochester
Syracuse

North Carolina
Charlotte
Greensboro

North Dakota
Fargo

Ohio
Cincinnati
Cleveland
Columbus
Dayton
Toledo

Oklahoma
Oklahoma City
Tulsa

Oregon
Eugene
Portland

Pennsylvania
Allentown
Erie
Philadelphia
Pittsburgh
Scranton

Rhode Island
Newport
Providence

South Carolina
Charleston

South Dakota
Sioux Falls

Tennessee
Knoxville
Memphis
Nashville

Texas
Austin
Dallas
Fort Worth
Houston
San Antonio

Utah
Salt Lake City

Vermont
Burlington
Montpelier
Rutland

Virginia
Richmond

Washington
Seattle
Spokane
Tacoma

Washington, D.C.

West Virginia
Charleston

Wisconsin
Green Bay
Madison
Milwaukee

Wyoming
Cheyenne

CANADA

Alberta
Calgary
Edmonton

British Columbia
Vancouver

Manitoba
Winnipeg

Newfoundland
St. John's

Nova Scotia
Halifax

Ontario
Hamilton
London
Ottawa
Toronto

Quebec
Montreal
Quebec

Saskatchewan
Regina
Saskatoon

Nashua
New Hampshire

Location and Topography

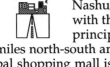

N

Located in southern New Hampshire, Nashua lies on the east bank of the Merrimack River with the Nashua River running east-west through the city. It is 4 miles north of the Massachusetts border, 40 miles northwest of Boston, and 15 miles south of Manchester. It is part of the Golden Triangle that extends toward Manchester and Salem, New Hampshire. The 14 communities of the Nashua region are known as the Gateways. Nashua has a gently rolling terrain characteristic of riverine towns. A number of ponds dot the landscape.

Layout of City and Suburbs

Nashua is a typical New England town with the Merrimack River serving as its principal artery. It extends about 20 miles north-south and 12 miles east-west. The principal shopping mall is the Pheasant Lane Mall, which, with 1 million square feet of space, is one of the largest shopping centers in New England. Its 250 stores attract over 100,000 shoppers every week. Downtown Nashua is the home of several specialty shops. The city's upscale residential buildings are found along Concord Street. Central Nashua contains only 3% of the land area but accounts for 46% of all jobs, 18% of housing, 14% of the population, 31% of the city's classrooms, and 64% of the banks.

Environment

Environmental Stress Index   NA
Green Cities Index: Rank   NA
                    Score   NA
Water Quality   Slightly acid, very soft
Average Daily Use (gallons per capita)   160
    Maximum Supply (gallons per capita)   400
Parkland as % of Total City Area   NA
% Waste Landfilled/Recycled   NA
Annual Parks Expenditures per Capita $15.41

Climate

Nashua has a typical New England climate with warm summers and cold winters. Humidity is moderate, making summers pleasant. Weather changes can be sudden due to the relatively close proximity to the ocean, about 30 miles away. Climatic hazards include fog, hail, thunderstorms, and floods.

Weather

Temperature

Highest Monthly Average °F   58.5
Lowest Monthly Average °F   34.3

Annual Averages

Days 32°F or Below   170
Days above 90°F   11

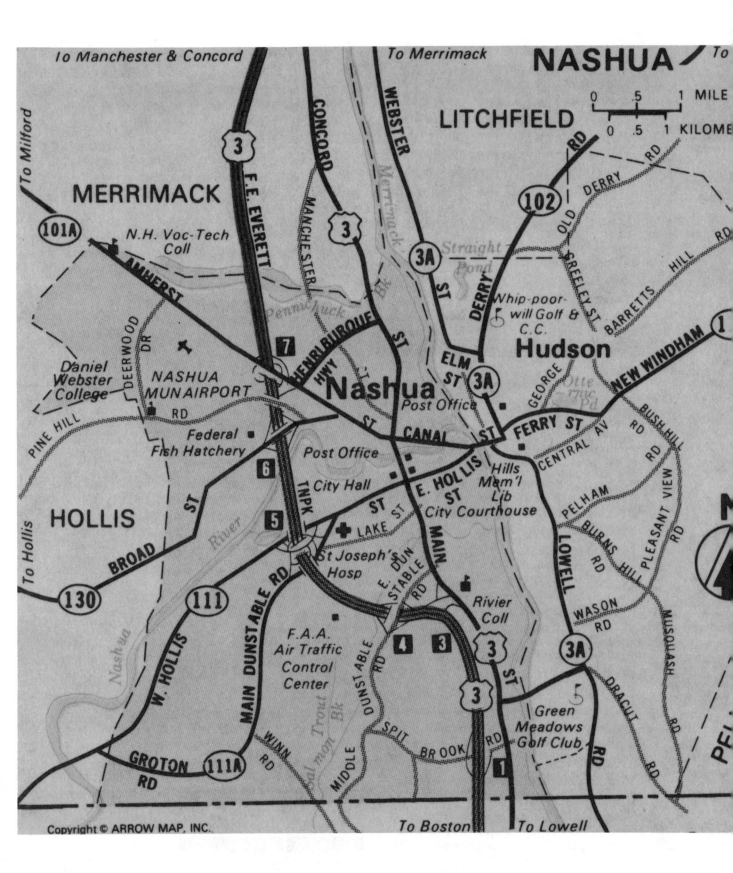

From the *Street Atlas of Metro Boston and Eastern Massachusetts* ©1993. Taunton, MA: Arrow Map, Inc.

Weather (continued)

Zero Degree Days   14
Precipitation (inches)   42.37
Snow (inches)   66.6
% Seasonal Humidity   NA
Wind Speed (m.p.h.)   NA
Clear Days   NA
Cloudy Days   NA
Storm Days   NA
Rainy Days   NA

Average Temperatures (°F)	High	Low	Mean
January	33.7	11.4	22.6
February	35.9	13.0	24.5
March	44.1	23.0	33.6
April	57.4	32.3	44.9
May	68.9	42.0	55.5
June	77.8	51.7	64.8
July	82.7	56.7	69.8
August	80.4	54.8	67.7
September	72.5	46.5	59.5
October	62.0	36.2	49.1
November	49.2	28.1	38.7
December	36.8	16.3	26.6

History

Nashua was home to the Algonquin Federation who lived in the Merrimack River Valley for centuries. The first white settlers were scouts from the Massachusetts Bay Colony who annexed some 200 square miles of the territory around Nashua in the middle 1600s. The first permanent white settlement was Dunstable, founded in 1673. Dunstable suffered as a result of the Indian wars and during the early 1700s had only fewer than 50 residents. In 1741 the town was placed within New Hampshire following a boundary settlement.

Dunstable's growth began in 1804 when the Middlesex Canal opened, connecting the town with Boston and making it the chief port on the Merrimack River. Shortly thereafter Daniel Abbot, a lawyer, and his partners formed the Nashua Manufacturing Company, a textile firm using the abundant water power to run its mills. Within a few years the firm became the largest producer of blankets in the world, employing about 20% of the city's work force, mostly Yankee farm girls and Irish and French-Canadian immigrants. As in other company towns, the streets, offices, and residential quarters were built by the textile firm.

In 1837 Dunstable merged with the nearby town of Indian Head, and the new town changed its name to Nashua, after one of the tribes of the Algonquin Federation. Nashua separated back into two towns in 1842 over a dispute as to where to locate the town hall, reuniting in 1853 when Nashua received its charter from the state. The city's economy received a boost during the Civil War when its mills helped to clothe the Union soldiers. The town prospered further when a new railroad from Boston to Concord put Nashua on the line. The new line also brought hundreds of new immigrants, mostly Greeks, Poles, and Lithuanians.

Nashua continued to maintain steady growth until after World War II. The advent of synthetics and com-

petition from abroad made the New England mills uneconomic and the Nashua Manufacturing Company closed its doors in 1948. The closure, along with that of Textron factories in the Merrimack River Valley, left thousands of workers jobless. Nashua faced the biggest economic crisis in its history. Disaster was averted only through the efforts of an organization called the Nashua Foundation. The foundation brought in Sanders Associates to occupy the mill space and diversify the city's economy. Heavy industry moved to take up the slack in the 1950s and 1960s, and high-tech industries followed in the 1970s and 1980s. Today Digital Equipment Corporation is the city's largest employer with Sanders Associates the second.

Historical Landmarks

The city's oldest historical structure is the Abbot-Spaulding House owned by the Nashua Historical Society. It is a restored Federal-style home built in 1804 by Daniel Abbot, owner of the Nashua Manufacturing Company. The home has several fine period artifacts on display, including china, glass, and portraits, one of which is of President Franklin Pierce.

Population

The 1990 population of the city of Nashua was 79,662. The Nashua PMSA (which includes the surrounding area of Amherst, Brookline, Hollis, Hudson, Litchfield, Londonderry, Merrimack, Milford, Mount Vernon, Nashua and Wilton) had in the same year a population of 180,557. Hillsborough County, of which Nashua is a part, had a population of 336,073. The city of Nashua accounts for 7.2% of the population of New Hampshire. Between 1970 and 1980 the city population grew by 22%, and between 1980 and 1990 by 17%, while the population of Nashua PMSA grew by 32% and 58%, respectively, during the two decades. The most interesting demographic characteristics are the predominance of females in the population and the relatively high median age. The city population is expected to grow slowly during the 1990s, because of the lack of housing within the city proper.

Population

	1980	1990
Central City	67,865	79,662
Rank	289	267
Metro Area	276,608	336,073
Pop. Change 1980–1990 +11,797		
Pop. % Change 1980–1990 +17.4		
Median Age 32.0		
% Male 49.1		
% Age 65 and Over 10.1		
Density (per square mile) 2,578		

Households

Number   31,051
Persons per Household   2.53

Chronology

1652	Settlers from the Massachusetts Bay Colony found a fur trading post on the site of present-day Nashua.
1673	First permanent settlement, called Dunstable, is founded.
1741	Boundary agreement places Dunstable within New Hampshire.
1804	The Middlesex Canal opens.
1823	Daniel Abbot founds the Nashua Manufacturing Company which dominates the city's economy for 125 years.
1837	Dunstable merges with the town of Nashua (formerly Indian Head) and adopts the latter's name.
1842	The town separates back into two towns over a dispute in locating the town hall.
1853	Nashua receives a city charter. The two towns are reunited.
1933	Rivier College is founded.
1948	Nashua Manufacturing Company closes its mills.

Population (continued)

% Female-Headed Households   9.3
% One-Person Households   24.8
Births—Total   1,118
    % to Mothers under 20   9.0
    Birth Rate per 1,000   15.4

Ethnic Composition

Nashua is a very homogeneous city with whites accounting for 95.2% of the population. Although there was heavy immigration in the 19th century, most of the immigrants were from Europe, particularly from Lithuania, Poland, and Greece, or from Canada. Blacks constitute less than 2%, and Hispanics a little over 3%. As a result, the city has been historically free of racial tensions.

Ethnic Composition (as % of total pop.)

	1980	1990
White	97.98	95.15
Black	0.99	1.62
American Indian	0.14	0.22
Asian and Pacific Islander	0.50	1.93
Hispanic	1.12	3.02
Other	NA	1.07

Government

Nashua operates under a mayor-council form of government. The mayor and the six at-large aldermen are elected to four-year terms (with three aldermen elected every three years). The nine ward aldermen are elected to two-year terms.

Nashua, like most of New Hampshire, is traditionally Republican, but has a Democratic mayor (James W. Donchess) and is represented in Congress by a Democrat (Dick Swett).

Government

Year of Home Charter   1969
Number of Members of the Governing Body   15
Elected at Large   6
Elected by Wards   9
Number of Women in Governing Body   3
Salary of Mayor $67,094
Salary of Council Members $283
City Government Employment Total   1,938
Rate per 10,000   253.3

Public Finance

The annual city budget showed revenues of $117.616 million and expenditures of $105.905 million. The total outstanding debt is $40.23 million. Through sound fiscal management Nashua has avoided many of the problems faced by New England cities in general. Nashua has no state or sales taxes.

However, property taxes are higher than the national average, eating up 5.6% of personal income compared to 3.5% nationwide.

Public Finance

Total Revenue (in millions) $117.616
Intergovernmental Revenue—Total (in millions) $16.23
Federal Revenue per Capita $2.16
% Federal Assistance   1.84
% State Assistance   11.92
Sales Tax as % of Total Revenue   NA
Local Revenue as % of Total Revenue   85.51
City Income Tax   no
Taxes—Total (in millions) $42.7

Taxes per Capita
    Total $559
    Property $550
    Sales and Gross Receipts $0
General Expenditures—Total (in millions) $63.6
General Expenditures per Capita $831
Capital Outlays per Capita $61

% of Expenditures for:
    Public Welfare   0.9
    Highways   7.8
    Education   46.7
    Health and Hospitals   0.8
    Police   8.7
    Sewerage and Sanitation   4.9
    Parks and Recreation   1.4
    Housing and Community Development   0.0

Public Finance (continued)

Debt Outstanding per Capita $354
   % Utility   0.0
Federal Procurement Contract Awards (in millions)
   $254.9
Federal Grants Awards (in millions) $2.8
Fiscal Year Begins   July 1

Economy (continued)

Hotels and Motels (in millions) $32.6
Health Services (in millions)   83.8
Legal Services (in millions) $20.3

Economy

Nashua's strong economy escaped the general downturn in the Northeast in the early 1990s. In 1987 Nashua was rated as the best place to live in the United States by Money magazine, which cited the presence of high-tech firms, such as Lockheed, Digital Equipment, Kollsman, and Nashua Corp, and the lack of sales tax or income tax. Grant Thornton, a national accounting firm, has ranked Nashua as the number one manufacturing town based on education, transportation, and wage rates. Nashua is also the major retail, service, and financial center for southern Hillsborough County. Two Nashua firms appear on the Fortune 500 list: Sanders, a subsidiary of Lockheed, and Nashua Corp.

Economy

Total Money Income (in millions) $1,034.5
% of State Average   116.0
Per Capita Annual Income $13,521
% Population below Poverty Level   6.5
Fortune 500 Companies   NA

Banks	Number	Deposits (in millions)
Commercial	9	498.0
Savings	2	234.7

Passenger Autos   259,314
Electric Meters   38,771
Gas Meters   18,901

Manufacturing

Number of Establishments   164
% with 20 or More Employees   37.8
Manufacturing Payroll (in millions) $553.5
Value Added by Manufacture (in millions) $1,617.3
Value of Shipments (in millions) $1,984.6
New Capital Expenditures (in millions) $58.7

Wholesale Trade

Number of Establishments   178
Sales (in millions) $1,129.0
Annual Payroll (in millions) $75.871

Retail Trade

Number of Establishments   860
Total Sales (in millions) $1,159.4
Sales per Capita $15,154
Number of Retail Trade Establishments with Payroll   645
Annual Payroll (in millions) $124.1
Total Sales (in millions) $1,142.6
General Merchandise Stores (per capita) $3,037
Food Stores (per capita) $2,208
Apparel Stores (per capita) $1,052
Eating and Drinking Places (per capita) $855

Service Industries

Total Establishments   679
Total Receipts (in millions) $324.1

Labor

The fastest growing employment sectors are finance, real estate, insurance, and retail. Jobs in these areas grew at twice the rate of other sectors. Much of the growth came in small firms of fewer than 20 employees. About 40% of the work force is in high-tech. Wage rates are competitive. Further, employees have the option of commuting to nearby Massachusetts, where electronics firms dot Routes 495 and 128.

Labor

Civilian Labor Force   47,183
% Change 1989–1990   1.3

Work Force Distribution
   Mining   NA
   Construction   2,200
   Manufacturing   28,900
   Transportation and Public Utilities   2,600
   Wholesale and Retail Trade   19,000
   FIRE (Finance, Insurance, Real Estate)   3,600
   Service   17,800
   Government   7,600
   Women as % of Labor Force   44.3
   % Self-Employed   3.7
   % Professional/Technical   17.5
Total Unemployment   3,074
Rate %   6.5
Federal Government Civilian Employment   743

Education

Nashua has a strong public as well as Catholic school system, both with a healthy teacher/pupil ratio, and high funding per pupil. The Catholic parochial school system consists of two elementary schools and one junior high school as well as two secondary schools: Mount Saint Mary, the oldest Catholic secondary school in the state, and Bishop Guertin High School. The privately run Mount Hope School enrolls physically and mentally impaired pupils.

Higher education is provided primarily in two colleges: Daniel Webster College, founded in 1965, and Rivier College, a Catholic institution founded in 1933. Satellite campuses of many larger area colleges are located in the city. The New England Aeronautical Institute is the largest technical institute.

Education

Number of Public Schools   16
Special Education Schools   NA
Total Enrollment   10,480
% Enrollment in Private Schools   9.7
% Minority   NA

Education (continued)

Classroom Teachers   443
Pupil-Teacher Ratio   18:1
Number of Graduates   NA
Total Revenue (in millions)   NA
Total Expenditures (in millions)   NA
Expenditures per Pupil $2,800
Educational Attainment (Age 25 and Over)   NA
   % Completed 12 or More Years   72.4
   % Completed 16 or More Years   18.4
Four-Year Colleges and Universities   2
   Enrollment   3,685
Two-Year Colleges   1
   Enrollment   476

Libraries

Number   11
Public Libraries   2
Books (in thousands)   194
Circulation (in thousands)   636
Persons Served (in thousands)   78
Circulation per Person Served   8.15
Income (in millions) $1,414
Staff   32

Four-Year Colleges and Universities
   Daniel Webster College
   Rivier College

Health

There are two large hospitals in the Nashua metro area: St. Joseph's Hospital, a federally designated trauma center, including the New England Rehabilitation Center; the Nashua Memorial Hospital, and two facilities specializing in out-patient surgery. Brookside Hospital offers psychiatric care.

Health

Deaths—Total   538
Rate per 1,000   7.4
Infant Deaths—Total   13
Rate per 1,000   11.6
Number of Metro Hospitals   2
Number of Metro Hospital Beds   382
Rate per 100,000   499
Number of Physicians   NA
Physicians per 1,000   NA
Nurses per 1,000   NA
Health Expenditures per Capita $10.97

Transportation

The city's major thoroughfares are Main Street, running north-south through downtown, and Hollis Street, running east-west. Both streets have heavy rush-hour traffic.

Nashua is linked to the outside world by two highways: I-93, which passes by the city to the east and is connected to Nashua by the east-west New Hampshire Route 111, and the F. E. Everett Turnpike or Route 3 running north-south through the western part of the city. Commercial bus lines operating out of the Nashua Bus Terminal include Trailways.

Before World War II, Nashua had four railway depots, but with the decline of rail travel, only the Boston and Maine rail line runs through the city. Most of the freight is hauled by five motor freight carriers.

Nashua Airport, located at Boire Field just outside the northwestern city limit, is New Hampshire's busiest facility, although its runways tend to be too short for larger-sized passenger planes. Airport traffic consists of over 600 departures and arrivals daily, most of them private, business, and training flights. Boire Field is the site of the Federal Aviation Control Center, serving all of New England and upstate New York. International flights are handled by Boston's Logan International Airport, about 60 miles to the southeast, connected to Nashua by daily bus services.

Transportation

Interstate Highway Mileage   NA
Total Urban Mileage   387
Total Daily Vehicle Mileage (in millions) $1.727
Daily Average Commute Time   43.6 min.
Number of Buses   NA
Port Tonnage (in millions)   NA
Airports   NA
Number of Daily Flights   NA
Daily Average Number of Passengers   NA

Airlines (American carriers only)
   See Boston

Housing

Of the 31,051 occupied housing units in 1990, 57.7% were owner-occupied. The median value of owner-occupied homes was $138,800 and the median monthly rent was $574.

Housing

Total Housing Units   33,383
% Change 1980–1990   23.8
Vacant Units for Sale or Rent   2,057
Occupied Units   31,051
% with More Than One Person per Room   1.6
% Owner-Occupied   57.7
Median Value of Owner-Occupied Homes $138,800
Average Monthly Purchase Cost $443
Median Monthly Rent $574
New Private Housing Starts   79
Value (in thousands) $5,744
% Single-Family   97.5
Nonresidential Buildings Value (in thousands) $17,957

Urban Redevelopment

Urban redevelopment programs are directed by the Nashua Downtown Development Corporation, supported by the Southern New Hampshire Planning Commission, the Nashua–New Hampshire Foundation, the Nashua Regional Planning Commission, and the Nashua Division of Community Development. These programs are targeted at improving the infrastructure and expanding existing corporate and industrial activity. The major programs include the Hillsborough County Court House, a second bridge across the Merrimack River, and the construction of the $145-million Circumferential Highway linking Routes 3 and 3A. Another major priority is the construction of industrial and commercial parks, such as the Gateway Center and the Southwood Park. The Airport Industrial Zone is another area of accelerated development, and it reached maximum capacity in 1991. Because there are few developable, commercially zoned properties left in downtown Nashua, most development is concentrated in the industrial zones.

Crime

 Nashua is the 20th safest metropolitan area in the country, according to the U.S. Department of Justice. According to *Money* magazine, even valuables left in unlocked cars are rarely stolen. Of the crimes known to police in 1991, there were 76 violent crimes and 2,686 property crimes.

Crime	
Violent Crimes—Total 76	
Violent Crime Rate per 100,000 73.4	
Murder 3	
Rape 18	
Robbery 23	
Aggravated Assaults 32	
Property Crimes 2,686	
Burglary 434	
Larceny 1,966	
Motor Vehicle Theft 286	
Arson 30	
Per Capita Police Expenditures $115.52	
Per Capita Fire Protection Expenditures $87.09	
Number of Police 137	
Per 1,000 1.85	

Religion

 Catholicism, professed by most of the later immigrants, predominates, but all major Protestant denominations are well represented.

Religion	
Largest Denominations (Adherents)	
Catholic	117,237
United Church of Christ	9,247
United Methodist	3,873
Independent Charismatics	1,600
Episcopal	3,693
American Baptist	2,457
Latter-Day Saints	1,375
Presbyterian	1,330
Jewish	3,500

Media

Nashua's sole daily newspaper is the *Nashua Telegraph*, published by the independent Telegraph Publishing Company. Because of Boston's proximity, no notable periodicals are published in the city. There are no television stations in Nashua, which is served by Boston's extensive facilities. A local firm provides cable television. Radio programs are provided by one AM and one FM station.

Media
Newsprint
Broadcaster, weekly
Nashua Telegraph, daily
Television
See Boston
Radio
WHOB (FM)   WSMN (AM)

Sports

 Golf is played on two 18-hole courses: the Sky Meadow Golf Club, a public facility, and the private Nashua Country Club.

Arts, Culture, and Tourism

 The Nashua Ballet and the Nashua Symphony Orchestra are the city's principal cultural institutions. The latter is a 60-member professional group performing at the Elm Street Auditorium. The American Stage Festival at Milford, ten miles from the city, is noted for its plays and musicals.

The Arts and Science Center is a complex of arts facilities including a children's museum, two galleries, and a theater for concerts, films, and lectures. It is the home of some of Nashua's best performing groups, such as Kids into Drama Players, the Merrimack Valley Folk Association, the Rasmussen Jazz Band, and the Granite Statesmen. The Rivier College has an art gallery located in its Memorial Hall and it presents six exhibits annually, along with lectures, workshops, and films.

Travel and Tourism
Hotel Rooms   2,768
Convention and Exhibit Space (square feet)   NA
Convention Centers
Sheraton Tara
Clarion-Somerset
Holiday Inn
Comfort Inn
Festivals
Summerfest

Parks and Recreation

 The principal recreational activities are fishing (in the Nashua River and the many ponds), whitewater rafting (on the Contoocook River), camping and hiking (in the Silver Lake State Park), skiing (in the nearby White Mountains), biking, swimming, and water-sports. Besides the Silver Lake State Park, the principal recreational areas are Benson's Wild Animal Farm in Hudson, about ten miles outside the city, and Canobie Lark Park in nearby Salem. Twelve Clydesdale horses are the star attractions in the Anheuser Busch Brewery in nearby Merrimack.

Sources of Further Information

Director
Nashua School District
6 Main Street
Nashua, NH 03061
(603) 881-4300

Nashua Center for the Arts
14 Court Street
Nashua, NH 03060
(603) 883-1506

Nashua Historical Society
5 Abbot
Nashua, NH 03060
(603) 883-0015

Nashua Public Library
2 Court Street
Nashua, NH 03060
(603) 883-4141

Nashua Regional Planning Commission
115 Main Street
Nashua, NH 03060
(603) 883-0366

Nashua–New Hampshire Foundation
Chestnut and Factory Streets
Nashua, NH 03060
(603) 883-3991

New Hampshire Association of Commerce and
    Industry
1 Tara Boulevard, Suite 211
Nashua, NH 03062
(603) 891-2471

Public Information Office
City of Nashua
229 Main Street
Nashua, NH 03061-2019
(603) 880-3391

Additional Reading

Nashua–New Hampshire Cross Reference Directory.
    Annual.
Nashua Employment Conditions. Monthly.

Nashville

Tennessee

Location and Topography

Nashville, one of the nation's largest cities in area, is located on both banks of the Cumberland River in central Tennessee. It is bounded on three sides by the escarpment of the Highland Rim. The rim rises 400 feet above the mean elevation of the basin, forming an amphitheater around the city from southwest to southeast. The J. Percy Priest Lake and the Old Hickory Lake lie to the east of the city.

Layout of City and Suburbs

As in every state capital, the capitol dominates the central city. Downtown Nashville is the most crowded part of the city, with the older business buildings on the public square, near the river. There are few exclusively industrial sections. Residential areas predominate in the north and east, spilling over into suburbs, such as Belle Meade, Green Hills, and Harpeth Hills.

Environment

Environmental Stress Index 2.8
Green Cities Index: Rank 38
               Score 30.38
Water Quality Alkaline, soft
Average Daily Use (gallons per capita) 239
   Maximum Supply (gallons per capita) 459
Parkland as % of Total City Area 1.9
% Waste Landfilled/Recycled 60:5 Incinerated 35
Annual Parks Expenditures per Capita $59.12

Climate

Nashville has a moderate climate with few extremes of temperatures. The humidity is moderate compared to other locations in the southeast. Nashville generally escapes severe storms and hurricanes, yet is subject to thunderstorms from March through September. Rainfall is heaviest in winter and early spring. Snowfall is not unusual in winter, but is rarely heavy.

Weather

Temperature

Highest Monthly Average °F 89.2
Lowest Monthly Average °F 29.0

Weather (continued)

Annual Averages

Days 32°F or Below 75
Days above 90°F 37
Zero Degree Days 1
Precipitation (inches) 46.0
Snow (inches) 10.7
% Seasonal Humidity 71
Wind Speed (m.p.h.) 7.9
Clear Days 103
Cloudy Days 155
Storm Days 55
Rainy Days 119

Average Temperatures (°F)	High	Low	Mean
January	47.6	29.0	38.3
February	50.9	31.0	41.0
March	59.2	38.1	48.7
April	71.3	48.8	60.1
May	79.8	57.3	68.5
June	87.5	65.7	76.6
July	90.2	69.0	79.6
August	89.2	67.7	78.5
September	83.5	60.5	72.0
October	72.2	48.6	60.9
November	59.0	37.7	48.4
December	49.6	31.1	40.4

History

The Cumberland Valley was the domain of the Shawnee Indians whose palisaded villages occupied the bluffs along the river. The first whites to reach the area were French fur traders who built trading posts in the dense woods. In 1767 five Long Hunters (so called because they spent months at a time on hunting) from East Tennessee entered the Cumberland Valley. Their glowing reports of a fertile and well-watered land inspired others to follow suit. Between 1765 and 1775 Henry Scaggs, James Smith, Kasper Mansker, Isaac Bledsoe, and others extensively explored this region. One of the parties found Timothe DeMonbreun, an Illinois Frenchman, operating a trading post in a cave on the Cumberland River. In 1775 Robert Henderson, one of the greatest land speculators of his time, acting through his agent Daniel Boone, purchased 20 million acres from the Cherokee, in what is known as the Transylvania Purchase. North Carolina and Virginia opposed the purchase and Henderson lost it. However, a tract of 200,000 acres, part of which lay in the Cumberland Valley, was granted to Henderson as compensation. In the spring of 1779 Henderson sent James Robertson, whom Andrew Jackson called the Father of Tennessee, into the valley. He selected a site at French Lick, or Big Lick, now Sulphur Dell Baseball Park, where he and his party built a few cabins and planted a field of corn at Sulphur Bottom near the Lick. Robertson then returned to the Watauga and bought the title to the site from the Transylvania promoters and made himself trustee for the new settlement. In the fall of 1779 Robertson led a team of 300 pioneers to the settlement. One party, led by Robertson, came overland, driving a herd of horses, cattle, and sheep. They reached the bluff on Christmas Day, 1779. The other party, bringing women and children and household goods, came by flatboat down the Tennessee to the Ohio and then up the Cumberland. The flotilla of 30-odd flatboats reached its destination on 24 April 1780. The new settlement consisted of seven stations or forts along the Cumberland River. The French Lock Station, called Fort Nashborough after General Francis Nash, a Revolutionary War hero, was the center community. The Cumberland Compact, signed by 256 of the 300 settlers, provided for a government by a council of representative notables or general arbitrators. Two men chosen from each station formed a Committee of Guardians of which Robertson was the head. Months later the settlers found themselves swept up in the Revolutionary War on its western front. Incited by the British, the Indians turned on the white settlers, and not until the end of the war did conditions return to normal. In 1784 the North Carolina State Legislature set aside a 250-acre site on the west side of the Cumberland River, including Fort Nashborough, renamed Nashville because of prejudice against the English-sounding borough. Settlers came in great numbers along the Wilderness Road to the new town. They faced hostile raids from the Chickamauga until an expedition under Major General James Ore crushed the tribe. James Robertson helped to establish the Davidson Academy, which eventually became the University of Nashville. In 1787 Nashville's first newspaper, the *Tennessee Gazette and Mero District Advertizer*, was established, followed two years later by the *Rights of Man or Nashville Intelligencer*. The town was chartered as a city in 1806 with a mayor and six aldermen. The state legislature met here from 1812 to 1817 and from 1827 onward. In 1843 Nashville officially became the state capital. With the coming of the first steamboat in 1818, Nashville entered on a profitable era of river trade. By 1825 when the population reached 3,460, a stone bridge went up over the Cumberland and the town became a shipping center for cotton. In 1850 a suspension bridge was built. The Nashville, Chattanooga and St. Louis Railway was completed in 1854. In 1843 construction began on a new state capitol on the summit of the city's highest hill. It was designed in neo-Classic style by William Strickland who designed a number of other distinguished buildings in Nashville. During this period, Nashville reached the zenith of its prosperity. A medical school was founded, the Adelphi Theater opened, and a Board of Education was established.

The Civil War brought the city's progress to a halt as it became a supply arsenal for the Confederate Army. It was captured by Union troops under General Don Carlos Buell on 24 February 1862. Within a month Andrew Johnson, then U.S. senator, was appointed military governor of Tennessee. When the mayor and the city council refused to take the oath of allegiance to the Union, they were replaced with Loyalists. The city was placed under martial law and newspapers were confiscated. In 1864 Confederate General Thomas E. Hood made a desperate attempt to retake the town. The ensuing Battle of Nashville was one of

Chronology

1767 Five Long Hunters visit the Cumberland Valley and return home with glowing tales of its fertility.

1770 Kasper Mansker and others lead another party to the region to scout for settlement sites.

1775 Richard Henderson makes one of the largest land purchases (20 million acres) through his agent Daniel Boone, which becomes known as the Transylvania Purchase. North Carolina and Virginia oppose the deal and Henderson is granted 200,000 acres in Cumberland Valley as compensation.

1779 Henderson sends James Robertson, called the Father of Tennessee by Andrew Jackson, to blaze the way for another land promotion scheme. Robertson selects a site at French Lick or Big Lick where he and his party build a few cabins and plant a field of corn in Sulphur Bottom. Robertson returns to Watauga where he purchases the site from the Transylvania promoters, with Robertson serving as trustee for the community. Robertson, along with the men driving a herd of horses, sheep, and cattle, returns to the bluff on Christmas Day.

1780 Women and children and household goods come to the settlement in a flotilla of 30 flatboats sailing down the Tennessee to the Ohio and then up the Cumberland. The settlers divide themselves into seven stations, or forts, along the Cumberland River, of which the French Lick station called Nashborough is the center. The settlers sign the Cumberland Compact, establishing a form of government with representative notables, or general arbitrators.

1784 Legislature of North Carolina sets aside 250 acres on the west side of the Cumberland River as a town to be known as Nashville, rather than Nashborough.

1787 Nashville's first newspaper, *Tennessee Gazette and Mero District Advertizer*, is established.

1789 Nashville's second newspaper, *Rights of Man or the Nashville Intelligencer* is founded.

1802 George Poyzer opens a cotton spinning mill.

1806 Nashville is chartered as a city.

1812 Seat of state legislature is moved to Nashville from Knoxville.

1817 Legislative seat returns to Knoxville.

1818 First steamboat reaches Nashville.

1825 First stone bridge spans the Cumberland River.

1827 Legislative seat returns to Nashville.

1843 Nashville is selected as state capital.

1850 Suspension bridge is built over the Cumberland. Southern Convention meets in Nashville in an effort to preserve the Union.

1854 Nashville, Chattanooga and St. Louis Railroad is completed.

1861 Tennessee secedes from the Union and Nashville becomes a Confederate supply arsenal.

1862 Union Army under General Don Carlos Buell captures Nashville. Senator Andrew Johnson is named Military Governor of Tennessee.

1864 Confederate attack on Nashville is repulsed by Union forces. In Battle of Nashville, Confederate Army is virtually wiped out.

1866 Nashville suffers first of two cholera epidemics.

1873 Fisk and Vanderbilt universities are founded.

1897 President McKinley opens the Centennial Exposition.

1963 Nashville City and Davidson County merge to form the first consolidated metro-government in the nation.

the bloodiest confrontations between North and South, and the last major conflict of the Civil War. After the Civil War recovery was slow because of the corrupt carpetbagger government and two cholera epidemics in 1866 and 1873. After 1875 the city regained lost ground and also made rapid strides. Vanderbilt and Fisk universities were established in 1873. The Maxwell Hotel was constructed. To celebrate the centennial of its founding, Nashville held a gigantic exposition that was opened by President McKinley in 1897. The exposition was visited by 6 million people. Nashville also became the Country Music Capital, and the Grand Ole Opry became the anchor of the new music recording and performing industry. In 1963 the city consolidated its government with that of Davidson County to become the first metro-government in the nation.

Historical Landmarks

 The State Capitol on Cedar Street is on Capitol Hill, the highest point in the city. The building follows the plan of an Ionic temple. The pedimented porticos on each facade are modeled after those of the Erectheum in Athens. William Strickland, who designed the capitol, also designed St. Mary's Roman Catholic Church on Fifth Avenue, completed in 1847. Surmounting the structure is an octagonal tower topped with a circular cupola. The First Presbyterian Church on the corner of Church Street and Fifth Street was also designed by William Strickland in a modified-Egyptian style with two 104-foot towers. It was built during the Civil War years to replace two earlier ones built in 1816 and 1832. The McKendree Methodist Church on Church Street is in Italian Renaissance style. It was completed in 1912, replacing earlier ones built in 1789 and 1812. The First Christian Science Church on Seventh Avenue, built in 1856–1871, is of pointed Gothic style. It was erected by the Episcopal Church of the Advent in 1866 and bought by the Christian Science congregation in the early 1900s. Christ Episcopal Church on Broadway is a Victorian Gothic built in 1887–1892 with exterior decorations resembling those of English cathedrals. The Roman Catholic Cathedral of the Incarnation on West End Avenue is a group of three buildings designed after famous Italian churches. The Holy Trinity Church on Sixth Avenue and Ewing Street was built in 1852 on the model of English parish churches. The First Lutheran Church on Fifth Avenue was built for a Baptist congregation in 1838 but purchased by the Lutherans in 1884. It is built in Gothic Revival style. Fort Nashborough on Church Street and First Avenue was built in 1930 on the model of the original built by James Robertson and his party on this site in 1780. The log blockhouses are inside a stockade of black locust logs. The John Bell Home on Broadway, built in 1857, was the home of the U.S. senator who was the presidential candidate of the Constitutional Union Party, defeated by Lincoln in the 1860 elections. The home of William Walker on the corner of Fourth Avenue and Commerce Street is indicated by a marker. Walker was a soldier of fortune who seized the government of Nicaragua in a filibustering expedition in the 1860s and became its president. When he invaded British Honduras he was captured by British marines and executed by a firing squad. Maxwell House, after which a popular brand of coffee was named, stands on the corner of Fourth Avenue and Church Street. Built by Colonel John Overton, and hence known also as Overton's Folly, it was one of the largest hotels in the state and its balcony, on a colonnaded portico, was used as a reviewing stand for all parades. In 1867 the Ku Klux Klan was founded here. Westwood on Westwood Drive, the home of Robert Woods, is built of large wooden blocks. Sunnyside on Kirkwood Lane and 12th Avenue was built in 1840 and is one of the finest examples of antebellum architecture in middle Tennessee. The house was in the line of fire during the Battle of Nashville. Fort Negley on Chestnut Street and Ridley Boulevard was erected by the Federal General James S. Negley in 1862 and restored in 1937 by WPA. The guns of Fort Negley opened the Battle of Nashville in 1864. During the Reconstruction, the abandoned fort was used as a meeting place for the Ku Klux Klan. The Natchez Trace Marker on West End Avenue facing Centennial Park is at the junction of the Old Wilderness Road from Knoxville and the Natchez Trace Road to Natchez, Mississippi. Originally the Natchez Trace Road was used by the Indian tribes to reach the rich hunting grounds of Tennessee and Kentucky. The Hume-Fogg High School on the corner of Broadway and Eighth Avenue is on the site of the first meeting place of the Tennessee Legislature in Nashville. The Vine Street Temple on Seventh Avenue is a Jewish synagogue built in 1876. The site of President Polk's home, on the corner of Union Street and Seventh Avenue, was built by Senator Felix Grundy who sold it to Polk in 1840. The War Memorial Building on Capitol Boulevard, completed in 1925, is a neo-Classic limestone structure bearing the names of the Tennessee dead in World War I. It includes the World War Museum and the State Historical Museum. The Hermitage, the home of President Andrew Jackson, is an 1819 plantation house designated as a national shrine. Belle Meade Mansion on the west side is a restored antebellum farm called the Queen of Tennessee Plantations.

Population

Nashville has expanded steadily in population since World War II. From 426,000 in 1970 it grew by 7% in the 1970s to reach 455,651 in 1980 and then by a further 7.2% to reach 488,374 in 1990. The formation of a consolidated city in 1963, including Davidson County, was one of the primary factors in the demographic expansion.

Population		
	1980	*1990*
Central City	455,651	488,374
Rank	25	25
Metro Area	850,505	985,026
Pop. Change 1980–1990 +32,723		
Pop. % Change 1980–1990 +7.2		
Median Age 32.3		
% Male 47.4		
% Age 65 and Over 11.4		
Density (per square mile) 1,065		

Households		
Number 198,585		
Persons per Household 2.35		
% Female-Headed Households 14.5		
% One-Person Households 30.7		
Births—Total 7,232		
% to Mothers under 20 14.9		
Birth Rate per 1,000 15.6		

Ethnic Composition

Whites make up 73.8%, blacks 24.3%, American Indians 0.2%, Asians and Pacific Islanders 1.4%, and others 0.3%.

Ethnic Composition (as % of total pop.)		
	1980	1990
White	75.69	73.77
Black	23.25	24.29
American Indian	0.12	0.23
Asian and Pacific Islander	0.48	1.4
Hispanic	0.80	0.95
Other	NA	0.3

Government

The consolidated city is governed by a metro mayor/council form of government. Voters elect 40 council members, 35 from wards and 5 at large.

Government

Year of Home Charter   1963
Number of Members of the Governing Body   40
Elected at Large   5
Elected by Wards   35
Number of Women in Governing Body   3
Salary of Mayor $75,000
Salary of Council Members $5,562
City Government Employment Total   18,040
Rate per 10,000   380.9

Public Finance

The annual budget consists of revenues of $1.546 billion and expenditures of $1.504 billion. Debt outstanding is $2.330 billion and cash and security holdings of $2.079 billion.

Public Finance

Total Revenue (in millions) $1,546.8
Intergovernmental Revenue—Total (in millions) $182.72
Federal Revenue per Capita $13.68
% Federal Assistance   0.88
% State Assistance   10.91
Sales Tax as % of Total Revenue   10.44
Local Revenue as % of Total Revenue   47.43
City Income Tax   no
Taxes—Total (in millions) $271.4

Taxes per Capita
   Total $573
   Property $273
   Sales and Gross Receipts $247
General Expenditures—Total (in millions) $561.4
General Expenditures per Capita $1,185
Capital Outlays per Capita $220

% of Expenditures for:
   Public Welfare   1.0
   Highways   3.2
   Education   33.0
   Health and Hospitals   8.0

Public Finance (continued)

   Police   7.1
   Sewerage and Sanitation   15.9
   Parks and Recreation   3.9
   Housing and Community Development   2.0
Debt Outstanding per Capita $2,485
   % Utility   35.2
Federal Procurement Contract Awards (in millions) $79.0
Federal Grants Awards (in millions) $352.2
Fiscal Year Begins   October 1

Economy

Nashville is a city of small businesses. Over the years some of its small businesses have gone on to become giants elsewhere, including American Express, Kentucky Fried Chicken, and Maxwell House Coffee. The insurance complex, American General Corporation (AGC), dominates the economic landscape and includes both the National Life and Accident Insurance Company and the Life and Casualty Insurance Company, whose corporate headquarters are the tallest buildings in the city. AGC also owns the entertainment empire that comprises Grand Ole Opry, Opryland Amusement Park, and Opryland Hotel. Nashville has a foothold in the brokerage and investment business through J. C. Bradford, Security Federal, and Massey-Burch Investment Group. Nashville is one of the largest centers in the South for printing and publishing. The city is the home of Thomas Nelson, one of the world's largest publishers of Bibles. Nashville's manufacturing output is varied and includes Nissan trucks, work clothes, shoes, lawnmowers, bicycles, telecommunications equipment, and aerospace products. The music industry, however, is what secures Nashville's fame. The mecca of country music and the recording industry, "Music Row" is represented by RCA, MCA, CBS, Warner Brothers, and Polygram (to name a few), and it brings in over half a billion dollars a year. It also brings in tourists and music lovers, generating further revenues.

Economy

Total Money Income (in millions) $5,330.2
% of State Average   121.1
Per Capita Annual Income $11,253
% Population below Poverty Level   12.6
Fortune 500 Companies   NA

Banks	Number	Deposits (in millions)
Commercial	8	6,800
Savings	7	NA

Passenger Autos   374,400
Electric Meters   NA
Gas Meters   NA

Manufacturing

Number of Establishments   827
% with 20 or More Employees   35.3
Manufacturing Payroll (in millions)   NA
Value Added by Manufacture (in millions)   NA
Value of Shipments (in millions)   NA
New Capital Expenditures (in millions)   NA

Economy (continued)

Wholesale Trade

Number of Establishments   1,454
Sales (in millions) $8,124.5
Annual Payroll (in millions) $552.492

Retail Trade

Number of Establishments   5,156
Total Sales (in millions) $4,481.1
Sales per Capita $9,460.0
Number of Retail Trade Establishments with Payroll   3,414
Annual Payroll (in millions) $538.6
Total Sales (in millions) $4,397.4
General Merchandise Stores (per capita) $1,383
Food Stores (per capita) $1,402
Apparel Stores (per capita) $474
Eating and Drinking Places (per capita) $1,067

Service Industries

Total Establishments   4,633
Total Receipts (in millions) $2,678.4
Hotels and Motels (in millions)   NA
Health Services (in millions) $670.3
Legal Services (in millions) $157.0

Labor

Nashville has a balanced employment market where all sectors are equally well represented. Trade and services make up nearly 50% of the labor force, but FIRE and manufacturing sectors claim larger than average shares. As the state capital, government figures prominently, with the city, state, and federal governments being the top three employers.

Labor

Civilian Labor Force   273,823
% Change 1989–1990   NA

Work Force Distribution
   Mining   NA
   Construction   20,500
   Manufacturing   86,300
   Transportation and Public Utilities   28,500
   Wholesale and Retail Trade   121,700
   FIRE (Finance, Insurance, Real Estate)   30,900
   Service   136,500
   Government   68,900
   Women as % of Labor Force   46.3
   % Self-Employed   4.6
   % Professional/Technical   17.4
Total Unemployment   NA
Rate %   NA
Federal Government Civilian Employment   6,295

Education

The Nashville metro public system supports 82 elementary schools, 20 junior high/middle schools, 13 senior high schools, and 5 special education schools. Forty-nine private and parochial schools enroll 20% of school-going children. The higher education sector is paced by Vanderbilt University, one of the South's foremost institu-

tions. The university was chartered in 1872 by the Methodist Episcopal Church South as the Central University, and continued under church control until 1914. In 1873 Cornelius Vanderbilt made a $1-million endowment, and the name was changed to Vanderbilt University. Subsequently the university received large endowments from the Rockefeller and Carnegie foundations. The George Peabody College for Teachers was founded in 1875 as a liberal arts college under the name of the University of Nashville. It has 12 buildings on a 50-acre campus. Belmont College was formed as a merger between Ward Seminary, established in 1865, and Belmont College, established in 1890. The college is located in Belmont, the former home of J. A. S. Acklen, built in 1850 and considered to be one of the finest homes in the South. Fisk University, chartered in 1867, is one of the largest black institutions in the nation. Meharry Medical College, adjoining Fisk University, is also an institution for blacks. The principal public institutions are the two campuses of the Tennessee State University.

Education

Number of Public Schools   120
Special Education Schools   5
Total Enrollment   68,452
% Enrollment in Private Schools   12.2
% Minority   41.2
Classroom Teachers   3,943
Pupil-Teacher Ratio   17.3:1
Number of Graduates   3,028
Total Revenue (in millions) $236.357
Total Expenditures (in millions) $284.243
Expenditures per Pupil $3,580
Educational Attainment (Age 25 and Over)
   % Completed 12 or More Years   65.4
   % Completed 16 or More Years   18.6
Four-Year Colleges and Universities   9
   Enrollment   25,675
Two-Year Colleges   6
   Enrollment   8,397

Libraries

Number   72
Public Libraries   17
Books (in thousands)   657
Circulation (in thousands)   1,820
Persons Served (in thousands)   510
Circulation per Person Served   3.56
Income (in millions) $7.813
Staff   205

Four-Year Colleges and Universities
   American Baptist University
   Vanderbilt University
   Fisk University
   Meharry Medical College
   Belmont University
   Tennessee State University
   David Lipscomb College
   Free Will Baptist Bible College
   Trevecca Nazarene College

Health

The Vanderbilt Medical Center and the associated Vanderbilt Children's Hospital, Baptist Hospital, and the St. Thomas

Hospital, run by the Daughters of Charity of St. Vincent de Paul, are the premier medical institutions in Nashville. There are also 14 other hospitals, including Hubbard Hospital of the Meharry Medical College, Veterans Administration Medical Center, the city-run Metropolitan Medical Hospital, and Nashville Memorial Hospital, a community hospital founded in 1965.

Health

Deaths—Total   4,213
Rate per 1,000   9.1
Infant Deaths—Total   90
Rate per 1,000   12.4
Number of Metro Hospitals   15
Number of Metro Hospital Beds   5,122
Rate per 100,000   1,081
Number of Physicians   2,313
Physicians per 1,000   2.72
Nurses per 1,000   9.62
Health Expenditures per Capita $35.56

Transportation

Nashville is approached by three major interstates: the north-south I-65 and I-40, and the east-west I-24. In addition, I-265 serves as an inner city loop and I-440 as an outer city loop. Rail freight services are provided by CSX and Southern. Nashville is a major river port on the Cumberland River, an artery of the Ohio River connected with the Mississippi and the Gulf of Mexico by the Tennessee-Tombigbee Waterway. The principal air terminal is the Metropolitan Nashville Airport, about eight miles from downtown.

Transportation

Interstate Highway Mileage   96
Total Urban Mileage   2,822
Total Daily Vehicle Mileage (in millions) $15.403
Daily Average Commute Time   49.3 min.
Number of Buses   81
Port Tonnage (in millions) $3.3
Airports   1
Number of Daily Flights   168
Daily Average Number of Passengers   10,264

Airlines (American carriers only)
American
Delta
Eastern
Northwest
Trans World
United
USAir

Housing

Of the total housing stock, 52.8% is owner-occupied. The median value of an owner-occupied home is $74,400 and the median monthly rent $358.

Housing

Total Housing Units   219,528
% Change 1980–1990   18.4
Vacant Units for Sale or Rent   17,844
Occupied Units   198,585
% with More Than One Person per Room   2.6
% Owner-Occupied   52.8
Median Value of Owner-Occupied Homes $74,400
Average Monthly Purchase Cost $307
Median Monthly Rent $358
New Private Housing Starts   1,597
Value (in thousands) $111,602
% Single-Family   75
Nonresidential Buildings Value (in thousands) $169,793

Tallest Buildings	*Hgt. (ft.)*	*Stories*
Third National Financial Center	490	30
American General Center	452	31
Landmark Center	409	30
Nashville City Center (1987)	402	27
James K. Polk State Office Bldg.	392	32
Stouffer Hotel (1987)	385	35
First American Center	354	28
One Nashville Plaza	346	23

Urban Redevelopment

Urban redevelopment programs are coordinated by the Nashville/Davidson County Planning Commission. The metro government has undertaken large renovation projects that are still in progress. Second Avenue, once a row of dilapidated turn-of-the-century warehouses, has become a bustling shopping district. The Hermitage Hotel has been refurbished. Renovation also has come to the Union Station on Broadway, one of Nashville's best known landmarks. The Nashville Convention Center was completed in the 1980s, a decade that also saw the building of the Third National Financial Center and the Nashville Place. Projects planned for the 1990s include the Ryman Center Project.

Crime

Nashville ranks low in public safety. Of the crimes known to police in 1991, there were 7,989 violent crimes and 35,969 property crimes.

Crime

Violent Crimes—Total   7,989
Violent Crime Rate per 100,000   1,014
Murder   88
Rape   514
Robbery   2,648
Aggravated Assaults   4,739
Property Crimes   35,969
Burglary   10,321
Larceny   21,807
Motor Vehicle Theft   3,841
Arson   NA
Per Capita Police Expenditures $112.72
Per Capita Fire Protection Expenditures $67.89
Number of Police   984
Per 1,000   2.04

Religion

Nashville has a high concentration of Southern Protestant denominations, such as Southern Baptists, who form 20% of the population. The Methodist and Church of Christ denominations each make up 10% of churchgoers. Catholics and other Protestant denominations are all represented in the city, but with less than 5%.

Religion	
Largest Denominations (Adherents)	
Catholic	23,514
Churches of Christ	41,607
Southern Baptist	101,508
Black Baptist	48,213
United Methodist	36,991
Presbyterian	11,287
Assembly of God	3,931
Church of the Nazarene	7,243
Independent Charismatics	4,325
Jewish	2,887

Media

The Nashville press consists of *The Tennessean* in the morning and the *Nashville Banner* in the evening. The electronic media consist of 6 television stations and 18 AM and FM radio stations, including WSM where Grand Ole Opry was born.

Media	
Newsprint	
Nashville Banner, daily	
Nashville Business Journal, weekly	
The Tennessean, daily	
Television	
WDCN (Channel 8)	
WKRN (Channel 2)	
WSMV (Channel 4)	
WTVF (Channel 5)	
WXMT (Channel 30)	
WZTV (Channel 17)	
Radio	
WAMB (AM)	WKDA (AM)
WKDF (FM)	WLAC (AM)
WLAC (FM)	WMDB (AM)
WNAH (AM)	WNAZ (FM)
WNQM (AM)	WPLN (FM)
WRVU (FM)	WSIX (FM)
WSM (AM)	WSM (FM)
WVOL (AM)	WYCQ (FM)
WYFN (AM)	WZEZ (FM)

Sports

In the absence of a major professional sports team, college teams supply most of the sports action. The Commodores of Vanderbilt University and the Tigers of the Tennessee State University are the local football teams. Vanderbilt has outstanding teams in basketball and tennis. The Nashville Sounds are a local AAA minor league

baseball club that is a farm team for the Detroit Tigers. The Iroquois Memorial Steeplechase heralds spring every year at Percy Warner Park. On weekends Nashville Raceway is the scene of stockcar races culminating in the Winston Cup Grand National in late October.

Arts, Culture, and Tourism

The cultural hub of Nashville is the Tennessee Performing Arts Center (TPAC), the home of the Nashville Symphony, the Circle Players, and Southern Stage Productions. TPAC is built in a distinctive cantilevered style without columns and houses three acoustically advanced theaters. One of the oldest companies in town is the Nashville Academy Theater, commonly known as the Children's Theater. The John Galt Westend Theater is a small experimental theater near the Vanderbilt. But Nashville's theater is overshadowed by its music, which bears its true signature. Musical groups appear on a variety of stages throughout the city. The Grand Ole Opry, the best known name in Nashville, is the nation's oldest and most listened-to country music radio show. What TPAC is to theater, the Cheekwood Fine Arts Center is to the visual arts. It is housed in a magnificent 60-room Georgian mansion on a 55-acre complex that once belonged to businessman Leslie Cheek. Fisk University's Van Vechten Gallery houses the Alfred Stieglitz Art Collection donated by Stieglitz's widow, Georgia O'Keeffe. The Country Music Hall of Fame and Museum, one of the South's most visited museums, is located in a chapel-like building. The State Museum on Capitol Plaza is noted for its Civil War collection. The state's natural history is showcased in the Cumberland Museum and Science Center.

Travel and Tourism
Hotel Rooms   22,046
Convention and Exhibit Space (square feet)
Convention Centers
Opryland Hotel
Nashville Convention Center
Ryman Auditorium
Vanderbilt Plaza Hotel
Maxwell House Hotel
Nashville Marriott
Festivals
Summer Lights Festival
Volunteer Jam (February)

Parks and Recreation

Nashville has 7,800 acres of city, state, and federal parks within city limits. The largest is the 2,665-acre Warner Park on the southwest, donated by Edwin and Percy Warner. Victory Park is a small park on Sixth Avenue. The 361-acre Shelby Park contains several log houses and iris gardens. In the Cherokee Park on 62nd Street is the

Treaty Oak under which, in June 1783, the white settlers under James Robertson met delegations from principal southern tribes in a peace council lasting three days.

Sources of Further Information

City Hall
107 Metropolitan Courthouse
Nashville, TN 37201
(615) 862-6000

Nashville Area Chamber of Commerce
161 Fourth Avenue
Nashville, TN 37219
(615) 259-4755

Additional Reading

Adams, George R. *Nashville: A Pictorial History.* 1988.
Blumstein, James F., and Benjamin Walter. *Growing Metropolis: Apects of Development in Nashville.* 1975.
Dick, Margaret E. *Upbeat and Down to Business.* 1990.
Doyle, Don H. *Nashville in the New South, 1880–1930.* 1985.
Durham, Walter T. *Reluctant Partners: Nashville and the Union.* 1987.
Goodstein, Anita S. *Nashville, 1789–1860. From Frontier to City.* 1989.
Hoss, E. E., and William B. Reese. *A History of Nashville, Tennessee.* 1970.
Lynch, Amy. *Nashville.* 1991.
Nashville Since the 1920s. 1985.
Pride, Richard A, and David J. Woodard. *The Burden of Busing: The Politics of Desegregation in Nashville.* 1985.
Sherman, Joe. *A Thousand Voices: The Story of Nashville's Union Station.* 1987.
Thomas, Jane H., and J. G. Ramsey. *Old Days in Nashville.* 1980.
Tipps, H. T. *Seven Early Churches of Nashville.* 1972.

New Haven

Connecticut

Location and Topography

New Haven is located in south-central Connecticut at the head of the New Haven Bay on Long Island Sound, and at the mouth of the Quinnipiac, Mill, and West rivers. It is bounded by the New Haven Harbor on the southeast, and the Merritt Parkway on the northwest. The downtown area near the harbor is flat land rising gradually to rolling hills and rocky outcroppings to the west.

Layout of City and Suburbs

New Haven is celebrated as the elm-lined city. The outstanding feature of the downtown area is the broad 16-acre Green, its trinity of churches standing in stately dignity with the Yale University buildings providing a backdrop to the west. Facing the other sides of the Green are large public office and commercial buildings. To the north and west of the Green are the principal residential districts with most of the university buildings and more congested dwelling areas broken by small parks and squares. New Haven's shore front is largely given over to business buildings and wharves. To the southeast there is considerable beach development at Nathan Hale Park, Morris Cove, and Lighthouse Point. The harbor entrance is protected by three strips of breakwater. The approaches to the harbor are difficult to navigate except at high tide.

Most of New Haven's residential districts were built in the earlier centuries and have undergone renovation. Typical is Wooster Square, where most of the houses were built in the 1840s as fashionable residences. It remained the exclusive domain of the wealthy until the late 1800s, when row houses were added, causing the wealthy to move out. At the turn of the century it became the settling place for Italian immigrants. By 1970 the neighborhood, now seriously run down, was chosen as the nation's first urban redevelopment project. By 1980 many of the old homes were restored to their former splendor and the wealthy began to move back. Upper State Street is another born-again neighborhood. A crude dirt road when New Haven was founded in 1638, it was a popular shopping center at the turn of the century, but then declined. A renaissance began in 1977 when the street was designated as a historic district. Much of its original character has been restored.

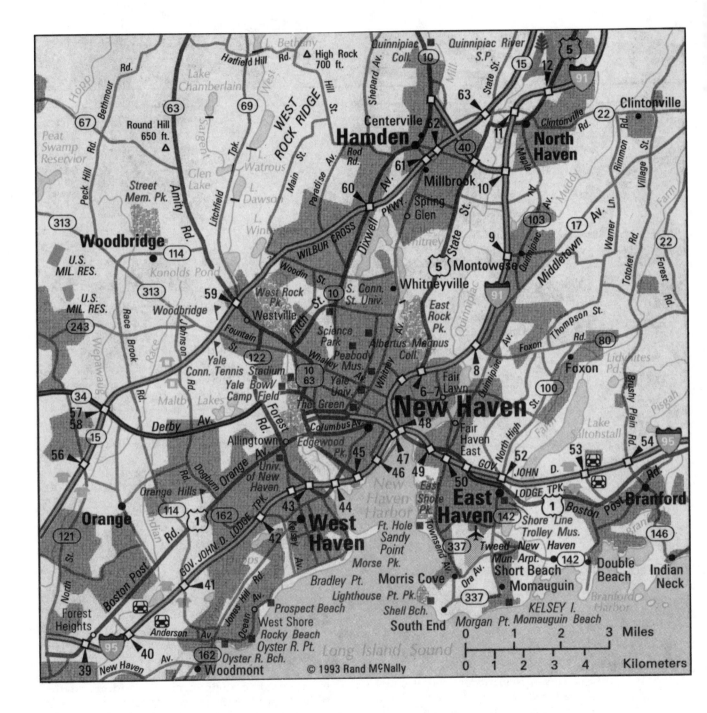

From the *Road Atlas* © 1993 by Rand McNally R.L. 93-S-92.

Environment

Environmental Stress Index   2.8
Green Cities Index: Rank   NA
                    Score   NA
Water Quality   Neutral, soft
     Average Daily Use (gallons per capita)   140
     Maximum Supply (gallons per capita)   413
Parkland as % of Total City Area   NA
% Waste Landfilled/Recycled   NA
Annual Parks Expenditures per Capita $60.60

Climate

 New Haven's climate is influenced by its location on Long Island Sound. Winters are generally mild with less snow accumulation while the summers are warm and humid. Rainfall is spread evenly throughout the year.

Weather

Temperature

Highest Monthly Average °F   60.5
Lowest Monthly Average °F   38.0

Annual Averages

Days 32°F or Below   145
Days above 90°F   4
Zero Degree Days   5
Precipitation (inches)   46.90
Snow (inches)   30.1
% Seasonal Humidity   NA
Wind Speed (m.p.h.)   NA
Clear Days   NA
Cloudy Days   NA
Storm Days   NA
Rainy Days   NA

Average Temperatures (°F)	High	Low	Mean
January	38.2	17.4	27.8
February	40.3	19.5	29.9
March	47.0	26.2	36.6
April	59.0	34.2	46.6
May	68.4	43.1	55.7
June	76.8	53.1	65.0
July	81.5	59.2	70.4
August	80.4	57.7	69.1
September	74.4	51.1	62.8
October	65.2	40.6	52.9
November	53.2	31.8	42.5
December	42.0	21.7	31.9

History

Discovered in 1614 by Adriaen Block, who called it Rodeberg (meaning Red Mount Place), New Haven was first settled by white men on 10 April 1638, when the Reverend John Davenport, a Puritan minister and Theophilius Eaton, a prominent merchant of his congregation, led a band of pioneers to this port from Boston. At first called Quinnipiac, after the local Native American tribe, the name was changed in August 1640 to New Haven, for the English seaport in Sussex. The initial land purchase included not only the site of the present city, but the districts now known as North Haven, Wallingford, Cheshire, Hamden, Bethany, Woodbridge, and Orange, for which the Indians were paid 23 coats, 12 spoons, 24 knives, 12 hatchets, scissors, some hoes, and porringers. The colony was laid out in nine squares. The central square was set aside as a common green for a daytime market and night pasture, and about this green the colonists built their homes. Shortly after their arrival, the settlers adopted a Plantation Covenant binding themselves to be governed solely by the law of Moses. On 4 June 1639, a constitution was adopted that ignored allegiance to the king, all statutes of common law, and trial by jury. The Word of God was to be the absolute rule. Seven Pillars were elected, to head both the church and the state government, and only members of the church were allowed to vote. On 25 October 1639, the Seven Pillars elected Theophilius Eaton as the first governor of the New Haven Colony. It was a theocracy, based on the strict laws of the Old Testament. Between 1643 and 1656 Guilford, Milford, Stamford, Southold (in Long Island) and Branford were admitted to the colony.

The boundaries of the Colony of Connecticut included all lands held by the New Haven Colony. After prolonged negotiations, New Haven surrendered its independence to Connecticut in 1664. The church held on to its privileges for a few more years. Hartford and New Haven were co-capitals of Connecticut from 1701 to 1873, when Hartford became the sole capital.

New Haven flourished as a port . Nine years after the founding of the colony, it was exporting shoes and beef. It also conducted a thriving trade with the West Indies. Later New Haven ships traveled to the Orient to import tea, porcelain, and silk. In 1716 the Collegiate School was transferred to New Haven as Yale College (in 1887 it was officially renamed Yale University). A newspaper began publication about this time. During the Revolutionary War the city was looted by British troops, but the residents celebrated the defeat of Cornwallis in 1781.

New Haven incorporated as a city in 1784. Its industrial history began shortly thereafter and is personified by the inventor Eli Whitney, the discoverer of the cotton gin that revolutionized the American economy. Whitney established the first company town in America at Mill Rock on the Hamden town line. The bridge spanning the millpond at the factory was the first lattice truss covered bridge in the country. Whitney is also credited with the mass manufacture of interchangeable parts. Elisha K. Root, another New Haven industrial pioneer, invented the first drop hammer, turret lathes, and automatic screw machines. Abel Buell, at one time jailed for counterfeiting, designed the dies for the first coins manufactured by the authority of the federal government. He also cast the first American printing type. By the early part of the 19th century, New Haven became the carriage-making capital of America, led by men like Jonathan Mix and George T. Newhall. Clockmaking was another prominent New Haven specialty, begun by Thomas Nash, the first clockmaker in the New World, and Chauncey Jerome, inventor of the first 34-hour brass movement.

Chronology

1638	Reverend John Davenport, Theophilius Eaton, and other Puritans found the Colony of Quinnipiac. The settlers adopt a Plantation Covenant binding themselves to be governed solely by the laws of Moses.
1639	Settlers adopt a theocratic Constitution entrusting both church and government to Seven Pillars. Eaton is elected first governor.
1640	Quinnipiac is renamed New Haven.
1643	Guilford, Milford, and Stamford are admitted to the Colony.
1651	Southold on Long Island is admitted to the Colony.
1656	Branford is admitted to the Colony.
1664	New Haven surrenders its independence and joins Connecticut.
1686	The first elms are planted in the parsonage of James Pierpont.
1701	New Haven is chosen as co-capital of Connecticut with Hartford.
1716	The Collegiate School, later Yale University, moves to New Haven.
1784	New Haven is incorporated as a city.
1789	New Haven is linked by rail with New York.
1873	New Haven is displaced from its co-capital status and Hartford becomes sole capital.
1957	New Haven embarks upon a large-scale urban redevelopment program.

New Haven's other great inventors included Charles Goodyear, who discovered the rubber vulcanization process when he accidentally spilled sulphur and rubber over a hot stove; Eli Whitney Blake, who invented the first successful stone crusher; Frank Sprague, inventor of the first electric elevator and who made the street railway possible; and Isaac Strouse, who invented the corset. The city's industrial firsts included the world's first commercial exchange, Aaron Beecher's first wooden match factory, and the first shirt factory in America. New Haven led the way in culture as well. Yale was the first university to confer the doctor of philosophy degree. In publishing, it was the home of the first Connecticut newspaper, *Connecticut Gazette*, and the first medical publication in the world.

Before and during the Civil War, New Haven was an important anti-Slavery Center. The Kansas Rifles were organized after Henry Ward Beecher delivered an address in the North Church. After the Civil War the city's carriage-making industry waned, but the slack was taken up by other industries, such as the Winchester Repeating Arms Company.

In 1957 New Haven became one of the first U.S. cities to begin a large-scale urban renewal of older downtown areas. Race riots ten years later accelerated the process and resulted in such structures as the Long Wharf Theater and the Veterans Memorial Coliseum.

Historical Landmarks

New Haven is 350 years old, yet the city has only seven buildings older than the middle of the 18th century. The city, throughout its history, is always renewing and rebuilding, but in patches. The street design imposed by the original arrangement still prevails, but photographs show how much New Haven has changed. One important legacy that has survived from the old days is the arrangement of the city in nine squares. Old buildings have been entirely altered to accommodate prevailing fashions. Examples are the Henry Farnham House, home of the Yale presidents, the John Sanford House, and St. Michael's Church in Wooster Square. As a result, the landscape of New Haven is constantly being redrawn without a grand plan or pattern. This does not imply that there have not been plans. A plan for city expansion along the lines of a Greek Revival was drawn up and partly implemented in the early decades of the 19th century. As a wealthy city, New Haven attracted eminent architects like Ithiel Town, Sidney Mason Stone, Henry Austin and J. Cleveland Cady. Town was the architect of the Trinity Church, and probably of the Exchange Building. St. Michael's Church and Perit House are examples of Stone's work; City Hall, the Willis Bristol House, and the Dana House of Austin's work; and the Othneil Marsh House of Cady's work. Early in the 20th century, New Haven abandoned its Greek Revival and went back to the Colonial-Federal style of red brick and white woodwork. Cass Gilbert introduced Colonial motifs into his design of the Public Library in 1908, and in Union Station in 1918. J. Frederick Kelly's John Pierpont House and Douglas Orr's New Haven Lawn Club and Quinnipiack Club are other examples of this trend. The end product of this erasing and revising is a patchwork of structures and styles.

The oldest house in New Haven is the Thomas Morris House in Morris Cove, built in 1680, burnt by the British in 1779, and reconstructed. The three churches on the Green are not only among the oldest, but also the best known landmarks of the city. Originally a swampland, the Green has been administered by a Proprietor's Committee since the ground was received as a town common in 1638. The Trinity Episcopal Church and the Center Church were both designed by Town while the United Church, formerly called the North Church, was designed by David Hoadley. Other buildings dating before 1900 are: City Hall, Church of the Redeemer (1870), Governor Ingersoll House (1830), Whitney Armory (c. 1800), Pierpont House (1767), John Cook House (1807), Bishop Homestead (1815), Bushnell House (1800), Tory Tavern (1775),

Elizabethan Club (1815), First Methodist Church (1854), Bacon Homestead (1760), Bowditch House (1815), Weir House (1810), Silliman Homestead (1809), Dana House (1849), Home of Noah Porter (1826), Elisha Hall or Bennett House (1812), and the Punderson Homestead (1787). On the eastern shore of the New Haven Harbor are the Black Rock Fort, used during the Revolutionary War, and Fort Nathan Hale, a Civil War fort.

Population

The population of New Haven has declined from 164,443 in 1950 to 130,474 in 1990 although it represents a decennial increase from the 126,089 reported for 1980. New Haven County in the same period has grown from 546,048 to 819,470.

Population

	1980	1990
Central City	126,089	130,474
Rank	115	125
Metro Area	761,325	804,219
Pop. Change 1980–1990 +4,385		
Pop. % Change 1980–1990 +3.5		
Median Age 29.2		
% Male 47		
% Age 65 and Over 12.3		
Density (per square mile) 6,903		

Households

Number 48,986
Persons per Household 2.41
% Female-Headed Households 21.6
% One-Person Households 34.0
Births—Total 2,204
    % to Mothers under 20 17.9
    Birth Rate per 1,000 17.7

Ethnic Composition

Before the Civil War, New Haven's population comprised mainly original Yankees, Irish, and German immigrants, and some blacks. The period before 1880 was characterized as the Old Immigration. A period of new immigration started in the 1880s with waves of arrivals from eastern and southern Europe, including large numbers of Italians, Poles, Russians, Romanians, and others. In 1900, 28% of the city's population of 100,000 was foreign-born. By 1910 one-third of the population was foreign-born, and another third had at least one foreign parent. Most of the new immigrants settled on the Hill, where cheap housing was available, but later moved to the suburbs. New Haven, like other American cities, has ethnic neighborhoods: the Irish are most numerous in Fair Haven; Jews in Woodbridge, Orange, and Bethany; Italians in Morris Cove and Wooster Square; and blacks in the Hill, Foxon Hill, and Dixon-Newhallville. In the early days blacks were scattered throughout the city, mostly as slaves or domestic servants. Around the turn of the century, there was a coherent black community in the Oak Street area of the

Hill, but they were crowded out by later immigrant arrivals, and many recongregated in a 20-block area around Dixwell Avenue west of the Green. Before World War II, blacks accounted for only 5% of the population, whereas they account for 32% in 1992. The percentage of whites has correspondingly declined to about 54%.

Ethnic Composition (as % of total pop.)

	1980	1990
White	62.11	53.85
Black	31.90	36.14
American Indian	0.25	0.31
Asian and Pacific Islander	1.08	2.41
Hispanic	7.96	13.22
Other	NA	7.29

Government

New Haven is governed by charter and has a mayor-aldermen form of government. The mayor is elected by general election for two-year terms and may succeed himself without limitation. He has the power of veto, but any veto may be overridden by a two-thirds majority vote of the Board of Aldermen. The city clerk serves a term concurrent with that of the mayor and is elected city-wide. The Board of Finance consists of the mayor, the controller, a representative of the Board of Aldermen and six citizens appointed for two-year terms by the mayor, not more than five of whom may be members of the same political party. The Board of Aldermen consists of 30 members who are elected to two-year terms.

Government

Year of Home Charter NA
Number of Members of the Governing Body 30
Elected at Large 30
Elected by Wards NA
Number of Women in Governing Body 5
Salary of Mayor $65,000
Salary of Council Members $2,000
City Government Employment Total 4,328
Rate per 10,000 350.6

Public Finance

The Board of Finance is responsible for preparing the annual city operating budget and capital budget and for setting the municipal tax rate and the tax levy for approval by the Board of Aldermen. The Board of Finance also adopts quarterly allotments for each city department appropriation. After holding public hearings, the Board of Aldermen must adopt the budget and tax rate by the first Monday of June. The Board of Aldermen may decrease or increase individual items of appropriation and decrease, but not increase, the tax rate. All financial transactions are audited by an independent accounting firm, currently Coopers and Lybrand.

The annual budget consists of revenues of $323.497 million and expenditures of $342.537 million. The debt outstanding was $209.613 million and cash and security holdings $170.250 million.

Public Finance

Total Revenue (in millions) $323.497
Intergovernmental Revenue—Total (in millions) $162.49
Federal Revenue per Capita $0.017
% Federal Assistance   5.32
% State Assistance   44.90
Sales Tax as % of Total Revenue   NA
Local Revenue as % of Total Revenue   43.82
City Income Tax   no
Taxes—Total (in millions) $86.7

Taxes per Capita
   Total $702
   Property $693
   Sales and Gross Receipts $0
General Expenditures—Total (in millions) $204.8
General Expenditures per Capita $1,659
Capital Outlays per Capita $380

% of Expenditures for:
   Public Welfare   6.8
   Highways   4.7
   Education   29.3
   Health and Hospitals   0.9
   Police   6.6
   Sewerage and Sanitation   10.0
   Parks and Recreation   2.0
   Housing and Community Development   8.8
Debt Outstanding per Capita $1,009
   % Utility   0.0
Federal Procurement Contract Awards (in millions) $23.4
Federal Grants Awards (in millions) $166.6
Fiscal Year Begins   July 1

Economy

New Haven has a post-industrial economy based on four sectors: biotechnology, health care, higher education, and communications. Until the 1960s New Haven had an economy dominated by manufacturing. After establishing itself as a mercantile port, New Haven was forced to switch to manufacturing after a series of shipping setbacks. Carriages, guns, rubber boots, clocks, and hardware became the mainstays of the city's wealth during the first half of the 18th century. Since the South had been New Haven's largest market, the Civil War took the bottom out of this economic boom. Again cut loose from its economic moorings, New Haven took the lead in another transition—the shift to railroads and smokestacks fueled by a large pool of cheap immigrant labor. By 1890 the city's economy was strong again, this time bolstered by four forces: the Winchester Repeating Arms Company, the New York and New Haven Railroad, the Southern New England Telephone Company (SNET), and the expansion of the Yale College, which became Yale University in 1887. In the 20th century the city suffered two major economical setbacks, first during the Great Depression, and then by the oil shock and the flight of manufacturing from the northeast seaboard during the 1970s. Many manufacturers left the city and manufacturing jobs decreased by 54% between 1968 and 1984. The drying up of the model cities project in the 1970s, after many older buildings had been demolished, contributed to a wasteland look in many areas.

New Haven entered a new economic era in the 1980s, shifting its focus to small technology and knowledge-based companies. The city has world-class scientists and research facilities that form the basis of a post-industrial economy. A major strength is biotechnology supported by one of the nation's top medical centers. Four of the world's top pharmaceutical firms are located near New Haven: Miles, Bristol Myers, Beringer Ingelheim, and Pfizer. Yale University is a major employer and reservoir of skills; in addition it is an integral part of the city's economy. Yale's 10,000 students spend over $40 million on goods and services every year, and the university directly accounts for a further $50 million. Yale also devotes a part of its investment funds on urban projects within the city. *Adweek* rates New Haven as the fifth-hottest market in the country.

Economy

Total Money Income (in millions) $1,157.7
% of State Average   66.6
Per Capita Annual Income $9,378
% Population below Poverty Level   23.2
Fortune 500 Companies   NA

Banks	Number	Deposits (in millions)
Commercial	31	24,472.6
Savings	14	9,699.4

Passenger Autos   460,617
Electric Meters   56,769
Gas Meters   95,258

Manufacturing

Number of Establishments   186
% with 20 or More Employees   37.1
Manufacturing Payroll (in millions) $193.7
Value Added by Manufacture (in millions) $390.0
Value of Shipments (in millions) $667.7
New Capital Expenditures (in millions) $20.7

Wholesale Trade

Number of Establishments   216
Sales (in millions) $1,732.2
Annual Payroll (in millions) $72.744

Retail Trade

Number of Establishments   1,106
Total Sales (in millions) $654.9
Sales per Capita $5,305
Number of Retail Trade Establishments with Payroll   852
Annual Payroll (in millions) $93.0
Total Sales (in millions) $637.8
General Merchandise Stores (per capita) $663
Food Stores (per capita) $667
Apparel Stores (per capita) $439
Eating and Drinking Places (per capita) $810

Service Industries

Total Establishments   1,209
Total Receipts (in millions) $634.4
Hotels and Motels (in millions) $20.6
Health Services (in millions) $197.0
Legal Services (in millions) $99.3

Labor

 New Haven is one of the few U.S. cities where the labor force is growing, and it is expected to grow for the rest of the century. Service, trade, and government account for roughly 71% of total nonagricultural employment. Although total nonagricultural employment has remained stable since 1985, there was a shift in employment from manufacturing to nonmanufacturing sectors. However, during the economic slowdown in the early 1990s, all employment sectors declined and the unemployment rate climbed to above the national average. Yale continues to be the city's largest employer followed by SNET, Yale–New Haven Hospital, St. Raphael's Hospital, and Southern Connecticut State University. The cost of living is slightly higher in New Haven than in the rest of the nation.

Labor

Civilian Labor Force   59,744
% Change 1989–1990   3.6

Work Force Distribution
  Mining   NA
  Construction   8,200
  Manufacturing   43,500
  Transportation and Public Utilities   16,100
  Wholesale and Retail Trade   51,600
  FIRE (Finance, Insurance, Real Estate)   16,200
  Service   75,700
  Government   31,600
  Women as % of Labor Force   47.6
  % Self-Employed   3.9
  % Professional/Technical   20.3
Total Unemployment   3,927
Rate %   6.6
Federal Government Civilian Employment   2,024

Education

For over two centuries New Haven has been synonymous with Yale. Founded in 1701 as the Collegiate School in Branford, with a gift of books from ten clergymen, Yale moved to New Haven in 1716 and was named Yale College, adopting the name Yale University in 1887. It consists of a graduate school, ten professional schools, and Yale College, which together enroll over 10,000 students in its downtown campus. The school is operated primarily according to a residential college system, each college being a small community with its own library and dining room. The Yale Library contains over 8 million volumes and is an outstanding research resources, as are the Yale Art Gallery, Peabody Museum of Natural History, and the Yale Center for British Art. Yale's cultural influence on the city is pervasive. The school's drama productions, adult lecture series, art galleries, and sporting events enrich the city's life. The school also dominates the city architecturally, with its fine buildings and towers, such as the Harkness Tower, the Sterling Memorial Tower, and the Payne Whitney Gymnasium.

Overshadowed by Yale are six other local colleges: Albert Magnus, located on a 50-acre site in a residential section, was founded in 1925 by Dominican Sisters as a private college for Catholic women. In 1985 it became coeducational. The University of New Haven enrolls 7,000 students on its 70-acre campus in West Haven. The Southern Connecticut State University is the city's second-oldest university, founded in 1893 as the New Haven Normal School. It achieved university status in 1983 and currently enrolls 6,600 students on its 200-acre campus. The other three colleges are the Quinnipiac College, with its three schools on a 132-acre campus at the foot of the Sleeping Giant Mountain State Park, Greater New Haven State Technical College, and Paier College of Art.

The public school system consists of 42 schools.

Education

Number of Public Schools   42
Special Education Schools
Total Enrollment   17,881
% Enrollment in Private Schools   14.8
% Minority   NA
Classroom Teachers   1,097
Pupil-Teacher Ratio   15.5:1
Number of Graduates   NA
Total Revenue (in millions) $127,061
Total Expenditures (in millions)   NA
Expenditures per Pupil $7,183
Educational Attainment (Age 25 and Over)
  % Completed 12 or More Years   60.9
  % Completed 16 or More Years   19.8
Four-Year Colleges and Universities   4
  Enrollment   31,416
Two-Year Colleges   1
  Enrollment   4,017

Libraries

Number   22
Public Libraries   4
Books (in thousands)   574
Circulation (in thousands)   266
Persons Served (in thousands)   126
Circulation per Person Served   2.11
Income (in millions) $2.188
Staff   NA

Four-Year Colleges and Universities
  Yale University
  University of New Haven
  Albert Magnus College
  Southern Connecticut State University

Health

New Haven is home to one of the ten top medical facilities in the nation—the Yale–New Haven Hospital with 875 beds and over 1,800 physicians. It is noted as the first hospital ever to make clinical use of penicillin, the first to use chemotherapy in cancer treatment, the first to transplant a number of organs, and the first to use in vitro fertilization.

St. Raphael's Hospital is equally distinguished and, after a $33-million expansion in the early 1990s, is the most modern in the state. St. Raphael's pioneered the first psychiatric unit for children, a faster and less expensive treatment for breast cancer, and the first radiation therapy center in New England. Both

Yale–New Haven and St. Raphael's are teaching hospitals for the Yale University Medical School.

Health

Deaths—Total   1,393
Rate per 1,000   11.2
Infant Deaths—Total   38
Rate per 1,000   17.2
Number of Metro Hospitals   5
Number of Metro Hospital Beds   1,413
Rate per 100,000   1,145
Number of Physicians   2,486
Physicians per 1,000   NA
Nurses per 1,000   NA
Health Expenditures per Capita $21.51

Transportation

 In road, rail, and sea transport, New Haven has established strengths. New Haven is one of the busiest Amtrak centers with the high-speed Metroliner linking the city with Boston, New York, Philadelphia, and Washington, D.C. The 70-year old Union Station has undergone major renovation.

Tweed Airport, located on the edge of the city, is primarily a commuter facility serving Kennedy, LaGuardia, and Logan. Tweed is served by three airlines: USAir, Continental Express, and United.

New Haven is strategically located at the intersection of several major highways. The major arteries serving the city are Interstate I-95 east-west and I-91 north-south. Another major highway is the Merritt/Wilbur Cross Parkway, also known as Route 15. This road, running northwest of the city, was the principal New York–New Haven route before the interstates were built. Less heavily traveled are Route 1 running along the shoreline, Route 10 connecting Hamden, Cheshire, and points north, and Route 34, connecting with Route 8 and the Naugatuck Valley. Ridesharing is heavily promoted by the transportation authorities. Rideworks, the ride-sharing brokerage, provides a free matching service for commuters.. A major transit component is the fixed 28-route radial bus system reaching Clinton, Wallingford, Waterbury, and Milford, and converging on New Haven. Nearly all the routes are accessible from the streets flanking the Green. The buses approach and leave the city through different thoroughfares, and thus service the city in such a way that no downtown building is more than 600 feet from a bus route.

Transportation

Interstate Highway Mileage   34
Total Urban Mileage   1,528
Total Daily Vehicle Mileage (in millions) $8.391
Daily Average Commute Time   42.9 min.
Number of Buses   100
Port Tonnage (in millions) $9.658
Airports   1
Number of Daily Flights   0.6
Daily Average Number of Passengers   2

Transportation (continued)

Airlines (American carriers only)
   USAir
   Continental Express
   United

Housing

 The Office of Housing and Neighborhood Development administers a variety of housing projects combining public and private investment. These programs have resulted in over 3,000 units of housing for both owners and renters at all income levels. The city receives Urban Development Action Grants for construction on scattered vacant sites in the Hill, Dixwell, Newhallville, and Dwight neighborhoods. Additionally, city-owned sites and surplus school buildings have been sold to developers for construction of apartment buildings.

Housing

Total Housing Units   54,057
% Change 1980–1990   6.3
Vacant Units for Sale or Rent   3,507
Occupied Units   48,986
% with More Than One Person per Room   4.9
% Owner-Occupied   31.8
Median Value of Owner-Occupied Homes $145,000
Average Monthly Purchase Cost $414
Median Monthly Rent $487
New Private Housing Starts   134
Value (in thousands) $5,123
% Single-Family   29.9
Nonresidential Buildings Value (in thousands) $3,957

Urban Redevelopment

 Since 1980 New Haven has witnessed a tide of urban development projects that have changed the urban landscape. From 1986 through 1990, approximately $221 million worth of development projects have been completed; $504.9 million are under construction and $171 million are now in the planning stage. In the entertainment district, the College Street Project has created retail, office, and residential space. Two historic theaters— the Shubert and the Palace—have been restored along with restaurants and shops. The last phase of this project involved the conversion of the Hyperion Theater into a hotel. In the Audubon Arts district, the $31.5-million Arts Council project has created 90,000 square feet of space (including 20,000 square feet of retail space), 56 residential townhouses and flats, and 387 parking spaces. The Century Tower has created 275,000 square feet of office space along with 550 parking spaces on the corner of Whitney Avenue and Grove Street. The Long Wharf Maritime Center is the signature building of the city skyline. Constructed right on the harbor and lit up at night, the building is visible from both I-95 and I-91. It contains offices, retail shops, a marina, and a hotel. Other projects include

Government Center, an $85-million, 25-story, 420,000-square-foot office adjacent to the Green, and complexes such as Whitney Grove, Arena Block, Ninth Square, and Harbor Landing, which include offices, shopping, and condominiums. The city has also completed the first plant of a district heating and cooling system.

The Volvo International Tennis Tournament recently selected New Haven as its permanent site. The state will construct a 15,000-seat stadium and a 3,000-seat stadium, both at a cost of $18 million, and will receive 50% of the net income from the tournament and all other events held at the facility.

Crime

Of the crimes known to police in 1991, there were 3,525 violent crimes and 4,146 property crimes.

Crime

Violent Crimes—Total	3,525
Violent Crime Rate per 100,000	782.4
Murder	118
Rape	1,355
Robbery	2,018
Aggravated Assaults	15,967
Property Crimes	4,146
Burglary	8,041
Larceny	8,780
Motor Vehicle Theft	136
Arson	68
Per Capita Police Expenditures	$172.18
Per Capita Fire Protection Expenditures	$179.01
Number of Police	351
Per 1,000	3.81

Religion

New Haven has little of its old Puritan heritage. Catholics and Protestants are both strongly represented and there is a sizable Jewish minority.

Religion

Largest Denominations (Adherents)	
Catholic	368,313
Episcopal	15,036
United Methodist	9,966
Black Baptist	19,391
United Church of Christ	26,033
Assembly of God	3,077
American Zion	7,705
Evangelical Lutheran	6,090
Jewish	34,250

Media

The city has two dailies, the morning *Journal-Courier* and the evening *New Haven Register*, two television stations, and one radio station. New York signals are easily picked up in the New Haven area and supplement local stations.

Media

Newsprint
  Journal-Courier, daily
  New Haven Advocate, weekly
  New Haven Register, daily
Television
  WEDY (Channel 65)
  WTNH (Channel 8)
Radio
  WYBC (FM)

Sports

The New Haven Nighthawks of the American Hockey League, the city's minor league hockey team, play at the Veterans Memorial Coliseum during the winter months. The team, part of the Northern Division, is jointly financed by the New York Rangers and Los Angeles Kings. The Teletrack provides horse-racing fans with simulcasts of some of the major races and permits betting. The Yale University football team plays at the 70,000-seat Yale Bowl.

Arts, Culture, and Tourism

New Haven offers cultural fare rarely found in a city of its size. The New Haven Symphony Orchestra is the fourth oldest in the country. Other musical groups include the Chamber Orchestra of New England, founded in 1975, the Philharmonic Orchestra of Yale University, and the Yale Opera. The Connecticut Ballet is based in New Haven but performs throughout the state. Barbara Feldman and Dancers is a professional ensemble dance troupe. The Long Wharf Theater was the city's first resident professional repertory company. It was followed by the Yale Repertory Theater, formed in 1967. The Palace and Shubert theaters, reopened in 1984, have spearheaded the city's cultural revival. The Veterans Memorial Coliseum is an 11,000-seat facility that occasionally hosts concerts and popular musicians. The Paul Mellon Arts Center at Chaote Rosemary Hall in Wallingford hosts a variety of concerts and plays in their theater.

The Yale University Art Gallery is considered one of the finest medium-sized museums in the country. Founded in 1832 to display John Trumbull's paintings of the American Revolution, it is the oldest university art museum in the Western Hemisphere. The Yale Center for British Art is the largest collection of British pictorial arts outside of the United Kingdom. Both these museums are housed in buildings designed by the noted architect Louis Kahn. Yale's Peabody Museum of Natural History annually attracts more than a quarter of a million adults and children to its Great Hall of dinosaur skeletons, Hall of Mammals, and other displays. The Yale Collection of Musical Instruments has over 800 exhibits. The Beinecke Rare Books and Manuscripts Library, also at Yale, is the largest building in the world devoted solely to rare books and manuscripts. On permanent display here are the

Guttenberg Bible and Audubon's Birds of America. The Museum of American Theater is a new museum, as is the Connecticut Afro-American Historical Society. The New Haven Colony Historical Society, founded in 1862, contains many interesting articles from the New Haven area, such as Eli Whitney's cotton gin and various firearms. Private galleries include John Slade Ely House, the Munson Gallery, Mona Berman Gallery, and the galleries of the Creative Arts Workshop and City Spirit Artists.

Travel and Tourism
Hotel Rooms   4,426
Convention and Exhibit Space (square feet)   NA
Convention Centers
Yale University
Festivals
East Shore Day (June)
Jazz Festival (summer)
Greek Festival (September)

Parks and Recreation

The major city parks are East Rock, a 446-acre park providing a wide panoramic view of the city. At the foot of the abrupt precipice, Mill River meanders, forming oxbows and little islands. At the summit, accessible by car, stands the 112-foot granite Soldiers and Sailors Monument, built in 1887. Edgewood Park on Chapel Street includes 121 acres of heavily wooded slopes and rolling meadowlands. West Rock Park on Blake Street contains the famous Judges Cave, the hiding place of the regicides Whalley and Goffe who, after signing the death warrant of Charles I, were forced to flee from England and seek asylum in New Haven in 1661.

Sources of Further Information

Main Library
133 Elm Street
New Haven, CT 06510
(203) 787-8130

Mayor's Office, City of New Haven
157 Church Street
New Haven, CT 06506
(203) 787-8200

New Haven Colony Historical Society–Whitney
  Library
114 Whitney Avenue
New Haven, CT 06510
(203) 562-4183

New Haven Convention and Visitors Bureau
900 Chapel Street
New Haven, CT 06510
(203) 787-8367

New Haven Economic Development Office
157 Church Street
New Haven, CT 06510
(203) 787-8031

Additional Reading

Brown, Elizabeth M. *New Haven: A Guide to Architecture and Urban Design.* 1976.

Dahl, Robert A. *Who Governs? Democracy and Power in an American City.* 1961.

Kagan, Myrna. *Vision in the Sky: New Haven's Early Years, 1638–1783.* 1989.

Philie, William L. *Change and Tradition: New Haven, Connecticut, 1780–1830.* 1990.

Sledge, Betsy, and Eugenia Fayen. *Enjoying New Haven.* 1985.

Warner, Robert A. *New Haven Negroes: A Social History.* 1970.

New Orleans

Louisiana

Name   New Orleans
Name Origin   For the Duke of Orleans
Year Founded   1718 Inc. 1805
Status: State   Louisiana
      County   Seat of Orleans Parish
Area (square miles)   180.7
Elevation (feet)   5
Time Zone   Central
Population (1990)   496,938
Population of Metro Area (1990)   1,238,816

Sister Cities
   Point Noire, Congo

Distance in Highway Miles To:

Atlanta	480
Boston	1,507
Chicago	919
Dallas	517
Denver	1,277
Detroit	1,070
Houston	352
Los Angeles	1,858
Miami	860
New York	1,335
Philadelphia	1,229
Washington, DC	1,099

Location and Topography

New Orleans, the largest city in Louisiana and the seat of Orleans Parish, is located in the eastern portion of the state between the Mississippi River and Lake Pontchartrain. The oldest section, the French Quarter, or the Vieux Carré (Old Square), lies on high ground—about 12 feet above sea level—but most of the city is marshland. Enclosed by levees, the city is 6 feet below sea level in some areas. New Orleans is about 130 miles south of the state capital, Baton Rouge.

Layout of City and Suburbs

Because New Orleans, also called the Crescent City, is shaped by the meandering Mississippi River, the pattern of its streets resembles a spiderweb cast outward from the city's center. The main divider is Canal Street, and the location of every landmark in the city is measured by its distance from this thoroughfare. One of the city's main sections is the French Quarter (also called the Vieux Carré), which is the site of the original colony. Other areas include the Fauborg Marigny (*fauborg* from the French word meaning suburb); the residential area of Algiers just across the Mississippi River; Bywater; Arabi; and Chalmette, the site of the Battle of New Orleans in 1815. Just across Canal Street, on the thin boundary that separates downtown and uptown, lies the central business district, called the CBD. The location of mass American migration following the Louisiana Purchase, the CBD is the main business activity center. Basin Street, just to the north of Canal Street, is the birthplace of jazz. New Orleans is surrounded by several communities in and around the parishes of Orleans, Jefferson, and St. Bernard that share the Mississippi River's resources, such as Kenner (the location of the New Orleans International Airport), Metairie, Gretna, and Westwego.

Environment

Environmental Stress Index   2.4
Green Cities Index: Rank   21
Score   24.79
Water Quality   Alkaline, soft, fluoridated
Average Daily Use (gallons per capita)   234
Maximum Supply (gallons per capita)   412
Parkland as % of Total City Area   NA
% Waste Landfilled/Recycled   NA
Annual Parks Expenditures per Capita $80.30

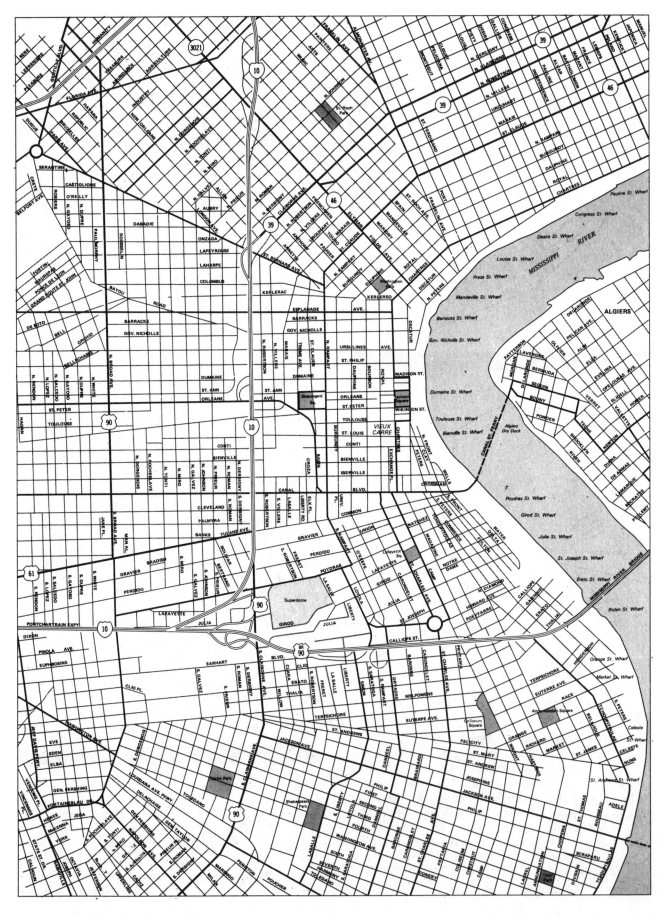

Climate

New Orleans has a humid, semitropical climate moderated by its proximity to the Gulf of Mexico. The city is exposed to the hurricanes and tornadoes that swing northwest from the Caribbean. Snowfall is negligible, but rainfall is heavy and frequent, with daily afternoon thunderstorms from mid-June through September. From December to March, precipitation is likely to be in the form of a steady rain of two or three days' duration. During winter and spring, fogs are common.

Weather

Temperature

Highest Monthly Average °F   90.6
Lowest Monthly Average °F   43.5

Annual Averages

Days 32°F or Below   13
Days above 90°F   67
Zero Degree Days   0
Precipitation (inches)   57.0
Snow (inches)   0.2
% Seasonal Humidity   77.0
Wind Speed (m.p.h.)   8.2
Clear Days   109
Cloudy Days   136
Storm Days   68
Rainy Days   113

Average Temperatures (F)	High	Low	Mean
January	62.3	43.5	52.9
February	65.1	46.0	55.6
March	70.4	50.9	60.7
April	78.4	58.8	68.6
May	84.9	65.3	75.1
June	89.6	71.2	80.4
July	90.4	73.3	81.9
August	90.6	73.1	81.9
September	86.6	69.7	78.2
October	79.9	59.6	69.8
November	70.3	49.8	60.1
December	64.2	45.3	54.8

History

New Orleans's beginnings can be traced to the early exploration of the Mississippi River. About 1682, Robert Cavelier, Sieur de La Salle, and a small band of explorers set out to trace the mighty Mississippi to its end. They rode the waterway from Canada to the Gulf of Mexico. La Salle claimed for Canada (then called New France) all the territory not belonging to the British and called it "Louisiane" in honor of France's King Louis XIV. Seventeen years later, two more Frenchmen, Pierre le Moyne, Sieur d'Iberville, and his younger brother, Jean-Baptiste le Moyne, Sieur de Bienville, started a small colony in what is now Ocean Springs, Mississippi, just to the east of Biloxi, Mississippi, which at that time was part of the Louisiana Territory. Eventually the two brothers established colonies at Natchez, Mobile, and Natchitoches. In 1717, Scotsman John Law worked his way into the favor of the French royal family. Louis XIV had died and was succeeded by his

grandson, Louis XV. Law persuaded the king's regent, the Duc (or duke) d'Orleans, to grant him a 25-year charter to set up colonies in the Louisiana Territory. The next year, on Law's orders, Jean-Baptiste le Moyne set up a colony on the site of what is now the French Quarter of New Orleans and named it La Nouvelle Orleans after the regent. He instructed his chief engineer, Adrien de Pauger, to lay out a town on the site.

Over the next century, New Orleans was populated by different cultures that contributed to much of today's mix of history and architecture. Ursuline nuns came in 1727 with "casket girls" (These girls were marriagable middle-class Catholics that immigrated to New Orleans following the French Revolution in order to find husbands. They were supervised by their parish priest or other religious. The French government provided each with a casket [small trunk] and suitable articles of clothing, hence the moniker.) and opened their convent three years later. In 1763, Acadians from Canada settled in Louisiana and added a new word to the emerging English dialect in the colonies—*Cajun*, a derivation of *Acadian*. A year later, France sold its stake in Louisiana to Spain, and Spanish troops oversaw the transition. The Spaniards intermarried with the locals and constructed buildings in the Spanish architectural style that can be seen today.

Although raging fires in 1788 and 1794 destroyed parts of the city, in 1795 the Treaty of Madrid opened the Port of New Orleans to Americans, making the city a major commercial center. The city reverted to French control in 1800, but Napoleon sold it to the United States three years later as part of the Louisiana Purchase, which doubled the territory of the United States.

In 1815, the city was the site of the last major battle of the War of 1812. By 1840, New Orleans was the fourth-largest city in the United States; in port business it was second only to New York. In 1861, it became part of the Confederacy when Louisiana seceded from the Union. A year later, Union Admiral David Farragut captured the city, and it remained in Union hands throughout the war. Since 1865, the ambience of New Orleans has come from its southern flavor, a mixture of being the birthplace of jazz and becoming the busiest port in the United States and second-busiest port in the world. In 1977, Ernest "Dutch" Morial became the city's first black mayor. In 1984, New Orleans hosted the World Exposition.

Historical Landmarks

New Orleans's historic atmosphere is marked by its French, Spanish, and early American influences. The plantations that line the Mississippi River west toward Baton Rouge are good examples of the city's Creole heritage, and include such showcases as the Destrehan Plantation, the Ormond Plantation, and the San Francisco Plantation. Closer to the city's core and marked by a combination of all three cultures are the Beauregard Keyes House and Garden, an 1826 cottage once the home of Confederate General P. G. T. Beauregard; the Gallier House Museum, former home of James Gallier, Jr., a major

Chronology

1682 The Mississippi River region is explored by Robert Cavalier, Sieur de La Salle, who names the area around the Gulf of Mexico "Louisiane" in honor of France's King Louis XIV.

1699 Two French brothers—Pierre le Moyne, Sieur d'Iberville, and Jean-Baptiste le Moyne, Sieur de Bienville—start a colony in the Louisiana Territory at what is now Ocean Springs, Mississippi. Over the next 20 years, they establish several other colonies in the territory.

1718 Under direction from Scotsman John Law, Jean-Baptiste le Moyne sets up a colony in the extreme eastern section of present-day Louisiana and calls it La Nouvelle Orleans after Philippe, duc d'Orleans, the regent of the king of France.

1723 New Orleans supplants Biloxi as the capital of the Louisiana Territory.

1762 King Louis XV of France secretly gives all the Louisiana Territory west of the Mississippi River to Spain. The Treaty of Paris (1783) makes the conversion official.

1788 Fire destroys most of the city. A second fire in 1794 is just as devastating.

1803 The United States purchases the Louisiana Territory, including New Orleans, from France.

1805 New Orleans is incorporated as a city.

1812 Louisiana is admitted to statehood with New Orleans as its capital.

1815 The Battle of New Orleans takes place between British forces, under General Sir Edward Pakenham, and Americans led by General Andrew Jackson.

1849 The permanent capital of Louisiana is moved to Baton Rouge.

1853– 1855 Yellow fever kills 11,000 residents.

1861– 1865 Louisiana is a member of the Confederate States; the city is captured (1862) by Admiral David Farragut.

1975 The Louisiana Superdome is built.

1977 Ernest "Dutch" Morial becomes the city's first black mayor.

1984 The World Exposition is held in New Orleans.

architect of the city; and the Hermann-Grima Historic House, with its original slave quarters. The city's historic area is the French Quarter, which is the site of the original city. In this area are sites such as the original Bank of Louisiana; the St. Louis Cathedral, a historic place of worship that is the third such building on this spot (rebuilt after a hurricane destroyed the first in 1722 and fire ruined the second in 1788); the Cabildo, one-time seat of the Spanish government; New Orleans City Hall; and the Louisiana Supreme Court, which was ruined by fire in 1988 but restored and reopened in 1992. The Garden District is noted for several landmarks, including the Women's Opera Guild Home, a Victorian house, and the Lafayette No. 1 Cemetery, where the city's yellow fever victims were buried up until 1852. On Esplanade Ridge is the Widow Castanedo's House, as well as the Musson-Degas House at 2306 Esplanade Avenue, home of French impressionist painter Edgar Degas.

Population

The flight to the suburbs continues unabated in New Orleans and is reflected in the steady loss of population through the 1970s and 1980s. The city's 1990 population of 496,938 is the lowest in many decades—10.9% lower than its 1980 population of 557,927 and still lower than its 1970 population of 593,000.

Population		
	1980	*1990*
Central City	557,927	496,938
Rank	22	24
Metro Area	1,256,668	1,238,816
Pop. Change 1980–1990 -60,989		
Pop. % Change 1980–1990 -10.9		
Median Age 31.9		
% Male 47.6		
% Age 17 and Under 27.9		
% Age 65 and Over 13.01		
Density (per square mile) 2,497		

Households		
Number 188,235		
Persons per Household 2.55		
% Female-Headed Households 24.1		
% One-Person Households 32.2		
Births—Total 10,432		
% to Mothers under 20 18.7		
Birth Rate per 1,000 18.7		

Ethnic Composition

Blacks constitute the majority of the city population with 61.9%, whites 34.9%, Hispanic 3.5%, Asian and Pacific Islanders 2%, American Indians 0.2%, and others 1.0%. Blacks have lived in the city since the first slaves were brought to the New World in the 1700s. Later their number was enlarged by free emigrants from the West Indies. Blacks have made a powerful contribution to the development of New Orleans as a center of jazz music. Among other ethnic groups there is an interesting remnant of French-speaking families from Acadia in the Canadian Maritime Provinces; the Acadians came to be called Cajuns. Descendants of early French-Spanish colonial settlers are known as Creoles, from the Spanish word *criollo,* or native.

Ethnic Composition (as % of total pop.)

	1980	1990
White	42.51	34.92
Black	55.27	61.92
American Indian	0.09	0.15
Asian and Pacific Islander	1.32	1.95
Hispanic	3.45	3.47
Other	NA	1.05

Government

New Orleans is governed by a mayor-council form of government. The mayor and the seven members of the council are elected to 4-year terms. The Democrats have controlled city hall since 1870. The mayor may not hold office for more than two consecutive terms.

Government

Year of Home Charter   1954
Number of Members of the Governing Body   7
Elected at Large   2
Elected by Wards   5
Number of Women in Governing Body   0
Salary of Mayor $85,880
Salary of Council Members $42,500
City Government Employment Total   11,217
Rate per 10,000   202.3

Public Finance

The annual budget consists of revenues of $715.547 million and expenditures of $750.453 million. The debt outstanding is $1.128 billion; cash and security holdings total $1.197 billion.

Public Finance

Total Revenue (in millions) $715.547
Intergovernmental Revenue — Total (in millions)
   $126.612
Federal Revenue per Capita $134.84
% Federal Assistance   10.46
% State Assistance   6.70
Sales Tax as % of Total Revenue   18.50
Local Revenue as % of Total Revenue   82.83
City Income Tax   no
Taxes—Total (in millions) $256.9

Taxes per Capita
   Total $463
   Property $133
   Sales and Gross Receipts $309
General Expenditures—Total (in millions) $567.6
General Expenditures per Capita $1,024
Capital Outlays per Capita $197

% of Expenditures for:
   Public Welfare   1.9
   Highways   9.0
   Education   0.0
   Health and Hospitals   2.3

Public Finance (continued)

   Police   10.2
   Sewerage and Sanitation   14.4
   Parks and Recreation   4.8
   Housing and Community Development   9.0
Debt Outstanding per Capita $1,436
   % Utility   4.1
Federal Procurement Contract Awards (in millions)
   $1,298.5
Federal Grants Awards (in millions) $130.7
Fiscal Year Begins   January 1

Economy

The economy of New Orleans is dominated by four sectors: tourism, construction, shipping, and petroleum. Tourism accounts for a large percentage of the city's economy, with an estimated 7 million visitors in 1990. Further, New Orleans is one of the top ten convention cities. In construction, employers such as Martin Marietta and Avondale Shipyards rank among the largest in the city. The shipping industry is among the largest in the nation, and is conducted from the port of New Orleans, which has more than 50 miles of port space on the Mississippi River alone. Shell Oil Company leads the way as the largest employer in the area of petroleum exploration and refinement.

Economy

Total Money Income (in millions) $4,976.6
% of State Average   101.6
Per Capita Annual Income   8,975
% Population below Poverty Level   26.4
Fortune 500 Companies   3

Banks	Number	Deposits (in millions)
Commercial	NA	NA
Savings	NA	NA

Passenger Autos   248,904
Electric Meters   195,591
Gas Meters   NA

Manufacturing

Number of Establishments   371
% with 20 or More Employees   31.0
Manufacturing Payroll (in millions) $431.0
Value Added by Manufacture (in millions) $1,133.9
Value of Shipments (in millions) $2,307.7
New Capital Expenditures (in millions) $72.9

Wholesale Trade

Number of Establishments   793
Sales (in millions) $4,180.7
Annual Payroll (in millions) $239.758

Retail Trade

Number of Establishments   4,264
Total Sales (in millions) $2,674.1
Sales per Capita $4,823
Number of Retail Trade Establishments with Payroll   2,920
Annual Payroll (in millions) $394.4
Total Sales (in millions) $2,611.6
General Merchandise Stores (per capita) $442
Food Stores (per capita) $992
Apparel Stores (per capita) $339
Eating and Drinking Places (per capita) $727

Economy (continued)

Service Industries

Total Establishments   3,920
Total Receipts (in millions) $2,318.1
Hotels and Motels (in millions) $400.1
Health Services (in millions) $511.2
Legal Services (in millions) $546.3

Labor

Trade and services account for half of the employment market. The third-largest sector is government, which employs twice as many workers as manufacturing. The share of manufacturing is slightly higher than that of transportation and public utilities. The work force is highly skilled, backed up by seven trade and vocational/technical schools. Louisiana is a right-to-work state. At 16.4%, union membership is low compared to the national average of 25.2%.

Labor

Civilian Labor Force   222,249
% Change 1989–1990   -2.5

Work Force Distribution
    Mining   14,600
    Construction   23,300
    Manufacturing   43,900
    Transportation and Public Utilities   43,200
    Wholesale and Retail Trade   136,500
    FIRE (Finance, Insurance, Real Estate)   32,900
    Service   147,600
    Government   88,800
    Women as % of Labor Force   45
    % Self-Employed   5.1
    % Professional/Technical   17.5
Total Unemployment   13,365
Rate %   6.0
Federal Government Civilian Employment   12,720

Education

The Orleans Parish School Board supports 81 elementary schools, 18 junior high/middle schools, 20 senior high schools, and 7 other schools. About 87% of public school students are black. The metro area also has 125 parochial schools, enrolling 60,000 students, and 53 other private institutions, including the noted Isidore Newman School.

The University of New Orleans, located on the lakefront, is the second-largest university in the Louisiana State University system. Other public universities include a branch of Southern University. Among the private universities, the oldest and most prestigious is Tulane University, with 11 academic schools and colleges. Jesuit-run Loyola University is the premier Catholic university. Xavier University is the only Catholic university in the nation with a predominantly black student body. Other Catholic institutions are Our Lady of Holy Cross College and Notre Dame Seminary Graduate School of Theology. The Baptists run the New Orleans Baptist Theological Seminary. Dillard University is one of the oldest historically black institutions in the South.

Education

Number of Public Schools   126
Special Education Schools   4
Total Enrollment   82,925
% Enrollment in Private Schools   27.3
% Minority   92.1
Classroom Teachers   4,644
Pupil-Teacher Ratio   17.8:1
Number of Graduates   3,435
Total Revenue (in millions) $275.152
Total Expenditures (in millions) $260.338
Expenditures per Pupil $2,904
Educational Attainment (Age 25 and Over)
    % Completed 12 or More Years   59.2
    % Completed 16 or More Years   17.7
Four-Year Colleges and Universities   8
    Enrollment   38,174
Two-Year Colleges   1
    Enrollment   1,094

Libraries

Number   58
Public Libraries   12
Books   923,853
Circulation (in thousands)   1,207
Persons Served (in thousands)   496.9
Circulation per Person Served   1.91
Income (in millions) $6.205
Staff   NA

Four-Year Colleges and Universities
    Southern University, New Orleans
    University of New Orleans
    Dillard University
    Loyola University
    Our Lady of Holy Cross College
    Tulane University of Louisiana
    Xavier University of Louisiana
    Louisiana State University Medical Center

Health

New Orleans has 21 hospitals providing three-fourths of the region's hospital beds. The OCHSNER Hospital, world famous for its excellence in medicine, is operated by the Alton Ochsner Foundation. Four of the largest hospitals in the central business district are the Veterans Administration Hospital, Charity Hospital, and hospitals affiliated with Louisiana State University and Tulane University. Other medical facilities include DePaul Hospital, United Medical Center, Eye and Ear

Health

Deaths—Total   5,798
Rate per 1,000   10.4
Infant Deaths—Total   167
Rate per 1,000   16.0
Number of Metro Hospitals   21
Number of Metro Hospital Beds   5,755
Rate per 100,000   1,038
Number of Physicians   3,433
Physicians per 1,000   3.22
Nurses per 1,000   7.14
Health Expenditures per Capita $20.41

Institute of Louisiana, Baptist Hospital, St. Charles General Hospital, and East Jefferson General Hospital.

Transportation

In a 1988 survey, New Orleans ranked ahead of Rotterdam, the Netherlands, as the number one port in the world in total cargo tonnage. It is the largest port in the United States (and, along with Amsterdam, the world's busiest). As the main harbor on the Mississippi River, the city provides shippers with unequaled access from the Gulf of Mexico. Highway access to New Orleans includes Interstate 10, U.S. 90, U.S. 61, and the Lake Pontchartrain Causeway, which connects the city with Baton Rouge to the north. Six major railroads serve the New Orleans area—Kansas City Southern, Louisiana & Arkansas Railway, Southern, Santa Fe, Southern Pacific, and Union Pacific—and connect the city and its port facilities to the nation. Air service, both passenger and commercial, is through New Orleans International Airport in nearby Kenner. The Alvin Callender Field at the U.S. Naval Air Station to the south acts as a military airfield.

Transportation
Interstate Highway Mileage   39
Total Urban Mileage   2,982
Total Daily Vehicle Mileage (in millions)   15.375
Daily Average Commute Time   55.9 min.
Number of Buses   400
Port Tonnage (in millions)   175.5
Airports   1
Number of Daily Flights   121
Daily Average Number of Passengers   8,687
Airlines (American carriers only)
American
Continental
Delta
Eastern
Midway
Northwest
Southwest
Trans World
United
USAir

Housing

About 44% of New Orleanians own their homes. The housing stock is quite old, half having been built before 1940 and about one-fourth built in the last century. Many of the older homes in the Garden District and the French Quarter have been restored. The median value of owner-occupied homes in 1990 was $69,600, and the median monthly rent was $277.

Urban Redevelopment

In the 1980s more than $300 million was invested in urban redevelopment projects. Notable among them were the International Trade Mart; the 53-story Place St. Charles, Louisiana's tallest building; and the Rivergate, a huge exhibition hall.

Housing
Total Housing Units   225,573
% Change 1985–1990   -0.4
Vacant Units for Sale or Rent   26,583
Occupied Units   188,235
% with More Than One Person per Room   7.9
% Owner-Occupied   43.7
Median Value of Owner-Occupied Homes $69,600
Average Monthly Purchase Cost $344
Median Monthly Rent $277
New Private Housing Starts   204
Value (in thousands) $16,537
% Single-Family   90.7
Nonresidential Buildings Value (in thousands) $27,036

Tallest Buildings:	Hgt. (ft.)	Stories
One Shell Square (1972)	697	51
Place St. Charles (1985)	645	53
Plaza Tower (1969)	531	45
Energy Centre (1984)	530	39
LL&E Tower (1987)	481	36
Sheraton Hotel (1985)	478	47
Marriott Hotel (1972)	450	42
Texaco Bldg. (1983)	442	33

Crime

New Orleans has a very high crime rate. In 1991 violent crimes totaled 10,969, property crimes totaled 43,269.

Crime
Violent Crimes—Total   10,969
Violent Crime Rate per 100,000   8,839.5
Murder   345
Rape   302
Robbery   5,969
Aggravated Assaults   4,353
Property Crimes   43,269
Burglary   12,400
Larceny   20,977
Motor Vehicle Theft   9,892
Arson   NA
Per Capita Police Expenditures $105.53
Per Capita Fire Protection Expenditures $82.99
Number of Police   1,378
Per 1,000   2.45

Religion

New Orleans is heavily Catholic, with 40% of its population belonging to the Roman Catholic Church. The Catholic

Religion	
Largest Denominations (Adherents)	
Catholic	171,328
Black Baptist	77,820
Southern Baptist	24,295
United Methodist	13,898
Lutheran-Missouri Synod	6,653
Episcopal	6,672
Presbyterian	4,650
Assembly of God	2,051
Jewish	4,814

share of the population is constantly increasing with emigration from Latin American countries.

Media

The city's daily newspapers are the *New Orleans Daily Record* and the *New Orleans Times-Picayune*. There are 7 television stations and 15 AM and FM radio stations.

Media
Newsprint
Black New Orleans, monthly
City Business, biweekly
New Orleans Business, weekly
New Orleans City Business, biweekly
New Orleans Daily Record, daily
New Orleans Times-Picayune, daily
Television
WDSU-TV (Channel 6)
WGNO (Channel 26)
WLAE-TV (Channel 32)
WNOL-TV (Channel 38)
WVUE (Channel 8)
WWL-TV (Channel 4)
WYES-TV (Channel 12)
Radio

WBOK (AM)	WBYU (AM)
WEZB (FM)	WNOE (AM)
WQUE (AM)	WQUE (FM)
WRNO (FM)	WSHO (AM)
WSMB (AM)	WTIX (AM)
WVOG (AM)	WWL (AM)
WYAT (AM)	WYLD (AM)
WYLD (FM)	

Sports

Louisiana boasts the Superdome, the largest indoor stadium in the world, with a capacity of 76,000. It is the home of the New Orleans Saints of the National Football League, as well as the USF&G Sugar Bowl, played annually on New Year's Day between top college football teams. Nearby Tulane University fields teams in college baseball, football, and basketball.

Arts, Culture, and Tourism

The city's culture ranges from jazz to voodoo. Jazz, born as a mixture of African chants, Negro spirituals, and modern sounds, began in Storyville, the red-light district closed by the city in 1917. The jazz scene gave rise to the careers of such notables as Louis Armstrong, Jelly Roll Morton (born Ferdinand Joseph La Menthe), King Oliver, Pete Fountain, and Al Hirt. Bourbon Street in the French Quarter is the home of jazz today. Visitors can hear this special music emanating from every club, including the New Storyville Jazz Hall, Pete Fountain's, and Tiptina's (known as Tip's). Voodoo is uniquely New Orleans—it was allegedly the religion of the African slaves brought to the city from the French Indies. Notable among the faithful was Marie Laveau, who lived at 1022 Ann Street, and practiced her craft until her death. Followers of voodoo, or the just plain curi-

ous, can visit her tomb in St. Louis Cemetery No. 2, where offerings are made to her spirit.

The city's museums include the Confederate Museum, the Historic New Orleans Collection, the New Orleans Museum of Art, the Louisiana Children's Museum, and the Museé Conti—a museum in the French Quarter featuring wax statues of the city's famous personages, including Jean Lafitte, Marie Laveau, and Andrew Jackson.

Travel and Tourism
Hotel Rooms   25,000
Convention and Exhibit Space (square feet)   733,360
Convention Centers
Ernest Morial Convention Center
Superdome
Rivergate
Municipal Auditorium
Festivals
Mardi Gras (February)
Jazz and Heritage Festival (April)
Spring Fiesta (April)
Festival of Food and Cooking (July)

Parks and Recreation

Wildlife abounds near New Orleans and is the attraction at the 22,770-acre Bayou Sauvage National Wildlife Refuge and the recently opened Freeport-McMoRan Audubon Species Survival and Research Center. Audubon Park encompasses approximately 340 acres from St. Charles Avenue to the Mississippi River and contains the Audubon Zoo, considered one of the top five in the nation. It was named after the famed nature artist John James Audubon, who once lived in New Orleans. City Park, between Merconi Drive and Wisner Boulevard, is the site of the New Orleans Museum of Art on LeLong Avenue. Other parks include the Chalmette National Historical Park, site of the Battle of New Orleans in 1815; the Washington Artillery Park; and the Wolfenberg River Park.

Sources of Further Information

City Hall
1300 Perdido Street
New Orleans, LA 70112
(504) 565-6000

Greater New Orleans Tourist and Convention
  Commission
1520 Sugar Bowl Drive
New Orleans, LA 70112
(504) 566-5011

The Chamber
New Orleans and River Region
301 Camp Street
New Orleans, LA 70130
(504) 527-6920

Additional Reading

Arnesen, Eric. *Waterfront Workers of New Orleans: Race, Class, and Politics, 1863–1923.* 1991.

Brasseaux, Carl A. *Denis-Nicolas Foucault and the New Orleans Rebellion of 1768.* 1987.

Bruce, Curt. *The Great Houses of New Orleans.* 1977.

Carter, Hodding, ed. *The Past as Prelude: New Orleans, 1718–1968.* 1968.

Carter, Samuel. *Blaze of Glory: The Fight for New Orleans, 1814–1815.* 1971.

Cary, Beth, and Liz McCarthy. *A Marmac Guide to New Orleans.* 1988.

Castellanos, Henry C. *New Orleans as It Was: Episodes of Louisiana Life.* 1961 (1st ed. 1895).

Clark, John G. *New Orleans, 1718–1812: An Economic History.* 1970.

Cowan, Walter G. *New Orleans Yesterday and Today.* 1983.

Davis, W. Hardy. *Aiming for the Jugular in New Orleans.* 1976.

Garvey, Joan B., and Mary L. Widmer. *Beautiful Crescent: A History of New Orleans.* 1988.

Gehman, Mary. *Women and New Orleans: A History.* 2nd ed. 1988.

Griffin, Thomas K. *The Pelican Guide to New Orleans.* 1978.

Haas, Edward F. *DeLesseps S. Morrison and the Image of Reform: New Orleans Politics, 1946–1961.* 1986.

Hermann, Bernard M. *New Orleans: Photography and Design.* 1980.

Jackson, Joy J. *New Orleans in the Gilded Age: Politics and Urban Progress, 1880–1896.* 1969.

Janssen, James S. *Building New Orleans: The Engineer's Role.* 1987.

Jumonville, Florence M. *Bibliography of New Orleans Imprints, 1764–1864.* 1989.

Kmen, Henry A. *Music in New Orleans: The Formative Years, 1791–1841.* 1966.

Mitchel, Osborne L. *Mardi Gras! A Celebration.* 1981.

———. *New Orleans: The Passing Parade.* 1980.

Niehaus, Earl F. *The Irish in New Orleans, 1800–1869.* 1965.

Reinders, Robert C. *End of an Era: New Orleans, 1850–1869.* 1964.

Reynolds, George M. *Machine Politics in New Orleans, 1897–1926.* 1936.

Siegel, Martin, ed. *New Orleans: A Chronological and Documentary History, 1539–1970.* 1975.

Starr, Frederick S. *Southern Comfort: The Garden District of New Orleans, 1800–1900.* 1989.

Swanson, Betsy. *Historic Jefferson Parish: From Shore to Shore.* 1975.

Vaughn, Howard L., and Robert S. Friedman. *Government in Metropolitan New Orleans.* 1959.

Vogt, Lloyd. *New Orleans Houses: A House-Watcher's Guide.* 1985.

New York

Basic Data

Name New York
Name Origin Duke of York
Year Founded 1624
Status: State New York
   County Bronx, New York, Queens, Kings, New
   York, Putnam, Richmond, Rockland, and Westchester
   counties
Area (square miles) 309
Elevation (feet) 25
Time Zone EST
Population (1990) 7,322,564
Population of Metro Area (1990) 8,546,846

Sister Cities
   Beijing, China
   Cairo, Egypt
   Madrid, Spain
   Santo Domingo, Dominican Republic
   Tokyo, Japan

Distance in Miles To:
Boston	222
Chicago	809
Dallas	1,559
Los Angeles	766
Norfolk	365
Philadelphia	101
Pittsburgh	379
Washington, DC	237

Location and Topography

New York is located on the southeastern tip of New York State, north of the Hudson estuary at the conjunction of the Hudson and East rivers with the New York Bay leading to the Atlantic Ocean. Of the city's five boroughs, four (Manhattan, Staten Island, Queens, and Brooklyn) are islands and only the Bronx is part of the mainland. The entrance to Lower New York Bay is defined on the west by Sandy Hook on the New Jersey shore, and on the east by Rockaway Point, the far southwestern corner of Queens, a part of Long Island. The Narrows, a strait between Staten Island to the west and Brooklyn to the east, separates Upper New York Bay from the Lower. Within the Upper Bay are three small islands, including Governors Island and Liberty (fomerly Bedloes) Island where the Statue of Liberty has welcomed immigrants for over a century. At the head of Upper New York Bay is Manhattan, only 12.5 miles long and 2.5 miles wide. West of Manhattan is the Hudson, or North River, with New Jersey on the opposite bank. Manhattan is separated from Queens and Brooklyn by the East River, which links Long Island Sound with the Upper Bay. Manhattan is divided from the Bronx by the Spuyten Duyvil Creek on the north and the Harlem River on the northwest. The Bronx, 41 square miles in area, is bordered by the Hudson River on the west and Westchester County on the north. It is separated from Queens and Brooklyn by Long Island Sound and the East River. In the Sound are a number of islands, such as Hart, City, Rikers, Randalls, Wards, and Franklin D. Roosevelt (formerly Welfare). South of the Sound is Queens, the largest of the boroughs, 108 square miles in extent. It ends in Rockaway Peninsula, which separates the marshy Jamaica Bay from the Atlantic Ocean. South of western and central Queens and bordering on Jamaica Bay is Brooklyn, 70 square miles in area, coextensive with Kings County. Brooklyn is the most populous of the boroughs. Across the Upper Bay, the Narrows, and the Lower Bay from Brooklyn, is Staten Island, coextensive with Richmond County. It is the only borough not connected directly with Manhattan. A triangular island with an area of 58 square miles, it is separated from New Jersey by Arthur Kill on the west and Newark Bay and Kill Van Kull on the north with Raritan Bay to the southeast.

Layout of City and Suburbs

Manhattan begins at Battery Park and Clinton National Monument at the southwestern tip. To its northeast is the Financial District of which Wall Street is a part. Further to the north is Foley Square where state, city, and federal offices are located. In this area the skyscraper canyons begin with the 792-foot Woolworth Building, 813-foot Chase Manhattan Bank, 900-foot 40 Wall Street, 950-foot 60 Wall Tower, and towering over them all, the 1,350-foot World Trade Center. The western edge of the Financial District is marked by the residential and office high rises of Battery Park City and by the Hudson riverfront esplanade. Around Mott Street in lower Manhattan is Chinatown, one of the city's more famous ethnic neighborhoods, which is slowly creeping into nearby Little Italy. Delancey Street is the main thoroughfare of the Lower East Side, which traditionally extends northward to 14th Street. The part of it north of Houston Street, centered about St. Mark's Place, is the East Village, a revered name in Hippie culture. Greenwich Village proper extends roughly from Houston Street northward to 14th Street and from Hudson River to Broadway. Here are found luxury buildings cheek by jowl with brick row houses. In the eastern part of the Village is Washington Square, dominated by the New York University. In the interwar years, Washington Square was synonymous with haute culture of uprooted artists and writers. More recently Soho (from So[uth of] Ho[uston]), a section of loft buildings with cast-iron facades, south of Houston Street below Greenwich Village, has become an American version of the Left Bank, with many artists' studios and galleries. Fourteenth Street is the big divide with respect to the street configuration. Below it the streets run pell mell, but above it a strict gridiron pattern has been imposed. The streets run east-west and the avenues north-south. The distance between avenues is three times that between streets. Avenues are numbered First to Twelfth from East River to the Hudson River with Lexington between Third and Park and Madison between Park and Fifth. Streets are numbered from First to 220th northward from Houston and are also named East and West with Fifth Avenue as the dividing line. The major exception to this pattern is Broadway, which runs diagonally from Ninth to 79th streets. Where it crosses major avenues it forms squares: Union Square at Park, Madison Square at Fifth, Herald Square at Sixth, Times Square at Seventh, Columbus Circle at Eighth, and Lincoln Square at Columbus. At the southwest corner of Madison Square is the Flatiron Building, one of the city's earliest skyscrapers. Northeast of Union Square is Gramercy Park and along the East River is the NYU-Bellevue Medical Center. North of West 14th Street is Chelsea, where the historic Chelsea Hotel is located.

Midtown Manhattan is the name applied to the area between 34th and 59th streets. It is the site of the largest cluster of skyscrapers in the world, including the 1,250-foot Empire State Building at 34th and Fifth, and close by at Herald Square is the Macy Department Store, claimed to be the largest in the world. The Garment District lies to the north of 34th Street in the west and Murray Hill to the east. The area also contains Madison Square Garden (where the 1992 Democratic Convention was held), Pennsylvania Station, and the General Post Office. Clinton, a working-class neighborhood, is in the west 40s. At the junction of Seventh Avenue, Broadway, and 42nd Street is Times Square (until 1904 Longacre Square), noted as much for its elegant theaters as for its sleazy pornography shops. Going east, 42nd Street passes Bryant Park, the New York Public Library (whose two lions face Fifth Avenue), Grand Central Terminal with the 808-feet Pan Am Building towering over it, and the 777-story art deco Chrysler Building with its 1,048-foot spire. Along the East River between 42nd and 48th streets is the United Nations Building. On Park Avenue in the low 50s are some of the masterpieces of modern architecture—such as Lever House and Seagram Building—as well as older classical structures such as the Waldorf-Astoria Hotel and St. Bartholomew's Church. Madison Avenue is noted for advertising just as Fifth Avenue is noted for shopping. Also on Fifth Avenue is St. Patrick's Cathedral. Close to the cathedral is Rockefeller Center, now owned by Japanese interests, a 25-acre complex of office buildings and plazas, stretching from 48th to 52nd streets and including the RCA Building and the Radio City Music Hall. Some of the more recent skyscrapers have risen up close by, including Citicorp on 53rd and Lexington, AT&T Building and IBM Building (both on Madison Avenue), and the Trump Tower on Fifth Avenue. Carnegie Hall, an equally famous name, is on 57th Street and Seventh Avenue.

In the heart of the city is the rectangular Central Park, extending from 59th to 110th streets and from Fifth Avenue to Eighth Avenue. At the southwest corner of the park is Columbus Circle and at the southeast corner the Grand Army Plaza. Facing Fifth Avenue is the Metropolitan Museum of Art, which stands in the center of Central Park. Temple Emanu-El stands at Fifth and 65th and Mount Sinai Hospital at Fifth and 100th. Yorkville is an old German community in the 80s east of Park Avenue. Overlooking the East River at 88th Street is Gracie Mansion, home of the city's mayors. On Central Park West from 77th to 81st streets are the American Museum of Natural History and the Hayden Planetarium. The area west of Central Park and north of 59th Street is known as the Upper West Side. It is a gentrified residential section, with many new apartment towers and renovated buildings. Some of the most elegant apartment buildings are found in Central Park West and along West End Avenue and Riverside Drive. The main commercial streets here are Broadway, Amsterdam Avenue, and Columbus Avenue. In the west 60s between Columbus and Amsterdam avenues are Lincoln Center for the Performing Arts and the campus of Fordham University. North of 110th

Chronology

1524 Giovanni de Verrazano sails into New York Bay.

1609 Henry Hudson sails his Half Moon into New York Harbor and then proceeds to sail up the river later named after him.

1613 Adriaen Block, shipwrecked near the island, spends a winter in Manhattan.

1621 A trade monopoly is granted to Dutch West India Company in the regions discovered by Henry Hudson, named New Netherland.

1624 Dutch West India Company sends first settlers into Manhattan.

1625 Dutch settlers erect fort, called Fort Amsterdam, at the island's southern tip and lay out a town.

1626 Peter Minuit buys Manhattan Island from the Indians for $24, paid in trinkets.

1628 The first church is erected, now the Collegiate Church.

1633 First school is opened by the Collegiate Church.

1636 First settlement is made in Breukelen (later Brooklyn).

1638 Ferry to Longe Eyelandt (Long Island) opens.

1641 First settlement is made in Bronx, named after Jonas Bronck, who establishes 500-acre farm there.

1642 First public tavern opens.

1645 First settlement is made in Queens.

1647 City receives first charter when Peter Stuyvesant becomes governor.

1648 Wharf is built on East River, marking New York's emergence as a port.

1653 As protection against Indian attacks, a waal or wall is erected which later becomes Wall Street. Governor Stuyvesant grants municipal charter to New York with sheriff, aldermen, and burgomasters.

1655 First Jewish synagogue is built.

1658 First hospital is established.

1660 A privately owned general post office begins operations.

1661 A permanent settlement is made at Oude Dorp on Staten Island.

1664 King Charles of England sends force under Captain Richard Nicholls to seize New York City from the Dutch. Governor Stuyvesant surrenders New York without struggle.

1665 Governor Nicholls reconstitutes municipal government on English lines under mayor, sheriff, and aldermen.

1672 Overland mail service between New York and Boston begins.

1673 City is recaptured by the Dutch but is returned to the English.

1678 New York is declared sole port of entry into the Crown Colonies.

1683 City is divided into six wards, each with an alderman.

1686 Governor Thomas Donggan issues charter authorizing annual election of aldermen.

1689 Jacob Leisler seizes control of the Provincial Government and authorizes election of Peter Delanoy as mayor.

1691 Leisler revolt is crushed.

1693 First bridge is built across the Harlem River. British build the Battery on the southern tip of the island.

1698 Trinity Church is built with help from leading citizens including the notorious pirate, William Kidd.

1727 William Bradford publishes first newspaper, the *New York Gazette*.

1731 Governor John Montgomery's Charter expands municipal powers.

1735 Peter Zenger is acquitted of libel, setting the legal basis for freedom of the press.

1736 Bellevue, the oldest hospital still functioning, opens doors.

1748 The first real estate firm, Cruikshank & Company, opens.

1754 The New York Society Library becomes city's first public library. Kings College, later Columbia University, is founded.

1756 Stage route from New York to Philadelphia begins.

1762 Street lighting is introduced. Fire patrol is established.

1766 St. Paul's Chapel, the oldest extant public building in the United States, is built.

1768 Chamber of Commerce begins functioning.

Chronology (continued)

1776 English forces under Lord Howe capture the city after beating George Washington's forces at the Battle of Long Island.

1783 British evacuate the city.

1784 The city's oldest bank, Bank of New York, is founded. James Duane is appointed the first mayor of the city under republican administration.

1785 New York is declared the capital of the United States and New York State.

1788 City Hall becomes Federal Hall and on its balcony George Washington takes oath of office as president of the United States.

1789 Tammany Hall is founded as a charitable society.

1790 National capital is moved from New York. Coast Guard is set up as Revenue-Marine Service.

1792 New York Stock Exchange is founded.

1797 State capital is moved from New York to Albany.

1801 *New York Post* begins publication.

1804 New York Historical Society is founded.

1807 Robert Fulton's steamboat, *Clermont,* leaves Hudson River pier at Cortlandt Street on her maiden voyage to Albany.

1811 City authorities direct that all streets above Houston should conform to the gridiron pattern.

1812 New City Hall is completed.

1824 Castle Garden is built, first as an auditorium, later becoming a center for immigrants.

1825 Erie Canal is completed. Illuminating gas is supplied to city homes.

1831 New York University is established.

1832 First horse-drawn street railroad car makes trip.

1835 City's largest fire in history destroys 670 buildings east of Broadway and south of Wall Street with losses estimated at $80 million.

1840 Hacks are introduced.

1842 Old Croton Aqueduct and Reservoir are completed.

1843 First insurance company, Mutual Life Insurance, opens door.

1844 Uniformed police force is organized.

1847 Associated Press is formed as first news agency by New York newspapers in conjunction with Magnetic Telegraph Company. Post offices begin selling stamps.

1848 Richard M. Hoe builds first high-speed printing press. James Bogardus builds first cast-iron building at Duane and Center streets.

1853 World's Fair is held at Crystal Palace. Elisha Otis of Yonkers introduces first safety hoisters, forerunners of elevators.

1854 Astor Library opens. Academy of Music is founded.

1858 First trans-Atlantic message sent by the newly laid Atlantic Cable is received in New York.

1859 Central Park, designed by Frederick Law Olmsted and Calvert Vaux, opens.

1863 In bloody draft riots, 1,200 are killed.

1865 First professional fire department is organized.

1869 The first apartments are constructed. On Black Friday, securities speculators Jay Gould and Jim Fisk lose vast fortunes.

1870 The first elevated railroad opens on Ninth Avenue. Metropolitan Museum of Art opens.

1871 Grand Central Station opens.

1875 Boss William Moxey Tweed is convicted of graft and embezzlement.

1878 First telephone exchange opens with a single-page phone directory of 271 names.

1881 On Pearl Street Thomas Edison builds first practical electrical power station.

1883 Brooklyn Bridge is completed. Metropolitan Opera House opens.

1886 Bartholdis's Statue of Liberty is unveiled.

1895 Bronx is annexed to the city.

1898 Brooklyn, Queens, Staten Island, Bronx, and Manhattan are consolidated into New York City.

1902 Flatiron Building is completed. Gimmsel Slocum burns as it passes Hell's Gate on East River with a loss of 1,201 lives.

1903 Williamsburg Bridge opens.

1904 First subway opens.

Chronology (continued)

1909 Queensborough-Manhattan Bridge opens.

1910 Theodore Roosevelt receives city's first ticker tape parade.

1913 Woolworth Building by Cass Gilbert is completed.

1920 Holland Tunnel is completed.

1921 Port of New York Authority is established.

1922 First radio station, WEAF, goes on the air.

1924 First municipal radio station, WNYC, goes on the air.

1927 Goethals Bridge and Outerbridge Crossing are completed. On triumphant return from Paris, Charles Lindbergh receives ticker tape parade.

1930 Chrysler Building is completed.

1931 George Washington Bridge is completed. Bayonne Bridge is completed. Empire State Building is completed. First municipal airfield, Floyd Bennett Field, opens for air traffic.

1932 Rockefeller Center opens. Mayor Jimmy Walker resigns after disclosures of malfeasance.

1934 Work begins on the Lincoln Tunnel.

1936 Henry Hudson Bridge is completed.

1938 City receives new charter.

1939 Whitestone Bridge is completed. LaGuardia Airport opens. World's Fair is held at Flushing Meadows.

1940 Queens Midtown Tunnel is completed.

1943 East River (later FDR) Drive opens.

1946 New York recives record 26 inches of snow. United Nations chooses New York as its world headquarters.

1948 Idlewild (later John F. Kennedy) International Airport opens. West Side Highway is completed.

1950 Brooklyn Battery Tunnel is completed.

1951 Lever House is completed.

1954 Ellis Island closes doors.

1960 New York Throughway opens to Buffalo.

1961 New zoning law takes effect.

1964 Verrazano Narrows Bridge opens.

1965 Idlewild is renamed JFK. Thirteen-hour power blackout shuts down city.

1966 John V. Lindsay becomes first Republican to be elected mayor in 60 years.

1971 Co-op City opens in Bronx.

1973 World Trade Center opens.

1975 New York City is rescued from bankruptcy by a $2.3-billion loan from commercial banks and federal authorities. Municipal Assistance Corporation is set up.

1985 World Financial Center is completed.

1989 David Dinkins becomes first black mayor of city.

Street, also known as Cathedral Parkway, and west of Morningside Park is the Morningside Heights section, site of Columbia University, the Cathedral of St. John the Divine, the Union Theological Seminary, Riverside Church, and Grant's Tomb, a noted landmark.

To the east of Morningside Heights is Harlem, the epicenter of Black America. Harlem stretches eastward to the Harlem and East rivers and south from 155th Street to 110th Street above Central Park and 96th Street east of Fifth Avenue. The main thoroughfare is 125th Street. Here most buildings are run-down. Harlem also has large low- income housing projects, especially around Marcus Gravey Park. East of Park Avenue is the Puerto Rican section of Harlem known as East, or Spanish, Harlem, where the Metropolitan Hospital Center is located. West of Harlem from 125th Street north to about 155th Street is Hamilton Heights, or West Harlem, a largely Hispanic section. Its lower part is known as Manhattanville. The City College of New York extends from Convent Avenue near 138th Street. The Museum of the American Indian and the American Numismatic Society are located at Audubon Terrace, on Broadway between 155th and 156th streets. To the north are Washington Heights and Inwood, both residential areas. Columbia-Presbyterian Medical Center extends from 165th to 168th streets between Broadway and Riverside Drive. Along the Hudson above 192nd Street is Fort Tryon Park, site of the Cloisters, a branch of the Metropolitan Museum of Art. The Inwood Hill Park occupies the northwesternmost tip of the island. The Bronx is essentially a residential borough, its neighborhoods varying from upscale ones, such as Williamsbridge and Riverdale, to middle-income apartment towers, such as Parkchester and Co-op City, to slums such as Morrisania, Mott Haven, and Hunts Point. The Bronx was the popular destination of many Irish, Italians, and Jews displaced from Manhattan's Lower East Side and Harlem in the 1920s. The main campus of Fordham University is at Fordham Road and Third Avenue. Fordham Road, which crosses the Grand Concourse toward the north, is the major shopping center in the borough. Since the 1960s blacks and Puerto Ricans have moved into the area, especially into South Bronx, Tremont, and East Tremont, as well as the north-south Grand Concourse running through West Bronx. Near the southern end of Grand Concourse is Yankee Stadium. At the southeastern corner of South Bronx is Hunts Point, the city's largest wholesale meat and produce market. In the center of the borough is Bronx Park, where the Bronx Zoo is located. The Van Cortlandt Park is in the northwestern Bronx while Pelham Bay Park fronts Long Island Park in the northeast. City Island lies east of the Bronx in Long Island Sound. Edgewater Park and Silver Beach are at the southeastern tip of the Bronx. Brooklyn was once a flourishing city until incorporated into Manhattan in 1897. Nicknamed "the City of Churches," it is known for its bustling downtown known as Civic Center, its tree-lined boulevards, and fine residential areas such as Brooklyn Heights. It has distinctive ethnic communities: the Italian Bensonhurst, the Jewish Borough Park, the black Bedford-Stuyvesant and Brownsville, and the Puerto Rican Sunset Park. Two of Brooklyn's oldest neighborhoods, Brooklyn Heights, and Cobble Hill, lie along East River, west of the downtown area. Flatbush Avenue, the main downtown street, begins at the Manhattan Bridge and runs through the heart of the borough. Its Prospect Park, established in the 1860s, adjoins the Brooklyn Botanic Garden, Brooklyn Museum, and the Brooklyn Public Library. At the southern tip of Brooklyn, fronting the Lower New York Bay, is Coney Island, in fact a peninsula, with its famous beach and boardwalk.

Queens is the oldest and the largest of the five boroughs. It has a number of ethnically distinct communities, such as Flushing, Jamaica, Forest Hills, Astoria, Jackson Heights, and Corona. Long Island City and Maspeth are the principal industrial areas. Both LaGuardia and Kennedy International Airport are located here. Its principal recreational areas are Flushing Meadow–Corona Park, site of the 1939 and 1964 New York World's Fair, Shea Stadium, Aqueduct Raceway, Jacob Riis Park, and Rockaway beachfront. Staten Island, the least populated borough, is essentially suburban with some prominent communities, such as Richmondtown and Tottenville. St. George is the site of the Staten Island Ferry Terminal. New York has 22 fine bridges and tunnels connecting the five boroughs or leading to New Jersey, 15 of them crossing the Harlem River. Among them are the Throgs Neck Bridge, Whitestone Bridge, Triborough Bridge, Queensboro Bridge, Queens Midtown Tunnel, Williamsburg Bridge, Manhattan Bridge, Brooklyn Bridge, Brooklyn Battery Tunnel, Verrazano Narrows Bridge, Holland Tunnel, Lincoln Tunnel, George Washington Bridge. and Third Avenue Bridge. The Harlem River is spanned by High Bridge, opened 1848, Harlem Bridge, Henry Hudson Bridge, and Alexander Hamilton Bridge.

Environment	
Environmental Stress Index	3.8
Green Cities Index: Rank	57
Score	38.29
Water Quality	NA
Average Daily Use (gallons per capita)	NA
Maximum Supply (gallons per capita)	NA
Parkland as % of Total City Area	NA
% Waste Landfilled/Recycled	NA
Annual Parks Expenditures per Capita	$61.09

Climate

The principal climatic influence is continental modified by proximity to the ocean. New York is close to the path of most storm systems that move across the continent as well as from the south. It therefore experiences higher temperatures in summer and lower temperatures in winter than would be expected from its location and latitude. The frequent passage of weather systems is beneficial in reducing the length of the warm and cold spells. Sea breezes help to moderate the heat of summer afternoons and also delay the onset of frigid weather. The normal annual precipitation is 40 inches distributed fairly evenly throughout the year and the average annual snowfall is 29 inches.

Weather			
Temperature			
Highest Monthly Average °F	85.2		
Lowest Monthly Average °F	25.9		
Annual Averages			
Days 32°F or Below	81		
Days above 90°F	16		
Zero Degree Days	0		
Precipitation (inches)	40		
Snow (inches)	29		
% Seasonal Humidity	65		
Wind Speed (m.p.h.)	9.4		
Clear Days	107		
Cloudy Days	133		
Storm Days	20		
Rainy Days	121		
Average Temperatures (°F)	*High*	*Low*	*Mean*
January	38.5	25.9	32.2
February	40.2	26.5	33.4
March	48.4	33.7	41.1
April	60.7	43.5	52.1
May	71.4	53.1	62.3
June	80.5	62.6	71.6
July	85.2	68.0	76.6
August	83.4	66.4	74.9
September	76.8	59.0	68.4
October	66.8	50.6	58.7
November	54.0	40.8	47.4
December	41.4	29.5	35.5

History

Before the arrival of the Europeans, greater New York City was occupied by about 100 Indian villages, inhabited by 29 Indian groups, mostly of Algonquian stock, although the Mohawk Iroquois were the overlords of the region. Twenty-eight years after Columbus arrived in the New World, Giovanni de Verrazano, a Florentine navigator in the service of France, became the first white man to sight New York. Another 85 years passed before Henry Hudson, an Englishman employed by the Dutch West India Company, explored the region and the Hudson River Valley. He named the Hudson River Mauritius River in honor of Prince Maurice of Orange, although the English called it the North River in distinction from the South, or Delaware, River. In 1613 Dutch trader and explorer Adriaen Block and his crew became the first Europeans to live on the island after their ship was destroyed by fire near the bay. Following this expedition, the Dutch government claimed the region and named it New Netherland. In 1621 a trade monopoly in the region was granted to the Dutch West India Company. During the next five years the Dutch were active in the area, building a fortified trading post named New Amsterdam. In 1626, there followed one of the most famous real estate transactions in history when Peter Minuit, the first director general of the company, bought Manhattan (Man-a-hat-ta, or Island of the Hills) Island for the equivalent of $24 in trinkets.

By the 1660s the new settlement had a population of 2,000. A defensive wall built at its northern limits as a barricade against Indian attacks is now Wall Street. During the provincial administration of Peter Stuyvesant (1647–1664) the settlement was granted municipal government with its own schout (sheriff), burgomasters, and schepens (sheriffs). Fire and police services were introduced in the 1650s. Meanwhile, the settlement spread beyond New Amsterdam into neighboring areas. Brooklyn (Breukelen) was settled by 1636; Bronx, named after Jonas Bronck, in 1641; Flushing, in what later became Queens in 1645; and Oude Dorp on Staten Island in 1661. On 8 September 1664, English forces under Captain Richard Nicholls, acting on orders of Charles II, seized the city without firing a shot. The city and colony were renamed New York in honor of the new proprietor, James, Duke of York, and it remained in English hands for the next 120 years with a brief interlude in 1673 when it reverted to Dutch hands. In 1665 Nicholls, the first English governor of the province, reconstituted the government on English lines with a mayor, aldermen, and sheriff. The Thomas Donggan charter of 1686 and the John Montgomery charter of 1731 substantially expanded the city's powers and authorized popular election of aldermen from the six wards into which the town had been divided in 1683. New York prospered under British rule. In 1678 New York was declared the sole port of entry into the colonies and its merchants dominated the trade on the Atlantic Seaboard and the Caribbean. The town's first newspaper, the *New York Gazette*, appeared in 1725 and Kings College, now Columbia University, was founded in 1754. Political life was as vigorous as the commercial one. Following Jacob Leisler's seizure of the provincial government in 1689, Peter Delanoy was elected mayor. In 1734 the popular party won the election for aldermen, and

opposition to royal rule gained a further boost when John Peter Zenger was acquitted in 1735 of libeling the governor. Opposition to British rule gained momentum after the end of the French and Indian Wars. A secret organization known as the Sons of Liberty sprang up in opposition to the Stamp Act, and fighting between them and the British soldiers was a daily occurrence. Delegates from nine colonies attended the Stamp Act Congress meeting in New York City Hall to protest British economic policies. In April 1774 the Sons of Liberty held their own tea party to signalize their opposition. In 1776 General George Washington moved his headquarters to New York City, but in the Battle of Long Island was worsted by the more seasoned British soldiers and forced to withdraw, leaving Manhattan in British hands for the next seven years. New York then became the headquarters of the British army and navy in the Colonies and a Loyalist haven. The last British troops were withdrawn on 25 November 1783 as Washington reentered the city.

From 1785 to 1790 New York was the capital of the United States and it was the state capital until 1796. On 30 April 1789, standing on the balcony of the Federal Hall, George Washington took the **oath** of office as president of the United States. With **the** end of the war New York resumed its economic growth, helped by the completion of the Erie Canal. It overtook Philadelphia and Boston as the principal metropolis of the nation, both in population and in economic power. In 1792 the New York Stock Exchange was founded. New York's population increased from about 12,000 in 1783 to 900,000 by the end of the Civil War and it soon became the first city in the nation with more than a million inhabitants. The demographic growth came not so much from natural increase or internal migration as from immigration from Europe. From the 1840s to the 1890s nearly half the residents were foreign-born, the majority from Russia, Germany, Italy, and Ireland. Tensions between the natives and the foreign-born often erupted in riots, as in 1834, 1835, and 1849. For most of this period, the City Hall was firmly in the hands of the Democratic Party, which enjoyed the support of immigrant voters. The party was the tool of Tammany Hall, an organization that evolved from a charitable society founded in 1789 into one of the most powerful political machines. In the 1860s, under Boss William M. Tweed, Tammany Hall became a synonym for graft, election fraud, bribery, and extortion and its power was not clipped until Tweed and his minions, known as the Tweed Ring, were exposed by Cartoonist Thomas Nast and others, and Tweed was eventually convicted in 1871. Tammany revived in the 1880s and late 1890s under Honest John Kelly and Richard Croker and again in the early 20th century under Charles Murphy. However, New York enjoyed brief interludes of good government under William L. Strong (1895–1897), Seth Low (1902–1903) and John P. Mitchell (1914–1917). The latter half of the 19th century and the early decades of the 20th century also witnessed dramatic changes in the city's infrastructure and in its cultural resources. Electric lighting became available by the 1880s. The Croton Aqueduct, completed in 1842, provided a good, clean water supply. The New York Police Department was organized in 1844 and the first professional fire department in 1865. Central Park, designed by Frederick Law Olmsted and Calvert Vaux, opened in 1859. Mass transit was improved with horsecars by the 1850s, elevated trains "the El" by the 1870s, electric trolleys by the 1890s, and the first subway in 1904. The first modern apartment building opened for tenants in 1869. The skyline began to change with the construction of the Flatiron Building in 1802. The Grand Central opened in 1871 and the Brooklyn Bridge, then called the Eighth Wonder of the World, in 1883. The World's Fair, held in Crystal Palace in 1853, made the city a world-class metropolis and an influential trendsetter in fashion, finance, communications, and culture. The Metropolitan Museum of Art was established in 1870, the Astor Library in 1854, the Academy of Music in 1874, and the Metropolitan Opera in 1883. In 1886, the Statue of Liberty rose on Bedloes (now Liberty) Island, a gift from the people of France. In the last decade of the 19th century, Chicago's impending status as the largest U.S. city increased favor for the proposal to consolidate Greater New York City. With this end in view, the Bronx was annexed in 1895, and three years later Brooklyn, by then the third-largest U.S. city, Queens, and Staten Island were annexed. Since then New York's status as the premier U.S. metropolis has never been challenged. The early part of the 20th century was marked by a flurry of bridge and tunnel building: The Williamsburg Bridge was completed in 1903, Queenborough Manhattan Bridge in 1909, Holland Tunnel in 1920, Goethals Bridge and Outerbridge Crossing linking Staten Island with New Jersey in 1927, the George Washington Bridge, with its 3,500-foot suspension span, and Bayonne Bridge in 1931, Lincoln Tunnel and Queens Midtown Tunnel in 1934, Henry Hudson Bridge in 1936, Whitestone Bridge in 1939, and Brooklyn Battery Tunnel, the world's lowest underwater tunnel, in 1950. The last bridge to be built was the Varrazano Narrows Bridge in 1964. The Port Authority of New York was established in 1921. In 1910 Theodore Roosevelt received the first ticker tape parade, a traditional New York salute to great Americans. He was followed in 1927 by Charles Lindbergh, who received a similar honor after crossing the Atlantic Ocean nonstop from New York to Paris in a solo flight. The skyline continued to change with the Woolworth Building by Cass Gilbert in 1913, Empire State Building in 1931, Chrysler Building in 1930, the Rockefeller Center in 1932, Lever House in 1951, World Trade Center in 1973, and the World Financial Center in 1985. The first Municipal Airport opened at Floyd Bennett Field (later sold to the Navy). It was followed by LaGuardia Airport in 1939 and Idlewild Airport in 1948 (renamed John F. Kennedy International in 1965). New York held two World's Fairs in the 20th century: in 1939 and in 1964, the latter at Flushing Meadows Park. In 1946 the city became a world capital of sorts when the United Nations established its headquarters here in a magnificent structure on the East River. In 1954 a historic institution came to an end when Ellis Island closed its doors as an immigrant reception area; it later reopened as a museum on the 100th anniversary of the Statue of Liberty. A decline in foreign legal immigration was offset by the in-migration of blacks, whose percentage of the population grew from 2% in 1840 to 29% in 1990, as well as Puerto Ricans. A succession of able mayors presided over the modernization of the city, notably Fiorello La Guardia (1934–1945), aided by his able park commissioner, Robert Moses, and John V. Lindsay (1966–1973), the first Republican in 60 years. During the administration of Edward Koch (1978–1989) the city was rescued from the verge of bankruptcy by sound financial maneuvers as well as commercial and federal loans. The crisis spurred the establishment of the Municipal Assistance Corporation as the financial watchdog for the city. In 1989, faced with a massive barrage of problems including crime, racial violence, homelessness, drugs, and deteriorating infrastructure, the city elected its first black mayor, David Dinkins. For the first time in its history New York's problems seemed to be beyond its resources.

Historical Landmarks

New York City contains fewer historical landmarks than Boston or Philadelphia, because as land values soared, many of the older buildings fell to the wrecker's ball. Although only a little more than a century old, the Statue of Liberty is the most visited site in the nation. Nearby Ellis Island, long the entry point for millions of European immigrants, is now a museum. The Browne House, in the Whitestone District of Queens, was built in 1661 and was used as a secret meeting place by the Quakers. The 1783 Dyckman House at 204th Street and Broadway is the only early extant farmhouse. Gracie Mansion, the official residence of the mayor, was originally the weekend home of Archibald Gracie, a merchant. The 1801 Hamilton Grange on Convent Avenue between 141st and 142nd streets was the country home of Alexander Hamilton. City Hall, built in 1826, has long been considered one of the most beautiful in the nation. Its front and sides are of marble and the back of red sandstone. According to one account, this resulted from the belief of the city fathers that the city had reached its limits of growth and would never grow beyond the building. Castle Clinton, which was Castle Garden for a time, was a fort built to defend the city in the War of 1812. The site of the Federal Hall is occupied by a 1842 Greek Revival Building. The birthplace of Theodore Roosevelt on East 20th Street and Grants Tomb near Riverside Drive and 122nd Street are other notable landmarks.

Population

New York is the most populous city in the United States, a status that it has enjoyed since the beginning of the 19th century and one it is not likely to lose in the near future.

Its population is more than twice that of the next largest city, Los Angeles. According to the 1990 census its population was 7,322,564, up by 3.5% from the 1980 total of 7,071,639, although still less than its 1970 population of 7,896,000. However, since hundreds of thousands of workers commute to the city every day, a more realistic population count would be that of the New York standard consolidated statistical area (including Putnam, Rockland, Westchester, Nassau, and Suffolk counties in New York; Bergen, Essex, Hudson, Middlesex, Monmouth, Morris, Passaic, Somerset, and Union counties in New Jersey; and Fairfield County in Connecticut), which is estimated at 17 million. Within New York City, 31.5% live in Brooklyn, 26.7% in Queens, 20.2% in Manhattan, 16.5% in the Bronx, and 4.1% on Staten Island. The population loss of the 1970s affected various boroughs differently. The Bronx and Brooklyn lost more, Manhattan and Queens lost less, and Staten Island gained.

Population		
	1980	1990
Central City	7,071,639	7,322,564
Rank	1	1
Metro Area	8,274,961	8,546,846
Pop. Change 1980–1990 +250,925		
Pop. % Change 1980–1990 +3.5		
Median Age NA		
% Male NA		
% Age 65 and Over 13.0		
Density (per square mile) 23,697		

Households	
Number 2,819,401	
Persons per Household 2.54	
% Female-Headed Households 18.0	
% One-Person Households 32.9	
Births—Total 109,610	
% to Mothers under 20 12.1	
Birth Rate per 1,000 15.3	

Ethnic Composition

Whites make up 52.3% of the population, blacks 28.7%, American Indians 0.4%, Asians and Pacific Islanders 7%, and others 11.7%. Hispanics make up 24.4%. Even in the 17th century New York was more heterogeneous than neighboring Boston or Philadelphia. However, when immigration began in earnest in the mid-19th century, racial riots became common, as in 1834, 1835, and 1849, and were directed principally against the Catholic Irish and East Europeans. By 1860 nearly half the residents were foreign-born. Blacks did not constitute a substantial minority until the early part of the century when legal limits were placed on immigration. The development of ghettoes tempered racial strife, since it introduced a de facto segregation into civic life. Harlem became a black city within the city, and it was by the 1970s 90% black. Since the end of World War II the black population has spilled over into other areas, particularly the Bedford-Stuyvesant, Brownsville, and Crown Heights sections of Brooklyn. Many of the newer black communities are comprised of more recent immigrants from the West Indies, notably Haiti. The largest concentration of Puerto Ricans is in East Harlem, the Lower East Side and Chelsea in Manhattan, Hunts Point, Tremont and South Bronx in the Bronx, and Williamsburg in Brooklyn. About 85% of nonwhites live in areas defined as poverty areas. Jews also have tended to make their home in New York more than in any other U.S. city. An estimated 1.5 million Jews live in the city and suburbs, making New York more Jewish than Tel Aviv. The Jews are widely dispersed, but there are major concentrations in the Upper West Side and Lower West Side in Manhattan and in Co-op City in the Bronx, and also in Williamsburg, Borough Park, and Crown Heights in Brooklyn, and in Queens. The Hasidic Jews are particularly conspicuous in Brooklyn and have tenaciously held on to their distinctive cultural and religious traditions. Dominicans and Cubans are most numerous in the Upper West Side, Lower Washington Heights, and Hamilton Heights. Cubans are also found mixed with other communities in Elmhurst and Jackson Heights in Queens. The Chinese are still remarkably cohesive within their bailiwick of Chinatown. The formerly distinct Italians, Irish, Germans, and other Europeans have become so completely assimilated that they have no clear geographical territories. Italians are almost as numerous as Jews. Vestiges of the formerly closely knit Italian communities survive in Little Italy between Canal Street and Washington Square, and also in East Harlem, once their stronghold. Bay Ridge in Brooklyn also has an Italian preserve. One in every ten New Yorkers is Irish (down from one in three in 1870), and there are still Irish neighborhoods in parts of Queens and the Bronx. Germans are even more assimilated than others, but Yorkville, centering on 86th Street and Third Avenue, remains a German enclave. Although New Yorkers historically have been very tolerant of ethnic diversity, violence tends to erupt periodically on the slightest provocation. Blacks have figured in most of such conflicts since the 1970s. In the late 1980s and early 1990s there were incidents pitting blacks against Koreans in Jamaica, Jews in Crown Heights, and Italians in Bensonhurst. However, since the election of a black mayor in 1989, ethnic violence appears to have been effectively contained.

Ethnic Composition (as % of total pop.)		
	1980	1990
White	60.72	52.26
Black	25.23	28.71
American Indian	0.17	0.38
Asian and Pacific Islander	3.27	7.0
Hispanic	19.88	24.36
Other	NA	11.65

Government

When a consolidated New York City was formed in 1898, it was hailed as the greatest experiment in municipal government.

In size, the city government is larger than many of the nation's states, and its mayor is accorded recognition throughout the nation. Under the 1990 charter the municipal government is highly centralized. The mayor, elected to four-year terms, has wide executive powers, including the authority to organize or disband administrative agencies, and to appoint or remove their heads, as well as strong veto power. The comptroller, also elected to four-year terms, recommends financial policies and advises the mayor and city council in formulating budgets. Each borough has an elected borough president, but no legislative body. Legislative authority is vested in the City Council made up of 51 members elected from individual districts, or wards, for four-year terms; its presiding officer is also chosen in city-wide elections to serve a four-year term. The council makes all laws and it can override mayoral vetoes by a two-thirds majority vote. There are nine major administrative agencies, called administrations, and two agencies that are in fact departments: police and fire. There are certain quasi-independent agencies, like the boards of education and of higher education, the housing authority, and the health and hospitals corporation. In addition, there are two bi-state or regional agencies: the Port Authority of New York and New Jersey, and the Metropolitan Transportation Authority. Politically the city is heavily Democratic with 70% of its voters regularly voting for Democrats and only 13% for Republicans. Although Tammany Hall is dead, the Democratic Party still suffers from the taint of corruption and machine politics. During the final term of Mayor Edward Koch, one borough president was jailed for graft and one committed suicide. Two small political groups, the Conservatives and the Liberals, are also active but have only symbolic influence. The 1990 charter is New York's eighth. The first charter was Nicholl's Charter of 1665, which Anglicized the municipal structure. The second, Donggan's Charter of 1686, authorized the popular election of aldermen. The third, the Montgomery Charter of 1731, was the last granted by a colonial governor, and it substantially expanded the city's powers. After the consolidation of Greater New York, the Charter of 1897 was issued. It created a strongly centralized city government concentrated in City Hall, not in the boroughs. The Charter of 1901 was a counterblast of the Republican establishment in Albany. It modified the 1897 Charter by increasing the power of the boroughs and reducing that of the mayor. It accomplished this by creating the all-powerful Board of Estimates, controlled by the borough presidents. The Charter of 1936 was a product of the LaGuardia administration. It restored to some degree the powers of the mayor and it introduced the City Planning Commission. The Charter of 1961 was a reaction to the growing power of the Board of Estimates, strengthening the mayor as chief executive and curbing the administrative powers of the Board of Estimates. In 1989, after the Supreme Court declared the Board of Estimates unconstitutional, the Board was abolished altogether and the 1990 Charter restored the mayor and council to their original importance in city government.

Government

Year of Home Charter   NA
Number of Members of the Governing Body   51
Elected at Large   16
Elected by Wards   35
Number of Women in Governing Body   14
Salary of Mayor $130,000
Salary of Council Members $55,000
City Government Employment Total   39,329
Rate per 10,000   541.5

Public Finance

The annual budget consists of revenues of $37.806 billion and expenditures of $37.630 billion. The debt outstanding is $26.005 billion and cash and security holdings $48.022 billion. New York has undergone a number of financial crises in the past two decades; the most severe was in the mid-1970s when it came close to bankruptcy. Since then, through rigorous cutbacks in public spending and through tighter fiscal policies, it has managed to avoid large-scale budgetary deficits. Its 1992 budget showed a small surplus.

Public Finance

Total Revenue (in millions) $37,806
Intergovernmental Revenue—Total (in millions) $12,333
Federal Revenue per Capita $994.4
% Federal Assistance   2.63
% State Assistance   29.69
Sales Tax as % of Total Revenue   9.40
Local Revenue as % of Total Revenue   52.46
City Income Tax   yes
Taxes—Total (in millions) $10,634.4

Taxes per Capita
  Total $1,464
  Property $588
  Sales and Gross Receipts $369
General Expenditures—Total (in millions) $20,590.1
General Expenditures per Capita $2.835
Capital Outlays per Capita $242

% of Expenditures for:
  Public Welfare   20.6
  Highways   2.8
  Education   21.0
  Health and Hospitals   10.5
  Police   5.7
  Sewerage and Sanitation   4.8
  Parks and Recreation   1.5
  Housing and Community Development   6.4
Debt Outstanding per Capita $1,781
  % Utility   18.5
Federal Procurement Contract Awards (in millions)
  $2,317.1
Federal Grants Awards (in millions) $6,510
Fiscal Year Begins   July 1

Economy

New York may be described as having a post-industrial economy in which invisibles like financial services and tourism account for a substantial part of the Gross City Product. Its economic base is so immense, so varied, and so global that it defies description in terms commonly used by urban economists. Even though each of its sectors remains vulnerable to national and regional down cycles, the whole maintains an astonishing degree of dynamism and vigor. There is no national economic sector in which New York does not have a strong impact. It is the third largest (after Los Angeles–Long Beach and Chicago) manufacturing center with 17,000 industrial plants. The largest manufacturing industries are printing, publishing, and the production of apparel. Other important industries are the electrical and food products industries. In the invisibles sector, tourism is the primary driving force, but there are a number of others, such as legal services, management services, membership organizations, entertainment services, and education services. New York is the headquarters of 69 of the leading 500 industrial corporations, and it is also the U.S. headquarters of some of the largest foreign industrial corporations. Although there has been a steady exodus of corporations from the city in recent years, the majority have found the city indispensable for their activities because it offers an array of services not provided elsewhere on the same scale. The presence of Wall Street financial firms and the New York Stock Exchange adds further sinews to the local economy. With a population of 7 million within city limits, and a consolidated metro population of 16 million, New York is the richest retail market in the nation. There are over 20,000 wholesale firms in the city employing over 240,000 people. New York also is a preeminent transportation center and the Port of New York and New Jersey is the second busiest in the nation.

Economy

Total Money Income (in millions) NA		
% of State Average 95.1		
Per Capita Annual Income $11,188		
% Population below Poverty Level 20.0		
Fortune 500 Companies 35		
Banks	*Number*	*Deposits (in millions)*
Commercial	79	155,321
Savings	9	26,913.3
Passenger Autos 2,051,332		
Electric Meters NA		
Gas Meters NA		

Manufacturing

Number of Establishments 14,595
% with 20 or More Employees 30.9
Manufacturing Payroll (in millions) $10,530.1
Value Added by Manufacture (in millions) $24,542.8
Value of Shipments (in millions) $44,693.6
New Capital Expenditures (in millions) $697.6

Wholesale Trade

Number of Establishments 20,062
Sales (in millions) $186,441
Annual Payroll (in millions) $6,707.4

Retail Trade

Number of Establishments 60,453
Total Sales (in millions) $33,735

Economy (continued)

Sales per Capita $4,645
Number of Retail Trade Establishments with Payroll 40,453
Annual Payroll (in millions) $4,586.5
Total Sales (in millions) $32,576.2
General Merchandise Stores (per capita) $501
Food Stores (per capita) $867
Apparel Stores (per capita) $496
Eating and Drinking Places (per capita) $627

Service Industries

Total Establishments 52,626
Total Receipts (in millions) $44,343
Hotels and Motels (in millions) $1,960
Health Services (in millions) $4,584.2
Legal Services (in millions) $7,786.6

Labor

 With a work force of 3.53 million and a payroll of over $120 billion, New York is the largest job market in the nation. However, New York offers the paradox of a thriving economy with a lagging employment market. The city has consistently had one of the highest unemployment rates in the nation, close to 10% on the average for the last ten years. The reason appears to lie in the downsizing of most establishments that suffered from overstaffing in the 1980s, the rise of less labor-intensive economic activities, and the changing manpower needs of the economy as a whole. Although big business dominates the economic landscape, small business employers are overwhelmingly in the majority. Of a total of 187,780 establishments, 164,078 employ fewer than 20 employees and only 4,375 employ over 100 workers. The labor participation rate at 57.6% is much lower than that of the national average of 66.7%. This indicates a mismatch between manpower quality and available jobs.

Labor

Civilian Labor Force 3,339,000
% Change 1989–1990 1.4

Work Force Distribution
Mining 1,300
Construction 152,000
Manufacturing 461,100
Transportation and Public Utilities 240,100
Wholesale and Retail Trade 762,100
FIRE (Finance, Insurance, Real Estate) 582,100
Service 1,250,700
Government 656,100
Women as % of Labor Force NA
% Self-Employed NA
% Professional/Technical NA
Total Unemployment 228,000
Rate % 6.8
Federal Government Civilian Employment 76,084

Education

 The New York public school system is the largest in the nation with an enrollment close to 1 million in close to 1000 schools.

Over 70% of the pupils are black or Hispanic. Another 350,000 students attend private and parochial schools. Nearly two-thirds of private school enrollment is white. Since 1969 local management of public elementary and middle schools has been vested in 32 community school boards, each headed by an elected superintendent. A seven-member Board of Education supervises the local boards and controls the high schools. Each of the five borough presidents nominates one member of the board and the mayor selects two. The board chooses its own president and appoints a professional as chancellor. New York is the only city in the nation to provide public education through the university level. The municipal City University of New York (CUNY) runs ten four-year colleges and 7 two-year colleges and also the John Jay College of Criminal Justice and the Mount Sinai School of Medicine. Among the two dozen private colleges, Columbia University is the oldest and the most prestigious. Fordham University, located in the Bronx, is the premier Jesuit institution in the nation. St. John's in Queens and Manhattan College and St. Vincent's in the Bronx are other distinguished Catholic institutions. Yeshiva University, founded in 1886, serves Orthodox Jews. Other institutions include Rockefeller University and New York University. In addition there are a number of specialized institutions, such as Juilliard School of Music, New School for Social Research, Cooper Union, and Pratt Institute.

Education

Number of Public Schools   1,000
Special Education Schools   52
Total Enrollment   943,969
% Enrollment in Private Schools   NA
% Minority   80.9
Classroom Teachers   55,343
Pupil-Teacher Ratio   17:1
Number of Graduates   35,982
Total Revenue (in millions)   NA
Total Expenditures (in millions)   NA
Expenditures per Pupil   NA
Educational Attainment (Age 25 and Over)
    % Completed 12 or More Years   60.2
    % Completed 16 or More Years   17.3
Four-Year Colleges and Universities   22
    Enrollment   153,087
Two-Year Colleges   14
    Enrollment   44,842

Libraries

Number   728
Public Libraries   82
Books (in thousands)   NA
Circulation (in thousands)   NA
Persons Served (in thousands)   NA
Circulation per Person Served   NA
Income (in millions) $198,130
Staff   NA

Four-Year Colleges and Universities
    Barnard College
    The Berkeley School of New York
    Boricua College
    City University of New York

Education (continued)

    City University of New York Bernard M. Baruch College
    City University of New York College
    City University of New York Hunter College
    City University of New York John Jay College of Criminal Justice
    College for Human Services
    The College of Insurance
    Columbia University in the City of New York
    Cooper Union
    Fashion Institute of Technology
    The Juilliard School
    Manhattan School of Music
    Marymount Manhattan College
    New School for Social Research
    New York Institute of Technology
    New York University
    School of Visual Arts
    State University of New York College of Optometry
    Yeshiva University

Health

 New Yorkers are served by over 88 hospitals and medical centers, including three dozen teaching hospitals and seven medical schools. The largest of these are the Columbia-Presbyterian Hospital, Mount Sinai Medical Center, Montefiore Hospital, and Albert Einstein Hospital. The New York City Health and Hospitals Corporation runs 11 acute-care hospitals, 5 long-term facilities, and a number of other clinics. The municipal hospitals provide medical care to all who need it and are subsidized by city, state, and federal funds. The quality of health care in New York is unmatched in the nation, but is also the most expensive. The biggest threat to the public care system is the rise and spread of the AIDS epidemic, which is already the leading cause of death among New Yorkers under 40. The medical sector accounts for over 13% of the city's gross product.

Health

Deaths—Total   74,762
Rate per 1,000   10.4
Infant Deaths—Total   1,420
Rate per 1,000   13.0
Number of Metro Hospitals   88
Number of Metro Hospital Beds   46,187
Rate per 100,000   636
Number of Physicians   NA
Physicians per 1,000   3.99
Nurses per 1,000   4.93
Health Expenditures per Capita   74.94

Transportation

 New York is the major hub of transportation in the Northeast. The city is approached by the New Jersey Turnpike (I-95) from the south, which becomes the New England Throughway north of the city, running to Boston and beyond. From the north the New York Thruway (I-87) connects with Major Deegan Expressway, which follows the east side of the Harlem River through the Bronx. Other major arteries are the Shore and Gowanus parkways in Brooklyn, and Grand Central Parkway and Long Island Expressway in Queens. Franklin D. Roosevelt Drive carries traffic along the eastern edge of the city and West Side Highway along the west. A much larger proportion of people use public transportation facilities in New York than in other American cities. On a normal day more than 5 million people use the subways and buses. Three major subway lines provide north-south service in Manhattan, the Bronx, Brooklyn, and Queens. They operate on about 230 miles of track. The Interborough Rapid Transit (IRT), the first subway, opened in 1904 followed by Independent Subway (IND) and Brooklyn Manhattan Transit Company (BMT). Despite the popularity of public transportation, more than 1 million cars enter the central business district each day, creating a gridlock on most intersections during rush hours. Parking is widely available in commercial garages, but is expensive. Alternate side of the road parking rules are enforced on working days. Two major railroad stations serve New York: Grand Central Terminal at 42nd Street and Park Avenue, and Pennsylvania Station on 31st Street and Seventh Avenue. In the mid-1960s the upper level of Penn Station was torn down and replaced by Madison Square Garden, but trains continue to operate beneath street level. Rail passenger services are provided by Amtrak, which runs the famous Metroliner to Washington and Boston. Commuter services include Metro North run by Metropolitan Transportation Authority, Long Island Railroad, and New Jersey Transit. The Port of New York and New Jersey is the nation's second-busiest port (after Los Angeles), and with 450 miles of waterfront, one of the longest. Activity at the port, however, has declined since 1959 as ships now travel up the St. Lawrence Seaway directly to the ports of the Great Lakes. The Port Authority of New York and New Jersey also operates the World Trade Center in New York. La Guardia Airport and Kennedy International Airport handle most of New York's commercial air traffic. The former serves domestic and Canadian traffic, and the latter domestic and international flights. Newark International Airport in New Jersey also serves the metro area. The Staten Island Ferry is the last major survivor of the major ferries that connected Manhattan with the other boroughs in the last century.

Transportation
Interstate Highway Mileage   431
Total Urban Mileage   35.341
Total Daily Vehicle Mileage (in millions)   224.22
Daily Average Commute Time   81.0
Number of Buses   3,279
Port Tonnage (in millions)   NA
Airports   3
Number of Daily Flights   NA
Daily Average Number of Passengers   NA

Transportation (continued)
Airlines (American carriers only)
American
American West
Continental
Delta
Eastern
Midwest Express
Northwest
Pacific Interstate
Trans World
United
USAir

Housing

Apartment living is the norm rather than the exception in New York City. About 65% of the families live in apartments and about 70% rent. About half of the housing was built before 1940, a larger percentage than in many other cities. The city has extensive laws protecting the tenant, requiring landlords to furnish basic and adequate services, and controlling rents. The city also has built many housing projects. About 170,000 low-income families live in public housing. Like other cities, New York has its slums and its upscale areas. The slums are found in Harlem, Bedford-Stuyvesant, Hamilton Heights, Mott Haven, Morrisania, and Hunts Point. Soho and Greenwich Village are the artsy and avant-garde districts, while Chelsea is becoming gentrified. Most professionals and wealthy natives live on the Upper East Side, the Upper West Side, and Gramercy Park in Manhattan; Riverdale in the Bronx; and Brooklyn Heights and Park Slope in Brooklyn. Of the total stock of housing, 28.6% is owner-occupied. The median value of an owner-occupied home is $189,600 and the median monthly rent $448.

Housing		
Total Housing Units 2,992,169		
% Change 1980–1990 1.5		
Vacant Units for Sale or Rent 130,092		
Occupied Units 2,819,401		
% with More Than One Person per Room 12.3		
% Owner-Occupied 28.6		
Median Value of Owner-Occupied Homes $189,600		
Average Monthly Purchase Cost NA		
Median Monthly Rent $448		
New Private Housing Starts 6,858		
Value (in thousands) $519,928		
% Single-Family 18.3		
Nonresidential Buildings Value (in thousands) $169,369		
Tallest Buildings	*Hgt. (ft.)*	*Stories*
World Trade Center (2 towers)	1,368	110/110
Empire State	1,250	102
Chrysler	1,046	77
American International	950	67
40 Wall Tower	927	71
Citicorp Center	927	71

Urban Redevelopment

 New York has arrived at a plateau in its physical development, the constraints on expansion becoming more evident every year. The skyscraper was the one engineering breakthrough that helped the city to grow in this century, but growth even in the vertical direction appears to have reached its limits. The 1980s saw an extraordinary surge in building programs, but the result was overbuilding, creating a glut in office space, which brought many big real estate firms to grief. New York may have reached the end of its skyscraper era, which began with the Flatiron Building in 1901. However, there are many plans on the drawing board calling for more and bigger structures to replace the dilapidated ones. Times Square and the murky 42nd Street are targeted for four large office towers designed to add new life into the heart of the city. Nearby developers plan a theater and entertainment complex. A cluster of low-rise office buildings is planned near Central Park on Columbus Circle. TriBeCa (short for Tri[angle] Be[low] Ca[nal] Street]) is another area targeted by developers, as is the Hunters Point Waterfront.

Crime

New York has earned a reputation for widespread crime, which is borne out by statistics. It ranks 332nd out of 333 cities in public safety, outranked only by Miami. Of crimes known to police in 1991, 170,390 were violent crimes and property crime numbered 508,465 cases. The three most characteristic features of the New York criminal scene are the high rate of drug-related crimes, the high rates of juveniles among the criminals, and the high rates of recidivists or returning criminals who are circling through the criminal justice system. Further, violent crimes increased by 22.7% from 1985 to 1990 while property crimes decreased by 1.2%. The distribution of violent crimes by boroughs showed Brooklyn leading by 37%, followed by Manhattan 27%, the Bronx 19%, Queens 16%, and Staten Island 1%. In property crimes Manhattan leads with 30%, Brooklyn with 27%, Queens with 24%, the Bronx with 15%, and Staten Island with 4%. The increase in crime has impacted heavily not only on judicial caseloads but also on correction facilities. The average daily inmate population of city jails in 1990 was 50% more than in 1985.

Crime

Violent Crimes—Total   170,390
Violent Crime Rate per 100,000   2,044
Murder   2,154
Rape   2,892
Robbery   98,512
Aggravated Assaults   66,832
Property Crimes   508,465
Burglary   112,015
Larceny   256,473
Motor Vehicle Theft   139,977
Arson   5,199

Crime (continued)

Per Capita Police Expenditures $239.32
Per Capita Fire Protection Expenditures $101.09
Number of Police   20,073
Per 1,000   36.3

Religion

New York has 3,600 churches, synagogues, temples, and mosques and other assorted religious buildings. The largest religious denomination is Roman Catholic, whose numbers are buttressed by the rising Hispanic migration. Some 23% of New Yorkers identify themselves as Protestants, 26% as Jewish, and 3% as other faiths or nonbelievers. Churches are among the most impressive landmarks in the city. The Cathedral of St. John the Divine on Amsterdam Avenue, the seat of the Episcopal Bishop of New York, is larger than Notre Dame in Paris and Westminster Abbey in London combined. The distance from one end to the other exceeds two football fields, and the great vaulted ceiling soars 12 stories. Among its outstanding features are an organ of 8,035 pipes, a pure marble baptistery, and a great rose window 40 feet in diameter, containing 10,000 pieces of glass. St. Patrick's Cathedral, on Fifth Avenue opposite Rockefeller Center, is the seat of the Roman Catholic Archbishop of New York. A light-colored Gothic Church built between 1858 and 1888, it is impressive because it stands against a setting of concrete canyons. Trinity Church, at the Broadway end of Wall Street, is the richest church in the United States with extensive real estate in lower Manhattan. Founded in 1698, it expanded with a land grant from Queen Anne in 1705. The present building, which dates from 1846, is surrounded on three sides by a cemetery. The oldest building in New York, completed in 1766, is St. Paul's Chapel on Broadway across from City Hall Park. As president of the new nation, President Washington often worshipped here. The second-oldest church is St. Mark's-in-the-Bowery. Its churchyard, constructed in 1799, contains the grave of Peter Stuyvesant, the last Dutch governor of New York. Among other places of worship are the interdenominational Riverside Church near Columbia University, Christ Church in Riverdale, Friends Meeting House in Flushing, St. George's Ukrainian Catholic Church on East Seventh Street, Marble Collegiate Church on Fifth Avenue and Twenty-ninth, Grace Church on Broadway at Tenth Street, John Street United Methodist Church in downtown where American Methodism began in 1768, and Henry Ward Beecher's Plymouth Church of the Pilgrims in Brooklyn Heights. The home of the oldest Jewish congregation in the country is Shearith Israel, founded by Spanish Sephardim in 1654. The oldest synagogue in continuous use is the Central Synagogue on 55th Street and Lexington Avenue, built in 1872. The largest synagogue is Temple Emanu-El at Fifth Avenue and 65th Street, which holds more people than St. Patrick's Cathedral.

Religion

Largest Denominations (Adherents)	
Catholic	564,969
Jewish	274,300
American Zion	80,018
Black Baptist	61,914
American Baptist	29,827
Episcopal	23,627
United Methodist	13,982
Presbyterian	11,042

Media

The New York press consists of five dailies: the *New York Times*, the *Daily News* and the *Post*, the *Wall Street Journal*, and *Newsday*. The *Wall Street Journal*, founded in 1882, is the best-selling newspaper in the United States, with a number of editions around the country. The *New York Times*, founded in 1851 as the *New York Daily Times* by Henry J. Raymond and George Jones, was bought by Adolph Ochs in 1896 and transformed into one of the most influential newspapers in the nation. The *New York Post* is one of the oldest newspapers now being published. It was begun in 1801 by William Coleman with the backing of Alexander Hamilton. The *New York Post* and the *Daily News* are tabloids. In addition there are 69 neighborhood newspapers, 15 daily trade newspapers, and 69 foreign language newspapers. The electronic media consist of 6 television stations, 3 radio networks, and 32 local AM and FM radio stations. The city is the headquarters for the 3 major television broadcasting networks, CBS, NBC, and ABC.

Media

Newsprint
- *Business Week*, weekly
- *New York Daily News*, daily
- *New York Magazine*, weekly
- *New York Perspective*, weekly
- *New York Times*, daily
- *The New Yorker*, weekly
- *Newsday*, daily
- *Newsweek*, weekly
- *Post*, daily
- *Wall Street Journal*, daily
- *The Wall Street Transcript*, weekly

Television
- WABC (Channel 7)
- WCBS (Channel 2)
- WNBC (Channel 4)
- WNET (Channel 13)
- WNYW (Channel 5)
- WPIX (Channel 11)

Radio

WABC (AM)	WADO (AM)
WBLS (FM)	WCBS (AM)
WCBS (FM)	WEVD (AM)
WHCR (FM)	WHTZ (FM)
WINS (AM)	WKCR (FM)
WKDM (AM)	WLIB (AM)
WLTW (FM)	WNCN (FM)
WNEW (AM)	WNEW (FM)

Media (continued)

WNSK (FM)	WNWK (FM)
WNYC (AM)	WNYC (FM)
WOR (AM)	WPLJ (FM)
WQCD (FM)	WQHT (FM)
WQXR (AM)	WQXR (FM)
WRKS (FM)	WSKQ (AM)
WSKQ (FM)	WXRK (FM)
WYNY (FM)	WZRC (AM)

Sports

New York is represented in every sport by one or more professional teams: the Knicks in basketball, the Giants and Jets in football, the Yankees and Mets in baseball, the Rangers and Islanders in hockey, and the Apples in tennis. The major sports arenas are Madison Square Garden in Manhattan, Shea Stadium in Queens, and Yankee Stadium in the Bronx. The Giants and the Jets play in the Giants Stadium in nearby East Rutherford in New Jersey. The major racetrack is the Aqueduct Race Track in Queens.

Arts, Culture, and Tourism

New York has long prided itself as the arbiter of American culture of both the high and pop varieties. Latest trends in music, dance, and stage first break in New York and then slowly make their way across the country. In fact, culture is one of the principal attractions of the city, whose quality of life has been deteriorating in other areas. New York may be described as the capital of the American stage as Hollywood is of the American cinema.

Between Broadway and the west 40s and 50s there are over 38 playhouses. There are hundreds of smaller off-Broadway and off-off-Broadway theaters, mostly in Greenwich Village and Chelsea. Between 350 and 400 motion picture theaters and countless bars, nightclubs, discotheques, and supper clubs enliven the after-dark Manhattan world. The most representative theater companies are Circle Repertory Company, Classic Stage Company, Ensemble Studio Theater, Hudson Guild Theater, Jewish Repertory Theater, Lincoln Center Theater, Manhattan Theater Club, Mirror Repertory Company, New Dramatists, New Federal Theater, New York Shakespeare Festival, New York Theater Workshop, Soho Repertory Theater, RAPP Arts Center, American Place Theater, New Theater of Brooklyn, and WPA Theater. Lincoln Center for the Performing Arts located north of the Theater District includes three performing arts auditoriums: Avery Fisher Hall, home of the New York Philharmonic; New York State Theater, home of the City Ballet, the City Opera, and the Metropolitan Opera House. Other facilities in the Lincoln Center are the Vivian Beaumont Theater, the Juilliard School, and the Alice Tully Hall. Other major music and dance facilities include the Carnegie Hall, New York City Center, and the Brooklyn Academy of Music. The major orchestral groups are American Symphony Orchestra, Bronx Symphony Orchestra, Brooklyn Philharmonic Symphony Orchestra,

Cosmopolitam Symphony Orchestra, National Orchestra, New York Chamber Players, New York City Symphony, New York Pops Orchestra, Staten Island Symphony, and West End Symphony. Opera is represented by Brooklyn Lyric Opera, New York Lyric Opera, and New York City Opera. Ballet is represented by Alvin Ailey American Dance Theater, American Ballet Theater, Ballet Manhattan, Dance Theater of Harlem, Joffrey Ballet, Martha Graham Dance Company, New York Theater Ballet, Metropolitan Opera Ballet, Rudolf Nureyev & Friends, and Twyla Tharp Dance. The flagship museum is the Metropolitan Museum of Art in Central Park with massive collections representing every age and culture. The Cloisters in Fort Tryon Park is a branch of the Metropolitan and is dedicated to the Middle Ages. At Fifth Avenue and 70th Street is the Frick Collection, primarily of European art. The Pierpont Morgan Library owns priceless illuminated manuscripts. Three museums with outstanding collections of modern art are the Museum of Modern Art on West 53rd Street; the Solomon R. Guggenheim Museum on Fifth Avenue, in a recently renovated cylindrical building designed by Frank Lloyd Wright; and the Whitney Museum of American Art on Madison Avenue. Other outstanding museums include the Brooklyn Museum, American Museum of Natural History, American Numismatic Society, Asia Society Galleries, Bronx County Historical Society, Bronx Museum of the Arts, Brooklyn Historical Society, Cooper-Hewitt Museum, China House Gallery, Cullom Davis Museum, City Island Museum, Fraunces Tavern Museum, Hall of Fame for Great Americans, Hispanic Society of America, International Center of Photography, Japan Society Gallery, Jewish Museum, Museum of American Folk Art, Museum of the American Indian, Museum of Primitive Art, New York Jazz Museum, South Street Seaport Museum, Studio Museum in Harlem, Museum of the City of New York, Nicholas Roerich Museum, National Academy of Design, and Staten Island Historical Society.

Travel and Tourism

Hotel Rooms   37,355
Convention and Exhibit Space (square feet)   NA

Convention Centers
Carnegie Hall
Grand Hyatt New York
Jacob K. Javits Convention Center of New York
Madison Square Garden
The Plaza
Shearson Lehman Brothers Conference Center
Sheraton New York Hotel & Towers
Waldorf-Astoria & Waldorf Towers
The World Trade Center

Festivals
Jazz Festival (February)
Snug Harbor Sculpture Festival (June-October)
New York Renaissance Festival (July-September)
Annual Autumn Craft Festival (August)
Richmond County Fair (August-September)
New York Film Festival (October)

Parks and Recreation

 New York has over 1,000 parks, covering 37,000 acres, of which the largest and best known is 843-acre Central Park. Designed by Frederick Law Olmsted and Calvert Vaux, it is 2.5 miles long and half a mile wide and occupies 5% of the city's land area. The 26,172-acre Gateway National Recreation Area lies along the Hudson River. Each borough has at least one major park. Brooklyn's Prospect Park was considered by Olmsted and Vaux as their finest achievement. Bronx's Van Cortlandt is the largest of the municipal parks. Flushing Meadow Park in Queens was the site of two World's Fairs, those of 1939 and 1964. Staten Island's La Tourette Park features the 96-acre Richmondtown Restoration.

Sources of Further Information

City Hall
New York, NY 10007
(212) 788-3000

New York Chamber of Commerce and Industry
One Battery Park Plaza
New York, NY 10004
(212) 493-7500

New York Convention and Visitors Bureau
Two Columbus Circle
New York, NY 10019
(212) 397-8200

New York Historical Society
170 Central Park West
New York, NY 10024
(212) 873-3400

New York Public Library
Fifth Avenue and 42nd Street
New York, NY 10018
(212) 221-7676

Additional Reading

Allen, Oliver E. *New York, New York. A History of the World's Most Exhilarating and Most Challenging City.* 1991.
Bayor, Ronald H. *Neighbors in Conflict: The Irish, Germans, Jews, and Italians of New York City, 1929–41.* 1988.
Bender, Thomas. *New York Intellect: A History of Intellectual Life in New York City from 1750 to the Beginnings of Our Own Time.* 1987.
Bookbinder, Bernie. *City of the World: New York and Its People.* 1989.
Bridges, Amy A. *A City in the Republic: Antebellum New York and the Origins of Machine Politics.* 1984.
Burnham, Alan. *New York City: The Development of the Metropolis. An Annotated Bibliography.* 1988.

Cheryn, Jerome. *New York as Myth, Marketplace and Magical Land.* 1987.

Cohen, Barbara. *New York Observed: Artists and Writers Look at the City, 1650 to the Present.* 1987.

Danielson, Michael N., and Jameson W. Doig. *New York: The Politics of Urban Regional Development.* 1982.

Diamondstein, Barbaralee. *The Landmarks of New York.* 1988.

Earle, Alice M. *Colonial Days in Old New York.* 1990.

Ellis, Edward R. *New York City: A Narrative History.* 1990.

Furer, Howard B. *New York: A Chronological and Documentary History, 1524–1970.* 1974.

Goldberger, Paul. *The City Observed: New York. A Guide to the Architecture of Manhattan.* 1979.

Goler, Robert I. *Capital City: New York After the Revolution.* 1987.

Hammack, David C. *Greater New York at the Turn of the Century.* 1982.

Howe, Irving. *World of Our Fathers.* 1989.

Kazin, Alfred. *Our New York.* 1990.

Kessner, Thomas. *Fiorello H. LaGuardia and the Making of Modern New York.* 1991.

Kieran, John. *A Natural History of New York City.* 1982.

London, Herbert. *The Broken Apple: New York in the 1980s.* 1989.

Lopez, Manuel D. *New York: A Guide to Information and Reference Sources.* 1980.

MacBean, J. P. *New York: Heart of the City.* 1990.

McDarrah, Fred W. *Museums in New York.* 1983.

McKay, Donald A. *The Building of Manhattan.* 1989.

Millstein, Gilbert. *New York.* 1977.

Mohl, Raymond A. *Poverty in New York, 1783–1825.* 1971.

Mollenkopf, John H. *Power, Culture and Place: Essays on New York City.* New York, 1989.

Nevins, Allan, and John A. Krout. *The Greater City: New York, 1898–1948.* 1981.

Pencak, William. *Immigration to New York City.* 1991.

Plunz, Richard A. *A History of Housing in New York City.* 1990.

Preato, Robert R. *New York: Empire City in the Age of Urbanism, 1875–1945.* 1992.

Rajs, Jake. *Manhattan: An Island in Focus.* 1985.

Reynolds, Donald M. *Manhattan Architecture.* 1988.

Rosenberg, Terry J. *Poverty in New York City, 1980–85.* 1987.

Rosenwalke, Ira. *Population History of New York City.* 1972.

Salins, Peter. *New York Unbound.* 1988.

Schachtman, Tom. *Skyscraper Dreams: The Great Real Estate Dynasties of New York.* 1991.

Spann, Edward K. *The New Metropolis: New York City, 1840–1857.* 1981.

Stewart, Frances, Todd. *City Grows Up: New York.* 1991.

Taylor, William R. *Inventing Times Square: Culture and Commerce at the Crossroads of the World.* 991.

White, E. B. *Here Is New York.* 1988.

Politics and Society

Bellush, Jewel, and Dick Netzer. *Urban Politics: New York Style.* 1990.

Bernstein, Blanche. *The Politics of Welfare: The New York Experience.* 1982.

Boggs, Vernon. *The Apple Sliced: Sociological Studies of New York City.* 1988.

Cole, William. *New York: A Literary Companion.* 1991.

Erenberg, Lewis A. *Steppin Out: New York Nightlife and the Transformation of American Life, 1890–1930.* 1984.

Gates, Robert A. *The New York Vision: Interpretations of New York City in the American Novel.* 1987.

Kivelson, Adrienne. *What Makes New York City Run?* 1990.

Mandelbaum, Seymour. *Boss Tweed's New York.* 1982.

Newfield, Jack, and Wayne Barrett. *New York for Sale: Ed Koch and the Betrayal of New York.* 1989.

Ryans, Herbert F. *New York City Politics: A Study of Delivery Systems.* 1989.

Sayre, Wallace S., and Herbert Kaufman. *Governing New York City.* 1960.

Wagner, Robert F. *New York Ascendant: The Report of the Commission on the Year 2000.* 1988.

Newark

New Jersey

Location and Topography

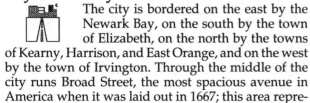

Newark is located in northeastern New Jersey along the west bank of the Passaic River and Newark Bay. Part of the Piedmont region, the Newark area is flat and marshy with some high ground in the southwest and northeast. The city is hemmed in by the sharply rising First Mountain to the west and the sinuous Passaic River that flows through sodden marshes to the east.

Layout of City and Suburbs

The city is bordered on the east by the Newark Bay, on the south by the town of Elizabeth, on the north by the towns of Kearny, Harrison, and East Orange, and on the west by the town of Irvington. Through the middle of the city runs Broad Street, the most spacious avenue in America when it was laid out in 1667; this area repre-sents the new Newark that dates from the 1950s. The rest of the city bears scars of urban blight with pockets of urban renewal. The city's earlier reputation for open space survives in the numerous parks. In addition to Broad Street, the major north-south thoroughfares are Washington, High, Turner, Bergen, and Clinton, as well as the McCarter Highway. Cutting across them are the east-west routes, such as Market and Raymond. Downtown is divided into four neighborhoods: Market Square, Four Corners, The Greens, and Riverfront.

Environment

Environmental Stress Index   3.6
Green Cities Index: Rank   58
               Score   38.67
Water Quality   Alkaline, soft to medium
Average Daily Use (gallons per capita)   NA
    Maximum Supply (gallons per capita)   NA
Parkland as % of Total City Area   NA
% Waste Landfilled/Recycled   25:50 Incinerated 25
Annual Parks Expenditures per Capita $30.49

Climate

Newark's continental weather patterns are influenced by its proximity to the ocean. Winds from the Atlantic moderate the temperatures in summer and winter. Average January temperature is 33.6°F and average July temperature is 77.9°F. Humidity is high in summer. The city receives generous rain and snow brought in by the northeasters. Average annual precipitation is 42.34 inches.

History

Newark was founded in 1666 by 30 Puritan families from Connecticut headed by Robert Treat of Milford and

Weather

Temperature

Highest Monthly Average °F   85.6
Lowest Monthly Average °F   24.2

Annual Averages

Days 32°F or Below   85
Days above 90°F   41
Zero Degree Days   0
Precipitation (inches)   42.34
Snow (inches)   28.0
% Seasonal Humidity   63.5
Wind Speed (m.p.h.)   10.2
Clear Days   95
Cloudy Days   159
Storm Days   27
Rainy Days   118

Average Temperatures (°F)	High	Low	Mean
January	41.1	26.0	33.6
February	47.2	29.9	38.6
March	52.6	36.2	44.4
April	63.8	45.7	54.8
May	79.5	58.3	68.9
June	84.6	63.7	74.2
July	86.6	69.2	77.9
August	87.1	68.3	77.7
September	77.3	88.6	68.0
October	67.5	49.1	58.3
November	55.1	40.1	47.6
December	46.3	31.2	38.8

the Reverend Abraham Pierson of Branford, and was named after Newark-on-Trent in England. The settlers bought the present-day Essex County, including the Passaic River valley and extending into the Watchung Mountains, from the Hackensacks and the Lenni Lenapes of the Delaware Indian tribe. Newark remained a stern Puritan town for over one generation, and the religious monopoly of the Old First Church founded by Pierson was not broken until Trinity Church was founded in 1733. The Puritans' traditional strengths in education and industry bore fruit in the establishment of the College of New Jersey (later Princeton University) in 1748, and in the creation of numerous forges and foundries.

The city's first elementary school was built in 1676, followed by the laying out of a market along Washington Square and a military training ground in Military Park. Just before the American Revolution, Newark was commercially important enough to warrant the building of roads and ferries connecting to New York. During the Revolutionary War, Newark was a supply base for Washington's forces and the scene of a number of skirmishes. After the war, growing commerce and industry transformed Newark into a prosperous business center. The first bank, the National Banking and Insurance Company, was organized in 1804, and six years later the Newark Fire Insurance Company wrote its first policies. In about 1790 Moses Combs founded the shoe industry, and within a few years one-third of the city's working population was engaged in some form of the leather trade. Abandoning its Puritan traditions, the town also supported three of the finest taverns in the country. After the War of 1812, new industries arose that made Newark the leading city of New Jersey. Epaphras Hinsdale began the manufacture of jewelry, and hatmaking and brewing were added to the list of industries. In the 1830s railroads and canals began to link the city with the rest of the eastern seaboard. The first rail line between Newark and Jersey City was completed in 1834 while the Morris Canal brought the markets of Philadelphia closer to Newark. In 1836, Newark, with a population of 20,000, was incorporated as a city. In 1848 the first theater was built. By 1855 Germans had settled in large numbers, making the city a center of German culture.

Modern Newark dates from the end of the Civil War in which 10,000 Newarkians fought on the Union side. Although leather, brewing, and jewelry remained the mainstays of the economy, the city was able to exploit new technological breakthroughs to establish new industries. The plastics industry, based on John Wesley Hyatt's invention of the celluloid; the electric power industry, based on Thomas A. Edison's invention of the electric bulb in nearby Menlo Park and Edward Weston's later discoveries in the same field, are two such examples. The chemical industry was established at this time and insurance became increasingly important. Newark also enjoyed strong municipal leadership under Mayor Joseph Haynes.

World War I heightened Newark's position as an industrial bellwether and laid the foundations of its future as a port. The first skyscrapers were built on Broad Street, giving the city a metropolitan appearance. The Hudson and Manhattan Railroad, between Manhattan and Newark, was completed in 1911. The Port of Newark opened in 1918 under the auspices of the Port Authority of New York and New Jersey. The Newark International Airport opened in the mid-1920s. In 1938, a new subway was built in the bed of the Morris Canal and a new Pennsylvania Railroad station was opened in 1933.

Beneath the facade of prosperity, Newark was entering a period of decline. The wealthier residents began to move into the suburbs near the Watchung Mountains, yielding the inner city to the blacks who had immigrated in large numbers during and after World War I. A corrupt municipal government began to neglect essential services, and the city's tax base eroded as many of the older industries relocated. Although a strong urban renewal program helped to stanch the outflow of residents, race riots erupted in 1967, resulting in 26 deaths and 300 fires. New disorders followed in 1968, triggered by the assassination of Martin Luther King, Jr. The worst hit in the riots was the Central Ward, and 10 of the city's 23 square miles were damaged. The riots resulted in a number of official actions relating to municipal housing, court procedure, welfare, and antipoverty measures. It also led to the election of Newark's first black mayor, Kenneth Gibson, in 1970. After serving four terms, Gibson was replaced by another black, Sharpe James.

Chronology

1666 Thirty Puritan families from Connecticut, led by Robert Treat and the Reverend Abraham Pierson, buy land from Indians and found settlement called Newark.

1676 First school is established.

1696 Newark Township is chartered, including the 22 municipalities in present-day Essex County. Bridge is built across the Passaic River.

1733 Trinity Church is founded by a breakaway group, thus ending the monopoly of the Old First Church.

1748 The College of New Jersey, later Princeton University, moves from Elizabethtown to Newark.

1776 Washington uses Newark as a supply base in war against the British.

1790 Moses Combs founds Newark's shoe industry.

1801 Epaphras Hinsdale begins jewelry manufacture.

1804 The first bank, Newark Banking and Insurance Company, is founded.

1834 The first railroad line linking Newark and Jersey City begins operations.

1836 Newark is incorporated as a city with William Halsey as first mayor.

1848 The first theater in Newark opens its doors.

1869 John Wesley Hyatt invents celluloid, thus founding the plastic industry.

1872 Newark holds industrial exposition.

1911 Hudson and Manhattan Railroad links Newark and New York.

1918 Port of Newark opens.

1929 Newark International Airport is designated eastern air mail terminal.

1933 The new Pennsylvania Railroad station opens.

1935 The city's subway system opens.

1967 Racial violence causes 26 deaths and $20 million damage to property.

1968 Blacks riot again on the assassination of Martin Luther King, Jr.

1970 Kenneth Gibson becomes the city's first black mayor.

1988 Sharpe James displaces Gibson as the city's second black mayor.

Historical Landmarks

The Newark City Hall on Broad Street, erected in 1906–1908, is a fine example of the beaux arts style of ornate architecture then in vogue in Europe. The Military Park, enclosed by Broad Street, Park Street, Rector Street, and Raymond Boulevard was laid out by the founders as a military training ground and was known for more than two centuries as the Lower Common. A large bronze statue, the Wars of America, by Gutzon Borglum, has 42 human figures on a granite base surrounded by a low fence of overlapping bronze swords. At the south end of the park is a bust of John F. Kennedy and a bronze howitzer. At the north end of the park stands the Trinity Episcopal Church, the city's second-oldest church, built in 1733. The oldest church, The First Presbyterian Church, is on Broad Street. It is the successor to the original church of the Puritan Congregationalist founders of the city. In 1719 the membership became Presbyterian. Other notable churches include the Grace Episcopal Church on Broad Street, built in 1848; St. Patrick's Pro-Cathedral on Washington Street, erected in 1849 as the city's first Roman Catholic cathedral; the Cathedral of the Sacred Heart between Park and Sixth avenues, which took 55 years to complete between 1899 and 1954 and is the fifth-largest cathedral in the United States; St. John's Roman Catholic Church on Mulberry Street, Newark's oldest Roman Catholic church; and the House of Prayer on Broad Street, an Episcopal church known for its unique steeple surmounted by a spire resembling a candle snuffer, built by Frank Wills in 1850. Adjoining it is the 18th-century Dutch colonial farmhouse, known as the John Plume House, which became a rectory for the church in 1850. The oldest house in Newark is the Sydenham House on Heller Parkway, which is traced back to 1712. The Essex County Courthouse, built by Cass Gilbert in 1906, is a modified Renaissance granite and marble structure. Newark's famous neigborhoods include the Ironbound, a Spanish-Portuguese enclave, and historic James Street, known for its Victorian row houses. Other landmark homes include: the William Clark Mansion, now known as the North Ward Center, an impressive 28-room mansion built in the 1870s; the Kreuger Mansion, the most expensive home ever built in Newark at a cost of $250,000 in 1888–1889; the Symington House on Ark Place, a red brick townhouse built in 1808 as the rectory of the Trinity Cathedral; the Polhemus House, built in 1859; and the Ballantine House on Washington Street, the last of the Victorian mansions built in 1885 by John Ballantine, a brewer.

Population

Newark's population has been falling more steeply than most cities. After peaking at 438,000 in 1950, it fell to 381,930 in 1970, 329,248 in 1980, and 275,221 in 1990. While still the largest city in New Jersey, its national rank has fallen to 56th in 1990 from 46th in 1980, 35th in 1970, and 30th in 1960.

Population

	1980	1990
Central City	329,248	275,221
Rank	46	56
Metro Area	1,879,147	1,824,321
Pop. Change 1980–1990 -54,027		
Pop. % Change 1980–1990 -16.4		
Median Age 29.6		
% Male 47.8		
% Age 65 and Over 9.3		
Density (per square mile) 11,420		

Households

Number 91,552
Persons per Household 2.91
% Female-Headed Households 28.6
% One-Person Households 27.5
Births—Total 5,500
   % to Mothers under 20 25.5
   Birth Rate per 1,000 17.5

Ethnic Composition

Newark's recent history is its transformation into a black metropolis. It has the 15th-largest black population among U.S. cities. Blacks make up almost 60% of the population, whites almost 30% (down from 44% in 1970), and other races the balance. Among ethnic white Americans, the largest group is Italian, followed by Cubans, Poles, and Irish.

Ethnic Composition (as % of total pop.)

	1980	1990
White	30.80	28.62
Black	58.24	58.46
American Indian	0.17	0.24
Asian and Pacific Islander	0.72	1.19
Hispanic	18.60	26.07
Other	NA	11.49

Government

Newark has a mayor-council form of government under Plan C of the Optional Municipal Charter Law. The mayor, who is not a voting member, serves a four-year term. The nine council members also serve four-year terms; five are elected at large and four by district. Newark is also the seat of Essex County.

Newark received its first charter as a town in 1713. From 1798 to 1806 it was a township divided into three districts: Newark, Bloomfield, and Orange. It was formally incorporated by charter as a city in 1836, and it received a supplementary charter in 1857. In 1917 voters discarded the mayor and council form of government in favor of a city commission under the Walsh Act. For the next 37 years the city was governed by a board of five commissioners. In 1947 the state adopted a new constitution calling for an enlargement of municipal powers. Under the new constitution the legislature enacted an Optional Municipal Charter Law. Plan C of the Charter Law provided for a nonpartisan mayor and a council of nine members and was over-whelmingly approved by the voters of Newark in 1953, with the board of commissioners being abolished in 1954.

Government

Year of Home Charter NA
Number of Members of the Governing Body 9
Elected at Large 4
Elected by Wards 5
Number of Women in Governing Body 1
Salary of Mayor $80,689
Salary of Council Members $37,655
City Government Employment Total 5,056
Rate per 10,000 159.9

Public Finance

The annual budget consists of revenues of $343.622 million and expenditures of $387.111 million. The debt outstanding was $150.114 million and cash and security holdings $121.029 million.

Public Finance

Total Revenue (in millions) $343.622
Intergovernmental Revenue—Total (in millions) $174.26
Federal Revenue per Capita $12.34
% Federal Assistance 3.59
% State Assistance 42.12
Sales Tax as % of Total Revenue 2.41
Local Revenue as % of Total Revenue 46.10
City Income Tax no
Taxes—Total (in millions) $73.2

Taxes per Capita
   Total $232
   Property $163
   Sales and Gross Receipts $16
General Expenditures—Total (in millions) $257.8
General Expenditures per Capita $815
Capital Outlays per Capita $23

% of Expenditures for:
   Public Welfare 13.8
   Highways 0.5
   Education 0.3
   Health and Hospitals 2.3
   Police 15.9
   Sewerage and Sanitation 11.0
   Parks and Recreation 1.4
   Housing and Community Development 7.1
Debt Outstanding per Capita $495
   % Utility 3.0
Federal Procurement Contract Awards (in millions) $78.4
Federal Grants Awards (in millions) $229.3
Fiscal Year Begins January 1

Economy

Newark has a many-faceted economy, and it has been said that as Newark fares, so does the rest of New Jersey. Like many other old cities, Newark was brought low in the 1960s and 1970s by a combination of factors that stripped it of its tax base, industrial prominence, and civic pride. Newark became better known for its riots and run-down buildings, and some sections of the town resembled the worst cities of the Third World. It began an economic comeback in the 1980s with a strong commitment from some of the largest insurance firms and industrial corporations to invest in its future. Among the Fortune 500 companies that now call Newark home are New Jersey Bell (telecommunications); Allied and BASF-Wynadotte (chemicals); Nabisco (food products); Merck, WarnerLambert, and Schering-Plough (pharmaceuticals); and Englehard (precious metals). In the FIRE sector, Prudential dominates the economic landscape as well as the skyline. The state's four biggest banks are all headquartered in the city, including First Fidelity Bancorp. It is estimated that more than half of all available New Jersey investment dollars are in Newark. Newark ranks second to New York in the writing of life insurance and third, behind New York and Hartford, in fire and casualty insurance.

Economy

Total Money Income (in millions) $2,053.6
% of State Average   49.5
Per Capita Annual Income $6,494
% Population below Poverty Level   32.8
Fortune 500 Companies   NA

Banks	Number	Deposits (in millions)
Commercial	16	50,229
Savings	104	3,190
(inc. Savings & Loan)		

Passenger Autos   NA
Electric Meters   324,991
Gas Meters   343,974

Manufacturing

Number of Establishments   644
% with 20 or More Employees   43.3
Manufacturing Payroll (in millions) $656.8
Value Added by Manufacture (in millions) $1,568.7
Value of Shipments (in millions) $3,150.7
New Capital Expenditures (in millions) $120.8

Wholesale Trade

Number of Establishments   509
Sales (in millions) $2,421.3
Annual Payroll (in millions) $185.426

Retail Trade

Number of Establishments   1,778
Total Sales (in millions) $824.2
Sales per Capita $2,606
Number of Retail Trade Establishments with Payroll   1,332
Annual Payroll (in millions) $119.1
Total Sales (in millions) $796.7
General Merchandise Stores (per capita) $245
Food Stores (per capita) $499
Apparel Stores (per capita) $233
Eating and Drinking Places (per capita) $488

Service Industries

Total Establishments   1,113
Total Receipts (in millions) $970.6
Hotels and Motels (in millions) $56.8
Health Services (in millions) $82.1
Legal Services (in millions) $227.4

Labor

 The Newark metropolitan area's million-strong work force is primarily employed in six sectors: services, trade, manufacturing, government, FIRE, and transportation sectors. Of these, services and trade employ over one-half. Of the over 5,000 employers, the largest are University of Medicine and Dentistry, Prudential Insurance, AT&T–Western Electric, Public Service, and Rutgers University.

Labor

Civilian Labor Force   127,046
% Change 1989–1990   1.1
Work Force Distribution
   Mining   600
   Construction   30,100
   Manufacturing   148,700
   Transportation and Public Utilities   74,600
   Wholesale and Retail Trade   174,100
   FIRE (Finance, Insurance, Real Estate)   69,100
   Service   258,900
   Government   134,500
   Women as % of Labor Force   46.8
   % Self-Employed   2.2
   % Professional/Technical   9.4
Total Unemployment   13,085
Rate %   10.3
Federal Government Civilian Employment   6,347

Education

The public school system is one of the oldest in the country, dating back to 1676. Nonwhites make up over 70% of the enrollment. Of the 90,000 students enrolled, 48,433 are in public schools. The Newark City School District operates 54 elementary, 6 middle schools, and 11 high schools, and 11 special schools. The private school system consists of 40 parochial and other schools.

There are five colleges within city limits: Essex County College (1966), New Jersey Institute of Technology (1881), Rutgers-Newark (1946), Seton Hall Law School (1971), and University of Medicine and Dentistry (1966). The Newark campus of Rutgers University is spread over 320 acres. The University of Medicine and Dentistry is the city's largest employer.

Education

Number of Public Schools   82
Special Education Schools   11
Total Enrollment   48,433
% Enrollment in Private Schools   14.2
% Minority   90.1
Classroom Teachers   3,418
Pupil-Teacher Ratio   14.16:1
Number of Graduates   1,915
Total Revenue (in millions) $354.248
Total Expenditures (in millions) $333.888
Expenditures per Pupil $6,173
Educational Attainment (Age 25 and Over)
   % Completed 12 or More Years   44.6
   % Completed 16 or More Years   6.3

Education (continued)

Four-Year Colleges and Universities 3
    Enrollment 19,119
Two-Year Colleges 1
    Enrollment 6,000

Libraries

Number 34
Public Libraries 12
Books (in thousands) 1,219
Circulation (in thousands) 1,500
Persons Served (in thousands) 329
Circulation per Person Served 4.55
Income (in millions) $9.7
Staff 260

Four-Year Colleges and Universities
    New Jersey Institute of Technology
    Rutgers University–Newark
    University of Medicine and Dentistry

Health

 The Newark area has nine hospitals providing a wide range of medical services: St. Michael's Medical Center, Beth Israel Medical Center, United Hospitals Medical Center (including Children's Hospital of New Jersey and the Eye Institute of New Jersey), University of Medicine and Dentistry, St. James Hospital, Center for Molecular Medicine and Immunology, Bayonne Hospital, and Columbus Hospital and Diabetes Center.

Health

Deaths—Total 2,936
Rate per 1,000 9.3
Infant Deaths—Total 103
Rate per 1,000 18.7
Number of Metro Hospitals 6
Number of Metro Hospital Beds 2,298
Rate per 100,000 727
Number of Physicians 4,651
Physicians per 1,000 2.97
Nurses per 1,000 7.93
Health Expenditures per Capita $20.23

Transportation

 With 13 miles of waterfront along Newark Bay and Passaic River, Newark is one of the busiest ports in the nation. Its main channel is 7,000 feet long and can berth 34 ships. As part of the largest containership port in the nation, Newark handles more than half the trade of the Port Authority of New York and New Jersey—about 50 million tons of cargo and 2,750 ships annually. Rail lines running to Newark include Amtrak, PATH, Conrail, New Jersey Transit, Central of New Jersey, and Erie Lackawanna. Some 450 commuter trains bring 24,000 passengers into the city on an average weekday and 6,000 buses on 50 lines carry 40,000 passengers. The 3.5-mile city subway, opened in 1935 on the old Morris Canal bed, carries an additional 2 million passengers annually. Newark is the hub of seven major highways. The major north-south route accessing

Newark is I-95, the New Jersey Turnpike. From the west Newark is approached by I-78 and I-80. Other major arteries include U.S. Highways 1, 9, and 22 and State Highways 21, 24, 25, 27, 78, 82, and 280. The Newark International Airport, opened in 1928, is one of the fastest growing in the nation. It handles 31 million passengers on 400,000 flights annually.

Transportation

Interstate Highway Mileage 431
Total Urban Mileage 35,341
Total Daily Vehicle Mileage (in millions) $224.2
Daily Average Commute Time 55.9 min.
Number of Buses 677
Port Tonnage (in millions) NA
Airports 2
Number of Daily Flights 904
Daily Average Number of Passengers 84,229

Airlines (American carriers only)
    USAir
    American West
    Delta
    United
    Continental
    Northwest

Housing

For a number of decades preceding the 1980s, Newark had one of the worst housing stocks in the nation and the deterioration of its residential areas was a frequent subject of commentators and cartoonists. More than half the houses predated 1950. A rebuilding program began in the early 1980s and has continued into the 1990s. Because of Newark's small size, most of the new housing is in the suburbs. Of the housing units, 72% are rented, 23.1% owner-occupied, and 9% vacant. Since 1965 more than 15,000 housing units have been built or renovated at a cost of over $450 million. Public housing consists of 15,000 apartments, including 4,000 for the elderly.

Housing

Total Housing Units 102,473
% Change 1980–1990 -18.5
Vacant Units for Sale or Rent 8,054
Occupied Units 91,552
% with More Than One Person per Room 13.6
% Owner-Occupied 23.1
Median Value of Owner-Occupied Homes $110,000
Average Monthly Purchase Cost $424
Median Monthly Rent $385
New Private Housing Starts 258
Value (in thousands) $8,834
% Single-Family 8.5
Nonresidential Buildings Value (in thousands) $65,322

Tallest Buildings	Hgt. (ft.)	Stories
Natl Newark & Essex Bldg.	465	36
Raymond-Commerce	448	37
Park Plaza Bldg.	400	26
Prudential Plaza	370	24
Public Service Elec. & Gas	360	26
Prudential Ins. Co.	360	26
AT&T Bldg.	359	31
Gateway 1	355	28

Urban Redevelopment

Urban redevelopment began soon after the demise of the commission form of government in 1954 when the Mutual Benefit Life Insurance Company and Prudential Insurance built their headquarter buildings in downtown Newark. The pace quickened thereafter, and the city skyline changed as other multistory buildings rose, including a YMCA-YWCA building, state and federal office buildings, and towering apartment buildings. The Port of New York Authority poured hundreds of millions of dollars into Port Newark and Newark International Airport. Rutgers and New Jersey Institute of Technology began work on nearly $100 million in new buildings. A 17-story medical center was built at a cost of $13 million. Since 1954 more than $1 billion has been spent on new construction. Recent development projects include the renovation of the Penn Station, renovation of the riverfront, and a $200-million performing arts center.

Crime

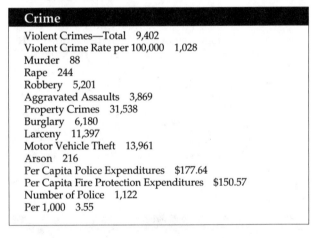

Newark is considered a high-crime area. Of the crimes known to police in 1991, there were 9,402 violent crimes and 31,538 property crimes.

Crime	
Violent Crimes—Total	9,402
Violent Crime Rate per 100,000	1,028
Murder	88
Rape	244
Robbery	5,201
Aggravated Assaults	3,869
Property Crimes	31,538
Burglary	6,180
Larceny	11,397
Motor Vehicle Theft	13,961
Arson	216
Per Capita Police Expenditures	$177.64
Per Capita Fire Protection Expenditures	$150.57
Number of Police	1,122
Per 1,000	3.55

Religion

Most of the Hispanics are Catholics and many of the historic churches are Roman Catholic. Blacks are divided among a number of Protestant churches, of which Holiness and Baptist are more prominent.

Religion	
Largest Denominations (Adherents)	
Catholic	308,459
American Baptist	16,622
American Zion	10,575
Episcopal	10,995
Presbyterian	12,865
Black Baptist	54,346
United Methodist	6,535
United Church of Christ	6,415
Jewish	76,200

Media

The city's daily newspaper is the *Star-Ledger*, publisher by the Newhouse Group. Weekly publications serve the city's Hispanic, black, and other communities. Newark has its own television and radio stations and also receives signals from New York.

Media
Newsprint
Star-Ledger, daily
Television
WHSE (Channel 68)
Radio
WBGO (FM)

Sports

The Meadowland Sports Complex in nearby East Rutherford is home to the New York Giants and the New York Jets of the National Football League, the New Jersey Nets of the National Basketball Association, and the Jersey Devils of the National Hockey League. Newark hosts the Hambletonian, the Wimbledon of harness racing.

Arts, Culture, and Tourism

The cultural bellwether of Newark is the Symphony Hall on Broad Street, a 2,800-seat art deco auditorium built in 1925. Among its resident groups are the New Jersey Symphony Orchestra, the New Jersey State Opera, and the Newark Boys Chorus. Classical music concerts are scheduled regularly at the Cathedral of the Sacred Heart, and free concerts at Washington Park and in the Gateway Complex. The major dance companies are the Garden State Ballet, the New Jersey Ballet, and the Newark Dance Theater. Local theater is represented by the Whole Theater Company of Montclair, the Paper Mill Playhouse of Milburn, and The Theater of Universal Images, a black group.

The principal museum is the Newark Museum, noted for its Schaeffer Collection of antique glass and Tibetan relics and its sculpture garden. Among art galleries the most active is the Paul Robeson Center at Rutgers.

Travel and Tourism
Hotel Rooms 10,265
Convention and Exhibit Space (square feet) NA
Convention Centers
Gateway Hilton
Festivals
Cherry Blossom Festival (April)

Parks and Recreation

The Branch Brook Park between Orange Street and city limits is the largest Essex County park covering 500 acres and is noted for its Japanese cherry trees. Lincoln Park, on Broad Street, and Clinton Park, on Washington and Clinton avenues, mark the end of the main downtown business district. The latter has a fine equestrian statue of Bartolomeo Coleono. Washington Park, enclosed by Broad Street, Washington Place, and Washington Street, was built in 1667 and was known for many years as Upper Green. It contains the statues of George Washington, Christopher Columbus, and Seth Boyden. Military Park is one of the oldest parks in the nation. Weequahic Park has a golf course.

Sources of Further Information

Greater Newark Chamber of Commerce
40 Clinton Street
Newark, NJ 07102
(201) CHAMBER

New Jersey Historical Society
230 Broadway
Newark, NJ 07104
(201) 483-3939

Newark Economic Development Corporation
744 Broad Street
Newark, NJ 07102
(201) 643-2790

Newark Public Information Office
City Hall
920 Broad Street
Newark, NJ 07102
(201) 733-8004

Newark Public Library
5 Washington Street
Newark, NJ 07101
(201) 733-7800

Additional Reading

Churchill, Charles W. *The Italians of Newark.* 1975.
Cunningham, John T. *Newark.* 1988.
Kolesar, John. *The Newark Experiment: A New Direction in Urban Healthcare.* 1975.
New Jersey Historical Society. *Records of the Town of Newark, New Jersey: From Its Settlement in 1666 to Its Incorporation as a City in 1836.* 1990.
Rice, Arnold S. *Newark: A Chronological and Documentary History, 1666–1970.* 1977.

Newport

Rhode Island

Basic Data

Name   Newport
Name Origin   NA
Year Founded   1639 Inc. 1784
Status: State   Rhode Island
        County   Seat of Newport County
Area (square miles)   7.7
Elevation (feet)   6
Time Zone   EST
Population (1990)   28,227
Population of Metro Area (1990)   87,194

Sister Cities
   Imperia, Italy
   Shimoda, Japan

Distance in Miles To:
   Providence   32
   Boston   65
   New York   200
   Hartford   99
   New Haven   115
   Waterbury   112

Location and Topography

N Bounded on the east by the Atlantic Ocean, Newport is located on a jagged peninsula at the southern end of Rhode Island (formerly called Aquidneck Island), in the state of Rhode Island, in Narragansett Bay. On the map the city looks like a boot, with its toe pointing westward into the Narragansett Bay and its sole to the Atlantic Ocean. The old center of town is, roughly, at the front of the ankle on the sheltered Newport Harbor.

Layout of City and Suburbs

There are three distinct Newports. The first is the Old Center, the second is the military and naval base, and the third is the resort occupied by the wealthy. The famous ten-mile drive that connects all three is a loop that winds nearly straight south from the center, swings west, and winds back to the center again. The main section of the city is built on a gentle slope, so that the houses and churches on the eastern side of the city are on much higher ground than those close to the harbor front. Many of these crooked and narrow streets are interesting because near the wharves the city has changed little in the past 200 years. Running parallel with the wharves is the Thames Street, or the Strand, as it was formerly called. Many side streets branch off from the artery of the business section and lead to Spring Street, another long thoroughfare also parallel to the waterfront, and Bellevue, which extends to the north as Broadway. The great mansions face the Atlantic Ocean.

Environment

Environmental Stress Index   NA
Green Cities Index: Rank   NA
                    Score   NA
Water Quality   Alkaline, soft
Average Daily Use (gallons per capita)   NA
   Maximum Supply (gallons per capita)   NA
Parkland as % of Total City Area   NA
% Waste Landfilled/Recycled   NA
Annual Parks Expenditures per Capita   NA

Climate

 Newport's climate is described as humid continental, because the Bay moderates the climate, making Newport somewhat warmer in winter and cooler in summer than places further inland. With an elevation of only six feet above sea level, the city is completely exposed to maritime influences. The average temperatures are 28.7°F in the winter and 69.0°F in the summer. Average annual precipitation is 48.49 inches.

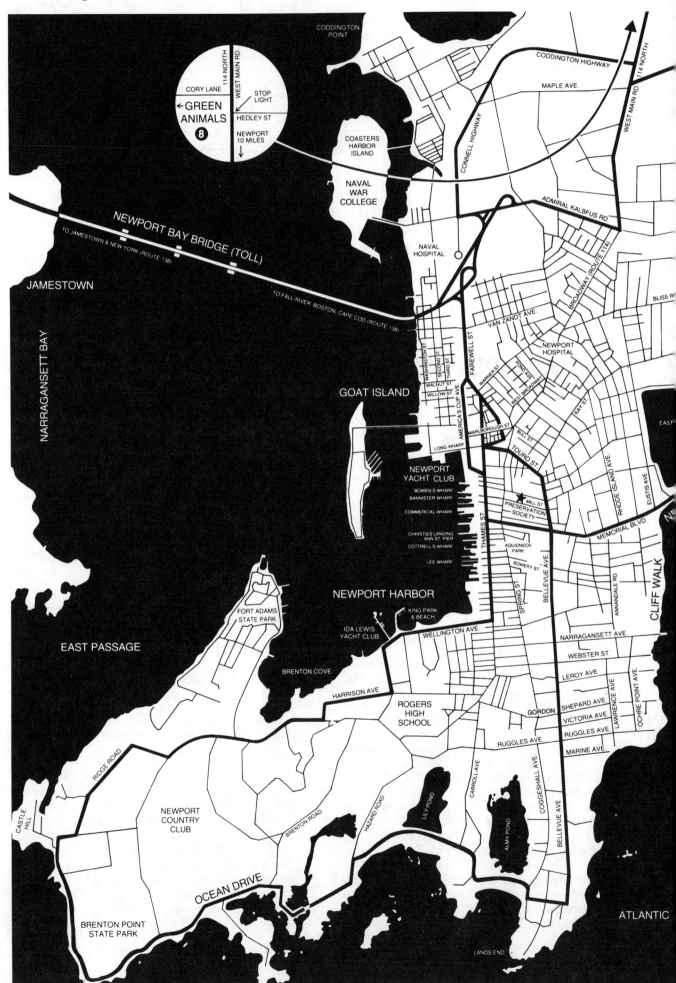

Weather			
Temperature			
Highest Monthly Average °F 59.6			
Lowest Monthly Average °F 38.8			
Annual Averages			
Days 32°F or Below 139			
Days above 90°F 4			
Zero Degree Days 5			
Precipitation (inches) 48.49			
Snow (inches) 32.5			
% Seasonal Humidity NA			
Wind Speed (m.p.h.) NA			
Clear Days NA			
Cloudy Days NA			
Storm Days NA			
Rainy Days NA			
Average Temperatures (°F)	*High*	*Low*	*Mean*
January	37.8	18.6	28.2
February	39.0	19.5	29.3
March	46.1	27.5	36.8
April	57.4	35.6	46.5
May	67.1	44.4	55.8
June	75.6	53.7	64.7
July	80.6	59.6	70.1
August	79.6	58.7	69.2
September	73.3	51.2	62.2
October	64.1	40.5	52.3
November	52.7	33.0	42.8
December	41.7	22.8	32.3

History

Newport was founded in the spring of 1639 by a small band of 17 men under the leadership of John Clarke and William Coddington. Earlier residents of Boston who had fallen into disfavor with the Massachusetts authorities for their antinomian beliefs, they had purchased Aquidneck (or Rhode) Island from the Indians with the help of Roger Williams. The group first settled near the north end of the island (in what is now Portsmouth), but on the arrival of Anne Hutchinson and her followers, decided to move to the southern end. On 16 May 1639, the new plantation was named Newport and its boundaries were determined. On 11 July the town was platted; the first four-acre house lots were laid out on the north side of Washington Square, and Thames Street was planned and made one mile long. In 1640 Newport and Portsmouth were joined with William Coddington as governor, assisted by a deputy governor and four magistrates called assistants. In the same year, the settlement's first school was established with Robert Lenthal as teacher. When Rhode Island secured its first English charter in 1644, John Coggeshall of Newport became the first chief executive (called president) of the colony. In 1663 the colony received its second charter, the King Charles Charter, through the efforts of John Clarke. Ostracized by the other colonies, Newport turned to the sea from its early days; shipbuilding began in 1646, and by the 1690s the city was one of the principal North American ports. Most of the trade was legitimate, but pirates also found a haven here. By 1675 the island farms, which

have the best soil in the state, were furnishing exports to the middle and southern colonies, the West Indies, and Europe. Newport's reputation as a center for religious nonconformism was instrumental in drawing the first Quakers and Jews to the New World. The first Quakers arrived in Newport in 1657, and soon many wealthy and influential persons, including William Coddington, William Brenton, and Nicholas Easton, embraced their doctrines. When George Fox came in 1671, he made Newport his headquarters. The first Jews to settle in the city were 15 families who came from Holland in 1658. They immediately formed a congregation, the Jeshuat Israel. Their first synagogue, built in 1763, still stands at 72 Touro Street. These Jews also brought with them the first degrees of Masonry, and established the first lodge of Freemasons in America. In 1726 the printer James Franklin, brother of Benjamin Franklin, left Boston and came to Newport, where he founded, in 1732, the state's first newspaper, the *Rhode Island Gazette*. In 1758 James Franklin, Jr., began the *Newport Mercury*, which survives as a weekly to this day. By the 1760s Newport gained notoriety as the chief slave-trading port in the British Empire. Great fortunes were made in the slave trade, in which more than 60 vessels were engaged. In addition to slave trade, the merchants of Newport were active in rum and molasses trade and the making of sperm oil and spermaceti candles. Newport's era of greatest prosperity was from 1740 to 1775, when hundreds of privateers sailed from the port annually. Newport became a mecca for many aristocratic families from the South and from the West Indies, who came here to spend the summer. This era also marked the beginning of the social Newport with its balls and other elegant festivities. The city appeared set to become the metropolis of the New World, rivaling New York, Philadelphia, and Boston.

Over this scene of commercial prosperity and social splendor, the dark shadow of the American Revolution fell. Troubles with the British began in 1764 when the British sent men-of-war to police Narragansett Bay against smuggling vessels. A number of violent incidents followed until 1776, when a British fleet under Sir Peter Parker landed about 9,000 British and Hessian troops in Middletown. The following day, soldiers commanded by General Henry Clinton and Lord Percy took possession of Newport and held it for three years. The occupation dealt a serious blow to the city, and the population declined from 9,209 in 1774 to 5,229 in 1776. The city's maritime trade collapsed and never recovered after the war. All the churches except two were turned into barracks or stables; wharves were ripped up, and nearly 500 buildings were destroyed. In October 1779 the Redcoats withdrew and the Americans reoccupied the city. From 1780 to 1781 the city was under French occupation headed by General Rochambeau.

After the Revolutionary War the city recovered very slowly. In 1784 Newport was incorporated as a city with George Hazard as mayor, but reverted soon to the town form of government. However, the population had de-

Chronology

1638 A small band of men led by John Clarke and William Coddington buy the Island of Aquidneck (Rhode Island) from the Indians and settle near its northern end, present-day Portsmouth.

1639 Settlers move to the southern end of the island as Anne Hutchinson and her followers take over Portsmouth. The new settlement is named Newport and platted.

1640 Newport and Portsmouth unite, with William Coddington as first governor. Robert Lenthal is appointed to teach the first school.

1644 Rhode Island receives its first charter. John Coggeshall of Newport becomes first executive of the colony.

1646 Newport builds its first ship.

1657 The first Quakers arrive in Newport.

1658 Fifteen Jewish families arrive from Holland.

1660 Governor William Brenton orders a day of thanksgiving to celebrate the restoration of Charles II to the British throne.

1663 Rhode Island receives its second charter from King Charles II.

1671 George Fox makes Newport the headquarters of the Quaker sect.

1681 A royal custom house is established in Newport.

1732 The printer, James Franklin, founds the state's first newspaper, the *Rhode Island Gazette*.

1743 The northern part of Newport is spun off into a separate town, named Middletown.

1769 The British authorities begin enforcing laws against smuggling and encounter opposition from the residents. The British ship *Liberty* is burned. In retaliation, a fleet under Captain James Wallace arrives to protect royal property.

1776 British fleet under Sir Peter Parker lands 9,000 English and Hessian troops and takes possession of Newport.

1778 The Battle of Rhode Island, between the British and the American Revolutionaries (supported by French allies), takes place.

1779 The British occupation forces depart.

1780 French fleet brings General Rochambeau and 5,088 men.

1781 General George Washington comes to confer with General Rochambeau.

1784 Newport is incorporated as a city.

1787 Town form of government is restored.

1806 Gas illumination is introduced in the house of one David Melville.

1845 Development begins on land lying south and east of Touro Street.

1853 Newport is incorporated as a city once again.

1857 City of Newport holds the first of its grand fetes.

1864 The first railway train arrives in Newport.

1881 The first National Championship tennis match is held in Newport.

1883 Telephones are introduced with about 175 subscribers.

1885 The office of the town crier is discontinued.

1886 The first international polo match is held in Newport.

1889 The first electric trolley runs crosstown from Commercial Wharf to Easton's Beach.

1895 The first National Open Golf Championship Tournament is held in Newport.

1899 Automobiles are introduced.

1970 The Newport Naval Base is closed.

clined to 4,000 and, as late as 1793, only six brick buildings were left standing. From 1775 to 1850 Newport achieved some success as a whaling center. During this time Newport entered a new phase in its history as the summer capital of the wealthy. In 1845 three real estate men purchased 300 acres of land lying south and east of Touro Street, laid out streets, and started building houses. By 1857 the city fathers began advertising the town, holding grand fetes during the summer for those who came. Following the Civil War, Newport's social life suddenly expanded through the efforts of residents like Mrs. Nicholas Beach, Mrs. August Belmont, and Ward McAllister, who began to invite wealthy northern families to their lavish fetes, dancing balls, and elaborate dinners. Other developments helped the trend. In 1864 the railways reached the town. The Naval Training Station and the Naval War College were established in the city in the 1880s, boosting the economy. The first national tennis championships were held in 1881. Telephones were introduced in

1882–1883. Polo was introduced in 1876 by James Gordon Bennett, and the first International Polo Match was held in 1886. The first National Open Golf Championship was held at the Newport Country Club in 1895. Automobiles were introduced in 1899. The first electric trolley cars ran crosstown in 1899.

During the so-called Gilded Years, 1890 to 1914, Newport summer society set standards of extravagance and opulence that have not been equalled since. Wealthy families, such as the Astors, Vanderbilts, and Morgans, built opulent mansions, which they called cottages, to entertain each other during the brief summer season. At the cottage of Mrs. William Astor, where the ballroom held exactly 400 people, America's Social Register of 400 people, was born. Huge sums were spent in the prevailing spirit of rivalry. Sometimes a single ball cost more than $100,000. Newport became a millionaire's playground from which all unacceptable intruders were excluded by a set of ironclad, though unwritten, rules. Town folks, called "our footstools" by the summer colonists, were excluded from the exclusive Bellevue Avenue or the Ocean Drive, as well as Bailey's Beach, the exclusive recreational club of the superrich.

World War I brought to an end this chapter of Newport's history. Most of the leaders of the 400 had dispersed or died. The new rich had less taste for ostentation. The stock market crash of 1929 dealt a final blow to the cottagers who had dominated the city for almost half a century. Until the 1970s the naval base more than counteracted the decline in the wealthy summer trade. The closing of the naval base in the 1970s damaged the city's economy.

Historical Landmarks

Newport has hundreds of historical landmarks. The most prominent among them are:

- Washington Square bounded by Touro Street and Broadway is in the heart of the old city.
- Old City Hall on Washington Square was built in 1761 on the site of a public granary.
- Oliver Hazard Perry House on Touro Street is a plain frame building (1755).
- The Old Colony House or Old State House in Washington Square (1739).
- Temple Jeshuat Israel on Touro Street is the oldest synagogue in America (1763).
- The Sabbatarian Meeting House, or Seventh Day Baptist Church (1729), is part of the Newport Historical Society Museum.
- The Tillinghast House on Mill Street is a three-story dwelling (1760).
- The Van Zandt House, on Pelham Street, a white frame Greek Revival structure (1846).
- Prescott House on Pelham Street is a three-story house (1767).
- The Champlin-Mason House on Thames Street, was built prior to 1760.
- The Maudsley House, one of the finest Georgian Colonial houses.

- The Trinity Church on Spring Street (1725) with a bell and communion service donated by Queen Anne.
- The Vernon House on Clarke Street is a Georgian structure (1756).
- The Central Baptist Church on Clarke Street (1733).
- The Henderson Home on Clarke Street was once a parsonage (1733).
- The Wanton-Lyman-Hazard House on Broadway is the oldest house in Newport (1675).
- The Friends Meeting House on Marlborough Street (1700).
- The Jonathan Nichols House on Marlborough Street was once the White Horse Tavern (1730).
- The Simeon Potter House on Washington Street was the site of Newport's first free school (1815).
- The Hunter House on Washington Street, one of the city's most celebrated residences, and since 1917 a convent of the Sisters of St. Joseph (1757).
- The Henry Collins House on Washington Street (1750).
- Robinson House on Washington Street (1760).
- The Breakers, originally owned by Cornelius Vanderbilt, a pretentious palace of Caen stone with red tiled roof. It is the most striking and magnificently furnished of Newport's cottages.
- The Marble Palace, a Renaissance building, with a Corinthian portico, ornate Louis XIV doors, and walls and floors of French and Numidian marble, was the home of Frederick Prince.
- Crossways, a large white Colonial-style mansion built by Stuyvesant Fish (1898).
- Fort Adams built in 1799 and named after President John Adams.
- The Malbone Town House on Thames Street (1744).
- The Stone Villa, on Bellevue Avenue, opposite the casino, was built by James Gordon Bennett before 1880.
- The Elms, a magnificent square stone mansion, once owned by Mrs. Bruen, corner of Bellevue Avenue and Dixon Street.

Population

Newport's population has been steadily declining during this century and is now estimated at 28,227.

Population		
	1980	*1990*
Central City	29,259	28,227
Rank	821	861
Metro Area	81,383	87,194
Pop. Change 1980–1990 -1,032		
Pop. % Change 1980–1990 -3.5		
Median Age NA		

Population (continued)

% Male   49.32
% Age 65 and Over   13.2
Density (per square mile)   3,665

Households

Number   11,196
Persons per Household   2.31
% Female-Headed Households   14.0
% One-Person Households   33.8
Births—Total   430
   % to Mothers under 20   12.6
   Birth Rate per 1,000   14.5

Ethnic Composition

Newport has more blacks than comparable towns in the state, making up 8% of the population, with whites at 89% and the remainder divided among a number of smaller racial groups.

Ethnic Composition (as % of total pop.)

	1980	1990
White	89.34	88.65
Black	7.66	8.08
American Indian	0.67	0.74
Asian and Pacific Islander	0.97	1.41
Hispanic	2.01	2.80
Other	NA	1.11

Government

Newport operates under a city-manager form of government. The city council consists of seven members elected for two-year terms, four from the four wards and three at-large. The mayor is elected by the three at-large councillors.

Government

Year of Home Charter   NA
Number of Members of the Governing Body   7
Elected at Large   3
Elected by Wards   4
Number of Women in Governing Body   NA
Salary of Mayor   NA
Salary of Council Members   NA
City Government Employment Total   963
Rate per 10,000   328.4

Public Finance

Total Revenue (in millions)   NA
Intergovernmental Revenue—Total (in millions)   NA
Federal Revenue per Capita   NA
% Federal Assistance   NA
% State Assistance   NA
Sales Tax as % of Total Revenue   NA
Local Revenue as % of Total Revenue   NA
City Income Tax   no
Taxes—Total (in millions) $20.3

Public Finance (continued)

Taxes per Capita
   Total $693
   Property $677
   Sales and Gross Receipts $0
General Expenditures—Total (in millions) $32.5
General Expenditures per Capita $1,109
Capital Outlays per Capita $4

% of Expenditures for:
   Public Welfare   0.3
   Highways   3.3
   Education   52.2
   Health and Hospitals   0.1
   Police   12.3
   Sewerage and Sanitation   7.3
   Parks and Recreation   1.8
   Housing and Community Development   3.0
Debt Outstanding per Capita $457
   % Utility   27.9
Federal Procurement Contract Awards (in millions) $52.5
Federal Grants Awards (in millions) $2.7
Fiscal Year Begins   NA

Economy

Newport's economy was historically dependent on the naval base and on summer tourists. Many of the naval base installations were closed in the 1970s and summer tourism has been declining. The rise of high-tech industries in Newport, as well as nearby Portsmouth and Middletown, has helped to offset the loss of employment and provide new directions for growth. Some light industry, fishing, and lobstering also contribute to the economy.

Economy

Total Money Income (in millions) $347.9
% of State Average   109.0
Per Capita Annual Income $11,867
% Population below Poverty Level   16.1
Fortune 500 Companies   NA

Banks	Number	Deposits (in millions)
Commercial	15	NA
Savings	10	NA

Passenger Autos   52,563
Electric Meters   25,246
Gas Meters   6,887

Manufacturing

Number of Establishments   NA
% with 20 or More Employees   NA
Manufacturing Payroll (in millions)   NA
Value Added by Manufacture (in millions)   NA
Value of Shipments (in millions)   NA
New Capital Expenditures (in millions)   NA

Wholesale Trade

Number of Establishments   31
Sales (in millions) $71.5
Annual Payroll (in millions) $4.451

Retail Trade

Number of Establishments   517
Total Sales (in millions) $211.6
Sales per Capita $7,217
Number of Retail Trade Establishments with Payroll   393

Economy (continued)

Economy (continued)

Annual Payroll (in millions) $34.4
Total Sales (in millions) $203.6
General Merchandise Stores (per capita)   NA
Food Stores (per capita) $958
Apparel Stores (per capita) $688
Eating and Drinking Places (per capita) $1,939

Service Industries

Total Establishments   218
Total Receipts (in millions) $119.3
Hotels and Motels (in millions) $24.9
Health Services (in millions) $18.6
Legal Services (in millions) $6.9

Labor

The largest industrial employer is Raytheon, whose work is related to the Naval Underwater Systems Center located in the city. During summer, the work force expands several times, as seasonal employees swell the local population.

Labor

Civilian Labor Force   15,271
% Change 1989–1990   -4.9

Work Force Distribution
   Mining   NA
   Construction   NA
   Manufacturing   5,968
   Transportation and Public Utilities   NA
   Wholesale and Retail Trade   7,951
   FIRE (Finance, Insurance, Real Estate)   1,083
   Service   10,089
   Government   4,461
   Women as % of Labor Force   NA
   % Self-Employed   NA
   % Professional/Technical   20.4
Total Unemployment   869
Rate %   5.7
Federal Government Civilian Employment   3,498

Education

The public school system consists of one high school, one junior high school, and six elementary schools. Six parochial schools supplement the public system. In addition, Newport has some prestigious private schools, including a day school, a college preparatory school, and a boys' school.

The only institution of higher education is Salve-Regina, The Newport College. A school of nursing is affiliated with the Newport Hospital.

Education

Number of Public Schools   8
Special Education Schools   NA
Total Enrollment   3,605

Education (continued)

Education (continued)

% Enrollment in Private Schools   NA
% Minority   NA
Classroom Teachers   360
Pupil-Teacher Ratio   10:1
Number of Graduates   NA
Total Revenue (in millions)   NA
Total Expenditures (in millions) $40.3
Expenditures per Pupil $3,336
Educational Attainment (Age 25 and Over)
   % Completed 12 or More Years   73.7
   % Completed 16 or More Years   26.1
Four-Year Colleges and Universities   1
   Enrollment   2,407
Two-Year Colleges   NA
   Enrollment   NA

Libraries

Number   11
Public Libraries   1
Books (in thousands)   81
Circulation (in thousands)   194
Persons Served (in thousands)   29.2
Circulation per Person Served   6.64
Income (in millions) $6.72
Staff   21

Four-Year Colleges and Universities
   Salve Regina College

Health

The 217-bed Newport Hospital is the principal medical facility.

Health

Deaths—Total   291
Rate per 1,000   9.8
Infant Deaths—Total   7
Rate per 1,000   16.3
Number of Metro Hospitals   2
Number of Metro Hospital Beds   347
Rate per 100,000   1,183
Number of Physicians   NA
Physicians per 1,000   NA
Nurses per 1,000   NA
Health Expenditures per Capita   NA

Transportation

Highway access is via I-95 from the west to Route 138 east; Route 138 from the east, and from the north via Route 24 south to the Sakonnet River Bridge and then via Route 138 or 114 into the city. The Theodore Francis Greene Airport in Warwick is approximately 40 minutes from Newport. The Newport State Airport handles only private and charter flights. The Providence and Worcester Railroad provides freight service. The Port of Providence is the nearest port for medium and deep-draft vessels. In the summer, ferries are often offered to Rhode Island. Newport offers docking facilities for yachts and smaller vessels.

Transportation

Interstate Highway Mileage   NA
Total Urban Mileage   NA
Total Daily Vehicle Mileage (in millions)   NA
Daily Average Commute Time   NA
Number of Buses   NA
Port Tonnage (in millions)   NA
Airports   NA
Number of Daily Flights   NA
Daily Average Number of Passengers   NA

Airlines (American carriers only)
    NA

Housing

Although known for its palatial mansions, Newport's housing stock is very old—38.7 years on average—and much of the newer housing activity is outside the city proper. Property taxes are high, and homes tend to be more expensive than in other towns the size of Newport.

About 52% of the homes have three or more bedrooms.

Housing

Total Housing Units   13,094
% Change 1980–1990   9.2
Vacant Units for Sale or Rent   1,018
Occupied Units   11,196
% with More Than One Person per Room   1.4
% Owner-Occupied   41.6
Median Value of Owner-Occupied Homes $155,000
Average Monthly Purchase Cost   NA
Median Monthly Rent $525
New Private Housing Starts   58
Value (in thousands) $2,182
% Single-Family   15.5
Nonresidential Buildings Value (in thousands) $140

Urban Redevelopment

Newport had a substantial urban redevelopment program in the 1980s but the recession of the early 1990s has slowed this activity.

Crime

Newport's total crime rate is low by national standards. One apparent reason is that Newport ranks high in both police presence and police expenditures: 3.5 policemen per 1,000 residents and $67 per capita. Of the crimes known to police in 1991, there were 127 violent crimes.

Crime

Violent Crimes—Total   127
Violent Crime Rate per 100,000   7,931
Murder   NA
Rape   NA
Robbery   NA

Crime (continued)

Aggravated Assaults   NA
Property Crimes   NA
Burglary   NA
Larceny   NA
Motor Vehicle Theft   NA
Arson   NA
Per Capita Police Expenditures $67
Per Capita Fire Protection Expenditures   NA
Number of Police   82
Per 1,000   3.5

Religion

Newport was a haven for religious pluralism in the early days and this tradition has persisted to this day. Catholics constitute the majority in the city but Epicopalians, Jews, and others are also represented.

Religion

Largest Denominations (Adherents)

Catholic	44,564
Episcopal	4,397
United Methodist	1,221
American Baptist	1,769
Latter-Day Saints	332
Jewish	700

Media

The city's only daily newspaper is *The Newport Daily News*. The weekly *Newport Mercury* is the oldest publication in the state. The electronic media is received from Providence, but there are two radio stations.

Media

Newsprint
    The Newport Daily News, daily
    Newport Mercury, weekly
    The Newport Navalog, weekly

Television
    See Providence

Radio
    WADK (AM)   WOTB (FM)

Sports

Newport is celebrated for its yacht racing. From 1951 to 1983 the America's Cup yacht races were held in Newport waters. The city still holds a mini–America's Cup yacht race in the summer. Professional tennis at the Newport Casino includes the Volvo Tournament in July. Jai Alai is played from February through December at the Newport Jai Alai.

Arts, Culture, and Tourism

The Swanhurst Theater is the home of the Rhode Island Shakespeare Theater. Newport holds a number of festivals each year, particularly the Newport Music Festival in mid-July, the Newport Folk Festival in late July or early August, the Newport Jazz Festival in August, and Christmas in Newport in December.

The Newport Historical Society Museum is the custodian of the city's heritage. There are three other notable museums: The Naval War College Museum, the Tennis Hall of Fame Museum, and the Newport Art Museum.

Travel and Tourism

Hotel Rooms   1,500
Convention and Exhibit Space (square feet)   NA

Convention Centers
  Newport Marriott
  Holiday Inn

Festivals
  Newport Music Festival (July)
  Newport Folk Festival (July)
  Newport Jazz Festival (August)
  Christmas in Newport

Parks and Recreation

The largest of the city parks is Miantonomi Park on the extreme northern end of the city, comprising 30 acres of land, including Miantonomi Hill. The most popular outdoor sport is sailing, with fishing a close second.

Sources of Further Information

City Hall
43 Broadway
Newport, RI 02840
(401) 846-9600

Newport County Chamber of Commerce
P.O. Box 237
Newport, RI 02840
(401) 847-1600

Newport Public Library
Aquidneck Park
Newport, RI 02840
(401) 847-8720

Preservation Society of Newport County
118 Mill Street
Newport, RI 02840
(401) 847-1000

Additional Reading

Dow, Richard A., and E. Andrew Mowbray. *Newport*. 1976.
Randall, Anne, and Robert Foley. *Newport: A Tour Guide*. 1983.
Warburton, Eileen. *In Living Memory: A Chronicle of Newport, Rhode Island, 1888–1988*. 1988.

Oklahoma City

Oklahoma

Location and Topography

Oklahoma City is located along the banks of the North Canadian River in a gently rolling prairie. The nearest mountains, the Arbuckle Mountains, are 80 miles to the south.

Layout of City and Suburbs

Altough located in the Mississippi Valley at the edge of the prairie plains, Oklahoma gives an impression of altitude and of being on a mountain slope. Bisected from east to west by Grand Avenue and from north to south by Broadway, the city falls into roughly four equal sections. To the north and east are the domeless capitol and the governor's mansion, located on rich oil wells that are pumped through angled shafts. To the east is the residential section and below 13th Street are the older homes. In the southeastern quarter is a forest of derricks that hide other structures. Southward along the Sante Fe railroad and slightly to the west is Capitol Hill and beyond lie suburban developments up to the South Canadian River. Almost directly southwest lies Will Rogers Park. To the west is Packingtown, an area of stockyards and meat-processing plants. The northwest is almost entirely residential. There are many lakes within city limits, the largest of which are Lake Hefner, Lake Stanley Draper, and Arcadia Lake.

Environment

Environmental Stress Index   2.6
Green Cities Index: Rank   4
                    Score   19.50
Water Quality   Alkaline, soft, fluoridated
Average Daily Use (gallons per capita)   104
   Maximum Supply (gallons per capita)   195
Parkland as % of Total City Area   5.0
% Waste Landfilled/Recycled   NA
Annual Parks Expenditures per Capita $57.39

Climate

The climate is continental, typical of the Great Plains cities. The result is pronounced daily and seasonal temperature changes and variations in seasonal and annual precipitation. Oklahoma City is one of the sunniest and windiest cities in the nation. The summers are long and hot and the winters are short and mild.

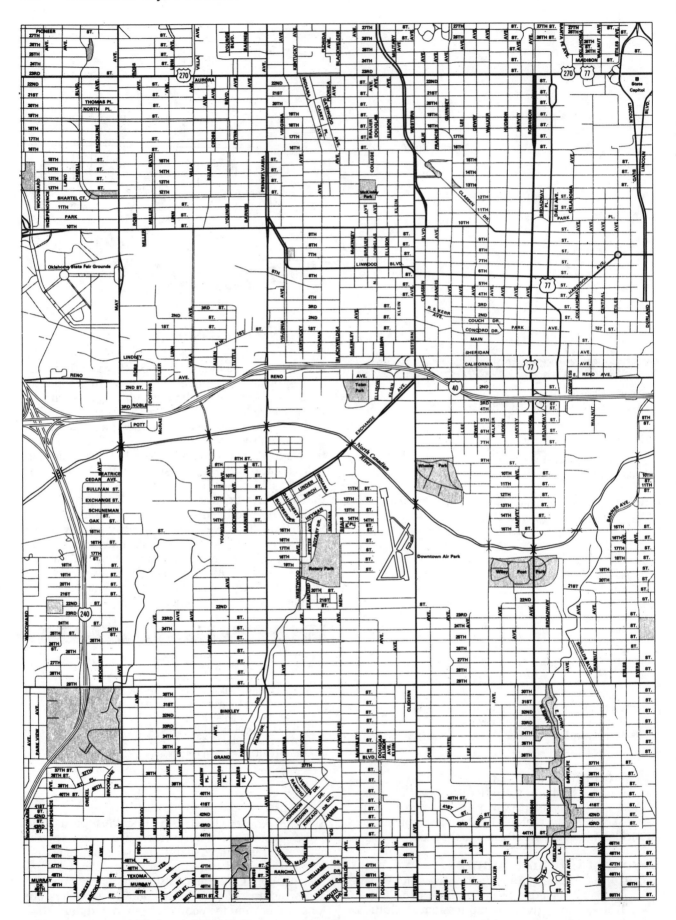

Weather

Temperature

Highest Monthly Average °F	92.6
Lowest Monthly Average °F	26.0

Annual Averages

Days 32°F or Below 80
Days above 90°F 64
Zero Degree Days 0
Precipitation (inches) 31.0
Snow (inches) 9.0
% Seasonal Humidity 65
Wind Speed (m.p.h.) 12.8
Clear Days 141
Cloudy Days 128
Storm Days 51
Rainy Days 81

Average Temperatures (°F)	High	Low	Mean
January	47.6	26.0	36.8
February	52.6	30.0	41.3
March	59.8	36.5	48.2
April	71.6	49.1	60.4
May	78.7	57.9	68.3
June	87.0	66.6	76.8
July	92.6	70.4	81.5
August	92.5	69.6	81.1
September	84.7	61.3	73.0
October	74.2	50.6	62.4
November	60.9	37.4	49.2
December	50.7	29.2	40.0

History

The region that is now Oklahoma City was part of the domain of the Plains tribes and was included in the Louisiana Purchase of 1803. Oklahoma was subsequently designated as Indian reservation, providing a new home for the tribes forced to relocate by the federal government from their ancestral lands in the southeastern United States. Many of these so forced were members of the so-called Five Civilized Tribes—Cherokee, Choctaw, Chickasaw, Creek, and Seminole. After the Civil War, the pressure of westward expansion brought railroads into the American Indian Territory where the U.S. government began to declare some land available for white settlement. Prairie land surrounding a Sante Fe railroad single-track boxcar station was designated as a town site when a presidential proclamation opened the central portion of the Indian Territory to claim-seekers at noon 22 April 1889. By nightfall 10,000 settlers had camped on the site of what was to become Oklahoma City. Within a month the settlers formed a city government. But only with the setting up of the Oklahoma territory on 2 May 1890 did the community enjoy legal municipal existence, and it was incorporated as Oklahoma City. The first provisional mayor was William L. Couch, who later died in an argument over a piece of real estate.

The Oklahoma and Indian territories were merged and were admitted to the Union as the State of Oklahoma in 1907, and within three years Oklahoma City became state capital. In 1928 the city economy changed dramatically when oil was discovered under the city.

A gigantic deposit at Mary Sudik well gushed wildly for 11 days in 1930, spewing 10,000 barrels of oil each day in a great geyser. Despite this accident, even the grounds beneath the capitol were opened for derricks.

Historical Landmarks

As one of the younger cities in the nation, Oklahoma City has only a few historical monuments. The State Capitol on Lincoln Boulevard is unusual in that it has no dome. Even though the original plans called for a central tower, it was left out for reasons of economy, causing much political debate, even after it was completed in 1917. Among the historical homes, the Overholser Mansion is notable as the first in the state.

Population

Oklahoma City has exhibited healthy growth since World War II, growing rapidly in many decades. Between 1970 and 1980 it grew by 9.5% from 368,000 to 404,014 and between 1980 and 1990 it grew by 10.1% to 444,719. Given the fact that the city is only 100 years old, it is possible that it will continue to grow for a number of decades to come.

Population

	1980	1990
Central City	404,014	444,719
Rank	31	29
Metro Area	860,969	958,839
Pop. Change 1980–1990 +40,705		
Pop. % Change 1980–1990 +10.1		
Median Age 32.4		
% Male 48.2		
% Age 65 and Over 11.9		
Density (per square mile) 731		

Households

Number 178,662
Persons per Household 2.44
% Female-Headed Households 12.6
% One-Person Households 30.0
Births—Total 8,357
    % to Mothers under 20 15.8
    Birth Rate per 1,000 18.9

Ethnic Composition

Whites make up 74.8% of the population, blacks 16%, American Indians 4.2%, Hispanic 4.95%, Asians and Pacific Islanders 2.4%, and others 2.7%.

Ethnic Composition (as % of total pop.)

	1980	1990
White	79.95	74.78
Black	14.56	15.98
American Indian	2.58	4.23
Asian and Pacific Islander	1.03	2.36
Hispanic	2.8	4.95
Other	NA	2.66

Chronology

1889 Presidential proclamation opens land around the Santa Fe railroad's single-track boxcar station to white settlement by noon of 22 April. By nightfall 10,000 settlers stake claims. Settlers form civil government with a mayor and a committee of 14.

1890 The western half of American Indian Territory is redesignated Oklahoma Territory. The new settlement is named Oklahoma City.

1907 Oklahoma and Indian territories are merged and admitted to the Union as the State of Oklahoma.

1910 Oklahoma City becomes state capital.

1928 Oil is discovered under the city.

Government

 Oklahoma City has a manager-council form of government. Its mayor and eight councilmen are elected to staggered terms of four years.

Government

Year of Home Charter   1911
Number of Members of the Governing Body   8
Elected at Large   NA
Elected by Wards   8
Number of Women in Governing Body   2
Salary of Mayor $2,000
Salary of Council Members $20
City Government Employment Total   4,928
Rate per 10,000   110.5

Public Finance

 The annual budget consists of revenues of $369.576 million and expenditures of $371.259 million. The debt outstanding is $504.139 million and cash and security holdings $474.068 million.

Public Finance

Total Revenue (in millions) $369.576
Intergovernmental Revenue—Total (in millions) $27.89
Federal Revenue per Capita $23.82
% Federal Assistance   6.44
% State Assistance   1.01
Sales Tax as % of Total Revenue   36.33
Local Revenue as % of Total Revenue   81.40
City Income Tax   no
Taxes—Total (in millions) $129.5

Taxes per Capita
   Total $290
   Property $53

Public Finance (continued)

Sales and Gross Receipts $226
General Expenditures—Total (in millions) $291.0
General Expenditures per Capita $652
Capital Outlays per Capita $195

% of Expenditures for:
   Public Welfare   0.0
   Highways   6.6
   Education   0.0
   Health and Hospitals   15.7
   Police   10.3
   Sewerage and Sanitation   23.2
   Parks and Recreation   7.6
   Housing and Community Development   4.3
Debt Outstanding per Capita $873
   % Utility   18.7
Federal Procurement Contract Awards (in millions)
   $104.1
Federal Grants Awards (in millions) $216.7
Fiscal Year Begins   July 1

Economy

 Oklahoma City's economy has been tied to oil since 1928. After booming for a number of years, the economy faltered when oil prices collapsed in the late 1980s. However, the dependence on oil has been reduced in recent years as the other sectors have come to the fore, and the city has attracted many large and small businesses. *Fortune* magazine has identified Oklahoma City as one of the top ten cities for business. A 25-year redevelopment plan drawn up by I. M. Pei is a blueprint for turning the city into a showcase.

Economy

Total Money Income (in millions) $5,142.4
% of State Average   118.2
Per Capita Annual Income $11,527
% Population below Poverty Level   12.0
Fortune 500 Companies   1

Banks	Number	Deposits (in millions)
Commercial	50	5,347.2
Savings	8	2,432.0

Passenger Autos   531,889
Electric Meters   360,917
Gas Meters   274,768

Manufacturing

Number of Establishments   727
% with 20 or More Employees   27.4
Manufacturing Payroll (in millions) $1,000.4
Value Added by Manufacture (in millions) $3,089.5
Value of Shipments (in millions) $8,216.6
New Capital Expenditures (in millions) $116.9

Wholesale Trade

Number of Establishments   1,471
Sales (in millions)   NA
Annual Payroll (in millions)   NA

Retail Trade

Number of Establishments   4,687
Total Sales (in millions) $3,164.9
Sales per Capita $7,094
Number of Retail Trade Establishments with Payroll   3,043

Economy (continued)

Annual Payroll (in millions) $391.9
Total Sales (in millions) $3,079.8
General Merchandise Stores (per capita) $884
Food Stores (per capita) NA
Apparel Stores (per capita) NA
Eating and Drinking Places (per capita) $810

Service Industries

Total Establishments 4,291
Total Receipts (in millions) NA
Hotels and Motels (in millions) $91.7
Health Services (in millions) NA
Legal Services (in millions) NA

Labor

Despite the collapse of the oil market, the Oklahoma City labor force has shown an upward trend in most years since 1980 and has exceeded national averages during all of these years, with the exception of one. The growth has been particularly impressive in the manufacturing sector, where most cities have been losing jobs. The unemployment rates are usually below the national average. Employment growth is expected to be moderate during the 1990s with gains anticipated in the health-care and service sectors.

Labor

Civilian Labor Force 233,789
% Change 1989–1990 0.2

Work Force Distribution
   Mining 10,700
   Construction 13,100
   Manufacturing 46,400
   Transportation and Public Utilities 21,100
   Wholesale and Retail Trade 105,900
   FIRE (Finance, Insurance, Real Estate) 25,000
   Service 107,700
   Government 102,200
   Women as % of Labor Force 44.2
   % Self-Employed 6.4
   % Professional/Technical 15.1
Total Unemployment 13,418
Rate % 5.7
Federal Government Civilian Employment 9,680

Education

The Oklahoma City Public School District supports 82 elementary, junior high/middle, and senior high schools. Seventeen parochial and private schools supplement the public school system. Four public universities maintain campuses in Oklahoma City: University of Oklahoma Health Sciences Center, Oklahoma State University Technical Institute, Langston University Urban Center, and Oklahoma City Community College. In addition, there are two private institutions: Oklahoma Christian College and Oklahoma City University.

Education

Number of Public Schools 82
Special Education Schools NA
Total Enrollment 36,066
% Enrollment in Private Schools 5.1
% Minority 37.0
Classroom Teachers 2,025
Pupil-Teacher Ratio 20.2
Number of Graduates 2,300
Total Revenue (in millions) $133.330
Total Expenditures (in millions) $132,597
Expenditures per Pupil $2,877
Educational Attainment (Age 25 and Over)
   % Completed 12 or More Years 72.4
   % Completed 16 or More Years 18.9
Four-Year Colleges and Universities 5
   Enrollment 12,917
Two-Year Colleges 2
   Enrollment 9,094

Libraries

Number 53
Public Libraries 21
Books (in thousands) 761
Circulation (in thousands) 3,082
Persons Served (in thousands) 517
Circulation per Person Served 5.96
Income (in millions) $7.361
Staff 201

Four-Year Colleges and Universities
   Langston University Urban Center
   Oklahoma Christian College
   Oklahoma City University
   Oklahoma State University Technical Institute
   University of Oklahoma Health Sciences Center

Health

The medical sector consists of Baptist Medical Center, Deaconess Hospital, Doctors General Hospital, Mercy Center, Presbyterian Hospital, St. Anthony Hospital, Community Hospital, O'Donoghue Rehabilitation Center, Oklahoma Memorial Hospital, Oklahoma Children's Hospital, and Hillcrest Osteopathic Hospital in addition to one federal and two specialty hospitals.

Health

Deaths—Total 3,897
Rate per 1,000 8.8
Infant Deaths—Total 96
Rate per 1,000 11.5
Number of Metro Hospitals 12
Number of Metro Hospital Beds 3,798
Rate per 100,000 851
Number of Physicians 1,174
Physicians per 1,000 2.41
Nurses per 1,000 8.51
Health Expenditures per Capita $2.41

Transportation

Oklahoma City is approached by three interstates: the north-south I-35 running east of the city, the northeast-south I-44 running west of the city, and the east-west I-40 running through the city. Interstate 240 links I-40 with the Will Rogers World Airport. Oklahoma City is also served by U.S. Highways 62, 77, 81, 270, and 277. Rail freight service is provided by Santa Fe, Burlington Northern, and Union Pacific. River transport is available through the Arkansas River Navigation Channel and through the Port of Muskogee, which is 140 miles away. The principal air terminal is the Will Rogers World Airport located 10 miles to the southwest. Two other municipal airports are available at Clarence Page and Wiley Post.

Transportation

Interstate Highway Mileage   9
Total Urban Mileage   3,696
Total Daily Vehicle Mileage (in millions) $19.506
Daily Average Commute Time   44.9 min.
Number of Buses   72
Port Tonnage (in millions)   NA
Airports   1
Number of Daily Flights   70
Daily Average Number of Passengers   3,947

Airlines (American carriers only)

American
Northwest
Trans World
Southwest
Delta
Continental
United

Housing

Of the total housing stock, 59.5% is owner-occupied. The median value of an owner-occupied home is $54,900 and the median monthly rent $282. The number of housing units increased by 16.6% from 1980 to 1990, while the population grew by 10.1%. As a result of this over-building, the housing market remains depressed. The construction of large executive-style houses has increased from 13.4% of the total new single-family construction in 1980 to 39% in 1990. The suburbs, particularly Norman, Yukon, Mustang, and Edmond, have higher housing growth rates than Oklahoma City.

Housing

Total Housing Units   212,367
% Change 1980–1990   16.6
Vacant Units for Sale or Rent   23,602
Occupied Units   178,662
% with More Than One Person per Room   4.1
% Owner-Occupied   59.5
Median Value of Owner-Occupied Homes $54,900
Average Monthly Purchase Cost $325
Median Monthly Rent $282
New Private Housing Starts   886
Value (in thousands) $72,547
% Single-Family   100
Nonresidential Buildings Value (in thousands) $35,015

Housing (continued)		
Tallest Buildings	*Hgt. (ft.)*	*Stories*
Liberty Tower (1971)	500	36
First National Center (1974)	493	33
City Place (1985)	440	32
First Oklahoma Tower (1982)	425	31
Kerr-McGee Center (1973)	393	30
Mid America Tower (1981)	362	19

Urban Redevelopment

The largest urban redevelopment project in recent years has been the Myriad Convention Center. Large-scale renovation projects are coordinated by the Metro Area Development Corporation.

Crime

Oklahoma City ranks low in public safety. Police reported 5,066 violent crimes in 1991 and 44,654 property crimes.

Crime

Violent Crimes—Total   5,066
Violent Crime Rate per 100,000   723.9
Murder   56
Rape   473
Robbery   1,499
Aggravated Assaults   3,038
Property Crimes   44,654
Burglary   11,825
Larceny   26,929
Motor Vehicle Theft   5,900
Arson   465
Per Capita Police Expenditures $108.68
Per Capita Fire Protection Expenditures $87.24
Number of Police   732
Per 1,000   1.65

Religion

Oklahoma City has 700 churches. Baptists constitute the largest denomination. One of the most notable churches in the city is the Church of Tomorrow, one of the largest in the nation.

Religion

Largest Denominations (Adherents)	
Catholic	40,378
Assembly of God	23,275
Christian Church (Disciples)	14,963
Southern Baptist	173,898
United Methodist	60,882
Black Baptist	33,813
Church of Christ	17,316
Church of the Nazarene	12,177
Presbyterian	9,381
Jewish	1,449

Media

The Oklahoma City press consists of the general morning daily, the *Oklahoman*, and the business daily, *Journal Record*. Electronic media consist of 9 television stations and 18 AM and FM radio stations.

Media	
Newsprint	
Journal Record, daily	
Oklahoman, daily	
Television	
KAUT (Channel 43)	
KETA (Channel 13)	
KFOR (Channel 4)	
KOCB (Channel 34)	
KOCO (Channel 5)	
KOKH (Channel 25)	
KSBI (Channel 52)	
KTBO (Channel 14)	
KWTV (Channel 9)	
Radio	
KBYE (AM)	KEBC (FM)
KKNG (FM)	KMGL (FM)
KNTL (FM)	KOKF (FM)
KRXO (FM)	KOCC (FM)
KOQL (FM)	KPRW (AM)
KATT (FM)	KQCV (AM)
KTOK (AM)	KJYO (FM)
KXXY (AM)	KXXY (FM)
KYIS (FM)	WKY (AM)

Sports

Oklahoma City does not have a major professional sports team. The most popular local sports teams are the 89ers, a Triple A farm team of the Texas Rangers in baseball, the University of Oklahoma Sooners in football, and the Oklahoma City University Chiefs in basketball. As befits a western city, rodeo and horse shows are prominent. The National Rodeo Finals are held here in the Myriad Convention Center.

Arts, Culture, and Tourism

The leading theater is the Oklahoma Theater Center. It is supplemented by the Black Liberated Arts Center, which showcases African-American artists, Lyric Theater of Oklahoma, Myriad Garden's Stage Center, and the Classen Theater. Music is represented by a number of groups, such as Oklahoma Symphony Orchestra, which performs at the Civic Center Music Hall; Chamber Orchestra of Oklahoma City, which performs at Christ the King Church; Blue Grass Music Society, which performs at the Midwest City Community Center; Oklahoma Oprey, which presents country music; and the Bowery, which presents rock and jazz. Dance

is represented by Ballet Oklahoma, which performs at the Civic Center Music Hall.

Oklahoma City's museums focus on western art and artifacts. Among the largest are the 1889er Harn Museum and the Kirkpatrick Center, which houses the Air Space Museum and the Omniplex Science and Arts Museum, along with extensive collections of Oriental, African, and Native American art; Sanamu African Gallery; Oklahoma Art Center; Oklahoma Firefighters Museum; Oklahoma Heritage Center; Oklahoma Museum of Art; and Oklahoma State Museum and Historical Society. The city also has three unusual halls of fame: the International Photography Hall of Fame in the Kirkpatrick Center, the National Softball Hall of Fame, and the Cowboy Hall of Fame and Western Heritage Center.

Travel and Tourism
Hotel Rooms   8,821
Convention and Exhibit Space (square feet)   NA
Convention Centers
Myriad Convention Center
Civic Center Music Hall
Festivals
Spring Festival of the Arts (April)
State Fair of Oklahoma (September)

Parks and Recreation

The city maintains 138 municipal parks. The largest is Lincoln Park in the northeast.

Sources of Further Information

City Hall
200 North Parker
Oklahoma City, OK 73102
(405) 297-2424

Oklahoma City Chamber of Commerce
1 Santa Fe Plaza
Oklahoma City, OK 73102
(405) 278-8900

Oklahoma City Convention and Tourism Bureau
4 Santa Fe Plaza
Oklahoma City, OK 73102
(405) 278-8912

Additional Reading

Byers, Lynn, and Kathleen Marks. *Visitors Guide to Oklahoma City.* 1991.
Polk's Oklahoma City Directory. 1991.

Omaha

Nebraska

Basic Data

Name   Omaha
Name Origin   From Omaha Indians
Year Founded   1854 Inc. 1857
Status: State   Nebraska
       County   Seat of Douglas County
Area (square miles)   100.7
Elevation (feet)   1,040
Time Zone   Central
Population (1990)   335,795
Population of Metro Area (1990)   618,262

Sister Cities
   Shizuoka, Japan

Distance in Miles To:

Atlanta	1,010
Boston	1,469
Chicago	479
Dallas	662
Denver	541
Detroit	734
Houston	864
Los Angeles	1,569
Miami	1,636
New York	1,252
Philadelphia	1,204
Washington, DC	1,135

Location and Topography

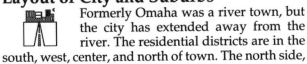

N   Omaha is located on the west bank of the Missouri River, stretching 12 miles north-south and extending 12 miles west, to rolling hills, and rising to over 300 feet.

Layout of City and Suburbs

Formerly Omaha was a river town, but the city has extended away from the river. The residential districts are in the south, west, center, and north of town. The north side,

inhabited mostly by African Americans, extends for several blocks from 24th Street. The bottoms, flooded by the river in 1881, have been filled in. Carter Lake, east of the city at Locust Street, was once a swamp. The surrounding bog was filled in, and is now occupied by the Municipal Airport and Levi Carter Park. The streets are arranged in a grid pattern, with Dodge Street dividing the city into north and south. Streets running north-south are numbered and east-west streets are named.

Environment

Environmental Stress Index   2.2
Green Cities Index: Rank   28
                    Score   26.46
Water Quality   Moderately alkaline, soft, fluoridated
Average Daily Use (gallons per capita)   206
   Maximum Supply (gallons per capita)   423
Parkland as % of Total City Area   NA
% Waste Landfilled/Recycled   NA
Annual Parks Expenditures per Capita $50.37

Climate

Omaha has a typical continental climate with warm summers and very cold, dry winters. Low pressure systems cause periodic and rapid changes, especially in winter. Most of the annual precipitation falls in summer. About 50% of days in winter and about 75% of days in summer are sunny. Omaha is also exposed to storms that cross the Nebraska plains.

Weather

Temperature

Highest Monthly Average °F   88.5
Lowest Monthly Average °F   10.2

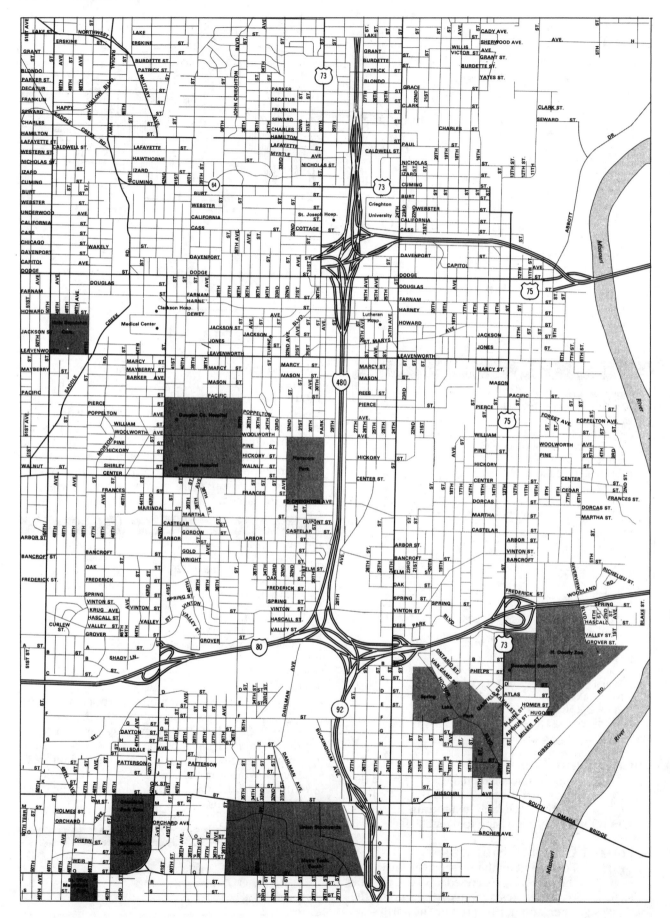

Weather (continued)

Annual Averages

Days 32°F or Below   138
Days above 90°F   38
Zero Degree Days   13
Precipitation (inches)   30.0
Snow (inches)   32.0
% Seasonal Humidity   68.0
Wind Speed (m.p.h.)   10.9
Clear Days   113
Cloudy Days   145
Storm Days   48
Rainy Days   99

Average Temperatures (°F)	High	Low	Mean
January	32.7	12.4	22.6
February	38.5	17.4	28.0
March	47.7	26.4	37.1
April	64.4	40.1	52.3
May	74.4	51.5	63.0
June	83.1	61.3	72.2
July	88.6	65.8	77.2
August	87.2	64.0	75.6
September	78.6	54.0	66.3
October	69.1	42.6	55.9
November	50.9	29.1	40.0
December	37.8	18.1	28.0

History

Before the 19th century, Omaha was inhabited by the Otoe, Missouri, and Maha tribes. The Mahas, a Nebraska plains group, lived on the present site of Omaha at the confluence of the Missouri and Platte rivers. Omaha was first visited by Lewis and Clark in 1804, the Hunt-Astor Party in 1810, and Stephen Long in 1819. A few fur traders were recorded in the area in 1820, notably Manuel Lisa, a Spaniard, and Jean Pierre Cabane, a Frenchman. In 1854, when the area was opened to settlers by treaty with the Maha Indians, immigration began. In the same year the Council Bluffs and Nebraska Ferry Company named the settlement after the dispossessed Mahas, and surveyed and platted the land. Within months, Omaha had a newspaper and about 20 buildings. The first Nebraska legislature met in the city in 1855. Among the early settlers were A. J. Poppleton, John M. Thayer, Andrew J. Hanscomb, George L. Miller, the Creightons, the Kountze brothers, William A. Paxton, Byron Reed, James M. Woolworth, James E. Boyd, and Joseph H. Millard. All of them played a major role in building the city, and in doing so built up enormous fortunes. Mormon pioneers set up camp in Winter Quarters, Florence, north of Omaha in 1846 and 1847. Six hundred of them died during the harsh winter of that year, and they are memorialized by a bronze sculpture by Avard T. Fairbanks in the Mormon Cemetery. Florence was later annexed by Omaha and served as a way station for Mormons on their way to Utah. Most of the early settlers did not care for the federal land laws, which restricted claims to 160 claims per family. They organized their own Claim Club to protect an allowance of 320 acres per person, and enforced this claim forcefully. Since each man was required to live upon his claim, a house on wheels was built and moved from one claim to another. Ruffians were hired to preempt land for absent claimants. Lawlessness flourished, and interlopers were expelled or summarily hanged. In 1857 the town was incorporated. Soon afterward a municipal hotel and a new capitol were built. By 1866 there was some semblance of law and order and the police force was increased from one to four policemen. In the late 1850s Omaha began to outgrow its small frontier-town origins. Gold seekers on their way to California arrived by steamboats daily, making the town their outfitting point. In 1865 the Union Pacific Railroad reached Omaha. The 1870s were a great decade for Omaha. The first gas works and a post office were built in 1870, followed by a new school in 1872, and a public library in 1877. Creighton University was established in 1878 and the Union Pacific Railroad bridged the Missouri River. The decade is also noted for the historic trial, *Standing Bear v. Crook,* that gave American Indians U.S. citizenship. The establishment of the Union Stockyards in the 1880s laid the foundation of Omaha's first distinctive industry. The great packing houses brought thousands of new immigrants, and in their wake came gamblers. After the flood of 1881 many Council Bluffs citizens moved to Omaha, triggering another real estate boom. Civic improvements followed, including an opera house, waterworks, asphalt paving, an electric light company, and an electric street railway. The city's 52 brickworks were producing 150 million bricks a year. The skyline also changed with the first skyscraper, the New York Life Insurance Company building. The suburbs of Dundee and Benson were added, and the Chamber of Commerce and the Knights of Ak-Sar-Ben (Nebraska spelled backwards) were founded. The Knights organized the Trans-Mississippi Exhibition, which brought national attention to Omaha. In the early 1900s the Omaha Grain Exchange was organized, and it helped to develop Omaha as a grain market. In 1917 the Reverend Edward J. Flanagan founded Boys Town, which soon became the city's best known institution. Between World Wars I and II, Omaha's political life was dominated by Tom Dennison, a gambler who became the political boss, and James C. Dahlman, who was mayor for 21 years.

Historical Landmarks

The site of the first territorial capitol is between Farnam and Douglas streets. The first capitol building was a gift to the town by the company that laid out the town site. Herndon House on Ninth and Farnam streets was the town's first hotel and headquarters of the Overland Stage. The Douglas House on 13th and Harney streets was one of the first hotels in Omaha. The City Hotel on 11th and Harney streets was the scene of a reception and grand ball in honor of Mark W. Izard in 1855. Florence, now a residential section, was occupied by the Mormons in 1846. Weber Mill on 30th Street was a gristmill built shortly after 1854. Mitchell House on 31st Street is

Chronology

1804	Lewis and Clark visit the site of Omaha.
1810	The Hunt-Astor party visit the site of Omaha.
1819	Stephen Long visits the site of Omaha.
1847	Mormon pioneers set up camp in Winter Quarters, Florence. Six hundred perish in harsh winter.
1854	Treaty dispossessing Maha Indians is followed by first white settlement. The Council Bluffs and Nebraska Ferry Company name the site Omaha and survey and plat the land.
1855	First territorial legislature meets in town.
1857	Omaha is incorporated.
1865	The Union Pacific Railroad reaches Omaha.
1867	Nebraska moves capital to Lincoln.
1870	New post office building is erected.
1872	New public school is built. Union Pacific Railroad builds bridge across Missouri River.
1877	Public library opens.
1878	Creighton University is founded.
1879	Historic *Standing Bear v. Crook* trial helps American Indians win U.S. citizenship.
1881	Disastrous Missouri River flood forces many Council Bluffs residents to move to Omaha.
1895	The Knights of Ak-Sar-Ben are organized.
1898	The Trans-Mississippi Exposition is held.
1913	Easter tornado causes heavy damage.
1917	Boys Town is founded.

claimed to be the oldest in the city, built about 1855. Fort Omaha, between Fort Street and Laurel Avenue, was built in 1868 as Sherman Barracks. St. Cecilia's Cathedral on 40th Street is the most imposing church in Omaha. Historic Bellevue includes an 1800s log cabin, church, and depot. The General Crook House is the restored Victorian quarters of General Crook in Fort Omaha.

Population

Omaha is a growing city. Between 1980 and 1990 it grew by 7% from 313,939 to 335,795. Its national ranking remains unchanged at 48th.

Population

	1980	1990
Central City	313,939	335,795
Rank	48	48
Metro Area	585,122	618,262
Pop. Change 1980–1990 +21,856		
Pop. % Change 1980–1990 +7.0		
Median Age 32.2		
% Male 47.8		
% Age 65 and Over 12.9		
Density (per square mile) 3,334		

Households

Number 133,842
Persons per Household 2.45
% Female-Headed Households 13.3
% One-Person Households 30.6
Births—Total 5,759
 % to Mothers under 20 13.4
 Birth Rate per 1,000 17.2

Ethnic Composition

Whites make up 83.86%, blacks 13.10%, American Indians 0.68%, Asians and Pacific Islanders 1.02%, Hispanics 3.06%, and others 1.35%.

Ethnic Composition (as % of total pop.)

	1980	1990
White	85.47	83.86
Black	12.05	13.10
American Indian	0.57	0.68
Asian and Pacific Islander	0.56	1.02
Hispanic	2.33	3.06
Other	NA	1.35

Government

Omaha is governed by a mayor and a council of seven members, all elected to four-year terms. The mayor is not a member of the council.

Government

Year of Home Charter 1956
Number of Members of the Governing Body 7
Elected at Large NA
Elected by Wards 7
Number of Women in Governing Body 1
Salary of Mayor $71,930
Salary of Council Members $18,627
City Government Employment Total 3,126
Rate per 10,000 89.5

Public Finance

The annual budget consists of revenues of $247.122 million and expenditures of $222.448 million. Debt outstanding is $179.238 million and cash and security holdings $265.669 million.

Public Finance

Total Revenue (in millions) $247.122
Intergovernmental Revenue—Total (in millions) $40.84
Federal Revenue per Capita $9.39
% Federal Assistance   3.89
% State Assistance   11.22
Sales Tax as % of Total Revenue   25.58
Local Revenue as % of Total Revenue   72.75
City Income Tax   no
Taxes—Total (in millions) $101.7

Taxes per Capita
    Total $291
    Property $140
    Sales and Gross Receipts $131
General Expenditures—Total (in millions) $176.0
General Expenditures per Capita $504
Capital Outlays per Capita $94

% of Expenditures for:
    Public Welfare   0.0
    Highways   14.2
    Education   NA
    Health and Hospitals   0.9
    Police   13.8
    Sewerage and Sanitation   19.2
    Parks and Recreation   7.7
    Housing and Community Development   7.2
Debt Outstanding per Capita $495
    % Utility   0.0
Federal Procurement Contract Awards (in millions)
    $124.1
Federal Grants Awards (in millions) $52.0
Fiscal Year Begins   January 1

Economy

 Omaha's staple industries are meat-packing, grain and livestock, and food processing. In recent decades Omaha has established additional strengths in insurance, telecommunications, and manufacturing. Over 40 insurance companies, including Mutual of Omaha and United of Omaha, are located in the city. Omaha's central location helped it to become a major railroad and truck distribution center and it is now emerging as a major telecommunications center—the base of operations of 800 numbers, telemarketing firms, travel industry reservation centers, and bank card processing centers (including First Data Resources, the nation's largest)—for the same reason. Omaha is the headquarters of some of the largest Fortune 500s, including ConAgra, U.S. West, Peter Kiewit Sons, Berkshire Hathaway, AG Processing, and Valmont Industries. In addition, the Strategic Air Command at Offut Air Force Base generates millions of dollars in support services and is a major player in the region's economy.

In the Grant Thornton study of general manufacturing climates, the Omaha region ranks fourth.

Economy

Total Money Income (in millions) $4,500.6
% of State Average   122.2
Per Capita Annual Income $12,886
% Population below Poverty Level   11.4

Economy (continued)

Fortune 500 Companies   3

Banks	Number	Deposits (in millions)
Commercial	40	6,281.7
Savings	6	4,644.2

Passenger Autos   270,938
Electric Meters   151,687
Gas Meters   152,338

Manufacturing

Number of Establishments   507
% with 20 or More Employees   40.0
Manufacturing Payroll (in millions) $651.2
Value Added by Manufacture (in millions) $2,004.1
Value of Shipments (in millions) $4,547.5
New Capital Expenditures (in millions) $100.3

Wholesale Trade

Number of Establishments   1,075
Sales (in millions) $7,333.4
Annual Payroll (in millions) $384.837

Retail Trade

Number of Establishments   3,420
Total Sales (in millions) $2,827.5
Sales per Capita $8,095
Number of Retail Trade Establishments with Payroll   2,526
Annual Payroll (in millions) $339.7
Total Sales (in millions) $2,783.9
General Merchandise Stores (per capita) $1,125
Food Stores (per capita) $1,528
Apparel Stores (per capita) $397
Eating and Drinking Places (per capita) $891

Service Industries

Total Establishments   3,130
Total Receipts (in millions) $1,772.6
Hotels and Motels (in millions) $66.8
Health Services (in millions) $453.5
Legal Services (in millions) $132.8

Labor

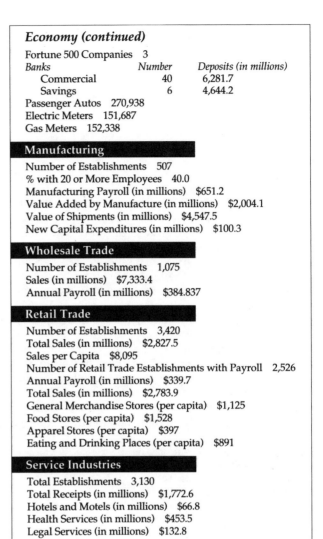 Between 1980 and 1990 employment in Omaha grew by 23.4%. The employment sector is well diversified with no industry accounting for over 30%. However, Omaha has a higher concentration of its employment in the FIRE, transportation, communications, and utilities (TCU) sectors than the national average. The region's 20 largest employers include 4 government institutions, 1 insurance, 5 medical facilities, 3 educational institutions, 2 distributors, 2 utilities, 2 communications firms, and 1 manufacturer.

Labor

Civilian Labor Force   186,525
% Change 1989–1990   3.5

Work Force Distribution
    Mining   200
    Construction   11,800
    Manufacturing   35,800
    Transportation and Public Utilities   24,100
    Wholesale and Retail Trade   81,800
    FIRE (Finance, Insurance, Real Estate)   28,600
    Service   99,100

Labor (continued)

    Government   48,100
    Women as % of Labor Force   45.1
    % Self-Employed   4.2
    % Professional/Technical   16.5
Total Unemployment   4,814
Rate %   2.6
Federal Government Civilian Employment   5,644

Education

Omaha Public Schools support 80 elementary schools, junior high schools, senior high schools, and special learning centers. The extensive parochial and private school system includes 33 elementary schools and 9 secondary schools run by the Catholic Archdiocese; the Bellevue Assembly of God Christian Academy, Brownell-Talbot (the oldest private school in Nebraska), Covenant Christian School, Friedel Jewish Academy, and the Seventh Day Adventist School are other private schools in Omaha. The city has two large universities: the Jesuit-run Creighton University and the University of Nebraska at Omaha. Other institutions include the College of St. Mary; Dana College, a Protestant liberal arts college; and Bellevue College, Nebraska's largest independent, nonsectarian college.

Education

Number of Public Schools   80
Special Education Schools   2
Total Enrollment   41,699
% Enrollment in Private Schools   15.1
% Minority   34.1
Classroom Teachers   2,505
Pupil-Teacher Ratio   16.6:1
Number of Graduates   2,200
Total Revenue (in millions) $176.596
Total Expenditures (in millions) $173.470
Expenditures per Pupil $4,058
Educational Attainment (Age 25 and Over)
    % Completed 12 or More Years   73.9
    % Completed 16 or More Years   18.4
Four-Year Colleges and Universities   5
    Enrollment   26,226
Two-Year Colleges   3
    Enrollment   9,020

Libraries

Number   43
Public Libraries   10
Books (in thousands)   619
Circulation (in thousands)   2,281
Persons Served (in thousands)   404
Circulation per Person Served   5.64
Income (in millions) $6.223
Staff   137

Four-Year Colleges and Universities
    Bishop Clarkson College
    University of Nebraska, Omaha
    University of Nebraska Medical Center
    Creighton University
    College of St. Mary

Health

The medical sector consists of 14 hospitals and two medical schools. Of the hospitals, the largest are St. Joseph Hospital, affiliated with the Creighton University School of Medicine, and the University of Nebraska Hospital and Clinic. Adjacent to St. Joseph Hospital is the Boys Town National Institute for Communication Disorders in Children. Other hospitals are the Bergen-Mercy Hospital, Lutheran Medical Center, Methodist Hospital, Clarkson Hospital, Douglas County Hospital, Immanuel Medical Center, Midlands Community Hospital, Nebraska Psychiatric Institute, and Veterans Administration Medical Center.

Health

Deaths—Total   3,247
Rate per 1,000   9.7
Infant Deaths—Total   84
Rate per 1,000   14.6
Number of Metro Hospitals   14
Number of Metro Hospital Beds   4,460
Rate per 100,000   1,277
Number of Physicians   1,531
Physicians per 1,000   2.73
Nurses per 1,000   8.82
Health Expenditures per Capita $0.71

Transportation

Omaha is approached by Interstates 80 and 29; U.S. routes 6, 30, 75, and 275; and state roads 36, 38, 50, 64, 85, 92, 131, 133, and 370. The Union Pacific, with headquarters in the city, and six other railroads provide freight service. The Port of Omaha is one of the largest inland ports, and it is linked to the Gulf of Mexico and the Atlantic Ocean through the Missouri River and the St. Lawrence Seaway. Eppley Airfield, four miles northeast of downtown Omaha, is served by 11 airlines. Millard Airport is a smaller commuter airport.

Transportation

Interstate Highway Mileage   42
Total Urban Mileage   2,315
Total Daily Vehicle Mileage (in millions) $9.088
Daily Average Commute Time   38.7 min.
Number of Buses   148
Port Tonnage (in millions)   NA
Airports   1
Number of Daily Flights   56
Daily Average Number of Passengers   2,758

Airlines (American carriers only)
    Trans World
    Delta
    Midway
    Northwest
    United
    American
    American West
    Continental
    USAir

Housing

Omaha has an abundant supply of affordable housing. The average sale price was $54,600 in 1991 and the average rent $326.

Housing

Total Housing Units   143,612
% Change 1980–1990   12.7
Vacant Units for Sale or Rent   6,845
Occupied Units   133,842
% with More Than One Person per Room   2.2
% Owner-Occupied   59.2
Median Value of Owner-Occupied Homes $54,600
Average Monthly Purchase Cost $334
Median Monthly Rent $326
New Private Housing Starts   2,309
Value (in thousands) $118,375
% Single-Family   58.5
Nonresidential Buildings Value (in thousands) $82,498

Tallest Buildings	Hgt. (ft.)	Stories
Woodmen Tower	469	30
Northwestern Bell Telephone	334	16
Masonic Manor	320	22
First Natl. Center	320	22

Urban Redevelopment

A three-year, $266-million downtown redevelopment program was completed in 1991. It included a new U.S. West computer center, new ConAgra facilities on the riverfront, renovation of the Union Pacific freighthouse, and conversion of the old First National Bank Building into apartment and retail space.

Crime

Omaha ranks above average in public safety. In 1991 violent crimes totaled 3,242, and property crimes totaled 20,762.

Crime

Violent Crimes—Total   3,242
Violent Crime Rate per 100,000   546.9
Murder   35
Rape   207
Robbery   634
Aggravated Assaults   2,366
Property Crimes   20,762
Burglary   3,986
Larceny   15,040
Motor Vehicle Theft   1,736
Arson   215
Per Capita Police Expenditures $92.05
Per Capita Fire Protection Expenditures $67.56
Number of Police   574
Per 1,000   1.58

Religion

Omaha has over 400 churches. Catholics make up the largest faith. Among the Protestants, the Lutheran, Baptist, and Methodist denominations rank highest.

Religion

Largest Denominations (Adherents)	
Catholic	119,453
Evangelical Lutheran	24,797
Lutheran-Missouri Synod	13,074
Presbyterian	12,440
Black Baptist	15,343
United Methodist	14,974
American Baptist	2,923
Christian and Missionary Alliance	4,400
Southern Baptist	4,366
Jewish	4,380

Media

The city dailies are the *Omaha World-Herald*, founded in 1885 by Gilbert M. Hitchcock, and *The Daily Record*. William Jennings Bryan was once editor of the paper. The electronic media consist of 5 television stations and 14 AM and FM stations.

Media

Newsprint
  The Daily Record, daily
  The Nebraska Observer, monthly
  Omaha World-Herald, daily

Television
  KETV (Channel 7)
  KMTV (Channel 3)
  KPTM (Channel 42)
  KYNE (Channel 26)
  WOWT (Channel 6)

Radio	
KCRO (AM)	KEFM (FM)
KEZO (AM)	KEZO (FM)
KFAB (AM)	KGOR (FM)
KGBI (FM)	KIOS (FM)
KKAR (AM)	KESY (FM)
KOIL (AM)	KVNO (FM)
WOW (AM)	WOW (FM)

Sports

Omaha has no major professional team in any of the sports. The Omaha Royals, Triple A farm team of the American League Kansas City Royals, play home games at the Rosenblatt Stadium, where the NCAA college baseball World Series is also held every June. The Omaha Racers of the Continental Basketball Association play 28 home games and the Omaha Lancers of the U.S. Hockey League play 24 home games at the Ak-Sar-Ben Coliseum. Ak-Sar-Ben is one of the nation's most popular racetracks, presenting thoroughbred racing since 1927.

Arts, Culture, and Tourism

The largest and oldest community theater in Omaha is the Omaha Community Playhouse, offering a year-round schedule of plays. Other theatrical groups include Centre

Stage, presenting African-American musicals and drama, Emmy Gifford Children's Theater, and Omaha Magic Theater. Joslyn Concert Hall presents a Chamber Music Series and a Tuesday Concert Series. Omaha Symphony Orchestra is the musical flagship, and Opera-Omaha offers three productions a year. Omaha Ballet presents four productions a year at the Orpheum Theater.

The Joslyn Art Museum is part of the Joslyn Memorial built in honor of George A. Joslyn, founder of the Nebraska Western Newspaper Union. It includes a concert hall and an art gallery, the largest in the city. The Western Heritage Museum and the Omaha Museum, opened in 1980, are housed in the Union Train Depot. The PhilaMatic Museum includes stamp, coin, and currency collections. The Strategic Air Command Museum in nearby Bellevue has displays of vintage and modern combat aircraft. Three other notable museums are the Great Plains Black Museum, Union Pacific Historical Museum, and the Omaha Children's Museum.

Parks and Recreation

 The city administers 6,300 acres of parks. The 38-acre Hanscom Park was donated to the city in 1872. The 41-acre Mandan Park offers a fine view of the Missouri River from its high bluffs. It is thought that Lewis and Clark camped

---

Travel and Tourism

Hotel Rooms 7,221
Convention and Exhibit Space (square feet) NA

Convention Centers
 Omaha Civic Auditorium
 Peter Kiewit Conference Center

Festivals
 Triumph of Agriculture (March)
 Ethnic Folk Festival (April)
 Summer Arts Festival (June)
 Sokol Set and Czechoslovakian Festival (June)
 Festa Italiana (Labor Day)
 Ak-Sar-Ben Rodeo and Livestock Exposition
  (September)
 Dickens in the Market (December)

---

here. Riverview Park between Funston and Homer streets has a statue of the German poet Schiller. The 1.7-acre Florence Park between Mormon and State streets is the oldest park in the city. Hummel Park on River Drive north of Florence affords panoramic views of the wooded Missouri River Valley. Fontenelle Park, acquired by the city in 1892, is named for Chief Logan Fontenelle. The 207-acre Elmwood Park on 60th Street contains an Alaskan Totem Pole. Miller Park between 24th and 30th streets is named for an early Omaha park commissioner. Kountze Park on 21st Street is the site of the Trans-Mississippi Exposition of 1904. The Levi Carter Park on the north shore of Carter Lake is Omaha's largest park. Other large parks include the Malcolm X Park, N. P. Dodge Memorial Park, and Standing Bear Lake.

Sources of Further Information

Douglas County Historical Society
General Crook House
30th and Fort Streets
Omaha, NE 68110
(402) 455-9990

Greater Omaha Chamber of Commerce
1301 Harney Street
Omaha, NE 68102
(402) 346-5000

Greater Omaha Convention and Visitors Bureau
1819 Farnam, Suite 1200
Omaha, NE 68183
(402) 444-4660

Omaha Public Library
215 South 15th Street
Omaha, NE 68102-1004
(402) 444-4800

Additional Reading

The Case for Omaha. 1991.
Guide to Omaha Educational System. 1991.

Peoria

Illinois

Basic Data

Name   Peoria
Name Origin   From the Peoria Indians
Year Founded   1819 Inc. 1845
Status: State   Illinois
     County   Seat of Peoria County
Area (square miles)   40.9
Elevation (feet)   470
Time Zone   Central
Population (1990)   113,504
Population of Metro Area (1990)   339,172

Sister Cities
   Friedrichshafen, Germany

Distance in Miles To:
Chicago	170
Carbondale	242
Springfield	72
St. Louis	166

Environment

Environmental Stress Index   2.4
Green Cities Index: Rank   NA
                Score   NA
Water Quality   Alkaline, hard, fluoridated
Average Daily Use (gallons per capita)   109
   Maximum Supply (gallons per capita)   263
Parkland as % of Total City Area   NA
% Waste Landfilled/Recycled   NA
Annual Parks Expenditures per Capita $2.56

Climate

 Peoria has a continental climate with a wide range of climatic and temperature variations. Temperatures over 100°F and below zero are not infrequent. Late spring and early fall are generally pleasant seasons, but summer may linger for an extended period. Rainfall is heaviest in the growing season and lowest in midwinter.

Location and Topography

N   Peoria is on the northwest bank of the Illinois River in rich north-central farming country. It is the oldest continuously inhabited community west of the Alleghenies. Its port is on Lake Peoria, a broad part of the Illinois River which flows from the Great Lakes to the Gulf of Mexico through the Mississippi River.

Layout of City and Suburbs

The city is defined by Lake Peoria, which shapes the contours of the city. The heart of the city is the space between War Memorial Drive (Highway 24/150) and Route 74. The Civic Center, a 20-acre entertainment and convention complex, is located downtown. The riverfront, with its Liberty Park, gives the city an appearance of spaciousness. West Peoria and Peoria Heights jut into the city to form one large metropolis.

Weather

Temperature

Highest Monthly Average °F   85.5
Lowest Monthly Average °F   13.3

Annual Averages

Days 32°F or Below   132
Days above 90°F   17
Zero Degree Days   11
Precipitation (inches)   35
Snow (inches)   23
% Seasonal Humidity   72
Wind Speed (m.p.h.)   10.3
Clear Days   97
Cloudy Days   168
Storm Days   49
Rainy Days   111

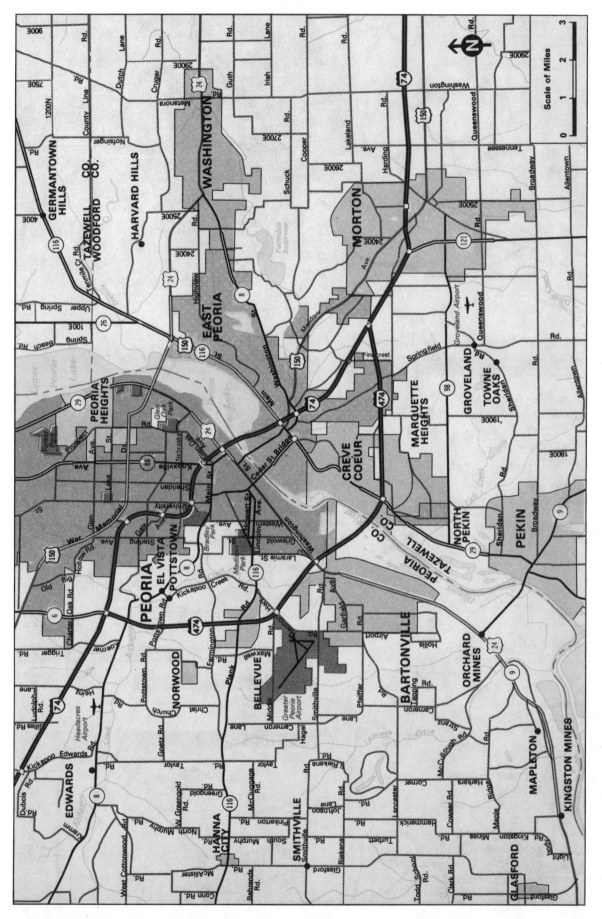

Weather (continued)

Average Temperatures (°F)	High	Low	Mean
January	31.9	15.7	23.8
February	36.0	19.3	27.7
March	46.5	28.1	37.3
April	61.7	40.8	51.3
May	72.3	50.7	61.5
June	81.7	60.9	71.3
July	85.5	64.6	75.1
August	84.0	62.9	73.5
September	76.4	54.6	65.5
October	65.9	44.0	55.0
November	48.7	31.1	39.9
December	35.7	20.3	28.0

History

The first white men in what is now Peoria were the legendary explorers Father Jacques Marquette and Louis Jolliet, who passed through Lake Peoria in 1673 on their way to the Mississippi. In 1680 they were followed by Robert Cavelier, Sieur de la Salle, leading a band of 33 men, who erected Fort Creve Coeur, the Refuge of the Broken Heart, on the left bank of Lake Peoria. Within three months it was plundered and abandoned. In 1691 a second settlement followed when Fort St. Louis, upstream from Peoria on Starved Rock, was moved to the west shore of Lake Peoria, where it was generally referred to as Fort Pimiteoui. Peorians date the establishment of their city from this date. In 1763 the British wrested control of the area from the French but the settlement remained abandoned until the French returned in 1778 under Jean Baptiste Maillet to a new village on the right bank of the river. The new village, officially called La Ville de Maillet, was commonly referred to as Au Pe, Le Pe, Opa, or Fort Le Pe, possibly derived from the French Au Pay (for country). By 1790 the name had become Piorias. The settlement was the scene of at least two destructive acts by American troops. During the Revolutionary War, a group of George Roger Clark's men destroyed the Indian village here. During the War of 1812, Illinois Governor Ninian Edwards led troops from Edwardsville and mistakenly destroyed the village of Black Partridge, who was in fact an American ally. In another incident, a French village was also destroyed by Americans. In 1813 the Americans erected Fort Clark on the site of Au Pe, and about it grew the nucleus of modern Peoria, although the name Fort Clark was used for another ten years. In 1819 the first American civilians arrived. In 1825 Peoria County was created with Peoria as its official seat. For the next six years Peoria, as the largest city in Illinois at that time, exercised jurisdiction over one-fourth of the state, including the stripling town of Chicago. Peoria was incorporated as a town in 1835 and as a city in 1845. Peoria achieved industrial prominence early in three areas: tractors, pork and beef packing, and liquors. It was in Peoria that Abraham Lincoln first clearly denounced the institution of slavery.

Historical Landmarks

The Pettengill-Morron House, located in the historic Moss-Bradley area, is on the National Register of Historic Places. The St. Mary's Cathedral's twin Gothic towers rise 192 feet in the air. Near its entrance is the Marquette-Jolliet Cross, a four-ton cross of New Hampshire granite. A reconstructed fort marks the site of the original Fort Creve Coeur, an 86-acre park overlooking the Illinois River. The Flanagan House, built circa 1837, is the city's oldest standing house.

Population

Both the central city population and the metro population have declined since 1980. In 1990 the former was 113,504, a decline of 8.6% compared to the 1980 population of 124,160, which itself was 2,400 less than the 1970 population of 126,560.

Population

	1980	1990
Central City	124,160	113,504
Rank	126	156
Metro Area	365,864	339,172
Pop. Change 1980–1990 -10,656		
Pop. % Change 1980–1990 -8.6		
Median Age 32.6		
% Male 47.2		
% Age 65 and Over 14.4		
Density (per square mile) 2,775		

Households

Number   44,976
Persons per Household   2.42
% Female-Headed Households   14.7
% One-Person Households   31.6
Births—Total   1,931
   % to Mothers under 20   18.6
   Birth Rate per 1,000   16.5

Ethnic Composition

Whites make up 76.5%, blacks 20.9%, American Indians 0.2%, Asian and Pacific Islanders 1.7%, and others 0.8%.

Ethnic Composition (as % of total pop.)

	1980	1990
White	81.49	76.52
Black	16.69	20.87
American Indian	0.16	0.18
Asian and Pacific Islander	0.85	1.68
Hispanic	1.39	1.6
Other	NA	0.75

Government

Peoria is governed under a council-manager system. The council consists of 11 members elected to four-year staggered terms, 5 members from each of the five wards and 6

Chronology

1673	Father Jacques Marquette and Louis Jolliet visit the site of present-day Peoria.
1680	Robert Cavelier, Sieur de la Salle, and a party of 33 establish a fort, Fort Creve Coeur, on the left bank of Lake Peoria.
1691	Fort St. Louis on Starved Rock is moved to Lake Peoria, where it is called Fort Pimiteoui.
1763	British wrest control of the region from the French.
1778	Jean Baptiste Maillet returns to area to found new settlement one mile farther down the river; although the settlement is officially called La Ville de Maillet, it is commonly referred to as Au Pe, Fort Le Pe, or Opa, and later Piorias with a silent s.
1812	Governor Ninian Edwards leads expedition and destroys the village of Black Partridge, an American ally, by mistake.
1813	Fort Clark is erected on the site of Au Pe.
1819	The first American civilian settlers arrive.
1825	Peoria County is organized with Peoria as county seat.
1835	Peoria is incorporated as a town.
1845	Peoria is incorporated as a city.
1854	In a public speech, Lincoln denounces slavery.

members at large. The mayor is elected at large in a nonpartisan election.

Government

Year of Home Charter   1970
Number of Members of the Governing Body   11
Elected at Large   6
Elected by Wards   5
Number of Women in Governing Body   1
Salary of Mayor $19,000
Salary of Council Members $7,200
City Government Employment Total   1,164
Rate per 10,000   105.5

Public Finance

 The annual budget consists of revenues of $82.665 million and expenditures of $69.141 million. The debt outstanding is $129.611 million and cash and security holdings of $200.495 million.

Public Finance

Total Revenue (in millions) $82.66
Intergovernmental Revenue—Total (in millions) $18.44
Federal Revenue per Capita $5.46
% Federal Assistance   6.60
% State Assistance   15.65
Sales Tax as % of Total Revenue   29.13
Local Revenue as % of Total Revenue   65.94
City Income Tax   no
Taxes—Total (in millions) $28.6

Taxes per Capita
  Total $259
  Property $134
  Sales and Gross Receipts $92
General Expenditures—Total (in millions) $69.1
General Expenditures per Capita $626
Capital Outlays per Capita $114

% of Expenditures for:
  Public Welfare   0.4
  Highways   15.2
  Education   0.0
  Health and Hospitals   0.1
  Police   13.1
  Sewerage and Sanitation   6.7
  Parks and Recreation   1.8
  Housing and Community Development   9.5
Debt Outstanding per Capita $1,286
  % Utility   0.0
Federal Procurement Contract Awards (in millions) $73.9
Federal Grants Awards (in millions) $13.2
Fiscal Year Begins   January 1

Economy

Historically, Peoria was one of the earliest industrial centers in Illinois, and its strength in this sector has been buttressed by the presence of Caterpillar, one of the largest manufacturers in the nation and the second-largest exporter of machinery. Peoria makes over 1,000 products, including wire and wire products, at Keystone Consolidated Industries and large trucking equipment at Komatsu Dresser Company. Peoria makes about 14% of all internal combustion engines, and 8% of construction machinery. It remains, as it was in the 19th century, one of the most important production centers for alcohol made from corn and grain. Located at the center of one of the richest farming regions in the nation, with corn and soybeans as principal crops, Peoria is a major grain and corn exporter and the fifth- or sixth-largest exporter of hogs. In addition, Peoria sits on one of the largest coal-bearing fields, and coal production makes a substantial contribution to the local economy. Peoria is a strong retail market and is often used as a test market for new products (hence the expression, "Does it play in Peoria?") because the demographics of the community closely mirror national statistics.

Economy

Total Money Income (in millions) $1,225.4
% of State Average   98.6
Per Capita Annual Income $11,140

Economy *(continued)*

% Population below Poverty Level   12.3
Fortune 500 Companies   1

Banks	Number	Deposits (in millions)
Commercial	35	2,896.5
Savings	19	NA

Passenger Autos   111,893
Electric Meters   80,697
Gas Meters   64,369

Manufacturing

Number of Establishments   121
% with 20 or More Employees   44.6
Manufacturing Payroll (in millions) $454.0
Value Added by Manufacture (in millions) $427.1
Value of Shipments (in millions) $961.0
New Capital Expenditures (in millions) $67.0

Wholesale Trade

Number of Establishments   316
Sales (in millions) $2,765.6
Annual Payroll (in millions) $106,675

Retail Trade

Number of Establishments   1,173
Total Sales (in millions) $938.3
Sales per Capita $8,508
Number of Retail Trade Establishments with Payroll   861
Annual Payroll (in millions) $108.9
Total Sales (in millions) $921.7
General Merchandise Stores (per capita) $1,399
Food Stores (per capita) $1,255
Apparel Stores (per capita) $486
Eating and Drinking Places (per capita) $834

Service Industries

Total Establishments   945
Total Receipts (in millions) $468.0
Hotels and Motels (in millions)   NA
Health Services (in millions) $151.1
Legal Services (in millions) $51.4

Labor

More than half of Peoria's employees are engaged in white-collar occupations despite the city's tradition of manufacturing. Medical and educational services are important employers in the nonmanufacturing sectors. Insurance, marketing, telecommunications, and advertising are among the growing service industries. Until the 1992 Caterpillar strike, Peoria enjoyed remarkable industrial peace through the efforts of the Peoria Area Labor Management Council.

Labor

Civilian Labor Force   54,697
% Change 1989–1990   1.2

Work Force Distribution
   Mining   NA
   Construction   7,400
   Manufacturing   32,000
   Transportation and Public Utilities   6,800
   Wholesale and Retail Trade   35,700

Labor *(continued)*

   FIRE (Finance, Insurance, Real Estate)   7,800
   Service   42,000
   Government   17,200
   Women as % of Labor Force   43.7
   % Self-Employed   4.5
   % Professional/Technical   18.2
Total Unemployment   3,825
Rate %   7.0
Federal Government Civilian Employment   1,535

Education

The Peoria Public School District supports 42 primary schools, middle schools, and senior high schools. The parochial system enrolls over 10,000 students in 2 high schools and 7 elementary schools. The bellwether of higher education is Bradley University, founded in 1897. Other colleges within or close to the city are Eureka College, a private liberal arts college about 40 miles from Peoria; Illinois Central College, a two-year junior college; and the University of Illinois College of Medicine.

Education

Number of Public Schools   42
Special Education Schools   2
Total Enrollment   17,378
% Enrollment in Private Schools   11.1
% Minority   NA
Classroom Teachers   NA
Pupil-Teacher Ratio   NA
Number of Graduates   NA
Total Revenue (in millions) $75.155
Total Expenditures (in millions) $79.053
Expenditures per Pupil $4,654
Educational Attainment (Age 25 and Over)
   % Completed 12 or More Years   69.6
   % Completed 16 or More Years   19.4
Four-Year Colleges and Universities   2
   Enrollment   6,558
Two-Year Colleges   NA
   Enrollment   NA

Libraries

Number   20
Public Libraries   5
Books (in thousands)   690
Circulation (in thousands)   901
Persons Served (in thousands)   124
Circulation per Person Served   7.26
Income (in millions) $2.529
Staff   82

Four-Year Colleges and Universities
   Bradley University
   Eureka College

Health

The medical sector includes three large hospitals: Proctor Community Hospital, Methodist Medical Center, and Saint Francis Medical Center. All are full-service hospitals with teaching facilities. Mental health care is provided by Zeller Zone Mental Health Center.

Health

Deaths—Total   1,146
Rate per 1,000   9.8
Infant Deaths—Total   21
Rate per 1,000   10.9
Number of Metro Hospitals   4
Number of Metro Hospital Beds   1,788
Rate per 100,000   1,621
Number of Physicians   610
Physicians per 1,000   NA
Nurses per 1,000   NA
Health Expenditures per Capita $0.56

Transportation

 Peoria is approached by Interstate 74, which bisects the city while the 474 bypass circles the city. U.S. Highways 24 and 150 are part of the metro area road network. Rail freight service is provided by Burlington Northern, C&NW, Illinois Central, Illinois Terminal N&W, Conrail, P&PU, Peoria Terminal, Santa Fe, Chicago Northwestern, Central and Gulf, Norfolk Southern Corporation, Norfolk and Western, and Pioneer. The Illinois River is a direct link from the Great Lakes to the Gulf of Mexico. Four barge lines transport over 650 million tons annually on the river. The Greater Peoria Regional Airport is the principal air terminal. There are two private air fields: Byerly Aviation and Mt. Hawley.

Transportation

Interstate Highway Mileage   29
Total Urban Mileage   1,231
Total Daily Vehicle Mileage (in millions) $4.512
Daily Average Commute Time   40.7 min.
Number of Buses   40
Port Tonnage (in millions)   NA
Airports   1
Number of Daily Flights   11
Daily Average Number of Passengers   299

Airlines (American carriers only)
   American
   Midway
   Trans World
   United

Housing

 Nearly 57% of houses are owner-occupied, which is below the national average. The median value of an owner-occupied home is $49,200 and the median monthly rent $277.

Housing

Total Housing Units   48,260
% Change 1980–1990   -5.4
Vacant Units for Sale or Rent   2,445
Occupied Units   44,976
% with More Than One Person per Room   2.2
% Owner-Occupied   56.5
Median Value of Owner-Occupied Homes $49,200

Housing (continued)

Average Monthly Purchase Cost $418
Median Monthly Rent $277
New Private Housing Starts   227
Value (in thousands) $23,512
% Single-Family   78.4
Nonresidential Buildings Value (in thousands) $50,662

Urban Redevelopment

 Peoria has developed a master redevelopment plan calling for an extensive revitalization of the central business district. Anchoring the plan are the 29-story Twin Towers, a residential and commercial complex, and the Boatworks, an entertainment complex along the west bank of the river.

Crime

 Peoria has an above national average public safety record. Property crimes totaled 9,193.

Crime

Violent Crimes—Total   NA
Violent Crime Rate per 100,000   NA
Murder   18
Rape   NA
Robbery   499
Aggravated Assaults   1,129
Property Crimes   9,193
Burglary   2,503
Larceny   6,362
Motor Vehicle Theft   328
Arson   88
Per Capita Police Expenditures $101.47
Per Capita Fire Protection Expenditures $71.22
Number of Police   194
Per 1,000   1.65

Religion

 Sixty-two denominations are represented in the city with 269 churches and two synagogues.

Religion

Largest Denominations (Adherents)

Catholic	34,713
United Methodist	12,749
Black Baptist	7,657
Presbyterian	4,738
Lutheran-Missouri Synod	5,835
Evangelical Lutheran	6,740
Assembly of God	1,203
Southern Baptist	3,949
Jewish	567

Media

 The Peoria press consists of the *Journal-Star*, which is published daily. The electronic media consist of three television stations and six AM and FM radio stations.

Media

Newsprint
  Journal-Star, daily
  Observer, weekly
  Peoria Heights Herald, weekly

Television
  WEEK (Channel 25)
  WMBD (Channel 31)
  WTVP (Channel 47)

Radio
  WIRL (AM)   WMBD (AM)
  WKZW (FM)   WVEL (AM)
  WWCT (FM)   WXCL (AM)

Sports

 Peoria has no major professional sports team. The Peoria Chiefs, a Class A minor league baseball team, and the Peoria Rivermen, a hockey team of the St. Louis Blues, are the two most popular teams. The Bradley Braves basketball team plays at the Civic Center. The Great Plains Sports Science and Training Center in Peoria offers athletic camps, sports seminars and exhibitions, and sports research and development.

Arts, Culture, and Tourism

 The performing arts scene includes the Peoria Symphony, Peoria Wind Ensemble, Peoria Civic Opera, Peoria Municipal Band, and Peoria Area Civic Chorale in music; the Peoria Civic Ballet in dance; and Broadway Theater League, Community Childrens Theater, Corn Stock Theater, Peoria Players, Illinois Central College Theater, and Bradley University Theater in drama. The Lakeview Museum for the Arts and Sciences is the flagship for the visual arts. It is also the headquarters of the Peoria Area Arts and Sciences Council.

Travel and Tourism

Hotel Rooms   2,240
Convention and Exhibit Space (square feet)   56,200

Convention Centers
  Peoria Civic Center

Festivals
  Heart of Illinois Fair
  Christmas Art & Craft Show

Parks and Recreation

 The Peoria Pleasure Driveway and Park District manages 8,200 acres of public parkland. Peoria has the seventh highest ratio of parkland per capita in the nation. Wildlife Prairie Park is located ten miles west of Peoria. It is an open zoo and nature conservancy that allows visitors to view native Illinois animals in their natural prairie habitat. The 106-acre Glen Oak Park on the Bluffs is one of the most popular parks. It includes the Boulder Monument commemorative of early settlers. The 440-acre McCutcheon Animal Park was established in 1970. The 756-acre Detweiller Park offers a variety of drives, trails, and picnic sites. The 500-acre Forest Park is a forest wildlife and nature center with a museum.

Sources of Further Information

City Hall
City Hall Building
Peoria, IL 61602
(309) 672-8512

Peoria Area Chamber of Commerce
124 SW Adams
Peoria, IL 61602
(309) 676-0755

Peoria Arts and Sciences Council
11125 West Lake Avenue
Peoria, IL 61614

Peoria Convention and Visitors Bureau
331 Fulton
Peoria, IL 61602
(309) 676-0303

Peoria Historical Society
942 NE Glen Oak
Peoria, IL 61603
(309) 674-1921

Peoria Public Library
107 NE Monroe Street
Peoria, IL 61602
(309) 672-8835

Additional Reading

Peoria-Pekin. *Illinois. Cross-Reference Directory.* 1991.
Polk's Peoria City Directory. 1991.

Philadelphia
Pennsylvania

Location and Topography

Philadelphia lies at the southeastern corner of Pennsylvania on the Delaware River, where it meets the Schuylkill River. The central city covers an area of 135 square miles. The metro area includes parts of southern New Jersey and northern Delaware, most notably the towns of Chester in Pennsylvania and Camden in New Jersey.

The city occupies fairly flat land along the banks of the Schuylkill River, which runs through it, and the Delaware River, which runs along the northern boundary. The terrain is more typical of the low flatlands of New Jersey and Delaware, rather than the mountainous interior of Pennsylvania.

Layout of City and Suburbs

Philadelphia is laid out in the classic rectangular pattern conceived by its founder, William Penn. "Let every house," Penn wrote in 1681, "be pitched in the middle of a plot so that there may be ground on each side for gardens or orchards or fields, that it may be a greene country towne that will . . . always be wholesome." Numbered streets run north and south, with the lowest numbers near the Delaware River. There is no 14th Street; in its place there is Broad Street, a wide boulevard that intersects the city in a north-south direction. Paralleling the Market Street are the streets named originally for famous persons, but changed by Penn for trees and flowers of the vicinity. From this originated the jingle :

High, Mulberry, Sassafras, Vine
Chestnut, Walnut, Spruce, and Pine

Across the Schuylkill River, the city spreads fan-shaped to Philadelphia International Airport and the Main Line suburbs. To the north, the city extends like a spreading hand along the banks of the two rivers.

Center City is the historical center of Philadelphia. To an extent remarkable in urban America, Center City is heavily residential and growing more so, with townhouses dating from the 18th and 19th centuries. Most of the historical sites and street patterns retain their original character. There is a center square at the midpoint and four other squares in each quadrant

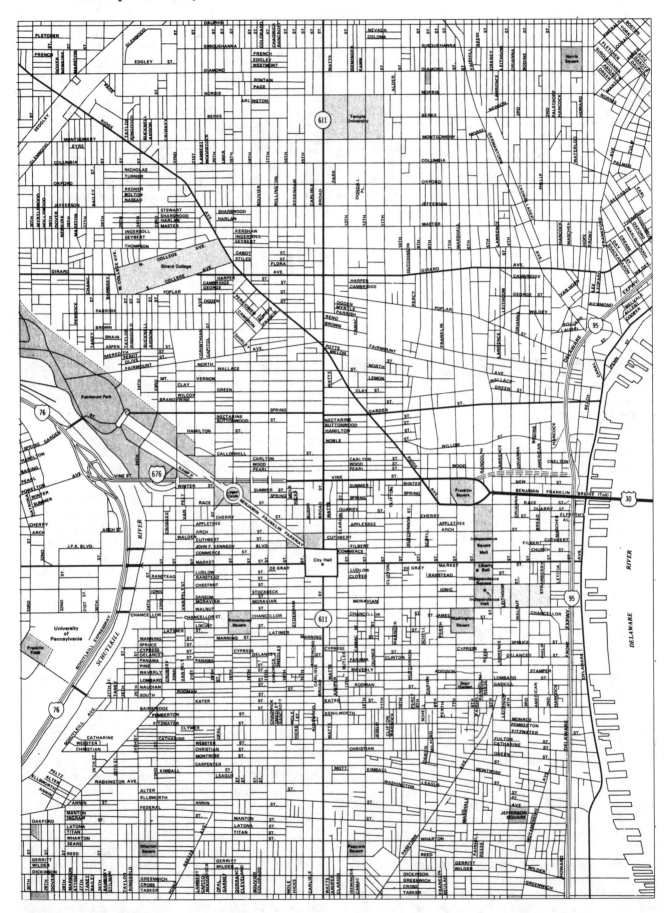

located on the diagonal from the center square in much the same manner as Penn designed them. Penn Square is dominated by City Hall, an imposing structure in the French Renaissance style. The city's tallest building is 548 feet and is topped by a 37-foot-high bronze statue of William Penn facing the Penn Treaty Park. To the west of the City Hall is Penn Center, a modern complex of tall office buildings. To the northwest of Penn Center lies another of the city's original squares, now Logan Circle. The Benjamin Franklin Parkway, a broad, tree-lined boulevard modeled on the Champs Elysees and designed by the French architect Jacques Greber, passes through the square. Most Philadelphians regard it as the most beautiful section of the city. Six blocks to the south is the Rittenhouse Square, named after the astronomer David Rittenhouse. Known in the 19th century for its wealthy homes, it still has tranquil, tree-lined walks that, in the summer, become a site for flower shows, art exhibits, and concerts. Eleven blocks to the east is Washington Square, the site of the memorial to the Unknown Soldiers of the American Revolution. It marks the western boundary of the Old City. The stretch of land between the waterfront and the Washington Square is a living museum of Colonial America, including the Independence National Historic Park. South of the Park is a residential area known as Society Hill, named for the Free Society of Traders, a stock company organized by William Penn. The area is a showcase of Colonial residential and ecclesiastical architecture. Queen Village, immediately to the south of Society Hill, contains the Gloria Dei (or the Old Swedes' Lutheran) Church, the oldest church in Pennsylvania.

The oldest section in Philadelphia is South Philadelphia, including the historic districts of Southwark and Moyamensing. West Philadelphia is located across the Schuylkill River from Center City, while the area just west of the Schuylkill River is known as the University City because it is dominated by the University of Pennsylvania and Drexel University. The area from Center City North to Somerset Street, including the historic districts of Northern Liberties and Spring Garden, is known as North Philadelphia. Northwest Philadelphia is connected to the Old City by the Germantown Road. Just north of Germantown are Mount Airy, Chestnut Hill, and Manayunk, all residential communities. Northeast Philadelphia is the largest geographical section of the city.

The city's residential areas have long been known for row houses—block after block of attached two-, three-, and four-story homes. This is particularly true of Society Hill, Kensington, Chestnut Hill, and Germantown.

Other communities in the metro area are bedroom towns. Upper Darby is one of the largest townships in the country. To the north of the city are Levittown, a planned residential development founded in 1952, and the artistic communities, such as Doylestown and New Hope in Bucks County. In New Jersey are the older suburbs of Haddonfield, Moorestown, and Merchantsville. A series of communities near Philadelphia is known as the Main Line, a name derived from the

main line of the old Pennsylvania Railroad. Today, Mainliners are wealthy suburbanites. Mainline communities include Merion, Ardmore, Wayne, Villanova, Bryn Mawr, and Haverford.

Environment	
Environmental Stress Index	3.4
Green Cities Index: Rank	55
Score	37.79
Water Quality	Slightly acid; moderately hard (Schuylkill River); moderately soft (Delaware River)
Average Daily Use (gallons per capita)	201
Maximum Supply (gallons per capita)	375
Parkland as % of Total City Area	12.8
% Waste Landfilled/Recycled	90.3:9.7
Annual Parks Expenditures per Capita	$46.60

Climate

The Appalachian Mountains to the west and the Atlantic Ocean to the east moderate the climate so that the winters are not too cold nor the summers too hot. However, humidity is high during the summer. Precipitation is fairly evenly distributed throughout the year, with a maximum in the summer when the Schuylkill is liable to flood. Snowfall is lighter in the city than in the northern, more elevated, suburbs. High winds are characteristic of the winter months.

Weather			
Temperature			
Highest Monthly Average °F	86.1		
Lowest Monthly Average °F	23.8		
Annual Averages			
Days 32°F or Below	101		
Days above 90°F	19		
Zero Degree Days	0		
Precipitation (inches)	40		
Snow (inches)	20		
% Seasonal Humidity	67		
Wind Speed (m.p.h.)	9.6		
Clear Days	92		
Cloudy Days	160		
Storm Days	27		
Rainy Days	116		
Average Temperatures (°F)	*High*	*Low*	*Mean*
January	40.1	24.4	32.3
February	42.2	25.5	33.9
March	51.2	32.5	41.9
April	63.5	42.3	52.9
May	74.1	52.3	63.2
June	83.0	61.6	72.3
July	86.8	66.7	76.8
August	84.8	64.7	74.8
September	78.4	57.8	68.1
October	67.9	46.9	57.4
November	55.5	36.9	46.2
December	43.2	27.2	35.2

Chronology

1682	William Penn founds the city on 1,280 acres with 80 families.
1700	The Old Swedes' Church is erected in Queen Village.
1723	Benjamin Franklin arrives in Philadelphia from Boston.
1730	The *Philadelphia Gazette* begins publication.
1732	Independence Hall is built as the State House of Pennsylvania.
1743	The American Philosophical Society is founded in Philadelphia.
1752	The Pennsylvania Hospital, the nation's first hospital, is founded in Philadelphia.
1774	The First Continental Congress meets in Carpenter's Hall.
1775	The Second Continental Congress meets in the State House.
1776	Thomas Jefferson drafts the Declaration of Independence.
1778	The British evacuate the city.
1781	The Bank of North America is organized in the city by Robert Morris, and is chartered by the Congress as the nation's first bank.
1790	Philadelphia is selected as the capital of the United States.
1793	A disastrous epidemic of yellow fever sweeps the city, claiming the lives of one-tenth of the population.
1800	National capital moves from Philadelphia to Washington, D.C.
1818	Philadelphia launches city-wide public school system.
1820	New York overtakes Philadelphia as the largest city in the country.
1854	City of Philadelphia merges with the County of Philadelphia.
1857	The Academy of Music is founded.
1876	Philadelphia holds the Centennial Exposition.
1917	The Benjamin Franklin Parkway is completed, connecting the City Hall and the Philadelphia Museum of Art.
1926	Philadelphia holds the Sesqui-Centennial Exposition.
1945	The Redevelopment Authority is established to direct an ambitious program of urban renewal.

Chronology

1951	Joseph S. Clark is elected mayor on the Democratic ticket, thus ending the Republican era in city politics; voters approve a home-rule charter replacing that of 1789.
1958	The Philadelphia Industrial Development Corporation is set up.
1972	Frank L. Rizzo is elected mayor.
1983	W. Wilson Goode is elected as the city's first black mayor; Police bomb the heavily fortified headquarters of the radical black group MOVE.

History

Philadelphia was built and christened by William Penn, the Quaker leader, who in 1681 received a grant of the territory now known as Pennsylvania from King Charles II of England. The town was platted in 1682 by Penn's cousin on the neck of the land between the Schuylkill and Delaware rivers. The early settlers were English Quakers, but a group of Palatinate Germans arrived in 1683 followed by immigrants from Scotland and Ireland, attracted by the city's reputation for religious tolerance. By the middle of the 18th century, Philadelphia became not only the largest city in the American colonies, but also the second largest in the British Empire. During this time the city developed into a manufacturing center, commercial entrepot, and port. Contributing to its prosperity were a number of factors. It was surrounded by rich farmlands and forests and had access to important raw materials. It possessed an excellent waterfront and was located at the crossroads of several trading routes. The colony's liberal immigration laws attracted skilled craftsmen and able merchants. The arts and sciences also flourished during this period, making the city the center of social, intellectual, artistic, and scientific activity. The genius of Benjamin Franklin dominated the city in this era and left an indelible impress upon it. Under his guiding hand, the city established the first institution in the colonies to be designated a university (the University of Pennsylvania), the first hospital (the Pennsylvania Hospital), and the first fire insurance company. He also was responsible for the founding of the American Philosophical Society and the Library Company. Franklin's newspaper, *Philadelphia Gazette*, became the mouthpiece of the radical elements of the colonial society. In addition to Franklin, a number of his contemporaries added to the city's eminence: John Morgan, the father of medical education; David Rittenhouse, the astronomer and mathematician; John Bartram, botanist; John James Audubon, painter and ornithologist; Benjamin Ruch, physician; and Benjamin West, painter.

Philadelphia was the natural choice of the American revolutionaries as the venue of the First and Second Continental congresses in 1774 and 1775, respectively. It became the birthplace of American independence when the Declaration of Independence was drafted by Thomas Jefferson and adopted on 4 July 1776 at the Independence Hall. The U.S. Constitution was written here, and the city was the capital of the new republic from 1790 until 1800.

After the Revolutionary War, Philadelphia rapidly expanded as the political center of the nation. In 1780 the first U.S.-organized bank was established in the city and, later, as the Bank of North America, it was the first to be chartered by Congress. In 1789 Philadelphia at last gave up its original Penn charter and received a new and more liberal one from the state.

After the transfer of the national capital to Washington, D.C., Philadelphia gradually lost its prominence. Cultural and commercial leadership passed to New York after the opening of the Erie Canal in 1825. Philadelphia, however, remained the second-largest city in the United States until 1890. With the decline in commerce, Philadelphia turned to manufacturing, particularly textiles, iron, and glass. The city also became a distribution center for coal mined in northeast Pennsylvania.

During the Civil War, Philadelphia, with its Quaker heritage, was strongly opposed to slavery, but not entirely pro-black. In fact, in the immediate decades before the Civil War, there were six race riots involving the city's small but segregated black community. Once the war began, however, Philadelphia actively supported President Lincoln, who had carried the city by a substantial majority in 1860. In 1854 the city was greatly enlarged by the incorporation of the remainder of Philadelphia County, including Germantown, Mayunk, Frankford, West Philadelphia, and South Philadelphia. Philadelphia was the site of the Centennial Exposition of 1876 and the Sesqui-Centennial Exposition of 1926.

After the Civil War, Philadelphia's population was swelled through the influx of large numbers of immigrants. These immigrants became the mainstay of post–Civil War machine politics, led by such figures as Senator Matthew Stanley Quay and Senator Boies Penrose. The era of machine politics lasted until the Great Depression of the 1930s, when labor strikes were frequent and bloody. After World War II, Philadelphia became increasingly Democratic and reform Democrats led by Joseph S. Clark and Richardson Dilworth finally broke the power of the Republican machine. In 1951 a new city charter was adopted and Clark began a vast urban renewal program. Slated for completion in the 21st century, the program is still under way.

Historical Landmarks

Philadelphia ranks third among U.S. cities in the number of historical landmarks and sites. The most notable of them is the Independence National Historic Park, often called the most historic square mile in America.

Among the park's 25 sites are the Independence Hall, the Liberty Bell Pavilion, the Second Bank of the United States, the City Tavern, the Carpenter's Hall, the meeting place of the First Continental Congress, Bishop White House, Philadelphia (Merchants) Exchange, and Todd House, the home of Dolly Madison.

Between the Independence Hall and the Delaware River are Elfreth's Alley, the oldest continuously occupied street in America, the Betsy Ross House, the 1804 Arch Street Friends' Meeting House, the 1724 Christ Church, the United States Mint, and the restored Philadelphia Bourse Building. Society Hill contains a number of 18th-century houses: the Roman Catholic St. Mary's and Old St. Joseph's, the Presbyterian Old Pine Street Church, and the Episcopal St. Peter's Church. Among the historic homes open to the public are: the Samuel Powell House, a red brick Georgian Colonial building built in 1765; the Wistar or Shippen House, a Georgian Colonial townhouse built in 1750; the Edgar Allan Poe House built in 1830; the Letitia Street House, built sometime before 1715; and the Woodford Mansion built in 1868.

Population

With a 1990 population of 1,585,577, Philadelphia is the fifth-largest city in the United States, having lost its fourth place to Houston in that year's census. Since 1980 it has shed 57,323 residents, or 3.5%. This is in keeping with the general demographic trends by which the South and the West have been gaining population at the expense of northeastern cities. However, Philadelphia still remains the second-most populous city on the Atlantic seaboard, a position it has retained since 1820. Demographics indicate that the loss in numbers will continue well into the 21st century. Another indicator pointing in the same direction is the fact that the central city population is aging faster than in comparable cities in the South and West.

Population		
	1980	*1990*
Central City	1,642,900	1,585,577
Rank	4	5
Metro Area	4,716,559	4,856,881
Pop. Change 1980–1990 -57,323		
Pop. % Change 1980–1990 -3.5		
Median Age 33.2		
% Male 46.5		
% Age 65 and Over 15.2		
Density (per square mile) 11,736		

Households
Number 603,075
Persons per Household 2.56
% Female-Headed Households 20.3
% One-Person Households 31.6
Births—Total 25,013
% to Mothers under 20 17.9
Birth Rate per 1,000 15.2

Ethnic Composition

Although the original Quaker settlers were all English and Scottish, Philadelphia's reputation as a liberal and tolerant community attracted immigrants from all over Europe, particularly Germany. They were followed in the early 1900s by Irish, Italian, and Polish immigrants who established many distinctive neighborhoods. Beginning in the 1880s thousands of east European Jews joined the ranks of immigrants. By 1900 virtually all major ethnic groups were represented in the city. Meanwhile, blacks began to move from the troubled southern cities just before the Civil War, but it was not until the beginning of the 20th century, and especially after World War II, that they had a significant impact on the racial composition.

As in other cities, each wave of immigration was followed by the creation of distinct ethnic neighborhoods. The residents of the Center City are largely white and middle class. South Philadelphia, site of a Swedish settlement in the 17th century, is heavily Italian with pockets of Jews, blacks, Poles, and Slavs. West Philadelphia was once a sparsely settled residential suburb for the city's wealthiest citizens. It became a working-class suburb in the 1920s and 1930s.

Today blacks form the largest group. North Philadelphia also is predominately black, and many of the black community's social, cultural, and religious institutions are found here. Germantown was settled in 1683 by a group of Germans who received a charter directly from William Penn. It contains some of the most famous 18th-century homes. Manayunk is the home of Irish, Italians, and Poles. The Northeast also is almost exclusively white, but less Anglo-Saxon.

Ethnic Composition (as % of total pop.)

	1980	1990
White	58.23	53.52
Black	37.84	39.86
American Indian	0.14	0.22
Asian and Pacific Islander	1.05	2.74
Hispanic	3.77	5.63
Other	NA	3.66

Government

Under the home-rule charter approved in 1951, the former weak mayor/strong council system was replaced by a strong mayor/weak council system. Under the charter, the mayor is the chief executive, and the council is the legislature of the city. The mayor serves for a term of four years and can be reelected only for one succesive term. He has the power to appoint and remove all principal administrative officials (with the exception of the city solicitor) with the approval of the city council, and he controls the city budget. His cabinet consists of four advisers—city solicitor, finance director, city representative/director of commerce, and city manager. Like the mayor, the city council is elected for four-year terms. The council consists of 17 members, 10 elected from geographical districts and 7 elected at large. The minority party (since 1951, the Republicans) is guaranteed two seats. The council votes appropriations based on the mayor's budget. Under the 1951 charter, the council has the power to legislate in a number of areas once the sole province of the state legislature, such as municipal salaries.

Between the Civil War and the New Deal, Republicans dominated city politics, and it was a virtual fiefdom of Republican leaders, such as James McManes and the Vares brothers—George, Edwin, and William. Philadelphia was the only city among the nation's 12 largest not carried by FDR in 1932. He won Philadelphia in 1936, but the Republicans continued as mayors until 1951, when Democrat Joseph S. Clark swept into office on a reform wave. The city was racially polarized under Mayor Frank L. Rizzo (1972–1980). He was beaten in the 1983 Democratic primary by W. Wilson Goode, who then became the city's first black mayor.

Government

Year of Home Charter   1951
Number of Members of the Governing Body   17
Elected at Large   7
Elected by Wards   10
Number of Women in Governing Body   6
Salary of Mayor $70,000
Salary of Council Members $40,000
City Government Employment Total   32,854
Rate per 10,000   200.0

Public Finance

Philadelphia's annual budget consists of revenues of $3.380 billion and expenditures of $3.498 billion. The debt outstanding is $3.796 billion and cash and security holdings total $2.866 billion.

Public Finance

Total Revenue (in millions) $3,380.2
Intergovernmental Revenue—Total (in millions) $610.5
Federal Revenue per Capita $151.5
% Federal Assistance   4.48
% State Assistance   12.15
Sales Tax as % of Total Revenue   1.01
Local Revenue as % of Total Revenue   59.9
City Income Tax   yes
Taxes—Total (in millions) $1,141.4

Taxes per Capita
   Total $695
   Property $139
   Sales and Gross Receipts $10
General Expenditures—Total (in millions) $1,839.2
General Expenditures per Capita $1,119
Capital Outlays per Capita $103

% of Expenditures for:
   Public Welfare   5.6
   Highways   4.1
   Education   1.1

Public Finance (continued)

Health and Hospitals   8.4
Police   12.8
Sewerage and Sanitation   9.4
Parks and Recreation   4.0
Housing and Community Development   6.1
Debt Outstanding per Capita $1,449
% Utility   34.5
Federal Procurement Contract Awards (in millions)
$1,230.8
Federal Grants Awards (in millions) $1,371.6
Fiscal Year Begins   July 1

Economy

 Philadelphia's economy was based until the 1960s on traditional manufacturing industries. No single industry dominated, but the more important ones were textiles, oil, paper, chemicals, electronics, pharmaceuticals, automobile and truck bodies, and rugs and carpets. The major plants in the area were those of GE, RCA, USX, Scott Paper, Sun Oil, Atlantic Richfield, Socony-Mobil, and Ford. Structural changes in manufacturing and the decline of steel led to the loss of many manufacturing jobs, as factories relocated to cheaper markets in the South. Since then, through a publicly funded urban revitalization program, the city has made a successful transition to a service economy. Services now make up the largest economic sector, accounting for 30% of the work force.

The city also has made a concerted effort to attract new businesses. While the center of business activities has moved to the western suburbs, corporate and law offices are moving into the Center City. Philadelphia ranks 17th among U.S. cities as a desirable corporate location. Middle-level corporations find Philadelphia attractive because of its location in the center of the nation's largest market, access to transportation, large reservoir of technical skills, and the availability of numerous industrial parks. Philadelphia has a thriving high-tech corridor in Route 202. The major economic development project in the city's 1989–1994 Capital Plan is the Penn's Landing Program on 33 acres along the Delaware River.

Economy

Total Money Income (in millions) $14,469.0
% of State Average   85.6
Per Capita Annual Income $8,807
% Population below Poverty Level   20.6
Fortune 500 Companies   4

Banks	Number	Deposits (in millions)
Commercial	36	145,091
Savings	NA	NA

Passenger Autos   490,892
Electric Meters   1,527,100
Gas Meters   872,400

Manufacturing

Number of Establishments   1,887
% with 20 or More Employees   38.4
Manufacturing Payroll (in millions) $2,425.1

Economy (continued)

Value Added by Manufacture (in millions) $5,084.5
Value of Shipments (in millions) $11,567.6
New Capital Expenditures (in millions) $213.3

Wholesale Trade

Number of Establishments   2,197
Sales (in millions) $12,518.2
Annual Payroll (in millions) $901.156

Retail Trade

Number of Establishments   12,793
Total Sales (in millions) $7,207.9
Sales per Capita $4,387
Number of Retail Trade Establishments with Payroll   8,388
Annual Payroll (in millions) $954.1
Total Sales (in millions) $6,958.1
General Merchandise Stores (per capita) $443
Food Stores (per capita) $936
Apparel Stores (per capita) $374
Eating and Drinking Places (per capita) $539

Service Industries

Total Establishments   8,633
Total Receipts (in millions) $6,132.5
Hotels and Motels (in millions) $256.0
Health Services (in millions) $1,043.6
Legal Services (in millions) $1,343.7

Labor

Services represent the largest employment sector, followed by retail and wholesale trade, manufacturing, government, FIRE (finance, insurance, real estate), construction, and transportation and public utilities. The growth rate in job opportunities during the 1990s is estimated at 6.05%.

Labor

Civilian Labor Force   732,351
% Change 1989–1990   0.3
Work Force Distribution
Mining   NA
Construction   NA
Manufacturing   326,800
Transportation and Public Utilities   100,700
Wholesale and Retail Trade   481,100
FIRE (Finance, Insurance, Real Estate)   156,300
Service   681,600
Government   301,100
Women as % of Labor Force   45.2
% Self-Employed   4.2
% Professional/Technical   15.5
Total Unemployment   44,110
Rate %   6.0
Federal Government Civilian Employment   48,799

Education

Philadelphia's public school system dates from 1818, when there were five schools in the city. The authority for the public school system is vested in a nine-member board of education with full administrative, but no fiscal, powers. The school population is overwhelmingly nonwhite with blacks making up 63%, Hispanics 7%, and Asians 2%. Roughly half of the teachers in the public school system also are black.

The private school system is largely white and heavily Roman Catholic. The system is attended by roughly a quarter of the students in the first- and second-level age groups. The Roman Catholic Archdiocese oversees one of the largest parochial systems in the United States with 278 schools. There are 372 other private schools.

Education

Number of Public Schools 257
Special Education Schools NA
Total Enrollment 190,979
% Enrollment in Private Schools 25.6
% Minority 76.9
Classroom Teachers 10,809
Pupil-Teacher Ratio 17.6:1
Number of Graduates 7,677
Total Revenue (in millions) $1,035.8
Total Expenditures (in millions) $999.204
Expenditures per Pupil $4,649
Educational Attainment (Age 25 and Over)
   % Completed 12 or More Years 54.3
   % Completed 16 or More Years 11.1
Four-Year Colleges and Universities 14
   Enrollment 89,658
Two-Year Colleges 9
   Enrollment 18,875

Libraries

Number 267
Public Libraries 50
Books (in thousands) 4,916
Circulation (in thousands) 4,912
Persons Served (in thousands) NA
Circulation per Person Served NA
Income (in millions) $42.214
Staff NA

Four-Year Colleges and Universities
   Temple University
   Chestnut Hill College
   Curtis Institute of Music
   Drexel University
   Hahnemann University
   Holy Family College
   La Salle University
   Moore College of Art & Design
   Philadelphia College of Textiles and Sciences
   Saint Joseph's University
   Spring Garden College
   Thomas Jefferson University
   University of Pennsylvania
   University of the Arts

Health

With an aging population, Philadelphia has a high crude mortality rate. Although the city is noted for its medical facilities and schools (six medical, two dental, and seven nursing), its physician and hospital bed ratios are less than those for comparable cities. The University of Pennsylvania houses a comprehensive cancer center and the $457-million Center for Health Care Sciences offers state-of-the-art pediatric care. Among the city's other well-known health-care facilities are the Will Eye Hospital and the Schie Eye Institute.

Health

Deaths—Total 20,090
Rate per 1,000 12.2
Infant Deaths—Total 388
Rate per 1,000 15.5
Number of Metro Hospitals 48
Number of Metro Hospital Beds 13,260
Rate per 100,000 807
Number of Physicians 12,465
Physicians per 1,000 3.02
Nurses per 1,000 7.10
Health Expenditures per Capita $143.20

Transportation

Philadelphia is the oldest planned city in the United States, and its streets are laid out on the grid system devised by William Penn. The city radiates from Broad Street and Market Street, the great north-south and east-west axes. Paralleling Market Street are other major east-west streets: Chestnut, Walnut, Locust, Spruce, Arch, Cherry, and Vine. Northwest from City Hall extends the Benjamin Franklin Parkway. Midway between the City Hall and the Art Museum is the Logan Circle, with sparkling fountains and flowerbeds. The city has two other public squares: Franklin and Washington.

Philadelphia is the hub of a system of radial expressways, particularly the New Jersey Turnpike, I-75 and I-95. Four bridges cross the Delaware River, linking Philadelphia and New Jersey. From north to south, they are the Tacony-Palmyra, the Betsy Ross, the Benjamin Franklin, and the Walt Whitman. The city is served by two subway lines: the Market-Frankford (east-west) and Broad Street (north-south). Local mass transit is operated by the Southeastern Pennsylvania Transportation Authority (SEPTA), created in 1964.

Two railroads, the Penn Central and the Reading, provide passenger and freight service. Some 13 rail commuter lines from across the region are linked through a $300-million commuter tunnel. The mass transit authorities operate 458 rapid rail cars, 1,112 buses, and 67 trolley coaches.

Philadelphia has two airports: the Northeast Philadelphia Airport, serving domestic flights, and the Philadelphia International Airport, serving international flights. The latter, located eight miles from the city, is served by 28 airlines offering 480 flights daily. There are 14 other smaller airports.

Philadelphia's harbor, one of the world's largest freshwater ports, is part of a complex known as Ameriport, and includes Chester in Pennsylvania, Camden and Gloucester in New Jersey, and Wilmington in Delaware. Located just 88 miles from the Atlantic Ocean, it handles the second-largest volume of tonnage in the United States. The port facilities are being modernized as part of the Penn's Landing project.

Transportation

Interstate Highway Mileage 173
Total Urban Mileage 10,839
Total Daily Vehicle Mileage (in millions) $66.774
Daily Average Commute Time 56.3 min.
Number of Buses 1,112
Port Tonnage (in millions) $37.863
Airports 1
Number of Daily Flights 227
Daily Average Number of Passengers 17,116

Airlines (American carriers only)
American
American Trans Air
Continental
Midway
Midwest
Northwest
Trans World
USAir

Housing

Philadelphia is known as the City of Homes, because unlike most U.S. cities, it has few tenements. The typical houses are townhouses, two- and three-story attached houses with common interior walls, or semidetached houses that are two homes attached by a common wall. Although home ownership has declined in the 1980s, more than 60% of Philadelphians live in their own homes. Philadelphia offers good value for home buyers because housing prices are lower and the homes are better built.

Housing

Total Housing Units 674,899
% Change 1980–1990 -1.6
Vacant Units for Sale or Rent 44,060
Occupied Units 603,075
% with More Than One Person per Room 4.7
% Owner-Occupied 61.9
Median Value of Owner-Occupied Homes $49,400
Average Monthly Purchase Cost $269
Median Monthly Rent $358
New Private Housing Starts 747
Value (in thousands) $46,205
% Single-Family 24.0
Nonresidential Buildings Value (in thousands) $53,831

Tallest Buildings	Hgt. (ft.)	Stories
One Liberty Place (1987)	960	61
Two Liberty Place (1989)	845	52
Mellon Bank Center (1989)	795	54
Bell Atlantic Tower (1991)	739	53
Blue Cross Tower (1990)	700	50
Commerce Sq., #1 (1990)	572	40
Commerce Sq., #2 (1992)	572	40
City Hall Tower, incl. 37-ft. statue of Wm. Penn. (1901)	548	7

Urban Redevelopment

After World War II Philadelphia launched an ambitious program of urban renewal with the establishment of the Redevel-opment Authority in 1945. Renewal efforts accelerated after 1949, when the federal government passed the Housing Act, providing two dollars for federal money for every dollar of state or city funds for this purpose. Under Mayors Joseph Clark and Richard Dilworth, the vision of a new Philadelphia became an architectural reality. Remaking the Center City involved more than three decades of effort. In 1953 the Broad Street Railway Station and the wall of elevated tracks that ran behind it were removed and replaced by Penn Center and the John F. Kennedy Boulevard. The historic government buildings and the surrounding areas of the Old City were restored. The Dock Street Food Wharf was relocated as the Food Distribution Center in South Philadelphia. In its place emerged an expensive housing area on Society Hill. Among other projects were waterfront development in Penn's Landing; Gallery I and II, a retail shopping mall and office building complex along East Market Street; a commuter tunnel linking the city's rail lines; and the building of satellite cities, such as Franklin Town, University City, and Queens Village.

Crime

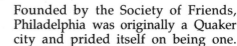

Violent crimes in 1991 totaled 22,481, property crimes totaled 86,658. An unusual feature is that the crime rate in the central city is not much higher than in the suburbs. One reason for Philadelphia's good showing on the crime rankings is that it leads the nation in per capita police personnel. When Frank Rizzo, a former policeman, was mayor in the 1980s, he revitalized the police department by adding thousands to the police rolls, particularly in high-risk areas.

Crime

Violent Crimes—Total 22,481
Violent Crime Rate per 100,000 759
Murder 440
Rape 904
Robbery 13,921
Aggravated Assaults 7,216
Property Crimes 86,658
Burglary 21,460
Larceny 40,880
Motor Vehicle Theft 24,318
Arson NA
Per Capita Police Expenditures $185.34
Per Capita Fire Protection Expenditures $69.22
Number of Police 6,966
Per 1,000 4.25

Religion

Founded by the Society of Friends, Philadelphia was originally a Quaker city and prided itself on being one. Quakers were more tolerant than Puritans, and the colony was one of the first to admit Jews and Catholics. The arrival of thousands of Irish, Italian, and Polish immigrants in the 19th and early 20th centuries helped to create a strong Catholic community. Catholics today constitute one-third of the population, followed by Baptists, Jews, and Episcopalians.

Religion

Largest Denominations (Adherents)

Catholic	537,699
Black Baptist	108,785
Assembly of God	7,847
American Zion	8,791
American Baptist	22,471
Evangelical Lutheran	24,450
Episcopal	24,450
Presbyterian	16,159
United Methodist	23,426
Jewish	106,303

Media

Philadelphia has two dailies: the *Philadelphia Inquirer*, published in the morning, and *Philadelphia Daily News*, published in the evening. Since both are owned by the Knight-Ridder Newspaper Group, Philadelphia may be said to be, in fact, a one-newspaper town. The principal city magazine is the *Philadelphia Magazine*. Philadelphia was an early center of book and magazine publishing, as well as printing, but little of this legacy survives. Philadelphia is served by 9 television and 18 radio stations.

Media

Newsprint
Focus-Metropolitan: *Philadelphia's Business News*
, monthly
Philadelphia Afri-American, weekly
Philadelphia Business Journal, weekly
Philadelphia Daily News, daily
Philadelphia Inquirer, daily
Philadelphia Magazine, monthly
Philadelphia Tribune, 3x/wk

Television
KYW (Channel 3)
WCAU (Channel 10)
WGBS (Channel 57)
WHYY (Channel 12)
WPHL (Channel 17)
WPVI (Channel 6)
WTGI (Channel 61)
WTXF (Channel 29)
WYBE (Channel 35)

Radio

KYW (AM)	WMMR (FM)
WDAS (AM)	WDAS (FM)
WFLN (FM)	WHAT (AM)
WHYY (FM)	WIP (AM)
WKDU (FM)	WOGL (AM)
WOGL (FM)	WPHE (AM)
WRTI (FM)	WTEL (AM)
WXPN (FM)	WURD (AM)
WUSL (FM)	WYSP (FM)

Sports

Philadelphia is represented in every major sport by a team: the Flyers in hockey, the 76ers in basketball, the Phillies in baseball, and the Eagles in football. The city also has two of the finest sports facilities in the country: the Spectrum and the Veterans Stadium. In suburban Philadelphia are a number of racetracks offering thoroughbred racing from summer through winter, and trotter racing in summer. A traditional regatta on the Schuylkill River is the highlight of the collegiate athletic season. Polo is popular at the Brandywine and Chukkar Valley polo clubs. The city has 134 golf courses, of which 72 are private, 49 daily fee, and 13 municipal.

Arts, Culture, and Tourism

The Philadelphia Museum of Art is considered one of the world's great art museums. The Barnes Foundation in Merion, just outside the city limits, has one of the world's finest collections of impressionist and post-impressionist paintings. The Rodin Museum, established in 1929, contains sculpture, paintings, and drawings by Auguste Rodin. The Pennsylvania Academy of the Fine Arts, founded in 1805, is the nation's oldest art museum and fine-arts school. Other museums include the Atwater-Kent, the Balch Institute, the Rosenbach, Museum of the University of Pennsylvania, and the Franklin Institute Science Museum.

Philadelphia has long been a theatrical center. The Walnut Street Theater, founded in 1809, is the oldest in continuous use in the English-speaking world. The Forrest Theater and the Society Hill Playhouse present Broadway and off-Broadway productions. The Zellerbach and the Harold Prince theaters are the city's newest at the Annenberg Center.

In music, the bellwether is the Academy of Music, the nation's oldest opera house in continuous use. It houses the Philadelphia Orchestra, the Philly Pops, Opera Company of Philadelphia, and the Pennsylvania Ballet. The Curtis Institute of Music, founded in 1924, is one of the nation's outstanding music conservatories. Among the many annual arts festivals in the city are the Luciano Pavarotti International Voice Competition and the Dance Celebration at the Annenberg Center.

Travel and Tourism

Hotel Rooms 24,615
Convention and Exhibit Space (square feet) 283,000

Convention Centers
Philadelphia Civic Center
Philadelphia Convention Center

Festivals
Freedom Festival (July)
International Theater Festival for Children
Mellon Jazz Festival
Native American Weekend Fall Festival

Parks and Recreation

 Philadelphia has more public parks than any other city in the United States. The Fairmount Park is considered one of the most beautiful landscaped gardens in the world. It stretches for 4,000 acres along the Schuylkill River, and is lined with walks, bridal paths, and picnic grounds. It also contains 15 restored colonial mansions, a functioning theater—the Playhouse in the Park—and America's oldest zoo.

Sources of Further Information

Greater Philadelphia Chamber of Commerce
1346 Chestnut Street, Suite 800
Philadelphia, PA 19107
(215) 545-1234

Greater Philadelphia Cultural Alliance
1718 Locust Street
Philadelphia, PA 19103
(215) 735-0570

Historical Society of Philadelphia
1300 Locust Street
Philadelphia, PA 19107
(215) 732-6201

Philadelphia City Planning Commission
23 North Juniper Street
Philadelphia, PA 19107
(215) 686-4607

Philadelphia Convention and Visitors Bureau
1515 Market Street, Suite 2020
Philadelphia, PA 19102
(215) 636-3300

Additional Reading

Allinson, E. P., and B. Penrose. *The City Government of Philadelphia*. 1988.
Blatzell, E. Digby. *Philadelphia Gentlemen*. 1979.
Bridenbaugh, Carl, and Jessica Bridenbaugh. *Rebels and Gentlemen: Philadelphia in the Age of Franklin*. 1978.
Cutler, William W., and Howard Gillette. *The Divided Metropolis: Social and Spatial Dimensions of Philadelphia, 1800–1815*. 1980.
Davis, Allen F., and Mark H. Haller. *The Peoples of Philadelphia: A History of Ethnic Groups and Lower Class Life, 1790–1940*. 1973.
Dowdle, Vincent P., and Anthony Dowdle. *The Philadelphia Sampler*. 1982.
Draper, Sarah. *Once Upon the Main Line*. 1980.
Lukacs, John. *Philadelphia: Patricians and Philistines, 1900–1950*. 1981.
Muller, Peter O. *Metropolitan Philadelphia: A Study of Conflicts and Social Cleavages*. 1976.
Siegel, Adrienne. *Philadelphia: A Chronological and Documentary History*. 1976.
Uhfielder, Eric. *Center City, Philadelphia: The Elements of Style*. 1984.
Warner, Sam B. *Private City: Philadelphia in Three Periods of Its Growth*. 1968.
Weigley, Russell F. *Philadelphia: A Three Hundred Year History*. 1982.

Directories

Cole's Directory of Philadelphia.
Dalton's Greater Philadelphia Directory.
Greater Philadelphia Women's Yellow Pages.
Philadelphia Business Journal-Book of Business Lists Issue.

Guides and Gazetteers

Arthur Frommer's Guide to Philadelphia. 1990.
Bendiner's Philadelphia. 1989.
Fodor's Philadelphia. 1990.
Marmac Guide to Philadelphia. 1984.
Women's Guide to Philadelphia. 1983.

Magazines

Focus: Philadelphia Business Newsweekly.

Statistics

Annual Economic Report of the Philadelphia Region.

Phoenix

Arizona

Basic Data

Name   Phoenix
Name Origin   From the mythological bird
Year Founded   1864 Inc. 1881
Status: State   Capital of Arizona
          County   Seat of Maricopa County
Area (square miles)   419.9
Elevation (feet)   1,090
Time Zone   Mountain
Population (1990)   983,403
Population of Metro Area (1990)   2,122,101

Sister Cities

　Chengdu, China
　Ennis, Ireland
　Grenoble, France
　Hermosillo, Mexico
　Himeji, Japan
　Taipei Municipality, China

Distance in Miles To:

Atlanta	1,827
Boston	2,670
Chicago	1,742
Dallas	1,002
Denver	813
Detroit	2,008
Houston	1,164
Los Angeles	376
Miami	2,348
New York	2,445
Philadelphia	2,374
Washington, DC	2,300

Location and Topography

Phoenix is located in the Salt River Valley in south-central Arizona on flat desert terrain. Surrounded by the Phoenix Mountain Preserve, it is bordered on the east by Superstition Mountain.

Layout of City and Suburbs

The heart of the city is the area between Maricopa Freeway and Glendale Avenue. The city has extended beyond I-17 on the west and the Salt River on the south. The northern boundary is formed by the Turf Paradise Race Track and the southern boundary by the South Mountain Park. The better residential sections are at Encanto, Palmcroft, Country Club Manor, Biltmore, and Arcadia. The poorer sections are found from Seventh Avenue westward.

Environment

Environmental Stress Index   4
Green Cities Index: Rank   47
　　　　　　　　　Score   34.31
Water Quality   Alkaline, hard, fluoridated
　Average Daily Use (gallons per capita)   175
　Maximum Supply (gallons per capita)   518
Parkland as % of Total City Area   NA
% Waste Landfilled/Recycled   NA
Annual Parks Expenditures per Capita $92.31

Climate

Phoenix is one of the sunniest cities in the nation with 86% sunshine. The climate is typical two-season desert, with low rainfall, low humidity, and high temperatures, well up to and above 100°F in the summer. Winters are mild although nighttime temperatures may drop to freezing. The region is windless except during the thunderstorm season in July and August, when gusts blow from the east.

History

Phoenix stands on the site of an ancient Indian settlement built by the now extinct Hohokam tribe, who flourished

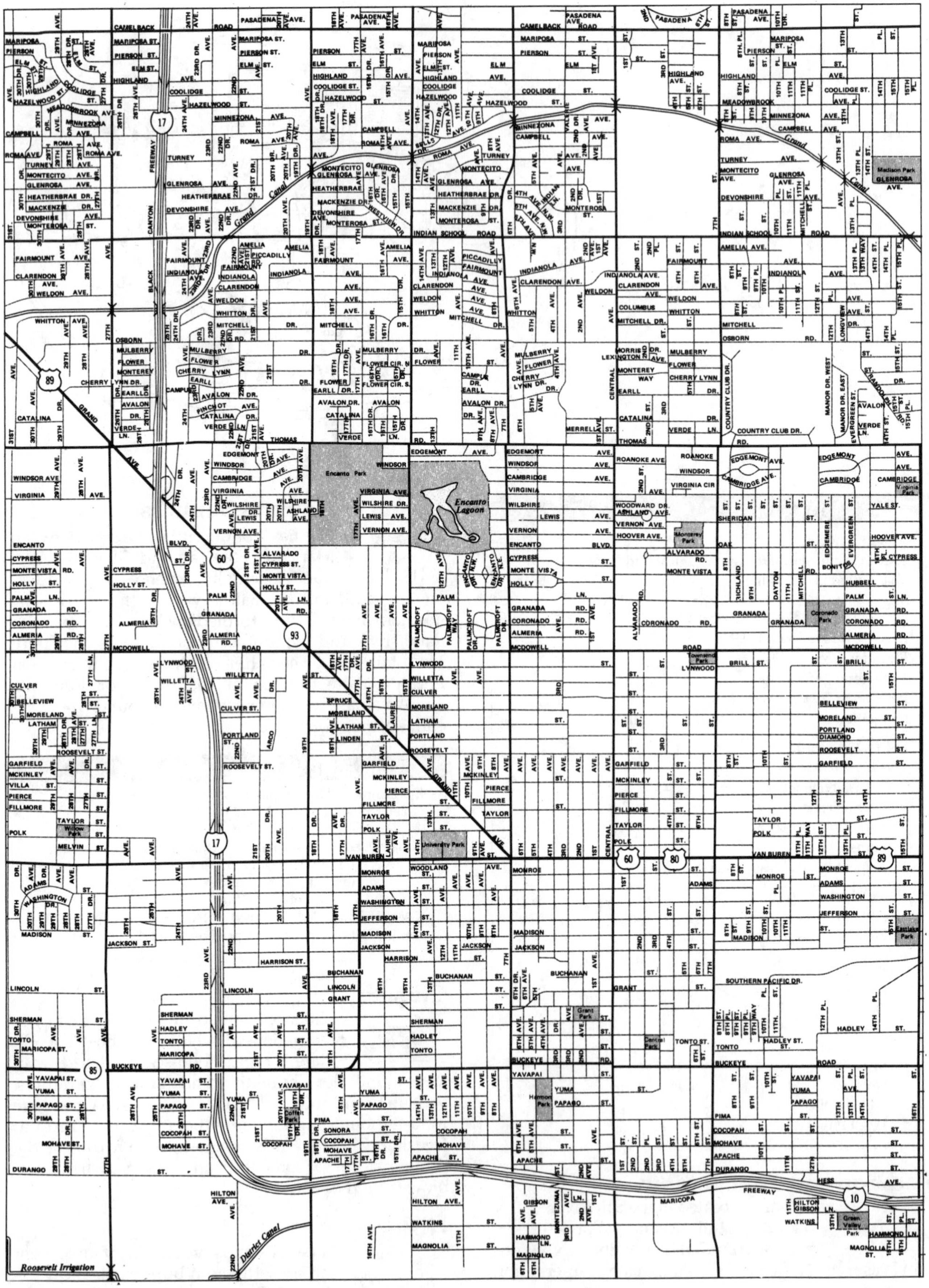
CAMELBACK ROAD
PASADENA AVE.
MARIPOSA ST.
PIERSON ST.
ELM ST.
HIGHLAND AVE.
COOLIDGE ST.
HAZELWOOD ST.
MINNEZONA AVE.
CAMPBELL AVE.
ROMA AVE.
TURNEY AVE.
MONTECITO AVE.
GLENROSA AVE.
HEATHERBRAE DR.
MACKENZIE DR.
DEVONSHIRE AVE.
MONTEROSA ST.
INDIAN SCHOOL ROAD
Grand Canal
BLACK CANYON FREEWAY
17
FAIRMOUNT AVE.
CLARENDON AVE.
WELDON AVE.
INDIANOLA AVE.
WHITTON AVE.
MITCHELL DR.
OSBORN RD.
MULBERRY
FLOWER
MONTEREY
CHERRY LYNN
EARLL
AVALON DR.
CATALINA
VERDE LN.
89
GRAND AVE.
THOMAS RD.
COUNTRY CLUB DR.
EDGEMONT AVE.
WINDSOR AVE.
VIRGINIA AVE.
CAMBRIDGE AVE.
Encanto Park
Encanto Lagoon
VERNON AVE.
ENCANTO BLVD.
CYPRESS ST.
MONTE VISTA RD.
HOLLY ST.
PALM LN.
GRANADA RD.
CORONADO RD.
ALMERIA RD.
Madison Park
Monterey Park
Coronado Park
60
93
MCDOWELL ROAD
Townsend Park
LYNWOOD
WILLETTA
CULVER ST.
MORELAND
LATHAM
PORTLAND
ROOSEVELT ST.
GARFIELD
MCKINLEY
PIERCE
FILLMORE
TAYLOR
POLK
Willow Park
University Park
VAN BUREN
80
MONROE
ADAMS
WASHINGTON
JEFFERSON
MADISON
JACKSON
HARRISON ST.
BUCHANAN
LINCOLN
GRANT
SOUTHERN PACIFIC DR.
SHERMAN
HADLEY
TONTO
MARICOPA
BUCKEYE ROAD
85
Eastlake Park
Grant Park
Central Park
YAVAPAI
YUMA
PAPAGO
PIMA
Harmon Park
Coffelt Park
COCOPAH
MOHAVE
APACHE
DURANGO
HILTON AVE.
WATKINS ST.
MAGNOLIA ST.
GIBSON LN.
HAMMOND LN.
FREEWAY
10
Green Valley Park
District Canal
Roosevelt Irrigation
CENTRAL AVE.

Weather			
Temperature			
Highest Monthly Average °F	105.0		
Lowest Monthly Average °F	39.4		
Annual Averages			
Days 32°F or Below	32		
Days above 90°F	164		
Zero Degree Days	0		
Precipitation (inches)	7.0		
Snow (inches)	0		
% Seasonal Humidity	36		
Wind Speed (m.p.h.)	6.2		
Clear Days	214		
Cloudy Days	70		
Storm Days	23		
Rainy Days	34		

Average Temperatures (°F)	High	Low	Mean
January	64.8	37.6	51.2
February	69.3	40.8	55.1
March	74.5	44.8	59.7
April	83.6	51.8	67.7
May	92.9	59.6	76.3
June	101.5	67.7	84.6
July	104.8	77.5	91.2
August	102.2	76.0	89.1
September	98.4	69.1	83.8
October	87.6	56.8	72.2
November	74.7	44.8	59.8
December	66.4	38.5	52.5

until 1450. They were followed by the Pima and Maricopa Indians, who inhabited the region at the time of the arrival of the first Spaniards in the 1500s in search of the Seven Cities of Cibola. After the U.S. annexation of the territory, conflicts with the Indians were frequent, making army intervention necessary. In 1864 a supply camp for nearby Camp McDowell was set up on the ruins of Hohokam settlement to supply the camp with hay and forage. John Y. T. Smith moved into the area, becoming the first white settler in 1864. In 1867, Jack Swilling, a pioneer prospector from Wickenburg, stopped for a few days at Smith's post. He noticed the lay of the land and the prospects of utilizing the easily accessible water from the Salt River. Upon his return to Wickenburg, he got others interested and formed the Swilling Irrigation Canal Company with a capital of $10,000. Within six months the canal was completed and within a year crops were harvested and several ranches established. Among the canal builders was one Lord Darrel Duppa, an English adventurer. He christened the settlement Phoenix and the name stuck and soon became official. Hancocks Store, a crude one-story adobe, was the first building constructed on the town site. It was at once the store, butcher shop, courthouse, and justice's office. The next building was Mike's Brewery, followed by the Phoenix Hotel. Soon the Main Street was lined with buildings on both sides. In 1878 the first newspaper, *Salt River Valley Herald*, made its debut. Phoenix soon became the supply point for the entire north-central Arizona Territory, which included rich mining districts being prospected by hundreds of prospectors. Large freighting outfits drawn by several teams of oxen, horses, and mules came in loaded with lumber and other merchandise in return for flour, grain, and other produce. The city was incorporated in 1881. The first railroad, the Maricopa and Phoenix, entered the city in 1887, the same year a narrow-gauge street railway began functioning. In 1888 the first city hall was built on Washington Street. In 1889 the territorial legislature meeting at Prescott passed a bill moving the seat of government to Phoenix. Two years later Phoenix suffered the worst flood disaster in its history when the Salt River broke its banks. The entire southern section of town was swept away in the raging torrent. The river waters rose so high that it reached the center of town, over a mile from the riverbed. Reclamation dams have removed the flood menace, and since the completion of the Bartlett Dam, the Salt River has ceased to exist in the area. The state capitol was formally occupied in 1901.

Historical Landmarks

The State Capitol on West Washington Street is in a ten-acre park. It is a neo-Classic structure designed by J. Reilly Gordon with additional wings by A. J. Gifford and Orville H. Bell. The Senate and House of Representatives wings were completed and occupied in 1960. The most notable churches are the First Presbyterian Church and the Trinity Episcopal Cathedral. Heritage Square near downtown is a city block of restored Victorian houses. In neighboring Scottsdale is Taliesin West, a national historic landmark built as the desert home of Frank Lloyd Wright.

Population

Phoenix has shared in the southwestern demographic explosion in the decades following World War II at the expense of the northern cities. From a population of 106,818 in 1950 it has grown every decade. It reached 581,562 in 1970, then grew by 35.2% to reach 789,704 in 1980 and then by a further 24.5% to reach 983,403 in 1990. Its population is expected to cross the million mark in 1994.

Population	1980	1990
Central City	789,704	983,403
Rank	9	9
Metro Area	1,509,227	2,122,101
Pop. Change 1980–1990	+193,699	
Pop. % Change 1980–1990	+24.5	
Median Age	31.1	
% Male	49.6	
% Age 65 and Over	9.7	
Density (per square mile)	2,341	

Households	
Number	369,921
Persons per Household	2.62
% Female-Headed Households	11.8
% One-Person Households	26.1
Births—Total	15,640
% to Mothers under 20	16.1
Birth Rate per 1,000	18.3

Chronology

1864 John Y. T. Smith sets up a supply camp for Camp McDowell.

1867 Jack Swilling, a pioneer prospector from Wickenberg, stops at the camp and is impressed with the agricultural potential of the Salt River Valley.

1868 Swilling sets up the Swilling Irrigating Canal Company, which builds a canal drawing water from Salt River for farming. An Englishman, Lord Darrel Duppa, christens the settlement Phoenix, a reference to the rebirth of the ancient Hohokam settlement that existed on the same site in the Middle Ages.

1878 The first newspaper, *Salt River Valley Herald*, debuts.

1881 Phoenix is incorporated.

1887 Maricopa and Phoenix Railroad reaches town. Narrow-gauge street railway is opened.

1888 City Hall is built on Washington Street.

1889 State capital is moved from Prescott to Phoenix.

1891 Flood washes away entire southern section of town and inflicts heavy damage on the rest.

1901 State Capitol opens.

1912 Arizona is admitted to the Union.

Ethnic Composition

Whites form the overwhelming majority with 81.69%, blacks make up 5.19%, American Indians 1.85%, Asians and Pacific Islanders 1.66%, and others 9.61%. Hispanics, both black and white, make up 20.04%.

Ethnic Composition (as % of total pop.)

	1980	1990
White	84.32	81.69
Black	4.79	5.19
American Indian	1.38	1.85
Asian and Pacific Islander	0.90	1.66
Hispanic	14.78	20.04
Other	NA	9.61

Government

Phoenix is governed under a council-manager form of government. The nine council members are elected to two-year terms, one at large and the others from wards. The mayor is also elected at large to two-year terms.

Government

Year of Home Charter 1913
Number of Members of the Governing Body 9
Elected at Large 1
Elected by Wards 8
Number of Women in Governing Body 1
Salary of Mayor $37,500
Salary of Council Members $18,000
City Government Employment Total 9,788
Rate per 10,000 109.5

Public Finance

The annual budget consists of revenues of $1.114 billion and expenditures of $1.347 billion. The debt outstanding is $2.061 billion and cash and security holdings $1.530 billion.

Public Finance

Total Revenue (in millions) $1,114.8
Intergovernmental Revenue—Total (in millions) $313.7
Federal Revenue per Capita $88.14
% Federal Assistance 7.90
% State Assistance 18.01
Sales Tax as % of Total Revenue 16.57
Local Revenue as % of Total Revenue 60.05
City Income Tax no
Taxes—Total (in millions) $197.2

Taxes per Capita
   Total $221
   Property $75
   Sales and Gross Receipts $131
General Expenditures—Total (in millions) $668.8
General Expenditures per Capita $748
Capital Outlays per Capita $252

% of Expenditures for:
   Public Welfare 0.1
   Highways 15.8
   Education 0.7
   Health and Hospitals 0.1
   Police 14.3
   Sewerage and Sanitation 14.2
   Parks and Recreation 8.3
   Housing and Community Development 4.5
Debt Outstanding per Capita $1,467
   % Utility 16.4
Federal Procurement Contract Awards (in millions) $262.4
Federal Grants Awards (in millions) $247.4
Fiscal Year Begins July 1

Economy

Phoenix's impressive demographic growth has been matched by economic growth. The three traditional bases of its economy were agriculture, manufacturing, and tourism, and they have not lost their importance. The city continues to be a major producer of agricultural commodities, industrial equipment, aircraft parts, chemicals, radios, leather goods, and air conditioning equipment. Among the largest Phoenix manufacturers are Motorola, Sperry, and Garrett Turbine. The pull of the sun brings thousands of tourists to the city, nicknamed the Valley of the Sun. The new players in the economy are the high-technology and service industries. Significantly, most of the city's 45 corporate headquarters are in the service sector, including Greyhound, Best Western, U-Haul, and Ramada. Major contributory factors in Phoenix's strong showing in the 1980s were low building costs, absence of a strong trade union movement, and abundance of land and water. Luke Air Force Base and William Air Force Base also contribute to the economy.

Economy

Total Money Income (in millions) $10,160
% of State Average   107.6
Per Capita Annual Income $11,363
% Population below Poverty Level   11.1
Fortune 500 Companies   1

Banks	Number	Deposits (in millions)
Commercial	38	30,335
Savings	6	7,642

Passenger Autos   1,038,051
Electric Meters   1,011,400
Gas Meters   250,000

Manufacturing

Number of Establishments   1,559
% with 20 or More Employees   32.1
Manufacturing Payroll (in millions) $1,928.5
Value Added by Manufacture (in millions) $4,665.3
Value of Shipments (in millions) $7,923.1
New Capital Expenditures (in millions) $299.1

Wholesale Trade

Number of Establishments   2,412
Sales (in millions) $12,583.2
Annual Payroll (in millions) $828.140

Retail Trade

Number of Establishments   8,427
Total Sales (in millions) $6,905.9
Sales per Capita $7,724
Number of Retail Trade Establishments with Payroll   5,503
Annual Payroll (in millions) $856.1
Total Sales (in millions) $6,758.7
General Merchandise Stores (per capita) $822
Food Stores (per capita) $1,652
Apparel Stores (per capita) $348
Eating and Drinking Places (per capita) $826

Service Industries

Total Establishments   9,130
Total Receipts (in millions) $5,049.9
Hotels and Motels (in millions) $339.4
Health Services (in millions) $958.0
Legal Services (in millions) $621.6

Labor

Job creation has kept with population growth and growth in housing. The work force has adjusted itself well to the new technological skills required in Phonenix's emerging industries. Phoenix is one of the few state capitals where the manufacturing sector is stronger in employment than the public sector.

Labor

Civilian Labor Force   595,354
% Change 1989–1990   1.1

Work Force Distribution
Mining   700
Construction   51,100
Manufacturing   132,200
Transportation and Public Utilities   57,300
Wholesale and Retail Trade   247,900
FIRE (Finance, Insurance, Real Estate)   74,000
Service   280,600
Government   140,500
Women as % of Labor Force   42.6
% Self-Employed   5.5
% Professional/Technical   15.8
Total Unemployment   26,639
Rate %   4.5
Federal Government Civilian Employment   10,553

Education

Phoenix is served by more than 18 separate public school districts, each with its own school board and superintendent. Together they run 435 elementary, middle, and senior schools. One of the districts, the Phoenix Union High School District, supports eight senior high schools, one vocational high school, and five alternative high schools. The public school system is supplemented by 130 private and parochial schools.

The city's largest universities are Grand Canyon University. Other institutions include Phoenix College, De Vry Institute of Technology, Maricopa Community Colleges, Phoenix Institute of Technology, Rio Salado Community College, and South Mountain College.

Education

Number of Public Schools   435
Special Education Schools   NA
Total Enrollment   18,297
% Enrollment in Private Schools   6.9
% Minority   NA
Classroom Teachers   NA
Pupil-Teacher Ratio   NA
Number of Graduates   NA
Total Revenue (in millions) $131.817
Total Expenditures (in millions) $158,963
Expenditures per Pupil $7,093
Educational Attainment (Age 25 and Over)
    % Completed 12 or More Years   73.3
    % Completed 16 or More Years   16.5
Four-Year Colleges and Universities   4
    Enrollment   48,384
Two-Year Colleges   11
    Enrollment   47,502

Libraries

Number   73
Public Libraries   11
Books (in thousands)   1,992
Circulation (in thousands)   5,574
Persons Served (in thousands)   971
Circulation per Person Served   5.74
Income (in millions) $13.553
Staff   290

Health

The largest hospitals in Phoenix are St. Joseph's Hospital and Medical Center, housing the Barrow Neurological Institute; Arizona State Hospital; Good Samaritan Medical Center; Phoenix Children's Hospital; Maricopa Medical Center; Humana Hospital; Phoenix General Hospital; Phoenix Indian Medical Center; and the Veterans Administration Medical Center.

Health

Deaths—Total	6,384
Rate per 1,000	7.5
Infant Deaths—Total	155
Rate per 1,000	9.9
Number of Metro Hospitals	18
Number of Metro Hospital Beds	5,364
Rate per 100,000	600
Number of Physicians	3,722
Physicians per 1,000	2.23
Nurses per 1,000	5.22
Health Expenditures per Capita	$1.75

Transportation

Phoenix is approached by I-10 (the Papago Freeway) entering from the west and I-17 (the Black Canyon Freeway) entering from the north. These highways join at Van Buren Street and 27th Avenue, becoming the Maricopa Freeway and then forming the Pima Freeway southwest of the city. State Route 69 (the Grand Avenue Expressway) enters diagonally from the northwest, joins State Route 60 at Van Buren Street downtown, then intersects the city laterally to the east, becoming the Superstition Freeway. Nevertheless, Phoenix ranks lowest of all major cities in freeway miles per capita. Rail passenger service is provided by Amtrak, which runs two trains daily through the city. The principal air terminal is the Skyharbor International Airport, located downtown.

Transportation

Interstate Highway Mileage	59
Total Urban Mileage	8,972
Total Daily Vehicle Mileage (in millions)	$41.422
Daily Average Commute Time	47.7 min.
Number of Buses	280
Port Tonnage (in millions)	NA
Airports	1
Number of Daily Flights	386
Daily Average Number of Passengers	27,852

Housing

Phoenix has one of the most affordable housing markets in the nation. The single-family house is the most popular. Of the total housing stock, 59.1% is owner-occupied. The median value of an owner-occupied home is $77,100 and the median monthly rent $374.

Housing

Total Housing Units	422,036
% Change 1980–1990	26.9
Vacant Units for Sale or Rent	41,553
Occupied Units	369,921
% with More Than One Person per Room	7.3
% Owner-Occupied	59.1
Median Value of Owner-Occupied Homes	$77,100
Average Monthly Purchase Cost	$375
Median Monthly Rent	$374
New Private Housing Starts	4,134
Value (in thousands)	$409,697
% Single-Family	81.2
Nonresidential Buildings Value (in thousands)	$170,089

Tallest Buildings	Hgt. (ft.)	Stories
Valley National Bank (1972)	483	40
Arizona Bank Downtown (1976)	407	31
Phoenix Plaza (1990)	397	25
First Interstate Bank Plaza (1971)	372	27
Phoenix Center (1979)	361	28
Citibank Plaza (1980)	356	27
One Renaissance Sq. (1987)	347	26
Two Renaissance Sq. (1989)	347	26

Urban Redevelopment

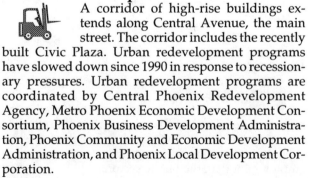

A corridor of high-rise buildings extends along Central Avenue, the main street. The corridor includes the recently built Civic Plaza. Urban redevelopment programs have slowed down since 1990 in response to recessionary pressures. Urban redevelopment programs are coordinated by Central Phoenix Redevelopment Agency, Metro Phoenix Economic Development Consortium, Phoenix Business Development Administration, Phoenix Community and Economic Development Administration, and Phoenix Local Development Corporation.

Crime

Phoenix ranks low in public safety. In 1991 violent crimes totaled 11,010, property crimes totaled 88,162.

Crime
Violent Crimes—Total 11,010
Violent Crime Rate per 100,000 771.4
Murder 128
Rape 480
Robbery 3,448
Aggravated Assaults 6,954
Property Crimes 88,162
Burglary 24,219
Larceny 47,338
Motor Vehicle Theft 16,605
Arson 405
Per Capita Police Expenditures $165.05
Per Capita Fire Protection Expenditures $84.90
Number of Police 1,704
Per 1,000 1.91

Religion

Historically, Catholic presence was strong in Phoenix because of its Spanish and Mexican roots, but this presence has tended to diminish over the years. With 325,438 adherents in 1990, Catholics continue to be well represented in Phoenix. Phoenix ranks third among cities in Mormon church members.

Religion	
Largest Denominations (Adherents)	
Catholic	325,438
Assembly of God	30,347
Latter-Day Saints	115,080
Evangelical Lutheran	38,723
Southern Baptist	90,877
United Methodist	37,538
Presbyterian	19,617
Lutheran-Missouri Synod	15,071
Episcopal	15,191
Jewish	50,000

Media

The city dailies are *The Arizona Republic* and *The Phoenix Gazette*. The electronic media consist of 9 television stations (8 commercial and 1 public) and 27 AM and FM radio stations.

Media
Newsprint
The Arizona Republic, daily
The Business Journal, weekly
The Phoenix Gazette, daily

Media (continued)	
Television	
KAET (Channel 8)	
KNXV (Channel 15)	
KPAZ (Channel 21)	
KPHO (Channel 5)	
KPNX (Channel 12)	
KTSP (Channel 10)	
KTVK (Channel 3)	
KTVW (Channel 33)	
KUTP (Channel 45)	
Radio	
KAMJ (AM)	KASA (AM)
KESZ (FM)	KFLR (FM)
KFNN (AM)	KFYI (AM)
KGRX (FM)	KHEP (AM)
KISP (AM)	KKLT (FM)
KLFF (AM)	KMEO (AM)
KMEO (FM)	KMXX (FM)
KONC (FM)	KOOL (AM)
KOOL (FM)	KOY (AM)
KOY (FM)	KPHF (FM)
KPHX (AM)	KRDS (AM)
KRDS (FM)	KSUN (AM)
KTAR (AM)	KVVA (AM)
KVVA (FM)	

Sports

Phoenix has two professional sports teams: the Phoenix Suns of the National Basketball Association, who play home games at the Veterans Memorial Coliseum, and the Phoenix Firebirds, an AAA baseball team that plays home games at the Municipal Stadium. The Phoenix Cardinals of the National Football League play at the Sun Devil Stadium in Tempe. The Phoenix International Raceway holds auto races and the Manzanita Speedway holds sprint, midget, and stockcar races. Thoroughbred racing is held at the Turf Paradise and greyhound races at the Phoenix Greyhound Park.

Arts, Culture, and Tourism

Performing arts have been the beneficiaries of the city's dramatic growth in recent years. In 1989 the Herberger Theater Center opened next to the Phoenix Civic Plaza Convention Center and Symphony Hall. It houses two theaters: the 820-seat Center Stage and the 330-seat Stage West. Herberger Theater houses the Arizona Theater Company, Black Theater Troupe, Childs Play, Ballet Arizona, and Musical Theater of Arizona. Also adjacent to the Civic Plaza is Mercato, a Mexican cultural center that includes a theater. The Phoenix Little Theater, founded in 1920, is the oldest theater in the city. Music is represented by the Phoenix Symphony Orchestra, which performs at the Symphony Hall, and the Arizona Opera.

The three principal museums are the Phoenix Art Museum, Arizona Historical Society Museum, and the Heard Museum of Anthropology. Other museums include Arizona Museum of Science and Technology, Arizona Hall of Fame Museum, and the Hall of Flame

Fire Museum. Arizona arts and crafts are showcased at the Craftsmen's Cooperative Gallery.

Travel and Tourism

Hotel Rooms   33,758
Convention and Exhibit Space (square feet)   223,000

Convention Centers
    Phoenix Civic Plaza and Convention Center

Festivals
    Rodeo of Rodeos (March)

Parks and Recreation

Phoenix has about 120 parks, including several desert parks. The 16,000-acre South Mountain Park is the largest city park in the nation. The 220-acre Encanto Park on 15th Avenue and Encanto Boulevard includes a boating lagoon.

Sources of Further Information

City Hall
251 West Washington Street
Phoenix, AZ 85003
(602) 262-7111

Phoenix Metropolitan Chamber of Commerce
34 West Monroe
Phoenix, AZ 85003
(602) 254-5521

Phoenix and Valley of the Sun Convention and
    Visitors Bureau
505 North Second Street
Phoenix, AZ 85004
(602) 254-6500

Additional Reading

Buchanan, J. E. *Phoenix: A Chronological and Documentary History, 1865–1976.* 1978.
Busch, Duffy. *Metro Phoenix: The Gold Book.* 1987.
Hardt, Athia. *Phoenix: America's Shining Star.* 1989.
Johnson, G. W. *Phoenix: Valley of the Sun.* 1982.
Luckingham, Bradford. *Phoenix: History of a Southwestern Metropolis.* 1989.
Sarda, Michael F. *Phoenix: From Legend to Reality.* 1991.
Singletary, Milly. *Finding Fabulous Phoenix.* 1987.

Pittsburgh

Pennsylvania

Basic Data

Name Pittsburgh
Name Origin From William Pitt
Year Founded 1758 Inc. 1816
Status: State Pennsylvania
      County Seat of Allegheny County
Area (square miles) 55.6
Elevation (feet) 745
Time Zone EST
Population (1990) 369,879
Population of Metro Area (1990) 2,056,705

Sister Cities
  Bilbao, Spain
  Wuhan, China
  Saarbrucken, Germany
  Sheffield, England
  Zagreb, Yugoslavia

Distance in Miles To:

Atlanta	683
Boston	574
Chicago	476
Dallas	1,208
Denver	1,427
Detroit	296
Houston	1,365
Los Angeles	2,430
Miami	1,180
New York	379
Philadelphia	308
Washington, DC	259

Location and Topography

N Pittsburgh is located at the foot of the Allegheny Hills on the fork where the Monongahela and Allegheny rivers unite to form the Ohio River. Except for the Golden Triangle and a few outlying sections, the city stretches over hills.

Layout of City and Suburbs

Adjoining the Triangle on the east is the cramped Hill District populated mostly by African Americans. Old Allegheny on the North Side with its red houses and public squares was once a German enclave. The South Side is a blue-collar district with many ethnic neighborhoods. Residential Oakland contains some of the city's most distinguished institutions: the Carnegie Institute and Library, the Historical Society, the Carnegie Institute of Technology, the Mellon Institute, the Stadium and Forbes Field, the Civic Center and the University of Pittsburgh's Cathedral of Learning. East Liberty is a town in itself, with small business houses and a residential section terminating at the Allegheny River in Highland Park. The Latimer Avenue district, toward the east, is populated mostly by African Americans. The city's upper crust lives along Beechwood Boulevard and the outer reaches of Fifth Avenue. Within the city, Highland, Schenley, Riverview, West, and Frick parks contribute green oases of spaciousness. South of Frick Park, across the curving Monongahela, lies the steel town of Homestead with its sooty steel factories that once gave Pittsburgh the pejorative nickname "Smoky City."

Environment

Environmental Stress Index 3.2
Green Cities Index: Rank 37
             Score 30.29
Water Quality Alkaline, soft, fluoridated
  Average Daily Use (gallons per capita) 85
  Maximum Supply (gallons per capita) 148
Parkland as % of Total City Area 7.2
% Waste Landfilled/Recycled 93:7
Annual Parks Expenditures per Capita $80.51

Climate

Pittsburgh has a humid continental climate moderated slightly by the influence of the Great Lakes and the Atlantic Ocean. In the winter the predominant cold air masses move in from Canada by way of storm tracks and in the summer warmer air moves in from the Gulf of Mexico. Precipitation is well distributed throughout the year.

Weather

Temperature

Highest Monthly Average °F	82.7
Lowest Monthly Average °F	19.2

Annual Averages

Days 32°F or Below	124
Days above 90°F	7
Zero Degree Days	5
Precipitation (inches)	36.0
Snow (inches)	45.0
% Seasonal Humidity	68.0
Wind Speed (m.p.h.)	9.4
Clear Days	59
Cloudy Days	204
Storm Days	36
Rainy Days	152

Average Temperatures (°F)	High	Low	Mean
January	35.3	20.8	28.1
February	37.3	21.3	29.3
March	47.2	29.0	38.1
April	60.9	39.4	50.2
May	70.8	48.7	59.8
June	79.5	57.7	68.6
July	82.5	61.3	71.9
August	80.9	59.4	70.2
September	74.9	52.7	63.8
October	63.9	42.4	53.2
November	49.3	33.3	41.3
December	37.3	23.6	30.5

History

The history of Pittsburgh begins in 1748 when George II of England granted one-half million acres in the upper Ohio River region to the Ohio Land Company, which was composed of gentlemen from Virginia and Maryland. The French, who also claimed this territory, sent forces to prevent the English from taking formal possession. In 1753 Governor Dinwiddie of Virginia, who had become a proprietor under the 1748 grant, sent a 21-year-old surveyor named George Washington with a letter to the French commandant at Fort Le Boeuf to notify him that the land belonged to the English.

The following February, Captain William Trent and 70 men began to erect a small fort on the site recommended by Washington, but it was captured before completion by a strong French force led by Sieur de Contrecoeur. Contrecoeur relocated and rebuilt the fort, christening it Fort Duquesne. In the four-year struggle between the two powers that followed, the British prevailed, and by 1758 British supremacy was established in the region.

On the site of the old French fort, the British built Fort Pitt, the largest British fort in the colonies. A cluster of log huts soon grew up around the fort but was torn down in 1763 when the settlement was attacked by the Indians led by Pontiac. After the Indians were defeated at Bushy Run, Colonel John Campbell laid out four new residential blocks bounded by Water, Second, Market, and Ferry streets. After the Fort Stanwix Treaty of 1768, civil courts were set up by Virginia, which claimed the region. The controversy between Pennsylvania and Virginia continued until 1780, when the Continental Congress decided in favor of the former.

After the Revolutionary War, Pittsburgh began to grow rapidly. The first stone house was built in 1783, and next year the land between Grant and 11th streets was platted and sold in lots. In 1786 John Scull and Joseph Hall began publication of the *Gazette*, the first newspaper west of the Alleghenies. The Pittsburgh Academy opened in a log house the same year, and next year a market house began operations. Allegheny Town was laid out across the Allegheny River and in 1788 Allegheny County was organized.

In 1794 Pittsburgh was incorporated as a borough— Pittsborough—and by then had 400 houses (up from 60 in 1783), a fire brigade, a post office, half a dozen taverns, a courthouse, stocks, and a pillory; it was already producing ropes, saddles, harnesses, breeches, textiles, salt, flour, cabinets, upholstery, shoes, hats, boats, and whiskey. By 1809, the town had 44 cotton-weaving establishments, a glass works, a large brewery, and several tanyards. In 1811, the *New Orleans*, built in a local shipyard, sailed to Louisiana, opening a new era of transportation. At about the same time, turnpikes were built to connect the town with Washington, D.C., and other places, beginning with the Pittsburgh-Harrisburg Turnpike in 1817.

Pittsburgh was incorporated as a city in 1816 with Ebenezer Denny as the first mayor. By the 1820s its population had exceeded 10,600. A bridge was built over the Monongahela and another over the Allegheny. The Pittsburgh Academy blossomed into the Western University of Pennsylvania and the first high school began meeting in a church. In 1829, with the opening of the Pennsylvania Canal, Pittsburgh could be reached within three days' travel from Philadelphia. The westward push of settlements stimulated industry. Foundries and rolling mills began spewing out smoke.

By the fourth decade of the century the city had 4 daily and 11 weekly newspapers, 10 other periodicals, and 18 printing houses. It had as well 76 churches, including four African-American churches, and the first high school was erected in 1845, the same year that a devastating fire razed 1,000 houses across 36 acres. B. F. Jones sold his profitable canal business to found a small puddling works that later grew into the giant Jones and Laughlin Steel Company. The Ohio and Pennsylvania Railroad entered the city in 1851 and in 1854 a rail link with Philadelphia was completed. In 1856 the Republican Party was organized during a

Chronology

1748 George II of England grants one-half million acres in the upper Ohio River region to the Ohio Land Company.

1753 Governor Dinwiddie of Virginia sends a young surveyor named George Washington to the commandant of the French Fort Le Boeuf notifying him of the grant.

1754 Captain William Trent and 70 men are sent from Virginia to erect a small fort on land in the fork.

1755 The British fort is captured by the French who rename it Fort Duquesne.

1758 British recapture the territory and build Fort Pitt.

1763 Indians under Pontiac attack the settlement but are decisively defeated at Bushy Run.

1764 Colonel John Campbell lays out four new residential blocks.

1768 After the Fort Stanwix Treaty civil courts are set by Virginia, which lays claim to the area.

1780 Continental Congress awards Pittsburgh to Pennsylvania.

1783 The first stone house is built in Pittsburgh.

1784 The land between the rivers, owned by the Penn family, is platted and sold in lots.

1786 John Scull and Joseph Hall publish the *Gazette*, the first newspaper west of the Alleghenies; the Pittsburgh Academy is founded.

1787 A market house begins operations.

1788 Allegheny County is organized.

1794 Pittsborough is incorporated as a borough.

1809 Oliver Evans puts the first steam engine to work in his gristmill.

1811 The *New Orleans* becomes the first ship to sail from Pittsburgh down the rivers to New Orleans.

1816 Pittsburgh is incorporated as a city with Ebenezer Denny as mayor.

1817 The Pittsburgh-Harrisburg Turnpike opens for traffic.

1829 The western division of the Pennsylvania Canal opens.

1845 The first high school is erected; fire destroys 1,000 houses over 36 acres.

1851 The Ohio and Pennsylvania Railroad reaches Pittsburgh.

1854 Rail link between Philadelphia and Pittsburgh is completed.

1877 Railroad workers go on strike.

1881 Samuel Gompers founds the Federation of Organized Trades and Labor Unions, later the American Federation of Labor.

1890 Mary E. Schenley donates land to build city's first public park.

1901 Allegheny, the third-largest city in state, is added to Pittsburgh.

1936 Disastrous flood causes $25 million in damage.

meeting of the Free Soil Party, and in 1858 the United Sons of Vulcan, parent body of the Amalgamated Association of Iron, Steel and Tin Workers, was formed.

The Civil War pushed the city's industrial capability to its maximum. The volume of business transactions grew so rapidly that a clearinghouse was established in 1865. By the end of the Civil War, Pittsburgh was manufacturing one-half of the nation's steel and one-third of its glass. In the 1870s 14 wards were added to the city. This was the era of the rise of the legendary captains of industry and steel magnates, such as Andrew Carnegie, Henry Clay Frick, and Charles M. Schwab. Workers became increasingly activist after a violent railroad strike in 1877, during which state troops fired on striking workers and 50 people were killed or injured. In 1881 eight national trade unions met in Pittsburgh under the chairmanship of Samuel Gompers to form the Federation of Organized Trades and Labor Unions, later renamed American Federation of Labor. In an effort to make the city more livable, the first public park took shape in 1890 on a tract donated by Mary E. Schenley.

In 1907 Allegheny, then the third-largest city in the state, was added to Pittsburgh, bringing with it 150,000 residents. By 1910 the city's population passed 534,000, with 80% of it foreign-born. The city continued to flourish until the Great Depression, when it was hard-hit because of its high concentration of industries, and a disastrous flood in 1936 caused $25 million in damage.

World War II restored Pittsburgh's prosperity, but within a few years of the war's end, the city's declining industries seemed poised on the brink of extinction. The demand for coal had fallen off, cheaper imported steel drove domestic steel out of the market, and many textile mills had relocated.

However, the city struggled vigorously to clean and rebuild itself. The urban renewal projects Renaissance I and II on the Golden Triangle represent the new Pittsburgh. The smokestacks have been cleaned up and Pittsburgh no longer smells or sounds like "Hell with Its Lid Off." Pittsburgh's efforts toward rejuvenation paid off by 1985 when *Places Rated Almanac* ranked it Most Livable City in the United States that year.

Historical Landmarks

The Gulf Refining Company Building, a modern 42-story skyscraper completed in 1932, marks the site where the petroleum industry was born in the United States. In 1849, Samuel Kier operated the first oil refinery here. The 20-story Frick Building, at the corner of Fifth Avenue and Grant Street, was erected in 1904. Its main lobby is embellished with a large stained glass window portraying Fortune at Her Wheel. The Allegheny County Courthouse on Grant Street, built in 1888, is the work of noted architect Henry Hobson Richardson. Above the center of its three main entrance arches rises a tall, turreted tower. The Trinity Episcopal Cathedral on Sixth Avenue is a Flemish Gothic structure erected during 1871 to 1872. It occupies the site of a church built in 1825 on part of a 2.5-acre tract granted by the Penns to the Church of England. Its tower rises 110 feet to the base of a 90-foot spire. The First Presbyterian Church on Sixth Avenue is the church of a congregation organized in 1784. Its first structure was erected in 1789 upon a Penn land grant.

The Schoenberger House on Penn Avenue was built before 1830; it became the Pittsburgh Club in 1884. The Fort Pitt Blockhouse on Penn Avenue is the last vestige of frontier Pittsburgh. It was erected by Colonel Henry Bouquet in 1764. Soldiers and Sailors Memorial Hall on the corner of Bigelow Boulevard and O'Hara Street, commemorating Civil War veterans, occupies an entire city block. The Allegheny Arsenal on the corner of 40th and Butler streets was designed between 1813 and 1815 by Benjamin Henry Latrobe, one of the architects of the Capitol in Washington, D.C. The Croghan House on Stanton Avenue was built about 1835 by the widow of William Croghan, Jr., who was an arbiter of Pittsburgh society. The Logan Community House on the corner of Lincoln and Allegheny avenues was constructed about 1843 by John T. Logan.

Other historical landmarks include the B. F. Jones House, the Byers-Lyons House, and the William Penn Snyder House, all on Ridge Avenue; Dowers Tavern on Becks Run Road; the Howe-Childs Gateway House and the Moreland-Hoffstat House on Fifth Avenue; the Pittsburgh and Lake Erie Railroad Station on Smithfield Street; the South Side Market House on 12th Street at Bigham; the Stanley Theater on Seventh Street; the Stephen Foster Center on Main Street; and the Woods House on Monongahela Street.

Population

Of U.S. cities, Pittsburgh is among those that have lost the most population in the 1970s and 1980s. From 520,000 in 1970, the population shrank to 423,959 in 1980 and 369,879 in 1990. Its rank among U.S. cities by population has correspondingly dropped from 30th to 40th.

Population		
	1980	1990
Central City	423,959	369,879
Rank	30	40
Metro Area	2,218,870	2,056,705
Pop. Change 1980–1990 -54,080		
Pop. % Change 1980–1990 -12.8		
Median Age 34.6		
% Male 46.4		
% Age 65 and Over 17.9		
Density (per square mile) 6,652		

Households
Number   153,483
Persons per Household   2.27
% Female-Headed Households   17.2
% One-Person Households   36.2
Births—Total   5,489
% to Mothers under 20   14.0
Birth Rate per 1,000   13.6

Ethnic Composition

Of the total population of 369,879 in 1990, whites numbered 266,791, blacks 95,362, American Indians and Eskimos 671, Asians and Pacific Islanders 5,937, and other races 1,118. Up to the 19th century, the population consisted chiefly of Irish and Scots supplemented by English. During the Civil War there was an influx of Germans, and after the 1880s the development of coal and steel industries brought thousands of Italians, Poles, Czechs, Slovaks, Hungarians, and Russians. The interwar decade was marked by an increase in the number of African Americans.

Ethnic Composition (as % of total pop.)		
	1980	1990
White	74.70	72.13
Black	24.02	25.78
American Indian	0.11	0.18
Asian and Pacific Islander	0.61	1.6
Hispanic	0.75	0.94
Other	NA	0.3

Government

The City of Pittsburgh operates under a mayor-council form of government, with the mayor and the council members elected by popular vote for four-year terms. City hall is traditionally dominated by Democrats.

Government
Year of Home Charter   1976
Number of Members of the Governing Body   9
Elected at Large   9
Elected by Wards   NA
Number of Women in Governing Body   2
Salary of Mayor $69,007
Salary of Council Members $39,347
City Government Employment Total   6,152
Rate per 10,000   158.8

Public Finance

The annual budget consists of revenues of $390.93 million and expenditures of $400.805 million. The outstanding debt is $603.811 million and cash and security holdings of $422.359 million.

Public Finance
Total Revenue (in millions) $390.93
Intergovernmental Revenue—Total (in millions) $89.47
Federal Revenue per Capita $25.09
% Federal Assistance   6.42
% State Assistance   8.04
Sales Tax as % of Total Revenue   5.63
Local Revenue as % of Total Revenue   76.89
City Income Tax   yes
Taxes—Total (in millions) $188.1
Taxes per Capita
Total $485
Property $215
Sales and Gross Receipts $38
General Expenditures—Total (in millions) $306.0
General Expenditures per Capita $790
Capital Outlays per Capita $129
% of Expenditures for:
Public Welfare   NA
Highways   11.6
Education   0.0
Health and Hospitals   1.9
Police   15.5
Sewerage and Sanitation   5.1
Parks and Recreation   6.7
Housing and Community Development   5.7
Debt Outstanding per Capita $976
% Utility   0.0
Federal Procurement Contract Awards (in millions) $285.8
Federal Grants Awards (in millions) $186.6
Fiscal Year Begins   January 1

Economy

Pittsburgh's industrial economy came to an abrupt halt in the 1960s with the collapse of the steel industry on which it was based and in which two out of three workers were employed. The city leaders charted a new direction for the faltering city based on high technology and service as the mainstays of a new economy.

Pittsburgh has also become one of the nation's leading financial and corporate centers. Among U.S. cities, it has the third-highest concentration of Fortune 500 companies, including USX, Westinghouse, Aluminum Company of America, PPG Industries, H. J. Heinz, and Bayer USA. Two of the nation's largest financial institutions—PNC Financial and Mellon Bank—are based in Pittsburgh.

Pittsburgh is also the headquarters of over 70 foreign firms. Research and development is the third-largest sector. The advanced technology sector consists of over 700 firms, including more than 200 founded in the 1980s.

Economy		
Total Money Income (in millions) $3,874.1		
% of State Average 97.2		
Per Capita Annual Income $9,998		
% Population below Poverty Level 16.5		
Fortune 500 Companies 8		
Banks	*Number*	*Deposits (in millions)*
Commercial	29	33,685
Savings	91	NA
Passenger Autos 692,724		
Electric Meters 1,110,016		
Gas Meters 763,033		

Manufacturing
Number of Establishments   607
% with 20 or More Employees   36.4
Manufacturing Payroll (in millions) $1,001.1
Value Added by Manufacture (in millions) $1,185.7
Value of Shipments (in millions) $2,383.3
New Capital Expenditures (in millions) $54.0

Wholesale Trade
Number of Establishments   1,138
Sales (in millions) $14,132.8
Annual Payroll (in millions) $467.974

Retail Trade
Number of Establishments   3,662
Total Sales (in millions) $2,584.2
Sales per Capita $6,669
Number of Retail Trade Establishments with Payroll   2,759
Annual Payroll (in millions) $360.5
Total Sales (in millions) $2,538.9
General Merchandise Stores (per capita) $745
Food Stores (per capita) $1,358
Apparel Stores (per capita) $492
Eating and Drinking Places (per capita) $900

Service Industries
Total Establishments   3,780
Total Receipts (in millions) $3,063.7
Hotels and Motels (in millions) $97.6
Health Services (in millions) $603.4
Legal Services (in millions) $450.1

Labor

Service and trade sectors together employ 55% of the total work force, whereas manufacturing employment has shrunk to 14.5%, compared to 28% in 1975. In 1990 services employed 311,100 persons, trade 219,700, government 103,200, FIRE 55,300, and transportation and public utilities 42,600. In the service sector, health services account for one-third of the employment. Workers in the fastest-growing occupations are computer programmers, paralegals, medical assistants, social welfare service aides, and computer system analysts. The largest private employers are Westinghouse Electric, USAir, Mellon Bank, and USX, in that order. Also among the ten largest employers are the federal government, the Commonwealth of Pennsylvania, and Allegheny County.

Labor

Civilian Labor Force   174,025
% Change 1989–1990   0.8

Work Force Distribution
   Mining   NA
   Construction   NA
   Manufacturing   115,800
   Transportation and Public Utilities   42,600
   Wholesale and Retail Trade   219,700
   FIRE (Finance, Insurance, Real Estate)   55,300
   Service   311,100
   Government   103,200
   Women as % of Labor Force   45.0
   % Self-Employed   4.2
   % Professional/Technical   18.5
Total Unemployment   7,895
Rate %   4.5
Federal Government Civilian Employment   11,704

Education

The Pittsburgh Public School System, administered by a City Board of Education, consists of 82 senior high schools, junior high/middle schools, and elementary schools. The Catholic Diocese of Pittsburgh administers an extensive network of grade schools and high schools. Pittsburgh also offers 15 private nonreligious schools.

The University of Pittsburgh is the city's oldest and largest institution of higher learning. It has two campuses in the city, with a school of medicine located in Oakland. Its central building is the Cathedral of Learning, a 42-story skyscraper dominating a 14-acre quadrangle on Bigelow Boulevard. The university had its beginnings in 1786 in a three-room log schoolhouse within gunshot of Fort Pitt. Known then as Pittsburgh Academy, it was rechartered in 1819 as the University of Western Pennsylvania, and received its present name in 1908. Cutting into the southwestern border of its 67-acre campus is the 70,000-seat Pitt Stadium. Equally well-known is Carnegie-Mellon University (CMU) and its affiliate, the Carnegie Institute of Technology. Duquesne University on Bluff Street overlooking the Golden Triangle was founded in 1878 by the Dominican Order. Other colleges within city limits include Carlow College, Robert Morris College, and Point Park College.

Education

Number of Public Schools   82
Special Education Schools   NA
Total Enrollment   39,896
% Enrollment in Private Schools   16.4
% Minority   53.6
Classroom Teachers   2,544
Pupil-Teacher Ratio   15.6:1
Number of Graduates   2,381
Total Revenue (in millions) $283.377
Total Expenditures (in millions) $291.739
Expenditures per Pupil $6,673
Educational Attainment (Age 25 and Over)
   % Completed 12 or More Years   61.1
   % Completed 16 or More Years   14.6

Education (continued)

Four-Year Colleges and Universities   7
   Enrollment   49,245
Two-Year Colleges   10
   Enrollment   15,065

Libraries

Number   123
Public Libraries   21
Books (in thousands)   2,913
Circulation (in thousands)   2,832
Persons Served (in thousands)   1,336
Circulation per Person Served   2.11
Income (in millions) $15.171
Staff   356

Four-Year Colleges and Universities
   University of Pittsburgh
   Carnegie-Mellon University
   Carlow College
   Chatham College
   Duquesne University
   La Roche College
   Point Park College

Health

Health care is one of the largest industries in the city. The 10 largest hospitals are the 830-bed Allegheny Hospital, the 789-bed Forbes Health System, the 750-bed St. Francis Medical Center, the 636-bed Presbyterian-University Hospital, the 568-bed West Penn Hospital, the 520-bed Montefiore Hospital, the 500-bed Mercy Hospital, the 496-bed McKeesport Hospital, the 488-bed Medical Center of Beaver, and the 464-bed Shadyside Hospital. The University Health Center comprises 2 general and 5 specialty hospitals and draws on the resources of the University of Pittsburgh and CMU. The region also includes some of the world's finest organ transplantation centers.

Health

Deaths—Total   5,457
Rate per 1,000   13.6
Infant Deaths—Total   83
Rate per 1,000   15.1
Number of Metro Hospitals   28
Number of Metro Hospital Beds   9,364
Rate per 100,000   2,417
Number of Physicians   5,275
Physicians per 1,000   2.88
Nurses per 1,000   22.37
Health Expenditures per Capita $17.34

Transportation

Pittsburgh is approached by a network of highways consisting of the east-west Interstates 70, 76, and 80 and the north-south Interstate 79. Parkway West and Parkway East traverse the county. The city also operates a ten-mile subway system linking the southern suburbs to the Golden Triangle. The Port Authority of Allegheny County runs buses and busways within the city.

The Pittsburgh International Airport, about 20 minutes from downtown, is the hub of the USAir system as well as 12 other major airlines. A new $550-million airport was completed in 1992. The Allegheny County Airport is one of the busiest corporate airfields in the country. Pittsburgh is the largest inland river port in terms of tonnage.

Transportation

Interstate Highway Mileage   138
Total Urban Mileage   7,566
Total Daily Vehicle Mileage (in millions) $33.168
Daily Average Commute Time   50.4 min.
Number of Buses   720
Port Tonnage (in millions) $34.373
Airports   2
Number of Daily Flights   NA
Daily Average Number of Passengers   NA

Airlines (American carriers only)
   American
   American West
   Continental
   Midway
   Northwest
   Trans World
   United
   USAir
   Westair

Housing

Many of Pittsburgh's residential areas are built on hills. As a result the city is noted for its thousands of frame dwellings clinging precariously to the slopes. Houses in the low-lying area are subject to floods.

Housing is one of the principal thrusts of the urban development programs initiated under Renaissance I and II. The Urban Redevelopment Authority's efforts to revitalize homes have affected 43,953 homes in the city's 88 neighborhoods. The Authority's goals are to provide affordable housing for very low- and moderate-income families; promote affordable homeownership opportunities; preserve the existing housing stock; stimulate construction of new housing; eliminate vacant and vandalized housing; and provide affordable housing for special populations, such as the aged. The neighborhoods benefiting most from these programs are Southside Flats, Mount Washington, Lower Lawrenceville, Hazelwood–Glenwood–Glen Hazel, Homewood North, North Oakland, Manchester, Central Lawrenceville, and Crawford-Roberts.

Housing

Total Housing Units   170,159
% Change 1980–1990   -5.3
Vacant Units for Sale or Rent   12,288
Occupied Units   153,483
% with More Than One Person per Room   2.0
% Owner-Occupied   52.3
Median Value of Owner-Occupied Homes $41,200
Average Monthly Purchase Cost $292
Median Monthly Rent $298

Housing (continued)

New Private Housing Starts   81
Value (in thousands) $5,039
% Single-Family   60.5
Nonresidential Buildings Value (in thousands) $31,677

Tallest Buildings	Hgt. (ft.)	Stories
USX Towers	841	64
One Mellon Bank Center	725	54
One PPG Place	635	40
Fifth Avenue Place (1987)	616	32
One Oxford Centre	615	46
Gulf, 7th Ave. and Grant St.	582	44
University of Pittsburgh	535	42
Mellon Bank Bldg.	520	41

Urban Redevelopment

Pittsburgh's rebirth began soon after World War II when the city was confronted with a host of overwhelming problems: pollution, floods, congestion, and rundown housing. A strong public-private partnership was formed to reverse the city's decline. Called Renaissance I, it featured smoke and flood control and construction of the Greater Pittsburgh International Airport, the Penn Lincoln Expressway, the Civic Arena, Three Rivers Stadium, USX Tower, Allegheny Center, Mellon Square, Oliver Plaza, and the demolition and rebuilding of the Point and Gateway Center in the Golden Triangle.

Some 20 years later, as the steel industry collapsed, Renaissance II was launched; it focused on the business and cultural resources of the Golden Triangle and the medical and educational resources of Oakland. Its highlights have included: David L. Lawrence Convention Center, PPG Place, One Mellon Bank Center, One Oxford Center, Chatham Center II, Liberty Center, Fifth Avenue Place, CNG Tower, Light Rail; Transit and Subway System, North Shore Development, Riverfront Center, and Station Square. The Downtown Development Strategy has brought over 7 million square feet of new and rehabilitated office space, the reclamation of two historic railroad stations, and construction of new hotels.

The capital budget through 1994 features a number of new projects, such as Washington's Landing on Herr's Island, the North Shore Project, the Three Rivers Stadium Project, the Pittsburgh Technology Center, and the expansion of the Convention Center. Also being developed are the Pittsburgh City Center and the $230-million expansion of the Oakland Medical Center. The conversion of the former J&L Strip Mill along Second Avenue to the Pittsburgh Technology Center is one of the most important of the ongoing projects. The center is expected to generate nearly $260 million in private investment, 11,000 direct and spinoff jobs, and more than $3 million in annual city tax revenues.

Crime

Pittsburgh is above-average in public safety. In 1991 violent crimes totaled 4,294, property crimes totaled 26,309

Crime

Violent Crimes—Total 4,294
Violent Crime Rate per 100,000 429.1
Murder 36
Rape 300
Robbery 2,704
Aggravated Assaults 1,254
Property Crimes 26,309
Burglary 5,891
Larceny 12,942
Motor Vehicle Theft 7,476
Arson 410
Per Capita Police Expenditures $112.21
Per Capita Fire Protection Expenditures $96.39
Number of Police 1,210
Per 1,000 3.02

Religion

Among U.S. cities, Pittsburgh has the sixth-highest Catholic population. Catholics make up nearly one-half of the population. Among Protestants, Presbyterians are most numerous, followed by Methodists, Lutherans, and Baptists. Among Jews, Reform Jews are the most prominent.

Religion

Largest Denominations (Adherents)

Catholic	695,911
Presbyterian	75,242
United Methodist	54,527
Black Baptist	34,787
Evangelical Lutheran	37,002
American Baptist	13,140
Episcopal	15,167
Lutheran-Missouri Synod	6,985
Assembly of God	6,337
Jewish	26,816

Media

Two daily newspapers are published in Pittsburgh: the *Pittsburgh Post-Gazette* in the morning and the *Pittsburgh Press* in the evening. The electronic media consist of 7 television stations and 23 FM and AM radio stations. Westinghouse KDKA is considered the pioneer radio station in the world, having received its license in 1920.

Media

Newsprint
  Pittsburgh, monthly
  Pittsburgh Business Journal, weekly
  Pittsburgh Business Review, bimonthly
  Pittsburgh Business Times, weekly
  The Pittsburgh Herald, weekly
  Pittsburgh Magazine, monthly
  Pittsburgh Post-Gazette, daily
  Pittsburgh Press, daily

Media (continued)

Television
  KDKA (Channel 2)
  KPGH (Channel 53)
  WPTT (Channel 22)
  WPXI (Channel 11)
  WQED (Channel 13)
  WQEX (Channel 16)
  WTAE (Channel 4)

Radio

KDKA (AM)	KQV (AM)
WAMO (FM)	WBZZ (FM)
WDUQ (FM)	WDVE (FM)
WEEP (AM)	WDSY (FM)
WJAS (AM)	WSHH (FM)
WLTJ (FM)	WORD (FM)
WPIT (AM)	WPIT (FM)
WPTS (FM)	WQED (FM)
WRCT (FM)	WTAE (AM)
WVTY (FM)	WWSW (AM)
WWSW (FM)	WYEP (FM)
WYJZ (AM)	

Sports

Pittsburgh is represented in three major national sports by strong teams: the National Football League's Pittsburgh Steelers, four-time Superbowl champions who play at Three Rivers Stadium from August through December; the National League's Pittsburgh Pirates, founded in 1877, who play baseball at Three Rivers Stadium from April through October; the Pittsburgh Gladiators, one of the nation's first professional football teams, who play at the Civic Arena April through July, as do the National Hockey League's Pittsburgh Penguins who play from September through April. The Civic Arena is one of the largest sports stadia in the nation and features a retractable dome.

Arts, Culture, and Tourism

The anchor of the city's performing and visual arts is Heinz Hall, the home of the Pittsburgh Symphony Orchestra, where Broadway plays are also presented. A second anchor is the Benedum Center for the Performing Arts, home of the Pittsburgh Opera, Civic Light Opera, Ballet, and Dance Council. Theatrical and dance performances are also staged at the Pittsburgh Playhouse Theater Center, which includes a Children's Theater Program. Other major arts facilities include the A. J. Palumbo Center, Civic Arena, Hazlett Theater, Manchester Craftsmen's Guild Auditorium, Soldiers and Sailors Memorial Hall, Stephen Foster Memorial Theater, and Syria Mosque. In per capita spending on the arts, Pittsburgh leads all cities in the nation at $17.03.

Andrew Carnegie's presence in the city in which he made his fortune is most conspicuous in the field of arts and museums. The Carnegie Building, constructed in two styles—Renaissance and Beaux Arts—includes the Carnegie Museum of Natural History, the Carnegie Museum of Art, and the Carnegie Music Hall as well as the Carnegie Library and the Buhl Science Center. Other local museums include the Fort Pitt Museum, Frick Art Museum, Pittsburgh Children's Museum, and the Westmoreland Museum of Art.

Travel and Tourism

Hotel Rooms   13,347
Convention and Exhibit Space (square feet)   131,000

Convention Centers
    David L. Lawrence Convention Center
    Civic Arena and Exhibit Hall

Festivals
    Three Rivers Arts Festival (June)
    Three Rivers Shakespeare Festival (May-August)
    Pittsburgh Children's Festival (May)
    Pittsburgh Folk Festival (May)

Parks and Recreation

Riverview Park on Perrysville Avenue and Watson Boulevard is a 350-acre tract of wooded hills and valleys containing the Allegheny Observatory. Schenley Park on Forbes Street and Bigelow Boulevard consists of 422 acres of beautifully landscaped woodlands and gardens, 300 acres of which were donated by Mary E. Schenley in 1890. The park contains the George Westinghouse Memorial and the Phipps Conservatory. Other parks include Frick Park and Point State Park, between which the Great Race is run in September.

Sources of Further Information

Carnegie Library of Pittsburgh
4400 Forbes Avenue
Pittsburgh, PA 15213
(412) 6223131

Greater Pittsburgh Chamber of Commerce
Three Gateway Center
Pittsburgh, PA 15222
(412) 392-4520

Greater Pittsburgh Convention and Visitors Bureau
4 Gateway Center
Pittsburgh, PA 15222
(412) 281-9222

Pennsylvania Economy League, Western Division
Two Gateway Center
Pittsburgh, PA 15222
(412) 565-5350

Additional Reading

Alberts, Robert C. *The Shaping of the Point: Pittsburgh's Renaissance Park.* 1980.

Baldwin, Leland D. *Pittsburgh: The Story of a City, 1750–1865.* 1981.

Couvares, Francis G. *The Remaking of Pittsburgh: Class and Culture in an Industrializing Society, 1877–1919.* 1984.

Gay, Vernon. *Discovering Pittsburgh's Sculpture.* 1983.

Hays, Samuel P. *City at the Point: Essays on the Social History of Pittsburgh.* 1990.

Lorant, Stefan. *Pittsburgh: The Story of an American City.* 1980.

Lubove, Roy. *Pittsburgh.* 1976.

Parlak, Rosemary, and Dorothy Miller. *Pittsburgh Walking Map and Guide.* 1991.

Rishel, Joseph F. *Founding Families of Pittsburgh: The Evolution of a Regional Elite, 1760–1910.* 1990.

Smith, Arthur G. *Pittsburgh, Then and Now.* 1990.

Van Trump, James D. *Life and Architecture in Pittsburgh.* 1983.

Vexler, Robert L. *Pittsburgh: A Chronological and Documentary History, 1682–1976.* 1977.

Portland

Maine

Basic Data

Name   Portland, ME
Name Origin   From Portland, England
Year Founded   1632 Inc. 1786
Status: State   Maine
        County   Seat of Cumberland County
Area (square miles)   22.6
Elevation (feet)   25
Time Zone   EST
Population (1990)   64,358
Population of Metro Area (1990)   243,135

Sister Cities

   Shinagawa, Japan

Distance in Miles To:

Atlanta	1,165
Boston	115
Chicago	1,086
Dallas	1,881
Denver	2,072
Detroit	899
Houston	1,959
Los Angeles	3,138
Miami	1,660
New York	317
Philadelphia	424
Washington, DC	557

Location and Topography

N

Portland lies on the southeast coast of Maine on the southern rim of Casco Bay, with its 365 islands. Portland itself was once almost an island, and even now access to the city without passing over water is possible only from the northwest.

Layout of City and Suburbs

The metropolitan area is clustered on a saddle-shaped arm almost surrounded by Casco Bay, Back Cove, and Fore River. Crowned by the Eastern and Western prome-

nades at opposite ends of the city, the central city extends in a general east-west direction. Portland owes much of its attractiveness to the tall elms lining its streets and parks.

Environment

Environmental Stress Index   2.4
Green Cities Index: Rank   NA
                    Score   NA
Water Quality   Neutral, very soft
Average Daily Use (gallons per capita)   135
    Maximum Supply (gallons per capita)   341
Parkland as % of Total City Area   NA
% Waste Landfilled/Recycled   NA
Annual Parks Expenditures per Capita $31.97

Climate

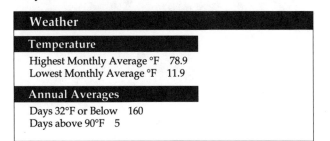

As a rule, Portland has very pleasant summers and falls and cold winters with frequent thaws. Winter begins late and often extends into spring; as a result, springs may be disagreeable. The White Mountains to the northwest keep heavy snow from reaching Portland; nevertheless winters can be severe and in many years snowfall exceeds 100 inches and temperatures well below zero are recorded frequently. Fall has the most number of sunny days. Rainfall tends to be uniform throughout the year.

Weather

Temperature

Highest Monthly Average °F   78.9
Lowest Monthly Average °F   11.9

Annual Averages

Days 32°F or Below   160
Days above 90°F   5

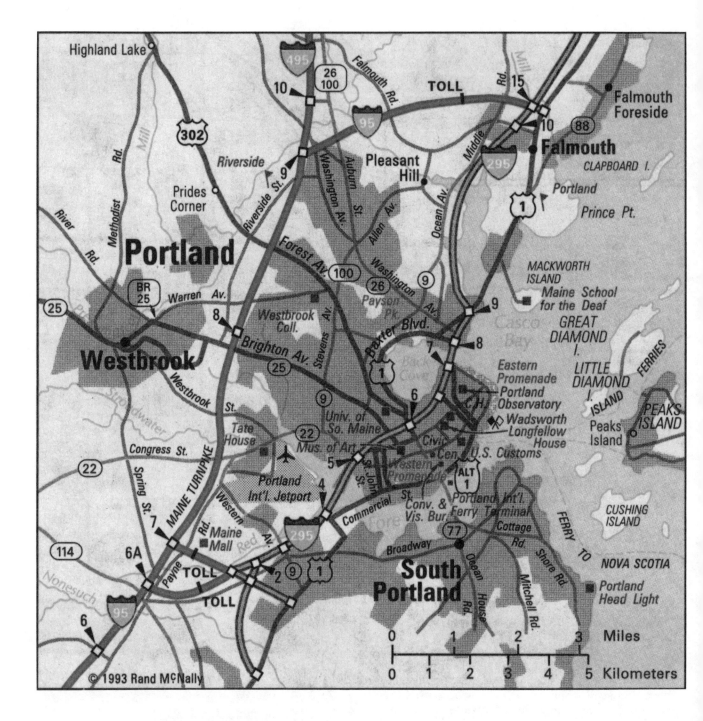

Weather (continued)

Zero Degree Days 15
Precipitation (inches) 41
Snow (inches) 74.0
% Seasonal Humidity 74
Wind Speed (m.p.h.) 8.8
Clear Days 107
Cloudy Days 160
Storm Days 18
Rainy Days 127

Average Temperatures (°F)	*High*	*Low*	*Mean*
January	31.2	11.7	21.5
February	33.3	12.5	22.9
March	40.8	22.8	31.8
April	52.8	32.5	42.7
May	63.6	41.7	52.7
June	73.2	51.1	62.2
July	79.1	56.9	68.0
August	77.6	55.2	66.4
September	69.9	47.4	58.7
October	60.2	38.0	49.1
November	47.5	29.7	38.6
December	34.9	16.4	25.7

History

It is said that Portland has risen and fallen not once but three times. Indians devastated it, the British burned it to the ground, and a great fire in 1866 left it in ashes. Nevertheless, it remains Maine's largest city.

The earliest recorded settlements of Portland were those of Christopher Levett from 1623 to 1624 and Walter Bagnall from 1628 to 1631. The place was known successively as Machigonne, Indigreat, Elbow, The Neck, Casco, and Falmouth. The name Portland was first given to Portland Head on Cape Elizabeth and to the sound between the head and Cushing's Island. In 1631 George Cleeve ingratiated himself with Maine proprietor Sir Ferdinando Gorges and was appointed deputy governor of the province. Soon ousted from that position, Cleeve went to England where he found a patron in Colonel Rigby, who purchased a patent to the province and put Cleeve in charge as deputy president. During 1643 and 1644 Cleeve summoned his first court in Casco, where he proclaimed his authority over the land from Sackadehock to Cape Corpus, about 13 leagues long. The claim was disputed by Gorges's agents but the Boston and English courts settled in favor of Rigby. Rigby died in 1650 and Massachusetts assumed control of the region in 1652. Cleeve himself died in poverty, ruined by the protracted litigation.

By 1675, Falmouth, as it was then known, had attained some prosperity. But next year, Indians attacked the settlement and virtually wiped it out. Only a few of the 400 inhabitants managed to escape. Another 40 years passed before a new settlement was planned at Falmouth by Samuel Moody with the permission of the Massachusetts government. At his own expense he built a fort here protected by three garrisons. The city was never again attacked by the Indians and by 1770 grew to be a prosperous shipbuilding center.

It also became a hotbed of Whig anti-royalist agitation in the years immediately preceding the Revolutionary War. In retaliation, on 16 October 1775, four British warships hove to off Portland and demanded its surrender. When the townfolk refused, the ships opened fire. Bombs, grapeshots, and cannonballs rained on the town; 414 buildings were burned to the ground and 2,000 people were left homeless. Only one tavern in the heart of the city escaped the flames. After the war, the city was slowly rebuilt and on 4 July 1786 took the name of Portland.

For the next two decades Portland experienced a surge of commercial activity. Maine's first bank was established here and the *Falmouth Gazette* appeared in 1785. When Commodore Edward Preble, a native son, subdued the Barbary pirates in 1803, Portland basked in his acclaim. However, with the two-year Jeffersonian embargo, the city went into decline. For the next two years the residents experienced the worst depression in Portland's history as the waterfront was deserted. Recovery came with the War of 1812, when the shipyards again hummed with work.

In 1813 Maine separated from Massachusetts and Portland became the capital of the new state until 1831, when Augusta was made capital. Chartered as a city in 1832, Portland expanded rapidly as a transportation center with the development of steam-driven boats and trains. The Portsmouth-Portland rail line opened in 1842. During the Civil War, the city, along with the state of Maine, was strongly pro-abolition and contributed one-fifth of its manpower to the Union armies.

After the war, the third great disaster in Portland's history struck. A fire, starting in a boat shop on Commercial Street and fanned by a strong southerly wind, swept diagonally across the Neck to Back Cove and up Munjoy Hill. Except for two lines of buildings, the most settled area of the city was burned flat, and most public buildings and half of the churches were razed.

Portland rebuilt itself the third time as a more modern city. During World War II Portland was the base of the North Atlantic fleet.

Historical Landmarks

 Although repeatedly destroyed and rebuilt, many historical monuments have survived and remain well preserved.

- The Wadsworth-Longfellow House was the childhood home of the poet Henry Wadsworth Longfellow. It was the first brick house in Portland.
- The First Parish (Unitarian) Church on Congress Street is successor to the Falmouth meetinghouse, originally built in 1674, burned by the Indians in 1690, and rebuilt in 1718, 1746, and 1826. It is Maine's oldest stone public building.
- The Civil War Monument was designed by Franklin Simmons.
- Tate House on Westbrook Street is of historical and architectural interest. Restored by the

Chronology

1623	Christopher Levett builds the first house on Hog (or House) Island.
1628	Walter Bagnall builds a hut near Richmond's Island where he lives for three years until he is killed by the Indians.
1631	George Cleeve is appointed deputy governor of the province by Sir Ferdinando Gorges, but is later dismissed.
1643	Cleeve returns as the agent of Colonel Rigby, who had purchased from the crown the patent to the land from Sackadehoc to Cape Corpus.
1652	On the death of Rigby, Massachusetts assumes control of the region.
1676	Indians wipe out the settlement of Falmouth.
1716	Samuel Moody receives permission from the Massachusetts government to resettle Falmouth.
1775	Falmouth, as a Whig stronghold, is shelled and bombed by British warships; 400 buildings are destroyed and 2,000 people are left homeless.
1785	The *Falmouth Gazette*, the city's first newspaper, debuts.
1786	Falmouth is renamed Portland.
1807	The Jeffersonian embargo halts trade and shipbuilding and triggers a two-year depression.
1813	Maine is separated from Massachusetts as a new state with Portland as the capital.
1831	State capital moves from Portland to Augusta.
1832	Portland is chartered as a city.
1842	The Portland-Portsmouth rail line opens.
1866	A great fire ravages the city, razing all public buildings, half the churches, and most residences.
1982–1990	Portland spends $143 million on downtown redevelopment.

Henry Austin. It is one of the finest examples of 19th-century domestic architecture.
- The Portland Observatory, built in 1807 by Captain Lemuel Moody, was closed at the turn of the century and reopened in 1939 by the city as a historical site.
- The Western Promenade is one of America's best preserved residential neighborhoods.
- Forts Preble, Scammel, Gorges, and McKinley are landmarks along Casco Bay.

Population

Portland's population in 1990 was 64,358—up from 61,572 in 1980, but down from 65,116 in 1970. Portland remains the largest city in Maine.

Population	1980	1990
Central City	61,572	64,358
Rank	327	355
Metro Area	215,789	243,135
Pop. Change 1980–1990 +2,786		
Pop. % Change 1980–1990 +4.5		
Median Age 32.9		
% Male 46.5		
% Age 65 and Over 15.0		
Density (per square mile) 2,847		

Households		
Number 28,235		
Persons per Household 2.21		
% Female-Headed Households 12.2		
% One-Person Households 35.3		
Births—Total 943		
% to Mothers under 20 14.1		
Birth Rate per 1,000 15.3		

Ethnic Composition

Whites constitute 97% of the residents, with only a sprinkling of other groups.

Ethnic Composition (as % of total pop.)	1980	1990
White	97.96	96.59
Black	0.85	1.12
American Indian	0.22	0.41
Asian and Pacific Islander	0.67	1.66
Hispanic	0.58	0.8
Other	NA	0.22

Government

Portland runs under a council-manager form of government, in which the city manager is the chief executive appointed by the council for an unspecified term. The legislative body is the council, composed of nine members, of whom five are elected from the voting districts and four are elected at large to serve staggered three-year terms. The mayor, who presides over council

Maine Society of Colonial Dames, it was the home of George Tate, mast agent for the English Navy, and much of its unusual wood paneling was said to have been brought from England. Believed to be Maine's oldest house, its exterior has never been painted.
- The Victoria Mansion on Danforth Street, also known as Morse-Libby House, was built in 1858 for Ruggles Sylvester Morse by architect

meetings, is selected by the council from among its own members to serve a one-year term. Portland also is the seat of Cumberland County.

Government

Year of Home Charter   1832
Number of Members of the Governing Body   9
Elected at Large   4
Elected by Wards   5
Number of Women in Governing Body   4
Salary of Mayor   NA
Salary of Council Members   NA
City Government Employment Total   2,563
Rate per 10,000   409.0

Public Finance

The city budget consists of revenues of $121.256 million and expenditures of $139.354 million. The total outstanding debt is $84.856 million and cash and security holdings are $29.662 million.

Public Finance

Total Revenue (in millions) $121.256
Intergovernmental Revenue—Total (in millions) $0.019
Federal Revenue per Capita $0.002
% Federal Assistance   2.10
% State Assistance   13.52
Sales Tax as % of Total Revenue   NA
Local Revenue as % of Total Revenue   84.38
City Income Tax   no
Taxes—Total (in millions) $45.4

Taxes per Capita
   Total $724
   Property $711
   Sales and Gross Receipts $0
General Expenditures—Total (in millions) $81.5
General Expenditures per Capita $1,300
Capital Outlays per Capita $159

% of Expenditures for:
   Public Welfare   2.8
   Highways   8.1
   Education   32.8
   Health and Hospitals   5.5
   Police   5.4
   Sewerage and Sanitation   7.3
   Parks and Recreation   5.3
   Housing and Community Development   0.5
Debt Outstanding per Capita $1,132
   % Utility   0.0
Federal Procurement Contract Awards (in millions) $10.0
Federal Grants Awards (in millions) $13.8
Fiscal Year Begins   NA

Economy

Historically, Portland was based on a marine economy in which shipbuilding was the most prominent activity. The city remains a major shipping center and oil terminal but has diversified into retailing, finance, fishing, manufacturing of food products, and medical services.

Economy

Total Money Income (in millions) $650.9
% of State Average   114.9
Per Capita Annual Income $10,386
% Population below Poverty Level   15.4
Fortune 500 Companies   NA

Banks	Number	Deposits (in millions)
Commercial	4	3,904.6
Savings	3	3,270.9

Passenger Autos   170,897
Electric Meters   86,000
Gas Meters   12,704

Manufacturing

Number of Establishments   133
% with 20 or More Employees   21.8
Manufacturing Payroll (in millions) $88.7
Value Added by Manufacture (in millions) $237.1
Value of Shipments (in millions) $442.1
New Capital Expenditures (in millions) $10.3

Wholesale Trade

Number of Establishments   255
Sales (in millions) $1,654.9
Annual Payroll (in millions) $117.183

Retail Trade

Number of Establishments   861
Total Sales (in millions) $606.4
Sales per Capita $9,676
Number of Retail Trade Establishments with Payroll   660
Annual Payroll (in millions) $85.6
Total Sales (in millions) $592.8
General Merchandise Stores (per capita) $424
Food Stores (per capita) $2,200
Apparel Stores (per capita) $562
Eating and Drinking Places (per capita) $1,389

Service Industries

Total Establishments   1,020
Total Receipts (in millions) $506.4
Hotels and Motels (in millions) $23.1
Health Services (in millions) $121.1
Legal Services (in millions) $97.9

Labor

Of the metropolitan labor force, 30% is employed in retail and wholesale trade, 24% in services, and 14% in manufacturing. The

Labor

Civilian Labor Force   39,298
% Change 1989–1990   2.8

Work Force Distribution
   Mining   NA
   Construction   5,300
   Manufacturing   15,000
   Transportation and Public Utilities   5,800
   Wholesale and Retail Trade   35,400
   FIRE (Finance, Insurance, Real Estate)   12,300
   Service   33,000
   Government   15,600
   Women as % of Labor Force   47.4
   % Self-Employed   49
   % Professional/Technical   18.1
Total Unemployment   1,646
Rate %   4.2
Federal Government Civilian Employment   1,421

largest employer is the Maine Medical Center. No industrial firm employs over 1,000 workers.

Education

The public school system consists of 2 senior high schools, 3 junior high/middle schools, 1 alternative school, 1 regional vocational school, and 12 elementary schools.

The University of Southern Maine, a unit of the University of Maine, is located in Portland. Westbrook College is a coeducational institution offering four-year degree programs in medical technology and business administration. The Portland School of Art offers a variety of programs in fine and applied arts.

Education

Number of Public Schools   19
Special Education Schools   NA
Total Enrollment   7,648
% Enrollment in Private Schools   8.9
% Minority   NA
Classroom Teachers   NA
Pupil-Teacher Ratio   NA
Number of Graduates   NA
Total Revenue (in millions)   NA
Total Expenditures (in millions)   NA
Expenditures per Pupil   NA
Educational Attainment (Age 25 and Over)
    % Completed 12 or More Years   72.9
    % Completed 16 or More Years   19.4
Four-Year Colleges and Universities   3
    Enrollment   11,315
Two-Year Colleges   3
    Enrollment   2,977

Libraries

Number   29
Public Libraries   5
Books (in thousands)   303
Circulation (in thousands)   469
Persons Served (in thousands)   62.5
Circulation per Person Served   7.50
Income (in millions) $2.143
Staff   50

Four-Year Colleges and Universities
    Portland School of Art
    Westbrook College
    University of Southern Maine

Health

The largest hospital in Portland is the Maine Medical Center, the most important referral center north of Boston. Other hospitals include the Portland City Hospital and Mercy Hospital.

Health

Deaths—Total   763
Rate per 1,000   12.3
Infant Deaths—Total   11
Rate per 1,000   11.7
Number of Metro Hospitals   3

Health (continued)

Number of Metro Hospital Beds   916
Rate per 100,000   1,462
Number of Physicians   612
Physicians per 1,000   3.40
Nurses per 1,000   NA
Health Expenditures per Capita $16.31

Transportation

The main artery is I-95 (also called the Maine Turnpike from Kittery to Portland). Canadian highways join the Maine Turnpike from the north. Interstate 295 branches off from I-95 and runs through the city before rejoining the interstate. The city also is served by Highway 1 running along the coast. The Maine Turnpike connects Portland with Auburn and Lewiston and points north.

The Portland International Jetport, ten minutes from downtown, is New England's fourth largest. The deepwater Port of Portland is the closest U.S. port to Europe and is one of the largest oil terminals on the East Coast.

Transportation

Interstate Highway Mileage   24
Total Urban Mileage   670
Total Daily Vehicle Mileage (in millions) $3.057
Daily Average Commute Time   37.6 min.
Number of Buses   17
Port Tonnage (in millions) $8.048
Airports   1
Number of Daily Flights   19
Daily Average Number of Passengers   1,185

Airlines (American carriers only)
    Continental
    Delta
    Northwest
    United
    USAir

Housing

Portland has been largely rebuilt three times and its houses are of markedly different vintages. Downtown has many Victorian buildings with cobblestone streets and gas street lamps. Congress Street, northeast of Monument Square, is another area of quaint houses from the past. Stroudwater Village is one of Portland's oldest neighborhoods, while the beautifully landscaped Eastern and Western promenades offer the best views of the city and Casco Bay's Calendar Islands.

Housing

Total Housing Units   31,293
% Change 1980–1990   10.6
Vacant Units for Sale or Rent   1,764
Occupied Units   28,235
% with More Than One Person per Room   1.3
% Owner-Occupied   42.1
Median Value of Owner-Occupied Homes $112,200
Average Monthly Purchase Cost $364

Housing (continued)

Median Monthly Rent $450
New Private Housing Starts 70
Value (in thousands) $4,570
% Single-Family 85.7
Nonresidential Buildings Value (in thousands) $5,138

Urban Redevelopment

 The city's redevelopment efforts have focused on the downtown area, on which $143 million were spent between 1982 and 1990. However, in 1987, voters approved a moratorium on further development in this area.

Crime

 Portland is above-average in public safety. Violent crimes reported to police in 1991 totaled 489, with property crimes totaling 7,014.

Crime

Violent Crimes—Total 489
Violent Crime Rate per 100,000 276.1
Murder 4
Rape 76
Robbery 120
Aggravated Assaults 289
Property Crimes 7,014
Burglary 1,837
Larceny 4,699
Motor Vehicle Theft 478
Arson 102
Per Capita Police Expenditures $89.40
Per Capita Fire Protection Expenditures $92.01
Number of Police 148
Per 1,000 2.36

Religion

Catholics represent the largest denomination in Portland, followed by United Church of Christ and United Methodist denominations.

Religion

Largest Denominations (Adherents)
Catholic 43,197
United Church of Christ 11,354
Episcopal 4,388
United Methodist 6,003
Evangelical Lutheran 1,578
Church of the Nazarene 1,546
American Baptist 3,029
Assembly of God 1,303
Jewish 3,900

Media

Portland media includes the morning *Portland Press Herald*, the *Evening Express*, and the *Maine Sunday Telegram*, four television stations, and nine FM and AM radio stations.

Media

Newsprint
Greater Portland Magazine, bimonthly
Maine Sunday Telegram, weekly
Evening Express, daily
Portland Press Herald, daily

Television
WCSH (Channel 6)
WGME (Channel 13)
WMEA (Channel 26)
WPXT (Channel 51)

Radio
WBLM (FM)   WGAN (AM)
WMGX (FM)   WLOB (AM)
WPOR (AM)   WPOR (FM)
WTHT (FM)   WYNZ (AM)
WYNZ (FM)

Sports

 The American Hockey League's Maine Mariners play at the 9,000-seat Cumberland County Civic Center from fall to spring. In August the Portland Yacht Club sponsors the Monhegan Island Yacht Race.

Arts, Culture, and Tourism

 Portland's cultural attractions have grown in the 1980s and now extend to all areas of the performing arts. The Portland Stage Company, a professional equity company, offers six plays each season. The Portland Performing Arts Center, opened in 1984, showcases the company's fall-through-spring productions and is also home to the Portland Players. The Maine Children's Theater caters to the young. The Ram Island Dance Company is the only professional contemporary dance company north of Boston. The Portland Ballet Company offers a full season of classical and contemporary dance between October and May. The Portland Symphony Orchestra features world-class artists at its concerts. The Portland String Quartet is the second-oldest running chamber group in the country.

The major museums are the Portland Museum of Art, designed by I. M. Pei; the Joan Whitney Payson Gallery of Art, located on the Westbrook College campus; the Baxter Gallery, located at the Portland School of Art; the Jones Museum of Glass and Ceramics, located on Douglas Hill in the nearby Sebago Lake region; the Children's Museum of Maine; and the Fireman's Museum.

Travel and Tourism

Hotel Rooms 3,056
Convention and Exhibit Space (square feet) NA

Convention Centers
Portland Exposition Building

Festivals
Old Port Festival (June)
Family Fest (July)
Maine Festival (August)

Parks and Recreation

The city maintains an extensive park system, including the Riverside Golf Course. The Great Maine Outdoors is close by, and includes Reid State Park and Popham Beach State Park, both located outside Bath; Camden Hills State Park, whose Mount Battie summit offers a spectacular view of Penobscot Bay; Wolf Neck Woods in Freeport, situated along a beautiful stretch of rocky coast; Acadia National Park on Mt. Desert Island; Sebago Lake, 30 miles west of Portland; Bradbury Mountain State Park in Pownal; Douglas Mountain in Sebago; the Rachel Carson Wildlife Refuge in Wells; Scarborough Marsh Nature Center; and Gilsland Farm in Falmouth, an Audubon bird sanctuary.

Sources of Further Information

City Hall and Economic Development Office
389 Congress Street
Portland, ME 04101
(207) 874-8680

Greater Portland Convention and Visitors Bureau
142 Free Street
Portland, ME 04101
(207) 772-4994

Portland Historical Society
485 Congress Street
Portland, ME 04101
(207) 774-1822

Portland Public Library
5 Monument Square
Portland, ME 04101
(207) 773-4761

Additional Reading

Barnes, Albert. *Portland Celebration: Three Hundred Fiftieth.* 1984.

Portland

Oregon

Basic Data

Name   Portland, OR
Name Origin   From Portland, ME, and England
Year Founded   1844 Inc. 1851
Status: State   Oregon
       County   Seat of Multnomah County
Area (square miles)   124.7
Elevation (feet)   77
Time Zone   Pacific
Population (1990)   437,319
Population of Metro Area (1990)   1,239,842

Sister Cities
   Ashkelon, Israel
   Corinto, Nicaragua
   Guadalajara, Mexico
   Kaohsiung, China
   Khabarovsk, Russia
   Sapporo, Japan
   Suzhou, China

Distance in Miles To:

Atlanta	2,664
Boston	3,144
Chicago	2,117
Dallas	2,043
Denver	1,261
Detroit	2,384
Houston	2,243
Los Angeles	962
Miami	3,257
New York	2,914
Philadelphia	2,859
Washington, DC	2,784

Location and Topography

N

Portland is located in northern Oregon on both banks of the Willamette River near its confluence with the Columbia River between two mountain ranges, the Cascade Range to the east and the lower Coast Ranges to the west. Portland is also the western portal of the Columbia Gorge, the only water-level passage through the Cascades. The topography is riverine, with hillsides and terraces.

Layout of City and Suburbs

The older part of the city, west of the Willamette River, occupies a comparatively narrow strip of bench land along the water's edge, backed by hills that extend toward the Coast Ranges, cutting the metropolis off from the fertile Tualatin Valley. These hills are segmented by the numerous winding drives and streets of Westover, Kings Heights, and Portland Heights, culminating in Council Crest at an elevation of nearly 1,100 feet above the business section.

The business section, characterized by short and narrow streets, is the oldest area of the city. Its tallest building is the 40-story First Interstate Bank. East of the river, long residential avenues extend to Mount Scott, Mount Tabor, Rocky Butte, and the snowy peaks of Mount St. Helens, Mount Adams, and Mount Hood. Four-fifths of the city lies east and north of the Willamette and is an area of spacious new developments. Newer residences are found in the eastern and southeastern sections of the city and along the western slopes of the hills backing the city. The principal residential sections lie east of the Willamette. Portland is divided into five areas—southwest, southeast, north, northeast, and northwest. The Willamette is crossed at 11 points. Downtown, most streets are one-way. The major streets are Grand Avenue, Union Avenue, Sandy Boulevard, and Southeast 82nd Street.

Climate

Portland has a mild and balmy maritime climate with rainy winters. Summers are pleasantly mild with northwesterly

749

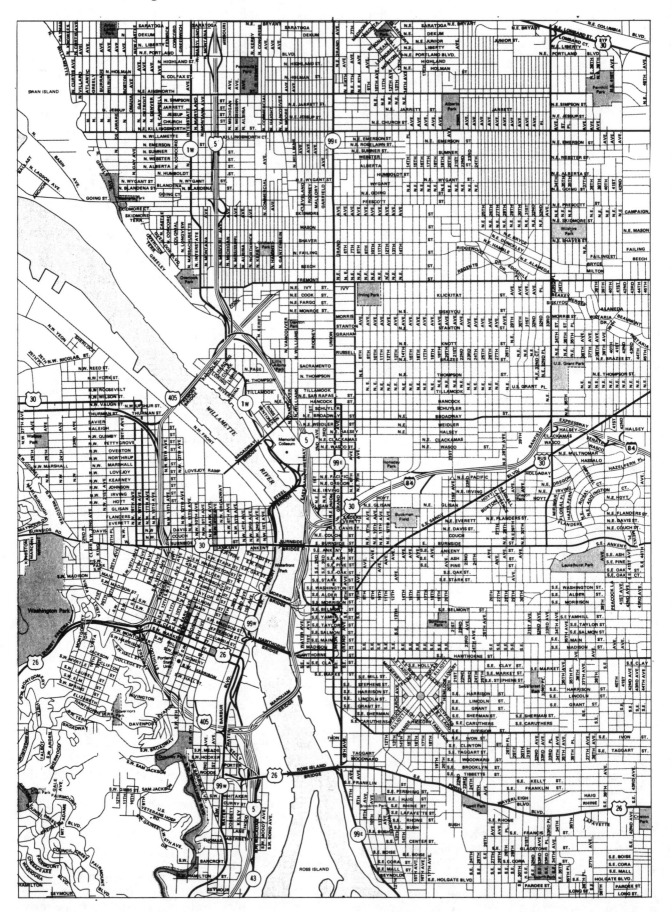

Environment

Environmental Stress Index   3.0
Green Cities Index: Rank   12
                Score   21.62
Water Quality   Neutral, very soft
    Average Daily Use (gallons per capita)   166
    Maximum Supply (gallons per capita)   363
Parkland as % of Total City Area   NA
% Waste Landfilled/Recycled   NA
Annual Parks Expenditures per Capita $85.72

winds and little precipitation. Winters are cloudy and foggy. The marine air keeps the climate moderate in all seasons.

Weather

Temperature

Highest Monthly Average °F   79.5
Lowest Monthly Average °F   33.5

Annual Averages

Days 32°F or Below   44
Days above 90°F   10
Zero Degree Days   0
Precipitation (inches)   38.0
Snow (inches)   7.0
% Seasonal Humidity   74.0
Wind Speed (m.p.h.)   7.8
Clear Days   69
Cloudy Days   228
Storm Days   7
Rainy Days   152

Average Temperatures (°F)	High	Low	Mean
January	43.6	32.5	38.1
February	50.1	35.5	42.8
March	54.3	37.0	45.7
April	60.3	40.8	50.6
May	67.0	46.3	56.7
June	72.1	51.8	62.0
July	79.0	55.2	67.1
August	78.1	55.0	66.6
September	73.9	50.5	62.2
October	62.9	44.7	53.8
November	52.1	38.5	45.3
December	46.0	35.3	40.7

History

Chinook Indians were the first to live on the site of Portland where Lewis and Clark found them in 1806. The first white person who settled in the area was Etienne Lucier, a French-Canadian and former Hudson Bay Company employee who built a small cabin in 1829 on the east side of the Willamette. In 1842, William Johnson, a British subject, built a small cabin in what is now South Portland, where he manufactured illegal liquor.

But the "official" history of white settlement begins in 1844 when William Overton, a Tennesseean, claimed a 640-acre tract on the west bank of the Willamette. The entire claim was covered by dense forest. Lacking the 25 cents needed for filing his claim, he sold a half-interest to Amos L. Lovejoy, a Bostonian, for the cost of filing. They made the tomahawk claim by blazing trees. Overton soon lost interest and traded his half-interest to Francis W. Pettygrove, a merchant from Portland, Maine, for $100. Lovejoy and Pettygrove cleared and platted the land for 4 streets and 16 blocks. Pettygrove erected a log store at the southeastern corner of Front and Washington streets in 1845 and built a wagon road to the hills. The settlement was known simply as "The Clearing" or "The Stumptown" until the two partners flipped a coin to decide on a new name. Pettigrove won the flip and named the settlement after his hometown of Portland.

Early settlers included James Terwilliger, a blacksmith; Daniel H. Lownsdale, a tanner; and John H. Couch, a salmon fisherman. By 1848, both Lovejoy and Pettygrove had sold their interests to Benjamin Stark and Daniel Lownsdale respectively, and the new claimholders added two partners, Stephen Coffin and W. W. Chapman, and formed the Townsite Promotion Company. Coffin established a canoe ferry service the same year.

The first entrepreneur to hit town was John Waymire, who built the first sawmill and the first hotel—a double log cabin—and also the first local transportation system, consisting of a wagon pulled by a team of Missouri oxen. By 1850 the town had a population of 500 that was served by churches, schools, stores, and a newspaper, the *Weekly Oregonian*, published by Thomas Dryer and printed on a hand press. Portland soon replaced Oregon City as the most populous town in the Northwest.

When the California gold rush began, Portland shared in the boom. The city was incorporated and the first elections were held in 1851 to elect Hugh D. O'Bryant as mayor. In the same year, a fire engine was purchased, a tax of .025% was authorized, a free school was opened, and the city jail received its first prisoner, one O. Traavaillot, jailed for riding furiously through the streets and endangering life and property.

By 1852 there were daily steamer arrivals from San Francisco. The first brick building was erected in 1853. Trade was stimulated by the Indian wars of the 1850s, with Portland outfitting the military forces. The city became the seat of Washington County in 1854. In the same year Portland was selected as the new West Coast terminal for the U.S. mail steamer *The Petonia*. The original town began expanding toward the south covering the later Multnomah Stadium area, then known as Goosetown.

The Civil War years were hard years for Portland, as the gold rush in eastern Oregon had ebbed, but the city was saved by the rise of the salmon industry beginning in 1864. People like John Quinn and Vincent Cook went into the salmon business and became immensely wealthy. The city suffered catastrophic fires in 1872 and 1873. In 1883 Portland became the terminus of the transcontinental railway, achieving a reputation as a solid town with potential equal to San Francisco. Late in the 1880s, franchises were granted to street-railway lines. In 1887 the Morrison Street

Chronology

1829 Etienne Lucier builds a small log cabin on the east side of the Willamette River.

1842 William Johnson builds a cabin in what is now South Portland.

1844 William Overton, a Tennesseean, claims a 640-acre heavily forested tract on the west bank of the Willamette, including the area called by Indians "The Clearing." Lacking the 25-cent filing fee, he sells a half-interest to Amos L. Lovejoy, a Bostonian. Overton soon sells his remaining half-interest to Francis W. Pettygrove, a merchant from Portland, Maine.

1845 Lovejoy and Pettygrove clear and lay down 4 streets and 16 blocks. The settlement is christened Portland when Pettygrove wins a coin-flip to name it after his hometown.

1846 Lovejoy sells his share to Benjamin Stark.

1848 Pettygrove sells his share to Daniel H. Lownsdale. Stark and Lownsdale add two new partners, Stephen Coffin and W. W. Chapman, and form the Townsite Promotion Company.

1849 John Waymire sets up the town's first hotel, sawmill, and wagon transportation system.

1850 Town has established schools, stores, churches, and a newspaper, the *Weekly Oregonian.*

1851 Portland is incorporated and Hugh D. O'Bryant is elected as the first mayor. First jail, free school, and firehouse are constructed.

1853 The city's first brick building is erected.

1854 Portland becomes the seat of Washington County and the West Coast terminal for *The Petonia*, a U.S. mail steamer.

1864 The salmon industry begins to take shape through the efforts of John Quinn and Vincent Cook.

1872 Fire destroys 3 city blocks.

1873 Second fire destroys 22 city blocks.

1883 Transcontinental railway reaches Portland.

1891 Portland annexes the towns of East Portland and Albina.

1905 Lewis and Clark Centennial Exposition draws thousands.

Bridge was built across the Willamette. In 1891 Portland annexed the towns of East Portland and Albina.

By the first decade of the 20th century, the population had grown to 207,314, spurred by the Alaskan gold rush and by the Lewis and Clark Centennial Exposition held in the city in 1905. World War I, World War II, and the building of the Bonneville Dam were important factors in further growth of the city.

Historical Landmarks

Among Portland's historical buildings are government offices, hotels, and saloons, all of which played a part in the opening up of the Northwest. A walking tour of downtown encompasses two separate national historical districts, including the largest example of 19th-century cast-iron architecture in the West. Among the city's official buildings are the Old Post Office Building on Morrison Street, built in 1875, and the U.S. Customhouse on Davis Street, built in 1901. Among the hotels are Hotel Portland, on Sixth Avenue, begun in the 1870s by Henry Villard, the railroad tycoon, and completed, after Villard's fortunes failed, in 1889; the Esmond Hotel, on Front Avenue; and the St. Charles Hotel on Front and Morrison streets. Two notable saloons dating from Portland's wild days are the Boss Saloon on Glisan Street, a flatiron building, and Erickson's, which stretches a full block on Burnside Street and was once the most widely known saloon in the Northwest.

The Skidmore Fountain in the Triangle at First Avenue, Ankeny, and Vine streets is a gift of Stephen Skidmore to the city. The New Market Block and Theater, erected in 1871, was the entertainment center of the city in the 1870s and 1880s. Lownsdale Square on Fourth Avenue, named after one of Portland's original settlers, contains the Elk Fountain and Soldiers Monument. The city's outstanding public statues include those of Abraham Lincoln, located in the square bounded by Main and Madison streets and Park and Ninth avenues; George Washington, on 57th Avenue facing Sandy Boulevard and looking eastward down the Old Oregon Trail; Joan of Arc on 29th Avenue and Glisan Street; and Theodore Roosevelt on Southwest Park Avenue, an equestrian statue standing 23 feet tall.

Population

After a decline of 3.6% in the 1970s—from 379,967 in 1970 to 368,148 in 1980—Portland rebounded in the 1980s by

Population		
	1980	*1990*
Central City	368,148	437,319
Rank	35	30
Metro Area	1,105,750	1,239,842
Pop. Change 1980–1990 +69,171		
Pop. % Change 1980–1990 +18.8		
Median Age 34.5		
% Male 48.5		

Population (continued)

% Age 65 and Over   14.6
Density (per square mile)   3,506

Households

Number   187,268
Persons per Household   2.27
% Female-Headed Households   11.0
% One-Person Households   34.9
Births—Total   6,116
    % to Mothers under 20   10.7
    Birth Rate per 1,000   16.7

growing 18.8% to 437,319. Its growth rate was higher than that of the metro area.

Ethnic Composition

Whites make up 84.6%, African Americans 7.7%, American Indians 1.2%, Asians and Pacific Islanders 5.3%, Hispanics, 3.2%, and others 1.2%. The Chinese presence is more than one century old and Portland's Chinatown is the second largest in the nation after San Francisco's.

Ethnic Composition (as % of total pop.)

	1980	1990
White	86.52	84.64
Black	7.57	7.67
American Indian	0.96	1.23
Asian and Pacific Islander	2.9	5.3
Hispanic	2.13	3.17
Other	NA	1.16

Government

Under its 1903 charter, Portland is governed by a commission form of government with five council members elected at large to four-year terms. Each member has administrative responsibilities for a group of city bureaus. The mayor is also elected to a four-year term and has considerable budgetary powers.

Government

Year of Home Charter   1903
Number of Members of the Governing Body   5
Elected at Large   5
Elected by Wards   NA
Number of Women in Governing Body   2
Salary of Mayor $72,595
Salary of Council Members $61,131
City Government Employment Total   4,805
Rate per 10,000   123.9

Public Finance

The annual budget consists of revenues of $440.611 million and expenditures of $441.141 million. The debt outstanding is $638.812 million and cash and security holdings total $469.140 million.

Public Finance

Total Revenue (in millions) $440.611
Intergovernmental Revenue—Total (in millions) $0.073
Federal Revenue per Capita $0.02
% Federal Assistance   4.58
% State Assistance   6.04
Sales Tax as % of Total Revenue   6.75
Local Revenue as % of Total Revenue   78.4
City Income Tax   no
Taxes—Total (in millions) $118.7

Taxes per Capita
    Total $306
    Property $220
    Sales and Gross Receipts $50
General Expenditures—Total (in millions) $256.4
General Expenditures per Capita $661
Capital Outlays per Capita $89

% of Expenditures for:
    Public Welfare   0.0
    Highways   6.9
    Education   0.0
    Health and Hospitals   4.4
    Police   18.8
    Sewerage and Sanitation   10.4
    Parks and Recreation   12.5
    Housing and Community Development   3.8
Debt Outstanding per Capita $1,305
    % Utility   29.8
Federal Procurement Contract Awards (in millions) $176.4
Federal Grants Awards (in millions) $84.7
Fiscal Year Begins   July 1

Economy

Portland is the financial, commercial, and industrial center of the Columbia River basin. The three pillars of Portland's economy are the harbor, lumber, and computer chips. The port of Portland is the third largest on the West Coast, and the easy access to river barges up the Columbia and Willamette rivers and to four transcontinental rail lines is an asset that few other cities can match. The port is also the export point for the lumber-rich hinterlands. Portland's association with high-technology began with the establishment of Tektronix in 1946. Today the city produces more than 50% of the computer chips sold in the nation. More than 2,800 manufacturing plants in the metropolitan area employ about half of all workers. Metal processing is the leading industry. Other industries include sportswear, furniture, and chemicals.

Economy

Total Money Income (in millions) $4,177.3
% of State Average   108.5
Per Capita Annual Income $10,770
% Population below Poverty Level   13
Fortune 500 Companies   3

Banks	Number	Deposits (in millions)
Commercial	10	17,285.5
Savings	5	7,805.9

Passenger Autos   412,318

Economy (continued)

Electric Meters   190,160
Gas Meters   59,904

Manufacturing

Number of Establishments   1,084
% with 20 or More Employees   28.1
Manufacturing Payroll (in millions) $806.1
Value Added by Manufacture (in millions) $1,831.0
Value of Shipments (in millions) $4,135.0
New Capital Expenditures (in millions) $78.1

Wholesale Trade

Number of Establishments   1,774
Sales (in millions) $14,411.2
Annual Payroll (in millions) $611.055

Retail Trade

Number of Establishments   4,286
Total Sales (in millions) $2,842.7
Sales per Capita $7,329
Number of Retail Trade Establishments with Payroll   2,993
Annual Payroll (in millions) $368.1
Total Sales (in millions) $2,773.3
General Merchandise Stores (per capita) $1,179
Food Stores (per capita) $1,111
Apparel Stores (per capita) $411
Eating and Drinking Places (per capita) $954

Service Industries

Total Establishments   4,696
Total Receipts (in millions) $2,240.0
Hotels and Motels (in millions) $108.8
Health Services (in millions) $NA
Legal Services (in millions) $343.0

Labor

Among the largest employers in Portland are James River Corporation, Tektronix, Bonneville Power Administration, and Pacific Northwest Bell. Job turnover rate is low and productivity higher than the national average.

Labor

Civilian Labor Force   212,783
% Change 1989–1990   0.7
Work Force Distribution
   Mining   600
   Construction   28,300
   Manufacturing   103,800
   Transportation and Public Utilities   38,500
   Wholesale and Retail Trade   165,700
   FIRE (Finance, Insurance, Real Estate)   52,800
   Service   164,600
   Government   85,500
   Women as % of Labor Force   44.7
   % Self-Employed   6.6
   % Professional/Technical   17.3
Total Unemployment   10,722
Rate %   5.0
Federal Government Civilian Employment   12,360

Education

The Portland Public School District supports 99 elementary, junior high, and senior high schools. Among the institu-

tions of higher education are the University of Portland, a private institution founded in 1901; the University of Oregon Health Sciences Center, chartered in 1974; Reed College, founded in 1909; Warner Pacific College, founded by the Church of God in 1937; Portland State University, a branch of the Oregon State University, founded as a college in 1955; Lewis and Clark College, founded in 1867 as Albany College; and the Columbia Christian College, affiliated with the Church of Christ, founded in 1956.

Education

Number of Public Schools   99
Special Education Schools   3
Total Enrollment   53,042
% Enrollment in Private Schools   8.2
% Minority   28.1
Classroom Teachers   2,714
Pupil-Teacher Ratio   19.5:1
Number of Graduates   2,432
Total Revenue (in millions) $289.096
Total Expenditures (in millions) $306.310
Expenditures per Pupil $5,622
Educational Attainment (Age 25 and Over)
   % Completed 12 or More Years   75.8
   % Completed 16 or More Years   22.1
Four-Year Colleges and Universities   9
   Enrollment   25,141
Two-Year Colleges   1
   Enrollment   23,255

Libraries

Number   82
Public Libraries   15
Books (in thousands)   1,206
Circulation (in thousands)   4,512
Persons Served (in thousands)   570
Circulation per Person Served   7.91
Income (in millions) $13.359
Staff   290

Four-Year Colleges and Universities
   Columbia Christian College
   Concordia College
   Lewis and Clark College
   Multnomah School of the Bible
   Oregon Health Science University
   Portland State University
   Reed College
   University of Portland
   Warner Pacific College

Health

With more than 2,000 physicians and 3,000 beds, Portland is the region's major health-care center. Among its 17 major hospitals are the Veterans Administration Medical Center, Oregon Health Sciences University Hospital, Emmanuel Hospital and Health Center, Good Samaritan Hospital and Medical Center, Providence Medical Center, and St. Vincent Hospital and Medical Center.

Health

Deaths—Total   4,318
Rate per 1,000   11.8
Infant Deaths—Total   73
Rate per 1,000   11.8
Number of Metro Hospitals   17
Number of Metro Hospital Beds   3,950
Rate per 100,000   1,018
Number of Physicians   2,859
Physicians per 1,000   2.85
Nurses per 1,000   NA
Health Expenditures per Capita   NA

Transportation

Portland is approached by two major interstate highways that intersect in the city: the north-south I-5 running from Canada to the Mexican border and the east-west I-84. I-405 bypasses the western edge of downtown and I-205 runs through the eastern suburbs. The city is also served by U.S. Highways 90, 30, and 26 and State Highways 2, 8, 10, 18, 43, 57, 84, 205, 213, 217, and 224. Rail passenger service is provided by Amtrak with five trains daily; rail freight service is provided by Southern Pacific, Union Pacific, and Burlington Northern. Portland is one of the most important freshwater ports in the nation, with 27 miles of deep-water frontage on both banks of the Willamette. The principal air terminal is Portland International, nine miles east of the city. Portland also boasts one of the most modern mass-transit systems, the showpiece of which is MAX, a light-rail system that connects downtown with the eastern suburbs. An area in the heart of downtown is designated as the fareless square. Vintage streetcars began service along Portland's original streetcar routes in 1988.

Transportation

Interstate Highway Mileage   85
Total Urban Mileage   5,123
Total Daily Vehicle Mileage (in millions) $23.089
Daily Average Commute Time   45.8 min.
Number of Buses   517
Port Tonnage (in millions) $31.970
Airports   1
Number of Daily Flights   196
Daily Average Number of Passengers   8,369

Airlines (American carriers only)
  Alaska
  American
  American West
  Continental
  Delta
  Eastern
  Horizon
  Trans World
  United

Housing

The population has been moving from the central city east and west toward the suburbs and to adjacent Clark County across state lines. Upper residential sections command magnificent views of Mount Hood and the river valley. Of the total housing stock 53% is owner-occupied. The median value of an owner-occupied home is $59,200 and the median monthly rent $340.

Housing

Total Housing Units   198,368
% Change 1980–1990   15.4
Vacant Units for Sale or Rent   7,344
Occupied Units   187,268
% with More Than One Person per Room   3.5
% Owner-Occupied   53.0
Median Value of Owner-Occupied Homes $59,200
Average Monthly Purchase Cost $357
Median Monthly Rent $340
New Private Housing Starts   1,323
Value (in thousands) $84,451
% Single-Family   55.1
Nonresidential Buildings Value (in thousands) $89,110

Tallest Buildings	*Hgt. (ft.)*	*Stories*
First Interstate Tower	546	41
U.S. Bancorp Tower	536	39
Koin Tower Plaza	509	35
Standard Insurance Center	367	27
Pacwest Center	356	31

Urban Redevelopment

Downtown Portland has a number of renovated historic shopping districts, such as Skidmore/Oldstown. The nearby Yamhill District features the Yamhill Marketplace. Morgan's Alley is an underground piazza of shops and eateries. As the home of some of the oldest urban malls, Portland provides rich shopping experiences at places like Water Tower at Johns Landing, a renovated furniture factory; Pioneer Place, which contains four tiers of unusual shops; and the multi-level Galleria.

After an ordinance prohibited buildings over 40 stories, Portland began experimenting with construction projects that innovatively blended green spaces and parks. The Tom McCall Waterfront Park, formerly an expressway, provides refreshing scenery. Pioneer Courthouse Square in the heart of Portland is an open plaza converted from a parking garage. Modern architecture is exemplified by Willamette Square with its extensive sky bridges and by the controversial Portland Building. Urban redevelopment programs are coordinated by the Association for Portland Progress, the Portland Planning Bureau, and the Portland Development Commission.

Crime

Portland ranks near the bottom in public safety. In 1991 violent crimes totaled 8,121 and property crimes totaled 42,160.

Crime

Violent Crimes—Total   8,121
Violent Crime Rate per 100,000   798.3
Murder   53

Crime (continued)

Rape   464
Robbery   2,723
Aggravated Assaults   4,881
Property Crimes   42,160
Burglary   9,503
Larceny   26,250
Motor Vehicle Theft   6,407
Arson   466
Per Capita Police Expenditures $175.87
Per Capita Fire Protection Expenditures $112.05
Number of Police   758
Per 1,000   2.06

Media (continued)

Television
KATU (Channel 2)
KGW (Channel 8)
KOIN (Channel 6)
KOPB (Channel 10)
KPDX (Channel 49)

Radio

KBBT (AM)	KBNP (AM)
KBOO (FM)	KBPS (AM)
KBPS (FM)	KBVM (FM)
KEZF (AM)	KEX (AM)
KFXX (AM)	KGON (FM)
KGW (AM)	KINK (FM)
KKEY (AM)	KKRZ (FM)
KKSN (AM)	KKSN (FM)
KLVS (AM)	KMXI (FM)
KNBP (FM)	KPDQ (AM)
KPDQ (FM)	KRRC (FM)
KUFO (FM)	KUPL (AM)
KUPL (FM)	KWJJ (AM)
KWJJ (FM)	KXL (AM)
KXL (FM)	KXYQ (FM)

Religion

The Portland area has more than 750 churches, with all major denominations represented. The Old Church, the city's oldest, is a fine example of Gothic architecture. The Sanctuary of Our Sorrowful Mother on Sandy Boulevard is an open-air grotto maintained by the Servite Fathers. It consists of an 18-acre landscaped lower level with a large altar and stations for prayer and a 40-acre upper level separated from the lower by a perpendicular cliff reached by an elevator. On the upper level are seven shrines and a monastery. Other religious edifices include the Trinity Episcopal Church on the corner of 19th Avenue and Everett Street; St. Mark's Cathedral on 21st Avenue and Northrup Street, an Italian Romanesque structure with a 75-foot tower built in 1874; Temple Beth Israel on 19th Avenue and Flanders Street; and the Sixth Church of Christ Scientist on Ninth Avenue.

Religion

Largest Denominations (Adherents)

Catholic	77,732
Presbyterian	13,291
Independent Charismatics	12,200
Latter-Day Saints	11,657
American Baptist	5,403
Evangelical Lutheran	9,590
Episcopal	6,930
United Methodist	7,716
Black Baptist	6,767
Jewish	3,704

Media

The city dailies are the *Oregonian* and the *Daily Journal of Commerce*. Electronic media consist of 5 television stations (3 commercial, 1 public, and 1 independent) and 30 AM and FM radio stations.

Media

Newsprint
  The Bee, weekly
  The Business Journal, weekly
  Daily Journal of Commerce, daily
  Portland Observer, weekly
  Oregonian, daily

Sports

Portland is represented in three sports by professional teams: the Portland Trail Blazers in basketball, the Portland Beavers in baseball, and the Portland Winter Hawks in hockey. Harness and thoroughbred racing is held at the Portland Meadows from October through April and greyhound racing at the Multnomah Kennel Club. Stock and Indy car racing takes place at the Portland International Raceway.

Arts, Culture, and Tourism

The cultural hub of Portland is the Portland Center for the Performing Arts. It features the Arlene Schnitzer Concert Hall and a four-theater complex in the New Theaters Building. Theater is represented by a number of theater companies, including Portland Repertory, New Rose Theater, Portland Civic Theater, and Storefront Theater; music by the Oregon Symphony Orchestra, the Little Orchestra of Portland, the Portland Youth Philharmonic, the West Coast Chamber Orchestra, Chamber Music Northwest, and the Portland Opera Association; and dance by Ballet Oregon and the Pacific Ballet Theater.

Portland supports a large number of museums. The principal ones are the Portland Art Museum and the Oregon Historical Center. Specialized museums include the American Advertising Museum, the Children's Museum, the Old Church Society, the Oregon Museum of Science and Industry, the World Forestry Center, the Oregon Maritime Center and Museum, the Northwest Film and Video Center, and the Mayhill Museum of Art. The Contemporary Arts Gallery is the nation's oldest nonprofit art gallery. Reed College Gallery is another outstanding gallery. Public art and fountains abound throughout the city. The most notable examples are Portlandia, a 35-foot-high hammered copper sculpture of a kneeling woman, and Iras Fountain, a cascading water sculpture dotted with islands and terraces, across from the Civic Auditorium.

Travel and Tourism
Hotel Rooms 12,549
Convention and Exhibit Space (square feet) NA
Convention Centers
Oregon Convention Center
Portland Memorial Coliseum Complex
Montgomery Park
Festivals
Portland Rose Festival (spring)
Hillsboro Happy Days Festival
Artquake (September)

Parks and Recreation

Portland has 148 parks. The 6,000-acre Forest Park has the largest woodland within a city in the nation. The Mill Ends Park, 24 inches in diameter, is the world's smallest park. The 20-acre Peninsula Park on Portland Boulevard contains the Sunken Rose Gardens that display 1,000 varieties of roses. The 3-acre Joseph Wood Hill Park covers the crest of Rocky Butte, one of the three cinder cones of volcanic origin on the east side of the city. Mount Tabor Park is on the summit of another cinder cone along the east edge of the city. The 30-acre Laurelhurst Park on 39th Avenue includes a lake. The 100-acre Washington Park crowns the hills directly west of the main business section. Near its entrance is the 34-foot shaft of granite erected in honor of Lewis and Clark and along the driveway is the statue of Sacajawea, the bird woman who guided Lewis and Clark through the mountains.

Sources of Further Information

City Hall
1220 SW Fifth Avenue
Portland, OR 97204
(503) 823-4120

Greater Portland Convention and Visitors Association
26 SW Salmon Street
Portland, OR 97204
(503) 222-2223

Portland Chamber of Commerce
10414 NE Sandy Boulevard
Portland, OR 97220
(503) 228-9411

Additional Reading

Abbott, Carl. *Portland: Planning Policies and Growth in a Twentieth Century City.* 1983.

Anderson, Patricia M. *Portland.* 1989.

Elwell, Edward H. *Portland and Vicinity.* 1975.

Gleason, Norma C. *Portland's Public Art: A Guide and History.* 1984.

Houle, Marcy C. *One City's Wilderness: Portland's Forest Park.* 1988.

Marlitt, Richard. *Matters of Proportion: The Portland Residential Architecture of Whidden and Lewis.* 1989.

Rule, Leslie. *Beautiful America's Portland.* 1989.

Snyder, Eugene E. *Early Portland: Stumptown Triumphant.* 1984.

Stein, Harry. *Portland: A Pictorial History.* 1980.

Will, Robin. *Beauty of Portland.* 1990.

Willoughby, Lee D. *Portland.* The Making of the Cities Series. 1991.

Portsmouth
New Hampshire

Location and Topography

Portsmouth, New Hampshire's first settlement, second-oldest city, only seaport, and first capital, is located in southeastern New Hampshire in Rockingham County.

Layout of City and Suburbs

Portsmouth lies on the banks of the Piscataqua River about three miles from the Atlantic Ocean facing a broad tidal basin of three inland rivers. Ideally located, Portsmouth has one of the deepest harbors in the world, a factor in its maritime preeminence in the 19th century. The land around the harbor is hilly, sloping down to the Piscataqua Bay.

The city has an old-world atmosphere with winding streets, fine old houses, and venerable trees that shade its narrow thoroughfares. Although ravaged by fires, the city still remains the Queen of the Piscataqua. The builders of the city had an eye for style and many houses show a delicacy of design. The side streets are narrow with shops located in small buildings.

Climate

Portsmouth has relatively mild winters because of its coastal location and the moderating influence of the Atlantic; average annual snowfall does not exceed 70 inches. The city is less subject to the storms that many cities on the Atlantic Coast face because the traditional northeasters are mostly spent by the time they reach Portsmouth. Summers tend to be occasionally hot and humid but tempered by sea breezes.

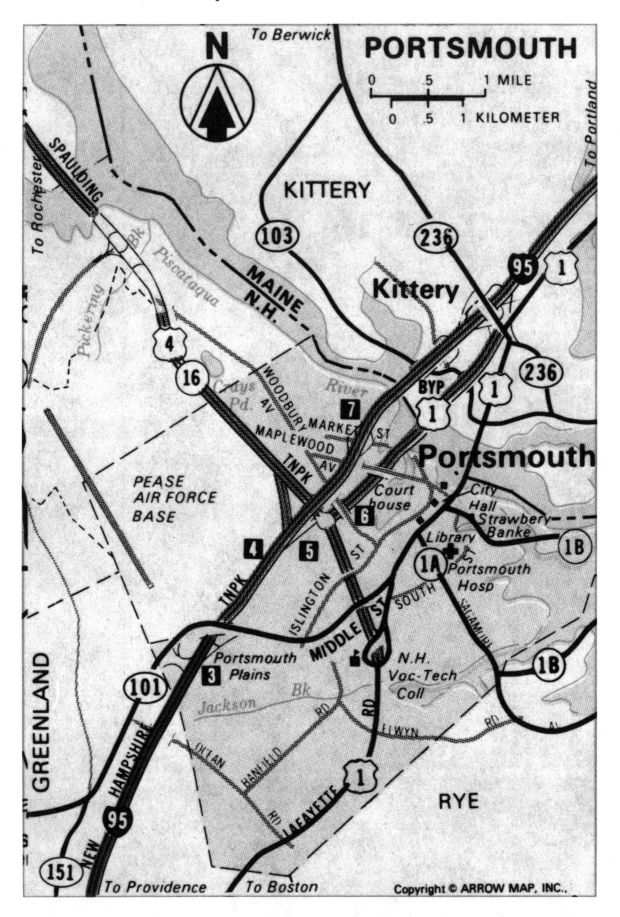

Weather (continued)			
Precipitation (inches) 36.53			
Snow (inches) 70			
% Seasonal Humidity 73			
Wind Speed (m.p.h.) 7.0			
Clear Days NA			
Cloudy Days NA			
Storm Days 20			
Rainy Days 127			
Average Temperatures (°F)	High	Low	Mean
January	31	16	24
February	34	14	26
March	42	27	35
April	54	37	45
May	65	47	56
June	74	56	66
July	80	62	71
August	78	66	69
September	70	52	62
October	60	42	51
November	48	34	41
December	36	22	29

History

The land around Portsmouth was settled in pre-colonial days by the Piscataquas, a tribe of the Algonquin federation. The Isle of Shoals, ten miles from the harbor, saw the first white people about four centuries ago. Among those early visitors was Captain John Smith, who discovered the Piscataqua River in 1614 and on his return to England published a description of the place, and Martin Pring, who in 1603 sailed the ships *Speedwell* and *Discoverer* up the Piscataqua.

In 1621 Captain John Mason procured a grant from the Plymouth Council of all land from Salem to the Merrimack River. The next year he shared with Sir Ferdinando Gorges a grant of the land from Merrimack north to Sagadahoc, extending to the Great Lakes. Under the authority of this grant, Mason and Gorges, with other merchants, formed the Company of Laconia, and in 1623 tried to establish a colony and fishery at Odiorne Point, two miles east of present-day Portsmouth.

In the spring of the following year, two groups came to the settlement under the authority of the Company of Laconia. One group landed on the southern shore of the Piscataqua, at its mouth, and named it Little Harbor. In 1629, scattered planters in the Massachusetts Bay Colony bought land here from the Indians. Granted as a township in 1631 with the name of Piscataqua, it was later renamed Strawbery Banke. In 1653 the name was again changed to Portsmouth on the petition of the 63 resident families. When New Hampshire was separated from the Massachusetts Bay Colony in 1679, Portsmouth was made the capital of the new colony. The town soon developed a strong economy based on shipbuilding, fishing, and trading with the West Indies.

Between the Revolutionary War and the Civil War the city flourished and attained its greatest glory. Private shipbuilding reached its acme during the first half of the 19th century when many of the famous clipper ships were launched on the Piscataqua Bay. Many new wharves were built, and in 1800 the U.S. Naval Shipyard was added to build and repair warships. Portsmouth formed one of the points in the brisk commercial trade between England, the West Indies, and the United States with lumber from New England, coal from England, and rum and molasses from the West Indies forming the staples. The profits of the trade helped to support the merchant class in opulent splendor and several ornate mansions were built during this time.

Portsmouth's decline as a city began when Concord became the state capital in 1808. Its fortunes suffered further with the invention of the steamship and the growing influence of Boston. Compensating for these developments was the rise of the brewing industry, which soon became one of the largest in the United States before Prohibition. The construction of the Little Bay–Dover Bridge in 1874 undermined the usefulness of the Piscataqua River as a transportation channel. Portsmouth became more and more dependent on the Naval Shipyard for its economic survival.

Although still an official port of entry and a foreign trade zone, the city today has only limited maritime activity. The commercial shipyard on Badger Island builds yachts and pleasure craft. Much of the waterfront has been transformed to parks and gardens, and condominiums and offices have taken the place of warehouses.

Historical Landmarks

Many buildings in the city date from the 1600s. Six of the historical landmarks are on the Portsmouth Trail, including the Governor John Langdon House and the John Paul Jones home. The oldest brick house is the Warner House, built in 1718 by Captain McPhaedris, whose daughter married Jonathan Warner. At the time of its building, this house was surpassed by few private residences in New England. Another magnificent private residence is the Wentworth Gardiner House, built in 1760 by Mrs. Wentworth as a wedding present for her son Thomas. There are a number of other Georgian and Federalist mansions of the old merchant princes and patricians, particularly the homes of Mark Wentworth, Jacob Wendrell, Fitz-John Porter, Nathan Walker, Tobias Lear, Thomas Bailey Aldrich, Samuel Larkin, and William Whipple.

Among the notable churches are the North Church, first built in 1712, the South Parish Church built in 1826, the Episcopal Church built in 1832, and St. John's Church built in 1807. The Old State House built in 1758 survives only in part. The Pitt Tavern was the site of Loyalist meetings before the Revolutionary War.

Population

The population of Portsmouth has remained fairly stable since World War II. In the 1990 census the city had nearly 26,000 residents, compared to 25,717 in 1970 and 26,254 in 1980.

Chronology

1603	Martin Pring sails up the Piscataqua on the *Discoverer* and *Speedwell*.
1614	Captain John Smith sails up the Piscataqua.
1622	Captain John Mason and Sir Ferdinando Gorges form the Company of Laconia to colonize the land between Salem and the Great Lakes.
1623	Gorges, Mason, and company make their first landing at Odiorne Point, two miles east of present-day Portsmouth, to establish a colony and fishery.
1624	One group, sponsored by the Company of Laconia, lands at the mouth of the Piscataqua name the spot Little Harbor.
1629	Some planters in the Massachusetts Bay Colony purchase land from Indians in the Piscataqua area.
1631	The settlement is named first Piscataqua and later Strawbery Banke.
1653	The name of the town is changed to Portsmouth.
1679	Portsmouth becomes capital of the newly formed state of New Hampshire.
1756	The *New Hampshire Gazette*, later the *Portsmouth Gazette*, begins publication.
1800	The U.S. Naval Shipyard is located in Portsmouth.
1808	Concord is named state capital.
1849	Portsmouth is incorporated as a city.
1870	Portsmouth is wired for electric lights.
1874	The Little Bay–Dover Bridge is built.
1887	Free postal delivery begins in city.
1990s	Redevelopment of municipal complex.

Population

	1980	1990
Central City	26,254	25,925
Rank	909	907
Metro Area	275,753	350,078
Pop. Change 1980–1990	-329	
Pop. % Change 1980–1990	-1.3	
Median Age	27.4	
% Male	49.6	
% Age 65 and Over	12.2	
Density (per square mile)	1,705	

Households

Number   10,329
Persons per Household   2.39
% Female-Headed Households   9.9

Population (continued)

% One-Person Households   28.6
Births—Total   442
    % to Mothers under 20   10.0
    Birth Rate per 1,000   15.9

Ethnic Composition

Portsmouth is one of the few New Hampshire towns where minorities make up more than 1% of the population. Whites account for 93%, blacks for 5%, and other ethnic groups for the balance.

Ethnic Composition (as % of total pop.)		
	1980	*1990*
White	94.32	92.63
Black	3.7	3.70
American Indian	0.25	0.27
Asian and Pacific Islander	0.86	1.72
Hispanic	1.43	2.00
Other	NA	0.77

Government

Portsmouth operates under a manager-council form of government. Nine council members are elected to two-year terms and they elect a mayor from among themselves. The administration is headed by a full-time professional city manager answerable to the council.

Government

Year of Home Charter   NA
Number of Members of the Governing Body   9
Elected at Large   9
Elected by Wards   NA
Number of Women in Governing Body   NA
Salary of Mayor   NA
Salary of Council Members   NA
City Government Employment Total   931
Rate per 10,000   358.5

Public Finance

Details of the city budget are given below.

Public Finance

Total Revenue (in millions)   NA
Intergovernmental Revenue—Total (in millions)   NA
Federal Revenue per Capita   NA
% Federal Assistance   NA
% State Assistance   NA
Sales Tax as % of Total Revenue   NA
Local Revenue as % of Total Revenue   NA
City Income Tax   no
Taxes—Total (in millions) $19.3

Taxes per Capita
    Total $742
    Property $728
    Sales and Gross Receipts $0

Public Finance (continued)

General Expenditures—Total (in millions) $36.8
General Expenditures per Capita $1,417
Capital Outlays per Capita $340

% of Expenditures for:
   Public Welfare   1.6
   Highways   3.9
   Education   42.4
   Health and Hospitals   0.1
   Police   5.7
   Sewerage and Sanitation   3.9
   Parks and Recreation   1.4
   Housing and Community Development   9.8
Debt Outstanding per Capita $458
   % Utility
Federal Procurement Contract Awards (in millions) $20.4
Federal Grants Awards (in millions) $3.0
Fiscal Year Begins   NA

Economy

The major economic sectors are the U.S. Naval Shipyard, tourism, retail and service, and fishing.

Economy

Total Money Income (in millions) $284.942
% of State Average   94.1
Per Capita Annual Income $10,972
% Population below Poverty Level   9.3
Fortune 500 Companies   NA

Banks	Number	Deposits (in millions)
Commercial	8	435.9
Savings	5	397.7

Passenger Autos   204,754
Electric Meters   13,772
Gas Meters   4,370

Manufacturing

Number of Establishments   51
% with 20 or More Employees   35.3
Manufacturing Payroll (in millions) $51.4
Value Added by Manufacture (in millions) $112.6
Value of Shipments (in millions) $243.4
New Capital Expenditures (in millions) $5.3

Wholesale Trade

Number of Establishments   78
Sales (in millions) $321.3
Annual Payroll (in millions) $23.165

Retail Trade

Number of Establishments   462
Total Sales (in millions) $555.6
Sales per Capita $21,394
Number of Retail Trade Establishments with Payroll   374
Annual Payroll (in millions) $63.4
Total Sales (in millions) $551.2
General Merchandise Stores (per capita) $2,727
Food Stores (per capita) $1,990
Apparel Stores (per capita) $1,067
Eating and Drinking Places (per capita) $1,929

Service Industries

Total Establishments   376
Total Receipts (in millions) $155.0

Economy (continued)

Hotels and Motels (in millions) $9.5
Health Services (in millions) $65.5
Legal Services (in millions) $15.0

Labor

The leading employer today, as it has been for the past 100 years, is the Naval Shipyard. However, a strong surge in summer tourism and the growth in retail and service sectors have helped to reduce the city's dependence on the shipyard. The occupational areas showing growth are computers, finance, and real estate. The scheduled closing of Pease Air Force Base may substantially reduce the city work force.

Labor

Civilian Labor Force   14,913
% Change 1989–1990   2.4

Work Force Distribution
   Mining   NA
   Construction   NA
   Manufacturing   2,200
   Transportation and Public Utilities   NA
   Wholesale and Retail Trade   6,318
   FIRE (Finance, Insurance, Real Estate)   NA
   Service   3,193
   Government   1,347
   Women as % of Labor Force   NA
   % Self-Employed   NA
   % Professional/Technical   16.9
Total Unemployment   646
Rate %   4.3
Federal Government Civilian Employment   416

Education

The Portsmouth Public School system comprises one high school, one junior high/middle school, and six elementary schools. The parochial school system is made up of two elementary schools. There is no higher education facility within the city other than an extension of the New Hampshire College.

Education

Number of Public Schools   8
Special Education Schools   NA
Total Enrollment   4,343
% Enrollment in Private Schools   6.3
% Minority   NA
Classroom Teachers   198
Pupil-Teacher Ratio   22:1
Number of Graduates   NA
Total Revenue (in millions)   NA
Total Expenditures (in millions)   NA
Expenditures per Pupil   NA
Educational Attainment (Age 25 and Over)   NA
   % Completed 12 or More Years   76.9
   % Completed 16 or More Years   17.5
Four-Year Colleges and Universities   NA
   Enrollment   NA
Two-Year Colleges   NA
   Enrollment   NA

Education (continued)

Libraries

Number 6
Public Libraries 1
Books (in thousands) 88.9
Circulation (in thousands) 223.3
Persons Served (in thousands) 27.9
Circulation per Person Served 8.0
Income (in millions) $0.681
Staff 19

Four-Year Colleges and Universities
   NA

Health

The principal medical facility is the Portsmouth Regional Hospital with 140 beds. The adjacent Portsmouth Pavilion is a psychiatric center. Long-term care is available at the Seacoast Hospice.

Health

Deaths—Total 197
Rate per 1,000 7.1
Infant Deaths—Total 4
Rate per 1,000 9.0
Number of Metro Hospitals 2
Number of Metro Hospital Beds 161
Rate per 100,000 620
Number of Physicians NA
Physicians per 1,000 NA
Nurses per 1,000 NA
Health Expenditures per Capita NA

Transportation

Portsmouth lies just west of I-95 (the Maine Turnpike) and is serviced by the north-south corridor of U.S. Route 1. Portsmouth is the eastern terminus of NH Route 101, an express highway for most of its length. Other routes running west from the city are U.S. Route 4 and NH Route 11 (the Spaulding Turnpike). Ferries are available between Portsmouth and Kittery, Maine, both also connected by the Memorial Bridge across the bay. Within the city the main thoroughfares converge at Market Square in downtown Portsmouth. The city is connected with Pierce Island by a bridge that crosses South Mill Pond.

Air travelers to and from Portsmouth have to use either Boston's Logan or Portland's International Airport. For domestic service the closest airport is in Manchester, about 47 miles away. Rail passengers and freight are carried by Boston and Maine Railroad.

Portsmouth is the only seaport in New Hampshire. Although not large by international standards, the port handles a variety of cargo, including salt, lobsters, scrap metal, gypsum, rock, and steel cable. The port is also designated as a foreign trade zone. Facilities include a 10-acre storage area and 50,000 square feet of warehouse space.

Transportation

Interstate Highway Mileage NA
Total Urban Mileage NA
Total Daily Vehicle Mileage (in millions) NA
Daily Average Commute Time 39.6 min.
Number of Buses 6
Port Tonnage (in millions) NA
Airports NA
Number of Daily Flights NA
Daily Average Number of Passengers NA

Airlines (American carriers only)
   See Boston and Portland, ME

Housing

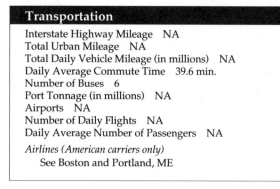

Modern housing is found only in the outskirts and suburbs of the city. A good part of downtown consists of houses built before 1940.

Housing

Total Housing Units 11,369
% Change 1980–1990 13.1
Vacant Units for Sale or Rent 780
Occupied Units 10,329
% with More Than One Person per Room 1.7
% Owner-Occupied 41.9
Median Value of Owner-Occupied Homes $137,600
Average Monthly Purchase Cost NA
Median Monthly Rent $497
New Private Housing Starts 5
Value (in thousands) $564
% Single-Family 100
Nonresidential Buildings Value (in thousands) $0

Urban Redevelopment

Portsmouth's major redevelopment project in the early 1990s was the new municipal complex including a new city hall, main library, and police headquarters.

Crime

Portsmouth has a low crime rate. Violent crimes reported to police totaled 171, property crimes totaled 1,301.

Crime

Violent Crimes—Total 171
Violent Crime Rate per 100,000 5,167
Murder NA
Rape NA
Robbery NA
Aggravated Assaults NA
Property Crimes 1,301
Burglary NA
Larceny NA
Motor Vehicle Theft NA
Arson NA
Per Capita Police Expenditures NA
Per Capita Fire Protection Expenditures NA
Number of Police 57
Per 1,000 20

Religion

Portsmouth is predominantly Catholic.

Religion	
Largest Denominations (Adherents)	
Catholic	57,763
United Church of Christ	5,789
United Methodist	4,217
American Baptist	4,876
Episcopal	3,359
Assembly of God	1,330
Southern Baptist	1,652
Unitarian	1,023
Jewish	1,100

Media

The city's only daily is the *Portsmouth Herald*, published weekday evenings and weekend mornings. No television signals originate in the city, but all major networks are received through the Boston channels. Radio broadcasting is conducted by two FM and AM stations.

Media	
Newsprint	
Portsmouth Herald, daily	
Portsmouth Press, weekly	
Television	
See Boston	
Radio	
WCQL (AM)	WHEB (FM)

Sports

There are no major sports facilities in Portsmouth.

Arts, Culture, and Tourism

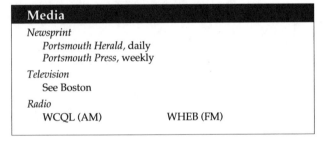

The city has two outstanding theater troupes. The Pontine Movement Theater, founded in 1977, is a professional mime group. Theater by the Sea, the resident professional troupe, presents a variety of programs, particularly during the Prescott Park Arts Festival. Ballet New England performs contemporary and traditional dance. Classical music is offered at the Strawbery Banke Chamber Music Festival.

Many of Portsmouth's historical homes are museums in their own right. In addition there are formal museums, such as the Athenaeum, the Portsmouth Historical Society Museum, and the Portsmouth Naval Shipyard Museum.

Travel and Tourism	
Hotel Rooms NA	
Convention and Exhibit Space (square feet) NA	
Convention Centers	
Sheraton Portsmouth Conference Center	
Festivals	
Naval Heritage Day (August)	
Blessing of the Fleet (June)	
Prescott Park Arts Festival	
Bow Street Fair	
Seacoast Jazz Festival (July)	

Parks and Recreation

The Odiorne Point State Park features a nature center. Prescott Park contains the Sheafe Warehouse where John Paul Jones outfitted the *Ranger*. Harbor cruises and whale watches are popular in the summer. Albacore Park, housing the Portsmouth Maritime Museum, includes Four Tree Island Park and Pierce Island Park. The city also maintains 12 tennis courts, indoor and outdoor pools, and 4 golf courses.

Sources of Further Information

City Manager
City of Portsmouth
Portsmouth, NH 03801
(603) 431-2000

Greater Portsmouth Chamber of Commerce
500 Market Street
Portsmouth, NH 03801
(603) 436-1118

Historic Dictrict
City of Portsmouth
Portsmouth, NH 03801
(603) 431-2000

Portsmouth Public Library
City of Portsmouth
Portsmouth, NH 03801
(603) 431-2000

Additional Reading

Greater Portsmouth Area Directory of Manufacturers and Products. Annual.
Lincoln, J. D., and Rosemary Lincoln. *People of Portsmouth and Some Who Came to Town.* 1982
Portsmouth Chamber of Commerce. *Community Profiles.* Irregular.

Providence

Rhode Island

Location and Topography

N

Providence, the capital of Rhode Island, is situated on the head of the Narragansett Bay on the Providence River. The city is intersected by two rivers.

Layout of City and Suburbs

The city is built on three hills, the most important of which is College (or Prospect) Hill rising steeply from the eastern border of the business district. The old city begins at the confluence of the Woonasquatucket and Moshassuck rivers, the former flowing from the west and the latter from the north. They unite to form the Providence River, but along the foot of College Hill the Providence is so walled up and covered over as to be nothing more than a sluggish underground canal. Although most of the original buildings in the old city have been torn down, fascinating relics survive, espe-

cially along Main Street, which runs along the east bank of the river from College Street to the North Burial Ground. Beyond College Hill the city sprawls without apparent plan or logic, yet Providence remains very compact, and no part is more than a 15-minute ride from the center. For the residents, the "city" is only the area radiating a few blocks from the intersection of Dorrance and Westminster streets. There is no financial district as such, although most of the banks and insurance companies lie east of Dorrance Street. The larger area to the west of Dorrance Street is known as the shopping district, yet it contains only run-of-the-mill establishments.

Climate

Providence has a pleasant maritime climate with mild summers and moderately cold winters. The ocean breezes temper extremes in both seasons. Spring and fall are balmy and sunny. Temperatures exceeding 90°F occur only 19 days in an average year, between late April and September. Temperatures dropping below zero occur two or three days a year between December and January, and freezing temperatures 119 days a year. Measurable precipitation falls on about one day in three, and is fairly evenly distributed throughout the year. There is no dry season but droughts occur occasionally. Every

five years or so the city is threatened by tropical storms or a hurricane, usually between late July and the end of October. Thunderstorms are responsible for much of the rainfall from May through August. The first winter snowfall comes near Thanksgiving, the last around mid-March. The record snowfall was 75.6 inches in the winter of 1947–1948.

Weather			
Temperature			
Highest Monthly Average °F	81.7		
Lowest Monthly Average °F	20.0		
Annual Averages			
Days 32°F or Below 119			
Days above 90°F 19			
Zero Degree Days 2			
Precipitation (inches) 45.32			
Snow (inches) 36.3			
% Seasonal Humidity 64.0			
Wind Speed (m.p.h.) 10.6			
Clear Days 100			
Cloudy Days 162			
Storm Days 18			
Rainy Days 121			
Average Temperatures (°F)	*High*	*Low*	*Mean*
January	38.7	20.5	29.6
February	44.8	25.3	35.1
March	50.2	32.3	41.3
April	62.4	41.2	51.8
May	75.6	52.2	63.9
June	80.5	58.1	69.3
July	84.5	63.8	74.2
August	82.9	64.2	73.6
September	72.7	53.5	63.1
October	65.7	46.5	56.1
November	53.1	37.6	45.4
December	45.1	27.4	36.3

History

The early history of Providence is closely allied to that of Rhode Island. The city was founded in 1636 by Roger Williams and his five companions: William Harris, John Smith, Francis Wickes, Joshua Verein, and Thomas Angell, all of whom had been expelled from Massachusetts for their espousal of the radical doctrine of separation of church and state. In 1638 Williams secured from Canonicus and Miantonomi, chiefs of the Narragansett tribe, a deed to the lands and meadows along the Moshassuck and Woonasquatucket rivers. The settlement was named Providence Plantations in acknowledgment of divine guidance in its selection. This piety was also expressed in the naming of streets, such as Hope, Benevolent, Benefit, Peace, Faith, and Friendship.

By 1664 the town had about 50 homesteads, most of them one-room structures of rough-hewn timbers with thatched or shingled roofs. Wells were dug in the streets, and orchards were planted with family burial plots in their middle. In addition to the home lot, each townsman was granted an acreage of pasture. In 1676, when the town had grown to a population of 1,000, a band of Indians descended and burned 29 of its 75 houses.

In 1680 another event launched the city into an era of great commercial prosperity. In that year Pardon Tillinghast built the first Providence wharf enabling the city's merchants to take part in the lucrative trade in West Indian and African molasses, rum, and slaves. Great fortunes were made, and within a century the city changed beyond recognition. In 1762 William Goddard founded the first newspaper, the *Providence Gazette and Country Journal.* In 1770 Rhode Island College (later Brown University), established at Warren in 1764, moved to Providence. The Market House was built in 1773. When the British began imposing restrictive laws against smuggling and illegal trade, the residents became increasingly restive. In 1772 a British ship was destroyed. In 1775 the city followed Boston's example and held its own Tea Party. In 1776 the Rhode Island Independence Act was signed in the Old State House. During the Revolutionary War, the city was spared actual fighting.

After independence, Providence resumed its commercial enterprises, with the China trade as its cornerstone. In 1790 the country's first water-powered cotton-spinning device was built by Samuel Slater in nearby Pawtucket, and Providence became the center of the nation's textile industry. The jewelry industry began in 1794 when a method was discovered for plating cheap metals with precious ones.

In 1815 the city suffered over $1 million worth of damage when it was struck by a great gale, and ships anchored below Weyboset Bridge broke their moorings and invaded the streets. Providence recovered quickly from this catastrophe. In 1831 the city was incorporated. By the middle of the 19th century, the city had become a full-blown industrial center, and steady streams of immigrants began to arrive, helping to swell the population. The vast majority of these immigrants were Italians, as a result of which the city became heavily Roman Catholic in stark contrast to its original nonconformist religious traditions. In 1900 Providence became the sole capital of the state. To mark this event, the new State House was completed on Smith Hill, permanently changing the city's skyline.

Although Providence prospered briefly during both world wars, it has declined economically since the 1950s as its old smokestack industries have been displaced by newer technologies.

Historical Landmarks

As one of the six oldest cities in the United States, Providence has numerous historical sites and buildings. Among the most notable are:

- The Old Market house (1773) was the site of the Providence Tea Party.
- Jabez Bowen House (1745), from the balcony of which were proclaimed the accession of George III and the Declaration of Independence. George Washington was entertained here in 1831.

Chronology

1636 Roger Williams founds a new settlement at the junction of the Woonasquatucket and Moshassuck rivers.

1638 Williams obtains a formal deed from the chiefs of the Narragansett tribe to the settlement, which is thereupon named Providence Plantations.

1676 Indians descend upon town and burn one-third of its houses.

1680 Pardon Tillinghast builds the first wharf, sparking an era of commercial prosperity and foreign trade.

1762 William Goddard establishes the first newspaper, the *Providence Gazette and Country Journal*.

1770 Rhode Island College (later Brown University) moves from Warren to Providence.

1773 The Market House is built.

1775 Providence holds its own Tea Party and rally against the British.

1776 Rhode Island Independence Act is signed in the Old State House.

1790 George Washington is granted an honorary degree by the Rhode Island College. Samuel Slater launches the city's industrial era with a textile mill in Pawtucket.

1815 Great storm devastates city.

1831 Providence is incorporated as a city.

1994 Scheduled year of completion for the Capital Center urban redevelopment project.

- The First Baptist Meeting House on Main Street, which dates from 1639. Designed by Joseph Brown, it is architecturally and historically one of the most famous buildings in New England.
- Shakespeare's Head House (1763) on Meeting Street, which was once one of the most important buildings in Providence. It was William Goddard's print shop for the *Providence Gazette and Country Journal*, and later the main post office under John Carter.
- The Brick School House (1769) was from 1800 one of the first free public schools in the nation.
- The Old State House (1758) was the meeting place for the State General Assembly for 138 years until 1900.
- The Samuel Bridgham House (1790) on Court Street is a Georgian colonial built by the first mayor of Providence.

- The Sullivan Dorr House (1810) is a three-story late Georgian colonial; behind it is the grave of Roger Williams.
- The Golden Bull Inn (1784) on Benefit Street was known at various times as the Daggett Tavern, Mansion House, and Roger Williams House. It was for many years the social center of the town. Five presidents of the United States were entertained here.
- The Edward Dexter House (1799) on Waterman Street is now Brown University's Rhode Island Hall.
- The Thomas Poynton Ives House (1811) on Power Street is one of the largest and most handsome of the Georgian colonial mansions.
- The John Carter Brown House (1792) on Benefit Street is one of the largest frame colonial houses.
- The John Brown House (1786) on Power Street was described by John Quincy Adams as the most magnificent and elegant mansion he had seen in the country. It was designed by Joseph Brown for his brother, John.
- The Unitarian Church (1723) at the corner of Benefit and Benevolent streets was originally the First Congregational Church. It is a fine example of early 19th-century ecclesiastical architecture.
- Stephen Hopkins House (1755) at the corner of Benefit and Hopkins streets was the home of Stephen Hopkins, ten times governor of the state and the first chancellor of Brown University. George Washington was a guest here twice.
- The Arcade (1828) traverses the block from 130 Westminster Street to 65 Weybosset Street. It is one of the most interesting remaining examples of the Greek Revival period in America. Its monolithic Ionic columns are the largest of any building in America except those in the Cathedral of St. John the Divine in New York City.
- Joseph Brown House (1774) on Main Street was for many years the home of the Providence Bank, the second-oldest in the United States.
- Old Friends Meeting House (1723) is a severely plain structure recalling the austerity of the early Quakers.
- St. Joseph's Church (1850) at the corner of Hope and Arnold streets is the oldest Catholic church in Providence.

Population

 After many years of population decline, the population of Providence rose by 3,924 from 156,804 in 1980 to 160,728 in 1990, yet its rank among U.S. cities dropped from 99 to 107.

Ethnic Composition

 Whites remain by far the largest racial group at 70%, but Hispanics have overtaken blacks as the second-largest group. Hispanics also had the second-highest growth rate

Population

	1980	1990
Central City	156,804	160,728
Rank	99	107
Metro Area	865,771	916,270
Pop. Change 1980–1990 +3,924		
Pop. % Change 1980–1990 +2.5		
Median Age 29.3		
% Male 47.6		
% Age 65 and Over 13.6		
Density (per square mile) 8,688		

Households

Number 58,905
Persons per Household 2.52
% Female-Headed Households 18.4
% One-Person Households 31.8
Births—Total 2,590
   % to Mothers under 20 15.3
   Birth Rate per 1,000 16.8

Ethnic Composition (as % of total pop.)

	1980	1990
White	81.20	69.93
Black	11.83	14.83
American Indian	0.67	0.93
Asian and Pacific Islander	1.08	5.94
Hispanic	5.78	15.54
Other	NA	8.37

among minorities at 132.2%, compared with 40.9% for blacks. The highest growth rate is claimed by Asians, because of the large influx of over 10,000 Southeast Asians, particularly Cambodians.

Government

 Providence operates under a mayor-council form of government. The mayor and the 15 council members are elected to four-year terms.

Government

Year of Home Charter 1980
Number of Members of the Governing Body 16
Elected at Large NA
Elected by Wards 16
Number of Women in Governing Body 3
Salary of Mayor $77,998
Salary of Council Members $7,586
City Government Employment Total 3,970
Rate per 10,000 252.5

Public Finance

 The annual budget consists of revenues of $286.828 million and expenditures of $314.804 million. Debt outstanding is $81.930 million and cash and security holdings $149.968 million.

Economy

 The economy is based partly on government services associated with the city's status as the state capital and partly on

Public Finance

Total Revenue (in millions) $286.828
Intergovernmental Revenue—Total (in millions) $94.73
Federal Revenue per Capita $14.3
% Federal Assistance 4.99
% State Assistance 27.63
Sales Tax as % of Total Revenue NA
Local Revenue as % of Total Revenue 55.44
City Income Tax no
Taxes—Total (in millions) $100.9
Taxes per Capita
   Total $642
   Property $635
   Sales and Gross Receipts $0
General Expenditures—Total (in millions) $182.1
General Expenditures per Capita $1,158
Capital Outlays per Capita $94
% of Expenditures for:
   Public Welfare 6.3
   Highways 3.2
   Education 41.0
   Health and Hospitals 0.1
   Police 6.8
   Sewerage and Sanitation 2.5
   Parks and Recreation 4.0
   Housing and Community Development 4.0
Debt Outstanding per Capita $614
   % Utility 9.4
Federal Procurement Contract Awards (in millions) $50.3
Federal Grants Awards (in millions) $143.2
Fiscal Year Begins July 1

Economy

Total Money Income (in millions) $1,493.5
% of State Average 87.2
Per Capita Annual Income $9,501
% Population below Poverty Level 20.4
Fortune 500 Companies 3

Banks	Number	Deposits (in millions)
Commercial	12	11,184.2
Savings	6	3,295.0

Passenger Autos 95,241 (city)
Electric Meters 357,056
Gas Meters 48,630 (city)

Manufacturing

Number of Establishments 844
% with 20 or More Employees 26.4
Manufacturing Payroll (in millions) $461.1
Value Added by Manufacture (in millions) $870.4
Value of Shipments (in millions) $1,608.3
New Capital Expenditures (in millions) $87.9

Wholesale Trade

Number of Establishments 438
Sales (in millions) $1,965.4
Annual Payroll (in millions) $155.061

Retail Trade

Number of Establishments 1,546
Total Sales (in millions) $830.0
Sales per Capita $5,280
Number of Retail Trade Establishments with Payroll 1,116
Annual Payroll (in millions) $108.2
Total Sales (in millions) $801.4
General Merchandise Stores (per capita) $353
Food Stores (per capita) $857
Apparel Stores (per capita) $300
Eating and Drinking Places (per capita) $603

Economy (continued)

Service Industries

Total Establishments   1,635
Total Receipts (in millions) $815.5
Hotels and Motels (in millions) $30.3
Health Services (in millions) $178.1
Legal Services (in millions) $181.6

manufacturing and finance. Among its manufacturing industries are jewelry and silverware. As a financial center, it is home to four of the largest financial concerns in the country. Tourism is an emerging industry supported by the city's role as a major convention center.

Labor

 Among the largest employers are Providence's three principal hospitals, as well as Brown University, New England Telephone, First National Bank, and Rhode Island Hospital Trust National Bank. Providence has one of the lowest percentages of private-sector unionized workers in New England—13%.

Labor

Civilian Labor Force   76,229
% Change 1989–1990   -1.1
Work Force Distribution
    Mining   100
    Construction   9,800
    Manufacturing   58,000
    Transportation and Public Utilities   11,200
    Wholesale and Retail Trade   60,100
    FIRE (Finance, Insurance, Real Estate)   21,500
    Service   95,700
    Government   45,200
    Women as % of Labor Force   46.4
    % Self-Employed   4
    % Professional/Technical   15.8
Total Unemployment   5,533
Rate %   7.3
Federal Government Civilian Employment   3,643

Education

The public school system consists of 35 senior high, junior high/middle, and elementary schools. Providence's best-known educational institution is Brown University, an Ivy League school, located on College Hill. It is the oldest college in New England and the seventh-oldest in the United States. It was founded by charter in 1764 as the Rhode Island College at Warren with the Reverend James Manning as first president. In 1770 it was moved to Providence into the College Edifice on an eight-acre tract of land. In 1804 the name was changed to Brown University, in recognition of a gift from Nicholas Brown. Brown is noted for its Medical School and its research programs in engineering, liberal arts, and science. Providence is also home to Rhode Island College, Johnson and Wales College, Providence College, and the Rhode Island School of Design (RISD).

Education

Number of Public Schools   35
Special Education Schools   NA
Total Enrollment   20,908
% Enrollment in Private Schools   14.3
% Minority   61.5
Classroom Teachers   786
Pupil-Teacher Ratio   26:1
Number of Graduates   747
Total Revenue (in millions) $92.735
Total Expenditures (in millions) $91.979
Expenditures per Pupil $4,586
Educational Attainment (Age 25 and Over)
    % Completed 12 or More Years   53.4
    % Completed 16 or More Years   15.7
Four-Year Colleges and Universities   5
    Enrollment   32,552
Two-Year Colleges   NA
    Enrollment   NA

Libraries

Number   46
Public Libraries   10
Books (in thousands)   1,017
Circulation (in thousands)   NA
Persons Served (in thousands)   956
Circulation per Person Served   NA
Income (in millions) $3.904
Staff   132

Four-Year Colleges and Universities
    Brown University
    Johnson and Wales College
    Providence College
    Rhode Island College
    Rhode Island School of Design

Health

 Providence is served by seven health-care facilities, all of them of the highest caliber. Five of them are affiliated with the Brown University Medical School: Rhode Island Hospital, the oldest medical facility in the state; Women's and Children's Hospital; Miriam Hospital; Roger Williams Hospital; and the Veterans Administration Medical Center. St. Joseph Hospital is the state's second-largest. Butler Hospital specializes in psychiatric and substance abuse treatment.

Health

Deaths—Total   1,850
Rate per 1,000   12.0
Infant Deaths—Total   30
Rate per 1,000   11.6
Number of Metro Hospitals   7
Number of Metro Hospital Beds   2,240
Rate per 100,000   1,425
Number of Physicians   2,029
Physicians per 1,000   3.64
Nurses per 1,000   NA
Health Expenditures per Capita $0.88

Transportation

 The principal interstates serving Providence are 95, 105, and 295. Interstate 95, the major north-south route, connects

Providence with Boston to the north and New York, Washington, D.C., and Philadelphia to the south. Interstate 295 is a 23-mile beltway. Interstate 195 connects Providence with southeastern Massachusetts and Cape Cod. Railroad freight service is provided by the Providence and Worcester Railroad and passenger service by Amtrak. A new railroad station was completed as part of the Capital Center project. The Port of Providence at the head of Narragansett Bay has a 40-foot-deep channel that is 600 to 1,300 feet wide. The port has 27 public and private docks. Municipal Wharf, owned and operated by the city, has 4,750 feet of berthing space. The Theodore Francis Green State Airport, nine miles south of the city, handles all of the city's commercial air traffic. It is served by 11 airlines providing 270 scheduled flights daily. For international flights, the nearest airport is Logan in Boston.

Transportation
Interstate Highway Mileage   71
Total Urban Mileage   4,345
Total Daily Vehicle Mileage (in millions) $17.707
Daily Average Commute Time   39.6 min.
Number of Buses   197
Port Tonnage (in millions) $7.837
Airports   1
Number of Daily Flights   37
Daily Average Number of Passengers   2,609
Airlines (American carriers only)
American
Continental
Delta
Eastern
Midway
Northwest
USAir
United

Housing

Buildable real estate is limited in Providence and most people who work in the city live in the suburbs. Because of the location of the city in the middle of the state, commuting is easy. Some 40% live in owner-occupied housing

Housing		
Total Housing Units 66,794		
% Change 1980–1990 -1.1		
Vacant Units for Sale or Rent 5,760		
Occupied Units 58,905		
% with More Than One Person per Room 6.0		
% Owner-Occupied 36.2		
Median Value of Owner-Occupied Homes $113,000		
Average Monthly Purchase Cost $392		
Median Monthly Rent $389		
New Private Housing Starts 313		
Value (in thousands) $8,848		
% Single-Family 34.5		
Nonresidential Buildings Value (in thousands) $2,496		
Tallest Buildings	*Hgt. (ft.)*	*Stories*
Fleet National Bank	420	26
Rhode Island Hospital		
Trust Tower	410	30
40 Westminster Bldg.	301	24

and 60% in rented dwellings and apartments. Major new apartment and condominium developments include the 290-apartment Providence Square, the 87-unit Renaissance Center just west of downtown, the 37-condo Conrad Building, the 97-condo Gateway Center, and the 595-unit Riverview Place. The upscale neighborhoods are Barrington, East Greenwich, and Lincoln, while the more affordable ones are Bristol-Warren, Cranston, East Providence, Warwick, and North Providence.

Urban Redevelopment

Providence's most ambitious redevelopment plan to date is the Capital Center project on 70 acres of previously undeveloped downtown property along which, until 1977, rail tracks wound their way. Scheduled for completion in 1994, the plan involves redirecting the two rivers and constructing commercial office space, one or more hotels, residential units, and parking at a cost of $100 million in public funds and $500 million in private funds. A $100-million convention center and a $300-million, 1.4–million-square-foot office/retail complex known as Providence Place will also be included in the Capital Center. Other redevelopment projects include:

- The $75-million adaptive reuse of the historic Union Station.
- Gateway Center, a $90-million office/hotel/condominium complex on 2.9 acres.
- Adaptive reuse of the 26-acre Brown and Sharpe Iron Foundry creating 1 million square feet of office space in eight modern buildings.

Crime

In 1991 violent crimes reported to police totaled 2,055 and property crimes totaled 14,275.

Crime
Violent Crimes—Total   2,055
Violent Crime Rate per 100,000   509.1
Murder   18
Rape   107
Robbery   804
Aggravated Assaults   1,126
Property Crimes   14,275
Burglary   3,707
Larceny   6,865
Motor Vehicle Theft   3,703
Arson   479
Per Capita Police Expenditures $131.31
Per Capita Fire Protection Expenditures $125.81
Number of Police   412
Per 1,000   2.66

Religion

Since the 19th-century immigration waves, which brought in thousands of Italians, Providence has been heavily Roman Catholic.

Religion

Largest Denominations (Adherents)	
Catholic	423,608
Episcopal	14,253
American Baptist	13,095
Armenian	9,000
United Church of Christ	6,535
United Methodist	4,708
Black Baptist	7,817
Jewish	10,267

Media

Providence's only daily is *The Providence Journal-Bulletin*. There are three television stations and eight AM and FM radio stations.

Media

Newsprint
    The New Paper, weekly
    The Providence Journal-Bulletin, daily

Television
    WJAR (Channel 10)
    WLNE (Channel 6)
    WPRI (Channel 12)

Radio

WALE (AM)	WBRU (FM)
WDOM (FM)	WLKW (AM)
WWLI (FM)	WRCP (AM)
WRBU (AM)	WWBB (FM)

Sports

College athletics and sports make up for the lack of franchised sports teams. The Civic Center is a large stadium that seats up to 13,000.

Arts, Culture, and Tourism

Theatrical performances began in the city in 1761 and have continued to this day. Both the Providence Performing Arts Center and the Providence Civic Center offer a

Travel and Tourism

Hotel Rooms   2,642
Convention and Exhibit Space (square feet)   NA

Convention Centers
    Providence Civic Center

Festivals
    Festival of Historic Homes (May)
    Annual Heritage Festival (September)

variety of concerts and plays. The Ocean State Center for the Performing Arts is home to the Rhode Island Philharmonic Orchestra and the Rhode Island State Ballet Company. The nationally acclaimed Trinity Repertory Company, the largest and the oldest permanent ensemble in the nation, presents 12 productions annually at the restored Lederer Theater.

The Museum of Rhode Island History is housed in an 1822 Federal mansion. The Museum of Art of the Rhode Island School of Design presents a wide-ranging collection, while the nearby Pendleton House presents a small collection of American furniture and silverware.

Parks and Recreation

The city has 104 parks and playgrounds of which the largest is Roger Williams Park.

Sources of Further Information

City Hall
25 Dorrance Street
Providence, RI 02903
(401) 421-7740

Greater Providence Convention and Visitors Bureau
30 Exchange Terrace
Providence, RI 02903
(401) 274-1636

Providence Public Library
150 Empire Street
Providence, RI 02903
(401) 521-7722

Rhode Island Department of Economic Development
7 Jackson Walkway
Providence, RI 02903
(401) 277-2601

Rhode Island Historical Society
121 Hope Street
Providence, RI 02906
(401) 331-8575

Additional Reading

Conley, Patrick, and Paul Campbell. *Providence: A Pictorial History*. 1983.
Gilkeson, John S. *Middle-Class Providence, 1820–1940*. 1986.
Woodward, W. McKenzie. *Providence: A City-Wide Survey of Historic Resources*. 1986.

Richmond

Virginia

Location and Topography

Richmond is located on both banks of the James River between Tidewater, Virginia, and the Piedmont. The Blue Ridge Mountain ranges lie to the east and the Chesapeake Bay to the west.

Layout of City and Suburbs

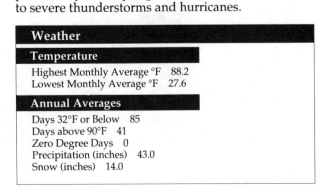

From Church Hill, the heart of Richmond, six long streets extend to the west of the city. Residences and apartment houses extend from Monroe Park to the city limits and south along the Boulevard. Across the river, South Richmond, formerly Manchester, has a large business district. Suburban areas extend westward along both banks of the river. The principal shopping district is concentrated on Broad, Grace, and Franklin streets between First and Ninth streets. The financial district is on Main Street between Seventh and Twelfth streets. Cary Street is primarily mercantile. Capitol Square is the center of Old Richmond where many historic buildings evoke the styles of an earlier age.

Environment

Environmental Stress Index   3.4
Green Cities Index: Rank   60
                     Score   23.57
Water Quality   Alkaline, soft, fluoridated
    Average Daily Use (gallons per capita)   131
    Maximum Supply (gallons per capita)   144
Parkland as % of Total City Area   5
% Waste Landfilled/Recycled   NA
Annual Parks Expenditures per Capita $77.87

Climate

Richmond has a continental climate with warm, humid summers and mild winters. Rainfall is distributed fairly evenly throughout the year, except for the fall when dry spells lasting for several weeks are common. Snowfall is generally light, less than 15 inches annually. The James River is subject to periodic flooding, particularly in the spring. Richmond is also vulnerable to severe thunderstorms and hurricanes.

Weather

Temperature

Highest Monthly Average °F   88.2
Lowest Monthly Average °F   27.6

Annual Averages

Days 32°F or Below   85
Days above 90°F   41
Zero Degree Days   0
Precipitation (inches)   43.0
Snow (inches)   14.0

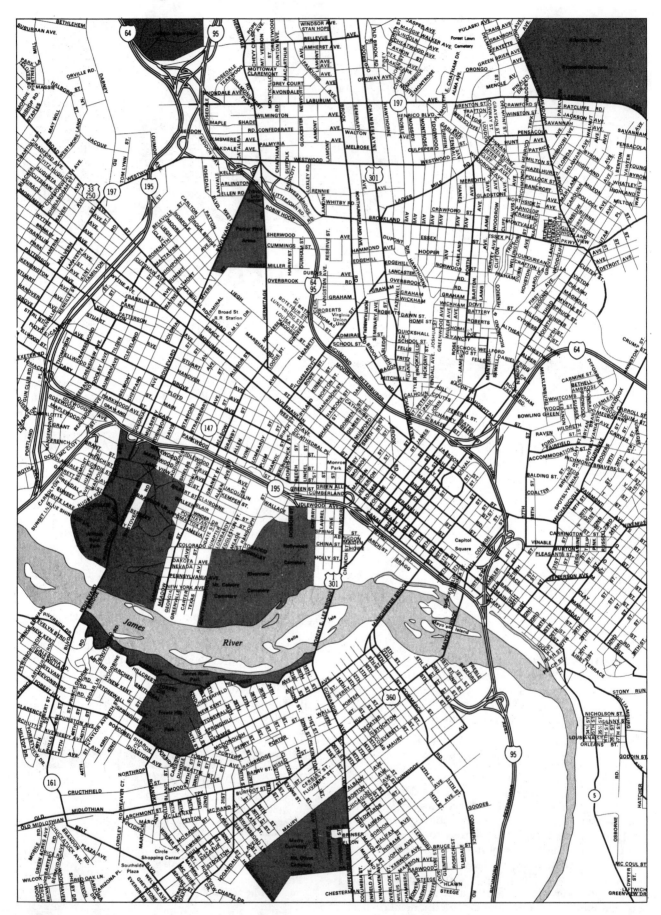

Weather (continued)			
% Seasonal Humidity 72			
Wind Speed (m.p.h.) 7.5			
Clear Days 103			
Cloudy Days 155			
Storm Days 37			
Rainy Days 113			
Average Temperatures (°F)	*High*	*Low*	*Mean*
January	47.4	27.6	37.5
February	49.9	28.8	39.4
March	58.2	35.5	46.9
April	70.3	45.2	57.8
May	78.4	54.5	66.5
June	85.4	62.9	74.2
July	88.2	67.5	77.9
August	86.6	65.9	76.3
September	80.9	59.0	70.0
October	71.2	47.4	59.3
November	60.6	37.3	49.0
December	49.1	28.8	39.0

History

A week after the English landed at Jamestown in 1607, Captain Christopher Newport sailed up the James River and set up a cross on a small island near the foot of present-day Seventh Street. Two years later Captain Francis West purchased a site at the falls from the Indians, and erected a fort that he named Fort West. Shortly thereafter the settlement was abandoned. In 1610 Lord Delaware returned briefly to the falls. After another 27 years passed, Thomas Stegg established a trading post on what is now Richmond. He was later granted land around the falls. His son, Thomas Stegg II, who had acquired property on both sides of the river, left his property to his nephew, William Byrd I. Since the settlement was in a region inhabited by the Algonquin Indians, there was constant conflict, which culminated in a massacre in 1644. After that incident, the settlers erected Fort Charles and offered freedom from taxation to anyone who would establish a home. Among those who did so was Nathaniel Bacon. The settlement at Fort Charles, also known as Byrd's Warehouse, became a trading post for furs, tobacco, and other commodities. Despite the hostility of the Indians leading to Bacon's Rebellion of 1676, the Byrd family continued to lay the foundations for new colonies. By 1733, Petersburg and Richmond were laid out, and by 1769 Shoccoes was added on the north bank of the James River and Manchester at Rocky Ridge on the south side. Of these settlements Richmond grew more rapidly than others. In the 1770s it became the site of four conventions: the First Virginia Convention of 1774, which elected delegates to the First Continental Congress; the Second Virginia Convention of March 1775 at St. John's Church, where Patrick Henry made his impassioned plea for liberty or death; the Third Convention of July 1775, which appointed the Committee of Safety; and a Fourth Convention, also in the same year. In 1779, Richmond, with a population of 684, was made the capital of Virginia. The town played an important role in the last days of the Revolution, suffered pillaging by the British under Benedict Ar-

nold, and was saved only by the arrival of LaFayette. With the end of the war, Richmond became an important political center in the new republic. Four newspapers were established, including the *Virginia Gazette*. In 1782 Richmond was chartered as a town. In 1788 the Jeffersonian capitol went up in Capitol Square. The town's growth was spurred by developments in transportation. In 1784 the James River Transportation Company was chartered, and six years later a canal was opened from Richmond to Westham. In 1836 the Richmond, Fredericksburg and Potomac Railway opened for business, and in 1840 the James River and Kanawha Canal was completed. In 1842 Richmond became a city. At the height of its prosperity, Richmond was plunged into the Civil War. Thousands of Richmonders celebrated the secession in the streets. In May 1861 the Confederate capital was moved from Montgomery, Alabama, to Richmond. As the capital, Richmond became the objective of Union generals, such as George McClellan, who came within sight of Richmond in 1862. In 1865, as the war was winding down, Richmond was burned by its own citizens. After the war, Richmond began the rebuilding of its economy. Within the next 50 years it emerged from the rubble to become one of the most influential banking and cultural centers in the new South.

Historical Landmarks

The state capitol is one of the oldest in the nation. Planned by Thomas Jefferson with the help of the French architect Charles Louis Clarisseau, it was begun in 1785 and completed in 1792. Inside French sculptor Houdon's life-size statue of George Washington stands in the Rotunda. The governor's mansion was built in 1813. St. Paul's Episcopal Church on the corner of Ninth and Grace streets, dedicated in 1845, was known as the Church of the Confederacy, since both Robert E. Lee and Jefferson Davis worshipped there. John Marshall's House on the corner of Ninth and Marshall streets was built soon after 1789 and was the home of Chief Justice John Marshall until his death in 1835. Grace House, on the corner of 19th and Grace streets, is a two-story, white frame house built by Adam Craig in the 18th century. St. John's Church on Broad Street is noted as the church where the Second Virginia Convention was held and where Patrick Henry made his impassioned plea for taking up arms in defense of liberty. It was built in 1741 on the grounds donated by William Byrd. The Edgar Allan Poe Shrine on Main Street is a little gray stone cottage. It is apparently the oldest house in Richmond, having been built in 1686. The Masonic Hall on Franklin Street is a white frame building erected in 1785 through the efforts of Chief Justice John Marshall. The Caskie House on the corner of Main and Fifth streets is a two-story red brick building built about 1815. Monument Avenue is dotted with statues of five distinguished Virginians, J. E. B. Stuart, General Lee, Jefferson Davis, Stonewall Jackson, and Commodore Matthew Fontaine Maury. The Confederate Memorial Institute, or Battle Abbey, on Boulevard is an

Chronology

1607 Captain Christopher Newport lands at Jamestown, sails up the James River, and sets up a cross on a small island.

1609 Captain Francis West purchases a site at the falls of the James River and erects Fort West.

1610 Lord Delaware leads an expedition to the falls seeking minerals.

1637 Thomas Stegg establishes a trading post at the site. His son, Thomas Stegg II, acquires land on both banks of the river.

1644 After a massacre of the settlers by Indians, Fort Charles is established as a protective stockade for settlers.

1670 Stegg leaves his holdings to his nephew, William Byrd I.

1676 Bacon's Rebellion is precipitated by settler-Indian conflicts.

1733 William Byrd II lays foundations of Richmond and Petersburg.

1769 William Byrd III founds Shoccoes and Manchester.

1774 First Virginia Convention meets in Williamsburg.

1775 Second, Third, and Fourth Virginia Conventions meet in town.

1779 Richmond is made capital of Virginia.

1781 Richmond is pillaged by the British under Benedict Arnold.

1782 Virginia is chartered as a town.

1788 The Jeffersonian capitol is erected in Capitol Square.

1790 A canal is opened from Richmond to Westham.

1836 Richmond, Fredericksburg, and Potomac Railway opens.

1840 James River and Kanawha Canal opens.

1842 Richmond becomes a city.

1861 Virginia secedes from the Union. The Confederate capital is moved to Richmond.

1865 Richmond is evacuated and burned by Confederates.

1887 Electric cars are introduced.

oblong windowless building of white marble completed in 1913. Other fine homes in Richmond include Ampthill, a red brick house built on Ampthill Road about 1732 and Reveille on Cary Street Road. Dabbs House is a pre–Civil War home that was used by General Lee as headquarters during the Seven Days Battle in 1862. The White House of the Confederacy, designed by Robert Mills, was the residence of Jefferson Davis during the Civil War. Marymont is a 100-acre late Victorian home with formal Japanese and Italian gardens and an arboretum. Agecroft Hall and Virginia House are medieval English manor houses transported from England and reconstructed in Richmond. The first was built in 1490, before America was discovered, and the second in the 16th century. The 17th-Century Market is a farmer's market that dates back 300 years.

Population

 Richmond has been steadily shedding population since the 1960s. From 249,000 in 1970 the population shrunk by 12.1% to 219,214 in 1980 and by a further 7.4% to 203,056 in 1990. The metro area, however, has gained by 13.7% during the 1980s.

Population		
	1980	*1990*
Central City	219,214	203,056
Rank	64	76
Metro Area	761,311	865,640
Pop. Change 1980–1990 -16,158		
Pop. % Change 1980–1990 -7.4		
Median Age 33.2		
% Male 45.7		
% Age 65 and Over 15.4		
Density (per square mile) 3,378		

Households		
Number 85,337		
Persons per Household 2.25		
% Female-Headed Households 19.8		
% One-Person Households 35.9		
Births—Total 3,414		
% to Mothers under 20 16.7		
Birth Rate per 1,000 15.6		

Ethnic Composition

Blacks make up the majority in Richmond with 55.22%, whites make up 43.35%, American Indians 0.23%, Asians and Pacific Islanders 0.88%, and others 0.32%.

Ethnic Composition (as % of total pop.)		
	1980	*1990*
White	47.78	43.35
Black	51.25	55.22
American Indian	0.16	0.23
Asian and Pacific Islander	0.45	0.88
Hispanic	1.01	0.93
Other	NA	0.32

Government

 Richmond is governed by a council-manager form of government. The city manager is the chief executive hired by a council of nine members elected to two-year terms. The city council also elects the mayor, a largely ceremonial position.

Government

Year of Home Charter   NA
Number of Members of the Governing Body   9
Elected at Large   NA
Elected by Wards   9
Number of Women in Governing Body   3
Salary of Mayor $17,000
Salary of Council Members $15,000
City Government Employment Total   10,061
Rate per 10,000   462.1

Public Finance

The annual budget consists of revenues of $654.730 million and expenditures of $682.684 million. The debt outstanding is $682.144 million and cash and security holdings of $495.768 million.

Public Finance

Total Revenue (in millions) $654.730
Intergovernmental Revenue—Total (in millions) $174.1
Federal Revenue per Capita $33.78
% Federal Assistance   5.16
% State Assistance   21.15
Sales Tax as % of Total Revenue   8.85
Local Revenue as % of Total Revenue   52.97
City Income Tax   no
Taxes—Total (in millions) $178.2

Taxes per Capita
   Total $819
   Property $489
   Sales and Gross Receipts $223
General Expenditures—Total (in millions) $365.6
General Expenditures per Capita $1,679
Capital Outlays per Capita $132

% of Expenditures for:
   Public Welfare   10.7
   Highways   4.2
   Education   35.7
   Health and Hospitals   1.5
   Police   7.4
   Sewerage and Sanitation   5.9
   Parks and Recreation   3.9
   Housing and Community Development   6.7
Debt Outstanding per Capita $1,808
   % Utility   21.5
Federal Procurement Contract Awards (in millions) $96.7
Federal Grants Awards (in millions) $677.1
Fiscal Year Begins   July 1

Economy

Richmond's economy are tobacco, chemicals, metals, and banking. Richmond has built up solid industrial leadership in these areas and is home to some of the largest corporations, such as Philip Morris, American Brands, RJR, Nabisco, E. I. du Pont, ICI, and CSX. A large number of European manufacturing operations are also based in Richmond. Its banking and insurance sector is one of the largest in the nation. Richmond is the headquarters of the Fifth Federal Reserve District as well as seven of the largest insurance companies.

Economy

Total Money Income (in millions) $2,383.1
% of State Average   92.0
Per Capita Annual Income $10,947
% Population below Poverty Level   19.3
Fortune 500 Companies   7

Banks	Number	Deposits (in millions)
Commercial & Savings	15	26,298.5
Savings & Loan	14	5,427.5

Passenger Autos   120,148
Electric Meters   352,861
Gas Meters   72,000

Manufacturing

Number of Establishments   428
% with 20 or More Employees   43.7
Manufacturing Payroll (in millions) $1,302.0
Value Added by Manufacture (in millions) $5,206.6
Value of Shipments (in millions) $8,280.4
New Capital Expenditures (in millions) $203.1

Wholesale Trade

Number of Establishments   896
Sales (in millions) $4,791.8
Annual Payroll (in millions) $279.334

Retail Trade

Number of Establishments   2,256
Total Sales (in millions) $1,945.0
Sales per Capita $8,934
Number of Retail Trade Establishments with Payroll   1,787
Annual Payroll (in millions) $245.5
Total Sales (in millions) $1,926.2
General Merchandise Stores (per capita) $345
Food Stores (per capita) $1,697
Apparel Stores (per capita) $403
Eating and Drinking Places (per capita) $910

Service Industries

Total Establishments   2,414
Total Receipts (in millions) $1,561.4
Hotels and Motels (in millions) $60.9
Health Services (in millions) $404.9
Legal Services (in millions) $199.5

Labor

 The largest employment sector is trade, followed by services, government, and manufacturing, in that order. The share of women is high as is the share of professional white-collar workers. As a right-to-work state, less than 10% of the workers are unionized. Richmond has a low work-stoppage record.

Labor

Civilian Labor Force   114,064
% Change 1989–1990   1.4

Work Force Distribution
    Mining   700
    Construction   28,100
    Manufacturing   64,100
    Transportation and Public Utilities   23,700
    Wholesale and Retail Trade   106,800
    FIRE (Finance, Insurance, Real Estate)   39,100
    Service   107,500
    Government   95,600
    Women as % of Labor Force   49.7
    % Self-Employed   3.3
    % Professional/Technical   17.7
Total Unemployment   6,008
Rate %   5.3
Federal Government Civilian Employment   9,713

Education

The Richmond Public Schools support 58 schools. Higher eduation is offered by six institutions. The Virginia Commonwealth University is the state's largest public university. The University of Richmond, founded in 1830 as Richmond College, is one of the largest private institutions in the state. It includes the T. C. Williams School of Law, Westhampton College, the Graduate School, and the E. Claiborne Robins School of Business. Other institutions are the Virginia Union University, Union Theological Seminary, Presbyterian School of Christian Education, and J. Sargeant Reynolds Community College.

Education

Number of Public Schools   58
Special Education Schools   7
Total Enrollment   27,021
% Enrollment in Private Schools   5.9
% Minority   0.0
Classroom Teachers   1,804
Pupil-Teacher Ratio   14.9
Number of Graduates   1,118
Total Revenue (in millions) $160.784
Total Expenditures (in millions) $159.264
Expenditures per Pupil $5,541
Educational Attainment (Age 25 and Over)
    % Completed 12 or More Years   57.1
    % Completed 16 or More Years   19.8
Four-Year Colleges and Universities   3
    Enrollment   27,921
Two-Year Colleges   2
    Enrollment   14,169

Libraries

Number   59
Public Libraries   9
Books (in thousands)   762
Circulation (in thousands)   833
Persons Served (in thousands)   213
Circulation per Person Served   3.91
Income (in millions) $3.209
Staff   126

Education (continued)

Four-Year Colleges and Universities
    Virginia Commonwealth University
    University of Richmond
    Virginia Union University

Health

Richmond has 19 general and specialized hospitals with over 4,000 beds. The largest is the 1,058-bed Medical College of Virginia, affiliated with the Virginia Commonwealth University. The second largest is the Hunter Holmes McGuire Veterans Administration Medical Center, followed by Chippenham, south of the James River; Richmond Memorial Hospital; St. Mary's Hospital, a Bon Secours facility; Henrico Doctor's Hospital; Johnston-Willis Hospital; St. Luke's Hospital, now part of the Humana network; Metropolitan Hospital; and Stuart Circle Hospital. Psychiatric treatment is offered in Westbrook Hospital; Tucker Pavilion, a part of Chippenham Hospital; and the Psychiatric Institute of Richmond. Richmond Eye and Ear Hospital is a specialized hospital.

Health

Deaths—Total   2,685
Rate per 1,000   12.3
Infant Deaths—Total   64
Rate per 1,000   18.7
Number of Metro Hospitals   19
Number of Metro Hospital Beds   4,730
Rate per 100,000   2,173
Number of Physicians   2,094
Physicians per 1,000   2.97
Nurses per 1,000   19.57
Health Expenditures per Capita $73.79

Transportation

Richmond is approached by I-95, the major north-south artery that runs through the middle of the city. It is intersected by I-64, an east-west route from St. Louis to Hampton Roads. Interstates 295 and 195 serve as belt parkways feeding the interstates. Richmond is also served by U.S. Highways 1, 33, 60, 250, 301, and 360 and State Highways 5, 6, and 10.

Rail passenger services are provided by Amtrak and freight transportation services by CSX, headquartered in Richmond; Southern; and Richmond, Fredericksburg, and Potomac. The Port of Richmond,

Transportation

Interstate Highway Mileage   62
Total Urban Mileage   2,373
Total Daily Vehicle Mileage (in millions) $14.219
Daily Average Commute Time   48.8 min.
Number of Buses   163
Port Tonnage (in millions) $2.574
Airports   1
Number of Daily Flights   50
Daily Average Number of Passengers   2,265

Transportation (continued)

Airlines (American carriers only)
Air Wisconsin
American
Delta
Eastern
United
USAir

recently modernized, has become a major facility with 250,000 square feet of warehouse space, 20,000 acres of open storage, multiple berths, and container handling facilities.

Housing

Of the total housing stock 46.3% is owner-occupied. The median value of an owner-occupied home is $66,600, and the median monthly rent $333.

Housing	
Total Housing Units	94,141
% Change 1980–1990	2.8
Vacant Units for Sale or Rent	6,457
Occupied Units	85,337
% with More Than One Person per Room	3.1
% Owner-Occupied	46.3
Median Value of Owner-Occupied Homes	$66,600
Average Monthly Purchase Cost	$369
Median Monthly Rent	$333
New Private Housing Starts	278
Value (in thousands)	$15,966
% Single-Family	92.8
Nonresidential Buildings Value (in thousands)	$18,450

Tallest Buildings	Hgt. (ft.)	Stories
James Monroe Bldg.	450	29
City Hall (incl. penthouse)	425	17
Crestar Bank Hdqt. Bldg.	400	24
Federal Reserve Bank	393	26
Sovran Center	333	25

Urban Redevelopment

Urban redevelopment programs are coordinated by a number of organizations, including Central Richmond Association, Richmond Economic Development Office, Richmond Regional Planning District Commission, and Richmond Renaissance.

Crime

Richmond ranks below national average in public safety. In 1991 violent crimes totaled 3,414 and property crimes totaled 20,503.

Crime	
Violent Crimes—Total	3,414
Violent Crime Rate per 100,000	591.6
Murder	116
Rape	150
Robbery	1,449
Aggravated Assaults	1,699
Property Crimes	20,503

Crime (continued)

Burglary	4,822
Larceny	12,941
Motor Vehicle Theft	2,740
Arson	207
Per Capita Police Expenditures	$172.04
Per Capita Fire Protection Expenditures	$128.11
Number of Police	612
Per 1,000	2.76

Religion

Richmond is one of the most important centers of Southern Baptists. Black Baptists rank next, followed by Methodists and Catholics.

Religion	
Largest Denominations (Adherents)	
Catholic	29,445
Southern Baptist	59,260
United Methodist	30,646
Black Baptist	45,718
Presbyterian	17,113
Episcopal	15,769
American Baptist	18,111
Assembly of God	2,018
Jewish	3,001

Media

The city's daily is the *Richmond Times-Dispatch*. The electronic media consist of 6 television stations (two network affiliates, two public and two independents) and 15 AM and FM radio stations.

Media	
Newsprint	
Richmond Times-Dispatch, daily	
Virginia Business, monthly	
Television	
WCVE (Channel 23)	
WCVW (Channel 57)	
WRIC (Channel 8)	
WRLH (Channel 35)	
WTVR (Channel 6)	
WWBT (Channel 12)	

Radio	
WCDX (FM)	WCLM (AM)
WCVE (FM)	WDYL (FM)
WFTH (AM)	WGGM (AM)
WKHK (FM)	WLEE (AM)
WMXB (FM)	WRNL (AM)
WRXL (FM)	WRVA (AM)
WTVR (AM)	WTVR (FM)
WXGI (AM)	

Sports

The 12,176-seat Richmond Coliseum is an air-conditioned dome where major sports events and games are held. The 12,500-seat Diamond is the home of the Richmond Braves, a Triple A team of the Atlanta Braves. In football, the Gold Bowl Classic is one of 21 college football games held every year. The Hermitage Country Club hosts a senior Professional Golfers Association Tournament every year. The state fair is held at the Virginia State Fairgrounds, where stock car and motorcycle races are popular features.

Arts, Culture, and Tourism

The umbrella organization for the performing arts in Richmond is the Arts Council of Richmond, which sponsors numerous arts programs. The cultural hub of Richmond is the Carpenter Center for the Performing Arts in the renovated old Loew's Theater, built in 1928. The Center is the home of the Richmond Symphony, which performs the Masterworks Series. Another musical arena is the Richmond Sinfonia, whose Weekend Ovation Series is performed at the Virginia Commonwealth University's Performing Arts Center. The Virginia Opera Association typically stages four productions every season. Other musical groups include the Richmond Pops/Great Big Band, Richmond Concert Band, Richmond Chamber Players, Richmond Community Orchestra, Richmond Classical Guitar Society, and the Richmond Renaissance Singers. Many groups offer outdoor performances including the Brookfield Concert Series, the Langley Air Force TAC Band performances, Out of the Bag Concerts sponsored by Sovran Bank, Terrace Concerts, Music At Noon at Second Presbyterian Church, and the Brandermill Chamber Series. In drama, the most active theaters are the Carpenter Center for the Performing Arts, Theatre Virginia at the Virginia Museum of Fine Arts, and Theater IV. The universities are very active in drama. Theater VCU of the Virginia Commonwealth University presents dramas and musicals at the Shafer Street Playhouse, the University Players at the University of Richmond perform four productions a year in the Camp Theater of the Modlin Fine Arts Center, the Virginia University Players perform in the Wall Auditorium, and the Randolph-Macon Drama Guild presents four plays a season in the Chapel Theater. The Children's Theater produces plays and marionette shows for children. Other theatrical groups include the Henrico Theater Company, the Chamberlayne Actors Theater, the John Rolfe Players, the Soweto Stage Company Board and Chancel Players, the Artists Alliance Theater Company, and the Brandermill's BCT Encore Players. Ballet is represented by the Richmond Ballet and the Concert Ballet of Virginia.

The Virginia Museum of Fine Arts, founded in 1936, is the leading art institution. There are several other fine museums, including the Museum of the Confederacy, displaying one of the largest collections of Civil War memorabilia; the Chesterfield County Museum, a replica of the original courthouse built in 1749; the Science Museum of Virginia; the Fire History Museum; the Edgar Allan Poe Museum; the Virginia E. Randolph Museum, dedicated to the pioneer black educator; the Valentine Museum and Heritage Square; the Virginia Museum for Black History and Archives;

and the Children's Museum. Among art galleries, the most visit-worthy are the Virginia Museum of Fine Arts, Virginia Commonwealth University's Anderson Gallery, Marsh Gallery of the University of Richmond, Neapolitan Gallery, and Last Stop of the National Conference of Artists. In addition there are a number of commercial galleries, such as Schindler, Mayo, Cudahy's, Amber, Isis Studio, Lordan, Baldridge, and Evelyn Christian Arts.

Travel and Tourism

Hotel Rooms   12,035
Convention and Exhibit Space (square feet)   NA

Convention Centers
   Richmond Center for Conventions and Exhibitions
   Richmond Coliseum
   The Mosque
   The Showplace
   Carpenter Center for the Performing Arts

Festivals
   June Jubilee
   Richmond Jazz Festival (fall)
   Dean's Invitational Jazz Festival (spring)
   Boys Club International Festival (September)
   Virginia State Fair (September)
   National Tobacco Festival (October)

Parks and Recreation

The Richmond area has 24,118 acres of parkland, and the city has 34 parks covering 2,000 acres. The James River Park is one of the few wilderness parks in the nation within an urban setting. The Chimbarazo Park on Broad Street is a landscaped promontory overlooking the city. It was purchased by the city in 1874. The 300-acre William Byrd Park at the south end of Boulevard dates from 1874. It contains the Carillon, a 240-foot tower of pink brick, erected in 1832 as a memorial to World War I victims.

Sources of Further Information

City Hall
900 East Broad Street
Richmond, VA 23219
(804) 780-7977

Metro Richmond Chamber of Commerce
201 East Franklin Street
Richmond, VA 23219
(804) 648-1234

Metropolitan Richmond Convention and Visitors
   Bureau
300 East Main Street
Richmond, VA 23219
(804) 782-2777

Richmond Economic Development Office
900 East Broad Street
Richmond, VA 23219

Additional Reading

Bill, Alfred H. *Richmond: The Beleaguered City, 1861–65.* 1980.

Byrd, Odell R. *Richmond: A City of Monuments and Statues.* 1988.

Chesson, Michael B. *Richmond After the War, 1865–1890.* 1981.

Duke, Maurice, and Daniel P. Jordan. *A Richmond Reader.* 1983.

Dulaney, Paul S. *The Architecture of Historic Richmond.* 1976.

Lutz, Francis E. *Richmond in World War II.* 1951.

Rouse, Parker, Jr. *Richmond in Color.* 1979.

Silver, Christopher. *Twentieth-Century Richmond: Planning, Policies, and Race.* 1984.

Ward, Harry M. *Richmond: An Illustrated History.* 1988.

Ward, Harry M., and Harold E. Greer. *Richmond During the Revolution.* 1977.

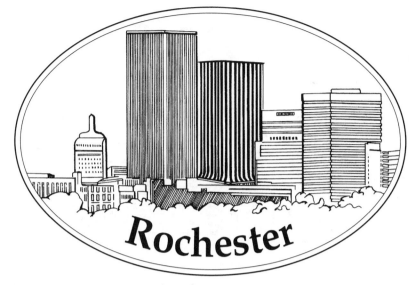

Rochester
New York

Basic Data

Name   Rochester
Name Origin   From Nathaniel Rochester
Year Founded   1811 Inc. 1834
Status: State   New York
      County   Seat of Monroe County
Area (square miles)   35.8
Elevation (feet)   515
Time Zone   EST
Population (1990)   231,636
Population of Metro Area (1990)   1,002,410

Sister Cities
  Bamako, Mali
  Caltanissetta, Italy
  Cracow, Poland
  Novogorod, Russia
  Rehovof, Israel
  Rennes, France
  Waterford, Ireland
  Wurzburg, Germany

Distance in Miles To:
  Albany   227
  New York   360
  Syracuse   97

Location and Topography

N Rochester is located at the mouth of the Genesee River, which bisects the city, at the approximate midpoint of the south shore of Lake Ontario. The city is located on a plateau between 500 and 697 feet above sea level. Three of the falls on the Genesee River are within the city.

Layout of City and Suburbs

The Four Corners—the junction of Main with State and Exchange streets—was for over a century the center of Rochester's city life. The Four Corners remains the financial center, but by the 1920s business moved eastward, following Main Street across the river. From this area

Rochester spreads out in every direction, blending into residential neighborhoods, such as East Avenue. The lakefront, seven miles north of Main Street is reached by Lake Avenue or St. Paul Boulevard. Running through the heart of the city is the Genesee River, spanned by 13 highway bridges.

Like many of the nation's cities, Rochester is looped. In fact, it has two loops: the inner loop roughly defines downtown, consisting mainly of offices, industrial buildings, and stores, but also a small and growing residential population mainly around Grove Place, St. Paul Street, and Manhattan Square Park. The outer loop roughly defines the city limits, curving down from East Ridge Road in Irondequoit to the barge canal, across the bottom of the city to the airport, then curving north to Lake Ontario Parkway. Between the inner and the outer loops are the city's neighborhoods, roughly divided into four major quadrants, split by the east-west Main Street and the north-south Genesee River. Rochester's cultural center is in the Southeast, with the University of Rochester, the Eastman School of Music, the Eastman Theater, the International School of Photography, and the George Eastman House. The Southeast contains Cobbs Hill and Highland Parks, the city's two reservoirs, and half of Genesee Valley Park. The major Southeast neighborhoods are Park Avenue, paralleling East Avenue; Monroe Avenue; South Wedge; Swillburg; Island Park-Strong; the Mount Hope Preservation District; Ellwanger-Barry; and Winto-Nunda-Castlebar. Across the River from the University lies the 19th Ward, or the Southwest, a place of great ethnic diversity. Its commercial heart is Thurston Road. The housing stock ranges from small cottages on Scottsville Road to mansions on West Avenue. Corn Hill is a preservation district with some of the oldest elegant brick houses in the city. Between Corn Hill and the 19th Ward is a very depressed area, and to its north is the Frederick Douglass

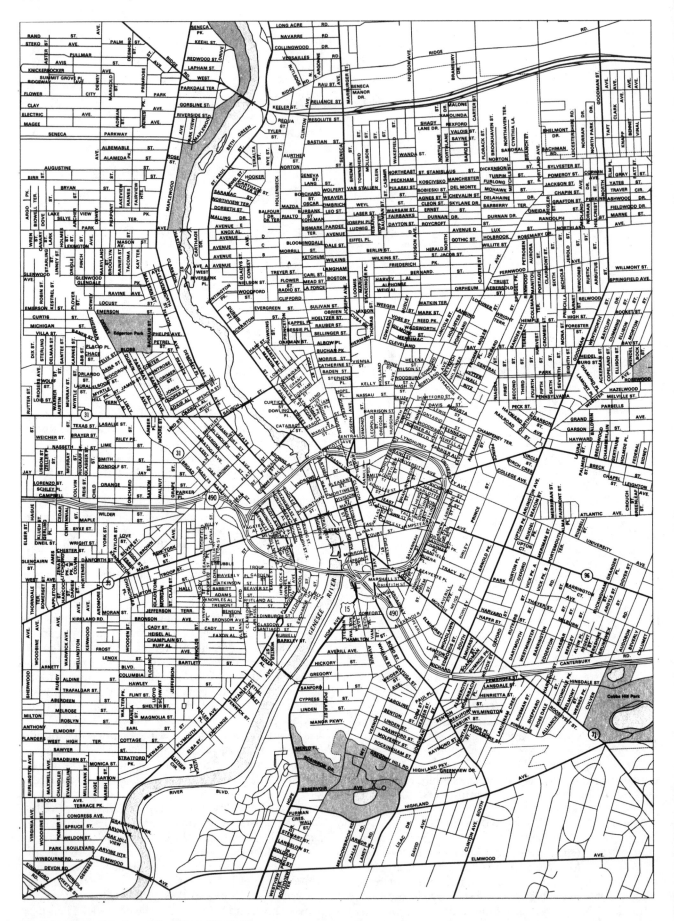

Historic Neighborhood. The Northwest officially begins at West Main Street and includes the Susan B. Anthony Preservation District off of West Main Street. Dutchtown, Brown Square, Lyell-Otis, and Edgerton share Lyell Avenue. Stretching to the north is Maplewood, which extends to Kodak Park. Beyond Kodak Park is Charlotte. The Northeast, more so perhaps than any other part of the city is Rochester's melting pot, where all races are strongly represented for the simple reason that the housing is affordable. Over to the west is a neighborhood known only by its zip code: 14621. Along the river there is Seneca Park, and on Norton Street there is Silver Stadium. On St. Paul Street, north of the old Bausch and Lomb factory, are stately old homes built by the Bausches. The area to the east of Marketview Heights, defined by University Avenue and Norton Street to the city line, is called North East Area Development, and includes Homestead Heights, Beechwood, the Northeast Triangle, and Browncroft. Browncroft has some of the largest and most expensive homes in the city.

Rochester has over 17 suburbs, most of them within minutes of downtown Rochester. They are as follows: Brighton (34,000); Brockport (9,000), the site of a SUNY; Chili (25,000); Churchville-Riga (1,500); Clarkson (4,500); East Rochester (6,900); Fairport-Perinton (43,000); Gates (28,000); Greece (90,000); Hamlin (9,200); Henrietta (36,000); Hilton-Parma (13,000); Honeoye Falls (2,400); Irondequoit (52,000); Mendon (6,800); Penfield (30,000); Pittsford (25,000); and Rush (3,200).

Environment

Environmental Stress Index	2.8
Green Cities Index: Rank	NA
Score	NA
Water Quality	Neutral, soft
Average Daily Use (gallons per capita)	144
Maximum Supply (gallons per capita)	219
Parkland as % of Total City Area	13.6
% Waste Landfilled/Recycled	NA
Annual Parks Expenditures per Capita	$83.81

Climate

Rochester's climate is temperate, moderated by Lake Ontario, which remains unfrozen in winter. Summer temperatures rarely rise above the 90s, and winter temperatures rarely fall below the teens. Precipitation is fairly evenly distributed throughout the year.

Weather

Temperature

Highest Monthly Average °F	82.3
Lowest Monthly Average °F	16.3

Annual Averages

Days 32°F or Below	134
Days above 90°F	7
Zero Degree Days	0
Precipitation (inches)	31.27

Weather (continued)

Snow (inches)	88.9
% Seasonal Humidity	71.5
Wind Speed (m.p.h.)	9.7
Clear Days	62
Cloudy Days	196
Storm Days	29
Rainy Days	159

Average Temperatures (°F)	High	Low	Mean
January	31.6	18.6	25.1
February	37.6	23.4	20.5
March	45.0	29.0	37.0
April	58.6	41.4	50.0
May	73.9	51.7	62.8
June	79.7	56.9	68.3
July	83.1	61.5	72.3
August	80.6	60.0	70.3
September	71.9	49.1	60.5
October	61.7	42.4	52.1
November	45.9	32.1	39.0
December	38.4	22.9	30.7

History

The Genesee River region was the home of the Five Nations of the Iroquois until 1779, when, much weakened by the destruction of their villages by the Revolutionary War general John Sullivan, they were induced to sell speculators a large tract of their land. This transaction became known as the Phelps and Gorham Purchase. The first settler was Ebenezer Indian Allen, who was granted a 100-acre tract of land at the falls of the Genesee on condition that he erect a mill near the site of the present Four Corners in 1789. After Allen moved away with his wives to Mount Morris, his 100-acre plot—a dismal swamp infested with snakes and mosquitoes—was purchased in 1803 by Colonel William Fitzhugh, Major Charles Carroll, and Colonel Nathaniel Rochester, all from Maryland. In 1811 Colonel Rochester offered lots for sale, and the following year Hamlet Scranton became the first settler when he moved with his family into a house on the site of the Powers Building. In 1813 Abelard Reynolds built a home, and in 1815 he opened a tavern. The first newspaper was published in 1816, the year prior to the town's incorporation as Rochesterville. By that time Rochester was one of eight settlements along the last 12 miles of the course of the Genesee. The construction of the Erie Canal through Rochester along what is now Broad Street helped Rochester to absorb all her rivals. By drastically reducing transportation costs, the canal opened eastern markets to the Genesee farmer. Flour mills multiplied along the river banks, and Rochester became known as the Flour City. It also became an important center of canal boat construction.

In 1822 the name *Rochester* was legally adopted and in 1833 Rochester applied for a city charter. Rochester also began to emerge from its early Puritan regime as newer immigrants introduced more liberal mores into city life. With the development of the railroads and the expansion of the West, the flour milling industry declined, and was succeeded in economic importance by the nursery industry. Rochester went from Flour City

Chronology

1788   The Five Nations of the Iroquois sell 2.6 million acres of land along the Genesee River to two Yankee traders, Phelps and Gorham.

1789   Ebenezer Indian Allen is granted a 100-acre tract at the falls of the Genesee to erect a mill for use by the Indians.

1792   Allen leaves for Mount Morris.

1803   Three Marylanders, Colonel William Fitzhugh, Major Charles Carroll, and Colonel Nathaniel Rochester buy Allen's property.

1811   Rochester offers lots for sale.

1812   Hamlet Scranton becomes the first permanent settler in Rochesterville.

1816   The first newspaper is published.

1817   Rochesterville is incorporated as a village.

1822   The village legally adopts the name *Rochester*.

1823   The completion of the Erie Canal through Rochester assures the city's future.

1833   Rochester applies for city charter.

1840   The nursery of Ellwanger and Barry is founded.

1844   Millerites assemble on Pinnacle Hills to witness the end of the world and to be gathered up to heaven.

1847   Frederick Douglass begins publication of the *North Star* from a church basement.

1848   The Fox sisters begin demonstrations of their spiritualist rappings.

1850   The University of Rochester is founded.

1853   Bausch and Lomb open an optical store, and they later began grinding their own lenses.

1880   George Eastman begins manufacturing photographic dry plates.

1887   Casper Pflauder begins manufacture of glass-lined steel tanks. Ellwanger and Barry present 20 acres of land to the city as the nucleus of Highland Park.

1888   The first Kodak camera is placed on the market.

1889   Frank Ritter produces the first dental chair; city electrification begins.

1916   City line is extended north to Lake Ontario.

1922   Strike by shoe workers cripples shoe industry.

1925   Rochester adopts city-manager form of government.

1931   Port of Rochester is enlarged, new piers are built, and the harbor is deepened.

1964   Violent race riot rocks the city.

to Flower City. By the 1840s two of the city nurseries, Ellwanger and Barry and James Vick, were among the largest in the world. The middle decade of the 19th century was noted for its religious and social ferment. In 1844 Millerites assembled on Pinnacle Hills to witness the end of the world; in 1848 the Fox sisters moved from nearby Hydeville to give their spiritualist seances; and in 1847 Frederick Douglass, a runaway slave, began publishing the *North Star* from a church basement, and Susan B. Anthony began preaching the equal rights of women. After the Civil War, Rochester's industrial direction shifted once again to shoes and clothes. By the last decade of the 19th century there were 64 shoe factories in the city. In the clothing industry, the arrival of large numbers of German Jews, skilled in the needle trades; the invention of the sewing machine; and improvements in transportation encouraged mass production of ready-made suits. Even more industries, however, were taking shape in the city, destined to dominate Rochester's industrial future. In 1853 John Jacob Bausch opened his optical store in which his friend Henry Lomb bought a half interest for $60. In 1880, after successful experiments in his mother's kitchen, George Eastman began the manufacturing of photographic dry plates. In 1888 the first Kodak camera was put on the market, placing photography within the reach of millions. In 1906 the Haloid Company, later to become Xerox Corporation, began in a loft above a shoe factory. In 1866 the Vacuum Oil Company, later to become Mobil, was founded. Casper Pfaudler began manufacturing glass-lined steel tanks in 1887, and in 1889 Frank Ritter produced the first dental chair. Industrial growth and Eastman's philanthropy brought a rapid expansion in the city's cultural and educational resources. In 1916 the city line was extended north in a long arm to Lake Ontario. The city-manager form of government was adopted in 1925. A prolonged strike crippled the shoe industry in 1922, yet by the 1930s Rochester became known for its peaceful labor-relations climate.

In 1931 the port of Rochester was expanded, the harbor was deepened, and the municipal piers were built. After World War II, the major event was the race riot of 1964, which galvanized efforts by civic leaders to rebuild the city's slums and ghettoes. The long-neglected Genesee River also was cleaned up. At the same time, developers lured middle-and upper-income residents back to the city.

Historical Landmarks

The Powers Building is an eight-story building, designed by Andrew Jackson Warner, on Main and State streets. It is typical of post–Civil War architecture. When erected in 1870 it was hailed as the first fireproof structure in the city and the only building with elevators. The Board of Education Building on Fitzhugh Street is a good example of Victorian Gothic architecture. It was built in 1874 on the site donated to the city by Colonel Nathaniel Rochester to build the city's first school in 1814. St. Luke's Episcopal Church on Fitzhugh Street, erected in 1824, is Rochester's oldest church. The City Hall on the corner of Fitzhugh and Broad streets is a five-story structure designed by Andrew Jackson Warner. The Jonathan Child House on Washington Street is an interesting example of Greek Revival style. It was built in 1837 by Jonathan Child, Rochester's first mayor. The Livingstone Park Seminary is a white, two-story, Federal style building. Rochester's fame as the birthplace of Spiritualism is evidenced by two buildings: the Fox Sisters' Home and the Plymouth Avenue Spiritualist Church on the corner of Plymouth Avenue and Troup streets. The Whittlesey House on the corner of Troup and Fitzhugh streets is a historical shrine that was erected in 1835. The Broad Street Bridge serves as a roof for what was once the Erie Canal aqueduct; it was considered an engineering marvel when erected in 1842. The Frederick Douglass Monument on Central Avenue and St. Paul Street was dedicated by Theodore Roosevelt in 1899 when he was New York governor. The Early Mission Monument on Blossom Road commemorates the first place of Christian worship in the region; it is a small cabin built of tree bark in 1679 by Franciscan Recollect missionaries. The Lomb Memorial on Bausch Street is a black granite shaft, 48 feet high, on a marble base. The Eastman Memorial at the Lake Avenue entrance of Kodak Park is a large circular plaza paved with Georgia rose marble. A circular pedestal in the center contains a bronze urn with the ashes of Eastman. The Old Charlotte Lighthouse off Lake Avenue was erected in 1822 on a bluff 2,000 feet from the mouth of the Genesee River. The East Avenue Preservation District contains the 49-room Georgian mansion built by George Eastman in 1905. The Woodside Mansion is the headquarters of the Rochester Historical Society. The Third Ward Preservation District on the west side is the site of the Susan B. Anthony Memorial.

Population

Rochester's population in 1990 was 231,636, down by 4.2% from 241,741 in 1980. Rochester's peak population was 324,694 just before World War II. Much of the population has been lost to the city's many suburbs.

Population

	1980	1990
Central City	241,741	231,636
Rank	57	66
Metro Area	971,230	1,002,410
Pop. Change 1980–1990	−10,105	

Population (continued)

Pop. % Change 1980–1990   −4.2
Median Age   29.7
% Male   47.2
% Age 65 and Over   12.1
Density (per square mile)   6,470

Households

Number   93,607
Persons per Household   2.37
% Female-Headed Households   20.6
% One-Person Households   35.3
Births—Total   5,164
    % to Mothers under 20   16.5
    Birth Rate per 1,000   21.3

Ethnic Composition

Whites make up 61% of the population, blacks 31%, and other races account for the remainder. Race relations reached their nadir during the race riot of 1964 but since then have improved. Among the whites, Italians are the most numerous, followed closely by Germans, and then by Canadians, Poles, Irish, and Russians. Rochester has few ethnic neighborhoods, and ethnicity never acquired political significance or caused social cleavages.

Ethnic Composition (as % of total pop.)

	1980	1990
White	69.54	61.09
Black	25.78	31.53
American Indian	0.42	0.48
Asian and Pacific Islander	0.64	1.76
Hispanic	5.44	8.66
Other	NA	5.15

Government

Rochester operates under a mayor-council form of government, first set up under the 1925 charter. The mayor and five council members are elected at large, and four members are elected by district. Rochester also is the seat of Monroe County. Democrats have controlled city government since 1974 and county government since 1987.

Government

Year of Home Charter   1907
Number of Members of the Governing Body   9
Elected at Large   5
Elected by Wards   4
Number of Women in Governing Body   4
Salary of Mayor $87,740
Salary of Council Members $22,714
City Government Employment Total   8,670
Rate per 10,000   367.4

Public Finance

The annual budget consists of revenues of $590.903 million and expenditures of $546.541 million. The outstanding debt is $213.125 million, and cash and security holdings $169.706 million.

Public Finance

Total Revenue (in millions) $590.903
Intergovernmental Revenue—Total (in millions) $317.03
Federal Revenue per Capita $62.23
% Federal Assistance   10.53
% State Assistance   31.78
Sales Tax as % of Total Revenue   1.74
Local Revenue as % of Total Revenue   53.74
City Income Tax   no
Taxes—Total (in millions) $125.9

Taxes per Capita
    Total $534
    Property $473
    Sales and Gross Receipts $6
General Expenditures—Total (in millions) $362.9
General Expenditures per Capita $1,538
Capital Outlays per Capita $194

% of Expenditures for:
    Public Welfare   0.2
    Highways   5.1
    Education   47.9
    Health and Hospitals   0.0
    Police   6.8
    Sewerage and Sanitation   2.8
    Parks and Recreation   1.9
    Housing and Community Development   4.4
Debt Outstanding per Capita $1,008
    % Utility   9.6
Federal Procurement Contract Awards (in millions)
    $138.1
Federal Grants Awards (in millions) $147.5
Fiscal Year Begins   July 1

Economy

Rochester prides itself as a high-technology town and its economy has been relatively recession-proof in the 1990s. The town is dominated by the giant $11.5 billion Eastman Kodak, which employs 45,530 residents—about 9% of the city's work force. In addition, hundreds of local companies are its suppliers. Rochester, however, is not a one-company town. It is the headquarters of two other multibillion dollar companies, Xerox and Bausch and Lomb, as well as many other Fortune 500 companies, such as Gleason Corporation, Pfaudler, Caldwell Manufacturing, and Wegmans. While the importance of the large companies can scarcely be overestimated, the underlying strength of the Rochester economy lies in the hundreds of small entrepreneurial high-technology companies, estimated to number over 450. Rochester's export rate is one of the highest per capita in the country, and the city is a foreign trade zone.

Economy

Total Money Income (in millions) $2,351.9
% of State Average   84.7
Per Capita Annual Income $9,967
% Population below Poverty Level   17.5
Fortune 500 Companies   6

Economy (continued)

Banks	Number	Deposits (in millions)
Commercial	10	NA
Savings	9	NA

Passenger Autos   441,777
Electric Meters   280,000
Gas Meters   240,000

Manufacturing

Number of Establishments   594
% with 20 or More Employees   35.7
Manufacturing Payroll (in millions) $2,331.7
Value Added by Manufacture (in millions) $5,249.2
Value of Shipments (in millions) $8,269.5
New Capital Expenditures (in millions) $521.8

Wholesale Trade

Number of Establishments   622
Sales (in millions) $2,292.1
Annual Payroll (in millions) $190.274

Retail Trade

Number of Establishments   2,022
Total Sales (in millions) $1,247.3
Sales per Capita $5,286
Number of Retail Trade Establishments with Payroll   1,453
Annual Payroll (in millions) $169.0
Total Sales (in millions) $1,213.6
General Merchandise Stores (per capita) $210
Food Stores (per capita) $1,048
Apparel Stores (per capita) $203
Eating and Drinking Places (per capita) $688

Service Industries

Total Establishments   2,029
Total Receipts (in millions) $1,017.8
Hotels and Motels (in millions) $30.4
Health Services (in millions) $178.4
Legal Services (in millions) $158.0

Labor

About one-third of the city's labor force is comprised of professional, skilled, or technical workers. As a result, the productivity rate is one of the highest in the nation. The city also has a remarkable track record for industrial peace. Xerox and Kodak particularly are noted as among the most socially conscious of large American corporations. The city's labor force has been shrinking because of demographic and age transitions, and a shortage of skilled workers is predicted for the rest of the 1990s.

Labor

Civilian Labor Force   118,045
% Change 1989–1990   -0.9

Work Force Distribution
    Mining   700
    Construction   17,800
    Manufacturing   130,400
    Transportation and Public Utilities   15,300
    Wholesale and Retail Trade   102,600
    FIRE (Finance, Insurance, Real Estate)   23,600

Labor (continued)

Service   127,600
Government   69,400
Women as % of Labor Force   46.0
% Self-Employed   3.3
% Professional/Technical   16.5
Total Unemployment   6,244
Rate %   5.3
Federal Government Civilian Employment   2,627

Education

The public school system consists of 54 senior high, junior/middle high, and elementary schools. Parochial and private schools enroll 13.2% of students.

Rochester's higher education is dominated by the University of Rochester and the Rochester Institute of Technology, both legacies of George Eastman. The university includes the Eastman School of Music, the School of Medicine and Dentistry, a graduate school of nursing, and the William E. Simon School of Business Administration. The Institute of Technology offers 234 technical and professional programs through its nine colleges, including the College of Graphic Arts and Photography. Other institutions include Rochester-Bexley-Crozer, Hobart/William Smith Colleges, Nazareth College, Roberts Wesleyan College, and St. John Fisher College.

Education

Number of Public Schools   54
Special Education Schools   1
Total Enrollment   32,730
% Enrollment in Private Schools   13.2
% Minority   72.0
Classroom Teachers   2,253
Pupil-Teacher Ratio   14.2
Number of Graduates   1,141
Total Revenue (in millions) $235.679
Total Expenditures (in millions) $236.650
Expenditures per Pupil $7,096
Educational Attainment (Age 25 and Over)
    % Completed 12 or More Years   58.0
    % Completed 16 or More Years   13.9
Four-Year Colleges and Universities   5
    Enrollment   28,121
Two-Year Colleges
    Enrollment

Libraries

Number   81
Public Libraries   12
Books (in thousands)   1,334
Circulation (in thousands)   1,624
Persons Served (in thousands)   241
Circulation per Person Served   6.73
Income (in millions) $9.369
Staff   NA

Four-Year Colleges and Universities
    University of Rochester
    Nazareth College
    Roberts Wesleyan College
    Rochester Institute of Technology
    St. John Fisher College

Health

The eight hospitals in the city provide a wide range of medical care. The largest is the 741-bed Strong Memorial Hospital, affiliated with the University of Rochester School of Medicine and Dentistry. The other hospitals include Rochester General, Genesee, Highland Park Ridge, and St. Mary's.

Health

Deaths—Total   2,741
Rate per 1,000   11.3
Infant Deaths—Total   68
Rate per 1,000   13.2
Number of Metro Hospitals   8
Number of Metro Hospital Beds   4,056
Rate per 100,000   1,719
Number of Physicians   2,269
Physicians per 1,000   2.85
Nurses per 1,000   12.34
Health Expenditures per Capita   NA

Transportation

Rochester is approached through I-90, which leads to the city through I-490 and the circular I-590 and I-390. Within the city, inner and outer loop arterial expressways facilitate traffic. Rail services are provided by Amtrak and Conrail. The Greater Rochester International Airport is just outside the city limits. It is served by seven major carriers and several feeder lines. The Port of Rochester has a dock wall extending 1,200 feet along the west bank of the Genesee River. The harbor accommodates regular lake traffic as well as coastal and ocean steamers. Passenger boats ply regularly between Rochester and Toronto.

Transportation

Interstate Highway Mileage   54
Total Urban Mileage   2,432
Total Daily Vehicle Mileage (in millions) $12,980
Daily Average Commute Time   42.9 min.
Number of Buses   196
Port Tonnage (in millions)   NA
Airports   1
Number of Daily Flights   67
Daily Average Number of Passengers   3,149

Airlines (American carriers only)
    American
    Continental
    Delta
    Midway
    Northwest
    United
    USAir

Housing

Cost of housing is consistently lower in Rochester than in comparable metro areas. There has been a recent trend of movement back into the downtown area with the advent of Old Rochesterville, a group of restored 19th-century office buildings transformed into loft apartments, office buildings and restaurants. In Cornhill, one of the oldest downtown areas, a large condominium complex has attracted a number of young urban professional residents. One of the most charming areas downtown is around Gibbs and Selden streets near the Eastman Theater. City neighborhoods along East and Park avenues on the east side are trendy places for professionals. The South Wedge, for years a rundown area, is being renovated as a multicultural neighborhood. Some of the choicest housing available in Monroe County is located in the suburbs to the east of the city in the Three P,s—Pittsford, Perinton, and Penfield. Certain other suburbs are associated with the industries located in or near them, like Webster with Xerox and Grace, Gates and Chili with Eastman Kodak. Brighton and Henrietta are more rural than the rest.

Housing

Total Housing Units   101,154
% Change 1980–1990   -1.5
Vacant Units for Sale or Rent   5,833
Occupied Units   93,607
% with More Than One Person per Room   2.9
% Owner-Occupied   44.0
Median Value of Owner-Occupied Homes $65,200
Average Monthly Purchase Cost $340
Median Monthly Rent $377
New Private Housing Starts   193
Value (in thousands) $7,635
% Single-Family   52.3
Nonresidential Buildings Value (in thousands) $43,605

Tallest Buildings	Hgt. (ft.)	Stories
Xerox Tower (1967)	443	30
Lincoln First Tower (1973)	392	27
Eastman Kodak Bldg. (1914)	340	19

Urban Redevelopment

 A determined program of urban renewal began in the 1950s and 1960s with the cleaning up of the Genesee. The pace quickened after 1970. Rochester's downtown has undergone massive change, the most obvious being the reconstruction of Main Street, which extends over six blocks. The Rochester Downtown Development Commission (RDDC) notes that since 1977 $140 million in public funds and $370 million in private funds have gone into improving the downtown area. The centerpiece of these efforts is the Riverside Convention Center. Zones such as the Cultural District, the Convention Center area and the Southeast loop area have undergone dramatic changes. Among the new developments are a new dormitory house for the Eastman School of Music; a townhouse development called Chestnut Court, the Sibley Music Library, including a winter garden; and an enclosed overhead bridge system called Skyway connecting tall buildings on East Avenue and Midtown Plaza.

Crime

 Rochester has a lower crime rate than most cities of its size. In 1991, of the crimes known to police, there were 2,409 violent and 23,621 property crimes.

Crime

Violent Crimes—Total   2,409
Violent Crime Rate per 100,000   342.2
Murder   64
Rape   166
Robbery   1,367
Aggravated Assaults   812
Property Crimes   23,621
Burglary   5,980
Larceny   15,644
Motor Vehicle Theft   1,997
Arson   315
Per Capita Police Expenditures $154.59
Per Capita Fire Protection Expenditures $104.94
Number of Police   570
Per 1,000   2.34

Religion

Rochester has a strong religious heritage derived from its Puritan background. Among Protestants, Methodists have a slight edge. Catholics make up 29% of the population, and Jews are strongly represented.

Religion

Largest Denominations (Adherents)

Catholic	233,718
Black Baptist	17,414
United Methodist	15,521
Presbyterian	18,015
Evangelical Lutheran	12,210
Episcopal	10,395
American Baptist	15,938
Lutheran-Missouri Synod	8,459
United Church of Christ	7,330
Jewish	16,382

Media

Gannett Company, founded in Rochester, publishes both of the city's dailies, the morning and Sunday *Sun Democrat and Chronicle* and the weekday afternoon *Times-Union*. The electronic media consist of five television stations, and 16 AM and FM radio stations.

Media

Newsprint
  Sun Democrat and Chronicle, daily
  Times-Union, daily
Television
  WHEC (Channel 10)
  WOKR (Channel 13)
  WROC (Channel 8)
  WUHF (Channel 31)
  WXXI (Channel 21)

Media (continued)

Radio

WBBF (AM)	WBEE (FM)
WCMF (FM)	WDKX (FM)
WHAM (AM)	WVOR (FM)
WIRQ (FM)	WKLX (FM)
WKQG (AM)	WPXY (FM)
WRMM (AM)	WRMM (FM)
WRUR (FM)	WWWG (AM)
WXXI (AM)	WXXI (FM)

Sports

Rochester is a baseball town. The Silver Stadium from April to September is crowded with fans watching the Red Wings, the first municipally owned team in the nation and an International League affiliate of the Baltimore Orioles. From October to April the War Memorial is the scene of hockey action when the Rochester Americans (Amerks), an American Hockey League affiliate of the Buffalo Sabres, take to the ice. The War Memorial also is the scene of the Rochester Basketball Classic, a collegiate competition. Rochester has two rugby teams that compete with Canadian teams each May during the Lilac Festival Tournament. In bowling the major events are the annual Olympic Bowl and a men's Professional Bowlers Tournament.

Arts, Culture, and Tourism

Rochester is a musical town thanks to the Eastman School of Music, which presents daily concerts at the Eastman Theater. This theater is also the home of the Rochester Philharmonic Orchestra, considered one of the 20 best professional orchestras in the United States. Choral music flourishes in the city with the Rochester Oratorio Society, the Eastman Rochester Chorus, the Bach Festival Choir, the Genesee Valley Chorale, Madigalia, the Swanne Alley Singers, and the Greece Cymphony and Chorus. Dance is another strong area, led by the Bucket Dance Theater, founded in 1970 by Garth Fagan. The Botsford School of Dance trains aspiring dancers for the American Dance Theater. In the world of theater, GeVa is the best known company, but a number of others perform regularly, including Shipping Dock Theater, the Blackfriars, and the Bristol Valley Playhouse. Art activities revolve around the Memorial Art Gallery, part of the University of Rochester, which holds a collection of over 9,500 works of art. There are two other world-class museums in the city: The International Museum of Photography/George Eastman House and the Margaret Woodbury Strong Museum with over 300,000 objects in its collections. The natural and cultural history of upstate New York is depicted in exhibits at the Rochester Museum and Science Center. Of the many smaller museums in the suburbs, the most noted is the Genesee Country Village and Museum in Mumford, a reconstructed 19th-century village. A free museum bus, sponsored by Goldome and the Regional Transit System, transports museum visitors from one museum to another.

Travel and Tourism
Hotel Rooms 5,989
Convention and Exhibit Space (square feet) 43,883
Convention Centers
Rochester Riverside Convention Center
War Memorial
Festivals
The Festival of Lilacs (May)
Rochester Harbor Festival (June)
Rochester Jazz Festival (July)
Carifest (August)
Bluegrass Festival (August)

Parks and Recreation

The county has nearly 11,000 acres of parks, including Highland Park, which features the world's largest collection of lilacs. The Durand-Eastman Park has 506 acres of rolling wooded terrain with a mile-long sandy beach along Lake Ontario and an 18-hole golf course. The Genesee Valley Park covers an area of 640 acres. At the entrance is a statue of Edward Mott Moore, father of Rochester's parks. Edgerton Park, 62 acres, is used for winter athletics. The Maplewood Park contains 145 acres bordering the west bank of the Genesee. The Seneca Park Zoo adjoins Letchworth Park, the Grand Canyon of the East. Many of these parks and ski areas offer a variety of winter recreational opportunities, such as cross-country and downhill skiing, luge, iceboating, icefishing, snowmobiling, winter camping, and snowshoeing.

Sources of Further Information

City Hall
30 Church Street
Rochester, NY 14614

Landmark Society
130 Spring Street
Rochester, NY 14610
(716) 473-7573

Rochester Convention and Visitors Bureau
126 Andrews Street
Rochester, NY 14604
(716) 546-3070

Rochester Historical Society
485 East Avenue
Rochester, NY 14607
(716) 271-2705

Additional Reading

Dobrovitz, Peter. *Rochestrivia: An Illuminating Look at Rochester*. 1984.

Johnson, Paul E. *A Shopkeeper's Millennium: Society and Revivals in Rochester, New York*. 1979.

Liebschutz, Sarah F. *Federal Aid to Rochester*. 1984.

McKelvey, Blake, *Rochester: A Brief History*. 1984.

Pula, James S. *Ethnic Rochester*. 1986.

Merrill, Arch. *Rochester Sketchbook*. 1986.

The Remaking of a City: Rochester, New York, 1964–1984. 1984.

Rutland

Vermont

Basic Data

Name   Rutland
Name Origin   From Duke of Rutland
Year Founded   1761 Inc. 1770
Status: State   Vermont
         County   Seat of Rutland County
Area (square miles)   5.1
Elevation (feet)   648
Time Zone   EST
Population (1990)   18,230
Population of Metro Area (1990)   NA

Distance in Miles To:

Boston	171
Burlington	67
Concord	101
Portsmouth	150
Nashua	130
Bennington	58

Environment

Environmental Stress Index   NA
Green Cities Index: Rank   NA
                    Score   NA
Water Quality   Alkaline, very soft
Average Daily Use (gallons per capita)   NA
     Maximum Supply (gallons per capita)   NA
Parkland as % of Total City Area   NA
% Waste Landfilled/Recycled   NA
Annual Parks Expenditures per Capita   NA

Climate

 The city enjoys a four-season climate with average temperatures in the teens in winter and in the seventies in summer. Average precipitation is 35 inches of rain and 65 inches of snow.

Location and Topography

 Rutland is located in the fertile Otter Creek Valley in south central Vermont, bounded by the Taconic and Green Mountains.

Layout of City and Suburbs

The tree-bordered streets of the residential district blend into the meadows of the fertile valley. Pico, Killington, and Shrewsbury, three of the most striking Green Mountain peaks, rise sharply to the east, and the Taconic Range stands to the west. The residential district flanks the Common, in early days known as the Federal Square but now known as the Main Street Park. Side streets dip westward down the hill to the business section, and beyond to the factories. To the north, near the country club, lies another residential district.

Weather

Temperature

Highest Monthly Average °F   56.9
Lowest Monthly Average °F   35.7

Annual Averages

Days 32°F or Below   155
Days above 90°F   4
Zero Degree Days   17
Precipitation (inches)   34.91
Snow (inches)   65.6
% Seasonal Humidity   NA
Wind Speed (m.p.h.)   NA
Clear Days   NA
Cloudy Days   NA
Storm Days   NA
Rainy Days   NA

Average Temperatures (°F)	High	Low	Mean
January	30.2	11.1	20.6
February	32.9	12.6	22.8

Weather (continued)			
Average Temperatures (°F)	High	Low	Mean
March	42.5	22.9	32.8
April	56.3	33.8	45.1
May	69.1	44.1	56.6
June	77.3	53.5	65.4
July	81.5	57.9	69.7
August	79.1	56.4	67.8
September	71.4	48.8	60.1
October	60.8	38.9	49.8
November	47.3	30.5	38.9
December	34.3	17.6	26.0

History

Otter Creek was a favorite route for Indian travel and was known as a rich beaver country. As early as 1730 a fur trader, James Cross, left a description of the territory. The site of the present city was a junction on the Crown Point military road, which General Amherst ordered built across the mountains to connect the Champlain forts with the Connecticut Valley. Rutland was chartered in 1761 by Governor Benning Wentworth of New Hampshire. The first grantee, John Murray of Rutland, Massachusetts, was responsible for the name of the town. Actual settlement was begun by James Mead, who brought his wife and ten children up over the mountains from Manchester in 1770 and established them in a log house near the falls that now bear his name. Shortly thereafter he built a sawmill and gristmill, and in a few years Rutland became an active frontier community. It also became an outpost of the Green Mountain Boys, celebrated for their resistance to royal authority. Within a few years of its founding, the town became the headquarters for state troops engaged in the Revolutionary War. Fort Rutland was built in 1775, and Fort Ranger in 1778. In 1784 Rutland was made the county seat, and one of the five post offices of the independent republic of Vermont was established. From 1784 to 1804 various sessions of the state legislature were held in the city. Vermont's admission to the Union was enthusiastically greeted by an all-day celebration in Federal Square. In 1794 Rutland's first newspaper, the *Rutland Herald*, was founded by Reverend Samuel Williams, author of the first history of the state. Between 1800 and 1880 the population of Rutland grew from 2,124 to 12,149, making it the largest town in Vermont. The population boom was due to two factors: the completion of the Rutland and Burlington Railroad connecting Vermont with Boston in 1849, and the post–Civil War development of the marble business by Colonel Redfield Proctor. The marble deposits in the western part of the town, owned by Proctor's Vermont Marble Company, were among the richest in the world. By 1886 Proctor (who had been governor from 1878 to 1880) was influential enough to persuade the legislature to create two townships, one West Rutland and the other, eponymously named Proctor, in which he held 97% of the property. In 1892 a further partition took place when the city of Rutland was organized. With the division,

Rutland lost its name as the Marble Capital of the World, but its economy was sustained by Howe Scales, which moved to Rutland from Brandon in 1877. The beginning of the ski industry brought a fresh wave of prosperity to Rutland, which now styles itself as the gateway to Vermont's ski resorts. Since the 1960s much of the downtown has been renovated.

Historical Landmarks

Colonial and Victorian Rutland still exist despite the rise of more modern architecture. Among the town's notable old residences are the Temple House (1812), Aiken House (1849), Sycamore Lodge, Pond House, Kilburn House (1794), Morse House, The Maples, and Gookin House (1781). The Congregational Church of 1860 dominates the hill with its impressive spire. The Downtown Historic District contains many interesting public buildings, such as the Opera House, the Gryphan Building, and Merchants Row. A second Historic District named after the Courthouse includes 85 buildings, including the post office.

Population

Rutland has a population of less than 20,000, and it experienced a declining population in the 1980s.

Population		
	1980	1990
Central City	18,436	18,230
Rank	690	NA
Metro Area (Rutland County)	58,347	62,142
Pop. Change 1980–1990 -206		
Pop. % Change 1980–1990 -1.1		
Median Age 35.1		
% Male 46.5		
% Age 65 and Over 18.06		
Density (per square mile) 3,574		

Households		
Number 7,009		
Persons per Household NA		
% Female-Headed Households NA		
% One-Person Households NA		
Births—Total NA		
% to Mothers under 20 NA		
Birth Rate per 1,000 NA		

Ethnic Composition

Rutland has one of the lowest percentages of blacks of any major city: 0.39%. Other minorities are even less well represented. Among the whites, Anglo-Saxons predominate with smaller groups of Italians, Poles, and Swedes.

Government

Rutland has a mayor-council form of government. The mayor and the 11 aldermen are elected for two-year terms.

Chronology

1730   Fur trader, James Cross, visits Otter Creek and leaves the first recorded description of the territory.

1761   Rutland is chartered as a town by Governor Wentworth of New Hampshire.

1770   The first settler, James Mead, arrives with wife and ten children and builds a gristmill and sawmill.

1775   Fort Rutland is built.

1778   Fort Ranger is built at Mead's Falls; the town is made headquarters for state troops.

1784   Rutland becomes the county seat and the location of one of the five post offices in the independent republic of Vermont.

1791   Vermont is admitted to the Union.

1794   Reverend Samuel Williams founds the *Rutland Herald*.

1836   Marble is quarried in Rutland and soon becomes a major industry.

1849   The Rutland and Burlington Railroad is completed.

1870   Redfield Proctor takes over the Sutherland Falls Marble Company and parlays it into the Vermont Marble Company, the largest marble producer in the world.

1886   Proctor persuades the state legislature to partition the town and create two new townships: Proctor and West Rutland.

1892   The city of Rutland is organized.

Ethnic Composition (as % of total pop.)

	1980	1990
White	99.59	98.93
Black	0.41	0.39
American Indian	0.10	0.13
Asian and Pacific Islander	0.20	0.46
Hispanic	0.47	0.45
Other	NA	0.09

Government

Year of Home Charter   1892
Number of Members of the Governing Body   12
Elected at Large   12
Elected by Wards   NA
Number of Women in Governing Body   2
Salary of Mayor   NA
Salary of Council Members   NA
City Government Employment Total   NA
Rate per 10,000   NA

Public Finance

Details of the city budget were unavailable at the time this book went to press.

Economy

Rutland is the commercial and financial center of south central Vermont. Its economy is based on a mixture of agriculture, tourist-related services, and small manufacturing businesses producing nontraditional durable goods. The largest private employer is General Electric, which maintains two defense contract plants in the region. Its presence has stimulated a thriving electronics industry.

Economy

Total Money Income (in millions)   NA
% of State Average   NA
Per Capita Annual Income $9,839
% Population below Poverty Level   NA
Fortune 500 Companies   NA

Banks	Number	Deposits (in millions)
Commercial	5	1,769.2
Savings	2	369.3

Passenger Autos   325,773 (Statewide)
Electric Meters   6,700
Gas Meters   NA

Manufacturing

Number of Establishments   NA
% with 20 or More Employees   NA
Manufacturing Payroll (in millions)   NA
Value Added by Manufacture (in millions)   NA
Value of Shipments (in millions)   NA
New Capital Expenditures (in millions)   NA

Wholesale Trade

Number of Establishments   NA
Sales (in millions)   NA
Annual Payroll (in millions)   NA

Retail Trade

Number of Establishments   NA
Total Sales (in millions)   NA
Sales per Capita $5,403
Number of Retail Trade Establishments with Payroll   NA
Annual Payroll (in millions)   NA
Total Sales (in millions)   NA
General Merchandise Stores (per capita)   NA
Food Stores (per capita)   NA
Apparel Stores (per capita)   NA
Eating and Drinking Places (per capita)   NA

Service Industries

Total Establishments   NA
Total Receipts (in millions)   NA
Hotels and Motels (in millions)   NA
Health Services (in millions)   NA
Legal Services (in millions)   NA

Labor

Rutland's labor force is highly regarded for its productivity and concern for quality. The town has had stable employment levels throughout the 1980s and is likely to maintain growth through the mid-1990s. Services and trade are the sectors absorbing most new workers.

Labor

Civilian Labor Force   34,554 (county)
% Change 1989–1990   NA

Work Force Distribution
    Mining   NA
    Construction   NA
    Manufacturing   NA
    Transportation and Public Utilities   NA
    Wholesale and Retail Trade   NA
    FIRE (Finance, Insurance, Real Estate)   NA
    Service   NA
    Government   NA
    Women as % of Labor Force   NA
    % Self-Employed   NA
    % Professional/Technical   NA
Total Unemployment   NA
Rate %   3.4
Federal Government Civilian Employment   NA

Education

The public school system consists of one senior high school, one junior high/middle school, and five elementary schools. The only local institution of higher education is the College of St. Joseph the Provider. Other institutions in the vicinity are Castleton State College, Green Mountain College, Middlebury College, Vermont Law School, and Vermont Technical College.

Education

Number of Public Schools   7
Special Education Schools   NA
Total Enrollment   2,936
% Enrollment in Private Schools   NA
% Minority   NA
Classroom Teachers   NA
Pupil-Teacher Ratio   NA
Number of Graduates   NA
Total Revenue (in millions)   NA
Total Expenditures (in millions)   NA
Expenditures per Pupil   NA
Educational Attainment (Age 25 and Over)   NA
    % Completed 12 or More Years   NA
    % Completed 16 or More Years   NA
Four-Year Colleges and Universities   1
    Enrollment   419
Two-Year Colleges   NA
    Enrollment   NA

Libraries

Number   6
Public Libraries   1
Books (in thousands)   82
Circulation (in thousands)   156
Persons Served (in thousands)   22
Circulation per Person Served   7.18
Income (in millions) $0.345
Staff   12

Four-Year Colleges and Universities
    College of St. Joseph the Provider

Health

Rutland has one general hospital: the Rutland Regional Medical Center. Residents also have access to the Porter Medical Center in Middlebury.

Health

Deaths—Total   NA
Rate per 1,000   10.6
Infant Deaths—Total   NA
Rate per 1,000   NA
Number of Metro Hospitals   1
Number of Metro Hospital Beds   NA
Rate per 100,000   384
Number of Physicians   NA
Physicians per 1,000   1.53
Nurses per 1,000   NA
Health Expenditures per Capita $2.0

Transportation

Rutland is strategically situated between Quebec and northeast United States, at the intersection of U.S. highways 4 and 7, providing east-west and north-south access and linking the city with Interstates 89, 91, and 87. Being on the U.S.-Canadian truck route, the town is the home of over 20 trucking firms. Vermont Rail provides full carrier service. The nearest international airport is in Burlington.

Transportation

Interstate Highway Mileage   NA
Total Urban Mileage   NA
Total Daily Vehicle Mileage (in millions)   NA
Daily Average Commute Time   15.9 min.
Number of Buses   NA
Port Tonnage (in millions)   NA
Airports   1
Number of Daily Flights   NA
Daily Average Number of Passengers   NA

Housing

The bulk of the housing stock dates to the early part of the 20th century, but there was some new construction in the 1980s.

Housing

Total Housing Units   8,083
% Change 1980–1990   NA
Vacant Units for Sale or Rent   NA
Occupied Units   53.4
% with More Than One Person per Room   NA
% Owner-Occupied   NA
Median Value of Owner-Occupied Homes $95,300
Average Monthly Purchase Cost   NA
Median Monthly Rent $387
New Private Housing Starts   NA
Value (in thousands)   NA
% Single-Family   NA
Nonresidential Buildings Value (in thousands)   NA

Urban Redevelopment

 Development projects in the region include new airport terminal facilities, the redevelopment of the Pifco Block, and the $20 million expansion of the Rutland Regional Medical Center.

Crime

 Rutland has a low crime rate. In 1991 violent crimes reported to the police totaled 42, property crimes totaled 1,226.

Crime
Violent Crimes—Total   42
Violent Crime Rate per 100,000   NA
Murder   0
Rape   5
Robbery   11
Aggravated Assaults   13
Property Crimes   1,226
Burglary   282
Larceny   884
Motor Vehicle Theft   50
Arson   NA
Per Capita Police Expenditures $21
Per Capita Fire Protection Expenditures $22
Number of Police   NA
Per 1,000   2.17

Religion

 Both Roman Catholics and Protestants are strongly represented in the community.

Religion	
Largest Denominations (Adherents)	
Catholic	19,188
American Baptist	1,326
United Church of Christ	2,461
United Methodist	2,451
Episcopal	1,107
Evangelical Lutheran	518
Jewish	550

Media

 The *Rutland Herald,* the oldest daily newspaper in the state, is published in the mornings. The electronic media consist of one television station and seven FM and AM radio stations.

Media	
Newsprint	
Rutland Herald, daily	
Television	
WVER (Channel 28)	
Radio	
WFTF (FM)	WHWB (AM)
WJJR (FM)	WRVT (FM)
WSYB (AM)	WZRT (FM)
WYOY (FM)	

Sports

 Rutland has no major facility for spectator sports.

Arts, Culture, and Tourism

 The Vermont Symphony Orchestra, the oldest state-supported symphony in the country, is the pride of the city. It presents over 70 concerts annually around the state. The Crossroads Arts Council presents 22 performances a year, including classical music, opera, dance jazz, and theater.

The Rutland Historical Society Museum is the principal custodian of the city's heritage. The Chaffee Art Gallery and the Moon Brook Arts Union Gallery display the works of local artists.

Travel and Tourism
Hotel Rooms   NA
Convention and Exhibit Space (square feet)   NA
Convention Centers
Holiday Inn Center
Festivals
Vermont State Fair (September)

Parks and Recreation

The Main Street Park is a quiet green dating back to the Revolutionary War days. Rutland is best known to skiers for its proximity to two outstanding ski areas at Pico Peak and Killington. The latter is the highest ski elevation in Vermont. A golf course is available at Rutland Country Club.

Sources of Further Information

City Hall
1 Strongs Avenue
Rutland, VT 05701
(802) 773-1800

Crossroads Arts Council
Rutland, VT 05701
(802) 775-5413

Rutland Chamber of Commerce
Rutland, VT 05701
(802) 773-2747

Rutland Free Library
Court Street
Rutland, VT 05701
(802) 773-1860

Rutland Historical Society
101 Center Street
Rutland, VT 05701
(802) 775-2006

Rutland Industrial Development Corporation
5 Court Street
Rutland, VT 05701
(802) 773-9147

Additional Reading

Regional Profile—Rutland Region. Irregular.

Sacramento

California

Basic Data

Name   Sacramento
Name Origin   From Spanish for "Holy Sacrament"
Year Founded   1839 Inc. 1850
Status: State   Capital of California
         County   Seat of Sacramento County
Area (square miles)   96.3
Elevation (feet)   30
Time Zone   Pacific
Population (1990)   369,365
Population of Metro Area (1990)   1,481,102

Sister Cities
    Hamilton, New Zealand
    Jinan, China
    Kishinev, Moldova
    Liestal, Switzerland
    Manila, Philippines
    Matsuyama, Japan
    Valencia, Spain

Distance in Miles To:

Los Angeles	387
Portland, OR	586
Reno	133
San Diego	511
San Francisco	91
San Jose	117

Location and Topography

Sacramento is located in a loop of the Sacramento River at its confluence with the American River in the center of California's broad Sacramento Valley. It is shielded by the Sierra Mountains to the east, the California Coast Ranges to the west, and the Siskiyou Mountains to the north. The land is flat.

Layout of City and Suburbs

The oldest part of town is along the banks of the river and it has high curbstones recalling the times when the river flooded its banks. The business section is set back from the older section and includes the Capitol Park. Just before entering the city, I-80 splits into two, forming a loop around the city, with the southern branch running parallel to Broadway. The domed capitol dominates the city.

Environment

Environmental Stress Index   3.8
Green Cities Index: Rank   40
                   Score   31.0
Water Quality   Soft to hard
Average Daily Use (gallons per capita)   350
    Maximum Supply (gallons per capita)   652
Parkland as % of Total City Area   NA
% Waste Landfilled/Recycled   85:15
Annual Parks Expenditures per Capita $121.97

Climate

Sacramento has a generally mild climate, but in the summer the northers from the Siskiyou Mountains create heat waves. Low humidity makes the heat tolerable. Winters are rainy but mild, and snow is rare.

Weather

Temperature

Highest Monthly Average °F   93.3
Lowest Monthly Average °F   37.9

Annual Averages

Days 32°F or Below   17
Days above 90°F   77
Zero Degree Days   0
Precipitation (inches)   17.0
Snow (inches)   0.1
% Seasonal Humidity   66.0
Wind Speed (m.p.h.)   8.3

Weather (continued)

Clear Days 193
Cloudy Days 100
Storm Days 5
Rainy Days 57

Average Temperatures (°F)	High	Low	Mean
January	53.0	37.1	45.1
February	59.1	40.4	49.8
March	64.1	41.9	53.0
April	71.3	45.3	58.3
May	78.8	49.8	64.3
June	86.4	54.6	70.5
July	92.9	57.5	75.2
August	91.3	56.9	74.1
September	87.7	55.3	71.5
October	77.1	49.5	63.3
November	63.6	42.4	53.0
December	53.3	38.3	45.8

History

Sacramento was founded when it was part of Mexico and named Sacramento in honor of the Holy Sacrament by José Moraga, comandante of the presidio of San Jose. The site drew the interest of John Augustus Sutter, the ex–Swiss Army officer who took a grant of 50,000 acres by swearing allegiance to the Mexican flag and built a principality named New Helvetia, in honor of his homeland. He ruled in baronial splendor from an adobe brick castle surrounded by a wooden fort with 12 guns mounted on its ramparts. He also constructed a landing on the Sacramento River called Embarcadero.

In 1848 an event happened that changed the history of the settlement and the life of its owner. On January 24, James W. Marshall, Sutter's boss carpenter, found a gold flake while building a mill for Sutter near Coloma on the south fork of the American River. It led to the great gold rush and to California's admission into the Union. It also led to Sutter's ruin, as the trampling hordes of gold seekers overran his fort and stole his cattle and his land. Even as millions of dollars of gold dust passed over his landing, Sutter moved to Pennsylvania in 1873 and died in Washington, D.C., in 1880 after vainly petitioning Congress for the restoration of his property. Meanwhile, the town of Sacramento was laid out on Sutter's property in 1848, and the first lots were sold in 1849. The town was hit by three disastrous floods between 1849 and 1853, and in 1852 a fire wiped out two-thirds of the town. In 1849 Sacramento offered $1 million to the state for the honor of being named state capital; not until 1854 was this honor bestowed. In 1856 Sacramento became the terminus of the first railroad built by Theodore Judah, the young engineer who planned the first transcontinental railroad through the passes of the Sierra Nevada. Judah's Central Pacific Railroad joined east and west in 1869. The Central Pacific branched out and became Southern Pacific, controlled by the Big Four tycoons: Leland Stanford, Collis P. Huntington, Mark Hopkins, and Charles Crocker. In the 1950s Sacramento embarked upon one of the first and most successful urban redevelopment programs in the nation.

Historical Landmarks

Along the banks of the Sacramento River is the Old Historic Sacramento Area, a national historic landmark. It includes the Old Sacramento Waterfront, the depots of the Central Pacific Railroad and California Steam Navigation Company, and Sutter's Fort. The Capitol Building is on a gently sloping terrace on Capitol Park. Begun in 1860 and completed in 1874, the E-shaped building was designed by F. M. Butler. In the center of the building is the rotunda topped with a great golden dome, 237 feet from the ground. On the walls of the rotunda are 12 murals by Arthur F. Mathews, and in its center is a statue of Columbus before Isabella.

The City Plaza on the corner of Ninth and I streets was given to the city by Sutter in 1849. The Tremont Hotel on J Street was one of Sacramento's early luxury hotels, built in the early 1850s. It had one of the largest gambling rooms in the West. Sutter's Fort on L and 26th streets is a complete restoration of Captain Sutter's original workshop, home fort, and ranch house, erected in 1839. The site of Sutterville, the town first projected by Captain Sutter in 1844, is just south of William Land Park. The first brick house in California was built here in 1847.

Population

After modest growth in the 1970s, Sacramento experienced explosive growth in the 1980s, partly as a result of the expansion of state services. From 257,105 residents in 1970 the city grew to 275,741 in 1980 and 369,365 in 1990. Metro growth has kept pace.

Population

	1980	1990
Central City	275,741	369,365
Rank	52	41
Metro Area	1,099,814	1,418,102
Pop. Change 1980–1990 +93,624		
Pop. % Change 1980–1990 +34.0		
Median Age 31.8		
% Male 48.4		
% Age 65 and Over 12.1		
Density (per square mile) 3,835		

Households

Number 144,444
Persons per Household 2.50
% Female-Headed Households 14.3
% One-Person Households 30.9
Births—Total 9,566
  % to Mothers under 20 13.6
  Birth Rate per 1,000 31.5

Ethnic Composition

Whites make up 60.1%, blacks 15.3%, American Indians 1.2%, Asians and Pacific Islanders 15.0%, and others 8.4%. Hispanics, both black and white, make up 16.2%.

Chronology

1839 Captain John Augustus Sutter takes a 50,000-acre grant after swearing allegiance to the Mexican flag and builds a principality named New Helvetia.

1848 James W. Marshall, Sutter's boss carpenter, discovers the first gold flake while building a mill on Sutter's property. The town of Sacramento is laid out on Sutter's farm.

1849 The first plots are sold in Sacramento. Flood causes extensive damage.

1852 Fire wipes out two-thirds of the business district.

1853 A second flood causes severe damage.

1854 Sacramento is named state capital in return for a gift of $1 million.

1856 Sacramento becomes the terminus for the first California railroad.

1869 The Central Pacific Railroad formed by Theodore Judah and four partners joins East and West in the first transcontinental rail system.

1911 The river channel is dredged to enable ships to reach the city from San Francisco.

Ethnic Composition (as % of total pop.)

	1980	1990
White	67.63	60.09
Black	13.37	15.30
American Indian	1.20	1.23
Asian and Pacific Islander	8.71	15.01
Hispanic	14.20	16.25
Other	NA	8.36

Government

Under its 1920 charter, Sacramento is governed by a mayor-council form of government. The mayor and the eight members of the council are elected to four-year terms. The city manager is appointed by the council.

Government

Year of Home Charter   1920
Number of Members of the Governing Body   8
Elected at Large   NA
Elected by Wards   8
Number of Women in Governing Body   2
Salary of Mayor $800
Salary of Council Members $800
City Government Employment Total   3,413
Rate per 10,000   105.5

Public Finance

The annual budget consists of revenues of $327.258 million and expenditures of $309.760 million. The debt outstanding is $308.696 million, and cash and security holdings $534.038 million.

Public Finance

Total Revenue (in millions) $327.258
Intergovernmental Revenue—Total (in millions) $27.14
Federal Revenue per Capita $0.614
% Federal Assistance   0.18
% State Assistance   5.92
Sales Tax as % of Total Revenue   25.63
Local Revenue as % of Total Revenue   76.86
City Income Tax   no
Taxes—Total (in millions) $89.6

Taxes per Capita
   Total $277
   Property $81
   Sales and Gross Receipts $159
General Expenditures—Total (in millions) $165.0
General Expenditures per Capita $510
Capital Outlays per Capita $83

% of Expenditures for:
   Public Welfare   0.0
   Highways   13.2
   Education   0.0
   Health and Hospitals   0.0
   Police   22.4
   Sewerage and Sanitation   16.2
   Parks and Recreation   12.1
   Housing and Community Development   2.1
Debt Outstanding per Capita $389
   % Utility   13.4
Federal Procurement Contract Awards (in millions) $285.4
Federal Grants Awards (in millions) $1,576.1
Fiscal Year Begins   July 1

Economy

A city built by the Gold Rush, Sacramento achieved economic stability when it became the state capital in 1854. As the state capital it became the center stage for railroad politics and a sink of railroad money. Productive mines still operate in the vicinity but do not significantly influence the economy. Located in the midst of a fertile valley, agriculture took up the slack soon after the gold rush fever subsided. Among its products are fruits and vegetables, rice and other grains, meat, beets, sugar, and almonds. As one of the earliest transportation centers in the state, Sacramento achieved prominence in rail as well as water transport. The city's deep-water port, connected with the San Francisco Bay via a 43-mile channel, provides an important outlet for northern California shippers. Rail facilities are equally strategic as the junction of two major historic railroads, Southern Pacific and Union Pacific. Three Defense installations—Mather Air Force Base, McClellan Air Force Base, and Sacramento Army Depot—not only pump millions of dollars into the local economy and provide thousands of jobs but also they are the reason for a cluster of defense-related industries making rockets, guided missiles, aircraft parts, weapons, and defense systems. Lumbering is a smaller sector but quite active. Above all, as the state capital, the city wields prestige and influence and plays a pre-eminent role in shaping the regional economy.

Economy

Total Money Income (in millions) $3,438.3
% of State Average   89.4
Per Capita Annual Income $10,627
% Population below Poverty Level   15.0
Fortune 500 Companies   NA

Banks	Number	Deposits (in millions)
Commercial	67	8,143
Savings	46	6,696

Passenger Autos   577,048
Electric Meters   450,000
Gas Meters   320,000

Manufacturing

Number of Establishments   448
% with 20 or More Employees   30.6
Manufacturing Payroll (in millions) $542.3
Value Added by Manufacture (in millions) $1,408.6
Value of Shipments (in millions) $2,703.4
New Capital Expenditures (in millions) $93.7

Wholesale Trade

Number of Establishments   792
Sales (in millions) $4,054.9
Annual Payroll (in millions) $311.964

Retail Trade

Number of Establishments   2,940
Total Sales (in millions) $2,395.7
Sales per Capita $7,404
Number of Retail Trade Establishments with Payroll   2,074
Annual Payroll (in millions) $302.6
Total Sales (in millions) $2,351.4
General Merchandise Stores (per capita) $1,262
Food Stores (per capita) $1,558
Apparel Stores (per capita) $285
Eating and Drinking Places (per capita) $888

Service Industries

Total Establishments   3,386
Total Receipts (in millions) $1,674.4
Hotels and Motels (in millions)   NA
Health Services (in millions) $393.7
Legal Services (in millions)   NA

Labor

Work force distribution is influenced by the city's status as the state capital. Government employees outnumber manufac-

Labor

Civilian Labor Force   175,542
% Change 1989–1990   0.6

Work Force Distribution
   Mining   900
   Construction   35,600
   Manufacturing   42,600
   Transportation and Public Utilities   29,900
   Wholesale and Retail Trade   150,700
   FIRE (Finance, Insurance, Real Estate)   43,500

Labor (continued)

   Service   149,400
   Government   184,000
   Women as % of Labor Force   45.2
   % Self-Employed   6.1
   % Professional/Technical   17.5
Total Unemployment   9,515
Rate %   5.4
Federal Government Civilian Employment   9,517

turing employees by four to one and account for 30% of the total work force. The state's financial problems may limit growth of this sector, but new jobs in the service and trade sectors are likely to take up the slack.

Education

The Sacramento City Unified School District, one of the largest in the state, supports 74 elementary schools, middle schools, and senior high schools. There are also more than 20 church-supported schools. Sacramento's higher education facilities include the California State University–Sacramento, Sacramento City College, Sierra College, American River College, and Cosumnes River College. The area is noted for a group of outstanding law colleges, including the McGeorge School of Law of the University of the Pacific, the University of California at Davis School of Law, and the Lincoln School of Law.

Education

Number of Public Schools   74
Special Education Schools   NA
Total Enrollment   49,557
% Enrollment in Private Schools   9.0
% Minority   64.9
Classroom Teachers   2,146
Pupil-Teacher Ratio   23.1:1
Number of Graduates   1,876
Total Revenue (in millions) $190.443
Total Expenditures (in millions) $177.310
Expenditures per Pupil $3,854
Educational Attainment (Age 25 and Over)
   % Completed 12 or More Years   71.6
   % Completed 16 or More Years   18.7
Four-Year Colleges and Universities   4
   Enrollment   26,339
Two-Year Colleges   5
   Enrollment   52,386

Libraries

Number   76
Public Libraries   25
Books (in thousands)   1,800
Circulation (in thousands)   NA
Persons Served (in thousands)   1,026
Circulation per Person Served   NA
Income (in millions) $16.1
Staff   227

Four-Year Colleges and Universities
   American River College
   California State University – Sacramento
   Cosumnes River College
   Sacramento City College

Health

Sacramento is home to 6 hospitals. The largest are the University of California at Davis Medical Center, Sutter General Hospital, Mercy Hospital, and Mercy San Juan.

Health	
Deaths—Total	4,569
Rate per 1,000	15.0
Infant Deaths—Total	83
Rate per 1,000	8.7
Number of Metro Hospitals	6
Number of Metro Hospital Beds	1,937
Rate per 100,000	599
Number of Physicians	2,731
Physicians per 1,000	2.32
Nurses per 1,000	8.92
Health Expenditures per Capita	$3.10

Transportation

Sacramento is approached by two interstates: the north-south I-5 (also known as the Pan-American Highway) and the east-west I-80. Also serving the city are U.S. 90 and U.S. 50. Other important roads within the city are the east-west Garden Highway and state road 99, which comes from the south to join 80. Downtown streets are named by letter when running east to west and by number when running north to south. Rail passenger service is provided by Amtrak and rail freight service by Southern Pacific, Union Pacific, Santa Fe, Sacramento Northern, and Central California Traction. Sacramento has one of the nation's largest switching yards. The Port of Sacramento serves oceangoing ships. The main airline terminal is Sacramento Metropolitan Airport, 12 miles northwest of downtown.

Transportation	
Interstate Highway Mileage	50
Total Urban Mileage	3,623
Total Daily Vehicle Mileage (in millions)	$23.947
Daily Average Commute Time	42.7 min.
Number of Buses	199
Port Tonnage (in millions)	$1.442
Airports	1
Number of Daily Flights	105
Daily Average Number of Passengers	4,931

Airlines (American carriers only)
American
American West
Continental
Delta
Northwest
Southwest
United
USAir

Housing

Of the total housing stock 51.3% is owner-occupied. The median value of an owner-occupied home is $115,800, and the median monthly rent is $429.

Housing

Housing	
Total Housing Units	153,362
% Change 1980–1990	19.6
Vacant Units for Sale or Rent	6,874
Occupied Units	144,444
% with More Than One Person per Room	8.5
% Owner-Occupied	51.3
Median Value of Owner-Occupied Homes	$115,800
Average Monthly Purchase Cost	$296
Median Monthly Rent	$429
New Private Housing Starts	2,181
Value (in thousands)	$174,145
% Single-Family	86.4
Nonresidential Buildings Value (in thousands)	$166,874

Tallest Buildings	Hgt. (ft.)	Stories
Wells Fargo Center	405	30
Park Plaza Tower	373	26
Renaissance Tower	372	28

Urban Redevelopment

The Sacramento Area Council of Governments has drawn up a Year 2010 Plan outlining development strategies for the next two decades. Development programs are coordinated by the Sacramento Planning and Development Department.

Crime

Sacramento ranks well below national average in public safety. In 1991 violent crimes totaled 4,896 and property crimes totaled 33,180.

Crime	
Violent Crimes—Total	4,896
Violent Crime Rate per 100,000	794.4
Murder	66
Rape	221
Robbery	2,280
Aggravated Assaults	2,329
Property Crimes	33,180
Burglary	7,753
Larceny	17,870
Motor Vehicle Theft	7,557
Arson	196
Per Capita Police Expenditures	$168.41
Per Capita Fire Protection Expenditures	$97.35
Number of Police	502
Per 1,000	1.6

Religion

Catholics make up 15% of the population, Baptists 4%, Methodists and Lutherans 3% each, and Presbyterians 2%. Latter-Day Saints have a significant showing, and, with a large Asian population, eastern religions are also well represented.

Religion	
Largest Denominations (Adherents)	
Catholic	147,882
Assembly of God	21,022

Religion (continued)	
American Baptist	7,230
Black Baptist	26,439
Southern Baptist	25,172
Latter-Day Saints	30,320
Evangelical Lutheran	10,374
Presbyterian	11,619
Independent Charismatic	17,950
Jewish	8,788

Media

The city's two daily newspapers are the *Sacramento Bee* and the *Sacramento Union*. The latter is California's oldest newspaper, first published in 1851. The electronic media consist of 6 television stations and 20 AM and FM radio stations.

Media

Newsprint
　Sacramento Bee, daily
　Sacramento Magazine, monthly
　Sacramento Observer, weekly
　Sacramento Union, daily

Television
　KCMY (Channel 29)
　KCRA (Channel 3)
　KRBK (Channel 31)
　KTXL (Channel 40)
　KVIE (Channel 6)
　KXTV (Channel 10)

Radio

KBER (AM)	KCTC (AM)
KFBK (AM)	KHYL (FM)
KNCI (FM)	KRAK (AM)
KRAK (FM)	KRCX (AM)
KRXQ (FM)	KSAC (AM)
KSEG (FM)	KSMJ (AM)
KSFM (FM)	KWOD (FM)
KWWN (FM)	KXOA (AM)
KXOA (FM)	KXPR (FM)
KYDS (FM)	KYMX (FM)

Sports

Sacramento's only major professional sports team is the Sacramento Kings, a member of the National Basketball Association. They play at the Arco Arena.

Arts, Culture, and Tourism

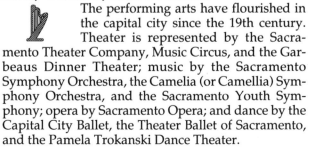

The performing arts have flourished in the capital city since the 19th century. Theater is represented by the Sacramento Theater Company, Music Circus, and the Garbeaus Dinner Theater; music by the Sacramento Symphony Orchestra, the Camelia (or Camellia) Symphony Orchestra, and the Sacramento Youth Symphony; opera by Sacramento Opera; and dance by the Capital City Ballet, the Theater Ballet of Sacramento, and the Pamela Trokanski Dance Theater.

The showpiece of cultural Sacramento is the Crocker Art Museum, which contains priceless artwork by Leonardo da Vinci, Michaelangelo, Rembrandt, Holbein, Dürer, Van Dyck, and Rubens. It was donated to the city in 1885 by the widow of Judge E. B. Crocker, brother of tycoon Charles Crocker. Other outstanding museums include the California State Capitol Museum, the California State Indian Museum, the California State Railroad Museum, the Sacramento History Center, the Towe Ford Museum, the Sacramento Museum and History Commission, and the Sacramento Science Center and Junior Museum.

Travel and Tourism

Hotel Rooms 15,086
Convention and Exhibit Space (square feet) NA

Convention Centers
　Sacramento Community Convention Center
　Memorial Auditorium
　California Exposition

Festivals
　Dixie Land Jazz Jubilee (Memorial Day)
　Sacramento Water Festival (July)
　California State Fair (August)

Parks and Recreation

Sacramento has 80 parks. The largest is the 236-acre William Land Park. The American River Bike Trail is a 33-mile trail along the river's edge.

Sources of Further information

City Hall
915 I Street
Sacramento, CA 95814
(916) 264-5407

Sacramento Convention and Visitors Bureau
1311 I Street
Sacramento, CA 95814
(916) 442-5542

Sacramento Metropolitan Chamber of Commerce
917 Seventh Street
Sacramento, CA 95814
(916) 443-3771

Additional Reading

Bachelis, Faren M. *The Pelican Guide to Sacramento and the Gold Country*. 1986.
Holden, William M. *Sacramento: Excursions into its History and Natural World*, 1991.
Leland, Dorothy K. *A Short History of Sacramento*. 1988.
———. *The Big Tomato: A Guide to the Sacramento Region*. 1990.

McGowan, Joseph A., and Terry R. Willis.
  Sacramento: Heart of the Golden State. 1983.
Zauner, Phyllis. *Sacramento and the California Delta.*
  1979.

St. Louis

Missouri

Basic Data

Name   St. Louis
Name Origin   From King Louis IX of France
Year Founded   1763 Inc. 1822
Status: State   Missouri
     County   (Independent)
Area (square miles)   61.9
Elevation (feet)   455
Time Zone   Central
Population (1990)   396,685
Population of Metro Area (1990)   2,444,099

Sister Cities

   Bologna, Italy
   Galway, Ireland
   Georgetown, Guyana
   Lyon, France
   Nanjing, China
   Stuttgart, Germany
   Suwa, Japan

Distance in Miles To:

Atlanta	565
Boston	1,207
Chicago	289
Dallas	655
Denver	863
Detroit	534
Houston	839
Los Angeles	1,836
Miami	1,226
New York	976
Philadelphia	904
Washington, DC	862

Location and Topography

N

St. Louis is located along a crescent-shaped bend of the Mississippi River about 10 miles downstream from the convergence of the Mississippi and the Missouri. The surrounding country is gently rolling with occasional high bluffs. St. Louis is spread along 19 miles of the Mississippi River shoreline and gently rises to the west to an elevation of 465 feet. St. Louis County, which surrounds the city on all sides except the east, has a more rolling topography. The metropolitan area includes three other Missouri counties and four Illinois counties. The Illinois counties are divided by bluffs that lie close to the river at Alton, recede about five miles inland at the boundary between East St. Louis and Belleville, and return to the river in the southern St. Clair and Monroe counties. The older suburban areas lie west of the bluffs, while some of the nation's richest farmland lies to the east.

Layout of City and Suburbs

The plan of the city has changed in the last 100 years. A wharf stretches for a mile and a half along the Mississippi; warehouses, commercial buildings, and factories dating from the period following the Great Fire of 1849 used to be located around this area. It was the former commercial core of the city that was abandoned when St. Louis turned its back on the river. The heart of the present city lies several blocks to the west, where the Jefferson National Expansion Memorial stands with its crowning showpiece—the Gateway Arch—between Twelfth Street Boulevard and Fifteenth Street. West from the end of Market Street, the main axis of the plaza, a highway runs to the suburbs. Formerly Fourth Street was the center of downtown. The principal older streets run north and south paralleling the river. As the city has expanded, additions have been made at haphazard angles so that streets spread fanwise away from the river, many of them following old trails. The chief business district extends roughly from Fourth Street almost to Grand Boulevard and from Chouteau Avenue to Franklin Avenue. The main shopping center is between Sixth and Eleventh and Olive and Washington. In the heart of the district extending to Grand Boulevard is the Vanderventer Place, two

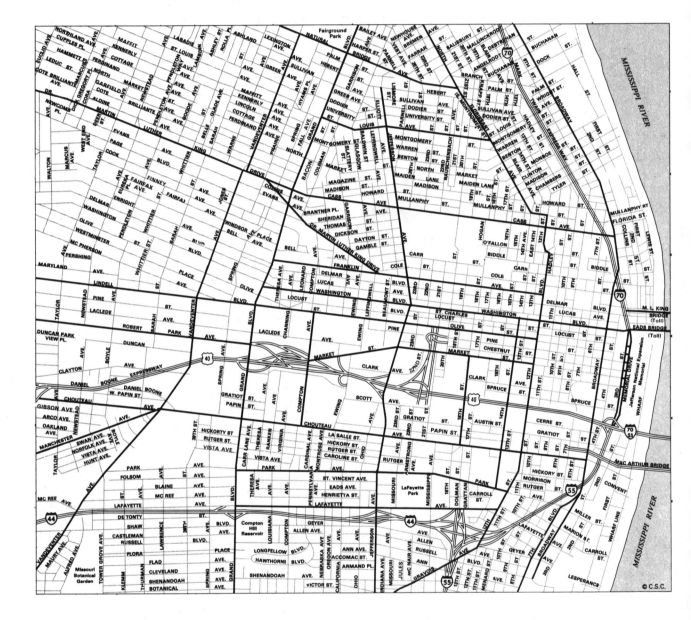

blocks of brick and stone mansions that were built between 1870 and 1890. Between Euclid and Maryland avenues is another exclusive shopping district. Forest Park, west of Kingshighway, is an upscale residential district. Along DaBaliviere and westward on Delmar are residential districts interspersed with hotels, small shops, and clinics. Directly to the north of this section is the Wellston shopping center along Easton Avenue. Enclosing this central swatch of the city are the North and South sides, each joined to the city along the business district by a depressed area. The German element is strong on the South Side. Each side has its own shopping center, the North Side at Grand and West Florissant, running north to the Water Tower; the South, on Grand from Cherokee to Gravois. The Italians are settled mainly between Sulphur Avenue and Kingshighway and between Manchester Road and Arsenel Street.

Environment

Environmental Stress Index   3.8
Green Cities Index: Rank   63
           Score   42.86
Water Quality   Alkaline, moderately hard, fluoridated
Average Daily Use (gallons per capita)   251
    Maximum Supply (gallons per capita)   536
Parkland as % of Total City Area   7.7
% Waste Landfilled/Recycled   NA
Annual Parks Expenditures per Capita $142.85

Climate

St. Louis has a modified continental, four-season climate without prolonged periods of extreme cold, heat, or humidity. The weather is influenced alternately by the warm moist air from the Gulf of Mexico and the cold Arctic air from Canada. Their encounters along the fractal zones produce a variety of weather conditions, so that St. Louisians rarely complain of climatic monotony. Winters, while brisk, are never severe, and snowfall rarely exceeds 20 inches a year. Summers are quite warm and often humid with at least five days over 100°F every year. The region also is exposed to severe storms or tornadoes, accompanied by damaging winds.

Weather

Temperature

Highest Monthly Average °F   89.0
Lowest Monthly Average °F   19.9

Annual Averages

Days 32°F or Below   107
Days above 90°F   37
Zero Degree Days   3
Precipitation (inches)   36.0
Snow (inches)   18
% Seasonal Humidity   70
Wind Speed (m.p.h.)   9.5
Clear Days   105
Cloudy Days   159
Storm Days   45
Rainy Days   108

Weather (continued)

Average Temperatures (°F)	High	Low	Mean
January	39.9	22.6	31.3
February	44.2	26.0	35.1
March	53.0	33.5	43.3
April	67.0	46.0	56.5
May	76.0	55.5	65.8
June	84.9	64.8	74.9
July	88.4	68.8	78.6
August	87.2	67.1	77.2
September	80.1	59.1	69.6
October	69.8	48.4	59.1
November	54.1	35.9	45.0
December	42.7	26.5	34.6

History

The region in which St. Louis is situated was once the home of the Kaskaskia Indians from the Illinois River and the Tamaroa Indians from the village of Cahokia. The first white settlement at this site was in 1700 when the Jesuit Order of St. Francis Xavier established a mission at the mouth of the *Riviere des Peres* (River of the Fathers) within the present city limits. The mission was abandoned after three years, and it remained deserted for the next 50 years. On 6 July 1763, Maxent, Laclede and Company of New Orleans was granted the exclusive rights to the Indian trade in the Missouri River Valley and the country west of the Mississippi as far north as St. Peter's River. On 3 August, Pierre Laclede Liguest, a junior partner in the firm, sailed up the Mississippi with 30 others and encamped near Fort Chartres on the east bank of the river below St. Louis. In December he moved upstream to the present site of St. Louis, which he predicted would become one of the finest cities on the continent. The first foundation was laid in February by 13-year-old Auguste Chouteau. The village, named for Louis IX, the crusader king of France, consisted of five streets: Rue Royale, now First Street, facing the river; behind it Rue de l'Eglise and Rue de Granges, now Second and Third Streets; and intersecting them, Rue Bonhomme and Rue de la Tour, now Market and Walnut streets. The village plan included La Place d'Armes, a public square, and a church site where the Old Cathedral is now. Laclede's own house was on the present First Street. Just above the town and slightly to the north on the second riverbank level was a group of Indian mounds in the shape of a parallelogram. The Big Mound at the northeast corner of the present Mound and Broadway was for many years a landmark. All of the large group of mounds, which once stood outside the wall of the original city, were leveled as St. Louis grew. For many years St. Louis remained the center of fur trade in the Mississippi Valley. In 1765 the Spanish government withdrew the fur-trading privileges of Maxent, Laclede and Company, and the region was thrown open to all settlers. During the Revolutionary War, France and Spain became allies of the colonists and helped to repel a British attack on the city. This victory preserved the important Mississippi-Ohio River route for the entry of American supplies. For a time, pirates made commerce dangerous on the

Chronology

1700 The Jesuit Mission of St. Francis Xavier establishes a mission at the mouth of the *Riviere des Peres*.

1763 Pierre Laclede, junior partner in Maxent, Laclede and Company of New Orleans, holders of exclusive trading rights in the Missouri River Valley, arrives at Fort Chartres on the east bank of the Mississippi below St. Louis. He selects the site of St. Louis as the most suitable location for his trading post.

1764 The foundation is laid for a village named after Louis IX of France, with five streets and a public square.

1765 Spanish government revokes the exclusive trading privileges granted to Maxent, Laclede and Company, and throws open the region to all settlers.

1780 With French and Spanish help, St. Louis repels British invaders.

1788 Ten boats sailing up the Mississippi from New Orleans put an end to piracy on the Mississippi River.

1803 St. Louis passes into the hands of the United States following the Louisiana Purchase.

1804 Lewis and Clark set out on their historic expedition.

1808 Joseph Charles founds the *Missouri Gazette*, the city's first newspaper. George Tompkins founds first English school. St. Louis is incorporated as a village with 1,400 inhabitants.

1809 The Missouri Fur Company is organized.

1817 *Zebulon M. Pike* is the first steamboat to dock at St. Louis.

1822 St. Louis is incorporated as a city.

1825 State capital is moved first to St. Charles then to Jefferson City.

1827 Fort Bellefontaine is replaced by Jefferson Barracks.

1832 St. Louis University is founded; an outbreak of cholera kills 4,060.

1837 Panic delays construction of railroad.

1849 Worst fire in St. Louis history destroys 15 business blocks.

1853 Washington University is founded.

1861 Union troops under General Nathaniel Lyon and Francis P. Blair force 800 pro-slavery state troopers to surrender at Camp Jackson and seize the St. Louis Arsenal.

1870 The *Natchez* and the *Robert E. Lee* race on the Mississippi from New Orleans to St. Louis.

1874 Eads Bridge and Union Station are completed.

1875 City purchases Forest Park, the largest park in St. Louis.

1876 Democratic party holds national convention in city.

1878 Joseph Pulitzer, a Hungarian immigrant, founds the *Post-Dispatch*; the first Veiled Prophet Festival is held.

1880 St. Louis Symphony Orchestra is founded.

1904 Louisiana Purchase Exposition is a resounding success; the city hosts the first Olympiad to be held in the United States; nine members of the municipal assembly are jailed for graft.

1910 The first international aviation meet is held in the city.

1955 Voters approve $110-million bond for rebuilding city; the Third Street Interregional Highway opens.

1958 A new four-lane expressway bridge opens across the Missouri River at St. Charles.

1961 The Mark Twain Highway from downtown to St. Charles opens.

1965 Gateway Arch is built on Laclede's landing place.

1968 The first black congressman is elected from the city.

Mississippi River until 1788, the Year of the Ten Boats, when they were driven out by ten boats traveling upstream from New Orleans. During the last decade of the 18th century St. Louis flourished and became the center of wealth and culture in the Upper Valley. In 1803, following the Louisiana Purchase, St. Louis became part of the United States and the gateway to the West. The immediate consequence of the change of government was a flood of immigrants, mostly brawlers, gamblers, and adventurers who found the riotous independence of the town appealing. After the expeditions of James Pursley in 1802 and of Lewis and Clark between 1804 and 1806, St. Louis-based fur traders and trappers were breaking trails over a far-flung territory extending to the Pacific. In 1809 the Missouri Fur Company was organized and managed to stave off John Jacob Astor's American Fur Company. In 1808 Joseph Charles founded the *Missouri Gazette*, the first newspaper west of the Mississippi River, and George Tompkins established one of the first English schools. In the same year, with its boundaries pushed back to

Seventh Street, St. Louis was incorporated as a village of 1,400 citizens. Fourteen years later it received its city charter. Until 1825 St. Louis was the seat of Missouri government, but the powerful rural bloc of voters persuaded Governor Alexander McNair to transfer the capital first to St. Charles and later to Jefferson City. In 1817 the first steamboat docked at St. Louis, signaling its rise as a river port. St. Louis began to spread back from the river as its population grew to 350,000 in 1880. By 1850 St. Louis had become an industrial city with tobacco factories, foundries, and flour mills. With industrial growth came a cultural renaissance. Roman Catholic and Episcopalian dioceses were established. A public library was built. The St. Louis University was organized in 1832, and Washington University in 1853. A public school system was instituted in the 1850s. The city had its share of disasters and reverses. Depressions in 1819, 1837, 1857, and 1873 dampened economic growth. The course of the Mississippi changed, threatening to leave the port of St. Louis a sandbar. The threat was removed only after jetties and revetments were constructed at the upper end of Bloody Island between 1837 and 1839. In 1849 the steamboat *White Cloud* caught fire. The flames spread rapidly to other boats and wharf buildings and, in the end, destroyed 15 business blocks. Cholera struck in 1832, killing over 4,000 residents. These tragedies, however, helped to promote a renovation of the city and an improvement in living conditions.

St. Louis shared the national prosperity in the 1850s after the Mexican War had added new territory to the United States, gold had been discovered in California, and railroads had begun to link cities together. St. Louis was in a position both geographically and commercially to benefit from the great westward movement. St. Louis traders and merchants were familiar with western markets and trails. The Pacific railroads had their eastern terminus in St. Louis. At the outbreak of the Civil War, St. Louis was divided in its sympathies. The older families were pro-slavery while the new immigrants, who made up two-thirds of the population, were pro-Union. A crisis came soon after the fall of Fort Sumter. General Nathaniel Lyon and Francis P. Blair, with about 10,000 German and U.S. soldiers, seized the St. Louis Arsenel and forced the surrender of 800 state troopers. Thereafter St. Louis served as a base of federal operations. St. Louis not only escaped damage but profited from the war, and its manufacturing output increased 296% during the decade of the 1860s. The postwar era saw the end of the steamboat traffic on the Mississippi but not before producing three of the largest craft to ply the river: *Natchez, Robert E. Lee,* and *J. M. White III.* The railroad era, which began soon after, saw the construction of the Eads Bridge and the first Union Station in 1874. Cultural growth kept pace. The Missouri Botanical Gardens and Tower Grove Park were presented to the city by Henry Shaw. The St. Louis Symphony Orchestra was founded in 1880. The Mercantile Library Association, founded in 1846, built up a fine collection of art objects. The press was joined by a new daily: the

Post-Dispatch, founded by Joseph Pulitzer. In 1877 a new charter for local government was adopted, providing for the separation of the city from the county. The city experienced a financial panic in 1873 and a railroad strike in 1877. The culmination of over one century of growth was the 1904 Louisiana Purchase Exposition, which was a tremendous success. The ice cream cone, the hot dog, and iced tea were introduced at this fair. The first Olympiad to be held in the United States took place in St. Louis in 1904. In 1910 the first international aviation meet was held at Kinloch Park in the city. But the first decade of the 20th century was marred by graft and corruption scandals in which nine members of the municipal assembly were convicted. St. Louis was hurt considerably by Prohibition and the Great Depression. An aggressive campaign against urban blight was launched in 1955. Several public housing projects were completed during the 1950s, including the redevelopment of Mill Creek Valley, a 465-acre depressed area. The city's transportation infrastructure was revamped through the construction of the Third Street Interregional Highway, opened in 1955; the Mark Twain Highway (Interstate 70) from downtown St. Louis to St. Charles opened in 1961; and a 4,028-foot, four-lane expressway bridge across the Missouri River at St. Charles, opened in 1958. In 1965 the Gateway Arch, the city's most famous landmark, designed by Eero Saarinen, was built on the spot where Laclede landed.

Historical Landmarks

The Gateway Arch, which rises 630 feet on Lacledes Landing, is the nation's tallest monument. Eads Bridge over the Mississippi at Washington Avenue, dedicated in 1874, is the world's first steel truss bridge and was designed and built by Captain James B. Eads at a cost of $10 million. Old Rock House on the corner of Wharf and Chestnut streets, facing the river, was a two-story building built in 1818 by Manuel Lisa, a noted fur trader for the Missouri Fur Company. The Merchants Exchange on Third Street was the largest trade hall with an unsupported ceiling when it was completed in 1875. The Old Courthouse on Fourth Street has a 198-foot-high cast-iron dome. Of cruciform Greek Revival design, its massive rotunda rises in four circular galleries to the dome. It was the scene of many of Missouri's historic events, including the *Dred Scott* case, which did much to precipitate the Civil War. The Old National Hotel occupies a historic site where, in 1818, the first Baptist church was built in St. Louis. The Old Cathedral of St. Louis of France on Walnut Street is one of the oldest buildings in the city, built on property given by Laclede. Since 1914, when the new St. Louis Cathedral was built, it has been known as the Church of St. Louis of France. The Eugene Field House on Broadway is a three-story red brick house built in 1845. It was dedicated as a museum in 1936. The John Woodward Johnson House on Market Street, the home of the third mayor of St. Louis, dates from the early 1830s. The Wainwright Building on Seventh Street was one of the earliest skyscrapers in St. Louis, built by Louis Sullivan. The Mercantile Library on Locust Street was first established in 1845; it was moved into the present location in 1885. The Dent-Grant House on Fourth and Cerre streets, built in 1845, was the home of the wife of Ulysses S. Grant. The Soldiers Memorial Building fills the central block of Memorial Plaza from Thirteenth Street to Fourteenth Street. In the center of the loggia is a cenotaph of Belgian marble bearing the names of 1,249 St. Louisians who died in World War I. Christ Church Cathedral on Thirteenth and Locust streets, a limestone structure in early English Gothic style, is the mother church of the Episcopal diocese. It was begun in 1859 and completed in 1867. The Robert Campbell House on Locust Street is an antebellum residence built in the 1850s by a rich fur trader. Union Station on Market Street is a four-story Romanesque building with a 230-foot clock tower, opened in 1896. Aloe Plaza, bounded by Market, Pine, Eighteenth, and Twentieth streets, is dominated by Carl Mille's fountain, The Meeting of the Waters. Unveiled in 1940, the 14 bronze figures of the fountain group symbolize the meeting of the Missouri and Mississippi rivers. The Old Arsenel on Second and Arsenel streets consists of a group of red brick and gray limestone buildings. It was established in 1827. Its capture by the Union forces in the Civil War proved to be decisive in keeping Missouri out of the Confederacy. The Jefferson Memorial on Lindell Boulevard is a two-story white limestone structure, consisting of two wings connected by a loggia. It is built on the site of the main entrance to the Louisiana Purchase Exposition. In the center of the loggia is an immense marble statue of Thomas Jefferson. North of Eads Bridge is Lacledes Landing, a former warehousing district, now a major tourist attraction. The Cathedral of St. Louis is a Byzantine structure dedicated in 1914. The nave is covered by a great dome flanked by two semidomes, all covered by mosaics. The remains of a major Indian trading village of the 17th century are preserved in Cahokia Mounds, on the Illinois side of the river.

Population

St. Louis, which was one of the ten largest cities in the United States in the 19th century, has been steadily losing population in the 20th century. In 1990 it ranked 34th with a population of 396,685, as against 26th with a population of 452,801 in 1980. In 1970 it had a population of 622,000, and it shed 27.2% of its residents in the 1970s and 12.4% in the 1980s.

Population		
	1980	1990
Central City	452,801	396,685
Rank	26	34
Metro Area	2,376,971	2,444,099
Pop. Change 1980–1990 -56,116		
Pop. % Change 1980–1990 -12.4		
Median Age 32.8		

Population (continued)
% Male 45.5
% Age 65 and Over 16.60
Density (per square mile) 6,408

Households
Number 164,931
Persons per Household 2.34
% Female-Headed Households 20.5
% One-Person Households 39.2
Births—Total 7,931
% to Mothers under 20 21.7
Birth Rate per 1,000 18.5

Ethnic Composition

Whites make up 51% of the population; blacks 48%; Hispanics 1%; and Asians, Pacific Islanders, and American Indians 1%. Blacks began moving into the city during the Civil War and by 1940 made up 11.4%. In the half century since then their share of the population has risen dramatically. They primarily live in a far-flung belt bounded by Chouteau, Cass, and Seventh Avenue and Marcus. The city's famous German community remains intact and is particularly strong on the south side. The historic Italian district is between Kingshighway and Sulphur Avenue and Manchester Road and Arsenel Street.

Ethnic Composition (as % of total pop.)		
	1980	1990
White	53.54	50.94
Black	45.55	47.50
American Indian	0.14	0.24
Asian and Pacific Islander	0.37	0.94
Hispanic	1.22	1.29
Other	NA	0.38

Government

The governmental structure of St. Louis is provided by its home-rule charter approved in 1914. The city is governed by a mayor and a council of 28 aldermen, all elected for four-year terms. Voters choose the mayor in April in odd-numbered years; half the number of aldermen are chosen from single wards every two years. St. Louis is one of the few cities not within a county. After withdrawing from St. Louis County in 1876, it became an independent city. It, however, has tried unsuccessfully to rejoin the county in recent years and to extend its territorial borders, meeting resistance from the county in both efforts. Unlike most cities, St. Louis does not control its own police department or its department of elections. Both these departments are run by commissions whose members are appointed by the governor. Since the city is expected to perform county functions within its borders, a complete line of county officers is elected and supported by public taxes. They include the recorder of deeds, sheriff, coroner, treasurer, public administrator, license collector, and collector of revenues. These individuals operate under state statutes and are outside the city's merit system. The Democrats have held power in St. Louis since 1949.

Government

Year of Home Charter   1914
Number of Members of the Governing Body   29
Elected at Large   1
Elected by Wards   28
Number of Women in Governing Body   8
Salary of Mayor $82,680
Salary of Council Members $21,465
City Government Employment Total   8,719
Rate per 10,000   204.5

Public Finance

The annual budget consists of revenues of $644.772 million and expenditures of $606.524 million. The debt outstanding is $709.001 million and cash and security holdings of $1.417 billion.

Public Finance

Total Revenue (in millions) $644.772
Intergovernmental Revenue—Total (in millions) $74.45
Federal Revenue per Capita $42.99
% Federal Assistance   6.66
% State Assistance   4.56
Sales Tax as % of Total Revenue   18.03
Local Revenue as % of Total Revenue   68.31
City Income Tax   yes
Taxes—Total (in millions) $235.2

Taxes per Capita
   Total $552
   Property $73
   Sales and Gross Receipts $247
General Expenditures—Total (in millions) $461.3
General Expenditures per Capita $1,082
Capital Outlays per Capita $214

% of Expenditures for:
   Public Welfare   0.4
   Highways   6.5
   Education   0.4
   Health and Hospitals   13.2
   Police   15.7
   Sewerage and Sanitation   2.6
   Parks and Recreation   4.0
   Housing and Community Development   8.3
Debt Outstanding per Capita $953
   % Utility   3.1
Federal Procurement Contract Awards (in millions)
   $5,248.5
Federal Grants Awards (in millions) $359.5
Fiscal Year Begins   May 1

Economy

$ St. Louis, having had flourishing industries even in the 19th century, has a rich industrial heritage. Despite heavy population losses and indifferent economic management, it has maintained this lead in many areas. It is a center for advanced technology with over 100,000 scientists and engineers employed by McDonnell Douglas, General Dynamics, and Monsanto, and

with high-technology facilities, such as St. Louis Technology Park and the Missouri Research Park. It is the headquarters of 10 Fortune 500 and 16 Forbes 500 firms and is the base of the Eighth Federal Reserve District. It is second only to Detroit in auto production with all the big three automakers operating assembly plants in the area. Besides automobiles, the major industrial products are jet aircraft, space capsules, foods, primary metals, fabricated metal products, nonelectrical machinery, and chemicals. It is one of the urban areas producing all the six basic metals—iron, lead, zinc, copper, aluminum, and magnesium. St. Louis also is a major wholesale center, a leading hog market, a major processor of raw furs, and one of the principal grain markets. The city is best known as the headquarters of Anheuser-Busch, the largest U.S. beermaker. Monsanto is another St. Louis-based firm that is an industrial leader. Formerly, St. Louis was an important shoe production center, and it is still the location of some of the most important shoe manufacturing firms.

Economy

Total Money Income (in millions) $3,748.3
% of State Average   85.6
Per Capita Annual Income $8,799
% Population below Poverty Level   21.8
Fortune 500 Companies   10

Banks	Number	Deposits (in millions)
Commercial	256	21,240.795
Savings	45	10,700.0

Passenger Autos   734,391
Electric Meters   505,000
Gas Meters   500,000

Manufacturing

Number of Establishments   980
% with 20 or More Employees   43.0
Manufacturing Payroll (in millions) $2,422.0
Value Added by Manufacture (in millions) $5,232.2
Value of Shipments (in millions) $11,964.0
New Capital Expenditures (in millions) $318.3

Wholesale Trade

Number of Establishments   NA
Sales (in millions)   NA
Annual Payroll (in millions)   NA

Retail Trade

Number of Establishments   3,422
Total Sales (in millions) $2,159.1
Sales per Capita $5,065
Number of Retail Trade Establishments with Payroll   2,532
Annual Payroll (in millions) $305.9
Total Sales (in millions) $2,124.0
General Merchandise Stores (per capita) $504
Food Stores (per capita) $1,038
Apparel Stores (per capita) $209
Eating and Drinking Places (per capita) $942

Service Industries

Total Establishments   2,673
Total Receipts (in millions) $2,060.3
Hotels and Motels (in millions) $139.8
Health Services (in millions) $249.3
Legal Services (in millions) $281.7

Labor

The largest sectors are services, trade, and manufacturing, in that order. Availability of skilled labor is one of the factors that favors St. Louis as an industrial site. Labor-management disputes are 22% or more below national average, principally as the result of the efforts of three labor management committees, PRIDE in the Missouri metro area and IMAGE in the Illinois counties, as well as the New Spirit of St. Louis Labor Management Committee.

Labor

Civilian Labor Force   187,334
% Change 1989–1990   -0.4

Work Force Distribution
    Mining   NA
    Construction   50,800
    Manufacturing   206,800
    Transportation and Public Utilities   78,700
    Wholesale and Retail Trade   276,100
    FIRE (Finance, Insurance, Real Estate)   73,600
    Service   327,800
    Government   144,200
    Women as % of Labor Force   48.4
    % Self-Employed   3.0
    % Professional/Technical   14.1
Total Unemployment   15,337
Rate %   8.2
Federal Government Civilian Employment   24,096

Education

St. Louis City School District, Missouri's largest school district, supports 130 elementary schools, junior high schools, and senior high schools. St. Louis has a strong parochial system with nearly 30 elementary and secondary schools.

St. Louis is the home of three private universities: St. Louis University, Washington University, and Webster University. There are two public universities as well: the University of Missouri at St. Louis, and the Southern Illinois University at Edwardsville. St. Louis University, founded in 1832, is the oldest university west of the Mississippi River. Founded as the St. Louis Academy in 1818, it became St. Louis College in 1820 and was placed under Jesuit direction in 1823. Washington University developed from the Elliot Seminary, chartered in 1853. Webster University is located in suburban Webster Groves. Four-year colleges include: Fontbonne College, Harris-Stowe State College, Maryville College, Metropolitan College of St. Louis University, Missouri Baptist College, St. Louis College of Pharmacy, and St. Louis Conservatory of Music. St. Louis is a center of theologial education with seven major institutions: Aquinas Institute, Cardinal Glennon College, Concordia Seminary, Covenant Theological Seminary, Eden Theological Seminary, St. Louis Rabbinical College, and St. Louis University Department of Theological Studies.

Education

Number of Public Schools   130
Special Education Schools   NA
Total Enrollment   43,284
% Enrollment in Private Schools   20.3
% Minority   NA
Classroom Teachers   3,309
Pupil-Teacher Ratio   13:1
Number of Graduates   1,457
Total Revenue (in millions) $248.664
Total Expenditures (in millions) $256.322
Expenditures per Pupil $5,396
Educational Attainment (Age 25 and Over)
    % Completed 12 or More Years   48.2
    % Completed 16 or More Years   10.0
Four-Year Colleges and Universities   10
    Enrollment   54,241
Two-Year Colleges   3
    Enrollment   18,109

Libraries

Number   128
Public Libraries   15
Books (in thousands)   1,630
Circulation (in thousands)   NA
Persons Served (in thousands)   396
Circulation per Person Served   NA
Income (in millions) $10.8
Staff   219

Four-Year Colleges and Universities
    University of Missouri, St. Louis
    Harris-Stowe State College
    Fontbonne College
    Maryville College
    Missouri Baptist College
    St. Louis College of Pharmacy
    St. Louis Conservatory of Music
    St. Louis University
    Washington University
    Webster University

Health

St. Louis has 26 hospitals. The Washington University Medical Center, comprised of Barnes Hospital, Jewish Hospital, and St. Louis Children's Hospital, is one of the best medical and teaching facilities in the nation. St. Louis University Medical Center is an outstanding regional facility, as is St. Louis Children's Hospital in pediatric care. Other major hospitals include St. John's Mercy Medical Center, St. Luke's Hospital, DePaul Health Center, St. Mary's Health Center, Deaconess Hospital, Cardinal Glennon Children's Hospital, and Missouri Baptist Medical Center.

Health

Deaths—Total   6,225
Rate per 1,000   14.5
Infant Deaths—Total   119
Rate per 1,000   15.0
Number of Metro Hospitals   26
Number of Metro Hospital Beds   9,637
Rate per 100,000   2,261
Number of Physicians   5,262
Physicians per 1,000   2.49
Nurses per 1,000   18.88
Health Expenditures per Capita $56.99

Transportation

St. Louis is approached by four interstate highways: I-44, I-55, I-64, and I-70, while I-270 rings the city. The Illinois and Missouri sections are linked by eight bridges spanning the Mississippi River. The oldest is Eads Bridge, and the others are MacArthur, Chain of Rocks, McKinley, Jefferson Barracks, Clark, Veterans Memorial, and Poplar Street. Rail transportation is provided by Amtrak for passengers, and ten trunk lines and three switching lines for freight. St. Louis is the nation's third-largest rail freight hub. All railroads use the Union Station, and the switching tracks are owned by St. Louis Terminal Railroad Association. Within the city, the road system is laid out on the grid system with numbered streets running north to south and streets named after trees running east to west. The numbered streets are bisected by Market Street on which the Union Station is located. A number of streets are one-way. Downtown Bistate runs a free bus zone, and the Levee Line also is free during summer months. The Metro Link is a light rail commuter trail line due for completion in 1993. It will run from Lambert Airport through downtown to East St. Louis. St. Louis is the country's busiest inland port. Barge services are available to New Orleans throughout the year and to Minneapolis and St. Paul for eight months of the year. The Chain of Rocks Canal has improved river traffic by bypassing a long curving stretch of the Mississippi River. The city airport is the municipally owned Lambert–St. Louis International Airport, one of the most modern facilities in the nation.

Transportation
Interstate Highway Mileage   214
Total Urban Mileage   7,187
Total Daily Vehicle Mileage (in millions) $45.279
Daily Average Commute Time   50.6 min.
Number of Buses   641
Port Tonnage (in millions) $29.011
Airports   2
Number of Daily Flights   379
Daily Average Number of Passengers   25,743
Airlines (American carriers only)
American
American West
Continental
Delta
Eastern
Northwest
Southwest
Trans World
United
USAir

Housing

The City Plan Commission estimates that 29% of the housing stock is in poor condition, 40% in fair condition, and 31% in good condition. The better housing is concentrated in South St. Louis, with an enclave of very spacious homes on broad, tree-lined streets at the west end. Most of the blighted areas and slums are found in the northern and central sections of the city. About two-thirds of the dwellings are single-family homes. Since the 1950s public housing projects have replaced hundreds of run-down homes.

St. Louis has distinctive neighborhoods that are being restored through regentrification programs. These include the Hill, which still retains a heavy Italian flavor; the Soulard Market area, still German; Lafayette Square, once an upper-class area, which declined after the 1950s but has been restored; Compton Heights, with homes modeled on those in 19th-century Berlin; Carondelet in South St. Louis, settled at first by the French and later by the Germans; Central West End, located next to Forest Park; Dog Town, once peopled by poor Irish workers who worked in the neighboring steel factory; Clayton, located in the Central Corridor, a strong central business district with a residential area; and Kirkwood and Webster Groves in West Louis County, known for their beautiful trees and historic frame houses. The city's Land Clearance and Redevelopment Authority has been responsible for many housing projects, such as the 465-acre Mill Creek Valley.

Housing		
Total Housing Units 194,919		
% Change 1980–1990 -3.7		
Vacant Units for Sale or Rent 19,858		
Occupied Units 164,931		
% with More Than One Person per Room 5.3		
% Owner-Occupied 45.1		
Median Value of Owner-Occupied Homes $50,700		
Average Monthly Purchase Cost $283		
Median Monthly Rent $252		
New Private Housing Starts 39		
Value (in thousands) $2,608		
% Single-Family 94.9		
Nonresidential Buildings Value (in thousands) $48,152		
Tallest Buildings	*Hgt. (ft.)*	*Stories*
Gateway Arch	630	NA
Metropolitan Square Tower	591	42
S.W. Bell Telephone Bldg.	587	44
Mercantile Center Tower	550	37
Centerre Plaza	433	31
Laclede Gas Bldg.	400	31
S.W. Bell Telephone Bldg.	398	31
Civil Courts	387	13

Urban Redevelopment

In the 1980s downtown St. Louis saw considerable redevelopment with the addition of three hotels and about 600,000 square feet of retail space at its two new malls, at St. Louis Centre and Union Station, and at the historic Lacledes Landing Area. The 1,500-acre Chesterfield Village will have more than 7.5 million square feet of office and research space by 2000. The I-44 Corridor, west of Lindbergh and Earth City (the region's largest business park), has experienced a building boom in recent years.

Crime

St. Louis ranks above average in crime rates. In 1991 violent crimes totaled 14,076, and property crimes totaled 50,027.

Crime	
Violent Crimes—Total	14,076
Violent Crime Rate per 100,000	937.5
Murder	260
Rape	342
Robbery	5,294
Aggravated Assaults	8,180
Property Crimes	50,027
Burglary	13,396
Larceny	27,381
Motor Vehicle Theft	9,250
Arson	867
Per Capita Police Expenditures	$221.06
Per Capita Fire Protection Expenditures	$72.49
Number of Police	1,627
Per 1,000	3.77

Religion

St. Louis has strong Catholic historical roots, and the city has numerous fine Catholic churches, including the St. Louis Cathedral, and many Catholic educational institutions. The largest denomination is Catholic. Jews also are well established and account for about 5% of the population. Among Protestants, Baptists are the strongest.

Religion	
Largest Denominations (Adherents)	
Catholic	317,562
Lutheran-Missouri Synod	41,026
Black Baptist	45,751
Southern Baptist	57,911
Evangelical Lutheran	6,243
United Church of Christ	24,807
United Methodist	27,995
Presbyterian	20,656
Jewish	21,689

Media

The St. Louis press includes the *St. Louis Daily Record*. The electronic media consist of 7 television stations and 29 AM and FM radio stations.

Media	
Newsprint	
St. Louis Business Journal, weekly	
St. Louis Commerce, monthly	
The St. Louis Crusader, weekly	
St. Louis Magazine, monthly	
St. Louis Daily Record, daily	

Media (continued)

Television
  KDNL (Channel 30)
  KETC (Channel 9)
  KMOV (Channel 4)
  KNLC (Channel 24)
  KPLR (Channel 11)
  KSDK (Channel 5)
  KTVI (Channel 2)

Radio

KATZ (AM)	KATZ (FM)
KBDY (FM)	KCFV (FM)
KDHX (FM)	KEZK (AM)
KEZK (FM)	KGLD (AM)
KHTK (FM)	KLOU (FM)
KMJM (FM)	KMOX (AM)
KSD (FM)	KSHE (FM)
KSTL (AM)	KSIV (AM)
KSIV (FM)	KSUA (AM)
KWMU (FM)	KWUR (FM)
KYKY (FM)	KYMC (FM)
WCBW (FM)	WEW (AM)
WFXB (FM)	WGNU (AM)
WKBQ (FM)	WKKX (FM)
WIL (FM)	

Sports

St. Louis is represented in two professional sports: in baseball by the St. Louis Cardinals, who compete in the National League and play their home games at Busch Stadium (in front of which stands a statue of Stan Musial); and in hockey by the St. Louis Blues, who play their home games in the Arena. There are two sports halls of fame in the city: the St. Louis Sports Hall of Fame and the National Bowling Hall of Fame. Every August St. Louis holds the Grand Prix power boat racing world championships.

Arts, Culture and Tourism

As befits the queen city of the Midwest, St. Louis is the regional leader in the performing arts. In music, it has the St. Louis Symphony Orchestra, based at the Powell Symphony Hall, and the Opera Theater; in dance, it has Dance St. Louis; in drama, it has the Fabulous Fox Theater; the Muny, a 12,000-seat, open-air amphitheater in Forest Park; the American Theater; the Repertory Theater; and the Theater Project Company. Other theater companies and groups include the Black Repertory Company, the Goldenrod Showboat, and the Westport Playhouse. The Loretto-Hilton Center at Webster University is a popular indoor stage. St. Louis is important in the history of jazz music as a place where some of its best exponents have played.

The St. Louis Art Museum in Forest Park was the Fine Arts Palace of the 1904 World's Fair. The Washington University Gallery of Art was the first museum west of the Mississippi. The Missouri Historical Society's Jefferson Memorial Museum is the custodian of the city's past. The Concordia Historical Institute maintains an authentic collection of documents and artifacts relating to Christianity in the United States.

The City Art Museum on Art Hill in Forest Park has an impressive art collection. Other museums include the Mercantile Money Museum, the Museum of Transport, the Dog Museum, the Golden Eagle River Museum of river lore and boats, the McDonnell Douglas Prologue Room of aerospace exhibits, and the Eugene Field House and Toy Museum.

Travel and Tourism

Hotel Rooms 22,848
Convention and Exhibit Space (square feet) 240,000

Convention Centers
  Alfonso J. Cervantes Convention & Exhibition Center
  The Kiel
  The Arena

Festivals
  Storytelling Festival (May)
  Fragrance Festival (May)
  American Indian Days (May)
  National Ragtime & Classic Jazz Festival (June)
  Stassenfest (July)
  Japanese Festival (August)
  Chocolate Rendezvous (January)

Parks and Recreation

St. Louis has about 70 parks. Forest Park, the largest, covers 1,374 acres and includes a number of lakes, a botanical garden and zoo, a theater, and a 6.2-mile bicycle/jogging trail. It was the site of the 1904 World's Fair. The 30-acre Lafayette Park, bounded by Mississippi, Missouri, Park, and Lafayette avenues, is the oldest park in St. Louis. Near the center of the park stands a statue of Thomas Hart Benton. Tower Grove Park (which, along with the Missouri Botanical Garden, was a gift from Henry Shaw) is noted for the variety of its trees and the beauty of its water lilies. Fairgrounds Park, between Grand and Fair, and Natural Bridge and Kossuth avenues, became a public park in 1909. It is the site of the annual St. Louis Fair. The Chain of Rocks Park is a stretch of wooded bluffs above the Mississippi River.

Sources of Further Information

Economic Development Corporation
1300 Convention Plaza
St. Louis, MO 63103
(314) 231-3500

Historical Association of Greater St. Louis
3601 Lindell Boulevard
St. Louis, MO 63108
(314) 658-2588

St. Louis Convention and Visitors Convention
10 South Broadway, Suite 300
St. Louis, MO 63102
(314) 421-1023

St. Louis County Economic Council
121 South Meramec
St. Louis, MO 63105
(314) 889-7663

The St. Louis Partnership
10 Broadway
St. Louis, MO 63102
(314) 231-5555

St. Louis Public Library
1301 Olive Street
St. Louis, MO 63103
(314) 241-2288

St. Louis Regional Commerce and Growth Association
100 South Fourth Street, Suite 500
St. Louis, MO 63102
(314) 231-5555

Additional Reading

Burnett, Betty. *St. Louis: Gateway to Tomorrow.* 1990.
Coyle, Elinor M. *St. Louis Treasures.* 1986.
Fifield, Barringer. *Seeing St. Louis.* 1991.
Horgan, James J. *City of Flight: The History of Aviation in St. Louis.* 1986.
McCue, George, and Frank Peters. *A Guide to the Architecture of St. Louis.* 1989.
Metro Files. *Cityfile: St. Louis.* 1991.
Mormino, Gary R. *Immigrants on the Hill: Italian-Americans in St. Louis.* 1982.
Scott, Quinta. *Images of St. Louis.* 1989.
Troen, Selwyn K. *St. Louis.* 1977.
Vexler, Robert I. *St. Louis: A Chronological and Documentary History, 1762–1970.* 1974.

St. Paul

Minnesota

Basic Data

Name   St. Paul
Name Origin   From Apostle St. Paul
Year Founded   1840 Inc. 1854
Status: State   Capital of Minnesota
         County   Seat of Ramsey County
Area (square miles)   52.8
Elevation (feet)   780
Time Zone   Central
Population (1990)   272,235
Population of Metro Area (1990)   2,464,124

Sister Cities

Changsha, China
Culiacan, Mexico
Modena, Italy
Nagasaki, Japan
Novosibirsk, Russia
Quito, Ecuador

Distance in Miles To:

Atlanta	1,121
Boston	1,390
Chicago	410
Dallas	949
Denver	920
Detroit	685
Houston	1,183
Los Angeles	1,857
Miami	1,769
New York	1,217
Philadelphia	1,195
Washington, DC	1,090

Location and Topography

St. Paul is located on the north bank of the Mississippi River at its confluence with the Minnesota River. The southeast end of the great bend in the river where St. Paul stands marks the merging of the two river valleys. On its way to this point, the Mississippi wanders diagonally through Minneapolis before the bluffs at Mendota force it to flow north again to the heart of St. Paul, after which it turns abruptly south once more. St. Paul, like Minneapolis, is a river town. The right or south bank rises steeply from 100 to 200 feet above alluvial flatlands. The left or north bank, about half as high, is a stone terrace backed by a series of plateaus, surrounded by hills. It was on these terraces that the city was founded, but it spread into the surrounding flat or rolling land dotted with lakes.

Layout of City and Suburbs

St. Paul, until recently, possessed an Old World appearance reminiscent of European cities, because of its hilly location with narrow, winding streets. It lacked the spaciousness of its neighbor, Minneapolis. Many of the streets seem to zigzag at unreasonable angles. Beginning in the early part of the 20th century, the city planners modernized the layout on a gridiron system, except where the hills and the natural bend in the river made it impossible. Most of the thoroughfares, particularly Kellogg Boulevard, Third Street, West Seventh and Eighth streets, and University Avenue, have been widened.

Environment

Environmental Stress Index   3.0
Green Cities Index: Rank   23
                    Score   25.50
Water Quality   Alkaline, soft, fluoridated
    Average Daily Use (gallons per capita)   129
    Maximum Supply (gallons per capita)   369
Parkland as % of Total City Area   NA
% Waste Landfilled/Recycled   NA
Annual Parks Expenditures per Capita $123.15

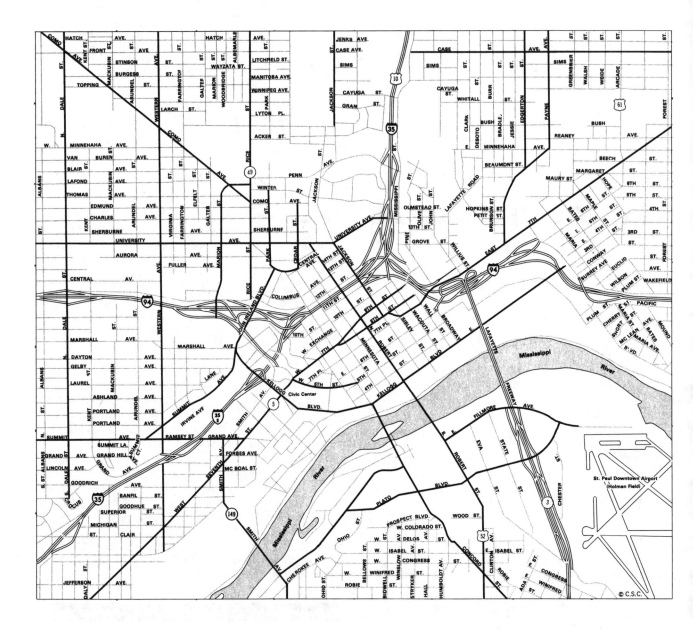

Climate

The climate is predominantly continental, marked by extreme variations in temperature, ranging from 30°F to 100°F. During spring, snowmelt and jammed ice on the Mississippi River pose the danger of flooding since St. Paul, unlike Minneapolis, is located downstream. Rain is abundant in summer. St. Paul, along with Minneapolis, is the second-coldest city in the nation after Anchorage, Alaska. For an average of 34 days a year the mercury remains below 0°F all day. Average temperature is 44°F. The summers are cool and dry with most days well below 90°F.

Weather

Temperature

Highest Monthly Average °F	83.4
Lowest Monthly Average °F	2.4

Annual Averages

Days 32°F or Below	155
Days above 90°F	15
Zero Degree Days	34
Precipitation (inches)	26.36
Snow (inches)	49.1
% Seasonal Humidity	109.5
Wind Speed (m.p.h.)	10.6
Clear Days	96
Cloudy Days	168
Storm Days	36
Rainy Days	113

Average Temperatures (°F)	High	Low	Mean
January	21.2	3.2	12.2
February	25.9	7.1	16.5
March	36.9	19.6	28.3
April	55.5	34.7	45.1
May	67.9	46.3	57.1
June	77.1	56.7	66.9
July	82.4	61.4	71.9
August	80.8	59.6	70.2
September	70.7	49.3	60.0
October	60.7	39.2	50.0
November	40.6	24.2	32.4
December	26.6	10.6	18.6

History

The area that is now St. Paul was inhabited by Sioux Indians before white men first appeared. In the winter of 1766–1767, a New Englander named Jonathan Carver sailed up the Mississippi and Minnesota rivers in search of a Northwest Passage to the Pacific Ocean. He stopped at the site of St. Paul to investigate an Indian burial ground. After the Louisiana Purchase, the U.S. government sent an expedition to the region in 1805 under Lieutenant Zebulon M. Pike. Pike bought land from the Indians around the confluence of the Minnesota and Mississippi rivers to build a military base. In 1819 Colonel Henry Leavenworth established a military post near the Minnesota River on the site of Mendota, now a suburb of St. Paul. The following year the post

was moved across the river to Fort St. Anthony, later renamed Fort Snelling. In the shadow of the fort a squatter settlement grew up, under the ministering eye of Roman Catholic and Protestant missionaries. In 1840 these settlers were evicted from the federal land. The evicted squatters, led by a French-Canadian fur trader named Pierre "Pigs' Eye" Parrant, moved to the Mississippi River landing, where they built a settlement named Pigs' Eye. The following year, Father Lucian Galtier built a log chapel and dedicated it to St. Paul. The name of the patron saint soon became the name of the settlement. In 1846 a post office was opened and next year the town was platted and a school opened. Shortly thereafter St. Paul became the headquarters of the American Fur Company, which had been based at Mendota since 1821. When the Minnesota Territory was created in 1849, St. Paul was named the capital, a status it retained after Minnesota became a state in 1858. It was incorporated as a town in 1849 and as a city in 1854. Two men dominated St. Paul in the latter half of the 19th century. James J. Hill, the railroad baron who controlled the Great Northern Railroad based in his adopted city of St. Paul, amassed immense wealth while creating a railroad empire. Hill came to St. Paul in 1856 and in 1878, with Canadian capital, gained control of the bankrupt St. Paul and Pacific Railroad. The second man was Archbishop John Ireland who built up one of the nation's largest Catholic dioceses in St. Paul, along with one of its finest cathedrals. He acquired 117,000 acres of railroad land on which he settled thousands of Irish and other immigrants.

Historical Landmarks

The Minnesota State Capitol on Wabasha Street is an imposing building topped by a cupola visible for miles. It is Minnesota's third capitol building, designed by Cass Gilbert, and built between 1896 and 1905. For his design Gilbert drew inspiration from the Italian High Renaissance. The main entrance is through three large arched openings in the rusticated base of the central pavilion. Above the entrances, at the second and third stories, is an arcaded loggia with Corinthian columns. The large central dome is a copy of Michelangelo's St. Peter's in Rome, from which it varies only in minor details. The Site of the Settler's Landing is at the Steamboat Wharf on the Mississippi River at the end of Jackson Street. The site of the log chapel of St. Paul, from which the city took its name, is between Minnesota and Cedar Streets. The Cherokee Heights Park and Lookout on Cherokee Boulevard overlooking the river valley mark the place where Pierre "Pigs' Eye" Parrant, St. Paul's first settler, erected a hovel after being expelled from federal lands at Mendota. The Church of the Assumption on Ninth and Franklin streets is the oldest German church in St. Paul, built in 1855. The largest church in the city is the Cathedral of St. Paul, begun in 1906 and dedicated in 1915. With a dome 175 feet high and 96 feet in diameter,

Chronology

1766	Jonathan Carver, attempting to find a Northwest Passage to the Pacific Ocean, visits the site of the future city of St. Paul.
1805	Lieutenant Zebulon M. Pike buys land on behalf of the Federal government from the Sioux Indians at the confluence of the Mississippi and Minnesota Rivers.
1819	Colonel Henry Leavenworth builds an army post on the Minnesota River on site of present day Mendota.
1840	Squatters on federal land at Mendota are expelled; under the leadership of Pierre "Pigs' Eye" Parrant, a French trader, they move to a new settlement called Pigs' Eye near Fort Snelling.
1844	Father Lucian Galtier builds a log church dedicated to St. Paul in the settlement, which soon adopts the name of the patron saint as its own.
1847	St. Paul is platted.
1849	St. Paul is named capital of Minnesota Territory and is incorporated as a town.
1854	St. Paul is incorporated as a city.
1858	Minnesota becomes a state with St. Paul as capital.
1873	James J. Hill gains control of the bankrupt St. Paul and Pacific Railroad and begins an outstanding career as a railroad magnate.
1876	Archbishop John Ireland begins work of establishing immigrant colonies on railroad land, building one of the great Catholic dioceses in the process.

it resembles St. Peter's in Rome. Other important churches include St. Luke's on Summit Avenue, considered the finest work of architect John T. Comes, and House of Hope Church, also on Summit Avenue. The James J. Hill House on Summit Avenue is a 32-room red stone house built in 1887 at a cost of $200,000. The Alexander Ramsey House was completed in 1872 by the first governor of the Minnesota Territory.

Population

In the 1990 census, St. Paul registered a modest 0.7% gain in population to 272,235 from a 1980 population of 270,230, reversing a ten-year 12.8% loss in population from 310,000 in 1970. Nevertheless, its overall rank fell from 54th to 57th.

Population

	1980	1990
Central City	270,230	272,235
Rank	54	57
Metro Area	2,137,133	2,464,124
Pop. Change 1980–1990 +2,005		
Pop. % Change 1980–1990 +0.7		
Median Age 31.3		
% Male 47.2		
% Age 65 and Over 13.70		
Density (per square mile) 5,155		

Households

Number 110,249
Persons per Household 2.37
% Female-Headed Households 13.0
% One-Person Households 34.7
Births—Total 5,040
   % to Mothers under 20 10.6
   Birth Rate per 1,000 19.0

Ethnic Composition

Whites make up 82.3% of the population, blacks 7.4%, American Indians 1.4%, and Asians and Pacific Islanders 7.1%.

Ethnic Composition (as % of total pop.)

	1980	1990
White	90.01	82.26
Black	4.92	7.38
American Indian	0.94	1.36
Asian and Pacific Islander	1.00	7.05
Hispanic	2.91	4.22
Other	NA	1.95

Government

St. Paul is governed under a strong mayor–weak council form of government. The mayor is elected for four-year terms while the seven members of the council are elected by wards for two-year terms.

Government

Year of Home Charter 1972
Number of Members of the Governing Body 7
Elected at Large NA
Elected by Wards 7
Number of Women in Governing Body 2
Salary of Mayor $70,014
Salary of Council Members $41,058
City Government Employment Total 3,403
Rate per 10,000 129.1

Public Finance

The budget consists of revenues of $460.758 million and expenditures of $432.116 million. The debt outstanding is $986.496 million and cash and security holdings $1.161 billion.

Public Finance

Total Revenue (in millions) $460.758
Intergovernmental Revenue—Total (in millions) $156.47
Federal Revenue per Capita $57.14
% Federal Assistance 12.4
% State Assistance 20.57
Sales Tax as % of Total Revenue 3.55
Local Revenue as % of Total Revenue 58.56
City Income Tax no
Taxes—Total (in millions) $68.1

Taxes per Capita
   Total $258
   Property $177
   Sales and Gross Receipts $68
General Expenditures—Total (in millions) $264.4
General Expenditures per Capita $1,003
Capital Outlays per Capita $201

% of Expenditures for:
   Public Welfare 0.0
   Highways 7.6
   Education 0.0
   Health and Hospitals 2.1
   Police 8.8
   Sewerage and Sanitation 10.1
   Parks and Recreation 10.2
   Housing and Community Development 5.3
Debt Outstanding per Capita $3,179
   % Utility 0.9
Federal Procurement Contract Awards (in millions)
$557.1
Federal Grants Awards (in millions) $336.7
Fiscal Year Begins January 1

Economy

The economy of St. Paul is intertwined with that of Minneapolis, and for all practical purposes, the two cities are considered a metropolitan area. Of the 25 largest employers in the region, 4 are located in St. Paul, including 3M, Unisys, Health East, and Burlington Northern. Among other large corporations are Northwest Airlines, The St. Paul Companies, Ecolab, H. B. Fuller, Andersen Corporation, Land O'Lakes, Control Data, Deluxe Check, Pentair, and Minnesota Life. Along with Minneapolis, St. Paul has one of the largest concentrations of high-technology firms, and it is one of the three largest meatpacking and livestock centers. St. Paul is also one of the nine World Trade centers in the United States, and its Foreign Trade Zone offers a number of benefits to firms engaged in international business. As the state capital, the public sector is larger than in Minneapolis.

Economy

Total Money Income (in millions) $3,051.0
% of State Average 103.3
Per Capita Annual Income $11,557
% Population below Poverty Level 10.9
Fortune 500 Companies 5

Banks	Number	Deposits (in millions)
Commercial	18	NA
Savings	6	8,000

Passenger Autos 284,991
Electric Meters 121,300
Gas Meters 90,600

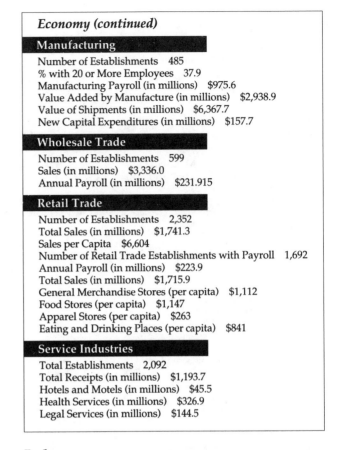

Economy (continued)

Manufacturing

Number of Establishments 485
% with 20 or More Employees 37.9
Manufacturing Payroll (in millions) $975.6
Value Added by Manufacture (in millions) $2,938.9
Value of Shipments (in millions) $6,367.7
New Capital Expenditures (in millions) $157.7

Wholesale Trade

Number of Establishments 599
Sales (in millions) $3,336.0
Annual Payroll (in millions) $231.915

Retail Trade

Number of Establishments 2,352
Total Sales (in millions) $1,741.3
Sales per Capita $6,604
Number of Retail Trade Establishments with Payroll 1,692
Annual Payroll (in millions) $223.9
Total Sales (in millions) $1,715.9
General Merchandise Stores (per capita) $1,112
Food Stores (per capita) $1,147
Apparel Stores (per capita) $263
Eating and Drinking Places (per capita) $841

Service Industries

Total Establishments 2,092
Total Receipts (in millions) $1,193.7
Hotels and Motels (in millions) $45.5
Health Services (in millions) $326.9
Legal Services (in millions) $144.5

Labor

The work force has an unusually large percentage of highly skilled technicians, engineers, and scientists. Trade is the largest among employment sectors, followed by services, manufacturing, and government.

Labor

Civilian Labor Force 145,191
% Change 1989–1990 1.6

Work Force Distribution
   Mining NA
   Construction 46,900
   Manufacturing 257,800
   Transportation and Public Utilities 77,800
   Wholesale and Retail Trade 85,300
   FIRE (Finance, Insurance, Real Estate) 99,400
   Service 368,100
   Government 189,700
   Women as % of Labor Force 47.1
   % Self-Employed 4.0
   % Professional/Technical 17.8

Education

The St. Paul Independent School District supports 52 elementary schools, junior high schools, and senior high schools. Private and parochial schools enroll over 12,000 students. They include Saint Agnes, Saint Bernards, and the St. Paul Academy.

The University of Minnesota at Minneapolis St. Paul dominates higher education. The only other public

Labor (continued)

Total Unemployment   6,932
Rate %   4.8
Federal Government Civilian Employment   6,068

institution is the Metropolitan State University. There are ten outstanding private colleges and universities, including Augsburg College, Bethel College, Concordia College, Hamline University, Macalester College, Northwestern College, College of St. Catherine, University of St. Thomas, Minneapolis College of Art and Design, and William Mitchell College of Law.

Education

Number of Public Schools   52
Special Education Schools   4
Total Enrollment   35,932
% Enrollment in Private Schools   12.5
% Minority   41.1
Classroom Teachers   1,856
Pupil-Teacher Ratio   18.7:1
Number of Graduates   1,856
Total Revenue (in millions) $190.641
Total Expenditures (in millions) $166.677
Expenditures per Pupil $5,128
Educational Attainment (Age 25 and Over)
   % Completed 12 or More Years   72.4
   % Completed 16 or More Years   19.8
Four-Year Colleges and Universities   14
   Enrollment   26,294
Two-Year Colleges   1
   Enrollment   2,918

Libraries

Number   85
Public Libraries   13
Books (in thousands)   835
Circulation (in thousands)   2,285
Persons Served (in thousands)   269
Circulation per Person Served   8.49
Income (in millions) $7.2
Staff   166

Four-Year Colleges and Universities
   Augsburg College
   Bethel College
   College of Associated Arts
   College of St. Catherine
   Concordia College
   Hamline University
   Macalester College
   Metropolitan State University
   Minneapolis College of Art and Design
   Northwestern College
   University of Minnesota at Minneapolis St. Paul
   University of St. Thomas
   William Mitchell College of Law

Health

Eight hospitals provide a wide range of medical care. The largest is the St. Paul–Ramsey Medical Center, a teaching and research hospital that also houses the Gillette Children's Hospital. Midway Hospital is affiliated with the International Diabetes Center. Other facilities include Children's Hospital, St, Joseph's Hospital, United Hospitals, and Bethesda Lutheran Medical Center.

Health

Deaths—Total   2,663
Rate per 1,000   10.0
Infant Deaths—Total   53
Rate per 1,000   10.5
Number of Metro Hospitals   8
Number of Metro Hospital Beds   1,791
Rate per 100,000   679
Number of Physicians   NA
Physicians per 1,000   NA
Nurses per 1,000   NA
Health Expenditures per Capita $25.86

Transportation

Principal access routes to St. Paul are I-94, intersecting the city from east to west, and I-35, intersecting it from north to south. I-494 and I-694 form a beltway circling the north, east, and west perimeters. Seven federal and 13 state highways serve the area. Rail passenger service is provided by Amtrak, and rail freight service by six railroads, including Burlington Northern, Chicago and Northwestern Transportation, and Soo Line, the last headquartered in Minneapolis. The ports of Minneapolis and St. Paul handle more than 11 million tons of cargo per year. Mass transit is operated by the Metropolitan Transit Commission. The Minneapolis–St. Paul International Airport is the major air gateway to the Upper Midwest. It is located about 11 miles from downtown St. Paul and Minneapolis and is served by 10 commercial airlines, 7 regional airlines, and 16 air cargo carriers. There are six reliever airports at St. Paul Downtown, South St. Paul Municipal, Anoka County, Flying Cloud, Lake Emo, and Crystal.

Transportation (Minneapolis St. Paul)

Interstate Highway Mileage   194
Total Urban Mileage   9,287
Total Daily Vehicle Mileage (in millions) $43.93
Daily Average Commute Time   44.2 min.
Number of Buses   925
Port Tonnage (in millions) $6.956
Airports   1
Number of Daily Flights   309
Daily Average Number of Passengers   23,178

Airlines (American carriers only)
   American
   American West
   Continental
   Delta
   Midway
   Midwest
   Northwest
   Trans World
   United
   USAir

Housing

The average price of a rental unit in the metropolitan area is $389. Downtown living is becoming a popular option, particularly in Lowertown. Away from downtown there are distinct neighborhoods. St. Paul exudes a small-town feeling, and this, along with affordable housing, was cited by *Newsweek* as reasons for making St. Paul one of the ten most livable cities in the nation. The average sale price of a home was $75,904. Most of the upscale housing is in the famed Summit Avenue–Crocus Hill area, along the shores of White Bear Lake, or in the rolling hills above the St. Croix River.

Housing		
Total Housing Units 117,583		
% Change 1980–1990 5.7		
Vacant Units for Sale or Rent 5,905		
Occupied Units 110,249		
% with More Than One Person per Room 4.0		
% Owner-Occupied 53.9		
Median Value of Owner-Occupied Homes $70,900		
Average Monthly Purchase Cost $362		
Median Monthly Rent $389		
New Private Housing Starts 102		
Value (in thousands) $6,569		
% Single-Family 72.5		
Nonresidential Buildings Value (in thousands) $12,193		
Tallest Buildings	*Hgt. (ft.)*	*Stories*
First Natl. Bank Bldg.	517	32
Minnesota World Trade Center	471	36
Galtier Plaza's Jackson Tower	440	46
Osborn Bldg., 320 Wabasha	368	20
Kellogg Square Apts.	366	32
Northwestern Bell Telephone (2 bldgs.)	340	16
Pointe of St. Paul	340	34
American National Bank Bldg.	335	25

Urban Redevelopment

 Downtown revitalization has been on an ongoing program since 1970, with an investment of over $1 billion. Neighborhood Development Program is a nationally acclaimed initiative. The showpiece of urban redevelopment is Energy Park, a 218-acre mixed-use project.

Crime

 St. Paul is above average in public safety. In 1991 violent crimes totaled 2,731, and property crimes totaled 19,034.

Crime	
Violent Crimes—Total 2,731	
Violent Crime Rate per 100,000 470	
Murder 12	
Rape 286	
Robbery 850	
Aggravated Assaults 1,583	
Property Crimes 19,034	
Burglary 4,583	
Larceny 12,124	
Motor Vehicle Theft 2,327	
Arson 269	
Per Capita Police Expenditures $118.37	
Per Capita Fire Protection Expenditures $87.76	
Number of Police 517	
Per 1,000 1.93	

Religion

 St. Paul is a city with a long Catholic heritage, which is still well preserved, both architecturally and spiritually. Sixty-six percent of the residents are churchgoers compared to 54% nationwide. Next to Catholics, the largest denomination is Lutheran.

Religion	
Largest Denominations (Adherents)	
Catholic	157,945
Evangelical Lutheran	66,037
Lutheran-Missouri Synod	10,749
Presbyterian	7,367
Episcopal	6,031
Assembly of God	5,050
United Methodist	9,526
Black Baptist	7,515
United Church of Christ	5,437
Jewish	6,604

Media

 The city dailies are the *St. Paul Dispatch* and *The Pioneer*. The electronic media consist of 4 television stations and 9 AM and FM radio stations.

Media	
Newsprint	
St. Paul Dispatch, daily	
The Pioneer, daily	
Television	
KLGT (Channel 23)	
KSTP (Channel 5)	
KTCA (Channel 2)	
KTCI (Channel 17)	
Radio	
KFAN (AM)	KLBB (AM)
KMTA (AM)	KNOF (FM)
KNOW (FM)	KSJN (FM)
KSTP (AM)	WMCN (FM)
WMIN (AM)	

Sports

 In sports, the Twin Cities share four professional sports teams: Minnesota Vikings in football, Minnesota Twins in baseball, Minnesota Timberwolves in basketball, and Minnesota North Stars in hockey. St. Paul shares the Hubert H. Humphrey Metrodome with Minneapolis. The St. Paul Derby is held at the Canterbury Downs Racetrack in Shakopee on the last weekend in June.

Arts, Culture, and Tourism

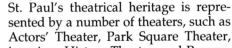 St. Paul's theatrical heritage is represented by a number of theaters, such as Actors' Theater, Park Square Theater, Great North American History Theater, and Penumbra Theater. In music, the Ordway Music Theater is the home of the St. Paul Chamber Orchestra, Minnesota Opera Company, and the Schubert Club. The Land-

mark Center, a Romanesque revival building with a south tower modeled after Boston's Trinity Church, hosts musical concerts and special events, and is also the location of the Schubert Piano Museum and a branch of the Minnesota Museum of Art. Recently renovated, the World Theater features a 915-seat hall in which no seat is more than 87 feet from the stage. The winner of the coveted Charlie Award for sustained excellence in the field of comedy, Dudley Riggs Theater presents comedies at two locations. The O'Shaughnessy Dance Series is a project of the College of St. Catherine.

St. Paul has a number of unusual and specialized museums, such as Children's Museum and Minnesota Awarehouse, Science Museum, and Historic Fort Snelling. The Minnesota Historical Society runs a museum devoted to the history of the state.

Travel and Tourism

Hotel Rooms   24,250
Convention and Exhibit Space (square feet)   NA

Convention Centers
   St. Paul Civic Center
   The Arena
   Roy Wilkins Auditorium

Festivals
   Winter Carnival
   Festival of Nations (April)
   Riverfest (July)
   Minnesota State Fair (Labor Day weekend)

Parks and Recreation

St. Paul's park system includes more than 50 recreational sites covering 2,000 acres. Como Park on East Como Boulevard and Hamline Avenue once marked the northern end of the city. Phalen Park and Lake on Phalen Parkway, named after St. Paul's third settler, Edward Phalen, is the city's largest park. Indian Mounds Park on Mounds Boulevard comprises 77 acres on a high bluff overlooking the Mississippi River. The 60-acre Battle Creek Park marks the site of a battle between two Indian tribes. Highland Park on Edgecumbe Road surrounds a 1,023-foot-high hill. The Hidden Falls Park adjoining Mississippi Boulevard has a wooded ravine with a 20-foot waterfall. Irvine Park in downtown is surrounded by historic homes.

Sources of Further Information

Ramsey County Historical Society
75 West Fifth Street
St. Paul, MN 55102
(612) 296-2747

St. Paul Chamber of Commerce
600 NCL Tower
St. Paul, MN 55101
(612) 223-5000.

St. Paul Convention and Visitors Bureau
44 Minnesota Street
St. Paul, MN 55101
(612) 297-6985

St. Paul Public Library
90 West Fourth Street
St. Paul, MN 55102-1668
(612) 228-5557.

Additional Reading

Benson, James K. *Irish and German Families and the Economic Development of Midwestern Cities, 1860–1895.* 1990.

Erwin, Jean. *Twin Cities Perceived: A Study in Words and Drawings.* 1980.

Jacob, Bernard, and Carol Morphew. *Pocket Architecture: A Walking Tour Guide to the Architecture of Downtown Minneapolis and St. Paul.* 1987.

Kunz, Virginia B. *St. Paul: A Modern Renaissance.* 1986.

Rich, Frieda, and Lael Berman. *Landmarks, Old and New. Minneapolis, St. Paul and Surrounding Areas.* 1987.

Sandeen, Ernest R. *St. Paul's Historic Summit Avenue.* 1988.

Smith, Robert T. *Minneapolis–St. Paul: The Cities, Their People.* 1988.

Williams, J. Fletcher. *A History of the City of St. Paul to 1875.* 1983.

St. Petersburg

Florida

Location and Topography

St. Petersburg is located in on the southern tip of Pinellas peninsula on the west coast of Florida, jutting into Tampa Bay and the Boca Ciega Bay on the Gulf of Mexico. It shares Tampa Bay with Tampa to the south and the Boca Ciega Bay with Clearwater to the north.

Layout of City and Suburbs

St. Petersburg's front yard is a series of landscaped parks paralleling Tampa Bay, a stretch of two miles embracing the harbor. North and west of the pier lie North Shore, the pioneer residential section, and Snell Isle. The latter, dredged from the bay, is reached by a short bridge over Coffee Pot Bayou. Further north is Shore Acres. Five miles around Pinellas Point another residential section occupies the site chosen by the town's first white settler and overlooks the main channel leading to the gulf.

Bordering the bay to the southwest is Gulfport. On the western border of the peninsula are homes, many of them built upon former Indian mounds. Citrus groves and open pine woods form the northern city border. Central Avenue, the city's White Way, extends seven miles across the peninsula, linking Tampa Bay with Boca Ciega Bay and dividing the north city from the south. The original business district is on the lower end of the avenue. To the west the skyline keeps mounting. Beyond Ninth Street, Central Avenue becomes more residential and passes through an area known as Goose Pond before ending at Sunset Park. A block paralleling railroad tracks on Second Avenue is the entertainment district. St. Petersburg advertises itself as the Sunshine City, and makes every effort to help residents and tourists absorb the maximum amount of that sunshine. More than 5,000 green benches were placed on the streets, giving the city the atmosphere of a permanent resort.

Environment

Environmental Stress Index   2.4
Green Cities Index: Rank   NA
             Score   NA
Water Quality   Alkaline, soft
Average Daily Use (gallons per capita)   NA
  Maximum Supply (gallons per capita)   NA
Parkland as % of Total City Area   NA
% Waste Landfilled/Recycled   NA
Annual Parks Expenditures per Capita $200.28

Climate

St. Petersburg, like neighboring Tampa, has a semitropical marine climate and it is one of the wettest cities in the nation, with frequent afternoon rains, as well as one of the most humid. Throughout summer from June through September thunderstorms are common.

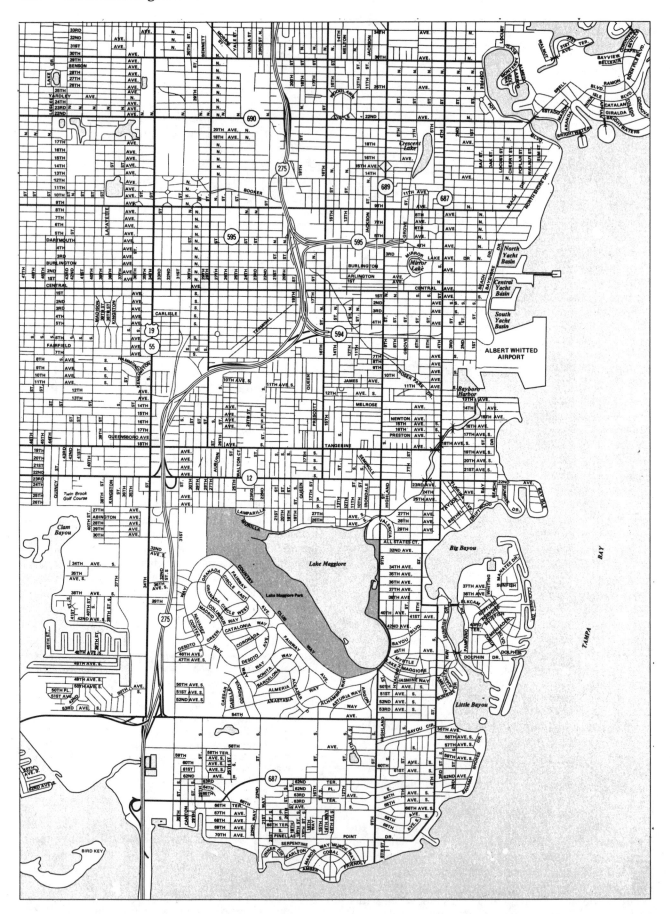

Weather			
Temperature			
Highest Monthly Average °F	81.3		
Lowest Monthly Average °F	65.8		
Annual Averages			
Days 32°F or Below	0		
Days above 90°F	81		
Zero Degree Days	0		
Precipitation (inches)	53.10		
Snow (inches)	0		
% Seasonal Humidity	NA		
Wind Speed (m.p.h.)	NA		
Clear Days	NA		
Cloudy Days	NA		
Storm Days	NA		
Rainy Days	NA		
Average Temperatures (°F)	*High*	*Low*	*Mean*
January	70.0	53.7	61.9
February	71.1	54.7	62.9
March	76.0	59.8	67.9
April	81.7	65.1	73.4
May	86.7	70.4	78.5
June	89.3	74.5	81.9
July	90.1	76.0	83.1
August	90.1	75.9	83.0
September	88.7	74.8	81.7
October	83.4	68.6	76.0
November	76.8	61.0	68.9
December	71.4	55.3	63.4

History

The Spanish explorer, Narvaez, is believed to have visited Tampa Bay in 1528, but the first white settler did not arrive until 1843, when Antonio Maximo set up a fish rancho on a point of land at the southern extremity of the peninsula, now called Maximo Point. His house was swept away in a hurricane. The next house was built in 1856 by James K. Hay, who came to look after hogs and cattle for Tampa stockmen. The place was shelled by Union forces during the Civil War, but the residents returned after the war was over. By 1856 a small community had sprung up around Big Bayou called Pinellas, some miles south of Central Avenue, and a post office was established. John Williams of Detroit, later given the honorary title of general, acquired several thousand acres in the area in 1876, which eventually became the nucleus of the town. He made a deal with railroad baron Piotr Alexeitch Dementieff, known by the Americanized name of Peter Demens, offering him an interest in the land in return for a rail line to the area. The line that Demens built, known as the Orange Belt Line, reached the area from Lake Monroe in 1888 when the community had a population of 30. According to popular accounts, the name St. Petersburg was chosen by Demens in honor of his birthplace in Russia, after a toss of the coin gave him the right to christen the new town. Later Williams built the town's first hotel, the Detroit, named for his hometown. St. Petersburg was incorporated in 1892. The Orange Belt Line was later absorbed by the Plant rail system and the Atlantic Coast Line. The city was part of Hillsborough County until 1911, when Pinellas County was created. The first land boom got under way shortly after the city extended its boundaries to Boca Ciega Bay. In 1914 a second railroad reached the town—the Tampa and Gulf Coast Railroad, later the Seaboard Air Line. By 1925 the population reached 50,000. Gandy Bridge was built connecting Tampa with St. Petersburg, and two causeways were built across Boca Ciega Bay. The city also gained thousands of acres when miles of the Tampa Bay waterfront were filled in and improved with sea walls.

Historical Landmarks

Jungle Prado Mounds on Park Street and Yellow Lane was the site of a large Indian village. Fort De Soto is at the southern end of the peninsula on Mullet Key. It was built during the Spanish-American War, but its guns have never been fired. The city's oldest church is St. Mary's on the corner of Fourth Street and Sixth Avenue.

Population

St. Petersburg lost exactly 18 persons from its census rolls between 1980 and 1990, when the population declined from 238,647 to 238,629. This decline was in contrast to its gain of 10.4% between 1970 and 1980, when its population was 216,000.

Population		
	1980	*1990*
Central City	238,647	238,629
Rank	58	65
Metro Area	1,613,600	2,067,959
Pop. Change 1980–1990 -18		
Pop. % Change 1980–1990 -0.01		
Median Age 38.6		
% Male 46.4		
% Age 65 and Over 22.19		
Density (per square mile) 4,030		
Households		
Number 105,703		
Persons per Household 2.19		
% Female-Headed Households 12.4		
% One-Person Households 35.1		
Births—Total 3,299		
% to Mothers under 20 16.7		
Birth Rate per 1,000 13.7		

Ethnic Composition

Whites make up 78%, blacks 19.6%, American Indians 0.3%, Asians and Pacific Islanders 1.7%, and others 0.5%. Hispanics, either black or white, account for 2.6%.

Ethnic Composition (as % of total pop.)		
	1980	*1990*
White	81.72	78.0
Black	17.18	19.58
American Indian	0.14	0.25
Asian and Pacific Islander	0.54	1.66
Hispanic	1.78	2.62
Other	NA	0.51

Chronology

1843	Antonio Maximo sets up a fish rancho at the southern extremity of Pinellas Peninsula, now called Maximo Point.
1848	Maximo's house is destroyed in a hurricane.
1856	James K. Hay builds first house within present city limits.
1876	Small community known as Pinellas springs up on the peninsula, and a post office is established. John C. Williams of Detroit buys several thousand acres and makes deal with railroad builder Piotr Alexeitch Dementieff, known as Peter Demens, to extend his rail line to Pinellas.
1888	Demens's line, known as the Orange Belt Line, reaches the area from Lake Monroe. Demens wins toss of coin to christen the settlement and chooses the name of his native city in Russia, St. Petersburg.
1892	St. Petersburg is incorporated.
1909	The first direct train arrives from New York.
1911	Pinellas County is created.
1914	Tampa and Gulf Coast Railroad reaches St. Petersburg.
1924	Gandy Bridge is built linking Tampa and St. Petersburg.
1925	Population reaches 50,000.

Government

St. Petersburg has a weak mayor-council form of government with an elected council and mayor who appoint the city manager as the effective chief executive.

Government

Year of Home Charter 1973
Number of Members of the Governing Body 8
Elected at Large 8
Elected by Wards NA
Number of Women in Governing Body 1
Salary of Mayor $23,500
Salary of Council Members $16,500
City Government Employment Total 3,160
Rate per 10,000 132.0

Public Finance

The annual budget consists of revenues of $278.125 million and expenditures of $285.549 million. Debt outstanding is $542.974 million and cash and security holdings of $664.358 million.

Public Finance

Total Revenue (in millions) $278.125
Intergovernmental Revenue—Total (in millions) $23.48
Federal Revenue per Capita $5.45
% Federal Assistance 1.96
% State Assistance 6.26
Sales Tax as % of Total Revenue 9.70
Local Revenue as % of Total Revenue 72.67
City Income Tax no
Taxes—Total (in millions) $44.7

Taxes per Capita
    Total $187
    Property $101
    Sales and Gross Receipts $78
General Expenditures—Total (in millions) $119.5
General Expenditures per Capita $499
Capital Outlays per Capita $81

% of Expenditures for:
    Public Welfare 0.0
    Highways 9.9
    Education 0.0
    Health and Hospitals 0.0
    Police 19.1
    Sewerage and Sanitation 13.8
    Parks and Recreation 14.3
    Housing and Community Development 5.6
Debt Outstanding per Capita $775
    % Utility 0.0
Federal Procurement Contract Awards (in millions) $235.4
Federal Grants Awards (in millions) $27.3
Fiscal Year Begins October 1

Economy

While tourism continues to be the bellwether sector, St. Petersburg has diversified its economy so that the fastest growing sectors are service industries like finance, health services, retailing, publishing, and real estate.

Economy

Total Money Income (in millions) $2,659.6
% of State Average 98.6
Per Capita Annual Income $11,109
% Population below Poverty Level 14
Fortune 500 Companies NA

Banks	Number	Deposits (in millions)
Commercial	26	9,355.6
Savings	29	7,835.6

Passenger Autos 622,740
Electric Meters 143,384
Gas Meters 31,120

Manufacturing

Number of Establishments 250
% with 20 or More Employees 23.6
Manufacturing Payroll (in millions) $202.8
Value Added by Manufacture (in millions) $402.5
Value of Shipments (in millions) $770.1
New Capital Expenditures (in millions) $40.5

Wholesale Trade

Number of Establishments 329
Sales (in millions) $680.4
Annual Payroll (in millions) $56.686

Economy (continued)

Retail Trade

Number of Establishments 2,229
Total Sales (in millions) $1,758.3
Sales per Capita $7,344
Number of Retail Trade Establishments with Payroll 1,411
Annual Payroll (in millions) $200.3
Total Sales (in millions) $1,721.2
General Merchandise Stores (per capita) $1,029
Food Stores (per capita) $1,392
Apparel Stores (per capita) $279
Eating and Drinking Places (per capita) $615

Service Industries

Total Establishments 2,336
Total Receipts (in millions) $956.5
Hotels and Motels (in millions) $54.1
Health Services (in millions) $376.7
Legal Services (in millions) $92.5

Labor

St. Petersburg offers considerable benefits to employers locating or relocating there, including a right-to-work law, skilled workers, savings in transportation, and a good climate. In terms of manpower and annual payroll, medical services are by far the largest employment sector with 34,518 workers and $740.3 million in wages, followed by business services with 14,941 workers and $205.4 million in wages, and engineering and management services with 10,392 workers and $239.7 million in wages.

Labor

Civilian Labor Force 139,129
% Change 1989–1990 2.6

Work Force Distribution
   Mining 400
   Construction 42,700
   Manufacturing 86,300
   Transportation and Public Utilities 39,600
   Wholesale and Retail Trade 229,200
   FIRE (Finance, Insurance, Real Estate) 63,900
   Service 277,700
   Government 116,700
   Women as % of Labor Force 47.4
   % Self-Employed 7.3
   % Professional/Technical 15.7
Total Unemployment 7,916
Rate % 5.7
Federal Government Civilian Employment 2,038

Education

The St. Petersburg Public School system supports 130 elementary, middle, and high schools. In addititon, 72 private and parochial schools complement the public system. There are three four-year colleges in the area: Eckerd College, Stetson University College of Law, and the Bayboro Campus of the University of South Florida.

Education

Number of Public Schools 130
Special Education Schools 6
Total Enrollment 91,393
% Enrollment in Private Schools 12.0
% Minority 20.8
Classroom Teachers 5,548
Pupil-Teacher Ratio 16.5:1
Number of Graduates 5,436
Total Revenue (in millions) $420.018
Total Expenditures (in millions) $409.041
Expenditures per Pupil $4,145
Educational Attainment (Age 25 and Over)
   % Completed 12 or More Years 65.7
   % Completed 16 or More Years 14.6
Four-Year Colleges and Universities 1
   Enrollment 1,359
Two-Year Colleges NA
   Enrollment NA

Libraries

Number 28
Public Libraries 6
Books (in thousands) 429
Circulation (in thousands) 1,077
Persons Served (in thousands) 243
Circulation per Person Served 4.43
Income (in millions) $2.492
Staff 61

Four-Year Colleges and Universities
   Eckerd College

Health

St. Petersburg has 9 hospitals, including 4 general hospitals, with a total of 2,045 beds. Downtown St. Petersburg contains All Children's Hospital, Bayfront Medical Center, and St. Anthony's Hospital. Humana maintains one hospital in St. Petersburg and another at Sun Bay. Three hospitals provide satellite medical campuses for the University of South Florida College of Medicine. Other facilities include the Veterans Administration Hospital and Palms of Pasadena Hospital.

Health

Deaths—Total 4,357
Rate per 1,000 18.1
Infant Deaths—Total 45
Rate per 1,000 13.6
Number of Metro Hospitals 9
Number of Metro Hospital Beds 2,045
Rate per 100,000 854
Number of Physicians NA
Physicians per 1,000 NA
Nurses per 1,000 NA
Health Expenditures per Capita $19.72

Transportation

St. Petersburg is approached by I-275, which connects with I-4 and I-275. U.S. 19 links St. Petersburg to the rest of Pinellas County and points north. The Sunshine Highway Bridge spans the mouth of Tampa Bay to join St. Petersburg with Manatee County, including Bradenton. St. Petersburg is linked to Tampa via Howard Frankland Bridge (I-275) and Gandy Bridge. Rail passenger service is provided by Amtrak. The principal air terminal is the St. Petersburg/Clearwater International Airport on the water's edge. However, the larger Tampa International Airport is preferred by most air travelers. Smaller planes use the Albert Whitted Airport downtown.

Transportation

Interstate Highway Mileage   32
Total Urban Mileage   4,239
Total Daily Vehicle Mileage (in millions) $18.961
Daily Average Commute Time   45.1 min. (inc. Tampa)
Number of Buses   279 (inc. Tampa)
Port Tonnage (in millions)   NA
Airports   2
Number of Daily Flights   162
Daily Average Number of Passengers   12,135

Airlines (American carriers only)
   American
   American Trans Air
   Continental
   Delta
   Midway
   Northwest
   United
   USAir
   Trans World

Housing

 Of the total housing stock, 63% is owner-occupied, which is higher than the national average. The median value of an owner-occupied home is $63,000 and the median monthly rent $353.

Housing

Total Housing Units   125,452
% Change 1980–1990   4.8
Vacant Units for Sale or Rent   10,299
Occupied Units   105,703
% with More Than One Person per Room   3.3
% Owner-Occupied   63.0
Median Value of Owner-Occupied Homes $63,000
Average Monthly Purchase Cost $282
Median Monthly Rent $353
New Private Housing Starts   463
Value (in thousands) $24,617
% Single-Family   30.9
Nonresidential Buildings Value (in thousands) $29,248

Urban Redevelopment

More than $900 million has been invested in private downtown redevelopment in the past decade. One of the largest was the Stouffer Vinoy Resort, a $93-million historic renovation of the Vinoy Park Hotel located on the bay at the northern tip of downtown. In 1990 Barnett Bank moved into the 26-story Barnett Building, the tallest building in the county. Plaza Parkway,

a streetscape project, has brightened up the look of downtown. Bay Plaza manages three of the municipal entertainment facilities in downtown: The Pier, Bayfront Center, and the Florida Suncoast Dome. The Pier is Florida's fifth-largest tourist attraction, drawing nearly 2 million visitors each year. The Dome is envisioned as the future site of major league baseball, and is already home to the Tampa Bay Storm and the Tampa Bay Lightning. The Bay Plaza is a private/public venture consisting of a large office/retail/entertainment complex.

Crime

 Violent crimes reported to police in 1991 totaled 5,824, and property crimes totaled 21,129.

Crime

Violent Crimes—Total   5,824
Violent Crime Rate per 100,000   1,264
Murder   33
Rape   184
Robbery   2,015
Aggravated Assaults   3,592
Property Crimes   21,129
Burglary   5,543
Larceny   13,116
Motor Vehicle Theft   2,510
Arson   241
Per Capita Police Expenditures $145.01
Per Capita Fire Protection Expenditures $55.45
Number of Police   419
Per 1,000   1.68

Religion

St. Petersburg has fewer churches than most cities of its size. About 43% of the residents are affiliated with established churches. Among these churches the largest are Catholics, Medthodists, and Baptists.

Religion

Largest Denominations (Adherents)	
Catholic	131,099
United Methodist	44,193
Southern Baptist	41,126
Black Baptist	19,670
Presbyterian	14,912
Evangelical Lutheran	11,929
Episcopal	13,150
Assembly of God	8,614
Lutheran-Missouri Synod	6,715
Jewish	9,500

Media

 The city's daily newspaper is the *St. Petersburg Times*. The electronic media consist of three television stations and ten AM and FM radio stations.

Media

Newsprint
 Pinellas County Review, biweekly
 St. Petersburg Times, daily
 The Weekly Challenger, weekly

Television
 WTOG (Channel 44)
 WTSP (Channel 10)
 WTTA (Channel 38)

Radio

WHVE (FM)	WQYK (AM)
WRBQ (AM)	WRXB (AM)
WSUN (AM)	WTIS (AM)
WTKN (AM)	WWRM (FM)
WYNF (FM)	WYUU (FM)

Sports

St. Petersburg's efforts to attract a major baseball league franchise have not yet been successful despite the building of the Dome. Greyhound racing is a big draw from January through May at Derby Lane, the world's oldest continuously operating dog track.

Arts, Culture, and Tourism

The Florida Orchestra is the best known cultural institution in the city. Broadway in the Sunshine performs at the Bay Center every winter season.

The Salvador Dali Museum on the waterfront houses the largest collection of the works of the Spanish artist. The St. Petersburg Museum of Fine Arts has a fine collection of European, American, Oriental, and pre-Columbian art. The St. Petersburg Historical Museum and the Haas Museum Complex are devoted to Florida history and culture.

Travel and Tourism

Hotel Rooms   32,044
Convention and Exhibit Space (square feet)   NA

Convention Centers
 Bayfront Center

Festivals
 International Folk Fair (February)
 Festival of State (April)

Parks and Recreation

St. Petersburg has 28 parks within city limits covering 2,400 acres. Mirror Lake Park between Fifth and Seventh streets is the city's liveliest playground. The 844-acre Fort De Soto Park stretches over six keys at the south end of the peninsula. On the south side of the city the Boyd Hill Nature Trail winds through six miles of swamp forest along an old Tamucuan Indian trail. On the other side of the town, Snowgrass Lake Park offers a one-mile nature trail through marshland.

Sources of Further Information

City Hall
175 Fifth Street North
St. Petersburg, FL 33701
(813) 893-7117

St. Petersburg Area Chamber of Commerce
401 Third Avenue South
St. Petersburg, FL 33731
(813) 821-4069

Tampa Bay Regional Planning Council
9455 Koger Boulevard
St. Petersburg, FL 33702
(813) 577-5151

Additional Reading

Polk's St. Petersburg City Directory. 1991.
St. Petersburg, Florida, Cross-Reference Directory. 1991.

Salt Lake City

Utah

Layout of City and Suburbs

Salt Lake City is a city of broad tree-lined streets, the first of many Utah towns laid out by the Mormons foursquare with the compass. Mountains can be seen in every direction—the Wasatch Range to the east and southeast, the Ensign Peak to the north, the Oquirrh and Stansbury Ranges to the southwest, and the Antelope Island to the west. The most conspicuous building is the copper-domed state capitol. South of it and lower down is the six-spired Temple of the Church of Jesus Christ of Latter Day Saints within the Temple Square. From the southeast corner of this square the city's streets radiate. Southward from the corner extends South Main Street through the principal business center of the Great Basin. To the west of the Temple Square is the industrial and railroad area. East of Main Street is primarily residential, although it is dominated by the tall tower of the City and County Building and the twin towers of the Roman Catholic Cathedral of the Madeleine. To the south is the suburb of Murray. North of South Temple Street the long city blocks are broken up into smaller squares by the east-west numbered avenues and lettered cross-streets. The more fashionable residential area is East Bench. The archi-

Environment

Environmental Stress Index   3.2
Green Cities Index: Rank   NA
                     Score   NA
Water Quality   Alkaline, hard
Average Daily Use (gallons per capita)   107
   Maximum Supply (gallons per capita)   250
Parkland as % of Total City Area   NA
% Waste Landfilled/Recycled   NA
Annual Parks Expenditures per Capita $75.04

Location and Topography

Salt Lake City lies in the Salt Lake Valley at the foot of the Wasatch Range of the Rocky Mountains, which surrounds it on three sides. The Jordan River flows just to the west of downtown.

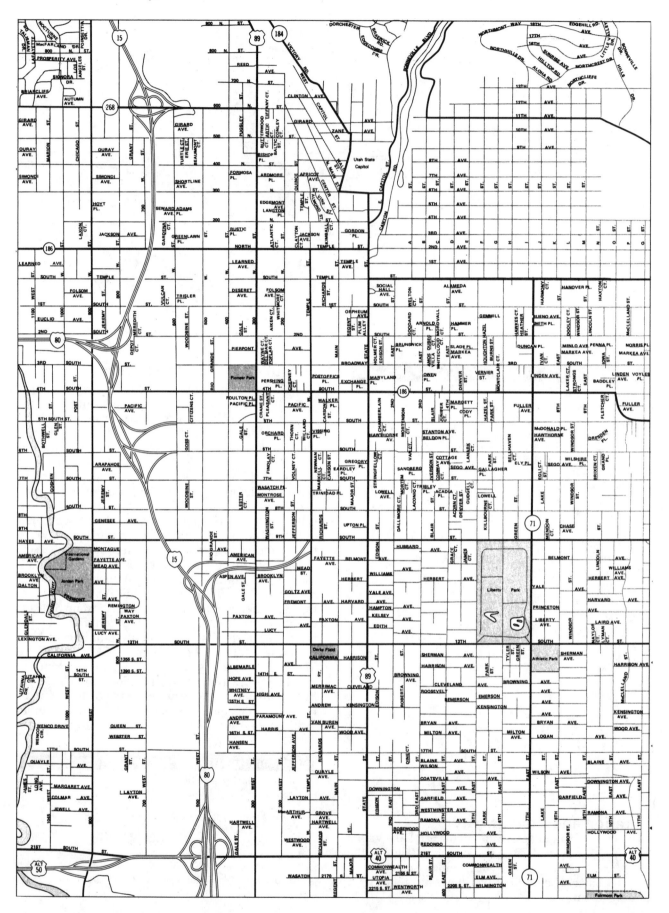

tectural styles reflect the various stages of Salt Lake City's history. Log houses are found in Temple Square and in Liberty Park; adobe houses in the first settled north and west sections; Norman, English colonial, Spanish mission, New England colonial, and other types occur beyond Ninth South Street, and modern styles in newer residential developments.

Weather			
Temperature			
Highest Monthly Average °F	93.2		
Lowest Monthly Average °F	19.7		
Annual Averages			
Days 32°F or Below	134		
Days above 90°F	58		
Zero Degree Days	3		
Precipitation (inches)	15.0		
Snow (inches)	58.0		
% Seasonal Humidity	54.0		
Wind Speed (m.p.h.)	8.7		
Clear Days	129		
Cloudy Days	133		
Storm Days	35		
Rainy Days	88		
Average Temperatures (°F)	*High*	*Low*	*Mean*
January	37.4	18.5	28.0
February	43.4	23.3	33.4
March	50.8	28.3	39.6
April	61.8	36.6	49.2
May	72.4	44.2	58.3
June	81.3	51.1	66.2
July	92.8	60.5	76.7
August	90.2	58.7	74.5
September	80.3	43.3	64.8
October	66.4	38.4	52.4
November	50.0	28.1	39.1
December	39.0	21.5	30.3

Climate

Mountains shield the city from the harsh winters and the lake moderates the temperatures in the summers, which are typically hot and dry. The winters are cold, but not severely so, and the snow remains on the ground until March. Spring is the season of high winds and heavy rains.

History

The history of Salt Lake City is inseparable from that of the State of Utah, (known earlier as the State of Deseret and the Territory of Utah), for which it has been the capital since 1847. It is also the headquarters for the Mormon Church; it has been from the time Brigham Young led his hardy followers into the desert region. Although the Fremont Indians lived and hunted in the vicinity for hundreds of years, it was a region that nobody wanted. The vanguard of the Mormon pioneers entered the site in July 1847. Four days after their arrival, Brigham Young called a Council of the Quorum of the Twelve, and they walked from the north camp to about the center between the two creeks where Young waved his hand and said that there were the 40 acres that would be the site of the Temple. By the time Captain Howard Stansbury came to the Great Basin to survey the Great Salt Lake in 1849, he was amazed to find a magnificent town, nearly four miles in length and three miles in width. The town was under ecclesisastical rule until 1851, when it was incorporated as the Great Salt Lake City by the Provisional State of Deseret. The religious titles of the city were in popular use for many years: New Jerusalem, City of the Saints, and Mormon Zion. Soon work began on the Temple Square and a wall around it. During the so-called Utah War, the Mormons were, according to the government, in a state of substantial rebellion, and there was little love lost between them and the U.S. troops. Great Salt Lake City became a Pony Express post in 1860, and the Pacific Telegraph Line was extended to the city in 1861. In 1863 following the passage of the federal antipolygamy laws, Brigham Young was under constant threat of arrest. Meanwhile, work began on the Temple in 1864. In 1868 the name Great Salt Lake City was shortened to Salt Lake City. The 1870s and 1880s were railroad years in which the city was connected by rail in all directions. Following the completion of the transcontinental railway in 1869, Young began the construction of the Utah Central Railroad connecting Salt Lake City with Ogden. Utah Southern was completed in 1873, connecting Salt Lake City with Provo; the Utah Southern Extension reached Milford and Frisco in 1880. The city was linked with Logan upon completion of the Utah Northern to Logan and Pocatello, Idaho, in 1874, and it was linked with Denver and other points east upon completion of the Denver and Rio Grande Western in 1886. Salt Lake Theater was opened in 1862 and the first presentation of Handel's Messiah was given there in 1875. In 1877 Brigham Young died and was buried with all the pomp and circumstance of a king. In 1890 polygamy was outlawed in the city, ending a long political conflict. In 1892 the Temple was completed, and it was dedicated the following year. Utah entered the Union in 1896 with Salt Lake City as capital. The city marked its semicentennial in 1897 with the unveiling of the Brigham Young Monument at Main and South Temple streets. In the early decades of the 20th century, the city began to assume its present character. The Capitol was built in 1915.

Historical Landmarks

The Temple Square is the heart of the Mormon Church and Salt Lake City. It is a 10-acre tract enclosed by a 15-foot wall. The grounds are landscaped with flower beds in geometric patterns. Closeby are other Mormon landmarks. The Great Salt Lake Base and Meridian Stone without the wall at the southeastern corner of the square was the starting point of Orson Pratt's original survey in 1847. The Bureau of Information and Museum is just inside the south entrance. On the first floor hall is *Torlief Knaphuss Hand-cart Family*, a bronze

Chronology

1847 Brigham Young and a band of Mormon pioneers reach the site of Salt Lake City, and plan a city to be built around a Temple.

1851 Ecclesiastical rule ends when Great Salt Lake City is incorporated by the Provisional State of Deseret.

1857–1863 The Federal government prohibits of polygamy. The Utah War breaks out; the Mormons remain in a state of substantial rebellion.

1860 Great Salt Lake City becomes a pony express post.

1861 The telegraph reaches Great Salt Lake City.

1862 The Salt Lake Theater is opened.

1864 Work begins on the Temple.

1868 The word *Great* is dropped from the name of the city.

1869 Transcontinental Railway is completed through Ogden.

1870 The Utah Central Railroad connects Ogden with Salt Lake City.

1873 The Utah Southern connects Salt Lake City with Provo.

1874 The Utah Northern connects Salt Lake City with Logan and Pocatello, Idaho.

1877 Brigham Young dies and is buried with great honors.

1880 Utah Southern extension links Salt Lake City with Frisco and Milford.

1886 The Denver and Rio Grande Western links Salt Lake City with Denver.

1890 A manifesto disavows polygamy and ends conflict with federal authorities.

1893 The Temple is dedicated.

1897 Salt Lake City celebrates its semicentennial.

1915 The Capitol is completed.

1934 The city experiences a major earthquake.

sculpture memorializing the Mormon hand-cart migration from the Missouri valley to Utah between 1856 and 1860. Many Mormon relics are on display, including Brigham Young's desk and safe, a brick and the bell from the Nauvoo Temple, personal memorabilia of church leaders, a wooden-cogged roadmeter used to measure mileage on the trek across the Great Plains, a battered plowshare, pioneer furniture, and the early press on which the *Deseret News* was printed. The oldest house, a log cabin protected by an iron fence and

a wooden canopy, is in the southeast corner of the square. The Three Witnesses Monument is northwest of the cabin. Statues of Joseph and Hyrum Smith, killed in Carthage, Illinois, in 1844, are mounted on square pedestals of Utah granite, west of the Three Witnesses Monument. The Temple is not open to non-Mormons. Facing east from the east central section of the square, it is a six-spired grey granite edifice, 186 feet long, 99 feet wide, and 167 feet high. The east center tower rises 210 feet, capped by the trumpet-bearing statue of the angel Moroni. The three spires on the east represent the Melchizedek order of priesthood, and the three spires on the west the Aaronic order of priesthood. The Temple took 40 years to build. The Tabernacle is a gigantic oval auditorium, 250 feet long and 150 feet wide, resembling the gray back of a huge tortoise. Its vaulted roof is an ellipsoid. A gallery, 30 feet wide, extends about three sides of the interior. It has a mammoth organ with 8,868 pipes varying in length from five-eighths of an inch to 32 feet. The Seagull Monument, east of the Assembly Hall, surrounded by a pool, is a memorial to the gulls that saved the crops of pioneers during the cricket invasion of 1848. The Brigham Young Monument at the intersection of Main and South Temple streets is a 25-foot bronze monument of the church leader set on a granite base. The Hotel Utah on the corner of Main and South Temple streets is a 10-story building owned by the Mormon Church and erected in 1911. It is a French Renaissance building with a cupola topped by the state emblem, the beehive. The Lion House on South Temple Street is an adobe structure named for the carved stone lion over the first floor portico. The building housed some of Brigham Young's numerous wives. The Beehive House on South Temple Street is a two-story adobe building that served for many years as the official residence of the presidents of the Mormon Church. Eagle Gate, spanning State Street at East South Temple Street, was erected in 1859 as an entrance to the private property of Brigham Young and City Creek Canyon. It displays a copperplated, wood-carved eagle, with outstretched wings measuring 16 feet, perched on a beehive. The state capitol at the end of North State Street is a classically styled four-story edifice on a bench of the Wasatch Foothills at the northern rim of the city, visible from all corners. Designed by Richard K. A. Kletting and built in a rectangle of Utah granite , it is 404 feet long, 240 feet wide, and 285 feet high at the tip of the dome, which is covered with copper. Southeast of the capitol is the Mormon Battalion Monument. Fort Douglas on Fort Douglas Boulevard and Gibbon Street occupies a 9,000-acre reservation on East Bench. This is The Place Monument north of Hogle Gardens Zoo on a dirt road is a simple square granite shaft with a buffalo skull carved in bas-relief near the top. It marks the spot where on 24 July 1847, Brigham Young marked out the spot where Salt Lake City was built. The Empey House on South Temple Street is a two-story buff adobe building. It was built about 1855 by Brigham Young for one of his wives, Ann Eliza Webb Young, who later divorced him. The house was later occupied by Bishop Nelson P. Empey, who married one of Brigham Young's daughters. The Pony Express Monument on South Main Street is a seven-foot granite marker commemorating the inauguration of the Pony Express service in 1860. The site of the Salt Lake Theater, razed in 1928, is on the corner of State and First South streets. The Ambassador Hotel on East Street is a large building erected under a congressional grant in 1889 to house women and children who were rescued from polygamy.

Population

Salt Lake City has been losing population since World War II. From a peak of 175,885 in 1970 it dropped by 7.3% to 163,034 in 1980 and then by a further 1.9% to 159,936 in 1990. The metro area, however, has been gaining substantially and now has 1,072,227 residents, compared to 684,000 in 1970.

Population		
	1980	*1990*
Central City	163,034	159,936
Rank	90	108
Metro Area	910,222	1,072,227
Pop. Change 1980–1990 -3,098		
Pop. % Change 1980–1990 -1.9		
Median Age 31.1		
% Male 49.3		
% Age 65 and Over 14.50		
Density (per square mile) 1,467		

Households
Number 66,657
Persons per Household   2.33
% Female-Headed Households   10.2
% One-Person Households   35.8
Births—Total 3,795
% to Mothers under 20   10.0
Birth Rate per 1,000   23.0

Ethnic Composition

Whites make up 87%, blacks 1.7%, American Indians 1.6%, Asians and Pacific Islanders 4.7%, and others 4.9%. Hispanics, both black and white, make up 9.7%.

Ethnic Composition (as % of total pop.)		
	1980	*1990*
White	89.76	87.02
Black	1.55	1.72
American Indian	1.30	1.59
Asian and Pacific Islander	2.04	4.73
Hispanic	7.55	9.7
Other	NA	4.94

Government

Salt Lake City is governed under a mayor-council form of government. The mayor is elected at large to a four-year term. The seven council members are elected from districts, also to four-year terms.

Government
Year of Home Charter   NA
Number of Members of the Governing Body   8
Elected at Large   1
Elected by Wards   7
Number of Women in Governing Body   3
Salary of Mayor $50,000
Salary of Council Members $10,000
City Government Employment Total   2,298
Rate per 10,000   145.0

Public Finance

The annual budget consists of revenues of $201.6 million and expenditures of $1.499 billion. Outstanding debt is $2.188 billion, and cash and security holdings $1.154 billion.

Public Finance
Total Revenue (in millions) $201.6
Intergovernmental Revenue—Total (in millions) $14.37
Federal Revenue per Capita $9.29
% Federal Assistance   4.6
% State Assistance   2.52
Sales Tax as % of Total Revenue   17.59
Local Revenue as % of Total Revenue   81.5
City Income Tax   no
Taxes—Total (in millions) $63.8
Taxes per Capita
Total $402
Property $171
Sales and Gross Receipts $212
General Expenditures—Total (in millions) $161.5
General Expenditures per Capita $1,019
Capital Outlays per Capita $316
% of Expenditures for:
Public Welfare   0.0
Highways   16.7
Education   0.0
Health and Hospitals   0.0
Police   12.1
Sewerage and Sanitation   6.7
Parks and Recreation   4.6
Housing and Community Development   10.5
Debt Outstanding per Capita $887
% Utility   18.0
Federal Procurement Contract Awards (in millions) $398.4
Federal Grants Awards (in millions) $261.0
Fiscal Year Begins   July 1

Economy

The economy has evolved from an agricultural one to one driven primarily by mining, finance, and manufacturing. Agriculture is still a major contributor to the economy, though, and a wide variety of crops is grown under irrigation. The surrounding desert is ideal for the production and testing of defense equipment, such as missiles and rocket engines. A number of high-technology firms also are located here. Although declining in size and output, mining is a major economic activity. The

Bingham Copper Mine is one of the nation's largest. Sugar, steel, and oil refining are also important industries. The sector showing greatest growth is artificial organ research and manufacture. Hence, Salt Lake City has earned the nickname "Bionic Valley." Supported by the University of Utah, firms such as Bonneville Pacific and Symbion produce a wide range of prosthetics, including the Jarvik artificial heart.

Economy

Total Money Income (in millions) $1,623.7
% of State Average   120.1
Per Capita Annual Income $10,248
% Population below Poverty Level   14.2
Fortune 500 Companies   NA

Banks	Number	Deposits (in millions)
Commercial	40	10,483.7
Savings & Credit Unions	206	9,892.1

Passenger Autos   317,032
Electric Meters   330,000
Gas Meters   340,000

Manufacturing

Number of Establishments   576
% with 20 or More Employees   34.7
Manufacturing Payroll (in millions) $663.5
Value Added by Manufacture (in millions) $1,495.0
Value of Shipments (in millions) $3,170.5
New Capital Expenditures (in millions) $80.1

Wholesale Trade

Number of Establishments   1,047
Sales (in millions) $6,279.1
Annual Payroll (in millions) $376.105

Retail Trade

Number of Establishments   2,270
Total Sales (in millions) $1,732.1
Sales per Capita $10,932
Number of Retail Trade Establishments with Payroll   1,632
Annual Payroll (in millions) $227.5
Total Sales (in millions) $1,702.5
General Merchandise Stores (per capita) $1,179
Food Stores (per capita) $1,926
Apparel Stores (per capita) $762
Eating and Drinking Places (per capita) $1,584

Service Industries

Total Establishments   2,787
Total Receipts (in millions) $1,513.8
Hotels and Motels (in millions) $125.0
Health Services (in millions) $281.7
Legal Services (in millions) $216.9

Labor

The employment market is dominated by the U.S. Department of Defense facilities and the University of Utah among public employers; and Hercules Aerospace, Morton Thiokol, and Union Pacific among private employers. Employment opportunities are projected to grow by 12% during the 1990s, with most of the growth occurring in service industries. A low cost of living is one of the city's biggest attractions.

Labor

Civilian Labor Force   100,325
% Change 1989–1990   -0.7

Work Force Distribution
   Mining   3,000
   Construction   21,400
   Manufacturing   68,200
   Transportation and Public Utilities   33,000
   Wholesale and Retail Trade   124,700
   FIRE (Finance, Insurance, Real Estate)   29,600
   Service   126,500
   Government   100,400
   Women as % of Labor Force   43.7
   % Self-Employed   5.5
   % Professional/Technical   21.0
Total Unemployment   4,338
Rate %   4.3
Federal Government Civilian Employment   6,819

Education

The Salt Lake City School District supports 39 elementary, intermediate, and senior high schools. Salt Lake City is the home of the University of Utah, the oldest university in the West, founded in 1850. The Westminster College, affiliated with the Methodist Church, is also located in the city.

Education

Number of Public Schools   39
Special Education Schools   2
Total Enrollment   24,766
% Enrollment in Private Schools   2.4
% Minority   22.7
Classroom Teachers   1,174
Pupil-Teacher Ratio   20.9:1
Number of Graduates   1,051
Total Revenue (in millions) $78.955
Total Expenditures (in millions) $78.829
Expenditures per Pupil $3,158
Educational Attainment (Age 25 and Over)
   % Completed 12 or More Years   76.7
   % Completed 16 or More Years   25.5
Four-Year Colleges and Universities   2
   Enrollment   26,390
Two-Year Colleges   3
   Enrollment   14,478

Libraries

Number   42
Public Libraries   6
Books (in thousands)   581
Circulation (in thousands)   1,961
Persons Served (in thousands)   152.7
Circulation per Person Served   12.8
Income (in millions) $5.640
Staff   121

Four-Year Colleges and Universities
   University of Utah
   Westminster College

Health

Salt Lake City's largest hospitals are the LDS Hospital, Holy Cross Hospital, and St. Mark's Hospital. The University Health Services Center is the teaching and research hospital for the University of Utah Medical School. Other hospitals include the Primary Children's Medical Center and the Veterans Administration Hospital.

Health
Deaths—Total   1,685
Rate per 1,000   10.2
Infant Deaths—Total   43
Rate per 1,000   11.3
Number of Metro Hospitals   10
Number of Metro Hospital Beds   2,300
Rate per 100,000   1,452
Number of Physicians   2,106
Physicians per 1,000   2.31
Nurses per 1,000   NA
Health Expenditures per Capita $0.15

Transportation

Salt Lake City is intersected by two major interstates: the north-south I-15 and the east-west I-80. Interstate 215 forms a commuter loop and bypass around the inner city. The city is also served by U.S. highways 40, 89, and 91 and state highways 111, 48, 171, 186, 65, 68, 71, 152, and 210. Amtrak provides rail passenger service with four trains daily. Rail freight service is provided by Union Pacific, Denver Rio Grande, and Southern Pacific. The principal air terminal is Salt Lake City International Airport, six miles west of downtown.

Transportation
Interstate Highway Mileage   80
Total Urban Mileage   2,856
Total Daily Vehicle Mileage (in millions) $15.928
Daily Average Commute Time   44.2 min.
Number of Buses   320
Port Tonnage (in millions)   NA
Airports   1
Number of Daily Flights   208
Daily Average Number of Passengers   14,367
Airlines (American carriers only)
American
American West
Continental
Delta
Northwest
United

Housing

Single-family detached homes are the norm, although more recently multifamily houses and condominiums have come into vogue. Of the total housing stock 49.4% are owner-occupied. The median value of an owner-occupied home is $67,200, and the median monthly rent is $282.

Housing		
Total Housing Units 73,762		
% Change 1980–1990 1.3		
Vacant Units for Sale or Rent 5,494		
Occupied Units 66,657		
% with More Than One Person per Room 4.4		
% Owner-Occupied 49.4		
Median Value of Owner-Occupied Homes $67,200		
Average Monthly Purchase Cost $370		
Median Monthly Rent $282		
New Private Housing Starts 69		
Value (in thousands) $7,401		
% Single-Family 89.9		
Nonresidential Buildings Value (in thousands) $96,889		
Tallest Buildings	*Hgt. (ft.)*	*Stories*
L.D.S. Church Office Bldg.	420	30
Beneficial Life Tower	351	21
Utah One Center (1992)	350	24

Urban Redevelopment

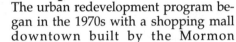

The urban redevelopment program began in the 1970s with a shopping mall downtown built by the Mormon Church. Later, private developers built a mall of the same size across the street, a commercial and industrial center near the Salt Lake Airport, and a shopping mall in a rundown area downtown. Urban redevelopment is coordinated by the Salt Lake City Department of Capital Planning and Programming and the Salt Lake City Department of Economic Development and Development Services.

Crime

Salt Lake City ranks below national average in public safety. In 1991, of crimes known to police, there were 1,319 violent crimes and 19,516 property crimes.

Crime
Violent Crimes—Total   1,319
Violent Crime Rate per 100,000   373.7
Murder   14
Rape   182
Robbery   474
Aggravated Assaults   649
Property Crimes   19,516
Burglary   3,460
Larceny   14,602
Motor Vehicle Theft   1,454
Arson   122
Per Capita Police Expenditures $125.89
Per Capita Fire Protection Expenditures $120.91
Number of Police   341
Per 1,000   2.08

Religion

Salt Lake City is uniqely associated with the Church of Jesus Christ of Latter-Day Saints. Mormons form about 63% of the population. Catholics make up about 6%, and most of the mainline Protestant denominations a smaller percentage. While no church compares with the Temple, the city has a number of other outstanding churches, such as the Cathedral of the Madeleine, St. Mark's Episcopal Cathedral, and the First Congregational Church.

Religion

Largest Denominations (Adherents)	
Catholic	38,480
Latter-Day Saints	466,551
Southern Baptist	5,255
United Methodist	4,179
Presbyterian	3,870
Evangelical Lutheran	3,299
Assembly of God	3,096
Lutheran-Missouri Synod	2,139
Jewish	1,997

Media

The Salt Lake City press consists of two dailies: the morning *Tribune* and the evening *Deseret News*. The electronic media consist of 6 television stations and 24 AM and FM radio stations.

Media

Newsprint
    Deseret News, daily
    Eagle, weekly
    Salt Lake Times, weekly
    Tribune, daily

Television
    KSL (Channel 5)
    KSTU (Channel 13)
    KTVX (Channel 4)
    KUED (Channel 7)
    KUTV (Channel 2)
    KXIV (Channel 14)

Radio

KALL (AM)	KALL (FM)
KCNR (AM)	KCPX (FM)
KCQQ (AM)	KDAB (FM)
KDYL (AM)	KFAM (AM)
KISN (AM)	KISN (FM)
KKAT (FM)	KKDS (AM)
KLZX (FM)	KMGR (FM)
KRSP (FM)	KRCL (FM)
KSFI (FM)	KSL (AM)
KSOP (AM)	KSOP (FM)
KTKK (AM)	KUER (FM)
KUTR (AM)	KZHT (FM)

Sports

Salt Lake City is the home of three major professional sports teams: Utah Jazz in basketball, the Salt Lake Trappers in baseball, and the Salt Lake Golden Eagles in hockey. A number of rodeo events also are held here.

Arts, Culture, and Tourism

Salt Lake City has a long tradition in the performing arts. In 1862 at Brigham Young's insistence, the Salt Lake Theater was built. Seating 1,500, it was the largest building in the West at the time it was completed. The Mormon Tabernacle Choir is an American institution. The Utah Symphony performs over 250 concerts annually, most of them at the Symphony Hall. Utah Opera stages a number of productions each year. Dance is represented by Ballet West, the Repertory Dance Theater, and the Ririe-Woodbury Dance Company. The Pioneer Theater Company, founded only two years after the city, is still active, as is the Salt Lake Acting Company.

The principal museum is the Utah Museum of Fine Arts on the campus of the University of Utah. The Pioneer Memorial Museum is located in a replica of the former Salt Palace. The Utah Historical Society is located in a restored 19th-century railroad station. Other museums include the Fort Douglas Military Museum, the Children's Museum of Utah, the Museum of Church History and Art, the Salt Lake Art Center, and the Utah Museum of Natural History.

Travel and Tourism

Hotel Rooms   11,914
Convention and Exhibit Space (square feet)   NA

Convention Centers
    Salt Palace Convention Center

Festivals
    Days of 47 Festival (July)
    Utah Arts Festival (June)
    Pioneer Harvest Days (September)
    Greek Festival (September)
    Jazz Festival (September)
    Utah State Fair (September)

Parks and Recreation

Salt Lake City maintains a number of parks; the largest are Liberty Park, which includes the 1852 Isaac Chase House and the Salt Lake City Relic Hall; and Pioneer Park between 3rd South and 2nd West streets, a landscaped one-block area upon which Mormon settlers built a fort and 17 log and adobe houses.

Sources of Further information

City Hall
451 South State Street
Salt Lake City, UT 84111
(801) 535-7704

Salt Lake Area Chamber of Commerce
175 East 400 South
Salt Lake City, UT 84111
(801) 364-3631

Salt Lake Valley Convention and Visitors Bureau
180 SW Temple
Salt Lake City, UT 84101
(801) 521-2822

Additional Reading

Burton, Richard F. *The City of the Saints.* 1990.

Haglund, Karl T. and Philip F. Notarianni. *The Avenues of Salt Lake City.* 1980.

Hamilton, Charles M. and Nina C. Cutrubus. *The Salt Lake Temple.* 1983.

McCormick, John S. *The Historic Buildings of Salt Lake City.* 1982.

Tomas, Charles. *Salt Lake City: The Center of Scenic America.* 1988.

Texas

Basic Data

Name   San Antonio
Name Origin   From Spanish Saint Anthony of Padua
Year Founded   1718 Inc. 1837
Status: State   Texas
        County   Seat of Bexar County
Area (square miles)   333
Elevation (feet)   650
Time Zone   Central
Population (1990)   935,933
Population of Metro Area (1990)   1,302,099

Sister Cities

   Guadalajara, Mexico
   Gwongju, Korea
   Kaohsiung, China
   Kumamoto, Japan
   Santa Cruz de Tenerife, Spain
   Monterrey, Mexico
   Las Palmas de Gran Canaria, Spain

Distance in Miles To:

Atlanta	995
Boston	2,018
Chicago	1,209
Dallas	270
Denver	946
Detroit	1,445
Houston	199
Los Angeles	1,387
New York	1,820
Philadelphia	1,737
Miami	1,385
Washington, DC	1,587

Layout of City and Suburbs

A bend in the San Antonio River encircles the center of the city, the heart of downtown San Antonio. Shops, restaurants and an open-air amphitheater line the river banks in an area called Paseo del Rio or River Walk. La Villita or Little Village occupies a square block along the downtown riverfront. It includes restored houses and shops built by early Spanish settlers. The Tower of the Americas rises 622 feet east of the river. The tower was originally built for HemisFair, a World's Fair that celebrated the city's 250th anniversary. North of the Tower stands the San Antonio Civic Center. The Civic Hall occupies the center of the Military Plaza, west of the river. The Alamo, a restored Roman Catholic mission and site of one of the most historic battles in U.S. history, stands in Alamo Plaza in downtown San Antonio. Other missions are located in the downtown area. Residential districts spread in all directions and include Hollywood Park, Kirby, Universal City, and Windcrest.

Environment

Environmental Stress Index   2.8
Green Cities Index: Rank   11
                   Score   21.58
Water Quality   Moderate mineral content
Average Daily Use (gallons per capita)   210
   Maximum Supply (gallons per capita)   812
Parkland as % of Total City Area   NA
% Waste Landfilled/Recycled   NA
Annual Parks Expenditures per Capita $61.52

Location and Topography

San Antonio is located in south central Texas between the Edwards Plateau to the northwest and the Gulf Coastal Plains to the southeast.

Climate

San Antonio has a tropical climate with hot summers and extremely mild winters. The city is ranked as the fourth-hottest in the nation with temperatures exceeding

90°F for over 111 days a year. Although the skies are mostly clear or only partly cloudy 60% of the time, the air is warm and muggy. In winter the temperatures drop below freezing for an average of only 22 days and snowfall is rare. Rainfall is abundant—28 inches annually—most of it falling in May and September. Because of the proximity to the gulf, severe tropical storms and thunderstorms are common. Winds are generally from the north in the winter and from the south and southeast in summer.

Weather

Temperature

Highest Monthly Average °F 94.9
Lowest Monthly Average °F 39.0

Annual Averages

Days 32°F or Below 22
Days above 90°F 111
Zero Degree Days 0
Precipitation (inches) 28.0
Snow (inches) 0.5
% Seasonal Humidity 67
Wind Speed (m.p.h.) 9.3
Clear Days 110
Cloudy Days 138
Storm Days 36
Rainy Days 81

Average Temperatures (°F)	High	Low	Mean
January	61.6	39.8	50.7
February	65.6	43.4	54.5
March	72.5	49.1	60.8
April	80.3	58.8	69.6
May	86.2	65.7	76.0
June	92.4	72.0	82.2
July	95.6	73.8	84.7
August	95.9	73.4	84.7
September	89.8	68.8	79.3
October	81.8	59.2	70.5
November	71.1	48.2	59.7
December	64.4	41.8	53.2

History

San Antonio is one of the oldest cities in North America. It is believed that Cabeza de Vaca visited the neighborhood in 1536 and discovered a place inhabited by friendly Indians. On 13 June 1691, Don Domingo Teran de los Rios, accompanied by Father Damian Massanet and an escort of 50 soldiers, found a large rancheria of Payayas at a village called Yanaguana by the Indians. It was rechristened San Antonio by Father Massanet after Saint Anthony of Padua. Don Martin de Alarcon, Captain General and Governor of the Province of Texas, and Fray Antonio de San Buenaventura Olivares, with 72 settlers, monks, and soldiers, reached the settlement in 1718, driving before them 200 cows, 548 horses, 1,000 sheep, and 200 oxen. Father Olivares founded the mission San Antonio de Vallero (later nicknamed the Alamo, from the Spanish word for cottonwood) and built a hut. Governor Alarcon founded the Villa de Bejar (later Bexar). This was the very nucleus of the settlement which, within the next 13 years, added four more missions. In 1724

the mission's huts were destroyed by a hurricane, but they were soon rebuilt. The first batch of new settlers reached the mission from Canary Islands, and they founded the Villa de San Fernando across the river. They built flat-roofed stone and adobe houses, dug irrigation ditches, and built a church and school. In 1786 Francisco Guadalupe Calaorra established a ferry across the San Antonio River. A presidio or fort was established near each mission to protect the missionaries. The missions prospered until the last decade of the 18th century, but then declined as epidemics and raids by the Comanches and Apaches reduced the population, and the soldiers, colonists, and friars quarreled among themselves. The mission was secularized in 1793 and the settlement was incorporated as San Antonio de Bexar, the capital of the Province of Texas. During the Mexican War of Liberation, a motley crew of Anglo-Americans, Indians, and Mexicans tried to free the town from Spanish rule in 1813, but they were overwhelmed by the Spanish general, Joaquin Arredondo. In retaliation, he imprisoned over 300 in an airless building on a street later named Dolorosa, or Street of Sorrow, where 18 suffocated. The remaining men were shot and the women forced to work as slaves. The town remained Mexican even after Moses Austin arrived in 1820 to open the Anglo-American chapter in its history. In 1834 a number of local Mexicans joined the cause of independence from the harsh rule of Santa Anna. The Battle of San Antonio began on 5 December 1835 when Texan revolutionaries, under Ben Milam, stormed the town and forced Mexican General Martin Perfecto de Cos to surrender. But the revolutionary success was short-lived. Santa Anna, with an army of more than 5,000, reached San Antonio in February 1836 and on 6 March took the Alamo fortress after every defender had been killed. Within a month the Mexicans were routed by Sam Houston's forces at San Jacinto and San Antonio became part of the Republic of Texas. In 1845 Texas joined the Union. In the late 1840s the arrival of German immigrants enlarged the population to nearly 8,000. During the Civil War, San Antonio contributed nearly 40 companies to the Confederate cause. After the Civil War, and especially after the coming of the first railroad in 1877, San Antonio grew rapidly to become the largest city in Texas by 1920, but lost this position to Houston and Dallas thereafter. During World War I San Antonio was a major military command center. The war also led to the eclipse of the German community and the rise of Hispanics in the city's political and social life. A destructive flood in 1921 spurred the rebuilding of the city and the city's first skyscrapers appeared soon thereafter. World War II brought further military activity, especially at the Lackland Air Force Base. In 1968 the city celebrated its 250th anniversary with HemisFair. The city also built the Tower of the Americas, a huge concrete and steel observation structure rising 622 feet, 67 feet taller than the Washington Monument. In the 1970s and 1980s, with the explosive growth of Hispanic immigration, San Antonio became the largest Hispanic city in the nation.

Chronology

1536 Explorer Cabeza de Vaca visits the neighborhood.

1691 Don Domingo de Teran de los Rios accompanied by Father Damian Massanet arrives at an Indian village called Yanaguana, which Father Damian rechristens San Antonio and where he sets up a cross and erects an arbor of cottonwood (alamo) boughs under which to say Mass.

1718 Don Martin de Alarcon, Captain General and Governor of the Province of Texas, and Fray Antonio de San Buenaventura Olivares, with 72 monks and soldiers reach settlement. Father Olivares founds Mission San Antonio de Vallero (later nicknamed the Alamo) and erects small hut. Governor Alarcon founds Villa de Bejar (later Bexar).

1724 Hurricane destroys the crude mission huts which are later rebuilt.

1731 Fifteen families from the Canary Islands establish the Villa de San Fernando across the river.

1746 First school is established in San Antonio.

1786 Francisco Guadalupe Calaorra establishes ferry across San Antonio River.

1793 The fort, the villa, and the settlement are secularized.

1809 San Antonio is incorporated.

1813 Insurrection against Spain is put down by General Joaquin Arredondo, and the male rebels are imprisoned and killed and the women forced into slavery.

1820 Moses Austin reaches San Antonio.

1821 As a result of the Mexican Revolution, San Antonio becomes a Mexican possession.

1834 Local revolutionaries take up arms against the harsh rule of dictator General Santa Anna.

1835 In the Battle of San Antonio, the Mexican governor Martin Perfecto de Cos is forced to surrender by revolutionaries under Ben Milam.

1836 General Santa Anna, with an army of 5,000, storms the city and seize the Alamo fortress after every defender is killed. With the rallying cry, "Remember the Alamo," Sam Houston's forces rout the Mexicans and retake the Alamo. Texas becomes an independent country.

1845 Texas joins the Union.

1861 Texas joins the Confederacy.

1877 Southern Pacific, the first railroad, reaches the city.

1921 Destructive flood causes massive damage.

1968 San Antonio celebrates its 250th anniversary with HemisFair.

1975 San Antonio elects first woman mayor, Lila Cockrell.

1981 San Antonio elects first Hispanic mayor, Henry Cisneros.

Historical Landmarks

The Alamo on Alamo Plaza is one of the nation's outstanding monuments and one of the oldest. The little gray chapel and the crumbling ivy-colored walls about the courtyard northwest of the chapel are all that remain of the building that was erected in 1756, the third on this spot. The mission-fort where 187 persons laid down their lives in 1836 had ceased to function as a church institution in 1793 and thereafter had been used as a fort, although it fell into decay, and at the time of the battle was a roofless ruin filled with debris. It had a high rock wall about three feet thick enclosing the cloisters/barracks. The Menger Hotel on the northeast corner of Alamo Plaza and Blum Street dates from 1859. The German-English School Building on South Alamo Street dates from 1859, and was in use until 1897. La Villita or Little Village is the site of a Spanish-Mexican village founded in the middle 18th century. Paseo del Rio San Antonio, 21 blocks long, has 31 stairways rising from the San Antonio River. Here the Fiesta Noche del Rio is held annually. Musquiz House on Commerce Street marked the site where Santa Anna received survivors of the Battle of the Alamo, and is near his headquarters. San Fernando Cathedral on Main Plaza between Trevino and Galan streets has the oldest parish church building in the state. Its dome once marked the geographic center of the city. Military Plaza between South Flores, Camaron, Commerce, and Dolorosa streets was established by settlers from the Canary Islands in 1731 as the Plaza de las Armas, or place of arms, for the protection of settlers against Indians. Among other Spanish-Mexican historical houses are two belonging to the signers of the Texas Declaration of Independence: the Navarro Homestead on Nueva and South Laredo streets, home of Jose Antonio Navarro, and Francisco Ruiz House, formerly on Dolores Street and now in Brackenridge Park, the home of Francisco Ruiz. The Spanish Governor's Palace on Military Plaza has the Hapsburg arms and the date 1749 on its entrance. The Grave of Ben Milam, the hero of resistance to Mexican rule, is in Milam Square between Commerce, Houston, and San Saba streets. St. Mary's Roman Catholic Church, on the corner of St. Mary's and College streets, is a modern building on the site of an earlier structure erected in 1855. St. Mark's Episcopal Church on the corner of Jefferson and Pecan streets was built in 1859 on grounds that once formed part of the Alamo property. Robert Lee was once a member of this parish. Fort Sam Houston covers 3,330 acres. Built in the 1870s, its distinguished alumni include Theodore Roosevelt, John Pershing, and Dwight Eisenhower. Mission Concepcion is the best preserved of the Texas Missions. It was built in 1716 of adobe and a porous gray rock called *tufa* in the usual cruciform pattern with identical twin towers and a slightly pointed cupola surmounting the dome. Among its rare frescoes is one called Our Lady of Seven Sorrows. Mission San Jose is known as the Queen of the Missions. A National Shrine, it is the most beautiful and the most fortified of all Texas missions. Among its noted features are a carved window, circular stairs to the belfry, a granary, and a mill. It was built in 1719 by Fray Antonio Margil de Jesus. The Indian pueblo of 84 compartments formed part of the immense quadrangle wall. Although of simple Moorish and Spanish design, its rich stone carvings reflect the influence of the Spanish baroque. The church has only one tower with a pyramid top and an open belfry reached through a round turret housing an ingeniously designed stairway. Mission San Francisco de la Espada was built at the same time as Mission Concepcion but it crumbled in 1758 and the present church was rebuilt in 1898. The baluarte, or fortified tower, is the only complete mission fort extant. It has a round bastion with vaulted roof, strongly buttressed. three-foot-thick stone walls, and portholes for rifles or cannon. The rough chapel has no tower but has a bell tower as an extension of the fort wall. Mission San Juan Capistrano was established in 1731. It does not have sculptured decoration or round arches, but the walls are thick and the rooms spacious with frescoes. It has a bell tower instead of a steeple.

Population

San Antonio is one of the fastest growing cities in the nation, with a population nearing 1 million. From 654,000 in 1970, its population grew by 20.1% to reach 785,940 and then by a further 19.1% to reach 935,933 in 1990. Its post–World War II growth reflects the continuing influx of Mexican immigrants from across the border.

Population		
	1980	*1990*
Central City	785,940	935,933
Rank	11	10
Metro Area	1,072,125	1,302,099
Pop. Change 1980–1990 +149,993		
Pop. % Change 1980–1990 +19.1		
Median Age 29.8		
% Male 48.2		
% Age 65 and Over 10.5		
Density (per square mile) 2,810		

Households		
Number 326,761		
Persons per Household 2.80		

Population (continued)		
% Female-Headed Households 15.7		
% One-Person Households 25.0		
Births—Total 16,838		
% to Mothers under 20 18.6		
Birth Rate per 1,000 20.0		

Ethnic Composition

Whites make up 72.2%, blacks 7%, American Indians 0.4%, Asians and Pacific Islanders 1.1%, and others 19.2%. Hispanics, both white and black, make up 55.59%.

Ethnic Composition (as % of total pop.)		
	1980	*1990*
White	78.64	72.24
Black	7.34	7.04
American Indian	0.23	0.35
Asian and Pacific Islander	0.65	1.14
Hispanic	53.69	55.59
Other	NA	19.23

Government

San Antonio has a council-manager form of government. The ten members of the council are elected by district for two-year terms while the mayor is elected at large. The city manager is appointed by the council.

Government
Year of Home Charter 1914
Number of Members of the Governing Body 10
Elected at Large NA
Elected by Wards 10
Number of Women in Governing Body 3
Salary of Mayor $50
Salary of Council Members $20
City Government Employment Total 12,761
Rate per 10,000 139.6

Public Finance

The annual budget consists of revenues of $1.433 billion and expenditures of $1.687 billion. The debt outstanding is $4.034 billion and cash and security holdings $1.374 billion.

Public Finance
Total Revenue (in millions) $1,433.918
Intergovernmental Revenue—Total (in millions) $96.24
Federal Revenue per Capita $38.96
% Federal Assistance 2.71
% State Assistance 2.10
Sales Tax as % of Total Revenue 5.87
Local Revenue as % of Total Revenue 32.39
City Income Tax no
Taxes—Total (in millions) $132.6

Public Finance (continued)

Taxes per Capita
    Total $145
    Property $71
    Sales and Gross Receipts $68
General Expenditures—Total (in millions) $407.4
General Expenditures per Capita $446
Capital Outlays per Capita $108

% of Expenditures for:
    Public Welfare 0.8
    Highways 7.3
    Education 0.8
    Health and Hospitals 5.3
    Police 13.8
    Sewerage and Sanitation 17.8
    Parks and Recreation 10.3
    Housing and Community Development 3.5
Debt Outstanding per Capita $2,470
    % Utility 75.0
Federal Procurement Contract Awards (in millions)
    $229.7
Federal Grants Awards (in millions) $148.1
Fiscal Year Begins October 1

Economy (continued)

Wholesale Trade

Number of Establishments 1,785
Sales (in millions) $8,702.4
Annual Payroll (in millions) $525.934

Retail Trade

Number of Establishments 9,041
Total Sales (in millions) $6,020.9
Sales per Capita $6,585
Number of Retail Trade Establishments with Payroll 5,743
Annual Payroll (in millions) $755.0
Total Sales (in millions) $5,895.4
General Merchandise Stores (per capita) $830
Food Stores (per capita) $1,440
Apparel Stores (per capita) $421
Eating and Drinking Places (per capita) $809

Service Industries

Total Establishments 6,974
Total Receipts (in millions) $3,109.8
Hotels and Motels (in millions) $188.5
Health Services (in millions) $913.8
Legal Services (in millions) $296.8

Economy

San Antonio is the southern end of the Austin–San Antonio Corridor, touted as one of the hottest high-tech zones in the nation. The city is ranked among the most business-friendly in the nation, with the most available manufacturing sites, and it also leads in labor availability, quality of life, and business climate. The city's expanding manufacturing base includes biomedical firms, semiconductor producers, optical manufacturers, and recyclers. San Antonio also has a special relationship with Mexico because of its large Spanish-speaking population and is emerging as one of the gateways of Latin American trade. It is also a favorite tourist destination with attractions such as Paseo del Rio, the Alamo and the Missions, Opryland, and Sea World. It draws an estimated 12 million visitors a year. San Antonio is also known as the Military City. Because of its strategic location it is one of the nerve centers of the defense network and is the headquarters of one of the largest military establishments in the nation. San Antonio's five military installations—Fort Sam Houston, Lackland, Brooks, Randolph, and Kelly Air Force bases—employ close to 150,000 people and pump $1.5 billion into the local economy. John Naisbitt, in his *Megatrends,* predicts a vigorous future for San Antonio based on its expanding high-technology economic base supplementing its traditional strengths in agriculture, retailing, and finance.

Labor

San Antonio's work force composition reveals the strengths of its economy. Manufacturing accounts for less than the national average for cities because the emerging high-technology sector is not labor-intensive. Government is a major employer because of the presence of the federal defense establishment. Services and trade dominate the economy, as it is heavily tourist-driven.

Economy

Total Money Income (in millions) $7,771.0
% of State Average 81.9
Per Capita Annual Income $8,499
% Population below Poverty Level 20.9
Fortune 500 Companies 3

Banks	Number	Deposits (in millions)
Commercial	29	2,788.6
Savings	14	NA

Passenger Autos 874,791
Electric Meters 468,890
Gas Meters 284,283

Manufacturing

Number of Establishments 927
% with 20 or More Employees 30.9
Manufacturing Payroll (in millions) $659.2
Value Added by Manufacture (in millions) $1,636.2
Value of Shipments (in millions) $3,474.1
New Capital Expenditures (in millions) $61.4

Labor

Civilian Labor Force 443,713
% Change 1989–1990 -1.6

Work Force Distribution
    Mining 1,900
    Construction 22,100
    Manufacturing 45,700
    Transportation and Public Utilities 22,900
    Wholesale and Retail Trade 130,600
    FIRE (Finance, Insurance, Real Estate) 38,600
    Service 145,100
    Government 119,500
    Women as % of Labor Force 43.4
    % Self-Employed 5.2
    % Professional/Technical 14.0
Total Unemployment 33,432
Rate % 7.5
Federal Government Civilian Employment 8,110

The manufacturing sector also benefits from the fact that only 8.5% of blue-collar workers are unionized.

Education

 San Antonio has 16 school districts in a decentralized system that has few parallels in the nation. Each school district is an independent entity with its own superintendent, board of education, and taxing authority, functioning outside of city or county jurisdiction. The largest school district, San Antonio ISD, supports 103 elementary schools, junior high/middle schools, and senior high schools. In addition, there are 50 parochial schools and over 100 private schools in the area.

The largest higher education facilities, the University of Texas at San Antonio and the University of Texas Health Science Center, are public; Catholic institutions, however, dominate private higher education. St. Mary's University, Our Lady of the Lake University, Incarnate Word College, and Oblate School of Theology are all Catholic, while Trinity University is Presbyterian. San Antonio College and St. Philip's College are junior colleges.

Education

Number of Public Schools   103
Special Education Schools   12
Total Enrollment   60,161
% Enrollment in Private Schools   8.1
% Minority   93.5
Classroom Teachers   3,548
Pupil-Teacher Ratio   16.9:1
Number of Graduates   2,695
Total Revenue (in millions) $219.534
Total Expenditures (in millions) $246.979
Expenditures per Pupil $3,233
Educational Attainment (Age 25 and Over)
  % Completed 12 or More Years   58.6
  % Completed 16 or More Years   13.6
Four-Year Colleges and Universities   6
  Enrollment   29,650
Two-Year Colleges   3
  Enrollment   31,385

Libraries

Number   70
Public Libraries   18
Books (in thousands)   1,907
Circulation (in thousands)   3,301
Persons Served (in thousands)   935
Circulation per Person Served   3.53
Income (in millions) $10.277
Staff   242

Four-Year Colleges and Universities
  University of Texas at San Antonio
  University of Texas Health Science Center
  Incarnate Word College
  Our Lady of the Lake University
  St. Mary's University
  Trinity University

Health

 The medical sector consists of 18 general hospitals, two psychiatric and rehabilitation hospitals, 2 DoD hospitals, a veterans hospital, and 2 state hospitals. The Saint Rosa Medical Center is the oldest and largest medical complex in San Antonio, consisting of four facilities that include a children's hospital and a long-term care center. The South Texas Medical Center is another large complex. The public medical sector includes the two DoD hospitals, the Brooke Army Medical Center at Fort Sam Houston, Wilford Hall Medical Center at Lackland Air Force Base, the Audie L. Murphy Memorial Veterans Administration Hospital, San Antonio State Hospital, and San Antonio State Chest Hospital. The other facilities include Baptist Medical Center, Lutheran General Hospital, Northeast Baptist Hospital, St. Benedict Health Care Center, St. Luke's Lutheran Hospital, Southeast Baptist Hospital, and Southwest Texas Methodist Hospital. Commercial for-profit hospitals include Charter Real, Colonial Hills, Nix Medical Center, Raleigh Hills, Southwest General, and Villa de Tejas.

Health

Deaths—Total   6,408
Rate per 1,000   7.6
Infant Deaths—Total   216
Rate per 1,000   12.8
Number of Metro Hospitals   24
Number of Metro Hospital Beds   7,352
Rate per 100,000   804
Number of Physicians   2,536
Physicians per 1,000   2.27
Nurses per 1,000
Health Expenditures per Capita $17.25

Transportation

San Antonio is approached by three interstates: I-35, I-10, and I-37. The city is encircled by Loop 410 (52.9 miles) and Loop 1604 (94.3 miles), facilitating easy access to the city. Supporting U.S. Highways are 90, 87, 81, 281, and 181, and State Highway 16. Rail freight service is provided by Union Pacific, Southern Pacific, and MKT. The principal air terminal is San Antonio International Airport, about 15 minutes from downtown. Stinson Field handles overflow aviation traffic.

Transportation

Interstate Highway Mileage   127
Total Urban Mileage   4,981
Total Daily Vehicle Mileage (in millions) $23,751
Daily Average Commute Time   44.9 min.
Number of Buses   385
Port Tonnage (in millions)   NA
Airports   1
Number of Daily Flights   99
Daily Average Number of Passengers   6,831

Transportation (continued)

Airlines (American carriers only)
- American
- Continental
- Northwest
- Southwest
- Trans World
- United
- USAir

Housing

Of the total housing stock 54% is owner-occupied. The median value of an owner-occupied home is $49,700 and the median monthly rent $308.

Housing

Total Housing Units	365,414
% Change 1980–1990	24.0
Vacant Units for Sale or Rent	29,506
Occupied Units	326,761
% with More Than One Person per Room	10.4
% Owner-Occupied	54.0
Median Value of Owner-Occupied Homes	$49,700
Average Monthly Purchase Cost	$263
Median Monthly Rent	$308
New Private Housing Starts	1,141
Value (in thousands)	$58,180
% Single-Family	93.0
Nonresidential Buildings Value (in thousands)	$103,114

Tallest Buildings	Hgt. (ft.)	Stories
Tower of the Americas (1968)	622	NA
Marriott Rivercenter (1988)	546	38
NBC Plaza (1988)	444	32
Tower Life (1929)	404	30
NCNB Plaza (1983)	387	28
Nix Professional Bldg. (1931)	375	23

Urban Redevelopment

San Antonio has experienced phenomenal urban redevelopment since 1968, when the HemisFair was held. In addition to Sea World, completed in 1989, a $100-million musical theme park known as Opryland opened in northwest San Antonio. Planned for completion in 1993 is the $160-million Alamodome, a 65,000-seat sports stadium and convention center.

Crime

San Antonio ranks low in public safety. In 1991 violent crimes reported to police totaled 7,573, and property crimes totaled 109,913.

Crime

Violent Crimes—Total	7,573
Violent Crime Rate per 100,000	712.2
Murder	208
Rape	698

Crime (continued)

Robbery	3,778
Aggravated Assaults	2,889
Property Crimes	109,913
Burglary	24,941
Larceny	70,559
Motor Vehicle Theft	14,413
Arson	1,015
Per Capita Police Expenditures	$101.41
Per Capita Fire Protection Expenditures	$63.04
Number of Police	1,273
Per 1,000	1.48

Religion

Almost all Hispanics belong to the Catholic Church, which has 55 churches. Baptists constitute the largest Protestant group with 130 churches, followed by Methodists, 51; Lutherans, 40; Church of Christ, 29; Pentecostals, 16; and Episcopalians, 13.

Religion

Largest Denominations (Adherents)	
Catholic	445,407
Southern Baptist	123,634
United Methodist	37,801
Black Baptist	36,117
Presbyterian	12,106
Independent Charismatics	20,680
Lutheran-Missouri Synod	8,944
Evangelical Lutheran	14,303
Episcopal	12,972
Assembly of God	8,897
Jewish	9,103

Media

The city press consists of two dailies: *San Antonio Express News* and *San Antonio Light*, as well as a business and legal daily, the *Commercial Recorder*. The electronic media consist of 8 television stations and 18 FM and AM radio stations.

Media

Newsprint
- *Commercial Recorder*, daily
- *North San Antonio Times*, weekly
- *San Antonio Express News*, daily
- *San Antonio Light*, daily
- *San Antonio Living*, bimonthly
- *San Antonio Monthly Magazine*, monthly
- *Windcrest Area Recorder Times*, weekly

Television
- KABB (Channel 29)
- KENS (Channel 5)
- KHCE (Channel 23)
- KMOL (Channel 4)
- KLRN (Channel 9)
- KSAT (Channel 12)
- KVDA (Channel 60)
- KWEX (Channel 41)

Radio

KAJA (FM)	KCHL (AM)
KCOR (AM)	KCYY (FM)
KDRY (AM)	KEDA (AM)
KISS (FM)	KKYX (AM)
KONO (AM)	KQXT (FM)
KSAQ (FM)	KSJL (AM)
KSLR (AM)	KSRR (FM)
KSYM (FM)	KTFM (FM)
KTSA (AM)	WOAI (AM)

Sports

The pride of the city is the San Antonio Spurs of the National Basketball Association, who play their home games at the Convention Center Arena in HemisFair Plaza. The San Antonio Dodgers, a farm team of the Los Angeles Dodgers, play minor league baseball at St. Mary's University. The city is also noted for its polo competitions held from April through August at the Retama Polo Center. Other sports attractions include the Vantage Golf Championships at the Oak Hill Country Club and stock car racing on the Raceway.

Arts, Culture, and Tourism

The San Antonio Performing Arts Association and the Arts Council of San Antonio are the two presiding organizations of cultural San Antonio. Many of the cultural events they present are held in the Majestic Performing Arts Center, an old vaudeville house restored in 1981. The showcase for black artists is the Carver Community Cultural Center, and a corresponding center for Hispanic artists is the Guadalupe Cultural Art Center. The Sunken Garden Theater at Brackenridge Park features Sunday afternoon concerts in the summer. San Antonio's higher education institutions are active promoters of the performing arts, and have one theater each, while Trinity University has two, Theater One and Attic Two. Avant garde and experimental theater is the fare at Our Lady of the Lake University's 24th Street Experiment. Other notable theatrical companies include Little Theater, founded in the 1930s; Salteens, a theater for children; Melodrama Playhouse; Harlequin Dinner Theater at Fort Sam Houston; and Alamo City Theater. In music the premier institution is the San Antonio Symphony Orchestra, which performs at the Lila Cockrell Theater for the Performing Arts at the Convention Center, and at Trinity University. Opera is staged at the Grand Opera House, built in 1886. Other musical groups are Tuesday Musical Club, the oldest musical organization in the city, San Antonio Chamber Music Society, and Texas Bach Choir. Ballet is represented by Ballet Folklorica de San Antonio, a Hispanic dance company performing at the Arneson River Theater, and the San Antonio Ballet.

The city's rich historical heritage is preserved in a number of museums, such as The San Antonio Museum of Art, Witte Memorial Museum at the Brackenridge Park, Institute of Texas Cultures, San Antonio Museum of Transportation, Pioneer Museum, Hertzberg Circus Collection, U.S. Army Medical Museum and the Fort Sam Houston Museum at Fort Sam Houston, Edward H. White Memorial Museum at Brooks Air Force Base, and History and Traditions Museum at Lackland Air Force Base. Among art galleries, the most notable are the Marion Koogler McNay Art Institute and the Mexican Cultural Institute. The former plant of the Lone Star Brewing Company includes collections of contemporary and early American as well as Latin American art.

Travel and Tourism

Hotel Rooms   18,406
Convention and Exhibit Space (square feet)   NA

Convention Centers
San Antonio Convention Center
Villita Assembly Hall
Municipal Auditorium
Joe Freeman Coliseum
Beethoven Hall

Festivals
Fiesta San Antonio (April)
Fiesta Noche del Rio (summer)
San Antonio Festival (June)
Carver Jazz Festival (June)
Texas Folk Life Festival (August)
Fiesta de las Luminarias (December)
Great Country River Festival (January)

Parks and Recreation

San Antonio has about 70 parks covering 4,300 acres. San Pedro Park, the oldest, includes the McFarlin Tennis Center. The 363-acre Brackenridge Park includes a theater, zoo, aquarium, skyride, miniature railroad, and riding stables. Overnight camping is available at the 850-acre McAllister Park. Outside city limits is Friedrich Park with wilderness trails for hikers.

Sources of Further Information

City Hall
P.O. Box 83966
San Antonio, TX 78283
(512) 299-7060

Greater San Antonio Chamber of Commerce
602 East Commerce Street
San Antonio, TX 78216
(512) 344-4848

San Antonio Convention and Visitors Bureau
210 South Alamo
San Antonio, TX 78298
(512) 299-8123

Additional Reading

Davis, John L. *San Antonio: A Historical Portrait.* 1978.

Foster, Nancy H. and Ben Fairbank, Jr. *The Texas Monthly Guide to San Antonio*. 1989.

Garcia, Richard A. *Rise of the Mexican-American Middle Class*. 1991.

Johnson, David R. *The Politics of San Antonio: Community, Progress and Power*. 1983.

Living Legacies. *The Businesses That Built San Antonio*. 1985.

Maguire, Jack. *A Century of Fiesta in San Antonio*. 1990.

San Antonio Bicentennial Heritage Committee. *San Antonio in the 18th Century*. 1976.

The San Antonio River. 1977.

Stebner, Werner. *San Antonio: A Photographic Fiesta*. 1990.

Toepperwein, Emily, and Fritz Toepperwein. *The Missions of San Antonio*. 1987.

Woods, Frances J. *Mexican American Leadership in San Antonio*. 1976.

San Diego

California

Basic Data

Name San Diego
Name Origin From Spanish Franciscan San Diego de
    Alcalá de Henares
Year Founded 1769 Inc. 1850
Status: State California
        County Seat of San Diego County
Area (square miles) 324.0
Elevation (feet) 20
Time Zone Pacific
Population (1990) 1,110,549
Population of Metro Area (1990) 2,498,016

Sister Cities
    Alcalá de Henares, Spain
    Cavite City, Philippines
    Edinburgh, Scotland
    Jeonju, Korea
    León, Mexico
    Perth, Australia
    Taichung, China
    Tema, Ghana
    Yantai, China
    Vladivostok, Russia
    Yokohama, Japan

Distance in Miles To:
Atlanta	2,146
Boston	2,984
Chicago	2,093
Dallas	1,348
Denver	1,095
Detroit	2,368
Houston	1,490
Los Angeles	124
Miami	2,678
New York	2,803
Philadelphia	2,773
Washington, DC	2,602

Location and Topography

N

San Diego, the oldest Spanish settlement in California, is in the extreme southwest corner of the United States, just 20 miles north of Mexico. Facing the Pacific Ocean, its terrain is characterized by rolling hills that gently rise to meet the Laguna Mountains to the east.

Layout of City and Suburbs

San Diego is dominated by its harbor, one of the finest natural harbors in the nation, facing the San Diego Bay. Broadway, the main artery, runs from the waterfront due east and divides the city into distinct sections. South of Broadway are the main commercial sections, particularly along Twelfth, Third, Fourth, and Fifth avenues. Balboa Park begins just northeast of the business district. Northwest of the business center is Mission Bay Aquatic Park, which houses Sea World Marine Park and Oceanarium. North and northwest of Balboa Park are newer residential districts, and to the west is Middletown, a narrow segment extending from the bay to the low hills. Old Town, the site of the original Spanish settlement, is northwest of Middletown. In the Logan Heights District, south and east of downtown, along the curved southern shore, sprawl the Mexican and African-American residential districts. The city includes about 40 residential communities. Bisecting the city from east to west along the San Diego River is Mission Valley. The center of San Diego's most popular area, the valley is lined with hotels, restaurants,

Environment

Environmental Stress Index 3.8
Green Cities Index: Rank 27
                Score 26.43
Water Quality Alkaline, hard
    Average Daily Use (gallons per capita) 184
    Maximum Supply (gallons per capita) 285
Parkland as % of Total City Area 1.7
% Waste Landfilled/Recycled 84:16
Annual Parks Expenditures per Capita $103.29

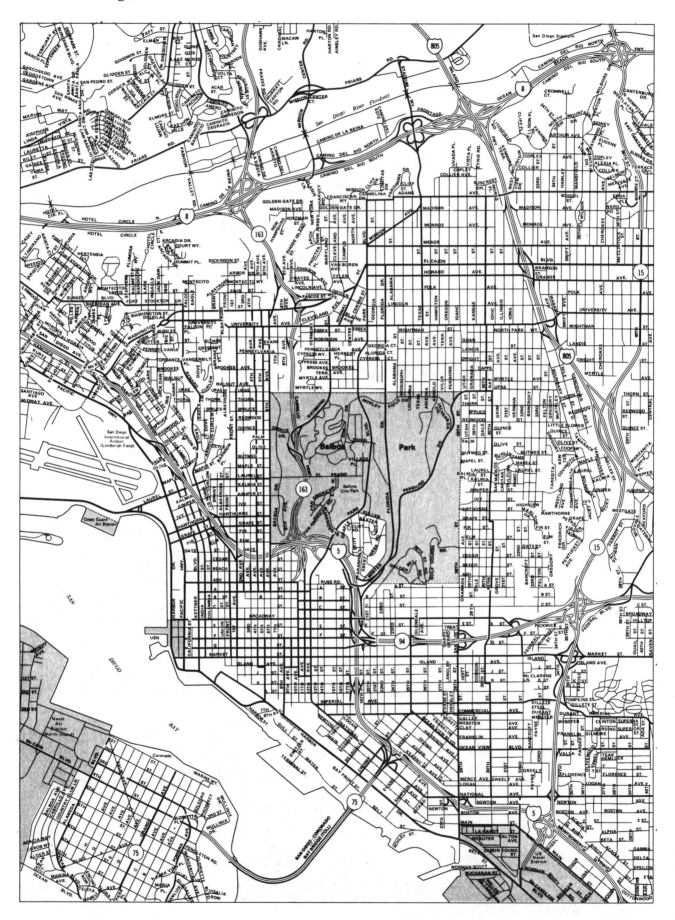

discos, and two large shopping malls. Overlooking the valley on the southern rim are newly built condos and the older luxury houses of Mission Hills. Extending to the east are the residential and academic communities of East San Diego and Kensington College Heights, Allied Gardens, and Del Cerro. Kearney Mesa, north of Mission Valley, is a city industrial park and home of a General Dynamics–Conair aerospace plant and Miramar Naval Air Station. Several residential communities, including Claremont and Linda Vista, are also located on the picturesque mesa. Northwest of the mesa are the academic communities of La Jolla and University City. Moving southward along the coast are the shore communities of Pacific Beach and Mission Beach and, south of Mission Bay, Ocean Beach. From this point the coast juts out in a rugged promontory to form the western flank of San Diego Bay. At the tip of the promontory is Cabrillo National Monument, named in honor of the harbor's 16th-century Spanish discoverer. Facing Point Loma across the water, at the end of San Diego Bay's eastern arm, are the U.S. Naval Air Station, North Island, and the independent resort city of Coronado. A two-mile toll bridge connects Coronado with the downtown area. The city extends south toward the Mexican border in a narrow corridor flanked on both sides by military installations and independent municipalities. This corridor connects the city to South San Diego, an agricultural community that is officially part of San Diego. At the foot of San Diego's business district near the harbor is the Charles C. Dail Community Concourse, which houses the city offices, a theater, a convention center, and an exhibition hall.

Climate

San Diego has a marine and partly Mediterranean climate, and one of the mildest coastal climates in North America. There are few extremes of weather, no freezing days and only a few days in which the mercury rises above 90°F. Sunshine is abundant, and sea breezes are cool even in the afternoon heat. Toward the interior, however, arid conditions prevail, and temperatures can

Weather
Temperature
Highest Monthly Average °F   75.6
Lowest Monthly Average °F   48.4
Annual Averages
Days 32°F or Below   0
Days above 90°F   3
Zero Degree Days   0
Precipitation (inches)   9.0
Snow (inches)   0
% Seasonal Humidity   68.0
Wind Speed (m.p.h.)   6.7
Clear Days   150
Cloudy Days   98
Storm Days   3
Rainy Days   41

Weather (continued)			
Average Temperatures (°F)	*High*	*Low*	*Mean*
January	64.6	45.8	55.2
February	65.6	47.8	56.7
March	66.0	50.1	58.1
April	67.6	53.8	60.7
May	69.4	57.2	63.3
June	71.1	59.9	65.5
July	75.3	63.9	69.6
August	77.3	65.4	71.4
September	76.5	63.2	69.9
October	73.8	58.4	66.1
November	70.1	51.5	60.8
December	66.1	55.4	62.9

fluctuate as much as 30°F in one day. In September and October hot winds from the interior create the hottest season of the year. Thunderstorms may number no more than three annually, but there is considerable fog along the coast and low clouds in the early mornings and in the evenings during summer.

History

The site of San Diego was visited in 1539 by Father Marcos from the desert side in his search for the Seven Cities of Cibola. In 1542 explorer Juan Rodriguez Cabrillo sailed into San Diego Bay and spent six days in the harbor after claiming the surrounding region for the king of Spain. The bay was named after a Spanish saint in 1602 by another Spanish navigator, Sebastian Vizaino. In 1769 Governor Portola, with soldiers and Franciscan friars, established a presidio here. It was one of 21 missions that the Franciscans built in California. In 1793 the British sloop *Discovery* visited the bay and ten years later the Yankee-owned *Lelia Byrd* was caught while smuggling otter skins. In 1834 the village, known as Old Town, was organized as a pueblo, but its population declined until it became another department of Los Angeles. After a brief period under Mexican rule, San Diego passed under U.S. rule with the Treaty of Guadalupe Hidalgo in 1846. In 1850 Old Town was incorporated as a city under the name *New Town* or *Davis's Folly*, after its first settler, William Heath Davis. For the next 20 years the town was an important whaling port. In 1867 San Francisco land developer Alonzo E. Horton bought a 1,000-acre plot in the center of town. He laid out streets, built a wharf and a hotel, and donated land to churches. After a fire wiped out Old Town's business district, New Town became the city center. By the time the Santa Fe Railroad made its transcontinental terminus, the town had 40,000 residents. It suffered a slump during the turn of the century when the population plunged to 17,000, but soon recovered after the completion of the Panama Canal and the rise of the aircraft industry. Since 1910 its population has doubled every decade. When Pearl Harbor was bombed by the Japanese at the start of World War II, San Diego took its place as the principal base of the Eleventh Naval District and the Naval Air Command. By the mid-1970s, it surpassed San Francisco as the second-largest city in California.

Chronology

1539	Father Marcos visits the site of San Diego.
1542	Juan Rodriguez Cabrillo sails into the San Diego harbor and claims the region for the king of Spain.
1602	Sebastian Vizaino charts the coast and names the bay San Diego.
1769	Governor Portola, Franciscan friars, and soldiers build a presidio.
1793	The British ship *Discovery* visits San Diego.
1834	San Diego is organized as a pueblo.
1846	San Diego becomes part of the United States.
1850	San Diego is incorporated as a city.
1867	Alonzo E. Horton buys 1,000 acres in the center of town and lays the foundation of New Town.
1885	The Santa Fe Railroad makes San Diego its terminus.
1915	The Panama-California Exposition is held in the city.
1942	San Diego becomes the headquarters of the Eleventh Naval District.

Historical Landmarks

Balboa Park, with its entrance on Laurel Street and Sixth Avenue, is the cultural and recreational center of San Diego. El Prado, the public walk, is a continuation of Laurel Street. The park contains many landmarks from the Panama-California Exposition of 1915–1916 and the California-Pacific International Exposition of 1935–1936, including the House of Pacific Relations, the Spreckels Organ Pavilion, the recreated Casa del Prado, and a reproduction of Shakespeare's Globe Theatre. To the north and inland is Presidio Park, the original site of San Diego de Alcala, Junipero Serra's first mission in upper California, founded in 1769. Here too is the Spanish presidio and Fort Stockton. Nearby is the terminus of El Camino Real, the king's highway, running north to Monterey, pioneered by Don Gaspar de Portola. Gaslamp Quarter is a restored Victorian district downtown. The Old Town Plaza on Calhoun and Wallace streets is the original center of town and retains its early Spanish color. It contains the Casa de Cabrillo, built in 1820; the Casa de Bandini, built in 1829; the Casa de Estudillo, built in 1825; Whaley House, built in 1856; and the Adobe Chapel, built in 1858. San Diego Bay harbors the *Star of India*, a 100–year-old sailing vessel that is now a maritime museum. It was built on the Isle of Man in 1863 and carried passengers between England and New Zealand for 30 years. The Cabrillo National Monument commemorates the spot where California was discovered and includes a restored lighthouse and whale overlook.

Population

San Diego has been a demographic success story. It has virtually doubled in population every decade since 1900. It reached 148,000 in 1940 and 697,000 in 1970. It grew by 25.5% in the 1970s to reach 875,538 in 1980, and then grew by 26.8% in the next decade to cross the million mark.

Population

	1980	1990
Central City	875,538	1,110,549
Rank	8	6
Metro Area	1,861,846	2,498,016
Pop. Change 1980–1990 +235,011		
Pop. % Change 1980–1990 +26.8		
Median Age 30.5		
% Male 51.0		
% Age 65 and Over 10.2		
Density (per square mile) 3,427		

Households

Number 406,096
Persons per Household 2.61
% Female-Headed Households 11.2
% One-Person Households 26.3
Births—Total 15,928
   % to Mothers under 20 9.6
   Birth Rate per 1,000 16.6

Ethnic Composition

Whites make up 67.1%, African Americans 9.4%, American Indians 0.6%, Asians and Pacific Islanders 11.8%, and others 11.1%. Hispanics, both black and white, make up 20.7%.

Ethnic Composition (as % of total pop.)

	1980	1990
White	76.17	67.12
Black	8.87	9.39
American Indian	0.58	0.61
Asian and Pacific Islander	6.53	11.79
Hispanic	14.92	20.67
Other	NA	11.09

Government

Under its charter of 1931, San Diego is governed by a council-manager form of government. The mayor and eight council members are elected to four-year terms.

Government

Year of Home Charter 1931
Number of Members of the Governing Body 8
Elected at Large 8
Elected by Wards NA

Government (continued)

Number of Women in Governing Body   4
Salary of Mayor $60,000
Salary of Council Members $49,000
City Government Employment Total   8,473
Rate per 10,000   83.5

Public Finance

The annual budget consists of revenues of $1.296 billion and expenditures of $1.08 billion. The debt outstanding is $1.406 billion, and cash and security holdings $2.756 billion.

Public Finance

Total Revenue (in millions) $1,295.7
Intergovernmental Revenue—Total (in millions) $195.3
Federal Revenue per Capita $66.26
% Federal Assistance   5.11
% State Assistance   6.59
Sales Tax as % of Total Revenue   14.35
Local Revenue as % of Total Revenue   72.18
City Income Tax   no
Taxes—Total (in millions) $211.7

Taxes per Capita
   Total $209
   Property $72
   Sales and Gross Receipts $118
General Expenditures—Total (in millions) $503.6
General Expenditures per Capita $496.0
Capital Outlays per Capita $100

% of Expenditures for:
   Public Welfare   NA
   Highways   6.0
   Education   0.0
   Health and Hospitals   NA
   Police   16.0
   Sewerage and Sanitation   14.3
   Parks and Recreation   12.1
   Housing and Community Development   10.6
Debt Outstanding per Capita $1,071
   % Utility   0.2
Federal Procurement Contract Awards (in millions)
   $2,342.4
Federal Grants Awards (in millions) $295.1
Fiscal Year Begins   July 1

Economy

San Diego's prosperity may be dated from the time it was chosen to be the headquarters of the Eleventh Naval District and the base for the U.S. Pacific Fleet. The base pumps in more than $6 billion every year into the local economy through wages and purchases. The naval presence has been a magnet drawing a variety of manufacturing industries involved in aerospace, transportation, shipbuilding, electronics, and machinery. The harbor, unmatched on the West Coast for its natural facilities, is another economic strength. The port is home to the largest tuna fleet in the nation. Tourism is a large industry, contributing several billions to the economy. Agriculture has been eclipsed in recent years by the other sectors but is still a substantial revenue-earner. San Diego County is one of the world's largest avo-

cado production centers. The production of eggs and dairy products is also important in the city's economy.

Economy

Total Money Income (in millions) $11,944.7
% of State Average   99.0
Per Capita Annual Income $11,766
% Population below Poverty Level   12.4
Fortune 500 Companies   NA

Banks	Number	Deposits (in millions)
Commercial	50	NA
Savings	27	NA

Passenger Autos   1,616,397
Electric Meters   886,395
Gas Meters   661,503

Manufacturing

Number of Establishments   1,397
% with 20 or More Employees   29.2
Manufacturing Payroll (in millions) $2,266.6
Value Added by Manufacture (in millions) $4,302.9
Value of Shipments (in millions) $7,398.8
New Capital Expenditures (in millions) $314.6

Wholesale Trade

Number of Establishments   1,832
Sales (in millions) $6,644.3
Annual Payroll (in millions) $606.323

Retail Trade

Number of Establishments   9,396
Total Sales (in millions) $6,790.1
Sales per Capita $6,689
Number of Retail Trade Establishments with Payroll   5,890
Annual Payroll (in millions) $873.0
Total Sales (in millions) $6,614.2
General Merchandise Stores (per capita) $766
Food Stores (per capita) $1,161
Apparel Stores (per capita) $436
Eating and Drinking Places (per capita) $868

Service Industries

Total Establishments   9,762
Total Receipts (in millions) $6,103.1
Hotels and Motels (in millions) $448.0
Health Services (in millions) $1,243.4
Legal Services (in millions) $583.0

Labor

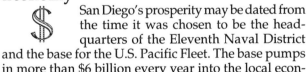

Government agencies, including the naval base establishment, employ about 25% of the work force, and the city's 2,000 manufacturing plants another 15%. About a fourth of the manufacturing work force is engaged in the aerospace industry. Despite being exposed to substantial immi-

Labor

Civilian Labor Force   556,688
% Change 1989–1990   0.2

Work Force Distribution
   Mining   600
   Construction   50,400
   Manufacturing   134,700
   Transportation and Public Utilities   36,800
   Wholesale and Retail Trade   230,800
   FIRE (Finance, Insurance, Real Estate)   64,300

Labor (continued)

    Service   277,300
    Government   179,500
    Women as % of Labor Force   45.2
    % Self-Employed   7.4
    % Professional/Technical   20.6
Total Unemployment   25,124
Rate %   4.5
Federal Government Civilian Employment   27,632

gration—both legal and illegal—unemployment has remained at acceptable levels. Small businesses with four or fewer employees comprise 49% of the employers, and those with fewer than 15 employees 76%.

Education

The San Diego Unified School District supports 158 elementary, middle, and high schools. About 90 private and parochial schools supplement the public school system. Four-year colleges and universities in the area include National University, San Diego State University, United States International University, Point Loma Nazarene College, and the University of San Diego. The University of California's world-renowned Scripps Institution of Oceanography is also in San Diego.

Education

Number of Public Schools   158
Special Education Schools   2
Total Enrollment   121,107
% Enrollment in Private Schools   9.3
% Minority   62.6
Classroom Teachers   5,215
Pupil-Teacher Ratio   23.2:1
Number of Graduates   5,958
Total Revenue (in millions) $500.989
Total Expenditures (in millions) $497.766
Expenditures per Pupil $4,282
Educational Attainment (Age 25 and Over)
    % Completed 12 or More Years   78.9
    % Completed 16 or More Years   24.0
Four-Year Colleges and Universities   6
    Enrollment   72,852
Two-Year Colleges   7
    Enrollment   75,411

Libraries

Number   101
Public Libraries   32
Books (in thousands)   1,642
Circulation (in thousands)   5,138
Persons Served (in thousands)   1,118
Circulation per Person Served   4.59
Income (in millions) $17.6
Staff   302

Four-Year Colleges and Universities
    San Diego State University
    University of California – San Diego
    University of San Diego
    National University
    Point Loma Nazarene College
    United States International University

Health

The area's medical sector includes over 40 hospitals, of which the largest are the Grassmont District Hospital, Alvarado Community Hospital, Mercy Hospital and Medical Center, Harborview Medical Center and Hospital, Sharp Memorial Hospital, Claremont Community Hospital, and Sharp Cabrillo Hospital. In addition, 70 nursing homes provide a variety of health-care services.

Health

Deaths—Total   6,622
Rate per 1,000   6.9
Infant Deaths—Total   155
Rate per 1,000   9.7
Number of Metro Hospitals   18
Number of Metro Hospital Beds   4,465
Rate per 100,000   440
Number of Physicians   4,755
Physicians per 1,000   2.51
Nurses per 1,000   NA
Health Expenditures per Capita $1.09

Transportation

San Diego is approached by two major north-south highways: I-5 from Los Angeles and I-15 from Los Angeles. They meet in San Diego and continue toward the Mexican border; I-8 enters San Diego from the east. Other routes serving San Diego include 52, 54, 94, 163, and 805. Rail passenger service is provided by Amtrak, which has seven daily trains. Rail freight service is provided by Santa Fe, San Diego, and Arizona and by Southern Pacific. The Port of San Diego is managed by the San Diego Unified Port District. The principal air terminal is the San Diego International Airport.

Transportation

Interstate Highway Mileage   139
Total Urban Mileage   5,836
Total Daily Vehicle Mileage (in millions) $50.734
Daily Average Commute Time   43.1 min.
Number of Buses   311
Port Tonnage (in millions) $2.016
Airports   1
Number of Daily Flights   193
Daily Average Number of Passengers   14,567

Airlines (American carriers only)
    Alaska
    American
    American West
    Continental
    Delta
    Northwest
    Southwest
    Trans World
    United
    USAir

Housing

There are a number of upscale neighborhoods, such as Point Loma, where the housing is expensive. Of the total housing stock 48.3% is owner-occupied. The median value of an owner-occupied home is $189,400, which is considerably higher than the national norm. The median monthly rent is also high at $560.

Housing

Total Housing Units   431,722
% Change 1980–1990   20.8
Vacant Units for Sale or Rent   20,212
Occupied Units   406,096
% with More Than One Person per Room   10.5
% Owner-Occupied   48.3
Median Value of Owner-Occupied Homes $189,400
Average Monthly Purchase Cost $416
Median Monthly Rent $560
New Private Housing Starts   8,312
Value (in thousands) $756,845
% Single-Family   26.1
Nonresidential Buildings Value (in thousands) $299,091

Tallest Buildings	Hgt. (ft.)	Stories
Symphony Tower (1989)	499	34
First Interstate Bank (1985)	398	23
Union Bank (1969)	388	27
First National Bank (1982)	379	27
The Meridien	375	27
Imperial Bank	355	24
Executive Complex (1963)	350	25
Wells Fargo Bldg. (1982)	348	20

Urban Redevelopment

Population growth and economic prosperity have spurred a decade-long urban renewal program. One of the largest developments is the new waterfront convention complex. Horton Plaza, built in the late 1980s is a large multilevel shopping and entertainment complex in bold and colorful architectural style. In the nearby Gaslamp Quarter, buildings and shops have been built to recreate the atmosphere of the 1890s.

Crime

San Diego ranks far below the national average in public safety. In 1991, 13,830 violent crimes and 82,951 property crimes were reported.

Religion

Catholics form 15% of the population, Baptists 3%, Lutherans 2%, Methodists 2%, Presbyterians 1.5% and Pentecostals 1%. In general religious membership is lower in San Diego than in comparable cities. Catholic churches are among the oldest and the most picturesque, including the Mission San Diego, where masses are still being held.

Crime

Violent Crimes—Total   13,830
Violent Crime Rate per 100,000   966.8
Murder   167
Rape   472
Robbery   5,331
Aggravated Assaults   7,860
Property Crimes   82,951
Burglary   17,088
Larceny   44,645
Motor Vehicle Theft   21,218
Arson   257
Per Capita Police Expenditures $128.01
Per Capita Fire Protection Expenditures $53.56
Number of Police   1,407
Per 1,000   1.42

Religion

Largest Denominations (Adherents)

Catholic	413,025
Black Baptist	42,478
Southern Baptist	30,304
Presbyterian	25,199
Latter-Day Saints	46,863
Assembly of God	15,982
Evangelical Lutheran	18,687
Episcopal	17,742
United Methodist	24,197
Jewish	70,000

Media

San Diego newspapers include the daily *San Diego Union-Tribune*. The electronic media consist of eight television stations and 21 AM and FM radio stations.

Media

Newsprint
San Diego Business Journal, weekly
San Diego Magazine, monthly
San Diego Reader, weekly
San Diego Union-Tribune, daily
The San Diego Voice News and Viewpoint, weekly

Television
KFMB (Channel 8)
KGTV (Channel 10)
KNSD (Channel 39)
KPBS (Channel 15)
KTTY (Channel 69)
KUSI (Channel 51)
XETV (Channel 6)
XEWT (Channel 12)

Radio

KCBQ (FM)	KFMB (AM)
KFMB (FM)	KFSD (FM)
KIFM (FM)	KIRS (AM)
KJQY (FM)	KKLQ (AM)
KKLQ (FM)	KKYY (FM)
KMJC (AM)	KPBS (FM)
KPOP (AM)	KGB (FM)
KSDO (FM)	KSDS (FM)
KSON (AM)	KSON (FM)
KYXY (FM)	XTRA (AM)
XTRA (FM)	

Sports

 All major sports, except basketball, are represented by local teams: the San Diego Padres in baseball, the San Diego Chargers in football, the San Diego Hawks in ice hockey, and the San Diego Sockers in soccer. The Padres and the Chargers play their home games at the Jack Murphy Stadium, and the San Diego Hawks in the San Diego Sports Arena. Thoroughbred racing is offered at the nearby Del Mar Thoroughbred Club.

Arts, Culture, and Tourism

San Diego's cultural landscape is as rich and varied as its natural one. Of the 13 performing arts facilities, the centerpiece is the Simon Edison Center of the Performing Arts, consisting of the Lowell Davies Festival Theater, a large outdoor arena, the Cassius Carter Center Stage, a theater-in-the-round, and the Old Globe Theatre, a replica of the Elizabethan theater in London. The La Jolla Playhouse is equally respected as a professional theater company. Other theaters include the San Diego Repertory Theater and the Gaslamp Quarter Theater. Dance is represented by the California Ballet Company, the San Diego Civic Youth Ballet, Grupo Folklorico de San Diego, the Mexicayotl Aztec Dance Company, and the Samahan Philippine Dance Company; music by the Pacific Chamber Ensemble, the San Diego Chamber Orchestra, the La Jolla Chamber Music Society, the North Coast Jazz Society, the Center for World Music, the San Diego Master Chorale, the San Diego Early Music Society, the San Diego Symphony Orchestra, and the San Diego Youth Symphony; and opera by the San Diego Opera and the San Diego Civic Light Opera.

Balboa Park is the site of 16 museums, such as the San Diego Museum of Art, the Timken Art Gallery, the Antique Auto Museum, the Aerospace Museum, the Hall of Champions, the Museum of Man, and the Natural History Museum. Other museums include the Allison Center for Study of Paleontology, the Cabrillo National Monument, the Junipero Serra Museum, the Museum of Photographic Arts, the Museum of San Diego History and Research Archives, the San Diego Art Center, the San Diego Historical Society, the San Diego Maritime Museum, the University Art Gallery at San Diego State University, the La Jolla Museum of Contemporary Art, the Mingei International Museum, the San Diego Model Railroad Museum, and the Villa Montezuma Museum at the Jesse Shepard House.

Parks and Recreation

San Diego has about 120 parks. Mission Bay Park, the largest, covers 4,600 acres and includes Sea World. The San Diego Zoo is in Balboa Park. The zoo also runs the San Diego Wild Animal Park, a wildlife preserve 30 miles north of downtown.

Sources of Further Information

City Hall
202 C Street
San Diego, California 92101
(619) 236-6330

Greater San Diego Chamber of Commerce
110 West C Street
San Diego, California 92101
(619) 232-0124

San Diego Convention and Visitors Bureau
1200 Third Avenue
San Diego, California 92101
(619) 232-3101

Additional Reading

Adams, John R. *Books and Authors of San Diego*. 1966.

Carrico, Susan H., and Kathleen Flanigan. *San Diego's Historic Gaslamp Quarter: Then and Now*. 1991.

Engstrand, Iris H. *Serra's San Diego: Father Junipero Serra and California's Beginnings*. 1982.

Federal Writers' Project. *San Diego: A California City*. 1973.

Fuller, Theodore W. *San Diego Originals: Profiles of the Movers and Shakers of California's First Community*. 1987.

Gray, Anne. *The Wonderful World of San Diego*. 1975.

Houlihan, William C. *San Diego: America's Finest*. 1991.

The Influence of German Immigrants on the Growth of San Diego. 1986.

Jensen, Peter. *San Diego on My Mind*. 1989.

Johl, Karen. *Timeless Treasures: San Diego's Victorian Heritage*. 1982.

McKeever, Michael A. *A Short History of San Diego*. 1985.

MacPhail, Elizabeth C. *The Story of New San Diego and of its Founder Alonzo E. Horton*. 1979.

Mayer, Robert. *San Diego: A Chronological and Documentary History, 1935–1936*. 1976.

Mendel, Carol. *San Diego: City and County*. 1990.

Mills, James R. *San Diego: Where California Began*. 1985.

Travel and Tourism

Hotel Rooms   36,636

Convention and Exhibit Space (square feet)   254,000

Convention Centers
  San Diego Convention Center
  Community Concourse

Festivals
  Oceanside Whale Festival (February)
  Cinco de Mayo Festival (May)
  Fiesta de la Primavera (May)
  Corpus Christi (May)
  Cabrillo Festival (September)

O'Connor, Karen. *San Diego*. 1990.

Peik, Leander, and Rosalie Peik. *Discover San Diego*. 1988.

Pryde, Philip R. *San Diego: An Introduction to the Region*. 1990.

Ross, Bill. *San Diego*. 1988.

San Francisco

California

Location and Topography

San Francisco is located at the tip of a peninsula in northern California, surrounded on three sides by the Pacific Ocean, the San Francisco Bay, and the Golden Gate. The city includes Farallones Islands in the Pacific Ocean and Alcatraz, Treasure, and Yerba Buena Islands in San Francisco Bay. Alcatraz was the site of a federal prison from 1934 to 1963. San Francisco is connected to the mainland by two of the longest bridges in the nation: the Golden Gate Bridge and the San Francisco–Oakland Bay Bridge. Behind the city the San Bruno Hills roll away to the south.

Layout of City and Suburbs

San Francisco is built on and around 40 hills. Three of the highest are in the northeastern section. Telegraph Hill rises abruptly from the shore to over 300 feet. The White Coit Tower, a famous landmark, stands on its top. North Beach, one of the oldest residential districts, occupies the western slope of Telegraph Hill. Just westward is Russian Hill, once a burying ground for Russian sailors. It includes what is known as the "Crookedest Street in the World," a section of Lombard Street that makes eight sharp turns in a single block. South of Russian Hill is Nob Hill, a shortened form of Nabob Hill, where Comstock millionaires once lived. Chinatown, home of 30,000 Chinese, lies east of Nob Hill, stretching eight blocks along the lively Grant Avenue. The northern boundary of Chinatown is Broadway, a bawdy district of restaurants and nightclubs. The hills are the reason for the fabled cable cars that crawl up and down the heights. Downtown San Francisco lies in the northeastern part of the city where Market Street runs diagonally southwest, cutting the city in half. South of Market is Mission District, one of the oldest and most densely populated sections of the city. The historic Mission Dolores stands in Mission District. The original mission, built by the Spanish in 1776, was destroyed by fire and replaced by another, built in 1782. Between the Mission and the bay lies Potrero District, largely industrial. The geographical center of the city is Twin Peaks, two hills of nearly equal

height. Southwest is Mount Davidson, the highest elevation, where, as also in St. Francis Woods and Ingleside Terrace, there are old palatial residences. Golden Gate Park, extending four miles to the ocean, divides two large residential districts, Richmond to the north and Sunset Parkside to the south. Overlooking the eastern end of Golden Gate Park is the 900-foot Mount Sutro. The main shopping area is Union Square. The Civic Center stands at Van Ness Avenue and McAlister Street, just north of Market Street. The financial district is east of Chinatown and centers on Montgomery Street, nicknamed the "Wall Street of the West." Dominating the financial district are the 853-foot TransAmerica Pyramid and the 52-story Bank of America building. The district also includes the Romanesque Mills Building and Hallidie Building. Farther east is a modern commercial and residential center known as the Golden Gateway near the bay. The Port of San Francisco borders the bay. A wide street called the Embarcadero parallels the shore. Across the Embarcadero from the Golden Gateway stands the Ferry Building, home of the World Trade Center, with its famous clock tower patterned after the Cathedral of Seville. At the northern end of Embarcadero lies Fishermens Wharf and nearby are two unusual shopping centers, the Cannery and Ghiradelli Square. The Western Addition, west of the downtown area, is noted for its restored Victorian houses. The Presidio, originally a Spanish army post, covers about 1,500 acres in northwestern San Francisco. It is the headquarters of the U.S. Sixth Army. The Officers Club, built in 1776, is the city's oldest building. To the west of Presidio lies Sea Cliff, a residential community. The city has its slums in the Tenderloin, a few blocks beyond Union Square, the theaters and hotels of Geary Street, and across Market Street. At the bottom of the western slopes of Nob and Russian hills is Polk Gulch, whose Polk Street is one of the city's two gay districts, the other being Castro Street, at the foot of Twin Peaks to the south. About 20% of the city's inhabitants are openly homosexual. Another typical San Francisco neighborhood is the Haight-Ashbury section, where the hippie culture was born in the 1960s. From Polk Gulch climbs Pacific Heights, one of the city's richest neighborhoods. Between Pacific Heights and the Bay is the Marina District, site of the 1915 Pacific Panama Exposition. Much of this area suffered during the 1989 earthquake. Principal areas in the southeast are Hunters Point–Bay View and Portal Visitación Valley neighborhoods.

Environment	
Environmental Stress Index	2.6
Green Cities Index: Rank	8
Score	20.33
Water Quality	Alkaline, very soft, fluoridated
Average Daily Use (gallons per capita)	NA
Maximum Supply (gallons per capita)	NA
Parkland as % of Total City Area	NA
% Waste Landfilled/Recycled	75/25
Annual Parks Expenditures per Capita	$164.91

Climate

San Francisco is generally described as an air-conditioned city because the Pacific air keeps temperatures moderate, rarely above 75°F or below 45°F. The climate is distinctly Mediterranean with nearly constant temperatures. Flowers bloom throughout the year and winter dress is not required. The rainy season corresponds to winter and most of the precipitation takes place between November and March. The most distinctive feature of the weather is the fog, which rolls in periodically from the ocean, only to quickly dissipate. It settles more in the valleys than on the hills. The fog is most common on summer mornings when it comes off the cooler ocean, and in winter when it comes from colder areas inland. On an average the city receives sunlight 66% of the time. Because of variations in elevation, there are wide constrasts in climate even within the city and between the city and the surrounding environs. Marin County, for example, enjoys warmer and sunnier weather than the city.

Weather			
Temperature			
Highest Monthly Average °F	64.0		
Lowest Monthly Average °F	46.2		
Annual Averages			
Days 32°F or Below	0		
Days above 90°F	1		
Zero Degree Days	0		
Precipitation (inches)	21		
Snow (inches)	0		
% Seasonal Humidity	75		
Wind Speed (m.p.h.)	8.7		
Clear Days	162		
Cloudy Days	100		
Storm Days	2		
Rainy Days	67		
Average Temperatures (°F)	*High*	*Low*	*Mean*
January	55.3	41.2	48.3
February	58.6	43.8	51.2
March	61.0	44.9	53.0
April	63.5	47.0	55.3
May	66.6	49.9	58.3
June	70.2	53.0	61.6
July	70.9	54.0	62.5
August	71.6	54.3	63.0
September	73.6	54.5	64.1
October	70.3	51.6	61.0
November	63.3	47.2	55.3
December	56.5	42.9	49.7

History

San Francisco and its outlying regions were originally inhabited by the Tamal Indians. The site was shielded by constant fog from the prying eyes of Spanish explorers for over one and a half centuries as they tried to find a good harbor to serve as a stop on the long voyage between the Philippines and Mexico. It was discovered quite accidentally from land by an expedition led north from San Diego by Don Gaspar de Portola. A

Chronology

1769 Spanish reconnoitering party under Sergeant Jose Ortega reaches San Francisco Bay, the first white men to do so.

1776 Don Juan Bautista de Anza with 30 soldiers and 200 colonists marches overland to the tip of the peninsula. A presidio and a mission are laid out, the latter established by Father Junipero Serra and christened San Francisco de Asis, later Mission Dolores.

1835 First brick building is erected by Captain William A. Richardson.

1836 Jacob Primer Leese opens first store. Jean Voiget lays out streets for a city that he names Yerba Buena.

1846 Captain John B. Montgomery lands marines from Portsmouth on the Plaza, hoists the Stars and Stripes, and takes possession of the city in the name of the United States. The plaza is renamed Portsmouth Square, its leading street Montgomery Street, and the city itself San Francisco. Mormon missionary Samuel Brannan unsuccessfully tries to persuade Brigham Young to locate in San Francisco rather than in Salt Lake City.

1847 Brannan founds town's first newspaper, *California Star*.

1848 Gold is discovered in Sutters Mill on the south fork of the American River, setting the stage for a mass influx of people into California. Great fortunes are made by miners and also local merchants profiteering in essential commodities.

1850 San Francisco is incorporated.

1851 First Vigilante Committee is organized.

1855 As the city swarms with swindlers, thieves, highwaymen, and thugs, U.S. Marshal George W. H. Richardson and crusading editor James King are killed and their assassins are lynched.

1873 Andrew Hallidies invents cable cars.

1906 Severe earthquake followed by fire destroys four square miles of the city, 30,000 buildings in 497 blocks. City begins rebuilding.

1908 Political power of Ruef-Schmitz machine is broken.

1914 City acquires Hetch-Hetchy watershed near Yosemite.

1915 Panama Pacific International Exposition is held at Rainbow City.

1936 San Francisco–Oakland Bay Bridge is opened.

1937 Golden Gate Bridge is opened.

1945 Delegates from 50 nations meet to sign U.N. Charter.

1974 Rapid Transit System opens.

1978 Mayor George Moscone and supervisor Harvey Milk are assassinated by a former supervisor.

1979 City elects first woman mayor, Diane Feinstein.

1989 Severe earthquake destroys parts of town and causes $3 billion in damages.

reconnoitering party from this expedition, under the command of Sergeant Jose Ortega and a handful of men, were the first white men to reach the shores of San Francisco Bay in November 1769. Settlement began seven years later when Don Juan Bautista de Anza with an army of 30 soldiers and 300 colonists marched to the tip of the peninsula, where they erected a village. A presidio and mission were immediately laid out by Father Junipero Serra, and named San Francisco de Asis, known later as Mission Dolores. For the next 70 years the sleepy little pueblo remained a collection of huts and tents, and its few residents carried on a halfhearted trade in pelts and hides. The first brick building was that of William A. Richardson, after whom Richardsons Bay is named. Jacob Primer Leese, an American, opened the first store, and Jean Vioget attempted to lay out streets in a colony that he named Yerba Buena (Good Herb). In July 1846, within three months of the outbreak of the Mexican War, Captain John B. Montgomery landed marines from the *Portsmouth* on the plaza, hoisted the Stars and Stripes, and took possession of the town in the name of the United States. Soon the plaza was renamed Portsmouth Square and the street passing along it Montgomery Street, and the town was rechristened San Francisco. Within two years, the arrival of the Mormon missionary Samuel Brannan galvanized the town. For the next 20 years Brannan was a powerful figure in the city as publisher of its first newspaper, the *California Star,* founded in 1847, and the principal organizer of its vigilante groups. The next event in the history of San Francisco was the discovery of gold in 1848 at Sutters Mill on the south fork of the American River. This event had an explosive impact on the demography and economy of California, and San Francisco was one of its main beneficiaries. It is said that Brannan himself ran through the muddy town shouting "Gold," when the news broke out. At first the news depopulated the town as every able-bodied man left to seek his fortune on Sutters property. Ships lay abandoned as crews joined in the gold hunt. As the news trickled slowly through the nation, thousands set out for California. By 1850 the city had a population of 25,000. Prices and rents soared as rooms rented for $300 a month, an apple sold for $5, and an egg for $1. Many huge fortunes were built by profiteering. The city was incorporated in 1850. As the transient population grew, so did vice and gambling. Dozens of saloons studded Portsmouth Square, each a gambling hall and a recruiting station for the brothels of the notorious Barbary Coast on Pacific Street from Sansome Street to Grant Avenue. Gangs flourished, as did crooked politicians backed by gangsters. The first vigilante committee was organized in 1851. In 1855 when a U.S. marshal, George W. H. Richardson, was shot and killed by Charles Cora, a mobster, and James King, the crusading editor, was shot and killed by his corrupt rival, James Casey, the vigilantes took the law into their own hands and lynched Cora and Casey in one of the last incidents of summary justice. The last Vigilantes Committee was disbanded in 1856. An era of expansion followed. During the Civil War California briefly considered declaring independence, but the legislature voted against secession. From the Comstock and Mather lodes, and from the Central Pacific Railroad, came the vast fortunes of Leland Stanford, Charles Crocker, Collis P. Huntington, Mark Hopkins, James Flood, William OBrien, John W. Mackay, James G. Fair, William C. Ralston, and others. San Francisco's development as a union town began with the formation of the Working Men's Trade and Labor Union. In 1873 Andrew Hallidies began operating his cable cars, thus beginning a unique San Francisco institution. In 1894 the city held its first great carnival, the Midwinter Exposition, at Opal City in Golden Gate Park. The city's growth was interrupted on 18 April 1906, when the San Andreas Fault settled violently and the greatest earthquake to hit the city shook it to its foundations. Fires broke out and for three days raged unchecked, as the water mains had been broken. Newspapers wrote epitaphs for the "City That Was." Four square miles, virtually all of the business district, were destroyed—30,000 buildings in 97 blocks. Within six days of the earthquake San Francisco began the task of rebuilding.

Between 1902 and 1906 city hall had been dominated by the notorious Ruef-Schmitz machine, controlled by mobsters and traction and utility corporations. Hearst newspapers, supported by Fremont Older, Rudolph Spreckels, and James D. Phelan, unleashed a campaign against the bosses and helped bring the criminal politicians to trial and to convict Ruef. In 1914 the city acquired the Hetch-Hetchy watershed to supply 400 million gallons of water a day. The opening of the Panama Canal was celebrated in 1915 by the Panama-Pacific International Exposition at Rainbow City. The San Francisco–Oakland Bay Bridge was completed in 1936, followed by the Golden Gate Bridge the next year. The Golden Gate International Exposition was held in 1939 at Treasure Island. After World War II, San Francisco was the site of the international meeting that drew up the Charter of the United Nations. A rapid transit system was introduced in 1974. In 1978 the city hit the headlines when its mayor George Moscone and supervisor Harvey Milk were killed by a former member of the Board of Supervisors, Dan White. In 1979 the city elected its first woman mayor. In 1989, San Francisco suffered its second major earthquake this century, causing $3 billion in property damage.

Historical Landmarks

The Ferry Building at the foot of Market Street is one of the city's best known landmarks. Completed in 1903, it has a 240-foot central tower topped with a four-faced clock and belfry, and cupola set back in four stages. Each dial of the clock is 22 feet in diameter. The Embarcadero, formerly East Street, is a crescent-shaped street paralleling the Bay Shore for three and a half miles. Lotta's Fountain at the intersection of Market, Kearney, and Geary streets was presented to the city in 1875 by actress Lotta Crabtree. The Palace Hotel on the corner of Market and New Montgomery streets is a seven-story yellow brick structure erected in 1910. President Warren G. Harding died in this hotel. The Native Son's Monument at the intersection of Market, Turk, and Mason streets is a tall granite shaft surmounted by a bronze figure holding an open book inscribed September 9, 1850, the date of California's admission to the Union. In the center of Union Square is the Victory Monument, commemorating Admiral Dewey's victory in Manila Bay. The Mark Hopkins Hotel on the corner of California and Mason streets is built on the site of the old residence of Mark Hopkins, one of the big four railroad tycoons. Fairmont Hotel on the corner of California and Mason streets was built in 1906 by Mrs. Herman Oelrichs, daughter of James G. Fair, one of the bonanza kings of the Comstock lode. Portsmouth Square, on Kearney Street between Washington and Clay streets, was Candelario Miramontes' potato patch in 1833; later it became the Spanish and Mexican plaza where the U.S. flag was raised in 1846. Jackson Square was the former Barbary Coast, the celebrated red light district of the 19th century. The Octagonal House on Gough Street was built in 1864 by Mrs. Harriet Sober McElroy. Fort Mason includes the former house of John C. Fremont built in 1853. The Presidio at Baker and Lombard streets was once the Spanish garrison. In front of the Officers Club, the oldest building in the city, stands two old Spanish guns, named Poder and San Pedro, inscribed Lima, Peru–1673. The Mission Dolores on Dolores Street was founded in 1776 by Father Juniper Serra and was so named after a nearby marsh known as *Laguna de Nuestra Senora de los Dolores* (Lagoon of Our Lady of Sorrows). Sutro Heights on Point Lobos Avenue and Great Highway was the home of Adolph Sutro, Nevada capitalist and former mayor of San Francisco. The Cliff House on Great Highway also was once owned by Sutro. On the summit of Mount Davidson, the highest point in the city, stands the Easter Cross.

Population

San Francisco's demographic history has had many ups and downs. After being a typical boomtown following the 1848 Gold Rush, its growth was interrupted by the 1906 earthquake and fire. After rebuilding, the population began to climb again though World War II. Then the physical constraints on the peninsula became more evident and a flight to the suburbs began in the 1960s. After peaking at 715,674 in 1970, the population declined by 5.1% to 678,974 in the 1980s and it lost the rank of the second–most-populous California city to San Diego. In the 1980s, however, it was able to regain some lost ground, growing by 6.6% to reach 723,959 by 1990, slightly higher than its 1970 figure. Every working day, however, the population in the central city grows by 250,000.

Population

	1980	1990
Central City	678,974	723,959
Rank	13	14
Metro Area	1,488,895	1,603,678
Pop. Change 1980–1990 +44,985		
Pop. % Change 1980–1990 +6.6		
Median Age 35.8		
% Male 50.1		
% Age 65 and Over 14.6		
Density (per square mile) 15,502		

Households

Number 305,584
Persons per Household 2.29
% Female-Headed Households 9.9
% One-Person Households 39.3
Births—Total 9,679
　% to Mothers under 20 8.1
　Birth Rate per 1,000 13.6

Ethnic Composition

San Francisco has had a significant proportion of non-Anglo population from its very founding. Today that proportion has risen to nearly 50%. Whites make up 53.6%, blacks 10.9%, American Indians 0.5%, Asians and Pacific Islanders 29.1%, and others 5.9%. Hispanics, both black and white, make up 13.9%. The Chinese are the predominant minority group, clustered in Chinatown, the largest Chinese settlement outside the Orient. Beside the Chinese, the largest Asian communities are Filipino, Japanese, and Korean. Blacks are found mainly in Hunters Point, south of Mission District and Potrero Hill, and in Western Addition and Fillmore District. Most Hispanics live in Mission District and Potrero Hill and Italians in North Beach.

Ethnic Composition (as % of total pop.)

	1980	1990
White	58.19	53.56
Black	12.73	10.92
American Indian	0.52	0.48
Asian and Pacific Islander	21.71	29.13
Hispanic	12.28	13.91
Other	NA	5.91

Government

San Francisco has a consolidated city and county government. Legislative powers are vested in an 11-member board of supervisors, 5 or 6 of them elected every two years for four-year terms. Other elected officials, including the mayor, also serve four-year terms. The mayor has veto power over legislation, and appoints the chief administrative officer, controller, and other officials.

San Francisco has had three charters in its history. The founding charter of 1850 remained in force until 1861 when a new charter was granted, which remained in force until 1898. The 1898 charter authorized the municipal ownership and operation of public utilities. The 1898 charter was replaced by a new charter in 1932.

Government

Year of Home Charter 1932
Number of Members of the Governing Body 11
Elected at Large 11
Elected by Wards NA
Number of Women in Governing Body 5
Salary of Mayor $13,083
Salary of Council Members $23,924
City Government Employment Total 24,914
Rate per 10,000 332.6

Public Finance

The annual budget consists of revenues of $2.914 billion and expenditures of $2.518 billion. The debt outstanding is $2.391 billion and cash and security holdings total $6.260 billion.

Public Finance

Total Revenue (in millions) $2,914.3
Intergovernmental Revenue—Total (in millions) $739.58
Federal Revenue per Capita $100.96
% Federal Assistance 3.46
% State Assistance 21.79
Sales Tax as % of Total Revenue 6.36
Local Revenue as % of Total Revenue 55.11
City Income Tax no
Taxes—Total (in millions) $563.5

Taxes per Capita
　Total $752
　Property $383
　Sales and Gross Receipts $190
General Expenditures—Total (in millions) $1,352.6
General Expenditures per Capita $1,806
Capital Outlays per Capita $207

% of Expenditures for:
　Public Welfare 12.1
　Highways 0.8
　Education 2.5
　Health and Hospitals 19.5
　Police 8.6
　Sewerage and Sanitation 9.5
　Parks and Recreation 6.1
　Housing and Community Development 3.6
Debt Outstanding per Capita $1,854
　% Utility 2.8
Federal Procurement Contract Awards (in millions)
　$556.8
Federal Grants Awards (in millions) $521.7
Fiscal Year Begins July 1

Economy

Since the time of the Gold Rush, San Francisco has remained a major financial center on the West Coast. San Francisco banks bankrolled the mining industry of the West. Today the city is the home of some 100 commercial banks, including the Bank of America and the Wells Fargo Bank, as well as a number of top insurance companies, such as TransAmerica and Firemans Fund. The Pacific Stock Exchange is also based in the city. San Francisco's financial clout is also reflected in its manufacturing base, which consists of 1,600 industrial plants, principally in food processing, electronic systems and equipment, clothing, and metal products. Another emerging field in which San Francisco has gained leadership is biotechnology, including bionics, genetic engineering, pharmaceuticals, and medical electronics. The region is estimated to employ nearly

one-third of the global work force in this sector. San Francisco, rather than Los Angeles, is the capital of West Coast publishing. More than 100 large U.S. corporations have their headquarters in or near the city. But the city's major asset is its port, which initially gained it prominence in international trade. Its 40 deep-water piers handle less volume than they did in the 19th century, but it is still one of the four or five largest ports on the West Coast. It remains the entrepot for a rich hinterland, including the San Joaquin Valley, and is the principal export center for a wide range of agricultural products. In the latter half of the 1980s high taxes and the growth of the anti-growth environmental lobby forced many large businesses to move out of the city. Further, in 1986, residents passed Proposition M to limit most new commercial development to 475,000 square feet per year. The proposition allows only one to two medium-size office buildings to be built in the city each year. While this is a disincentive to large corporations, small businesses have thrived and now make up about 90% of all businesses.

Labor

The ethnic diversity that is a feature of San Francisco's culture is also reflected in its work force. With one of the largest concentrations of new immigrants, the city has a continuous supply of skills at all levels. Diversity is also reflected in the variety of work opportunities. The large Asian population has sustained strong economic ties with Pacific Rim countries. While employment in large corporations has declined, small businesses (employing four or fewer people) have risen significantly. The city's work force is also becoming more white-collar and small business oriented.

Economy

Total Money Income (in millions) $9,828		
% of State Average 114.2		
Per Capita Annual Income $13,575		
% Population below Poverty Level 13.7		
Fortune 500 Companies 6		
Banks	*Number*	*Deposits (in millions)*
Commercial	175	42,052.9
Savings	28	32,200
Passenger Autos 331,876		
Electric Meters 1,686,588		
Gas Meters 1,448,139		

Manufacturing

Number of Establishments 1,695
% with 20 or More Employees 27.8
Manufacturing Payroll (in millions) $1,174.9
Value Added by Manufacture (in millions) $2,745
Value of Shipments (in millions) $4,727.9
New Capital Expenditures (in millions) $84.3

Wholesale Trade

Number of Establishments 2,257
Sales (in millions) $13,943.4
Annual Payroll (in millions) $759,142

Retail Trade

Number of Establishments 10,194
Total Sales (in millions) $5,726.7
Sales per Capita $7,646
Number of Retail Trade Establishments with Payroll 6,884
Annual Payroll (in millions) $910.3
Total Sales (in millions) $5,513
General Merchandise Stores (per capita) $766
Food Stores (per capita) $1,307
Apparel Stores (per capita) $674
Eating and Drinking Places (per capita) $1,494

Service Industries

Total Establishments 10,538
Total Receipts (in millions) $8,794.5
Hotels and Motels (in millions) $794.6
Health Services (in millions) $829.4
Legal Services (in millions) $1,706.6

Labor

Civilian Labor Force 393,245
% Change 1989–1990 -1.8
Work Force Distribution
    Mining 700
    Construction 32,600
    Manufacturing 80,100
    Transportation and Public Utilities 78,700
    Wholesale and Retail Trade 204,600
    FIRE (Finance, Insurance, Real Estate) 107,400
    Service 307,800
    Government 138,800
    Women as % of Labor Force 45.2
    % Self-Employed 8
    % Professional/Technical NA
Total Unemployment 15,695
Rate % 4
Federal Government Civilian Employment 23,185

Education

The San Francisco Unified School District supports 110 elementary, middle, and senior high schools. There are also some 140 private schools enrolling nearly 26,000 students. The San Francisco State University is the flagship institution of higher education, with an enrollment of 18,000. Other facilities include Golden Gate University and the University of San Francisco. Specialized institutions include the Hastings School of Law, California School of Professional Psychology, San Francisco Art Institute, and the San Francisco Conservatory of Music.

Education

Number of Public Schools   110
Special Education Schools   1
Total Enrollment   61,688
% Enrollment in Private Schools
% Minority   86.1
Classroom Teachers   3,052
Pupil-Teacher Ratio   20.2:1
Number of Graduates   4,757
Total Revenue (in millions) $268.059
Total Expenditures (in millions) $268.031
Expenditures per Pupil $4,148
Educational Attainment (Age 25 and Over)
    % Completed 12 or More Years   74
    % Completed 16 or More Years   28.2
Four-Year Colleges and Universities   8
    Enrollment   53,313
Two-Year Colleges   5
    Enrollment   37,604

Libraries

Number   140
Public Libraries   27
Books (in thousands)   1,937
Circulation (in thousands)   3,395
Persons Served (in thousands)   741
Circulation per Person Served   4.58
Income (in millions) $20.176
Staff   406

Four-Year Colleges and Universities
    Academy of Art College
    San Francisco State University
    Golden Gate University
    New College of California
    San Francisco Art Institute
    University of California – Hastings School of Law
    University of California – San Francisco
    University of San Francisco

Health

The health sector is strong in the breadth of the services offered as well as the number of facilities. The largest hospital is the 532-bed San Francisco General Hospital. Other facilities include Medical Center at the University of

Health

Deaths—Total   7,984
Rate per 1,000   11.2
Infant Deaths—Total   85
Rate per 1,000   8.8
Number of Metro Hospitals   19
Number of Metro Hospital Beds   6,131
Rate per 100,000   819
Number of Physicians   6,273
Physicians per 1,000   4.97
Nurses per 1,000   5.84
Health Expenditures per Capita $197.34

California, San Francisco; St. Francis Memorial Hospital; St. Marys Hospital and Medical Center; and Seton Medical Center. Laguna Honda Hospital is a 1,000-bed long-term care facility.

Transportation

San Francisco is approached by Interstate 80, with north-south loops I-580 and I-680 providing access to I-5, which connects Canada with Mexico. U.S. 101 and State Road 1 converge on the city from north and south. Also serving the city is U.S. 50. The publicly owned Bay Area Rapid Transport (BART) operates a 25-station electric rail system in the region. One BART route passes through the Trans-Bay Tube, a tunnel that runs under the San Francisco Bay between San Francisco and Oakland. The cable car system, a national historic landmark, has three lines and covers ten miles. The cable cars run on rails and are pulled by a moving cable under the street. Four ferry services connect the city with Oakland and Berkeley across the Bay. Rail passenger service is provided by Amtrak, with seven trains daily, and CalTrain, a commuter line from San Francisco to San Jose. Rail freight service is provided by Southern Pacific, Santa Fe, and Union Pacific. The Port of San Francisco is still a major trans-Pacific port, although with diminished importance. The principal air terminal is the San Francisco International Airport, about 12 miles south of the city.

Transportation

Interstate Highway Mileage   195
Total Urban Mileage   9,166
Total Daily Vehicle Mileage (in millions) $76.482
Daily Average Commute Time   55.2 min.
Number of Buses   1,082
Port Tonnage (in millions) $2.274
Airports   3
Number of Daily Flights   565
Daily Average Number of Passengers   42,228

Airlines (American carriers only)
    Alaska
    American
    American Trans Air
    American West
    Continental
    Delta
    Northwest
    Trans World
    United
    USAir

Housing

San Francisco is noted for its row houses, mostly two-story wood or stucco buildings with a common wall. Each row house may have two or more apartments. About two-thirds of the housing was built before 1939 and is run-down in many cases. Most of the slums are found in Hunters Park and Fillmore District, while the more expensive communities are found in Sea Cliff, Pacific Heights, and Twin Peaks. There are a number of strong middle-class communities, such as Bayshore, Buena Vista (including the

Haight-Ashbury and Ashbury Heights sections), Mission District, Richmond District, and Sunset District. Lake Merced is a recent development.

San Francisco's housing is one of the most expensive in the nation. The median value of an owner-occupied home is $298,900 and the median monthly rent is $613. Of the total housing stock, 34.5% is owner-occupied.

Housing

Total Housing Units   328,471
% Change 1980–1990   3.6
Vacant Units for Sale or Rent   15,836
Occupied Units   305,584
% with More Than One Person per Room   10.7
% Owner-Occupied   34.5
Median Value of Owner-Occupied Homes $298,900
Average Monthly Purchase Cost $394
Median Monthly Rent $613
New Private Housing Starts   1,077
Value (in thousands) $143,432
% Single-Family   14.9
Nonresidential Buildings Value (in thousands) $164,032

Tallest Buildings	Hgt. (ft.)	Stories
Transamerica Pyramid	853	48
Bank of America	778	52
101 California St.	600	48
5 Fremont Center	600	43
Embarcadero Center, No. 4	570	45
Security Pacific Bank	569	45
One Market Plaza, Spear St.	565	43
Wells Fargo Bldg.	561	43

Urban Redevelopment

 Between 1950 and 1980 San Francisco went through a boom cycle, resulting in a dramatically new skyline with towering office buildings, such as the TransAmerica Building and huge commercial and residential complexes such as Golden Gateway. In 1985 an ordinance called the Downtown Plan was passed, limiting the size of future structures. This has put large-scale development within the city on hold. The 1989 earthquake necessitated some rebuilding in the Marina District in the north. Redevelopment plans are coordinated by San Francisco Redevelopment Agency, Downtown Association of San Francisco, and Market Street Development Project.

Crime

 In 1991, violent crimes reported to police totaled 12,160, and property crimes totaled 57,190.

Crime

Violent Crimes—Total   12,160
Violent Crime Rate per 100,000   983.7
Murder   95
Rape   400
Robbery   7,020
Aggravated Assaults   4,645
Property Crimes   57,190
Burglary   10,604
Larceny   34,679
Motor Vehicle Theft   11,907
Arson   429

Crime (continued)

Per Capita Police Expenditures $190.2
Per Capita Fire Protection Expenditures $129.32
Number of Police   1,929
Per 1,000   2.63

Religion

Although Christian fundamentalists have described San Francisco as a modern Sodom and Gomorrah (because about 20% of San Franciscans are self-confessed gays), religion flourishes in the city in sometimes unconventional forms. San Francisco is noted for its tolerance of heterodoxy and has been the scene of the rise (and fall) of many fringe cults. The presence of a large Asian population also adds to the impression of a religious mosaic. Nevertheless, San Francisco has made its distinct contribution to American religious heritage. There are a number of notable religious structures in the city, including St. Patricks Church on Mission Street (called the Most Irish Church on the continent), erected in 1851 by Father Maginnis, then the only English-speaking priest in the city. Built of brick, with a slender tower and steeple, its interior is finished in green translucent Connemara marble. Other churches include Grace Cathedral on the corner of California and Jones Street, a gift of the Crocker family to the Episcopal diocese; the Old St. Marys Church on the corner of Grant Avenue and California Street in the heart of Chinatown, built in 1854; Saints Peter and Paul Church on Filbert Street in the heart of the Italian section, built in 1924 with two 191-foot turreted towers of terra cotta; St. Brigids Church on the corner of Van Ness Avenue and Broadway, built of old paving blocks; and St. Marys Cathedral on the corner of Van Ness Avenue and O'Farrell Street, the seat of the Roman Catholic Diocese of San Francisco, built in 1891. Among non-Christian places of worship, the most notable are the Kong Chow Temple, dedicated to Quan Dai, and Temple Emanu-el on First Avenue, erected in 1925.

Religion

Largest Denominations (Adherents)	
Catholic	195,160
Black Baptist	19,350
American Baptist	6,714
Episcopal	6,456
United Methodist	6,360
Presbyterian	4,644
Southern Baptist	4,499
Jewish	45,500

Media

 Two San Francisco dailies consist of the morning *San Francisco Chronicle* and the evening *San Francisco Examiner* which combine on Sunday to produce the *San Francisco Examiner and Chronicle*. The *San Francisco Daily Journal* is another daily newspaper. The electronic media consist of 10 television stations, and 34 AM and FM radio stations.

Media

Newsprint
- *California Business Magazine*, monthly
- *San Francisco Bay Guardian*, weekly
- *San Francisco Business*, weekly
- *San Francisco Chronicle*, daily
- *San Francisco Daily Journal*, daily
- *San Francisco Examiner*, daily
- *San Francisco Focus Magazine*, monthly
- *San Francisco Post*, biweekly
- *Sun Reporter*, weekly

Television
- KBHK (Channel 44)
- KCNS (Channel 38)
- KDTV (Channel 14)
- KGO (Channel 7)
- KMTP (Channel 32)
- KOFY (Channel 20)
- KPIX (Channel 5)
- KOED (Channel 9)
- KRON (Channel 4)
- KTSF (Channel 26)

Radio

KABL (AM)	KABL (FM)
KALW (FM)	KCBS (AM)
KDBX (FM)	KDFC (AM)
KDBK (FM)	KDFC (AM)
KDFC (FM)	KEAR (FM)
KEST (AM)	KFRC (AM)
KFRC (FM)	KGO (AM)
KIOI (FM)	KIQI (AM)
KITS (FM)	KKHI (AM)
KKHI (FM)	KKSF (FM)
KMEL (FM)	KNBR (AM)
KFOG (FM)	KOIT (AM)
KOIT (FM)	KNEW (AM)
KPOO (FM)	KQED (FM)
KRQR (FM)	KSAN (FM)
KSFO (AM)	KYA (FM)
KUSF (FM)	WILD (FM)

Sports

San Francisco is the home of three major professional sports teams: the Giants in baseball, the Golden State Warriors in basketball, and the FortyNiners in football. Thoroughbred racing is held at Golden Gate Fields and auto racing at the Baylands Raceway Park. The city holds the annual San Francisco Marathon, a major event on the local sports calendar.

Arts, Culture, and Tourism

San Francisco has 26 major performing arts facilities. The cultural hub is the San Francisco Performing Arts Center in Civic Center Plaza, consisting of the War Memorial Opera House, home of the San Francisco Opera; the Louise M. Davies Symphony Hall, where the San Francisco Ballet performs; and the Herbst Theater. The city's opera company, founded in 1923, is the oldest in the western United States, and the ballet company, founded in 1933, the oldest in the nation. Theater is represented by the American Conservatory Theater, Eureka Theater Company, and Magic Theater; dance by Arabesque Concert Dance, Dancers Stage Company, Eugene Ballet, Lines Dance Company, London Ballet Theater, Margaret Jenkins Dance Company, ODC, Pacific Ballet, San Francisco Ballet, and Theater of San Francisco; opera by Lamplighters/Opera West, Merola Opera Program, Opera Center Singer's Ensemble, San Francisco Pocket Opera, and Western Opera Theater; and music by Chamber Symphony of San Francisco, Philharmonia Baroque Orchestra, San Francisco Chamber Orchestra, San Francisco Chamber Players, San Francisco Conservatory of Music Orchestra, San Francisco University Symphony Orchestra, and San Francisco Symphony Youth Orchestra.

The city's best known museum is the San Francisco Museum of Modern Art in the Civic Center. The California Palace of the Legion of Honor in Lincoln Park displays French art. The M. H. de Young Memorial Museum features European paintings, and the Asian Art Museum, the Brundage Collection of Oriental art. There are scores of specialized museums, of which a few are the National Maritime Museum, Old Mint, American Carousel Museum, Museum of Modern Mythology, San Francisco International Toy Museum, San Francisco African-American Historical and Cultural Society Museum, Wells Fargo History Museum, Natural History Museum of the California Academy of Sciences, San Francisco Crafts and Folk Art Museum, Chinese Culture Center Museum, Galeria de la Raza (the Mexican Museum), Museo Italo Americano, Josephine D. Randall Junior Museum, Museum of Russian Culture, Presidio Army Museum, Museum of Ophthalmology, San Francisco Fire Department Museum, Telephone Museum, Treasure Island Museum, California Crafts Museum, and the Fine Arts Museum of San Francisco.

Travel and Tourism

Hotel Rooms 40,010
Convention and Exhibit Space (square feet) 260,560

Convention Centers
- Civic Center
- Civic Auditorium
- Brooks Exhibit Hall
- Moscone Center

Festivals
- Chinese New Year (February)
- St. Patrick's Day (March)
- Cherry Blossom Festival (April)
- Cinco de Mayo (May)
- Carnaval (June)
- Summer Festival (June–July)
- International Film Festival (October)

Parks and Recreation

San Francisco has 160 parks and playgrounds covering 4,000 acres. The 72,815-acre Golden Gate National Recreation Area covers part of San Francisco and Marin Counties. The 1,013-acre Golden Gate Park, created in the 1870s from bare sand dunes, is the most popular recreation area. Pioneer Park is on the crest of Telegraph Hill. Lincoln Park, on 33rd Avenue and Clement Street, extends northwest almost to the ocean.

Sources of Further Information

City Hall
Room 200
San Francisco, CA 94102
(415) 554-6141

San Francisco Chamber of Commerce
465 California Street
San Francisco, CA 94104
(415) 392-4511

San Francisco Convention and Visitors Bureau
201 Third Street
San Francisco, CA 94103
(415) 974-6900

Additional Reading

Becker, Howard S. *Culture and Civility in San Francisco.* 1971.

Bernhardi, Robert C. *Great Buildings of San Francisco.* 1980.

Caen, Herbert. *Baghdad-by-the-Sea.* 1987.

———. *One Man's San Francisco.* 1978.

Cherny, Robert W. and William Issel. *San Francisco.* 1981.

Chow, Willard T. *The Reemergence of an Inner City: The Pivot of Chinese Settlement in the East Bay Region of San Francisco Bay Area.* 1977.

Cockle, George R. *Frisco in Transition.* 1985.

Elliott, Virgil L. *San Francisco Statistical Abstract.* 1988.

Gold, Herbert. *Travels in San Francisco.* 1990.

Hunter, Samuel F. *The San Francisco Almanac.* 1991.

Irion, Christopher and James Shay. *New Architecture of San Francisco.* 1989.

Jones, Proctor. *Side Street: San Francisco.* 1990.

Regnery, Dorothy F. *An Enduring Heritage. Historic Buildings of San Francisco Peninsula.* 1976.

San Francisco. 1991.

Scott, Mel. *The San Francisco Bay Area: A Metropolis in Perspective.* 1985.

Sunset Magazine. *San Francisco.* 1986.

Verran, Roger. *The Fog and San Francisco.* 1982.

Watkins, T. H. *San Francisco in Color.* 1968.

History

Asbury, Herbert. *Barbary Coast: An Informal History of the San Franciso Underworld.* 1990.

Barnhart, Jacqueline. *Fair but Frail: Prostitution in San Francisco, 1849–1900.* 1986.

Barth, Gunther. *Instant Cities: Urbanization and the Rise of San Francisco and Denver.* 1988.

Bowman, J. N., and Robert F. Heizer. *Anza and the Northwest Frontier of New Spain.* 1967.

Bronson, William. *The Earth Shook, the Sky Burned: A Moving Record of America's Great Earthquake and Fire, San Francisco, April 18, 1906.* 1986.

Chandler, Arthur B. *Old Tales of San Francisco.* 1989.

Clary, Raymond H. *Making of Golden Gate Park: The Growing Years, 1906–1950.* 1987.

Cole, Tom A. *A Short History of San Francisco.* 1981.

Daniels, Douglas H. *Pioneer Urbanites: A Social and Cultural History of Black San Francisco.* 1991.

Dickson, Samuel. *Tales of San Francisco.* 1955.

Dillon, Richard H. *San Francisco: Adventures and Visionaries.* 1983.

Dwinelle, John W. *The Colonial History: City of San Francisco.* 1978.

Gentry, Curt. *Madams of San Francisco.* 1977.

Gordo, Mark. *Once Upon a City: A Wild Ride through San Francisco's Past.* 1988.

Gumina, Deanna. *The Italians of San Francisco.* 1985.

Hamilton, Sue. *San Francisco Earthquake.* 1992.

House, James, and Steffens, Bradley. *The San Francisco Earthquake.* 1989.

Jewett, Marsha C. *Coit Tower, San Francisco: Its History and Art.* 1983.

Kahn, Judd. *Imperial San Francisco: Politics and Planning in an American City, 1897–1906.* 1980.

Kao, George. *Cathay by the Sea: San Francisco Chinatown in 1950.* 1989.

Kazin, Michael. *Barons of Labor: The San Francisco Building Trades and Union Power in the Progressive Era.* 1989.

Kennard, Charles. *San Francisco Bay Area Landmarks.* 1987.

Levinsohn, John L. *Cow Hollow: Early Days of San Francisco Neighborhood from 1776.* 1976.

Lewis, Oscar. *San Francisco: Mission to Metropolis.* 1980.

Lotchin, Roger W. *San Francisco, 1846–1856: From Hamlet to City.* 1979.

Mayer, Robert. *San Francisco: A Chronological and Documentary History.* 1974.

Morris, Charles. *The San Francisco Calamity by Earthquake and Fire.* 1986.

Moses, B. *The Establishment of Municipal Government in San Francisco.* 1985.

Palmer, John W. *Pioneer Days in San Francisco.* 1977.

Perry, Stewart E. *San Francisco Scavengers: Dirty Work and the Pride of Ownership.* 1978.

Robin, Ron. *Signs of Change: Urban Iconographies in San Francisco, 1880–1915.* 1990.

Roszak, Theodore. *From Salon to Silicon Valley: San Francisco and the American Counter Culture.* 1986.

Saul, Eric, and Don DeNevi. *The Great San Francisco Earthquake and Fire, 1906.* 1989.

Senkewicz, Robert M. *Vigilantes in Gold Rush San Francisco.* 1985.

Taubert, Everett O. *San Francisco: Vignette of History.* 1989.

Wollenberg, Charles. *Golden Gate Metropolis: Perspectives on Bay Area History.* 1985.

Zauner, Phyllis. *San Francisco: The Way It Was Then and Now.* 1980.

Politics and Society

Bean, Walton. *Boss Ruef's San Francisco: The Story of the Union Labor Party, Big Business and the Graft Prosecution.* 1952.

Burchell, B. A. *The San Francisco Irish.* 1980.

Fine, Doris. *When Leadership Fails: Desegregation and Demoralization in San Francisco Schools.* 1986.

Jain, Usha. *The Gujeratis of San Franciso.* 1989.

McDonald, Terence J. *The Parameters of Urban Fiscal Policy: SocioEconomic Change and Political Culture in San Francisco, 1891–1906.* 1986.

Mollenkopf, John H. *The Contested City.* 1983.

Narell, Irena. *The Jews of San Francisco.* 1981.

Radin, Paul. *The Italians of San Francisco.* 1975.

Wirt, Frederick M. *Power in the City: Decision Making in San Francisco.* 1975.

San Jose

California

Basic Data

Name   San Jose
Name Origin   From the Spanish for St. Joseph
Year Founded   1777 Inc. 1850
Status: State   California
         County   Seat of Santa Clara County
Area (square miles)   171.3
Elevation (feet)   90
Time Zone   Pacific
Population (1990)   782,248
Population of Metro Area (1990)   1,497,577

Sister Cities

Dublin, Ireland
Okayama, Japan
San Jose, Costa Rica
Tainan City, China
Vera Cruz, Mexico

Distance in Miles To:

San Francisco	44
San Diego	468
Sacramento	117
Reno	259
Portland, OR	675
Los Angeles	347

Location and Topography

 San Jose is located in Santa Clara Valley at the southern tip of San Francisco Bay, bounded by the Santa Cruz Mountains on the west and the Diablo Mountain Range on the east. The Coyote and Guadalupe rivers run through the city.

Layout of City and Suburbs

The city lies eight miles from the bay, separated by low ground and marshes. Mountains are visable from every point in the city. The business district is roughly in the form of a cross, with its arms running north-south, and east-west. The geographical center of town is the crossing of Park Avenue and Market Street where the Convention Center and the principal public buildings are located. West of First Street the business district merges with the industrial area. East of First Street is the older residential district, and on northern First Street is another residential district. Santa Clara is a separate city northwest of San Jose but the two, due to their close proximity, for all intents and purposes comprise one metropolitan area.

Environment

Environmental Stress Index   3.4
Green Cities Index: Rank   53
                    Score   37.23
Water Quality   Alkaline, very hard
Average Daily Use (gallons per capita)   NA
    Maximum Supply (gallons per capita)   NA
Parkland as % of Total City Area   15.1
% Waste Landfilled/Recycled   75:25
Annual Parks Expenditures per Capita $79.75

Climate

 San Jose has a mild but arid climate, very similar to San Francisco. Winter is short, lasting only for two months.

Weather

Temperature

Highest Monthly Average °F   73.6
Lowest Monthly Average °F   41.2

Annual Averages

Days 32°F or Below   0
Days above 90°F   1
Zero Degree Days   0

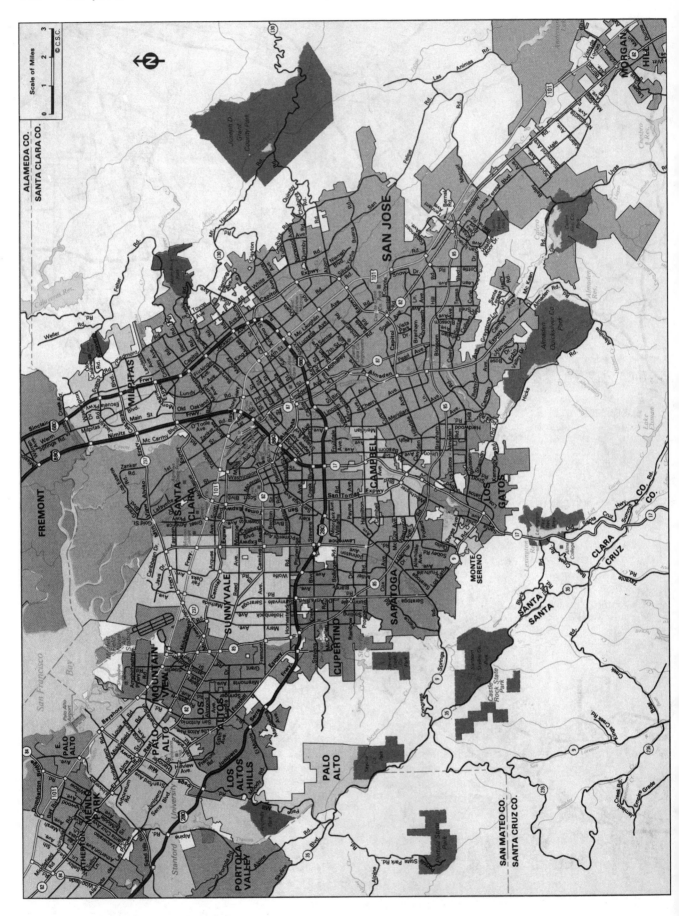

Weather (continued)

Precipitation (inches)   21.0
Snow (inches)   0
% Seasonal Humidity   75.0
Wind Speed (m.p.h.)   8.7
Clear Days   162
Cloudy Days   100
Storm Days   2
Rainy Days   67

Average Temperatures (°F)	High	Low	Mean
January	55.3	41.2	48.3
February	58.6	43.8	51.2
March	61.0	44.9	53.0
April	63.5	47.0	55.3
May	66.6	49.9	58.3
June	70.2	53.0	61.6
July	70.9	54.0	62.5
August	71.6	54.3	63.0
September	73.6	54.5	64.1
October	70.3	51.6	61.0
November	63.3	47.2	55.3
December	50.5	42.9	49.7

History

The Olhone Indians lived in the area before the white settlers. In 1777, in response to orders from the viceroy of Mexico, nine soldiers, five *pobladores*, or settlers, their families, and one cowboy founded the village of Pueblo de San Jose de Guadalupe. This was the first non-mission town founded in California. When Mexico broke from Spanish rule in 1821, San Jose passed on to Mexican rule. By 1831 the village had 524 residents. By the 1840s, the first wave of emigration from the east began to add to the population. When Captain Thomas Fallon arrived in 1846 to raise the U.S. flag, he found a sleepy little town. Within two years the Gold Rush changed the small town into a vigorous city that was chosen to be state capital in 1849; the city was incorporated in 1850. Accommodations proved to be so poor, however, that the legislators moved the capital to Benicia in 1851. The railroad came through in 1864, spurring the first real estate boom, which lasted until 1887. Meanwhile, the Gold Rush was ending and the residents turned to farming with extraordinary results. The surrounding countryside became a large farming center, noted particularly for its prunes and apricots.

San Jose's greatest expansion occurred after World War II. From 95,000 in 1950, the population rose to 200,000 in 1960. Between 1950 and 1980 the city annexed an additional 140 square miles, as orchards and pastures were turned into housing developments. In 1989 San Jose suffered in the major earthquake that devastated the San Francisco Bay area.

Historical Landmarks

San Jose contains a number of historic homes. Two of the most interesting are the Edwain Markham Home on Eighth Street, where the poet lived from 1857 to 1899, and the 160-room Winchester Mystery House built by the eccentric widow of the maker of Winchester rifles.

Population

San Jose, like many other California cities, has never suffered a slippage of population in this century. From 200,000 in 1960, the population rose to 460,000 in 1970, rising again by 36.9% to 629,400 in 1980, and then by a further 24.3% to 782,248 in 1990. The population is expected to cross the million mark by 2000.

Population

	1980	1990
Central City	629,400	782,248
Rank	17	11
Metro Area	1,295,071	1,497,577

Pop. Change 1980–1990   +152,848
Pop. % Change 1980–1990   +24.3
Median Age   30.4
% Male   50.8
% Age 65 and Over   7.2
Density (per square mile)   4,566

Households

Number   250,218
Persons per Household   3.08
% Female-Headed Households   11.9
% One-Person Households   18.4
Births—Total   14,598
 % to Mothers under 20   10.7
 Birth Rate per 1,000   21.3

Ethnic Composition

Whites make up 62.8%, blacks 4.7%, American Indians 0.7%, Asians and Pacific Islanders 19.5%, and others 12.3%. Hispanics, both black and white, make up 26.6%.

Ethnic Composition (as % of total pop.)

	1980	1990
White	73.61	62.8
Black	4.64	4.7
American Indian	0.76	0.69
Asian and Pacific Islander	8.26	19.54
Hispanic	22.33	26.64
Other	NA	12.27

Government

Under the 1916 charter, San Jose is governed by a council-manager form of government. The ten council members serve staggered four-year terms and the mayor also serves a four-year term. The city manager, appointed by the council, serves an open-ended term.

Government

Year of Home Charter   1916
Number of Members of the Governing Body   10
Elected at Large   NA
Elected by Wards   10
Number of Women in Governing Body   8
Salary of Mayor $80,000
Salary of Council Members $52,800
City Government Employment Total   4,966
Rate per 10,000   69.7

Chronology

1777 On orders from the viceroy of Mexico, Pueblo de San Jose de Guadalupe is founded as the first non-mission settlement in California.

1821 Mexico breaks from Spain and San Jose passes on to Mexican rule.

1846 San Jose passes to U.S. rule as Captain Thomas Fallon raises the Stars and Stripes over the pueblo.

1848 San Jose's population grows due to the Gold Rush.

1849 San Jose is chosen as the first state capital.

1850 San Jose is incorporated.

1851 Legislature leaves San Jose and moves to Benicia.

1864 The first railroad reaches town.

1880 Real estate boom peaks.

1989 Strong earthquake hits San Francisco Bay area.

Public Finance

 The annual budget consists of revenues of $700.479 million and expenditures of $720.710 million. The debt outstanding is $1.042 billion, and cash and security holdings $1.677 billion.

Public Finance

Total Revenue (in millions) $700.479
Intergovernmental Revenue—Total (in millions) $79.26
Federal Revenue per Capita $7.38
% Federal Assistance   1.05
% State Assistance   7.71
Sales Tax as % of Total Revenue   19.54
Local Revenue as % of Total Revenue   77.54
City Income Tax   no
Taxes—Total (in millions) $213.5

Taxes per Capita
   Total $300
   Property $99
   Sales and Gross Receipts $139
General Expenditures—Total (in millions) $416.0
General Expenditures per Capita $584
Capital Outlays per Capita $167

% of Expenditures for:
   Public Welfare   0.0
   Highways   20.8
   Education   0.0
   Health and Hospitals   1.3
   Police   13.9
   Sewerage and Sanitation   12.8
   Parks and Recreation   6.9
   Housing and Community Development   8.5

Public Finance (continued)

Debt Outstanding per Capita $717
   % Utility   NA
Federal Procurement Contract Awards (in millions) $1,027.8
Federal Grants Awards (in millions) $120.3
Fiscal Year Begins   July 1

Economy

San Jose is the crown of the Silicon Valley and its remarkable prosperity during the 1970s and 1980s was a fallout from the Silicon Valley's rise as the computer chip capital. But the economy of San Jose is based on more than computer chips. There are over 500 manufacturing facilities, including large aerospace plants, some of which build space vehicles for NASA. San Jose also is one of the largest food-processing centers on the West Coast. The city is the main distribution point for the agricultural products of the fertile Santa Clara Valley.

Economy

Total Money Income (in millions) $8,960.1
% of State Average   105.9
Per Capita Annual Income $12,583
% Population below Poverty Level   8.2
Fortune 500 Companies   2

Banks	Number	Deposits (in millions)
Commercial	226	NA
Savings	161	NA

Passenger Autos   953,666
Electric Meters   569,597
Gas Meters   465,405

Manufacturing

Number of Establishments   1,056
% with 20 or More Employees   31.7
Manufacturing Payroll (in millions) $2,335.7
Value Added by Manufacture (in millions) $4,645.1
Value of Shipments (in millions) $7,864.4
New Capital Expenditures (in millions) $384.2

Wholesale Trade

Number of Establishments   1,132
Sales (in millions) $7,687.3
Annual Payroll (in millions) $551.823

Retail Trade

Number of Establishments   5,977
Total Sales (in millions) $4,031.3
Sales per Capita $5,661
Number of Retail Trade Establishments with Payroll   3,308
Annual Payroll (in millions) $515.2
Total Sales (in millions) $3,893.5
General Merchandise Stores (per capita) $657
Food Stores (per capita) $1,240
Apparel Stores (per capita) $290
Eating and Drinking Places (per capita) $560

Service Industries

Total Establishments   4,970
Total Receipts (in millions) $2,722.8
Hotels and Motels (in millions) $78.1
Health Services (in millions) $579.9
Legal Services (in millions) $271.1

Labor

The dominance of manufacturing in San Jose is unusually high for a large city. San Jose workers in manufacturing are not blue-collar but white-collar, due to the presence of high-tech industries, thus blurring the distinction between the two. The workers are also highly mobile, as most California workers tend to be. Of the top ten employers eight are in the high-tech electronics or computer business, including Hewlett-Packard, IBM, Lockheed, National Semiconductor, Apple, and Advanced Micro Devices.

Labor

Civilian Labor Force   381,968
% Change 1989–1990   -3.9

Work Force Distribution
   Mining   300
   Construction   30,100
   Manufacturing   258,500
   Transportation and Public Utilities   23,100
   Wholesale and Retail Trade   164,400
   FIRE (Finance, Insurance, Real Estate)   32,400
   Service   219,900
   Government   88,900
   Women as % of Labor Force   43.4
   % Self-Employed   4.9
   % Professional/Technical   18.3
Total Unemployment   18,088
Rate %   4.7
Federal Government Civilian Employment   3,829

Education

The San Jose Unified School District supports 42 elementary, junior high/middle, and senior high schools. In addition there are 20 private and parochial schools. San Jose's local university is the San Jose State University. San Jose City College is part of the San Jose Community College District.

Education

Number of Public Schools   42
Special Education Schools   NA
Total Enrollment   29,630
% Enrollment in Private Schools   11.1
% Minority   56.9
Classroom Teachers   1,427
Pupil-Teacher Ratio   20.3:1
Number of Graduates   1,854
Total Revenue (in millions) $139.112
Total Expenditures (in millions) $133.182
Expenditures per Pupil $4,516
Educational Attainment (Age 25 and Over)
   % Completed 12 or More Years   76.4
   % Completed 16 or More Years   21.1
Four-Year Colleges and Universities   3
   Enrollment   32,337
Two-Year Colleges   5
   Enrollment   12,993

Education *(continued)*

Libraries

Number   46
Public Libraries   18
Books (in thousands)   1,364
Circulation (in thousands)   3,905
Persons Served (in thousands)   749
Circulation per Person Served   5.21
Income (in millions) $13.604
Staff   320

Four-Year Colleges and Universities
   The National Hispanic University
   San Jose City College
   San Jose State University

Health

San Jose has six major hospitals of which the largest are the Valley Medical Center, Good Samaritan Hospital, and O'Connor Hospital. Within driving distance are some of the finest hospitals in the state, including the Stanford University Medical Center.

Health

Deaths—Total   3,865
Rate per 1,000   5.6
Infant Deaths—Total   115
Rate per 1,000   7.9
Number of Metro Hospitals   6
Number of Metro Hospital Beds   1,802
Rate per 100,000   253
Number of Physicians   3,307
Physicians per 1,000   2.85
Nurses per 1,000   NA
Health Expenditures per Capita   NA

Transportation

San Jose is approached by three interstates: the north-south I-680, which becomes the east-west I-280; the north-south I-880; and the northeast-southwest I-101. Travel within the city is facilitated by the light rail transit and the Transit Mall, both part of the Guadalupe Corridor project completed in 1990. Rail passenger service is provided by Amtrak and rail freight service by Southern Pacific and Western Pacific. The principal air terminal is the San Jose International Airport, ten miles from downtown, served by 11 airlines.

Transportation

Interstate Highway Mileage   41
Total Urban Mileage   3,685
Total Daily Vehicle Mileage (in millions) $32.876
Daily Average Commute Time   50.2 min.
Number of Buses   745
Port Tonnage (in millions)   NA
Airports   1
Number of Daily Flights   140
Daily Average Number of Passengers   8,475

Transportation (continued)

Airlines (American carriers only)
- Alaska
- American
- American West
- Continental
- Delta
- Northwest
- Trans World
- United
- USAir

Housing

Of the total housing stock 61.3% is owner-occupied. The median value of an owner-occupied home is $259,100 and the median monthly rent is $692.

Housing

Total Housing Units	259,365
% Change 1980–1990	16.5
Vacant Units for Sale or Rent	7,715
Occupied Units	250,218
% with More Than One Person per Room	14.9
% Owner-Occupied	61.3
Median Value of Owner-Occupied Homes	$259,100
Average Monthly Purchase Cost	$478
Median Monthly Rent	$692
New Private Housing Starts	1,725
Value (in thousands)	$117,052
% Single-Family	21.3
Nonresidential Buildings Value (in thousands)	$118,559

Urban Redevelopment

In 1968 work began on a downtown urban renewal project called Park Central Plaza. The project, scheduled for completion in the 1990s, includes several office buildings, banks, and a hotel. Another urban renewal project, the Silicon Valley Financial Center, covering a decaying eight-block area, started in 1985 and is scheduled for completion in the late 1990s. Urban development projects are coordinated by Downtown Development Corporation.

Crime

San Jose ranks above national average in public safety. In 1991 5,258 violent crimes and 37,578 property crimes were reported to the police.

Crime

Violent Crimes—Total	5,258
Violent Crime Rate per 100,000	522.4
Murder	53
Rape	445
Robbery	1,382
Aggravated Assaults	3,432
Property Crimes	37,578

Crime (continued)

Burglary	7,403
Larceny	25,663
Motor Vehicle Theft	4,512
Arson	327
Per Capita Police Expenditures	$123.90
Per Capita Fire Protection Expenditures	$64.62
Number of Police	976
Per 1,000	1.38

Religion

Catholics form over one-half of the population with particular strength in the Hispanic community. Baptists, Lutherans, Presbyterians, and Methodists compose less than 5% of San Jose's population. Eastern religions are strongly represented in the Asian community.

Religion

Largest Denominations (Adherents)

Catholic	368,611
Southern Baptist	21,153
Black Baptist	14,868
United Methodist	16,651
Presbyterian	11,228
Evangelical Lutheran	11,866
Episcopal	9,593
Latter-Day Saints	23,595
Assembly of God	10,532
Jewish	32,000

Media

The city daily is the *San Jose Mercury News*. The electronic media consist of 5 television stations and 10 FM and AM radio stations.

Media

Newsprint
- *The Business Journal*, weekly
- *San Jose Mercury News*, daily

Television
- KICU (Channel 36)
- KLXV (Channel 65)
- KNTV (Channel 11)
- KSTS (Channel 48)
- KTEH (Channel 54)

Radio

KEEN (AM)	KBAY (FM)
KEZR (FM)	KLEL (FM)
KLIV (AM)	KLOK (AM)
KOME (FM)	KSJS (FM)
KSJX (AM)	KUFX (FM)

Sports

Although dwarfed by nearby San Francisco and Oakland in professional sports, San Jose has two minor league or semiprofessional teams: the San Jose Giants (a farm team of the San Francisco Giants) in baseball, and the San Jose Earthquakes in soccer. The Giants play at the

Municipal Stadium and the Earthquakes at the San Jose State University's Spartan Stadium.

Arts, Culture, and Tourism

San Jose's cultural activities revolve around three outstanding facilities: the Center for Performing Arts, the Civic Auditorium, and the Montgomery Theater. Theater is represented by San Jose Stage Company, San Jose Repertory Company, City Lights Theater Company, San Jose Musical Theater, and Northside Theater Company. Music is represented by the San Jose Symphony Orchestra and the San Jose Chamber Music Society; opera by Civic Light Opera and Opera San Jose; and dance by San Jose Cleveland Ballet, Margaret Wingrove Dancers and San Jose Dance Theater, as well as the Mexican troupes, Xocipilli and Los Lupenos.

The principal museum is the San Jose Museum of Art. In addition there are a number of specialized museums, such as the American Museum of Quilts and Textiles, Military Medal Museum, Rosicrucian Egyptian Museum and Art Gallery, San Jose Historical Museum, and Science Museum. The new Technology Museum of Silicon Valley is a complex of science museums on a 12-acre site next to the Convention Center. Among the art galleries, the most notable are the Union Gallery, Art Department Galleries of San Jose State University, San Jose Art League, Institute of Contemporary Arts, and the Works Gallery.

Travel and Tourism
Hotel Rooms   14,985
Convention and Exhibit Space (square feet)   NA
Convention Centers
San Jose Convention & Cultural Center
Santa Clara County Exposition Center
Festivals
International Fair (March)
VITA Shakespeare Festival (April)
Nikkei Matsuri (Japanese) (May)
Obon Festival (July)
Santa Clara County Fair (July)

Parks and Recreation

San Jose has about 75 parks. Alum Rock Park, the largest, features unusual rock formations and 22 mineral springs. Kelley Park includes a Japanese tea garden, a museum, and a zoo. St. James Park, between St. John and St. James streets, was the site of a notorious lynching in 1933. The San Jose Municipal Rose Garden features 7,500 plants, including 158 varieties of roses. Other parks include Almaden Quicksilver Park, Lake Cunningham Regional Park, and Vasona Lake Park.

Sources of Further Information

City Hall
801 North First Street
San Jose, CA 95110
(408) 277-4237

San Jose Chamber of Commerce
1 Paseo de San Antonio
San Jose, CA 95150
(408) 998-7000

San Jose Convention and Visitors Bureau
1 Paseo de San Antonio
San Jose, CA 95150
(408) 998-7000

Additional Reading

Brackway, Edith. *San Jose Reflections.* 1977.
Farrell, Harry. *San Jose and Other Famous Places.* 1983.
Loomis, Patricia. *Signposts II.* 1985.
Muller, Kathleen. *San Jose: City with a Past.* 1988.
Peyton, Wes. *San Jose: A Personal View.* 1989.
Pierce, Marjorie. *San Jose and Its Cathedral.* 1988.

Scranton

Pennsylvania

Basic Data

Name   Scranton
Name Origin   From the Scranton family
Year Founded   1786 Inc. 1866
Status: State   Pennsylvania
      County   Seat of Lackawanna County
Area (square miles)   25.2
Elevation (feet)   725
Time Zone   EST
Population (1990)   81,805
Population of Metro Area (1990)   734,175

Distance in Miles To:

Baltimore	199
Erie	295
Trenton	139
Pittsburgh	290
Philadelphia	129
New York	136

Location and Topography

N

Scranton lies in the narrow, crescent-shaped Lackawanna Valley in northeastern Pennsylvania, hemmed by the Moosic Mountains to the north, the West Mountains to the west, and the Pocono Mountains to the southeast.

Layout of City and Suburbs

Scranton is historically a company town built by the Scranton brothers and the Lackawanna Iron and Steel Company. Known for many years as the Anthracite Capital of the World, its carries the legacy of coal in its soot, the angular skyline formed by coal breakers and factory stacks, and the occasional building resting askew on sunken foundations. Close to the Lackawanna River, which winds in a southwesterly direction through the city, lies the downtown district. To the east is the hill section with clapboard and stuccoed buildings pre-dominating. More imposing buildings are found in the Green Ridge to the north.

Environment

Environmental Stress Index   NA
Green Cities Index: Rank   NA
              Score   NA
Water Quality   Slightly acid, very soft, neutral
Average Daily Use (gallons per capita)   NA
    Maximum Supply (gallons per capita)   NA
Parkland as % of Total City Area   NA
% Waste Landfilled/Recycled   NA
Annual Parks Expenditures per Capita $11.64

Climate

Scranton has pleasant summers with frequent showers. Winter temperatures are moderate, but occasional snowstorms approach blizzard conditions. The surrounding mountains protect the city from high winds. The city's elevation is a major factor influencing weather patterns.

Weather

Temperature

Highest Monthly Average °F   73.4
Lowest Monthly Average °F   27.5

Annual Averages

Days 32°F or Below   114
Days above 90°F   17
Zero Degree Days   0
Precipitation (inches)   35.06
Snow (inches)   33.9
% Seasonal Humidity   59
Wind Speed (m.p.h.)   8.3
Clear Days   89
Cloudy Days   177
Storm Days   26
Rainy Days   125

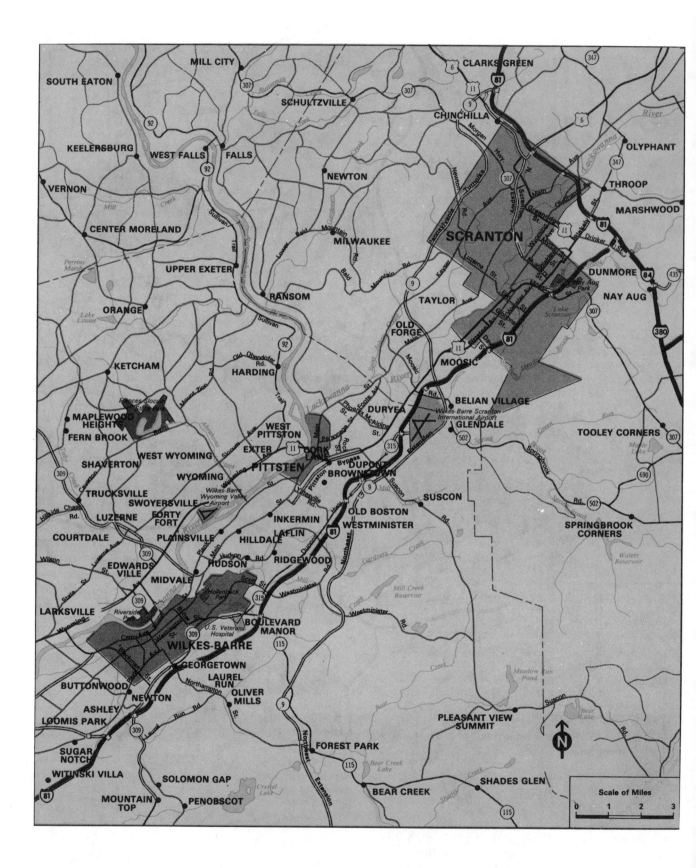

Weather (continued)

Average Temperatures (°F)	High	Low	Mean
January	35.3	19.7	27.5
February	41.4	25.4	33.4
March	49.3	31.5	40.4
April	61.2	42.1	51.7
May	77.8	53.5	65.7
June	81.6	57.3	69.5
July	84.3	62.4	73.4
August	82.6	61.8	72.2
September	72.4	51.2	61.8
October	63.7	42.8	53.3
November	49.2	33.5	41.4
December	40.4	25.3	32.9

History

The region was inhabited until 1771 by the Munsee Indians, who had their wigwams along both sides of the Susquehanna River. The first white settlers came about the middle of the 18th century and, between 1758 and 1771, moved westward to the Ohio Valley. The Wyoming Massacre at Forty Fort in 1778 spread panic among these settlers, and they withdrew for the next ten years. The settlement renewed in 1788 when Philip Abbott, a former settler, returned and built a log hut and gristmill beside the Roaring Brook. He was followed ten years later by Ebenezer and Benjamin Slocum. The brothers acquired property in the settlement, which they named Unionville, although some settlers called its Skunk's Misery. In 1816 the name was changed to Slocum's Hollow. The Slocums built a forge and distillery in 1800. In 1840 two other brothers, George W. and Selden T. Scranton, came to the settlement from New Jersey. At that time it was a community of five weather-beaten houses. Attracted by the abundance of iron ore in the region, the Scrantons and their partners—William Henry, Sanford Grant, and Philip Mattes—organized the firm of Scranton, Grant and Company, constructing a forge. The firm became the nucleus of the Lackawanna Iron and Steel Company. In 1845 the Scrantons named the place Harrison in honor of President William Henry Harrison. With a view to expanding the plant, the Scrantons borrowed $10,000 from their cousin, Joseph Hand Scranton of Georgia. In 1847 Joseph Scranton bought out Sanford Grant's interest and assumed leadership of the Lackawanna Iron Works. In 1851 the name of the town was changed once again to Scranton. In 1853 the first train of the Delaware and Lackawanna Railroad came in, helping to promote the development of coal mines. In 1866 Scranton absorbed the two boroughs of Providence and Hyde Park and also the township of Providence; Scranton received its town charter that year. By 1886 the town had a population of over 50,000. In 1891 the Scranton Steel Company merged with the Lackawanna Iron and Coal Company to become the Lackawanna Iron and Steel Company. In 1902 this company moved to a site near Buffalo, New York, to be closer to the Great Lakes ore supply, but by then coal mining had already superseded iron as the main industry. For the next 30 years, the city was the scene of some of the bloodiest clashes between coal mine workers and the owners. The first dispute in 1877 resulted in much bloodshed, the imposition of martial law, and the intervention of troops. By 1897 the miners were effectively organized into the powerful United Mine Workers of America under the leadership of John Mitchell. They struck in 1900 and 1902, winning substantial wage concessions. Another strike in 1923 resulted in an eight-hour workday. The longest and the most disastrous strike occurred in 1925–1926. It lasted for 170 days and its effects were felt for over a decade. Gradually, the coal mining industry declined and the economy was forced to diversify under the so-called Scranton Plan, devised in 1945.

Historical Landmarks

The Courthouse Square on Spruce Street is the site of the Lackawanna County Courthouse, built in Romanesque style in 1881–1884. The Elm Park Methodist Church, on a triangle formed by Linden Street and Jefferson and Madison avenues, was built in 1892. The Historic Scranton Iron Furnaces in the heart of the city, last fired in 1909, were rededicated in the 1980s. The Steamtown National Historic Site has been restored by the National Park Service. Among its displays are the 1.2-million-pound Big Boy, one of the largest locomotives ever built.

Population

After peaking at 103,564 in 1970, the population of Scranton has been declining. It reached 88,117 in 1980 and 81,805 in 1990.

Population	1980	1990
Central City	88,117	81,805
Rank	199	258
Metro Area	728,796	734,175
Pop. Change 1980–1990 -6,312		
Pop. % Change 1980–1990 -7.2		
Median Age 37.2		
% Male 45.8		
% Age 65 and Over 21.92		
Density (per square mile) 3,246		

Households		
Number 32,637		
Persons per Household 2.37		
% Female-Headed Households 13.8		
% One-Person Households 34.0		
Births—Total 1,128		
% to Mothers under 20 11.7		
Birth Rate per 1,000 13.5		

Ethnic Composition

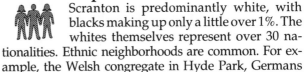

Scranton is predominantly white, with blacks making up only a little over 1%. The whites themselves represent over 30 nationalities. Ethnic neighborhoods are common. For example, the Welsh congregate in Hyde Park, Germans

Chronology

1778   The Wyoming Massacre at Forty Fort wipes out white settlement along the Lackawanna River.

1788   Philip Abbott builds a log cabin and gristmill beside Roaring Brook.

1798   Ebenezer and Benjamin Slocum acquire property called Unionville.

1800   The Slocum Brothers build a forge and distillery.

1816   The settlement is renamed Slocum Hollow.

1840   George W. and Selden T. Scranton migrate to the settlement and, in collaboration with three partners, build a forge that eventually becomes the Lackawanna Iron and Steel Company.

1845   The settlement is named Harrison.

1847   Joseph Hand Scranton, cousin of George and Selden, assumes leadership of the iron and steel company.

1851   The name of the settlement is changed to Scranton.

1853   The railroad reaches Scranton.

1866   Scranton absorbs the two boroughs of Providence and Hyde Park, and the township of Providence, and receives a city charter.

1877   Bloody clashes between miners and mine owners result in collapse of workers union.

1883   The Scranton Steel Company rolls first steel rails.

1886   Streetcars are introduced.

1891   Scranton Steel Company merges with Lackawanna Iron and Coal Company to become Lackawanna Iron and Steel Company.

1897   Miners reorganize as the United Mine Workers of America under John Mitchell.

1900   Workers gain concessions after UMW-led strike.

1902   Lackawanna Iron and Steel Company moves to Buffalo, New York. After a 165-day strike, miners gain further concessions.

1923   Miners strike and win benefits.

1925   Disastrous 170-day strike cripples coal industry.

and Irish in South Scranton, and Poles, Russians, and Italians in outlying areas.

Ethnic Composition (as % of total pop.)		
	1980	*1990*
White	98.26	97.18
Black	1.08	1.58
American Indian	0.04	0.9
Asian and Pacific Islander	0.39	0.91
Hispanic	0.45	0.67
Other	NA	0.24

Government

Scranton runs under a mayor-council form of government. The mayor and five council members are elected to four-year terms. Scranton also is the seat of Lackawanna County.

Government
Year of Home Charter   1976
Number of Members of the Governing Body   5
Elected at Large   5
Elected by Wards   NA
Number of Women in Governing Body   0
Salary of Mayor $45,900
Salary of Council Members $11,000
City Government Employment Total   854
Rate per 10,000   103.8

Public Finance

The annual budget consists of revenues of $35.485 million and expenditures of $37.081 million. Debt outstanding is $9.249 million and cash and security holdings $13.790 million.

Public Finance
Total Revenue (in millions) $35.485
Intergovernmental Revenue—Total (in millions) $6.2
Federal Revenue per Capita   NA
% Federal Assistance   NA
% State Assistance   8.04
Sales Tax as % of Total Revenue   NA
Local Revenue as % of Total Revenue   88.54
City Income Tax   yes
Taxes—Total (in millions) $17.1
Taxes per Capita
Total $208
Property $69
Sales and Gross Receipts $0
General Expenditures—Total (in millions) $39.7
General Expenditures per Capita $483
Capital Outlays per Capita $70
% of Expenditures for:
Public Welfare   0.0
Highways   10.9
Education   0.0
Health and Hospitals   1.3
Police   10.1
Sewerage and Sanitation   11.3
Parks and Recreation   2.3
Housing and Community Development   3.8

Public Finance (continued)

Debt Outstanding per Capita $26
  % Utility 0.0
Federal Procurement Contract Awards (in millions) $22.0
Federal Grants Awards (in millions) $16.1
Fiscal Year Begins January 1

Economy

The economy of Scranton was reborn in 1945 as a result of the Scranton Plan. Scranton was historically a company town, dependent on its coal industry. The collapse of coal mining deprived the city of its mainstay and forced it to diversify. Its efforts in this direction were so successful that it emerged as one of the most important manufacturing centers in the Northeast. The city now claims some of the most active industrial firms in the region, including RCA, Specialty Records, Owen-Illinois, Weston Controls, Gentrex, Haddon Craftsmen, and The Trane Company. The region is ranked second in the nation for silk, rayon, and nylon weaving. Defense industries are also prominent, led by General Dynamics and Chamberlain Corporation.

Economy

Total Money Income (in millions) $700.1
% of State Average 82.7
Per Capita Annual Income $8,511
% Population below Poverty Level 12.9
Fortune 500 Companies NA

Banks	Number	Deposits (in millions)
Commercial	20	6,525
Savings	NA	NA

Passenger Autos 114,604
Electric Meters 100,000
Gas Meters 45,000

Manufacturing

Number of Establishments 168
% with 20 or More Employees 44.6
Manufacturing Payroll (in millions) $137.5
Value Added by Manufacture (in millions) $321.3
Value of Shipments (in millions) $551.9
New Capital Expenditures (in millions) $12.0

Wholesale Trade

Number of Establishments 208
Sales (in millions) $729.6
Annual Payroll (in millions) $52.493

Retail Trade

Number of Establishments 1,027
Total Sales (in millions) $658.8
Sales per Capita $8,009
Number of Retail Trade Establishments with Payroll 623
Annual Payroll (in millions) $68.5
Total Sales (in millions) $637.4
General Merchandise Stores (per capita) $1,710
Food Stores (per capita) $1,402
Apparel Stores (per capita) $508
Eating and Drinking Places (per capita) $496

Service Industries

Total Establishments 641
Total Receipts (in millions) $280.0
Hotels and Motels (in millions) $16.3
Health Services (in millions) $108.6
Legal Services (in millions) $27.9

Labor

Scranton's successful transition to manufacturing has sustained the labor market for over 45 years, but now appears to be on the wane. The apparel industry is threatened by foreign competition. In the late 1980s services overtook manufacturing as the largest employment sector, with trade following as a close third. Tourism in the Poconos provides additional employment. Once mining employed almost every able-bodied person in town but has now shrunk to less than 500 workers.

Labor

Civilian Labor Force 39,664
% Change 1989–1990 0.8
Work Force Distribution
  Mining 600
  Construction 12,700
  Manufacturing 70,800
  Transportation and Public Utilities 16,300
  Wholesale and Retail Trade 69,900
  FIRE (Finance, Insurance, Real Estate) 13,000
  Service 74,300
  Government 42,600
  Women as % of Labor Force 43.9
  % Self-Employed 6.0
  % Professional/Technical 12.1
Total Unemployment 2,691
Rate % 6.8
Federal Government Civilian Employment 738

Education

The public school system consists of 3 senior high, 3 junior high/middle, and 13 elementary schools. The Diocese of Scranton administers an extensive parochial school system, including the Jesuit-run Scranton Preparatory School.

The three major institutions of higher education are the Jesuit-run University of Scranton, the Worthington Scranton Campus of the Pennsylvania State University, and Marywood College. Scranton also is home to the International Correspondence Schools, founded in 1890, the Johnson Technology Institute, and Northeast Institute of Education.

Education

Number of Public Schools 19
Special Education Schools NA
Total Enrollment 9,175
% Enrollment in Private Schools 16.3
% Minority NA
Classroom Teachers NA
Pupil-Teacher Ratio NA
Number of Graduates NA
Total Revenue (in millions) NA
Total Expenditures (in millions) NA
Expenditures per Pupil NA
Educational Attainment (Age 25 and Over)
  % Completed 12 or More Years 61.4
  % Completed 16 or More Years 9.6
Four-Year Colleges and Universities 3
  Enrollment 8,202
Two-Year Colleges 3
  Enrollment 4,413

Education (continued)

Libraries

Number 17
Public Libraries 4
Books (in thousands) 184.6
Circulation (in thousands) NA
Persons Served (in thousands) NA
Circulation per Person Served NA
Income (in millions) $1.151
Staff NA

Four-Year Colleges and Universities
University of Scranton
Marywood College
Pennsylvania State University – Worthington Scranton

Health

The Scranton area has 5 general hospitals, of which the largest are the Clarks Summit State Hospital, Mercy Hospital, and Community Medical Center.

Health

Deaths—Total 1,368
Rate per 1,000 16.3
Infant Deaths—Total 15
Rate per 1,000 13.3
Number of Metro Hospitals 5
Number of Metro Hospital Beds 1,239
Rate per 100,000 1,506
Number of Physicians 1,120
Physicians per 1,000 NA
Nurses per 1,000 NA
Health Expenditures per Capita $0.06

Transportation

Scranton is approached by the north-south I-81, connecting with both Canada and Maryland; I-84, extending to the Massachusetts Turnpike and running south to Philadelphia and west to Ohio; and I-380, linking it to the Poconos and then to I-80, the transcontinental route. Scranton shares the Wilkes-Barre/Scranton International Airport in Avoca, seven miles from downtown. Rail access is provided by four carriers.

Transportation

Interstate Highway Mileage 33
Total Urban Mileage 1,449
Total Daily Vehicle Mileage (in millions) $6.010
Daily Average Commute Time 40.9
Number of Buses 102
Port Tonnage (in millions) NA
Airports 1
Number of Daily Flights 9
Daily Average Number of Passengers 376

Airlines (American carriers only)
Eastern
USAir
Westair

Housing

Because of a declining population, housing construction has declined since 1990. About one-third of housing units are renter-occupied. The major suburbs are Old Forge, Taylor, Dunmore, Dickson City, Blakely, and Olyphant.

Housing

Total Housing Units 35,357
% Change 1980–1990 -2.3
Vacant Units for Sale or Rent 1,708
Occupied Units 32,637
% with More Than One Person per Room 1.2
% Owner-Occupied 53.7
Median Value of Owner-Occupied Homes $57,100
Average Monthly Purchase Cost $305
Median Monthly Rent $252
New Private Housing Starts 60
Value (in thousands) $3,660
% Single-Family 100
Nonresidential Buildings Value (in thousands) $6,656

Urban Redevelopment

Urban redevelopment programs are coordinated by SLIBCo and MetroAction. SLIBCo was instrumental in building the Office Park at Montage. New corporations expanding into Scranton are JC Penney Telemarketing and Prudential. MetroAction has sponsored a number of restoration projects, including Steamtown USA.

Crime

Scranton is the sixth-safest city in the United States with police reporting 175 violent crimes and 2,546 property crimes.

Crime

Violent Crimes—Total 175
Violent Crime Rate per 100,000 3,174
Murder NA
Rape NA
Robbery NA
Aggravated Assaults NA
Property Crimes 2,546
Burglary NA
Larceny NA
Motor Vehicle Theft NA
Arson NA
Per Capita Police Expenditures $72.31
Per Capita Fire Protection Expenditures $100.68
Number of Police 143
Per 1,000 1.67

Religion

Catholics and Methodists form the most prominent religious groups in the city.

Media

The media consist of *The Scranton Tribune* on weekday mornings, *The Scranton Times* on weekday evenings and Sunday

Religion

Largest Denominations (Adherents)

Catholic	125,510
United Methodist	13,310
Presbyterian	4,776
American Baptist	2,672
Episcopal	2,332
Evangelical Lutheran	1,921
United Church of Christ	2,030
Assembly of God	1,292
Jewish	1,984

Media

Newsprint
    The Scranton Times, daily
    The Scranton Tribune, daily
    The Scrantonian, weekly

Television
    WBRE (Channel 28)
    WOLF (Channel 38)
    WWLF (Channel 56)
    WYOU (Channel 22)

Radio

WBCR (AM)	WCDL (AM)
WEJL (AM)	WEZX (FM)
WGBI (AM)	WGBI (FM)
WICK (AM)	WWDL (FM)
WTSS (AM)	WVMW (FM)

mornings, *The Scrantonian* on Sundays, 4 television stations, and 10 radio stations.

Sports

For Scranton sports fans, 1989 was a big year when the Red Barrons, affiliates of the Philadelphia Phillies, opened their first season at the new Lackawanna County Multipurpose Stadium near Montage. Horse racing, skiing, and auto racing are some of the most popular sports in Lackawanna County and the nearby Poconos.

Arts, Culture, and Tourism

The Masonic Temple's Scottish Rite Cathedral in downtown is home to Community Concerts, the Broadway Theater League, and the Northeast Pennsylvania Philharmonic. The Scranton Public Theater performs at the Lucan Arts Center from fall through spring.

The Everhart Museum at Nay Aug Park was established in 1908. It has an interesting collection of North American birds and mammals, and a collection of paintings, ceramics, glass, lacquer, and ivory as well as Aztec, Pompeian, Indian, and Mexican crafts. To the

rear of the museum is the Brooks Coal Mine. The Marine Corps League Museum presents artifacts dealing with the Marine Corps. The Pennsylvania Anthracite Heritage Museum at McDade Park and Catlin House has exhibits featuring Scranton's great legacy of coal.

Travel and Tourism

Hotel Rooms   7,856
Convention and Exhibit Space (square feet)   NA

Convention Centers
    The Hilton at Lackawanna Station

Festivals
    Fall Arts Festival

Parks and Recreation

The 116-acre Nay Aug Park, between Arthur Avenue and Roaring Brook in East Scranton, has memorials to the pioneers, relics of the city's founding days, a museum, a conservatory, a zoo, a swimming pool, and the attractive Nay Aug Falls, where Philip Abbott erected his gristmill and dam in 1788.

Sources of Further Information

City Hall, Municipal Building
340 North Washington Avenue
Scranton, PA 18503
(717) 348-4113

Greater Scranton Chamber of Commerce
P.O.B. 431
Scranton, PA 18501
(717) 342-7711

Lackawanna Historical Society
232 Monroe Avenue
Scranton, PA 18510
(717) 344-3841

Scranton Public Library
Washington at Vine
Scranton, PA 18503
(717) 348-3000

Additional Reading

Community Profile. Annual.

Seattle

Washington

Basic Data

Name   Seattle
Name Origin   From Indian Chief Seattle
Year Founded   1851 Inc. 1869
Status: State   Washington
     County   Seat of King County
Area (square miles)   83.9
Elevation (feet)   10
Time Zone   Pacific
Population (1990)   516,259
Population of Metro Area (1990)   1,972,961

Sister Cities

  Beersheba, Israel
  Bergen, Norway
  Chongging, China
  Christchurch, New Zealand
  Kobe, Japan
  Galway, Ireland
  Limbe, Cameroon
  Mazatlan, Mexico
  Mombasa, Kenya
  Nantes, France
  Pecs, Hungary
  Reykjavik, Iceland
  Taejon, Korea
  Taskent, Uzbekistan

Distance in Miles To:

Atlanta	2,625
Boston	3,016
Chicago	2,052
Dallas	2,131
Denver	1,341
Detroit	2,327
Houston	2,369
Los Angeles	1,134
Miami	3,303
New York	2,841
Philadelphia	2,816
Washington, DC	2,721

Location and Topography

N

Seattle is located along Elliott Bay, on the east shore of Puget Sound, 128 miles from the Pacific Ocean. Built on seven hills, with intervening lowlands, the city extends from Puget Sound to Lake Washington, which are joined by two canals and Lake Union. The Olympic Mountains lie to the west and the Cascade Mountains to the east.

Layout of City and Suburbs

Seattle is built on many hills. By using pressurized water, the city washed some sections of the hills into Elliott Bay, thus expanding the land area and reducing the height of the hills at the same time. The central business district extends eastward from the bay. The tallest building here is the 76-story Columbia Seafirst Center. The Pike Place Market is a popular shopping area. The Seattle Center, north of the business district, includes buildings from the 1964 Expo Century 21, including the 607-foot Space Needle. The main residential areas are east of Lake Washington and include Bellevue, Kirkland, and Mercer Island. Auburn, Kent, and Renton lie to the south of the city. Within the city, the better residential areas are found in First and Capitol Hills as well as Queen Hill, the highest point north of Smith

Environment

Environmental Stress Index   2.8
Green Cities Index: Rank   24
             Score   25.54
Water Quality   Alkaline, very soft
    Average Daily Use (gallons per capita)   143
    Maximum Supply (gallons per capita)   20
Parkland as % of Total City Area   NA
% Waste Landfilled/Recycled   64:36
Annual Parks Expenditures per Capita $135.27

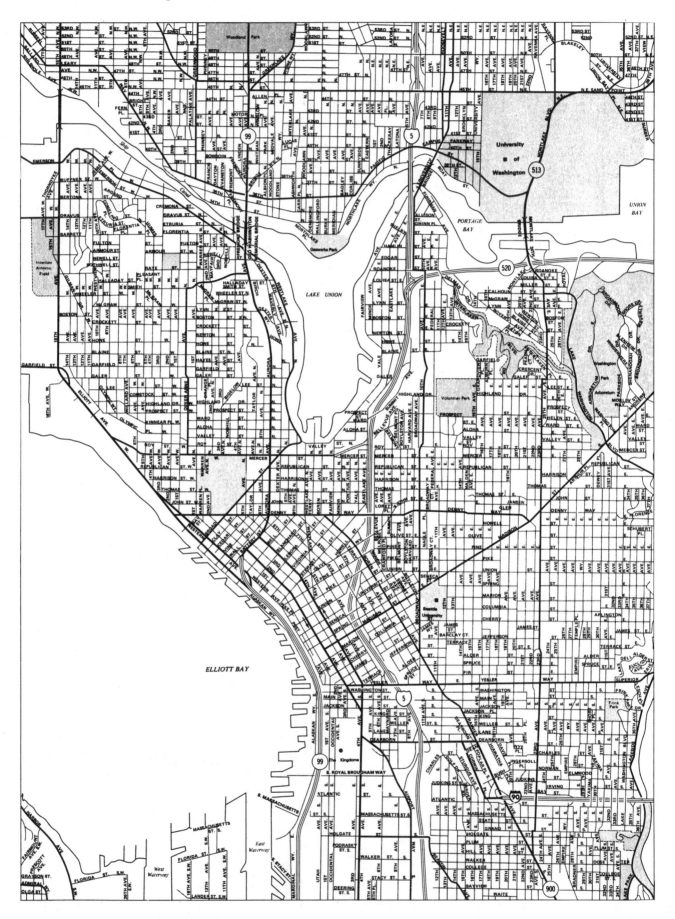

Cove. The city, when viewed from the air, is impressively beautiful. From Smith Cove to the left, north of the metro area, to Alki Point at the right runs a rim of piers, docks, and wharves, broken only to the south by the Duwamish River, which forks around man-made Harbor Island. Along the waterfront is the Alaskan Freeway, a broad commercial avenue.

Climate

Seattle climate combines the best of a maritime climate with that of a mountainous one. Westerly air currents from the ocean and the shielding effects of the Cascade Range produce a mild and moderately moist climate with warm winters and cool summers. Extremes of temperature are rare or of short duration. Occasionally severe winter storms come in from the north, but do not disrupt normal life. Frequent overcast days give the city the reputation for being rainy, but annual precipitation is only 39 inches and the annual snowfall 15 inches.

Weather

Temperature

Highest Monthly Average °F   74.6
Lowest Monthly Average °F   35.9

Annual Averages

Days 32°F or Below   32
Days above 90°F   3
Zero Degree Days   0
Precipitation (inches)   39
Snow (inches)   15
% Seasonal Humidity   74
Wind Speed (m.p.h.)   9.3
Clear Days   57
Cloudy Days   229
Storm Days   7
Rainy Days   160

Average Temperatures (°F)	High	Low	Mean
January	43.4	33.0	38.2
February	48.5	36.0	42.3
March	51.5	36.6	44.1
April	57.0	40.3	48.7
May	64.1	45.6	54.9
June	69.0	50.6	59.8
July	75.1	53.8	64.5
August	73.8	53.7	63.8
September	68.7	50.4	59.6
October	59.4	44.9	52.2
November	50.4	38.8	44.6
December	45.4	35.5	40.5

History

Many Indian tribes, including the Duwamish, Snohomish, and Suquamish, once hunted and fished in what is now Seattle. In 1851 a group of Illinois pioneers led by Arthur A. Denny settled on Alki Point on Puget Sound, moving to Elliott Bay the next year. At first the settlement was named New York in the hope that one day it would rival its namesake on the east coast. By 1852, lumbering had begun but the difficulty in getting the logs on ship convinced the settlers to move up to the present site of the city. The new settlement was named Seattle after the friendly chief of the Duwamish tribe. Other settlers soon arrived: Dr. David S. Maynard, who opened the first store and ventured into salmon fishing, and Thomas Mercer, whose horse and wagon provided the settlements transportation service. In 1853 the plat of the Town of Seattle was filed with the territorial government. Henry Yesler from Portland was given a tract of land to build the first steam sawmill. The Reverend David E. Blaine formed the first church and the next year his wife, Catherine, was appointed teacher in the first school. Hostility from the Klickitat Indians slowed the town's growth. During the Civil War the village was little more than a collection of a few log houses, stores, and sawmills, yet its citizens were able to persuade the territorial government, in 1861, to allow the building of a university, the University of Washington. The first newspaper, the *Seattle Gazette* (now the *Seattle Post-Intelligencer*), appeared in 1863 and Dr. Maynard left his salmon business to open a hospital. In 1864 the telegraph reached Seattle, and the coal mines opened at Coal Creek. The village, like many other frontier settlements, suffered from a shortage of females. Of the 182 residents, 96 were bachelors. To remedy this situation Asa Mercer, the university president, went south and succeeded in persuading Civil War widows and orphan girls to return with him. The so-called Mercer Girls, who were eagerly welcomed by the town's bachelors, helped to increase the town's population. The town was reincorporated by court order in 1869. Next year the census showed it had a population of 1,107. The town held its first elections to choose a mayor, and the first bank opened its doors. Seattle lost out to Tacoma as the terminus of the Great Northern Railroad, and to compensate for that loss the city organized the Seattle and Walla Walla Railroad and Construction Company to build a line over Snoqualmie Pass. In 1875 regular steamship services began with San Francisco. The town became so prosperous that two opera houses were built: Watson C. Squire in 1879 and Frye in 1880. In 1883 Seattle was linked with the Puyallup Valley by the Columbia and Puget Sound Railroad. As in tacoma, there was popular agitation against the employment of cheap Chinese coolie labor. When mobs tried to deport the Chinese forcibly, martial law was declared until the violence subsided. In 1888 the first public library was established. Toward the end of the 1880s, horse-drawn streetcars were replaced by cable cars, and electric lighting was introduced. In 1889 a great fire broke out at First Avenue and Madison Street and soon spread, destroying over 50 blocks. Within the next few years the entire business district was rebuilt. In 1893 the Great Northern Railroad entered Seattle from Everett. In 1894 the university moved from its downtown location to the shores of Lake Washington. The depression of 1893 caused a slump in the city's lumber and shipping industries, but within four years the discovery of gold in Alaska helped it to enter another growth trajectory. Seattle became the supply

Chronology

1851 A group of pioneers, led by Arthur A. Denny, sail into Elliott Bay and build a cabin on the south headland. Other members of their families, 12 adults and 12 children, join them in a settlement called New York. Difficulties in loading and unloading ships force them to move up to the present site, which they name Seattle after the Duwamish Indian chief.

1852 Plat of the Town of Seattle is filed with the territorial government at Olympia. Henry Yesler from Portland is given land to erect first steam sawmill on Puget Sound.

1853 First shipment to China is a cargo of ship spars. First church is organized by the Reverend David E. Blaine.

1854 First school opens.

1856 First and last Indian attack on Seattle settlers is repulsed.

1861 University of Washington is founded, with Asa Mercer as instructor.

1863 The first newspaper, *Gazette*, debuts.

1864 Coal mines open at Coal Creek. Asa Mercer recruits southern girls for the town's bachelors.

1869 Seattle is reincorporated.

1870 Seattle elects first mayor, Henry A. Atkins. First bank opens doors. Central School opens.

1873 Failing to be named terminus of the Northern Pacific Railroad, Seattle organizes Seattle and Walla Walla Railroad.

1874 Gas streetlights are installed.

1875 Regular steamship service begins between Seattle and San Francisco.

1879 Watson C. Squire Opera House opens.

1880 Frye Opera House opens.

1883 Seattle and Puyallup Valley are linked by the Columbia and Puget Sound Railroad.

1888 First public library is established. Cable cars are introduced.

1889 Fire destroys 50 blocks of the business district.

1893 Depression causes slump in lumber and shipping.

1894 University of Washington moves from downtown to new site on shores of Lake Washington.

1897 News of gold strike in Alaska spurs boom as Seattle becomes the Gateway to the Klondike.

1903 Symphony Orchestra holds first concert.

1907 West Seattle, Ballard, and Columbia City are annexed.

1909 Alaska-Yukon-Pacific Exposition draws 3.75 million people.

1910 Georgetown is annexed.

1916 Boeing Aircraft Company is founded.

1918 City acquires control of the upper waters of the Skagit River.

1919 Sixty thousand workers stage five-day general strike, the nation's first.

1962 Seattle holds World's Fair Century 21 Exposition

1985 Columbia Seafirst Center is completed.

center and point of departure for gold seekers, and Seattle interests controlled 95% of the Alaskan trade. The census of 1900 gave the city a population of 80,671, double that of 1890. In the same year the first horseless carriage appeared. The method of sluicing employed in Alaskan mining to remove hills caught the imagination of Seattle engineers. Soon Jackson Street and Dearborn Street hills and part of Denny Hill were washed away to fill in 1,400 acres of Elliott Bay. During the next 30 years 41.5 million cubic yards of dirt were thus dumped into the bay. The cultural life in Seattle began to reflect its new prosperity. The public library was enlarged and the first symphony orchestra was organized. The Alaska-Yukon Exposition of 1909 drew 3.75 million. The city limits were extended to include West Seattle, Ballard, Columbia City, and Georgetown. Another transcontinental railroad, the Chicago, Milwaukee, and St. Paul, arrived in 1909 followed by the Union Pacific in 1910, and both lines began running out of the newly built Union Station. The Duwamish River Channel was dredged to accommodate oceangoing ships, and the Sound-to-Lake Washington Canal was dug in 1911–1916. World War I carried the industrial boom to its peak with the shipyards working double time. In 1918 the city acquired control of the upper waters of the Skagit River in order to develop its hydroelectric potential. The end of the war was followed by a collapse of the lumber market and the closing of the war industries. Unemployment led to labor unrest, culminating in a five-day general strike, the first in the United States. Seattle returned to prosperity during World War II, and the Boeing Company, established in 1916, became the driving force of the economy. In 1962 Seattle hosted the World's Fair, Century 21, and it helped to define the future of the city as one of the primary urban centers on the Pacific Rim.

Historical Landmarks

Pioneer Square on First Avenue and Yesler Way is the site of Yesler's Mill, where the social life of Seattle centered in the early days. It includes the original Skid Road as well as the five-block underground city left standing after the 1889 fire. The Pike Place Public Market at First Avenue and Pike Street, extending three blocks to the north and two blocks to the west, is one of the few remaining authentic farmers markets. The Chief Seattle Monument in the center of Denny Place is a bronze statue of the Indian chief with hands outstretched in a gesture of peace and friendship. Fort Lawton is a 640-acre army reservation off Magnolia Bluff overlooking Puget Sound; established in 1897, it was named for Major General Henry W. Lawton, an American officer killed in the Philippines. Alki Point on the beach front at Alki and 59th avenues is the site of the first Seattle settlement. A more recent landmark is the 605-foot Space Needle, constructed for the 1962 World's Fair.

Population

After peaking at 530,831 in 1970, Seattle's population declined by 7% in the 1970s to 493,846, reflecting the troubles of Boeing during this decade. As the sales of aircraft rebounded, so did the population, gaining by 4.5% to reach 516,259.

Population

	1980	1990
Central City	493,846	516,259
Rank	23	21
Metro Area	1,607,618	1,972,961
Pop. Change 1980–1990	+22,413	
Pop. % Change 1980–1990	+4.5	
Median Age	34.9	
% Male	48.8	
% Age 65 and Over	15.2	
Density (per square mile)	6,153	

Households

Number	236,702
Persons per Household	2.09
% Female-Headed Households	9.0
% One-Person Households	39.8
Births—Total	6,685
% to Mothers under 20	8.9
Birth Rate per 1,000	13.7

Ethnic Composition

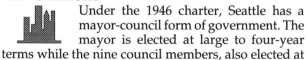

Whites make up 75.3%, Asians and Pacific Islanders 11.8%, blacks 10.1%, Hispanics 3.5%, American Indians 1.4%, and others 1.4%.

Government

Under the 1946 charter, Seattle has a mayor-council form of government. The mayor is elected at large to four-year terms while the nine council members, also elected at large, serve staggered four-year terms.

Ethnic Composition (as % of total pop.)

	1980	1990
White	79.53	75.32
Black	9.47	10.06
American Indian	1.27	1.42
Asian and Pacific Islander	7.41	11.78
Hispanic	2.56	3.55
Other	NA	1.42

Government

Year of Home Charter	1946
Number of Members of the Governing Body	9
Elected at Large	9
Elected by Wards	NA
Number of Women in Governing Body	4
Salary of Mayor	$95,398
Salary of Council Members	$63,892
City Government Employment Total	10,001
Rate per 10,000	205.7

Public Finance

The annual budget consists of revenues of $1.011 billion and expenditures of $944.949 million. The debt outstanding is $903.878 million and cash and security holdings are $854.712 million.

Public Finance

Total Revenue (in millions)	$1,011.299
Intergovernmental Revenue—Total (in millions)	$93.33
Federal Revenue per Capita	$27.16
% Federal Assistance	2.68
% State Assistance	5.76
Sales Tax as % of Total Revenue	13.94
Local Revenue as % of Total Revenue	53.85
City Income Tax	no
Taxes—Total (in millions)	$213.6

Taxes per Capita
Total	$439
Property	$131
Sales and Gross Receipts	$205
General Expenditures—Total (in millions)	$379.5
General Expenditures per Capita	$781
Capital Outlays per Capita	$67

% of Expenditures for:
Public Welfare	0.0
Highways	3.9
Education	0.0
Health and Hospitals	1.0
Police	14.6
Sewerage and Sanitation	13.3
Parks and Recreation	13.1
Housing and Community Development	4.3
Debt Outstanding per Capita	$1,310
% Utility	61.0
Federal Procurement Contract Awards (in millions)	$1,863.8
Federal Grants Awards (in millions)	$300.2
Fiscal Year Begins	January 1

Economy

Seattle is so often associated with Boeing that the city's other thriving sectors are often overlooked. These sectors, fundamental to the city's economy, are the Port of Seattle, lumber, food processing, computer software (led by Microsoft), and other advanced technology. Seattle competes with Los Angeles, San Francisco, and Vancouver for trans-Pacific maritime trade. Tourism is a staple revenue-earner. Seattle is the major supplier of food products to Alaska and a major distributor of Alaskan products, especially canned salmon. Seattle's own large fishing fleet is noted for its halibut catch. Shipbuilding, a huge industry during World Wars I and II, is now limited to fishing boats, barges, and pleasure craft.

Economy

Total Money Income (in millions) $6,281.2
% of State Average   118.9
Per Capita Annual Income $12,919
% Population below Poverty Level   11.2
Fortune 500 Companies   2

Banks	Number	Deposits (in millions)
Commercial	30	13,009
Savings	30	8,284

Passenger Autos   979,608
Electric Meters   281,893
Gas Meters   193,989

Manufacturing

Number of Establishments   1,261
% with 20 or More Employees   27.8
Manufacturing Payroll (in millions) $902.5
Value Added by Manufacture (in millions) $1,852.2
Value of Shipments (in millions) $3,726.0
New Capital Expenditures (in millions) $85.6

Wholesale Trade

Number of Establishments   2,004
Sales (in millions) $13,085.1
Annual Payroll (in millions) $645.317

Retail Trade

Number of Establishments   5,834
Total Sales (in millions) $3,976.3
Sales per Capita $8,178
Number of Retail Trade Establishments with Payroll   4,076
Annual Payroll (in millions) $558.7
Total Sales (in millions) $3,898.6
General Merchandise Stores (per capita) $1,008
Food Stores (per capita) $1,510
Apparel Stores (per capita) $686
Eating and Drinking Places (per capita) $1,158

Service Industries

Total Establishments   6,533
Total Receipts (in millions) $3,415.7
Hotels and Motels (in millions) $181.5
Health Services (in millions) $553.3
Legal Services (in millions) $588.7

Labor

Boeing is the largest employer and has more employees than the other 1,261 manufacturers in the area. The Seattle employment market is thus extremely sensitive to Boeing's fortunes and to the market demands for aircraft worldwide. Since the end of the 1980s, this demand has been very strong, and there is a backlog of orders that will keep Seattle buoyant well into 2000. Weyerhauser is another large employer, and it has weathered the assaults of environmentalists on its tree-cutting programs.

Labor

Civilian Labor Force   349,689
% Change 1989–1990   1.7

Work Force Distribution
   Mining   600
   Construction   59,400
   Manufacturing   216,800
   Transportation and Public Utilities   68,300
   Wholesale and Retail Trade   262,900
   FIRE (Finance, Insurance, Real Estate)   72,200
   Service   278,700
   Government   152,100
   Women as % of Labor Force   45.5
   % Self-Employed   6.3
   % Professional/Technical   21.5
Total Unemployment   12,965
Rate %   3.7
Federal Government Civilian Employment   15,521

Education

Seattle School District is the largest in the state, supporting 108 elementary, junior high/middle, and senior high schools. About 15,000 students attend 70 private and parochial schools, many of them nationally known, such as Helen Bush-Parkside School, St. Nicholas School, Forest Ridge Convent, Holy Names Academy, Lakeside School, and St. Joseph's School. The University of Washington, which opened just 10 years after the city was founded, occupies a 640-acre campus overlooking Lake Washington and Lake Union. The Roman Catholic Seattle University, founded in 1892, and the Free Methodist Seattle Pacific University, founded in 1893, are also in the city.

Education

Number of Public Schools   108
Special Education Schools   6
Total Enrollment   40,917
% Enrollment in Private Schools   11.1
% Minority   56.5
Classroom Teachers   2,221
Pupil-Teacher Ratio   18.4:1
Number of Graduates   NA
Total Revenue (in millions) $232.458
Total Expenditures (in millions) $227.573
Expenditures per Pupil $4,531
Educational Attainment (Age 25 and Over)
   % Completed 12 or More Years   79.7
   % Completed 16 or More Years   28.1
Four-Year Colleges and Universities   5
   Enrollment   40,874
Two-Year Colleges   5
   Enrollment   18,331

Libraries

Number   94
Public Libraries   17
Books (in thousands)   1,884
Circulation (in thousands)   576
Persons Served (in thousands)   516

Health

Seattle has 19 hospitals with over 4,000 beds. The largest facilities are the University Hospital, Swedish Hospital, Virginia Mason Medical Center, Providence Medical Center, Children's Orthopedic Hospital, and Group Health Cooperative, the nation's largest cooperative health-care organization.

Health

Deaths—Total   5,225
Rate per 1,000   10.7
Infant Deaths—Total   81
Rate per 1,000   12.1
Number of Metro Hospitals   19
Number of Metro Hospital Beds   4,205
Rate per 100,000   865
Number of Physicians   4,579
Physicians per 1,000   3.0
Nurses per 1,000   8.89
Health Expenditures per Capita $22.11

Transportation

Seattle is approached by two interstates: the north-south I-5, connecting the West Coast cities, and the east-west I-90. Seattle is also on U.S. Highway 99 and U.S. Highway 10, the latter entering the city from the east across the Lake

Transportation

Interstate Highway Mileage   107
Total Urban Mileage   6,707
Total Daily Vehicle Mileage (in millions) $43.098
Daily Average Commute Time   50.8
Number of Buses   1,248
Port Tonnage (in millions) $18.645
Airports   2
Number of Daily Flights   319
Daily Average Number of Passengers   19,346

Airlines (American carriers only)
  Alaska
  American
  American West
  Continental
  Delta
  Eastern
  Hawaiian
  Horizon
  Northwest
  Trans World
  United
  USAir

Washington Floating Bridge, erected in 1940. The bridge, spanning the lake on floating pontoons, is an outstanding engineering feat. The Washington State Ferries, the world's most extensive automobile ferry system, connects Seattle with the Olympic Peninsula, several islands in Puget Sound, and the city of Victoria, British Columbia. Seattle is the southern terminus of the Alaska Marine Highway system. Rail passenger service is provided by Amtrak, which runs four trains daily, and rail freight service by Burlington Northern. The Port of Seattle handles about 9 million tons of cargo yearly, mainly to Alaska and the Far East. Seattle is about 1,500 miles closer to Far Eastern ports than San Francisco or Los Angeles. The principal air terminal is the Seattle-Tacoma International Airport, served by 29 airlines.

Housing

A characteristic architecture of generous picture windows and sundecks has developed in Seattle, with many houses built on hills overlooking Puget Sound, Lake Union, and Lake Washington. There are also over 400 houseboats on the lakes. Over the years the typical Seattle houseboat has evolved from a one-room barn floating on logs into a multiroom house suppported by styrofoam floats, complete with fireplace and sundeck. Clusters of houseboats are moored to walkways running out into Lake Union and Portage Bay. Exclusive residential areas are found on Mercer Island. Of the total housing stock, 48.9% is owner-occupied. The median value of an owner-occupied home is $137,900 and the median monthly rent $425.

Housing

Total Housing Units   249,032
% Change 1980–1990   7.6
Vacant Units for Sale or Rent   9,058
Occupied Units   236,702
% with More Than One Person per Room   4.0
% Owner-Occupied   48.9
Median Value of Owner-Occupied Homes $137,900
Average Monthly Purchase Cost $331
Median Monthly Rent $425
New Private Housing Starts   3,162
Value (in thousands) $228,135
% Single-Family   18.5
Nonresidential Buildings Value (in thousands) $144,807

Tallest Buildings	Hgt. (ft.)	Stories
Columbia Seafirst Center (1985)	954	76
Two Union Square (1989)	740	56
Washington Mutual Tower (1988)	730	55
AT&T Gateway Tower (1990)	722	62
1001 4th Pl. (1969)	609	50
Space Needle (1962)	605	NA
Pacific First Center (1989)	580	44
First Interstate Center (1983)	574	48

Urban Redevelopment

Recent civic projects have included the King Dome in downtown Seattle, completed in 1976. In 1985 the 76-story Columbia Seafirst Center was completed. In 1988 the Washington State Convention and Trade Center opened. Urban development projects are coordinated by the Downtown Seattle Development Association.

Crime

Seattle ranks below the national average in public safety. Violent crimes known to police in 1991 numbered 468 and property crimes numbered 7,156.

Crime

Violent Crimes—Total 7,221
Violent Crime Rate per 100,000 596.4
Murder 43
Rape 398
Robbery 2,761
Aggravated Assaults 4,019
Property Crimes 57,987
Burglary 10,639
Larceny 40,502
Motor Vehicle Theft 6,846
Arson 285
Per Capita Police Expenditures $140.64
Per Capita Fire Protection Expenditures $96.13
Number of Police 1,039
Per 1,000 2.10

Religion

Catholics make up the largest population, followed by Lutherans, Mormons, Presbyterians, and Jews. St. James Cathedral on Ninth Avenue, built in 1907, is the seat of the Roman Catholic archdiocese, and St. Marks Cathedral on Tenth Avenue is the seat of the Episcopal dicocese.

Religion

Largest Denominations (Adherents)
Catholic	211,528
Assembly of God	18,586
Latter-Day Saints	38,195
Evangelical Lutheran	38,704
Presbyterian	25,101
Episcopal	17,552
United Methodist	21,564
Black Baptist	19,906
Southern Baptist	11,334
Jewish	21,975

Media

Seattle press consists of two dailies: *Seattle Times* and the *Seattle Post-Intelligencer.* The electronic media consist of 7 television stations and 34 AM and FM radio stations.

Sports

Seattle supports professional teams in all major sports: Seattle Seahawks in football, Seattle Mariners in baseball, SuperSonics in basketball, and Seattle Breakers in hockey. The Seahawks and Mariners play home games

Media

Newsprint
  Argus Weekend, weekly
  Seattle Post-Intelligencer, daily
  Seattle Times, daily
  Fact News, weekly
  Highline Times, 3x/wk
Television
  KBGE (Channel 33)
  KCTS (Channel 9)
  KCWT (Channel 27)
  KING (Channel 5)
  KIRO (Channel 7)
  KOMO (Channel 4)
  KTZZ (Channel 22)
Radio
KBLE (AM)	KBRD (FM)
KBSG (AM)	KBSG (FM)
KCIS (AM)	KCMU (FM)
KCMS (FM)	KEZX (FM)
KING (AM)	KING (FM)
KIRO (AM)	KISW (FM)
KIXI (AM)	KJR (AM)
KLTX (FM)	KKFX (AM)
KKNW (FM)	KMGI (FM)
KMPS (AM)	KMPS (FM)
KMTT (FM)	KNHC (FM)
KOMO (AM)	KPLC (FM)
KRIZ (AM)	KSER (FM)
KTAC (AM)	KUBE (FM)
KUOW (FM)	KVI (AM)
KWMX (FM)	KXRX (FM)
KZOK (AM)	KZOK (FM)

in the King Dome, the SuperSonics in Seattle Center Coliseum, and the Seattle Breakers in Seattle Center Arena.

Arts, Culture, and Tourism

The Seattle Center is the headquarters of many major performing arts organizations. The Seattle Opera Association is based in the 3,100-seat Opera House, staging five operas between September and May. Wagner's *Ring Cycle* is performed annually. The Opera House is also home to the Pacific Northwest Ballet and Seattle Symphony. Other music groups include Northwest Chamber Orchestra, Olympic Youth Symphonies, Thalia Symphony, and Chamber Symphony. Dance is represented by the Cornish Dance Theater and the Seahurst Ballet. The number of equity theaters in Seattle is exceeded only by that of New York. One of the most outstanding is Seattle Repertory Company, which stages its productions at the Bagley Wright Theater. Visiting Broadway plays are staged at Fifth Avenue Theater, a historic landmark. Live theater is represented by ACT (A Contemporary Theater), Empty Space, Intiman, Seattle Group Theater, Seattle Gilbert and Sullivan Society, Seattle Mime Theater, Children's Theater, and Bathhouse Theater.

Seattle has over 20 major museums. Among the larger general ones are the Seattle Art Museum, which opened in a new facility in 1990; the Charles and Emma Frye Art Museum; the Henry Art Gallery at the University of Washington, the oldest museum in the state; and the Bellevue Art Museum in Bellevue Square. Specialized museums include Center for Wooden Boats, King Dome Sports Museum, Museum of Flight, Museum of History and Industry, Nordic Heritage Museum, Pacific Arts Center, Pacific Science Center, Seattle Children's Museum, Shoreline Historical Museum, Thomas Burke Memorial Washington State Museum, and Suquamish Museum.

Travel and Tourism

Hotel Rooms 20,191
Convention and Exhibit Space (square feet) 102,000

Convention Centers
  Seattle Center
  King Dome

Festivals
  Northwest Regional Folklife Festival (May)
  Seafair (July-August)
  Pacific Northwest Wagner Festival (July-August)
  Seattle Arts Festival (Labor Day)

Parks and Recreation

 Seattle's 140 parks cover 3,800 acres. The 107-acre Lincoln Park on Puget Sound is a wooded saltwater recreational area. Seward Park on Lake Washington Boulevard was once an island. A Japanese *torii* forms the Gateway of Welcome. Volunteer Park on East Prospect to East Galer streets includes a statue of William Henry Seward and an observation tower. The 188-acre Woodland Park, flanked by Phinney Avenue, 50th Street, 59th Street, and Greenlake Way is the largest of Seattle's parks. It includes the War Garden, Rose Gardens, Harding Memorial, and the Zoological Gardens. Denny Park at the intersection of Battery Street, Denny Way, and Dexter Avenue is on the site of the city's first park donated in 1884 by David Denny. Other popular city parks include Golden Gardens Park, Discovery Park, Klondike Gold Rush National Historical Park, Magnuson Park, Washington Park, and Glen Lake Park.

Sources of Further Information

City Hall
600 Fourth Avenue
Seattle, WA 98104-1873
(206) 684-4000

Greater Seattle Chamber of Commerce
1200 One Union Square
Sixth and University streets
Seattle, WA 98101
(206) 447-7200

Seattle/King County Convention and Visitors
  Bureau
1815 Seventh Avenue
Seattle, WA 98101
(206) 447-4200

Additional Reading

Andrews, Mildred. *Seattle Women: A Legacy of Community Development.* 1984.
Binns, Archie. *The Northwest Gateway: The Story of the Port of Seattle.* 1949.
Brambilla, Roberto, and Gianni Longo. *Learning from Seattle.* 1980.
Buerge, David, and Stuart R. Grover. *Seattle in the Eighteen Eighties.* 1986.
Daniel, Jack. *Seattle: World Class City.* 1991.
Dorpat, Paul. *Seattle: Now and Then.* 1984.
Kriesman, Lawrence. *Historic Preservation in Seattle.* 1985.
McIntyre, Cindy. *Seattle, Tacoma and Puget Sound Region.* 1988.
Morgan, Murray. *Skid Road: An Informal Portrait of Seattle.* 1982.
Morrow, Theresa. *Seattle Survival Guide.* 1990.
Rapp, James M. *Art in Seattle's Public Places: An Illustrated Guide.* 1991.
Satterfield, Archie. *Seattle Guidebook.* 1989.
Sayre, J. Willis. *Early Waterfront of Seattle.* 1982.
Warren, James R. *A Century of Seattle's Business.* 1989.
Warren, James R., and William R. McCoy. *Highlights of Seattle's History.* 1989.

Sioux Falls
South Dakota

Location and Topography

N

Sioux Falls is located in the Big Sioux River Valley in southeast South Dakota. The natural beauty of the city contrasts with the rather monotonous plains of the surrounding country. The nearest hills are approximately 100 miles to the northeast and the south.

Layout of City and Suburbs

The Big Sioux River, called The Thick-Wooded River by early settlers, and Wakpa-Ipaktan or the Winding River by American Indians, meanders in the form of a gigantic "S" through the center of the city. The business section follows the river flats, from which the residential districts rise up in a gradual slope. The landscape is dominated by the State Penitentiary on the northern hills, and the twin spires of the St. Joseph's Cathedral to the west. The river itself dominates the city as it tumbles and roars over a series of cascades. The city has acquired a red hue over

the years from the quartzite, great deposits of which underlie the city. Almost all the big buildings are built of this stone. The residential districts are spacious with great trees and attractive gardens.

Environment

Environmental Stress Index   3.4
Green Cities Index: Rank   NA
                    Score   NA
Water Quality   Alkaline, hard, fluoridated
Average Daily Use (gallons per capita)   NA
    Maximum Supply (gallons per capita)   NA
Parkland as % of Total City Area   5.5
% Waste Landfilled/Recycled   NA
Annual Parks Expenditures per Capita $49.01

Climate

Sioux Falls has a continental climate with frequent weather variations as differing air masses move into the area. During the late fall and winter strong winds cause the temperature to abruptly drop, but cold spells are generally short. Typically the city receives one or two heavy snowfalls each year, comprising most of the annual 39 inches of snow. Thunderstorms are common in late spring and summer, and tornadoes in July. Flooding from the spring runoff has been a major problem in the past.

Weather

Temperature

Highest Monthly Average °F   86.2
Lowest Monthly Average °F   1.9

Annual Averages

Days 32°F or Below   171
Days above 90°F   28

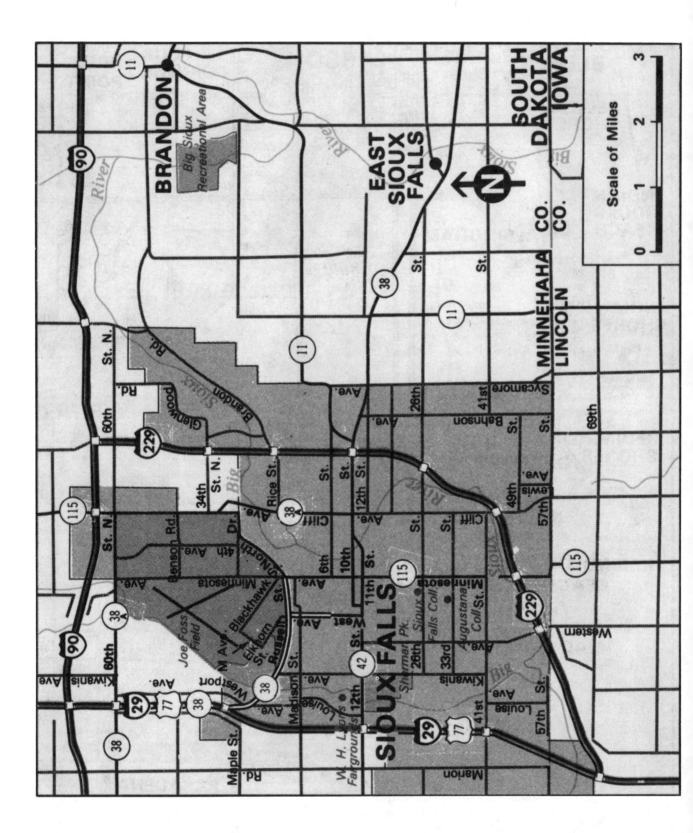

Weather (continued)

Zero Degree Days 33
Precipitation (inches) 25
Snow (inches) 39.0
% Seasonal Humidity 69
Wind Speed (m.p.h.) 11.2
Clear Days 105
Cloudy Days 155
Storm Days 43
Rainy Days 93

Average Temperatures (°F)	*High*	*Low*	*Mean*
January	24.6	3.7	14.2
February	29.7	9.0	19.4
March	39.7	20.2	30.0
April	57.8	34.4	46.1
May	69.7	45.7	57.7
June	78.9	56.3	67.6
July	85.1	61.5	73.3
August	83.8	59.8	71.8
September	73.0	48.7	60.9
October	62.7	37.6	50.2
November	43.5	22.7	33.1
December	29.6	10.4	20.0

History

The history of white settlement in Sioux Falls began with Jean Nicollet, an agent of the Canadian government, who in 1839 visited the area and published a report. A copy of this book fell into the hands of Dr. George M. Staples of Dubuque, Iowa, who in 1856 organized the Western Land Company to scout for a town site near the falls of the Big Sioux River.

He followed the east bank of the river from Sioux City and took possession of the site. Meanwhile, the Legislature of Minnesota Territory also became interested in the venture. In 1856–1857 it chartered the Dakota Land Company to establish a city at Sioux Falls. For a while both the Western Land Company and the Dakota Land Company had agents in the settlement and, although rivals, they lived amicably, fearing only their common enemy, the Sioux. When threatened by the Indians, the settlers would withdraw discreetly, but return when the danger was over. In 1857 a sawmill was built along with a stone house and a store. By 1858 there were 35 inhabitants in the well-fortified settlement. In the same year the territory's first newspaper, *The Democrat*, appeared using an old Smith printing press from St. Paul. The first elections were held to select members of a territorial legislature. Soon afterwards, the legislature was convened and a governor and a speaker were chosen. In 1862 the Sioux rose against the settlers and some were killed, while others were forced to flee. The Sioux destroyed everything, setting fire to the buildings and throwing the printing press into the river. (The press was retrieved later and is now on display at the Pettigrew Museum and Minnesota Historical Society.) For nearly three years the Sioux Valley remained abandoned. On 1 May 1865, a military post, Fort Dakota, was established on what is now Phillip's Avenue, between Seventh and Eighth streets. Gradually the settlers returned and a town took shape around the fort. In 1868 the Minnehaha County was reorganized and a post office was established. In 1870 the military reservation was vacated. The settlement received a boost when the power of the falls was harnessed in 1873. In 1871 the first church opened its doors and the first public school two years later. Surviving a scourge of grasshoppers in 1874, the population grew to 600. Incorporation as a town followed in 1877 and as city in 1883. The first railroad came into town in 1878 and street lampposts were erected. In the last decades of the 19th century, the city prospered as new immigrants came to develop the city's resources. Two church-related schools were founded during this period to serve the educational needs of the frontier community: Augustana College, founded by the Lutherans in 1860, and the Sioux Falls College, founded by the Baptists in 1883. During World War II Sioux Falls was the site of the Air Force Radio Technical School.

Historical Landmarks

The Minnehaha County Courthouse on Main Avenue was built in 1890 and is a good example of the Romanesque style of architecture. The State Penitentiary on Main Avenue is one of the most imposing buildings in the city. Among the churches, the most notable are the Episcopal Calvary Cathedral on Main Avenue, completed in 1889 with funds from John Jacob Astor, and the Catholic St. Joseph Cathedral on Duluth Avenue, built in 1918. The Memorial to the Pioneers at the junction of North Drive and North Cliff Avenue marks the spot where pioneers from Iowa first saw the falls from the Sioux.

Population

For the first time Sioux Falls joined the Census Bureau's list of cities with over 100,000 inhabitants. Its 1990 population of 100,814 registered a 23.9% increase over 1980.

Population	1980	1990
Central City	81,343	100,814
Rank	NA	192
Metro Area	109,435	123,809
Pop. Change 1980–1990 +19,471		
Pop. % Change 1980–1990 +23.9		
Median Age 31.3		
% Male 47.6		
% Age 65 and Over 11.7		
Density (per square mile) 2,230		

Households

Number 39,790
Persons per Household 2.43
% Female-Headed Households 9.4
% One-Person Households 28.7
Births—Total 1,599
  % to Mothers under 20 8.5
  Birth Rate per 1,000 18.2

Ethnic Composition

Sioux Falls is 96.8% white, 0.7% black, 1.6% American Indian, 0.7% Asian or Pacific Islander, 0.6% Hispanic, and 0.2% other.

Chronology

1856 George M. Staples of Dubuque organizes the Western Town Company to establish a settlement on the Big Sioux River falls. Dakota Land Company is authorized by the Legislature of the Minnesota Territory for the same purpose. Indians threaten the settlements of the two companies, forcing the settlers to leave.

1857 A new settlement is made by the two companies. Settlers build a sawmill, stone house, and store.

1858 Settlers hold an election to select members of the Territorial Legislature.

1859 *The Democrat*, the first newspaper, appears.

1860 Augustana College opens.

1862 Indians attack the settlement, burning the buildings and throwing the newspaper press into the river. Settlers flee.

1865 A military post, Fort Dakota, is established to safeguard a new effort to settle the Sioux Valley.

1868 The first post office opens for business.

1870 The military reservation is vacated as the population grows.

1871 The first church is organized.

1873 The first public school begins holding classes. A gristmill is built using the power of the falls.

1874 A grasshopper plague forces many inhabitants to leave town.

1877 Sioux Falls is incorporated as a town.

1878 The first railroad reaches the town.

1883 Street lighting, using kerosene lamps, is introduced. Sioux Falls College opens.

1884 Sioux Falls is incorporated as a city.

1942 War Department builds Air Force Technical Radio School.

Ethnic Composition (as % of total pop.)

	1980	1990
White	97.68	96.84
Black	0.31	0.73
American Indian	1.19	1.56
Asian and Pacific Islander	0.38	0.68
Hispanic	0.46	0.57
Other	NA	0.19

Government

Sioux Falls operates under a mayor and a commission of four members, all of them elected to five-year terms.

Government

Year of Home Charter   NA
Number of Members of the Governing Body   5
Elected at Large   5
Elected by Wards   NA
Number of Women in Governing Body   2
Salary of Mayor $42,804.10
Salary of Council Members $41,729.20
City Government Employment Total   928
Rate per 10,000   95.1

Public Finance

The annual budget consists of revenues of $85.892 million and expenditures of $77.282 million. The debt outstanding is $61.392 million and cash and security holdings $132.913 million. South Dakota does not have a personal property, corporate income, or inventory tax.

Public Finance

Total Revenue (in millions) $85.892
Intergovernmental Revenue—Total (in millions) $5.6
Federal Revenue per Capita $3.05
% Federal Assistance   3.55
% State Assistance   2.96
Sales Tax as % of Total Revenue   29.05
Local Revenue as % of Total Revenue   71.85
City Income Tax   no
Taxes—Total (in millions) $28.5

Taxes per Capita
   Total $292
   Property $129
   Sales and Gross Receipts $153
General Expenditures—Total (in millions) $46.0
General Expenditures per Capita $472
Capital Outlays per Capita $183

% of Expenditures for:
   Public Welfare   0.1
   Highways   16.1
   Education   0.0
   Health and Hospitals   2.1
   Police   8.7
   Sewerage and Sanitation   27.4
   Parks and Recreation   10.6
   Housing and Community Development   2.8
Debt Outstanding per Capita $215
   % Utility   0.0
Federal Procurement Contract Awards (in millions) $11.4
Federal Grants Awards (in millions) $6.1
Fiscal Year Begins   January 1

Economy

Set in one of the most fertile agricultural regions in the nation, Sioux Falls has historically been a leader in farm-related manufacturing and trade, including dairy and bakery items, livestock feed milling, and farm implements and equipment. It is also the home of some of the largest stockyards in the Midwest, such as that of John Morrell and Company. The medical industry has made considerable strides in recent years and its top two hospitals are among the largest employers in the metro area. The most spectacular growth has been in the financial sector. The credit card and financial operations of Citibank (South Dakota), First City Bank of Houston, Dial Bank, and Sears Payment Systems are located in Sioux Falls.

Economy

Total Money Income (in millions) $1,122.6
% of State Average   134.5
Per Capita Annual Income $11,508
% Population below Poverty Level   8.6
Fortune 500 Companies   NA

Banks	Number	Deposits (in millions)
Commercial	8	1,833.8
Savings	5	360.5

Passenger Autos   111,652
Electric Meters   43,700
Gas Meters   32,186

Manufacturing

Number of Establishments   112
% with 20 or More Employees   38.4
Manufacturing Payroll (in millions) $156.7
Value Added by Manufacture (in millions) $444.7
Value of Shipments (in millions) $1,462.7
New Capital Expenditures (in millions) $19.8

Wholesale Trade

Number of Establishments   321
Sales (in millions) $1,354.1
Annual Payroll (in millions) $79.171

Retail Trade

Number of Establishments   1,069
Total Sales (in millions) $879.5
Sales per Capita $9,016
Number of Retail Trade Establishments with Payroll   768
Annual Payroll (in millions) $102.0
Total Sales (in millions) $869.9
General Merchandise Stores (per capita)   NA
Food Stores (per capita) $1,518
Apparel Stores (per capita) $423
Eating and Drinking Places (per capita) $882

Service Industries

Total Establishments   843
Total Receipts (in millions) $328.1
Hotels and Motels (in millions)   NA
Health Services (in millions) $131.1
Legal Services (in millions) $21.1

Labor

 Sioux Falls has one of the lowest unemployment rates in the country. Manufacturing is a relatively smaller sector than in older industrialized areas, accounting for only 12% of employment. Services and trade form the first and second ranking sectors. The three largest employers are John Morrell and Company, Citibank (South Dakota), and Sioux Valley Hospital.

Labor

Civilian Labor Force   57,863
% Change 1989–1990   0.8

Work Force Distribution
  Mining   NA
  Construction   3,700
  Manufacturing   9,600
  Transportation and Public Utilities   5,000
  Wholesale and Retail Trade   22,000
  FIRE (Finance, Insurance, Real Estate)   8,200
  Service   21,800
  Government   7,900
  Women as % of Labor Force   46.2
  % Self-Employed   5.9
  % Professional/Technical   15.3
Total Unemployment   1,601
  Rate %   2.8
Federal Government Civilian Employment   1,780

Education

The Sioux Falls Public School System, the largest in the state, supports 35 elementary, junior high, and senior high schools, as well as 2 special education facilities. The two largest institutions of higher education are both church-related: Augustana College, founded in 1860, and the Sioux Falls College, affiliated with the Baptist Church. Other smaller colleges include Nettleton College and National College.

Education

Number of Public Schools   35
Special Education Schools   2
Total Enrollment   16,092
% Enrollment in Private Schools   14.7
% Minority   NA
Classroom Teachers   NA
Pupil-Teacher Ratio   NA
Number of Graduates   NA
Total Revenue (in millions)   NA
Total Expenditures (in millions)   NA
Expenditures per Pupil   NA
Educational Attainment (Age 25 and Over)   NA
  % Completed 12 or More Years   77.1
  % Completed 16 or More Years   18.8
Four-Year Colleges and Universities   4
  Enrollment   3,050
Two-Year Colleges   NA
  Enrollment   NA

Libraries

Number   15
Public Libraries   1
Books (in thousands)   192
Circulation (in thousands)   746
Persons Served (in thousands)   90.5
Circulation per Person Served   8.24
Income (in millions) $1.552
Staff   59

Four-Year Colleges and Universities
  Augustana College
  National College
  Nettleton College
  Sioux Falls College

Health

South Dakota ranks ninth in quality of medical care among 333 cities. The five hospitals in the area are noted for the range and sophistication of their services. They are the Sioux Valley Hospital, McKennan Hospital, Veterans Hospital, Royal C. Johnson Memorial Veterans Hospital, and the Crippled Children's Hospital and School. The Good Samaritan is one of the leading health providers for senior citizens. Charter Hospital serves people with mental and emotional disorders. An important factor in the high level of medical care is the University of South Dakota School of Medicine.

Health	
Deaths—Total	722
Rate per 1,000	8.2
Infant Deaths—Total	8
Rate per 1,000	5.0
Number of Metro Hospitals	4
Number of Metro Hospital Beds	1,304
Rate per 100,000	1,337
Number of Physicians	319
Physicians per 1,000	2.86
Nurses per 1,000	NA
Health Expenditures per Capita	$16.14

Transportation

East-west I-90, joining Boston and Seattle, and north-south I-29, connecting Kansas City and Winnipeg, intersect northwest of Sioux Falls.

Interstate 229, a beltway around the eastern sector of the city, links I-90 and I-29. Other routes accessing Sioux Falls are U.S. Highways 18 and 81, and state roads 38 and 42. Costello Terminal at the regional airport at Joe Foss Field is the largest airport in South Dakota and has recently been enhanced with a $4-million renovation. Within the city, Sioux Falls Transit provides mass transit while Paratransit provides on-demand door-to-door service for the disabled and elderly. From its beginnings rail service has played a major role in linking Sioux Falls with the rest of the nation. The city is served by the Chicago and Northwestern, Burlington and Northern, and Illinois Central Gulf railroads.

Transportation	
Interstate Highway Mileage	27
Total Urban Mileage	553
Total Daily Vehicle Mileage (in millions)	$1.580
Daily Average Commute Time	32.3 min.
Number of Buses	22
Port Tonnage (in millions)	NA
Airports	1
Number of Daily Flights	16
Daily Average Number of Passengers	604
Airlines (American carriers only)	
Delta	
Northwest	
Trans World	
United	

Housing

As a growing city, Sioux Falls' neighborhoods are expanding with new homes, and these are available at prices far lower than in metropolitan areas in the East and West. The average price in 1991 was $65,000 for a three-bedroom home. The older homes are found in the Historic District, and more modern homes in places like Prairie Tree. New housing construction is expected to follow the overall trends in average household size, which will decline through the year 2015. Demand for single-family housing is expected to be strong over the next ten years and then decline. Demand for apartment houses is expected to grow, as the senior population grows. Almost half of all new housing units constructed through 2015 will be apartments.

Housing	
Total Housing Units	41,568
% Change 1980–1990	20.7
Vacant Units for Sale or Rent	1,306
Occupied Units	39,790
% with More Than One Person per Room	1.6
% Owner-Occupied	58.8
Median Value of Owner-Occupied Homes	$59,100
Average Monthly Purchase Cost	$378
Median Monthly Rent	$336
New Private Housing Starts	587
Value (in thousands)	$38,395
% Single-Family	69.0
Nonresidential Buildings Value (in thousands)	$31,059

Urban Redevelopment

To encourage economic expansion, the Sioux Falls Development Foundation and the Chamber of Commerce have jointly undertaken a long-range marketing program entitled Forward Sioux Falls. The heart of the program is the Downtown Development Plan, adopted as part of the Sioux Falls 2000 Comprehensive Development Plan. Downtown Sioux Falls lies near the geographic center of the city, principally on the west bank of the Big Sioux River. It covers 435 acres with a strong linear north-south orientation. It contains 1.540 million square feet of office space with 22 restaurants, 11 night clubs, 3 movie theaters, the Community Playhouse, the Civic Fine Arts Center, the Old County Courthouse Museum, and the Coliseum Theater. The number of downtown retail establishments has declined over the past 20 years. Today the retail district is concentrated on Phillips Avenue between Tenth and Twelfth streets. The majority of the buildings are in good physical condition with run-down buildings principally located in the south and southeastern portion of the Central Business District. The Downtown Development Plan will build on existing strengths. An additional half million square feet of office space will be added during the next 30 years, primarily along First Avenue. Other plans call for a new convention center and performance theater. During the middle years of the plan (1995–2005) redevelopment activities will concentrate on the east bank of the Big Sioux, creating an exciting urban waterfront. A major indoor place is planned to host public events. The property between downtown and Falls Park will be improved by extending Phillips Avenue as a tree-lined boulevard to Falls Park.

Crime

The crime rate in Sioux Falls is below the national average. Violent crimes reported in 1991 totaled 378, and property crimes totaled 4,806.

Crime
Violent Crimes—Total   378
Violent Crime Rate per 100,000   319.7
Murder   2
Rape   88
Robbery   32
Aggravated Assaults   256
Property Crimes   4,806
Burglary   800
Larceny   3,837
Motor Vehicle Theft   169
Arson   35
Per Capita Police Expenditures $60.01
Per Capita Fire Protection Expenditures $62.34
Number of Police   125
Per 1,000   0.26

Religion

Of the 115 churches in the city, denominations with the most churches are: Lutheran, 20; Baptist, 13; Catholic, 8; Full Gospel, 7; United Methodist, 5; Reformed Church, 5; Presbyterian, 4; Episcopal, 3; Church of Christ, 3; Southern Baptist, 3; Mennonite, 3; Assemblies of God, 2; American Baptist, 2; Independent Baptist, 2; Christian Reformed, 2; Church of God, 2; Congregational, 2; United Church of Christ, 2; Lutheran Missouri Synod, 2; and Eastern Orthodox, 2.

Religion	
Largest Denominations (Adherents)	
Catholic	23,364
Evangelical Lutheran	28,404
United Methodist	6,414
Lutheran-Missouri Synod	3,971
Presbyterian	2,436
Reformed Church	2,173
United Church of Christ	1,654
American Baptist	2,938
Assembly of God	1,413
Jewish	135

Media

The city's daily newspaper is *Argus Leader,* part of the Gannett chain. Electronic media consist of 4 television stations and 14 radio stations.

Media
Newsprint
Argus Leader, daily
Television
KDLT (Channel 5)
KELO (Channel 11)
KSFY (Channel 13)
KTTW (Channel 17)

Radio	
KAUR (FM)	KCFS (FM)
KCSD (FM)	KELO (AM)
KELO (FM)	KJIA (AM)
KNWC (AM)	KNWC (FM)
KRSD (FM)	KSOO (AM)
KPAT (FM)	KTWB (FM)
KWSN (AM)	KXRB (AM)

Sports

Sioux Falls has no professional sports team. Both Augustana College and Sioux Falls College have strong teams in most collegiate sports.

Arts, Culture, and Tourism

The South Dakota Symphony is based in Sioux Falls and presents classical and pop concerts. The Sioux Falls College's Jeschke Fine Arts Center and the Sioux Falls Coliseum mount frequent cultural events. The Sioux Falls Community Playhouse presents theater productions ranging from Broadway plays to children's shows. The principal museums are the Pettigrew Museum, formerly the residence of U.S. Senator R. F. Pettigrew, Siouxland Heritage Museum, and Courthouse Museum. The Civic Fine Arts Center holds frequent exhibitions of contemporary regional artists. The Jim Savage Western Art Gallery holds works of Jim Savage and more than 50 of the nation's top western artists.

Travel and Tourism
Hotel Rooms   2,032
Convention and Exhibit Space (square feet)   NA
Convention Centers
Sioux Falls Arena
Ramkota Exhibit Hall/Rushmore Conference Center
Convention Center
Coliseum
Festivals
Dakotas Traditional Folk Arts Festival (June)
Sioux Empire Fair (August)
Sidewalk Arts Festival (September)

Parks and Recreation

Sioux Falls has over 50 parks and recreation centers. McKennan Park on 21st Street includes a 20-acre tract of which 7 acres are wooded. Sherman Park and Zoo on Kiwanis Avenue comprise 200 acres set aside in early 1900, including many prominent mounds associated with an early Indian tribe of mound-builders. Terrace Park at Covell Lake has 52 acres of woodland. Elmwood Park on North Kiwanis Avenue is heavily wooded.

Sources of Further Information

Minnehaha County Historical Society
200 West Sixth Street
Sioux Falls, SD 57102
(605) 338-7090

Sioux Falls Area Chamber of Commerce
315 South Phillips
Sioux Falls, SD 57101
(605) 336-1620

Sioux Falls Convention and Visitors Bureau
Box 1425
Sioux Falls, SD 57101
(605) 336-1620

Sioux Falls Public Library
201 North Main Avenue
Sioux Falls, SD 57102-0386
(605) 339-7081

Additional Reading

Guide to Sioux Falls. 1992.
Sioux Falls Community Data Profile. 1992.

South Bend

Indiana

Indiana

Just where the drive leads off the highway is the spot where Pierre Navarre built his first log cabin in 1820. Among the city's many spots of natural beauty is the Rum Village Park on the southern edge, named for Chief Rum of the Potawatomi Indians.

Basic Data	
Name South Bend	
Name Origin From the South Bend of St. Joseph River	
Year Founded 1823 Inc. 1865	
Status: State Indiana	
County St. Joseph County	
Area (square miles) 36.4	
Elevation (feet) 710	
Time Zone EST	
Population (1990) 105,511	
Population of Metro Area (1990) 247,052	
Distance in Miles To:	
Indianapolis	140
Louisville	258
Gary	59
Muncie	140
Evansville	326
Chicago	96

Environment
Environmental Stress Index   2.4
Green Cities Index: Rank   NA
Score   NA
Water Quality   Neutral, hard, fluoridated
Average Daily Use (gallons per capita)   192
Maximum Supply (gallons per capita)   600
Parkland as % of Total City Area   NA
% Waste Landfilled/Recycled   NA
Annual Parks Expenditures per Capita $64.48

Location and Topography

South Bend is located in the valley of St. Joseph River in northern Indiana at the crest of the watershed dividing St. Lawrence Basin from the Mississippi Basin. It covers St. Joseph River at its southernmost bend, hence the name of the city.

Layout of City and Suburbs

Downtown South Bend is a bustling business center, locally called Michiana because it is the trade and financial heart of southern Michigan and northern Indiana. The center of activity lies at Michigan and Washington streets. The southern and western sections are mainly industrial with hundreds of factories. The north and east sections are residential. In the northern section along Michigan Street are many stately old houses, particularly along Navarre Place. The North Shore Drive along the northern bank also has many fine houses.

Climate

Located within 20 miles of Lake Michigan, South Bend has a moderate continental climate. Both summers and winters are less severe than in most places on the same latitude. However, winters tend to be cloudy and humid with frequent periods of heavy snow brought in by cold northwest winds passing over Lake Michigan. Distribution of precipitation is relatively even throughout the year with greater than normal amounts during the growing season.

Weather		
Temperature		
Highest Monthly Average °F 82.7		
Lowest Monthly Average °F 15.9		
Annual Averages		
Days 32°F or Below 122		
Days above 90°F 37		

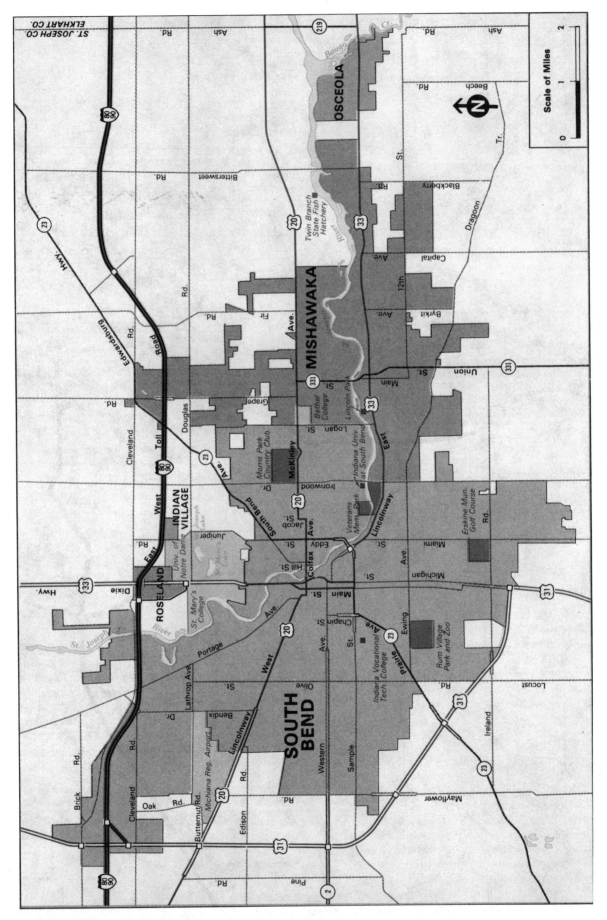

Weather (continued)

Zero Degree Days 2
Precipitation (inches) 38.16
Snow (inches) 72.0
% Seasonal Humidity 72.5
Wind Speed (m.p.h.) 10.3
Clear Days 72
Cloudy Days 193
Storm Days 52
Rainy Days 140

Average Temperatures (°F)	High	Low	Mean
January	30.4	17.9	24.2
February	39.4	25.1	32.3
March	50.9	32.0	41.5
April	62.2	42.9	52.6
May	78.0	56.9	67.5
June	85.7	62.2	74.0
July	87.2	64.1	75.7
August	84.1	62.3	73.2
September	74.4	52.0	63.2
October	64.1	45.7	54.9
November	44.7	28.5	36.6
December	39.0	25.2	32.1

History

South Bend was among the places visited by René-Robert Cavelier, Sieur de La Salle in 1679 and 1681. During his second visit La Salle met with the chiefs of the Miami and Illinois confederations under a tree later known as the Council Oak. This meeting is reported to have forged an alliance between the two nations against the Iroquois. The first white man to make a permanent home in St. Joseph County was Pierre Freischutz Navarre, a French agent of the American Fur Company who established the first trading post here in 1820. He married a Potawatomi woman. However, the founder of the town was Alexis Coquillard, who named the site the Big St. Joseph Station to distinguish it from a trading station run by his relatives on the Little St. Joseph River near the present site of Fort Wayne.

Settlers soon dubbed the post the Bend or South Bend. In 1823 Coquillard persuaded his father, Francis Comparet, to become his partner, and invest $75,000 to purchase John Jacob Astor's American Fur Company for the region of the Upper Lakes. Four years later Colonel Lathrop M. Taylor opened a trading post here for Samuel Hanna and Company and renamed the settlement St. Josephs. In 1829 the name was changed again to Southold, but in 1830 the post office adopted the name of South Bend. Coquillard and Taylor helped to lay out the city, and in 1831 brought about its selection as the county seat. It was incorporated in 1835 and chartered in 1865. The town grew slowly until Henry and Clement Studebaker came to South Bend in 1852. With $68 and two forges, they opened a blacksmith and wagon shop. The Studebaker Corporation, which grew out of the wagon shop, together with the Oliver Chilled Plow Works, founded by James Oliver in 1855, became the basis of South Bend's industrial future. Another significant event was the arrival in 1842 of Father Edward Sorrin and seven brothers of the Congregation of the Holy Cross, to found the University of Notre Dame on 600 acres granted to them by Bishop Hailandiere of the diocese of Vincennes. Rebuilt after a fire destroyed the campus in 1879, the university has become the city's most famous institution.

Historical Landmarks

St. Joseph County's Original Courthouse on Lafayette Boulevard is an excellent example of colonial architecture. It is now a museum. La Salle's First Portage between St. Joseph and Kankakee rivers is designated by a marker. At this point, in 1679, La Salle became the first white man to cross the region. The La Salle Monument in Riverview Cemetery also commemorates the event. Historic mansions open to the public are the Tippecanoe Place, a feudal castle that was the home of Clement Studebaker, and Beiger Mansion, home of Martin Beiger, founding partner of Mishawaka Wollen Manufacturing Company. The University of Notre Dame has a number of historic buildings. The golden-domed Administration Building has Luigi Gregori's mural of Christopher Columbus, and reproductions of the Grotto of Lourdes and of the Log Chapel, in which the first ordination of a university president took place.

Population

South Bend lost population in the 1980s. Its 1990 population of 105,511 was 3.8% smaller than its 1980 population of 109,727. As a result its ranking has dropped precipitously from 143rd to 180th.

Population		
	1980	1990
Central City	109,727	105,511
Rank	143	180
Metro Area	241,617	247,052
Pop. Change 1980–1990 -4,216		
Pop. % Change 1980–1990 -3.8		
Median Age 33.2		
% Male 47.2		
% Age 65 and Over 16.81		
Density (per square mile) 2,898		

Households		
Number 42,260		
Persons per Household 2.45		
% Female-Headed Households 14.9		
% One-Person Households 30.7		
Births—Total 1,862		
% to Mothers under 20 16.5		
Birth Rate per 1,000 17.4		

Ethnic Composition

Blacks are well represented in South Bend and make up 21% of the population. The proportion of whites has declined from 80% to 76% between 1980 and 1990.

Chronology

1820 Pierre Navarre builds trading post on the site of the future South Bend.

1821 Alexis Coquillard establishes second trading post and names the site Big St. Joseph Station.

1823 With funds from his father in law, Coquillard purchases John Jacob Astor's American Fur Company for the Upper Lakes.

1827 Colonel Lathrop M. Taylor opens trading post for Samuel Hanna and Company and renames the settlement St. Joseph's.

1829 The name of the settlement is changed to Southold.

1830 The Post Office settles on the name of South Bend.

1831 Coquillard and Taylor plat the town and engineer its selection as county seat.

1842 Father Edward Sorrin of the Congregation of the Holy Cross founds the University of Notre Dame.

1852 Henry and Clement Studebaker come to South Bend and open a wagon shop.

1855 James Oliver founds Oliver Chilled Plow Works after inventing process for chilling and hardening steel.

1879 Fire destroys campus of the University of Notre Dame.

1963 Studebaker closes doors, leaving 8,000 people unemployed.

Ethnic Composition (as % of total pop.)

	1980	1990
White	79.5	76.03
Black	18.29	20.9
American Indian	0.23	0.37
Asian and Pacific Islander	0.46	0.87
Hispanic	2.36	3.36
Other	NA	1.84

Government

South Bend is governed by a mayor and council. The mayor and nine council members are elected to four-year terms. The mayor is not a member of the council.

Government

Year of Home Charter   1981
Number of Members of the Governing Body   9
Elected at Large   3
Elected by Wards   6
Number of Women in Governing Body   3
Salary of Mayor $64,004

Government (continued)

Salary of Council Members $14,035
City Government Employment Total   1,259
Rate per 10,000   117.5

Public Finance

The annual budget consists of revenues of $96.737 million and expenditures of $79.282 million. The outstanding debt is $29.913 million and cash and security holdings are $21.942 million.

Public Finance

Total Revenue (in millions) $96.737
Intergovernmental Revenue—Total (in millions) $21.36
Federal Revenue per Capita $7.95
% Federal Assistance   8.22
% State Assistance   13.54
Sales Tax as % of Total Revenue   0.0
Local Revenue as % of Total Revenue   57.03
City Income Tax   no
Taxes—Total (in millions) $20.7

Taxes per Capita
  Total $193
  Property $188
  Sales and Gross Receipts $2
General Expenditures—Total (in millions) $54.9
General Expenditures per Capita $512
Capital Outlays per Capita $35

% of Expenditures for:
  Public Welfare   0.0
  Highways   6.1
  Education   0.1
  Health and Hospitals   0.8
  Police   14.0
  Sewerage and Sanitation   19.6
  Parks and Recreation   10.8
  Housing and Community Development   17.7
Debt Outstanding per Capita $262
  % Utility   0.2
Federal Procurement Contract Awards (in millions) $275.1
Federal Grants Awards (in millions) $11.1
Fiscal Year Begins   January 1

Economy

Historically, South Bend entered the industrial age with the establishment of the Studebaker Wagon Company and its further progress was the result of the establishment of a number of other manufacturing companies, such as Oliver Chilled Plow and Singer Cabinet Works. The economy faced a severe blow in the 1960s when the Studebaker Corporation folded, followed by other older manufacturers. The city had to rebuild its economic base and diversify. Manufacturing still remains an important sector, but has been overtaken by both services and trade. South Bend is a major retail center for the Michiana region. It is also a center for business, financial, and professional support services, such as marketing, telecommunications, and data processing.

Economy

Total Money Income (in millions) $1,088.4
% of State Average   101.8
Per Capita Annual Income $10,154
% Population below Poverty Level   12.1
Fortune 500 Companies   1

Banks	Number	Deposits (in millions)
Commercial	9	NA
Savings	3	NA

Passenger Autos   144,372
Electric Meters   79,000
Gas Meters   36,500

Manufacturing

Number of Establishments   235
% with 20 or More Employees   40.0
Manufacturing Payroll (in millions) $367.5
Value Added by Manufacture (in millions) $719.5
Value of Shipments (in millions) $1,606.9
New Capital Expenditures (in millions) $55.9

Wholesale Trade

Number of Establishments   309
Sales (in millions) $1,085.7
Annual Payroll (in millions) $103.322

Retail Trade

Number of Establishments   1,111
Total Sales (in millions) $790.9
Sales per Capita $7,378
Number of Retail Trade Establishments with Payroll   790
Annual Payroll (in millions) $99.7
Total Sales (in millions) $780.2
General Merchandise Stores (per capita) $832
Food Stores (per capita) $1,548
Apparel Stores (per capita) $225
Eating and Drinking Places (per capita) $792

Service Industries

Total Establishments   1,037
Total Receipts (in millions) $517.9
Hotels and Motels (in millions) $19.2
Health Services (in millions) $164.2
Legal Services (in millions) $28.6

Labor

With a total labor force of 123,150, South Bend is a medium-range labor market. The unemployment rate at 6.2% is slightly below the national average. However, the labor force is expected to grow, particularly in health and human services. Small firms with fewer than 100 employees account for two-thirds of new job openings. The largest employers are Allied-Signal/Bendix, LTV Missiles and Electronics, Uniroyal Plastics, Allied Products, RACO, Dodge/Reliance Electric, and Koontz Wagner Electric, among industrial companies; University of Notre Dame, South Bend Community Schools, and Indiana University at South Bend among educational institutions; Memorial Hospital and St. Josephs Care Group among medical services; and 1st Source and Associates Bancorp among financial services.

Labor

Civilian Labor Force   58,622
% Change 1989–1990   -0.9
Work Force Distribution
   Mining   NA
   Construction   NA
   Manufacturing   20,800
   Transportation and Public Utilities   5,600
   Wholesale and Retail Trade   30,000
   FIRE (Finance, Insurance, Real Estate)   6,500
   Service   35,800
   Government   12,200
   Women as % of Labor Force   44.3
   % Self-Employed   4.3
   % Professional/Technical   15.5
Total Unemployment   3,643
Rate %   6.2
Federal Government Civilian Employment   953

Education

The South Bend Community School system supports 36 schools. The parochial school system consists of 18 schools and the private school system of 3, including a Hebrew school. The premier institution of higher education is the University of Notre Dame, known as well for its academic excellence as for its legendary football team. Its growth since World War II was a personal achievement of its former president, Theodore Hesburgh. It maintains a special relationship with St. Mary's College, a liberal arts college for women. South Bend has a third Catholic institution in Holy Cross Junior College, located near the University of Notre Dame. The major public university is the Indiana University at South Bend, the third largest in the state's eight-university system.

Education

Number of Public Schools   36
Special Education Schools   NA
Total Enrollment   21,435
% Enrollment in Private Schools   16.6
% Minority   34.7
Classroom Teachers   1,243
Pupil-Teacher Ratio   17.3:1
Number of Graduates   1,257
Total Revenue (in millions) $83.024
Total Expenditures (in millions) $89.829
Expenditures per Pupil $3,936
Educational Attainment (Age 25 and Over)
   % Completed 12 or More Years   65.6
   % Completed 16 or More Years   14.7
Four-Year Colleges and Universities   3
   Enrollment   7,469
Two-Year Colleges   NA
   Enrollment   NA

Libraries

Number   20
Public Libraries   8
Books (in thousands)   420
Circulation (in thousands)   195
Persons Served (in thousands)   167
Circulation per Person Served   1.16

Health

South Bend has four general and intensive care hospitals with 388 doctors and 1,148 beds. They are Memorial Hospital, Michiana Community Hospital, St. Joseph Medical Center, and Healthwin Hospital for chronic care. The Northern Indiana State Hospital has a special disabilities center. The National Center for Senior Living offers a state-of-the-art residential program for older persons including medical care.

Health	
Deaths—Total	1,261
Rate per 1,000	11.8
Infant Deaths—Total	24
Rate per 1,000	12.9
Number of Metro Hospitals	4
Number of Metro Hospital Beds	1,148
Rate per 100,000	1,071
Number of Physicians	388
Physicians per 1,000	NA
Nurses per 1,000	NA
Health Expenditures per Capita	$5.00

Transportation

South Bend is approached by Interstates 80 and 90; U.S. 20 and 31/33; and state routes 2, 23, 123, and 331. Within the city the main thoroughfares are the north-south Main Street and Michigan Street, and the east-west Colfax Avenue. Rail passenger services are provided by Amtrak. The South Shore Line connects the city with the Chicago Loop. Rail freight services are provided by Conrail and two smaller private railroads. The Michiana Regional Airport, with 112 flights daily, is the nearest air terminal to South Bend for all domestic flights, but the closest international airport is in Chicago, 96 miles away.

Transportation	
Interstate Highway Mileage	10
Total Urban Mileage	1,301
Total Daily Vehicle Mileage (in millions)	$3.242
Daily Average Commute Time	38.1 min.
Number of Buses	48
Port Tonnage (in millions)	NA
Airports	1
Number of Daily Flights	19
Daily Average Number of Passengers	668

Airlines (American carriers only)
  Midway
  Northwest
  United
  USAir

Housing

The total number of housing units is 45,757. The flurry of construction activity in the 1980s led to the building of a number of modern apartment complexes, such as at Pointe at St. Joseph.

Housing	
Total Housing Units	45,757
% Change 1980–1990	2.1
Vacant Units for Sale or Rent	2,641
Occupied Units	42,260
% with More Than One Person per Room	2.4
% Owner-Occupied	65.9
Median Value of Owner-Occupied Homes	$40,300
Average Monthly Purchase Cost	$227
Median Monthly Rent	$325
New Private Housing Starts	175
Value (in thousands)	$12,880
% Single-Family	60.6
Nonresidential Buildings Value (in thousands)	$16,282

Urban Redevelopment

The rebuilding of South Bend following the closure of its major industrial employers began in the 1970s. The Scottsdale Mall opened in 1971; Block Six, including the Karl King Towers, in 1973; Century Center in 1977; Commerce Center in 1980; East Race Waterway in 1984; One Michiana Square and Old Lathe Works in 1986; the Valley American Bank building in 1987; Coveleski Regional Stadium in 1988; and Pointe at St. Joseph apartment complex in 1990. The Downtown Development Plan, which is expected to be in effect until 2000, has a number of goals. Among them are the revitalization of the Michigan Street Corridor, the central core of the downtown area consisting of 11 city blocks bounded by La Salle, Monroe, St. Joseph, and Main streets. It will include the development of Morris Civic Park, and rehabilitation and conversion of LaSalle Hotel, Inwoods Building, Commerce Building, Robertsons Building, and Center City Place. A number of other buildings have been renovated under this plan, such as Lafayette Building, Trigon Building, JMS Building, Bath Building and Wayne Place, and Union and St. Joseph stations. Plans were begun in 1988 for the creation of an entertainment district involving renovation of Morris Civic Auditorium and Palais Royale as well as the State Theater.

Crime

The crime rate is above the national average in Southbend.

Religion

Roman Catholicism is strong in South Bend, helped by its French roots and the 19th and early–20th-century immigration of Poles and Hungarians. There are over 120 churches.

Crime

Crime	
Violent Crimes—Total	NA
Violent Crime Rate per 100,000	NA
Murder	NA
Rape	NA
Robbery	NA
Aggravated Assaults	NA
Property Crimes	NA
Burglary	NA
Larceny	NA
Motor Vehicle Theft	NA
Arson	NA
Per Capita Police Expenditures	$75.66
Per Capita Fire Protection Expenditures	$54.99
Number of Police	230
Per 1,000	2.15

Religion

Largest Denominations (Adherents)	
Catholic	62,723
United Methodist	11,731
Evangelical Lutheran	3,909
Black Baptist	8,001
Presbyterian	3,757
Assembly of God	1,666
Episcopal	1,097
United Church of Christ	1,949
Jewish	1,800

Media

South Bend Tribune is the city's only daily. The electronic media consist of two local television stations and seven FM and four AM stations. South Bend also receives television and radio signals from Chicago.

Media
Newsprint
Tri-County News, weekly
South Bend Tribune, daily
Television
WNDU (Channel 16)
WSBT (Channel 22)
Radio
WAMJ (AM)   WETL (FM)
WHME (FM)   WNDU (AM)
WNDU (FM)   WSBT (AM)
WNSN (FM)

Sports

Although South Bend does not have a professional team in any sports, this lack is more than made up by the presence of the Fighting Irish football team of the University of Notre Dame. Built up by Knut Rockne in the 1920s with the Four Horsemen and the Seven Mules, the team is legendary. Their home schedule is played on Saturday afternoons in the Knut Rockne Stadium at the university. The Stanley Coveleski Regional Stadium is the home field of the Chicago White Sox Class A Minor League. The East Race Waterway is the only artificial white water course in North America.

Arts, Culture, and Tourism

Century Center includes a theater, art center, and the Discovery Hall Museum. The South Bend Symphony and the Broadway Theater League perform at the Morris Civic Auditorium, Indiana's oldest historic theater. The Studebaker National Museum houses a collection of over 100 carriages, wagons, cars, and trucks, including the one used by Lincoln on the night of his assassination. The Northern Indiana Historical Society, founded in 1867, maintains a collection of over 200,000 artifacts from St. Joseph County.

Travel and Tourism
Hotel Rooms 2,414
Convention and Exhibit Space (square feet) 37,190
Convention Centers
Century Center
Morris Civic Auditorium
Athletic and Convocation Center, University of Notre Dame
Festivals
Firefly Festival (summer)
Summerfest
Autumnfest

Parks and Recreation

Leeper Park, the location of the Pierre Navarre log cabin, is located just north of downtown at Michigan Street and the river. Howard Park is located along the East Bank of the river. Rum Village is a 160-acre park that also houses the Indiana Wildlife Rehabilitation Center. The Potawatomi Park Zoo and Botanical Gardens is a 60-acre facility including Muessel Ellison Tropical Gardens. In addition, there are 67 smaller parks.

Sources of Further Information

City of South Bend
1400 County-City Building
South Bend, IN 46601
(219) 284-9261

Northern Indiana Historical Society
112 South Lafayette Boulevard
South Bend, IN 46601
(219) 284-9664

South Bend/Mishawaka Chamber of Commerce
401 East Colfax Avenue
South Bend, IN 46634-1677
(219) 234-0079

South Bend Public Library
122 West Wayne Street
South Bend, IN 46601
(219) 282-4600

Additional Reading

Polk's South Bend Directory. 1992.

Spokane

Washington

Basic Data

Name   Spokane
Name Origin   From Spokane Indians
Year Founded   1810 Inc. 1881
Status: State   Washington
         County   Seat of Spokane County
Area (square miles)   55.9
Elevation (feet)   1,890
Time Zone   Pacific
Population (1990)   177,196
Population of Metro Area (1990)   361,364

Sister Cities
   Jilin, China
   Limerick, Ireland
   Lubeck, Germany
   Makhach Kala, Russia
   Nishinomiya, Japan

Distance in Miles To:
   Seattle   282
   Portland, OR   351
   Vancouver, BC   348
   Tacoma   295
   Coeur d'Alene   33

Location and Topography

Spokane is located in eastern Washington near the Idaho border on the eastern edge of the Columbia Basin, a wide sloping plain that rises sharply to the east toward the Rocky Mountains. This uneven plateau, ranging from 400 feet to 5,000 feet in height, extends beyond the Coeur d'Alene Mountains on the east, spreads southward along the rolling Palouse and Walla Walla districts into Oregon, and circles through the Big Bend country to the Columbia River on the west.

Layout of City and Suburbs

Concentrated around the falls of the Spokane River, the city spreads outward toward the east over the level valley floor and stretches upward on the north and south beyond the rocky rim of steep, pine-covered hills. The river, which bisects the city, flows west until it reaches Havermale Island, a huge rock just above the 150-foot falls, where it divides. Below the falls the stream sweeps in a broad curve between the railway embankment on the right and the narrow flat of the Peaceful Valley on the left below the canyon walls. Then, it turns north, flowing past parks, avenues, and buildings, as well as Fort George Wright, until it passes beyond the northwestern limits of the city. Running approximately north and south, at the west end of town, is Latah Creek, or Hangman Creek, spanned by the Latah Creek Bridge. South of the river is the city proper, centered on Riverside Avenue and bounded by Trent Avenue on the north, First Avenue on the south, Division Street on the east, and Monroe Street on the west. Bordering on the river is the main industrial district with a smaller industrial area lying south of First Avenue along the Northern Pacific Railroad. Beyond the rail tracks the streets begin to gradually climb to Canon Hill, a residential area. Other residential districts are Manitou Park, Cliff Drive, Rockwood Boulevard, Coeur d'Alene Park, and North Hill. Within the city, east-west thoroughfares are known as avenues, and north-south thoroughfares are streets. Major east-west avenues are Francis, Wellesley, Sprague, and 29th, and

Environment

Environmental Stress Index   3.0
Green Cities Index: Rank   NA
                    Score   NA
Water Quality   Alkaline, hard
Average Daily Use (gallons per capita)   350
   Maximum Supply (gallons per capita)   1,575
Parkland as % of Total City Area
% Waste Landfilled/Recycled   72:28
Annual Parks Expenditures per Capita $53.75

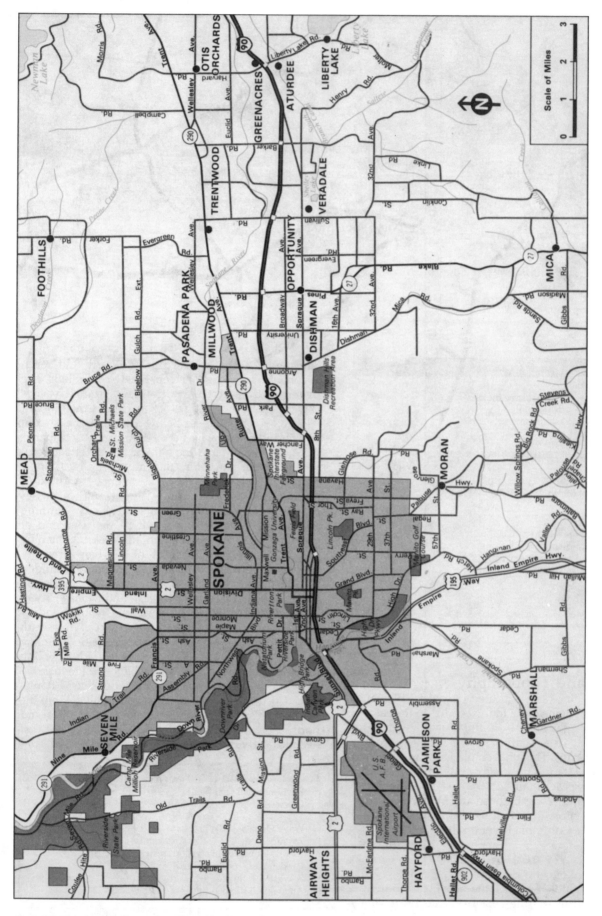

north-south streets are Maple, Monroe, Division, and Nevada.

Climate

Generally, Spokane has a mild arid climate in the summer and a cold, coastal climate in the winter. Snowfall can total as much as 55 inches but rarely accumulates to more than one foot. Most air masses coming from the west or southwest lose their moisture during their passage over the Cascade ranges.

Weather			
Temperature			
Highest Monthly Average °F 84.0			
Lowest Monthly Average °F 20.0			
Annual Averages			
Days 32°F or Below 141			
Days above 90°F 21			
Zero Degree Days 5			
Precipitation (inches) 17.0			
Snow (inches) 53.0			
% Seasonal Humidity 63			
Wind Speed (m.p.h.) 8.7			
Clear Days 89			
Cloudy Days 189			
Storm Days 11			
Rainy Days 114			
Average Temperatures (°F)	*High*	*Low*	*Mean*
January	31.9	19.6	25.4
February	39.0	25.3	32.2
March	46.2	28.8	37.5
April	57.0	35.2	46.1
May	66.5	42.8	54.7
June	73.6	49.4	61.5
July	84.3	55.1	69.7
August	81.9	54.0	68.0
September	72.5	46.7	59.6
October	58.1	37.5	47.8
November	41.8	29.2	35.5
December	33.9	24.0	29.0

History

Spokane was the domain of the Indian tribe of the same name for centuries, and remained unsettled by white men until the first decade of the 19th century. Between 1810 and 1830 it was the scene of considerable activity by fur traders of the Northwest Fur Company and the Pacific Fur Company, the latter owned by John Jacob Astor. In 1810 Finan McDonald and Joco Finlay of the Northwest Fur Company built the Spokane House, about ten miles below the falls at the junction of the Spokane and Little Spokane rivers. About two years later, John Clarke of the Pacific Fur Company built Fort Spokane nearby. In 1813 both companies merged, and eight years later the Hudson's Bay Company took over the combined operation. However, in 1826, Hudson's Bay decided to close their operations at Fort Spokane and moved to Fort Colville. After a brief interregnum, the missionaries took over where the fur traders had left. The Reverend Samuel Parker in 1835, and the Rever-

ends Cushing Ells and Elkanah Walker in 1838, established temporary missions with meager results. On the settlement of the boundary dispute between the United States and Canada in 1846, there was a sudden flurry of migration, but the hostility of the Indians, culminating in the Whitman Massacre, led to a virtual closing of the settlement of the country east of the Cascade Mountains. Settlers did not return until the creation of Washington Territory in 1853. In 1851 Antoine Plante established a ferry a few miles above the falls and in 1853 Pelletier settled on the old mission. Also in the same year, Francis B. Owens, a cattleman, came to the valley with 500 horses and 600 head of cattle. With the discovery of the Colville mines in 1855, a small trickle of migrants began to move in. The first to locate claims on the banks of the river were J. J. Downing and S. R. Scranton, two cattlemen, in 1871. They were joined by Richard M. Benjamin, who purchased a third of their interest. In 1872 a post office was established. Within two years Benjamin, Scranton, and Downing were bought out by James Nettle Glover, J. N. Metheny, and Cyrus F. Yeaton. Slowly, the settlement began to take roots. A school was organized under the Reverend H. T. Cowley. The Reverend S. G. Havermale, after whom the river island is named, set up a church in Glover's store. The same year the town witnessed its first baseball game. On 13 February 1878, the town was officially born when Glover filed the plat of Spokane Falls at Colville. Shortly thereafter, J. J. Browne and A. M. Canon bought half-interest in the town site from Glover. A schoolhouse was built, the first Methodist and Congregational churches were organized, and the first newspaper, *Spokane Times*, made its debut. In 1881 the Jesuits, who had established St. Michael's Mission east of Spokane Falls in 1887, began construction of Gonzaga University. The school opened in 1887 with an enrollment of eight students. The year 1881 was a landmark in Spokane's history: the first theater, the Globe, opened; the first train on the Northern Pacific Railroad arrived; the first bank opened; and the town was incorporated as Spokane Falls with a population of 1,000. The following year Joy's Opera House opened, and Spokane was taking on all the trappings of a major urban center. In 1883 the Northern Pacific Railroad was completed through Montana, thus linking Spokane with all major cities in the nation. The immediate result was a big stampede to the town, which became the supply point and promotion center for the putative gold mines on the North Fork of the Coeur d'Alene River. Every train brought hundreds of people, and by 1884 the population doubled. As white settlers became more numerous, the Indians were dispossessed of their land, despite the plaintive protests of Chief Garry. By 1885 Spokane had four newspapers, one library, and 17 churches in addition to several variety halls and less reputable entertainment centers. The city suffered a setback in 1889 when a fire broke out on Railroad Avenue and, fanned by a brisk wind, soon consumed the entire section of the city from the Northern Pacific Railway tracks to the river, and from Lincoln to Washington streets. The

Chronology

1810 Finan McDonald and Joco Finlay of the Northwest Fur Company build the Spokane House, ten miles below the falls.

1812 John Clarke of the Pacific Fur Company builds Fort Spokane in the vicinity.

1813 Northwest Fur Company buys Pacific Fur Company.

1821 Hudson's Bay Company buys Northwest Fur Company.

1826 Hudson's Bay Company abandons operations in Spokane.

1835 The Reverend Samuel Parker establishes mission in Spokane Valley.

1838 The Reverends Cushing Ells and Elkanah Walker establish mission in Walkers Prairie.

1846 New immigration follows delimitation of boundary between United States and Canada at the 49th parallel, but the Whitman Massacre leads to a virtual closing of settlements.

1851 Antoine Perry establishes ferry a few miles north of the falls.

1853 Washington Territory is created. Pelletier settles on the abandoned Walker Ells mission site. Francis B. Owens brings 500 horses and 500 cattle from Montana.

1871 J. J. Downing and S. R. Scranton locate claims on the banks of the river.

1872 Richard M. Benjamin buys a third interest in the Downing-Scranton claim.

1873 James Nettle Glover, J. N. Metheny, and Cyrus F. Yeaton buy out Scranton and Downing.

1875 A school district is organized with the Reverend H. T. Cowley as teacher. The Reverend S. G. Havermale holds first church service in Glover's store. First baseball game is played.

1878 Glover files plat of the town of Spokane Falls. J. J. Browne and A. M. Canon buy half of Glover's interest. Schoolhouse is built.

1879 The first newspaper, *Spokane Times*, debuts. First Congregational and first Methodist churches are organized. Population jumps to 75.

1881 Foundation stone of Gonzaga University is laid by Jesuit Father J. M. Cataldo. The first theater, the Globe, opens.

1882 Joy's Opera House opens.

1883 The first train on the Northern Pacific Railroad steams into town. Spokane Falls is incorporated as a town by an act of Territorial Legislature with a population of 1,000 and an area of 1.5 square miles. Town limits expanded to four square miles.

1885 Public library is founded.

1889 Fire destroys entire section of 32 blocks from the Northern Pacific Railway tracks to the river, and from Lincoln to Washington streets, with an estimated loss of $6 million.

1890 Spokane Falls is reincorporated as Spokane and city limits are expanded by an additional 16 square miles.

1893 *The Spokesman* merges with *Review* to become *The Spokesman-Review*. Panic of 1893 brings slump to the local economy.

1900 First automobiles appear on the streets.

1909 Spokane, Flathead, and Coeur d'Alene Indian reservations are thrown open to settlement.

1910 Population crosses 100,000 mark. City's first skyscraper, the 15-story Old National Bank, is completed.

1913 The saloons and taverns close as the state prohibits alcohol.

1914 Three new transcontinental railroads, Union Pacific, Canadian Pacific, and Chicago, Milwaukee, and St. Paul railroads, effect junction in city.

1933 Work begins on the Grand Coulee Dam.

1974 Spokane hosts World's Fair Expo.

entire 32-block business district was destroyed with an estimated loss of $6 million. Within a year the city was rebuilt. In rebuilding, the business district shifted from Front (Trent) Avenue, along the river, to Riverside, two blocks south. In 1890, when Washington was admitted to the Union, Spokane Falls was reincorporated as Spokane, and the city limits were extended to include another 16 square miles to the original 4. Civic improvements accompanied this expansion. New bridges were built at Howard and Division streets. A cable-car line was started in the Fort Wright District. Horseracing, baseball, and tennis became widely popular sports. *The Spokesman* merged with *Review* to become *The Spokesman-Review*. Variety theaters and dance halls flourished, defying attempts to suppress them by the mayor and the local ministers. Despite periodical slumps, such as the Depression of 1893, Spokane entered upon a period of unprecedented expansion. New silver and lead mines were opened in the Coeur d'Alenes. An extensive construction program from 1904 to 1910 resulted in hundreds of new buildings. A city beautifying campaign was begun and 80,000 shade trees were planted. The population was growing in proportion to economic prosperity. Emigrants from Germany, Poland, Russia, and the Scandinavian countries came in a steady stream. The influx reached its peak in 1909 when the Spokane, Flathead, and Coeur d'Alene Indian reservations were thrown open to settlement. From a population of 36,848 in 1900 the city reached 104,402 in 1910. This era also saw the passing of the vestiges of the old mining town. Most of the saloons and variety theaters closed when the state passed prohibition into law in 1913. By 1914 three new transcontinental railroads—the Union Pacific, Canadian Pacific, and the Chicago, Milwaukee, and St. Paul—reached the city. Spokane was hit hard by the slump that followed World War I, and even more so by the Great Depression. The most important factor in the recovery of Spokane from these crises was the building of the Grand Coulee Dam.

Historical Landmarks

The 1,400-acre Fort George Wright on Government Way was established in 1894 on a plateau overlooking the river and named in honor of Colonel George Wright, whose troops camped here after defeating the Indians in the Battle of Spokane Plains. The Spokane County Courthouse was built in 1895 and has a massive square tower with a conical roof. Campbell House, built in 1898, has been restored and is open for tours.

Population

Spokane has shown modest population gains since 1970. It grew by 0.5% in the 1970s, from 171,000 to 171,300 in 1980, and then by a slightly higher rate in the 1980s to reach 177,196 in 1990.

Population		
	1980	*1990*
Central City	171,300	177,196
Rank	82	94
Metro Area	341,835	361,364
Pop. Change 1980–1990 +5,896		
Pop. % Change 1980–1990 +3.4		
Median Age 33.4		
% Male 47.7		
% Age 65 and Over 16.2		
Density (per square mile) 3,169		

Households
Number 75,147
Persons per Household 2.29
% Female-Headed Households 12.4
% One-Person Households 33.8
Births—Total 2,989
% to Mothers under 20 11.1
Birth Rate per 1,000 17.2

Ethnic Composition

Whites make up 93.3%, blacks 1.9%, American Indians 2%, Asians and Pacific Islanders 2.1%, and others 0.7%.

Ethnic Composition (as % of total pop.)		
	1980	*1990*
White	94.34	93.28
Black	1.62	1.93
American Indian	1.57	2.04
Asian and Pacific Islander	1.36	2.08
Hispanic	1.49	2.08
Other	NA	0.67

Government

Under its 1910 charter Spokane has a mayor-council-manager form of government. The mayor and six members of the council are elected to four-year terms. The council appoints a city manager as chief operating officer.

Government
Year of Home Charter 1910
Number of Members of the Governing Body 6
Elected at Large 6
Elected by Wards NA
Number of Women in Governing Body 1
Salary of Mayor $25,000
Salary of Council Members $12,500
City Government Employment Total 2,010
Rate per 10,000 116.3

Public Finance

The annual budget consists of revenues of $149.409 million and expenditures of $196.910 million. The debt outstanding is $200.932 million and cash and security holdings $210.168 million.

Public Finance
Total Revenue (in millions) $149.409
Intergovernmental Revenue—Total (in millions) $17.45
Federal Revenue per Capita $2.86
% Federal Assistance 1.91
% State Assistance 9.46
Sales Tax as % of Total Revenue 19.49
Local Revenue as % of Total Revenue 71.97
City Income Tax no
Taxes—Total (in millions) $41.7
Taxes per Capita
Total $241
Property $68
Sales and Gross Receipts $152
General Expenditures—Total (in millions) $87.1
General Expenditures per Capita $504
Capital Outlays per Capita $89
% of Expenditures for:
Public Welfare 0.0
Highways 13.4
Education 0.0
Health and Hospitals 1.6
Police 12.7
Sewerage and Sanitation 14.6
Parks and Recreation 11.7
Housing and Community Development 3.5
Debt Outstanding per Capita $241
% Utility 37.6
Federal Procurement Contract Awards (in millions) $64.7
Federal Grants Awards (in millions) $16.3
Fiscal Year Begins January 1

Economy

Spokane is the industrial and trade capital of the region, known as the Inland Empire. It has unmatched natural resources, particularly lumber and mining. Inland Empire is the only source for certain rare minerals, such as antimony and vermiculite, and it also accounts for about 40% of the silver mined in the nation. Most manufacturing is based on natural resources. Agriculture is still an important revenue-earner. The region produces a wide range of farm produce, such as apples, peas, pears, hops, asparagus, and sweet cherries. Spokane is also a center of Washington's brewing industry.

Economy

Total Money Income (in millions) $1,690.3
% of State Average   89.7
Per Capita Annual Income $9,751
% Population below Poverty Level   13.9
Fortune 500 Companies

Banks	Number	Deposits (in millions)
Commercial	7	1,843
Savings	41	1,528

Passenger Autos   204,098
Electric Meters   138,264
Gas Meters   48,479

Manufacturing

Number of Establishments   323
% with 20 or More Employees   20.1
Manufacturing Payroll (in millions)   NA
Value Added by Manufacture (in millions)   NA
Value of Shipments (in millions)   NA
New Capital Expenditures (in millions)   NA

Wholesale Trade

Number of Establishments   573
Sales (in millions) $1,816.1
Annual Payroll (in millions) $148.814

Retail Trade

Number of Establishments   2,015
Total Sales (in millions) $1,556.5
Sales per Capita $9,003
Number of Retail Trade Establishments with Payroll   1,396
Annual Payroll (in millions) $190.5
Total Sales (in millions) $1,527.8
General Merchandise Stores (per capita) $1,576
Food Stores (per capita) $1,670
Apparel Stores (per capita) $535
Eating and Drinking Places (per capita) $907

Service Industries

Total Establishments   1,880
Total Receipts (in millions) $663.2
Hotels and Motels (in millions) $33.0
Health Services (in millions) $247.2
Legal Services (in millions) $66.8

Labor

The employment market is dominated by state government, Fairchild AFB, Eastern Washington University, Sacred Heart Hospital, and public utilities. Among private employers, the largest are Kaiser Aluminum, Hewlett-Packard, Burlington Northern, and Cowles Publishing.

Labor

Civilian Labor Force   87,415
% Change 1989–1990   1.0

Work Force Distribution
Mining   NA
Construction   NA
Manufacturing   NA
Transportation and Public Utilities   NA
Wholesale and Retail Trade   26,097
FIRE (Finance, Insurance, Real Estate)   NA
Service   13,986
Government   4,597
Women as % of Labor Force   44.1
% Self-Employed   6.5
% Professional/Technical   16.0
Total Unemployment   4,789
Rate %   5.5
Federal Government Civilian Employment   2,587

Education

Spokane School District enrolls 27,965 students in its 64 schools. Spokane is home to an outstanding Jesuit university, Gonzaga University. Eastern Washington University, a state-run school, is located about 15 miles away at Cheney. Whitworth College, a private school affiliated with the Presbyterian Church, is also located in Spokane.

Education

Number of Public Schools   64
Special Education Schools   5
Total Enrollment   27,965
% Enrollment in Private Schools   8.0
% Minority   11.0
Classroom Teachers   1,386
Pupil-Teacher Ratio   20.2:1
Number of Graduates   NA
Total Revenue (in millions) $107.395
Total Expenditures (in millions) $110.236
Expenditures per Pupil $3,770
Educational Attainment (Age 25 and Over)
   % Completed 12 or More Years   76.2
   % Completed 16 or More Years   17.8
Four-Year Colleges and Universities   2
   Enrollment   6,275
Two-Year Colleges   1
   Enrollment   6,881

Libraries

Number   26
Public Libraries   6
Books (in thousands)   596
Circulation (in thousands)   1,505
Persons Served (in thousands)   177
Circulation per Person Served   8.5
Income (in millions) $4.482
Staff   140

Four-Year Colleges and Universities
   Gonzaga University
   Whitworth College

Health

 Spokane has 8 metro hospitals, with 1,770 beds and eight specialized facilities with 1,400 beds offering a variety of services.

Health
Deaths—Total   2,080
Rate per 1,000   12.0
Infant Deaths—Total   34
Rate per 1,000   11.4
Number of Metro Hospitals   8
Number of Metro Hospital Beds   1,770
Rate per 100,000   1,024
Number of Physicians   758
Physicians per 1,000   2.49
Nurses per 1,000   9.15
Health Expenditures per Capita $12.95

Transportation

 Spokane is approached by I-90, which passes through the middle of the city. It is also served by U.S. Highway 2, which approaches the city from the west and then turns north. U.S. 395 continues north into Canada and U.S. 195 continues south. Rail freight service is provided by Burlington Northern and Union Pacific. The principal air terminal is Spokane International Airport, a few miles from downtown, served by five airlines.

Transportation
Interstate Highway Mileage   22
Total Urban Mileage   1,632
Total Daily Vehicle Mileage (in millions) $5.316
Daily Average Commute Time   40.5 min.
Number of Buses   99
Port Tonnage (in millions)   NA
Airports   1
Number of Daily Flights   68
Daily Average Number of Passengers   1,982
Airlines (American carriers only)
Alaska
Continental
Delta
Horizon
Northwest
United

Housing

 Of the total housing stock 57.2% is owner-occupied. The median value of an owner-occupied home is $51,000 and the median monthly rent $278.

Housing
Total Housing Units   79,875
% Change 1980–1990   4.8
Vacant Units for Sale or Rent   3,470
Occupied Units   75,147
% with More Than One Person per Room   2.5
% Owner-Occupied   57.2
Median Value of Owner-Occupied Homes $51,000
Average Monthly Purchase Cost $315
Median Monthly Rent $278

Housing (continued)
New Private Housing Starts   812
Value (in thousands) $62,237
% Single-Family   53.4
Nonresidential Buildings Value (in thousands) $45,519

Urban Redevelopment

 Riverfront Park, the site of the 1974 World's Fair Expo, has been developed into a multipurpose cultural and recreational complex. It includes a convention center and theater. The Spokane Coliseum and the Joseph A. Albi Stadium are two large projects that have been completed in recent years. Urban development programs are coordinated by Spokane Regional Planning Conference and Spokane Unlimited.

Crime

 Spokane ranks average in public safety. In 1991, violent crimes totaled 1,283, property crimes totaled 14,935.

Crime
Violent Crimes—Total   1,283
Violent Crime Rate per 100,000   424.1
Murder   7
Rape   98
Robbery   372
Aggravated Assaults   806
Property Crimes   14,935
Burglary   3,298
Larceny   10,916
Motor Vehicle Theft   721
Arson   61
Per Capita Police Expenditures $106.78
Per Capita Fire Protection Expenditures $84.66
Number of Police   236
Per 1,000   1.34

Religion

Catholics form the largest population, followed by Mormons and Lutherans. Our Lady of Lourdes Cathedral, built in 1908, is the oldest existing Roman Catholic church in the Inland Empire. The Episcopal Cathedral of St. John the Evangelist is an outstanding architectural landmark designed in Gothic style.

Religion	
Largest Denominations (Adherents)	
Catholic	41,095
Latter-Day Saints	11,976
Evangelical Lutheran	10,781
United Methodist	6,102
Presbyterian	8,277
Episcopal	4,673
Southern Baptist	5,758
Assembly of God	4,089
Lutheran-Missouri Synod	3,995
Jewish	1,378

Media

Spokane daily press consists of the *Spokane Spokesman-Review* and the *Spokane Chronicle*. The electronic media consist of 5 television stations and 25 AM and FM radio stations.

Media

Newsprint
    Spokane Chronicle, daily
    Spokane Spokesman-Review, daily
    Spokane Valley Herald, weekly

Television
    KAYU (Channel 28)
    KHQ (Channel 6)
    KREM (Channel 2)
    KSPS (Channel 7)
    KXLY (Channel 4)

Radio

KAGU (FM)	KAQQ (AM)
KDRK (FM)	KEYF (AM)
KEYF (FM)	KEZE (FM)
KGA (AM)	KHDL (AM)
KISC (FM)	KJRB (AM)
KKPL (FM)	KMBI (AM)
KMBI (FM)	KPBX (FM)
KSBN (AM)	KSFC (FM)
KSVY (AM)	KTRW (AM)
KUDY (AM)	KZZU (FM)
KKZX (FM)	KVXO (FM)
KWRS (FM)	KXLY (AM)
KXLY (FM)	

Sports

Spokane has no major professional sports team but Gonzaga University sports and athletic teams are popular. Spokane Indians are a minor league baseball team. Thoroughbred racing is held at Playfair Race Course.

Arts, Culture, and Tourism

The Riverfront Park Center, Spokane Civic Theater, and Spokane Coliseum are the principal venues for cultural performances. Music is represented by Spokane Symphony, Spokane Jazz Society, Connoisseur Concerts, and Spokane Opera House; dance by Spokane Ballet and theater by Spokane Interplayers Ensemble. Spokane has four major museums, including the Spokane Public Museum, founded in 1916; Spokane Arts Center; Museum of Native American Culture on the campus of Gonzaga University; and the Cheney Cowles Museum.

Travel and Tourism

Hotel Rooms   3,469
Convention and Exhibit Space (square feet)   60,000

Convention Centers
    Riverpark Center
    Spokane Coliseum

Festivals
    Music and Allied Arts Festival
    Lilac Festival

Parks and Recreation

The city maintains over 100 parks of which the most attractive are the 93-acre Down River Park, on Summit Boulevard and Mission Avenue northward along the Spokane River; the 4.5-acre Cliff Park on 13th Avenue located on a rocky bluff and including Review Rock; and the 90-acre Manito Park and Flower Gardens, bounded by Bernard Street, Grand Boulevard, and 17th and 25th avenues.

Sources of Further Information

City Hall West
808 Spokane Falls Boulevard
Spokane, WA 99201
(509) 456-2665

Spokane Area Chamber of Commerce
West 1020 Riverside Avenue
Spokane, WA 99201
(509) 624-1393

Spokane Area Convention and Visitors Bureau
301 West Main
Spokane, WA 99201
(509) 624-11341

Additional Reading

Cochran, Barbara. *Exploring Spokane's Past*. 1984.
Glover, James N. *Reminiscences of James N. Glover*. 1985.
Hook, Harry H., and Francis J. Maguire. *Spokane Falls Illustrated*. 1984.
Schmeltzer, Michael. *Spokane: The City and the People*. 1988.

Springfield

Illinois

Basic Data

Name   Springfield, IL
Name Origin   From local springs
Year Founded   1818 Inc. 1840
Status: State   Capital of Illinois
         County   Seat of Sangamon County
Area (square miles)   42.5
Elevation (feet)   610
Time Zone   Central
Population (1990)   105,227
Population of Metro Area (1990)   189,550

Sister Cities
   Ashikaga, Japan

Distance in Miles To:
   Chicago   202
   St. Louis   96
   Peoria   72
   Champaign   87
   Rockford   194
   Moline   164

Location and Topography

 Springfield is located in central Illinois, south of the Sangamon River. The terrain is gently sloping, but rolling terrain is found near Sangamon River and Spring Creek. The city is surrounded by rich agricultural land.

Layout of City and Suburbs

Springfield is a planned city laid out in a grid pattern. Washington Street bisects the city from east to west, and the parallel Fifth and Sixth streets bisect it north to south. All three of these streets intersect in the center of downtown. The capitol is located between Washington Park and Pasfield Park. The city is dominated by two Lincoln monuments: his home between Eighth and Jackson streets and his tomb to the north of the city near Lincoln Park. Just outside the city limits to the south is

Lake Springfield with the Sangamon State University on its shores.

Environment

Environmental Stress Index   2.2
Green Cities Index: Rank   NA
                    Score   NA
Water Quality   Neutral, soft
Average Daily Use (gallons per capita)   145
     Maximum Supply (gallons per capita)   268
Parkland as % of Total City Area   NA
% Waste Landfilled/Recycled   NA
Annual Parks Expenditures per Capita $26.41

Climate

Springfield has a typically continental climate with warm to hot summers and cold winters. Summers are sunny and often uncomfortably warm and humid, while the winters, though milder than in cities to the north, are subject to chilly prairie winds. Relative humidity is 64% annually. Annual snowfall averages 22 inches.

Weather

Temperature

Highest Monthly Average °F   87.1
Lowest Monthly Average °F   16.3

Annual Averages

Days 32°F or Below   119
Days above 90°F   28
Zero Degree Days   8
Precipitation (inches)   35
Snow (inches)   22
% Seasonal Humidity   71
Wind Speed (m.p.h.)   11.4
Clear Days   108
Cloudy Days   165

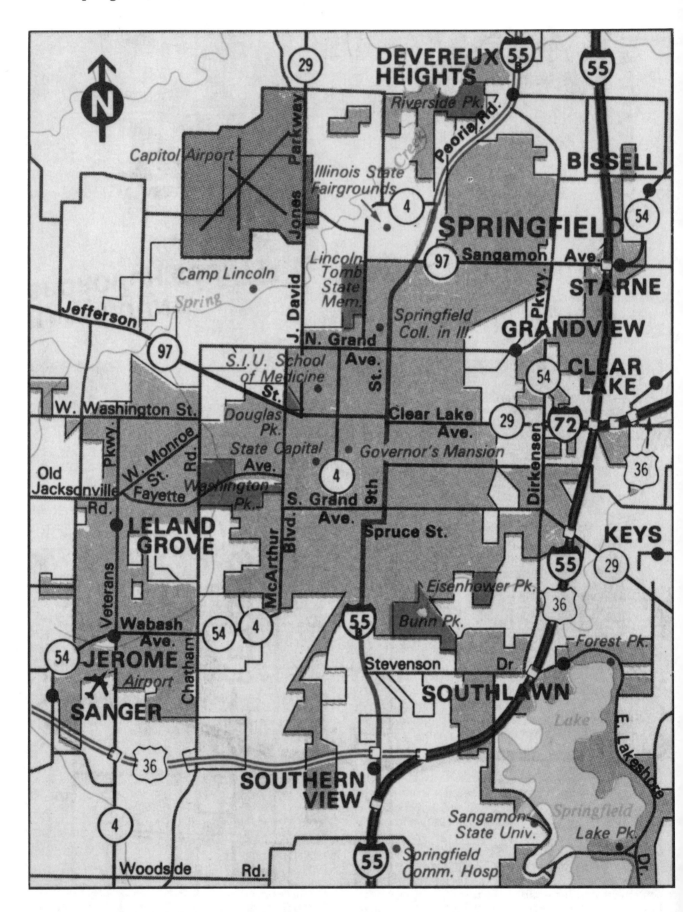

Weather (continued)

Storm Days 50
Rainy Days 112

Average Temperatures (°F)	High	Low	Mean
January	34.8	18.6	26.7
February	38.9	21.8	30.4
March	48.7	30.1	39.4
April	63.6	42.6	53.1
May	74.1	52.6	63.4
June	83.3	62.5	72.9
July	86.6	65.6	76.1
August	85.0	63.7	74.4
September	78.7	55.6	67.2
October	68.1	45.0	56.6
November	51.0	32.7	41.9
December	38.2	22.7	30.5

History

Springfield has two founders. The first was Elisha Kelly who arrived from North Carolina in 1818 and settled there with his father and brothers. Sangamon County was organized in 1821 and the temporary county seat was located in Kelly's field near a spring, which led to the name Springfield. The *Sangamon Journal* began publication in 1831 in Springfield, which was incorporated as a town the following year. The second founder was Abraham Lincoln, because it was through his efforts (as well as those of his fellow legislators) that the capital of Illinois was moved from Vandalia to Springfield in 1837. The city was incorporated in 1840.

After Lincoln's assassination, the city became a living monument to him. A new capitol was completed in 1868.

Historical Landmarks

Monuments to Abraham Lincoln dot the city. His home on the northeast corner of Eighth and Jackson streets is a national historic site. It is the only house that he owned, and he lived there from 1844 until his departure for Washington in 1861. In 1881 Robert Lincoln gave the property to the State of Illinois, when it became the first state memorial. The Lincoln law offices on Fifth Street; the C. M. Smith Store on Adams Street, where he drafted his first inaugural address; the First Presbyterian Church on Capitol Avenue, which Lincoln attended and where his pew is preserved; the Abraham Lincoln Museum on South Eighth Street; the Ninian Edwards House, where the Lincolns were married; and the Lincoln Depot, where he said farewell to his fellow Springfield citizens on 11 February 1861 upon leaving for Washington, are all historical landmarks associated with Lincoln. The Lincoln Tomb at the end of Monument Avenue in Oak Ridge Cemetery is one of the most visited sites in Springfield. The marble monument stands on a landscaped area of 12.4 acres. Two staircases lead to the balustraded roof from which rises the 117-foot obelisk.

The State Capitol is an imposing structure completed in 1868 at a cost of $4.5 million. Its dome rises 451 feet above the city. Directly west of the capitol stands the Illinois State Office Building completed in 1956 in the form of an "H." The Centennial Building, facing the south side of the capitol, was completed in 1923 to commemorate the centennial of Illinois as a state. The Old State Capitol, occupying the historic square, bounded by Fifth, Sixth, Washington, and Adams streets, is a new structure that incorporates original walls and columns of the old. It was dedicated as a Lincoln historic shrine in 1968. The Vachel Lindsay Home on South Fifth Street is maintained by the Vachel Lindsay Association and is filled with his books and papers. The Dana-Thomas House, designed by Frank Lloyd Wright in 1902, is a good example of the architect's Prairie style.

Population

Springfield crossed the 100,000 population mark in 1980 and grew by 5.2% in the next decade to reach 105,227 in 1990.

Population	1980	1990
Central City	100,054	105,227
Rank	171	181
Metro Area	187,770	189,550
Pop. Change 1980–1990 +5,173		
Pop. % Change 1980–1990 +5.2		
Median Age 34.0		
% Male 46.0		
% Age 65 and Over 14.9		
Density (per square mile) 2,475		

Households
Number   45,006
Persons per Household   2.29
% Female-Headed Households   12.7
% One-Person Households   35.0
Births—Total   1,817
% to Mothers under 20   13.0
Birth Rate per 1,000   17.9

Ethnic Composition

Whites make up 86% of the population, African Americans 13%, Asians and Pacific Islanders 1%, American Indians 0.2%, and Hispanics 0.8%.

Ethnic Composition (as % of total pop.)	1980	1990
White	88.04	85.59
Black	10.79	13.01
American Indian	0.11	0.16
Asian and Pacific Islander	0.69	0.98
Hispanic	0.66	0.83
Other		0.25

Government

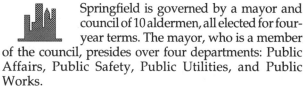

Springfield is governed by a mayor and council of 10 aldermen, all elected for four-year terms. The mayor, who is a member of the council, presides over four departments: Public Affairs, Public Safety, Public Utilities, and Public Works.

Chronology

1818   Elisha Kelly of North Carolina settles in Springfield with his father and brothers.

1821   Sangamon County is organized and the temporary county seat is located on Kelly's property.

1831   *Sangamon Journal* debuts.

1832   Springfield is incorporated as a town.

1837   Through the efforts of Abraham Lincoln and his fellow legislators, the capital of Illinois is moved from Vandalia to Springfield.

1840   Springfield is incorporated as a city.

1868   New capitol building is completed.

Government

Year of Home Charter
Number of Members of the Governing Body   10
Elected at Large   10
Elected by Wards   NA
Number of Women in Governing Body   0
Salary of Mayor $62,000
Salary of Council Members $8,000
City Government Employment Total   1,776
Rate per 10,000   177.1

Public Finance

 The annual budget consists of revenues of $162.061 million and expenditures of $157.280 million. The debt outstanding is $263.234 million, and cash and security holdings total $232.225 million.

Public Finance

Total Revenue (in millions) $162.061
Intergovernmental Revenue—Total (in millions) $11.28
Federal Revenue per Capita $2.02
% Federal Assistance   1.25
% State Assistance   5.67
Sales Tax as % of Total Revenue   15.5
Local Revenue as % of Total Revenue   33.3
City Income Tax   no
Taxes—Total (in millions) $25.0

Taxes per Capita
   Total $249
   Property $102
   Sales and Gross Receipts $125
General Expenditures—Total (in millions) $44.0
General Expenditures per Capita $439
Capital Outlays per Capita $10

% of Expenditures for:
   Public Welfare   0.0
   Highways   11.1
   Education   0.0
   Health and Hospitals   5.8
   Police   19.6
   Sewerage and Sanitation   1.8
   Parks and Recreation   4.1
   Housing and Community Development   8.0

Public Finance (continued)

Debt Outstanding per Capita $2,182
   % Utility   58.5
Federal Procurement Contract Awards (in millions) $86.1
Federal Grants Awards (in millions) $413.9
Fiscal Year Begins   March 1

Economy

Springfield's economy is dominated by the public sector. There is, however, a strong private sector that is supplemented by the professional activities of numerous lobbying groups and over 150 state, regional, and national associations. Because of the city's central location and well-developed transportation and distribution facilities, manufacturing has become increasingly important in the economy.

Economy

Total Money Income (in millions) $1,164.2
% of State Average   103.0
Per Capita Annual Income $11,642
% Population below Poverty Level   10.5
Fortune 500 Companies   NA

Banks	*Number*	*Deposits (in millions)*
Commercial	10	1,415
Savings	5	425

Passenger Autos   110,307
Electric Meters   56,500
Gas Meters   50,012

Manufacturing

Number of Establishments   93
% with 20 or More Employees   32.3
Manufacturing Payroll (in millions) $73.6
Value Added by Manufacture (in millions) $173.8
Value of Shipments (in millions) $424.1
New Capital Expenditures (in millions)   NA

Wholesale Trade

Number of Establishments   229
Sales (in millions) $1,271.4
Annual Payroll (in millions) $73.375

Retail Trade

Number of Establishments   1,255
Total Sales (in millions) $1,113.1
Sales per Capita $11,099
Number of Retail Trade Establishments with Payroll   923
Annual Payroll (in millions) $126.8
Total Sales (in millions) $1,100.8
General Merchandise Stores (per capita) $1,921
Food Stores (per capita) $1,791
Apparel Stores (per capita) $482
Eating and Drinking Places (per capita) $1,191

Service Industries

Total Establishments   1,013
Total Receipts (in millions) $502.7
Hotels and Motels (in millions) $44.3
Health Services (in millions) $163.2
Legal Services (in millions) $36.3

Labor

Nearly one-third of the city's work force is engaged in the public sector, about 25% in services, 20% in trade, and 4% in manufacturing. The distribution of the work force in Sangamon County and Greater Springfield is more diverse. The proportion of workers commuting to the city from outlying suburbs is much greater in Springfield than in comparable cities. The largest private manufacturer employs only 450 workers, whereas the State of Illinois employs 20,000.

Labor	
Civilian Labor Force 61,534	
% Change 1989–1990 0.2	
Work Force Distribution	
Mining NA	
Construction 3,900	
Manufacturing 4,000	
Transportation and Public Utilities 4,800	
Wholesale and Retail Trade 25,200	
FIRE (Finance, Insurance, Real Estate) 7,800	
Service 29,200	
Government 34,300	
Women as % of Labor Force 48.7	
% Self-Employed 5.0	
% Professional/Technical 18.0	
Total Unemployment 3,356	
Rate % 5.5	
Federal Government Civilian Employment 1,873	

Education

Springfield Public School District supports 32 elementary, junior high, and senior high schools. The only university in the area is Sangamon State University, founded in 1970 on a 1,000-acre campus, which it shares with Lincoln Land Community College. The oldest junior college is the Springfield College in Illinois, conducted by the Ursuline Order. The Southern Illinois University (SIU) School of Medicine is located in Springfield.

Education	
Number of Public Schools 32	
Special Education Schools NA	
Total Enrollment 15,813	
% Enrollment in Private Schools 18.2	
% Minority NA	
Classroom Teachers NA	
Pupil-Teacher Ratio NA	
Number of Graduates NA	
Total Revenue (in millions) NA	
Total Expenditures (in millions) NA	
Expenditures per Pupil NA	
Educational Attainment (Age 25 and Over) NA	
% Completed 12 or More Years 71.9	
% Completed 16 or More Years 20.8	
Four-Year Colleges and Universities 1	
Enrollment 4,347	
Two-Year Colleges 2	
Enrollment 7,717	

Education (continued)	
Libraries	
Number 26	
Public Libraries 4	
Books (in thousands) 365	
Circulation (in thousands) 1,043	
Persons Served (in thousands) 101	
Circulation per Person Served 10.32	
Income (in millions) $2.21	
Staff 90	
Four-Year Colleges and Universities	
Sangamon State University	

Health

Springfield's three primary medical care facilities are St. John's Hospital, Memorial Medical Center, and Doctors Hospital. The SIU School of Medicine is a major medical resource in teaching and research.

Health	
Deaths—Total 1,213	
Rate per 1,000 11.9	
Infant Deaths—Total 27	
Rate per 1,000 14.9	
Number of Metro Hospitals 4	
Number of Metro Hospital Beds 1,594	
Rate per 100,000 1,589	
Number of Physicians 544	
Physicians per 1,000 NA	
Nurses per 1,000 NA	
Health Expenditures per Capita $20.91	

Transportation

Springfield is accessed by three interstate freeways, a limited access highway, and several state routes. Interstate 55 intersects Sangamon County and runs north-south along the eastern boundary of Springfield; I-72 links the city with Champaign-Urbana to the east; U.S. 36 connects with I-55 south of Springfield and continues west to Jacksonville. State routes include the east-west 29, 54, and 97, and north-south 4. Passenger rail services are provided by Amtrak, and freight services are provided by Southern Pacific Railroad, Illinois Central Railroad, Norfolk and Southern Railroads, Chicago and Northwestern Transportation Company, and Chicago and Illinois Midland Railway. The city airport is Capital Airport, served by four commercial airlines.

Transportation	
Interstate Highway Mileage 14	
Total Urban Mileage 587	
Total Daily Vehicle Mileage (in millions) $2.524	
Daily Average Commute Time 38.1 min.	
Number of Buses 37	
Port Tonnage (in millions) NA	
Airports 1	
Number of Daily Flights 71	
Daily Average Number of Passengers NA	

Transportation (continued)

Airlines (American carriers only)
    American
    Continental Express
    Midway
    Trans World

Housing

Most Springfield workers live in the suburbs and commute to the city. As a result, there has been only limited housing construction activity in the city in recent decades, and most houses are over 50 years old. Of total housing stock, 58.3% is owner-occupied. The median value of owner-occupied homes is $59,200, and the median rent is $316.

Housing

Total Housing Units	48,534
% Change 1980–1990	9.3
Vacant Units for Sale or Rent	2,692
Occupied Units	45,006
% with More Than One Person per Room	2.0
% Owner-Occupied	58.3
Median Value of Owner-Occupied Homes	$59,200
Average Monthly Purchase Cost	$362
Median Monthly Rent	$316
New Private Housing Starts	944
Value (in thousands)	$48,515
% Single-Family	35.8
Nonresidential Buildings Value (in thousands)	$26,481

Urban Redevelopment

Most construction activity in Springfield is in the private commercial sector. Local investors have helped to expand the city to its southern and western sides. Many of them are mixed-use developments, combining office, residential, and retail space.

Crime

Springfield has a crime rate above the national average. Police reported 933 violent crimes and 9,202 property crimes in 1991.

Crime

Violent Crimes—Total	933
Violent Crime Rate per 100,000	NA
Murder	2
Rape	NA
Robbery	324
Aggravated Assaults	768
Property Crimes	9,202
Burglary	2,475
Larceny	6,332
Motor Vehicle Theft	395
Arson	81
Per Capita Police Expenditures	$90.55
Per Capita Fire Protection Expenditures	$82.43
Number of Police	198
Per 1,000	1.95

Religion

While Catholics are the largest denomination, Springfield has a rich Presbyterian history. Other Protestant denominations are also well represented.

Religion

Largest Denominations (Adherents)	
Catholic	35,589
United Methodist	12,438
Black Baptist	4,424
Southern Baptist	4,228
Evangelical Lutheran	3,811
Church of Christ	8,757
Assembly of God	7,967
American Baptist	4,424
Lutheran-Missouri Synod	7,759
Presbyterian	5,186
Jewish	1,000

Media

The city's daily newspaper is the *State Journal-Register*. Electronic media consist of four television stations and eight AM and FM stations.

Media

Newsprint
    State Journal-Register, daily

Television
    WCFN (Channel 49)
    WICS (Channel 20)
    WRSP (Channel 55)
    WSEC (Channels 14 & 65)

Radio

WCVS (AM)	WFMB (FM)
WNNS (FM)	WQNA (FM)
WSSU (FM)	WTAX (AM)
WVEM (FM)	WYMG (FM)

Sports

Springfield's only professional sports team is the Springfield Cardinals, a class A minor league team of the National League St. Louis Cardinals, who play at the Lanphier Stadium.

Arts, Culture, and Tourism

The Springfield Theater Guild in drama, the Springfield Symphony Orchestra in music, and the Ballet Company in dance provide the institutional settings for performing arts in the city. During the summer months, the Great American People Show stages outdoor drama in a natural amphitheater in New Salem State Park. The Illinois State Museum has changing and permanent exhibits on Illinois history. The Vachel Lindsay Home and the Edwards Place (the city's oldest home) are also museums open to the public.

Travel and Tourism

Hotel Rooms   3,176
Convention and Exhibit Space (square feet)   NA

Convention Centers
   Prairie Capital Convention Center

Festivals
   International Carillon Festival (June)
   Lincolnfest (July)
   Old Capitol Art Fair (May)
   Illinois State Fair (August)
   International Ethnic Festival (September)
   Air Rendezvous (August)

Parks and Recreation

The largest recreation area is the 150-acre Washington Park, located in the west-central part of the city. It is noted for its flower gardens and a carillon on a hilltop. The 60-acre Abraham Lincoln Memorial Garden on the northeast shore of Lake Springfield has numerous woodland trails and bridges. Lake Springfield, a 4,040-acre man-made reservoir, is surrounded by eight parks.

Sources of Further Information

The Greater Springfield Chamber of Commerce
3 Old State Capitol, Suite 100
Springfield, IL 62701
(217) 525-1173

Sangamon County Historical Society
308 East Adams
Springfield, IL 62701
(217) 522-2500

Springfield Convention and Visitors Bureau
115 North Seventh Street
Springfield, IL 62705
(217) 789-2360

Springfield Public Library
326 South Seventh Street
Springfield, IL 62701
(217) 753-4900

Additional Reading

Polk's Springfield City Directory. 1991.
Retail Trends and Opportunities, Springfield/Sangamon County. 1991.

Springfield

Massachusetts

Basic Data

Name   Springfield, MA
Name Origin   From Springfield, England
Year Founded   1636 Inc. 1852
Status: State   Massachusetts
     County   Seat of Hampden County
Area (square miles)   32.1
Elevation (feet)   85
Time Zone   EST
Population (1990)   156,983
Population of Metro Area (1990)   602,878

Distance in Miles To:

Boston	90
Albany	86
Hartford	29
Manchester	113
New York	136
Portsmouth	152
Providence	88
Worcester	51
Pittsfield	50
Lowell	99

Location and Topography

Springfield is located on the east bank of the Connecticut River, in Pioneer Valley, about 92 miles southwest of Boston and 3 miles from the Connecticut border. Springfield is the seat of Hampden County and the third-largest city in Massachusetts.

Springfield occupies a plateau between the Holyoke Range of the White Mountains to the east and the Green Mountains to the west. As a riverine town, it has a flat terrain.

Layout of City and Suburbs

Downtown Springfield is composed of eight different districts, each with its own physical, social, and economic characteristics. The mix of buildings and activities varies from district to district, as does the height and density of buildings, the width of the streets, and the amount of open space.

The Downtown Core is the primary shopping area and office district, and it houses the largest employers and the majority of the financial businesses. It includes the shopping malls of BayState West and Center Square, Steiger's Department Store, and the shops of Market Place, Columbus Center, and Bridge Street.

Court Square is the institutional and government center comprising such landmarks as the City Hall, the Campanile, Symphony Hall, the Hall of Justice, and the Civic Center.

The North Blocks is a mixed-use district of late–19th-century, four- to six-story buildings.

New North is a 1960s commercial district of low-density buildings surrounded by large surface parking lots.

State-Union area is a transition area between downtown and the South End neighborhood. Nearly every conceivable type of business is found here, including law firms and professional service businesses, attracted by the proximity to the courthouse and city and county offices.

The Quadrangle residential area is the cultural core of the city, marked by high-quality architecture.

The Lyman-Taylor area is a fringe area east of Chestnut Street. Its most characteristic feature is the predominance of automotive businesses.

The city has many places for people to meet. Stearns Square, Court Square, and the Quadrangle are historic public parks. Cobblestones and brick walkways at Market Place, Columbus Center, and Duryea Way have made Springfield a pedestrian's haven. The Armory Commons, Morgan Square, and Stockbridge Court are residential parks. The indoor courts at BayState West and Center Square are filled many evenings with

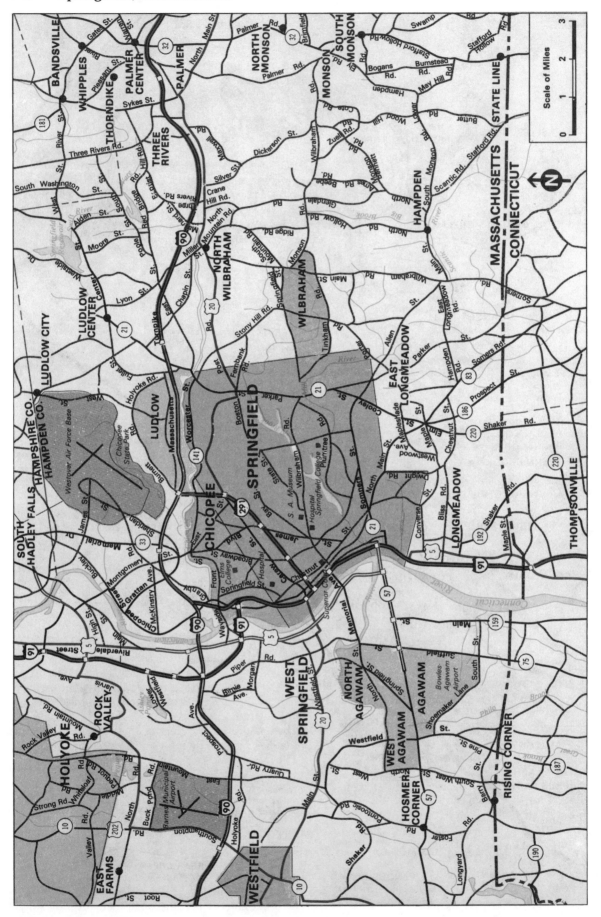

concerts and community events. Keep America Beautiful, the national civic beautification program, featured Court Square in its television program in 1987.

Environment

Environmental Stress Index	2.6
Green Cities Index: Rank	NA
Score	NA
Water Quality	Acid, very soft
Average Daily Use (gallons per capita)	152
Maximum Supply (gallons per capita)	384
Parkland as % of Total City Area	9.9
% Waste Landfilled/Recycled 82:14	Composted 4
Annual Parks Expenditures per Capita	$20.83

Climate

Springfield has a typical New England climate with generous snowfall of about 45 inches annually, cold winters, and fairly warm summers in which the average temperature is about 73°F in July and 27°F in January.

Weather

Temperature

Highest Monthly Average °F	73.6
Lowest Monthly Average °F	26.6

Annual Averages

Days 32°F or Below	126
Days above 90°F	16
Zero Degree Days	4
Precipitation (inches)	44.87
Snow (inches)	44.5
% Seasonal Humidity	NA
Wind Speed (m.p.h.)	NA
Clear Days	NA
Cloudy Days	NA
Storm Days	NA
Rainy Days	NA

Average Temperatures (°F)	High	Low	Mean
January	35.0	18.1	26.6
February	37.3	19.7	28.5
March	46.5	28.2	37.4
April	60.3	38.1	49.2
May	71.4	47.7	59.6
June	79.8	56.8	68.3
July	84.6	62.5	73.6
August	82.9	60.9	71.9
September	75.0	52.6	63.8
October	64.5	42.8	53.7
November	51.4	34.4	42.9
December	38.3	22.5	30.5

History

The first white settlement in Springfield was made on the west side of the Connecticut River in the spring of 1636 by a group of 12 families led by William Pynchon, one of the original founders of the Massachusetts Bay Colony. Fear of clashes with the Indians caused the settlers to move to the less fertile east side of the river on the present-day site of Springfield. In 1640 the settlement's name was changed from Agawam to Springfield, after Pynchon's birthplace in England. Springfield was established as a town in 1641. Pynchon remained its leader until 1652 when he was forced to leave for England after being publicly condemned and deprived of his magistracy by the Massachusetts General Court for his heretical writings. During King Philip's War in 1675, the settlement was virtually destroyed by the Agawam Indians, but was soon rebuilt.

At the outset of the Revolutionary War Springfield's numerous gunsmith shops were transformed into factories to supply arms to the colonial forces. In 1777 the town's small arsenal was enlarged under George Washington's orders, and Springfield became an important supply point for the Continental Army. In 1786 followers of Daniel Shays made an abortive attack on the arsenal to secure arms for Shays' army. The town's industrial growth was determined by the establishment of a federal armory in 1794. Development was further stimulated by the opening of the railroad between Worcester and Springfield in 1839. In 1852 Springfield became a city. Skilled artisans and inventors flocked to Springfield, leading to the establishment of a diverse industrial base that included paper, machinery, textiles, and swords. In 1892 Charles E. Duryea and his brother Frank invented what is considered the first gasoline-powered automobile in the United States. It was a two-cycle, one-cylinder model. In 1895 the brothers founded the nation's first automobile company, the Duryea Motor Wagon Company. Springfield also was the site of the invention of the motorcycle by George Hendee in 1901. James Naismith, the father of basketball, was another native son of the city.

During the Civil War era, abolitionist John Brown lived in Springfield and made it an important stop on the Underground Railroad. The Springfield rifles were used by the Union Army in the Civil War and by both sides in the Franco-Prussian War. The town's arms industry was immortalized by the poet Henry Wadsworth Longfellow in his poem "The Arsenal at Springfield."

Springfield's population grew rapidly during what is described as the second colonization of New England. The turn of the century witnessed a massive influx of immigrants—first the Irish, followed by the French-Canadians, Germans, Scots, Italians, Jews, Russians, Poles, Portuguese, Greeks, Blacks, and Hispanics roughly in that order. The Springfield Armory played an important role in both world wars, supplying the Springfield rifles in World War I and Garand semiautomatic rifles in World War II. Although the Armory closed in the 1960s, the tradition lives on through other small arms makers, such as Smith & Wesson and Dan Wesson Arms.

Historical Landmarks

Downtown Springfield has two local historic districts, a designation that protects historic properties and sites from indiscriminate developers. These districts boast some architectural landmarks and a fine collection of late–19th- and early 20th-century architecture. City Hall, the Campanile (a 300-foot carillon bell tower), and Symphony Hall are Springfield's signature buildings. The

Chronology

1636 William Pynchon leads a group of 12 families from Boston to a site on the west bank of the Connecticut River in the Pioneer Valley. Faced with Indian attacks, the settlers withdraw to the eastern bank.

1640 The town is named Springfield in honor of Pynchon's hometown in England.

1641 Springfield is established as a town.

1675 Springfield is burned by the Indians during King Philip's War.

1777 George Washington selects Springfield as the site for a national arsenal.

1786 Daniel Shays and his followers make an abortive attempt to seize the arsenal.

1794 Federal government establishes the arsenal as the Springfield Armory.

1843 The first Merriam-Webster Dictionary is published in Springfield.

1852 Springfield receives city charter.

1891 John Naismith nails two peach baskets at either end of a YMCA gym and plays the world's first game of basketball.

1892 The Duryea, the nation's first successful gasoline-powered automobile, makes its trial run in Springfield.

1895 The Duryea Motor Wagon Company is founded.

1901 George Hendee invents the motorcycle.

1968 The Springfield Armory stops manufacturing operations.

1971 BayState West, a hotel-office-retail complex, opens.

1972 The Civic Center is completed.

1982 One Financial Plaza and Center Square open for business.

real personality of the city, however, comes from the commercial buildings lining Main Street; the brownstones and the gas lamps in the Mattoon and Pearl Street neighborhoods; the industrial buildings of the North Blocks; the McKnight district, with nearly 900 Victorian homes; and the small park resulting from the collaboration of sculptor Augustus St. Gaudens and the architect Sanford White. City Hall in Court Square boasts Corinthian columns and 27 varieties of marble.

Springfield's most famous historic landmark is the Springfield Armory National Historic Site, a large firearms museum housed in the original arsenal. The collection, started by the Army in 1870, is now one of the most extensive in the world and includes the Organ of Guns immortalized by Longfellow.

Population

Springfield has experienced a slight increase in population since the 1980s. In the 1990 census Springfield reported a population of 156,983 compared to 152,319 in 1980. Nine neighborhoods reported growth: East Springfield (3.6%), Memorial Square (7.5%), Metro Center (32.2%), Six Corners (18.2%), Old Hill (4.6%), McKnight (0.7%), Bay (20.9%), Pine Point (4.9%), and Boston Road (16.8%). Eight neighborhoods reported decline: Indian Orchard (-0.3%), Liberty Heights/Atwater (-0.2%), Brightwood (-0.6%), South End (-2.8%), Upper Hill (-2.4%), Sixteen Acres (-0.3%), East Forest Park (-3.2%), and Forest Park (-0.2%).

Population		
	1980	*1990*
Central City	152,319	156,983
Rank	103	111
Metro Area	581,831	602,878
Pop. Change 1980–1990 +4,664		
Pop. % Change 1980–1990 +3.1		
Median Age 30.6		
% Male 47.1		
% Age 65 and Over 13.74		
Density (per square mile) 4,890		

Households		
Number 57,769		
Persons per Household 2.60		
% Female-Headed Households 21.2		
% One-Person Households 27.8		
Births—Total 2,604		
% to Mothers under 20 19.4		
Birth Rate per 1,000 17.3		

Ethnic Composition

Blacks and Hispanics are well represented in the city, making up 19.15% and 16.9% of the population respectively. American Indians constitute 0.21% and Asians and Pacific Islanders 1.04%. Whites are drawn from various stocks, such as Germans, Scots, Italians, Jews, Russians, Poles, Portuguese, and Greeks. Blacks constitute a majority in Old Hill, McKnight, Bay, Upper Hill, and a substantial minority in Metro Center and Six Corners. Hispanics dominate Memorial Square and Brightwood, while whites dominate all other neighborhoods. Whites have been losing numbers in virtually all neighborhoods except Bay and Boston Road, while blacks have been gaining in the white neighborhoods.

Ethnic Composition (as % of total pop.)		
	1980	*1990*
White	76.07	68.56
Black	16.56	19.15
American Indian	0.14	0.21
Asian and Pacific Islander	0.34	1.04
Hispanic	9.06	16.9
Other	NA	11.04

Government

The city is governed by a mayor-council form of government. The mayor is elected to two-year terms, while the nine council members serve coinciding two-year terms. The major city agencies are the Springfield Redevelopment Authority, Springfield Planning Board, and the Springfield Parking Authority.

Government

Year of Home Charter   1961
Number of Members of the Governing Body   9
Elected at Large   9
Elected by Wards   NA
Number of Women in Governing Body   2
Salary of Mayor $55,000
Salary of Council Members $7,500
City Government Employment Total   6,706
Rate per 10,000   448.8

Public Finance

Springfield's annual budget in 1990 comprised revenues of $290.542 million and expenditures of $320.330 million. Total debt outstanding was $99.445 million and cash and security holdings $20.927 million. The largest item under revenues was state government subsidies, and the largest item under expenditures was education.

Public Finance

Total Revenue (in millions) $290.542
Intergovernmental Revenue—Total (in millions) $160.36
Federal Revenue per Capita $7.84
% Federal Assistance   2.70
% State Assistance   52.49
Sales Tax as % of Total Revenue   NA
Local Revenue as % of Total Revenue   40.7
City Income Tax   no
Taxes—Total (in millions) $55.4

Taxes per Capita
   Total $371
   Property $367
   Sales and Gross Receipts $0
General Expenditures—Total (in millions) $163.2
General Expenditures per Capita $1,092
Capital Outlays per Capita $18

% of Expenditures for:
   Public Welfare   0.4
   Highways   3.3
   Education   47.6
   Health and Hospitals   7.4
   Police   8.3
   Sewerage and Sanitation   5.3
   Parks and Recreation   3.3
   Housing and Community Development   0.0
Debt Outstanding per Capita $287
   % Utility   6.5
Federal Procurement Contract Awards (in millions) $13.0
Federal Grants Awards (in millions) $17.2
Fiscal Year Begins   July 1

Economy

Historically, manufacturing is the mainstay of Springfield's economy, supported by strong financial and service sectors. As the transportation hub and largest town of western Massachusetts, it has drawn skilled workers into the city and surrounding areas, just as it did in the days of the Armory. The mature manufacturing industries, such as fabricated metals, nonelectrical machinery, paper, printing, publishing, chemicals, and plastics, have been joined by high-tech and computer industries in the 1980s. The service industry is anchored by two major insurance companies: Massachusetts Mutual Insurance and Monarch Insurance. Among the institutions promoting business development in Springfield are Springfield Central Business Inc., the city's Community Development Department, and the Springfield Economic Development Corporation. While Springfield, like most Massachusetts towns, was hard hit by the recession of the late 1980s, its robust economic base is expected to help it to

Economy

Total Money Income (in millions) $1,357.8
% of State Average   72.6
Per Capita Annual Income $9,088
% Population below Poverty Level   17.8
Fortune 500 Companies   NA

Banks	Number	Deposits (in millions)
Commercial	10	2,698.3
Savings	27	4,129.2

Passenger Autos   279,146
Electric Meters   NA
Gas Meters   NA

Manufacturing

Number of Establishments   200
% with 20 or More Employees   36.0
Manufacturing Payroll (in millions) $299.5
Value Added by Manufacture (in millions) $631.1
Value of Shipments (in millions) $1,251.4
New Capital Expenditures (in millions) $52.1

Wholesale Trade

Number of Establishments   285
Sales (in millions) $1,168.8
Annual Payroll (in millions) $103,106

Retail Trade

Number of Establishments   1,379
Total Sales (in millions) $1,196.4
Sales per Capita $8,007
Number of Retail Trade Establishments with Payroll   1,034
Annual Payroll (in millions) $146.8
Total Sales (in millions) $1,175.6
General Merchandise Stores (per capita) $1,080
Food Stores (per capita) $1,331
Apparel Stores (per capita) $434
Eating and Drinking Places (per capita) $731

Service Industries

Total Establishments   1,129
Total Receipts (in millions) $533.6
Hotels and Motels (in millions)   NA
Health Services (in millions) $166.3
Legal Services (in millions) $66.5

emerge from the downturn much faster than other towns in the area.

Labor

Of the 66,000 jobs added to western Massachusetts employment during 1986–1991, over one-half were created in Springfield and Hampden County. The share of manufacturing employment, which was 30.7% in 1971, is expected to shrink to 23.9% in 1996, while that of the manufacturing sector is expected to gain correspondingly. The most rapid growing positions in the workforce in the area are for computer specialists, health professionals, teachers, writers and artists, scientists and technical professionals, managers, and clerical workers. Within the service sector, education is a significant source of economic opportunity. The 16 colleges and universities in the Springfield region employ over 8,000 people and serve as an important reservoir of skills. Wage rates in Springfield are much lower than the averages for Massachusetts and for the nation.

Labor

Civilian Labor Force 68,674
% Change 1989–1990 0.4

Work Force Distribution
    Mining 200
    Construction 5,900
    Manufacturing 43,300
    Transportation and Public Utilities 9,000
    Wholesale and Retail Trade 49,600
    FIRE (Finance, Insurance, Real Estate) 14,600
    Service 59,900
    Government 37,000
    Women as % of Labor Force 46.2
    % Self-Employed 3.5
    % Professional/Technical 13.9
Total Unemployment 4,939
Rate % 7.2
Federal Government Civilian Employment 3,031

Education

The city's 42 public schools are overseen by the School Committee. Its showpiece is the Central School, a $25 million facility believed to be the most modern in the Northeast. The Community Service Learning Program involves every child from kindergarten through high school in volunteer community work. Special schools include the Bridge Academy, an alternative secondary school, and the OWL Adult Learning Center. Private nonparochial schools include the Putnam Vocational Technical High School and the MacDuffie School for Girls.

Springfield is the educational hub of western Massachusetts. In and around Springfield are 14 colleges and universities that together enroll 63,000 students. Four of these institutions are in the city proper: Springfield Technical Community College, the only technical community college in Massachusetts; Western New England College, which offers the only law school in

the state outside of Boston; American International College; and Springfield College, which opened its doors in 1885 as the School for Christian Workers and today is a private nonsectarian institution. It was here that in 1891 faculty member James Naismith invented the game of basketball, and a few years later one of his students, William Morgan, invented the game of volleyball. Today, Springfield College has one of the largest intercollegiate athletic programs in the nation.

Education

Number of Public Schools 42
Special Education Schools 1
Total Enrollment 24,194
% Enrollment in Private Schools 14.9
% Minority 61.1
Classroom Teachers NA
Pupil-Teacher Ratio NA
Number of Graduates NA
Total Revenue (in millions) $106.919
Total Expenditures (in millions) $91.669
Expenditures per Pupil $3,565
Educational Attainment (Age 25 and Over)
    % Completed 12 or More Years 63.5
    % Completed 16 or More Years 11.8
Four-Year Colleges and Universities 3
    Enrollment 10,511
Two-Year Colleges 1
    Enrollment 3,424

Libraries

Number 24
Public Libraries 9
Books (in thousands) 706
Circulation (in thousands) 1,906
Persons Served (in thousands) 152
Circulation per Person Served 7.21
Income (in millions) $3.4
Staff NA

Four-Year Colleges and Universities
    American International College
    Springfield College
    Western New England College

Health

Springfield has four major health-care facilities: The Baystate Medical Center; the Shriner's Hospital for Crippled Children, operated by the Melha Temple; Mercy Hospital, run by the Sisters of Providence; and the Municipal Hospital.

Health

Deaths—Total 1,592
Rate per 1,000 10.6
Infant Deaths—Total 35
Rate per 1,000 13.4
Number of Metro Hospitals 4
Number of Metro Hospital Beds 1,592
Rate per 100,000 1,066
Number of Physicians 1,099
Physicians per 1,000 2.48
Nurses per 1,000 NA
Health Expenditures per Capita $8.50

Transportation

Two major New England highways intersect in Springfield—the east-west Massachusetts Turnpike, or I-90, and the north-south I-91 and its branch I-291, running through downtown. Springfield's downtown is located on the east bank of the Connecticut River, which provides a major channel for the transport of freight. Amtrak trains run between Springfield and other large cities, as far as Chicago and Montreal. In addition, three commercial bus lines serve the city. Bradley, 18 miles to the south of the city in Windsor Locks, is the city's nearest international airport. It is served by 19 airlines with 250 daily scheduled commercial flights. Corporate planes make use of a number of private airfields, such as Barnes and Westover.

Transportation	
Interstate Highway Mileage	68
Total Urban Mileage	2,580
Total Daily Vehicle Mileage (in millions)	$11.038
Daily Average Commute Time	39.8 min.
Number of Buses	25
Port Tonnage (in millions)	NA
Airports	NA
Number of Daily Flights	85
Daily Average Number of Passengers	6,212

Housing

Springfield is known as the City of Homes, and this reputation was sustained through the difficult housing markets of the late 1980s. It is one of the few cities in the nation with nearly 50% of its housing owner-occupied and nearly 40% single-family dwellings. It was the first in the state to offer a Home Ownership Opportunity program and the first with a City Housing Authority. Many of the city's neighborhoods have undergone a remarkable revival, including Upper Hill, Bay, McKnight, and Maple High-Six.

According to published reports there are between 350 and 500 homeless people in Springfield. The Friends of the Homeless run a shelter for the homeless on Worthington Street with 101 beds. The Greater

Housing		
Total Housing Units	61,320	
% Change 1980–1990	4.3	
Vacant Units for Sale or Rent	2,833	
Occupied Units	57,769	
% with More Than One Person per Room	4.1	
% Owner-Occupied	49.4	
Median Value of Owner-Occupied Homes	$105,500	
Average Monthly Purchase Cost	$328	
Median Monthly Rent	$418	
New Private Housing Starts	256	
Value (in thousands)	$12,812	
% Single-Family	39.1	
Nonresidential Buildings Value (in thousands)	$5,255	
Tallest Buildings	*Hgt. (ft.)*	*Stories*
Valley Bank Tower	370	29

Springfield Coalition for Homelessness runs three downtown shelters with 192 beds.

Urban Redevelopment

City revitalization efforts, under the aegis of the Springfield Redevelopment Authority, began in the mid-1970s. New construction and renovation projects have produced over 2 million square feet of office space since then. The Economic Development Partners (EDP), a consortium of economic development agencies and public policymakers, is leading the effort to create a regional development policy integrating Springfield and the surrounding region. New development projects taking shape in 1991 included Springfield's tallest building, a 32-story condominium in Columbus Place; the Civic Center arena; and Riverfront North.

Crime

Springfield's crime rate is slightly below the national average. In 1991, police reported 2,944 violent crimes and 14,536 property crimes.

Crime	
Violent Crimes—Total	2,944
Violent Crime Rate per 100,000	884.2
Murder	13
Rape	146
Robbery	807
Aggravated Assaults	1,978
Property Crimes	14,536
Burglary	4,024
Larceny	6,794
Motor Vehicle Theft	3,718
Arson	NA
Per Capita Police Expenditures	$119.33
Per Capita Fire Protection Expenditures	$93.25
Number of Police	446
Per 1,000	2.9

Religion

Springfield is predominantly Catholic, reflecting the strength of its Polish, Portuguese, Irish, Italian, and Hispanic communities.

Religion	
Largest Denominations (Adherents)	
Catholic	152,254
United Church of Christ	14,827
American Baptist	6,037
Episcopal	5,657
Black Baptist	8,288
United Methodist	5,478
Assembly of God	3,187
Evangelical Lutheran	2,032
Lutheran-Missouri Synod	2,024
Jewish	8,875

Media

Springfield media include one daily newspaper, *Union News;* one Sunday newspaper, *Sunday Republican;* two commercial television stations, one PBS station, one channel franchise, and seven AM and FM stations.

Media
Newsprint
Union News & Sunday Republican, daily
Television
WGBY (Channel 57)
WGGB (Channel 40)
WWLP (Channel 22)
Radio

WAIC (FM)	WMAS (AM)
WMAS (FM)	WNEK (FM)
WNNZ (AM)	WSCB (FM)
WTCC (FM)	

Sports

The Springfield Indians of the American Hockey League are the city's best-known sports team. The Civic Center hosts their home games as well as the annual NBA Hall of Fame game and the Collegiate Tip-Off Classic. There are two golf courses: Franconi and Veteran's. Boatmen, skiers, campers, hikers, and cyclists have prime facilities close to the city.

Arts, Culture, and Tourism

The city's major performing arts centers are the Civic Center, Symphony Hall, and the Paramount Performing Arts Center. The Civic Center presents touring concert and musical performances. Symphony Hall, dedicated in 1913 and renowned for its acoustics and ornate architecture, is the home of the Springfield Symphony Orchestra and the Children's Theater of Mars. The Paramount, built in 1929, hosts concerts and plays. StageWest, which performs at the Blake Theater and the Arms Studio Theater, is western Massachusetts' only resident professional theater company. Dance troupes include the Berkshire Ballet, the New England Dance Theater, and City Dancers.

The city's four museums are located on the Quadrangle. They are the Museum of Fine Arts, the George Walter Vincent Smith Art Museum, the Connecticut Valley Historical Museum, and the Springfield Science Museum and Planetarium. Local artists are showcased at the Avis Neigher Gallery at BayState West and the Zone Center for the Arts. The Springfield Armory Museum houses one of the most extensive collections of weapons in the world. The Indian Motorcycle Museum and the Naismith Memorial Basketball Hall of Fame commemorate Springfield's contributions to American industry and sports respectively.

Travel and Tourism
Hotel Rooms   2,722
Convention and Exhibit Space (square feet)   NA
Convention Centers
Springfield Civic Center
Festivals
International Festival (May)
Harambee Holiday Festival (August)
Mattoon Street Art Festival (September)
Winter Highlight Festival (November)

Parks and Recreation

Springfield has the distinction of having more public park space per capita than any other U.S. city. Fifty-four parks and playgrounds, a total of over 2,500 acres, are landscaped and maintained by the Park Department. For this reason, Springfield received the Keep America Beautiful's first Vision Award in 1986. The most notable of the city parks are the Forest Park and the Riverfront Park.

Sources of Further Information

Connecticut Valley Historical Museum
194 State Street
Springfield, MA 01103
(413) 732-3080

Mayor's Office
36 Court Street
Springfield, MA 01103
(413) 787-6100

Pioneer Valley Convention and Visitors Bureau
56 Dwight Street
Springfield, MA 01103
(413) 787-1548

Springfield Central Business District
338 Worthington Street
Springfield, MA 01103
(413) 732-7467

Springfield Central Library
220 State Street
Springfield, MA 01103
(413) 739-3871

Additional Reading

Greater Springfield Cross-Reference Directory. Annual.
Visitor Guide. Annual.

Springfield
Missouri

Location and Topography

N

Known as the Gateway to the Ozark Mountains, Missouri is located on the crest of Ozark Mountain Plateau. It is surrounded by flat or gently rolling tableland. The average elevation is 1,300 feet.

Layout of City and Suburbs

The business district is concentrated around the public square, which lies near the center of the city. Within the square is the pie, a slightly raised concrete safety zone approximately 75 feet in diameter around which traffic moves. Just north of the square is the Civic Center. Around Commercial Street—the principal industrial and commercial street—extends a tier of railroad tracks. The middle-income residential district is on the eastern side of the city, and the more expensive homes on the southeast.

Climate

Springfield has a four-season plateau climate, with milder seasons than in the upland plains or prairie sections of the state. The climate is characterized by an abundance of sunshine, low wind velocity, mild temperatures, and favorable humidity. Normal temperature ranges are 46°F to 83°F in spring, 59°F to 87°F in summer, 38°F to 55°F in fall, and 24°F to 55°F in winter. Average annual precipitation is 40 inches with 15 inches in the form of snow.

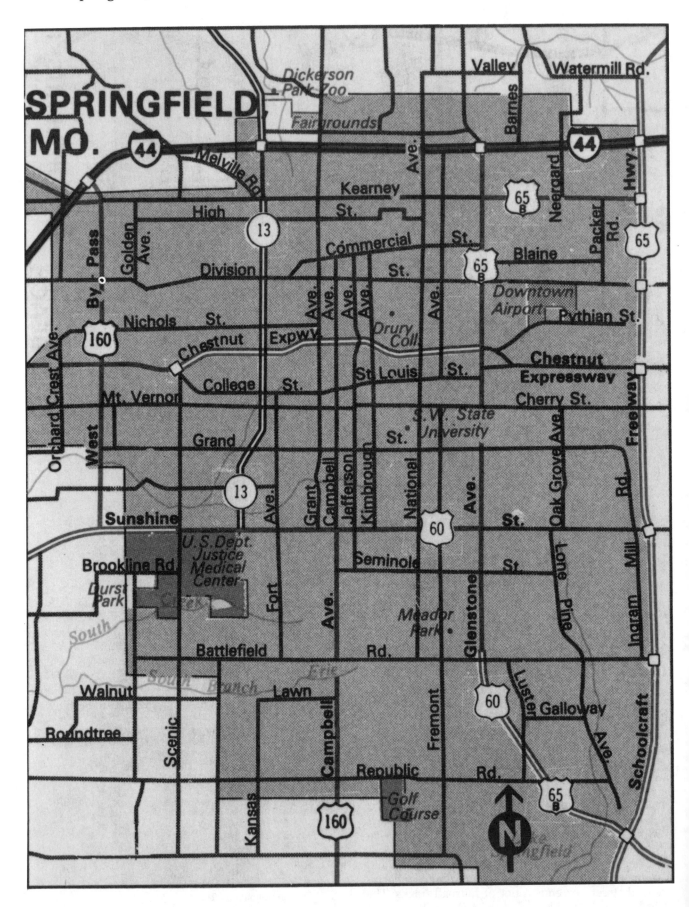

Weather (continued)

Clear Days 117
Cloudy Days 149
Storm Days 58
Rainy Days 107

Average Temperatures (°F)	High	Low	Mean
January	43.2	22.6	32.9
February	47.5	26.5	37.0
March	55.1	32.8	44.0
April	68.0	45.0	56.5
May	76.1	54.0	65.1
June	84.2	62.9	73.6
July	89.0	66.5	77.8
August	88.9	65.2	77.1
September	81.2	57.3	69.3
October	71.1	46.8	59.0
November	56.4	34.5	45.5
December	45.7	26.3	36.0

History

The first attempt to establish a permanent settlement in Springfield was made in 1821 by Thomas Patterson, who brought his family up the James River in 1821 and purchased the claim of the John C. Pettijohn family. Five hundred Delaware Indians arrived the next year claiming the land as their reservation; and two villages, one Delaware and one Kickapoo, were built on the present site of Springfield. Subsequently, all the white settlers abandoned the village except James Wilson, who married an Indian woman and moved in with her. When the Delaware finally left the village, he sent his Indian wife with them, married a white woman from St. Louis, and then returned to develop a farm on the creek that now bears his name. In 1830 the government began moving all Indian tribes westward and white families began to move in. Among the first were James Polk Campbell and his brother Madison, who staked their claim by carving their names on a tree near the present Public Square. In 1833 Greene County was organized with Campbell as clerk. Two years later Campbell and his wife deeded 50 acres between what are now Jefferson and Campbell avenues and Pershing and Mill streets to the county as the site for a new town. Campbell had planned the town with a square in the center and all roads converging on it. Named Springfield, the town was incorporated in 1838 and reincorporated in 1846, a year before it received its charter. Springfield grew rapidly, being strategically located at the intersection of the region's two most important roads. The settlers primarily were stockbreeders looking for good grazing land. When the Civil War began, the centrally located town became a military objective for both Union and Confederate forces. The Battle of Wilson's Creek was fought 11 miles south of the town on 10 August 1861. The Confederates held the town until February 1862. In 1870 an extension of the Atlantic and Pacific Railroad through a high divide between the Missouri and White river basins led to the creation of a new town one and a half miles north of Springfield. The new town, called North Springfield, competed with Springfield for seven years until they merged. The establishment of the Southwest Missouri State Teachers College in 1905 gave Springfield a new impetus for growth.

Historical Landmarks

The John Polk Campbell Home on Mary Avenue, built in 1851, is the oldest home in Springfield. The site of General Nicholas Smith's Tavern is marked by a granite tablet at a building on Boonville Avenue. The tavern was a station on the Butterfield Stage Line, which carried the first overland mail from Missouri to San Francisco in 1858. The city's major sightseeing attraction is Wilson's Creek National Battlefield, the site of the first Civil War battle between Union and Confederate armies in Missouri.

Population

Springfield is a growing city. During the 1980s it grew 5.5%—from a population of 133,116 in 1980 to 140,494 in 1990. Its national rank, however, fell during the same period from 118th to 126th.

Population	1980	1990
Central City	133,116	140,494
Rank	118	126
Metro Area	207,704	240,593
Pop. Change 1980–1990 +7,378		
Pop. % Change 1980–1990 +5.5		
Median Age 31.8		
% Male 47.3		
% Age 65 and Over 15.9		
Density (per square mile) 2,066		

Households		
Number 57,353		
Persons per Household 2.28		
% Female-Headed Households 10.1		
% One-Person Households 31.5		
Births—Total 1,923		
% to Mothers under 20 13.8		
Birth Rate per 1,000 14.0		

Ethnic Composition

Whites constitute 96% of the population; blacks 2.5%; and American Indians, Asians and Pacific Islanders, and other races 1.8%.

Ethnic Composition (as % of total pop.)	1980	1990
White	96.48	95.65
Black	2.15	2.51
American Indian	0.53	0.67
Asian and Pacific Islander	0.55	0.9
Hispanic	0.73	0.95
Other	NA	0.27

Chronology

1821 The first white settler, Thomas Patterson, establishes a permanent home on the site of present-day Springfield.

1822 Government grants the land to the Delaware Indians as a reservation, and a Delaware and a Kickapoo village are built. Subsequently, all white settlers leave except James Wilson, married to an Indian woman.

1830 Government moves all Indian tribes westward and white settlers begin to move into the area, among them John Polk Campbell, his brother Madison, and his brother-in-law Joseph Miller.

1833 Greene County is organized with Campbell as clerk.

1835 Campbell deeds 50 acres to the county as the site for a new town, Springfield. The town is platted and a courthouse is built on the square. A government land office is established.

1838 Springfield is incorporated as a town.

1847 Springfield receives its charter.

1861 In the Battle of Wilson's Creek, Confederate forces win a Pyrrhic victory.

1870 North Springfield is founded by a group of land speculators taking advantage of the new depot of the Atlantic and Pacific Railroad located 1.5 miles north of Springfield.

1873 Drury College is founded.

1877 Springfield and North Springfield merge.

1881 Kansas City, Fort Scott, and Memphis Railroad completes extension to North Springfield.

1905 Southwest Missouri State Teachers College is founded.

Government

Springfield is governed by a council-manager form of government. The nine members of the council are elected to four-year terms. One of them is then chosen to serve as a mayor for two years.

Government

Year of Home Charter 1847
Number of Members of the Governing Body 9
Elected at Large 5
Elected by Wards 4
Number of Women in Governing Body 2
Salary of Mayor $2,400
Salary of Council Members $0.0
City Government Employment Total 2,269
Rate per 10,000 162.8

Public Finance

The annual budget consists of revenues of $239.093 million and expenditures of $243.277 million. The debt outstanding is $209.732 million, and cash and security holdings total $212.839 million.

Public Finance

Total Revenue (in millions) $239.093
Intergovernmental Revenue—Total (in millions) $14.25
Federal Revenue per Capita $3..29
% Federal Assistance 1.37
% State Assistance 4.09
Sales Tax as % of Total Revenue 12.09
Local Revenue as % of Total Revenue 33.11
City Income Tax no
Taxes—Total (in millions) $27.0

Taxes per Capita
Total $194
Property $27
Sales and Gross Receipts $155
General Expenditures—Total (in millions) $55.6
General Expenditures per Capita $399
Capital Outlays per Capita $74

% of Expenditures for:
Public Welfare 7.6
Highways 13.7
Education 0.0
Health and Hospitals 4.2
Police 13.6
Sewerage and Sanitation 16.3
Parks and Recreation 7.2
Housing and Community Development 1.3
Debt Outstanding per Capita $1,213
% Utility 78.7
Federal Procurement Contract Awards (in millions) $10.1
Federal Grants Awards (in millions) $6.5
Fiscal Year Begins July 1

Economy

As an area still rich in natural resources, Springfield is an agribusiness center. The Springfield Regional Stockyards is the sixth-largest feeder cattle operation in the nation with sales of over $100 million annually. The manufacturing sector is highly diversified, including Littons Advanced Circuitry Division, General Electric, Kraft, Zenith, and Gospel Publishing House. Retailing, health care, and financial services are other economic activities in which Springfield has established strength. The metro area is the third-largest market in the state. Springfield also is the shipping and distribution hub for the Ozarks region. The

Economy

	Number	Deposits (in millions)
Total Money Income (in millions) $1,339.1		
% of State Average 93.7		
Per Capita Annual Income $9,634		
% Population below Poverty Level 14.3		
Fortune 500 Companies 1		
Banks	*Number*	*Deposits (in millions)*
Commercial	40	1,510
Savings	25	897
Passenger Autos 122,780		
Electric Meters 64,198		
Gas Meters 57,050		

Economy (continued)

Manufacturing

Number of Establishments   278
% with 20 or More Employees   37.1
Manufacturing Payroll (in millions) $371.4
Value Added by Manufacture (in millions) $859.8
Value of Shipments (in millions) $2,781.8
New Capital Expenditures (in millions) $49.6

Wholesale Trade

Number of Establishments   504
Sales (in millions) $3,132.9
Annual Payroll (in millions) $144.269

Retail Trade

Number of Establishments   1,958
Total Sales (in millions) $1,506.5
Sales per Capita $10,810
Number of Retail Trade Establishments with Payroll   1,349
Annual Payroll (in millions) $181.2
Total Sales (in millions) $1,480.6
General Merchandise Stores (per capita) $2,028
Food Stores (per capita) $1,654
Apparel Stores (per capita)   NA
Eating and Drinking Places (per capita) $1,069

Service Industries

Total Establishments   1,512
Total Receipts (in millions) $576.5
Hotels and Motels (in millions)   NA
Health Services (in millions) $196.5
Legal Services (in millions) $39.9

Ozarks also provide Springfield with millions of tourist dollars and sustain a large services sector.

Labor

Employment opportunities have not kept pace with the growing population, yet the city's unemployment rate is below state and national averages. The largest employers are medical institutions, distributors, and food processing firms. Because Springfield, relative to other cities, is not very dependent on manufacturing, its economy is less vulnerable to cyclical fluctuations, and its labor force distribution is more stable.

Labor

Civilian Labor Force   82,024
% Change 1989–1990   2.5
Work Force Distribution
   Mining   NA
   Construction   4,800
   Manufacturing   21,200
   Transportation and Public Utilities   7,500
   Wholesale and Retail Trade   34,300
   FIRE (Finance, Insurance, Real Estate)   5,400
   Service   33,700
   Government   15,300
   Women as % of Labor Force   44.9
   % Self-Employed   6.3
   % Professional/Technical   15.0
Total Unemployment   3,648
Rate %   4.4
Federal Government Civilian Employment   1,545

Education

The public school system supports 56 schools. Seven private and parochial schools are attended by over 1,400 students. The largest institution of higher learning is the Southwest Missouri State University. Religious colleges are strong in Springfield; they include Drury College, Assemblies of God Theological Seminary, Baptist Bible College, Evangel College, and Central Bible College. In 1991 the Heart of the Ozarks Technical Community College opened as a public institution offering technical education.

Education

Number of Public Schools   56
Special Education Schools   NA
Total Enrollment   23,631
% Enrollment in Private Schools   4.6
% Minority   0.0
Classroom Teachers   1,334
Pupil-Teacher Ratio   17.4:1
Number of Graduates   1,494
Total Revenue (in millions) $83.072
Total Expenditures (in millions) $77.537
Expenditures per Pupil $3,087
Educational Attainment (Age 25 and Over)
   % Completed 12 or More Years   70.2
   % Completed 16 or More Years   16.2
Four-Year Colleges and Universities   6
   Enrollment   25,131
Two-Year Colleges   1
   Enrollment   650

Libraries

Number   20
Public Libraries   6
Books (in thousands)   416
Circulation (in thousands)   NA
Persons Served (in thousands)   207.9
Circulation per Person Served   7.26
Income (in millions) $3.196
Staff   96

Four-Year Colleges and Universities
   Assemblies of God Theological Seminary
   Southwest Missouri State University
   Central Bible College
   Baptist Bible College
   Drury College
   Evangel College

Health

Springfield has 6 hospitals with a combined total of 2,677 beds: the Lester E. Cox Medical Center (with two branches), St. John Regional Health Center, Springfield Community Hospital, Springfield General Hospital, and Springfield Park Central Hospital.

Health

Deaths—Total   1,387
Rate per 1,000   10.1
Infant Deaths—Total   21
Rate per 1,000   10.9
Number of Metro Hospitals   6

Health (continued)

Number of Metro Hospital Beds   2,677
Rate per 100,000   1,921
Number of Physicians   436
Physicians per 1,000   2
Nurses per 1,000   NA
Health Expenditures per Capita $19.02

Transportation

Springfield is approached by I-44; U.S. 60, 65, 66, 160, and 266; and Missouri 13. Rail service is provided by Burlington Northern and Missouri Pacific. The Springfield Regional Airport provides air access through six airlines, including Trans World and United.

Transportation

Interstate Highway Mileage   8
Total Urban Mileage   810
Total Daily Vehicle Mileage (in millions) $3.4
Daily Average Commute Time   39.2 min.
Number of Buses   21
Port Tonnage (in millions) $
Airports   1
Number of Daily Flights   6
Daily Average Number of Passengers   256

Airlines (American carriers only)
American West
Northwest
Trans World
United

Housing

Springfield has affordable housing and apartments. The average value of an older house is $65,000, and that for a new three-bedroom house between $70,000 and $90,000. There are over 1,000 apartment units, both public and private, for lower-income people and retirees. Apartments rent for between $250 and $300 a month.

Housing

Total Housing Units   62,472
% Change 1980–1990   10.2
Vacant Units for Sale or Rent   3,874
Occupied Units   57,353
% with More Than One Person per Room   2.1
% Owner-Occupied   55.5
Median Value of Owner-Occupied Homes $53,900
Average Monthly Purchase Cost $284
Median Monthly Rent $280
New Private Housing Starts   668
Value (in thousands) $30,052
% Single-Family   51
Nonresidential Buildings Value (in thousands) $46,756

Urban Redevelopment

The Square downtown is undergoing redevelopment under the auspices of the Downtown Association and with private funds. Also in the planning stages is the creation of an urban district by converting existing older buildings into malls and offices. Neighborhood preservation plans have been developed for Westside, Walnut, and Roundtree, as well as plans for development of South National Avenue, South Springfield, and Southwest Springfield.

Crime

Springfield is the 105th safest city in the United States. Police in 1991 reported 635 violent crimes and 11,270 property crimes.

Crime

Violent Crimes—Total   635
Violent Crime Rate per 100,000   300.6
Murder   4
Rape   54
Robbery   151
Aggravated Assaults   426
Property Crimes   11,270
Burglary   2,560
Larceny   8,275
Motor Vehicle Theft   435
Arson   935
Per Capita Police Expenditures $61.01
Per Capita Fire Protection Expenditures $46.75
Number of Police   181
Per 1,000   1.32

Religion

Springfield is the national headquarters of the Assemblies of God, the largest Pentecostal denomination in the United States, and the site of its two theological colleges and publishing operations. Most other Protestant denominations are well represented.

Religion

Largest Denominations (Adherents)

Catholic	10,920
Assembly of God	12,068
Southern Baptist	46,633
United Methodist	13,098
Presbyterian	4,625
Churches of Christ	4,102
Independent non-Charismatic	7,983
Lutheran-Missouri Synod	2,458
Jewish	246

Media

Springfield's only daily newspaper is *The News-Leader*. Electronic media consist of 5 television stations (3 network, 1 public, and 1 independent) and 10 FM and AM radio stations.

Media

Newsprint
The News-Leader, daily

Television
KDEB (Channel 27)
KOLR (Channel 10)
KOZK (Channel 21)

Media (continued)

KSPR (Channel 33)
KYTV (Channel 3)

Radio

KGBX (AM)	KGBX (FM)
KIDS (AM)	KLFJ (AM)
KSMU (FM)	KTOZ (AM)
KTOZ (FM)	KTTS (FM)
KTXR (FM)	KWTO (AM)

Sports

 Springfield has no local professional sports teams. Both Drury College and Southwest Missouri State University have strong basketball teams.

Arts, Culture, and Tourism

A number of institutions serve and promote cultural interests: Springfield Symphony Orchestra and Springfield Regional Opera in music, Springfield Civic Ballet in dance, and Little Theater in drama. The Shepherd of the Hills is an outdoor theater. In addition, there are 15 country music theaters. Among museums the largest is the Museum of Ozarks History, located in the Bentley House.

Travel and Tourism

Hotel Rooms   3,321
Convention and Exhibit Space (square feet)   NA

Convention Centers

Shrine Mosque
University Plaza Trade Center

Festivals

Ozark Empire Fair

Parks and Recreation

 The city maintains 41 parks. Nearby is the Mark Twain National Forest and the Mincy Wildlife area.

Sources of Further Information

Greene County Historical Society
2214 Cherryvale
Springfield, MO 65804
(417) 883-8396

Springfield Area Chamber of Commerce
320 North Jefferson
Springfield, MO 65806-1109
(417) 862-5567

Springfield Convention and Visitors Bureau
320 North Jefferson
Springfield, MO 65806-1109
(417) 862-5501

Springfield-Greene County Library
397 East Central
Springfield, MO 65801
(417) 869-4621

Additional Reading

Polk's Springfield Directory. 1992.
Springfield Cross-Reference Directory. 1992.

Stamford

Connecticut

Basic Data

Name   Stamford
Name Origin   From Stamford, England
Year Founded   1641 Inc. 1893
Status: State   Connecticut
           County   Fairfield
Area (square miles)   37.7
Elevation (feet)   35
Time Zone   EST
Population (1990)   108,056
Population of Metro Area (1990)   827,645

Sister Cities
    NA

Distance in Miles To:
    Hartford   79
    New Haven   41
    Providence   147
    Waterbury   55
    Bridgeport   22

Location and Topography

N

Stamford is located in Fairfield County in southeastern Connecticut at the mouth of the Rippowam River on Long Island Sound.

Layout of City and Suburbs

The city is built around a wide bay crossed by two tidal inlets, and its harbor borders a finger of land jutting into the bay. The terrain is relatively flat. There are numerous bridges across the serrated shoreline.

Environment

Environmental Stress Index   3.0
Green Cities Index: Rank   NA
                    Score   NA
Water Quality   Slightly acid, moderately soft, fluoridated

Environment (continued)

Average Daily Use (gallons per capita)   NA
    Maximum Supply (gallons per capita)   NA
Parkland as % of Total City Area   NA
% Waste Landfilled/Recycled   NA
Annual Parks Expenditures per Capita $66.63

Climate

Stamford has a typical New England climate tempered by its proximity to Long Island Sound. The summers are warm with moderate humidity, while the winters are mild with less snow than inland Connecticut.

Weather

Temperature

Highest Monthly Average °F   72.7
Lowest Monthly Average °F   28.0

Annual Averages

Days 32°F or Below   130
Days above 90°F   11
Zero Degree Days   2
Precipitation (inches)   46.90
Snow (inches)   28.2
% Seasonal Humidity   NA
Wind Speed (m.p.h.)   NA
Clear Days   NA
Cloudy Days   NA
Storm Days   NA
Rainy Days   NA

Average Temperatures (°F)	High	Low	Mean
January	37.3	18.7	28.0
February	39.0	19.8	29.5
March	47.1	28.4	37.8
April	59.4	38.0	48.7
May	69.0	46.7	57.9
June	78.2	56.1	67.2
July	83.6	61.7	72.7

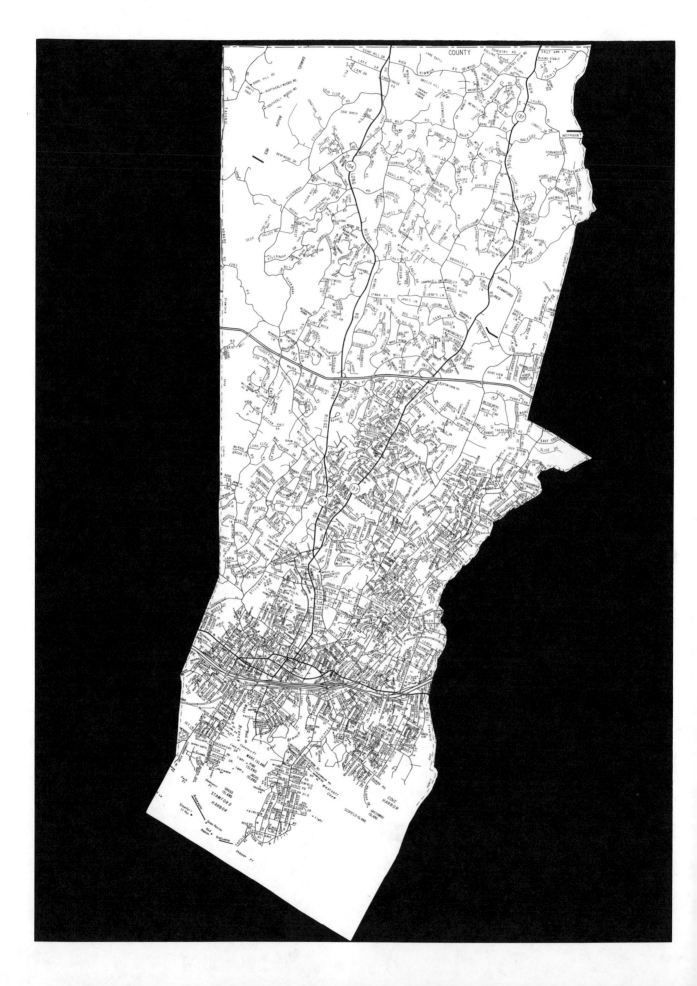

Weather (continued)			
August	82.1	60.2	71.2
September	75.3	52.7	64.1
October	64.8	41.3	53.1
November	53.3	33.4	43.4
December	41.3	23.2	32.3

History

Captain Nathaniel Turner, agent for the New Haven Colony, explored the Rippowam area in 1640, and purchased land from Ponus, sachem of the Siwanoy Indian tribe. Turner sold the land in 1641 to 28 families who had left Wethersfield in a church-related dispute. In 1642 the new settlers named the place Stamford. Soon afterward some of them crossed the Long Island Sound and founded the settlement of Hempstead. Stamford was in the New Haven Colony until 1662, when it joined Connecticut. The railroad came in 1848, and the city was incorporated in 1893.

Stamford's rise as a commercial and industrial center began in 1844 with the founding of the Stamford Manufacturing Company. Four years later, Linus Yale invented the first cylinder lock here, thus launching a new American industry. From 1868 until 1959 the Yale and Towne Company was the largest employer in the city. In the last decade of the 19th century, three inventions of Simon Ingersoll expanded the industrial stature of the city: the friction clutch, the spring scale, and the steam-driven wagon.

Until World War II Stamford grew primarily as a bedroom suburb of New York, but since then it has become the home of some of the largest U.S. corporations. The city boasts some of the finest research and development facilities on the East Coast.

Historical Landmarks

The Hoyt Barum House, built in 1699 and refurbished in 1738, represents three centuries of Stamford life. Fort Stamford is a reconstructed Revolutionary War fort that also contains a perennial garden. The gray stone Town Hall, built in 1907, was designed by Mellon and Jocelyn.

Population

Stamford has experienced a steady and healthy population growth since 1950 and now ranks 175th among all U.S. cities with a population of 108,056. Its growth rate in the 1980s was 5.5%.

Population		
	1980	1990
Central City	102,466	108,056
Rank	161	175
Metro Area	807,143	827,645
Pop. Change 1980–1990 +5,590		
Pop. % Change 1980–1990 +5.5		
Median Age 34.9		
% Male 47.8		

Population (continued)	
% Age 65 and Over 13.3	
Density (per square mile) 2,866	

Households	
Number 41,945	
Persons per Household 2.54	
% Female-Headed Households 12.4	
% One-Person Households 26.5	
Births—Total 1,462	
% to Mothers under 20 8.5	
Birth Rate per 1,000 14.3	

Ethnic Composition

The ethnic composition of Stamford has changed considerably in recent decades. The city was originally almost entirely Anglo-Saxon. The Irish were the first ethnic immigrants to arrive; they settled in sections appropriately called Dublin and Kerrytown. The Polish arrived in the last decades of the 19th century, and they were followed by virtually all major ethnic groups. The city has a large black population estimated at over 17%. Whites make up about 76%, and other races account for the remainder.

Ethnic Composition (as % of total pop.)		
	1980	1990
White	81.48	76.28
Black	14.97	17.78
American Indian	0.07	0.12
Asian and Pacific Islander	1.32	2.6
Hispanic	5.62	9.77
Other	NA	3.21

Government

Stamford operates with a mayor-council system of government. The mayor and the 50-member Board of Representatives are elected in odd-numbered years to two-year terms. The city has 20 districts and each district elects two representatives.

Government	
Year of Home Charter 1949	
Number of Members of the Governing Body 50	
Elected at Large 10	
Elected by Wards 40	
Number of Women in Governing Body 14	
Salary of Mayor $45,000	
Salary of Council Members $0.0	
City Government Employment Total 3,347	
Rate per 10,000 331.1	

Public Finance

Stamford's annual budget consists of revenues of $274.987 million and expenditures of $259.838 million. The total debt outstanding is $158.244 million, and cash and security holdings $230.780 million.

Chronology

1640 Nathaniel Turner purchases land on the Rippowam River from the sachem of the Siwanoy Indians.

1641 Turner sells the land to 28 families from Wethersfield.

1642 The new settlers choose the name of Stamford for their town.

1662 Stamford leaves the New Haven Colony and joins Connecticut.

1844 Stamford Manufacturing Company is set up.

1848 The New York–New Haven rail line runs through Stamford; Linus Yale invents the cylinder lock.

1893 Stamford is incorporated as a city.

Public Finance

Total Revenue (in millions) $274.987
Intergovernmental Revenue—Total (in millions) $32.64
Federal Revenue per Capita   NA
% Federal Assistance   NA
% State Assistance   11.87
Sales Tax as % of Total Revenue   NA
Local Revenue as % of Total Revenue   80.44
City Income Tax   no
Taxes—Total (in millions) $117.3

Taxes per Capita
   Total $1,161
   Property $1,141
   Sales and Gross Receipts $0
General Expenditures—Total (in millions) $168.0
General Expenditures per Capita $1,662
Capital Outlays per Capita $167

% of Expenditures for:
   Public Welfare   5.7
   Highways   5.7
   Education   38.6
   Health and Hospitals   2.0
   Police   7.9
   Sewerage and Sanitation   5.6
   Parks and Recreation   3.1
   Housing and Community Development   1.6
Debt Outstanding per Capita $1,203
   % Utility   0.0
Federal Procurement Contract Awards (in millions) $18.4
Federal Grants Awards (in millions) $3.8
Fiscal Year Begins   July 1

Economy

The economy of Stamford was transformed in the 1980s when it became the sixth-largest center of Fortune 500 companies in the nation. Among these companies are Xerox, Champion International, Combustion Engineering, Great Northern Nekoosa, Pitney Bowes, Olin Corporation, The Singer Company, General Signal, Amstar, American Maize, and Sprague Technologies. Of the Fortune 1000 Industrial and Service Companies, 11 are headquartered in Stamford. However, manufacturing, most of it defense-related, still remains important. Stamford also is the major retail center of Fairfield County.

Economy

Total Money Income (in millions) $1,846.1
% of State Average   129.5
Per Capita Annual Income $18,246
% Population below Poverty Level   7.7
Fortune 500 Companies   8

Banks	Number	Deposits (in millions)
Commercial	9	NA
Savings	4	NA

Passenger Autos   539,057
Electric Meters   41,945
Gas Meters   16,077

Manufacturing

Number of Establishments   313
% with 20 or More Employees   37.7
Manufacturing Payroll (in millions) $848.4
Value Added by Manufacture (in millions) $1,529.2
Value of Shipments (in millions) $2,268.9
New Capital Expenditures (in millions) $55.2

Wholesale Trade

Number of Establishments   370
Sales (in millions) $11,030.3
Annual Payroll (in millions) $208.450

Retail Trade

Number of Establishments   1,106
Total Sales (in millions) $1,138.8
Sales per Capita $11,266
Number of Retail Trade Establishments with Payroll   780
Annual Payroll (in millions) $142.6
Total Sales (in millions) $1,111.7
General Merchandise Stores (per capita) $2,073
Food Stores (per capita) $1,405
Apparel Stores (per capita) $1,097
Eating and Drinking Places (per capita) $749

Service Industries

Total Establishments   1,448
Total Receipts (in millions) $1,467.2
Hotels and Motels (in millions) $65.0
Health Services (in millions) $99.0
Legal Services (in millions) $91.8

Labor

Stamford has become a very attractive town for both employers and employees. The work force is well trained and educated, especially in the corporate and R&D sectors. The largest labor sector is services, followed by trade and

Labor

Civilian Labor Force   62,907
% Change 1989–1990   0.1

Work Force Distribution
   Mining   NA
   Construction   3,700

Labor *(continued)*

Manufacturing   18,500
Transportation and Public Utilities   6,000
Wholesale and Retail Trade   26,900
FIRE (Finance, Insurance, Real Estate)   14,100
Service   37,100
Government   10,400
Women as % of Labor Force   44.8
% Self-Employed   6.6
% Professional/Technical   16.5
Total Unemployment   2,762
Rate %   4.4
Federal Government Civilian Employment   1,021

then by manufacturing. The largest employer is Pitney Bowes.

Education

The public school system comprises 2 senior high schools, 3 junior high/middle schools, and 11 elementary schools. There are 14 private and parochial schools enrolling about 16% of schoolgoers.

Stamford has no local university, but branches of the Bridgeport Engineering Institute and the University of Connecticut are located there. St. Basil's College is a seminary that trains for the ministry.

Education

Number of Public Schools   16
Special Education Schools   NA
Total Enrollment   11,316
% Enrollment in Private Schools   16.4
% Minority   NA
Classroom Teachers   1,088
Pupil-Teacher Ratio   10.4:1
Number of Graduates   NA
Total Revenue (in millions)   NA
Total Expenditures (in millions)   NA
Expenditures per Pupil   NA
Educational Attainment (Age 25 and Over)   NA
   % Completed 12 or More Years   72.7
   % Completed 16 or More Years   25.6
Four-Year Colleges and Universities   1
   Enrollment   1,817
Two-Year Colleges   NA
   Enrollment   NA

Libraries

Number   29
Public Libraries   4
Books (in thousands)   443
Circulation (in thousands)   947
Persons Served (in thousands)   102
Circulation per Person Served   9.28
Income (in millions) $4.766
Staff   102

Four-Year Colleges and Universities
   St. Basil's College

Health

The city's principal medical facilities are Stamford Hospital and St. Joseph Hospital, with 485 and 260 beds respectively.

Health

Deaths—Total   873
Rate per 1,000   8.6
Infant Deaths—Total   13
Rate per 1,000   8.9
Number of Metro Hospitals   2
Number of Metro Hospital Beds   745
Rate per 100,000   480
Number of Physicians   NA
Physicians per 1,000   NA
Nurses per 1,000   NA
Health Expenditures per Capita $65.28

Transportation

Stamford is historically part of New York City's transportation network, and its road, rail, and air services are oriented toward New York rather than Connecticut. By road Stamford is approached via I-95, running north-south along the coastline; the Merritt Parkway, or Connecticut Route 15, running parallel to I-95 farther inland. Interstate 287 connects the Connecticut Turnpike with White Plains. Route 7 leads to Danbury and to I-84.

Commuters to New York City use Amtrak Metro North, which runs 60 trains daily, or the Bridgeport–Port Jefferson Long Island ferry, which runs from mid-May through the end of December. Conrail handles rail freight. The closest international airport is JFK in New York City.

Transportation

Interstate Highway Mileage   13
Total Urban Mileage   711
Total Daily Vehicle Mileage (in millions) $4.064
Daily Average Commute Time   53.2 min.
Number of Buses   25
Port Tonnage (in millions) $1.034
Airports   NA
Number of Daily Flights   NA
Daily Average Number of Passengers   NA

Airlines (American carriers only)
   See New York City

Housing

Most of Stamford's better residential communities lie outside the city proper. The most exclusive residential area is Shippan Point. Long Ridge Road and High Ridge Road are the most sought-after business areas. Some sections of the city are impoverished ghettoes.

Housing

Total Housing Units   44,279
% Change 1980–1990   9.5
Vacant Units for Sale or Rent   1,874
Occupied Units   41,945
% with More Than One Person per Room   4.9
% Owner-Occupied   57.9
Median Value of Owner-Occupied Homes $295,700
Average Monthly Purchase Cost $616
Median Monthly Rent $716

Housing (continued)
New Private Housing Starts   408
Value (in thousands) $22,367
% Single-Family   17.4
Nonresidential Buildings Value (in thousands) $7,681

Urban Redevelopment

 Stamford has undergone a more dramatic facelift in recent years than many comparable cities. Of the hundreds of office/residential complexes, the most impressive is The Classic, built in the late 1980s. The city has an urban redevelopment commission and an urban redevelopment committee.

Crime

 Stamford has an above average crime rate with 567 violent crimes reported in 1991. Property crimes totaled 5,936.

Crime

Violent Crimes—Total   567
Violent Crime Rate per 100,000   304.2
Murder   10
Rape   25
Robbery   297
Aggravated Assaults   235
Property Crimes   5,936
Burglary   1,236
Larceny   3,741
Motor Vehicle Theft   959
Arson   55
Per Capita Police Expenditures $197.18
Per Capita Fire Protection Expenditures $167.88
Number of Police   268
Per 1,000   2.77

Religion

 Catholics are predominant in Stamford, but Protestants are well represented.

Religion

Largest Denominations (Adherents)

Catholic	347,526
Episcopal	27,705
United Church of Christ	27,805
United Methodist	18,431
Black Baptist	19,196
Presbyterian	7,625
American Baptist	12,656
Evangelical Lutheran	7,733
Lutheran-Missouri Synod	5,429
Jewish	45,800

Media

 Stamford media consist of the daily newspaper *The Advocate* and two AM and FM radio stations. Stamford receives all New York television signals clearly.

Media

Newsprint
   The Advocate, daily

Television
   None

Radio
   WSTC (AM)   WQQQ (FM)

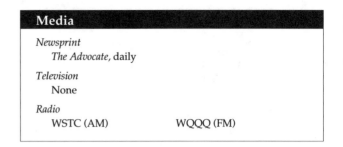

Sports

 The city has no local professional sports team, but Hartford, Bridgeport, and New York facilities are close.

Arts, Culture, and Tourism

 Stamford's major cultural facilities are the Palace Theater of the Arts and the Stamford Center for the Arts. The Hartman Theater and the Connecticut Grand Opera perform at the former. The Kweskin Barn is a community theater. In music and ballet the city has four established companies: the Stamford Symphony Orchestra, the Young Artists Philharmonic, the Pro Ante Chamber Singers, and the Connecticut Ballet Theater.

The Stamford Historical Society Museum is the custodian of the city's heritage. The Whitney Museum of American Art of New York City maintains a branch in Stamford.

Travel and Tourism

Hotel Rooms   6,675
Convention and Exhibit Space (square feet)   NA

Convention Centers
   Stamford Marriott
   Stamford Sheraton
   Crowne Plaza Hotel
   Westin Hotel

Festivals
   Stamford Festival of the Arts (June)
   North Atlantic Sailboat Show (September)

Parks and Recreation

The 118-acre Stamford Museum and Nature Center is a 19th-century park containing a working farm with farm animals and early colonial furniture. The Cummings Park at the end of Elm Street was named for U.S. Attorney General Homer S. Cummings. There are 39 other parks covering more than 1,000 acres, including beaches. The city maintains two public golf courses: E. Gaynor Brennan and Sterling Farms.

Sources of Further Information

Ferguson Library
One Public Library Plaza
Stamford, CT 06901
(203) 964-1000

Southwestern Area Commerce and Industry
  Association
One Landmark Square
Stamford, CT 06901
(203) 359-3220

Stamford Historical Society
1508 High Ridge Road
Stamford, CT 06903-4107
(203) 329-1183

Additional Reading

Stamford Cross-Reference Directory. Annual.

Syracuse
New York

Basic Data

Name   Syracuse
Name Origin   From Syracuse, Sicily
Year Founded   1786 Inc. 1848
Status: State   New York
      County   Seat of Onondaga County
Area (square miles)   25.1
Elevation (feet)   400
Time Zone   EST
Population (1990)   163,860
Population of Metro Area (1990)   659,864

Sister Cities
   Tampere, Finland

Distance in Miles To:

Albany	148
Buffalo	154
Montreal	253
New York	269
Rochester	91
White Plains	253
Binghamton	75
Kingston	197
Rome	42
Utica	56
Poughkeepsie	221
Plattsburgh	230

Location and Topography

N Syracuse, known as the Salt City and Crossroads of New York State, is located south of Lake Ontario at the south end of Onondaga Lake. To the north is the rolling Lake Plain, and to the south are the hills and the deep-cut valleys of the Allegheny Plateau. In earlier days it was a port at the junction of the Oswego and Erie canals.

Layout of City and Suburbs

Clinton Square, the heart of the city, is where 19th-century freight and passengers were transferred to canal boats at Packet Dock. Traversing the square, wide Erie Boulevard is built on the fill of the old Erie Canal. The main business district, south of the square, is dominated by Salina Street with its mixture of old and new buildings. From downtown, newer residential sections push south and east into the valleys between the Onondaga Hills. James Street is an exclusive residential thoroughfare and its homes represent architectural styles of every kind from Greek Revival to Georgian Colonial. West Genesee Street was once part of the original Genesee Turnpike. Large industrial plants are scattered throughout the city, but principally along Erie Boulevard and around the lakeshore. The city is crossed by routes I-81 and 11 north to south and I-90 east to west.

Environment

Environmental Stress Index   2.8
Green Cities Index: Rank   NA
              Score   NA
Water Quality   Slightly alkaline, moderately hard,
   fluoridated
Average Daily Use (gallons per capita)   218
   Maximum Supply (gallons per capita)   285
Parkland as % of Total City Area   5.6
% Waste Landfilled/Recycled   NA
Annual Parks Expenditures per Capita $49.17

Climate

The Syracuse area enjoys a four-season continental climate with marked seasonal changes. The winters are cold, as the cyclonic systems move from the interior of the country through the St. Lawrence Valley, and cold air masses advance down from the Hudson Bay through the Great Lakes region. During the summer and parts of autumn, temperatures cutomarily rise rapidly during daytime to fall as rapidly after sunset, so nights are

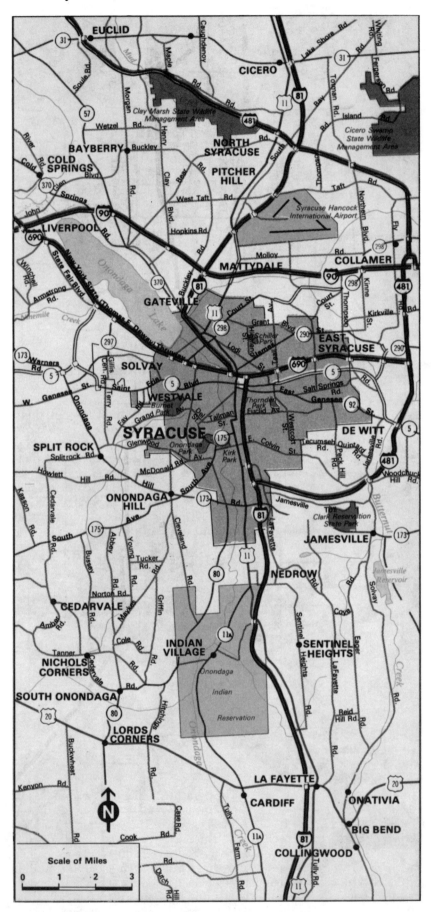

relatively cool. The area averages only six days annually with temperatures above 90°F. Rainfall is evenly distributed, with monthly averages close to three inches.

Weather			
Temperature			
Highest Monthly Average °F	81.6		
Lowest Monthly Average °F	15.0		
Annual Averages			
Days 32°F or Below	138		
Days above 90°F	6		
Zero Degree Days	9		
Precipitation (inches)	36.0		
Snow (inches)	109.0		
% Seasonal Humidity	73.0		
Wind Speed (m.p.h.)	9.8		
Clear Days	64		
Cloudy Days	201		
Storm Days	29		
Rainy Days	168		
Average Temperatures (°F)	*High*	*Low*	*Mean*
January	31.4	15.8	23.6
February	32.7	16.5	24.6
March	41.5	24.8	33.2
April	56.5	36.4	46.5
May	67.6	46.0	56.8
June	77.7	56.1	66.9
July	82.0	61.0	71.5
August	80.2	59.2	69.7
September	73.3	52.3	62.8
October	62.4	42.5	52.5
November	48.3	33.6	41.0
December	35.0	21.2	28.1

History

Syracuse occupies an important place in the history of American Indians as the domain of the Iroquois Confederacy. In 1654 it was visited by French soldiers and Jesuits, who found salt springs in the swampy place. The first white settler was Ephraim Webster, who came from Oriskany in 1786 and opened a trading station near the mouth of Onondaga Creek. Webster persuaded Major Asa Danforth and his family to emigrate in 1788. Asa was followed by his brother John, who began the manufacture of salt on the lakeshore. In 1794 James Geddes settled on the west shore of the lake and in 1796 dug the first salt well in the present township of Geddes. Soon other settlers came and little clusters of salt houses were built around the scattered salt works along the lakeshore. The most important of these settlements was Salina, now the north section of Syracuse. In 1797 the state took over the salt fields and established a reservation. In 1804 Geddes, then a member of the state legislature, interested Governor Clinton in a plan to sell 250 acres of the reservation and use the proceeds to build a road to the salt springs. The land, now the central portion of Syracuse, was bought by Abraham Walton for $6,650. It was an unhealthy, almost impassable swamp, but it was cleared, drained, and settled. A gristmill, sawmill, tannery, and tavern

were built, and around these grew up a village, variously known through the years as Bogardus Corners, Milan, Cossit's Corners, Corinth, and finally Syracuse. The last name was suggested by John Wilkinson, the postmaster, in honor of the Sicilian city. Across Walton's land Geddes laid out a ten-mile corduroy road, which later became part of the Genesee Turnpike. Within a few years Syracuse became the largest salt-production center in the United States. Salt was made by pumping brine either into salt blocks, where it was boiled in huge kettles, or into vats, where it was exposed to the sun and precipitated by evaporation. Other manufactures began to take shape. Thomas Wiard began to make wooden plows with iron staves and Nicholas Mickles built the Onondaga Furnace to manufacture kettles for the salt industry. The next event was the building of the Erie Canal in an effort to facilitate the transport of salt. Heavily promoted by Geddes and Joshua Forman, both of them Syracuse manufacturers and state legislators, the 363-mile canal became a reality in 1825, the year in which Syracuse was incorporated as a village. The canal followed a course through present-day downtown Syracuse. The impact of the canal had a dramatic effect on Syracuse's population, which rose from 250 in 1820 to 11,000 in 1830. In 1830 the first bank opened. A further stimulus came when the Auburn and Syracuse Railroad was opened for traffic in 1838, the Syracuse and Utica Railroad in 1839, the Oswego and Syracuse Railroad in 1848, the Rochester and Syracuse Railroad in 1853, and the Syracuse and Binghamton Railroad in 1854. In 1848 Syracuse was joined with Salina and Lodi and incorporated as a city. In 1869 Charles Dickens described Syracuse as a most wonderful out-of-the-world place, and the 1857 *Appleton's Handbook for American Travel* described Syracuse as a large and elegant city. Syracuse soon became a center for factional politics. Following the Jerry Rescue, one of the most dramatic events in the anti-slavery movement in which a former slave was freed from jail and smuggled into Canada, a series of meetings in the city led to the birth of the Republican Party. After the Civil War waves of immigrants, particularly the Irish and Germans, helped to expand the skilled labor force serving the new manufacturing plants. Anthony Will started candlemaking in 1855, James D. Gray started shoemaking in 1866, William Sweet founded the first steel mill in 1871, Harry Wiard began production of improved plows in 1876, William and Lyman Smith began making typewriters, H. H. Franklin opened a diecasting shop in 1894, and the first Franklin stock car appeared in 1902. Social progress kept pace. The first high school building was erected in 1868, the first public hospital in 1870, the Syracuse University opened its doors in 1871, and the first park was completed in 1886. The 1920s brought the days of mule-powered Erie Canal boats running through downtown to an end. It also brought the salt industry to an end. The last salt-production facility closed in 1926. Syracuse then entered on a new phase of its history.

Chronology

1654	French soldiers and Jesuits visit the site of Syracuse and discover the salt springs.
1658	The French build Fort Sainte Marie de Gannentaha on the lakeshore.
1786	The first white settler, Ephraim Webster, opens a trading station near the mouth of the Onondaga.
1788	Major Asa Danforth and family immigrate and erect the first Christian home in the county.
1794	James Geddes settles on the west shore of the lake.
1796	Geddes digs first salt well in the present town of Geddes.
1797	State takes over the salt mines and establishes reservation.
1804	Geddes, as member of the state legislature, interests Governor Clinton in a plan to sell 250 acres of the State Reservation to Abraham Walton, and use the proceeds to build a road to the salt springs.
1825	The Erie Canal is completed. Syracuse is incorporated as a village.
1838	The Bank of Syracuse is organized. Auburn-Syracuse rail line is opened.
1839	Syracuse-Utica rail line is opened.
1848	Oswego-Syracuse rail line is opened. Syracuse is incorporated as a city with Lodi and Salina.
1851	In the Jerry Rescue, one of the most dramatic incidents in the abolitionist movement, Jerry, a former slave, is freed from jail and smuggled into Canada.
1853	Rochester-Syracuse rail line is opened.
1854	A historic conference attended by Horace Greeley and Thurlow Weed is the forerunner of the Republican Party. Binghamton-Syracuse rail line is opened.
1868	The first high school building is erected.
1869	Charles Dickens visits Syracuse.
1870	The first hospital is built.
1871	The Syracuse University opens its doors.
1886	The first city park is opened.
1926	The last salt production facility closes.

Historical Landmarks

The Plymouth Congregational Church was built in 1859 by architect Horatio N. White. Close by on Columbus Circle is the Cathedral of Immaculate Conception, founded in 1841. The 11-foot bronze Columbus statue was created by the Italian sculptor Renzo Baldi in 1934. The Wesleyan Methodist Church, erected in 1845, is the oldest religious building in the city. Another landmark church is St. Paul's Cathedral, erected in 1885 and designed by Henry Dudley. The Courier Building on East Washington Street was known as Frazee Block when built in 1844. The City Hall was designed by Charles E. Colton and opened in 1892. It is an Onondaga limestone building typical of the Romanesque and Gothic styles popular in the 1880s. It was completely renovated in 1979. The Weighlock Building and Canal Museum is the only extant weighlock of the seven original ones on the Erie Canal. The S. A. and K Building, known earlier as the Granger Block, is a unique triangular building filling a whole block. The Hanover Square Historical Preservation District includes the oldest structures in downtown Syracuse, including the Larned Building (1869), the Old Post-Standard Building (1884), Snow Drug Company Building (1870), Franklin Building (1834), Bank of Syracuse (1896), Dana Building (1837), Phoenix Buildings (1834), Gere Building (1894), Gridley Building (1869), Syracuse Savings Bank (1875), the Third National Bank Building (1885), Onondaga Savings Bank (1896), The White Memorial Building (1876), and the University Building (1897). The Landmark Theater Loew Building, on South Salina Street, is an Indo-Persian fantasy theater, opened in 1928 and completely renovated in 1975.

Population

Like most cities in the Northeast, Syracuse has shed population steadily since World War II. Its 1990 population was 163,860 compared with 170,105 in 1980 and 190,000 in 1970. The metropolitan population on the other hand has experienced a slight gain in population during the same period.

Population	1980	1990
Central City	170,105	163,860
Rank	87	106
Metro Area	642,971	659,864
Pop. Change 1980–1990 -6,245		
Pop. % Change 1980–1990 -3.7		
Median Age 30.0		
% Male 46.6		
% Age 65 and Over 14.9		
Density (per square mile) 6,528		

Households		
Number 64,945		
Persons per Household 2.33		
% Female-Headed Households 16.9		
% One-Person Households 35.8		
Births—Total 2,895		
% to Mothers under 20 17.0		
Birth Rate per 1,000 17.6		

Ethnic Composition

Whites make up 75% of the city population, blacks 20%, and other races 5%. The proportion of whites is significantly higher in the suburbs of Madison and Oswego counties.

Ethnic Composition (as % of total pop.)		
	1980	1990
White	81.26	74.98
Black	15.74	20.33
American Indian	1.01	1.26
Asian and Pacific Islander	0.72	2.17
Hispanic	1.66	2.89
Other	NA	1.25

Government

The Syracuse City Charter provides for a mayor-council form of government. The mayor is elected for four-year terms. The Common Council consists of ten members—five district representatives elected to two-year terms, and four at-large members and the council president elected to two-year terms. The city auditor and the five city court judges also are elected to four-year terms.

Government
Year of Home Charter 1960
Number of Members of the Governing Body 10
Elected at Large 5
Elected by Wards 5
Number of Women in Governing Body 3
Salary of Mayor $72,100
Salary of Council Members $15,000
City Government Employment Total 5,911
Rate per 10,000 367.7

Public Finance

The annual budget consists of revenues of $316.682 million and expenditures of $356.631 million. The outstanding debt is $217.026 million and cash and security holdings $145.729 million.

Public Finance
Total Revenue (in millions) $316.682
Intergovernmental Revenue—Total (in millions) $192.5
Federal Revenue per Capita $29.58
% Federal Assistance 9.34
% State Assistance 36.10
Sales Tax as % of Total Revenue 0.76
Local Revenue as % of Total Revenue 51.89
City Income Tax no
Taxes—Total (in millions) $56.8
Taxes per Capita
Total $353
Property $333
Sales and Gross Receipts $14
General Expenditures—Total (in millions) $249.4
General Expenditures per Capita $1,552
Capital Outlays per Capita $284

Public Finance (continued)
% of Expenditures for:
Public Welfare 0.0
Highways 5.0
Education 41.2
Health and Hospitals 0.0
Police 6.4
Sewerage and Sanitation 2.8
Parks and Recreation 1.8
Housing and Community Development 15.6
Debt Outstanding per Capita $963
% Utility 0.0
Federal Procurement Contract Awards (in millions) $344.2
Federal Grants Awards (in millions) $45.5
Fiscal Year Begins January 1

Economy

Syracuse has a highly diversified economy with no single industry or firm dominating. Once known as the Salt City, it made a successful transition to manufacturing in the early decades of the 20th century, and is now making another transition to a 21st-century economy based on finance, high technology, and service. General Electric is the largest company; other Fortune 500 companies include Carrier, General Motor's Fisher Division, Bristol-Myers, and Agway. Overall Syracuse has 25 manufacturing and service industries employing over 1,000 people each. An abundant water supply has attracted two major breweries: Miller Brewing and Anheuser-Busch. A 100-block section near West Side has been designated as one of the ten development zones in New York State.

Economy		
Total Money Income (in millions) $1,550.2		
% of State Average 82.0		
Per Capita Annual Income $9,644		
% Population below Poverty Level 18.4		
Fortune 500 Companies 1		
Banks	Number	Deposits (in millions)
Commercial	NA	NA
Savings	7	NA
Passenger Autos 268,756		
Electric Meters 200,136		
Gas Meters 158,295		

Manufacturing
Number of Establishments 233
% with 20 or More Employees 39.1
Manufacturing Payroll (in millions) $678.6
Value Added by Manufacture (in millions) $1,069.5
Value of Shipments (in millions) $2,056.1
New Capital Expenditures (in millions) $64.6

Wholesale Trade
Number of Establishments 476
Sales (in millions) $4,344.4
Annual Payroll (in millions) $174.453

Retail Trade
Number of Establishments 1,507
Total Sales (in millions) $989.3
Sales per Capita $6,154
Number of Retail Trade Establishments with Payroll 1,126

Economy (continued)
Annual Payroll (in millions) $124.2
Total Sales (in millions) $969.1
General Merchandise Stores (per capita)   NA
Food Stores (per capita) $1,068
Apparel Stores (per capita) $258
Eating and Drinking Places (per capita) $750

Service Industries

Total Establishments   1,577
Total Receipts (in millions) $843.8
Hotels and Motels (in millions) $38.3
Health Services (in millions) $206.9
Legal Services (in millions) $105.4

Labor

 Services and trade dominate the employment market, with government and manufacturing closely behind. During the 1990s five occupational groups are expected to achieve above-average growth—technicians, service workers, professional workers, sales workers, and executives and managerial workers. Although layoffs have cut the number of factory jobs, there remains an acute shortage of skilled workers.

Labor

Civilian Labor Force   82,952
% Change 1989–1990   0.6

Work Force Distribution
   Mining   NA
   Construction   14,100
   Manufacturing   49,100
   Transportation and Public Utilities   19,800
   Wholesale and Retail Trade   74,200
   FIRE (Finance, Insurance, Real Estate)   20,700
   Service   78,600
   Government   53,500
   Women as % of Labor Force   47.0
   % Self-Employed   3.8
   % Professional/Technical   18.9
Total Unemployment   3,529
Rate %   4.3
Federal Government Civilian Employment   3,596

Education

The public school system consists of 34 senior high, junior high, and elementary schools. In addition, the Catholic archdiocese maintains an extensive parochial system.

Of the seven higher education institutions, the largest is the University of Syracuse, the nation's largest private residential university, noted for its Syracuse Challenge Program. It crowns the area known as the Hill. Among its 14 schools and colleges are the prestigious Samuel I. Newhouse School of Public Communications and the Maxwell School of Citizenship and Public Affairs. Le Moyne College, identified by *U.S. News and World Report* as one of the best colleges in the country, overlooks Syracuse from the east from its 150-acre campus known as the Heights. It was founded in 1946 by the Society of Jesus. The other institutions include Regina College, SUNY Health Science Center, and SUNY College of Environmental Science and Forestry.

Education

Number of Public Schools   34
Special Education Schools   1
Total Enrollment   22,561
% Enrollment in Private Schools   7.7
% Minority   42.2
Classroom Teachers   1,922
Pupil-Teacher Ratio   11.4
Number of Graduates   888
Total Revenue (in millions) $146.365
Total Expenditures (in millions) $138.534
Expenditures per Pupil $6,065
Educational Attainment (Age 25 and Over)
   % Completed 12 or More Years   63.6
   % Completed 16 or More Years   17.9
Four-Year Colleges and Universities   3
   Enrollment   24,385
Two-Year Colleges   4
   Enrollment   10,060

Libraries

Number   40
Public Libraries   9
Books (in thousands)   1,568
Circulation (in thousands)   1,378
Persons Served (in thousands)   463
Circulation per Person Served   2.97
Income (in millions) $10.538
Staff   212

Four-Year Colleges and Universities
   Le Moyne College
   Regina College
   SUNY College of Environmental Science and Forestry
   SUNY Health Sciences Center
   University of Syracuse

Health

The leading health-care center is the 359-bed SUNY Health Science Center whose 62 clinics and two emergency rooms draw patients from all over the Northeast. Crouse-Irving Memorial Hospital, an inner-city teaching and community hospital founded in 1887, is noted for its Child Development Center and the Soule Clinic for Alcoholics. St. Joseph's Hospital Health Center is a 457-bed general acute hospital with one of the busiest emergency rooms in the region. Other major medical facilities include the Veterans Administration Medical Center and Community General Hospital. Psychiatric care is provided by Hutchings Psychiatric Center and the Benjamin Rush Center.

Health

Deaths—Total   1,943
Rate per 1,000   11.8
Infant Deaths—Total   39
Rate per 1,000   13.5
Number of Metro Hospitals   7
Number of Metro Hospital Beds   2,306
Rate per 100,000   1,435
Number of Physicians   1,422
Physicians per 1,000   2.60
Nurses per 1,000   NA
Health Expenditures per Capita   NA

Transableportation

Two major four-lane highways bisect the city. The north-south I-81 passes through the center of the city, while the east-west I-90 passes just a mile north of the city. Routes 11 and 690 also pass through downtown while 490 skirts it to the east. CENTRO provides bus service through and between the city and the surrounding area. Hancock Airport, located ten miles from downtown, is the third-largest airport in New York State and is served by over ten airlines. Thirty-five miles to the south, the deep-water port of Oswego and the New York Barge Canal system provide access to the Great Lakes. Conrail and Amtrak handle train and freight services. The *Places Rated Almanac* ranks Syracuse 14th in the nation in accessibility of transportation.

Transportation	
Interstate Highway Mileage	54
Total Urban Mileage	1,593
Total Daily Vehicle Mileage (in millions)	$6.885
Daily Average Commute Time	41.4 min.
Number of Buses	161
Port Tonnage (in millions)	NA
Airports	1
Number of Daily Flights	91
Daily Average Number of Passengers	3,484

Airlines (American carriers only)
- American
- Continental
- Delta
- Northwest
- Trans World
- United
- USAir

Housing

Syracuse has a rich tradition of neighborhoods, each with its own cachet. They range from Radisson, a totally planned community, to Hawley apartments and mansions on James Street. The University Hill area has a mix of old homes and new student dorms. One of the city's best known and most closely knit neighborhoods is Tipperary Hill. Neighborhood revitalization became a major thrust of city renewal in the 1970s. It

Housing	
Total Housing Units	71,502
% Change 1980–1990	-2.3
Vacant Units for Sale or Rent	5,148
Occupied Units	64,945
% with More Than One Person per Room	2.7
% Owner-Occupied	41.1
Median Value of Owner-Occupied Homes	$67,600
Average Monthly Purchase Cost	$342
Median Monthly Rent	$347
New Private Housing Starts	63
Value (in thousands)	$2,967
% Single-Family	68.3
Nonresidential Buildings Value (in thousands)	$74,486

includes projects like Syracuse Hill, Cherry Hill, and McCarthy Manor. Surrounding residential communities in Cazenovia, Skaneateles, and Baldwinsville offer a wide range of handsome homes in lushly landscaped settings. Residents also continue to move back into the city based on the growth of downtown housing units. Many of these units are located on Presidential Plaza. The century-old Nettleton Building has been renovated into a housing complex.

Urban Redevelopment

The centerpiece of downtown development is the Galleries of Syracuse, a $48 million mixed-use complex. It contains the Onondaga County Public Library, a 150,000-square-foot shopping center, a soaring atrium, and office space. The Franklin Square Project is expected to feature a $100 million shopping mall. Other development projects include the $110 million War Memorial/Convention Center Complex, the renovation of the Armory Square, and the construction of the $25 million MONY III complex and the AT&T Signature Building. Salina and Warren streets in downtown are being revitalized, creating a new anchor for traditional retail shops. Another ambitious magnet project is the 800-acre, $1 billion Lakefront Project featuring a 1.4 million-square foot mega-mall. Surrounding the mall will be 2,000 housing units, hotels, marinas, offices, and a light industrial park. Graystone Square is a $4.8 million renovation of 125,000 sq. feet of office space. Expansion is also the order of the day in medical facilities and universities. Examples are the $52 million rehabitation of the SUNY Health Science Center, the $30 million Sports Medicine Center, and Syracuse University's $60 million Science and Technology Center.

Crime

Violent crimes for 1991 were 321.3 per 100,000. Property crimes totaled 11,148.

Crime	
Violent Crimes—Total	1,559
Violent Crime Rate per 100,000	321.3
Murder	13
Rape	86
Robbery	608
Aggravated Assaults	852
Property Crimes	11,148
Burglary	3,328
Larceny	7,108
Motor Vehicle Theft	712
Arson	134
Per Capita Police Expenditures	$126.03
Per Capita Fire Protection Expenditures	$116.59
Number of Police	423
Per 1,000	2.57

Religion

Catholics are the largest denomination, with United Methodists second. All of the other major Protestant denominations are also represented.

Religion	
Largest Denominations (Adherents)	
Catholic	159,183
United Methodist	27,027
American Baptist	7,491
Episcopal	7,127
Evangelical Lutheran	7,642
Presbyterian	7,226
Black Baptist	7,717
Assembly of God	2,414
Jewish	6,396

Media

Syracuse media consists of two daily newspapers: *The Post-Standard* in the morning, and the *Syracuse Herald-Journal* in the evening, 4 commercial television stations, and 13 radio stations.

Media
Newsprint
Syracuse Business, monthly
Syracuse Herald-Journal, daily
Syracuse Record, weekly
Syracuse New Times, weekly
The Post-Standard, daily
Television
WCNY (Channel 24)
WSTM (Channel 3)
WSYT (Channel 68)
WTVH (Channel 5)
Radio
WAER (FM)   WAQX (AM)
WCNY (FM)   WFBL (AM)
WJPZ (FM)   WMHI (FM)
WMHR (FM)   WNDR (AM)
WNTQ (FM)   WOLF (AM)
WSIV (AM)   WSYR (AM)
WYYY (FM)

Sports

Syracuse has strong teams in both collegiate and professional sports. Syracuse University teams perform at the 50,000-seat Carrier Dome, the only domed stadium in the Northeast. Lacrosse teams compete from March through May, football teams from September through November, and Orangemen play basketball from November through March. The Dome also is the scene of the Empire State Games (which return to Syracuse every other year), New York Special Olympics, and the AAU Junior Olympics. In the world of professional sports, MacArthur Stadium is home to baseball's Syracuse Chiefs, the AAA affiliate of the Toronto Blue Jays, and one of the few community-owned teams in the nation. Crowds also throng to Onondaga Lake to watch the Miller American Thunderboat Classic, a hydroplane race.

Arts, Culture, and Tourism

The focal point of arts in Syracuse is the John H. Mulroy Civic Center, home of the Syracuse Opera Company, the Syracuse Symphony Orchestra, and two theaters. The Syracuse Opera Company stages three performances every year and the Syracuse Symphony Orchestra has a 44-week season. The Syracuse Area Landmark Theater hosts performances by popular entertainers and touring companies. The Regent Theater Complex at Syracuse University is attached to the Drama Department. The Famous Artists Series, established by Rose and Murray Bernthal in 1940, brings Broadway performances to Syracuse. Syracuse Stage is one of the outstanding professional regional theaters, founded by Arthur Storch in 1974, and it performs at the 500-seat John D. Archbold Theater. The Salt City Center for Performing Arts is an outlet for local theatrical talent along with Paul Robeson Performing Arts Company, the Contemporary Theater, Syracuse Talent Company, and Sheila Shattuck Productions. The Syracuse Friends of Chamber Music, affiliated with the Music Department of Syracuse University, holds chamber music concerts.

Syracuse has over 40 museums, of which the most outstanding are the Everson Museum of Art, Syracuse University's Lowe Art Gallery, the Erie Canal Museum, the Onondaga History Society Museum, and the Discovery Center of Science and Technology. The Everson Museum, designed by I. M. Pei, with ten galleries on three levels, is considered a work of art in itself. The lower level is the home of the China Center for the Study of American ceramics, the most complete American Ceramics collection in the world.

Travel and Tourism	
Hotel Rooms 5,987	
Convention and Exhibit Space (square feet) 70,000	
Convention Centers	
Convention Center Complex	
Sheraton Syracuse Convention Center	
Hotels at Syracuse Square	
Syracuse Marriott	
Festivals	
Syracuse Arts and Crafts Festival (July)	
Winterfest	
New York State Fair (Labor Day)	
Festival of Nations (November)	

Parks and Recreation

Syracuse has 33 community and neighborhood parks, 12 downtown parks, 8 open spaces, and 6 natural areas covering 865 acres. The Schiller Park of 23.5 acres was designed by David Campbell in 1811; the Thornden Park of 76 acres was once the Haskins estate, and later the Davis estate when it was bought by the city in 1921. The Lower Onondaga Park is an extension of the Onondaga Park, the first Historic Landscape to achieve local protected site designation. The 15.6-acre park was planned and designed by George Kessler in 1907. Onondaga State Park, in the suburb of Liverpool, contains the original Le Moyne Salt Spring, the Jesuit well, the Salt Museum, and the French fort, Sainte Marie de Gannentaha. The smallest park is 1.2-acre Fayette Park built in 1827 as Centre Square. Elmwood Park is a historic site traced back to 1796, and it was once a First Class Temperance Pleasure Resort. Academy Green, also known as Sabine Park, originally housed a school building and now a Presbyterian church.

Sources of Further Information

Bureau of Research
City Hall
Syracuse, NY 13202
(315) 449-8020

Onondaga County Public Library
447 South Salina Street
Syracuse, NY 13202
(315) 448-INFO

Onondaga Historical Association
321 Montgomery Street
Syracuse, NY 13202
(315) 428-1862

Syracuse Convention and Visitors Bureau
100 East Onondaga Street
Syracuse, NY 13202
(315) 470-1343

Additional Reading

Martin, Roscoe C. *Decisions in Syracuse*. 1966.
O Neill, Alexis. *Syracuse: The Heart of New York*. 1988.

Tacoma

Washington

Location and Topography

Tacoma is located on Commencement Bay, an inlet of Puget Sound, at the foot of Mount Rainier in the Puyallup River Valley. The Olympic Mountains rise to the west and the Cascade Mountains to the east. The terrain rises steeply from the bay to more than 300 feet above sea level. The Puyallup River flows through the city from Mount Rainier, 40 miles to the southeast.

Layout of City and Suburbs

Few cities have a more beautiful setting than Tacoma with the serene, snow-capped Mount Rainier looming majesti-

cally in the background. On the waterfront is the industrial district, Bayside Drive, which follows along the edge of Commencement Bay, giving a good view of the harbor. Rising above the industrial district is the business district. To the north, west, and south are the residential districts, the upscale ones being found in the north, especially in Prospect Hill. To the west the Tacoma Narrows Bridge crosses The Narrows, and Point Narrows Park occupies the jutting promontory. From the park Ruston Way skirts the western side of Commencement Bay to become the southbound Pacific Avenue. Coming from the north, I-5 crosses the heart of the city. Dash Point and Browns Point are to the north of Commencement Bay, with Marine View Highway hugging the shores to meet East 11th Street. There are seven small inlets in Commencement Bay, providing an extensive coastline to the city.

Environment

Environmental Stress Index   3.6
Green Cities Index: Rank   NA
               Score   NA
Water Quality   Neutral, very soft, fluoridated
   Average Daily Use (gallons per capita)   370
   Maximum Supply (gallons per capita)   660
Parkland as % of Total City Area   NA
% Waste Landfilled/Recycled   70:30
Annual Parks Expenditures per Capita $36.33

Climate

Tacoma has a mild maritime climate. The surrounding mountains protect the city from severe winters, and the sea helps to keep the temperature down in summer. Tacoma has a reputation for being rainy, but most of the rain falls in winter.

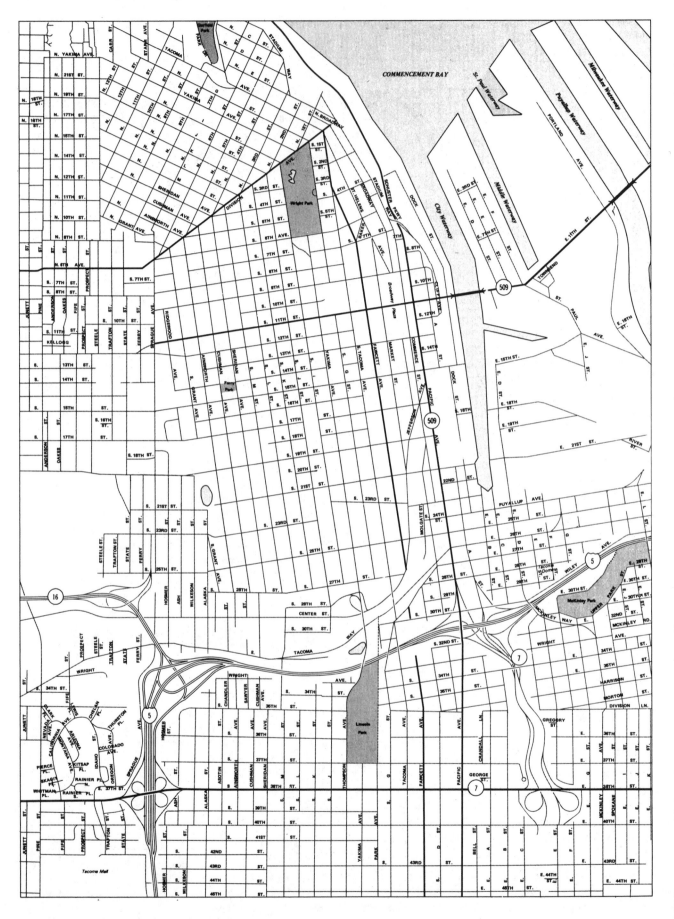

Weather

Temperature

Highest Monthly Average °F 65.0
Lowest Monthly Average °F 40.3

Annual Averages

Days 32°F or Below 33
Days above 90°F 2
Zero Degree Days 0
Precipitation (inches) 37.17
Snow (inches) 9.3
% Seasonal Humidity 72
Wind Speed (m.p.h.) 9.0
Clear Days 71
Cloudy Days 201
Storm Days 7
Rainy Days 160

Average Temperatures (°F)	High	Low	Mean
January	45.6	35.0	40.3
February	50.3	37.2	43.8
March	52.8	37.6	45.2
April	58.8	40.9	49.8
May	65.9	45.8	55.8
June	70.4	50.8	60.6
July	76.0	53.9	65.0
August	74.9	54.4	64.7
September	70.1	51.3	60.7
October	61.3	45.7	53.5
November	51.8	39.5	45.7
December	47.3	36.6	42.0

History

The Puyallup Valley was the home of the Nisqually and Puyallup Indian tribes when Captain George Vancouver became the first white to explore the area in 1792. Vancouver sailed up Puget Sound and named the mountain, which the American Indians called *Tacoma*, Mount Rainier. Half a century passed before the Charles Wilkes expedition arrived in 1841 and named another landmark—Commencement Bay. The first settlement of the region waited until 1852, when a Swedish immigrant, Nicholas De Lin, and his companions built a sawmill at Gallaghers' Gulch between the two creeks. De Lin worked his mill until 1861 when he sold it and moved to Portland. He was followed by Job Carr in 1864, who homesteaded on a site called Chebaulip, now Old Town. Carr was bought out by General Morton Matthew McCarver, a land promoter. He named the settlement Tacoma and proceeded to sell tracts to new settlers. The new town received its first break when the San Francisco lumbering concern Hanson and Ackerman decided to open a lumber mill in Tacoma. Construction workers for the project were followed by mill hands, lumberjacks, loggers, mechanics, shopkeepers, and others. By 1870 Tacoma appeared on a map of Washington. The first church, St. Peters, opened at the same time as a saloon and a hotel. In 1873, Northern Pacific Railway selected Tacoma as its terminus, just as McCarver had planned. The event sparked a flurry of civic activity, including the incorporation of the town, the establishment of a newspaper, *The Pacific Tribune,* and the opening of several stores. During the next decade, coal mining and lum-

ber industries were established, along with a flour mill, salmon cannery, and machine shops. In 1887 the city received direct transcontinental rail connections, and the new tie-up resulted in an era of phenomenal growth for the lumber industry. Rail transportation further improved in 1888 when the Stampede Pass Tunnel was completed. Great Northern and Union Pacific soon extended competing lines to the city. Between 1885 and 1890, the population increased from 7,000 to 36,000, making it necessary to build more homes and schools. In 1888 alone 1,016 buildings were built, including Tacoma Hotel, designed by Sanford White. In 1893 the city suffered from the stock market crash, from which it received a brief respite as a result of the Alaskan Gold Rush and the creation of the Weyerhauser Timber Company in 1900. World War I enabled Tacoma to recapture some of its lost economy, but generally it was eclipsed by Seattle, because of the latter's rise as a port. Commencement Bay was declared an official U.S. Port of Entry in 1918. The Great Depression caused further slowing of the economy, and it did not recover until after World War II.

Historical Landmarks

The Pierce County Courthouse on the corner of 11th and G streets was completed in 1893. The Tacoma Theater Building on the corner of Ninth Street and Broadway Avenue was designed by Stanford White in 1890 in the manner of a Norman Chateau. The City Hall, on Seventh Street, an adaptation of an Italian town hall with an attached campanile, is a National Historic Landmark. Union Station, built in the days when rail transportation was king, is also a National Historic Landmark. Other area attractions include Fort Nisqually, a restored trading post, Camp Six, a re-creation of a logging camp, and the Narrow Bridge, spanning the Sound between Tacoma and Gig Harbor Peninsula, one of the longest suspension bridges in the nation.

Population

Tacoma has had a slow, steady growth since the end of World War II. From 154,000 in 1970, it grew by 2.7% to reach 158,501 in 1980, and then by a further 11.5% to reach 176,664 in 1990.

Population		
	1980	1990
Central City	158,501	176,664
Rank	98	95
Metro Area	485,667	586,203
Pop. Change 1980–1990 +18,163		
Pop. % Change 1980–1990 +11.5		
Median Age 31.8		
% Male 48.4		
% Age 65 and Over 13.7		
Density (per square mile) 3,672		

Chronology

1852	Nicholas De Lin clears the land near the end of Gallaghers Gulch and erects a sawmill. New settlers join Lin.
1855	Indian uprising in the White River Valley forces the settlers to abandon settlement.
1861	De Lin sells his mill and moves to Portland.
1864	Job Carr homesteads on site called Chebaulip by Indians.
1866	General Morton Matthew McCarver buys Carr's homestead, renames it Tacoma, and proceeds to promote settlement.
1869	Hanson and Ackerman build lumber mill in town.
1870	Name of Tacoma first appears on a map.
1873	St. Peters Church is built. Northern and Pacific Railway select Tacoma as its terminus. Tacoma city government begins functioning. The first newspaper, *The Pacific Tribune*, debuts.
1875	Coal mines are opened at Wilkeson.
1884	Old Tacoma and New Tacoma are consolidated as Tacoma.
1885	Anti-Chinese feelings lead to illegal deportation of Chinese workers.
1887	Tacoma is linked to the transcontinental rail systems by a route through the Cascade Range.
1888	Stampede Pass Tunnel is completed. Foundation stone is laid for the College of Puget Sound.
1893	Crash of 1893 halts city's progress.
1900	Weyerhauser Lumber Company is created.
1918	Tacoma is declared a U.S. Port of Entry.

Population (continued)

Households

Number   69,939
Persons per Household   2.44
% Female-Headed Households   13.3
% One-Person Households   31.3
Births—Total   3,053
    % to Mothers under 20   14.3
    Birth Rate per 1,000   19.1

Ethnic Composition

Whites make up 78.1%, blacks 11.4%, American Indians 2%, Asians and Pacific Islanders 6.9%, and others 1.5%.

Ethnic Composition (as % of total pop.)

	1980	1990
White	84.21	78.14
Black	9.15	11.38
American Indian	1.83	2.02
Asian and Pacific Islander	2.99	6.91
Hispanic	2.44	3.78
Other	NA	1.54

Government

Under its 1953 charter, Tacoma has a council-manager form of government. The mayor and the nine council members, four at large and five by district, are all elected to four-year terms.

Government

Year of Home Charter   1953
Number of Members of the Governing Body   9
Elected at Large   4
Elected by Wards   5
Number of Women in Governing Body   1
Salary of Mayor $40,000
Salary of Council Members $12,164.30
City Government Employment Total   2,995
Rate per 10,000   188.4

Public Finance

The annual budget consists of revenues of $398.672 million and expenditures of $399.021 million. The debt outstanding is $413.381 million and cash and security holdings are $383.068 million.

Public Finance

Total Revenue (in millions) $398.672
Intergovernmental Revenue—Total (in millions) $16.51
Federal Revenue per Capita $2.16
% Federal Assistance   0.54
% State Assistance   3.55
Sales Tax as % of Total Revenue   11.77
Local Revenue as % of Total Revenue   39.03
City Income Tax   no
Taxes—Total (in millions) $52.6

Taxes per Capita
    Total $331
    Property $99
    Sales and Gross Receipts $160
General Expenditures—Total (in millions) $124.5
General Expenditures per Capita $783
Capital Outlays per Capita $74

% of Expenditures for:
    Public Welfare   0.3
    Highways   11.4
    Education   0.0
    Health and Hospitals   5.6
    Police   10.7
    Sewerage and Sanitation   14.7
    Parks and Recreation   7.8
    Housing and Community Development   2.3
Debt Outstanding per Capita $1,810

Public Finance (continued)
% Utility 78.3
Federal Procurement Contract Awards (in millions) $53.3
Federal Grants Awards (in millions) $70.0
Fiscal Year Begins January 1

Economy (continued)
Total Receipts (in millions) $632.5
Hotels and Motels (in millions) $22.9
Health Services (in millions) $251.0
Legal Services (in millions) $67.3

Economy

 Tacoma once considered itself as the City of Destiny in terms of its economic potentials. These expectations have been scaled down in the 20th century, but it has exceptional strengths in three areas: shipping, lumber, and tourism. The Port of Tacoma generates over $1 billion a year and is the sixth-busiest container-handling port in the nation, receiving over 1,300 ships annually. Lumber, once the city's green gold, is still a major asset although hedged with environmental concerns. Tacoma has a rich agricultural hinterland that produces more than lumber; for example, it is noted for flower bulbs, berries, rhubarb, and other produce. Tourism is a major revenue earner, with Mount Rainier as its calling card. The McChord Air Force Base and Fort Lewis also pump millions of dollars into the local economy.

Economy

Total Money Income (in millions) $1,489.0
% of State Average 86.2
Per Capita Annual Income $9,365
% Population below Poverty Level 14.1
Fortune 500 Companies 1

Banks	Number	Deposits (in millions)
Commercial	11	1,453.3
Savings	14	1,264.0

Passenger Autos 312,752
Electric Meters 116,987
Gas Meters 20,233

Manufacturing

Number of Establishments 339
% with 20 or More Employees 35.7
Manufacturing Payroll (in millions) $338.8
Value Added by Manufacture (in millions) $761.4
Value of Shipments (in millions) $1,866.8
New Capital Expenditures (in millions) $66.7

Wholesale Trade

Number of Establishments 362
Sales (in millions) $2,240.2
Annual Payroll (in millions) $140.356

Retail Trade

Number of Establishments 1,616
Total Sales (in millions) $1,430.8
Sales per Capita $9,002
Number of Retail Trade Establishments with Payroll 1,180
Annual Payroll (in millions) $179.8
Total Sales (in millions) $1,409.9
General Merchandise Stores (per capita) $1,620
Food Stores (per capita) $1,262
Apparel Stores (per capita) $637
Eating and Drinking Places (per capita) $919

Service Industries

Total Establishments 1,539

Labor

 The composition of the labor force is constantly changing. The Port of Tacoma is a major employer, as are McChord Air Force Base and Fort Lewis. Lumbering is losing workers because of environmental pressures, but Weyerhauser still remains the largest employer. Most of the other employers are service companies.

Labor

Civilian Labor Force 85,888
% Change 1989–1990 0.9
Work Force Distribution
Mining NA
Construction NA
Manufacturing 13,400
Transportation and Public Utilities NA
Wholesale and Retail Trade 22,034
FIRE (Finance, Insurance, Real Estate) NA
Service 13,986
Government 6,100
Women as % of Labor Force 42.4
% Self-Employed 5.4
% Professional/Technical 15.3
Total Unemployment 4,509
Rate % 5.2
Federal Government Civilian Employment 3,083

Education

Tacoma School District supports 73 schools, which enroll 29,465 students. Among the private and parochial schools are the Annie Wright and Charles Wright academies and Bellermine Catholic preparatory school. Tacoma is home to two four-year colleges: the private Pacific Lutheran University and the University of Puget Sound.

Education

Number of Public Schools 73
Special Education Schools NA
Total Enrollment 29,465
% Enrollment in Private Schools 6.3
% Minority 33.0
Classroom Teachers 1,620
Pupil-Teacher Ratio 18.2:1
Number of Graduates NA
Total Revenue (in millions) $154.407
Total Expenditures (in millions) $154.468
Expenditures per Pupil $4,737
Educational Attainment (Age 25 and Over)
% Completed 12 or More Years 71.1
% Completed 16 or More Years 13.6
Four-Year Colleges and Universities 2
Enrollment 6,934
Two-Year Colleges 2
Enrollment 12,998

Education (continued)

Libraries

Number 31
Public Libraries 10
Books (in thousands) 949
Circulation (in thousands) 2,733
Persons Served (in thousands) 174
Circulation per Person Served 15.7
Income (in millions) $6.653
Staff 110

Four-Year Colleges and Universities
  Pacific Lutheran University
  University of Puget Sound

Health

Tacoma has ten major medical facilities, including the Veterans Administration Medical Center and two children's hospitals.

Health

Deaths—Total 1,799
Rate per 1,000 11.3
Infant Deaths—Total 38
Rate per 1,000 12.4
Number of Metro Hospitals 8
Number of Metro Hospital Beds 2,150
Rate per 100,000 1,353
Number of Physicians 779
Physicians per 1,000 NA
Nurses per 1,000 NA
Health Expenditures per Capita $15.91

Transportation

Tacoma is approached by the north-south I-5, which links it with all Pacific coast cities. East-west access is provided by State Highway 16. Rail passenger service is provided by Amtrak and rail freight service by Burlington Northern and Union Pacific. A ferry service serves Puget Sound. The Port of Tacoma has grown to become one of the nation's ten largest deep-water harbors. The principal air terminal is Seattle-Tacoma International Airport, 16 miles north of the city.

Transportation

Interstate Highway Mileage 23
Total Urban Mileage 2,258
Total Daily Vehicle Mileage (in millions) $12.166
Daily Average Commute Time 47.1 min.
Number of Buses 104
Port Tonnage (in millions) $20.667
Airports 1
Number of Daily Flights 319
Daily Average Number of Passengers 19,346

Airlines (American carriers only)
  Alaska
  American
  American West
  Continental
  Delta

Transportation (continued)

  Eastern
  Hawaiian
  Northwest
  Trans World
  United

Housing

Of the total housing stock, 52.7% is owner-occupied. The median value of an owner-occupied home is $66,200 and the median monthly rent $350.

Housing

Total Housing Units 75,147
% Change 1980–1990 9.8
Vacant Units for Sale or Rent 3,753
Occupied Units 69,939
% with More Than One Person per Room 4.9
% Owner-Occupied 52.7
Median Value of Owner-Occupied Homes $66,200
Average Monthly Purchase Cost $316
Median Monthly Rent $350
New Private Housing Starts 817
Value (in thousands) $52,324
% Single-Family 43.1
Nonresidential Buildings Value (in thousands) $47,797

Urban Redevelopment

One of the major urban development projects in recent years has been the Tacoma Dome, a multi-use facility with a convention hall. Urban development programs are coordinated by Downtown Tacoma Association.

Crime

In 1991 violent crimes reported to police totaled 3,583, property crimes totaled 16,977.

Crime

Violent Crimes—Total 3,583
Violent Crime Rate per 100,000 947.5
Murder 31
Rape 277
Robbery 1,100
Aggravated Assaults 2,175
Property Crimes 16,977
Burglary 3,752
Larceny 11,677
Motor Vehicle Theft 1,548
Arson 185
Per Capita Police Expenditures $118.05
Per Capita Fire Protection Expenditures $106.26
Number of Police 276
Per 1,000 1.71

Religion

All major denominations are represented in Tacoma. Catholics make up the largest population, followed by Mormons and Lutherans. The oldest church is St. Peter's Episcopal Church, built in 1873, with a bell tower on the top of a fir tree. Holy Communion Church on South Street is also a large Episcopal church. Among the Roman Catholic churches are the Holy Rosary Church on Tacoma Avenue, St. Patrick's Church, and the Church of the Immaculate Conception. The Presbyterian Church on 14th Street is an architectural jewel.

Religion	
Largest Denominations (Adherents)	
Catholic	53,259
Assembly of God	13,485
Latter-Day Saints	16,534
Evangelical Lutheran	15,804
Black Baptist	11,565
United Methodist	8,750
Southern Baptist	7,657
Presbyterian	8,826
Lutheran-Missouri Synod	6,611
Jewish	1,100

Media

The city daily is the *Tacoma News Tribune*. Electronic media consist of two television stations, and nine AM and FM radio stations. In addition Tacoma receives clear signals from Seattle-based television and radio stations.

Media	
Newsprint	
Tacoma Area Progress, monthly	
Tacoma Facts, weekly	
Tacoma News Tribune, daily	
Television	
KTBW (Channel 20)	
KTPS (Channel 28)	
Radio	
KBSG (FM)	KDFL (AM)
KKMO (AM)	KPLU (FM)
KRPM (FM)	KTAC (AM)
KTPS (FM)	KUPS (FM)
KVTI (FM)	

Sports

Tacoma does not have any major professional sports team. The Tacoma Tigers, a minor baseball league, play at Cheney Stadium, and the Tacoma Stars, a soccer team, play at the Tacoma Dome.

Arts, Culture, and Tourism

The Tacoma Arts Commission has been actively engaged in the promotion of performing arts in the city. Most of the cultural events take place at the Pantages Center for the Performing Arts. Music is represented by the Tacoma Symphony Orchestra and the Tacoma Youth Symphony, theater by the Tacoma Actors Guild, and dance by the Tacoma Performing Dance Company and Balletacoma.

The premier museums are Tacoma Art Museum and the Washington State Historical Society. There are a number of smaller, more specialized museums, such as the Fort Nisqually Historic Site, Bing Crosby Historical Society, James R. Slater Museum of Natural History, Western Forest Industries Museum, and the Thomas Handforth Art Gallery.

Travel and Tourism	
Hotel Rooms 2,871	
Convention and Exhibit Space (square feet) NA	
Convention Centers	
Tacoma Dome	
Festivals	
Annual Daffodil Show (April)	
Holiday Food and Gift Festival (October)	
Western Washington Fair (September)	
Scandinavian Festival (October)	
Tidefest (December)	

Parks and Recreation

Of the city's numerous parks, the most popular is the 640-acre Point Defiance Park on the northern tip of the Tacoma Peninsula. In addition to a lake and landscaped gardens, it includes Job Carr's Cabin and a reconstructed Fort Nisqually, built in 1833 and moved to its present site in 1934. The 15-by-20-foot house of handhewn logs was built by Archibald McDonald of Hudsons Bay Company in Dupont, about 17 miles south of Tacoma. A stockade of 250 feet square was built in 1847 as a protection against Indian attack. The 27-acre Wright Park, bounded by G and I streets and Sixth and Division avenues, is in the very center of the city. Its arboretum is one of the oldest in the nation.

Sources of Further Information

City Hall
747 Market Street
Tacoma, WA 98402
(206) 591-5100

Tacoma–Pierce County Chamber of Commerce
735 St. Helens Avenue
Tacoma, WA 98401
(206) 627-2175

Additional Reading

Morgan, Murray, and Rosa Morgan.
  Tacoma, Washington: South on the Sound. 1984.
Snyder, Wilma. *Tacoma: Voice from the Past*. 1988.

Tampa

Florida

Location and Topography

Tampa is located midway down Florida's west coast, bordered by the Hillsborough Bay on the south and the Old Tampa Bay on the west. Hillsborough River runs through the city from the northeast into Hillsborough Bay.

Layout of City and Suburbs

Tampa has a distinctively Spanish atmosphere. The Maritime district faces the horseshoe-shaped estuary of the Hillsborough River. The principal shopping district is along Franklin Street. Many firms on this street date back to the 19th century. The street is also the location of the City Hall and the courthouse. Hyde Park, adjoining the University of Tampa, was the original residential section. South of Hyde Park are Davis Islands. Bayshore Boulevard, sweeping south along Hillsborough Bay, is in the midst of another large residential section. West Tampa and Ybor City are both within Tampa city limits. Tampa roads are laid out in a grid pattern with Florida Avenue dividing east and west and John F. Kennedy Boulevard and Frank Adamo Drive dividing north and south.

Environment

Environmental Stress Index   3.0
Green Cities Index: Rank   6
              Score   20.29
Water Quality   Alkaline, moderately hard
  Average Daily Use (gallons per capita)   150
  Maximum Supply (gallons per capita)   350
Parkland as % of Total City Area   NA
% Waste Landfilled/Recycled   NA
Annual Parks Expenditures per Capita $256.71

Climate

A remarkable feature of the Tampa weather is the prevalence of thunderstorms. On an average there are 88 days of thunderstorms per year, mostly in the afternoons from July to September, causing the temperatures to drop by almost 20 degrees. Although in a tropical zone, Tampa's temperature is modified by the waters

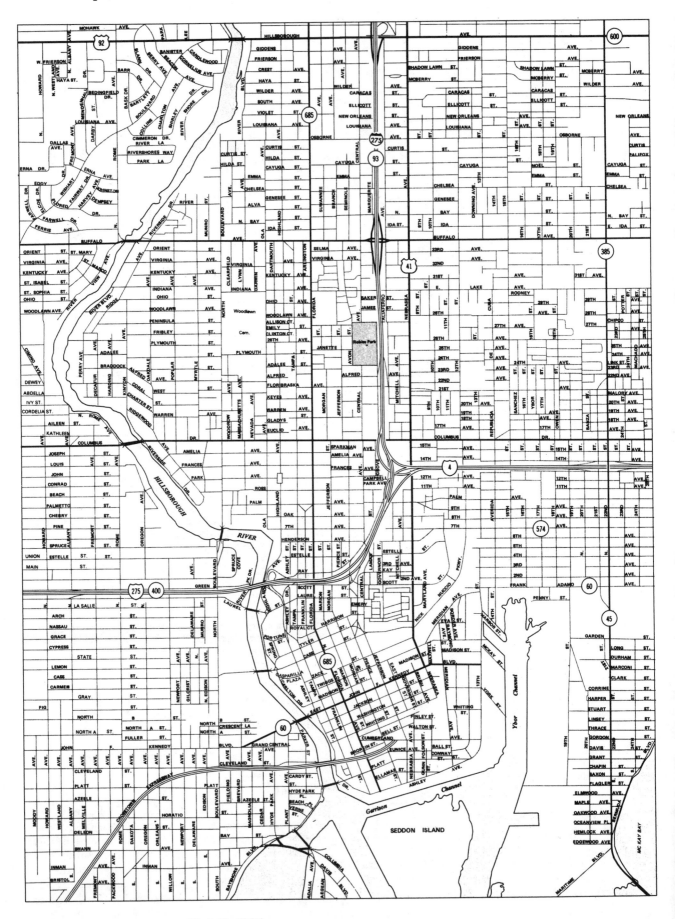

of the Gulf of Mexico. There is virtually no snow or freezing temperatures, but fog is common.

Weather			
Temperature			
Highest Monthly Average °F	90.0		
Lowest Monthly Average °F	49.5		
Annual Averages			
Days 32°F or Below	4		
Days above 90°F	81		
Zero Degree Days	0		
Precipitation (inches)	49.0		
Snow (inches)	NA		
% Seasonal Humidity	74.0		
Wind Speed (m.p.h.)	8.5		
Clear Days	98		
Cloudy Days	127		
Storm Days	88		
Rainy Days	107		
Average Temperatures (°F)	*High*	*Low*	*Mean*
January	70.6	50.1	60.4
February	71.9	51.7	61.8
March	76.1	55.9	66.0
April	82.4	61.6	72.0
May	87.5	66.9	77.2
June	89.9	72.0	81.0
July	90.1	73.7	81.9
August	90.4	74.0	82.2
September	89.0	72.6	80.8
October	83.9	65.5	74.7
November	77.1	56.4	66.8
December	72.0	51.2	61.6

History

The origin of Tampa is uncertain. De Soto had originally christened Tampa Bay as Espiritu Santo Bay. Tampa first appears in 1580 in Fontenado's list of Indian towns and in De Laet's map of 1625. It was believed to be inhabited by the Calusa Indians, who along with the Ticobaga, Timucua, and Apalachee, had lived in the region for hundreds of years. The first white presence dates from 1528 when Navarez, commissioner general of Florida, headed an expedition through Tampa to the north. Later de Soto sailed into Tampa Bay in 1539 and took possession of an Indian village. The pioneer American settlement in the region had to wait for another 184 years until 1823, when Fort Brooke, named after George Brooke, its first commander, was established. The presence of the garrison encouraged immigration and the settlement grew throughout the Seminole Wars.

A post office called Tampa Bay was established in 1831 and the name was shortened to Tampa three years later. The government donated 40 acres for the construction of a courthouse. With the vast pastures in its hinterland, Tampa became the center of a flourishing cattle industry. Trade with Cuba was also a factor in the town's growth. Florida joined the Confederacy in 1861. The town was blockaded and shelled in 1863 and was occupied by federal troops. In 1873 yellow fever swept the area and the population dwindled. For a number of years Tampa was merely a port of call for schooners operating between Cedar Keys and Key West. The comparative isolation of the town lasted until 1884 when the South Florida Railroad, later the Atlantic Coast Line, reached Tampa; it was later extended to Port Tampa, where piers were built to berth ocean steamships. In 1889 a wooden bridge across the Hillsborough River at Lafayette Street supplanted the ferry and a second railroad, the Florida Railway and Navigation Company—later the Seaboard Air Line—entered the city. From then on, expansion was rapid. By 1890 the population grew to 5,000 and by the end of the century to 15,000. Meanwhile the cigar industry moved from Key West to Ybor City. In 1891 Henry Plant completed the building of the Tampa Bay Hotel, determined to make the city a fashionable winter resort and to outdo developer Henry Flagler on Florida's east coast. Plant spent more than $3 million on the hotel. During the Spanish-American War, Tampa was the staging ground for 30,000 U.S. troops and their commanders, including Theodore Roosevelt and his Rough Riders. Clara Barton, founder of the U.S. Red Cross, also maintained headquarters in the city. Following the Spanish-American War there was a spurt of growth for the "squalid, sand-blighted city," as Richard Harding Davis called it. The harbor was dredged and improved and new steel bridges replaced the old wooden ones over the Hillsborough River. Cigar manufacturing reached its peak before World War I. Gandy Bridge was completed in 1924, spanning Tampa Bay and connecting with St. Petersburg, and Davis Causeway opened in 1934, connecting with Clearwater. During the next 50 years Tampa experienced a series of downturns during the Depresssion and in the immediate postwar years, but always managed to come back. An urban renewal program under Mayor Dick Greco (1968–1974) turned the city once more into a place where, as the city slogan describes it, the good life gets better every day.

Historical Landmarks

The site of Fort Brooke on the corner of Platt and Franklin streets is indicated by a bronze plaque. The Sacred Heart Roman Catholic Church on the corner of Twiggs Street and Florida Avenue was dedicated in 1905. Above the central entrance is a marble statue of the risen Christ. The Orange Grove Hotel Building on Madison Street, built in 1843, was the home of William Hooker, one of the cattle kings of south Florida. Plant Hall, the administration building of the University of Tampa, opened in 1891 as the Tampa Bay Hotel, a 511-room ornate building in Moorish style built for railroad baron Plant by J. A. Wood. Never a commercial success, the hotel was deeded to the city in 1904 and taken over by the university in 1930. Opposite the east entrance of the university is the de Soto Oak under which, according to legend, de Soto parlayed with the Indians. Tampa's Latin American quarter is Ybor City, a National Historic Register District. Ybor City developed around two cigar factories built in the 1880s by Cubans. Historic buildings in the city include El Pasaje Hotel, Ritz Theater, and Ferlita Bakery.

Chronology

1823	Fort Brooke is established near Tampa Bay.
1831	Post office called Tampa Bay is established in settlement around Fort Brooke.
1834	The name is shortened to Tampa.
1863	Tampa is shelled and blockaded and later occupied by Union troops.
1873	Yellow fever sweeps Tampa.
1877	Stagecoach line begins operation between Tampa and Gainesville.
1884	Henry Plant builds South Florida Railroad to Tampa.
1889	Wooden bridge supplants ferry across the Hillsborough River.
1891	Plant completes building the extravagant Tampa Bay Hotel.
1899	On the outbreak of the Spanish-American War, 30,000 troops camp in and around Tampa.
1924	Gandy Bridge is completed linking Tampa and St. Petersburg.
1934	Davis Causeway is built, providing direct route to Clearwater.

Population

Tampa has gained population in the 1980s, in contrast to its loss of population in the 1970s. In 1990 its population was 280,015, a gain of 3.1% over its 1980 population of 271,577. During the preceding decade it had declined by 2.2% from its 1970 population of 278,000. Some of its growth in the last decade has been from heavy Cuban migration.

Population

	1980	1990
Central City	271,577	280,015
Rank	53	55
Metro Area	1,613,600	2,067,959
Pop. Change 1980–1990 +8,438		
Pop. % Change 1980–1990 +3.1		
Median Age 33.3		
% Male 48.0		
% Age 65 and Over 14.6		
Density (per square mile) 2,576		

Households

Number 114,800
Persons per Household 2.35
% Female-Headed Households 15.5
% One-Person Households 32.3
Births—Total 5,163
　% to Mothers under 20 18.5
　Birth Rate per 1,000 18.7

Ethnic Composition

Whites make up 70.9%, blacks 25%, American Indians 0.3%, Asians and Pacific Islanders 1.4%, and others 2.4%. Hispanics, both black and white, make up 15% of the population.

Ethnic Composition (as % of total pop.)

	1980	1990
White	75.48	70.9
Black	23.42	25.0
American Indian	0.22	0.3
Asian and Pacific Islander	0.7	1.35
Hispanic	13.18	15.0
Other	NA	2.40

Government

Tampa adopted a mayor-council form of government in 1945. The mayor and the seven council members are elected in nonpartisan elections every four years.

Government

Year of Home Charter
Number of Members of the Governing Body 7
Elected at Large 7
Elected by Wards NA
Number of Women in Governing Body 1
Salary of Mayor $110,000
Salary of Council Members $19,928
City Government Employment Total 3,964
Rate per 10,000 142.8

Public Finance

The annual budget consists of revenues of $429.337 million and expenditures of $435.877 million. The debt outstanding is $1.216 billion, and cash and security holdings total $1.175 billion.

Public Finance

Total Revenue (in millions) $429.337
Intergovernmental Revenue—Total (in millions) $54.21
Federal Revenue per Capita $15.27
% Federal Assistance 3.5
% State Assistance 6.42
Sales Tax as % of Total Revenue 13.46
Local Revenue as % of Total Revenue 66.76
City Income Tax no
Taxes—Total (in millions) $76.3

Taxes per Capita
　Total $275
　Property $96
　Sales and Gross Receipts $155
General Expenditures—Total (in millions) $250.2
General Expenditures per Capita $901
Capital Outlays per Capita $349

% of Expenditures for:
　Public Welfare 0.0
　Highways 5.7
　Education 0.0

Public Finance (continued)

Health and Hospitals   NA
Police   13.7
Sewerage and Sanitation   35.9
Parks and Recreation   8.2
Housing and Community Development   2.5
Debt Outstanding per Capita $2,059
  % Utility   23.0
Federal Procurement Contract Awards (in millions)
  $203.1
Federal Grants Awards (in millions) $53.2
Fiscal Year Begins   October 1

Economy

Tampa was known as the cigar capital of the nation well until the end of World War II. It was a one-industry town whose 100-plus cigar factories produced more cigars than Havana. The fall of Cuba to the Communists led to a crisis in the industry and posed a serious threat to Tampa's prosperity. It spurred a push to diversify. When heavy industry was found to be an unattractive option, Tampa turned to service industries. Within two decades the city was transformed into a commercial and financial hub on Florida's west coast, successfully competing with other Florida cities, such as Miami, St. Petersburg, and Jacksonville. Tourism became a major revenue-earner along with insurance, banking, and brokerage. The city also has expanded into medical and aerospace technology and electronics. Tampa is also a thriving agribusiness center with a heavy stake in citrus fruits, beef, dairy products, eggs, vegetables, ornamental plants and flowers, and tropical fish. Two breweries, Anheuser-Busch and Pabst, have production facilities here. Overall, there are 800 manufacturing firms today, including cigar makers.

Economy

Total Money Income (in millions) $2,748.6
% of State Average   87.9
Per Capita Annual Income $9,902
% Population below Poverty Level   18.7
Fortune 500 Companies   2

Banks	Number	Deposits (in millions)
Commercial	27	6,869.743
Savings	19	1,277.895

Passenger Autos   608,824
Electric Meters   335,000
Gas Meters   14,489

Manufacturing

Number of Establishments   610
% with 20 or More Employees   31.3
Manufacturing Payroll (in millions) $492.5
Value Added by Manufacture (in millions) $1,087.9
Value of Shipments (in millions) $2,459.7
New Capital Expenditures (in millions) $77.9

Wholesale Trade

Number of Establishments   1,352
Sales (in millions) $10,959.0
Annual Payroll (in millions) $499.754

Economy (continued)

Retail Trade

Number of Establishments   3,614
Total Sales (in millions) $3,118.3
Sales per Capita $11,234
Number of Retail Trade Establishments with Payroll   2,679
Annual Payroll (in millions) $374.9
Total Sales (in millions) $3,073.5
General Merchandise Stores (per capita) $1,548
Food Stores (per capita) $1,590
Apparel Stores (per capita) $437
Eating and Drinking Places (per capita) $1,230

Service Industries

Total Establishments   4,015
Total Receipts (in millions) $2,752.4
Hotels and Motels (in millions) $132.9
Health Services (in millions) $526.7
Legal Services (in millions) $281.2

Labor

More than half the work force is engaged in services and trade, compared to 12% in manufacturing and 15% in government. As a point of arrival for Latin American immigrants, Tampa possesses an ethnically diverse labor force. The MacDill Air Force Base is also a major employer. Finance and tourism-related industries are expected to provide strong employment potential in the 1990s.

Labor

Civilian Labor Force   188,769
% Change 1989–1990   2.2

Work Force Distribution
  Mining   400
  Construction   42,700
  Manufacturing   86,300
  Transportation and Public Utilities   39,600
  Wholesale and Retail Trade   229,200
  FIRE (Finance, Insurance, Real Estate)   63,900
  Service   277,700
  Government   116,700
  Women as % of Labor Force   46.1
  % Self-Employed   5.7
  % Professional/Technical   13.5
Total Unemployment   10,069
Rate %   5.3
Federal Government Civilian Employment   6,323

Education

The Hillsborough District Public School System supports 149 schools. In addition, 122 private and parochial schools operate in the district.

Five institutions provide higher education: The University of South Florida, headquartered in Tampa with campuses in Fort Myers, Lakeland, St. Petersburg, and Sarasota, has nine colleges with 33,000 students. The University of Tampa is a private liberal arts institution with an enrollment of 2,400. The other institutions are Tampa College, Florida College, and Hillsborough College.

Education

Number of Public Schools 149
Special Education Schools 12
Total Enrollment 123,900
% Enrollment in Private Schools 12.0
% Minority 35.4
Classroom Teachers 7,526
Pupil-Teacher Ratio 16.4:1
Number of Graduates 6,187
Total Revenue (in millions) $535.699
Total Expenditures (in millions) $521.448
Expenditures per Pupil $3,902
Educational Attainment (Age 25 and Over)
   % Completed 12 or More Years 61.0
   % Completed 16 or More Years 12.8
Four-Year Colleges and Universities 5
   Enrollment 36,363
Two-Year Colleges 4
   Enrollment 20,988

Libraries

Number 50
Public Libraries 18
Books (in thousands) 1,160
Circulation (in thousands) 3,128
Persons Served (in thousands) 825
Circulation per Person Served 3.79
Income (in millions) $12.340
Staff 279

Four-Year Colleges and Universities
   Florida College
   Hillsborough College
   Tampa College
   University of South Florida
   University of Tampa

Health

Tampa has 15 major hospitals in Hillsborough County of which the largest is the Tampa General Hospital, the primary teaching hospital for the University of South Florida College of Medicine. Other facilities are James A. Haley Veterans Hospital, St. Joseph's Hospital, University Community Hospital, Humana Hospital and Humana Women's Hospital, AMI Memorial Hospital, H. Lee Moffitt Cancer Center, Charter Hospital, Centurion Hospital, USF Psychiatry Center, South Florida Baptist Hospital, South Bay Hospital, Centro Espanol Memorial Hospital, Vensor Westshore Hospital, Shriner's Hospital for Crippled Children, MacDill USAF Regional Hospital, and Northside Community Mental Health Center.

Health

Deaths—Total 3,355
Rate per 1,000 12.2
Infant Deaths—Total 68
Rate per 1,000 13.2
Number of Metro Hospitals 15
Number of Metro Hospital Beds 3,855
Rate per 100,000 1,389
Number of Physicians 3,447

Health (continued)

Physicians per 1,000 2.11
Nurses per 1,000 13.08
Health Expenditures per Capita $12.47

Transportation

Tampa is approached by the north-south I-75, which becomes I-275 as it passes through the city; and I-4 from the northeast, which merges with I-275 downtown. U.S. Highways 41 (a coastal road also known as Tamiami Trail) and 301 parallel I-75 on the west and east. The principal state road is 60. CSX Transportation provides rail service. The Port of Tampa is the seventh largest in the nation and the largest in Florida. It is also the home of one of the world's largest shrimp fleets and has extensive shipbuilding and ship-repair facilities. The Tampa International Airport is located five miles from downtown. A second and smaller terminal is the Peter O. Knight Airport on Davis Islands.

Transportation

Interstate Highway Mileage 46
Total Urban Mileage 1,854
Total Daily Vehicle Mileage (in millions) $12.232
Daily Average Commute Time 45.1 min.
Number of Buses 279
Port Tonnage (in millions) $50.252
Airports 2
Number of Daily Flights 162
Daily Average Number of Passengers 12,135

Airlines (American carriers only)
   American
   American Trans Air
   Continental
   Delta
   Midway
   Northwest
   Trans World
   United
   USAir

Housing

About 55.5% of total housing stock is owner-occupied. The median value of an owner-occupied home is $59,000 and the median monthly rent is $334.

Housing

Total Housing Units 129,681
% Change 1980–1990 11.9
Vacant Units for Sale or Rent 11,234
Occupied Units 114,800
% with More Than One Person per Room 6.0
% Owner-Occupied 55.5
Median Value of Owner-Occupied Homes $59,000
Average Monthly Purchase Cost $276
Median Monthly Rent $334
New Private Housing Starts 1,106
Value (in thousands) $87,522
% Single-Family 38.3

Housing (continued)

Nonresidential Buildings Value (in thousands)		$30,344

Tallest Buildings	Hgt. (ft.)	Stories
Barnett Plaza (1986)	577	42
Tampa City Center (1981)	537	39
First Financial Tower (1973)	458	36
NCNB Plaza (1988)	454	33

Urban Redevelopment

Urban redevelopment began in the 1960s and has been continuing ever since at a fast pace. Most of it is in the form of private developments and corporate facilities, but also includes public projects such as the Tampa Convention Center. Among the major private developments are the Renaissance Park, Barnett Plaza, Enterprise Plaza, Florida Building, Landmark Building, Landmark Center, One Harbor Place, Riverside Plaza, and Tampa City Center. Harbor Island is a 177-acre mixed-use project. Further development is taking place at Westshore and along Tampa Parkway.

Crime

Tampa ranks quite near the bottom in public safety. In 1991 violent crimes totaled 10,362 and property crimes totaled 37,214.

Crime

Violent Crimes—Total	10,362
Violent Crime Rate per 100,000	1,264.5
Murder	64
Rape	347
Robbery	3,094
Aggravated Assaults	6,857
Property Crimes	37,214
Burglary	11,239
Larceny	20,072
Motor Vehicle Theft	5,903
Arson	62
Per Capita Police Expenditures	$148.16
Per Capita Fire Protection Expenditures	$66.97
Number of Police	692
Per 1,000	2.43

Religion

Tampa has 428 places of worship, of which 240 are Protestant, 50 Catholic, 8 Jewish, and 130 other.

Religion

Largest Denominations (Adherents)	
Catholic	120,722
Southern Baptist	92,554
Black Baptist	35,093
United Methodist	33,282
Assembly of God	9,285
Presbyterian	10,828
Episcopal	8,242
Churches of Christ	7,459
Church of God	7,561
Jewish	11,110

Media

The city daily is the *Tampa Tribune*. Electronic media consist of 6 television stations and 16 AM and FM radio stations.

Media

Newsprint
Bay Area Business Analyst, monthly
Tampa Bay Business, weekly
Tampa Bay Magazine, monthly
Tampa Florida Sentinel-Bulletin, semiweekly
Tampa Magazine, monthly
Tampa News Reporter, weekly
Tampa Tribune, daily

Television
WBHS (Channel 50)
WEDU (Channel 3)
WFLA (Channel 8)
WFTS (Channel 28)
WTVT (Channel 13)
WUSF (Channel 16)

Radio

WAMA (AM)	WBVM (FM)
WDAE (AM)	WUSA (FM)
WFLA (AM)	WFLZ (FM)
WGUL (AM)	WGUL (FM)
WMNF (FM)	WMTX (AM)
WQBN (AM)	WQYK (AM)
WRBQ (FM)	WTIS (AM)
WTMT (AM)	WUSF (FM)

Sports

Tampa is the home of two professional teams, the Tampa Bay Buccaneers of the National Football League and the Tampa Bay Rowdies of the North American Soccer League. Both play at the Tampa Stadium, the former from August through December and the latter from March through July. The Tampa Tarpons are a Class A team of the Cincinnati Reds. Another popular spectator sport is jai alai, played at the Tampa Jai Alai Fronton. Both horse racing and dog racing are popular. The Tampa Bay Downs and Turf Club is the only thoroughbred track on Florida's west coast. The Tampa Greyhound Track is located north of downtown.

Arts, Culture, and Tourism

The performing arts have received considerable institutional and public support. There are 13 major entertainment centers including the restored Tampa Theater, Tampa Bay Performing Arts Center, USF Sun Dome, Curtis Dixon Hall, Bayfront Center, Richard B. Baumgardner Center, Asolo Theater, Ven Wezel Performing Arts Hall, Tampa Convention Center, Loft Theater, University of South Florida Theater, Suncoast Dome, and Ruth Eckerd Hall. The Tampa Players and the Playmakers of Ybor City are the best-known professional theater groups. Other groups include Spanish Little Theater and Bits 'n' Pieces Theater. The Tampa Ballet in residence at the University of Tampa stages four ballets in a season. Musical entertainment is provided by the Florida Orchestra, performing ten concerts, Florida Gulf Coast Symphony, Community Concert Association, and the San Carlos Opera.

Among the major museums and art galleries in Hillsborough County are the Tampa Museum of Art, Museum of Science and Industry, Henry B. Plant Museum, County Historical Museum, Seminole Culture Center, Florida Center for Contemporary Art, Lee Scarfone Gallery, University of South Florida Art Galleries, Ybor City State Museum, Salvador Dali Museum, The John and Mable Ringling Museum, Florida Museum of Holography, Museum of Natural History, Museum of African-American Art, and Children's Museum.

Parks and Recreation

Tampa has 87 parks covering 832 acres and 52 picnic areas. To the northeast of the city is the Hillsborough River State Park Picnic Island, a park where Teddy Roosevelt and the Rough Riders camped during the Spanish-American War.

Travel and Tourism

Hotel Rooms   32,044
Convention and Exhibit Space (square feet)   NA

Convention Centers
  Tampa Convention Center
  Curtis Hixon Convention Center

Festivals
  Florida State Fair (February)
  Gasparilla Pirate Invasion and Parade (February)

Sources of Further Information

City Hall
306 East Jackson Street
Tampa, FL 33602
(813) 223-8251

Greater Tampa Chamber of Commerce
801 West Kennedy Boulevard
Tampa, FL 33602
(813) 228-7777

Tampa/Hillsborough Convention and Visitors
  Association
100, South Ashley Drive
Tampa, FL 33602
(813) 223-1111

Tampa Office of Economic Development
315, West Kennedy Boulevard
Tampa, FL 33602
(813) 223-8381

Additional Reading

Bane, Michael, and Ellen More. *Tampa: Yesterday, Today and Tomorrow.* 1982.
Polk's Tampa City Directory. 1991.

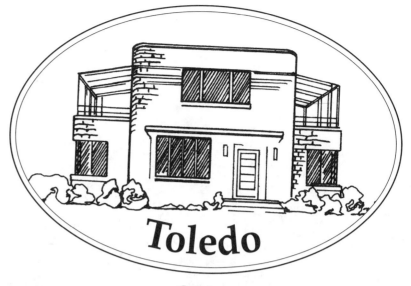

Toledo

Ohio

Basic Data

Name   Toledo
Name Origin   From Toledo, Spain
Year Founded   1817 Inc. 1837
Status: State   Ohio
         County   Seat of Lucas County
Area (square miles)   80.6
Elevation (feet)   585
Time Zone   EST
Population (1990)   332,943
Population of Metro Area (1990)   614,128

Sister Cities

   Londrina, Brazil
   Poznan, Poland
   Qinhuangdao, China
   Szeged, Hungary
   Toledo, Spain

Distance in Miles To:

Cincinnati	210
Columbus	144
Dayton	157
Springfield	128
Zanesville	191
Detroit	55
Chicago	234
New York	610

Location and Topography

N

Toledo stretches for 15 miles along both sides of the Maumee River, southwest of Maumee Bay on the westernmost tip of Lake Erie. The city is surrounded by fairly level terrain.

Layout of City and Suburbs

The heart of the city is the curving Maumee River that widens into the bay. The main section of Toledo lies on the west side of the Maumee, connected with East Toledo by seven bridges. The business district is a short distance from the west bank, about eight miles south of the Maumee Bay. Westward from the river and the business district are the middle-class residential areas. The better residential sections are found south, near the vicinity of the Ottawa Hills and in Collingwood.

Environment

Environmental Stress Index   3.2
Green Cities Index: Rank   16
                   Score   23.46
Water Quality   fluoridated
   Average Daily Use (gallons per capita)   169
   Maximum Supply (gallons per capita)   399
Parkland as % of Total City Area   NA
% Waste Landfilled/Recycled   NA
Annual Parks Expenditures per Capita $29.59

Climate

The close proximity of Lake Erie has a moderating influence on climate; extreme temperatures are rarely recorded. Snowfall is light, but humidity and cloudiness are high throughout the year. During winter the sun shines for only 30% of daylight hours, and from December through January the percentage drops to only 16%. Severe storms are frequent and heavy rains often cause flooding.

Weather

Temperature   °

Highest Monthly Average °F   83.4
Lowest Monthly Average °F   15.5

Annual Averages

Days 32°F or Below   145
Days above 90°F   13
Zero Degree Days   8

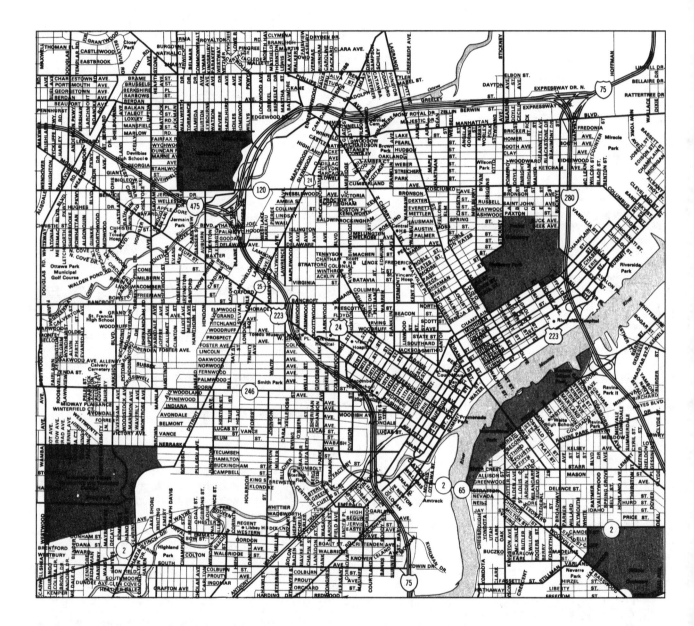

History

The area around Toledo was first visited by Europeans as early as 1615 when Etienne Brule, a guide for Samuel de Champlain, found the Erie Indians living among the swamps and dense forests at the mouth of the Maumee. In 1689 Robert Cavelier, Sieur de la Salle, claimed the territory in the name of King Louis XIV. Following the French and Indian War of 1763, France ceded the territory to the British, who annexed it to the Canadian province of Quebec in 1774. At the end of the American Revolution the region became a part of the United States and was designated part of the Northwest territory in 1787. Opposition from Indians continued until General "Mad" Anthony Wayne's victory in the Battle of Fallen Timbers, fought a few miles to the southwest of Toledo in 1794, opened the area for permanent settlement. Settlers began to move northward from the Ohio River and westward from the Allegheny Mountains. Under orders from Wayne, a stockade called Fort Industry was erected on the present site of the city. The first settlers fled with the outbreak of the War of 1812. In 1813, General William Henry Harrison, later president, erected Fort Meigs, nicknamed Gibraltar of the Northwest because of its massive size. With the defeat of the British in the Battle of Lake Erie and the Battle of the Thames, the Northwest Territory was permanently secured against invasion. After the Treaty of 1817 conveyed to the government all remaining lands in Indian hands, a Cincinnati syndicate purchased a 974-acre tract at the mouth of the Swan Creek on the northwest side of the Maumee River. Named Port Lawrence, it went into limbo when the syndicate failed in 1820, but was revived in 1832 when it was consolidated with Vistula, a river settlement to the north, under the name of Toledo. It included a number of small communities: Manhattan, Marengo, and Miami on the west bank; Lucas City, Mendota, Oregon, and Orleans on the east.

The settlers faced numerous hardships, particularly a cholera epidemic, drought, financial panic, and not least of all, a dispute over the town between Ohio and Michigan, known as the Toledo War of 1835–1836. Because early maps of the Northwest Territory were ill-drawn, both Michigan and Ohio claimed the northern cape of the Maumee River, including Toledo. Michigan's 21–year-old acting governor, Stevens T. Mason, and Ohio governor Robert Lucas called their state troops to enforce their respective jurisdictions over Toledo. Before any actual fighting began, emissaries from President Jackson arrived and persuaded the governors to subscribe to a temporary truce. The truce notwithstanding, minor raids continued. Michigan troops entered Toledo, pulled down the Ohio flag and dragged it through the streets, arrested the Ohio boundary commissioners, and marched them into Michigan. Governor Lucas called a special session of the Ohio legislature to create Lucas County out of the disputed territory. The new county was directed to hold its court in Toledo, but under the threat of a Michigan invasion, the court was held at night by the light of a tallow candle. Having hastily appointed new county commissioners, the judges fled, but the minutes of the meeting were claimed as documentary proof of Ohio's jurisdiction. President Jackson and Congress, who favored Ohio's claims, laid down Michigan's acceptance of Ohio's jurisdiction over Toledo as a condition for its entrance into the Union in exchange for the Upper Peninsula. The end of the Toledo War was celebrated in the city with parades, bells, and guns. The opening of the Erie Canal in New York spurred the building of the Wabash and Erie Canal in 1843 and the Miami and Erie Canal in 1845. The two canals, joining at Defiance, extended to the lake along the Maumee River. As Toledo prospered from the canal trade, it began to expand along the riverbank. In 1836 the Erie and Kalamazoo Railroad was completed with Toledo as its southern terminus. The Maumee was bridged at Cherry Street in 1865, joining the eastern and western sections of town. In 1869 new rail lines came into town with the completion of the Wheeling & Lake Erie, and the Toledo, Ann Arbor, and Northern railroads. The rail network continued with the completion of the Toledo and Woodville in 1873 and the Toledo, Columbus, and Hocking Valley in 1875. The decades following the Civil War brought sustained growth to the city, both economically and culturally. The first unit of the park system was laid out in 1871. The Toledo University was established in 1872 and in the same year a public library was opened. The 1880s brought a new industrial epoch based on glass and oil. The glass industry was developed by Edward Libbey, who closed his East Cambridge, Massachusetts, glass factory and, bringing 100 glass craftsmen with him, founded the Libbey Glass Company in Toledo. There he was joined by a master craftsman, Michael Owens. Later Edward Ford founded his plate-glass plant on the east side of the Maumee in the model industrial town of Rossford. By 1890 Toledo's docks totaled 18 miles, its manufacturing

Chronology

1615	Etienne Brule, a French-Canadian guide for Samuel de Champlain, visits Erie Indians living in the Maumee River valley.
1689	La Salle claims the territory on behalf of the king of France.
1763	France cedes the territory to the British at the end of the French and Indian Wars.
1774	The region is incorporated in the Canadian province of Quebec.
1787	The region is designated as part of the Northwest Territory and it becomes part of the United States.
1794	General "Mad" Anthony Wayne defeats Indian chief Little Turtle at the Battle of Fallen Timbers and establishes American control. Under Wayne's orders a stockade named Fort Industry is built on the present site of Toledo.
1812	American settlers flee Toledo on the outbreak of the War of 1812.
1813	General William Henry Harrison builds Fort Meigs, named Gibraltar of the Northwest.
1817	Treaty conveys to the government all Indian lands in the region. A Cincinnati syndicate purchases a 974-acre tract at the mouth of Swan Creek and names it Port Lawrence.
1820	The Port Lawrence syndicate fails.
1832	Port Lawrence is revived, and survives an epidemic of Asiatic cholera.
1833	Port Lawrence merges with another river settlement called Vistula, under the name of Toledo.
1835–1836	Toledo War breaks out between Ohio and Michigan, with each state using its militia to occupy the town and arrest the officials of the other. Ohio creates Lucas County out of the disputed territory and holds court there to prove its rights. Congress awards Toledo to Ohio and in exchange offers Michigan the Upper Peninsula. The Erie and Kalamazoo Railroad is completed.
1837	City of Toledo is incorporated.
1838	Drought destroys crops and trees.
1843	The first canal barge arrives from Lafayette, Indiana, on the Wabash and Erie Canal.
1845	The Miami and Erie Canal opens.
1865	The first bridge over the Maumee opens.
1869	Three new railroads reach Toledo.
1871	The first unit of the park system is set up.
1872	The University of Toledo is founded. The public library opens.
1873	Toledo and Woodville Railroad opens.
1875	Toledo, Columbus, and Hocking Valley Railroad opens.
1888	Edward Libbey founds the Libbey Glass Company.
1893	The Wheeler Opera House burns to the ground. Oil is struck in East Toledo.
1896	Edward Ford founds a plate-glass plant in the industrial town of Rossford.
1897	Samuel M. Jones becomes mayor and gains national fame through his fight against corruption and for good management.
1898	St. Johns College is founded by the Jesuits.
1899	Toledo Zoo opens.
1900	Toledo Museum of Art opens.
1905	Brand Whitlock succeeds Jones as mayor and continues the struggle for reform and good government.
1908	John Willys acquires the Toledo-Pope plant and moves his Overland plant from Indianapolis to found Willys-Overland.
1914	Champion Spark Plug establishes plant.
1928	Transcontinental Airport is dedicated.
1930	Presque Isle's $20-million dock opens.
1934	Violent strike at Electric Auto-Lite heralds unionization of the automotive industry.
1935	The Industrial Peace Board is set up to prevent recurrence of violent strikes. Toledo adopts the city-manager form of government.

plants numbered 750, and the number of passenger trains was 184. Toledo also became the largest oil-refining center between New York and Chicago after oil wells were dug in East Toledo. The turn of the century also witnessed the rise of two famous reform leaders as mayors of Toledo. Samuel M. Jones became mayor in 1897. Known as Golden Rule Jones, he warred against misuse of public funds, favoritism, and the political machine; he also established one of the first municipal utilities, the Toledo Municipal Gas Company, as well as organizing the city's first band concerts and kindergartens. His successor, Brand Whitlock, carried on Jones's crusade and was instrumental in securing the passage of a state law providing for the election of judges on a nonpartisan ticket. The city's cultural resources were enhanced during this era with the founding of St. Johns College in 1898, the Toledo Zoo in 1899, and the Toledo Museum of Art in 1900. The first decade of the 20th century saw the expansion of the glass industry with the invention of a bottlemaking machine, and also the introduction of the new gasoline buggy when John Willys moved his Overland automobile factory from Indianapolis and acquired the Toledo-Pope plant. Automobile spare parts manufacture also flourished. Champion Spark Plug established its plant in 1914 and Warner Manufacturing Company was turning out automobile gears. Just before the Great Depression, Toledo was at the height of its prosperity. In 1928 the Trancontinental Airport was dedicated. Presque Isle's $20-million coal and iron ore docks were opened and Libby-Owens and Edward Ford merged. In 1934 the Electric Auto-Lite strike heralded the unionization of the automotive industries. To avoid industrial violence in the future, the Toledo Industrial Peace Board came into being in 1935, and was soon copied by other cities. In the same year Toledo adopted the city-manager form of government.

Historical Landmarks

The site of Fort Industry built on the orders of General Wayne, on the corner of Monroe and Summit streets, is marked by a bronze tablet. The Oliver House on Broadway was once considered the city's finest hotel with 170 rooms, each with its own fireplace. The St. Francis de Sales Cathedral was erected in 1861 on the site of Toledo's first church. At the rear of the cathedral stands Toledo's oldest building, built in 1838 as a Presbyterian meeting house. Fort Meigs, on the southern bank of the Maumee River west of Perrysburg, was the largest walled fortification in America. Old West End, covering 25 blocks, has one of the largest collections of late Victorian architecture. The restored freighter, *William B. Boyer*, first launched in 1911, is docked at International Park.

Population

Toledo has been steadily losing population since the 1960s. Its 1990 population was 332,943, compared to its 1980 population of 354,635, and its 1970 population of 383,000. Its loss of population was 7.4% during the 1970s and 6.1% during the 1980s. As a result, its overall population rank has fallen from 40th to 49th.

Population		
	1980	*1990*
Central City	354,635	332,943
Rank	40	49
Metro Area	616,864	614,128
Pop. Change 1980–1990 -21,692		
Pop. % Change 1980–1990 -6.1		
Median Age 31.7		

Population (continued)	
% Male 47.4	
% Age 65 and Over 13.6	
Density (per square mile) 4,130	
Households	
Number 130,883	
Persons per Household 2.50	
% Female-Headed Households 15.7	
% One-Person Households 29.7	
Births—Total 5,594	
% to Mothers under 20 17.0	
Birth Rate per 1,000 16.3	

Ethnic Composition

Whites make up 77%, blacks 19.7%, American Indians 0.3%, Asians and Pacific Islanders 1%, and others 2%. Among the whites, Germans make up one-third and Polish one-fourth.

Ethnic Composition (as % of total pop.)		
	1980	*1990*
White	80.11	76.97
Black	17.44	19.7
American Indian	0.28	0.28
Asian and Pacific Islander	0.57	1.05
Hispanic	3.10	3.97
Other	NA	2.01

Government

Since 1935 Toledo has been governed by a city manager form of government. Nine council members, one of whom serves as the mayor, are elected to two-year terms. The mayor and council appoint the city manager.

Government
Year of Home Charter   1914
Number of Members of the Governing Body   9
Elected at Large   9
Elected by Wards   NA
Number of Women in Governing Body   3
Salary of Mayor $36,900
Salary of Council Members $7,800
City Government Employment Total   3,384
Rate per 10,000   99.3

Public Finance

The annual budget consists of revenues of $254.352 million and expenditures of $266.913 million. The debt oustanding is $193.762 million and cash and security holdings are $75.572 million.

Public Finance

Total Revenue (in millions) $254.352
Intergovernmental Revenue—Total (in millions) $45.4
Federal Revenue per Capita $13.1
% Federal Assistance   5.1
% State Assistance   10.95
Sales Tax as % of Total Revenue   NA
Local Revenue as % of Total Revenue   76.15
City Income Tax   yes
Taxes—Total (in millions) $103.7

Taxes per Capita
   Total $304
   Property $32
   Sales and Gross Receipts $1
General Expenditures—Total (in millions) $195.8
General Expenditures per Capita $575
Capital Outlays per Capita $111

% of Expenditures for:
   Public Welfare   0.0
   Highways   9.4
   Education   0.0
   Health and Hospitals   1.9
   Police   19.7
   Sewerage and Sanitation   20.1
   Parks and Recreation   4.1
   Housing and Community Development   8.2
Debt Outstanding per Capita $554
   % Utility   6.1
Federal Procurement Contract Awards (in millions) $61.1
Federal Grants Awards (in millions) $40.4
Fiscal Year Begins   January 1

Economy

Total Money Income (in millions) $3,427.0
% of State Average   96.9
Per Capita Annual Income $10,050
% Population below Poverty Level   13.6
Fortune 500 Companies   3

Banks	Number	Deposits (in millions)
Commercial	10	NA
Savings	5	NA

Passenger Autos   285,096
Electric Meters   283,750
Gas Meters   150,000

Manufacturing

Number of Establishments   560
% with 20 or More Employees   38.4
Manufacturing Payroll (in millions) $1,366.0
Value Added by Manufacture (in millions) $3,355.6
Value of Shipments (in millions) $9,198.1
New Capital Expenditures (in millions) $184.4

Wholesale Trade

Number of Establishments   656
Sales (in millions) $3,096.3
Annual Payroll (in millions) $219.782

Retail Trade

Number of Establishments   2,881
Total Sales (in millions) $2,042.6
Sales per Capita $5,996
Number of Retail Trade Establishments with Payroll   2,194
Annual Payroll (in millions) $262.5
Total Sales (in millions) $2,018.6
General Merchandise Stores (per capita) $1,249
Food Stores (per capita) $1,217
Apparel Stores (per capita) $356
Eating and Drinking Places (per capita) $816

Service Industries

Total Establishments   2,395
Total Receipts (in millions) $1,117.8
Hotels and Motels (in millions) $18.1
Health Services (in millions) $344.0
Legal Services (in millions) $91.1

Economy

Manufacturing is the key to Toledo's economy, comprising nearly one-fourth of the gross city product. The sector consists of more than 600 facilities, many of them automobile-related. It includes many firms that have played a historic role in the growth of the city, such as Libby-Owens-Ford, Champion Spark Plug, Jeep/Eagle Division of Chrysler (formerly Willys-Overland) Owens-Illinois, and Owens-Corning Fiberglass. In addition to these firms, Toledo is the headquarters for A. P. Parts Company, The Andersons, Bostwick-Braun Company, Dana Corporation, Glasstech, Seaway Foodtown, and Trinova Corp. Of the total 982 manufacturing plants, the largest number are in nonelectrical machinery (189), fabricated metal products (158), printing and publishing (135), rubber and plastics (58), food (47), and stone, clay, and glass (46). With 12 major financial institutions, Toledo also is a financial center for northern Ohio. Among the largest banks are Capital Bank, Farmers and Merchants State Bank, Fifth Third Bank of Toledo, Huntington National Bank, Mid-American National Bank and Trust Company, Ohio Citizens Bank, and Society Bank. Between 1988 and 1991 the number of new businesses grew at a rate of 6.5% overall. Most growth was achieved by companies employing between 100 and 500. Toledo has worked to strengthen its technology base. It is home to a growing number of small to mid-size companies on the cutting edge of research and product development, especially in ceramics, polymers, industrial systems, pharmaceuticals, and tooling and precision components. Among the older industries, automotive industries are declining but glass is holding up well. Among the new growth areas are plastics, control devices, and computer software.

Labor

Since 1987, the employment distribution has changed. Decreases in manufacturing employment (particularly durable goods and automotive-related products) were offset partially in the nonmanufacturing sector. In the durable goods sector, rubber and plastics proved to be exceptions to the rule by posting an employment growth of 37% during this period. In the nonmanufacturing sector, most of the new jobs were created in health and business services.

Labor

Civilian Labor Force   174,118
% Change 1989–1990   -0.6

Work Force Distribution
   Mining   200
   Construction   10,500
   Manufacturing   53,600
   Transportation and Public Utilities   13,200
   Wholesale and Retail Trade   15,600
   FIRE (Finance, Insurance, Real Estate)   11,900
   Service   75,100
   Government   44,300
   Women as % of Labor Force   43.1
   % Self-Employed   3.6
   % Professional/Technical   15.8
Total Unemployment   13,898
Rate %   8.0
Federal Government Civilian Employment   1,823

Education

The Toledo City School District supports 43 elementary schools, 8 junior high schools, 10 senior high schools, and 1 special education school. The Diocese of Toledo operates an extensive parochial school system.

The major institution of higher education is the University of Toledo, founded in 1872 as a municipal institution, becoming a state institution in 1957. It is the fastest growing university in Ohio. The Medical College of Ohio is the only other four-year institution in Toledo. The University of Toledo Community and Technical College and Owens Technical College offer two-year programs. The Stautzenberger College offers business training and Davis College offers associate degrees in business and computing. Within commuting distance is the Bowling Green State University.

Education

Number of Public Schools   62
Special Education Schools   1
Total Enrollment   40,452
% Enrollment in Private Schools   16.9
% Minority   44.0
Classroom Teachers   2,262
Pupil-Teacher Ratio   17.8:1
Number of Graduates   2,218
Total Revenue (in millions) $186.729
Total Expenditures (in millions) $198.029
Expenditures per Pupil $4,297
Educational Attainment (Age 25 and Over)
   % Completed 12 or More Years   63.9
   % Completed 16 or More Years   12.2
Four-Year Colleges and Universities   2
   Enrollment   25,608
Two-Year Colleges   3
   Enrollment   8,524

Libraries

Number   42
Public Libraries   19
Books (in thousands)   1,900
Circulation (in thousands)   5,432
Persons Served (in thousands)   462
Circulation per Person Served   11.75

Education (continued)

Income (in millions) $16.551
Staff   274
Four-Year Colleges and Universities
   University of Toledo
   Medical College of Ohio, Toledo

Health

Nine medical facilities in the area provide the Toledo area with some of the finest health care in the state. The largest are the Toledo Hospital, Medical College Hospital, St. Vincent Medical Center, St. Charles Hospital, Flower Memorial Hospital, Mercy Hospital, Riverside Hospital, St. Lukes Hospital, and Parkview Hospital. Medical College of Ohio is an important resource for the medical community. In addition, 56 clinical facilities, including the Toledo Clinic, operate specialized programs.

Health

Deaths—Total   3,548
Rate per 1,000   10.3
Infant Deaths—Total   51
Rate per 1,000   9.1
Number of Metro Hospitals   7
Number of Metro Hospital Beds   2,915
Rate per 100,000   856
Number of Physicians   1,347
Physicians per 1,000   2.52
Nurses per 1,000   9.31
Health Expenditures per Capita $16.21

Transportation

The city's main transportation arteries are the north-south I-75, extending south to Florida, and the east-west I-80 and I-90, extending from New York to San Francisco. Toledo is also approached through U.S. Highways 20, 23, and 24, and State Highways 2, 51, 65, and 120. Within the city, downtown streets are tilted on a northwest-southeast axis following the Maumee River. In 1992 additional access to the industrial area was realized through two new interchange projects: the Airport Highway and I-80/90, were connected by an interchange at Toledo Express Airport. Also, I-75, I-80/90, and State Highway 795 were connected through a comprehensive interchange system in southeastern Toledo. Rail passenger service is provided by Amtrak and rail freight service by CSX, Conrail, Norfolk and Southern, Detroit, Toledo and Ironton, Detroit and Toledo Shoreline, and Ann Arbor Railroad. The Port of Toledo on the Maumee River is a domestic and international shipping facility. The principal air terminal is Toledo Express Airport, served by eight commercial airlines. Additional services are available at Metcalf Field, south of the city.

Transportation

Interstate Highway Mileage   61
Total Urban Mileage   1,986
Total Daily Vehicle Mileage (in millions) $9.268
Daily Average Commute Time   39.4
Number of Buses   175
Port Tonnage (in millions) $14.741
Airports   1
Number of Daily Flights   14
Daily Average Number of Passengers   642

Airlines (American carriers only)
   Air Wisconsin
   Delta
   Trans World

Housing

 Toledo has a rich mix of neighborhoods of every conceivable architectural style. The city's oldest section is bounded by the river on the east, Cherry Street and Old West End on the north, and Monroe Street on the southwest. Until 1970 there was a steady exodus of residents from this neighborhood, but successful downtown redevelopment has halted this flight. The Old West End is in an area of several distinct neighborhoods from the Central Business District to the University of Toledo. The homes in this area are remnants of a vanished era. The Westmoreland Historic District was also once the home of the old rich, but now its inhabitants are a more diverse group. West Toledo has homes of all sizes and price ranges. It is bounded by Monroe Street on the east, Alexis Road on the north, Ottawa Hills and Sylvania on the west, and Dorr Street on the south. Included in this area are Trilby, annexed to the city in the late 1960s, and Old Orchard and Westgate, in which the University of Toledo is located. East Toledo is settled mainly by Hungarians, Czechs, and other southeastern Europeans. Old South End is the older part of the city bounded by Airport Highway, Broadway Avenue, River Road, and Byrne Road. New South End is comprised of much of the former Adams Township. This has been Toledo's major growth area during the past decade. North Toledo is characterized by small neighborhood businesses. Bounded by I-75, Cherry Street, and Buckeye Basin, this neighborhood is dominated by single-family homes. The northernmost section of the city, Shoreland and Point Place, is bounded by the Maumee Bay and Ottawa River marinas, and yacht clubs and boat docks abound. The median value of a owner-occupied home in Toledo is $48,900.

Housing

Total Housing Units   142,125
% Change 1980–1990   -0.8
Vacant Units for Sale or Rent   7,550
Occupied Units   130,883
% with More Than One Person per Room   1.9
% Owner-Occupied   60.7
Median Value of Owner-Occupied Homes $48,900

Housing (continued)

Average Monthly Purchase Cost $329
Median Monthly Rent $286
New Private Housing Starts   208
Value (in thousands) $6,077
% Single-Family   37.5
Nonresidential Buildings Value (in thousands) $22,887

Tallest Buildings	Hgt. (ft.)	Stories
Owens-Illinois Corp. Headquarters	411	32
Owens-Corning Fiberglas Tower	400	30
Ohio Citizens Bank Bldg.	368	27
Toledo Govt. Center	327	22

Urban Redevelopment

Toledo is in the midst of a second phase of a master development plan for its central business district. Toledo's skyline has changed with the new Summit Center, a $34-million building with over 200,000 square feet of office and retail space. A new condominium complex was developed at Commodore Island. The Spitzer Arcade, Toledo's first shopping mall, was renovated as part of the revitalization of downtown. The Madison Building at Huron and Madison was also refurbished.

Crime

Toledo is above-average in crime rates. Violent crimes totaled 3,486 in 1991. Property crimes totaled 28,421.

Crime

Violent Crimes—Total   3,486
Violent Crime Rate per 100,000   671.7
Murder   36
Rape   418
Robbery   1,807
Aggravated Assaults   1,225
Property Crimes   28,421
Burglary   5,885
Larceny   17,743
Motor Vehicle Theft   4,793
Arson   301
Per Capita Police Expenditures $130.33
Per Capita Fire Protection Expenditures $87.75
Number of Police   758
Per 1,000   2.21

Religion

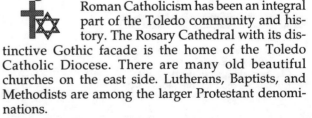 Roman Catholicism has been an integral part of the Toledo community and history. The Rosary Cathedral with its distinctive Gothic facade is the home of the Toledo Catholic Diocese. There are many old beautiful churches on the east side. Lutherans, Baptists, and Methodists are among the larger Protestant denominations.

Religion

Largest Denominations (Adherents)	
Catholic	88,991
Evangelical Lutheran	35,165
United Methodist	17,707
Black Baptist	23,467
Presbyterian	5,054
United Church of Christ	5,547
Southern Baptist	4,311
Episcopal	5,810
American Baptist	4,299
Jewish	4,635

Media

 The city daily is the *The Toledo Blade*, which has the right to carry the Spanish royal coat of arms. Electronic media consist of 6 television stations and 13 AM and FM radio stations.

Media

Newsprint
   Anthony Wayne Herald, weekly
   The Sun, weekly
   The Toledo Blade, daily
   Toledo Business News, monthly
   Toledo Business Report, irregular
   Toledo Economic Report, quarterly

Television
   NEW (Channel 40)
   WGTE (Channel 30)
   WNWO (Channel 24)
   WTOL (Channel 11)
   WTVG (Channel 13)
   WUPW (Channel 36)

Radio
WCWA (AM)	WIOT (FM)
WGTE (FM)	WOTL (FM)
WSPD (AM)	WLQR (FM)
WTOD (AM)	WKKO (FM)
WVKS (FM)	WVOI (AM)
WWWM (AM)	WXTS (FM)
WXUT (FM)	

Sports

 Toledo has no major professional sports team. The Toledo Mud Hens, a Triple A farm team of the Detroit Tigers, play their home games at the Ned Skeldon Stadium in Maumee. The University of Toledo Rockets field strong teams in the Mid-American Conference sports. Raceway Park holds harness racing from March through December.

Arts, Culture, and Tourism

The Toledo Opera, founded in 1960 and based at the Toledo Masonic Auditorium, is the city's premier cultural institution. The Toledo Symphony Orchestra, founded in 1943, presents a Classics series, Mozart series, Music Today series, and Neighborhood concerts. The Toledo Ballet delights area audiences with the annual performance of *The Nutcracker* and also brings world-famous choreographers and dancers as guest artists. The dramatic arts are represented by the Toledo Repertoire Theater, the Village Players, the University of Toledo's Center for the Performing Arts, and the Theater for Children. The Toledo Museum of Art, founded in 1912, is one of Edward Libbey's many contributions to the city. In attendance it ranks among the top ten museums in the nation. Its Peristyle in the East Wing is a colonnaded arena with 1,500 seats and a huge stage, the scene of most of Toledo's concerts. Of its many galleries, several are devoted to a glass collection, rated as one of the largest in the nation. Its Gothic Hall has stained-glass windows dating from the Middle Ages. Toledo's pioneer past is exhibited in the Wolcott House Museum Complex in Maumee. The center of the complex is the restored James Wolcott Home, built in 1836. The Balir Museum contains a large collection of wax carvings. The Toledo Firefighter's Museum exhibits antique fire equipment.

Travel and Tourism

Hotel Rooms 5,539
Convention and Exhibit Space (square feet) NA
Convention Centers
   Seagate Center
Festivals
   Old West End Spring Festival (June)
   Crosby Gardens Festival of the Arts (June)
   International Folk Festival

Parks and Recreation

Established in 1928, the Metroparks of Toledo include nine parks covering 6,400 acres. They include the Wildwood Preserve, Swan Creek Preserve, Providence Park, Bend View Park, Farnsworth Park, Side Cut Park, Secor Park, Pearson Metropark, and Oak Openings Preserve. There are 147 city parks of various sizes. Among the larger ones are Promenade Park in the Central Business District; Ottawa Park in Westmoreland; Woodsdale Park and Highland Park in East Toledo; Heatherdowns Park, Sleepy Hollow Park, Walbridge Park and Hawkins Park in Southwyck; and Riverside Park, Bayview Park, Detwiler Park, Danny Thomas Park, and Joe E. Brown Park in North Toledo.

Sources of Further Information

City Hall
1 Government Center
Toledo, OH 43604
(419) 245-1001

The Greater Toledo Office of Tourism and
   Conventions
281 Huron Street
Toledo, OH 43604
(419) 243-8191

Toledo Area Chamber of Commerce
218 North Huron Street
Toledo, OH 43604
(419) 243-8191

Toledo-Lucas County Public Library
325 Michigan Street
Toledo, OH 43624-1614
(419) 255-7055

Additional Reading

Illman, Harty R. *Unholy Toledo*. 1986.
Parry, Evelyn P. *Pictorial Toledo, Then and Now*. 1983.

Topeka

Kansas

Location and Topography

Topeka is on both banks of the Kansas River about 60 miles upriver from the junction of the Kansas and Missouri rivers. Two tributaries of the Kansas River, Soldier and Shunganunga creeks, flow through the city. The river valley is bordered by rolling prairie uplands, 2 to 4 miles wide and 200 to 300 feet high.

Layout of City and Suburbs

Kansas Avenue, the main street, extends from the northern to the southern limits of the city. The industrial district, near the river, is the oldest part of town where the streets were laid out parallel to the riverbank, while in the later sections they follow the cardinal points of the compass. South from Third Street to Fifth Street, Kansas Avenue is on a rise, bordered by shops, hotels, and theaters. Between Fifth and Tenth streets and on

Quincy and Jackson streets are modern business and professional establishments. At Tenth Street, the commercial aspect of Kansas Avenue changes to a residential one. The principal residential districts are in the south and west. Westboro in the southwest is the only section that does not follow a formal street plan, but is laid out in lanes, courts, terraces, and drives. With its tree-lined avenues, Topeka gives the appearance of a spacious city.

Climate

Summers are generally hot, but are made tolerable by low humidity and southerly winds. There are occasional short spells of very hot and humid weather. About 70% of the annual precipitation falls from April through September. Winter is mild with only brief spells of cold weather accompanied by snow or sleet. Topeka is also free from the severe storms common in the midwestern plains.

History

The first white settlers in what is now Shawnee County were two French-Canadians, Joseph and Louis Pappan, who were married to Kaw women and who established a ferry across the Kaw River at the site of Topeka, which they operated until the river was

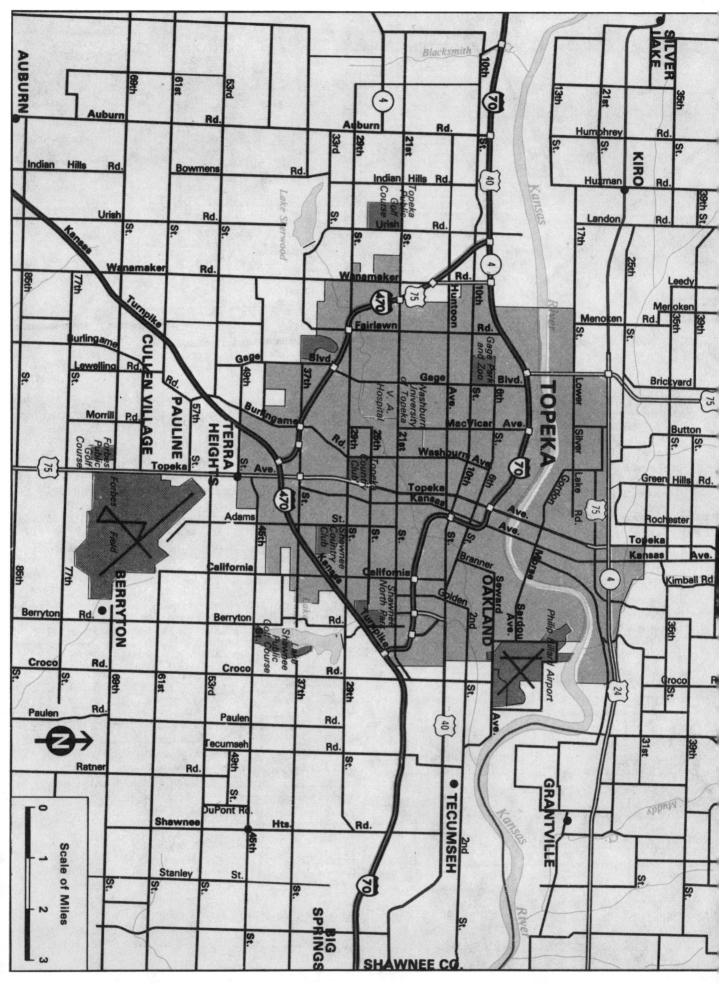

Weather

Temperature

Highest Monthly Average °F	89.6
Lowest Monthly Average °F	15.7

Annual Averages

Days 32°F or Below 112
Days above 90°F 64
Zero Degree Days 2
Precipitation (inches) 33.38
Snow (inches) 21.7
% Seasonal Humidity 71.0
Wind Speed (m.p.h.) 10.1
Clear Days 113
Cloudy Days 155
Storm Days 56
Rainy Days 109

Average Temperatures (°F)	High	Low	Mean
January	34.9	15.5	25.2
February	55.0	27.6	41.3
March	60.9	35.5	48.2
April	68.3	47.1	57.7
May	79.0	59.7	69.4
June	87.2	67.0	77.1
July	92.8	67.6	80.2
August	90.9	63.6	77.3
September	82.2	56.3	69.3
October	71.6	45.5	58.6
November	47.3	28.4	37.9
December	46.2	28.5	37.4

bridged in 1857. Topeka, however, owes its origin to Colonel Cyrus K. Holliday, a young Pennsylvanian who came to Kansas Territory in 1854 with $20,000 and a dream to build a railroad. Together with his New England partners, Holliday picked a site, 26 miles up the Kaw River from Kansas City, which they christened Topeka, an Indian word meaning potatoes. The following year a large contingent of New Englanders arrived, and Topeka began to grow into a sizable settlement. By 1856 plans had been completed for building the railroad envisioned by Robinson, one that eventually became the Santa Fe. The first Kansas Constitution was framed by a convention of Free-Staters who met in Topeka in 1855. In 1857, the city was incorporated and the first bridge across the Kaw was completed. The bridge was rebuilt after high waters carried it away in the summer. In 1858 Topeka was chosen as the county seat over Tecumseh. When Kansas was admitted to the Union under the Wyandotte Constitution in 1861, Lawrence and Topeka competed in the election to become the capital city. Topeka won, and within a decade of its founding grew from a village to become the state capital. Meanwhile, the Atchison, Topeka and Santa Fe Railway established its general offices and machine shops in Topeka in 1878, thus ensuring its continued economic growth. During the Civil War, Topeka was the scene of a bloody resistance against Price's raid in 1864. During the late 1880s Topeka went through a period of boom that ended with a crash in real estate prices. In 1903 the city experienced a disastrous flood of the Kaw River, prompting the construction of dikes to prevent a recurrence of the disaster.

Historical Landmarks

The site of the first building in Topeka is marked by a bronze marker on the corner of Kansas Avenue and First Street. The site of the Old Stockade, called Fort Folly by its detractors, on the corner of Sixth Street and Kansas Avenue is marked by a plate on the sidewalk. Potwin Place is an exclusive section with Italian and Victorian farm-style homes. Memorial Building on Tenth and Jackson streets is a French Renaissance–style white-marble structure dedicated in 1911 to the soldiers and sailors of Kansas. It includes the State Historical Library and Museum. The Kansas State Capitol is in the center of a ten-acre landscaped park extending from Jackson Street to Harrison Street. Based upon the design of the national Capitol, it has four wings extended in the form of a Greek cross with a large rotunda in the middle. It was completed in 1869. The dome, rising to a height of 304 feet on an octagonal drum, is more slender in proportion than that of the national Capitol, and is sheathed in copper. The Executive Mansion on Eighth and Buchanan streets was built as a private residence in 1889 by Erastus Bennett and purchased by the state in 1901. Grace Cathedral on Eighth and Polk streets is the cathedral of the Kansas Diocese of the Protestant Episcopal Church. Its exterior is patterned after the medieval cathedrals of England and Normandy. The Charles Curtis Home on the corner of Topeka Boulevard and 11th Street is a three-story late-Victorian structure. Curtis, the grandson of a Kaw Indian chief, was vice president under Herbert Hoover.

Population

From a peak of 125,000 in 1970, the population declined to 118,690 in 1980 and rose slightly to 119,883 in 1990.

Population

	1980	1990
Central City	118,690	119,883
Rank	132	149
Metro Area	154,916	160,976
Pop. Change 1980–1990 +1,193		
Pop. % Change 1980–1990 +1.0		
Median Age 33.6		
% Male 47.6		
% Age 65 and Over 14.7		
Density (per square mile) 2,171		

Households

Number 49,936
Persons per Household 2.33
% Female-Headed Households 11.9
% One-Person Households 32.0
Births—Total 1,914
　% to Mothers under 20 12.8
　Birth Rate per 1,000 16.1

Ethnic Composition

Whites make up 85% of the population, blacks 11%, American Indians 1%, Asians and Pacific Islanders 1%, and others 3%.

Chronology

1842 Joseph and Louis Pappan establish a ferry across the Kaw River.

1854 Colonel Cyrus K. Holliday and associates propose building a railroad from Kansas to the West; with the aid of Charles Robinson, agent of the New England Emigrant Aid Company in Lawrence, they pick out a site for a new town 26 miles from Lawrence, which they name Topeka.

1855 Free-Staters meet in a convention at Topeka and pass first Kansas Constitution, which is declared illegal by the federal government.

1857 Topeka is incorporated. First bridge across the Kaw is completed.

1858 New bridge across the Kaw is swept away in a flood. Topeka is named seat of Shawnee County.

1860 Topeka suffers in drought.

1861 Kansas is admitted to the Union. In first election, Topeka is chosen as state capital and Robinson as state governor.

1864 Topekans erect stockade against Price's raid. The Second Regiment and Kansas State Militia inflict heavy losses on Price's troops.

1878 General offices of the Atchison, Topeka and Santa Fe Railroad are located in Topeka.

1889 Land speculation boom ends in crash.

1903 In disastrous flood, the Kaw overflows its banks and causes heavy damage in north Topeka.

1925 Karl and Charles Menninger found the Menninger Clinic.

Ethnic Composition (as % of total pop.)

	1980	1990
White	86.64	84.71
Black	9.54	10.64
American Indian	1.04	1.28
Asian and Pacific Islander	0.53	0.79
Hispanic	4.24	5.78
Other	NA	2.57

Government

Topeka adopted a new charter in 1984 providing for a mayor-council-administrator form of government. The nine council members are elected from districts to staggered four-year terms. The mayor, who is a member of the council, is likewise selected to four-year terms. The administrator is responsible to the mayor.

Government

Year of Home Charter	1984
Number of Members of the Governing Body	9
Elected at Large	NA
Elected by Wards	9
Number of Women in Governing Body	2
Salary of Mayor	$50,000
Salary of Council Members	$6,000
City Government Employment Total	1,580
Rate per 10,000	133.2

Public Finance

The annual budget consists of revenues of $106.703 million and expenditures of $118.575 million. The debt outstanding is $321.592 million and cash and security holdings $238.436 million.

Public Finance

Total Revenue (in millions)	$106.703
Intergovernmental Revenue—Total (in millions)	$11.82
Federal Revenue per Capita	$3.55
% Federal Assistance	3.32
% State Assistance	5.55
Sales Tax as % of Total Revenue	18.57
Local Revenue as % of Total Revenue	80.66
City Income Tax	no
Taxes—Total (in millions)	$33.5
Taxes per Capita	
Total	$283
Property	$138
Sales and Gross Receipts	$140
General Expenditures—Total (in millions)	$84.5
General Expenditures per Capita	$713
Capital Outlays per Capita	$146
% of Expenditures for:	
Public Welfare	0.0
Highways	10.9
Education	0.0
Health and Hospitals	4.0
Police	12.1
Sewerage and Sanitation	18.5
Parks and Recreation	7.9
Housing and Community Development	6.2
Debt Outstanding per Capita	$1,851
% Utility	9.7
Federal Procurement Contract Awards (in millions)	$12.8
Federal Grants Awards (in millions)	$139.9
Fiscal Year Begins	January 1

Economy

Topeka's public services account for 25% of the gross city product. Services and trade account for a slightly lower share of the economy. Manufacturing, however, claims a share of only 10%. Among the Fortune 500 companies in the city are American Bakeries; Armco; Atchison, Topeka and Santa Fe Railway; Essex Group; Frito-Lay; Georgia Pacific; and Hills Pet Products.

Economy

Total Money Income (in millions) $1,338.5
% of State Average 105.3
Per Capita Annual Income $11,248
% Population below Poverty Level 9.3
Fortune 500 Companies NA

Banks	Number	Deposits (in millions)
Commercial	14	1,357.1
Savings	2	3,529.8

Passenger Autos 96,919
Electric Meters 70,000
Gas Meters 52,000

Manufacturing

Number of Establishments 118
% with 20 or More Employees 40.7
Manufacturing Payroll (in millions) NA
Value Added by Manufacture (in millions) NA
Value of Shipments (in millions) NA
New Capital Expenditures (in millions) NA

Wholesale Trade

Number of Establishments 244
Sales (in millions) NA
Annual Payroll (in millions) NA

Retail Trade

Number of Establishments 1,428
Total Sales (in millions) $1,056.5
Sales per Capita $8,910
Number of Retail Trade Establishments with Payroll 1,035
Annual Payroll (in millions) $124.0
Total Sales (in millions) $1,038.0
General Merchandise Stores (per capita) $1,288
Food Stores (per capita) $1,683
Apparel Stores (per capita) NA
Eating and Drinking Places (per capita) $898

Service Industries

Total Establishments 1,092
Total Receipts (in millions) $412.6
Hotels and Motels (in millions) NA
Health Services (in millions) $137.6
Legal Services (in millions) $38.5

Labor

About 25% of Topekans are employed in public agencies, with 20% in services, and 20% in trade. Unemployment, which was in the 4% range for most of the 1980s, has climbed into the 5% range in the 1990s.

Labor

Civilian Labor Force 69,133
% Change 1989–1990 0.7

Work Force Distribution
  Mining NA
  Construction 3,400
  Manufacturing 9,400
  Transportation and Public Utilities 6,100
  Wholesale and Retail Trade 20,100
  FIRE (Finance, Insurance, Real Estate) 6,500
  Service 23,500
  Government 22,200

Labor (continued)

  Women as % of Labor Force 47.1
  % Self-Employed 5.2
  % Professional/Technical 17.8
Total Unemployment 3,464
Rate % 5.0
Federal Government Civilian Employment 2,941

Education

Topeka's Unified School District 504 supports 35 elementary schools, middle schools, and senior high schools. There are 13 private and parochial schools. Topeka has only one major higher education institution: the publicly funded Washburn University, comprised of a college of arts and sciences, and schools of law, business, nursing, and continuing education.

Education

Number of Public Schools 35
Special Education Schools NA
Total Enrollment 15,165
% Enrollment in Private Schools 11.0
% Minority NA
Classroom Teachers NA
Pupil-Teacher Ratio NA
Number of Graduates NA
Total Revenue (in millions) NA
Total Expenditures (in millions) NA
Expenditures per Pupil NA
Educational Attainment (Age 25 and Over) NA
  % Completed 12 or More Years 76.6
  % Completed 16 or More Years 20.9
Four-Year Colleges and Universities 1
  Enrollment 6,492
Two-Year Colleges NA
  Enrollment NA

Libraries

Number 17
Public Libraries 1
Books (in thousands) 355
Circulation (in thousands) 1,236
Persons Served (in thousands) 118
Circulation per Person Served 10.47
Income (in millions) $3.7.7
Staff 102

Four-Year Colleges and Universities
  Washburn University of Topeka

Health

The Topeka area has seven metro hospitals. The general hospitals are Memorial Hospital, St. Francis Hospital and Medical Center, and Stormont-Vail Regional Medical Center. The Colmery-O'Neill Veterans Administration Medical Center is a general care facility. Topeka's most famous medical institution is the C. F. Menninger Memorial Hospital, known as the Menninger Clinic, a world-renowned center for mental health care. Also in the mental health field are two other facilities: the Topeka State Hospital and the Kansas Neurological Institute.

Health

Deaths—Total 1,217
Rate per 1,000 10.2
Infant Deaths—Total 21
Rate per 1,000 11.0
Number of Metro Hospitals 7
Number of Metro Hospital Beds 2,265
Rate per 100,000 1,910
Number of Physicians NA
Physicians per 1,000 NA
Nurses per 1,000 NA
Health Expenditures per Capita $42.06

Transportation

Topeka is approached by two interstates: I-70, running northeast to south through the city, and I-470, an outer belt running through the western boundary of the city. U.S. highway access routes are U.S. Highway 24, linking Topeka with Omaha; the east-west U.S. Highway 40, which becomes Sixth Street within the city; and the north-south U.S. Highway 75, which becomes Topeka Boulevard. The state routes are 4 and 10. Within the city, streets are laid out in a grid pattern with numbered east-west streets and named north-south ones. Rail freight service is provided by the Santa Fe, Union Pacific, and St. Louis Southwestern railroads. The major commercial airport is Forbes, seven miles south of downtown. The terminal for general business traffic is Phillip Billard Field, three miles northeast of the city.

Transportation

Interstate Highway Mileage 25
Total Urban Mileage 693
Total Daily Vehicle Mileage (in millions) $2.329
Daily Average Commute Time 40.5 min.
Number of Buses 22
Port Tonnage (in millions) NA
Airports 1
Number of Daily Flights NA
Daily Average Number of Passengers 49

Airlines (American carriers only)
   Trans States

Housing

Between 1985 and 1991, 3,591 single-family dwellings and 2,065 multifamily dwellings were built in Topeka. The average price of a owner-occupied home is $48,800.

Housing

Total Housing Units 54,664
% Change 1980–1990 7.9
Vacant Units for Sale or Rent 3,527
Occupied Units 49,936
% with More Than One Person per Room 2.2
% Owner-Occupied 60.8
Median Value of Owner-Occupied Homes $48,800
Average Monthly Purchase Cost $319
Median Monthly Rent $304

Housing (continued)

New Private Housing Starts 287
Value (in thousands) $20,449
% Single-Family 69.0
Nonresidential Buildings Value (in thousands) $18,189

Urban Redevelopment

Since 1986 Topeka has witnessed a construction boom in downtown, including a regional shopping mall, a shopping center, and office buildings along the Wanamaker Corridor in west Topeka. The Topeka Industrial Business Park and Topeka Air Industrial Park have expanded with help from the Topeka–Shawnee County Development Corporation.

Crime

Topeka has an above-average crime rate. In 1991 violent crimes totaled 1,427, property crimes totaled 11,171.

Crime

Violent Crimes—Total 1,427
Violent Crime Rate per 100,000 929.6
Murder 16
Rape 79
Robbery 332
Aggravated Assaults 1,000
Property Crimes 11,171
Burglary 3,524
Larceny 7,148
Motor Vehicle Theft 499
Arson 56
Per Capita Police Expenditures $112.75
Per Capita Fire Protection Expenditures $79.00
Number of Police 221
Per 1,000 1.85

Religion

There are over 200 churches in Topeka, the majority of which are Protestant. Baptists are particularly strong in Topeka.

Religion

Largest Denominations (Adherents)

Catholic	30,716
United Methodist	13,192
Black Baptist	4,450
Southern Baptist	6,875
Presbyterian	4,653
Lutheran-Missouri Synod	4,716
American Baptist	5,605
Episcopal	2,332
Assembly of God	1,340
Jewish	500

Media

The city daily is *Topeka-Capital Journal*. Electronic media consist of four television stations (three commercial and one public) and eight FM and AM radio stations.

Media

Newsprint
    Topeka Capital-Journal, daily

Television
    KSNT (Channel 27)
    KTKA (Channel 49)
    KTWU (Channel 11)
    KIBW (Channel 13)

Radio

KJTY (FM)	KMAJ (AM)
KMAJ (FM)	KTOP (AM)
KDVV (FM)	KTPK (FM)
WIBW (AM)	WIBW (FM)

Sports

Topeka has no major professional sports team. Spectator sports revolve around the Washburn University basketball team. The university also hosts an annual regatta in rowing.

Arts, Culture, Tourism

The most prominent musical institutions are the Topeka Symphony Orchestra, performing a six-concert season at Washburn University; Tosca Opera Club, staging one opera in the fall; Topeka Jazz Workshop, presenting seven performances annually; and the Topeka Chamber Music Series, hosting five concerts a season. In dance, Ballet Midwest presents classical ballet. The theatrical fare includes the Topeka Civic Theater, Washburn University Theater, Helen Hocker Theater, and the Showcase Comedy Dinner Theater. The prin-

Travel and Tourism

Hotel Rooms   1,885
Convention and Exhibit Space (square feet)   NA

Convention Centers
    Kansas Expocenter

Festivals
    Go 4th Festival (July)
    Apple Festival

cipal museums are the Mulvane Art Museum on the campus of Washburn University, the Kansas Museum of History, and the Combat Air Museum at Forbes Field. Notable art also is displayed in public buildings, such as Louis Comfort Tiffany's Ascension Window in the sanctuary of the First Presbyterian Church, and Peter Felton's Amelia Earhart in the rotunda of the State Capitol.

Parks and Recreation

Historic Meade Park overlooks the Kansas River Valley from its position on a bluff. On park grounds are a log cabin, a restored 1900s Kansas town called Prairie Crossings, and botanical gardens. The 160-acre Gage Park on Gage Boulevard contains the Reinisch Rose Garden and the Old Settlers' Memorial Cabin.

Sources of Further Information

Greater Topeka Chamber of Commerce
120 East Sixth Street
Topeka, KS 66603
(913) 234-2644

Kansas State Historical Society
120 West Tenth Street
Topeka, KS 66612
(913) 296-3251

Shawnee County Historical Society
1205 West 29th Street
Topeka, KS 66611
(913) 267-0309

Topeka Convention and Visitors Bureau
120 East Sixth Street
Topeka, KS 66603
(913) 234-2644

Topeka Public Library
1515 West Tenth Street
Topeka, KS 66604-1374
(913) 233-3040

Additional Reading

Holman, Charles. *North Topeka*. 1987.
Richmond, Robert W. *A Souvenir Album of Topeka.* 1988.

Trenton

New Jersey

Basic Data

Name   Trenton
Name Origin   From William Trent
Year Founded   1679 Inc. 1792
Status: State   Capital of New Jersey
    County   Seat of Mercer County
Area (square miles)   7.7
Elevation (feet)   35
Time Zone   EST
Population (1990)   88,675
Population of Metro Area (1990)   325,824

Sister Cities
  Jundiai, Brazil
  Lenin District, Moscow
  Stoke on Trent, England

Distance in Miles To:

Atlantic City	74
Camden	32
Wilmington	62
New York	74
Newark	50
Jersey City	56

Location and Topography

N Trenton is located in west-central New Jersey, on a plateau on the east bank of the Delaware River at its navigable head. The city is bisected by the Assunpink Creek.

Layout of City and Suburbs

 The heart of Trenton is State Street, which broadens for a short stretch before reaching the State Capitol building. It is a congested shopping district, spilling over into Warren and Broad streets. In the western residential area, once a farming area, are historic colonial homes. The manufacturing districts lie chiefly to the south and east of the business center. A number of highways pass through the city or immediately around it, particularly I-95, I-295, I-206, and U.S. Route 1. The major suburbs are White Horse, Hamilton Square, Mercerville, Blackwood, and Ewing.

Environment

Environmental Stress Index   NA
Green Cities Index: Rank   NA
               Score   NA
Water Quality   Alkaline, soft, fluoridated
  Average Daily Use (gallons per capita)   NA
  Maximum Supply (gallons per capita)   NA
Parkland as % of Total City Area   NA
% Waste Landfilled/Recycled   NA
Annual Parks Expenditures per Capita $10.68

Climate

Trenton has a continental climate subject to the influence of winds blowing from the west. The Appalachian Mountains are another strong climatic influence. Average temperatures are 32°F in January and 76°F in July. Annual precipitation is 40.2 inches with snowfall about 24 inches.

Weather

Temperature

Highest Monthly Average °F   73.9
Lowest Monthly Average °F   32.1

Annual Averages

Days 32°F or Below   87
Days above 90°F   17
Zero Degree Days   0
Precipitation (inches)   40.17
Snow (inches)   24.3
% Seasonal Humidity   NA
Wind Speed (m.p.h.)   7.0
Clear Days   100

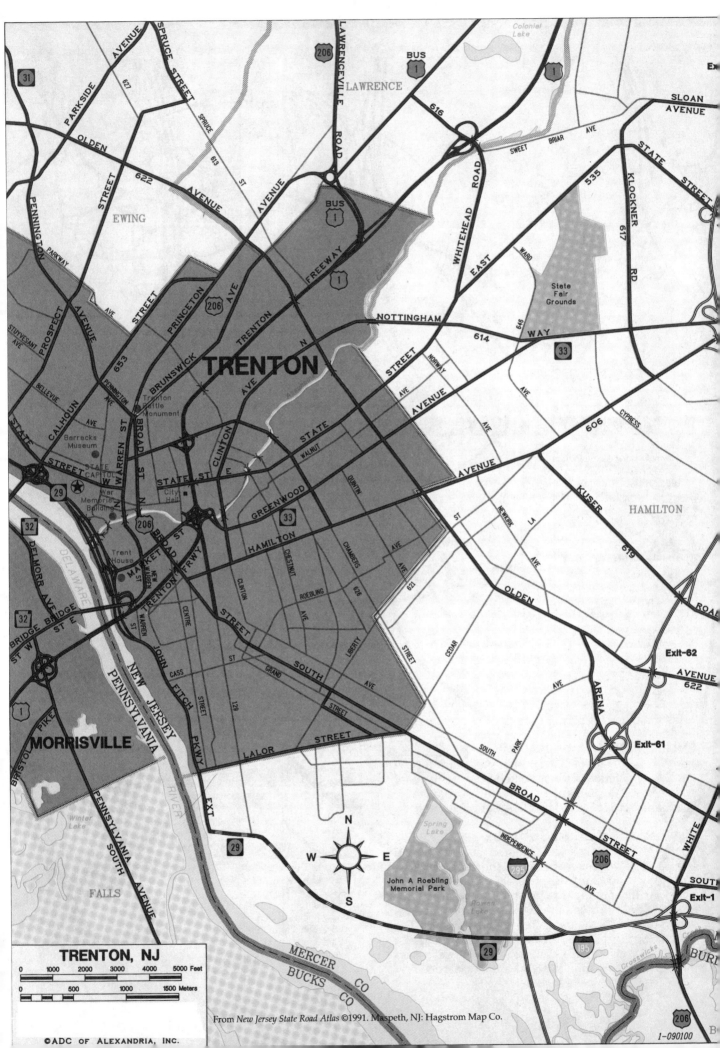

TRENTON, NJ

From *New Jersey State Road Atlas* ©1991. Maspeth, NJ: Hagstrom Map Co.

©ADC OF ALEXANDRIA, INC.

1-090100

Weather (continued)

Cloudy Days 150
Storm Days NA
Rainy Days 121

Average Temperatures (°F)	High	Low	Mean
January	38.8	25.3	32.1
February	40.6	26.1	33.4
March	49.2	33.1	41.2
April	61.8	42.5	52.2
May	72.0	52.2	62.1
June	80.9	61.6	71.3
July	84.9	66.8	75.9
August	82.8	65.0	73.9
September	76.2	55.1	67.2
October	66.2	48.2	57.2
November	53.9	38.7	46.3
December	41.5	28.3	34.9

History

Before the arrival of the white man, the area was inhabited by Sanhicans, a clan of the Unami subdivision of the Lenape Indians. The first white settler was Mahlon Stacy, an English Quaker, who took up a grant of land in 1679 at "ye ffalles of ye De La Warr" (the falls of Delaware). In 1714 a Philadelphia merchant, William Trent, bought out the Stacy farmstead of 800 acres on Assunpink Creek and built a fine mansion called Bloomsbury Court, now the oldest in the city. Trent's town, as the settlement came to be known, soon entered a period of steady growth. Its location at the head of sloop navigation on the Delaware made the town a shipping point for grain and other produce, and a depot for merchandise bound for Philadelphia or New York. Overland travelers found the village a convenient stopping place on the King's Highway. In 1745 the town received a royal charter as a borough and a town, but the charter was voluntarily surrendered five years later. Ferry service with Philadelphia began in 1727, and from 1746 rafts began to carry merchandise on the Delaware. In 1774 John Adams described Trenton as a pretty village, the largest in the Jerseys. By 1776 the town had about 100 hip or gable-roofed houses clustered along King and Queen (now Warren and Broad) streets.

Trenton figured prominently in the Revolutionary War and was the scene of one of Washington's early victories. His famous crossing of the ice-choked Delaware formed the subject of one of the most famous paintings in American history. Trenton was chosen as the state capital in 1790, and although little more than a village, by 1792 was incorporated as a city. Between 1794 and 1798 many of the federal government offices were moved to Trenton from Philadelphia, and even President Adams and his wife were temporary residents. Trenton's growth thereafter was helped by the construction of the bridge across the Delaware in 1806, the construction of the Delaware and Raritan Canal, and the Camden and Amboy Railroad. Potterymaking, a colonial industry, flourished in the city, making Trenton the Staffordshire of America. Walter Lenox laid the foundation of the Lenox Pottery. The city's greatest expansion occurred between 1880 and 1920, when the population passed the 100,000 mark, and the adjacent boroughs of Chambersburg and Wilbur, Milham Township, and parts of Ewing Township were annexed. In the first half of the 20th century, Trenton came to be a major industrial center, producing handcrafted Mercer motor cars, Goodyear tires, and steel wire.

Although the Delaware was dredged in 1932 to make Trenton accessible to oceangoing vessels, the city never gained importance as a port. Further, many of the key industries moved out after World War II, and so did most of the middle class. A redevelopment effort in the 1970s and 1980s helped to slow the city's decline, but Trenton's future appears to lie almost entirely in its status as the state capital.

Historical Landmarks

Although much diminished in importance since the 18th century, Trenton is noted for its historical landmarks, many of them going back to the colonial times. Among them are:

- The Capitol building, facing State Street and extending west to the Delaware River. The first state building was erected in 1795, five years after Trenton was made the state capital. It has been rebuilt a number of times and extended by several additions.
- The Old Barracks on Willow Street is the only remaining unit of the five barracks erected in 1758–1759 to house colonial troops during the French and Indian Wars that were previously billeted in private houses.
- The Old Masonic Lodge House, on the corner of South Willow and Lafayette streets, is one of the oldest Masonic houses, built in 1793.
- The Douglass House in the extreme easterly part of Mahlon Stacy Park was the meeting place of Washington and his officers on 2 January 1777.
- Trent House on Warren Street, a two-story brick building with a cupola, is the oldest private house in Trenton. It was built in 1719 by William Trent, the town's eponymous founder.
- The Eagle Tavern, built as a residence circa 1760, was later expanded and converted into a tavern.
- St. Michael's Episcopal Church, erected 1747–1748, although the parish dates back to 1703. It was used as a barracks by Hessian troops during the American Revolution.
- First Presbyterian Church, established in 1726, and rebuilt twice, the last time in 1839. President James Monroe worshiped here.
- Friends' Meeting House, erected in 1739. Thomas Cadwalader, first chief burgess, is buried here.

Chronology

1679	Mahlon Stacy, an English Quaker, takes up a grant of land near the falls and builds a log mill and a clapboard house.
1714	William Trent, a Philadelphia merchant, buys the property from Stacy's son, and builds a house called Bloomsbury Court.
1727	Ferry is chartered between Trenton, or Trent's town, and Philadelphia.
1745	Trenton receives royal charter.
1750	Dr. Thomas Cadwalader, the first chief burgess, gives £500 to found the Trenton Library Company.
1776	George Washington crosses the Delaware River to launch a surprise attack on Trenton, one of the key battles of the American Revolution.
1790	Trenton is made state capital.
1792	Trenton is incorporated as a city.
1806	A covered bridge is built across the Delaware.
1932	The Delaware River is dredged, making Trenton a port for seagoing vessels.

Population

Trenton has shed population in the last decade, declining from 92,124 in 1980 to 88,675 in 1990. As a result, its population rank has dropped, among New Jersey cities, from third to seventh. Trenton is likely to continue losing population for the rest of the century.

Population		
	1980	*1990*
Central City	92,124	88,675
Rank	158	228
Metro Area	307,863	325,824
Pop. Change 1980–1990	−3,449	
Pop. % Change 1980–1990	−3.7	
Median Age	31.4	
% Male	48.5	
% Age 65 and Over	12.7	
Density (per square mile)	11,516	

Households	
Number	30,744
Persons per Household	2.76
% Female-Headed Households	24.6
% One-Person Households	28.8
Births—Total	1,861
% to Mothers under 20	26.0
Birth Rate per 1,000	20.2

Ethnic Composition

Whites and blacks are almost evenly divided among the residents, the former accounting for 42% and the latter for 49%. Hispanics make up most of the remaining population, with few people of other races.

Ethnic Composition (as % of total pop.)		
	1980	*1990*
White	48.94	42.17
Black	45.44	49.27
American Indian	0.12	0.25
Asian and Pacific Islander	0.36	0.66
Hispanic	7.99	14.13
Other	NA	7.65

Government

Trenton operates under a mayor-council form of government. The seven council members and the mayor are elected for four-year terms. Of the council members, four are elected at large and three by ward. Trenton is also the state capital and the seat of Mercer County.

Government	
Year of Home Charter	NA
Number of Members of the Governing Body	7
Elected at Large	3
Elected by Wards	4
Number of Women in Governing Body	1
Salary of Mayor	$63,972
Salary of Council Members	$12,061
City Government Employment Total	1,718
Rate per 10,000	188.5

Public Finance

The annual budget consists of revenues of $176.706 million and expenditures of 187.180 million. Outstanding debt is

Public Finance	
Total Revenue (in millions)	$176.706
Intergovernmental Revenue—Total (in millions)	$106.7
Federal Revenue per Capita	$0.10
% Federal Assistance	NA
% State Assistance	60.3
Sales Tax as % of Total Revenue	NA
Local Revenue as % of Total Revenue	33.39
City Income Tax	no
Taxes—Total (in millions)	$22.5
Taxes per Capita	
Total	$247
Property	$239
Sales and Gross Receipts	$0
General Expenditures—Total (in millions)	$57.2
General Expenditures per Capita	$627
Capital Outlays per Capita	$47
% of Expenditures for:	
Public Welfare	3.8
Highways	3.6
Education	0.0
Health and Hospitals	4.6
Police	20.4
Sewerage and Sanitation	16.0
Parks and Recreation	3.1
Housing and Community Development	2.0

Public Finance (continued)

Debt Outstanding per Capita $722
   % Utility   20.8
Federal Procurement Contract Awards (in millions) $37.4
Federal Grants Awards (in millions) $370.6
Fiscal Year Begins   January 1

$90.887 million and cash and security holdings total $29.182 million.

Economy

Even with a falling population, Trenton was ranked by Dun & Bradstreet in 1988 as the fifth fastest growing of the nation's 200 large cities, based on the dollar value of construction grants issued by the city. Trenton is a desirable site for many reasons, particularly its location in the middle of the New York–Washington, D.C. corridor and its low costs, taxes, and rents. Its status as the state capital is another feature promoting its growth. State, county, and city employees form a sizable segment of the economic base.

Economy

Total Money Income (in millions) $793.0
% of State Average   66.3
Per Capita Annual Income $8,699
% Population below Poverty Level   21.2
Fortune 500 Companies   NA

Banks	Number	Deposits (in millions)
Commercial	7	NA
Savings & Loan	12	1,892.4

Passenger Autos   NA
Electric Meters   122,950
Gas Meters   87,316

Manufacturing

Number of Establishments   135
% with 20 or More Employees   38.5
Manufacturing Payroll (in millions) $208.9
Value Added by Manufacture (in millions) $360.8
Value of Shipments (in millions) $608.9
New Capital Expenditures (in millions) $19.5

Wholesale Trade

Number of Establishments   145
Sales (in millions) $560.0
Annual Payroll (in millions) $52.604

Retail Trade

Number of Establishments   674
Total Sales (in millions) $252.4
Sales per Capita $2,769
Number of Retail Trade Establishments with Payroll   451
Annual Payroll (in millions) $31.4
Total Sales (in millions) $237.8
General Merchandise Stores (per capita) $136
Food Stores (per capita) $559
Apparel Stores (per capita) $125
Eating and Drinking Places (per capita) $457

Service Industries

Total Establishments   463
Total Receipts (in millions) $203.0
Hotels and Motels (in millions) $0.9
Health Services (in millions) $70.4
Legal Services (in millions) $19.3

Labor

The state of New Jersey, the city of Trenton, and Mercer County are the largest employers in Trenton. The next three large employers are medical facilities. There are two industrial firms among the top ten employers. Growth areas in employment in the 1980s included services, construction, research and development, and high-tech manufacturing.

Labor

Civilian Labor Force   43,816
% Change 1989–1990   3.0
Work Force Distribution
   Mining   NA
   Construction   4,100
   Manufacturing   25,500
   Transportation and Public Utilities   6,900
   Wholesale and Retail Trade   30,300
   FIRE (Finance, Insurance, Real Estate)   11,800
   Service   59,300
   Government   54,600
   Women as % of Labor Force   47.9
   % Self-Employed   3.5
   % Professional/Technical   11.9
Total Unemployment   3,198
Rate %   7.3
Federal Government Civilian Employment   2,491

Education

The public school system consists of 1 senior high school, 5 junior high/middle schools and 18 elementary schools. The public system is supplemented by an extensive parochial and private school system. One of the leading institutions in higher education is the Thomas Edison State College, founded in 1972. Within commuting distance are Princeton University and the Trenton State College in Ewing.

Education

Number of Public Schools   24
Special Education Schools   NA
Total Enrollment   12,222
% Enrollment in Private Schools   22.9
% Minority   NA
Classroom Teachers   NA
Pupil-Teacher Ratio   28:1
Number of Graduates   NA
Total Revenue (in millions) $100.293
Total Expenditures (in millions) $95.420
Expenditures per Pupil $7,807.23
Educational Attainment (Age 25 and Over)
   % Completed 12 or More Years   49.6
   % Completed 16 or More Years   7.7
Four-Year Colleges and Universities   2
   Enrollment   15,232
Two-Year Colleges   1
   Enrollment   8,779

Libraries

Number   25
Public Libraries   5
Books (in thousands)   300

Education (continued)

Circulation (in thousands) 110
Persons Served (in thousands) 95
Circulation per Person Served 1.15
Income (in millions) $2.079
Staff 56

Four-Year Colleges and Universities
Thomas Edison State College
Trenton State College

Health

Trenton has five major hospitals, which include St. Francis Medical Center, with 443 beds; Helen Fuld Hospital, with 350 beds; and Mercer Medical Center, with 344 beds.

Health

Deaths—Total 1,109
Rate per 1,000 12.0
Infant Deaths—Total 33
Rate per 1,000 17.7
Number of Metro Hospitals 5
Number of Metro Hospital Beds 1,572
Rate per 100,000 1,724
Number of Physicians 745
Physicians per 1,000 NA
Nurses per 1,000 NA
Health Expenditures per Capita $19.49

Transportation

Trenton is located on historic Route 1, which bisects the city diagonally, running northeast-southwest. Also running through the city is Route 206. Interstate 95 skirts the city to the north, while I-295 circles the eastern part of the city and I-295 splits off east, toward the coast. Within the city, the thoroughfares with the heaviest traffic are John Fitch Parkway and Olden Avenue Extension, running east-west, and Calhoun Street and Princeton Avenue, running north-south.

Rail connections are provided by New Jersey Transit, SEPTA, and Amtrak, which together operate 43 trains daily. The Mercer County Airport in nearby Ewing Township handles small commuter planes and helicopters. The nearest international airports are at Newark and Philadelphia, both an hour's drive away.

Transportation

Interstate Highway Mileage 29
Total Urban Mileage 1,215
Total Daily Vehicle Mileage (in millions) $7.465
Daily Average Commute Time 47.7 min.
Number of Buses 58
Port Tonnage (in millions) $0.936
Airports NA
Number of Daily Flights NA
Daily Average Number of Passengers NA

Airlines (American carriers only)
See Philadelphia

Housing

Because of the declining population, housing has not been a major priority with city planners. Most workers in the city commute from nearby towns in Mercer County as well as from Pennsylvania across the Delaware River.

Housing

Total Housing Units 33,578
% Change 1980–1990 -6.7
Vacant Units for Sale or Rent 1,887
Occupied Units 30,744
% with More Than One Person per Room 8.0
% Owner-Occupied 51.1
Median Value of Owner-Occupied Homes $71,300
Average Monthly Purchase Cost $330
Median Monthly Rent $387
New Private Housing Starts 10
Value (in thousands) $547
% Single-Family 100.0
Nonresidential Buildings Value (in thousands) $137

Urban Redevelopment

The City of Trenton has established a Corridor Development Plan with four areas of emphasis: the Route 1 corridor, the State Street corridor, the Southeast corridor, and the Riverfront corridor.

Crime

In 1991 violent crimes reported to police totaled 1,833, and property crimes totaled 7,837.

Crime

Violent Crimes—Total 1,833
Violent Crime Rate per 100,000 689.1
Murder 7
Rape 111
Robbery 693
Aggravated Assaults 1,022
Property Crimes 7,837
Burglary 1,904
Larceny 3,227
Motor Vehicle Theft 2,706
Arson 13
Per Capita Police Expenditures $152.05
Per Capita Fire Protection Expenditures $129.12
Number of Police 367
Per 1,000 3.92

Religion

The strongest established churches belong to the mainline Protestant denominations.

Religion	
Largest Denominations (Adherents)	
Catholic	112,756
Black Baptist	14,477
Presbyterian	11,512
United Methodist	6,195
American Baptist	5,652
Episcopal	7,647
Evangelical Lutheran	4,612
Assembly of God	2,957
Jewish	9,000

Media

Trenton has two daily newspapers: *The Trenton Times,* published in the evening, and *The Trentonian,* published in the morning. Trenton is within range of television and radio signals from Philadelphia and, to a lesser extent, from New York City.

Media	
Newsprint	
Mercer Business Magazine, monthly	
Mercer County Messenger, weekly	
Trenton Evening Times, daily	
The Trentonian, daily	
Television	
WNJT (Channel 52)	
See also Philadelphia	
Radio	
WBUD (AM)	WKXW (FM)
WIMG (AM)	WNJT (FM)
WPST (FM)	WTSR (FM)
WTTM (AM)	WCHR (FM)
WWFM (FM)	

Sports

Sports fans generally travel to Philadelphia or New York City to watch their favorite teams.

Arts, Culture, and Tourism

Trenton's cultural life is sustained by a number of performance groups: Pennington Players, playing at the Open Air Theater at Washington Crossing State Park; Shakespeare 70, playing at the Open Air Theater and the Artists Showcase Theater; the Greater Trenton Symphonic Orchestra, presenting classical concerts at the War Memorial Auditorium; and the Trenton Civic Opera.

The city's fine museums include the State Museum at the New Jersey Cultural Center, the Old Barracks devoted to colonial military memorabilia, Trenton City Museum at the restored Ellarslie Mansion in Cadwalader Park, Contemporary Club Victorian Museum, Meredith Havens Fire Museum, and Flag Museum. The Library Gallery at Mercer County Com-

munity College and the Art Porcelain Studio hold periodic exhibitions.

Travel and Tourism	
Hotel Rooms 2,867	
Convention and Exhibit Space (square feet) NA	
Convention Centers	
National Conference Center (East Windsor)	
Festivals	
Eyes on Trenton	
St. Hedwig's Festival	
Heritage Days Festival	

Parks and Recreation

The Mahlon Stacy Park on Memorial Drive, bordering the Delaware, has 19 wooded acres close to the State House. The Washington Crossing State Park, Eldridge Park, Roebling Memorial Park, and Mercer County Park are close-by, offering a full range of outdoor activities, including camping.

Sources of Further Information

Department of Arts, Culture, and History
City of Trenton
City Hall
319 East State Street
Trenton, NJ 08608
(609) 989-3632

Free Public Library
120 Academy Street
Trenton, NJ 08608
(609) 392-7188

Mercer County Chamber of Commerce
214 West State Street
Trenton, NJ 08608
(609) 393-4143

Trenton Historic Landmarks Commission
Department of Housing
City Hall Annex
319 East State Street
Trenton, NJ 08608
(609) 989-3582

Additional Reading

Ciecolella, Erasmo S. *Vibrant Life: Trenton's Italian Americans, 1866–1942.* 1986.
Gummere, Barker. *Street Railways of Trenton.* 1986.
Quigley, Mary A., and David E. Collier. *A Capital Place: The Story of Trenton.* 1984.
Washington, Jack. *In Search of a Community's Past: The Black Community in Trenton.* 1990.

Tucson

Arizona

Basic Data

Name   Tucson
Name Origin   From Papago Indian name
Year Founded   1775 Inc. 1853
Status: State   Arizona
       County   Seat of Pima County
Area (square miles)   125.4
Elevation (feet)   2,390
Time Zone   Mountain
Population (1990)   405,390
Population of Metro Area (1990)   666,880

Sister Cities

   Alma-Ata, Kazakhstan
   Ciudad Obregon, Mexico
   Guadalajara, Mexico
   Santo Domingo, Nicaragua
   Taichung, China
   Trikkala, Greece

Distance in Miles To:

Atlanta	1,740
Boston	2,652
Chicago	1,744
Dallas	927
Denver	856
Detroit	1,983
Houston	1,052
Los Angeles	494
Miami	2,212
New York	2,429
Philadelphia	2,376
Washington, DC	2,244

Location and Topography

Tucson is located at the foothills of the Catalina Mountains in the valley of the Sonoran Desert in southeastern Arizona. It is surrounded by the Sierrita and Santa Rita mountain ranges to the south, and the Rincon mountains to the east.

Layout of City and Suburbs

The heart of downtown is the Convention Center. Also downtown is La Placita, a complex of office buildings, shops, and restaurants in a plaza designed to look like a Mexican village. Tucson is a sprawling city, with only half a dozen skyscrapers built in recent decades. Stone Avenue divides the east-west streets, and Congress Street divides the north-south ones. The largest residential area surrounds the university campus. The more impressive homes are in the Catalina Foothills Estates, the El Encanto Estates, and the Paseo Redondo, two blocks from the Main Street. Most Mexicans live in the Old Town, called El Bario Libre. The Davis-Monthan Air Force Base is to the east of the city via Broadway.

Environment

Environmental Stress Index   3.0
Green Cities Index: Rank   15
            Score   22.86
Water Quality   Alkaline
   Average Daily Use (gallons per capita)   149
   Maximum Supply (gallons per capita)   346
Parkland as % of Total City Area   3.7
% Waste Landfilled/Recycled   NA
Annual Parks Expenditures per Capita $100.75

Climate

Tucson is one of the sunniest and hottest cities in the nation. It has a typical desert climate characterized by long, hot, and dry summers and extremely mild winters. The mercury hits 100°F over 40 days in a year on an average. The high temperature is made tolerable by low humidity and relatively cool nights.

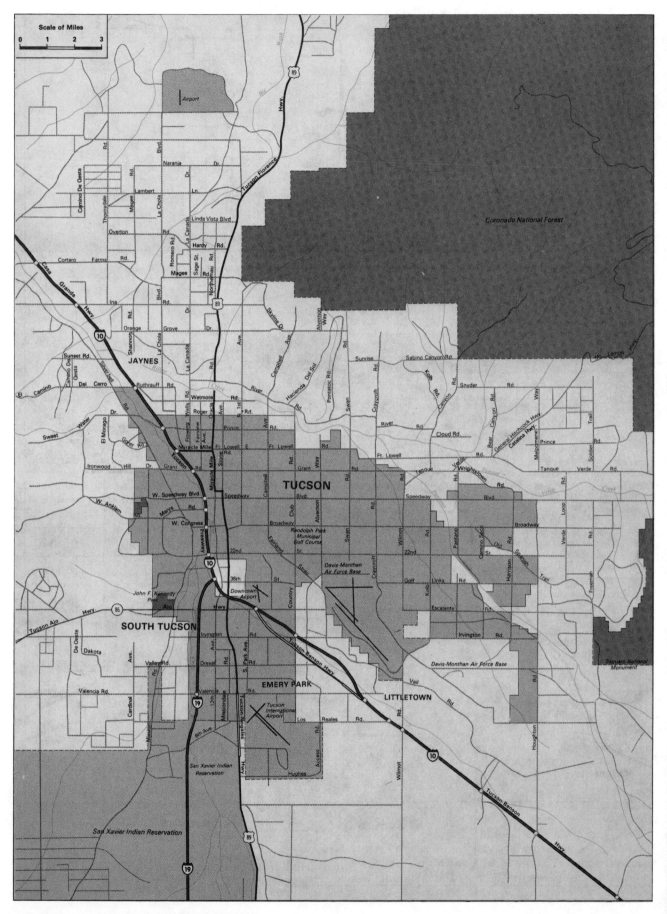

Weather

Temperature

Highest Monthly Average °F   98.5
Lowest Monthly Average °F   38.1

Annual Averages

Days 32°F or Below   21
Days above 90°F   139
Zero Degree Days   0
Precipitation (inches)   11.14
Snow (inches)   2.0
% Seasonal Humidity   38.5
Wind Speed (m.p.h.)   8.2
Clear Days   198
Cloudy Days   78
Storm Days   40
Rainy Days   50

Average Temperatures (°F)	High	Low	Mean
January	63.5	38.2	50.9
February	67.0	39.9	53.5
March	71.5	43.6	57.6
April	80.7	50.3	65.5
May	89.6	57.5	73.6
June	97.9	66.2	82.1
July	98.3	74.2	86.3
August	95.3	72.3	83.8
September	93.1	67.1	80.1
October	83.8	56.4	70.1
November	72.2	44.8	58.5
December	64.8	39.1	52.0

History

An extensive civilization existed in the Santa Cruz Valley for centuries. The first white man to venture into the desert was Padre Eusebio Francisco Kino, a Jesuit priest, who arrived in 1687 and has left a detailed record of the culture of the Pima and Sobaipuri Indians. At that time, the settlement was known as *Stjukshon*, anglicized as Tucson, translated to mean "dark spring at the foot of a black hill." In 1700 Padre Kino started to build the lovely mission San Xavier. The work of the mission came to an end in 1751, when the Pima plundered San Xavier. In 1767 when the Jesuits were expelled from the Spanish provinces, the Franciscans took over the work under Padre Francisco Tomas Garces. In 1775 the Spanish garrison at Tubac was moved to Tucson where, according to legend, Padre Garces built a new mission called San Jose del Tucson. The Royal Presidio of Tucson was built in 1776. There the Spanish settlers flourished, despite intermittent Apache raids. With the termination of Spanish rule in Mexico, Tucson came under the rule of the province of Sonora. In 1846 Tucson was briefly visited by the Mormon Battalion under Lieutenant Colonel Philip St. George Cooke. In 1854 Tucson came within the territory acquired by the United States through the Gadsden Purchase. The overland stage service from San Antonio to San Diego and later from St. Louis to San Francisco began in 1857 and it passed through Tucson. During the Civil War the town changed hands a number of times, but in general Tucson was sympathetic to the Confederacy, which prevented its selection as the capital of the Arizona Territory in 1864. It was the territorial seat from 1867 to 1877. After the Civil War, the Apaches were pacified. In 1870 the first permanent public school was established and in 1876 the first Protestant church. A few years later the University of Arizona was given to the town as compensation for the loss of its capital status. With the arrival of the Southern Pacific in 1880, the future of the town was well established.

Historical Landmarks

Tucson's most famous landmark is the San Xavier Mission, known as the White Dove of the Desert. The Mission San Xavier Del Bac stands on a slight eminence and faces south across the Santa Cruz Valley. In front of the church, which dominates the other buildings, lies a long narrow atrium with a chapel at one end and low dormitories at the other. Founded by Father Kino in 1700, the mission was abandoned and plundered many times before it was rebuilt and finally dedicated in 1797. The mission was again deserted when the mission lands were secularized during the Mexican regime and it was restored by Bishop Granjon in 1906. Built of burned adobe brick and lime plaster, the mission is a fine example of the late–Spanish Renaissance style of architecture. San Augustin on Stone Avenue is a Catholic cathedral with double towers built in 1897. The Kino Memorial on Main Street is in a small park. Erected in 1936, the oblong block of black volcanic rock honors Eusebio Francisco Kino, the Jesuit missionary who is considered the founder of Tucson. The Wishing Shrine, El Tiradito, on Simpson and Main streets, is a parapet of weathered adobe bricks. According to legend, it is the resting place of Juan Oliveras, a Mexican youth murdered by his father-in-law for an illicit affair with his mother-in-law. Olivares was buried without church rites in 1890. Thereafter, Mexican women burned candles over Juan's grave, and the shrine came to be used by parents praying for their wayward daughters. Eventually, it became a place of pilgrimage and it was believed that anyone who placed a lighted candle on Juan Oliveras's grave and made a wish would have the wish granted by dawn, provided the candle burned to its base. A few blocks away at the edge of the Armory Park District is the site of the printing office of a Spanish language newspaper founded in 1878. Tucson has three historical districts, El Presidio, Armory Park, and Barrio Historico. Around El Presidio are many historical structures dating from the early Spanish rule.

Population

Tucson is typical of the population gains made by the Southwest since 1970. From a population of 262,933 in 1970, it grew by 25.7% to reach 330,537 in 1980, and then by a further 22.6% to reach 405,390 in 1990. The metro area also has grown by 25.5% between 1980 and 1990.

Chronology

1687	Father Eusebio Francisco Kino, a Jesuit missionary, visits *Stjukshon*, or Tucson, inhabited by the Pima and Sobaipuri Indians.
1700	Father Kina builds the San Xavier Mission.
1751	The Pima plunder the San Xavier.
1767	On the expulsion of Jesuits, Franciscans take over mission work in the province.
1768	Father Francisco Tomas Garces is placed in charge of San Xavier and other missions.
1775	Captain Juan Bautista de Anza, the Spanish commander, moves his garrison to Tucson, where he builds a military post.
1776	Royal Presidio is built.
1822	With the termination of Spanish rule in Mexico, Tucson comes under the jurisdiction of the Province of Sonora.
1846	Mormon Battalion passes through Tucson.
1854	Tucson comes within U.S. territory as a result of the Gadsden Purchase.
1857	Tucson becomes a stop in the overland stage service from San Antonio to San Diego.
1864	Tucson is made a district of the Arizona Territory.
1867	Tucson is made Territorial Capital of Arizona.
1870	First public school is founded.
1876	The first Protestant church services are held.
1877	State capital is moved to Prescott.
1880	Southern Pacific reaches town.
1885	The University of Arizona is founded.

Population

	1980	1990
Central City	330,537	405,390
Rank	45	33
Metro Area	531,443	666,880

Pop. Change 1980–1990   +74,853
Pop. % Change 1980–1990   +22.6
Median Age   30.6
% Male   48.7
% Age 65 and Over   12.63
Density (per square mile)   2,232

Households

Number   162,685
Persons per Household   2.42
% Female-Headed Households   12.4

Population (continued)

% One-Person Households   31.3
Births—Total   6,878
    % to Mothers under 20   12.9
    Birth Rate per 1,000   18.8

Ethnic Composition

Whites make up 75.3% of the population, blacks 4.3%, American Indians 1.6%, Asians and Pacific Islanders 2.2%, and others 16.7%. Hispanics, both black and white, make up 29.3%.

Ethnic Composition (as % of total pop.)

	1980	1990
White	83.12	75.25
Black	3.51	4.28
American Indian	1.39	1.59
Asian and Pacific Islander	1.04	2.20
Hispanic	24.84	29.25
Other	NA	16.68

Government

Tucson has a council-manager form of government with a seven-member council. The mayor and the council members are elected to four-year terms.

Government

Year of Home Charter   NA
Number of Members of the Governing Body   7
Elected at Large   NA
Elected by Wards   7
Number of Women in Governing Body   0
Salary of Mayor $24,000
Salary of Council Members $12,000
City Government Employment Total   4,776
Rate per 10,000   133.1

Public Finance

The annual budget consists of revenues of $436.866 million and expenditures of $472.698 million. The debt outstanding is $773.404 million and cash and security holdings of $712.378 million.

Public Finance

Total Revenue (in millions) $436.866
Intergovernmental Revenue—Total (in millions) $120.4
Federal Revenue per Capita $26.53
% Federal Assistance   6.07
% State Assistance   20.03
Sales Tax as % of Total Revenue   22.46
Local Revenue as % of Total Revenue   53.95
City Income Tax   no
Taxes—Total (in millions) $93.5

Taxes per Capita
    Total $261
    Property $34

Public Finance *(continued)*

Sales and Gross Receipts $212
General Expenditures—Total (in millions) $249.3
General Expenditures per Capita $695
Capital Outlays per Capita $168

% of Expenditures for:
Public Welfare   0.8
Highways   13.8
Education   0.0
Health and Hospitals   0.0
Police   13.3
Sewerage and Sanitation   6.5
Parks and Recreation   9.5
Housing and Community Development   6.4
Debt Outstanding per Capita $1,746
   % Utility   18.7
Federal Procurement Contract Awards (in millions)
   $1,288.7
Federal Grants Awards (in millions) $94.4
Fiscal Year Begins   July 1

Economy

 Tucson's economy is said to be based on the four Cs: climate, copper, cotton, and cattle. Although copper has faced a shrinking market, the industry has bottomed out and is showing promising signs of growth with two major mining companies, Phelps Dodge and Magma Copper, resuming active operations in the late 1980s. Tourism, based on Tucson's climate, has remained the mainstay of the economy, bringing over $1 billion a year. The fine Pima cotton grown here sustains a healthy agricultural sector, which also produces many other dry-weather crops. Tucson's impressive economic growth in recent decades has come from its high-technology sector, transforming it into a Silicon Desert. The high-technology sector is led by established giants, such as Hughes Aircraft and IBM, as well as newer players, such as Gates Learjet, National Semiconductor, Garrett Controls, General Instruments, Krieger, Hamilton Test Systems, Unitronics, Burr Brown, and TEC. Tucson also parlays its proximity to Mexico by encouraging the establishment of *maquiladora* industries with Mexican labor and U.S. capital. The University of Arizona, Fort Huachuca, and the Davis-Monthan Air Force Base also make significant contributions to the economy.

Economy

Total Money Income (in millions) $3,383.9
% of State Average   89.3
Per Capita Annual Income $9,430
% Population below Poverty Level   14.7
Fortune 500 Companies   1

Banks	Number	Deposits (in millions)
Commercial	10	32,621
Savings	4	NA

Passenger Autos   419,999
Electric Meters   280,082
Gas Meters   223,318

Manufacturing

Number of Establishments   497

Economy *(continued)*

% with 20 or More Employees   24.9
Manufacturing Payroll (in millions) $692.2
Value Added by Manufacture (in millions) $1,745.3
Value of Shipments (in millions) $3,231.3
New Capital Expenditures (in millions) $106.5

Wholesale Trade

Number of Establishments   682
Sales (in millions) $1,270.0
Annual Payroll (in millions) $130.779

Retail Trade

Number of Establishments   3,840
Total Sales (in millions) $3,277.0
Sales per Capita $9,132
Number of Retail Trade Establishments with Payroll   2,897
Annual Payroll (in millions) $388.6
Total Sales (in millions) $3,231.1
General Merchandise Stores (per capita) $1,329
Food Stores (per capita) $1,715
Apparel Stores (per capita) $409
Eating and Drinking Places (per capita) $875

Service Industries

Total Establishments   3,768
Total Receipts (in millions) $1,570.2
Hotels and Motels (in millions) $81.6
Health Services (in millions) $530.4
Legal Services (in millions) $134.7

Labor

Tucson's work force composition has shown significant changes since 1970, when copper was king. Since then, employment in copper mining has declined, as has employment in agriculture. The majority of the work force added since 1970 are employed in such leading-edge industries as computers, biotechnology, electronics, and aerospace. High-tech employment accounts for 63% of all employment, and Tucson accounts for 20% of Arizona's total high-tech employment. Among the largest employers are Hughes Aircraft and IBM.

Labor

Civilian Labor Force   203,475
% Change 1989–1990   -0.2

Work Force Distribution
Mining   2,300
Construction   14,100
Manufacturing   24,800
Transportation and Public Utilities   10,000
Wholesale and Retail Trade   61,700
FIRE (Finance, Insurance, Real Estate)   11,600
Service   75,600
Government   59,000
Women as % of Labor Force   43.9
% Self-Employed   5.4
% Professional/Technical   19.0
Total Unemployment   8,426
Rate %   4.1
Federal Government Civilian Employment   4,376

Education

Tucson Unified School District supports 108 elementary, middle, and senior high schools. Tucson has a strong parochial school system, in addition to 6 private schools. The largest higher education institution is the University of Arizona, with an enrollment of 35,000. Other colleges include Pima Community College and a branch of the University of Phoenix.

Education

Number of Public Schools   108
Special Education Schools   3
Total Enrollment   56,174
% Enrollment in Private Schools   7.7
% Minority   46.9
Classroom Teachers   2,668
Pupil-Teacher Ratio   21:1
Number of Graduates   3,372
Total Revenue (in millions) $217.648
Total Expenditures (in millions) $248.533
Expenditures per Pupil $3,579
Educational Attainment (Age 25 and Over)
    % Completed 12 or More Years   72.7
    % Completed 16 or More Years   19.2
Four-Year Colleges and Universities   1
    Enrollment   35,735
Two-Year Colleges   4
    Enrollment   29,513

Libraries

Number   53
Public Libraries   18
Books (in thousands)   820
Circulation (in thousands)   4,452
Persons Served (in thousands)   666
Circulation per Person Served   6.68
Income (in millions) $11.254
Staff   254

Four-Year Colleges and Universities
    University of Arizona

Health

Tucson has built up a reputation as one of the most healthful cities in the nation, with a warm dry air that is ideal for those suffering from respiratory illnesses. Of the city's 12 hospitals the largest is the University of Arizona Medical Center, which provides health care to all of southern Arizona. Other facilities include St. Mary's

Health

Deaths—Total   3,371
Rate per 1,000   9.2
Infant Deaths—Total   74
Rate per 1,000   10.8
Number of Metro Hospitals   12
Number of Metro Hospital Beds   2,498
Rate per 100,000   696
Number of Physicians   2,530
Physicians per 1,000   3.03
Nurses per 1,000   6.92
Health Expenditures per Capita $1.78

Hospital, Cerelle Center for Womens Health, and Thomas Davis Birth Center.

Transportation

Tucson is approached by two interstates: I-10, which links the city with Los Angeles and El Paso; and I-19, which originates at the Mexican border and joins with I-10 inside city limits. Rail passenger service is provided by Amtrak and rail freight service by Southern Pacific. The principal air terminal is Tucson International Airport, served by 14 major airlines.

Transportation

Interstate Highway Mileage   23
Total Urban Mileage   1,564
Total Daily Vehicle Mileage (in millions) $8.752
Daily Average Commute Time   46.4 min.
Number of Buses   124
Port Tonnage (in millions)   NA
Airports   1
Number of Daily Flights   56
Daily Average Number of Passengers   3,591

Airlines (American carriers only)
    Alaska
    American
    American West
    Continental
    Delta
    Trans World
    United
    USAir

Housing

Of the total housing stock, 51.4% is owner-occupied. The median value of an owner-occupied home is $66,800 and the median monthly rent $327. Nearly 12% of all homes are mobile homes, which are popular with the older population.

Housing

Total Housing Units   183,338
% Change 1980–1990   25.1
Vacant Units for Sale or Rent   14,838
Occupied Units   162,685
% with More Than One Person per Room   7.3
% Owner-Occupied   51.4
Median Value of Owner-Occupied Homes $66,800
Average Monthly Purchase Cost $307
Median Monthly Rent $327
New Private Housing Starts   477
Value (in thousands) $32,215
% Single-Family   92.2
Nonresidential Buildings Value (in thousands) $40,401

Urban Redevelopment

Most urban redevelopment took place in the 1970s and 1980s, when the number of high-rise office buildings doubled. The new structures include the Great Western Bank Building and the United Bank Tower. The number of new industrial parks has grown to over 50. Redevelopment programs are coordinated by Tucson Local Development Corporation, Tucson Economic Development Corporation, and Tucson Downtown Development Corporation.

Crime

Tucson ranks low in public safety. In 1991 violent crimes totaled 3,896, property crimes totaled 39,243.

Crime	
Violent Crimes—Total	3,896
Violent Crime Rate per 100,000	668.8
Murder	24
Rape	332
Robbery	889
Aggravated Assaults	2,651
Property Crimes	39,243
Burglary	7,493
Larceny	28,281
Motor Vehicle Theft	3,469
Arson	180
Per Capita Police Expenditures	$128.29
Per Capita Fire Protection Expenditures	$59.66
Number of Police	647
Per 1,000	1.70

Religion

Tucson is heavily Catholic, reflecting its Spanish and Mexican heritage. Catholics form the largest population. The next strongest denominations are Baptist, Jewish, and Mormon.

Religion	
Largest Denominations (Adherents)	
Catholic	178,448
Southern Baptist	27,428
Evangelical Lutheran	9,216
Assembly of God	5,580
Latter-Day Saints	14,064
Episcopal	6,872
Presbyterian	9,568
United Methodist	11,439
Black Baptist	5,540
Jewish	20,000

Media

The daily city press consists of three publications: the *Tucson Arizona Daily Star*, published mornings, and the *Tucson Citizen*, published evenings, and the *Daily Territorial*. The electronic media consist of 8 television stations and 24 AM and FM radio stations.

Sports

Tucson has no major professional sports team. Most of the sports action revolves around the University of Arizona Wildcats and the Tucson Toros (the Houston Astro's farm team), who play their home games at Hi Corbett Field.

Media		
Newsprint		
Daily Territorial, daily		
Tucson, monthly		
Tucson Arizona Daily Star, daily		
Tucson Business Digest, quarterly		
Tucson Citizen, daily		
Television		
KGUN (Channel 9)		
KMSB (Channel 11)		
KOLD (Channel 13)		
KPOL (Channel 40)		
KTTU (Channel 18)		
KUAS (Channel 27)		
KUAT (Channel 6)		
KVOA (Channel 4)		
Radio		
KCDX (FM)		KCEE (AM)
KWFM (FM)		KCRZ (FM)
KCUB (AM)		KIIM (FM)
KFLT (AM)		KGMS (FM)
KGVY (AM)		KJYK (AM)
KKLD (FM)		KMRR (AM)
KNST (AM)		KRQQ (FM)
KSAZ (AM)		KTKT (AM)
KLPX (FM)		KTUC (AM)
KTZR (AM)		KUAT (AM)
KUAT (FM)		KUAZ (FM)
KXCI (FM)		KXEW (AM)

Arts, Culture, and Tourism

Tucson is a cultural showcase of the Southwest. The Downtown Arts District includes the Music Hall, Tucson Community Center Little Theater, and the Temple of Art and Music. The Arizona Theater Company in Tucson is the state's only professional resident theater company. The Gaslight Theater offers Victorian plays. In music, the Tucson Symphony offers an eight-month season in classical music. Other musical groups include the Arizona Opera and the Southern Arizona Light Opera. In dance the principal group is the Arizona Ballet.

The principal museums are the Arizona State Museum, which specializes in southwestern ethnology and archeology; and the Tucson Museum of Art, which specializes in southwestern, particularly pre-Columbian, arts and crafts. The Arizona Historical Society administers three museums: its own museum, which includes a mining exhibit; Fort Lowell Museum, a reconstruction of the 1865 fort and its military equipment; and the 1858 John C. Fremont House, one of the oldest adobe houses

Travel and Tourism	
Hotel Rooms 11,048	
Convention and Exhibit Space (square feet) NA	
Convention Centers	
Tucson Convention Center	
Festivals	
Tucson Festival (March)	
Cinco de Mayo Festival (May)	
Fiesta San Augustin (August)	
Summer Arts Festival	

in Tucson. Other museums include the Pima Air Museum, Amerind Foundation Museum, Arizona–Sonora Desert Museum, and the University of Arizona Center for Creative Photography.

Parks and Recreation

Tucson maintains 200 parks. The largest are the Emery Park, near the Tucson International Airport, and the John F. Kennedy Park in southern Tucson.

Sources of Further Information

City Hall
255 West Alameda Street
Tuscon, AZ 85701
(602) 791-4201

Tucson Convention and Visitors Bureau
450 West Paseo Redondo
Tuscon, AZ 85705
(602) 624-1817

Tucson Metropolitan Chamber of Commerce
435 West St. Marys Road
Tuscon, AZ 85701
(602) 792-7388

Additional Reading

Cosulich, Bernice. *Tucson.* 1987.
Diamos, Kerson D. *Remembrance of Tucson's Past.* 1985.
Dobnys, Henry F. *Spanish Colonial Tucson: A Demographic History.* 1976.
Getty, Harry T. *Interethnic Relationships in the Community of Tucson.* 1976.
Lockard, Peggy H. *This Is Tucson: Guidebook to the Old Pueblo.* 1988.
Polzer, Charles W. *Tucson: A Short History.* 1986.
Row, A. Tracy. *Frontier Tucson: Hispanic Contributions.* 1987.
Sheaffer, Jack. *Jack Sheaffer's Tucson, 1945–1965.* 1985.
Sonnichsen, C. L. *Tucson: The Life and Times of an American City.* 1987.

Tulsa

Oklahoma

Basic Data

Name   Tulsa
Name Origin   From Creek name
Year Founded   1836 Inc. 1898
Status: State   Oklahoma
          County   Seat of Tulsa County
Area (square miles)   183.5
Elevation (feet)   804
Time Zone   Central
Population (1990)   367,302
Population of Metro Area (1990)   708,954

Sister Cities
   Beihai, China
   Kaohsiung, China
   San Luis Potosi, Mexico
   Tiberias, Israel

Distance in Miles To:
   Oklahoma City   105
   Wichita   174
   Dallas   263
   Norman   122
   Amarillo   360
   Fort Smith   116

Location and Topography

N

Tulsa is located on the Arkansas River at an elevation of 804 feet above sea level, surrounded by the Ozark foothills.

Layout of City and Suburbs

Tulsa is a city of contrasts. The Old Tulsa, north of Third Street, coexists with the modern city. The industrial sections flank the railroad tracks between First Street and Archer Avenue, and West Tulsa across the river. The Civic Center forms the heart of downtown Tulsa. The buildings cover eight square blocks and include the City Hall, Courthouse, and Assembly Center.

Environment

Environmental Stress Index   2.2
Green Cities Index: Rank   26
                    Score   26.36
Water Quality   Alkaline, soft, fluoridated
Average Daily Use (gallons per capita)   276
   Maximum Supply (gallons per capita)   422
Parkland as % of Total City Area   5.8
% Waste Landfilled/Recycled   NA
Annual Parks Expenditures per Capita $51.88

Climate

Tulsa has a continental climate with mild winters and hot summers, and temperatures frequently over 100°F, moderated by low humidity and southerly breezes. Spring and early summer bring tornadoes and windstorms, but sunny days and cool nights characterize early fall. Rainfall is heaviest in spring.

Weather

Temperature

Highest Monthly Average °F   93.9
Lowest Monthly Average °F   24.8

Annual Averages

Days 32°F or Below   85
Days above 90°F   70
Zero Degree Days   1
Precipitation (inches)   37
Snow (inches)   9
% Seasonal Humidity   67
Wind Speed (m.p.h.)   10
Clear Days   127
Cloudy Days   137
Storm Days   52
Rainy Days   90

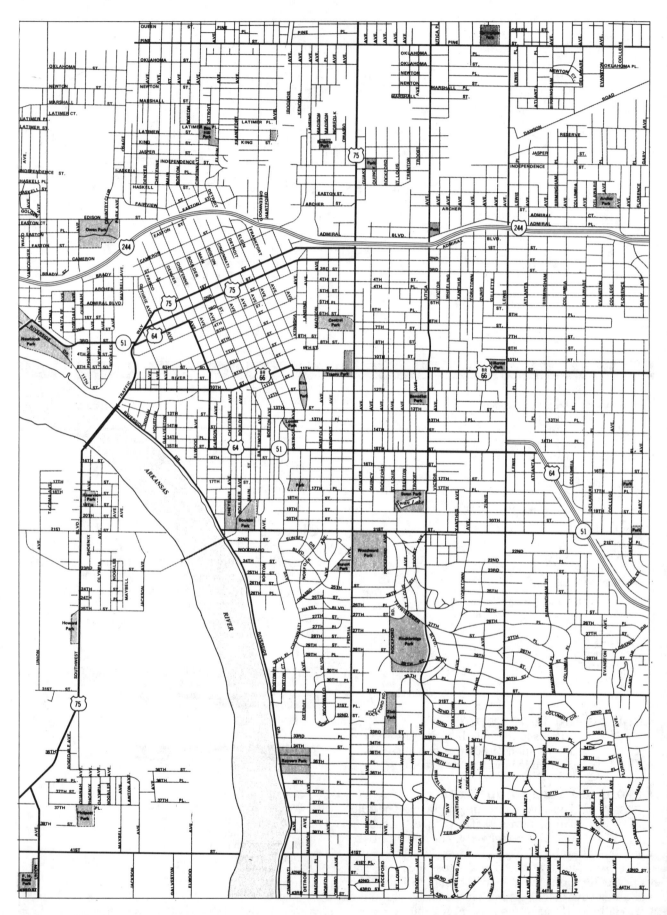

Weather (continued)

Average Temperatures (°F)	High	Low	Mean
January	47.0	26.1	36.6
February	52.2	30.2	41.2
March	59.7	36.9	48.3
April	71.8	49.7	60.8
May	79.2	58.4	68.8
June	87.3	67.3	77.3
July	92.8	71.4	82.1
August	92.7	70.0	81.4
September	84.8	61.7	73.3
October	75.0	50.8	62.9
November	60.8	38.0	49.4
December	50.1	29.5	39.8

History

Tulsa existed as early as 1879 on the Pony Express mail route through Indian Territory. The post office was in the home of a Creek rancher, George Perryman, whose brother was the first postmaster. It first appeared on the map when the Atlantic and Pacific Railroad built a depot on the site. Originally the builders planned to stop in the Cherokee Nation about a mile from the riverbank, but since Cherokee laws forbade trading by non-natives, the railroad had to go through the Creek Nation, where the laws were less stringent. The terminal, with a roundhouse and large loading pen, was established on the site of the present business district. Local cattle, which formerly had to be driven to Vinita, were now loaded in Tulsa for shipments to the stockyards of St. Louis and Chicago. The town was first called Tulsey Town by the Creek Indians, who had originally lived in Tallassee, Alabama. Within a few years the first church had been set up by the Presbyterian Home Mission Board, near the old cattle trail. Nevertheless, the town experienced a number of problems that retarded development: insurgent Indians, muddy and poorly designed roads, alcoholics and gamblers, and a dearth of drinking water. As a result the railroad shifted its terminus to Sapulpa and it looked as if Tulsa, incorporated as a town in 1898, might never amount to much more than a tiny town in Indian Territory. Then, on 25 June 1901, it catapulted into fame and its history changed forever. Across the river at Red Fork, now within city limits, oil was dug. For some time it seemed as if Tulsa might merely be a suburb of Red Fork, until three residents agreed to build a toll bridge across the river with their own funds. Tulsa then began to invite the horde of oilmen to come and develop the natural resource. The Enabling Act of 1906 merged Indian Territory and Oklahoma Territory and removed the last barrier to full-scale white settlement. By 1910 a building boom was in full swing. Pipelines with the Gulf of Mexico were laid, and hotels, banks, and office buildings sprouted. The population leaped from 1,390 in 1900 to 18,182 in 1910, 72,075 in 1920, 141,258 in 1930, and 182,740 in 1950. The city experienced its first serious race riot in 1921.

Historical Landmarks

The Old Council Tree on Cheyenne Avenue is marked by a bronze tablet nailed to the trunk. The ground under the tree branches was the traditional meeting place for the heads of Creek families composing the Tallassee *lochapokas* (towns) for their councils, or *busks*. The Tulsa County Courthouse on the corner of Sixth Street and Boulder Avenue marks the site of the first post office of the town headed by George Perryman, the Creek chief.

Population

Tulsa maintained steady demographic growth in the past three decades when many other cities were losing their population. From 330,000 in 1970 it grew by 9.3% to 360,919 in 1980, and then by a further 1.8% to 367,302 in 1990.

Population	1980	1990
Central City	360,919	367,302
Rank	38	43
Metro Area	657,173	708,954
Pop. Change 1980–1990 +6,383		
Pop. % Change 1980–1990 +1.8		
Median Age 33.1		
% Male 47.8		
% Age 65 and Over 12.7		
Density (per square mile) 2,001		

Households		
Number 155,447		
Persons per Household 2.31		
% Female-Headed Households 11.8		
% One-Person Households 32.7		
Births—Total 6,376		
% to Mothers under 20 14.2		
Birth Rate per 1,000 17.0		

Ethnic Composition

Whites make up 79.4%, blacks 13.6%, American Indians 4.7%, Asians and Pacific Islanders 1.4%, and others 1.0%. Many whites have varying degrees of Indian blood but are not identified as Indians unless they have more than one-fourth Indian blood.

Ethnic Composition (as % of total pop.)	1980	1990
White	82.82	79.35
Black	11.87	13.57
American Indian	3.83	4.65
Asian and Pacific Islander	0.82	1.4
Hispanic	1.74	2.6
Other	NA	1.04

Government

Tulsa moved from a commission form of government to a council form of government in 1990. The mayor, elected to four-year terms, is the chief executive. The nine council members are elected every two years from districts.

Chronology

1879 George Perryman's home is the first post office in the Creek settlement, called Tulsey Town or Tulsa.

1882 Atlantic and Pacific Railroad brings rail lines into Tulsa and builds a terminal with a roundhouse and loading pen.

1884 The Presbyterian Home Mission Board builds first church and small mission school near the old cattle trail.

1898 Tulsa is incorporated as a town.

1901 Oil is discovered in Red Creek, catapulting Tulsa into a major metropolis.

1905 Glenn Pool oil well is discovered.

1906 Congress passes Enabling Act, merging Indian Territory and Oklahoma Territory.

Government

Year of Home Charter   1908
Number of Members of the Governing Body   9
Elected at Large   0
Elected by Wards   9
Number of Women in Governing Body   0
Salary of Mayor $50,000
Salary of Council Members $38,500
City Government Employment Total   NA
Rate per 10,000   NA

Public Finance

The annual budget consists of revenues of $437.098 million and expenditures of $414.931 million. The debt outstanding is $1.450 billion and cash and security holdings $1.448 billion.

Public Finance

Total Revenue (in millions) $437.098
Intergovernmental Revenue—Total (in millions) $20.16
Federal Revenue per Capita $6.94
% Federal Assistance   1.58
% State Assistance   2.97
Sales Tax as % of Total Revenue   29.84
Local Revenue as % of Total Revenue   82.10
City Income Tax   no
Taxes—Total (in millions) $138.7

Taxes per Capita
  Total $371
  Property $45
  Sales and Gross Receipts $319
General Expenditures—Total (in millions) $299.3
General Expenditures per Capita $801
Capital Outlays per Capita $250

% of Expenditures for:
  Public Welfare   0.0
  Highways   12.1
  Education   NA
  Health and Hospitals   1.2
  Police   10.0

Public Finance (continued)

  Sewerage and Sanitation   13.8
  Parks and Recreation   6.8
  Housing and Community Development   3.0
Debt Outstanding per Capita $2,270
  % Utility   4.7
Federal Procurement Contract Awards (in millions) $191.8
Federal Grants Awards (in millions) $28.1
Fiscal Year Begins   July 1

Economy

Tulsa was known as the Oil Capital during the the oil boom, which began in 1901. The oil boom is long over, but oil still drives the economy and more than 1,000 petroleum-based companies are headquartered in the city. In trying to devise a post-oil economic strategy, Tulsa has focused on three sectors: aerospace, data processing, and medical services. The city's Sunbelt location and its low energy, construction, and living costs are strong business incentives, especially considering the low taxes. The company most closely identified with Tulsa is American Airlines, which maintains a large central organization here. The American Airlines Saber Computer Complex is the largest nonmilitary computer system in the world. Also located in Tulsa are two of the largest defense contractors: McDonnell Douglas and Rockwell International.

Economy

Total Money Income (in millions) $4,735.4
% of State Average   129.9
Per Capita Annual Income $12,670
% Population below Poverty Level   10.4
Fortune 500 Companies   2

Banks	Number	Deposits (in millions)
Commercial	29	4,296.2
Savings	3	1,876.6

Passenger Autos   384,916
Electric Meters   160,323
Gas Meters   186,126

Manufacturing

Number of Establishments   868
% with 20 or More Employees   27.2
Manufacturing Payroll (in millions) $966.9
Value Added by Manufacture (in millions) $1,864.9
Value of Shipments (in millions) $3,836.7
New Capital Expenditures (in millions) $112.8

Wholesale Trade

Number of Establishments   1,345
Sales (in millions)   NA
Annual Payroll (in millions)   NA

Retail Trade

Number of Establishments   4,384
Total Sales (in millions) $3,073.1
Sales per Capita $8,222
Number of Retail Trade Establishments with Payroll   2,940
Annual Payroll (in millions) $371.7
Total Sales (in millions) $3,007.2
General Merchandise Stores (per capita) $944
Food Stores (per capita)   NA

Economy *(continued)*

Apparel Stores (per capita) $574
Eating and Drinking Places (per capita)   NA

Service Industries

Total Establishments   3,985
Total Receipts (in millions) $1,841.6
Hotels and Motels (in millions) $98.4
Health Services (in millions) $450.0
Legal Services (in millions) $199.4

Labor

 Although the growth of the labor force is less than that of the population at large, the city's employment market survived the difficult recession of the early 1990s rather well. Mining claims a larger share of the employment pie than is the case with other cities, but other employment sectors follow the typical urban profile.

Labor

Civilian Labor Force   200,929
% Change 1989–1990   1.4

Work Force Distribution
  Mining   NA
  Construction   11,200
  Manufacturing   57,500
  Transportation and Public Utilities   26,900
  Wholesale and Retail Trade   77,000
  FIRE (Finance, Insurance, Real Estate)   17,500
  Service   84,100
  Government   39,800
  Women as % of Labor Force   43.7
  % Self-Employed   5.8
  % Professional/Technical   16.7
Total Unemployment   9,893
Rate %   4.9
Federal Government Civilian Employment   3,603

Education

Tulsa Public Schools support 54 elementary schools, 14 junior high/middle schools, and 9 senior high schools. Higher education is provided by four public and two private institutions. The public institutions are Oklahoma Tulsa Medical College, Oklahoma Osteopathic College of Medicine and Surgery, Tulsa Junior College, and University Center at Tulsa. The private institutions are the University of Tulsa and the Oral Roberts University (ORU).

Education

Number of Public Schools   77
Special Education Schools   1
Total Enrollment   40,732
% Enrollment in Private Schools   5.5
% Minority   38.2
Classroom Teachers   2,192
Pupil-Teacher Ratio   18.5:1
Number of Graduates   2,300
Total Revenue (in millions) $133.330

Education *(continued)*

Total Expenditures (in millions) $132.597
Expenditures per Pupil $2,877
Educational Attainment (Age 25 and Over)
  % Completed 12 or More Years   77.3
  % Completed 16 or More Years   21.7
Four-Year Colleges and Universities   3
  Enrollment   8,171
Two-Year Colleges   2
  Enrollment   22,763

Libraries

Number   54
Public Libraries   21
Books (in thousands)   864
Circulation (in thousands)   3,270
Persons Served (in thousands)   517
Circulation per Person Served   6.3
Income (in millions) $9.623
Staff   201

Four-Year Colleges and Universities
  University of Tulsa
  Oral Roberts University
  University Center at Tulsa

Health

 The medical sector consists of nine hospitals, including the City of Faith Research and Medical Center (associated with ORU), Doctor's Medical Center, Hillcrest Medical Center, St. Francis Hospital, St. John Medical Center, and Oklahoma Osteopathic Center. Also in Tulsa County is the Children's Medical Center.

Health

Deaths—Total   3,246
Rate per 1,000   8.7
Infant Deaths—Total   69
Rate per 1,000   10.8
Number of Metro Hospitals   9
Number of Metro Hospital Beds   2,985
Rate per 100,000   799
Number of Physicians   1,174
Physicians per 1,000   1.84
Nurses per 1,000   5.83
Health Expenditures per Capita $19.12

Transportation

Tulsa is approached from the east and south by I-44, which merges with U.S. Highways 66, 75-Alternate, and State Highway 33 a few miles southwest of the city; from the east by I-244, which intersects with I-44 a few miles east of Tulsa and leads directly into the city, merging with U.S. 75 southwest of the city; from the south by U.S. Highway 66; from north and south by 75; from the southeast by 64, which merges with 51 southeast and northwest of the city and 169 from the northeast; and by the east-west State Highways 33 and 51. Four toll roads radiate from the city: Red Fork and Crosstown (I-244), Cherokee (U.S. 75), and Broken Arrow (U.S. 64/State 51). Rail freight service is provided by Burlington Northern, Santa Fe, MK&T, and Texas South Pacific. Tulsa became a major inland river port with the opening in 1971 of the Port of Catoosa, on the Verdigris River, along the 445-mile McClellan-Kerr Navigation System connected by the Mississippi River with the Gulf of Mexico. The principal air terminal is Tulsa International Airport, nine miles from downtown. A smaller facility, the Richard Lloyd Jones, Jr. Airport, exists south of the city.

Transportation
Interstate Highway Mileage   40
Total Urban Mileage   2,559
Total Daily Vehicle Mileage (in millions) $13.344
Daily Average Commute Time   44.7 min.
Number of Buses   80
Port Tonnage (in millions)   NA
Airports   1
Number of Daily Flights   70
Daily Average Number of Passengers   3,947
Airlines (American carriers only)
American
Continental
Delta
Northwest
Trans World
United
USAir

Housing

Of the total housing stock, 55.8% is owner-occupied. The median value of an owner-occupied home is $60,500 and the median monthly rent $293.

Housing		
Total Housing Units 176,211		
% Change 1980–1990 11.3		
Vacant Units for Sale or Rent 15,096		
Occupied Units 155,447		
% with More Than One Person per Room 2.8		
% Owner-Occupied 55.8		
Median Value of Owner-Occupied Homes $60,500		
Average Monthly Purchase Cost $325		
Median Monthly Rent $293		
New Private Housing Starts 984		
Value (in thousands) $78,468		
% Single-Family 69.5		
Nonresidential Buildings Value (in thousands) $78,248		
Tallest Buildings	*Hgt. (ft.)*	*Stories*
Bank of Oklahoma Tower	667	52
City of Faith Clinic Tower	640	60
1st National Tower	516	41
Mid-Continent Tower	513	36
4th Natl. Bank of Tulsa	412	33
320 South Boston Bldg.	400	24
Occidental Place	388	28
Univ. Club Tower	377	32

Urban Redevelopment

Tulsa's 41-story First National Bank and Trust Company Building was completed in 1973. In 1977 the 52-story Bank of Oklahoma Tower replaced it as Tulsa's tallest structure. This tower forms part of the Williams Center, a project covering 11 square blocks in downtown Tulsa. It includes the Tulsa Performing Arts Center, completed in 1977. Development efforts are coordinated by Downtown Tulsa Unlimited, Tulsa Department of Development, Tulsa Economic Development Commission, and Tulsa Economic Development Corporation.

Crime

Tulsa ranks low in public safety. In 1991 violent crimes reported to police totaled 4,923, and property crimes totaled 28,024.

Crime
Violent Crimes—Total   4,923
Violent Crime Rate per 100,000   829.8
Murder   42
Rape   414
Robbery   1,469
Aggravated Assaults   2,998
Property Crimes   28,024
Burglary   8,724
Larceny   13,688
Motor Vehicle Theft   5,612
Arson   247
Per Capita Police Expenditures $99.84
Per Capita Fire Protection Expenditures $81.06
Number of Police   694
Per 1,000   1.85

Religion

Tulsa is noted as the center of the Pentecostal movement, represented by Oral Roberts University and its City of Faith. In addition to Pentecostals, other strong denominations are Baptists, Methodists, and Presbyterians.

Religion	
Largest Denominations (Adherents)	
Catholic	35,032
Assembly of God	12,112
Black Baptist	19,000
Independent Charismatic	15,262
Southern Baptist	111,802
United Methodist	60,172
Church of Christ	9,179
Presbyterian	11,401
Episcopal	5,156
Jewish	1,925

Media

The daily city press consists of the *Tulsa World* and the *Tulsa Daily Business Chronicle*, both published daily. The electronic media consist of 8 television stations and 13 AM and FM radio stations.

Sports

Tulsa has no major professional sports team. The most popular local teams are the Roughnecks of the North American Soccer League, who play at the Metro Christian Acad-

Media

Newsprint
  Tulsa Business Chronicle, weekly
  Tulsa County News, weekly
  Tulsa Daily Business Journal, daily
  Tulsa Magazine, monthly
  The Tulsa Oklahoma Eagle, semiweekly
  Tulsa Star, weekly
  Tulsa World, daily

Television
  NEW (Channel 53)
  KJRH (Channel 2)
  KOED (Channel 11)
  KOKI (Channel 23)
  KOTV (Channel 6)
  KTFO (Channel 41)
  KTUL (Channel 8)
  KWHB (Channel 47)

Radio
  KAKC (AM)   KMOD (FM)
  KBEZ (FM)   KCFO (AM)
  KGTO (AM)   KRAV (FM)
  KQLL (AM)   KRMG (AM)
  KWEN (FM)   KTFX (FM)
  KVOO (AM)   KVOO (FM)
  KWGS (FM)

Travel and Tourism

Hotel Rooms   8,821
Convention and Exhibit Space (square feet)   NA

Convention Centers
  Tulsa Convention Center
  Tulsa Exposition Center

Festivals
  Mayfest
  Tulsa Powwow (July)
  Tulsa State Fair (September)
  Jubilee Art Festival
  Square Dance Festival

emy; the Tulsa Drillers, a Class AA team of Texas League Baseball who play at the Drillers Stadium; the Golden Hurricanes football and basketball teams of the University of Tulsa; and the Titans baseball and basketball teams of ORU. Tulsa sponsors the International Finals Rodeo, a top event on the rodeo circuit.

Arts, Culture, and Tourism

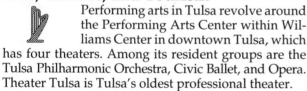

Performing arts in Tulsa revolve around the Performing Arts Center within Williams Center in downtown Tulsa, which has four theaters. Among its resident groups are the Tulsa Philharmonic Orchestra, Civic Ballet, and Opera. Theater Tulsa is Tulsa's oldest professional theater.

Among the major city museums are the Thomas Gilcrease Institute of American History and Art, Tulsa County Historical Society Museum, Gershon and Rebecca Fenser Gallery of Jewish Art, Philbrook Art Center, and the Alexandre Hogue Gallery of Art at Tulsa University.

Parks and Recreation

Tulsa has one of the nation's largest municipal parks, the 2,800-acre Mohawk Park. The Tulsa Municipal Rose Garden, in Woodward Park, features about 12,000 rose plants.

Sources of Further Information

City Hall
200 Civic Center
Tulsa, OK 74103
(918) 596-7777

Metropolitan Tulsa Chamber of Commerce
616 South Boston
Tulsa, OK 74103
(918) 585-1201

Tulsa Convention and Visitors Bureau
616 South Boston
Tulsa, OK 74119
(918) 585-1201

Additional Reading

Blakey, Ellen Sue et al. *Tulsa Spirit.* 1979.
Dunn, Nina L. *Tulsa's Magic Roots.* 1979
Vaughn-Roberson, Courtney Ann and Vaughn-Roberson, Glen. *City in the Osage Hills, Tulsa, Oklahoma.* 1984.

Washington

District of Columbia

Basic Data

Name   Washington, D.C.
Name Origin   From George Washington
Year Founded   1790 Inc. 1790
Status: State   District of Columbia
      County   Capital of the United States
Area (square miles)   61.4
Elevation (feet)   25
Time Zone   EST
Population (1990)   606,900
Population of Metro Area (1990)   3,923,574

Sister Cities
  Bangkok, Thailand
  Beijing, China
  Dakar, Senegal

Distance in Miles To:

Atlanta	618
Boston	448
Chicago	709
Dallas	1,307
Denver	1,616
Detroit	516
Houston	1,365
Miami	1,057
New York	237
Philadelphia	143
St. Louis, MO	862
Los Angeles	2,646

Location and Topography

Washington, D.C., is located at the confluence of the Potomac and Anacostia rivers. It stands on the western edge of the Atlantic coastal plain about midway between the Blue Ridge Mountains and Chesapeake Bay.

Layout of City and Suburbs

Unlike most cities, Washington was designed before it was built. Its first architect, French engineer Pierre Charles L'Enfant, visualized the city as a rectangular network of streets intersected diagonally by broad avenues. The avenues were to be named after the states, and where they met there were to be squares and circles with statues, fountains, and other monuments. At Thomas Jefferson's suggestion, a mile-long Mall extending westward from the future capitol, was made part of L'Enfant's plan. Today the Mall, along with three streets that lead from the capitol—North, East, and South Capitol—divide the city into four sections: Northeast, Southeast, Southwest, and Northwest. Alphabetical streets run east-west, and numbered streets go north-south. Most of the city's government buildings, monuments, and museums are found on Capitol Hill, on or near the Mall, and in the northwest section of the city.

Legally mandated restrictions on building heights have kept the skyline low, with no tall skyscrapers. Much of downtown has undergone rebuilding and renovation in the last decade or two. The areas around Metro Center and Gallery Place and along Pennsylvania Avenue, as well as buildings such as the Convention Center and Union Station, have become showcases. Office buildings at Connecticut Avenue and K Street, NW, have proliferated and spread northwestward toward the residential districts.

Although a planned city, much of modern Washington's growth has been anything but planned. The city was expected to grow eastward from the Capitol, but instead developed westward.

Northwest Washington is the city's largest section and includes nearly half its residents. It encompasses the downtown shopping district, the White House, Washington Monument, Lincoln Memorial, Smithsonian museums, and the Kennedy Center—the city's premier performing arts center. Residential areas representing all income levels are also located here, lying

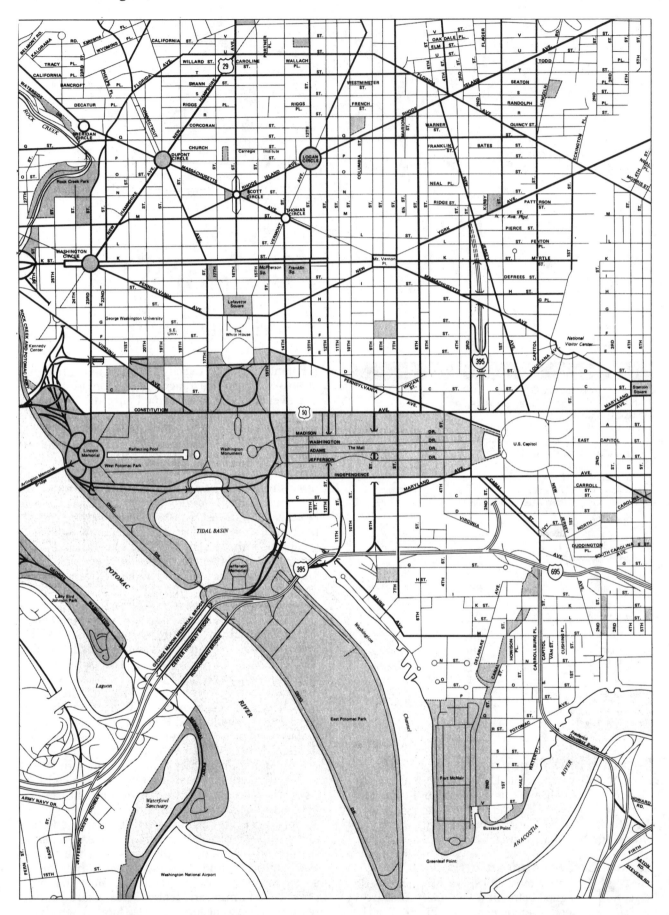

east and west of Rock Creek Park, which divides northwest Washington in half.

Georgetown, to the west of Rock Creek, is an affluent neighborhood of historic homes, some dating back to the 1700s. Upscale bars and nightclubs, small boutiques, and elegant shops line its commercial streets. Once a thriving 18th-century tobacco shipping port at the head of navigation on the Potomac, Georgetown degenerated into a slum a century later; only in about 1930 did it begin to be rehabilitated.

Northeast Washington encompasses about a fourth of the city and is mainly a residential section, home to about a quarter of the city's residents in both middle-class and low-income brackets. Southeast is about the same size as northeast, and includes a wealthy residential section near the Capitol and low-income housing south of the Anacostia River. Southwest Washington is the city's smallest section, with only about 4% of its residents living in what constitutes about an eighth of the entire city. Most of southwest Washington was razed in the 1950s, its old businesses, dilapidated warehouses, and piers replaced by apartments, townhouses, waterfront marinas, restaurants, and the architecturally acclaimed shop, office, and hotel complex called L'Enfant Plaza.

Environment	
Environmental Stress Index 3.0	
Green Cities Index: Rank 49	
Score 35.36	
Water Quality Slightly alkaline, medium soft	
Average Daily Use (gallons per capita) 240	
Maximum Supply (gallons per capita) 210	
Parkland as % of Total City Area NA	
% Waste Landfilled/Recycled 73:8 Incinerated 19	
Annual Parks Expenditures per Capita $97.43	

Climate

Politics, not climate, determined the location of the capital city. Washington is notorious for its muggy weather in summer, when temperatures average in the upper 80s, accompanied by high humidity. Winters are generally mild, with average temperatures in the high 30s and infrequent snows. Falls and springs are generally pleasant.

Weather	
Temperature	
Highest Monthly Average °F 87.9	
Lowest Monthly Average °F 27.5	
Annual Averages	
Days 32°F or Below 75	
Days above 90°F 37	
Zero Degree Days 0	
Precipitation (inches) 39.0	
Snow (inches) 16.0	
% Seasonal Humidity 64.0	
Wind Speed (m.p.h.) 9.3	
Clear Days 101	

Weather (continued)			
Cloudy Days 158			
Storm Days 29			
Rainy Days 111			
Average Temperatures (°F)	*High*	*Low*	*Mean*
January	43.5	27.7	35.6
February	46.0	28.6	37.3
March	55.0	35.2	45.1
April	67.1	45.7	56.4
May	76.6	55.7	66.2
June	84.6	64.6	74.6
July	88.2	69.1	78.7
August	86.6	67.6	77.1
September	80.2	61.0	70.6
October	69.8	49.7	59.8
November	57.2	38.8	48.0
December	45.2	29.5	37.4

History

The Algonquian Indians were the first known residents of the area that became Washington, D.C. In the late 1600s, white settlers moved in and built farms and plantations in the region.

From the the 1780s, when Congress decided that there should be a permanent government center, the choice of a site for the national capital was a cause of great dissension between the North and South. In 1790, Treasury Secretary Alexander Hamilton and Secretary of State Thomas Jefferson worked out a compromise that resulted in a southern site. That same year, Congress authorized President Washington to choose a location for the capital somewhere along the Potomac. The site the president chose was a sparsely settled area, except for the port of Georgetown in Maryland and the city of Alexandria, Virginia.

George Washington engaged Pierre Charles L'Enfant, a French architect, to design the city. L'Enfant's magnificent plan was Baroque in inspiration and enhanced by Thomas Jefferson's guidance. Much of the concept copied Versailles with its great ceremonial open spaces, broad diagonal avenues, and magnificent vistas. Although L'Enfant was eventually dismissed, those who came after him essentially built on his plans and did not radically alter them.

In 1800, President John Adams and his wife Abigail moved south, trading the comforts of Philadelphia for this raw, untamed village where game was shot in fields near the White House and people slogged through swamps and woods. In 1801, Thomas Jefferson was inaugurated as president here. Gradually more homes were built, but the city remained a small, rural town for many years. During the War of 1812 the British, in October 1814, torched almost all the government buildings, including the Capitol and the White House. The city was poorly defended—many had assumed that the enemy would go after a more important place, such as Baltimore. It took some five years for the city to rebuild.

Even in the 1840s Washington remained comparatively small, its population numbering only about 50,000. Economically, it could not compete with Boston, New

Chronology

1790 Alexander Hamilton and Thomas Jefferson establish a compromise for the site of a capital. Congress authorizes its location along the Potomac.

1791 George Washington chooses the exact site of the capital city and appoints French engineer Pierre Charles L'Enfant as the architect.

1792 Construction of the President's House (White House) begins. L'Enfant is dismissed.

1800 John and Abigail Adams move from Philadelphia to Washington to live in the unfinished White House; Congress meets for the first time in the new capitol building.

1801 President Thomas Jefferson is inaugurated in the new capitol.

1814 British capture Washington, burning the White House and most of the other government buildings in the city.

1855 Smithsonian "Castle" Building is completed; it houses laboratories, offices, lecture hall, art gallery, and science museum.

1865 On 14 April, Abraham Lincoln is shot while watching a play at Ford's Theater. He is carried to a house across the street, where he dies the following morning. His body lies in state in the Capitol.

1871 Washington is named federal territory, administered by a governor and council appointed by the president. Only a lower house is to be elected.

1874 Congress establishes new municipal government for Washington consisting of three commissioners appointed by the president.

1884 Washington Monument is completed.

1963 In August Martin Luther King, Jr., leads a march on Washington protesting racial inequities in the country and delivers his now-famous "I Have a Dream" speech. On 22 November, President John F. Kennedy is assassinated in Dallas. His body is brought back to Washington where it lies in state in the Capitol. The city witnesses his somber funeral procession and burial at Arlington National Cemetery.

1968 Riots break out in Washington after the assassination of Martin Luther King, Jr. Ralph Abernathy, Jr., leads the Poor People's March on Washington, protesting the government's attitude toward poverty, welfare, and related issues.

1969– 1970 Protesters pour into Washington to rally against the U.S. government's involvement in the Vietnam War.

1975 Home rule is restored to Washington.

York, or Philadelphia. However, the Civil War, from 1861 to 1865, spurred unprecedented growth. The number of government workers increased the city's population, and added to that were thousands of Union troops and slaves freed by the Emancipation Proclamation. By 1865, Washington's population had reached about 120,000.

In the 1870s, the capital city finally added modern amenities such as sewer, water, and gas lines, as well as improved roads and sidewalks graced by many newly planted trees. In the last decades of the century, a building program resulted in the completion of the Washington Monument, the Old Executive Office Building, and the Library of Congress. At the turn of the century, completion of the neglected Mall was undertaken, with plans for building the Lincoln and Jefferson memorials and for removing railroad tracks and a train depot from the site. But with World War I and yet another growth spurt, the Mall was turned into a parking lot for workers who flocked into the city to help the war effort. It was not until the 1930s that it was finally completed.

The New Deal era and World War II brought another expansion as the city's growth again paralleled the ever-growing role of the federal government. By 1950, Washington's population had reached more than 800,000.

In the past several decades, the capital has been the focus of much of the country's social and economic turbulence. In 1963 a march on Washington protesting racial inequality was led by Martin Luther King, Jr., who delivered his famous "I Have a Dream" speech to more than 100,000 people at the Lincoln Memorial. Five years later, when King was assassinated, riots engulfed much of the inner city, forcing President Lyndon Johnson to call out federal troops. In 1969 and 1970, thousands came to Washington to participate in organized protests and rallies against U.S. involvement in Vietnam.

In recent decades, like many large American cities, Washington has seen many families, both white and black, move to the suburbs to escape an ever-spiraling plague of inner-city drug-related homicides and violence. Nonetheless, the city's world-class museums, active cultural life, and elegant monuments continue to draw thousands of tourists annually.

Historical Landmarks

The Capitol sits atop Jenkins Hill, a high site overlooking the city, deliberately chosen by L'Enfant so the building would dominate the city. It is a magnificent building constructed of white sandstone and marble, crowned by an immense dome atop which stands a bronze

19.5-foot Statue of Freedom. Among its magnificent rooms is the Rotunda. Lying directly beneath the dome, this is where many leaders have lain in state, including Presidents Lincoln and Kennedy.

The Supreme Court Building faces the east side of the Capitol. It was designed by Cass Gilbert and completed in 1935. Also facing the east side of the Capitol is the main building of the Library of Congress—the Thomas Jefferson Building, completed in 1897. It represents the Gilded Age's exuberant architectural style with painted, gilded, and stenciled decor. The Folger Shakespeare Library, a block east of the Capitol, has the biggest collection of Shakespearean items in the world.

Down Pennsylvania Avenue from Capitol Hill lies the White House, at 1600. It was once called the President's House and later the Executive Mansion; not until President Theodore Roosevelt's day was it dubbed the White House. Designed in Neoclassic style by James Hoban and built of sandstone, the 132-room building has been enlarged and renovated a number of times. It consists of a main building flanked by west and east wings. The main building has two columned porticoes; the north portico is the main entrance. The White House stands on a landscaped area bounded on the north by the seven-acre Lafayette Square, an elegant landscaped park with five statues, and on the south by the Ellipse, a grassy expanse of playing fields.

Several historic buildings border Lafayette Square, including St. John's Church, the first building erected here in 1816, and designed by Benjamin Henry Latrobe. It is called the Church of the Presidents, because every president since James Madison has worshipped here at one time or another.

In the Blair-Lee House at 1651 Pennsylvania Avenue, at the beginning of the Civil War, Robert E. Lee was offered command of the Union armies by Montgomery Blair. Lee refused, later taking command of Virginia's forces. Decatur House, designed by Benjamin Henry Latrobe, was built by naval hero Stephen Decatur. Two floors are open to the public.

Nearby is the Old Executive Office Building, a grand Beaux–Arts-style edifice dating to 1888 and once used for cabinet members' offices. Today, presidential staffers work there.

Between the White House and the Capitol is the Federal Triangle with a number of federal buildings. Perhaps most impressive is the Pavilion at the Old Post Office Building, regally restored and replete with shops, eateries, and offices. Nearby is the National Archives, where the Declaration of Independence, Constitution, and Bill of Rights are displayed.

Another nearby historic landmark is Ford's Theater, the playhouse where Abraham Lincoln was shot on 14 April 1865. Petersen House, where he died the following morning, is across the street from the theater.

The mile-long Mall, stretching from the Capitol to the Lincoln Memorial, is rich in historical landmarks, including the original Smithsonian building, the red-brick "Castle" erected in 1855. The most visible structure on the Mall is the Washington Monument, a white marble obelisk just over 555 feet high. The monument overlooks West Potomac Park with its reflecting pool. Beyond is the Lincoln Memorial, a white marble structure with a colonnade of 36 Doric columns resembling a classic Greek temple. Inside is a seated statue of Lincoln, the work of Daniel Chester French. The texts of Lincoln's Gettysburg address and his second inaugural address are inscribed on bronze plaques on the walls.

North of the Lincoln Memorial is the Vietnam Veterans Memorial, designed by Maya Lin and dedicated in 1982. Its black granite walls are inscribed with the names of the 58,000 U.S. military men and women who died or never returned from the Vietnam War.

Southeast of the Washington Monument is the Jefferson Memorial, a small but elegant domed, colonnaded marble building. A 19-foot bronze statue of Jefferson stands beneath the rotunda, and excerpts from his Declaration of Independence and the Virginia Statute for Religious Freedom adorn the walls. The memorial stands amid a grove of Japanese cherry trees, some of the 3,000 given to the United States by Japan in 1912 and planted here along the tidal basin.

Other sites of interest in or around Washington are those in Georgetown, such as the Federal-style houses lining N Street and the Old Stone House at 3051 M Street, the city's oldest building, erected in 1764. Pierce Mill, at Tilden and Beach Drive in Rock Creek Park, is a restored and working grain mill dating to the 1820s. Closer to Dupont Circle is the Woodrow Wilson House at 2340 S Street, NW, the former president's retirement home, built in Georgian Revival style in 1921. Nearby is Anderson House-Society of the Cincinnati at 2118 Massachusetts Avenue. Built in 1902 by Ambassador and Mrs. Larz Anderson, it belongs to the Society of the Cincinnati and is open to the public.

Washington Cathedral, at Wisconsin Avenue and Woodley Road, is a Gothic-style Episcopal church. It was only recently completed, having been under construction since 1907. The grounds were designed by Frederick Law Olmsted. The National Shrine of the Immaculate Conception, at Fourth and Michigan Avenue, NE, is a blend of contemporary, Byzantine, and Romanesque styles, and is the largest Roman Catholic church in the United States.

Across the Potomac in Arlington, Virginia, lies the Pentagon Building, headquarters of the Department of Defense. Nearby are the hills of Arlington National Cemetery, which includes the Tomb of the Unknown Soldier and the grave of John F. Kennedy.

Population

Washington's population has declined since the 1970s as living and social conditions in the city have deteriorated. From 757,000 in 1970 it shrank by 15.6% to 638,333 in 1980, and fell an additional 4.9% to 606,900 in 1990. The median age also rose between 1980 and 1990 from 31.1 years to 33.5. However, the metro population grew by 20.7% between 1980 and 1990, from 3.250 million to 3.924 million.

Population

	1980	1990
Central City	638,333	606,900
Rank	15	19
Metro Area	3,250,921	3,923,574
Pop. Change 1980–1990	-31,433	
Pop. % Change 1980–1990	-4.9	
Median Age 33.5		
% Male 46.6		
% Age 65 and Over 12.8		
Density (per square mile) 9,884		

Households

Number 249,634
Persons per Household 2.26
% Female-Headed Households 19.5
% One-Person Households 41.5
Births—Total 9,666
  % to Mothers under 20 18.0
  Birth Rate per 1,000 15.5

Ethnic Composition

In 1990 blacks composed 65.8% of the population of the district; whites made up 29.6%, Hispanics 5.4%, Asians and Pacific Islanders 1.9%, and American Indians 0.2%.

Ethnic Composition (as % of total pop.)

	1980	1990
White	26.91	29.60
Black	70.32	65.84
American Indian	0.16	0.24
Asian and Pacific Islander	1.04	1.85
Hispanic	2.77	5.39
Other	NA	2.46

Government

The governing of Washington was originally assumed by Congress under the Constitution and the Residence Bill of 1790. A temporary government was established by an act of Congress in 1801. In 1802 Washington received a charter under which the mayor was appointed by the president, and a council was popularly elected. In 1812 the charter was amended to provide for an elected board of aldermen; together with the council, they chose the mayor. From 1820 the mayor also was popularly elected.

After the Civil War, Congress repealed the municipal charter and made the District of Columbia a federal territory. This was replaced in 1874 by a commission form of government, which prevailed until 1967 when

Government

Year of Home Charter 1973
Number of Members of the Governing Body 13
Elected at Large 5
Elected by Wards 8
Number of Women in Governing Body 1
Salary of Mayor $88,065
Salary of Council Members $69,500
City Government Employment Total 43,839
Rate per 10,000 700.3

Congress authorized a new city government headed by a commissioner, or mayor, and a nine-member city council, all of whom were appointed by the president.

In 1975 a new charter went into effect under which voters popularly elect the mayor and a city council of 13 members, 8 from wards and 5 at large, for four-year terms.

While the city may levy taxes and regulate zoning, its budget and laws remain subject to congressional approval. The 23rd Amendment to the Constitution, passed in 1961, gives city residents the right to vote in presidential elections, and a 1970 federal law gives the district one non-voting delegate to the House of Representatives.

Public Finance

The annual budget consists of revenues of $4.323 billion and expenditures of $4.512 billion. The debt outstanding is $3.422 billion, and cash and security holdings are $2.500 billion.

Public Finance

Total Revenue (in millions) $4,323.4
Intergovernmental Revenue—Total (in millions) $1,306.16
Federal Revenue per Capita $1,233.5
% Federal Assistance 28.53
% State Assistance NA
Sales Tax as % of Total Revenue 15.59
Local Revenue as % of Total Revenue 65.83
City Income Tax yes
Taxes—Total (in millions) $1,574.4

Taxes per Capita
  Total $2,515
  Property $727
  Sales and Gross Receipts $789
General Expenditures—Total (in millions) $2,834.7
General Expenditures per Capita $4,528
Capital Outlays per Capita $349

% of Expenditures for:
  Public Welfare 17.2
  Highways 3.2
  Education 16.7
  Health and Hospitals 9.4
  Police 6.4
  Sewerage and Sanitation 4.2
  Parks and Recreation 1.4
  Housing and Community Development 5.8
Debt Outstanding per Capita $3,819
  % Utility 3.8
Federal Procurement Contract Awards (in millions) $2,759.2
Federal Grants Awards (in millions) $1,912.2
Fiscal Year Begins October 1

Economy

The major economic activity in Washington is within the service and business sectors, although the principal activity in Washington remains government, which engages a large portion of the population. Other strong economic sectors are trade, tourism, and construction.

Economy

Total Money Income (in millions) $8,469.7
% of State Average 100.0
Per Capita Annual Income $13,530
% Population below Poverty Level 18.6
Fortune 500 Companies 3

Banks	Number	Deposits (in millions)
Commercial	160	31,720.0
Savings	NA	NA

Passenger Autos 252,452
Electric Meters 1,180,000
Gas Meters 658,000

Manufacturing

Number of Establishments 564.6
% with 20 or More Employees 25.5
Manufacturing Payroll (in millions) $494.1
Value Added by Manufacture (in millions) $1,525.4
Value of Shipments (in millions) $2,128.3
New Capital Expenditures (in millions) $43.6

Wholesale Trade

Number of Establishments 554
Sales (in millions) $2,846.2
Annual Payroll (in millions) $231.591

Retail Trade

Number of Establishments 4,478
Total Sales (in millions) $3,464.9
Sales per Capita $5,534
Number of Retail Trade Establishments with Payroll 3,681
Annual Payroll (in millions) $575.4
Total Sales (in millions) $3,423.0
General Merchandise Stores (per capita) $502
Food Stores (per capita) $943
Apparel Stores (per capita) $521
Eating and Drinking Places (per capita) $1,336

Service Industries

Total Establishments 7,486
Total Receipts (in millions) $7,882.5
Hotels and Motels (in millions) $679.4
Health Services (in millions) $584.6
Legal Services (in millions) $2,992.4

Labor

Washington has the largest concentration of government workers in the nation; government workers make up 25% of the work force. Manufacturing is the second-lowest employment sector. Nearly 40% of the work force is highly skilled. Washington is also home to an important group of employers made up of lobbyists, com-

Labor

Civilian Labor Force 298,000
% Change 1989–1990 -5.4

Work Force Distribution
Mining 1,000
Construction 106,500
Manufacturing 83,100
Transportation and Public Utilities 104,400

Labor (continued)

Wholesale and Retail Trade 416,300
FIRE (Finance, Insurance, Real Estate) 130,900
Service 748,700
Government 595,900
Women as % of Labor Force 51.1
% Self-Employed 4.2
% Professional/Technical 23.9
Total Unemployment 20,000
Rate % 6.6
Federal Government Civilian Employment 215,926

munications and media firms, lawyers, accountants, public relations firms, and public affairs research organizations. Numerous labor unions and trade associations are also located in the city.

Education

The District of Columbia Board of Education supports 181 elementary, junior high/middle, senior high, and special education schools. About 95% of the public school population is black, resulting in de facto segregation. Many whites send their children to the 80 private or parochial schools. The only public higher-education institution is the University of the District of Columbia. Gallaudet College for the Deaf, founded in 1857, and Howard University, an African American institution founded in 1867, receive appropriations from Congress. Washington's oldest university is Georgetown, the first Roman Catholic college in the United States, founded in 1789 and directed by Jesuits since 1805. George Washington University was founded in 1821 as Columbian College. Catholic University of America, founded in 1889, is directly controlled by the church hierarchy. American University was established in 1893 by the Methodists. Two specialized institutions are National War College and Industrial College of the Armed Forces at Fort McNair. Other colleges include Southeastern University, Trinity College, Strayer College, and Wesley Theological Seminary.

Education

Number of Public Schools 181
Special Education Schools 12
Total Enrollment 80,694
% Enrollment in Private Schools 13.5
% Minority 96.1
Classroom Teachers 4,666
Pupil-Teacher Ratio 17.2:1
Number of Graduates 3,626
Total Revenue (in millions) $483.940
Total Expenditures (in millions) $561.167
Expenditures per Pupil $5,872
Educational Attainment (Age 25 and Over)
    % Completed 12 or More Years 67.1
    % Completed 16 or More Years 27.5
Four-Year Colleges and Universities 13
    Enrollment 79,675
Two-Year Colleges NA
    Enrollment NA

Education (continued)

Libraries

Number 447
Public Libraries 26
Books (in thousands) 1.620
Circulation (in thousands) 1.979
Persons Served (in thousands) 628
Circulation per Person Served 3.15
Income (in millions) $18.517
Staff 437

Four-Year Colleges and Universities
The American University
Catholic University of America
Corcoran School of Art
Gallaudet University
George Washington University
Georgetown University
Howard University
Mount Vernon College
Oblate College
Southeastern University
University of the District of Columbia
Trinity College
Strayer College

Health

There are 17 hospitals in the city, the largest of which is D.C. General Hospital, affiliated with Howard University and Georgetown University. Both Georgetown University and George Washington University have hospitals. The major psychiatric facility is St. Elizabeth Hospital, founded in 1852.

Health

Deaths—Total 6,762
Rate per 1,000 10.9
Infant Deaths—Total 203
Rate per 1,000 21.0
Number of Metro Hospitals 17
Number of Metro Hospital Beds 8,309
Rate per 100,000 1,327
Number of Physicians 10,172
Physicians per 1,000 3.39
Nurses per 1,000 9.02
Health Expenditures per Capita $253.98

Transportation

Washington is encircled by a beltway, I-495. Also providing access to the city are I-95, I-270, I-395, and I-66. In the 1950s and 1960s, Washington embarked on an ambitious network of freeways and radial highways, but this plan was gradually replaced with a rapid-transit system. Construction of Metro—a subway—began in the early 1970s, and the first section of a proposed 100-mile system with 86 stations opened in 1976. The subway links the city with the suburbs of Virginia and Maryland.

Washington has one of the most impressive train terminals in the nation in Union Station, completed in 1907. After a period of decline, rail passenger traffic has been revived with Amtrak's Metroliner service to New York and other cities.

Three major airports serve the Washington area: Washington National, across the Potomac in Virginia, minutes from downtown by car or the Metro; Dulles International, also in Virginia; and Baltimore-Washington International, midway between Washington and Baltimore.

Transportation

Interstate Highway Mileage 163
Total Urban Mileage 8,452
Total Daily Vehicle Mileage (in millions) $62.980
Daily Average Commute Time 64.5 min.
Number of Buses 1,433
Port Tonnage (in millions) $0.536
Airports 3
Number of Daily Flights 461
Daily Average Number of Passengers 31,339

Airlines (American carriers only)
American
American West
Continental
Delta
Northwest
Trans World
United
USAir

Housing

About 50% of the people live in one-or two-family homes and others in apartments. About 40% own their own homes, compared to a national average of 48%. The city faces a shortage of good housing for low income as well as moderate-income families. Since the 1960s the cost of housing has risen faster in Washington than in comparable cities.

Housing

Total Housing Units 278,489
% Change 1980–1990 0.5
Vacant Units for Sale or Rent 19,907
Occupied Units 249,634
% with More Than One Person per Room 8.2
% Owner-Occupied 38.9
Median Value of Owner-Occupied Homes $123,900
Average Monthly Purchase Cost $399
Median Monthly Rent $441
New Private Housing Starts 368
Value (in thousands) $20,801
% Single-Family 48.9
Nonresidential Buildings Value (in thousands) $19,378

Urban Redevelopment

Urban blight in residential areas and business districts has affected Washington more than most other cities, although the well-kept condition of public buildings obscures that fact. Development has been rapid in areas beyond the city line, where housing developments, shopping centers, and apartment buildings have taken up land originally set aside as parks. Renovation projects have involved Union Station and the Pennsylvania Avenue corridor, including the Old Post Office Building and Willard Hotel. Metro has encouraged redevelopment near its stations, such as the new campus of the University of the District of Columbia.

Crime

 Washington has achieved a kind of notoriety in recent decades as a crime capital. Violent crimes in 1991 totaled 14,665, including 482 murders. Crimes involving property numbered 49,654, including 12,403 burglaries.

Crime	
Violent Crimes—Total	14,665
Violent Crime Rate per 100,000	785.1
Murder	482
Rape	214
Robbery	7,265
Aggravated Assaults	6,704
Property Crimes	49,654
Burglary	12,403
Larceny	29,119
Motor Vehicle Theft	8,132
Arson	256
Per Capita Police Expenditures	$446.88
Per Capita Fire Protection Expenditures	$158.22
Number of Police	3,837
Per 1,000	6.13

Religion

 Washington has a number of imposing religious buildings, among them the Episcopal Cathedral Church of St. Peter and St. Paul, generally known as Washington Cathedral. Begun in 1907 and completed only in the 1980s, its Gloria in Excelsis Central Tower is the highest point in Washington. The National Shrine of the Immaculate Conception is the largest Catholic church in the nation. St. John's Episcopal Church, located near the White House, is known as the Church of the Presidents because a number of presidents have worshiped there.

Religion	
Largest Denominations (Adherents)	
Catholic	77,532
Southern Baptist	17,597
Episcopal	16,273
American Zion	39,500
American Baptist	33,744
Black Baptist	102,897
United Methodist	18,321
Presbyterian	9,629
Jewish	25,400

Media

As the capital, Washington is the nerve center of national and international communications. Foreign correspondents from almost every nation are stationed here. There are two general daily newpapers: the *Washington Post* and *The Washington Times. USA Today,* a national paper published by Gannett, is based in Arlington, Virginia. The electronic media consist of 6 television stations and 19 AM and FM radio stations.

Media	
Newsprint	
Washington Afro-American Newspaper, weekly	
Washington Informer, weekly	
Washington News Observer, weekly	
Washington Post, daily	
The Washington Times, daily	
The Washingtonian, monthly	
Television	
WDCA (Channel 20)	
WHMM (Channel 32)	
WJLA (Channel 7)	
WRC (Channel 4)	
WTTG (Channel 5)	
WUSA (Channel 9)	
Radio	
WAMU (FM)	WAVA (FM)
WDCU (FM)	WHUR (FM)
WJZE (FM)	WKYS (FM)
WMAL (AM)	WMMG (FM)
WPGC (AM)	WPGC (FM)
WRQX (FM)	WMZQ (AM)
WMZQ (FM)	WOL (AM)
WPFW (FM)	WTOP (AM)
WASH (FM)	WUST (AM)
WYCB (AM)	

Sports

 Washington is home to three major league professional sports teams, although only one is actually resident. The Washington Redskins of the National Football League carry the hopes of the city at Robert F. Kennedy Memorial Stadium. The Washington Capitals of the National Hockey League and the Washington Bullets of the National Basketball Association both play at Capital Center in nearby Largo, Maryland.

Arts, Culture, and Tourism

 Washington offers cultural attractions on a grand scale. Performing arts revolve around the John F. Kennedy Center for the Performing Arts, the capital's cultural showpiece. It is the home of the National Symphony Orchestra, American Ballet Theater, and Washington Opera. The Arena Stage and Kreeger Theater are nationally known for their fine productions. The National Theatre serves primarily as a rehearsal stage for productions destined for New York. The historic Ford's Theater was restored in 1968 and is used for theatrical productions. Other performing arts centers include Folger Theater and Warner Theater. Local theater groups perform at Source Theatre and Studio Theatre. Lisner Auditorium at George Washington University presents various kinds of performances.

The Smithsonian Institution, nicknamed America's Attic, administers more than a dozen museums. Most are on the Mall, including the National Air and Space Museum, Joseph H. Hirshhorn Museum and Sculpture

Garden, Arts and Industries Building, National Museum of Natural History, National Museum of American History, National Museum of African Art, Arthur M. Sackler Gallery, and Freer Gallery of Art. The National Gallery of Art is under the Smithsonian, but has its own administration. Off the Mall, the Smithsonian oversees the National Museum of American Art, National Portrait Gallery, Renwick Gallery, the Anacostia Neighborhood Museum, and the Holocaust Museum.

Other museums include the Corcoran Gallery of Art, which houses a fine collection of American paintings; National Museum of Women in the Arts; National Building Museum; Phillips Collection; and specialized museums such as the Textile Museum, the D.A.R.'s Decorative Arts Collection, and the collections of Byzantine and pre-Columbian art and history at Dumbarton Oaks.

Travel and Tourism

Hotel Rooms 60,569
Convention and Exhibit Space (square feet) 381,000

Convention Centers
  Washington Convention Center
  DC Armory Starplex

Festivals
  Potomac Riverfest (June)
  Festival of American Folk Life (June)
  Cherry Blossom Festival (spring)

Parks and Recreation

Washington was planned by L'Enfant to be a city of parks, and his original design included a number of them. Foremost among them is the Mall, running west from the Capitol to the Potomac and its cross-axis running from the tidal basin to the White House. The largest of the formal parks is Rock Creek Park, which follows the course of Rock Creek through the northwestern part of the city.

Sources of Further Information

D.C. Chamber of Commerce
1301 Pennsylvania Avenue, NW, Suite 309
Washington, DC 20004
(202) 347-7201

Office of the Mayor
441 Fourth Street, NW, 11th floor
Washington, DC 20001
(202) 727-6319

Washington, D.C., Convention and Visitors
  Association
1212 New York Avenue, NW
Washington, DC 20005
(202) 789-7000

Additional Reading

Capitol

Aikman, Lonnelle. *We the People: The Story of the United States Capitol.* 1991.
Brown, Glenn. *History of the United States Capitol.* 1st ed. 1900–1903. 1970.

Description

Daniels, Jonathan. *Frontier on the Potomac.*1946.
Highsmith, Carol M., and Ted Landphair. *Embassies of Washington.*1992.
*Union Station: A Decorative History of Washington's Grand Terminal.*1988.

Guidebooks

Applewhite, E. J. *Washington Itself: An Informal Guide to the Capital of the United States.*1981.
Chapin, Isolde. *Writer's Guide to Washington.*1983.
Duffield, Judy. *Washington, D.C.: The Complete Guide.*1991.
Fitzpatrick, Sandra, and Maria R. Goodwin. *The Guide to Black Washington.*1990.
Kennon, Donald R., and Richard Striner. *Washington, Past and Present: A Guide to the Nation's Capital.* 2nd ed. 1983.
Pratson, Frederick John. *Guide to Washington, D.C. and Beyond.*1989.

Directories

Arden, Lorraine, Carolyn Blakeslee, and Drew Steis. *Washington Art: A Guide to Galleries, Art Consultants, and Museums.*1988.
Congressional Quarterly. *Washington Information Directory, 1992–1993.*1991.
Russell, John J., ed. *Washington 91.*1991.

History

Arnebeck, Bob. *Through a Fiery Trial: Building Washington 1790–1800.*1991.
Bowling, Kenneth R. *The Creation of Washington, D.C.: The Idea and Location of the American Capital.*1990.
Furer, Howard B. *Washington, D.C.: A Chronological & Documentary History.*1975.
Green, Constance McLaughlin. *Washington: A History of the Capital.*4 vols. 1962–1963.
Junior League of Washington. *The City of Washington: An Illustrated History.*1977.
Lewis, David L. *District of Columbia: A Bicentennial History.*1976.
Porter, John A. *The City of Washington, Its Origin and Administration.*1st ed., 1885. 1973.

White House

The White House: An Historic Guide. 1987.

Waterbury

Connecticut

Basic Data

Name   Waterbury
Name Origin   From the Waugatuck River
Year Founded   1674 Inc. 1853
Status: State   Connecticut
         County   New Haven County
Area (square miles)   28.6
Elevation (feet)   260
Time Zone   EST
Population (1990)   108,961
Population of Metro Area (1990)   804,219

Distance in Miles To:

New York	85
Hartford	32
Kingston, RI	105
Boston	130
Providence	117
New Haven	38

Location and Topography

Waterbury is located in New Haven County in west-central Connecticut. Built on a rocky plain in the Naugatuck River Valley, the city is bounded by granite hills to the east and west. The Mad River runs through the east side, curves to the west, and joins the Naugatuck River.

Layout of City and Suburbs

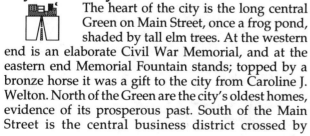

The heart of the city is the long central Green on Main Street, once a frog pond, shaded by tall elm trees. At the western end is an elaborate Civil War Memorial, and at the eastern end Memorial Fountain stands; topped by a bronze horse it was a gift to the city from Caroline J. Welton. North of the Green are the city's oldest homes, evidence of its prosperous past. South of the Main Street is the central business district crossed by

Meadow, State, Church, Leavenworth, Bank, and South Main streets. The city's Clock Tower on Meadow Street is visible for miles. The city's religious heritage is evident in the large number of churches.

Environment

Environmental Stress Index   2.2
Green Cities Index: Rank   NA
                    Score   NA
Water Quality   Neutral, moderately soft, fluoridated
Average Daily Use (gallons per capita)   NA
      Maximum Supply (gallons per capita)   NA
Parkland as % of Total City Area   NA
% Waste Landfilled/Recycled   NA
Annual Parks Expenditures per Capita $47.20

Climate

Waterbury has a typically inland Connecticut climate with breezy springs and autumns, warm humid summers, and cold dry winters. Snowfall averages 38 inches a year.

Weather

Temperature

Highest Monthly Average °F   72.5
Lowest Monthly Average °F   27.4

Annual Averages

Days 32°F or Below   121
Days above 90°F   7
Zero Degree Days   2
Precipitation (inches)   50.10
Snow (inches)   38.1
% Seasonal Humidity   NA
Wind Speed (m.p.h.)   NA
Clear Days   NA
Cloudy Days   NA
Storm Days   NA
Rainy Days   NA

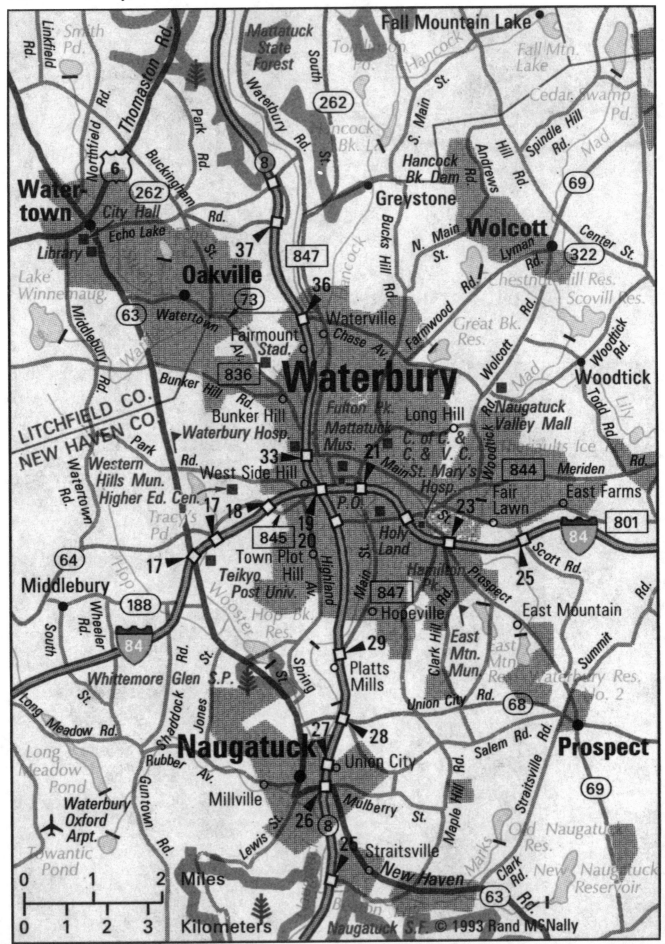

Weather (continued)			
Average Temperatures (°F)	High	Low	Mean
January	35.1	19.8	27.4
February	37.1	20.9	29.1
March	45.5	28.9	37.2
April	58.4	38.3	48.4
May	69.2	47.6	58.5
June	78.1	56.9	67.5
July	82.7	62.3	72.5
August	80.4	61.1	70.7
September	72.4	53.6	63.0
October	62.3	43.8	53.1
November	51.2	35.2	43.2
December	39.1	24.5	31.8

History

Known to the Indians as Mattatuck (a corruption of Matetcoke, or "land without trees") the tract of land on which Waterbury stands was purchased by settlers from Farmington in 1674 for $38. The town was incorporated and renamed Waterbury in 1686. The area was so rugged and barren that the settlers believed that it could not accommodate more than 30 families. The town suffered much from the Great Flood of 1691 and an epidemic in 1712. For the next 35 years the town did not grow much beyond the original population of 150. It was chartered as a city in 1853, and the surrounding area merged with Waterbury in 1901.

Waterbury's rise to industrial eminence as the brass capital of the world began in the early decades of the 19th century. The early braziers bought scrap brass, bronze, copper, and zinc, and melted their own metal. Early button shops flourished in 1790. In 1802 James Harraison built a water wheel and applied hydropower to the manufacture of clocks. By 1814 there were four clock makers in the city. Sundries were added to the city's production by 1820. Waterbury furnished much of the stock for Yankee peddlers for the remainder of the century. The brass industry owed much to imported English labor. James Croft was hired from England by Leavenworth, Hayden, and Scovill in 1820 to produce the striking orange tint that Americans then favored in their brass buttons. A variety of better finishes became possible after electroplating was developed in 1837. Isaac Holmes invented methods for making pins with drawn wire in 1831, and for producing brazed tubing in 1836. The disks for U.S. nickels were blanked by Waterbury mills, and coins for many South American countries were produced here. Cartridge brass formed a large percentage of the city's production, along with shell cases, time fuses, and the hydraulic speed gears that turned battleship turrets. While the men worked in the brass factories, their wives and daughters were employed in the production of watches. The Waterbury Clock Company, formed in 1857, manufactured 500,000 watches annually until 1922. The American Brass Association, formed in 1853, was the first trade association in America. Among its members, all located in Waterbury, were the American Brass Company (unit of Anaconda Copper Company since 1922), A. S. Chase (unit of Kennecott Copper Company since 1929), Scovill, Somers Brass, and Waterbury Rolling Mills. At its peak during World War II, 10,000 people worked at Scovill, and all the mills in the city's east end occupied more than 2 million square feet and more than 90 buildings.

After World War II, the brass manufacturing industry faltered. The city's last brass mill closed in the 1970s. Since then, the city has rebuilt itself by diversifying into other industries and embarking on an aggressive construction and remodeling program.

Historical Landmarks

As one of the original towns of the Connecticut Colony, Waterbury displays a proud architectural heritage of which the following are most notable:

• The Cooke Homestead, a white gabled house with green trim, is the city's only remaining old house. Some of its timbers are from the original 1741 structure.

• The brick and limestone Chase Brass and Copper Company office building on the corner of Grand and Leavenworth streets, an entire city block wide, was designed by Cass Gilbert and erected in 1917. The Municipal Building, the Chase Infirmary, the Waterbury Bank, and Waterbury Club also were designed by Gilbert, making the city an unusual showcase of one of America's great architects.

Population

With a population of 108,961 in 1990, Waterbury is among the few cities in the northeast that have grown in numbers, growing by 5.5% from its 1980 population of 103,266.

Population		
	1980	1990
Central City	103,266	108,961
Rank	158	170
Metro Area	761,325	804,219
Pop. Change 1980–1990 +5,695		
Pop. % Change 1980–1990 +5.5		
Median Age 33.1		
% Male 47.3		
% Age 65 and Over 16.5		
Density (per square mile) 3,809		

Households
Number 43,164
Persons per Household 2.48
% Female-Headed Households 15.4
% One-Person Households 29.7
Births—Total 1,631
% to Mothers under 20 15.1
Birth Rate per 1,000 15.9

Ethnic Composition

While the original stock of Waterbury residents were from the British Isles, they were joined in the 19th and early-20th centuries by Italians, Poles, French, Lithuanians, and Russians. The black presence is smaller than in other

Chronology

1674	Settlers from Farmington buy a tract of land in Mattatuck for $38.
1686	Mattatuck is renamed Waterbury, and is admitted as the 26th town in the Colony of Connecticut.
1691	The Great Flood devastates town.
1712	Epidemic strikes town.
1802	James Harraison builds water wheel and applies technology to manufacture clocks.
1853	Waterbury is incorporated as a city.
1901	The areas surrounding Waterbury are merged with the city.
1902	Fire burns the entire business section of Waterbury.
1955	A flood of the Naugatuck River kills 87 people and buries much of the city under mud.

Connecticut cities, such as New Haven and Hartford with only 13%. Whites make up 80%, and other races 7%.

Ethnic Composition (as % of total pop.)

	1980	1990
White	83.53	79.55
Black	11.64	12.97
American Indian	0.20	0.32
Asian and Pacific Islander	0.31	0.72
Hispanic	6.69	13.38
Other	NA	6.44

Government

Waterbury operates under a mayor-council form of government The mayor and the 15 aldermen are elected to two-year terms.

Government

Year of Home Charter 1957
Number of Members of the Governing Body 15
Elected at Large 15
Elected by Wards NA
Number of Women in Governing Body 2
Salary of Mayor $85,300
Salary of Council Members $4,000
City Government Employment Total 3,372
Rate per 10,000 329.6

Public Finance

Waterbury's budget consists of revenues of $211.338 million and expenditures of $232.569 million, leaving a deficit of $21.231 million. The debt outstanding is $71.548 million and cash and security holdings $73.411 million.

Public Finance

Total Revenue (in millions) $211.38
Intergovernmental Revenue—Total (in millions) $97.39
Federal Revenue per Capita $16.67
% Federal Assistance 7.89
% State Assistance 38.17
Sales Tax as % of Total Revenue NA
Local Revenue as % of Total Revenue 43.7
City Income Tax no
Taxes—Total (in millions) $61.0
Taxes per Capita
   Total $596
   Property $582
   Sales and Gross Receipts $0
General Expenditures—Total (in millions) $114.3
General Expenditures per Capita $1,117
Capital Outlays per Capita $28
% of Expenditures for:
   Public Welfare 6.2
   Highways 2.3
   Education 45.5
   Health and Hospitals 1.1
   Police 8.1
   Sewerage and Sanitation 5.2
   Parks and Recreation 2.1
   Housing and Community Development 1.0
Debt Outstanding per Capita $674
   % Utility 4.5
Federal Procurement Contract Awards (in millions) $30.6
Federal Grants Awards (in millions) $9.1
Fiscal Year Begins July 1

Economy

Economically, the middle decades of this century were the worst in Waterbury's history. The city came to the brink of disaster as its brass mills, on which its prosperity was based, were closed. City hall faced a shrinking tax base and the central business district became a shell of its former glory. A revitalization effort, begun in the 1980s, helped to stay the slide to economic failure. Many historic buildings were renovated and the infrastructure was modernized. The industrial base was diversified. The city also has emerged as the second largest retail market in the state. Scovill, one of the Fortune 500 companies, remains the bellwether of the corporate sector. Colonial Bank, Century Brass Products, and McDermaid are among the other corporations headquartered in the city. The tax base has

Economy

Total Money Income (in millions) $1,042.1
% of State Average 72.3
Per Capita Annual Income $10,187
% Population below Poverty Level 14.1
Fortune 500 Companies NA

Banks	Number	Deposits (in millions)
Commercial	5	4,949.4
Savings	4	2,111.9

Passenger Autos 460,617
Electric Meters 82,813
Gas Meters 29,607

Economy *(continued)*

Manufacturing

Number of Establishments   242
% with 20 or More Employees   38.8
Manufacturing Payroll (in millions) $261.8
Value Added by Manufacture (in millions) $631.1
Value of Shipments (in millions) $1,087.3
New Capital Expenditures (in millions) $35.4

Wholesale Trade

Number of Establishments   166
Sales (in millions) $428.2
Annual Payroll (in millions) $47.374

Retail Trade

Number of Establishments   1,061
Total Sales (in millions) $855.6
Sales per Capita $8,364
Number of Retail Trade Establishments with Payroll   713
Annual Payroll (in millions) $93.8
Total Sales (in millions) $833.4
General Merchandise Stores (per capita) $1,296
Food Stores (per capita) $1,803
Apparel Stores (per capita) $637
Eating and Drinking Places (per capita) $506

Service Industries

Total Establishments   765
Total Receipts (in millions) $350.7
Hotels and Motels (in millions)   NA
Health Services (in millions) $149.9
Legal Services (in millions) $35.5

doubled between 1980 and 1988. Waterbury has become one of the striking examples of urban renewal in the United States.

Labor

Waterbury's economy created 12,000 new jobs between 1980 and 1990. Of the 88,000 workers in the city, 27.5% are employed in manufacturing, 24.1% in services, and 19.3% in trade. The largest employers are the city's two hospitals, St. Mary's and Waterbury.

Labor

Civilian Labor Force   50,958
% Change 1989–1990   1.6

Work Force Distribution
　Mining   NA
　Construction   2,800
　Manufacturing   18,400
　Transportation and Public Utilities   3,300
　Wholesale and Retail Trade   16,600
　FIRE (Finance, Insurance, Real Estate)   4,000
　Service   23,100
　Government   12,700
　Women as % of Labor Force   44.9
　% Self-Employed   3.4
　% Professional/Technical   12.0
Total Unemployment   4,465
Rate %   8.8
Federal Government Civilian Employment   604

Education

The Waterbury public school system consists of 27 senior high, junior high/middle, and elementary schools. The parochial school system consists of two high schools and 11 elementary schools.

Waterbury has no independent institution of higher education, but is served by three extension campuses: University of Connecticut – Waterbury, University of New Haven, and Teikyo Post College. Two-year institutions include Mattatuck Community College and Waterbury State Technical College.

Education

Number of Public Schools   27
Special Education Schools   NA
Total Enrollment   13,000
% Enrollment in Private Schools   19.4
% Minority   NA
Classroom Teachers   NA
Pupil-Teacher Ratio   15.1:1
Number of Graduates   NA
Total Revenue (in millions)   NA
Total Expenditures (in millions)   NA
Expenditures per Pupil   NA
Educational Attainment (Age 25 and Over)   NA
　% Completed 12 or More Years   55.4
　% Completed 16 or More Years   9.4
Four-Year Colleges and Universities   3
　Enrollment   2,082
Two-Year Colleges   2
　Enrollment   5,772

Libraries

Number   10
Public Libraries   2
Books (in thousands)   166
Circulation (in thousands)   274
Persons Served (in thousands)   111
Circulation per Person Served   2.46
Income (in millions) $1.431
Staff   61

Four-Year Colleges and Universities
　Teikyo Post University
　University of Connecticut – Waterbury
　University of New Haven – Waterbury

Health

The city's major medical institutions are the Waterbury Hospital and St. Mary's Hospital, with a combined total of 829 beds.

Health

Deaths—Total   1,210
Rate per 1,000   11.8
Infant Deaths—Total   16
Rate per 1,000   9.8
Number of Metro Hospitals   2
Number of Metro Hospital Beds   848
Rate per 100,000   829
Number of Physicians   NA
Physicians per 1,000   NA
Nurses per 1,000   NA
Health Expenditures per Capita $30.01

Transportation

The city's transportation lifeline is the north-south I-84 which connects it with Hartford to the northeast and New York and Pennsylvania to the southwest. It is bisected by the north-south Route 8 which links the city with I-95.

Daily bus services connect the city with Bradley International Airport at Windsor Locks and the New York airports. There are 26 buses serving commuters within the city. Waterbury suffers from the lack of a navigable waterway. Much of the freight is handled by Conrail.

Transportation

Interstate Highway Mileage   9
Total Urban Mileage   672
Total Daily Vehicle Mileage (in millions) $2.751
Daily Average Commute Time   42.9 min.
Number of Buses   26
Port Tonnage (in millions)   NA
Airports   NA
Number of Daily Flights   NA
Daily Average Number of Passengers   NA

Airlines (American carriers only)
   American
   Continental
   Delta
   Eastern
   Midway
   United
   USAir

Housing

Waterbury led all Connecticut cities in new housing starts from 1985 through 1990. Many of the older residential buildings are in need of repair, and are targeted by the city's development programs for special assistance.

Housing

Total Housing Units   47,205
% Change 1980–1990   13.5
Vacant Units for Sale or Rent   3,387
Occupied Units   43,164
% with More Than One Person per Room   3.3
% Owner-Occupied   49.0
Median Value of Owner-Occupied Homes $131,800
Average Monthly Purchase Cost $364
Median Monthly Rent $404
New Private Housing Starts   354
Value (in thousands) $13,041
% Single-Family   81.4
Nonresidential Buildings Value (in thousands) $2,312

Urban Redevelopment

In 1978 the city's major downtown redevelopment program came into being. The 50,000 square feet, $3.5 million First Federal Savings Bank Plaza opened at the corner of Bank Street and Grand Street. In 1979 a new city police station was opened on East Main Street, and 1980 saw the completion of the largest new development in decades, the 155,000 square foot Plaza on the Green. This $15 million commercial/residential complex re-

defined the appearance of Exchange Place, where North, South, East and West Main Streets converge. After 1980, the city's economic recovery accelerated the renovation programs. In 1982 the central Green was fully renovated with $300,000 worth of new sidewalks, benches, lighting, and landscaping. In 1982 the $9-million Exchange Place Tower was built in the southeast corner of Exchange Place. The major renovation projects that followed were: the Center Street Apartment/Retail Complex in 1983, renovations of the 1900 Corbo Building, the 1898 Carriage House, and the 1830 Miller and Peck Building, all in 1984; the conversion of the 1904 Margaret Croft School into a professional and office space, the Buckingham Square project in 1985, and renovations to the 1865 Tuscon Villa, the 1930 Farrington Building, the 1894 Apothecary Hall, the 1905 Moriarty Building, the 1930 Brown Building, the 1906 Frederick Building, and the 1889 Rectory Building, all between 1986 and 1990. Two industrial parks have helped to enlarge Waterbury's industrial capacity: the 120-acre Captain Neville Industrial Park, and the 119-acre Reidville Drive Industrial Park. New development projects include the Renaissance Mall, the largest enclosed shopping mall in New England, North Square Plaza in the North Square, the River Edge Square shopping plaza, and the Gateway Center Business Park.

The master plan initiated 20 years ago is being continued in two major projects planned for the next 15 years: the Heritage Park along the banks of the Naugatuck River and the Crossroads Center on 50 acres in the Enterprise Zone, west of the Central Business District.

Crime

The crime rate in Waterbury is half that of the large cities in Connecticut: 49% below New Haven, 45% below Bridgeport, and 55% below Hartford.

Crime

Violent Crimes—Total   845
Violent Crime Rate per 100,000   503.1
Murder   9
Rape   32
Robbery   388
Aggravated Assaults   416
Property Crimes   9,329
Burglary   2,920
Larceny   4,985
Motor Vehicle Theft   1,424
Arson   13
Per Capita Police Expenditures $145.73
Per Capita Fire Protection Expenditures $142.05
Number of Police   251
Per 1,000   2.42

Religion

Catholicism is strong in Waterbury, which has over 100 churches.

Religion	
Largest Denominations (Adherents)	
Catholic	368,313
United Church of Christ	26,033
Episcopal	15,036
American Baptist	10,770
Black Baptist	19,391
United Methodist	9,966
Evangelical Lutheran	6,090
Assembly of God	3,077
Jewish	34,250

Media

 The Waterbury Republican is published in the morning and *The Waterbury American* in the evening. Residents can pick up New Haven and Hartford television and radio signals. In addition there is one local television station and four AM and FM stations.

Media	
Newsprint	
The Waterbury Republican-American, daily	
Television	
WTXX (Channel 20)	
Radio	
WATR (AM)	WWYZ (FM)
WQQW (AM)	WWCO (AM)

Sports

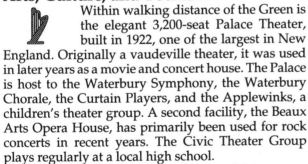 The Waterbury Indians, a double A farm team of the Cleveland Indians of the American League East, play at the Municipal Stadium April through November. The Municipal Stadium is the home of the NCAA sponsored Connecticut Yankees of the ACBL, the Mickey Mantle World Series, and the Stan Musial State Tournament.

Arts, Culture, and Tourism

Within walking distance of the Green is the elegant 3,200-seat Palace Theater, built in 1922, one of the largest in New England. Originally a vaudeville theater, it was used in later years as a movie and concert house. The Palace is host to the Waterbury Symphony, the Waterbury Chorale, the Curtain Players, and the Applewinks, a children's theater group. A second facility, the Beaux Arts Opera House, has primarily been used for rock concerts in recent years. The Civic Theater Group plays regularly at a local high school.

The principal museum is the Mattatuck Museum, a rich treasure house of Waterbury history. Other museums include the Museum of American Political Life, Carousel Museum, Canton Historical Museum, American Clock and Watch Museum, and the American Indian Archeological Institute.

Travel and Tourism	
Hotel Rooms NA	
Convention and Exhibit Space (square feet) NA	
Convention Centers	
Sheraton Waterbury	
Festivals	
Italian Heritage Festival	
Traditional Folk Music Festival	
September Festival	

Parks and Recreation

The Mattatuck State Forest and the Black Rock State Forest are close to the city. There are bathing, fishing, and boating facilities at Lakewood within the city and and at Lake Quassapaug and Hitchcock Lake outside city limits. There are two 18-hole golf courses, East Mountain and Western Hills. The city maintains 35 parks and playgrounds, offering a variety of recreational opportunities.

Sources of Further Information

Waterbury UP Committee
101 South Main Street
Waterbury, CT 06722-2122
(203) 757-9621

Silas Bronson Library
267 Grand Street
Waterbury, CT 06702
(203) 574-8200

Greater Waterbury Chamber of Commerce
83 Bank Street
Waterbury, CT 06721
(203) 757-0701

Additional Reading

Anderson, Joseph. *The Town and City of Waterbury.* 1896.

Pape, William J. *History of Waterbury and the Naugatuck Valley.* 3 vols. 1918.

Quinn, Elizabeth. *The Story of Waterbury, 1917–1938.* 1953.

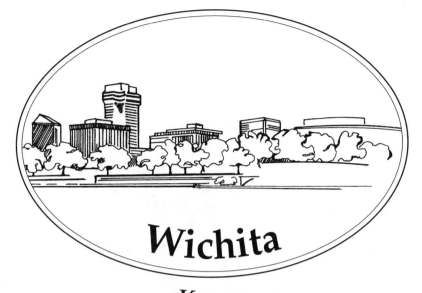

Wichita

Kansas

Location and Topography

N Wichita is located on the Arkansas River at its confluence with the Little Arkansas in the Central Great Plains. The topography is gentle and there are no prominent features.

Layout of City and Suburbs

 A fifth of the city is built west of the Arkansas River, a small portion on the tongue of land between the junction of the rivers, and the remainder of the city east of the rivers with a drainage canal bisecting it. The city is connected by concrete bridges, 6 across the Arkansas, 8 across the Little Arkansas, and 24 across the drainage canal. The area west of the Arkansas River, called West Wichita, is a residential district. It also is the home of the Friends University, Mount Carmel Academy, and the Masonic Home. The attractive residential section, called Riverside, is on the peninsula between the rivers and extends from the river banks to Sim Park and Central Riverside Park. East of the river Wichita consists of residential, industrial, and business blocks.

The business district is centered around the junction of Main Street and Douglas Avenue. On Wichita Street, between Louis and English streets, is Tractor Row, an area two blocks long, so called because it is occupied by dealers in farm power equipment and tractors. The avenues north and south of the business district are lined with elm and cottonwood trees. This neighborhood is bounded on the east by the tracks of the Santa Fe Railway. East of the tracks to the drainage canal is a low-income section. Beyond the drainage canal the streets rise gradually to the slopes that flank the eastern section of the city. On the crest of the slope is the residential area known as College Hill. The eastern fringe of the College Hill district is residential. At the extremity of Douglas Avenue is Eastborough,

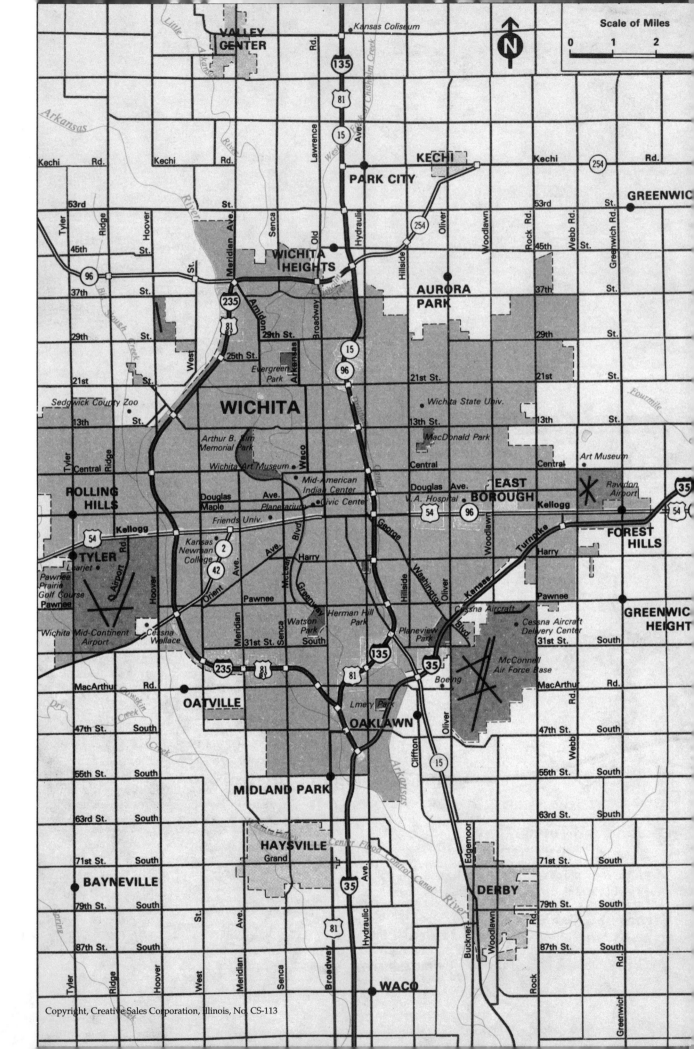

developed in the 1920s as an exclusive residential area, but where oil was discovered in 1930. Oil derricks later overshadowed the Georgian mansions. The buffer section between the Santa Fe Railroad and the drainage canal trails off to the north in an industrial area that includes stockyards, grain elevators, and oil tanks.

Climate

Wichita is located in an area where the moist air from the Gulf of Mexico collides with the cold air from the Arctic. As a result abrupt weather changes are common. Summers are usually warm and humid, and occasionally hot with over 60 days when the mercury hits 90°F. Winters are mild and snowfalls are light with an average of 17 inches annually.

Spring and summer thunderstorms can be severe, accompanied by heavy rain, hail, strong winds, and tornadoes.

Weather			
Temperature			
Highest Monthly Average °F	92.9		
Lowest Monthly Average °F	19.4		
Annual Averages			
Days 32°F or Below	34		
Days above 90°F	62		
Zero Degree Days	2		
Precipitation (inches)	28.61		
Snow (inches)	17.0		
% Seasonal Humidity	68.0		
Wind Speed (m.p.h.)	12.3		
Clear Days	127		
Cloudy Days	142		
Storm Days	55		
Rainy Days	84		
Average Temperatures (°F)	*High*	*Low*	*Mean*
January	41.4	21.2	31.3
February	47.1	25.4	36.3
March	55.0	32.1	43.6
April	68.1	45.1	56.6
May	77.1	55.0	66.1
June	86.5	65.0	75.8
July	91.7	69.6	80.7
August	91.0	68.3	79.7
September	81.9	59.2	70.6
October	71.3	47.9	59.6
November	55.8	33.8	44.8
December	44.3	24.6	34.5

History

Wichita was named for the Wichita Indians who returned to their native Kansas from Texas in 1863 (where they had been driven by the Osage Indian's invasion of Kansas) and built a village at the mouth of the Little Arkansas River. In 1864, James R. Mead and Jesse Chisholm established a trading village near this settlement. Chisholm was responsible for blazing the trail named after him. Following the removal of the Wichita tribe to the Oklahoma Territory in 1865, Mead's trading post became the nucleus of a settlement. It grew to be a watering hole for the herd-driving cowboys on the Chisholm Trail driving Texas longhorns to the Union Pacific Railroad at Abilene. In 1870 Wichita was platted, and in 1871 it was incorporated as a town. . When the Santa Fe Railroad was extended to Wichita in 1872, it became the center of the cattle market in the country. A government land office was established and the Wichita Eagle began publication. Shops, cafes, saloons, and dance halls were hastily built. Wichita soon gained notoriety as a rough, dangerous town. By 1880 the Chisholm Trail was fenced off with barbed wire by settling farmers and sown with wheat. The cattle trail consequently shifted to Dodge City and Wichita entered a period of decline which did not last long, soon becoming an important grain-milling center. During harvest seasons, wheat laden wagons waited in files 10 blocks or longer for 36 hours before the grain could be weighed and emptied at the mills. The new wealth was used, not for gambling as in the cattle days, but to build churches and schools; Wichita was quickly able to rid itself of its reputation as a raucous town. The population exceeded 24,000 by 1900 and 86,000 by 1920. Soon after World War I, oil was discovered. Wichita was also able to attract airplane manufacturers to build their plants in the city. As the Air Capital of America, Wichita had 15 plane manufacturers by 1928. Four of these 15 survived the Great Depression and still bolster the area economy.

Historical Landmarks

Wichita is noted for its outdoor sculptures and murals, numbering over 125. They include such classics as Joan Miro's mosaic at Wichita State University. The Hiker, on the corner of Nims and Murdock avenues, is a heroic bronze figure of a soldier designed by Newman Allen to honor Spanish-American War veterans. The Carry A. Nation Memorial Fountain on Douglas Avenue was dedicated in 1918; it commemorates the barroom raid by Nation at the old Carey (now Eaton) Hotel in December 1900. The McKnight Memorial on the corner of Grove Street and Douglas Avenue was designed by Alexander Proctor and erected in 1931. It consists of a lifesized-bronze figure of a trapper leaning on his rifle beside the seated figure of an Indian with a bow and arrow in hand. The Soldiers and Sailors Monument on the south lawn of the courthouse was designed by Viquesney and erected in 1912 in memory of the Union soldiers in the Civil War. It consists of a bronze figure of Liberty flanked by figures representing soldiers and sailors. The Old Munger House on Back Bay Boulevard is generally believed to be the first house in Wichita. It was constructed of plaster reinforced with buffalo hair in 1868. On Mead Island, south of Minisa Bridge, is a grass house of the type in which the Wichita Indians formerly lived.

Population

Wichita is the 51st most populous city in the nation with a population of 304,011 compared to 279,838 in 1980. Its population gain during the 1980s was 8.6%.

Chronology

1863 Wichita Indians build a village near the mouth of the Little Arkansas River.

1864 John R. Mead and Jesse Chisholm establish a trading post near the Wichita village.

1865 The Wichita Indians are forcibly removed to Oklahoma Territory and Mead's trading post becomes the nucleus of a white settlement.

1870 Wichita is platted.

1871 Wichita is incorporated as a town.

1872 Santa Fe Railroad is extended to Wichita. *Wichita Eagle* begins publication.

1886 Wichita is chartered as a city.

1892 Wichita Municipal University is founded.

1898 Friends University is founded.

1915 Oil is discovered close to town limits.

1917 Wichita adopts city manager-commission form of government.

1987 Wichita's tallest building, the 20-story, 325 foot Epic Center, opens.

Population

	1980	1990
Central City	279,838	304,011
Rank	51	51
Metro Area	442,401	485,270
Pop. Change 1980–1990 +24,173		
Pop. % Change 1980–1990 +8.6		
Median Age 31.7		
% Male 48.6		
% Age 65 and Over 12.4		
Density (per square mile) 2,641		

Households

Number 123,249
Persons per Household 2.43
% Female-Headed Households 11.1
% One-Person Households 30.0
Births—Total 6,239
  % to Mothers under 20 13.2
  Birth Rate per 1,000 22.0

Ethnic Composition

Whites make up 82% of the resident population; blacks 11%; Hispanics, of any race 5%; and Asians and Pacific Islanders and American Indians 4%.

Ethnic Composition (as % of total pop.)

	1980	1990
White	84.44	82.29
Black	10.81	11.28
American Indian	0.92	1.16
Asian and Pacific Islander	1.39	2.56
Hispanic	3.55	5.02
Other	NA	2.71

Government

Wichita operates under a council-manager form of government. Five council members are elected to four-year terms and appoint the city manager.

Government

Year of Home Charter 1964
Number of Members of the Governing Body 5
Elected at Large 5
Elected by Wards NA
Number of Women in Governing Body 0
Salary of Mayor $12,500
Salary of Council Members $7,500
City Government Employment Total 2,929
Rate per 10,000 101.4

Public Finance

The annual budget consists of revenues of $303.713 million and expenditures of $237.302 million. The debt outstanding is $558.604 million and cash and security holdings are $587.300 million.

Public Finance

Total Revenue (in millions) $303.713
Intergovernmental Revenue—Total (in millions) $41.11
Federal Revenue per Capita $0.0
% Federal Assistance 0.0
% State Assistance 4.31
Sales Tax as % of Total Revenue 6.94
Local Revenue as % of Total Revenue 76.7
City Income Tax no
Taxes—Total (in millions) $62.6

Taxes per Capita
  Total $217
  Property $145
  Sales and Gross Receipts $64
General Expenditures—Total (in millions) $246.3
General Expenditures per Capita $853
Capital Outlays per Capita $165

% of Expenditures for:
  Public Welfare 0.0
  Highways 9.5
  Education 0.0
  Health and Hospitals 1.7
  Police 6.5
  Sewerage and Sanitation 7.0
  Parks and Recreation 8.9
  Housing and Community Development 1.9
Debt Outstanding per Capita $4,091
  % Utility 2.7
Federal Procurement Contract Awards (in millions) $1,588.8
Federal Grants Awards (in millions) $24.6
Fiscal Year Begins January 1

Economy

Wichita ranks as the thirtieth most affluent market in the nation. Its economy is based on aircraft, wheat growing, meat packing, flour milling, grain storage, oil refining, high technology, and telecommunications. Although its agricultural and oil refining sectors declined in the 1980s, the other sectors grew sufficiently fast to offset the decline. According to the Center for Economic Development and Business Research at the Wichita State University, the national economy does not necessarily influence the Wichita economy. National growth is driven primarily by consumer demand, while the Wichita area economy is driven by a strong manufacturing/export base. Aircraft industries have experienced impressive growth. Boeing Military Airplanes is the second largest division of the Boeing Company and the largest employer in Kansas. Boeing alone plans to invest about $150 to $200 million a year for several years in Wichita for new and improved facilities. These projects will add 880,000 square feet of office space. Boeing Wichita currently occupies over 11 million square feet and employs 23,000 people. The other three aviation firms are Learjet, Cessna, and Beech. The nearby McConnell Air Force Base also affects the economy positively. Several Wichita companies are among the leaders of their industries. Cargill is one of the nation's top agribusiness corporations and its subsidiary, Excel Corporation, is the second largest beefpacker. Vulcan Chemicals is among the largest producers of chlorinated solvents. Other megacompanies include NCR Engineering and Manufacturing; Coleman Company, pioneering producers of outdoor recreational gear; Pizza Hut; and Chance Rides.

Economy

Total Money Income (in millions) $3,398.2
% of State Average   110.1
Per Capita Annual Income $11,764
% Population below Poverty Level   10.2
Fortune 500 Companies   0

Banks	Number	Deposits (in millions)
Commercial	13	3,290.0
Savings	6	1,450.6

Passenger Autos   258,082
Electric Meters   130,625
Gas Meters   105,000

Manufacturing

Number of Establishments   509
% with 20 or More Employees   36.5
Manufacturing Payroll (in millions) $1,620.6
Value Added by Manufacture (in millions) $3,554.5
Value of Shipments (in millions) $6,684.4
New Capital Expenditures (in millions) $240

Wholesale Trade

Number of Establishments   805
Sales (in millions) $3,453.2
Annual Payroll (in millions) $217.040

Economy (continued)

Retail Trade

Number of Establishments   3,379
Total Sales (in millions) $2,449.4
Sales per Capita $8,479
Number of Retail Trade Establishments with Payroll   2,304
Annual Payroll (in millions) $298.8
Total Sales (in millions) $2,399.2
General Merchandise Stores (per capita) $1,305
Food Stores (per capita) $1,563
Apparel Stores (per capita) $421
Eating and Drinking Places (per capita) $925

Service Industries

Total Establishments   2,596
Total Receipts (in millions) $1,319.8
Hotels and Motels (in millions)   NA
Health Services (in millions) $519.4
Legal Services (in millions) $95.0

Labor

Wichita has a stable employment market less affected by the recession in the early 1990s than comparable cities. One reason is that the aviation industry has remained sufficiently strong with a heavy backlog of orders from other nations. The other core industries also have proved less vulnerable to cyclical fluctuations: food, computers, recreation, and chemicals. Manufacturing remains the largest sector in terms of employment.

Labor

Civilian Labor Force   167,594
% Change 1989–1990   1.0

Work Force Distribution
Mining   1,800
Construction   10,600
Manufacturing   62,800
Transportation and Public Utilities   11,400
Wholesale and Retail Trade   56,300
FIRE (Finance, Insurance, Real Estate)   10,900
Service   60,900
Government   29,300
Women as % of Labor Force   43.5
% Self-Employed   5.2
% Professional/Technical   16.5
Total Unemployment   7,936
Rate %   4.7
Federal Government Civilian Employment   3,136

Education

Unified School District 259 of Wichita Public Schools is the largest elementary and secondary system in the state and supports 100 elementary, junior high, and senior high schools. In addition, Sedgwick County is served by over 40 parochial and public schools.

The largest institution of higher education is the Wichita State University, formerly the Wichita Municipal University, founded in 1892 as Fairmount College. The University of Kansas Medical School, formerly affiliated with the Wichita State University, is now a separate institution. The largest private universities are Friends University, affiliated with the Quakers, and the Kansas Newman College, a Roman Catholic institution.

Education

Number of Public Schools   100
Special Education Schools   2
Total Enrollment   47,222
% Enrollment in Private Schools   10.4
% Minority   31.3
Classroom Teachers   2,748
Pupil-Teacher Ratio   17.1:1
Number of Graduates   2,333
Total Revenue (in millions) $169.769
Total Expenditures (in millions) $171.918
Expenditures per Pupil $3,577
Educational Attainment (Age 25 and Over)
  % Completed 12 or More Years   75.9
  % Completed 16 or More Years   19.0
Four-Year Colleges and Universities   4
  Enrollment   19,522
Two-Year Colleges   NA
  Enrollment   NA

Libraries

Number   31
Public Libraries   12
Books (in thousands)   616
Circulation (in thousands)   1,542
Persons Served (in thousands)   288
Circulation per Person Served   5.35
Income (in millions) $4.525
Staff   107

Four-Year Colleges and Universities
  Wichita State University
  Friends University
  Kansas Newman College
  University of Kansas Medical School

Health

Wichita has three of the four largest medical institutions in Kansas: St. Francis Regional Medical Center, HCA Wesley Medical Center, and St. Joseph Medical Center, with a total of 1,617 beds. Other medical care facilities include Riverside Hospital, Veterans Administration Medical Center, 384th Strategic Hospital at McConnell Air Force Base, Charter Hospital, and CPC Great Plains Hospital. Wichita is also home to the Women's Research Institute and the Research Center

Health

Deaths—Total   2,583
Rate per 1,000   9.1
Infant Deaths—Total   74
Rate per 1,000   11.9
Number of Metro Hospitals   6
Number of Metro Hospital Beds   2,074
Rate per 100,000   718
Number of Physicians   960
Physicians per 1,000   2.07
Nurses per 1,000   7.68
Health Expenditures per Capita $4.51

for Molecular Medicine. The University of Kansas Medical School maintains training programs at four local hospitals.

Transportation

Wichita is literally at the crossroads of America. A network of interstate, federal, and state highways link Wichita with the West and East coasts and with the Canadian and Mexican borders. Interstates 35 and 135 pass directly through Wichita, connecting the city with I-40, I-44, and I-70. Major U.S. highways are 54 and 81, while state routes include K-42, K-2, K-15, K-254, K-96 and the Kansas Turnpike. Rail passenger service is available through Amtrak, and rail freight service through Union Pacific, Burlington Northern, and Atchison, Topeka and Santa Fe. The airport is the Midcontinent Airport, about 12 miles from downtown. In addition, there are general aviation airports within a 40-mile radius.

Transportation

Interstate Highway Mileage   46
Total Urban Mileage   1,557
Total Daily Vehicle Mileage (in millions) $6.034
Daily Average Commute Time   39.4 min.
Number of Buses   45
Port Tonnage (in millions)   NA
Airports   1
Number of Daily Flights   40
Daily Average Number of Passengers   1,623

Airlines (American carriers only)
  American
  American West
  Continental
  Northwest
  Trans World
  United
  USAir

Housing

Wichita has 135,069 housing units of which 22,113 are in a state of disrepair and 20,701 have been rehabilitated in recent years. There are 49,030 renter-occupied units

Housing

Total Housing Units   135,069
% Change 1980–1990   13.6
Vacant Units for Sale or Rent   9,508
Occupied Units   123,249
% with More Than One Person per Room   3.9
% Owner-Occupied   58.9
Median Value of Owner-Occupied Homes $56,700
Average Monthly Purchase Cost $316
Median Monthly Rent $299
New Private Housing Starts   1,609
Value (in thousands) $89,809
% Single-Family   62.8
Nonresidential Buildings Value (in thousands) $65,677

Tallest Buildings	Hgt. (ft.)	Stories
Epic Center	325	20

with a median rent of $299. Owners occupy 58.9% of Wichita's housing.

Urban Redevelopment

 Downtown development is coordinated by WI/SE (Wichita-Sedgwick County), a group of businessmen and public officials. For some time there was controversy over groundwater pollution in the business district, but it was settled. The City Council has endorsed a plan to create a streetscape of rebuilt brick streets, period sidewalks, and decorative lighting in the historic Old Town warehouse district. WI/SE is developing a proposal to consolidate all Wichita-area offices of the State of Kansas in one downtown location. Among the large development projects in the late 1980s were the Epic Center, the state's tallest building, which houses the Mid-America World Trade Center. Another added an exhibition hall to the Century II Convention Center. Corporate construction has kept pace. A recent survey identified 50 Wichita area companies planning expansion, including Chance Industries, Koch Industries, Vulcan Chemicals, Great Plains Industries, and Flight-Safety International.

Crime

Of the crimes known to police in 1991, 2,672 were violent and 23,829 involved property.

Crime
Violent Crimes—Total   2,672
Violent Crime Rate per 100,000   655.5
Murder   24
Rape   284
Robbery   1,404
Aggravated Assaults   960
Property Crimes   23,829
Burglary   7,459
Larceny   17,089
Motor Vehicle Theft   2,893
Arson   NA
Per Capita Police Expenditures $77.19
Per Capita Fire Protection Expenditures $52.39
Number of Police   474
Per 1,000   1.66

Religion

Over 46 religious denominations are represented in Wichita. Of these those with the most churches are: Roman Catholic, Baptist, Methodist, Presbyterian, Lutheran and Orthodox.

Religion	
Largest Denominations (Adherents)	
Catholic	56,513
Southern Baptist	30,807
United Methodist	28,278
Black Baptist	12,303

Religion (continued)	
Presbyterian	9,194
Lutheran-Missouri Synod	7,303
Christian Church (Disciples)	6,759
American Baptist	5,572
Assembly of God	4,584
Jewish	831

Media

 The city's daily newspaper is the *Wichita Eagle*, published mornings and Sundays. Electronic media consist of five television stations and 13 AM and FM stations.

Media	
Newsprint	
Wichita Business Journal, weekly	
Wichita Eagle, daily	
Television	
KAKE (Channel 10)	
KPTS (Channel 8)	
KSAS (Channel 24)	
KSNW (Channel 3)	
KWCH (Channel 12)	
Radio	
KFDI (FM)	KFH (AM)
KICT (FM)	KKRD (FM)
KMUW (FM)	KNSS (AM)
KQAM (AM)	KEYN (FM)
KRBB (FM)	KSGL (AM)
KWKL (FM)	KXLK (FM)
KZSN (FM)	

Sports

 Wichita is represented in two professional sports: in indoor soccer by the Wichita Wings, and in double-A minor league baseball by the Wichita Pilots. The latter play their home games in the Lawrence Dumont Stadium. Since 1931 Wichita has held the National Baseball Congress, the nation's largest amateur baseball tournament. Among major special tournaments hosted by Wichita are drag racing at the Wichita International Raceway, auto races on the 81 Speedway, the Virginia Slims Tennis championships, Kansas Special Olympics, and Grand Prix Automobile racing at Lake Afton.

Arts, Culture, and Tourism

Wichita supports over 50 organizations in the performing and visual arts, many of them housed in the Century II Convention Center. Music groups include the Wichita Symphony Orchestra, Wichita Choral Society, Wichita Jazz Festival, Opera Kansas, Music Theater of Wichita, and the Singing Quakers from Friends University. The major dance groups are the Metropolitan Ballet and Mid-American Dance Company. The most active theater groups are Kechi Playhouse, Summer Shakespeare in the Park, Wichita Children's Theater, Wichita Community Theater, and Wichita State University Theater.

Wichita Art Museum at the south entrance to Sim Park is the city's largest museum. Other major museums are the Natural History Museum, Children's Museum, Edwin A. Ulrich Museum of Art, Fellow-Reeve Museum of History and Science, Friends University Garvey Art Center, Great Plains Transportation Museum, Kansas Aviation Museum, Museum of Anthropology, Old Cowtown Museum, Wichita Center for the Arts, Wichita Gallery of Fine Art, and Wichita/Sedgwick County Historical Museum.

Travel and Tourism

Hotel Rooms 4,584
Convention and Exhibit Space (square feet) NA

Convention Centers
 Century II Convention Center

Festivals
 Wichita River Festival (May)
 Kansas Pokatennial (May)
 Wichita Arts Festival (September)
 Wichita Asian Festival (October)
 Oktoberfest
 International Holiday Festival (November)

Parks and Recreation

Wichita's public park system includes about 75 parks that cover over 3,000 acres. Pawnee Prairie, the largest park, covers 700 acres. Chisholm Creek Park includes native and restored prairie habitats. The Botanica, or Wichita Gardens, is located on the banks of the Arkansas River. Price Woodward Park is located between Century II and the Arkansas River. The 183-acre Sim Memorial Park is located beside the Arkansas River.

Sources of Further Information

Wichita Convention and Visitors Bureau
100 South Main
Wichita, KS 67202
(316) 2652800

Wichita Public Library
223 South Main
Wichita, KS 67202
(316) 262-0611

Wichita Area Chamber of Commerce
350 West Douglas Avenue
Wichita, KS 67202-2970
(316) 2652-2095

Wichita Sedgwick County Historical Museum
 Library
204 South Main Street
Wichita, KS 67202
(316) 265-9314

Additional Reading

Kirkman, Kay. *Wichita: A Pictorial History.* 1981.
Miller, Glenn W., and Jimmy M. Skaggs.
 Metropolitan Wichita: Past, Present and Future. 1978.
Miner, H. Craig. *Wichita: The Magic City.* 1988.
Wichita: The Early Years. 1982.

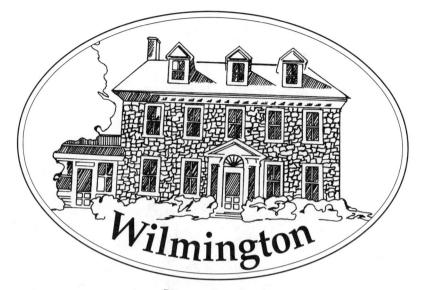

Wilmington

Delaware

ing numbers. Market Street, the chief business thoroughfare, is the dividing line between east and west. Other business streets run parallel with this street: King to the east, and Shipley, Orange, and Tatnall to the west. From Market Street business has spread along many of the cross streets, particularly West Ninth and West Tenth streets. A number of avenues, generally wider than streets, crisscross various sections of the city. Baynard Boulevard extends from the north end of Washington Street Bridge to the city line. Near the western end of town, Bancroft Parkway extends from Union Park Gardens to the south.

Location and Geography

N

Wilmington is located in the northeast corner of Delaware on the western bank of the Delaware River at the junction of the Christina River and Brandywine Creek. It is bounded by the Delaware River on the east and the Chesapeake Bay on the southwest. There are highlands to the north and lowlands to the south.

Layout of City and Suburbs

The center of the city is Rodney Square, a few blocks from the Brandywine Creek Bridge. Wilmington's main streets run at right angles, with north-south streets bearing the names of persons or trees, and east-west streets bear-

Climate

Wilmington, like the rest of Delaware, has warm, humid summers and mild winters. During the summer, relative humidity reaches 75%, accompanied by fog. Average annual snowfall is about 20 inches, but snow rarely remains on the ground for more than a few days and winter precipitation is more often in the form of rain or sleet. Rainfall is abundant in summer, mostly as thundershowers. Although hurricanes rarely reach Wilmington in full force, strong easterly and southeastern winds cause high tides and floods along the Delaware River.

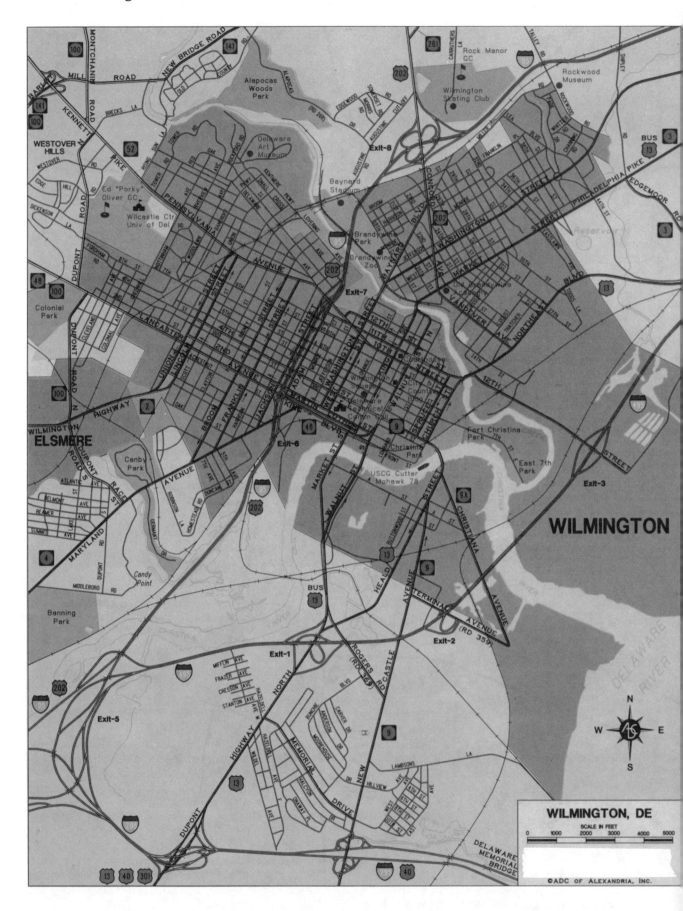

From *Maryland/Delaware State Road Atlas* ©1991. Alexandria, VA: ADC.

Weather			
Temperature			
Highest Monthly Average °F	85.6		
Lowest Monthly Average °F	23.2		
Annual Averages			
Days 32°F or Below	101		
Days above 90°F			
Zero Degree Days			
Precipitation (inches)	41.38		
Snow (inches)	21.3		
% Seasonal Humidity	66.5		
Wind Speed (m.p.h.)	9.2		
Clear Days	97		
Cloudy Days	164		
Storm Days	NA		
Rainy Days	NA		
Average Temperatures (°F)	*High*	*Low*	*Mean*
January	40.1	24.4	32.3
February	42.2	25.5	33.9
March	51.2	32.5	41.9
April	63.5	42.3	52.9
May	74.1	52.3	63.2
June	83.0	61.6	72.3
July	86.8	66.7	76.8
August	84.8	64.7	74.8
September	78.4	57.8	68.1
October	67.9	46.9	57.4
November	55.5	36.9	46.2
December	43.2	27.2	35.2

History

The Delaware region was the domain of the Lenni-Lenape Indians, known to Europeans as a peaceful tribe. In March 1638, a Swedish expedition led by Peter Minuit entered Delaware Bay. They sailed up the river two miles and cast anchor opposite a natural stone wharf called The Rocks which still stands at the foot of Seventh Street. Minuit purchased the surrounding land, which he called New Sweden, from the Lenni-Lenape, and after building a fort there called Christina, he departed for Sweden bearing a rich cargo. Twelve successive Swedish expeditions arrived under commanders Peter Hollander Ridder, Johan Printz, and Johan Classon Rising, and with each expedition the settlement grew. In 1654 the little town had a building boom spurred by a town plan made by Peter Lindestrom, but before it was completed the Dutch, under Governor Stuyvesant, besieged the town and seized it without firing a shot. The name of the fort was changed to Fort Altena, but life changed little for the Swedish settlers who kept their land, their officers, and their clergy. In 1665 the fort changed hands once again as English soldiers under Sir Robert Carr occupied the land in the name of James, Duke of York. In 1690 a young visitor from Sweden, Andrew Printz, was so impressed by their flourishing colony that he returned to Sweden and enlisted the support of King Charles X. The king sent three ministers in 1697, one of whom, Eric Bjorck, remained at Christina and built the Old Swedes Church near the fort in 1698. In 1671 all the land from Christina to Brandywine was owned by two Swedes, Johan Andersson Stalcop and Tymen Stidham. Stalcop, who died in 1685, granted half his land to Samuel Peterson and Lars Cornelison. Peterson's land was later sold to Andrew Justison while Cornelison sold his land to Matthias de Foss, who sold it to Charles Pickering. These two tracts are the nucleus of the present Wilmington. Justison began platting his land in 1730 assisted by Thomas Willing, his son-in-law, and the town was initially called Willingtown. Willingtown was designed as a farmer's or market town for the service of ships and mills. A markethouse was erected by the lot-owners on the free ground offered by Willing. The town's phenomenal growth in the next few decades is attributable to the arrival of an English Quaker, William Shipley, who, in 1735, bought all of the land west of Market Street (bounded by Market and West, Christina Creek, and Fifth Street). In the fall he moved with his family from Ridley Township in Pennsylvania. An influential Quaker of considerable means, Ridley was responsible for attracting numerous Quaker families to the town. Thus Willingtown became a Quaker town. Until 1739, there was no formal government. The new town was embroiled in a dispute over two markets: the one built by Shipley near his own land on High Street (Fourth) between Shipley and Market, and the one built on land donated by Thomas Willing on Second Street. Each side in the dispute appealed to Thomas Penn. In 1739 Penn sent a charter for the borough prescribing the market days for both markets and their regulation by all those who paid an annual rent of five pounds or more. At this time, either as a result of misspelling or in honor of Penn's friend, Spencer Compton, Earl of Wilmington, the name of the town was changed to its present one. In 1740 William Shipley became the chief burgess following the first election. Soon after, Wilmington began to compete with New Castle for the West Indies trade and smuggling operations. A jail was built, in 1740, to house rowdy sailors out on the town. By 1754 there was a subscription library, and in 1761 James Adams established the first printing press. Within a few years the Wilmington Academy came into existence, headed by Lawrence Girelius, the last Swedish-speaking minister of Old Swedes. In addition to the Willing and Shipley markets, a new one grew that dealt solely in imported slaves, many of whom were bought by plantation owners. On the outbreak of the American Revolution, Wilmington became a frontline theater of operations. George Washington, along with General "Mad" Anthony Wayne, established the Revolutionary Army headquarters in Wilmington, but were unable to prevent its capture by Lord Howe following the Battle of Brandywine in 1777. When the British left after one month, the city suffered an economic slump. Living conditions worsened as a result of heavy immigration, first the Irish, and then the French who had been driven out of Santo Domingo. Scarcely had these immigrants settled when hundreds more poured in from Philadelphia in 1793, where a yellow fever epidemic was rampant. With the Philadelphia economy crippled, Delaware was forced to found the Bank of Delaware in 1795. The years be-

Chronology

1638 Commander Peter Minuit sails up the Delaware River and lands at The Rocks, purchases land from the Lenni-Lenape Indians, and builds Fort Christina.

1654 Engineer Peter Lindestrom's town plan spurs building boom in Christina.

1655 The Dutch, under Governor Stuyvesant, seize Christina, which they rename Fort Altena.

1665 The English, under Sir Robert Carr, drive out the Dutch and claim the settlement in the name of James, Duke of York.

1698 The Old Swedes Church is built by Minister Eric Bjorck, sent by King Charles X of Sweden.

1730 Andrew Justison and his son-in law, Thomas Willing, begin platting a town, called Willingtown, on land obtained from Johan Andersson Stalcop, one of the original landholders in Christina.

1735 William Shipley, an English Quaker, buys all of the town lots west of Market Street and brings in numerous Quaker associates and relatives to live in the settlement.

1739 Thomas Penn gives a charter to the town of Wilmington.

1740 First borough elections take place. William Shipley is elected chief burgess. The brig, *Wilmington,* sails for the West Indies, launching Wilmington's maritime trade.

1754 Public library is founded.

1761 James Adams founds town's first printing press.

1776 One of the first naval battles of the Revolutionary War is fought in Wilmington.

1777 The British capture Wilmington following the Battle of Brandywine.

1793 The yellow fever scare drives hundreds of Philadelphians to take refuge in Wilmington.

1795 The Bank of Delaware opens its doors.

1802 E. I. du Pont de Nemours buys the shell of a cotton mill two miles up the Brandywine from Jacob Broom and begins powder manufacturing.

1812 Fort Union is built on the site of the old Fort Christina.

1815 Five new turnpikes are built to handle the increased traffic.

1831 The Newcastle and Frenchtown Railway opens.

1832 Wilmington is chartered as a city.

1835 *Ceres,* Wilmington's first whaling ship, is launched.

1883 Wilmington Park Commission is created to conserve the banks of the Brandywine.

1917 Wilmington Board of Harbor Commissioners is created.

1968 Blacks erupt in riots following the assassination of Martin Luther King, Jr.

---

tween the end of the Revolutionary War and the War of 1812 were prosperous for Wilmington. It was home to some of the most distinguished minds of the age: Rober Coram, teacher and librarian; Willard Hall, father of public education in the state; Benjamin H. Latrobe, architect; Hezekiah Niles, printer and publisher; John Dickinson, governor; Archibald Hamilton Rowan, Irish patriot; William Cobbett, the banished Duke of Orleans; and Louis Philippe, the future king of France. Meanwhile, Jacob Broom became the town's first postmaster and started the first cotton factory in the Old Academy, and later, two miles up the Brandywine, he founded a mill. When the mill burned down in 1802 he sold the shell to E. I. du Pont, who started his powder making there. During this time Joshua and Thomas Gilpin started their papermill on the Brandywine. In 1812, Fort Union was built on the site of the old Fort Christina as a defense against British ships during the War of 1812. In 1815, after the war was over and as the population and trade grew, five new turnpikes were built to handle the traffic. Steamboats and stagecoaches plied regularly between Philadelphia and Wilmington. One of the earliest railroads in the nation—the Newcastle and Frenchtown Railway—opened in 1831 and soon after it came the Wilmington and Susquehanna Railroad. In recognition of its growing status the town was incorporated as a city in 1832, and Richard H. Bayard was elected as first mayor. Between 1835 and 1845 a picturesque chapter was added to Wilmington's industrial history when a whaling fleet was stationed at the port. Whenever a whaling vessel returned a shot was fired from Whaler's Wharf and most of the town stopped work. The Civil War did not seriously interrupt the city's growth. In 1883 a Wilmington Park Commission was created to preserve the community from industrial pollution. In 1917 the Wilmington Board of Harbor Commissioners was created to operate the Marine Terminal. After World War I, the E. I. du Pont de Nemours Company became even more powerful in the city than it had been before, and finally emerged as one of the largest industrial holdings in the nation, controlling the chemical and automobile industries.

Historical Landmarks

The oldest building in the city is the Old Swedes, or Holy Trinity Church, on the corner of Seventh and Church streets. It is a modest gray stone church with a massive gabled side porch and an arcaded belfry topped with a low onion-shaped dome, built in 1698. The site of Fort Christina, near The Rocks, at the foot of Seventh Street, is now a state park. During the Swedish Tercentenary in 1938, a monument was erected here. The Alrichs House, on an embankment on the south side of the Christina River is a two and-a-half story brick and frame structure built by the Alrichs family during the Dutch occupation. The site of Crane Hook Church, built in 1667, is marked by a granite tablet. The Rodney Square, covering the block bounded by Market, King, 10th, and 11th streets, is named for Caesar Rodney, one of the signers of the Declaration of Independence. The Old Brandywine Walk on Market Street is part of an old, fashionable neighborhood. Among its residences are the John Marot Twin Houses and the four Price Houses, built from 1825 to 1835 by James Price for his daughter and three sons. The Jacob Starr House built about 1806, was the residence of shipping magnate Captain Thomas Starr. Bishopstead on 14th Street is a long gabled house built in 1742 by Oliver Canby who bought the old gristmill site from the son of one of the original Swedish settlers. Later it became the residence of the bishops of Delaware. The Colonial Dames House at Park Drive is a small Dutch Colonial red brick building with a gambrel roof, built in 1740 as the First Presbyterian Church. The approximate site of the Old Barley Mill on Park Drive at Adams Street is designated by a large flat millstone. This is the site of the first Brandywine mill for cleaning barley, built by Tymen Stidham, who came with the Swedish governor in 1654. Later it became a calico printing and dyeing establishment owned by the Irish expatriate, Archibald Hamilton Rowan. The Augustine Bridge, crossing the Brandywine near Lovering Avenue and Dupont Street, was built by the Baltimore and Ohio Railroad Company and ranks as one of the finest stone arch structures in the nation. Derickson House on Market Street is a two-and-a-half-story native stone house, built about 1771 by James Marshall. Joseph Tatnall House on Market Street was built in 1770 by an English Quaker of the same name, a friend of both Washington and Lafayette. Edward Tatnall House on Market Street was also built by Joseph Tatnall in 1790 for the use of his son. William Lea House on Market Street is a Quaker post-Colonial home of the Leas, Brandywine Flour Mill proprietors. The Episcopal Cathedral of St. John on the corner of Concord Avenue and Market Street is an Early English Gothic erected in 1857. The Old Brandywine Academy on Vandever Avenue was founded in 1798 according to the datestone above the door. The land was donated by John Dickinson and John Walsh. The Dr. Didier House on French Street, a three-story mansion, was the home of Dr. Pierre Didier, a French physician who fled from Santo Domingo at the time of the black revolt and settled in Wilmington as the family physician of the du Ponts. The Old Town Hall on Market Street, built in 1798, was designed by Peter Bauduy. The Dr. Simms House on the corner of Fourth and King streets, erected about 1820, was the apothecary shop and residence of Dr. John Simms and his son Dr. John Henry Simms. The Sign of the Ship Tavern on the corner of Third and Market streets was one of the most popular inns of the pre-Revolutionary days, erected in 1738. The Asbury Methodist Episcopal Church on the corner of Third and Walnut streets was the first Methodist church in the city and was met with considerable opposition in its early days. St. Andrew's Protestant Episcopal Church, on the corner of Eighth and Shipley streets, was built in 1829, totally destroyed by fire in 1840, and rebuilt in the same year. Washington's headquarters on West Street is a three-story brick building where Washington lived from August 25 to September 8, 1777 before the Battle of Brandywine on September 11. The Friends Meeting House occupies the whole of the block bounded by West, Washington, Fourth, and Fifth streets. It was erected in 1816 to replace the meeting place built in 1748 on the same spot, and an earlier one built in 1738. The St. Peter's Roman Catholic Pro-Cathedral on the corner of Sixth and West streets, erected in 1816, was the first Catholic church in Wilmington. The two Woodward Houses were built in 1745 and 1760 respectively. The Tilton House on the corner of Ninth and Broom streets stands on Federal Hill, so called because it was once a candidate for the federal capitol. Dr. James Tilton, its owner, and surgeon general of the U. S. Army in the War of 1812, built the house in 1802. The Banning House on Broom Street is a large two-and-a-half-story mansion built in 1812. Latimeria, on Maryland Avenue, was built in 1815 by William Warner, on whose death it passed on to John R. Latimer.

Population

Wilmington is the largest city in Delaware, but its population has never exceeded the 85,000 mark. After peaking at 80,386 in 1970, it declined to 70,195 in 1980 and then rose slightly to 71,529 in 1990. Because Wilmington's population had been expected to drop even further in 1990, the slight increase was taken as a sign of the city's revival.

Population		
	1980	*1990*
Central City	70,195	71,529
Rank	284	307
Metro Area	523,221	578,587
Pop. Change 1980–1990 +1,334		
Pop. % Change 1980–1990 +1.9		
Median Age 32.7		
% Male 46.5		
% Age 65 and Over 14.8		
Density (per square mile) 6,623		

Population (continued)

Households

Number   28,556
Persons per Household   2.44
% Female-Headed Households   21.8
% One-Person Households   36.4
Births—Total   1,732
   % to Mothers under 20   20.6
   Birth Rate per 1,000   24.9

Ethnic Composition

 Wilmington has a black majority. Blacks make up 52.4%, whites 42.1%, American Indians 0.2%, Asians and Pacific Islanders 0.4%, and others 4.9%.

Ethnic Composition (as % of total pop.)

	1980	1990
White	45.2	42.13
Black	51.18	52.35
American Indian	0.12	0.22
Asian and Pacific Islander	0.2	0.44
Hispanic	4.71	7.09
Other	NA	4.86

Government

 Wilmington has a mayor-council form of government. The mayor and the 13 members of the city council are elected to four-year terms. Nine members of the council are elected by district and four members at large.

Government

Year of Home Charter   1964
Number of Members of the Governing Body   13
Elected at Large   4
Elected by Wards   9
Number of Women in Governing Body   2
Salary of Mayor   NA
Salary of Council Members   NA
City Government Employment Total   1,385
Rate per 10,000   198.7

Public Finance

The annual revenues consist of revenues of $125.911 million and expenditures of $135.901 million. The debt outstanding is $205.941 million and cash and security holdings are $130.137 million.

Public Finance

Total Revenue (in millions) $125.911
Intergovernmental Revenue—Total (in millions) $10.69
Federal Revenue per Capita $6.81
% Federal Assistance   5.44
% State Assistance   3.09

Public Finanace (continued)

Sales Tax as % of Total Revenue   1.01
Local Revenue as % of Total Revenue   74.98
City Income Tax   yes
Taxes—Total (in millions) $31.8

Taxes per Capita
   Total $457
   Property $15
   Sales and Gross Receipts $12
General Expenditures—Total (in millions) $86.6
General Expenditures per Capita $1,243
Capital Outlays per Capita $248

% of Expenditures for:
   Public Welfare   0.0
   Highways   2.3
   Education   0.0
   Health and Hospitals   0.0
   Police   13.0
   Sewerage and Sanitation   24.9
   Parks and Recreation   3.6
   Housing and Community Development   1.9
Debt Outstanding per Capita $1,972
   % Utility   26.5
Federal Procurement Contract Awards (in millions) $37.4
Federal Grants Awards (in millions) $26.5
Fiscal Year Begins   July 1

Economy

 Wilmington is the chemical capital of America. It is the headquarters of four of the largest chemical companies, including the giant Du Pont, which has been identified with the city for almost two centuries. The others are Hercules, ICI Americas, and W. L. Gore. Chemical firms are not the only institutions anchoring the economy. More than a dozen credit card companies and banks have moved into Wilmington since 1981, when the government removed the ceiling on interest rates. Other regulations favorable to business, including the absence of sales and inventory tax, have helped to bring in a host of companies, many of which maintain only token operations here.

Economy

Total Money Income (in millions) $655.7
% of State Average   82.7
Per Capita Annual Income $9,410
% Population below Poverty Level   24.6
Fortune 500 Companies   2

Banks	Number	Deposits (in millions)
Commercial	NA	NA
Savings	50	26,000

Passenger Autos   266,577
Electric Meters   165,000
Gas Meters   110,600

Manufacturing

Number of Establishments   128
% with 20 or More Employees   34.4
Manufacturing Payroll (in millions) $785.2
Value Added by Manufacture (in millions) $245.0
Value of Shipments (in millions) $473.0
New Capital Expenditures (in millions) $29.6

Economy (continued)

Wholesale Trade

Number of Establishments   199
Sales (in millions) $3,061.8
Annual Payroll (in millions) $99.302

Retail Trade

Number of Establishments   792
Total Sales (in millions) $678.4
Sales per Capita $9,735
Number of Retail Trade Establishments with Payroll   605
Annual Payroll (in millions) $73.9
Total Sales (in millions) $666.6
General Merchandise Stores (per capita)   NA
Food Stores (per capita) $1,232
Apparel Stores (per capita) $310
Eating and Drinking Places (per capita) $901

Service Industries

Total Establishments   967
Total Receipts (in millions) $580.1
Hotels and Motels (in millions) $28.6
Health Services (in millions) $160.9
Legal Services (in millions) $142.3

Labor

Nearly five out of every six Wilmington workers commute from New Jersey, Pennsylvania, or Maryland. The city has escaped much of the downsizing woes of the neighboring cities and states. Another unusual feature of the Wilmington workforce is the dominance of the chemical industry, as well as the more recent dominance of banking and financial services. As a city with a modest population, Wilmington has been very innovative in pumping resources to keep existing companies happy and active by providing them with well trained labor.

Labor

Civilian Labor Force   34,247
% Change 1989–1990   1.9

Work Force Distribution
   Mining   200
   Construction   15,700
   Manufacturing   60,700
   Transportation and Public Utilities   16,800
   Wholesale and Retail Trade   57,900
   FIRE (Finance, Insurance, Real Estate)   29,100
   Service   72,500
   Government   37,800
   Women as % of Labor Force   48.3
   % Self-Employed   3.6
   % Professional/Technical   17.3
Total Unemployment   2,610
Rate %   7.6
Federal Government Civilian Employment   2,070

Education

In 1976 the Newcastle County School District was reorganized into four school districts: Brandywine, Red Clay Consolidated, Christina, and Colonial. Together these districts support 56 elementary schools, 14 junior high and middle schools, and 12 senior high schools. Wil-

mington has three institutions of higher learning: Goldey Beacom College, Delaware Technical and Community College, and Widener University with four constituent schools, Brandywine College, University College, School of Hotel and Restaurant Management, and Delaware Law School. The University of Delaware maintains a campus downtown.

Education

Number of Public Schools   82
Special Education Schools   NA
Total Enrollment   16,798 (Christina District)
% Enrollment in Private Schools   21.1
% Minority   NA
Classroom Teachers   NA
Pupil-Teacher Ratio   NA
Number of Graduates   NA
Total Revenue (in millions) $104.669
Total Expenditures (in millions) $112.692
Expenditures per Pupil $6,708.66
Educational Attainment (Age 25 and Over)
   % Completed 12 or More Years   55.2
   % Completed 16 or More Years   13.1
Four-Year Colleges and Universities   2
   Enrollment   1,784
Two-Year Colleges   NA
   Enrollment   NA

Libraries

Number   3
Public Libraries   3
Books (in thousands)   320
Circulation (in thousands)   NA
Persons Served (in thousands)   400
Circulation per Person Served   0.31
Income (in millions) $1.91
Staff   33

Four-Year Colleges and Universities
   Goldey Beacom College
   Widener University

Health

Wilmington's six medical facilities include two of the state's largest: the Medical Center of Delaware and the Alfred I. du Pont Institute. The Medical Center is a complex consisting of Christina Hospital, Eugene du Pont Memorial Hospital, and Wilmington Hospital. The Alfred I. du Pont Institute treats crippled children and the Nemours Health Clinic serves the elderly. Other medical facilities include St. Francis Hospital, Riverside

Health

Deaths—Total   1,130
Rate per 1,000   16.2
Infant Deaths—Total   26
Rate per 1,000   15.0
Number of Metro Hospitals   6
Number of Metro Hospital Beds   2,001
Rate per 100,000   2,871
Number of Physicians   1,001
Physicians per 1,000   1.99
Nurses per 1,000   NA
Health Expenditures per Capita   NA

Hospital, Rockford Center, and Veteran's Administration Medical Center.

Transportation

Wilmington is on the Boston–Washington corridor served by a number of highways. The principal artery is I-95 which cuts through the western portion of the city and connects with downtown through the Wilmington Bypass or I-495. The New Jersey Turnpike crosses the Delaware River and becomes I-295. U.S. routes 13, 40, 41, and 202 also provide access to the city. Amtrak provides daily service to Washington D.C. to the south, and New York and Boston to the north. Rail freight services are provided by Conrail, Chessie Systems, Wilmington and Western, and Delaware Coastline. The Port of Wilmington on the Christina River, about 65 miles from the Atlantic Ocean, is one of the busiest in the nation. The principal air terminal is the Greater Wilmington Airport, about ten miles from downtown.

Transportation	
Interstate Highway Mileage	47
Total Urban Mileage	1,669
Total Daily Vehicle Mileage (in millions)	$9.578
Daily Average Commute Time	45.5 min.
Number of Buses	85
Port Tonnage (in millions)	$3.715
Airports	1
Number of Daily Flights	NA
Daily Average Number of Passengers	6

Housing

Of the total housing stock 53.2% is owner-occupied. The median value of an owner-occupied home is $77,800 and the median monthly rent $374.

Housing	
Total Housing Units	31,244
% Change 1980–1990	2.4
Vacant Units for Sale or Rent	1,827
Occupied Units	28,556
% with More Than One Person per Room	4.3
% Owner-Occupied	53.2
Median Value of Owner-Occupied Homes	$77,800
Average Monthly Purchase Cost	$287
Median Monthly Rent	$374
New Private Housing Starts	144
Value (in thousands)	$6,562
% Single-Family	98.6
Nonresidential Buildings Value (in thousands)	$29,101

Urban Redevelopment

Downtown revitalization is spearheaded mainly by new corporate building. The American Life Insurance Company's world headquarters is in Christina Gateway, an impressive complex on the eastern section of the waterfront. Chase Manhattan and the Bank of Delaware have invested millions of dollars in new downtown offices.

Crime

Wilmington ranks below national average in public safety. The crimes reported to police in 1991 consisted of 1,351 violent and 7,283 property crimes.

Crime	
Violent Crimes—Total	1,351
Violent Crime Rate per 100,000	642.2
Murder	15
Rape	124
Robbery	661
Aggravated Assaults	551
Property Crimes	7,283
Burglary	1,698
Larceny	4,775
Motor Vehicle Theft	810
Arson	54
Per Capita Police Expenditures	$210.75
Per Capita Fire Protection Expenditures	$141.48
Number of Police	255
Per 1,000	3.52

Religion

Catholics have the strongest representation in Wilmington with %50 of the church-going population. The principal Protestant denominations are Baptist, Episcopalian, Lutheran and Methodist. Catholics form a significant minority.

Religion	
Largest Denominations (Adherents)	
Catholic	105,069
Episcopal	9,216
Presbyterian	13,075
United Methodist	30,690
Black Baptist	27,298
Evangelical Lutheran	5,816
Southern Baptist	3,655
American Baptist	3,179
Jewish	8,850

Media

The city press consists of *The News Journal*. The electronic media consist of one public and one commercial station and seven AM and FM radio stations.

Media	
Newsprint	
The News Journal, daily	
The Defender, weekly	
Television	
NA	
Radio	
WAMS (AM)	WDEL (AM)
WSTW (FM)	WILM (AM)
WJBR (FM)	WJBR (AM)
WMPH (FM)	

Sports

 Wilmington has no major professional sports team. Other sports, however, flourish here, such as horseriding in the 300-acre Bellevue State Park, tennis in the Delcastle Tennis Center, golf in the Delcastle Golf Club and Rock Manor Golf Course, ice skating in the Ice Skating Club, birdwatching and fishing in Brandywine State Park, and canoeing on Brandywine Creek. The Delaware Park Racecourse and Brandywine Raceway present thoroughbred racing and harness racing, respectively.

Arts, Culture, and Tourism

Philanthropic and state support for the performing arts is a long tradition in Wilmington. At least three major official organizations are involved in the promotion of arts: The Delaware State Arts Council, the Mayor's Office of Cultural Affairs, and the Wilmington Arts Commission. The Grand Opera House, built in 1871 and restored recently, is the home of the Center for the Performing Arts as well as Delaware Symphony and OperaDelaware. The Delaware Theater Company, the state's only professional theater company, plays in its downtown location from November through April. Broadway plays are offered at the Playhouse Theater in the Hotel du Pont. Dance is represented by Wilmington Academy of the Dance.

The du Pont philanthropy is responsible for two of the finest museums in Wilmington. The Winterthur Museum is the legacy of Henry Francis du Pont and includes his vast collections of American furniture and decorative arts. The Hagley Mills was also built and endowed by the du Pont family, and it recreates 19th century industrial life and machinery. Other museums include the Delaware Museum of Natural History, founded by John du Pont, with its Hall of Birds and fine shell collection. Brandywine River Museum and the Delaware Art Museum are devoted to contemporary American art.

Travel and Tourism
Hotel Rooms   4,012
Convention and Exhibit Space (square feet)
Convention Centers
Wilmington Hilton
Hotel du Pont
Festivals
Waterfest
Brandywine Arts Festival

Parks and Recreation

Of Wilmington's 500 acres of Parkland, almost 200 acres are in the Brandywine Park, designed by Frederick Law Olmstead. The 13-acre Eden Park on Newcastle Avenue is a historic park known as Monckton Park before 1783. Cool Spring Park, bounded by Tenth Street, Park Place, Van Buren, and Jackson streets, has many varieties of rare trees.

Sources of Further Information

Greater Wilmington Convention and Visitors Bureau
1300 Market Street
Wilmington, DE 19801
(302) 652-4088

Newcastle County Chamber of Commerce
P.O. Box 11247
Wilmington, DE 19850
(302) 737-8450

City Hall, 800 French Street, 19801 (302) 571-4100

Additional Reading

Hoffecker, Carol E. *Corporate Capital: Wilmington in the 20th Century.* 1983.
Prather, H. Leon. *We Have Taken A City: Wilmington Racial Massacres and Coup.* 1984.

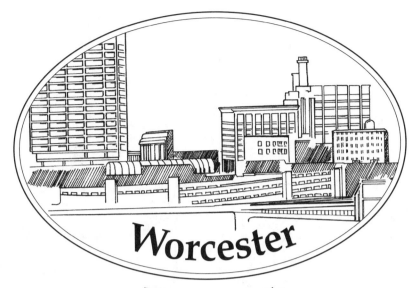

Worcester

Massachusetts

Basic Data

Name   Worcester
Name Origin   From Worcester, England
Year Founded   1673 Inc. 1848
Status: State   Massachusetts
        County   Seat of Worcester County
Area (square miles)   37.6
Elevation (feet)   475
Time Zone   EST
Population (1990)   169,759
Population of Metro Area (1990)   709,705

Sister Cities
   Pushkin, Russia
   St. Vincent, West Indies

Distance in Miles To:
Albany	129
Boston	42
Hartford	66
Lowell	41
Manchester	65
New York	172
Portsmouth	99
Providence	44

Location and Topography

Worcester is located in the geographic center of Massachusetts on a series of rolling hills overlooking the Blackstone River. Lake Quinsigamond, seven miles long, marks the eastern boundary of the city.

Layout of City and Suburbs

Worcester is a city of lakes and ponds. In addition to Lake Quinsigamond, there are scores of lakes, such as Indian Lake, and ponds, such as Flint Pond. The city is bisected by expressways I-190 and I-290. Running in a north-south direction are Main Street and Park Avenue, and in an east-west direction are Chandler, Highland, and others. The landscape is hilly. Holy Cross College is located on Mt. St. James, and Assumption College is located on another hill. The Common, near City Hall, occupies 5 acres out of the 20 acres set aside for this purpose in 1669.

Environment

Environmental Stress Index   2.4
Green Cities Index: Rank   NA
                    Score   NA
Water Quality   Neutral, very soft
Average Daily Use (gallons per capita)   NA
    Maximum Supply (gallons per capita)   NA
Parkland as % of Total City Area   5.1
% Waste Landfilled/Recycled   NA
Annual Parks Expenditures per Capita $21.77

Climate

Worcester is noted for its rapidly changing weather because of the influence of the Berkshire Mountains to the west/northwest and the Atlantic coastline to the east. Occasional storms may dump rain, snow, or sleet. Summer is relatively mild. Average temperatures are 23.8°F for January, and 70.0° F for July. The average annual precipitation is 47.6 inches

Weather

Temperature	
Highest Monthly Average °F	79
Lowest Monthly Average °F	15.6

Annual Averages	
Days 32°F or Below	143
Days above 90°F	5
Zero Degree Days	2

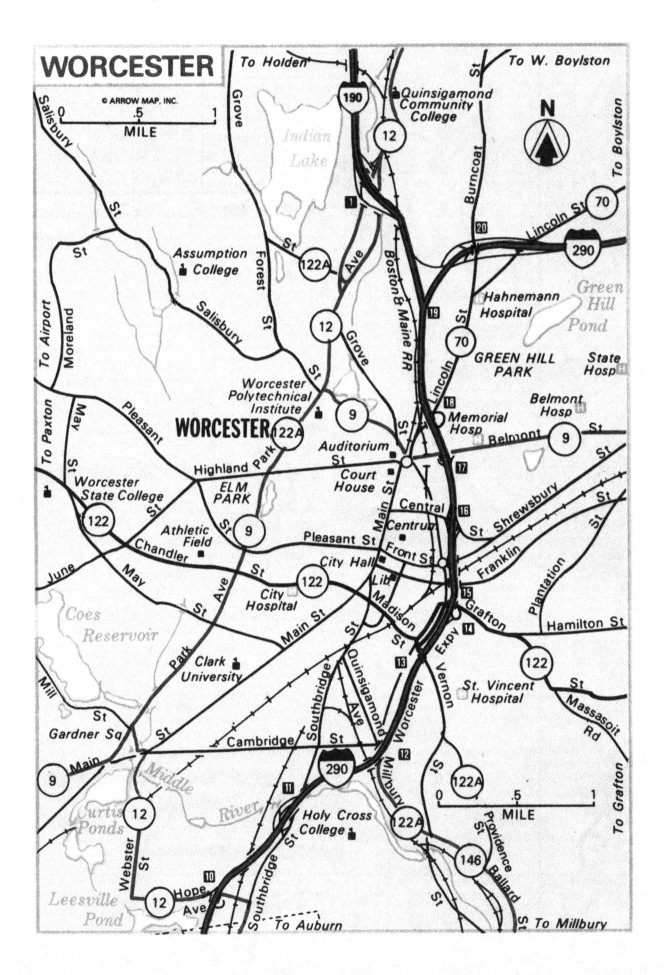

Weather (continued)

Precipitation (inches) 47.61
Snow (inches) 69.7
% Seasonal Humidity 65.5
Wind Speed (m.p.h.) 10.1
Clear Days 90
Cloudy Days 168
Storm Days 19
Rainy Days 135

Average Temperatures (°F)	*High*	*Low*	*Mean*
January	31.6	16.0	23.8
February	38.8	21.8	30.3
March	44.5	28.4	36.5
April	57.9	38.5	48.2
May	72.7	49.7	61.2
June	74.8	54.6	64.7
July	78.8	61.1	70.0
August	78.2	59.9	69.1
September	67.8	49.5	58.7
October	61.3	42.5	51.9
November	47.0	33.4	40.2
December	37.8	21.5	29.7

History

The first European to arrive in the area was Daniel Gookin, who visited the Nipmuck Indians in 1674. Eight years laters he returned with a small group and bought eight square miles of land along Lake Quinsigamond for £12, two coats, and four yards of cloth. The settlers called the place Quinsigamond Plantation. In 1684 the settlement was abandoned because of Indian hostility, but the settlers returned. In 1702 these settlers were again driven out by the Indians during Queen Anne's War. A second successful attempt at colonization came in 1713, when Jonas Rice built a home atop Union Hill. By 1722 the settlement was large enough to incorporate itself as a town, renamed Worcester. Worcester grew to be a major transportation center of the Massachusetts Colony, initially as a stagecoach stop between Boston and the interior. Its political stature also grew after the patriot publisher, Isaiah Thomas, escaped from the Boston Tories in 1775 to Worcester with his printing press and continued printing his paper *The Massachusetts Spy*. The broadsides and pamphlets which poured from his presses helped to consolidate the revolutionary elements throughout New England. He is believed to have given the first public reading of the U.S. Constitution in 1776. After the war, Thomas built up the new nation's largest publishing house and produced the first dictionary.

Worcester continued its liberal, anti-authoritarian traditions after the birth of the United States. Worcester played an active role in the Shay's Rebellion, the formation of the Free Soil Party (which paved the way for the Republican Party), the launching of the Equal Suffrage Movement, and the organization of the Emigrant Aid Company to help Kansas join the union as a free state.

Worcester's industrial history began with the advent of the steam power and the opening of the Blackstone Canal. Within 50 years of the end of the Civil War, four major industries were established in the city.

Ichabod Washburn developed wire manufacturing, William Crompton revolutionized the textile industry with the invention of a fancy loom in 1837, F. B. Norton began producing grinding wheels by a vitrification process in 1875, and Russell Hawes laid the foundations of the United States Envelope Company. The city is credited with a number of other firsts: the first carpet loom, the first valentine, the first steam calliope, the first roll of barbed wire, the first bolt of corduroy, and the first bicycle. The railroads arrived in 1835 providing a fresh impetus to industrialization.

Historical Landmarks

The City Hall was erected in 1898. It was designed by Richard Howland Hunt in a modified Italian Renaissance style. Its Florentine campanile towers rise 205 feet. The Municipal War Memorial Auditorium occupies one entire block between Highland, Salisbury, and Harvard streets and Institute Road. The Mechanics Hall is a Victorian structure erected as an exhibition Hall by the Mechanics Association in 1857 and restored in 1977. The 1772 Salisbury Mansion, restored under the auspices of the Worcester Historical Museum, is one of the best-documented mansions in New England. The Home of Timothy Paine is on Lincoln Street. The Davis Tower, a gift of a former mayor, offers a fine view of the Quinsigamond Lake.

The Trumbull Mansion was originally the second court house, which Daniel Shay's army tried to seize. The Grand Army of the Republic Hall of 1876 was designed by Calvert Vaux.

Population

Worcester's population peaked in 1950 at 203,000 but since then has declined. In the 1990 census the population was 169,759, an increase of 7,960 from the 1980 population of 161,799. Worcester is the second most populous city in Massachusetts.

Population

	1980	*1990*
Central City	161,799	169,759
Rank	91	101
Metro Area	646,352	709,705

Pop. Change 1980–1990 +7,960
Pop. % Change 1980–1990 +4.9
Median Age 31.8
% Male 47.6
% Age 65 and Over 16.1
Density (per square mile) 4,514

Households

Number 63,884
Persons per Household 2.46
% Female-Headed Households 15.7
% One-Person Households 30.1
Births—Total 2,407
  % to Mothers under 20 13.0
  Birth Rate per 1,000 15.1

Chronology

1674	Daniel Gookin arrives in the area to visit the Nipmuck Indians.
1682	Daniel Gookin returns with small band of settlers and buys eight square miles of land from the Nipmuck Indians for £12, two coats, and four yards of cloth.
1684	Settlement is abandoned because of Indian hostility, but settlers return.
1702	Settlement again abandoned during Queen Anne's War.
1713	Jonas Rice founds first permanent settlement which is renamed Worcester.
1722	Town of Worcester is incorporated.
1731	Worcester named shire town of Worcester County.
1738	First schoolhouse is built on Lincoln Square.
1775	First newspaper published by Isaiah Thomas.
1776	The first post office established with Isaiah Thomas as postmaster.
1783	First stage line opens.
1786	Shays's Rebellion begins with the occupation of the court house by a company of armed men.
1788	The first dictionary is published by Isaiah Thomas.
1807	Road is built linking Boston and Worcester.
1812	American Antiquarian Society is founded.
1828	The Blackstone Canal opens.
1835	The first railroad train arrives in Worcester from Boston.
1840	The first valentine is made by Esther Howland.
1842	Charles Dickens visits Worcester.
1843	The first typewriter is developed by Charles Thurber.
1848	Worcester is chartered as a city with Levi Lincoln as mayor; Abraham Lincoln gives speech at City Hall.
1850	The first woman's suffrage national convention is held.
1853	Russell Hawes invents first envelope-making machine.
1854	City purchases land for Elm Park, the first public park in the nation.
1857	Mechanics Hall is dedicated.
1861	Free public library opens.
1864	First public hospital, St. Elizabeth's, opens.
1879	The first telephones are installed.
1883	Electric street lights are installed.
1887	Clark University is founded.
1898	Present City Hall is dedicated.
1924	The first radio station in city goes on air.
1926	Robert H. Goddard, launches first liquid fuel rocket on Pakachoag Hill in Auburn.
1938	Hurricane strikes Worcester, causing great damage.
1945	Worcester Airport is opened.
1947	The city constitution is adopted.
1948	Cruiser U.S.S. *Worcester* is commissioned.
1970	Interstate 290 completed.
1977	Ground is broken for new Civic Center complex.

Ethnic Composition

Whites make up 87% of the population, blacks 4.5%, and Hispanics and others the remainder. The whites are drawn from many nationalities, the most prominent being Swedes, Irish, Canadians, Italians, Lebanese, Lithuanians, Greeks, and Armenians.

Ethnic Composition (as % of total pop.)		
	1980	*1990*
White	93.94	87.08
Black	2.86	4.52
American Indian	0.25	0.32
Asian and Pacific Islander	0.60	2.81
Hispanic	4.25	9.58
Other	NA	5.27

Government

Worcester operates with a council-city manager form of government. Of the 11 council members elected to two-year terms, 6 are elected at large and 5 are elected by district. A largely ceremonial mayor presides over the council meetings, and is elected at large separately. The city manager is appointed by the council and serves under them. Worcester is also the county seat of Worcester county.

Government	
Year of Home Charter	1950
Number of Members of the Governing Body	11
Elected at Large	6
Elected by Wards	5
Number of Women in Governing Body	1

Government (continued)

Salary of Mayor $20,000
Salary of Council Members $17,500
City Government Employment Total   6,562
Rate per 10,000   415.9

Public Finance

The annual budget consists of $311.513 million and expenditures of $322.299 million. The outstanding debt is $99.978 million and cash and security holdings $9.349 million.

Public Finance

Total Revenue (in millions) $311.513
Intergovernmental Revenue—Total (in millions) $136.69
Federal Revenue per Capita $14.16
% Federal Assistance   4.54
% State Assistance   39.33
Sales Tax as % of Total Revenue   0.15
Local Revenue as % of Total Revenue   52.22
City Income Tax   no
Taxes—Total (in millions) $68.3

Taxes per Capita
    Total $433
    Property $423
    Sales and Gross Receipts $0
General Expenditures—Total (in millions) $230.8
General Expenditures per Capita $1,463
Capital Outlays per Capita $114

% of Expenditures for:
    Public Welfare   2.1
    Highways   4.2
    Education   32.8
    Health and Hospitals   13.8
    Police   5.4
    Sewerage and Sanitation   5.9
    Parks and Recreation   2.3
    Housing and Community Development   2.4
Debt Outstanding per Capita $527
    % Utility   12.1
Federal Procurement Contract Awards (in millions) $21.9
Federal Grants Awards (in millions) $51.4
Fiscal Year Begins   July 1

Economy

As the second largest city in Massachusetts, Worcester is a major manufacturing, distribution, service, retail, and trading center with a diverse economic base. Of its 3,500 firms, nearly 800 are manufacturing firms producing a wide range of products. While the focus of the city's economy has changed to the service sector, manufacturing remains significant. While industrial employment has declined by 21% since 1980, it still represents 20% of the employment base. In the 1980s a major new industry emerged in the area: biotechnology research and development. The Massachusetts Biotechnology Research Park is located on 75 acres of land and represents an investment of over $320 million of which BASF Corporation alone accounts for $200 million. Worcester is home to two Fortune 500 companies: Norton and Idle Wild Foods.

Economy

Total Money Income (in millions) $1,649.3
% of State Average   83.6
Per Capita Annual Income $10,454
% Population below Poverty Level   14.4
Fortune 500 Companies   2

Banks	Number	Deposits (in millions)
Commercial	13	2,944.5
Savings	28	3,374.5

Passenger Autos   421,966
Electric Meters   59,304
Gas Meters   34,845

Manufacturing

Number of Establishments   342
% with 20 or More Employees   38.6
Manufacturing Payroll (in millions) $472.2
Value Added by Manufacture (in millions) $964.4
Value of Shipments (in millions) $1,578.0
New Capital Expenditures (in millions) $80.6

Wholesale Trade

Number of Establishments   347
Sales (in millions) $1,839.1
Annual Payroll (in millions) $146.787

Retail Trade

Number of Establishments   1,647
Total Sales (in millions) $1,498.7
Sales per Capita $9,499
Number of Retail Trade Establishments with Payroll   1,165
Annual Payroll (in millions) $157.1
Total Sales (in millions) $1,469.1
General Merchandise Stores (per capita) $875
Food Stores (per capita) $1,230
Apparel Stores (per capita) $474
Eating and Drinking Places (per capita) $848

Service Industries

Total Establishments   1,356
Total Receipts (in millions) $718.7
Hotels and Motels (in millions) $17.4
Health Services (in millions) $214.8
Legal Services (in millions) $78.3

Labor

Worcester provides the Metropolitan Statistical Area with over 56% of its available jobs. The local economy is extremely diversified and robust. As a result the unemployment rate has been lower than both the state and national rates for the past decade. Manufacturing employs over one-fifth of the work force although it has steadily lost ground as an employer since 1980 to the other sectors. The arrival of BASF and other biotechnology firms has helped Worcester to avoid the severe employment downturn that other Northeast cities have experienced. All the top employers have over 1,500 workers on their payrolls; two are in manufacturing, two in retail trade, two in insurance, three in healthcare, and one in government. To meet the labor requirements of the local industry, the city has developed an extensive network of vocational training programs through the Office of Employment and Training.

Labor

Civilian Labor Force   79,387
% Change 1989–1990   -0.9

Work Force Distribution
   Mining   100
   Construction   5,300
   Manufacturing   37,200
   Transportation and Public Utilities   9,000
   Wholesale and Retail Trade   42,500
   FIRE (Finance, Insurance, Real Estate)   13,500
   Service   48,600
   Government   23,400
   Women as % of Labor Force   45.4
   % Self-Employed   3.9
   % Professional/Technical   17.3
Total Unemployment   5,661
Rate %   7.1
Federal Government Civilian Employment   1,062

Education

The Worcester public school system is considered one of the top 30 in the nation and is administered by a School Committee presided over by the mayor. The system consists of 50 high, junior high/middle, and elementary schools. Supplementing these schools are publicly supported vocational schools and some 23 parochial schools.

The Worcester Consortium for Higher Education is a voluntary association of the area's 10 universities and colleges: Anna Maria College, Assumption College, Becker Junior College, Clark University, College of the Holy Cross, Quinsigamond Community College, the Tufts School of Veterinary Medicine, University of Massachusetts Medical School, Worcester Polytechnic Institute and Worcester State College. Business programs are offered at the New England School of Accounting/Salter Secretarial and Computer School, and at nearby Nichols College.

Education

Number of Public Schools   50
Special Education Schools   NA
Total Enrollment   21,066
% Enrollment in Private Schools   11.2
% Minority   33.3
Classroom Teachers   NA
Pupil-Teacher Ratio   NA
Number of Graduates   NA
Total Revenue (in millions) $101.271
Total Expenditures (in millions) $98.820
Expenditures per Pupil $4,728
Educational Attainment (Age 25 and Over)
   % Completed 12 or More Years   62.6
   % Completed 16 or More Years   14.8
Four-Year Colleges and Universities   8
   Enrollment   15,849
Two-Year Colleges   2
   Enrollment   5,580

Libraries

Number   33
Public Libraries   8
Books (in thousands)   523
Circulation (in thousands)   848

Education (continued)

Persons Served (in thousands)   161
Circulation per Person Served   5.2
Income (in millions) $3.279
Staff   136

Four-Year Colleges and Universities
   Anna Maria College
   College of the Holy Cross
   Worcester State College
   Assumption College
   Central New England College
   Clark University
   Worcester Polytechnic Institute
   University of Massachusetts–Worcester

Health

The linchpin of the healthcare system is the University of Massachusetts Medical Center, consisting of a medical school and a 353-bed teaching hospital with over 350 resident physicians. Other facilities include the Memorial Hospital, Worcester City Hospital, and St. Vincent Hospital.

Health

Deaths—Total   1,926
Rate per 1,000   12.0
Infant Deaths—Total   27
Rate per 1,000   11.2
Number of Metro Hospitals   8
Number of Metro Hospital Beds   2,458
Rate per 100,000   1,558
Number of Physicians   1,599
Physicians per 1,000   4.46
Nurses per 1,000   NA
Health Expenditures per Capita $17.68

Transportation

Worcester is located at the center of New England at a point where all major transportation routes intersect or are easily accessible by the interstate highway network and other thoroughfares. This system includes Interstates 290, 190, and 146, as well as State Routes 9, 12, and U.S. 20. All of these routes pass through the city and provide access to I-90, I-395, and I-495, resulting in an integrated north, south, east, and west network. Interstate 146 leads directly into the Central Business District. Rail passenger service is provided by Amtrak and Conrail, while the Boston & Maine Railroad and the Providence and Worcester Railroad handle freight. Commuter rail service to and from Boston is being explored by the Massachusetts Bay Transit Authority. The Worcester Regional Transit Authority serves the city and 12 surrounding towns on 29 routes. Interstate bus travel is provided by Greyhound, Trailways, Peter Pan, and Marathon Lines.

The Worcester Airport has grown in recent years and has been upgraded by the Federal Aviation Administration from a commercial service airport to a primary airport, the highest FAA classification. Many of the region's frequent air travellers prefer the

Worcester Airport over Boston's Logan. A total of 17 commercial passenger flights arrive and depart from Worcester Airport daily. A master plan for the airport calls for the construction of a $13 million terminal building.

Transportation	
Interstate Highway Mileage	58
Total Urban Mileage	1,637
Total Daily Vehicle Mileage (in millions)	$7.490
Daily Average Commute Time	41.1 min.
Number of Buses	62
Port Tonnage (in millions)	NA
Airports	1
Number of Daily Flights	7
Daily Average Number of Passengers	352
Airlines (American carriers only)	
USAir	

Housing

Residential development has been substantial during the past decade. Nearly 5,000 permits were issued since 1988 adding over 4,000 units to the city's housing stock. In the downtown area the most significant new projects have been the 59-unit Lynden House in the Central Business District, the 75-unit Illyrian Gardens, the 155-unit Royal Worcester Apartments, and the 196-unit Franklin Square complex. The total housing stock has grown from 61,645 in 1980 to 69,263 in 1990. The vacancy rate is 8.3%. Total property valuations exceed $7 billion.

Housing	
Total Housing Units	69,336
% Change 1980–1990	11.1
Vacant Units for Sale or Rent	4,116
Occupied Units	63,884
% with More Than One Person per Room	3.3
% Owner-Occupied	43.3
Median Value of Owner-Occupied Homes	$128,900
Average Monthly Purchase Cost	$364
Median Monthly Rent	$451
New Private Housing Starts	405
Value (in thousands)	$22,428
% Single-Family	68.1
Nonresidential Buildings Value (in thousands)	$19,481

Urban Redevelopment

In the period 1985–1990 approximately $500 million had been invested in the Central Business District. Approximately 24,000 square feet of office space is being absorbed per month. The vacancy rate of 10.27% in Class A office space is much lower than the national vacancy rate of 21%. According to a study by Leggatt McCall Advisors the city could support a building program of between 1 and 1.5 million square feet of office space during the next five years. The new construction projects in response to this need are:

- Chestnut Plaza, 175,000 square feet.
- City Plaza, 300,000 square feet of office tower, 100,000 square feet of retail space, and a 15-story residential tower.
- Worcester Market Building, 45,000 square feet.
- Clubland, the former E. M. Loew's Theater, a night club, concert hall, and dance floor with a 26 x 30-foot video wall.
- Renovation of the Worcester Center Galleria at a cost of $45 million.
- The City Hall/Worcester Common Streetscape, a $16 million public works plan for the Main Street portion of the Downtown area from Franklin Square to Lincoln Square.
- Liberty Square, 730,000-square-foot, $140 million, four-building office/retail complex.

Crime

Worcester's crime rate is average, with 416 violent crimes and 3,582 property crimes known to police in 1991.

Crime	
Violent Crimes—Total	416
Violent Crime Rate per 100,000	NA
Murder	NA
Rape	NA
Robbery	NA
Aggravated Assaults	NA
Property Crimes	3,582
Burglary	NA
Larceny	NA
Motor Vehicle Theft	NA
Arson	NA
Per Capita Police Expenditures	$120.97
Per Capita Fire Protection Expenditures	$115.20
Number of Police	368
Per 1,000	2.29

Religion

There are 110 churches in the city of which 29 are Roman Catholic. A number of churches serve ethnic minorities, such as Armenians, Russians, Koreans, and others.

Religion	
Largest Denominations (Adherents)	
Catholic	325,686
Episcopal	11,639
American Baptist	8,484
United Church of Christ	20,753
Evangelical Lutheran	8,287
Assembly of God	3,639
Unitarian	3,957
United Methodist	9,228
Jewish	13,700

Media

Worcester has two daily newspapers— *The Worcester Telegram* in the morning and *The Evening Gazette* in the afternoon.

The city picks up major television networks from Boston. Six AM and FM stations, including two National Public Radio stations, conduct radio broadcasting.

Media

Newsprint
  Worcester Telegram, daily
  The Evening Gazette, daily

Radio
  WCUW (FM)   WICN (FM)
  WORC (AM)   WTAG (AM)
  WSRS (FM)   WXLO (FM)

Sports

Worcester's only sports franchise is the New England Blazers of the Major Indoor Lacrosse League. They play at the 15,500-seat Centrum from January through March.

Arts, Culture, and Tourism

The leading theater company is the Worcester Foothills Theater Company, founded in 1974. This residential troupe stages seven productions annually. Other companies include the Worcester Forum Theater Ensemble, the Clark University Center for Contemporary Performance and Theater Program, Worcester Children's Theater, and Theater Unlimited. The Pyramid Gypsy Dance Company, founded in 1978, is the premier dance group, and its repertory ranges from mime to ballet. Opera is staged by Opera Worcester, the Worcester Chorus, and the Worcester County Light Opera. The Worcester Orchestra plays two concert series, one in winter spring and the other in summer. The Central Massachusetts Symphony Orchestra performs many of its concerts at Mechanics Hall and its summer offerings at Institute Park. Medieval music is presented by the Salisbury Concert of Early Music, and and traditional American music by the Worcester Area Folk Society. The city's Music Festival, founded in 1858, draws large crowds each fall. The All Saints Choir of Men and Boys, founded in 1868, is the country's oldest choir. The most famous choral group is the Worcester Chorus, which performs with the Worcester Orchestra.

Worcester has a number of distinguished performing arts centers, including the Mechanics Hall on Main Street, founded in 1867, Centrum on Foster Street, founded in 1982, and the Worcester Memorial Auditorium on Lincoln Square, built in 1932.

The Worcester Art Museum is one of the largest in the country and is noted for its fine collection of European masters; stained glass windows from Chartres, Strasbourg and Borsham House; Japanese prints and American furniture. The Worcester Historical Museum, founded in 1877, has many exhibits illustrating the city's history, including Charles Thurber's first typewriter, invented in 1843. The Higgins Armory Museum has the largest collection of western armor.

Travel and Tourism

Hotel Rooms   3,475
Convention and Exhibit Space (square feet)

Convention Centers
  Centrum
  Mechanics Hall
  Worcester Memorial Auditorium

Festivals
  Abbott's Mime Festival
  Annual Music Festival
  Harvest Fest
  Albanian/Greek Orthodox Festival (June)

Art galleries include Summer's World Center for the Arts, the Grove Street Art Gallery, Gallery 69A, the University of Massachusetts Medical Center Gallery, the Cantor Gallery at the College of the Holy Cross, and the Little Center Gallery at Clark University.

Parks and Recreation

Worcester has 47 parks covering 1,200 acres. The oldest (1854) is Elm Park, the first park in the nation purchased with public funds. Green Hill Park, opposite Burncoat Park, is named after Andrew H. Green, the Worcester native who later became known as the "Father of Greater New York." It includes an 18-hole golf course, picnic groves, a skating pond, a ski run, and a petting zoo. Lake Quinsigamond Park, bordered on the east and west by the hills of Shrewsbury and Worcester, stretches nearly nine miles.

Sources of Further Information

City Hall
445 Main Street
Worcester, MA 01608
(508) 799-1033

Main Library
City of Worcester, Salem Square
Worcester, MA 01608
(508) 799-1655

Worcester Area Chamber of Commerce
33 Waldo Street
Worcester, MA 01608
(508) 753-2924

Worcester County Convention and Visitors Bureau
33 Waldo Street
Worcester, MA 01608
(508) 753-2920

Worcester Cultural Commission
55 Pearl Street
01608
(508) 799-1994

Worcester Heritage Society
321 Main Street
Worcester, MA 01608
(508) 754-8760

Additional Reading

Brooke, John L. *The Heart of the Commonwealth: Society and Political Culture in Worcester County, Massachusetts, 1713–1861.* 1990.

Glassman, Alfred. *Universal Atlas of Central Massachusetts and Metropolitan Worcester.* 1984.
Goyer, Jane. *So Dear to My Heart: Memories of a Gentler Time.* 1990.
Konigburg, Lisa. *Rendering from Worcester's Past: Nineteenth-Century Architectural Drawings from the American Antiquarian Society.* 1987.
Worcester: An All-American City. Irregular.

Calgary

Alberta

Location and Topography

Calgary is in the eastern foothills of the Canadian Rocky Mountains in Alberta, and is thus known sometimes as the Foothills City. It is located at the junction of the Bow and Elbow rivers, which run through the heart of the city.

Layout of City and Suburbs

Situated on the meeting point of the western prairies and the mountain foothills, Calgary is one of the most picturesque cities in North America and the highest city in Canada. The city is framed against the backdrop of the Rocky Mountains, and in many respects retains its old frontier landscape. The Bow River curves around the city and forms its northern border. Two smaller rivers, the Elbow River and Nose Creek, flow through the city into the Bow, creating valleys and bluffs. The main

business district is compressed between the Bow River and the Canadian Pacific rail tracks. Railroads enter the city from all four directions. Residential developments follow the river valleys to the northwest and southeast. The University of Calgary and the International Airport lie to the north, and the Glenmore Reservoir, Fish Creek Provincial Park, and Sarcee Indian Reserve are to the south. The main manufacturing district is located to the east in the suburb of Ogden, while assorted commercial and manufacturing establishments follow the rail lines southward in the direction of Fort MacLeod and northward toward Edmonton. Across the Elbow River to the east are the stockyards and refineries that sustain Calgary's economy.

The streets within the city run north and south, with avenues running east and west. The intersection of Centre Street and the Bow River is the starting point of the numbering system for both streets and avenues. Centre Street divides the east and west numbers and the Bow River divides the north and south numbers. The intersection of Bow River and Centre Street also divides the city into quarters.

The principal architectural landmarks are the City Hall, the 626-feet Calgary Tower with an observation deck and revolving restaurant, and the twin buildings of the Petro Canada Center, whose 55-story tower is the tallest in Calgary.

Climate

Although Calgary is a northern city with short summers and cold winters, its proximity to the mountains tends to moderate its temperatures. The severity of the winter is tempered by the chinook, a warm dry wind blowing from the Rocky Mountains that raises temperatures by as much as 40° F within a few hours on an average of 25 days a year. Precipitation averages about 17.5 inches

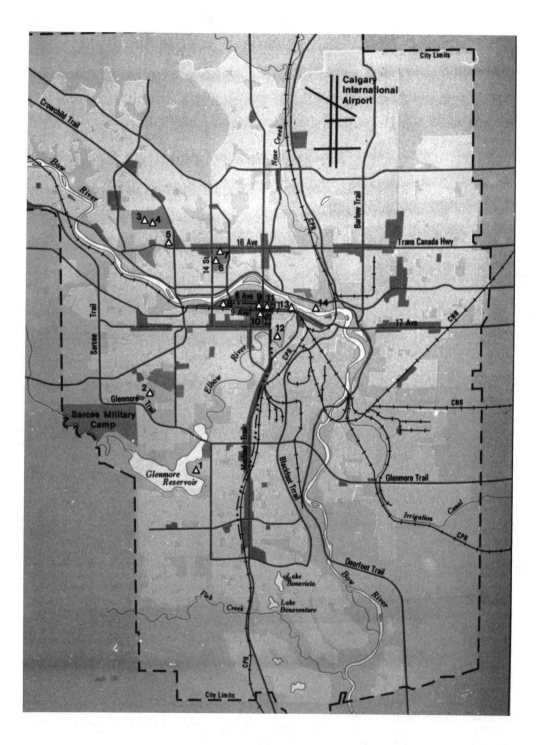

annually of which 5.9 inches fall as snow. From May to September the mean rainfall averages 11.8 inches. July is the month of maximum thunderstorm and hail activity. The number of days with measurable snowfall is 62 and the number of rainy days 58. There are 112 frost-free days annually, on average. The average hours of sunshine per day is 6.34. The mean daily temperature is 61.5°F in July and 10.7°F in January.

Weather	
Annual Averages	
January °F	10.7
July °F	61.5
Precipitation (inches)	17.5
Sunshine (hours)	2,314

History

Spearpoints found in the region are evidence of a human settlement in the area as early as 12,000 years ago. Over the next 10,000 years many successive waves of nomadic hunting peoples settled here, the last of whom were the Blackfoots, the Sarcees, and the Stoneys. The westward movement of the fur trade brought the first white men into the area in the late 18th century. Among the early fur traders who visited Calgary were two employees of the Northwest Company: David Thompson, in 1787, and Peter Fidler, in 1792. Illegal activities by buffalo hunters and whisky traders led to the establishment in 1875 of a North West Mounted Police post here known as Fort Calgary. The first railroad reached Fort Calgary in 1883 and Canadian Pacific subsequently laid out its first townsite west of the Elbow and south of the Bow rivers. Calgary was incorporated in 1884 as the first town in what is now Alberta, receiving city status in 1893, when its population approached 4,000.

As large ranches developed in southern Alberta, Calgary became the center of the Canadian meat-packing industry. In 1886 the city held its first annual agricultural exhibition, and in 1912 its first annual rodeo known as the Calgary Stampede, which merged in 1923 to become the Calgary Exhibition and Stampede. Oil was discovered in nearby Turner Valley in 1914, and oil became the basis of the city's prosperity and the heart of its economy, which it remains until today.

Historical Landmarks

Calgary's skyline is dominated by the Calgary Tower, adjacent to the Palliser Hotel. In the shadow of the Tower are the Glenbow-Alberta Institute and the Centre for the Performing Arts. Downtown features the Devonian Gardens, in Toronto Dominion Square, with its 20,000 terraced plants. To the east, where the Bow River meets the Elbow River, stands the Calgary Interpretive Center. The city's northwest quadrant is dominated by the University of Calgary and other educational insti-

tutions. A few blocks south of the downtown area are the exhibition grounds of the Calgary Exhibition and Stampede. The grounds also contain the Olympic Saddledome, built in 1988 for the Winter Olympics. Calgary's most visible links with its historic past are found in the Heritage Park, a recreated frontier town built on the shore of Glenmore Lake, southwest of the city. Fort Calgary, at the confluence of the Bow and Elbow rivers, is the original site of the North West Mounted Police Post, built in 1875. McDougall Centre is one of Calgary's early sandstone buildings built in 1806. The Deane House Historic Site and Tea Room, across from Fort Calgary, was built in 1906, and was opened to the public in 1986.

Population

The population of Calgary in the 1990 census was 710,677. Population growth has been high throughout the 20th century, rising from 43,000 in 1911 to 87,000 in 1941; 469,917 in 1976 to 592,246 in 1981, and then to 636,105 in 1986. Calgary's growth has been due primarily to immigration rather than to natural increase. The large immigration of young adults keeps the average age well below the national level. Nevertheless, the median age rose from 27 to 32 in 1976. Both the 0–14 and the 15–24 age groups are declining in size while the 65+ age group has grown to 8%.

Population		
City Population	*1986*	*1990*
	636,105	710,677
% Male 49.91		
Age		
% Under 14 21.40		
% Over 65 6.92		
Vital Statistics		
Births (1989) 12,284		
Deaths (1989) 3,313		
Natural Increase (1986–1991) 8,971		
Marriages (1989) 5,783		
Married (1989) 311,710		
Single (1989) 140,150		
Widowed/Divorced (1989) 48,105		
Households and Families		
Household Total 167,775		
Average Persons per Household 3.1		
Average Children per Household 1.2		
Mother Tongue		
English 81.6		
French 1.4		
Chinese 2.5		
German 2.3		

Ethnic Composition

By ethnic origin, Anglo-Saxons and Irish constitute the dominant majority with 595,200. French number 74,035, Germans 119,215, Dutch 36,295, Ukrainians 41,145, other

Chronology

1787   David Thompson of the Northwest Company visits the site of Calgary.

1792   Peter Fidler of the Northwest Company visits the site of Calgary.

1875   A North West Mounted Police post known as Fort Calgary is established to combat buffalo poachers and whiskey traders.

1883   The Canadian Pacific Railway selects Fort Calgary as its principal station in Alberta.

1884   Calgary is incorporated as a town.

1886   Calgary holds its first annual agricultural exhibition.

1893   Calgary is raised to the status of a city.

1912   Calgary holds its first annual rodeo known as Calgary Stampede.

1914   Oil is discovered in Turner Valley.

1923   Agricultural exhibition and rodeo are combined to form Calgary Exhibition and Stampede.

1988   Calgary becomes the first Canadian city to host the Winter Olympics.

Europeans 141,205, Jews 7,359, Middle Easterners 6,435, East Indians and Pakistanis 15,361, Chinese 26,175, other Asians 15,525, blacks 4,880, American Indians 16,125, and others 7,660.

Government

Under the Municipal Government Act of 1968, Calgary has a mayor-council form of government. The mayor, who is elected to a three-year term, appoints a four-member board of commissioners, including a chief commissioner. The council consists of 14 aldermen, each elected from a ward for three-year terms.

Public Finance

The 1992 municipal budget consists of $Can 846.7 million compared to $Can 793.3 million in 1991. Of the municipal services provided for in the budget, 28% is spent on transportation, 28% on police, 12% on parks and recreation, 9% on staff and support, 9% on public works, 8% on capital financing, 3% on social services, and 3% on public library. Of the revenues, 39% is derived from property tax; 16% from user fees, licenses, and penalties; 14% from utilities and franchise fees; 13% from business tax; 12% from grants and subsidies; and 6% from investment income and reserves. The 1992 Capital Budget was $Can 392.2 million, of which 55% went to transportation, 16% to public works, 16% to parks

and recreation, 7% to protective services, and 6% to administrative services. The outstanding debt is $Can 885 million for tax-supported operations; and $Can 643 million, incurred before 1983 for self-supporting utilities.

Economy

Calgary is an oil city, much as Houston is in the United States. More than 640 oil companies have their headquarters in Calgary as well as 73% of Canada's geological, geophysical, and surveying consultant firms. Many Canadian banks, as well as 11 multinational banks, also maintain their western head offices in the city. The Alberta Stock Exchange, founded in 1914 as the Calgary Stock Exchange, has grown to become the premier stock exchange in the West with the volume of trade over $Can 800 million. Calgary's historical distinction as Canada's leading cattle center and meat processor has survived the oil boom. The city's location also makes it a natural center for transportation. Ten airlines, two transcontinental railways, four branch railways, and numerous transcontinental truck lines serve the city. The headquarters of Canadian Pacific have been located here for over a century. The Trans-Canada Highway runs through the city. Calgary has more than 940 industrial plants, most of them using natural gas and electricity rather than fossil fuels. Calgary exceeds the national average in per capita income and percentage of population in the work force. Yet, despite the phenomenal growth rate, Calgary remains overly dependent on oil and suffers accordingly whenever there is a slump in the oil market. The manufacturing industry is diversifying, notably into food processing, clothing, furniture, and high technology. Calgary is home to the largest concentration of research facilities in western Canada. There are two research parks, the 105-acre University Research Park and the 1,100-acre Calgary Research and Development Park, which is administered by the Calgary Research and Development Authority. More than two-thirds of Alberta's advanced technology companies are based in Calgary and they generate annual revenues of over $Can 2 billion.

Labor

Calgary has a work force of 381,000 with a participation rate of 74.2%, the highest in Canada. This high rate is attributable to the fact that Calgary has the largest percentage of post-secondary level workers—over 55%. The work force is heavily oriented toward the professional management and commercial sectors. Blue-collar occupations are dominated by the building, railway, and more recently, the oil supply trades. Within industry 22.7% of employees are engaged in the primary sector, including manufacturing and construction; and 77.3% in the secondary sector, including services, FIRE, trade, transportation, and public services. The largest employer is the City of Calgary and the following seven largest are also in the public sector. The largest private employers are Safeway Canada, Calgary Cooperative, Amoco Canada, Petro Canada, and Transalta Utilities.

Labor

Work Force	Male	Female
Total Work Force	206,285	165,860
Employed	184,920	149,605
Employment Rate	84.0	66.60
% of 15–24 Year Olds	75.29	72.10

Occupation	Male	Female
Managerial	31,255	14,745
Education	4,955	8,655
Health	3,030	12,900
Technical and Cultural	30,565	12,460
Clerical	15,640	63,650
Sales	22,695	16,240
Service	23,720	25,475
Manufacturing	24,100	4,315
Construction	19,660	585
Transportation	11,485	1,050
Other	16,350	2,790

Income

Male ($Can) 36,684
Female ($Can) 22,553
Average Household Income ($Can) 40,533
Average Family Income ($Can) 45,624
Average Tax ($Can) 7,094
Average Household Expenditure ($Can) 49,545
Number of Banks 9
  Branches 337

Manufacturing

Plants 898
Employees 22,653
Value of Shipments ($Can) 3,343,641,000
Total Value Added ($Can) 1,284,887,000

Education

The Calgary Board of Education supports 204 schools with an enrollment of 91,000 students. The Calgary Roman Catholic Separate School District administers 69 schools with an enrollment of 30,000. The post-secondary education sector is represented by four major institutions, of which the largest is the University of Calgary with an enrollment of over 20,000. Its medical faculty is located in the Health Sciences Centre at the Foothills Medical Complex.

Mount Royal College, established in 1910, is the city's oldest college. It has two campuses, one at Lincoln Park in southwest Calgary and one downtown. It provides extensive credit-free programs for professional development and personal enjoyment. The Southern Alberta Institute of Technology is Canada's oldest polytechnical

Education

Population (over 15 years old) 494,835
Less than Grade 9 35,210
Grades 9–13 183,075
Trade Certificate 139,510
University Degree 74,710

Four-Year Universities and Colleges
  University of Calgary

school and offers more than 60 full-time certificate and diploma programs in the applied arts, engineering technologies, and medical sciences. Other post-secondary institutions include the Alberta College of Art, Alberta Vocational College, and a branch of the U.S.-based DeVry Institute of Technology.

Health

Medical services are provided in seven hospitals. These facilities are anchored by three major groups: the Foothills Medical Centre, Calgary General Hospital, and the Calgary District Hospital Group. Included in the Foothills Medical Centre are the Thomas Baker Cancer Centre, the Provincial Lab, the University of Calgary Faculty of Medicine and Medical Clinic, the Alberta Heritage Medical Research Centre, and the Foothills Provincial General Hospital. The Calgary General Hospital operates the Bow Valley Centre in conjunction with the new Peter Lougheed Centre. The Calgary District Hospital Group manages three hospitals: the Holy Cross Hospital, the Rockyview General Hospital, and the Colonel Belcher Hospital, including the Southern Alberta Regional Geriatric Centre. Two other hospitals also serving Calgary are the Alberta Children's Hospital and the Salvation Army Grace Hospital.

Transportation

Calgary is located on the Trans-Canada and secondary highways, providing efficient access to the east-west and north-south markets. Historically, railroads have played a major role in the development of Calgary, particularly the Canadian Pacific Railway, which first established a station here in 1883. Today CP Rail and Canadian National Railways provide comprehensive freight services while Via Rail Canada provides passenger services. Citywide passenger bus and light rail (C-Rail) transit service is provided by Calgary Transit with 97 bus routes. The city has three light rail lines. The principal air terminal is the Calgary International Airport, located about six miles from downtown. The airport is used by eight airlines: Air BC, Air Canada, American Airlines, Canadian Airlines International, Delta Airlines, KLM Royal Dutch Airlines, Time Air, and United Airlines. Twenty-five percent of all corporate aircrafts in Canada are based in Calgary. In addition there is a satellite airport at Springbank, eight miles west of city limits beside the Trans-Canada Highway.

Housing

Housing stock consists of 281,939 units of which 59.3% are owner-occupied. Prices for detached two-story executive homes range from $Can 310,000 in Mount Royal to $Can 145,000 in the northeast. Standard two-story homes are available in the $Can 112,000–to–$Can 135,000 range in Beddington, The Properties, Silver Springs, and Woodlands.

Housing

Total Housing Stock   281,939
Owned   135,360
Rented   102,205
Single, Detached   129,515
Apartments   20,610
Homes Built 1990   6,892
Building Permits Value ($Can)   946,310,000

New Automobiles

Domestic   18,421
Imported   8,266
Trucks   17,353

Tallest Buildings	Hgt. (ft.)	Stories
Petro-Canada Tower #2	689	52
Benkers Hall (1989)	645	50
Calgary Tower	626	NA
Canterra Tower (1988)	580	46
First Canadian Centre	547	44
Scotia Centre	504	38
Nova Bldg.	500	37
Petro-Canada Tower #1	469	33

Media

Newsprint
  The Calgary Herald, daily
  The Calgary Sun, daily
Television
  CBRT (Channel 9)
  CFCN (Channel 4)
  CKXX (Channel 2)
Radio

CBR (AM)	CBR (FM)
CFAC (AM)	CFCN (AM)
CFFR (AM)	CHFM (FM)
CHQR (AM)	CISS (AM)
CJAY (FM)	CKIK (FM)
CKRY (FM)	

Urban Redevelopment

In 1964–1967 Calgary announced plans for a major urban renewal in the downtown area. The seventies and the eighties were the boom construction years, changing the skyline as well as the architecture of the city. Among the major buildings built during this period were the University of Calgary Medical School (1970), Calgary Convention Centre (1974), Bow Valley Square (1982), Olympic Saddledome (1983), and the Calgary Centre for the Performing Arts (1984).

Crime

There were 90,921 Criminal Code violations in 1991, of which homicides numbered 25, sexual offenses 874, assaults 7,311, robbery 1,151, breaking and entering 12,916, thefts 42,694, drug trafficking 632, and others 12,318. The Calgary Police Force has a strength of 1,147 sworn officers, a ratio of 1 police officer for every 421 residents.

Religion

Calgary has 430 churches. With Anglo-Saxons in the majority, mainline Protestant denominations are dominant.

Media

Calgary has two mass-circulation dailies: *The Calgary Herald* with a circulation of 140,000 and *The Calgary Sun* with a circulation of 75,000. The Toronto-based *Globe and Mail* is printed in Calgary via satellite. The electronic media consist of three television stations broadcasting on three channels, and 11 AM and FM radio stations.

Sports

Calgary has two major professional sports teams: The Canadian Stampeders of the Canadian Football League, who play in McMahon Stadium; and the Calgary Flames of the National Hockey League, who play in the Olympic Saddledome. The Calgary Olympic venues continue to provide athletes with quality facilities. These include the Olympic Oval, a fully enclosed speed skating rink; Olympic Park; and Olympic Plaza. Other facilities include the Father David Bauer Arena, Max Bell Arena, and the Stampede Corral.

Arts, Culture, and Tourism

The hub of Calgary's cultural life is the Calgary Centre for the Performing Arts, which opened in 1985. It houses the Max Bell Theatre, Pumphouse Theatre, Lunchbox Theatre, Martha Cohen Theatre, Alberta Theatre Projects, and Jack Singer Concert Hall. The Calgary Philharmonic Orchestra also performs here under Conductor Mario Bernardi. The Southern Alberta Jubilee Auditorium hosts various concerts. In addition, there are numerous active theatrical groups, such as the Pleiades Theatre, Loose Moose Theatre, and the University Theatre. Music is represented by the Calgary Opera Company, Chamber Music Society, Calgary Festival Chorus, and the Early Music Society.

The Glenbow Museum, part of the Glenbow-Alberta Institute, is the largest museum in western Canada. Other museums include the Nickle Arts Museum; the Muttart Gallery; Aero Space Museum; Alberta Science Centre; Alberta Sports Hall of Fame; Canadian Western Natural Gas, Light, Heat and Power Company Museum; Energeum; Grain Academy; Museum of Movie Art; Museum of the Regiments; Naval Museum of Alberta; Olympic Hall of Fame; Sarcee People's Museum; Stockmen's Memorial Foundation; Royal Tyrrell Museum of Paleontology; and Whyte Museum of the Canadian Rockies.

Parks and Recreation

Calgary has over 100 public parks. The most popular are the Devonian Gardens, a glass-enclosed downtown park;

Century Gardens; Princes Island Park, a downtown island park; Fish Creek Provincial Park, one of the world's largest urban parks located on the southern limits of the city; Bowness Park; and Carburn Park.

Sources of Further Information

Calgary Chamber of Commerce
517 Centre Street S.
Calgary, Alberta T2G 2C4

City Hall
Post Office Box 2100, Station M
Calgary, Alberta T2P 2M5

Additional Reading

Baine, R P. *Calgary: An Urban Study.* 1973.
Barr, B. M. *Calgary: Metropolitan Structure and Influence.* 1975.
Foran, Max L. *Calgary: An Illustrated History.* 1978.
McEwan, J. W. Grant. *Calgary Cavalcade.* 1975.
Ward, Tom. *Cow Town: An Album of Early Calgary.* 1975.

Edmonton

Alberta

Basic Data

Name   Edmonton
Year Founded   1795 Inc. 1892
Status: Province   Capital of Alberta
Area (square miles)   271
Elevation   2,200 ft.
Time Zone   Mountain
Population (1990)   616,741

Distance in Miles to:

Calgary	186
Chicago	1,691
Montreal	2,339
New York	2,500
Ottawa	2,221
Quebec	2,507
Regina	488
Toronto	2,147
Vancouver	773
Winnipeg	843

Location and Topography

Edmonton, the capital of Alberta, is located on the North Saskatchewan River near the geographical center of the province. It is the northernmost major city in North America and is called the Gateway to the North.

Layout of City and Suburbs

Edmonton is a sprawling city spread over 268 square miles, making it the largest Canadian city in area. The North Saskatchewan River winds through the city for 38 miles and is crossed by numerous bridges. Downtown is bounded by 104 Avenue on the north and 100 Avenue on the south, 95 Street on the east and 109 Street on the west. Streets running north-south and avenues running east-west are numbered rather than named.

Most government buildings are on the north bank of the river at 109 Street. The major shopping center and tourist attraction is the Edmonton Mall in the west, completed in 1986 with 800 stores and a vast entertainment and recreation complex. The city's focal point is Sir Winston Churchill Square, the largest ornamental park in the world. To its east and north is the Civic Centre, including City Hall, public library, art gallery, and Citadel Theatre Complex. Nearby is Chinatown Gate, donated by Edmonton's sister city of Harbin, China, and the Edmonton Convention Centre, built into the valley wall in a series of terraces. The Aviation Hall of Fame is also located here. A pedestrian mall, Rice-Howard Way, leads from the Civic Centre into the business district, where it connects with an extensive network of enclosed walkways, called pedways. Another walkway, known as the Heritage Trail, links historic buildings. Downstream, Fort Saskatchewan has developed into an industrial zone, the largest in Alberta.

Climate

Edmonton has a very cold mid-continental climate. The average temperature is 5°F in January and 63°F in July. The weather is generally dry and rainfall averages only 17.5 inches annually. The hours of sunshine are 2,263 per year.

Weather	
Annual Averages	
January °F	5
July °F	63
Annual Precipitation (inches)	17.5
Annual Sunshine (hours)	2,263

History

The Blackfoot and Cree Indians lived in the area preceding the arrival of the first Europeans. The first white men to reach the area were agents of the Hudson's Bay Company, who built a fur-trading post on North Saskatchewan River in 1795 called Fort Edmonton. The fort was moved four times before being relocated in 1830 on the north bank of the river near the present site of the Legislative Building. By 1869, when Hudson's Bay Company agreed to transfer title to the area to the Canadian government as part of its sale of Rupert's Land, the fort had grown into a town. It was incorporated in 1892 and chartered as a city in 1904.

When the province of Alberta was established in 1905, Edmonton became the capital. In the same year the Canadian Northern (later Canadian National) Railway reached town. Strathcona, a settlement on the south bank, was annexed in 1912. Homesteaders flooded the northern prairie lands, swelling Edmonton's population to 75,000 by 1914. In the interwar years, the population boom collapsed with the decline in the wheat market, but Edmonton remained important as a base for bush pilots on the air route to Alaska. The first airport was built in 1926. Later, as the terminus of the Alaska Highway, the city gained further commercial importance. But the city did not hit its stride until the discovery of oil at nearby Leduc in 1947. As oil wealth flowed into the city, its skyline changed, and its population grew by leaps and bounds.

The city held the Commonwealth Games in 1978. In 1981 it annexed 139 square miles of surrounding land in order to make room for further orderly growth.

Historical Landmarks

Fort Edmonton Historical Park contains a reconstruction of the original Fort Edmonton. The Strathcona Town Center is designated as a historic heritage area. The Heritage Trail links sites and buildings of historical importance.

Population

Edmonton is one of Canada's fastest-growing cities with a sixfold increase between 1941 and 1991. Its 1990 population of 616,741 makes it Canada's fifth largest city, only slightly smaller than Winnipeg. From a total of 461,361 in 1976 it grew to 532,246 in 1981 and 573,980 in 1986. Until 1971 natural increase accounted for much of the growth, but since that time migration has supplied a majority of the new residents.

Population		
City Population	1986	1990
	573,980	616,741
% Male 49.55		
Age		
% Under 14 20.83		
% Over 65 8.25		

Population (continued)		
Vital Statistics		
Births (1989) 10,527		
Deaths (1989) 3,409		
Natural Increase (1986–1991) 7,118		
Marriages (1989) 5,157		
Married (1989) 271,750		
Single (1989) 134,965		
Widowed/Divorced (1989) 27,715		
Households and Families		
Households Total 149,060		
Average # Persons per Household 3.1		
Average # Children per Household 1.2		
Mother Tongue		
English 74.8		
French 2.3		
Ukrainian 3.4		
German 2.8		
Chinese 2.7		

Ethnic Composition

About 45% of the inhabitants are of English origin. Of the remaining, the largest groups are Scottish, German, Irish, Ukrainian, and French.

Government

Edmonton has a mayor-council form of government. The mayor and the twelve aldermen (two from each of the six wards) are elected to three-year terms. The city manager, the chief executive, is appointed by the council for five-year terms.

Public Finance

Edmonton receives its revenues from taxes and from provincial grants.

Economy

Edmonton's dependence on oil exploration and production is substantial, and it has been called the "Houston of Canada." However, unlike Calgary, it has few petroleum-related companies located in the city. Until the oil market collapsed in the mid-1980s, oil wealth generated construction and service activities. The Inter-Provincial Pipeline begins in Edmonton, and the city has many refineries processing crude oil. Traditional industries include clothing, fabricated metal products, lumber, and food and beverages.

Labor

The oil industry is not labor-intensive and therefore does not generate many jobs within the city. Nevertheless, Edmonton historically has had a very low unemployment rate. Public administration accounts for 10% of the work force, same as manufacturing. Services are the largest sector with 37%, followed by trade with 20%.

Chronology

1795	Hudson's Bay Company builds Fort Edmonton as a fur trading post on the North Saskatchewan River.
1830	Fort Edmonton is moved to the present site of the Legislative Building.
1870	Hudson's Bay Company agrees to relinquish Rupert's Land to the Canadian government.
1892	Fort Edmonton is incorporated as the Town of Edmonton.
1902	The North Saskatechewan River is bridged.
1904	Edmonton is chartered as a city.
1905	Edmonton is chosen as capital of the new province of Alberta. The Canadian Northern Railway reaches town.
1912	Edmonton annexes Strathcona on the southern bank of the river.
1915	The original Fort Edmonton is demolished.
1926	First airport is built.
1942	U.S. Army Corps of Engineers builds the Alaska Highway to Edmonton.
1947	Oil is discovered at Leduc.
1978	Rapid transit system opens. Commonwealth Games are held.
1981	Edmonton annexes 139 square miles of surrounding land.
1987	Tornado strikes Edmonton causing widespread damage.

Labor

Work Force	Male	Female
Total Work Force	179,480	147,205
Employed	157,845	132,905
Employment Rate	81.40	64.60
% of 15–24 Year Olds	76.40	62.09

Occupation	Male	Female
Managerial	22,395	11,730
Education	5,215	8,120
Health	3,960	14,090
Technical and Cultural	18,910	9,205
Clerical	13,885	52,900
Sales	18,620	15,005
Service	24,040	24,880
Manufacturing	23,814	4,505
Construction	20,070	425
Transportation	11,140	955
Other	18,070	2,590

Labor (continued)

Income

Male ($Can)   32,298
Female ($Can)   21,437
Average Household Income ($Can)   35,516
Average Family Income ($Can)   40,465
Average Tax ($Can)   5,931
Average Household Expenditure ($Can)   44,089

Manufacturing

Plants   795
Employees   19,132
Value of Shipments ($Can)   2,411,687,000
Total Value Added ($Can)   1,109,524,000

Education

The Edmonton School Board supports 185 public schools with a total enrollment of about 68,000, and the Catholic Separate School Board supports 90 schools serving 27,500 students. Both systems are publicly funded. The principal institution of higher education is the University of Alberta, which opened in 1908 in nearby Strathcona, annexed by Edmonton in 1912. Other institutions include the Northern Alberta Institute of Technology, Alberta College, Concordia College, and King's College.

Education

Population (over 15 years old)   448,570
Less than Grade 9   45,945
Grades 9–13   174,405
Trade Certificate   123,065
University Degree   57,250

Four-Year Universities and Colleges
   University of Alberta

Health

Healthcare is provided by seven hospitals: Charles Camsell Hospital, Dr. W. W. Cross Cancer Institute, Edmonton General Hospital, Glenrose Provincial Hospital, Misericordia Hospital, Royal Alexandra Hospital, and University of Alberta Hospital.

Transportation

Edmonton is approached by the Yellowhead Interprovincial Highway. Other provincial roads include 2, 16, 14, 17, 15, and 28. A Light Rapid Transit (LRT) system was built in 1978. CPR and CNR provide rail passenger and freight service. The Edmonton International Airport at Leduc is the northernmost major air terminal on the

Transportation

New Automobiles

Domestic   13,742
Imported   6,139

continent. Built in 1926 as the Edmonton Municipal Airport, it was Canada's first licensed commercial airport.

Housing

Residential communities completely ring the city, their curving streets in marked contrast to the rectangular grid of the older sections. Southwest of the university and the city center, exclusive residential areas line the bluffs along both sides of the river. High-rise apartments are most numerous in the Oliver district west of downtown.

Housing		
Total Housing Stock 218,820		
Owned 109,620		
Rented 109,205		
Single, Detached 109,960		
Apartments 20,155		
Homes Built 1990 3,479		
Building Permits Value ($Can) 615,436,000		
Tallest Buildings	*Hgt. (ft.)*	*Stories*
Manulife Place (1983)	479	39
Royal Trust Tower (1973)	476	30
AGT Tower (1971)	441	34
Canada Trust Tower (1982)	440	34
Metropolitan Place (1980)	370	30
Scotia Place (1983)	366	30
CN Tower (1966)	365	26
Phipps McKinnon (1977)	359	21

Urban Redevelopment

The first city planning department was established in 1950 and has been successful in managing orderly redevelopment programs. The central core city has been in a state of continuous rebuilding since 1960 and now includes numerous skyscrapers.

Religion

Edmonton is predominantly Protestant with a Catholic minority, the latter including many ethnic French, Irish, and Ukrainians.

Media

Edmonton has two daily newspapers: the *Edmonton Journal* and the *Edmonton Sun*. The electronic media include 4 television stations and 15 radio stations.

Media
Newsprint
The Edmonton Journal, daily
The Edmonton Sun, daily
Television
CBXFT (Channel 11)
CBXT (Channel 5)
CFRN (Channel 3)
CITV (Channel 13)

Media (continued)	
Radio	
CBX (AM)	CBX (FM)
CFRN (AM)	CFCW (AM)
CJKE (FM)	CHED (AM)
CKNG (FM)	CHFA (AM)
CHMG (AM)	CHQT (AM)
CISN (FM)	CJCA (AM)
CIRK (FM)	CKER (AM)
CKRA (FM)	

Sports

Edmonton has two major professional sports teams: the Edmonton Eskimos of the Canadian Football League, who play their home games in Commonwealth Stadium, and the Edmonton Oilers of the National Hockey League, who play their home games in the Northlands Coliseum. There are two smaller teams: the minor-league Edmonton Trappers of the Pacific Coast Baseball League and the Edmonton Brickmen of the Canadian Soccer League.

Arts, Culture, and Tourism

Edmonton has three of the largest performing arts organizations in Canada: the Edmonton Symphony Society, the Edmonton Opera Association, and the Citadel Theatre. The Symphony Orchestra performs in the Northern Alberta Jubilee Auditorium. Dance is represented by the Alberta Ballet Company. In 1987 the city hosted the Fringe Theatre Event, which attracted 175,000 people from all over the world. The principal museum is the Provincial Museum and Archives. The City of Edmonton Archives specializes in the history of the city. The Edmonton Art Gallery showcases northern Alberta artists. Other museums include the Strathcona Science Park, Canadian Aviation Hall of Fame, Ukrainian Village, Muttart Conservatory, the Space Sciences Centre, and Fort Edmonton Historical Park.

The Klondike Days Festival celebrates the city's pioneer heritage every July.

Parks and Recreation

Edmonton has about 11,000 acres of parklands. The largest park is the 3,000-acre Capital City Recreation Park along the North Saskatchewan River. Also near Edmonton are the Polar Park and the Alberta Wildlife Park.

Sources of Further Information

City Hall
Edmonton, Alberta T5J 2R7
(403) 428-5448

Edmonton Chamber of Commerce
10123 99 Street #600
Edmonton, Alberta T5J 3G9
(403) 426-4620

Additional Reading

MacGregor, J. G. *Edmonton: A History.* 1967.
Smith, P. J. *Edmonton: The Emerging Metropolitan Pattern.* 1978.

Halifax

Nova Scotia

Halifax

Basic Data

Name Halifax
Year Founded 1749 Inc. 1841
Status: Province Capital of Nova Scotia
Area (square miles) 23.94
Elevation 105
Time Zone Atlantic
Population (1990) 114,455

Distance in Miles to:

Yarmouth	217
St. John	149
St. John's	838
Amherst	171
Charlottetown	144

Location and Topography

N

Halifax, the capital city of Nova Scotia, is located on a small peninsula on the west side of the harbor midway along the southeastern coast of the province. Halifax Harbour, known formerly as Chebucto Bay, is 14 miles long and among the finest in North America; the outer harbor is 6 miles long and 1 mile wide, and its inner harbor, Bedford Basin, is 10 square miles in area. It is called the "Warden of the North" because of its strategic location.

Layout of City and Suburbs

Most of Halifax lies on a peninsula between the harbor and an inlet called the North West Arm. The cityscape of Halifax has changed considerably over the years. Early Halifax stretched along the harbor, flanked to the west by the Halifax Citadel and the Common. The Naval Dockyard, built in 1758, was located in the northern suburbs, while the southern suburbs and large estates on the Northwest Arm were elite residential areas.

Point Pleasant Park, built in 1866, is a preserve created by the military. Since World War II, particularly after the building of the Angus L. McDonald Bridge in 1954 and the A. Murray McKay Bridge in 1970, the city has spilled over into Dartmouth. Dartmouth is its sister city, which is separated from Halifax by The Narrows, a small strait connecting the inner and outer harbors on Halifax's northeast border. The suburb of Bedford lies on the opposite end of Bedford Basin to the northwest, with the town of Sackville nearby.

Climate

Halifax has a maritime climate with mild summers and winters. The average temperature is 26°F in January and 65°F in July. The average annual precipitation is 50 inches.

Weather

Annual Averages

January °F 26
July °F 65
Annual Precipitation (inches) 50.47
Annual Sunshine (hours) 1,872

History

Micmac Indians lived in the present Halifax area in pre-colonial times. In the early 18th century the French established various settlements along the Nova Scotia coast, particularly in Louisbourg. The British government, in order to combat French predominance in the region, sent Colonel Edward Cornwallis with 2,500 settlers to establish a new town on the east coast of Nova Scotia in the summer of 1749. The town that Cornwallis established was first named Chebucto, but was renamed Halifax, in honor of George Dunk, Earl of Halifax, and chief lord of trade and plantations, who

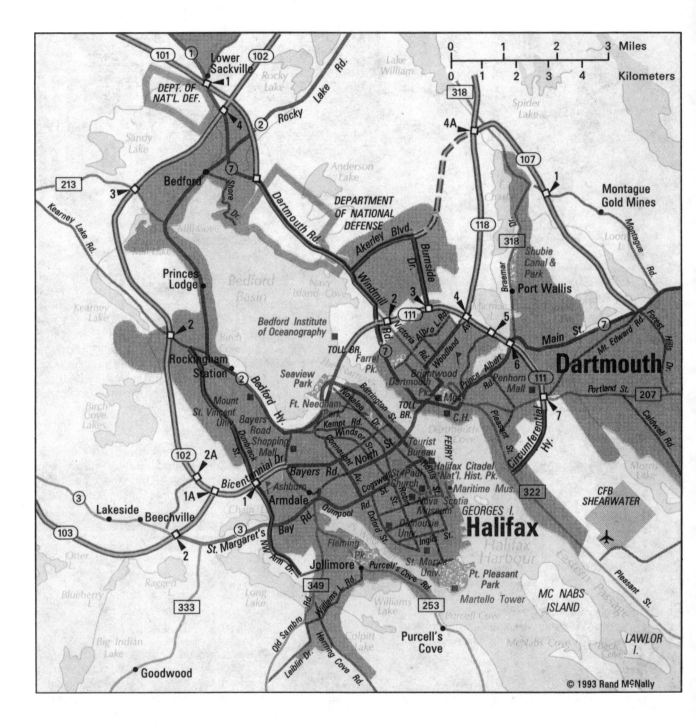

masterminded the settlement. It became the capital of Nova Scotia that same year. The town was built on a grid plan with a central square, one that was widely copied later in the American colonies.

Settlers drew lots for free land, but before homes were built, many fled to the southern colonies. Dartmouth was first settled in 1750, but Indian threats restricted growth. With few resources other than fishing, Halifax grew mainly as a naval base, thriving during times of war. Military officers governed the city until 1841, when Joseph Howe led a campaign that brought Halifax incorporation and self government. In the mid-19th century trade to the West Indies led to a golden age of prosperity. Railways reached the city after 1850, linking the city to the rest of Canada. In 1867, when Nova Scotia joined the Federation, Halifax became the capital of the Province of Nova Scotia. In 1917 Halifax experienced one of the worst disasters in North American history when a French ammunition ship exploded in the harbor, resulting in the deaths of over 2,000 and the destruction of much of the peninsula.

Historical Landmarks

As the oldest city in Canada, Halifax is rich in historical monuments. Province House, Canada's oldest parliament building, completed in 1818, stands in downtown Halifax. The Citadel, a stone fortress built in 1828, overlooks the downtown area from a hilltop. On the slope below the main entrance to the Citadel is the Old Town Clock, built in 1803. York Redoubt, a defense post on the North West Arm, dates from 1793. The Prince of Wales Martello Tower, a fortification built in 1796, stands in Point Pleasant Park. St. Paul's Church is Canada's oldest Anglican church built in 1750. Nearby Government House was built in 1827 with materials from every section of the province, as well as some from England and Scotland. The Carleton Hotel was built in 1760 as a private residence with stones from the ruins of Louisbourg. The National School, now the National School of Art, was built in 1818. A number of historic buildings are also found in the Historic Properties in the original Central Square.

Population

The population of Halifax in the 1990 census was 114,455. It represents a decline from the 1976 high of 117,882, and the 1981 total of 114,594, but a modest gain from the 1986 total of 113,575. The reasons for Halifax's demographic decline are many. Most newcomers are tran-

Population		
City Population	*1986*	*1990*
	113,575	114,455
% Male 47.02		
Age		
% Under 14 14.84		
% Over 65 10.57		

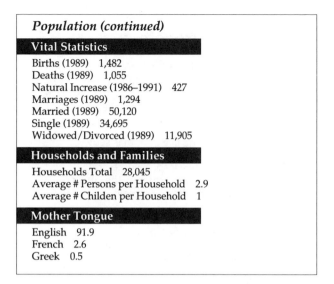

Population (continued)		
Vital Statistics		
Births (1989) 1,482		
Deaths (1989) 1,055		
Natural Increase (1986–1991) 427		
Marriages (1989) 1,294		
Married (1989) 50,120		
Single (1989) 34,695		
Widowed/Divorced (1989) 11,905		
Households and Families		
Households Total 28,045		
Average # Persons per Household 2.9		
Average # Childen per Household 1		
Mother Tongue		
English 91.9		
French 2.6		
Greek 0.5		

sients, such as military personnel. There is little immigration from overseas, and the rate of natural increase is low.

Ethnic Composition

People of Anglo-Saxon origin make up 80% of the population. The original settlers were English, Irish, and Scots. Later they were joined by Germans. This ethnic mix has remained constant.

Government

Halifax has a council-manager form of government. The mayor and 10 aldermen are elected to three-year terms. The council appoints the city manager who serves as the principal administrative officer. Until 1968, a century-old gentleman's agreement alternated the mayoral office between Catholics and Protestants.

Economy

Halifax is generally regarded as the most dynamic city in the Maritimes. The economy is sustained by the Port of Halifax, six military bases, and a small manufacturing sector consisting of over 100 plants. The discovery of offshore oil in the 1970s was considered as a harbinger of a bright economic future, but the promise has not been fulfilled. Nevertheless, the city has strengths in research, health, and tourism comparable to such larger cities as Toronto and Montreal.

Labor

About 5,000 civilians and 10,000 enlisted men and women work in the six military bases. About 12% of the work force is in public employment, 37% in services, particularly tourism, 21% in trade, and about 7% in manufacturing. Fishing, previously the staple occupation of most Nova Scotians until the 20th century, now accounts for only a small percentage of the workforce.

Chronology

1749	Colonel Edward Cornwallis, sent by the British government along with 2,500 settlers, founds a town on the east coast of Nova Scotia. Halifax is named capital of Nova Scotia.
1750	Neighboring Dartmouth is settled.
1841	Joseph Howe leads a successful campaign to incorporate the city and introduce self-government.
1867	Nova Scotia is admitted to the Federation with Halifax as capital.
1917	French ammunition ship explodes in harbor, wrecking much of the city and killing 2,000 people.
1970	Halifax Container Terminal opens.
1971	Oil is struck off Sable Island.

Labor

Work Force	Male	Female
Total Work Force	34,440	30,850
Employed	31,480	27,930
Employment Rate	77.70	61.00
% of 15–24 Year Olds	79.1	75.29

Occupation	Male	Female
Managerial	4,585	2,700
Education	1,490	2,090
Health	1,170	3,985
Technical and Cultural	4,215	2,205
Clerical	3,000	10,815
Sales	3,325	2,705
Service	6,910	4,675
Manufacturing	2,575	415
Construction	2,595	55
Transportation	1,660	105
Other	2,380	460

Income

Male ($Can)   31,152
Female ($Can)   20,403
Average Household Income ($Can)   35,164
Average Family Income ($Can)   41,005
Average Tax ($Can)   6,378
Average Household Expenditure ($Can)   44,304
Banks   9

Manufacturing

Plants   83
Employees   3,071
Value of Shipments ($Can)   397,926,000
Total Value Added ($Can)   140,522,000

Education

The first free public school in Canada was established in Halifax. The Halifax District School Board supports 50 public schools. There are two private schools. Halifax has a number of distinguished institutions of higher learn-ing. The best known is the Dalhousie University, founded in 1818. It was followed in 1841 by St. Mary's University, the oldest English-speaking Roman Catholic university in Canada. King's College University was founded in 1789 at Windsor and moved to Halifax in 1929. Mount St. Vincent, a university since 1966, was founded in 1873 by the Sisters of Charity. The Technical University of Nova Scotia, the Nova Scotia Institute of Technology, and the Nova Scotia College of Art and Design are other specialized institutions. The famous Bedford Institute of Oceanography is one of the world's leading institutions in this field.

Education

Population (over 15 years old)   94,875
Less than Grade 9   9,945
Grades 9–13   30,705
Trade Certificate   21,140
University Degree   19,045

Four-Year Universities and Colleges
University of King's College
Dalhousie University
Technical University of Nova Scotia
Nova Scotia College of Art and Design
Mount St. Vincent University
St. Mary's University

Health

Medical care is provided by seven hospitals: Camp Hill Hospital, Halifax Civic Hospital, Grace Maternity Hospital, Halifax Infirmary Hospital, Izaak Walton Killam Hospital for Children, Nova Scotia Rehabilitation Centre, and Victoria General Hospital.

Transportation

Halifax may be approached from the south by Highway 103, from the north by highway 107 or 215, and from the west by highway 101; numerous secondary highways also allow access to the city. Two major railroads, Canadian Pacific Railway and Canadian National Railroad, have terminals in Halifax. Halifax Harbour is one of the finest in the world and was known to the Micmac Indians as *Chebucto,* or the "great long harbor." It handles about 12 million tons of cargo annually. The Halifax International Airport lies about 25 miles northwest of the city.

Transportation

New Automobiles

Domestic   4,879
Imported   2,295
Trucks   1,933

Housing

Of the total housing stock of 45,059 units, 18,655 are owner-occupied.

Housing

Total Housing Stock	45,095
Owned	18,655
Rented	26,440
Single, Detached	14,970
Apartments	9,220
Homes Built 1990	904
Building Permits Value ($Can)	156,801,000

Religion

Halifax is the seat of the Roman Catholic archbishop of Halifax and the Anglican bishop of Nova Scotia. The Irish population is heavily Catholic, while the German and English population is predominantly Protestant. Halifax has the oldest Anglican church in Canada, St. Paul's Church, built in 1750. The Round Church, built in 1800, is a fine example of the Byzantine style. The Old Dutch Church was built in 1755 by German settlers.

Media

Among the many firsts in Canada that Halifax claims is the first newspaper, the first printing press, and the first printed book. *The Halifax Gazette* was first founded in 1752 and was published for many years until it closed. Halifax has two dailies: *The Chronicle-Herald* and *The Mail-Star*. *The Daily News* is published in nearby Sackville and *Free Press* in Dartmouth. The electronic media consist of three AM radio stations, six FM radio stations, and three television stations.

Media

Newsprint
  The Chronicle-Herald, daily
  The Mail-Star, daily

Television
  CBHT (Channel 3)
  CIHF (Channel 8)
  CJCH (Channel 5)

Radio
  CBHA (FM)   CFDR (AM)
  CFRQ (FM)   CIEZ (FM)
  CNHA (FM)   CHNS (AM)
  CHFX (FM)   CJCH (AM)
  CIOO (FM)

Sports

Amateur sports, rather than professional, are dominant in Halifax. The Wanderers Amateur Athletic Association, founded in 1882, conducts a number of events. As in other maritime cities, yachting, canoeing, rowing, and swimming are popular.

Arts, Culture, and Tourism

Halifax is the cultural center of the province. The Neptune Theatre, in drama, and the Atlantic Symphony, in music, are the most active cultural institutions. Halifax has about ten art galleries, including the Dalhousie University Arts Centre. The principal museums are the Nova Scotia Museum, the Maritime Museum, and the Public Archives of Nova Scotia.

Parks and Recreation

Halifax park system includes the 175-acre Point Pleasant Park at the tip of the peninsula, and the 17-acre Public Gardens.

Sources of Further Information

City Hall
Box 1749
Halifax, Nova Scotia B3J 3A5
(902) 426-6430

Halifax Board of Trade, 402
1800 Argyle Street
Halifax, Nova Scotia B3J 3N8
(902) 420-0223

Additional Reading

Bird, M. J. *The Town that Died.* 1962.
Blakeley, Phyllis. *Glimpses of Halifax.* 1973.
Heritage Trust of Nova Scotia. *Founded Upon a Rock: Historic Buildings of Halifax and Vicinity.* 1967.
Payzant, Joan. *Halifax.* 1985.
Raddall, Thomas H. *Halifax: Warden of the North.* 1965.
Roache, Gordon. *Halifax Book.* 1987.
Rompkey, Ronald. *Expeditions of Honor.* 1982.

Hamilton

Ontario

Location and Topography

Hamilton is located on the western end of Lake Ontario, on Burlington Bay, 42 miles southwest of Torotno and 41 miles west of Niagara Falls.

Layout of City and Suburbs

Hamilton is built on a narrow plain between the Hamilton Harbour and the Niagara Escarpment, where it extends for 13 miles from west to east. The escarpment, which is known as the Mountain, rises abruptly to a height of 300 to 400 feet above Lake Ontario. Hamilton Harbour, which is accessed by way of the Burlington Canal, is a landlocked body of water of about 10 square miles, and is separated from Lake Ontario by Lake Hamilton Beach, a sand and gravel strip that is 4 miles long and 200 to 300 yards wide. The beach is almost entirely residential. The Burlington Skyway Bridge traverses the harbor. The intersection of James and King streets at Gore Park is the heart of the business district. City Hall stands a few blocks west at Main and Bay streets, and next to it is the Canadian Foot-

ball Hall of Fame. Across the street from City Hall is the Lloyd D. Jackson Square, and close by is Hamilton Place, a theater-auditorium complex. The Art Gallery of Hamilton and the Hamilton Trade and Convention Centre adjoin Hamilton Place, and two blocks away is the 18,000-seat Copps Coliseum. For a city of its size, Hamilton has relatively few office towers. Residential areas include the old elite Durand District between James and Queen streets, the westend middle-class community of Westdale, and working class areas to the east and northeast. Most of the steel mills and factories are along the waterfront.

Climate

Hamilton shares the same climatic features as Toronto and other cities on the Great Lakes. The climate is tempered by the proximity of the lakes with the average temperature being 20.4°F in January and 69°F in July. Precipitation is about 32 inches annually. Hours of sunshine are 2,044.6 per year

Weather

Annual Averages

January °F   20.4
July °F   69
Annual Precipitation (inches)   32
Annual Sunshine (hours)   2,044.6

History

Huron Indians lived in the region when the first white men, French fur traders, arrived in the 17th century. It was first settled in 1778 by Robert Land and Richard Beasley, United Empire Loyalists, after fleeing from the United

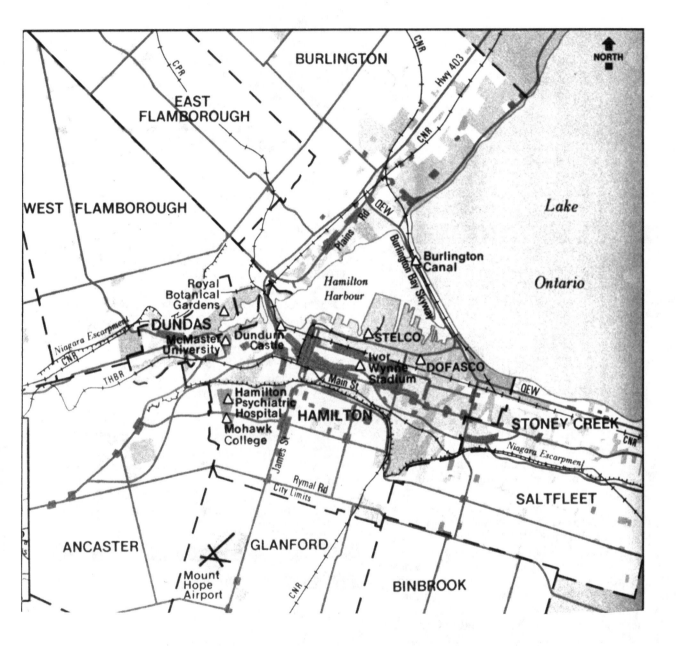

States. Then called the Head of the Lake, the village was later renamed Hamilton in 1813, after George Hamilton who bought land in the village, and surveyed and platted it. The town grew slowly until the completion of a ship channel in 1832 made it an important transshipment point. It was incorporated as a city in 1846. In the early 1850s the Great Western Railway was brought into the city by Sir Allan McNab. Though the railway boom collapsed in 1857, it had brought foundries and other industries. These industries prospered until 1890 when a new boom, based on national railroad construction, led to another two decades of growth. In the 1890s the Hamilton Blast Furnace Company began to produce pig iron which led to the development of a strong steel industry. During World War I and World War II, Hamilton experienced economic stability from supplying various war materiel. After World War II, manufacturing converted to appliances, automobiles, and textiles. The city's economy, however, became more and more reliant on the steel industry, and the 1980s brought many plant closings.

Historical Landmarks

Hamilton Historical Board administers a number of historical landmarks and monuments, including Dundurn Castle (1835), the home of Sir Allan Napier McNab, and Whitehern (1848). Many 19th-century buildings were demolished during the construction boom of the 1960s and 1970s, but some remain, such as the Commercial Block (1858), Sandyford Place (1858) and St. Paul's Church (1857).

Population

Hamilton is Canada's seventh most-populous city, estimated at the 1990 census at 318,499. As a steel town, Hamilton's demographic history followed its economic fortunes. After reaching 312,003 in 1976, its population declined to 306,434 in 1981 but rebounded slightly to 306,730 in 1986.

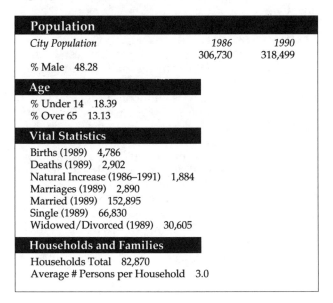

Population		
City Population	*1986*	*1990*
	306,730	318,499
% Male 48.28		
Age		
% Under 14 18.39		
% Over 65 13.13		
Vital Statistics		
Births (1989) 4,786		
Deaths (1989) 2,902		
Natural Increase (1986–1991) 1,884		
Marriages (1989) 2,890		
Married (1989) 152,895		
Single (1989) 66,830		
Widowed/Divorced (1989) 30,605		
Households and Families		
Households Total 82,870		
Average # Persons per Household 3.0		

Population (continued)	
Average # Children per Household 1.2	
Mother Tongue	
English 75.3	
French 1.4	
Italian 5.5	
Portuguese 1.6	
Polish 1.5	

Ethnic Composition

Originally the population was almost entirely Anglo Saxon. The growth of the steel industry between 1900 and 1913 brought workers from Poland and Italy and, later during the 1920s, they were joined by emigrants from Central Europe and the Baltic states. After World War II, Dutch, German, Italian and Polish immigration reached a peak in the early 1950s. The 1960s and 1970s saw more Portuguese, South Asian, and West Indian immigrants. Ethnic neighborhoods abound, usually centering around churches and small-business districts. About 60% of the population is of British origin. Italians make up 8%. There are also sizable German and Polish minorities.

Government

Hamilton has a mayor-council form of government. The mayor and 16 aldermen are elected to three-year terms. In 1974 the Regional Municipality of Hamilton-Wentworth was inaugurated in order to manage social services, police, and water and sewage facilities.

Economy

Despite the worldwide slump in steel, steel still drives Hamilton's economy. Two of Canada's four largest steel firms have their plants here, although one of them, Stelco, moved its head offices to Toronto in 1968. Together they produce about nine million tons of steel a year from iron ore brought from northern Quebec by the St. Lawrence Seaway. Westinghouse, International Harvester, Dominion Glass, Otis Elevator, National Steel Car, Canada Canners, and Procter & Gamble also have large plants here. There are 750 other factories producing over $2 billion worth of goods annually. Hamilton plants also process beef, dairy products, fruits, tobacco, and vegetables.

Labor

Industry employs about 28% of the workers, services 32%, and trade 18%. Hamilton is a highly unionized city. The nine-hour workday movement began first in Hamilton in 1872, and the Knights of Labor and AFL had substantial memberships until recently. The last major strike occurred at Stelco in 1981.

Chronology

1778	Robert Land and Richard Beasley, United Empire Loyalists, settle in the area and found a village called Head of the Lake.
1813	George Hamilton buys property in the village and surveys and plats the land for the town which is renamed Hamilton.
1832	Canal is completed through Burlington Beach, permitting steamers and schooners entry into Burlington Bay.
1846	Hamilton is incorporated as a city.
1850s	Great Western Railroad reaches Hamilton early in the decade.
1890	National railroad construction begins, heralding two decades of economic growth.
1890s	Hamilton Blast Furnace Company begins to produce pig-iron.
1910	Steel Company of Canada is formed here, laying the foundations of Hamilton's rise as the "Pittsburgh of Canada."
1912	Hamilton's second steel company, Dominion Foundries and Steel, is formed.
1921	Population passes the 100,000 mark.
1951	Population passes the 200,000 mark.
1985	Slater Steel Mills close, marking the decline of Hamilton's great steel era.

Labor

Work Force	Male	Female
Total Work Force	87,610	68,960
Employed	80,995	62,520
Employment Rate	74.20	53.59
% of 15–24 Year Olds	71.50	68.50

Occupation	Male	Female
Managerial	6,880	3,745
Education	2,150	3,380
Health	1,215	6,690
Technical and Cultural	6,105	3,290
Clerical	6,425	20,845
Sales	6,230	7,265
Service	7,930	13,400
Manufacturing	21,025	5,520
Construction	8,390	175
Transportation	5,160	485
Other	14,730	2,715

Income

Male ($Can) 29,409
Female ($Can) 18,802
Average Household Income ($Can) 31,073
Average Family Income ($Can) 35,175
Average Tax ($Can) 5,873

Labor (continued)
Average Household Expenditure ($Can) 44,142
Number of Banks 137

Manufacturing

Plants 386
Employees 45,778
Value of Shipments ($Can) 6,845,400,000
Total Value Added ($Can) 3,010,133,000

Education

The Hamilton Board of Education supports 90 public elementary schools and 12 public high schools with a student enrollment of 55,000. The Separate Roman Catholic School Board supports 45 elementary and high schools. The leading institution of higher education is McMaster University with an enrollment of 15,000 students. It is the only Canadian university with a nuclear reactor on its campus. It also runs the Health Sciences Centre, a combined hospital and medical school. Hamilton is also the home of the Mohawk College of Applied Arts and Technology.

Education

Population (over 15 years old) 246,685
Less than Grade 9 46,730
Grades 9–13 108,415
Trade Certificate 58,040
University Degree 17,480

Four-Year Universities and Colleges
McMaster University
Mohawk College of Applied Arts and Technology

Health

The Health Sciences Centre of McMaster University is the largest medical facility in Hamilton. There are five other hospitals, including Hamilton General Hospital, Civic Hospital, Henderson General Hospital, St. Joseph's Hospital, and St. Peter's Centre.

Transportation

Hamilton is the fourth largest port in Canada in tonnage, and its port has not lost the preeminence it had in the early decades of this century. A number of highways lead into the city. The Chedoke Expressway, or Route 403, and Routes 2, 6, and 5 skirt the city to the north while Centennial Parkway, or Route 56, and Routes 53, 8, and 20 enter the city from the south or southeast. The Canadian National Railway maintains industrial freight services and a limited passenger service to Toronto and Niagara Falls. The Toronto, Hamilton, and Buffalo Railway, now merged with Canadian Pacific Railway, maintains business loops within the city. A rail commuter service also operates between Hamilton and Burlington. Bus services have expanded in recent years. Hamilton's Civic Airport is a local air terminal with flights to Canadian and U.S. cities. Most plane passengers use Toronto's Lester B. Pearson International Airport, one hour away.

Transportation
New Automobiles
Domestic 7,394
Imported 2,602
Trucks 2,959

Housing

Of the total housing stock of 117,925, 66,755 are owner-occupied.

Housing
Total Housing Stock 117,925
Owned 66,755
Rented 51,170
Single, Detached 61,485
Apartments 27,875
Homes Built 1990 1,273
Building Permits Value $Can 384,231,000

Urban Redevelopment

In the 1960s and 1970s, Hamilton's city fathers began an ambitious program of construction. The program has had only limited success as most corporations prefer to be in Toronto, and most families prefer to live in suburban houses rather than central-city apartments. The major success has been the Lloyd D. Jackson Square downtown, where there are large office and store complexes. Buildings in Jackson Square are connected to the Convention Centre and Hamilton Place Theatre by enclosed above-ground walkways.

Religion

Mainline Protestant, especially Anglican and United Church denominations, claim the largest membership in Hamilton with Roman Catholics forming a sizable minority. The oldest religious landmark is St. Paul's Church, built in 1857.

Media

The city daily is *The Hamilton Spectator*, the Southam chain's first newspaper, founded in 1846. Electronic media consist of one television station, CHCH, one of Canada's few unaffiliated television stations, and five radio stations, including CKOC, Ontario's oldest, founded in 1922.

Media
Newsprint
The Hamilton Spectator, daily
Television
CHCH (Channel 11)

Media (continued)
Radio
CHAM (AM) CHML (AM)
CKOC (AM) CKLH (FM)
CKDS (FM)

Sports

Hamilton has one professional sports team, the Tiger-Cats of the Canadian Football League who play their home games in Ivor Wynne Stadium. Hamilton is home to the Canadian Football Hall of Fame.

Arts, Culture, and Tourism

The Hamilton Philharmonic Orchestra plays in Hamilton Place, with the Mohawk College Singers, McMaster Chamber Orchestra, Bach Elgar Choir, and Opera Hamilton combining to make Hamilton a strong musical town. Until 1981, when it was closed for lack of funding, the Royal Hamilton Conservatory of Music was also located here. Theater is represented by small groups playing in Hamilton Place and by Theatre Aquarius at McMaster. The Cockpit Theater and Children's Theater are in Dundurn Park.

The principal art gallery is the Art Gallery of Hamilton. Dundurn Castle includes a museum of 19th century period costumes and furniture. Just outside city limits are the Historical Society Museum and the Brant Museum.

Parks and Recreation

Hamilton has about 80 parks covering 2,500 acres. The largest is the Royal Botanical Gardens. Parts of the garden, including the Rock Garden, are formally developed, but other parts are maintained in their natural state. Smaller parks within city limits include King's Forest Park and Gage Park.

Sources of Further Information

City Hall
71 Main Street West
Hamilton, Ontario L8N 3T4
(416) 526-2700

Hamilton Chamber of Commerce
555 Bay Street Nort
Hamilton, Ontario L8L 1H1
(416) 522-1154

Additional Reading

Katz, M. *The People of Hamilton, Canada West.* 1975.
Weaver, John C. *Hamilton: An Illustrated History.* 1982.

London

Ontario

Basic Data	
Name London	
Year Founded 1826 Inc. 1847	
Status: Province Ontario	
Area (square miles) 68.32	
Elevation 912	
Time Zone EST	
Population (1990) 303,165	
Distance in Miles to:	
Ottawa	361
Toronto	113
Quebec	166

Weather	
Annual Averages	
January °F 20	
July °F 68	
Annual Precipitation (inches) 35.83	
Annual Sunshine (hours) 1,894.6	

Location and Topography

London, the seat of Middlesex County, is located on the Thames River in the southwestern peninsula of Ontario midway between Toronto and Windsor.

Layout of the City and Suburbs

London's older central area is a grid of wide streets laid out on level ground between the north and south branches of the Thames River. After World War II the city expanded to higher ground to the north, south, and west. London is known as the Forest City after its streets lined with silver maples.

Climate

London has a mild climate with average temperatures of 68°F in July and 20°F in January. The average annual precipitation is 36 inches.

History

Originally a part of the Attiwandaronk nation, London was reserved in 1793 by John Graves Simcoe as a 510-acre site for the future capital of the province. The site, however, was not settled until 1826 when a fort-like masonry courthouse with crenellated towers was built. The settlement was named London, probably because the river than ran through it had already been named Thames. There was a wave of settlers in the 1830s and the town grew beyond its original limits. During the Rebellion of 1837 a large garrison of troops was stationed here, earning it the nickname of "Garrison Town." Fire destroyed most of the city in 1845, but it was soon rebuilt. The opening of the Great Western Railway in 1854 ensured the city's economic future. It was incorporated as a village in 1840, as a town in 1847, and as a city in 1855, when it was also made the seat of the Roman Catholic and Anglican dioceses. Its later development as a financial center followed the discovery of oil to the west of the city. In 1910 London became one of the first towns to receive electrical power from the Niagara Falls.

Historical Landmarks

Eldon House, a home built in the 1830s, is one of the most popular landmarks in the city.

Population

The population of London in 1991 was 303,165. Population growth has been steady, if unspectacular—from 240,392 in 1976 to 254,280 in 1981, and 269,140 in 1986. Immigra-

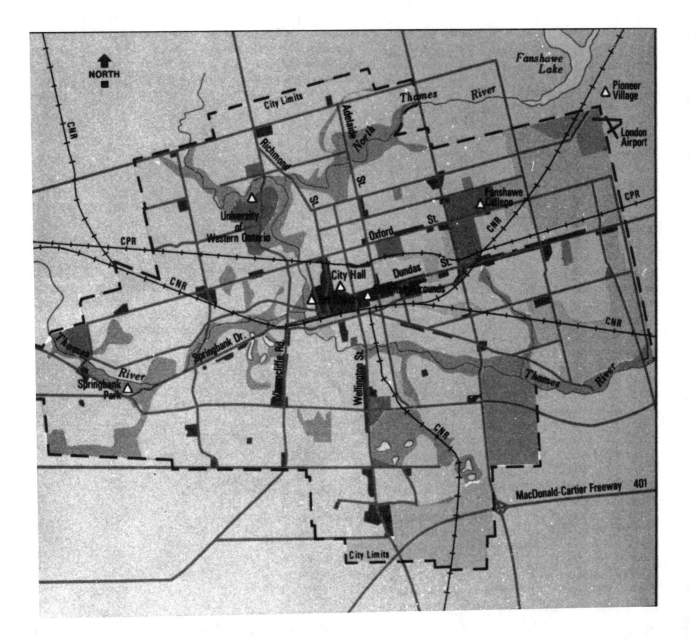

tion, rather than a growth in the birth rate, accounts for most of the increase.

Population

City Population	1986	1990
	269,140	303,165
% Male 47.85		

Age

% Under 14 19.68
% Over 65 11.14

Vital Statistics

Births (1989) 4,312
Deaths (1989) 2,269
Natural Increase (1986–1991) 2,043
Marriages (1989) 2,587
Married (1989) 135,245
Single (1989) 58,710
Widowed/Divorced (1989) 22,195

Households and Families

Households Total 72,050
Average # Persons per Household 3.0
Average # Children per Household 1.2

Mother Tongue

English 85.9
French 1.1
German 1.3
Italian 1.3
Portuguese 1.2

Ethnic Composition

 The majority of the population, 85%, are of Anglo-Saxon heritage. The rest of the population is divided among French, German, Italian, and Portugese.

Government

London has a mayor-council form of government. After the 1961 annexation of surrounding municipalities, the number of wards rose from three to seven. Each ward elects two aldermen. In addition, there is a board of control consisting of the mayor plus four directly elected councillors. The Public and Separate School boards are also elected, as is the Public Utilities Commission, which is responsible for utilities as well as parks.

Economy

London is a major manufacturing center with over 300 plants. The principal products include beverages, chemicals, electrical products, diesel vehicles, food, hosiery, and telephone equipment. Since the 19th century it has been a financial center, although quite overshadowed by Toronto. Many nationwide companies, such as London Life Insurance, Canada Trust Company, and Avco Finance, are located in London. Brewing has developed here. Both John Labatt and John Carling were noted brewers with their headquarters located in London.

Labor

 Despite London's importance as a manufacturing town, its work force is dominated by the service and trade sectors, which employ 38% and 20.6% respectively. Manufacturing is third with 19%.

Labor

Work Force	Male	Female
Total Work Force	80,085	69,545
Employed	74,550	64,020
Employment Rate	79.8	61.7
% of 15–24 Year Olds	77.8	74.4
Occupation	*Male*	*Female*
Managerial	10,780	5,475
Education	3,400	4,020
Health	2,345	8,115
Technical and Cultural	6,985	3,765
Clerical	5,755	21,700
Sales	8,545	7,455
Service	9,315	10,915
Manufacturing	12,715	4,035
Construction	7,180	190
Transportation	4,235	390
Other	7,870	2,415

Income

Male ($Can) 31,389
Female ($Can) 20,153
Average Household Income ($Can) 34,462
Average Family Income ($Can) 39,975
Average Tax ($Can) 6,571
Average Household Expenditure ($Can) 48,557
Number of Banks 81

Manufacturing

Plants 338
Employees 19,744
Value of Shipments ($Can) 2,547,849,000
Total Value Added ($Can) 1,399,108,000

Education

Public and parochial schools are administered by the London School Board and the Separate School Board, respectively. Of the 17 private schools, two are Hebrew schools. The principal higher education institution is the University of Western Ontario, founded in 1878. London is also the home of Fanshawe College of Applied Arts and Technology. Two provincial teacher colleges are also located here.

Education

Population (over 15 years old) 213,100
Less than Grade 9 22,860
Grades 9–13 86,900
Trade Certificate 54,475
University Degree 27,985

Four-Year Universities and Colleges
Fanshawe College of Applied Arts and Technology
University of Western Ontario

Chronology

1793 John Graves Simcoe reserves a 510-acre site in southern Ontario as the future provincial capital.

1826 British settlers locate here following the building of the courthouse. Town is named London after the capital of England.

1837 Large garrison is stationed here to suppress rebels.

1840 London is incorporated as a village.

1845 Fire destroys most of the city. Great Western Railway reaches London.

1847 London is incorporated as a town.

1855 London is incorporated as a city.

1910 London receives power from the Niagara Falls.

Health

Medical care is provided by five hospitals: Parkwood Hospital, St. Joseph's Hospital, St. Mary's Hospital, University Hospital and Victoria Hospital

The Provincial Asylum, founded in 1870, was the first regional hospital. The University Hospital is famous for its neurosurgery.

Transportation

London is an important transportation hub and is connected by freeways to Windsor, Sarnia, and Hamilton-Toronto through Highways 2, 4, 401, and 402. The London and Port Stanley Railway provided connections with Lake Erie, but stopped service in 1976. Eleven daily trains run between London and Toronto. The principal air terminal is the London Airport, just outside of the city.

Transportation

New Automobiles

Domestic   6,696
Imported   3,008
Trucks   4,048

Housing

Total Housing Stock   104,325
Owned   56,180
Rented   48,140
Single, Detached   52,715
Apartments   20,670
Homes Built 1990   4,095
Building Permits Value ($Can)   444,881,000

Religion

Mainline Protestant denominations have a slight edge in London in terms of the number of churches and believers. Among Protestants, the Anglicans are particularly strong.

Media

The city daily is *The London Free Press*. Electronic media consist of one television station and five radio stations.

Media

Newsprint
    The London Free Press, daily
Television
    CFPL (Channel 10)
Radio
    CFPL (AM)   CFPL (FM)
    CJBX (FM)   CKSL (AM)
    CIQM (FM)

Sports

London has no major professional sports team. The Knights compete in Junior A hockey.

Arts, Culture, and Tourism

The University of Western Ontario Faculty of Music has contributed much to musical activity in the city, as has the Orchestra London. Theater is represented by the Grand Theatre, which has two stages and presents six plays per season. Museums include a pioneer village and an Indian site.

Parks and Recreation

Springbank Park, along the Thames River, is the principal municipal park. The park includes Storybook Gardens, a children's amusement center.

Sources of Further Information

City Hall
300 Dufferin Avenue
London, Ontario N6A 4L9
(519) 679-4500

London Chamber of Commerce
244 Pall Mall Street
London, Ontario N6A 5P6
(519) 432-7551

Additional Reading

Armstrong, F. H. *The Forest City: An Illustrated History of London*. 1986.

Montreal

Quebec

Basic Data

Name   Montreal
Year Founded   1642 Inc. 1832
Status: Province   Quebec
Area (square miles)   68
Elevation   100 ft.
Time Zone   EST
Population (1990)   1,017,666

Distance in Miles to:

Anchorage	4,300
Calgary	2,326
Chicago	847
Edmonton	2,339
New York	382
Ottawa	118
Regina	1,851
San Francisco	2,959
Toronto	335
Vancouver	2,983

Location and Topography

Montreal is located on the Ile de Montreal, between the St. Lawrence River and the Rivière des Prairies near the confluence of the Ottawa and St. Lawrence rivers. The roughly triangular island is about 32 miles long and 10 miles wide at its widest point, with a total area of 182 square miles, of which the city proper occupies 78 square miles. The metropolitan area spreads across the St. Lawrence to the mainland on the south and to Jesus Island on the north. In the center of the island is Mount Royal, known simply as the Mountain, which rises sharply on its eastern slope to a height of 763 feet but descends gently on the other side. On the upper slopes is Mount Royal Park.

Layout of City and Suburbs

Montreal was built on a series of terraces rising steeply from the banks of the St. Lawrence. Old Montreal lies on the lowest terraces, near the riverfront, where the Boulevard St. Laurent runs. The Boulevard, one of the city's chief east-west streets, divides the city center into two sections—East End and West End—although geographically they might more accurately be described as north and south, respectively. Old Montreal, also known as Le Quartier, borders the St. Lawrence between Berri and McGill streets. Some of Montreal's most historic buildings are in this area, which includes the Place d'Armes (Parade Ground) and the Place Royale (Royal Square). Government buildings, including the Hôtel de Ville (City Hall), line the Rue Notre Dame, a few blocks north of the Place d'Armes. The major thoroughfares between the river and the mountain are Notre Dame, St. James, Craig, Dorchester, St. Catherine, Ontario, Sherbrooke, and Pine. The north-south René Levesque Boulevard, crossing the heart of downtown through Dominion Square, is noted for its skyscrapers, including Montreal's tallest and most distinctive landmark, the Royal Bank of Canada Building at René Levesque and University streets, which towers over the Place Ville Marie, an office complex. Flanking Dominion Square are the buildings of the Canadian Imperial Bank of Commerce and the Sun Life Assurance Company of Canada. Mountain Street in downtown has some of the city's most charming restaurants. The southern part of Dominion Square, renamed Place du Canada, is surrounded by the Archbishop's Palace, the Place du Canada Building, St. George's Anglican Church, and the Cathedral Basilica of Mary, Queen of the World. Beneath the Place Ville Marie is a 50-acre underground city consisting of hotels, offices, theaters, stores, restaurants, and the city's two main railroad stations. Parts of this underground complex are linked by the Metro. On the southern side of the Place Ville Marie is the Place Bonaventure, a merchandise mart, international trade

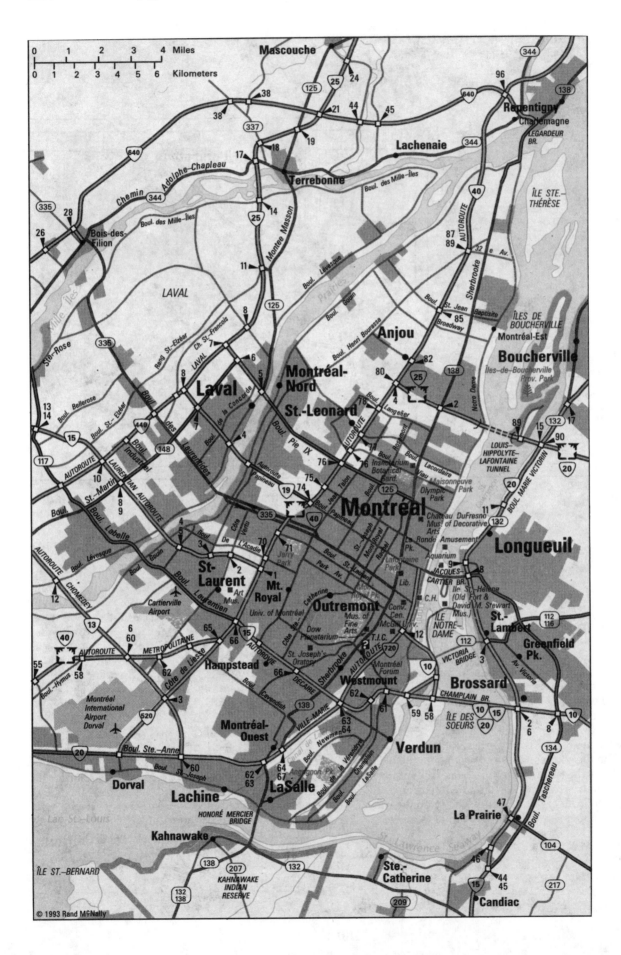

center, and convention hall, topped by a modern hotel. In Victoria Square, near the Old Financial District, is the Place Victoria, where the Montreal Stock Exchange is located. It is linked by an escalator with the Commerce House. The residential suburbs spread to the south and north and into Ile de Laval. In the middle of the St. Lawrence is Ile Ste. Hélène, site of Expo '67 and the Man and His World annual exhibition. Next to it is the man-made Ile Notre Dame, also site of Expo '67 and now a park. Farther east, the imposing Olympic Stadium dominates the district of Maisonneuve.

Climate

 Montreal has a variable climate with extremes of heat and cold. The average temperature in January, the coldest month, is 14°F, but temperatures often fall below zero. Winters are characterized by bitterly cold winds and heavy snow. Montreal generally receives more snow than Moscow. July, the hottest month, has an average temperature of 70°F. The average annual precipitation is 40 inches. The hours of sunshine are 2,054 per year.

Weather
Annual Averages
January °F   14
July °F   70
Annual Precipitation (inches)   40
Annual Sunshine (hours)   2,054

History

The Montreal region was inhabited by Algonquian and Iroquois Indians at the time of contact. In 1535 Jacques Cartier, sailing up the St. Lawrence, became the first white man to reach the island. He found the Iroquois town of Hochelaga at the foot of the mountain he named Mont Real (Mount Royal). Samuel de Champlain visited the site in 1603 but found no sign of the town. He returned in 1611 to found a trading post named Place Royale. In 1639, Jérôme Le Royer, Sieur de la Dauversière, formed a company in Paris to establish a colony on the island of Mont Real and sent a Roman Catholic missionary group, led by Paul de Chomedey, Sieur de Maisonneuve, in 1642 to convert the Indians to Christianity. Maisonneuve established the settlement of Ville-Marie and built a fort in Old Montreal at what is now the Place Royale. In 1663 the entire island was granted as a seigneury to the religious order of the Gentlemen of St. Sulpice. The early decades of the city were marked by almost continual conflicts with the Iroquois, which did not end until the peace treaty of 1701. In the second half of the 17th century, Montreal became the center of French exploration of North America and of the lucrative fur trade. It served as a base for Antoine de la Mothe Cadillac, Louis Jolliet, Father Jacques Marquette, Louis Hennepin, René-Robert Cavelier de La Salle, and others.

During the Seven Years' War, after the fall of Quebec in 1759, the capital of New France was moved to Montreal. Montreal, however, also fell to the British when it was captured by General Jeffrey Amherst in 1760. When the Treaty of Paris was signed, all of New France came under the British flag. During the American Revolution, Montreal was occupied briefly by American forces under General Richard Montgomery. Montreal's economy continued to depend almost entirely on the fur trade for many decades. The English gradually gained control of the town's economy. British and Scottish merchants like Alexander Mackenzie, the Frobisher Brothers, Simon McTavish, and William McGillivray established a dynamic trading class and laid the foundations of Montreal's commercial greatness. This group created the Bank of Montreal in 1817 and the Committee of Trade in 1822 and invested in shipping and railways. A large wave of emigration from the British Isles began in 1815 and accelerated the social transformation of the city. The population grew from 9,000 in 1800 to 22,540 in 1825, and 44,591 in 1844. In 1832 Montreal was incorporated as a city, and from 1844 until 1849 it served as the capital of the Province of Canada. By 1831 residents of British origin became the majority, leading to conflicts with the native French Catholics that erupted in the Rebellions of 1837. After the defeat of the Patriotes, changes in transportation and industry overshadowed politics. The first steamboat, *Accommodation*, sailed from Quebec to Montreal in 1809. The building of the Lachine Canal in 1825 and the dredging of the St. Lawrence River made Montreal the principal seaport for British North America. Rail construction, particularly of the Grand Trunk Railway, made the city the hub of the rail system as well. Meanwhile, industrial growth kept pace and made the city the leading industrial center of French Canada. The city expanded by annexing 22 suburbs between 1883 and 1914. French Canadians living in rural areas poured into the city, and from 1867 they once again became the majority. The Canadian Pacific established its headquarters in Montreal in the 1880s. St. James Street became the financial center of the Dominion, a place it occupied until the 1970s when Toronto displaced it. The population grew from 50,000 in 1850 to 107,000 in 1871, 267,730 in 1901, and 467,986 in 1911. It passed the 1 million mark in 1931. During World War II, many Montrealers led by Mayor Camillien Houde opposed Canadian participation in the war. Houde was arrested and imprisoned until 1944. The opening of the St. Lawrence Seaway in 1959 spurred another period of rapid growth for the city. Under Mayor Jean Drapeau, Montreal embarked upon monumental projects: the Metro begun in 1966, the 1967 Expo, the 1976 Summer Olympic Games, and the 1980 Floralies Internationales. During the 1960s the separatist organization FLQ (Front de Liberation du Québec) was sporadically active in Montreal. In 1969 the building of the Montreal International Airport began. In 1982 the city annexed Pointe-aux-Trembles, a suburb, increasing the city area by 10%.

Chronology

1535 Jacques Cartier, sailing up the St. Lawrence and unable to pass Lachine Falls, stops at the Iroquois village of Hochelaga on the present island of Montreal.

1607 Samuel de Champlain visits the island but finds no trace of the Indian village.

1611 On second visit, Champlain founds trading post known as Place Royale.

1639 Jérôme Le Royer, Sieur de la Dauversiere, founds company in Paris to colonize Mont Real.

1642 Paul de Chomeday, Sieur de Maisonneuve, arrives on island, leading a group of settlers and Roman Catholic missionaries. He founds Ville Marie and builds a fort on Place Royale.

1663 Gentlemen of St. Sulpice are granted the island as a seigneury.

1701 Peace is made with Iroquois Indians.

1759 On the fall of Quebec, Montreal becomes capital of New France.

1760 Montreal is captured by British forces led by General Jeffrey Amherst.

1775 American troops under General Richard Montgomery seize Montreal briefly.

1809 Steamboat *Accommodation* sails from Quebec to Montreal.

1815 Large–scale British immigration begins.

1817 Bank of Montreal is founded.

1822 Committee of Trade is founded.

1825 Lachine Canal is built, making it possible for ships to sail up the St. Lawrence to the Great Lakes.

1831 Persons of British origin become the majority in the city.

1832 Montreal is incorporated as a city.

1837 The Francophone Patriotes are defeated in the Rebellions of 1837.

1844–1849 Montreal is capital of the Province of Canada.

1867 The French Canadians are again the majority in the city.

1885 Canadian Pacific completes transcontinental railroad.

1940 Mayor Camillien Houde is imprisoned for antiwar efforts.

1959 St. Lawrence Seaway opens.

1966 The Metro is begun.

1967 Expo '67 is held, attracting 20 million visitors.

1969 Building of the Montreal International Airport begins.

1976 Montreal hosts Summer Olympics.

1980 Floralies Internationales is held.

1982 City annexes Pointe-aux-Trembles.

Historical Landmarks

Montreal is a living museum with many reminders of its history in its Old Town. Across Rue Notre Dame is Place d'Armes where the first clash between the new settlers and Iroquois Indians took place in 1644. An obelisk marks the spot where the first settlers landed in 1642. In Jacques Cartier Square are the Lord Nelson Monument, built in 1809, the old court house, and the city hall. The Maisonneuve Monument in the square honors the city's founder. A few blocks to the east on Rue St. Paul is Place Royale. First named by Samuel de Champlain, it is where Fort Montreal was built in 1642. Across from the city hall is Château de Ramezay, built in 1705 by the eleventh governor of Montreal. On St. Paul Street, is the historic Bonsecours Market. Other landmarks include the Old Custom House on St. Paul Street West; the Old Fort, built in 1822 on the orders of the Duke of Wellington; and the former Dalhousie Station, the Canadian Pacific station in Montreal from 1883 to 1898.

Population

In terms of city population, Montreal is the largest city in Canada with a 1991 total of 1,017,666. In metro population, however, it trails Toronto. Montreal's recent population growth has been rather uneven. From 1986 to 1991 it gained only about 2,000 people and, although its population rose from 980,354 in 1981, the increase only made up the numbers lost between 1976 and 1981. Cycles of rise and decline are not unusual in Montreal's demographic history. The periods of growth were 1851–1861, 1901–1911, and 1951–1961. Since 1966 the number of city inhabitants has decreased in direct proportion to the growth of the suburbs. In 1931, 80% of the metro population lived in the city proper, but only 35% in 1981. Between 1883 and 1983 the city annexed 26 suburbs.

Population		
City Population	*1986*	*1990*
	1,054,420	1,017,666
% Male 47.59		
Age		
% Under 14 14.28		
% Over 65 13.75		

Population (continued)

Vital Statistics

Births (1989)   13,763
Deaths (1989)   9,961
Natural Increase (1986–1991)   3,802
Marriages (1989)   7,524
Married (1989)   444,560
Single (1989)   307,985
Widowed/Divorced (1989)   117,815

Households and Families

Households Total   251,810
Average # Persons per Household   2.9
Average # Children per Household   1.1

Mother Tongue

English   11.7
French   64.2
Italian   5.6
Greek   2.1

Ethnic Composition

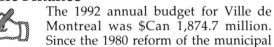

Montreal has been predominantly French since 1867. At the turn of the century, contingents of Jews from Eastern Europe arrived, beginning the process of ethnic diversification, which persists to this day. In the late 1980s the French formed 66% of the population (making it the largest French-speaking city in the world after Paris), British 11%, Jews 5%, and others 18%. Others include the earlier arrivals from Italy, Germany, the Ukraine, Poland, and the Netherlands, as well as later arrivals from the West Indies and South Asia. In addition, about 3% of the population is listed as having multi-ethnic origins.

Government

Montreal has a mayor-council form of government. The mayor and 57 members of the city council are elected to four-year terms. A seven-member city executive committee prepares the city budget and proposes statutes. Since 1970 all municipalities on the island have been represented in the Montreal Urban Community whose responsibilities include police protection, urban planning, sewerage, and environment. In the 20th century Montreal politics have been dominated by populist mayors: Mederic Martin, Camillien Houde (who was in jail during wartime for anti-British activities) and the flamboyant Jean Drapeau. Drapeau's Parti Civic was in power from 1960 until 1986 when Drapeau's extravagance was challenged successfully by Jean Doré's Montreal Citizens' Movement.

Public Finance

The 1992 annual budget for Ville de Montreal was $Can 1,874.7 million. Since the 1980 reform of the municipal tax system, 84.5% of the revenues has come from taxes. The remaining 15.5% comes from other sources, such as income from permits, fines, and transfer payments. The main source of revenue is property tax, bringing in 46.6 cents on every tax dollar. The residential sector accounts for 59.2% of taxable property, and commercial and industrial sectors for 38.4%. Of the expenditures, 37.9% goes to transportation, 38.5% to recreation and culture, 1.4% to public security, 6.1% to health and welfare, 6.4% to urban planning and development, 6.2% to sanitation and ecology, and 4.9% to general administration.

Economy

Montreal has a multifaceted economy like most world-class cities, and its strength arises from a synergy of all the sectors rather than from a single sector alone. Manufacturing, transportation, agriculture, trade, finance, and communications all contribute to the versatile economy. Despite significant decentralization, the manufacturing sector remains large. The principal products include food and beverages, clothing, metal products, transportation equipment, and chemicals. Although manufacturing remains vigorous in terms of output, its share of the work force has declined to 20.7%. International trade is important, and Montreal companies handle 20% of all Canadian imports and 10% of the exports. These companies also account for 12% of national trade and 65% of Quebec trade. Montreal has some of Canada's largest department stores, such as Place Bonaventure with 3 million square feet of display space. Although overshadowed by Toronto since 1970, Montreal remains a major financial center with 40% of the nation's finance companies, including the Bank of Montreal. The Montreal Stock Exchange, opened in 1874, is the oldest stock exchange in the country.

Labor

Services account for 35% of the work force, manufacturing 21%; retail and wholesale trade 18%; public administration 5%; FIRE 7%; transportation, communications, and utilities 9%; construction 4%; and other 1%.

Labor

Work Force	Male	Female
Total Work Force	290,470	236,470
Employed	250,140	203,130
Employment Rate	72.20	52.40
% of 15–24 Year Olds	68.40	65.40
Occupation	*Male*	*Female*
Managerial	30,680	18,670
Education	9,140	12,835
Health	8,470	20,740
Technical and Cultural	31,280	19,325
Clerical	29,480	73,465
Sales	24,180	17,075
Service	39,990	27,040
Manufacturing	44,610	28,485
Construction	18,185	455
Transportation	14,950	605
Other	25,750	6,795

Labor (continued)

Income

Male ($Can)   26,127
Female ($Can)   19,224
Average Household Income ($Can)   26,338
Average Family Income ($Can)   31,783
Average Tax ($Can)   3,435
Average Household Expenditure ($Can)   36,158

Manufacturing

Plants   2,937
Employees   110,622
Value of Shipments ($Can)   11,836,505,000
Total Value Added ($Can)   5,395,336,000
Number of Banks   500 (Branches)

Education

Montreal has an unusual four-tiered school system divided by both language and religion. The four categories of schools are: Roman Catholic English-language, Roman Catholic French-language, Protestant French-language, and Protestant English-language. Jewish students attend either Protestant schools or their own yeshivas. Of the total of 300 schools, the Roman Catholic school boards control 225. Montreal is home to two of the nation's finest universities: the all-French University of Montreal and the all-English McGill University. Both of them are privately run. Both the French and English sectors have a second university: the state-run Université du Québec at Montreal in the former and Concordia University in the latter. There are also 16 public colleges, 12 French-teaching and 3 English-teaching, and 19 private colleges, 15 French-teaching, 2 English-teaching, and 2 bilingual.

Education

Population (over 15 years old)   853,475
Less than Grade 9   226,446
Grades 9–13   265,825
Trade Certificate   178,690
University Degree   101,195

Four-Year Universities and Colleges
   University of Montreal
   McGill University
   MacDonald College
   Concordia University

Public Colleges, French
   Ahuntsic
   André-Laurendeu
   Bois-de-Boulogne
   Maisonneuve
   Rosemont
   Saint-Laurent
   Edouard-Montpetit
   Lionel-Groulx
   Vieux-Montreal
   Montmorency
   Institut de Tourisme et d'Hôtellerie
   Conservatoire de Musique

Education (continued)

Public Colleges, English
   Dawson
   Champlain Regional
   John Abbott

Private Colleges, French
   Stanislas
   Marie-de-France
   Français
   Jean-de-Brébeuf
   Marie-Victorin
   Ecole de Musique Vincent-d'Indy
   Andre-Grasset
   Institut Teccart
   College LaSalle
   Conservatoire Lassalle
   Beth-Jacob
   Centre Specialise de Conception et Fabrication
   Centre Specialise de la Môde

Private Colleges, English
   Marianopolis
   Centennial Academy

Health

Medical care is provided in more than 20 hospitals and 56 clinics. Every neighborhood has its own community health center. The major hospitals are Saint-Luc, Sacré-Coeur, Hôtel-Dieu, Sainte-Justine, Jewish General (Sir Mortimer B. Davis), Julius Richardson's, Montreal Children's, Montreal General, Institut de Cardiologie, Shriner's, Bellechasse, Jean-Talon, La Visitation, Hôpital Juif de Readaptation, Louis-H. Lafontaine, Marie-Clarac, Reine Elizabeth, Marie-Claret, Marie-Enfant, Hôpital Neurologique, Notre-Dame, Notre-Dame-de-la-Merci, Notre-Dame-des-Lourdes, Reddy Memorial, Saint-Joseph-de-la-Providence, Santa Cabrini, Institut de Readaptation, Sainte-Jeanne-d'Arc, St. Mary's, Maisonneuve-Rosemont, Catherine-Booth, Guy-Laporte, Rivière-des-Prairies, Hôpital Chinois, Trés-Saint-Redempteur, Bourget, Fleury, Royal Victoria, and Saint-Michel.

Transportation

More than 10 major highways serve Montreal. The Trans-Canada Highway, which runs from coast to coast, crosses downtown Montreal. Twenty railroad and highway bridges connect Montreal with Ile de Laval and the east shore of the St. Lawrence River. The city's subway, the 38.5-mile Metro, built between 1962 and 1967, has trains that run almost soundlessly, following each other at three-minute intervals during rush hours. It has four lines interconnecting downtown. The 65 stations, each designed by a different architect, are works of art with abstract murals, stained glass, and ceramic bas-reliefs. Montreal is closely associated with the history of Canadian railways. As the hub of the transcontinental system, it is at the head of major lines running south to the United States, east to the Maritimes, and west to Vancouver. Both CN and CP have their headquarters here. The Montreal Harbor stretches 15 miles along the west bank of the St. Lawrence River. Annually its 17 berths handle over 3,000 ships and 21 million tons of cargo, of which between 6 and 7 million tons are grain. Montreal's two international airports are Dorval, for Canadian and American domestic flights, and Mirabel for international flights. Saint Hubert is used mainly by private and military aircraft. Both Air Canada and the International Civil Aviation Organization have their headquarters in Montreal.

Transportation
New Automobiles
Domestic   19,706
Imported   17,367
Trucks   8,662

Housing

Montreal has a lower proportion of single-family houses and a higher proportion of apartments than other major Canadian cities. Most of the poorer houses and apartments are in East End, and middle-class homes in West End. Upscale houses and mansions are generally on the slopes of Mount Royal. The most distinctive dwellings are two- or three-story apartment buildings with outside staircases. In the 1960s, the city redeveloped a 107-acre area below downtown called Little Burgundy, building 1,200 new apartments at a cost of $Can 30 million. One of the most impressive developments is the Habitat on Cité du Havre, a strip of land extending into the St. Lawrence River.

Housing
Total Housing Stock   443,560
Owned   113,225
Rented   330,335
Single, Detached   22,835
Apartments   52,340
Homes Built 1990   3,403
Building Permits Value ($Can)   1,054,665,000

Urban Redevelopment

After the heavy building programs in the 1960s and 1970s construction of massive structures slowed down and the recession of the early 1990s put a further damper on high rises. Nevertheless, many major buildings have were built between 1985 and 1992: the $Can 280 million IBM Tower, the $Can 140 million McGill College Tower, the $Can 200 million Eaton Center, the $Can 169 million World Trade Center, the $Can 250 million 1000 de la Gauchetiere, the $Can 115 million Montreal Trust Tower, the $Can 75 million La Laurentienne Tower, the $Can 185 million Les Cours Mont Royal, and the $Can 60 million Scotia Bank Tower.

Crime

With a murder rate of only 4.1 per 100,000 Montreal ranks as one of the safest cities in North America.

Religion

Montreal, founded as Ville Marie, is perhaps the most Catholic city in North America. Once a seigneury of the Order of St. Sulpice, religious landmarks are strewn around the city and constitute its richest heritage. Of the more than 300 churches, the most famous is the Notre Dame parish church in Old Montreal facing the Place d'Armes. The church, first built in 1656, has two towers, one of which houses a huge bell called Le Gros Bourdon and weighing 12 tons. Also facing the square is St. Sulpice Seminary, dating from 1685. Notre Dame de Bon Secours, also known as the Sailor's Church, is another well-known church. The Cathedral Basilica of Mary, Queen of the World, stands in the heart of downtown. It is patterned after St. Peter's in Vatican City. Saint Joseph's Oratory, built in 1675 on the west slope of Mount Royal, is a place of pilgrimage, visited by more than 2 million annually. St. Patrick's Church serves English-speaking Roman Catholics. Other Catholic churches include St. Jean-Baptiste Church, which holds almost 3,000 people, and St. Joachim Church, built by the architect Victor Bourgeau. The major Protestant churches are Christ Church, the seat of the Anglican diocese; St. George's Anglican Church; and the Presbyterian Church of St. Andrew and St. Paul.

Media

Four daily newspapers are published in Montreal: One—*The Gazette*, founded in 1778—is published in English and three—*La Presse, Le Devoir*, and *Le Journal de Montreal*—are published in French. *Le Journal de Montreal* has the largest circulation. The electronic media consist of thirteen radio stations and four television stations. Seven of the radio stations and three of the television stations are in French, and the others are in English. Radio station CFCF, founded in 1919, was Canada's first, and television station CBFT was one of Canada's first two.

Media
Newsprint
Le Devoir, daily
The Gazette, daily
Le Journal de Montreal, daily
Montreal, weekly
Montreal Ce Mois-Ci, monthly
Montreal Magazine, 10 issues
Montreal Scope
La Presse, daily

Media (continued)

Television
    CBFT (Channel 2)
    CBMT (Channel 6)
    CFCF (Channel 12)
    CFTM (Channel 10)

Radio

CFMB (AM)	CIBL (FM)
CINQ (FM)	CITE (FM)
CJAD (AM)	CJFM (FM)
CJMS (AM)	CKMF (FM)
CKAC (AM)	CKIS (AM)
CHOM (FM)	CKVL (AM)
CKOI (FM)	

Sports

Montreal has two major professional sports teams: the Montreal Canadiens of the National Hockey League, who play in the Forum, and the Montreal Expos of the National Baseball League, who play at the Olympic Stadium. The Olympic Stadium is one of the city's most impressive landmarks and features a retractable dome. The Montreal Alouettes (Concordes) football team was disbanded in 1987. The city hosts the annual Canadian Grand Prix Formula I automobile race and the Montreal International Marathon.

Arts, Culture, and Tourism

Montreal's most famous cultural institutions are the International Theatre, La Poudriere on Ile Ste.-Helene, and Place des Arts, a large performing arts complex. The complex includes the 3,000-seat Salle Wilfrid-Pelletier concert hall, and the smaller Maisonneuve and Port Royal theaters. Music is represented by the Montreal Opera and the Montreal Symphony Orchestra; dance by Les Feux-Follets and Les Grands Ballets Canadiens; and theater by Le Theatre du Nouveau Monde and Le Theatre du Rideau-Vert.

The Museum of Fine Arts, founded in 1860, is one of the oldest museums in Canada. The Museum of Contemporary Arts stands in Cite du Havre. The Château de Ramezay is a history museum housed in a historical building constructed in 1705. The McCord Museum specializes in the ethnology and the history of Canada. Other major museums include the Montreal Museum of Decorative Arts, Saint-Laurent Art Museum, Montreal History Centre, David M. Stewart Museum, Marguerite d'Youville Museum (also called the Grey Nuns Museum), Lachine Museum, Redpath Museum, Post Office House, and Canadian Railway Museum.

Parks and Recreation

The Montreal park system includes over 400 parks covering 5,000 acres. The largest is the 295-acre Mount Royal Park in the center of the island, which includes Beaver Lake. It was designed by Frederick Law Olmsted. Lafontaine Park at Sherbrooke and Amherst also has a lake. Maisonneuve Park at Sherbrooke and Pie IX Boulevard includes the Botanical Gardens. St. Helen's Park is located on St. Helen's Island. The Ile Notre-Dame includes the Floral Park, a legacy of the 1980 Floralies Internationales. Other parks include Jeanne-Mance Park, between Mount Royal and Duluth Avenue; the 267-acre Angrignon Park; René-Lévesque Park, the 926-acre Cap Saint Jacques Regional Park; Bois-de-Liesse Regional Park; Ile-de-la-Visitation Regional Park, and Bois-de-la-Reparation Regional Park.

Sources of Further Information

City Hall
333 Saint-Antoine Street East
Montreal, Quebec H2X 1R9
(514) 872-5321

Montreal Board of Trade
1080 Beave Hall Hill, #710
Montreal, Quebec H2Z 1S9
(514) 871-4000

Additional Reading

Leonard, Jean Francois, and Jacques Leveillee. *Montreal after Drapeau*. 1986.
Toker, Franklin. *The Church of Notre Dame in Montreal: An Architectural History*. 1991.
Marsan, Jean-Claude. *Montreal in Evolution: Historical Analysis of the Development of Montreal's Architecture and Urban Environment*. 1981.

Ottawa

Ontario

Basic Data

Name Ottawa
Year Founded 1826 Inc. 1855
Status: Province Capital of Canada
Area (square miles) 42.5
Elevation 259 ft.
Time Zone EST
Population (1990) 313,987

Distance in Miles to:

Calgary	2,208
Chicago	736
Edmonton	2,221
Montreal	118
New York	430
Quebec	286
Regina	1,733
San Francisco	2,865
Toronto	248
Vancouver	2,886

Location and Topography

N

Ottawa, the capital of Canada, is located on a rugged limestone ridge on the south bank of the Ottawa River on Ontario's eastern boundary with Quebec. The river separates Ottawa from the city of Hull, Quebec, on the north bank. The Rideau River plunges 37 feet over a cliff into the Ottawa River at the northeastern end of the city, forming the Rideau Falls. The Rideau Canal cuts through the city on its way from the Ottawa River to Lake Ontario. The terrain is generally hilly.

Layout of City and Suburbs

The principal physical attractions of the city are the rapids and falls punctuating the course of the Ottawa River. Parliament Hill borders the Ottawa River just west of the Rideau Canal. The original core of the city is the Lower Town, east of the Rideau Canal, where Ottawa was founded in the 19th century, and which includes the restored Mile of History along Sussex Drive and the By Ward Market. In the 1860s, when Ottawa became the capital, the Upper Town became the center of government buildings.

Ottawa's open space areas include the large Central Experimental Farm in the southwestern part of the city and a green belt girdling the riverine area. Since the 1920s, the core area of the city has been considerably developed with parks, such as Confederation Square, and major national buildings, such as the National Arts Center. The skyline began to change after 1973, when the limit on the height of buildings was removed. The Rideau Center, a downtown convention, hotel, and shopping complex, opened in 1983. Much of the beautification of the city was carried out by the National Capital Commission. The chief shopping districts are the Sparks Street Mall in Upper Town and Byward Market and Rideau Street in Lower Town. The municipalities of Rockcliffe Park and Vanier, each with its own government, lie entirely within Ottawa.

Climate

Ottawa is one of the coldest national capitals of the world. It has a continental climate with a mean annual temperature of 42°F and a mean annual precipitation of 32.5 inches. Snowfall is heavy, ranging from an annual low of 84.5 inches to a high of 174.8 inches. The summers are warm, but not excessively hot.

Weather

Annual Averages

January °F 12
July °F 69
Annual Precipitation (inches) 32.5
Annual Sunshine (hours) 2,008

History

The Ottawa River was used for thousands of years by American Indians as a highway between the east and west. Recorded history began in 1613, when the French explorer Samuel de Champlain first sailed up the river, pausing on the northern shore of Ottawa to watch his native guides make sacrifices of tobacco to the falls he named "Chaudiere" (French for *cauldron*). In the 18th century, French traders, or *voyageurs*, portaged three times where Hull now stands before continuing their journey to the Great Lakes.

In 1800 the first settlers, headed by Philemon Wright, arrived from Woburn, Massachusetts. They settled on the northern shore of the Ottawa River, near Chaudiere Falls, in a village called Wright's Town. The building of the Rideau Canal (1826–1832) shifted the focus of development from Wright's Town to the southern shore of the Ottawa River. The canal was designed in the wake of the War of 1812 to provide a military supply route from Montreal to the Great Lakes well away from the U.S. border. Built by British Ordnance under the command of Lieutenant Colonel John By, the Rideau Canal was completed in six years, connecting the Ottawa River and Lake Ontario at Kingston. To house his workers, By surveyed and laid out a new town, named Bytown, on the south shore of the Ottawa River. Many streets in Ottawa still run exactly as he had planned them. Bytown soon acquired a reputation for violence as hundreds of rowdy raftsmen came into town on their way back from winter camps and stopped to celebrate noisily in the streets and taverns of Lower Town. At the same time new immigrants from Europe began to add to the diversity of residents and to provide the basis for a stable community.

In the 1830s timber became the principal economic activity in the region and by the 1850s Bytown was one of the largest sawing and milling centers in the world. In 1855 Bytown was raised to the status of a city and renamed Ottawa, after the Outaouais Indian tribe. In 1857, Queen Victoria chose Ottawa as the capital of the Province of Canada. Construction of Parliament buildings began in 1859 and they were officially opened in 1866. In 1867 the city was made the capital of the new Dominion of Canada. Ottawa grew slowly in the last part of the 19th century and in 1900 was damaged heavily in a fire. It was not until the turn of the century, when Sir Wilfred Laurier embarked on a plan to create a "Washington of the North," that the new Ottawa began to take shape. In 1896 the Ottawa Improvement Commission was formed to carry out the building program. It was replaced by the Federal District Commission in 1927. Ten years later, Prime Minister W. L. Mackenzie King appointed Jacques Greber to replan the city. His plan was accepted by Parliament in 1951. Its highlights included the removal of rail tracks from the center of the city and the development of a belt of parks, including the 88,000-acre Gatineau Park. The National Capital Commission replaced the Federal District Commission in 1959. It created a National Capital Region of 1,800 square miles, half in Ontario and half in Quebec Province.

Historical Landmarks

The Parliament buildings are Ottawa's most historic attractions. They consist of three buildings: the Centre Block, the East Block, and the West Block on a 35-acre square. They were completed in 1865, but the Centre Block was destroyed by fire in 1916 and was rebuilt in 1920. The Centre Block includes the House of Commons, the Senate Chamber, and the Peace Tower. During July and August the Governor General's Foot Guards and the Canadian Grenadier Guards perform a daily changing-the-guard ceremony in front of the Peace Tower. Other government buildings are the Royal Canadian Mint, the National Library and Public Archives, and the Canadian Supreme Court. Rideau Hall, also called the Government House, stands near the mouth of the Rideau River. It is the official residence of the Canadian Governor General. The National War Memorial at Confederation Square honors Canadian war dead. It consists of a granite arch with bronze figures underneath. Confederation Boulevard, also known as the Discovery Route, is the city's major heritage trail. It begins on Parliament Hill and passes through historic districts. Since 1840 the By Ward Market has served as the heart of Lower Town. Laurier House is a large Victorian dwelling that served as home to two prime ministers: Sir Wilfrid Laurier and William Lyon Mackenzie King. The Ottawa Locks on the Rideau Canal mark the northern entrance of the Rideau Canal. These consist of eight locks rising more than 80 feet from the Ottawa River. The Voyageur Portage in nearby Hull contains a statue of Jean de Brebeuf, a 17th-century Jesuit missionary who traveled up the Ottawa River to work among the Iroquois Indians.

Population

The population of Ottawa in 1990 was 313,987, highest in its history. After rising steadily from 268,206 in 1961 to 302,341 in 1971 and 304,462 in 1976, the population dipped in 1981 to 295,163, but then rose again to 300,763 in 1986.

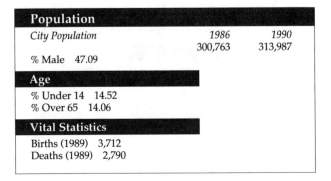

Population		
City Population	*1986*	*1990*
	300,763	313,987
% Male 47.09		
Age		
% Under 14 14.52		
% Over 65 14.06		
Vital Statistics		
Births (1989) 3,712		
Deaths (1989) 2,790		

Chronology

1613 Samuel de Champlain sails up the Ottawa River and pauses near the present site of Ottawa to name the Chaudiere Falls.

1800 Philemon Wright, a Tory from Massachusetts, settles on the present site of Hull on the northern bank of the Ottawa River. The new village becomes known as Wright's Town.

1826 Construction begins on the Rideau Canal under the leadership of Lieutenant Colonel John By. By lays out a village on the southern bank of the Ottawa River, later called Bytown.

1832 Rideau Canal is completed.

1855 Bytown is raised to the status of a city and renamed Ottawa.

1857 Queen Victoria names Ottawa as the capital of the Province of Canada.

1859 Construction begins on Parliament buildings.

1866 Parliament buildings open.

1896 Sir Wilfrid Laurier establishes the Ottawa Improvement Commission.

1900 A fire does extensive damage in the city.

1927 The Federal District Commission replaces the Ottawa Improvement Commission.

1937 Jacques Greber is named architect to direct the redevelopment of the capital.

1951 The Greber Plan is approved by Parliament.

1959 The National Capital Commission replaces the Federal District Commission. The National Capital Region is created encompassing 1,800 square miles in Ontario and Quebec provinces.

Population (continued)

Natural Increase (1986–1991) 922
Marriages (1989) 3,655
Married (1989) 139,850
Single (1989) 85,650
Widowed/Divorced (1989) 31,575

Households and Families

Households Total 75,125
Average # Persons per Household 2.9
Average # Children per Household 1.0

Mother Tongue

English 66.6
French 16.7
Italian 2.1

Ethnic Composition

 Most Ottawans are native Canadians, about half of them of English ancestry. Ethnic French-Canadians compose about one-fourth of the population. Most of the English live in Upper Town and most of the French in Lower Town.

Government

 Ottawa has a mayor-council form of government. Voters elect a mayor and 15 council members to three-year terms. In 1968 Ontario established the Regional Municipality of Ottawa-Carleton, combining Ottawa and Carleton counties under a single government. It is made up of a council consisting of elected officials from six cities, one village, and four townships. The regional government has taxing powers and controls health and welfare services, water supply, roads, and sewage. In addition, the National Capital Commission wields considerable influence as autonomous landowner and developer of public works. The federal government, the city's largest landowner, is exempt from city by-laws and taxes. The result is that Ottawa has a weak municipal government, further complicated by the electoral ward system designed to balance the interests of Upper and Lower Towns. The Irish and French Catholic communities generally vote liberal while the Anglo-Protestant community votes conservative.

Public Finance

 Taxes on property, sales, and businesses provide the bulk of municipal revenue. Ottawa also receives federal and provincial grants.

Economy

 Until the late–19th-century the economy was dominated by the lumber industry. After Ottawa became the national capital, however, the economy shifted to become heavily oriented to the public sector. One of the last vestiges of the traditional economy, a pulp and paper mill at Chaudiere Falls, ceased operation in the 1980s. Next to government, the largest economic sector is the growing tourism industry. Manufacturing in the region is essentially limited to light industries, which employ 12,300 people in 355 manufacturing and processing plants. Few corporate offices have been established in Ottawa, with the notable exception of Metropolitan Life Insurance. Ottawa is also an important center of scientific research.

Labor

The dramatic change in Ottawa's labor distribution came about in the mid-19th century when the dominant employment sector shifted from lumbering and milling to government. In 1861, lumber mills engaged about 48% of the work force and government 10%. By 1990 the ratio had reversed to 25% government and 6% manufacturing.

About 100,000 Ottawans work for the government, 24,000 in electronics industries, and another 24,000 in tourism.

Labor

Work Force	Male	Female
Total Work Force	91,530	80,815
Employed	84,850	74,590
Employment Rate	77.50	60.00
% of 15–24 Year Olds	76.10	56.42

Occupation	Male	Female
Managerial	16,795	11,050
Education	2,895	4,285
Health	2,120	6,335
Technical and Cultural	16,115	8,985
Clerical	10,170	28,685
Sales	7,285	5,820
Service	13,610	11,025
Manufacturing	6,155	1,550
Construction	6,355	160
Transportation	3,830	260
Other	4,880	1,320

Income

Male ($Can)   34,139
Female ($Can)   23,900
Average Household Income ($Can)   35,154
Average Family Income ($Can)   45,883
Average Tax ($Can)   7,543
Average Household Expenditure ($Can)   51,533
Number of Banks   170

Manufacturing

Plants   245
Employees   8,330
Value of Shipments ($Can)   1,629,524,000
Total Value Added ($Can)   505,479,000

Education

Two school boards operate in Ottawa. About two-thirds of school-age children attend schools run by the Ottawa Board of Education, which also serves part of the population of Vanier and Rockcliffe Park Village. The Ottawa Roman Catholic Separate School Board administers its own schools, which until 1987 were limited by statute to grades 10 and under. Centers of higher education include the University of Ottawa and Carleton University. Although formally secular, the former embodies some of the traditions of the Oblate Order, which operated the university for many years. St. Paul's University is an affiliate of the University of Ottawa. The major community institution is the Algonquin College of Applied Arts and Technology.

Education

Population (over 15 years old)   252,825
Less than Grade 9   25,040
Grades 9–13   84,880
Trade Certificate   54,910
University Degree   55,090

Four-Year Universities and Colleges
   University of Ottawa
   Carleton University

Health

The medical care system consists of 11 major hospitals, including Ottawa Civic Hospital, Ottawa General Hospital, Royal Ottawa Hospital, Queensway-Carleton Hospital, Salvation Army Grace General Hospital, St. Vincent Hospital, The Perley Hospital, Riverside Hospital, Hospital Montfort, Children's Hospital of Eastern Ontario, and Elisabeth Bruyere Hospital.

Transportation

Ottawa is on the Trans-Canada Highway. East-west highway routes are linked through the city by Queensway, a freeway of four to six lanes that bisects the city for most of its length. The highway system includes scenic drives running parallel to the Rideau Canal on both sides, and extending across the Ottawa River to the Gatineau Hills. Five automobile bridges and one rail bridge connect Ottawa with Hull. The Ottawa River links the city with Montreal and the Rideau Canal connects it with Kingston. Passenger rail services are provided by VIA, a merger of the Canadian National and the Canadian Pacific railways. Ottawa is one of Canada's busiest air terminals owing largely to its location. The two principal airports are Uplands, at the southern edge of the city, and Rockcliffe. However, most international flights use Mirabel Airport, northwest of Montreal, about 90 minutes by road from Ottawa.

Transportation

New Automobiles

Domestic   10,214
Imported   6,043
Trucks   4,039

Urban Redevelopment

The rebuilding of Ottawa has continued under the direction of the National Capital Commission. The National Aviation Museum was completed in 1985, the National Gallery of Canada and headquarters of the Regional Municipality of Ottawa-Carleton in 1988, Central Mortgage and Housing Corporation Headquarters and Public Health Laboratory in 1989, the Riverside Medical Building in 1990, Photographic Museum in 1991, and the Post Office Complex and extension facilities of the Childrens Hospital of

Housing

Total Housing Stock   128,615
Owned   50,590
Rented   78,025
Single, Detached   38,600
Apartments   44,730
Homes Built 1990   1,390
Building Permits Value ($Can)   507,656,000

Tallest Buildings	Hgt. (ft.)	Stories
Place de Ville, Tower C	368	29
R.H. Coats Bldg.	326	27

Eastern Ontario in 1992. The Ottawa City Hall is presently under construction.

Crime

In 1990, 45,973 criminal offenses were reported in Ottawa, of which 4,199 were violent offenses. Offenses that showed an increase were attempted murder, sexual assaults and other assaults.

Religion

Nearly half the population is Roman Catholic. The next two largest denominations are the United Church, claiming 16% of the population, and the Anglican Church, claiming 15%. No other denomination has a membership of over 5% of the population. The most prominent religious landmark in Ottawa is the Cathedral-Basilica of Notre Dame on Sussex Drive. It is built on land originally given to the parish of Bytown in 1832. Construction began in 1840 and was completed in 1890. Other notable churches include Christ Church Cathedral on Queen Street, built in 1873; St. Bartholomews Church on McKay Street, outside the gates of Rideau Hall, the parish church of over 20 governors general; St. Matthews Church on Glebe Avenue; and St. Francois-de-Sales Church, on Jacques Cartier Street, built in 1886.

Media

The city press consists of three dailies: *Le Droit* in French, and *The Ottawa Citizen* and *The Ottawa Sun* in English. *The Ottawa Sunday Herald* appears every Sunday. Electronic media consist of 3 television stations and 12 radio stations.

Media

Newsprint
  The Ottawa Citizen, daily
  Le Droit, daily
  The Ottawa Sun, daily
  Ottawa Centretown News, bi-weekly

Television
  CBOFT (Channel 9)
  CBOT (Channel 4)
  CJOH (Channel 13)

Radio

CBO (FM)	CBOF (AM)
CBOF (FM)	CFGO (AM)
CFRA (AM)	CFMO (FM)
CHEZ (FM)	CKBY (FM)
CKCU (FM)	CIWW (AM)
CBO (AM)	CKO (FM)

Sports

Ottawa is represented in professional sports by three teams: the Ottawa Rough Riders in football, the Ottawa Senators in hockey, and the Ottawa Lynx, who began competing in Triple A baseball in 1993.

Arts, Culture, and Tourism

The National Arts Center, which opened in 1969, is the focal point of Ottawa's cultural life. It contains a 2,300-seat opera house, 1,100-seat theater, and a smaller 350-seat theater. The lead museum is the National Gallery of Canada with extensive collections of Canadian and world art. Other museums include the National Museum of Science and Technology, the National Museum of Man and the Natural Sciences, the Canadian War Museum, the National Aviation Museum, the National Postal Museum, the Canadian Museum of Contemporary Photography, the Bytown Museum, the Currency Museum, the Ski Museum, and the Canadian Museum of Caricature.

Parks and Recreation

Ottawa maintains an extensive park system, much of it converted to playing fields in summer or skating rinks in winter. Major parks include Britannia Bay and Mooney's Bay on the waterfront and Landsdowne Park. The Rideau Canal becomes a five-mile-long skating rink in winter. The National Capital Commission maintains a network of pathways and parkways along the Ottawa and Rideau rivers. The park system extends to the 88,000-acre Gatineau Park, northwest of Hull.

Sources of Further Information

City Hall
111 Sussex
Ottawa K1N 5A1
(613) 564-1429

Ottawa Area Board of Trade
185 Sparks Street
Ottawa K1P 5B9
(613) 236- 3631

Additional Reading

Bernard, Andre. *Profile: Ottawa-Hull.* 1974.
Bond, C. C. J. *City on the Ottawa.* 1967.
———. *Where Rivers Meet: An Illustrated History of Ottawa.* 1984.
Eggleston, W. *The Queen's Choice.* 1961.
Haig, Robert. *Ottawa: City of the Big Ears.* 1970.
Maitland, Leslie and Louis Taylor. *Historical Sketches of Ottawa.* 1990.

Quebec

Quebec

Basic Data

Name   Quebec
Year Founded   1608 Inc. 1833
Status: Province   Quebec
Area (square miles)   34.2
Elevation   321
Time Zone   EST
Population (1990)   167,517

Distance in Miles To:

Calgary	2,494
Chicago	1,010
Edmonton	2,507
Montreal	168
New York	566
Ottawa	286
Regina	2,119
San Francisco	3,122
Toronto	503
Vancouver	3,151

Location and Topography

Quebec, the capital of the province of the same name, is located on the north shore of the St. Lawrence River where it meets the Rivière St. Charles. Here the St. Lawrence narrows to a width of less than one mile. Navigation of the river here, once made difficult by a group of islands of which the largest is the Ile d'Orleans, is today made safe and easy by dredging of a shipping channel. Cap Diamant, a rocky promontory, dominates the city earning Quebec the nickname of Gibraltar of North America.

Layout of the City and Suburbs

Quebec is the only walled city in North America. With its crooked cobblestone streets, old stone houses, and numerous churches, it resembles European cities more than it does New World ones. The Château Frontenac, a castle-like hotel with towers, red brick walls, and steep copper roof built by Canadian Pacific in its heyday, adds to the medieval atmosphere of the town.

Quebec has two sections: Old and New. The former, about four square miles in area, has two districts: Upper Town and Lower Town. The Citadel, Quebec's signature landmark, overlooks the city protectively from a height of 347 feet. It stands at the highest point of Cap Diamant, which drops sharply toward the St. Lawrence and more gently toward the St. Charles River. Massive walls and cannons surround the fort and its 140-acre parade ground, completed by the British in 1832.

North of the Citadel is Upper Town encircled by a stone wall averaging 35 feet in height. It has three ornate entrance gates. These walls enclose many parks, colleges, shops, restaurants, and hotels. A 60-foot-wide planked walkway extends along the cliffs from the Citadel to the Château Frontenac. Lower Town, northeast of Upper Town, lies 19 feet above sea level on a strip of land between the rivers and the cliffs of Cap Diamant.

Lower Town is one of the oldest city quarters in North America and is distinguished by its old, narrow, crooked streets. Sous-le-Cap, for instance, measures only 8 feet 10 inches at its narrowest, and is the narrowest street in North America. Because the military installations and the religious institutions crowded out residential construction in the old section, the town broke out of its fortified confines in the 19th century and early 20th century and stretched westward along the banks of the St. Charles. Particularly since 1950, there has been expansion to the north and west around Sillery, Ste.-Foy, Charlesbourg, Cap-Rouge, and Ancienne Lorette.

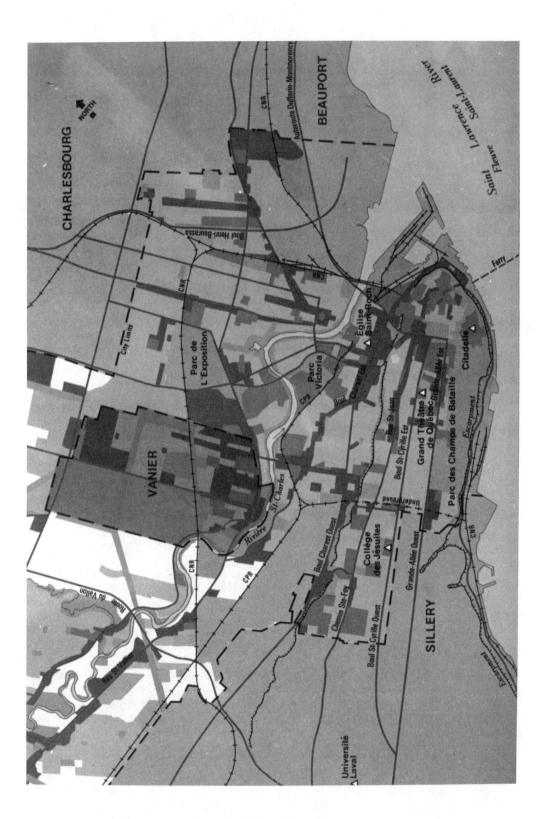

Climate

Given its northern location, Quebec has extremely cold winters but mild summers. The average temperature is 10°F in January and 66°F in July. The average annual precipitation is 42 inches. Hours of sunshine are 1,851.7 per year.

Weather
Annual Averages
January °F   10.2
July °F   66
Annual Precipitation (inches)   42
Annual Sunshine (hours)   1,852

History

The site of Quebec was once the hunting grounds of Angonquian and Iroquois Indians. The first white man to visit the region was the French explorer Jacques Cartier, who spent the winter of 1535 near the Iroquois village of Stadacona. Seventy-three years later, in 1608, Samuel de Champlain established the first French settlement here. The first Canadian farmer, Louis Hébert, set up a farmstead here in 1617. In 1620, Champlain built Fort St. Louis on the site where the Château Frontenac now stands. The first of the many clashes between the English and French over Quebec began in 1629, when an English fleet under Admiral David Kirke captured the settlement, when it had only 60 inhabitants. France regained the settlement in 1632 through the Treaty of St. Germaine-en-Laye. In 1659, Monsignor François Xavier de Laval de Montmorency arrived in Quebec. More than any other man, he helped to transform Quebec into the Cradle of New France, as it came to be called. In 1674 he became the first bishop of Quebec. In 1690 the English made another attempt to capture Quebec under General Sir William Phips, but were warded off by Louis de Buade, Comte de Frontenac, governor-general of New France. A third effort also failed when in 1711 a British fleet under Admiral Hovenden Walker was forced to turn back from a planned attack when a storm wrecked many of his ships. The fourth and decisive attempt was made in 1759 when a large British fleet set sail from Halifax charged with the capture of Quebec. Aboard the 250 ships were Major General James Wolfe and a force of 8,000 soldiers and 18,000 seamen. The city's defender this time was the Marquis de Montcalm, commanding 2,900 soldiers and 13,000 reservists and Indians. Montcalm believed that the British could not attack the city by climbing the steep cliffs leading to the Plains of Abraham so he left them undefended.

Wolfe decided to attack the city from that very quarter. During the cloudy, calm night of 12–13 September 1759, the tide bore the British flatboats to the foot of the cliffs. By dawn 5,000 British regulars had scaled the cliffs and were ranged for battle on the plains. The French, after a hasty attack, fled in disar-ray. Both Wolfe and Montcalm were fatally wounded. The battle, which lasted only 15 minutes, decided the fate not only of Quebec but also of the French empire in North America. The following year the French tried to recapture Quebec and defeated the British at Ste.-Foy. But large British reinforcements from Lake Champlain cheated the French of their victory. The Treaty of Paris of 1763 stripped France of all its possessions in North America except for the tiny islands of St. Pierre and Miquelon, which are still in its hands. The Quebec Act of 1774 enlarged the boundaries of the Province of Quebec and guaranteed religious freedom to the province's Roman Catholic majority. The act established French civil law and British criminal law and provided for the continued use of the seigneurial system. During the Revolution, American troops led by Richard Montgomery and Benedict Arnold attacked Quebec, but suffered an ignominious defeat in which Montgomery was killed. When Upper and Lower Canada were formed in 1791, Quebec City became the capital of Lower Canada. In 1820–1831 the Quebec Citadel was built encircling the Upper Town cliff with four martello towers on the Plains of Abraham. Quebec received its city charter in 1832. Quebec served twice as the capital of the Province of Canada: from 1851 to 1855 and from 1859 to 1865. When the Dominion of Canada was established in 1867 Quebec City, with a population of 60,000, was named as the capital of the new province of Quebec. Quebec's importance began to diminish in the 19th century in proportion to the rise of Montreal as the principal port of the St. Lawrence River. However, industrialization and expansion of provincial government services helped its population to grow from 80,000 in 1911 to 164,016 in 1951. In the 1970s the city annexed four suburbs and its area increased from eight square miles to 36 square miles.

Historical Landmarks

Within the ramparts of the old walled city are some of the oldest buildings in North America, including the Seminary (1668), the monastery and convent of the Ursuline Order (1639), the Hôtel-Dieu Hospital, and the fortifications of Artillery Park. Along the narrow streets are old stone houses as well as restaurants, boutiques, and galleries. In the Harbor District in Lower Town are other historic buildings, such as the Chevalier House; the Notre Dame des Victoires chapel, completed in 1688, standing on a site once occupied by Champlain's first log cabin; and the Place Royale, where Champlain originally built his Abitation. Lower and Upper Town are connected by steep streets and stairways. In the house where Louis Jolliet lived in the 16th century there is an elevator to carry people to Upper Town. Near the mouth of the St. Charles River are the Exhibition Grounds and Talon's Vaults, on the site of the first brewery built during the administration of Jean Baptiste Talon, intendant of New France from 1665 to 1672. East of Quebec are some of French Canada's oldest rural settlements: Giffard, Beauport, Beaupré,

Chronology

1735	Jacques Cartier quarters in the Iroquois village of Stadacona.
1608	Samuel de Champlain establishes permanent settlement at Quebec.
1617	Louis Hébert becomes first settler and farmer.
1620	Champlain builds Fort St. Louis on the site of present Château Frontenac.
1629	British fleet under Admiral David Kirke captures the city.
1632	Treaty of St. Germaine-en-Laye restores Quebec to France.
1659	Monsignor François Xavier de Laval arrives and begins the transformation of Quebec into the center of New France.
1674	Laval is made bishop.
1690	Sir William Phips makes abortive attempt to capture the city and is repulsed by Louis de Buade, Comte de Frontenac.
1711	British fleet under Admiral Hovenden Walker is turned back from a planned attack on the city after a storm wrecks many of his ships.
1759	General James Wolfe captures the city after his troops heroically scale the cliffs of Cap Diamant by night and surprise the French defenders under the Marquis de Montcalm on the Plains of Abraham. Both Wolfe and Montcalm are killed.
1760	French defeat the English at Ste.-Foy but are foiled in their efforts to recapture Quebec by British reinforcements.
1763	By the Treaty of Paris, France cedes its dominions in North America to Britain.
1774	The Quebec Act grants religious freedom to Roman Catholics and enlarges the boundaries of Quebec Province.
1775	American troops under Richard Montgomery and Benedict Arnold attack Quebec but are repulsed.
1791	Quebec is named capital of Lower Canada.
1820–1831	The Citadel is built.
1832	Quebec receives city charter.
1851–1855	Quebec is capital of Province of Canada.
1859–1865	Quebec is again capital of Province of Canada.

1867	The Dominion of Canada is formed with Quebec as capital of the province of Quebec.
1879	The Quebec, Montreal, Ottawa and Occidental Railway reaches the city.
1900	Building of the Quebec Bridge begins.
1907	Southern cantilever span of the Quebec Bridge falls into St. Lawrence River, killing 75 workers.
1919	Quebec Bridge is opened by the Prince of Wales.
1970	Quebec Urban Community is formed. Quebec annexes four suburbs. A second bridge across St. Lawrence, Pierre Laporte, opens.

and St.-Joachim. The Ste. Anne Boulevard leads to the famous pilgrimage shrine of Ste.-Anne-de-Beaupré.

Population

The population of Quebec in the 1991 census was 167,517, representing a slight upturn from a slow decline that began in 1976 when its population was 177,082. By 1981 it was 166,474 and by 1986 164,580. At the time of the Conquest, it was little more than a small village with 8,000 inhabitants. Growth was rapid in the first half of the 19th century and by 1861 it had 60,000 people. The population stabilized in the second half of the 19th century. In the 20th century its population growth has been the result of annexation of surrounding suburbs: St. Sauveur (1889), St. Malo (1908), Limoilou (1909), Montcalm (1913), Notre-Dame-des-Anges (1924), Les Saules (1969), Duberger (1970), Neufchatel(1971), and Charlesbourg Ouest (1973).

Population		
City Population	*1986*	*1990*
	164,580	167,517
% Male 46.59		

Age
% Under 14   14.68
% Over 65   14.03

Vital Statistics
Births (1989)   1,702
Deaths (1989)   1,707
Natural Increase (1986–1991)   -5
Marriages (1989)   1,527
Married (1989)   69,565
Single (1989)   52,320
Widowed/Divorced (1989)   18,520

Households and Families
Households Total   40,700
Average # Persons per Household   2.9
Average # Children per Household   1.0

Population (continued)

Mother Tongue

English 1.8
French 94.5
Other 3.7

Ethnic Composition

About 95% of the people have French ancestry. This was not always so. The population was 41% British in 1851 and 51% British in 1861. But the percentage of Francophones rose to 68.5% in 1871, 90% by 1921 and 95% by 1981.

Government

Quebec has a mayor-council form of government. The mayor and the 16 council members are elected to four-year terms. Quebec received its first charter in 1832 and a second one in 1840.

Public Finance

Taxes on property, sales, and businesses provide a substantial part of the revenues. A third of the city property is exempt from property taxes, but provincial and federal properties pay amounts in lieu of taxes.

Economy

Quebec has experienced a number of cycles of growth and decline in its history. It was the premier commercial port in Canada until the mid–19th century, and the timber resources of its hinterland provided it with an unmatched source of wealth. However, beginning in the second half of the 19th century, many factors militated against it in favor of Montreal — the decline of the timber trade, the development of railway networks that bypassed it, the dredging of the St. Lawrence River between Quebec and Montreal, and the growing importance of trade with the United States. After World War II, Quebec's economy got a second wind through the expansion of manufacturing. Today more than 500 manufacturing plants are located in the Quebec area, employing 17,000 workers and producing nearly $Can 800 million annually. Most of the industrial sites are along the St. Charles River. The leading industries are papermaking, cement, manufacturing and shipbuilding. Tourism is also important, drawing over 1 million visitors annually.

Labor

Work Force	Male	Female
Total Work Force	45,690	36,370
Employed	39,350	30,825
Employment Rate	71.79	48.70
% of 15–24 Year Olds	69.90	65.10
Occupation	Male	Female
Managerial	6,020	3,100
Education	1,825	2,245

Labor (continued)

Occupation	Male	Female
Health	1,200	3,445
Technical and Cultural	5,655	3,110
Clerical	4,680	12,200
Sales	4,060	3,000
Service	7,665	5,390
Manufacturing	4,510	1,225
Construction	2,390	85
Transportation	2,450	100
Other	2,915	335

Income

Male ($Can) 26,877
Female ($Can) 19,683
Average Household Income ($Can) 26,697
Average Family Income ($Can) 32,276
Average Tax ($Can) 3,219
Average Household Expenditure ($Can) 36,085
Number of Banks 11

Manufacturing

Plants 208
Employees 8,392
Value of Shipments ($Can) 1,144,991,000
Total Value Added ($Can) 526,901,000

Labor

Most jobs are concentrated in public administration, defense, and the service sector, and only 10% are in manufacturing.

Education

Quebec's public school system consists of 75 Roman Catholic and 15 Protestant schools with a total of 75,000 pupils. Most of the Catholic schools teach in French. The premier higher education institution is the historic Université Laval, Canada's oldest French-language university, in Ste.-Foy. It traces its beginnings to the Seminary of Quebec, which was founded by François Xavier de Laval de Montmorency, the first Roman Catholic bishop of Quebec, in 1668. It was granted university status by royal decree in 1852. Private schools include the Seminary, the College des Jesuites, and Merici College.

Education

Population (over 15 years old) 138,305
Less than Grade 9 32,010
Grades 9–13 47,205
Trade Certificate 33,735
University Degree 15,455

Four-Year Universities and Colleges
Université Laval

Health

Health care is provided by several hospitals: L'Hôtel Dieu, Hôpital de l'Enfant Jesus, Hôpital de St.-Sacrement, Centre Hospital Jeffrey Hale, Centre Hospital Courchesne, Hôpital St.-François-d'Assise, L'Hôtel

Dieu Sacré-Coeur-de-Jesus, Hôpital General, Hôpital Ste. Monique, Hôpital Fleur de Lys, Hôpital Civique, and Centre Hospitalier Notre Dame du Chemin.

Transportation

 Quebec is approached from the south by Route 73, which crosses the Quebec Bridge and the city before turning into Charlesbourg and points north. From the east it is approached by Route 40, which merges with Route 73 within the city before moving west. The city has many Parisian boulevards, such as Metropolitain, Laurentien, Charest, Wilfrid Laurier, and Wilfrid Hamel. Grande Allée, the most significant street, runs south from the 17th-century gate of St. Louis, past the Parliament buildings into the campus of Université Laval. The pride of Quebec is its harbor, which, although overshadowed by Montreal, is one of the major ports of North America and one that is open all year to ocean-going vessels. The harbor extends six miles along the east and west sides of the cape, and into the mouth of the St. Charles River. A ferry and two bridges—Quebec Bridge and Pierre Laporte Bridge—cross the St. Lawrence River. The city is served by three freight lines and by Via Rail passenger service. The principal air terminal is the Quebec International Airport 10 miles from downtown. The Ancienne Lorette Airport accommodates medium-size jet aircraft.

Transportation
New Automobiles
Domestic   3,627
Imported   3,563
Trucks   1,915

Urban Redevelopment

 Three underground garages were built in 1971 and 1972 to relieve the city's acute shortage of parking spaces. In 1974 a $Can 50 million convention center was built at Place Quebec, opposite Parliament.

Housing
Total Housing Stock   70,030
Owned   21,395
Rented   48,635
Single, Detached   10,100
Apartments   7,110
Homes Built 1990   1,637
Building Permits Value ($Can)   206,403,000

Religion

Quebec is a citadel of Roman Catholicism. The Catholic presence is everywhere, from schools and universities to churches and hospitals. The city is the seat of a Catholic as well as an Anglican archbishopric. Of the over 100 Catholic basilicas the premier one is Basilique Notre Dame, with walls built in 1647. Also important

in the religious history of the city is the Ursuline Convent, founded in 1639. The Anglican Cathedral of the Holy Trinity, the first Anglican cathedral built outside Great Britain, was completed in 1804.

Media

 Quebec has two dailies, both in French: *Le Journal de Québec*, and *Le Soleil*. Electronic media consist of three French-language television stations, one English-language television station, eleven French-language radio stations, and one English-language radio station.

Media	
Newsprint	
Le Journal de Québec, daily	
Le Soleil, daily	
Television	
CBVT (Channel 11)	
CFAP (Channel 2)	
CFCM (Channel 4)	
CKMI (Channel 5)	
Radio	
CBV (AM)	CBV (FM)
CBVE (FM)	CFLS (AM)
CHRC (AM)	CHOI (FM)
CITF (FM)	CJMF (FM)
CJRP (AM)	CHIK (FM)
CKIA (FM)	CKRL (FM)

Sports

 Quebec's only major professional sports team is the Nordiques, members of the National Hockey League since 1979. Downhill and cross-country skiing centers are found in Mont Saint-Anne and Lac Beauport.

Arts, Culture, and Tourism

Cultural activity centers around the Grand Theater, a combined 1,800-seat concert hall and 800-seat theater. Among musical groups the most notable is the Quebec Symphony Orchestra. The Trident Theater Company presents performances throughout the year.

Old Quebec is included in the United Nations list of world heritage sites. The three principal museums are the Musée du Quebec, Musée Historique, and the Seminary Museum. The Provincial Museum is located in Battlefield Park, and the Wax Museum in Upper Town.

Parks and Recreation

The park system includes 45 parks covering 350 acres. The major parks include Victoria Park and Cartier-Brebeuf Park on the St. Charles River, Exposition Park, and Artillery Park. The National Battlefields Park includes the historic Plains of Abraham. Northeast of Quebec is the Montmorency Falls, where the waters plunge 274 feet (80 feet higher than Niagara Falls) into the St. Lawrence River.

Sources of Further Information

City Hall
CP 700
Québec, Québec G1R 4S9
(418) 694-6024

Additional Reading

Fitzmaurice, John. *Quebec and Canada: Past, Present and Future*. 1985.
Ruddel, David T. *Quebec City, 1765–1832*. 1988.

Regina

Saskatchewan

Basic Data

Name   Regina
Year Founded   1882 Inc. 1903
Status: Province   Capital of Saskatchewan
Area (square miles)   43
Elevation   1,893
Time Zone   Mountain
Population (1990)   179,178

Distance in Miles to:

Calgary	475
Chicago	1,149
Edmonton	488
Montreal	1,851
New York	1,968
Ottawa	1,733
Quebec	2,019
Toronto	1,659
Vancouver	1,132
Winnipeg	355

Location and Topography

Regina, the capital of Saskatchewan, is located on a wide, level alluvial plain in the southern part of the province.

Layout of City and Suburbs

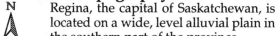

Wascana Creek winds through the city. Southeast of the downtown area, the creek widens into the man-made Wascana Lake. Surrounding the lake is the Wascana Centre, a 2,273-acre area, where the Legislative Building, the University of Regina, the Museum of Natural History, and the Saskatchewan Centre of the Arts are located. The Canadian Pacific Railway runs through the middle of the city. Running east-west are the avenues, of which the most notable are Victoria and Dewdney, and running north-south are the streets, of which the most notable is Albert. The city limits are the TransCanada Highway to the south and Ninth Avenue to the north.

Climate

Regina has a typical continental climate characterized by a wide variability of temperatures and low precipitation. The average temperature is 0°F in January and 66°F in July. Annual rainfall is 15 inches. In general, the climate, like the landscape, is arid and dry.

Weather

Annual Averages

January °F   0
July °F   66
Annual Precipitation (inches)   15.8
Annual Sunshine (hours)   2,331

History

The Cree Indians inhabited the area on which Regina stands. It was visited in 1857 by the British explorer, John Palliser, who reported the land unsuitable for farming. His report was contradicted in 1880 by Canadian botanist John Macoun, who found excellent potential here for wheat farming. He succeded in persuading the Canadian Pacific Railway to select a townsite near the meandering Wascana Creek and to lay out the streets in 1882. It was named by the governor general, the Marquess of Lorne, after his mother in law, Queen Victoria. In the same year it was selected by the North West Mounted Police (now the Royal Canadian Mounted Police) as its headquarters. It was made the capital of the North West Territories in 1883 and incorporated as a city in 1903 with a population of 3,000. When the Province of Saskatchewan was created in

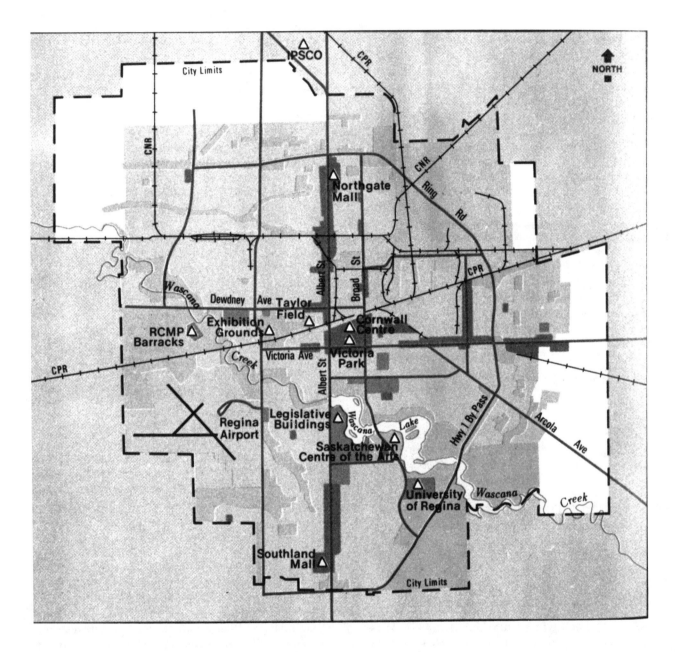

1905, Regina became its capital. By 1911 the population jumped to 30,000. A tornado in 1912, an economic depression in 1913, and the outbreak of World War I halted the growth of the city. The slump continued after World War I because of the drop in wheat prices. The city was hit hard by the Great Depression and about a fifth of the residents were on welfare by 1937. This created the conditions for the rise of the radical socialist party, the Cooperative Commonwealth Federation (CCF), which held is first national convention in Regina. Later it adopted the famous Regina Manifesto, calling for an end to capitalism. In 1944 CCF captured the provincial government, making Saskatchewan the first socialist-run province in Canada. After the 1950s the economy improved as potash and petroleum were discovered and many new industries were established. During the 1970s and 1980s the city experienced steady if unspectacular growth, although facing chronic financial deficits.

Historical Landmarks

The Diefenbaker homestead, the home of the former prime minister, is located here. Saskatchewan House is a landmark on Dewdney Avenue.

Population

The population of Regina in the 1990 census was 179,178, slightly higher than its 1986 population figure of 175,060. The city has shown steady growth in each quinquennial census, rising from 149,593 in 1976 to 162,613 in 1981. The population has more than doubled since the end of World War II, in part through emigration from outside the province and in part through a general population shift from farm to city within the province.

Population		
City Population	*1986*	*1990*
	175,060	179,178
% Male 48.67		
Age		
% Under 14 23.05		
% Over 65 9.89		
Vital Statistics		
Births (1989) 3,102		
Deaths (1989) 1,064		
Natural Increase (1986–1991) 2,038		
Marriages (1989) 1,327		
Married (1989) 83,425		
Single (1989) 38,125		
Widowed/Divorced (1989) 13,155		
Households and Families		
Households Total 45,255		
Average # Persons per Household 3.2		
Average # Children per Household 1.3		
Mother Tongue		
English 85.0		
French 1.3		
German 3.7		
Ukrainian 1.6		
Chinese 1.0		

Ethnic Composition

Nearly half the population are of Anglo Saxon origin. Other major ethnic groups include Germans, Ukrainians, and Scandinavians.

Government

Regina has a council-mayor form of government. The voters elect a mayor and 10 council members for three-year terms. The present wards were established in 1973. The powers of the city council are set out in the Urban Municipality Act.

Economy

Once almost entirely dependent on wheat, Regina has diversified its economy and thus managed to achieve a measure of stability. The city has more than 280 manufacturing plants which account for more than a third of the provincial industrial production. The principal industrial products include cement, steel, and fertilizer. Farming is still important and Regina is the headquarters of the Saskatchewan Wheat Pool, the largest grainhandling cooperative in the world, with a membership of over 70,000. Regina is also a major distribution center for farm machinery. The third bastion of the economy is oil. The oil fields of Southern Saskatchewan supply the local refinery. Along with Saskatoon, it remains an important retail trade and service center for the entire province. The provincial government and the Royal Canadian Mounted Police are also major factors in the urban economy.

Labor

Almost a fourth of the city workforce is engaged in trade and a seventh in city, provincial, and federal government agencies.

Labor		
Work Force	*Male*	*Female*
Total Work Force	51,525	43,650
Employed	47,300	40,115
Employment Rate	80.6	63.3
% of 15–24 Year Olds	76.1	72.8
Occupation	*Male*	*Female*
Managerial	8,085	3,815
Education	1,430	2,130
Health	920	4,085
Technical and Cultural	5,285	2,595
Clerical	4,390	17,320
Sales	5,635	3,965
Service	6,040	7,055
Manufacturing	6,240	765
Construction	5,565	140
Transportation	2,890	190
Other	4,210	655
Income		
Male ($Can) 32,711		
Female ($Can) 21,622		
Average Household Income ($Can) 36,573		

Chronology

1857 John Palliser visits the region and reports unfavorably on its farming potentials.

1880 Botanist John Macoun visits the region and reports favorably on settlement prospects.

1882 Macoun persuades Canadian Pacific Railway to select a townsite near the Wascana Creek and to lay out the streets. The North West Mounted Police establishes its headquarters in Regina.

1883 Regina is selected as the capital of the North West Territories.

1903 Regina is incorporated as a city.

1905 Regina is named capital of the Province of Saskatchewan.

1912 Tornado hits Regina, causing widespread damage.

1924 Buffeted by falling wheat prices, Saskatchewan farmers form the Saskatchewan Wheat Pool.

1933 Cooperative Commonwealth Federation (CCF), a radical socialist party, holds first its first convention in Regina.

1944 CCF gains statehouse in elections.

Labor (continued)

Average Family Income ($Can)   41,894
Average Tax ($Can)   6,184
Average Household Expenditure ($Can)   44,171
Number of Banks, Savings, Trust and Credit Unions   104

Manufacturing

Plants   178
Employees   4,239
Value of Shipments ($Can)   1,012,374,000
Total Value Added ($Can)   351,403,000

Education

Regina's public school system supports 60 elementary schools and 10 high schools. The Separate Roman Catholic School Board oversees 10 high schools. Higher education facilities include the University of Regina, the Wascana Institute of Applied Arts and Sciences, and the Regina Plains Community College.

Education

Population (over 15 years old)   132,825
Less than Grade 9   15,240
Grades 9–13   52,390
Trade Certificate   30,455
University Degree   50,165

Four-Year Universities and Colleges
University of Regina

Health

Healthcare is provided by six area hospitals: Regina General Hospital, Pasqua Hospital, South Saskatchewan Hospital Centre, Wascana Hospital, Plains Health Centre, and Community Health Services Association.

Transportation

Regina is approached from east and west by the Trans-Canada Highway, from which a highway partially encircles the city. Rail services are provided by Canadian Pacific Railroad and Canadian National Railways. The principal air terminal is Regina Airport, just outside the city limits.

Transportation

New Automobiles

Domestic   3,915
Imported   1,330
Trucks   3,252

Housing

Of the total housing stock of 64,030, 41,280 are owner-occupied.

Housing

Total Housing Stock   64,030
Owned   41,280
Rented   22,755
Single, Detached   43,930
Apartments   3,410
Homes Built 1990   484
Building Permits Value ($Can)   102,011,000

Tallest Bulidings	Hgt. (ft.)	Stories
Lloyds Bank tower	NA	22
Saskatchewan Government Insurance Tower	NA	20
Avord Tower	NA	16
Canadian Imperial Bank of Commerce	NA	16
City Hall	NA	15
Saskatchewan Power Building	NA	13

Urban Redevelopment

The construction boom that changed Regina's skyline began in the 1960s. Three of the city's tallest buildings went up during this period: the 16-story Avord Tower, the 16-story Canadian Imperial Bank of Commerce, and the 13-story Saskatchewan Power Building. Another construction boom began in the 1970s and continued into the 1980s. A new 15-story City Hall opened in 1976. Two provincial government office buildings were built in 1979—the sprawling three-story T. C. Douglas Building, and the 20-story Saskatchewan Government Insurance Tower. In 1980 a huge enclosed shopping mall called the Cornwall Centre was completed followed by the 13-story Bank of Montreal Building in 1983. In 1985 Regina's tallest building, the 22-story Lloyds Bank Tower, opened.

Religion

 Regina is very much a main-line denominational city. Roman Catholics have a strong presence and the Greek Orthodox Church is well represented. The largest Protestant denominations are United Church, Lutheran, and Anglican. The oldest church in Regina, built in 1885, is the Little Chapel on the Square, part of the Royal Canadian Mounted Police Museum.

Media

 The city daily is *The Leader-Post*. Electronic media consists of one French-language and two English-language television stations, and nine radio stations.

Media
Newsprint
The Leader-Post, daily
Television
CBKT (Channel 9)
CFRE (Channel 11)
CKCK (Channel 2)
Radio

CBK (AM)	CBK (FM)
CBKF (FM)	CJME (AM)
CIZL (FM)	CKCK (AM)
CKIT (FM)	CKRM (AM)
CFMQ (FM)	

Sports

 Regina's principal professional sports team is the Saskatchewan Rough Riders of the Canadian Football League who play at the 27,600-seat Taylor Field. The Lawson Aquatic Centre, next to Taylor Field, holds swimming events, and Exhibition Park holds horse races. An annual festival called Buffalo Days is held in late July and early August, to celebrate Regina's wild west days.

Arts, Culture, and Tourism

 The Saskatchewan Centre of the Arts is the hub of Regina's cultural life. It includes the Centennial Centre Concert Hall, the Jubilee Theatre, and a convention facility called Hanbidge Hall. The Regina Symphony Orchestra also performs at the center. The Globe Repertory Theatre stages productions in the Globe Theater downtown.

The principal musuem is the Norman Mackenzie Art Gallery in Wascana Centre. The Royal Canadian Mounted Police Museum features historical exhibits that show how the Mounties brought law and order to the Canadian west. The Museum of Natural History is also in the Wascana Centre.

Parks and Recreation

The Waterfowl Park affords an opportunity to view numerous species of birds and mammals in their natural habitat. The smaller Victoria Park is on Victoria Avenue.

Sources of Further Information

City Hall
Regina, Saskatchewan S4P 3C8
(306) 569-7262

Regina Chamber of Commerce
2145 Albert Street
Regina, Saskatchewan S4P 2V1
(306) 757-4658

Additional Reading

Dale, E. H. *Regina: Regional Isolation and Innovative Development*. 1980.
Drake, E. G. *Regina: The Queen City*. 1955.

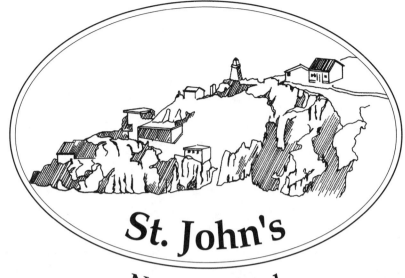

St. John's

Newfoundland

Basic Data

Name   St. John's
Year Founded   1497 Inc. 1888
Status: Province   Capital of Newfoundland
Area (square miles)   39.22
Elevation   459
Time Zone   Newfoundland Time Zone
Population (1990)   95,770

Distance in Miles to: (by ferry)

Charlottetown	804
Halifax	838
St. John	977
Monckton	885

Location and Topography

N

St. John's is located on the eastern side of the Avalon Peninsula of southeast Newfoundland. It is the eastern-most city in Canada.

Layout of City and Suburbs

St. John's is built on high hills. Its harbor is almost landlocked, admitting ships through the Narrows, flanked by cliffs 500 feet high. The old business section borders the harbor, while the newer part stretches to the Confederation Building, which houses the provincial government. In the eastern part of the city are the Colonial buildings, Government House and, on the site of Old Fort William, the Newfoundland Hotel. Until 1964, when the government completed a wharf along the north side of the harbor, numerous private finger piers jutted out from the merchants' warehouses on the south side of Water Street. The city's streets, generally narrow and winding, run east-west parallel to the harbor. The older architectural styles are log cabins or frame buildings with cottage roofs. After the 1892 fire,

the style shifted to Gothic or International Second Empire. Most modern buildings date from after the 1960s.

Climate

St. John's has a maritime climate with mild winters and summers. The average daily temperature is 60°F in July and 29°F in January. The average annual rainfall is 60 inches and the hours of sunshine are 1,497.

Weather

Annual Averages

January °F   29
July °F   60
Annual Precipitation (inches)   59.64
Annual Sunshine (hours)   1,497

History

The area was inhabited by Beothuk Indians before the arrival of Europeans. The Italian explorer John Cabot claimed the site for England in 1497, naming it after Saint John the Baptist. In the 1500s, European fishing crews started coming to the nearby fishing grounds. In 1583 English claim to the settlement was renewed by Sir Humphrey Gilbert. The Dutch attacked St. John's in 1665 and the French captured it three times, in 1696, 1708, and 1762. Each time the English recaptured it. During the Revolutionary War and the War of 1812, St. John's was a major naval base for the British. Afterwards, the settlement became a center for sailmaking, shipbuilding, and the drying and smoking of fish. In 1832 St. John's became the seat of the government when Newfoundland was granted a colonial legislature by England. In 1888 it received its own municipal council. The city was ravaged by fires in 1816, 1817, 1819, 1846, and again in 1892. It was rebuilt each time in a haphazard manner because much

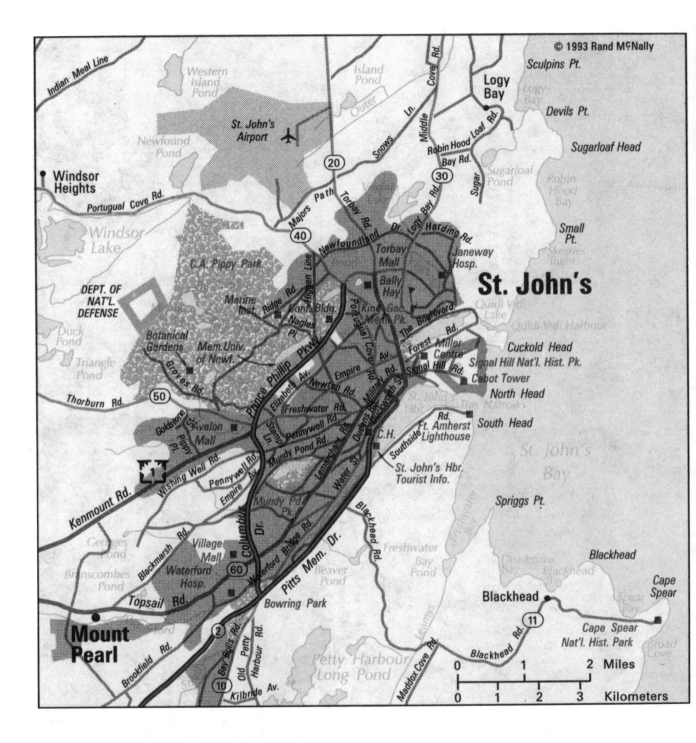

© 1993 Rand McNally

From the *Road Atlas* © 1993 by Rand McNally R.L. 93-S-92.

of the land in the main commercial-residential area was owned by British absentee landlords. After 1870, small manufacturing industries were established, and a dry dock opened in 1882. In 1897 St. John's became the headquarters of the Trans-Island Railway, completed by Robert Reid. Poor world markets for fish and the Great Depression combined to make the early part of the 20th century one of great hardship for St. John's. However, with the arrival of U.S. forces in 1941 to build Fort Pepperell, some measure of prosperity returned. The construction boom continued with the creation of St. John's Housing Corporation in 1944 and the subsequent building of new suburbs which lasted until well after 1946. Newfoundland became a province in 1949 with St. John's as its capital. Federal funds helped to build a number of new office buildings, such as the Confederation Building in 1959 and the City Hall in 1970.

Historical Landmarks

There are a suprising number of historic buildings still standing, considering the unusually large number of fires that ravaged the city throughout the nineteenth century. Signal Hill, now part of Signal Hill National Historic Park, offers a breathtaking view of the city. It includes the Cabot Tower, now a museum, built in 1897 to commemorate the 400th anniversary of Cabot's landing. It was here in 1902 that Guglielmo Marconi received the world's first transatlantic message from Cornwall, England. Fort Amherst, below Signal Hill on the opposite side of the Narrows, has protected St. John's for over 400 years. Old Fort William now houses the Newfoundland Hotel. The Murray Premises in Beck's Cove is a National Historic Site. They are the only remaining 19th-century fishery premises (for drying and packing fish). The courthouse is an imposing structure dating from 1899–1901. It replaced a smaller structure, built in 1849, that contained a produce market, jail and post office in addition to court rooms. On Duckworth Street is the Bank of British North America, built circa 1885. Other landmarks include the Masonic Temple on Cathedral Street, built in 1897; Victoria Hall, a meeting place for the Ulstermen on Gower Street, built in 1895; Kelvin House (1884); Sunnyside (1845); Rothwell House and Winterholme (1907); and Lodge (1890) on Rennies Mill Road; Bannerman House (1849); Sir Robert Bond House (1885); Bartra (1906) on Circular Road; Sutherland Place (1884); and Commissariat (1821) on Kings Bridge Road; Devons Place (1844) on Forest Road; Rendell-Shea House (1897) on Cochrane Street; and Martin McNamara House (1849) on Brine Street. The Colonial Building on the north side of Military Road served as the seat of Newfoundland legislature from 1850 to 1959. Also on Military Road is the Government House, completed in 1831.

Population

The population of St. John's in 1990 was 95,770, a decline of 446 from the 1986 total of 96,215. It followed a spurt of rapid growth from 1981, when the population was 83,770, and a slow decline from 1976, when the population was 86,576. Such fluctuations are typical of St. John's demographic history. St. John's experienced slow growth until the Napoleonic Wars, when substantial Irish Roman Catholic immigration nearly tripled the population to 10,018 by 1815. The growth slowed after 1832, but even so taxed St. John's resources until relieved by natives emigrating to the United States and Canada. The population again doubled between 1946 and 1971 as St. John's status as provincial capital added job opportunities in construction, services, and government. Between 1971 and 1981 the city again experienced a decline, which was reversed in the first half of the 1980s.

Population		
City Population	*1986*	*1990*
	96,215	95,770
% Male 48.06		

Age		
% Under 14 20.56		
% Over 65 10.64		

Vital Statistics		
Births (1989) 1,348		
Deaths (1989) 784		
Natural Increase (1986–1991) 564		
Marriages (1989) 957		
Married (1989) 42,075		
Single (1989) 27,005		
Widowed/Divorced (1989) 7,370		

Households and Families		
Households Total 23,410		
Average # Persons per Household 3.4		
Average # Children per Household 1.5		

Mother Tongue		
English 97.9		
French 0.3		
Other 1.8		

Ethnic Composition

The population is predominantly Anglo-Saxon and Irish.

Government

St. John's has a mayor-council form of government. The mayor and the eight council members are elected to four-year terms.

Economy

Since World War II, St. John's has lost its traditional role as a fish exporter, although codfish remains a staple industrial catch. Much of the port's revenues are now derived from supplying and repairing local and international fishing fleet. The port is now called the service station of the North Atlantic. Close proximity to the

Chronology

1497	John Cabot sails into the harbor and names it St. John's.
1583	Sir Humphrey Gilbert officially declares Newfoundland as an English colony.
1665	Dutch forces attack St. John's.
1696	French capture St. John's, but the English retake it.
1708	French capture St. John's for a second time, but the English again retake it.
1762	French capture St. John's for a third time, but the English retake it.
1816	Fire damages parts of town.
1817	Fire again burns parts of town.
1819	Fire burns parts of town.
1832	Newfoundland is granted colonial legislature with St. John's as its seat.
1846	Fire destroys parts of St. John's.
1870s	Small manufacturing industries are established.
1882	Dry dock opens in St. John's harbor.
1888	St. John's receives its own municipal council.
1892	Great Fire destroys many buildings
1897	St. John's becomes headquarters for the Trans-Island Railway.
1902	St. John's is incorporated as a city, with a population of 30,000.
1941	U.S. forces arrive to build Fort Pepperell; economic prosperity begins to return to the city.
1944	St. John's Housing Corporation is created and new suburb construction begins.
1949	Newfoundland becomes a province in the Confederation with St. John's as capital.
1959	Confederation Building opens.
1970	City Hall opens.

offshore oil wells in Grand Banks holds some promising potential for future growth. The federation has not been an unmixed blessing for St. John's economy. Cheaper manufactured goods from other provinces have depressed the market for local manufacturers, and the completion of a paved trans-island highway has enabled distributors to bypass the city and use Corner Brook and Channel-Port Aux Basques.

Labor

Since 1949 St. John's employment market has left its traditional mooring in fishing and become almost entirely public-service oriented. About a fourth of the work force is in trade. In 1991 the work force numbered 83,000, of whom 72,000 were employed and 11,000 or 13.1% were unemployed. The employment rate was 65.6%.

Labor

Work Force	Male	Female
Total Work Force	26,040	21,785
Employed	22,235	18,655
Employment Rate	73.79	55.20
% of 15–24 Year Olds	63.79	62.40
Occupation	*Male*	*Female*
Managerial	4,125	1,570
Education	1,160	1,860
Health	855	2,655
Technical and Cultural	2,780	1,445
Clerical	2,175	7,555
Sales	2,465	1,930
Service	3,265	3,180
Manufacturing	2,575	440
Construction	2,085	35
Transportation	1,500	75
Other	2,220	285

Income

Male ($Can) 30,458
Female ($Can) 19,613
Average Household Income ($Can) 36,273
Average Family Income ($Can) 38,132
Average Tax ($Can) 6,114
Average Household Expenditure ($Can) 45,422
Banks 39

Manufacturing

Plants 61
Employees 2,685
Value of Shipments ($Can) 278,779,000
Total Value Added ($Can) 148,167,000

Education

St. John's elementary and secondary education are administered by the Avalon Consolidated School Board as well as the Catholic School Board. In addition there are two smaller school boards: the Pentecostal School Board and the Seventh Day Adventist School Board. These boards support 50 schools. The principal institutions of higher education are the Memorial University of Newfoundland, with an enrollment of 14,000, the College of Trades and Technology, and the College of Fisheries, Navigation, Marine Engineering, and Electronics.

Health

Health services are provided by nine hospitals: Children's Rehabilitation Centre, Charles A. Janeway Child Health Centre, Grace General Hospital, Health Science

Education

Population (over 15 years old)   74,790
Less than Grade 9   10,950
Grades 9–13   26,760
Trade Certificate   16,415
University Degree   9,375

Four-Year Universities and Colleges
   Memorial University of Newfoundland
   College of Trades and Technology
   College of Fisheries, Navigation, Marine Engineering
      and Electronics

Complex, St. Clare's Mercy Hospital, St. Luke's Home, St. John's General Hospital, St. Patrick's Mercy Home, and Waterford Hospital.

Transportation

St. John's is the eastern starting point of the Trans-Canada Highway which ends at Victoria, B.C. The harbor, modernized in 1966, handles mostly fishing boats and tourist ships. The principal air terminal is St. John's Airport.

Transportation

New Automobiles

Domestic   3,357
Imported   1,276
Trucks   1,721

Housing

Before 1944, the residential and commercial districts were mixed. After the creation of St. John's Housing Corporation in that year, planned suburbs were built in the valleys to west, north, and northeast of the city. Average home prices for a standard detached bungalow range from $Can 98,300 in Mount Pearl to $Can 117,000 in St. John's East. St. John's has the highest rate of home ownership in Canada at 68.4%.

Housing

Total Housing Stock   29,750
Owned   17,725
Rented   12,020
Single, Detached   12,885
Apartments   560
Homes Built 1990   467
Building Permits Value ($Can)   109,508,000

Religion

Roman Catholics made up the majority of the population until 1911. The city has a number of beautiful churches. St. Thomas's Anglican Church, also known as the Old Garrison Church, is the oldest surviving church building in St. John's, opened in 1836. On Military Road is the Roman Catholic Basilica of St. John the Baptist, a

National Historic site. The Anglican Cathedral of St. John the Baptist is a Gothic Revival structure built by Sir George Gilbert Scott in 1847 on land provided by Queen Victoria. It was completed in 1885, destroyed by fire in 1892, and rebuilt. The Gower Street United Church was the first Methodist chapel in the city. It was begun in 1816, rebuilt in 1856, destroyed by fire in 1892 and later rebuilt. On Water Street is St. Patrick's Roman Catholic Church, begun in 1864 and completed in 1881.

Media

The city's daily is *The Evening Telegram*. The electronic media consists of two television stations and eight AM and FM radio stations.

Media

Newsprint
   The Evening Telegram, daily

Television
   CBNT (Channel 8)
   CJON (Channel 6)

Radio

CBN (AM)	CBN (FM)
CHMR (FM)	CHOZ (FM)
CJYQ (AM)	CKIX (FM)
VOCM (AM)	VOCM (FM)

Sports

St. John's most famous sporting event is the Regatta, the oldest continuous sporting event in North America, held annually on the first Wednesday in August since 1818. St. John's was the site of the 1977 Canada Summer Games, which left the city with many sporting facilities.

Arts, Culture, and Tourism

The Arts and Culture Centre houses a 1,000-seat auditorium, a 100-seat theater, the Memorial University Art Gallery, and the Newfoundland Symphony Orchestra. The principal museum is the Newfoundland Museum featuring historical naval, maritime, and military exhibits.

Parks and Recreation

There are four major city parks: Bannerman Park, Bowring Park, Victoria Park and the Harborside Park. In addition, the city is close to the 34,500-acre C. A. Pippy Provincial Park.

Sources of Further Information

City Hall
St. John's, Newfoundland A1C 5M2
(709) 726-8820

St. John's Board of Trade
P.O. Box 5127
St. John's, Newfoundland A1C 5V5

Additional Reading

Baker, Melvin. *Aspects of Nineteenth Century St. John's Municipal History.* 1982.

Copes, P. *St. John's and Newfoundland: An Economic Survey.* 1961.
Noel, S. J. R. *Politics in Newfoundland.* 1971.
O'Dea, Shane. *The Domestic Architecture of St. John's.* 1974.
O'Neill, Paul. *The Story of St. John's, Newfoundland.* 2 vols. 1975–1976.
Pearson, R. E. *Atlas of St. John's, Newfoundland.* 1969.

Saskatoon

Saskatchewan

Basic Data

Name Saskatoon
Year Founded 1883 Inc. 1906
Status: Province Saskatchewan
Area (square miles) 51.04
Elevation 1,690 ft.
Time Zone Mountain
Population (1990) 186,058

Distances: Mi

Calgary	385
Edmonton	328
Regina	160
Winnipeg	515

ter by as much as 20°F in a few hours. Annually, there are 105 days of rain or snow in a year with an average precipitation of 36 inches.

Weather

Annual Averages

January °F   -1.8
July °F   79
Annual Precipitation (inches)   36
Annual Sunshine (hours)   2,449

Location and Topography

 Saskatoon is located on both banks of the South Saskatchewan River in Saskatchewan Province. Saskatoon has an attractively variable topography although the general terrain is flat. The Moon and Pike oxbow lakes provide recreational opportunities closeby.

Layout of City and Suburbs

 The south Saskatchewan River dominates the city's layout. The river is spanned by seven bridges, including the Traffic Bridge (1907) and the 42nd Street Bridge, which completes the Ring Road. Prominent on the low west bank are the chateau-style Bessborough Hotel and several historic churches.

Climate

Saskatoon has a typical continental climate with short, warm summers and long, cold winters. Average temperaures range from -2°F in January to 79°F in July. Warm chinook winds may raise temperatures in win-

History

The region was first inhabited by hunting tribes about 6,000 years ago. When the first Europeans arrived, they found the Cree and Metis Indians living with the Sioux at Moose Woods. White settlement began after the site was chosen by the Temperance Society of Toronto as a colony. John Lake's survey party selected an east bank site in 1882, and the first settlers arrived in 1883. Construction of a railway from Regina in 1890 caused the commercial center to shift to the more level west bank. The new west bank community called itself Saskatoon (after a local berry) whereas the original settlement was called Nutana (from Latin, for *first-born*). A third settlement, known as Riverdale, rose south of the railyards. Between 1901 and 1905 all three were incorporated as villages, and in 1906 they combined to form the city of Saskatoon. The coming of the railroads and the location of the provincial university in the city in 1909 helped Saskatoon to become one of the fastest growing cities in the Canadian West. The interwar years were hard ones for Saskatoon, as they were for Regina and other western cities. However, after World War II, the resurgence of the farm and the

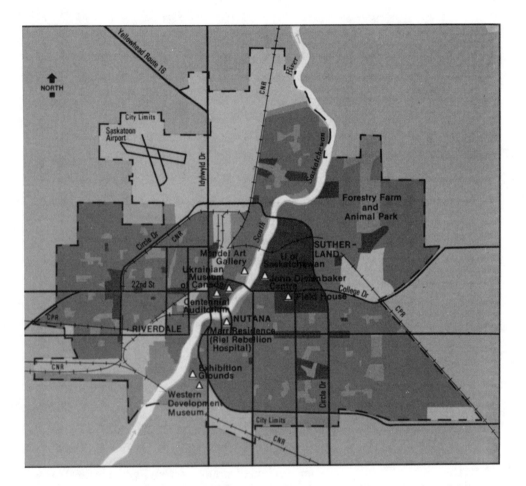

discovery of potash and uranium in northern Saskatchewan brought prosperity once again.

Historical Landmarks

Saskatoon has few historical buildings remaining, except a few sites associated with the Northwest Rebellion of 1885, such as the Marr Residence.

Population

Saskatoon has benefited from the shift of population from the farm to the city. Its demographic growth has been steady: from 133,750 in 1976 to 154,210 in 1981, and then to 186,058 in 1990.

The population of Saskatoon in 1990 was 186,058, making it the largest city in Saskatchewan.

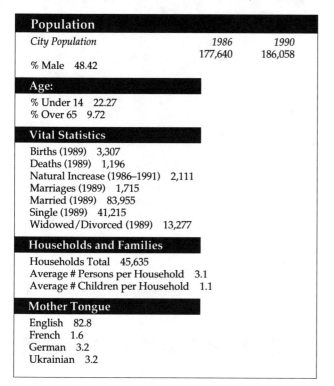

Population

City Population	1986	1990
	177,640	186,058
% Male 48.42		

Age:

% Under 14 22.27
% Over 65 9.72

Vital Statistics

Births (1989) 3,307
Deaths (1989) 1,196
Natural Increase (1986–1991) 2,111
Marriages (1989) 1,715
Married (1989) 83,955
Single (1989) 41,215
Widowed/Divorced (1989) 13,277

Households and Families

Households Total 45,635
Average # Persons per Household 3.1
Average # Children per Household 1.1

Mother Tongue

English 82.8
French 1.6
German 3.2
Ukrainian 3.2

Ethnic Composition

The original population was almost entirely Anglo-Saxon, but later migrants came from all parts of Europe, particularly Ukraine and Scandinavia. Since the 1980s, the arrival of Vietnamese, Filipino, Chilean, and East Indian immigrants has helped to create a broader ethnic mix.

Government

Saskatoon has a mayor-council form of government. The 1906 city charter specified a commissioner form of government with a mayor and a commissioner. The strong rule of Commissioner C. J. Yorath (1913–1921) made the system popular. The ward system was first introduced in 1906 but was abolished in 1920, reintroduced in 1973, and approved by voters in 1979. At present each of the 10 wards elect one alderman. Relations between the municipality and the province are governed by Urban Municipalities Act of 1984.

Economy

Saskatoon is in the midst of one of the largest wheat-growing prairies in Canada. Its economy is not exclusively tied to agriculture, however, but also to mining, manufacturing, and distribution. During the 1960s Saskatoon became an important supply center for the mining industry, developing some of the world's largest potash and uranium deposits north of the city. The leading manufacturing industries are food processing and electronic equipment.

Labor

The largest employers are the university, the city, and Intercontinental Packers. The mining industry provides hundreds of jobs within the city.

Labor

Work Force	Male	Female
Total Work Force	52,505	43,235
Employed	47,715	38,455
Employment Rate	80.7	61.0
% of 15–24 Year Olds	76.7	69.6
Occupation	*Male*	*Female*
Managerial	6,795	2,850
Education	1,995	2,730
Health	1,200	4,870
Technical and Cultural	5,060	2,740
Clerical	3,290	13,730
Sales	6,105	4,135
Service	5,770	8,405
Manufacturing	7,860	1,445
Construction	5,980	165
Transportation	3,025	305
Other	4,550	805

Income

Male ($Can) 31,665
Female ($Can) 26,970
Average Household Income ($Can) 33,604
Average Family Income ($Can) 38,852
Average Tax ($Can) 5,891
Average Household Expenditure ($Can) 41,488
Number of Banks, Savings, Credit Unions and Trusts 88

Manufacturing

Plants 216
Employees 6,820
Value of Shipments ($Can) 926,771,000
Total Value Added ($Can) 392,150,000

Education

The Saskatoon Board of Education oversees all public schools. In addition, there are three private church-supported schools. The major institution of higher education is the University of Saskatchewan, which is affiliated with Thomas Moore College, College of Emmanuel, St. Chad, Lutheran Theological Seminary, and St. Andrew's

Chronology

1882   Survey party from the Temperance Society of Toronto chooses east bank site for colony.

1883   Thirty-five members from the Temperance Society of Toronto, led by John Lake, found a settlement known as Nutana on the east bank of the South Saskatchewan River.

1890   Canadian Pacific Railway reaches the west bank of the river, causing the commercial center to shift from the east bank. The new settlement is called Saskatoon. A third settlement, called Riverdale, is built south of the railroad yards.

1906   Nutana, Sasktaoon, and Riverdale merge into a city called Saskatoon.

1909   Provincial legislature picks Saskatoon as site of new university.

1956   Town of Sutherland is annexed.

College, all within the city. Co-operative College of Canada, Kelsey Institute, and Saskatoon Region Community College are other educational institutions.

Education

Population (over 15 years old)   135,915
Less than Grade 9   15,485
Grades 9–13   50,445
Trade Certificate   32,550
University Degree   18,010

Four-Year Universities and Colleges
   University of Saskatchewan

Health

Medical care is provided by four hospitals: Community Health Services Association, St. Paul's Hospital, Saskatoon City Hospital, and University Hospital.

Transportation

Saskatoon is called the Hub City because it is at the junction of several highways: the interstate Route 16 (Yellowhead Route) from Portage La Prairie passes through the city on its way north, as does Route 11 from Regina on its way to Prince Albert. Other state routes approaching Saskatoon include 7, 5, 41, and 12. The Canadian Pacific railway and Canadian National railways operate freight rail services, and Via Rail offers passenger service. The principal air terminal is Saskatoon Airport, located to the north of the city.

Transportation

New Automobiles
Domestic   3,323
Imported   1,352
Trucks   2,309

Housing

Of the total housing stock of 67,075 units, approximately 38,345 are owner-occupied.

Housing

Total Housing Stock   67,075
Owned   38,345
Rented   28,730
Single, Detached   40,320
Apartments   3,935
Homes Built 1990   362
Building Permits Value ($Can)   164,467,000

Religion

The religious composition reflects Saskatoon's ethnic heritage. Roman Catholicism is strong, as is Greek Orthodox among the Ukrainians; United Church and Anglicanism among the Anglo-Saxons; and Lutheranism among the Germans and Scandinavians. Eastern religions have been introduced by more recent Asian immigrants.

Media

The city daily is the *Star-Phoenix*. Electronic media consist of 3 television stations and 6 radio stations.

Media

Newsprint
   Star-Phoenix, daily

Television
   CBKST (Channel 11)
   CFQC (Channel 8)
   CFSK (Channel 4)

Radio
   CBKF (AM)   CBKS (FM)
   CFMC (FM)   CFQC (AM)
   CJWW (AM)   CKOM (AM)

Sports

Saskatoon does not have a major professional sports franchise. The principal sports facilities are the Arena, Saskatchewan Place, the Field House on the campus of the University of Saskatchewan, and the Harry Bailey Aquatic Centre.

Arts, Culture, and Tourism

The Yevshan Ukrainian Folk Ballet is the most prominent among numerous dance groups. Music is represented by a symphony orchestra, an opera group, and a jazz society.

Saskatoon has numerous museums. The Western Development Museum features one of the largest collections of antique cars and early farm equipment. The Mendel Art Gallery features Eskimo art and sculpture. The Ukrainian Museum of Canada presents Ukrainian art and culture through hundreds of original exhibits. The John Diefenbaker Centre has a large collection of memorabilia associated with the native son and former prime minister.

Parks and Recreation

The largest public park is Holiday Park on the western bank of the South Saskatchewan River.

Sources of Further Information

City Hall
Saskatoon, Saskatchewan S7K OJ5
(306) 644-9240

Saskatoon Board of Trade
306 24th Street East
Saskatoon, Saskatchewan S7K 4R2
(306) 244-2151

Additional Reading

Clubb, S. P. *Saskatoon: The Serenity and the Surge.* 1966.
Delainey, W. P., J. H. Duerkop, and William A. S. Sarjeant. *Saskatoon: A Century in Pictures.* 1982.
Delainey, W. P. and William A. S. Sarjeant. *Saskatoon: The Growth of a City.* 1975.
Kerr, D., and S. Hanson. *Saskatoon: The First Half Century.* 1982.
McConnell, G. *Saskatoon: Hub City of the West.* 1983.

Toronto

Ontario

Location and Topography

Toronto is located on the northwestern shore of Lake Ontario, on the neck of the Ontario Peninsula. Central Toronto is built on flatlands bordering the harbor and the lakeshore on each side of the harbor. About 2 miles to the north the land rises from about 50 to 75 feet to a second plain, which continues northward for about 30 miles. Two rivers, the Don to the east and the Humber to the west, occupy northwest-southeast valleys created during the last ice age.

Layout of City and Suburbs

Metropolitan Toronto, Canada's largest municipality, comprises the cities of Toronto, North York, Scarborough, York, Etobicoke, and the borough of East York. The shore plain by the harbor is the downtown area. The main business and shopping area is concentrated within a mile of the lakefront. Residential areas surround the city core in a great crescent extending about 20 miles east and 40 miles west from Yonge Street, the city's original main street, which divides the city in half. Paralleling Yonge Street to the west is University Avenue, a wide boulevard lined with major commercial buildings and leading to Queen's Park, where the provincial parliament and the campus of the University of Toronto are located. In the older, southerly part of Toronto the main east-west arteries are King and Queen streets, which traverse the central commercial area. On Queen Street, between Yonge and University, is the 12-acre Nathan Phillips Square with its impressive City Hall, which opened in 1965. This unusual structure consists of two curved office towers and between them the oyster-shaped city chambers. Along nearby Bay Street is the financial district and Osgoode Hall, built in 1829 to house the provincial law courts. The Eaton Centre, a huge downtown complex on Yonge Street, includes Eaton's, the city's largest department store. It also has some 300 other stores, a 36-story office building, and a 26-story office building. Downtown Toronto has three of the world's tallest buildings: the 72-story Bank of Montreal Tower, the 68-story Scotia Plaza Building, and the 57-story Commerce Court West. Nearby is the 1,815-foot CN Tower, the world's tallest freestanding structure. It includes a large antenna and an observation deck. Next to the CN Tower is the 8-acre Sky-dome, a sports arena with a rectractable roof. Ontario Place, a recreation center in the harbor, has an exhibition area, a marina, and a theater.

Climate

Toronto has a continental temperate climate with a mean January temperature of 24°F and July temperature of 71°F.

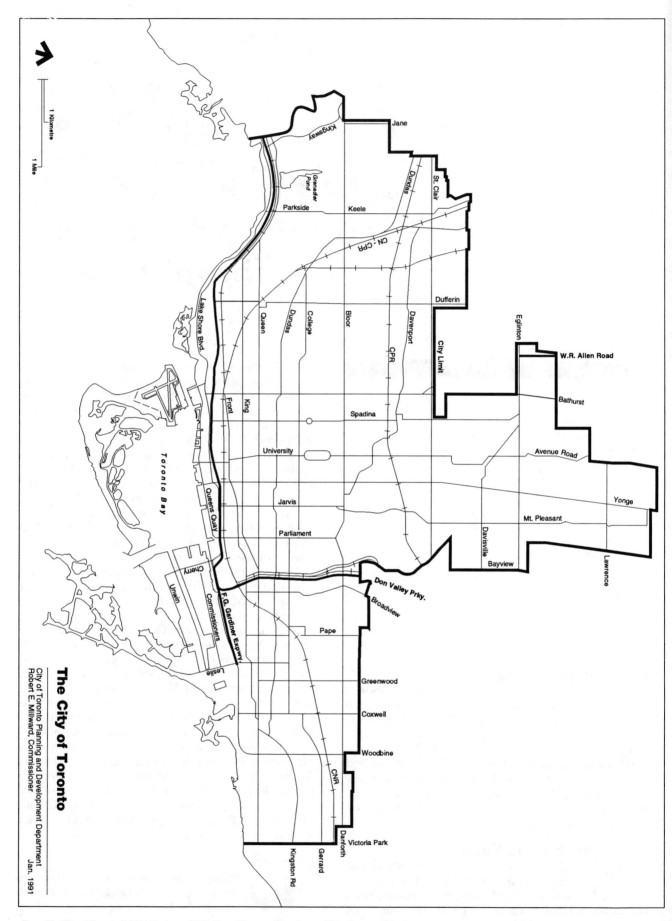

From *The City of Toronto* © 1991. Toronto, ONT: City of Toronto Planning and Development Dept.

The average annual precipitation of 32 inches is distributed fairly evenly throughout the year. Because the city is located in the lee of the prevailing northwest winds blowing from the Great Lakes, its average annual snowfall of 55.5 inches is considerably less than that of surrounding regions.

Weather
Annual Averages
January °F   24
July °F   71
Annual Precipitation (inches)   32
Annual Sunshine (hours)   2,045

History

Iroquois Indians were the earliest historically known inhabitants of the Toronto area, which marked the southern end of the trail that ran between Lake Huron and Lake Ontario. The place was named "Toronto," or "the Place of Meeting," by the Indians. The Toronto Passage, used as early as 1615 by Étienne Brûle, became well known to French traders. During the early 1700s, the French built a trading store here and later a fort called Fort Toronto or Fort Rouillé, but they burned it down in 1759 to prevent the British from seizing it.

Canada was ceded to the British by the Treaty of Paris in 1763. In 1787 the Canadian government bought the peninsula from the Mississauga Indians. No permanent settlement was made until 1793, when Governor John Graves Simcoe chose it to replace Newark as the capital of the colony of Upper Canada. The new settlement was named York after the Duke of York. In 1813, with a population of only 700, it suffered its first disaster when it was raided and pillaged by U.S. forces, an act that prompted the British to retaliate by burning Washington, D.C.

In 1834 the fast-growing town of 9,000 was incorporated as the city of Toronto, with an elected civic government. Its first mayor, William Lyon Mackenzie, a prominent printer and journalist, tried to seize the city by force during the Upper Canada Rebellion of 1837, and upon collapse of the revolt was forced to flee to the United States. The city expanded rapidly through the 1840s, and by 1850 the railroads linked the city to New York, Montreal, Detroit, and Chicago. The city was made capital of the new province of Ontario in 1867. Industrialization was aided by federal tariff policies and by industrialists, such as Hart Massey; railroad builders like Casimir Gzowski; and department store tycoons, notably Timothy Eaton. The settlement of the Canadian West and the tapping of the northern Ontario forests opened further markets and fueled Toronto's growth as a banking and transportation center. World War I helped to establish strong munitions and meat-processing industries under the auspices of Sir Joseph Flavelle. From 1911, hydroelectric power from the nearby Niagara Falls provided cheap electricity for the industrial sector. The Great Depression did not hit Toronto as hard as other Canadian cities and in any case the city's fortunes took off once more after World War II. However, a flood of new immigrants after the war pointed up numerous problems, including housing and water shortages and a poor transportation system. These problems led to the creation of the Municipality of Metropolitan Toronto in 1953. A federation of Toronto and 12 of its suburbs came into being on 1 January 1954. In 1967 these 13 units were merged into 6: Toronto and 5 boroughs.

Historical Landmarks

Toronto has a number of old historic landmarks, although modern buildings dominate the central city. Historic sites include the original Fort York Complex (rebuilt in 1813–1815); the Grange, a mansion built about 1817; the Osgoode Hall, rebuilt in 1857; St. Lawrence Hall of 1850; the Parliament Buildings, constructed in 1892; the City Hall, completed in 1899; the Royal Alexandra Theater of 1907; and the Union Station of 1927. The Queen's Wharf Lighthouse at the corner of Fleet Street and Lake Shore Boulevard played an important role in Toronto's maritime heritage. Spadina is a historic home built by financier James Austin in 1866. Home to four generations of the Austin family, Spadina offers visitors a glimpse into the elegant world of Toronto high society at the turn of the century. The Mackenzie House, which belonged to the rebel mayor, William Lyon Mackenzie, is an 1857 Victorian townhouse. It includes a reconstructed 19th-century print shop. The Colborne Lodge, the home of John George Howard and his wife Jemima, is one of the oldest surviving Regency villas in North America.

Population

The population of Toronto in 1990 was 635,395, almost 100,000 below its historical high of 699,130 in 1942. As in most large cities, the suburbs have siphoned off much of the central city population in recent years, and with natural increase at an all-time low, the city is sustained largely by strong immigration. Nevertheless, the city's overall population gain has been only about 100,000 since 1919, when its population was 499,278. Since then the demographic totals at the five-year censuses were as follows:

1921 - 522,666	1956 - 643,791
1926 - 556,691	1961 - 647,749
1931 - 627,231	1966 - 659,689
1936 - 645,462	1971 - 688,803
1941 - 655,751	1976 - 678,103
1946 - 696,555	1981 - 599,217
1951 - 653,499	1986 - 612,290

By age groups, the largest are the 20–39 group with 42%, the 40–64 group with 26%, the 0–19 group with 12%, and the over-65 group with 12%. The largest growth is occurring in the 20–44 group while the size of the school age population is declining.

Chronology

1615	Étienne Brûlé visits the Toronto Passage.
1720	French fur traders build a small store on the site.
1750	The store is enlarged into a fort, known as Fort Rouille.
1759	Fort Rouille is burned to the ground by the French to prevent its capture by the British in the Seven Years' War.
1763	By the Treaty of Paris all Canada passes into British hands.
1787	The Canadian government buys the land on the Toronto peninsula from the Mississauga.
1793	Governor John Graves Simcoe selects the site as capital of Upper Canada and names it York.
1812	York is captured by the United States and burnt.
1834	York is incorporated as a city and renamed Toronto.
1837	William Mackenzie King, Toronto's first elected mayor, tries to seize the city and, on the collapse of his revolt, flees to the United States.
1867	Toronto is made capital of Ontario.
1911	Hydroelectric power from Niagara Falls reaches Toronto.
1949	Toronto subway system opens.
1953	Toronto and 12 of its suburbs merge into the Municipality of Metropolitan Toronto.
1967	Constituent units of the Municipality of Metropolitan Toronto are reduced to six.

Population

City Population	1986	1990
	612,290	635,395
% Male 48.53		

Age

% Under 14   14.56
% Over 65   11.97

Vital Statistics

Births (1989)   10,154
Deaths (1989)   5,477
Natural Increase (1986–1991)   4,677
Marriages (1989)   8,808
Married (1989)   263,730
Single (1989)   197,230
Widowed/Divorced (1989)   62,190

Households and Families

Households Total   139,025
Average # Persons per Household   3.0

Population (continued)

Average # Children per Household   1.1

Mother Tongue

English   61.9
French   1.6
Chinese   5.5
Portuguese   7.0
Italian   4.1

Ethnic Composition

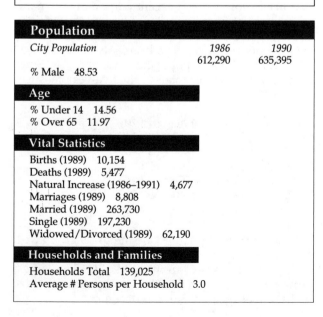

About 40% of Torontoans can trace English ancestors, and there are many people of Scots and Irish descent, as well. Toronto was a favorite destination of European immigrants after World War I and this is reflected in large numbers of Italians, Portuguese, French, Germans, and Jews. More recently Chinese, East Indians, and West Indians have helped to diversify the racial mix. Of the 2,364,987 immigrants to Canada from 1971 to 1988, 1,188,722 settled in Ontario and of these 703,618 settled in metropolitan Toronto. The city thus receives nearly 30% of all immigrants to Canada. In the 1980s, 37% of the emigrants were from Asia, 22% from Europe, 16% from the Caribbean and Guyana, 6% from the United Kingdom, 5% from the Middle East, 5% from Africa, 5% from Latin America, and 4% from the United States. The result of sustained immigration for nearly a century is that neither the Anglo-Saxons nor any other ethnic group forms a majority in the city as a whole, although many neighborhoods have their own ethnic majority. There are, for example, Italian neighborhoods in a belt extending from the city proper west of Bathurst Street northward into the boroughs of York and North York; German Canadians east of High Park in Toronto and in the outer boroughs; and many Jewish people in the Forest Hill section and in North York. There are Ukrainian and Polish neighborhoods in the central city and in Etobicoke.

Government

Metropolitan Toronto has a two-level system of government. The top level consists of the Metropolitan Council of the Municipality of Metropolitan Toronto, and the lower level comprises the separate city and borough councils. The former provides most of the area's major government services, including ambulance, highway, police, public transportation, urban development, and welfare. The separate Toronto City Council handles other services, including fire protection, garbage collection, and public health. The Metropolitan Council consists of 34 elected members, plus six mayors—one from each city and borough. The Toronto City Council has a mayor and 22 council members, all elected to three-year terms. The mayor heads the Executive Committee, which includes 4 other members of the City Council. The mayors of Toronto have often been powerful political figures and have included such notables as William Lyon Mackenzie, William Howland, Tommy Church, Nathan Phillips, and David Crombie.

Today, however, the chairman of the Metropolitan Council wields more power than the mayor of the city of Toronto.

Public Finance

The 1991 municipal budget includes revenues of $Can 2,904,718,300, of which 35.1% was derived from the tax levy on municipalities, 41.3% from provincial grants, 23.1% from operating and sundry revenues, and 0.5% from surplus from prior years. The budget was balanced with 44.7% of the expenditures going to social and family services, 19.3% to law and order, 13.7% to transportation services, 8.3% to environmental services, 3.9% to recreation and cultural services, 2.4% to ambulance services, 3% to general government, and 4.7% to other services.

Economy

Metro Toronto is Canada's principal industrial center, although it is increasingly buffeted by foreign competition. More than 8,400 industrial plants produce $Can 50 billion in value of manufactured goods. A total of 196 firms, or 39% of the top 500 industrials listed by the Financial Post, have their head offices in the Toronto region. By value of shipments, transport equipment leads with 19.9%, followed by food at 10.4%, electronic products at 10.2%, metal fabrication at 8.5%, and chemicals at 8.2%. Overall, there are some 81,837 businesses in the city, of which 1,208 have over 100 employees. Toronto is also Canada's principal financial and banking center, outranking Montreal in this respect. It is the headquarters for 5 of Canada's 10 chartered banks. Of the 55 foreign banks in Canada, 46 have head offices in Toronto. Ten of the top 20 insurance companies are located in Toronto, as are 7 of the top 10 investment dealers. The Toronto Stock Exchange ranks as the fourth largest in North America in volume of shares traded. The earlier bases of its economy, as transportation, remain strong. Like New York, Toronto is strong in media and communications and is the headquarters for such national media leaders as Southam and Thomson and the Maclean Hunter group. With 4.2% of the population of Canada, Toronto receives 13% of the national disposable income, and as a result has the highest average standard of living of any metro area in the country. The average household income is $Can 73,803 and the average per capita income $Can 26,017. At the same time, Toronto is an expensive city in which to live. The average annual cost of living for a typical family is $Can 53,282. Toronto is Canada's largest metropolitan retail market with $Can 26 billion in total retail sales. It is also Canada's wealthiest retail market with a total personal income exceeding $Can 87 billion. With approximately 4,500 stores and 10 million square feet of retail space, Toronto's downtown is second only to New York and Chicago. The largest shopping centers are Eaton Centre, Yorkdale Shopping Centre, Scarborough Town Centre, and Dufferin Mall. Toronto is

headquarters to at least half of Canada's top service companies, 90% of top advertising agencies, 50% of accounting firms, and 60% of law firms. More than 60% of the top 50 foreign-owned companies in Canada operate out of Toronto.

Labor

Toronto is Canada's largest employment market with a metro work force estimated at 1.93 million, 37% of the provincial labor force and 14% of the national labor force. The employment rate was 77.9% for males and 60.7% for females. The unemployment rate of 5.3% in 1990 was significantly lower than the national average of 8.1%. Employment projections indicate employment growth to 3 million by the year 2011, mostly in the outer regions and in the office sector. The work force is heavily concentrated in the office, manufacturing, and retail sectors. Manufacturing engages 17.3%, services 11.1%, retail trade 11.5%, office 45.5%, and institutional 12.1%. Government employs some 100,000 persons or 5% of the total work force. The government of Ontario alone employs 33,000 persons. Labor is widely unionized in Toronto, particularly in the public sector, large private enterprises, and skilled trades. From the York Printers Union of 1832, organized labor has exerted a powerful political and economic influence on the city. Toronto's largest corporate employers are, in descending order by size: General Motors of Canada, Bell Canada, Canadian Imperial Bank of Commerce, Bank of Nova Scotia, Toronto Dominion Bank, Royal Bank of Canada, Sears Canada, Magna International, IBM Canada, and Bank of Montreal.

Labor		
Work Force	*Male*	*Female*
Total Work Force	195,575	171,555
Employed	182,410	160,475
Employment Rate	78.60	64.10
% of 15–24 Year Olds	72.60	72.20
Occupation	*Male*	*Female*
Managerial	29,020	21,860
Education	6,320	9,440
Health	4,650	12,145
Technical and Cultural	30,985	19,725
Clerical	17,625	48,605
Sales	17,725	15,080
Service	26,120	22,085
Manufacturing	22,000	13,435
Construction	14,690	490
Transportation	6,990	505
Other	16,990	6,105

Income	
Male ($Can)	34,699
Female ($Can)	22,924
Average Household Income ($Can)	39,118
Average Family Income ($Can)	46,623
Average Tax ($Can)	8,880
Average Household Expenditure ($Can)	52,948
Number of Banks	67

Labor (continued)

Manufacturing

Plants 1,716
Employees 65,815
Value of Shipments ($Can) 7,055,724,000
Total Value Added ($Can) 3,393,174,000

Education

The public school system of the Municipality of Metropolitan Toronto supports 550 elementary and high schools with about 280,000 students. Another 94,000 students attend Roman Catholic parochial and private schools. The largest institution of higher learning is the University of Toronto, founded in 1827. It has a current enrollment of over 50,000. Other schools include Ryerson Polytechnical Institute, National Ballet School, Ontario College of Art, and the Royal Conservatory of Music. York University is located in nearby North York.

Education

Population (over 15 years old) 516,530
Less than Grade 9 92,305
Grades 9–13 157,865
Trade Certificate 95,155
University degree 110,145

Four-Year Universities and Colleges
University of Toronto
Erindale College
Innis College
New College
Scarborough College
University College
Woodsworth College
University of St. Michael's College
University of Trinity College
Victoria University
Emmanuel College
Knox College
Regis College
Wycliffe College
Massey College
Ryerson Polytechnical Institute

Health

Toronto has over 50 hospitals with 18,012 beds and 7,900 physicians. The health industry employs about 130,000 persons. Among the larger hospitals in the metro area are: Centenary Hospital, Central Hospital, Clarke Institute of Psychiatry, The Doctors' Hospital, the Donwood Institute, Etobicoke General Hospital, Hillcrest Hospital, Hospital for Sick Children, Hugh MacMillan Medical Centre, Institute of Traumatic Plastic and Restorative Surgery, Lyndhurst Hospital, Mount Sinai Hospital, Northwestern General Hospital, North York General Hospital, North York Branson Hospital, Ontario Cancer Treatment and Research Foundation, Orthopaedic and Arthritic Hospital, Princess Margaret Hospital, Providence Hospital, Queen Elizabeth Hospital, Queen Street Mental Health Centre, Queensway

General Hospital, Riverdale Hospital, Runnymede Hospital, St. Joseph's Health Centre, St. Michael's Hospital, Salvation Army Scarborough Grace General Hospital, Scarborough General Hospital, Sunnybrook Health Sciences Centre, Toronto East General and Orthopaedic Hospital, Toronto Eye Bank, Toronto General Hospital, Toronto General Division, Toronto Western Division, Toronto Rehabilitation Centre, Wellesley Hospital, West Park Hospital, and Women's College Hospital.

Transportation

Until the late–20th-century, most Toronto streets were laid out in a rectangular grid that required extensive bridging. In recent years a network of expressways has been designed to follow natural contours of the terrain. The Don Valley Parkway, for example, follows the Don River north from the lakefront. This parkway connects with the Macdonald-Cartier Freeway (Highway 401), the major east-west road through southern Ontario, which crosses north-central Toronto as a 12-lane, limited-access artery. A second major east-west route is the Gardiner Expressway, which skirts the lakefront from the Don Valley Parkway to the Humber River and connects with the Macdonald-Cartier Freeway to the north. In 1989 the Ontario Ministry of Transportation unveiled a $Can 1.24-billion transportation capital program for the Toronto region. It includes plans for new highways, such as Highways 407, 410, and 403.

The 34-mile Toronto Subway, which opened in 1954, was Canada's first underground rapid transit railway. It consists of the east-west Bloor-Danforth line, which crosses the south-central and the Yonge Street line, which in turn follows University Avenue south from the Bloor-Danforth line and then loops northward under Yonge Street, extending into the city of North York. Several new rapid transit lines opened in the 1960s and 1970s. A line serving Scarborough opened in 1985 and several others are planned for construction during the next 20 years.

Toronto is one of the major North American Great Lakes ports, handling about 2 million tons of cargo annually. Via Rail Canada offers intercity, regional, and transcontinental rail passenger service out of Union Station. Rail freight services are provided by Canadian National and CP Rail. A provincially owned commuter system links Toronto with Pickering, Hamilton, Oshawa, Newmarket, Barrie, and Milton, making use of the facilities of the Canadian National. The principal air terminal is the Lester B. Pearson International Airport, about 15 miles northwest of downtown. The Toronto Island Airport in Lake Ontario has a

Transportation

New Automobiles

Cars, Domestic 11,024
Imported 9,021
Trucks 6,646

seaplane base. Buttonville Airport, near the northeast perimeter of the city, is Canada's fourth busiest, and serves private and executive aircraft.

Housing

Until after World War II most Torontoans owned or rented houses. However, multiple-unit buildings now constitute more than half the total number of dwellings, as soaring land prices have driven detached homes out of the reach of all but the rich. Toronto has one of the most expensive housing markets in Canada, and the fourth highest in North America. In 1991 home prices averaged $Can 254,400, compared to a national average of $Can 148,700. In 1990 housing construction exceeded $Can 2.7 billion or 23% of Canada's $Can 12-billion residential construction activity. Within the metro area, 70% of residential development activity took place outside the city of Toronto. Because of high home prices, the apartment rental market is extremely tight with a vacancy rate of only 1.8%. Rental rates in Toronto are significantly higher than in other major Canadian cities, except Vancouver. The average monthly rent for a one-bedroom apartment in 1990 was $Can 557. Rent controls were first legislated in 1975, and rents can be increased only once a year by a maximum of 5.1%.

Housing

Total Housing Stock 253,150		
Owned 100,080		
Rented 153,075		
Single, Detached 46,325		
Apartments 87,910		
Homes Built 1990 2,866		
Building Permits Value ($Can) 1,290,636,000		

Tallest Buildings	Hgt. (ft.)	Stories
CN Tower, World's tallest self-		
supporting structure (1976)	1,821	NA
First Canadian Place (1979)	970	72
Bay/Adelaide Project (1991)	951	57
Scotia Plaza (1988)	902	68
Canada Trust Tower (1990)	869	52
Bay-Wellington Tower (1990)	705	47
Commerce Court West (1972)	784	57
Toronto-Dominion Tower		
(TD Centre) (1967)	758	56

Urban Redevelopment

Despite the recession, Toronto's vertical growth has continued unchecked throughout the 1980s and early 1990s. Some new high-rise building projects, either completed after 1985 or slated in the first half of the 1990s are (with costs in $Can million): B.C.E. office and stores (124.5), Marriott Hotel (49.5), St. Michael's Hospital (55.6), Scotia Plaza (127.3), Temperance Street (225.9), CBC office and stores (158.6), Convention Centre (85), Dome Stadium (280.7), and Metro Hall (79.5).

Crime

Canada, in general, has a much lower crime rate than the United States: a murder rate of 2.2 per 100,000 versus 8.3 in the United States. Toronto, known as Toronto the Good, has a much lower rate of both violent and property crimes than U.S. cities of comparable size: per 100,000 a rate of 2 for murder, 208 for robberies, and 1,080 for breaking and entering. The total number of criminal code offenses was 292,180 (compared to 234,693 in 1987) with a clearance rate of 43.3% (compared to 48.4% in 1987). All kinds of reported crimes increased in 1991. The strength of the uniformed police force was 5,666, which is close to the authorized strength of 5,695. Actual expenditures on law enforcement grew substantially to $Can 547 million (compared to $Can 379.6 million in 1987). Per capita cost was $Can 254.43.

Religion

Toronto has over 1,000 churches, synagogues, and other places of worship, representing 80 religions. Roman Catholicism is the dominant religion with over 1.1 million members, followed by United Church (427,195), Anglican (404,885), Presbyterian (165,535), Jewish (123,725), Eastern Orthodox (118,890), and Baptist (88,720).

Media

Toronto has more daily newspapers than most cities in North America of comparable size. The press includes the national newspaper, the *Globe and Mail;* two local newspapers, the *Toronto Star* and the *Toronto Sun;* and a business newspaper, *The Financial Post.* More than half of Canada's 800 business publications originate in Toronto. Toronto is the head office of the Thomson Corporation, the sixth-largest publishing firm in the world, as well as the largest business magazine publishers in Canada, Maclean Hunter, and Southam Business Communications. The electronic media consist of 7 television stations and 16 AM and FM radio stations.

Media

Newsprint	
The Financial Post, daily	
Globe and Mail, daily	
Toronto Star, daily	
Toronto Sun, daily	
Television	
CBLFT (Channel 25)	
CBLT (Channel 5)	
CFMT (Channel 47)	
CFTO (Channel 9)	
CICO (Channel 19)	
CIII (Channel 41)	
CITY (Channel 57)	
Radio	
CBL (AM)	CBL (FM)
CKFM (FM)	CFRB (AM)
CFTR (AM)	CHFI (FM)

Media (continued)

CHIN (FM)	CHUM (AM)
CHUM (FM)	CILQ (FM)
CIRV (FM)	CJBC (AM)
CJCL (AM)	CJEZ (FM)
CJRT (FM)	CKYC (AM)

Sports

Toronto has three professional sports teams. The Toronto Maple Leafs of the National Hockey League play their home games in the Maple Leaf Gardens. The Canadian Argonauts of the Canadian Football League play in the Skydome. The Toronto Blue Jays of the American League play baseball in the Skydome. The Hockey Hall of Fame is in Exhibition Park. Toronto is home to two racetracks. Downtown's Greenwood Race Track offers both thoroughbred and harness racing. Woodbine Racetrack, northwest of the city near the airport, holds the Queen's Plate and Rothman International.

Arts, Culture, and Tourism

Toronto has a number of major performing arts centers, including the Roy Thomson Hall, O'Keefe Centre for the Performing Arts, St. Lawrence Center for the Arts, St. Lawrence Hall, Royal Conservatory of Music, and the Canadian Music Centre. The Toronto Symphony Orchestra and Mendelssohn Choir perform in the Roy Thomson Hall. The O'Keefe Centre for the Performing Arts presents programs by the Canadian Opera Company and the National Ballet of Canada. Toronto is the third-largest English-language theater center in the world after New York and London. Toronto is also home to several acclaimed dance companies, including the Toronto Dance Theater and the Desrosiers Dance Theater.

Toronto's largest museum is the renowned Royal Ontario Museum with its McLaughlin Planetarium. The George R. Gardiner Museum of Ceramic Art is the only specialized museum of its kind in North America. The McMichael Canadian Collection is devoted exclusively to Canadian art. Other art galleries include the Art Gallery of Canada and the Canadian Gallery. The Marine Museum of Upper Canada shows the development of shipping on the Great Lakes and the St.

Lawrence River. Other attractions include the Ontario Science Centre and Casa Loma, a 98-room castle built in the early 1900s by Sir Henry Pellatt, a Toronto stockbroker.

Parks and Recreation

Toronto's park system includes over 100 parks covering 6,000 acres. The largest, the 612-acre Toronto Islands Park, is in Lake Ontario. Further west is the hilly High Park, privately donated to the city in 1890.

Sources of Further Information

City Hall
Toronto, Ontario M5H 2N2
(416) 392-6990

Metro Toronto Board of Trade
1 First Canadian Place
Toronto, Ontario M5X 1C1
(416) 366-6811

Metropolitan Toronto Convention and Visitors Association
Eaton Centre
220 Yonge Street
Toronto, Ontario M5B 2H1
(416) 979-3133

Additional Reading

Armstrong, Frederick H. Toronto: The Place of Meeting. 1983.
Arthur, Eric R. *Toronto: No Mean City.* 1986.
Atkinson, Tom. *Housing and Mobility in Metropolitan Toronto and Its Boroughs.* 1982.
Firth, Edith G. *The Town of York, 1793–1834.* 2 vols. 1970.
Goheen, Reter G. *Victorian Toronto, 1850 to 1900: Pattern and Process of Growth.* 1970.
Russell, Victor L., ed. *Forging a Consensus: Historical Essays on Toronto.* 1984.
Sharma, Raghubar D. *Trends in Demographic and Socio-Economic Characteristics of the Metropolitan Toronto Population.* 1982.

Vancouver

British Columbia

by a shallow inlet called False Creek. Stanley Park is on the shorter, northern ridge.

Basic Data

Name   Vancouver
Year Founded   1885 Inc. 1886
Status: Province   British Columbia
Area (square miles)   44
Elevation   258 ft.
Time Zone   Pacific
Population (1990)   471,844

Distance in Miles to:

Anchorage	2,237
Calgary	657
Chicago	2,176
Edmonton	773
Montreal	2,983
New York	2,943
Ottawa	2,865
Quebec	3,151
San Francisco	954
Toronto	2,791

Location and Topography

N

Vancouver lies on a peninsula on the southwest corner of the mainland of British Columbia. It is surrounded by the Burrard Inlet and the Fraser River, and connected to the Pacific Ocean by the Strait of Georgia, the English Bay, and the Juan de Fuca Strait. The city is built on low rolling land.

Layout of City and Suburbs

Vancouver has one of the most beautiful physical settings of any city in the world. To the north across the harbor, two forested snowcapped peaks, known as the Lions, rise majestically 3,000 to 4,000 feet above sea level. The flat green delta lands of the Fraser River Basin spread south of the Fraser River. The city lies between two ridges separated by a shallow inlet called False Creek. Stanley Park is on the shorter, northern ridge. To the south and east of this ridge is West End and downtown. The broader, southern ridge, ending in Point Grey and jutting into the Strait of Georgia, includes the East End, the main residential area. The heart of downtown is the intersection of Georgia and Granville streets. It is dominated by the 30-story Toronto Dominion Bank Tower in the Pacific Center. The city's tallest building, the 38-story Royal Bank Tower, stands in Royal Centre between Georgia and Burrard streets. Several streets in downtown reflect Vancouver's ethnic heritage, particularly Robsonstrasse, or Robson Street, where German and other European traditions still survive; and Chinatown, the second-largest Chinese community in North America, on Pender Street. Gastown, the original center of Vancouver, named after "Gassy" Jack Deighton, is just north of Chinatown. The largest suburb is Surrey. Other suburbs include Burnaby, Coquitlam, Richmond, Delta, North Vancouver, and West Vancouver.

Climate

The protective Coast Mountains and the warm winds blowing from the Pacific guarantee Vancouver a mild climate, despite its northern latitude. The temperatures average 37° F in January and 62° F in July. Vancouver is famous for its heavy rainfall of about 47 inches, falling mainly between November and March. The hours of sunshine per year number 1,872.

Weather

Annual Averages

January °F   37
July °F   62
Annual Precipitation (inches)   47
Annual Sunshine (hours)   1,872

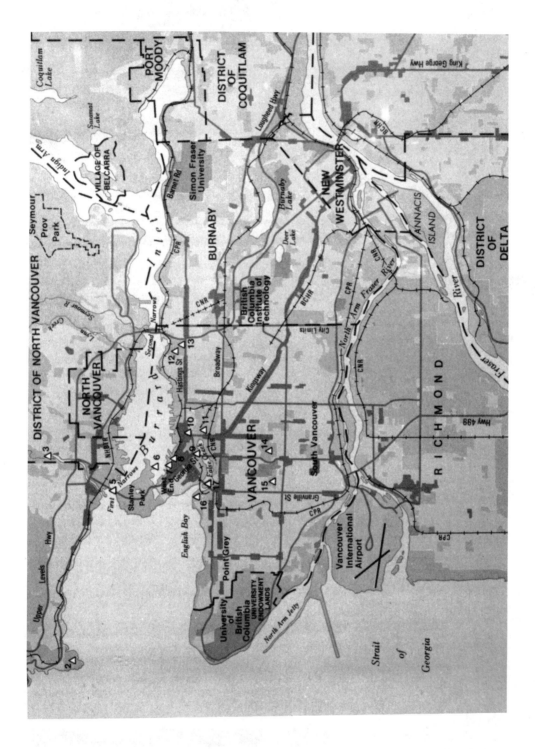

History

The Vancouver region was inhabited by coastal Salish Indians since circa 500 B.C. The Spanish sailor Don Jose Marie Narvaez in 1791, and the English sailor Captain George Vancouver in 1792, were the first Europeans to visit the bay. No further attention was paid to the area until Hudson's Bay Company founded a fur trading post on the Fraser River at Fort Langley in 1827. In 1849 the company relinquished its exclusive control over Vancouver Island and agreed to colonize it on behalf of the crown for a rental fee of seven shillings a year. Between 1855 and 1858 gold rather than furs attracted Europeans to the area. Thousands flocked to the Cariboo and cleared the wilderness in their search for gold. In 1858 the crown assumed direct control of the area and the Colonial Office sent a corps of Royal Engineers. Under the command of Richard Clement Moody, these men established the city of Queensborough (later New Westminster) in 1859. Disillusioned goldseekers were the first settlers on Burrard Inlet where, in the early 1860s, three Englishmen built an unsuccessful brickyard. They were followed in 1865 by lumbermen who built Hastings Mill on the site, and in 1867 by an English sailor, John Deighton, who built a saloon nearby to serve the loggers. Deighton was nicknamed "Gassy Jack" because he was talkative and the community was named Gastown after him. The city, however, did not appear on the map until 1884 when William Van Horne, manager of the Canadian Pacific Railroad, announced that CPR would extend its line 16 miles westward from its statutory terminus, Port Moody, in order to take advantage of the harbor facilities offered by the Burrard Inlet. Van Horne named the place Vancouver, after Captain George Vancouver, and the city was incorporated in 1885 with M. A. MacLean as the first elected mayor. In the same year a fire blew out of control and wrecked most of the ramshackle buildings, but the city was rebuilt soon after. The first CPR train reached Vancouver in 1887. Its history as a port began in 1891 when the CPR-owned Canadian Pacific Steamship Company inaugurated regular sailings between Vancouver and the Orient. By the turn of the century, Vancouver displaced Victoria, the provincial capital, as the leading commercial center on the west coast. In 1904 the Great Northern Railway linked Vancouver with Seattle. The opening of the Panama Canal in 1914 was a tremendous boost to Vancouver's seaborne commerce as the canal provided a cheaper shipping route from western Canada to the east. In the 1920s Vancouver displaced Winnipeg as the leading Canadian city in the west. In 1929, neighboring communities of Point Grey and South Vancouver were annexed to the city. By this time Vancouver was one of the fastest-growing cities in Canada. Its population had grown from 2,000 at the time of incorporation to 8,000 in 1889, 42,000 in 1901, 86,000 in 1911, 163,220 in 1921, and 250,000 in 1931. The Great Depression hit the city hard, and unrest among the unemployed caused several incidents, but it recov-

ered and resumed its growth trajectory quickly after World War II. In 1970 a new cargo-loading terminal was built to handle the heavy volume of shipping. By 1963 Vancouver ranked first in tonnage among Canadian ports. The three decades from 1960 to 1990 included much heavy construction. In 1986 an international exposition of communication and transportation technology was held in Vancouver, attracting more than 22 million visitors. The impending transfer of Hong Kong to China in 1996 brought a heavy influx of rich Chinese entrepreneurs into the city, providing a new stimulus for economic growth.

Historical Landmarks

There are 2,846 historical buildings in Vancouver that are a part of the city's heritage program. Of these, 227 are in the top A category, and 1,099 in the B category, with the remainder in the C category. Among the most notable of these buildings are the Lions Gate Bridge, CP Roundhouse, and CP Station.

Population

The population of Vancouver in 1990 was 471,844, up from 431,145 in 1986, 414,281 in 1981, and 410,188 in 1976. Vancouver's population over the past century has grown in spurts, responding to cycles of prosperity. The largest increase took place in the 1920s when it annexed Point Grey and South Vancouver. Thereafter immigration, both internal and external, supplied most of the increase, except in the early 1970s when there was a slight decline.

Population		
City Population	*1986*	*1990*
	431,145	471,844
% Male 48.76		
Age		
% Under 14 13.97		
% Over 65 15.01		
Vital Statistics		
Births (1989) 5,997		
Deaths (1989) 4,253		
Natural Increase (1986–1991) 1,744		
Marriages (1989) 4,513		
Married (1989) 189,760		
Single (1989) 129,225		
Widowed/Divorced (1989) 51,945		
Households and Families		
Households Total 100,620		
Average # Persons per Household 2.9		
Average # Children per Household 1.1		
Mother Tongue		
English 62.3		
French 1.5		
Chinese 13.0		
German 2.5		

Chronology

1791	Don Jose Marie Narvaez becomes the first European to visit the area.
1792	Captain George Vancouver sails into the Burrard Inlet.
1827	Hudson's Bay Company establishes trading post at Fort Langley on the Fraser River.
1849	Hudson's Bay Company relinquishes control over the region and agrees to colonize it on behalf of the crown.
1858	Crown assumes direct control of British Columbia and sends a corps of Royal Engineers who establish the town of Queensborough (later New Westminster).
1860	Disillusioned goldseekers settle near Burrard Inlet, where three Englishmen build an unsuccessful brickyard.
1865	Lumbermen arrive, erecting the Hastings lumber mill.
1867	John Deighton, nicknamed "Gassy Jack," builds a saloon to serve the loggers. The saloon becomes the nucleus of Gastown.
1884	Canadian Pacific Railroad selects the settlement as its western terminus. William Van Horne, CPR general manager, christens the terminus Vancouver, after Captain George Vancouver.
1886	Vancouver is incorporated with M. A. MacLean as the first elected mayor. Fire destroys most of the town but is quickly rebuilt.
1887	First Canadian Pacific Railroad train reaches Vancouver from the east.
1891	The Canadian Pacific Steamship Company inaugurates regular sailings between Vancouver and the Orient.
1904	Great Northern Railway links Vancouver with Seattle.
1914	Opening of the Panama Canal makes shipping goods by sea to the east cheaper than rail.
1986	Vancouver holds Expo '86, an international exposition of communication and transportation technology.

Ethnic Composition

For the first 50 years of this century, Anglo Saxons formed the dominant majority of the population. The first major wave of non-European immigration began after World War II. By 1979 the School Board reported that nearly 40% of the pupils in elementary schools did not speak English as their first language. Among ethnic minorities the most prominent are Chinese, Italian, and East Indian. Historically, there has been active prejudice against Asians, evidenced by such incidents as the anti-Chinese and anti-Asian riots of 1887 and 1907, the Komagata Maru incident of 1914, and the evacuation of Japanese residents in 1942. Of the people belonging to a single ethnic group in the metro area, 95,945 are British, 8,375 French, 14,745 German, 70,505 Chinese, 15,870 South Asian, 3,970 Dutch, and others 92,145. In addition, persons of multiple origins number 123,115. Vancouver is the third most popular city for immigrants and absorbs 11% of Canada's migrants.

Government

Vancouver has a mayor-council form of government. The mayor and ten members of the council are elected to two-year terms. Vancouver is unique among British Columbia municipalities in having its own charter, but it remains within provincial control under the Municipalities Act. The Non-Partisan Association, a loose association of liberals and conservatives, has been in power for many decades. The Greater Vancouver Regional District was created in 1967 and has taken over a number of municipal functions, such as sewerage, capital finance, building regulations, housing, and air pollution control.

Public Finance

Property taxes and grants from the provincial government provide most of the city's revenues. The 1992 municipal budget was $Can 486.4 million, of which 63% came from property taxes; 15% from fees, fines, and penalties; 13% from other sources; 5% from revenue sharing; and 4% from reserves. Of the expenditures, 33% went to law enforcement, 22% to community services, 20% to engineering, 14% to debt servicing, 7% to general government, and 4% to capital works.

Economy

Vancouver prides itself as the Pacific Rim Gateway. Its position as the undoubted leader of the Canadian West has not been challenged in this century, and has, in fact, grown considerably since World War II. The city is the headquarters of 123 corporations (including major firms such as Macmillan Bloedel, Cominco, and BC Forest Products) with total revenues of close to $Can 55 billion. Its financial sector is vigorous. Every major Canadian bank is represented, in addition to 35 foreign banks and other institutions. Together they have assets of nearly $Can 500 billion. Trading on the Vancouver Stock Exchange totals $Can 500 million annually. Another strong sector is tourism with total revenues of nearly $Can 4 billion. Consumer buying power, estimated at $Can 25 billion, sustains a broadly based retailing sector. Vancouver also benefits from the abundance of energy resources in British Columbia, which is self-sufficient in all forms of energy, except oil, and which exports electricity, natural gas, and coal. Businesses face lower electricity costs than Toronto or Montreal. Oil from Alberta is refined in and around Vancouver. While manufacturing does not play as large a role in the economy as it does in other major cities, both basic production and advanced technology manufacturing are important. The city has over 700 manufacturing establishments led by food and beverages, machinery, plastics, printing and publishing, garment production, and telecommunications.

Labor

 The metro labor force was estimated in 1991 at 887,000, yielding a employment rate of 68.4%. Of this total, 813,000 were employed and 74,000 unemployed, yielding an unemployment rate of 13.2%. Historically, Vancouver had a high unemployment rate because of the influx of unemployed workers from other parts of western Canada in search of jobs. Within the city, 12.9% were employed in primary manufacturing; 4.6% in construction; 8.4% in transportation, communication, and utilities; 16% in wholesale and retail trade; 7.5% in FIRE; 7.9% in other business services; 4.9% in government; 6.4% in education; 9.4% in health services; 11.2% in tourism and hospitality; and 10.7% in other industries. By occupation, 10.7% were in managerial professions, 14% in knowledge-related professions, 5.8% in

Labor		
Work Force	*Male*	*Female*
Total Work Force	132,530	112,750
Employed	113,430	100,665
Employment Rate	75.00	60.10
% of 15–24 Year Olds	75.20	73.0
Occupation	*Male*	*Female*
Managerial	15,345	9,825
Education	3,675	5,245
Health	3,740	9,835
Technical and Cultural	16,015	8,785
Clerical	11,070	33,910
Sales	13,110	10,100
Service	21,395	21,615
Manufacturing	16,070	6,865
Construction	9,895	210
Transportation	6,420	395
Other	10,015	2,345

Income
Male ($Can) 32,137
Female ($Can) 21,316
Average Household Income ($Can) 32,384
Average Family Income ($Can) 39,905
Average Tax ($Can) 7,300
Average Household Expenditure ($Can) 41,453
Number of Banks 88

Manufacturing
Plants 831
Employees 22,721
Value of Shipments ($Can) 2,641,326,000
Total Value Added ($Can) 1,240,384,000

health, 47.1% in clerical and sales, 18% in blue-collar professions, and 4.3% in other occupations.

Education

 The Vancouver School District supports 100 public elementary schools and 20 public high schools, with a total enrollment of 70,000. The Separate School Board oversees about 40 church-supported schools. The University of British Columbia is situated on a large campus on Point Grey overlooking the Pacific Ocean. The Simon Fraser University, opened in 1965, is located on a mountaintop site in suburban Burnaby. A third institution, Capilano College, enrolls about 2,000 students. In addition, four institutions offer technical programs: B. C. Institute of Technology, Kwantlen College, Vancouver Community College, and Douglas College.

Education
Population (over 15 years old)   364,450
Less than Grade 9   49,970
Grades 9–13   120,010
Trade Certificate   84,405
University Degree   59,410
Four-Year Universities and Colleges
Capilano College
Simon Fraser University
University of British Columbia

Health

 Medical care is provided in 12 local hospitals: B. C. Cancer Agency, B. C. Rehabilitation Society, Children's Hospital, Grace Hospital, Holy Family Hospital, Mount St. Joseph Hospital, St. Paul Hospital, St. Vincent Hospital, Shaughnessy Hospital, Sunny Hill Hospital for Children, University Hospital, and Vancouver General Hospital.

Transportation

The Trans-Canada Highway passes through the heart of Vancouver and is the principal approach to the city from other major regions. The city is linked to the United States by U.S. Highway 5. The city's longest street is Marine Drive, which encircles the peninsula and extends to West Vancouver. Most of the city streets are laid out in a rectangular pattern, with the exception of the Shaughnessy area where the roads are curved. The east-west thoroughfares are called avenues and the north-south ones are called streets. The principal streets are Granville, Oak, Cambie, Main, and Knight. In 1974 the city prohibited automobile traffic on a part of Granville Street and turned the section into an attractive mall. Local transportation systems include a bus system and an elevated rapid transit system, Skytrain, connecting downtown with New Westminster, Burnaby, and Surrey. Ferries link Vancouver with nearby Vancouver Island. The 1,550-foot Lions Gate Bridge spans the Burrard Inlet. Vancouver serves as the western terminus of both CPR and CNR. In addition, the British Columbia government owns the British Columbia Railway. The Burlington Northern connects Vancouver with cities in the United States. The port of Vancouver is the busiest in Canada, handling about 65 million tons annually, most of it in trans-Pacific shipping. More than 50 steamship lines serve the port. In 1970 a coal-loading terminal opened south of Vancouver at Roberts Bank. The principal air terminal is the Vancouver International Airport, served by all three major Canadian airlines as well as U.S. foreign airlines.

Transportation	
New Automobiles	
Domestic	9,611
Imported	12,168
Trucks	7,666

Housing

In general, the larger and more expensive houses are to the west of Cambie Street, and the more modest homes are to the east. In the metro area there are 532,240 houses, of which 299,840, or 56.3%, are owner-occupied. Apartments number 184,685 with an average monthly rent of $Can 723.

Housing		
Total Housing Stock 185,790		
Owned 78,570		
Rented 107,225		
Single, Detached 70,190		
Apartments 24,900		
Homes Built 1990 4,329		
Building Permits Value ($Can)	851,480,000	
Tallest Buildings	*Hgt. (ft.)*	*Stories*
Royal Centre Tower (1973)	460	36
Canada Trust Tower	454	35
Scotiabank Tower	451	36
Bentall IV (1981)	450	35
Vancouver Center (1977)	450	36
Park Place (1984)	450	35
T-D Bank Tower (1978)	440	30
200 Granville Square (1973)	438	28

Urban Redevelopment

Vancouver changed dramatically after World War II. The original core of the city, east of the Canadian Pacific Railroad Station, became a derelict area when stores and businesses migrated to Granville Street. This section was restored in the 1960s under its original name of Gastown. On the north side of False Creek a 60,000-seat sports stadium opened in 1983. Downtown, 20- and 40-story-high office and hotel towers, including Bentall, Royal, Pacific, and Vancouver centers, have replaced the two- and three-story shops of pre–World

War I vintage. Architecturally, the most interesting new buildings are the Provincial Court House, Robson Square Conference Center, Canada Place, and Vancouver Art Gallery. Canada Place includes the 500-room Pan Pacific Hotel, built for the 1986 Expo and now a World Trade Center, and a cruise ship terminal. Other major buildings constructed since 1985 include the BC Pavilion and the Science World. The city's oldest residential neighborhood, east-end Strathcona, has been largely rehabilitated. In the West End, high-rise apartment complexes have replaced the single-family detached homes of the 19th century.

Crime

Vancouver has the highest crime rate of any city in Canada, with an average of 17 offenses per 1,000 compared to 12 in Toronto. In 1991 there were 42 murders, 38 attempted murders, 2,182 robberies, 624 sexual assaults, 4,464 other assaults, and 26 abductions.

Religion

Religious influences are less strong in the West than in the East. Until the arrival of Asian ethnic groups in the 1970s, mainline Protestant denominations were the dominant presence with a smaller Roman Catholic minority.

Media

Vancouver has two major dailies: *The Province* and *The Sun*, both owned by Pacific Press, the leading media group in western Canada. Electronic media consist of 4 television stations and 14 radio stations. The Canadian Broadcasting Corporation has its regional headquarters in Vancouver.

Media	
Newsprint	
The Province, daily	
The Sun, daily	
Vancouver, monthly	
Vancouver Magazine, monthly	
Television	
CBUFT (Channel 26)	
CBUT (Channel 2)	
CHAN (Channel 8)	
CKVU (Channel 10)	
Radio	
CBU (AM)	CBU (FM)
CBUF (FM)	CFUN (AM)
CHQM (AM)	CHRX (AM)
CJJR (FM)	CIMA (AM)
CITR (FM)	CJVB (AM)
CKLG (AM)	CFOX (FM)
CKWX (AM)	CKKS (FM)

Sports

Vancouver has two major professional sports teams: the British Columbia Lions of the Canadian Football League, who

play their home games in the domed BC Place Stadium, and the Vancouver Canucks of the National Hockey League, who play their home games in the Pacific Coliseum on the Pacific National Exhibition Grounds.

Arts, Culture, and Tourism

Vancouver's cultural resources include the Vancouver Opera Association performing in the Queen Elizabeth Theatre, dramatic performances in the Playhouse Theatre next door, and the Vancouver Symphony Orchestra performing at the Orpheum Theatre. Ballet is represented by Ballet BC and 14 other dance companies. In honor of its 1958 centennial, Vancouver built a new museum called the Centennial Museum and, with funds from H. R. Macmillan, the lumber magnate, a planetarium at the mouth of False Creek. On the waterfront is the Maritime Museum, which displays the famous ship *St. Roch*, which was the first to sail the Northwest Passage both ways between 1940 and 1944. In addition there are two other notable museums, Museum of Anthropology and the Transportation Museum, and two art galleries, the Vancouver Art Gallery, and the Contemporary Art Gallery.

Parks and Recreation

The city's extensive park system is administered by an elected Board of Parks and Recreation, the only such elected body in North America. The city has 158 parks covering 2,700 acres. The largest is the 1,000-acre Stanley Park, including a zoo and an aquarium. Queen Elizabeth Park includes an arboretum and the Bloedel Conservatory. Other parks include the Vanier Park, John Hendry Park, and Jericho Park within the city, and Confederation Park and Central Park just outside city limits.

Sources of Further Information

City Hall
453 West 12th Avenue
Vancouver, British Columbia V5Y 1V4
(604) 873-7011

Tourism Vancouver
1055 Dunsmuir Street
Vancouver, British Columbia V7X 1L3
(604) 693-2000

Vancouver Board of Trade
999 Canada Place #400
Vancouver, British Columbia V6C 3C1
(604) 681-2111

Additional Reading

Davis, C. *The Vancouver Book*. 1976.
Evenden, L. J. *Vancouver: Western Metropolis*. 1978.
Kalman, H. *Exploring Vancouver*. 1978.
McDonald, R. A. J., and J. Burman. *Vancouver's Past: Essays in Social History*. 1986.
Pethick, Derek. *Vancouver Recalled*. 1983.
Petrie, Anne. *Ethnic Vancouver*. 1983.
Roy, Patricia E. *Vancouver: An Illustrated History*. 1980.
Yee, Paul. *Saltwater City: The Chinese in Vancouver*. 1989.

Winnipeg
Manitoba

Basic Data

Name   Winnipeg
Year Founded   1812 Inc. 1873
Status: Province   Capital of Manitoba
Area (square miles)   221
Elevation   784 ft.
Time Zone   Central
Population (1990)   616,790

Distance in Miles to:

Calgary	830
Chicago	862
Edmonton	843
Montreal	1,496
New York	1,660
Ottawa	1,378
Quebec	1,664
Regina	355
Toronto	1,304
Vancouver	1,487

Location and Topography

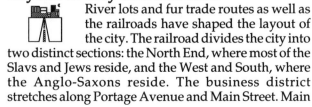

Winnipeg, the capital of Manitoba, is located at the confluence of the Red River and Assiniboine River, midway between the Atlantic and Pacific oceans, about 60 miles north of the U.S. border. The city, called the "Bull's Eye of the Dominion" and the "Gateway to the West" is situated where the prairie begins and the Canadian Shield ends.

Layout of City and Suburbs

River lots and fur trade routes as well as the railroads have shaped the layout of the city. The railroad divides the city into two distinct sections: the North End, where most of the Slavs and Jews reside, and the West and South, where the Anglo-Saxons reside. The business district stretches along Portage Avenue and Main Street. Main Street, once an important settlers trail, is the chief north-south street, and Portage Avenue, the beginning of the old overland route to Edmonton, is the chief east-west street. The 34-story Richardson Building, Winnipeg's tallest, rises at Main and Portage. Most of the 19th century buildings were built in the so-called Red River Frame style, with vertical and horizontal logs. Much of the city had to be rebuilt after the disastrous Red River flood of 1950. During the 1960s and 1970s, Winnipeg changed steadily, although not as dramatically as Calgary.

Climate

Winnipeg is noted as one of the coldest and windiest North American cities. The average temperature is -2.7°F in January and 67°F in July. The average annual precipitation is 20.6 inches. However, the climate is dry and healthy, with 2,321 hours of sunshine and 195 frost free days annually.

Weather	
Annual Averages	
January °F	-2.7
July °F	67
Annual Precipitation (inches)	20.6
Annual Sunshine (hours)	2,321

History

The Assiniboine and Cree Indians lived in the region when the first Europeans arrived in the 18th century. Sieur de la Verendrye, a French-Canadian fur trader, was the first person to visit the site of the city in 1738. He built Fort Rouge at the junction of the Red and Assiniboine rivers. In 1812, Lord Selkirk of the Hudson's Bay Company persuaded Scottish and Irish farmers to settle in

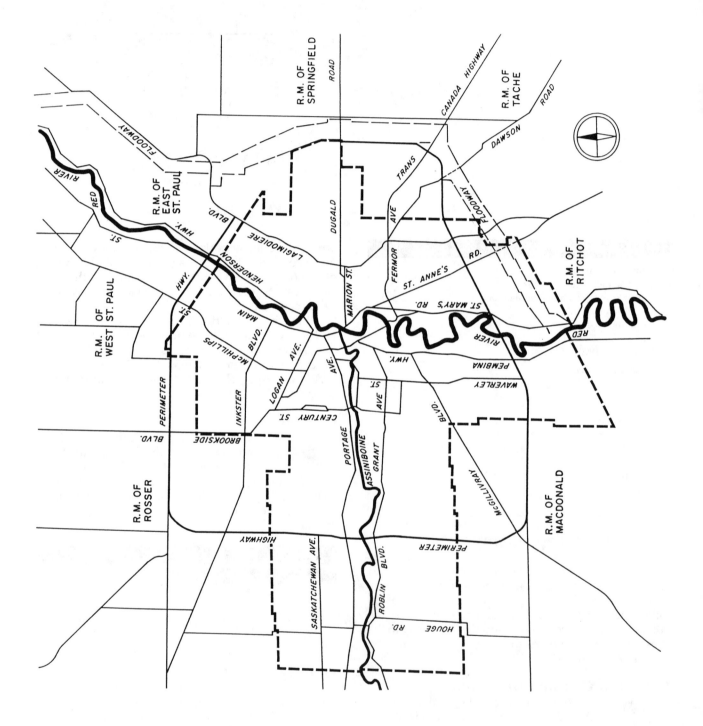

the area. In 1820 St. John's College, the oldest college in western Canada, was founded. There followed a period of intense rivalry between Hudson's Bay Company and its chief rival, the Northwest Company, which ended with the merger of the two in 1821. Thereupon, in 1822, Hudson's Bay Company enlarged its earlier post called Fort Gibraltar and renamed it Fort Garry. It rebuilt the fort in 1832, calling it Upper Fort Garry to distinguish it from the trading post north of Winnipeg called Lower Fort Garry. Upper Fort Garry became the center of the Red River Settlement. In 1862, Henry McKenney built a general store on a site which later became the corner of Portage and Main. In 1870, when Manitoba entered the Dominion of Canada, Red River Settlement was renamed Winnipeg, meaning "muddy water" in the Cree language, and it became the capital of the new province. When it was incorporated as a city in 1873, it had a population of 3,700 and was little more than a collection of shacks. In 1878 Manitoba's first railroad linked Winnipeg with St. Paul, Minnesota. Winnipeg's strategic location astride the continent made it a natural focus for the westward extension of the transcontinental railroads. When the Canadian Pacific was completed in 1885, the city became a magnet for immigrants hungry for land. The period of growth lasted until World War I, when Winnipeg's fortunes began to slide. The opening of the Panama Canal in 1914, the general strike of 1919, and the Great Depression were among the factors that kept its economy weak. The Red River flood of 1950 devastated many parts of the city. Conditions improved greatly after the 1950s, but it never regained its earlier monopoly of western commerce. Sharp increases in the demand for livestock, lumber, metals, and wheat helped to sustain the economy. Since the 1960s Winnipeg has lost population. In 1960 Winnipeg was Canada's fourth largest city; by the end of the decade it had dropped to the eighth. In 1960 the Manitoba legislature established the Metropolitan Corporation of Greater Winnipeg to administer a number of services for Winnipeg and its suburbs. Because of constant bickering in the metropolitan agency, the corporation was converted into one city called UniCity. As a result Winnipeg once again became the third largest city, falling back to fourth place in 1981. A downtown building boom that began in the 1960s continued through the next two decades. In 1981 the city launched the Core Area Initiative to rebuild the inner city.

Historical Landmarks

Two provincial plaques in La Verendrye Park commemorate the formal proclamation of the Red River Colony by Miles McDonell, the first governor of Assiniboia in 1812. Two plaques commemorate the beginning of the St. Boniface Settlement—the arrival of Jean-Baptiste Lagimodiere and Marie Anne Gaboury to settle on Seine River lots in 1817 and the establishment of the first permanent mission and school in the west by Fathers Provencher and Dumoulin in 1818–1819. A provincial plaque on Mount Royal Road at Trail Avenue marks the original site of Silver Heights, a well-known stopping place on the Portage Trail. Historic buildings include the Barber House on Euclid Street, built in 1862; A. A. Heaps Building, the former Bank of Nova Scotia; Dalnavert, the home of the son of Sir John A. MacDonald, Canada's first prime minister; Garry Telephone Exchange, the former Great-West Life building; and Seven Oaks House, one of the oldest homes in Manitoba built by John Inkster in 1851. The Manitoba Legislative Building, formally opened in 1920, was designed by an English architectural firm in classical style. Its 240-foot dome is topped by Manitoba's best known symbol, the Golden Boy. Winnipeg has a historic area in the central city known as the Warehouse District containing renovated warehouse buildings built in the 19th and early-20th centuries. The Red River Settlement's first known water mill, Grant's Old Mill, built in 1829, stands on Sturgeon Creek on Portage Avenue. The Forks National Historic Site at the junction of the Red and Assiniboine rivers salutes all those who played a part in the opening of the Canadian West.

Population

The population of Winnipeg was 616,790 in 1990, making it the fourth largest in Canada. After its dramatic growth in the last decades of the 19th century to 1911, Winnipeg's population fell back until well after World War II. Its demographic rank had fallen to eighth until 1972 when, through its merger with outlying suburbs in the UniCity, it managed to regain third place. It was, however, outstripped by Calgary in 1981. Since 1976 its growth has been steady but unspectacular: from 560,874 in 1976, to 564,473 in 1981, and 594,555 in 1986.

Population

City Population	1986	1990
	594,555	616,790
% Male 48.26		

Age

% Under 14 19.81
% Over 65 12.31

Vital Statistics

Births (1989) 9,363
Deaths (1989) 4,812
Natural Increase (1986–1991) 4,551
Marriages (1989) 4,817
Married (1989) 289,820
Single (1989) 134,315
Widowed/Divorced (1989) 52,640

Households and Families

Households Total 156,695
Average # Persons per Household 3.1
Average # Children per Household 1.2

Mother Tongue

English 72.7
French 4.1
German 4.1
Ukrainian 3.6

Chronology

1670	Charter is granted by King Charles II to Hudson's Bay Company deeding the latter all territory draining into the rivers flowing into Hudson Bay.
1738	Fur trading post of Fort Rouge established by Sieur de la Verendrye.
1812	Lord Selkirk's colonists reach the banks of the Red River.
1820	St. John's College, the oldest college in western Canada, is founded.
1821	Hudson's Bay Company and North West Company end long period of rivalry by merging.
1822	Fort Garry (Formerly Fort Gibraltar) is built.
1832	Fort Garry is rebuilt and renamed Upper Fort Garry.
1835	First government of Red River Settlement is organized.
1855	First post office in western Canada opens in Winnipeg.
1859	First steamboat plies the Red River.
1862	Henry McKenney builds general store on a site that later became the corner of Portage and Main.
1870	Manitoba becomes fifth province of Canada and Red River Settlement, renamed Winnipeg, is named the capital.
1873	Winnipeg is incoporated as a city with four wards.
1874	First city council meeting is held.
1876	First City Hall and theater are built.
1877	University of Manitoba is founded.
1878	Rail links are established with St. Paul, Minnesota. First telephone service begins.
1882	First public water supply systems begins operation in Winnipeg. Horse-drawn cars appear on city streets.
1884	Work begins on new City Hall.
1886	The first train completes Montreal to Vancouver run on the Canadian Pacific. Second City Hall is completed.
1892	First electric street cars begin operation.
1919	General Strike from 15 May to 26 June helps to win workers' rights but paralyzes the economy.
1950	Red River flood inflicts heavy damage on city.
1960	The Metropolitan Corporation of Greater Winnipeg is established.
1972	UniCity, combining Winnipeg and its suburbs into one municipality is inaugurated.
1975	Winnipeg Convention Centre opens.
1981	Core Area Initiative is launched in an effort to revive downtown.
1987	North Portage Development opens in downtown Winnipeg, including shopping malls connected by pedestrian bridges.

Ethnic Composition

People of British origin make up 34% of the population. With the exception of the French and the Italians, all ethnic groups are represented with a greater percentage in the city than nationwide. Ukrainians make up 7.7%, Germans 7.2%, French 5.3%, Anglo-French 3.7%, other Eastern Europeans 3.5%, Pacific Islanders 2.7%, American Indians 4.7%, and Jews 2.3%.

Government

Winnipeg has a mayor-council form of government. The mayor and the 29 councillors, representing wards, are elected to serve three-year terms. A five-member board of commissioners, headed by a chief commissioner, supervises the municipal departments.

Public Finance

In 1992 the total government revenues were $Can 654,507,905, of which taxation provided $Can 445,398,605 and provincial grants $Can 120,283,505. Total expenditures were balanced at $Can 654, 507,905. By function, 6% went to general government departments, 12% to operations, 20% to fire and police, 7% to health and social services, 10% to parks and recreation, 8% to other departments, 19% to debt and finance charges, and 18% to corporate charges.

Economy

Winnipeg dominates Manitoba's economy, producing 83% of its manufactured goods and accounting for 62% of its retail sales. Winnipeg is one of the principal manufacturing regions in western Canada. More than 1,000 factories produce goods estimated at $Can 5 billion annually, the chief products being buses, clothing, cement, farm machinery, furniture, metal products, and processed foods. The Winnipeg Commodity Exchange is Canada's major grain market. The Canadian

Wheat Board is located here. Winnipeg is also one of the most important transportation and trading centers between Toronto and Vancouver, although it has been overtaken by Calgary in both respects. Winnipeg is active in promoting its own industrial advantages.

Labor

The labor force is estimated at 338,400 with a participation rate of 67.9%. The employed number 304,300 and the unemployment rate is 12.2%, slightly higher than that of Canada. The three largest work sectors are services at 35%, trade at 20%, and manufacturing at 14%. Although Winnipeg is the provincial capital, public administration accounts for less than 10%.

Labor

Work Force	Male	Female
Total Work Force	175,135	145,845
Employed	161,575	133,870
Employment Rate	78.20	59.29
% of 15–24 Year Olds	74.60	71.10
Occupation	Male	Female
Managerial	22,980	10,265
Education	5,620	8,265
Health	4,135	14,295
Technical and Cultural	15,740	9,070
Clerical	15,695	50,470
Sales	17,250	13,990
Service	20,160	22,600
Manufacturing	25,385	9,240
Construction	15,990	450
Transportation	10,880	870
Other	18,680	3,495

Income

Male ($Can) 30,151
Female ($Can) 19,188
Average Household Income ($Can) 33,295
Average Family Income ($Can) 38,647
Average Tax ($Can) 5,705
Average Household Expenditure ($Can) 43,384
Number of Banks 11
  Branches 193

Manufacturing

Plants 911
Employees 40,495
Value of Shipments ($Can) 4,012,082,000
Total Value Added ($Can) 1,862,968,000

Education

Winnipeg's public school system supports 180 elementary schools and 55 high schools with a total enrollment of about 115,000. The city also has about 30 parochial and private schools. The University of Manitoba, founded in 1877, has an enrollment of over 20,000. The University of Winnipeg is located downtown. St. Boniface College is a small institution with an enrollment of about 430.

Education

Population (over 15 years old) 469,885
Less than Grade 9 62,490
Grades 9–13 193,455
Trade Certificate 103,495
University Degree 53,820

Four-Year Universities and Colleges
  St. Boniface College
  University of Winnipeg
  University of Manitoba

Health

Winnipeg has seven general hospitals and seven specialized hospitals with 1,085 physicians and 4,598 beds. The general hospitals are Victoria General Hospital, Grace General Hospital, Concordia Hospital, Misericordia General Hospital, St. Boniface General Hospital, Health Sciences Centre, and Seven Oaks Hospital. The specialized hospitals are St. Amant Centre, Deer Lodge Hospital, Rehabilitation Centre for Children, King Edward Memorial Hospital, King George Hospital, Princess Elizabeth Hospital, and Tache Nursing Centre Hospital.

Transportation

Major arterial thoroughfares within Winnipeg are designated as routes. These routes, in general, form a grid pattern with the north-south routes ending in even numbers and the east-west ones in odd numbers. Provincial highways entering Winnipeg form direct connections with the route system which is linked with the Trans Canada Highway. Both of Canada's transcontinental railroads have their western headquarters in Winnipeg, which is also connected by rail with St. Paul, Minnesota. The principal air terminal is Winnipeg International Airport.

Transportation

New Automobiles

Domestic 9,832
Imported 4,040
Trucks 6,261

Housing

The housing stock consists of 132,645 single detached homes 29,935 apartments, and 64,570 other types. Of the total 59.5% is owner-occupied. The average home price in 1990 was $Can 81,740 ($Can 52,656 in 1981) 42.9% above the national average. The difference between city and national averages has widened sharply since 1981. However, prices in Winnipeg are much lower than in the eastern cities and Winnipeg remains the fourth most affordable of all major Canadian cities.

Housing

Total Housing Stock   227,145
Owned   135,265
Rented   91,880
Single, Detached   132,645
Apartments   29,935
Homes Built 1990   2,686
Building Permits Value ($Can)   467,297,000

Media

Newsprint
   The Winnipeg Free Press, daily
   The Winnipeg Sun, daily

Television
   CBWT (Channel 6)
   CHMI (Channel 13)
   CKND (Channel 9)
   CKY (Channel 7)

Radio

CBW (AM)	CBW (FM)
CIFX (AM)	CHIQ (FM)
CJOB (AM)	CJKR (FM)
CKJS (AM)	CKRC (AM)
CHZZ (FM)	CKY (AM)
CITI (FM)	

Urban Redevelopment

Winnipeg has changed steadily since World War II, although not as dramatically as Calgary. In the 1970s numerous high-rise hotels, banks, and office buildings altered the skyline. New urban redevelopment programs were initiated in 1985 by North Portage Development Corporation. It has constructed more than 1,000 units of housing and over 2 million square feet of office space. The agency has also unveiled plans to revitalize the CN East Yards waterfront area. A 900-unit residential and multi-use complex has opened on Fort Garry Place. Winnipeg's largest shopping center opened in Polo Park, and the Royal Winnipeg Ballet acquired a new home on Graham Avenue in the late 1980s.

Religion

Winnipeg's religious mosaic is as varied as its ethnic one. Both mainline and Catholic churches are strong but not dominant. There are a number of historical churches of which Anthony on the Red is perhaps the most famous. The Kildonan Presbyterian Church was the first Presbyterian church in western Canada, erected in 1854. St. James Church, built in 1853, is the oldest log church in Manitoba. The first Protestant church in the Red River Settlement was St. John's Cathedral, built in 1822 by John West. It was followed three years later in 1825 by St. John's Middlechurch at Image Plain. The principal Roman Catholic cathedral is St. Boniface Basilica in St. Boniface. The original cathedral was constructed by Father Provencher in 1818, but was rebuilt several times after being destroyed by fire. There are a number of Ukrainian churches, both Catholic and Greek Orthodox, serving the large Ukrainian community. The three largest are St. Nicholas Ukrainian Catholic Church at the corner of Arlington Street and Bannerman Avenue; St. Vladimir and Olga Cathedral on McGregor Street; and the Holy Trinity Ukrainian Orthodox Cathedral on Main Street. Until 1982, when it burned down, Winnipeg had the only Trappist monastery in western Canada, Our Lady of the Prairies, in St. Norbert.

Media

Winnipeg has two daily newspapers: *The Winnipeg Free Press* and *The Winnipeg Sun.* The electronic media consist of 5 television stations and 11 radio stations.

Sports

Winnipeg has two professtional sports teams: the Winnipeg Blue Bombers of the Canadian Football League, who play their home games in Winnipeg Stadium, and the Winnipeg Jets of the National Hockey League, who play their home games in the Winnipeg Arena. Winnipeg was host to the 1967 Pan-American Games whose legacies are an Olympic size swimming pool (home of the National Aquatic Hall of Fame), a cycling velodrome, and a track and field facility.

Arts, Culture, and Tourism

The city's acclaimed Royal Winnipeg Ballet and the Winnipeg Symphony Orchestra perform at the Centennial Centre. Nearby is the Manitoba Theatre Centre, one of the most important regional theaters in Canada. Known as the Music City, Winnipeg holds the Manitoba Music Festival and Folklorama, a festival of ethnic culture. Other cultural groups include Le Cercle Moliere, Contemporary Dancers, Manitoba Opera Association, Actors' Showcase, Prairie Theatre Exchange, Manitoba Chamber Orchestra, Winnipeg Singers, Les Danseurs de la Riviere Rouge, and Alliance Chorale Manitoba. In summer, the Rainbow Stage in Kildonan Park comes alive with two Broadway musical productions.

Winnipeg's premier museum, the Museum of Man and Nature, is located in the Manitoba Centennial Centre. It has seven major galleries interpreting Manitoba's natural and human history. Other museums include the Aquatic Hall of Fame; and Museum of Canada on Poseidon Bay, which includes the Pan-Am Natatorium, the largest indoor pool in the world measuring 75 feet by 225 feet; Manitoba Children's Museum; Crafts Guild of Manitoba Museum; Ivan Franko Museum, dedicated to the noted Ukrainian poet and writer; the Living Prairie Museum, a 12-acre outdoor museum, one of the last remaining examples of tallgrass prairie; Oseredok, the Ukrainian Cultural and Educational Centre; La Musee de Saint-Boniface, housed in the oldest building in the city erected for the Grey Nuns in 1846; Ross House Museum, the first post office in western Canada, built in 1854; the Royal Winnipeg Rifles Museum, depicting the history of the oldest militia unit in western Canada; the Historical Museum of St. James Assiniboia, including the William Brown House, Seven Oaks House Museum, Transcona Historical Museum, Ukrainian Museum of Canada, Stewart-Hay Memorial Zoological Museum, and the Western Canada Aviation Museum. The Winnipeg Art Gallery houses over 14,000 works of art in its nine major galleries, including the largest collection of Inuit sculpture.

Parks and Recreation

Winnipeg has over 300 parks covering 8,044 acres. The largest is the 375-acre Assiniboine Park, including a conservatory and zoo. Another popular park is the 98.2-acre Kildonan Park, which includes a swimming pool and Grimm's Brothers Fairy Tale House. Other major regional parks (defined as those over 15 acres in size) include Birds Hill, Polo, Sargent, Juba, Bonnycastle, Bunns Creek, Centennial, Blumberg, Heubach, Kings, Kilcona, Lyndale Drive, Whittier, Sturgeon Creek, Munson, Caron, Crescent Drive, Churchill Drive, La Barriere, St. Vital, Maple Grove, Fraser's Grove, Little Mountain, and Westview.

Sources of Further Information

City Hall
Civic Centre
510 Main Street
Winnipeg, Manitoba R3B 1B9
(204) 986-2171

Winnipeg Chamber of Commerce
500-167 Lombard Avenue
Winnipeg, Manitoba R3B 3E5
(204) 944-8484

Additional Reading

Brownstone, Meyer and T. J. Plunkett. *Metropolitan Winnipeg: Politics and the Reform of the Local Government.* 1983.
Kidd, Peter. *The Winnipeg General Strike.* 1987.